KOREAN

WAR

A Tribute To Those Who Served

VETERANS

Turner Publishing Company

MEMORIAL

TURNER PUBLISHING CO.

P.O. Box 3101

Paducah, Kentucky 42002-3101

(502) 443-0121

Korean War Veteran's Memorial was compiled using available information. The Publisher is not responsible for errors or omissions.

Korean War Veteran's Memorial Editor:
Korean War Veterans Memorial Advisory Board:
Colonel Rosemary T. McCarthy, USA (Ret.)
Colonel William E. Weber, USA (Ret.)
Robert L. Hansen, Executive Director

Layout and design concept developed by
Louis Nelson Associates, Inc.

Turner Publishing Company's Staff:
Chief Editor: Robert J. Martin
Designer: Trevor W. Grantham

Library of Congress Catalog
Card Number: 95-60326
ISBN: 1-56311-192-6

Printed and produced in the
United States of America.
Limited Edition. Additional books may be purchased
from Turner Publishing Company.

Photo caption: From the doorway of a Korean house near Seoul, Pfc. Richard Coate (New York Post 18) of the 3d Infantry Division scans the surrounding hills for enemy activity in this 1951 photograph by James E. Martenhoff of Associated Press. (AP/Wide World Photo, Courtesy of Richard Coate)

Contents

Publisher's Message

It is a great honor to be able to publish the book on the *Korean War Veterans Memorial*, since we have had the privilege of publishing the Korean War Veterans Association history titled *Korean War Veterans- The Forgotten War Remembered*; *Chosin Few, North Korea- November-December 1950*; *Korean War Ex-Prisoners of War*; as well as many others. Of all the wars our nation has fought in the cause for peace, the Korean War has been one designated as "The Forgotten War." There were 325,270 United States veterans who served in Korea during the War with 54,236 deaths.

To those who gave so much, it is only fitting that their heroic deeds be remembered. The *Korean War Veterans Memorial* is at last a tribute to those who answered the call to serve. It is my sincere hope that those who have not had the opportunity to visit the Memorial itself will be able to remember through this book. Remember those who fought, who bled, who died in the battles of the Pusan Perimeter, Inchon, the Chosin Reservoir, along the 38th parallel, and in the many others.

Willard A. Matthews, a Korean War veteran with Company A, 19th Infantry Regiment, 24th Infantry Division, wrote in his poem titled *Combat In Korea (A Soldier's Prayer)*,

"When I die God will erase, the things that hurt me yet, Then will I have peace of mind, only then will I forget."

Dave Turner, President
Turner Publishing Company

May those Korean War Veterans who remain today also be remembered along with their fallen comrades. May the surviving families, the subsequent generations, and all of us who enjoy the freedom that these patriots have secured through their dedication echo the same sentiment, "Only then will I forget."

4

Dedication
by Col. William E. Weber, USA (Ret)

Col. William E. Weber, USA (Ret)

As with the Korean War Veterans Memorial, dedicated to the honor and memory of those Americans who served so nobly in "The Forgotten War," so too is this book dedicated. And, to those hundreds of thousands, those who died on the battlefield, in captivity, who lie in unmarked graves, or who survived the war but did not live to see their Memorial, the Nation's final debt to you has been paid!

Though you cannot physically survey the Memorial, we know you can see it in a way that will come as well to us who now walk the pathways. And, we sense you by our side, as you were when we faced the trials of armed conflict. Your face, your being, is in the line of sculptures, in the images on the wall, is reflected in the still waters of the pool and shadowed by the colors that fly proudly over one and all.

For we each are the one that is all. In each is the comrade that fell, the husband that did not return, the son or daughter that bled, the friend that never again will share a handclasp. Though we were once forgotten, it was not from each other. That we are now remembered is but a Nation's belated acknowledgment of that which we honored from the beginning.

There are many to whom credit is due for our Memorial. Your sacrifices manifested justification for such, the efforts of those responsible gave substance to such. To one among these must go credit for the leadership, perseverance and dedication he displayed, without which the Memorial would have suffered. General Richard G. Stilwell, USA (Ret), deceased, is also a casualty of the war, for those who worked with him well know his life was cut short by the stress and trials of the Memorial project.

FREEDOM IS NOT FREE!
ALL HAVE SACRIFICED!
ALL HAVE PAID THE PRICE!

Acknowledgements

In any great and lasting design there are many hands and many thoughts that play a role in its shaping. There were hundreds who contributed to the final development of the Korean War Veterans Memorial. We would like to pay tribute to a few of those who were most influential.

Those whose creative talents shaped the three-dimensional reality of the Memorial: Kent Cooper, William Lecky, Jim Clark, Rob Smedley, Jim Cummings, Karen Murray, Louis Nelson, Jennifer Stoller, Robert Hansen, Frank Gaylord, Jeff Howard, Claude Engel, John Woods, Henry Arnold, Steve Lederach, William Hobbs, Greg Blair, James Madison Cutts, Tom McElwain, Joe Mensch, Massoud Nadjmabadi.

Those whose words, thoughtfulness, and influence had significant impact on the Memorial: Gen. Richard Stilwell, Gen. Ray Davis, Col. William Weber, Col. Rosemary McCarthy, Col. Fred Cherry, Mike McKevitt, John Staum, Carlos Rodriguez, William McSweeney, Thomas Dehne, Jake Comer, Edward Brocherdt, John Curcio, John Phillips, Conrad Hausman, Robert Hansen, Gen. P.X. Kelley, Col. Ken Pond , Col. Fred Badger, Col. William Ryan, Gen. Joseph Laposata , J. Carter Brown, Charles Atherton, John Parsons, John Beardsley, John Triano, William Taylor, Glen DeMarr, Sean McCabe, Veronica Burns Lucas, John Paul Lucas, Don Alvaro Leon, Eliza Pennypacker Oberholtzer

Those fabricators, artisans, and builders whose management, skilled hands, and in many cases, strong backs, put all the pieces together: Major Pete Taylor, Rick Dean, Don Sansing, Jon Sadler, Jerry Bell, Dick Polich, Chuck Mortenson, Dan Rae, Pat Mitchell, Ann Hawkins, Larry Cooper, Rinaldo Lopez, John Theis, Joe Theis, Ken Viere.

Photo Credits

Author's Note

I met Robert L. Hansen, Executive Director of the Korean War Veterans Memorial Advisory Board in August 1993. A one-hour meeting turned into a several day briefing. As a life-long resident of Washington, DC, and a 25-year enthusiast for American public monuments, I had read the newspaper accounts detailing this project's trials and tribulations. Bob offered and I accepted the invitation to tell the story of the making of this memorial.

I must acknowledge the help of all participants, particularly that graciously offered by Kent Cooper and Bill Lecky, who permitted me access to their files. Equally important was the discovery, among the Board's minutes, of verbatim transcripts of KWVMAB's first five meetings. The Corps of Engineers (Baltimore District) and the American Battle Monuments Commission also made their records available. In every instance, I was able to examine relevant (and controversial) records.

I have spoken with nearly all, and interviewed many, members of the Board, as well as tape-recorded the architects, the 1989 designer winners and representatives of the various agencies mentioned in the text. All citations come from either original documents or recorded conversations.

I am grateful for help extended in preparing the initial draft of the manuscript and generously offered during the excruciatingly necessary task of rewriting and editing, by Bob Hansen, William Weber and Rosemary McCarthy.

Michael Richman
Takoma Park, MD
April, 1995

Prologue
by Col. William E. Weber, USA (Ret.)

There are those moments in time when events, which are of major import, pass unheralded and forgotten by those who view them from a distance. The nature of mankind is to view events from the perspective of whatever direct impact they have on one's life, family and surroundings. The less the impact, the more remote is awareness, and the passage of time condemns the event to an almost total absence of recall. So it is with people and so it is with nations. SO IT WAS WITH "THE FORGOTTEN WAR"!

Those who are players in these events are branded by such, and the searing marks them personally and bonds them collectively as a group, part of and yet distinct from their countrymen. Absent from the consciousness of their countrymen, in the subconscious they constitute a buried memory, sensed, though not manifested, that silently preys on the conscience of their people and nation. SO IT WAS WITH THE SOLDIERY OF "THE FORGOTTEN WAR"!

Forty-five years in the past, a minority of a generation of Americans embarked on a conflict of which few were forewarned and for which all were unprepared. Thrust into an event, then relatively insignificant to the mass of their countrymen, they served a cause few perceived and even fewer could comprehend.

They fought: for the freedom of a land most had never heard of; for a people they did not then know; in a cause that did not threaten their nation; and, against a foe espousing a philosophy that would endanger the free world, though such threat was perceived to be elsewhere than at the point of conflict.

They answered the call of their people who were not threatened by the conflict and who were only remotely aware of the cause that was embraced by their nation's leaders. That cause, succored by a soldiery largely unknown and destined to be forgotten, engendered the most brutal and bloody foreign war of our history. One of 10 who served in Korea would give their life or shed their blood on that foreign soil.

Absorbed by other events, their countrymen ignored that which was done in their stead by those they sent to Korea. Those that returned to premature graves and those that lie in unmarked and uneasy graves were mourned only by their families and those with whom they served. Those who returned to take up interrupted lives were melded back into the fabric of their country as if they had never left. Few knew of their departure. Fewer heralded their return. And, even fewer knew what they had faced. SO WERE THE SACRIFICES OF "THE FORGOTTEN WAR"!

The true nature of the war was not presented to, or understood by, the nation. Encouraged by a policy that defined the conflict as limited and distracted by the pursuit of the good life, the nation viewed the event with disinterest. A war, so far away, fought by so few, and one that seemed not to embrace the concept of victory, but rather a return to status quo, was too foreign a concept to be understood by a nation acclimated by the nature of its previous wars.

And thus, because of the remoteness of the land in which it transpired, the absence of a perceived national interest and the non-event it was portrayed to be, Korea has been characterized in our history as a "five-paragraph war." This, even though the protracted land campaigns exceeded in length those in either the European or Pacific Theaters in W.W.II. This, even though the enemy faced was as tenacious, numerous and ferocious as any faced in all our previous wars! This, even though we sent our soldiery on a cause as honorable as any embraced in our past! SO IT WAS WE JUDGED "THE FORGOTTEN WAR"!

But, events do register in the subconscious of a people and nation and, in time, they rise to the surface in the conscious to be relived and remembered. The catalyst to awaken the past may take a single major or a multiplicity of minor forms, but the surfacing is inevitable when a people are stimulated to remember their past.

Time, the ability to place the past in perspective with the events of the 90s, and the resurgence of patriotism which suffered so in the decade of Vietnam, has awakened the long dormant memory of Korea. The nation has now chosen to remember and to acknowledge the need to do now that which was then undone. SO IT IS NOW WITH "THE FORGOTTEN WAR"!

In retrospect we can now accept that, that which seemed but a footnote in world history is, instead, a benchmark. In the 42 years that have passed since the war terminated in a truce, the world has changed dramatically, and for the better. The events bringing about this change are many, but ranked among the primary of these and perhaps the most significant, is "The Forgotten War"!

It was in Korea that the line was drawn signifying that conquest by arms would be resisted and subjugation of freedom by force would not be tolerated. This personification of resolve in a small and distant point of confrontation signaled a like response in all parts of the world, minor or major. It also signaled a willingness to expend wealth, resources and people to match and surpass any threat and any disruption of world order. Therein lay the beginning of the demise of the attempt to rule the world by force.

Belatedly, but most appropriately, this nation now acknowledges the long dormant memory of what was achieved by those it sent to fight for a cause only now appreciated. That cause and story of the Memorial portrayed in this volume gives substance to that memory just as their now being remembered finally gives honor to those who served. Their legacy to the world and an everlasting memorial of this generation is the impact their sacrifice gave to the change in world order.

SO IT IS WE SHALL NOW REMEMBER
"THE FORGOTTEN WAR"!
THE FORGOTTEN WAR SHALL
BE FORGOTTEN NO MORE!
"FREEDOM IS NOT FREE
SOME PAY THE PRICE!"
A VICTORY REMEMBERED.

The Korean War . . .
The Forgotten War, A Remembered Victory.
By D. Randall Beirne, Ph.D.

Chapter One: Justification of the Korean War

Forty-five years have passed since the early morning hours of 25 June, 1950 when thousands of North Korean troops crossed the 38th Parallel into South Korea. The Korean War or "Forgotten War" had begun, and it was to become a turning point in post World War II history with world-wide repercussions. It was the first time that the United States used military force to halt Communist military expansion. It ultimately became the determining factor in the struggle with Communism.

This "police action" as President Harry Truman called the conflict in Korea became the stimulus that awoke the West. It motivated the West into consolidating the international anti-Communist coalition and turned NATO from a paper tiger into a real military force. To the world it proved that America had a will to stand up to the Communists.

The Korean conflict initiated a contest known as the "Cold War," a term originated by the newspaperman, Walter Lippman, that was to last over forty years. The term specifically implied a power struggle between the two great super powers: the United States and the Soviet Union.

The "Forgotten War" eventually turned out to be the decisive conflict that started the collapse of Communism. Over the next forty-one years America and the Soviet Union challenged each other in the arms race. The economics of the two powers was tested to the fullest. By 1989 the economy of the Soviet Union had begun to crack. Premier Gorbachev attempted to ease the economic crisis by ending "Cold War" competition with the United States. Opposition to Gorbachev along

Courtesy of Hermes, Walter G. Truce Tent and Fighting Front, *U.S. Army in the Korean War. Office of the Chief of Military History, U.S. Army, Washington, DC, 1966.*

with the failed coup-putsch in August 1991 brought about the crumbling of Soviet Communism. By December 1991 communism had been overthrown, and the Soviet Union was broken into fourteen independent Russian republics. The forty-one year "Cold War" came to an end, and the United States remained the only super power.

The clash between the Soviet and American power systems had actually begun at the end of World War II. After 1945 the United States adopted a new strategic theory that initiated an active, global diplomacy. Concurrently in both Europe and Asia the unsettled international environment brought on by war gave the communists an opportunity to instigate and support national revolutions. As early as May 1945 Winston Churchill cabled President Harry Truman that "communist expansion must be handled firmly before our strength is dispersed-otherwise our fruits of victory will be cast away."

Between 1945 and 1950 this power struggle was mostly verbal, although several clashes almost led to armed conflict. Negotiation finally settled the Iranian conflict between the West and the Soviet Union in 1946. Since the allied powers could not agree on the unification of Germany in 1945, independent occupation zones were established. In 1947 when Communist political pressure threatened Greece and Turkey, American foreign aid rescued these nations. As the Communists continued to try to become dominant in Europe, America responded with its Marshall Plan to increase foreign aid and stimulate economic growth.

The "Cold War" almost escalated to a military conflict in June 1948 when the Russians cut off their allies access to Berlin from Western Germany. The Allies responded with a massive airlift of food and fuel that lasted until May, 1949, when the blockade was lifted

As a result of these conflicts the two German Republics of East Germany (German Democratic Republic) and West Germany (The Federal Republic of Germany) were formed. In addition to the earlier Marshall Plan of economic aid to Europe, the Allies now felt they needed some military defense against Soviet aggression. Out of this fear came the North Atlantic Treaty Organization. Under NATO the United States and the West European countries agreed upon a common defense for Western Europe to thwart Communism that was to last almost forty years.

The Korean War demonstrated that in spite of Soviet nuclear power, the United States could for the first time oppose localized communist aggression by use of military force. Localized response could now be used to try to achieve objectives such as Vietnam. Military response would not escalate into a nuclear war

The Korean War of 1950-1953 presented Americans with a clear cut victory. After achieving victory in World War II, Americans felt that all American wars should be victories. When the Korean War became a stalemate, most Americans wanted to forget it. Yet the Korean War should not be called a defeat or "Forgotten War." The economic affluence and success of South Korea today compared to North Korea is a direct result of American action in June 1950. From a longer point of view the failure of Communism in the Soviet Union and other countries, and economic changes in China may be the results of the Korean War which acted as a catalyst by projecting the resolve of America and her allies to stop the spread of Communism.

The National Korean War Veterans Memorial has been erected in honor of those servicemen who gave their lives to stop the expansion of World Communism. In 1953 when hostilities ceased, it may have seemed that these men gave their lives in vain. The peace settlement at Panmonjon was not clear cut, and there was no victory. With the fall of Communism in the Soviet Union in 1991, their sacrifice in 1950-1953 may seem justified. General Omar Bradley, Chairman of the Joint Chiefs of Staff at that time, characterized the war as, "the wrong war, at the wrong time and in the wrong place." Had he lived to 1995 and witnessed the changes that have led to the dedication of this memorial, he might have changed his mind. This "Forgotten War" in Korea from 25 June 1950 until 27 July 1953, may have been the decisive conflict that started the collapse of Communism.

Chapter Two: American Military Policy In Post World War II Period

The victory of the United States and its allies over the Axis Powers in World War II created a United States confident of its own strength. The war and its devastating economic effect on former world powers formed a post war power vacuum into which the United States moved to consolidate its advantage. American overseas interests expanded and sought to create a peace on American terms. Economic well-being at home depended on an active foreign policy. Economic expansion, aided by limited competition from the other powers, continued as a central feature of post war foreign relations.

Concurrent with this economic expansion a new strategic theory developed that promoted a globalist diplomacy. To protect against military challenges in the post war, military planners selected defenses far beyond American borders. The U.S. thus selected bases throughout the world from which they could launch swift attacks.

While President Truman and his administration pushed for this global expansion, many conservative critics of this policy, such as Senator Robert Taft, urged America to reduce its overseas commitments and draw its defense line in the Western Hemisphere. This concerned many Americans who remembered the isolationist policies of the post World War I era that led to the rise of Adolph Hitler.

Not wanting to test the willingness of the American voters and Congress to pay for this global policy, the Truman administration stretched resources to cover this expanded policy. President Truman's new Secretary of Defense, Louis A. Johnson, produced a budget in May 1949 of $12.3 billion. This was a tremendous drop from the World War II budget of approximately $350 billion. The lion's share of this budget, $4.4 billion, went to the new Air Force to support forty-eight groups of which a third were targeted for strategic delivery of atom bombs. The Army, which employed the most people, received only $4.4 billion to support nine divi-

sions while the Navy received $3.9 billion for 238 warships.

The military were furious , and Johnson was disliked by all in uniform. President Truman, however, supported Johnson and stubbornly refused to listen to Pentagon pleas. General Eisenhower commented at the time that the results of this cutback would not show up until the United States got itself in serious trouble.

American military planners were acutely concerned about the military cutbacks. Since Germany and Japan had been stripped of their military forces, America was now responsible for their defense. When the Soviet threat developed after 1947, American planners had to make certain assumptions. One major assumption made by these planners was that the Soviet threat to Europe was greater than the Soviet threat to Japan.

By 1949, however, the political situation in the Far East began to change. In that year the Chinese Communists defeated Chiang Kai-shek and the American supported Nationalists. For the first time Japan and South Korea were threatened by a new and enormous Communist power.

The outcome of the defense debates in Congress in the late 1940s was to compromise on strategic planning and the use of military resources. American troops would be left to defend overseas bases in Europe and Asia , but the size and strength of units would be diminished. By early 1950 the National Security Council delivered to the President a document, NSC-68, that asked for a larger military budget to counter Soviet expansion. The Truman Administration, however, was not sure that this appeal would ever pass the budget conscious Congressional Representatives.

Strategic military thinking had changed in the years following World War II. The new Air Force was created and emphasis was placed on strategic bombing as an alternative to a large ground force and navy. The atom bombs at Hiroshima and Nagasaki had convinced many Congressmen that the day of the foot soldier was over. In spite of bombing studies of Germany in World War II that questioned the dominance of air power, Congressmen were still swayed by the savings in costs. Studies in cost analysis showed that air power at strategic locations throughout the world was a much cheaper investment by the taxpayer than stationing thousands of ground troops worldwide.

In Europe where 100,000 United States servicemen were stationed, units were able to meet full strength. In the occupation of Germany and Austria the American units were supplemented by the British and the French.

As a result of the Berlin Airlift of 1948, relations with the Soviet Union became tense. In 1949 the North Atlantic Treaty Organization was founded to meet the new Soviet threats. By supporting this treaty, initiated by the Europeans, President Harry Truman hoped that the United States could save money. The U.S. would give air and naval support while withdrawing some U.S. ground forces. Under this plan the Europeans were to furnish the bulk of the ground forces.

The Navy was particularly reduced in strength after World War II. By December, 1948 the Navy had cut from 3.3 million sailors to 428,000, and its 40 aircraft carriers were reduced to 11. The Navy tried to fight these cuts, and a rebellion almost ensued. In the summer of 1949, when Lewis Johnson became the Secretary of Defense, the Navy was cut even more to 238 warships and 7 carriers. At the same time the Marine Corps had dropped from 480,000 men in World War II to 86,000. These cuts were to be felt drastically when naval forces were needed in the early days of the Korean War.

Other military units throughout the world were greatly reduced in strength. In the United States in order to keep military posts open, many combat troops were used in housekeeping chores. In Coronado, California, for example, when the 5th Marines were alerted in June 1950 to go to Korea, men on housekeeping duties had to be collected throughout California to bring the unit up to strength. In Hawaii the Army made an exception in letting the 5th RCT have three infantry battalions and three artillery batteries. Even these were at two thirds strength. When the unit was called up to go to Korea in June 1950, replacements came from service units and staff of the large Army Headquarters at Fort Schafter and some volunteers from the Reserves. Even weapons in this combat unit were limited and many, such as recoilless rifles, had to be requisitioned from the Hawaiian National Guard.

The reduction limitations in funds for defense fell harder in the Far East on the Army than on the Air Force. Military units of each service were stretched from the Philippines, the Marianas and Okinawa to South Korea and across all Japan. Although the Allies occupied their former colonies in other parts of Asia after 1945, the responsibility for occupation of Japan and some of her former colonies fell to the United States.

The Air Force component (FEAF) of the Far East Theatre Command under General MacArthur (CINCFE) had the formidable task of defending an area of operations that stretched from Siberia to Indo -China. The largest unit of FEAF was the Fifth Air Force which had five major bases in Japan. South of Japan was the Twentieth Air Force with bases on Okinawa and Guam. Southwest of Japan covering the South China Sea was the Thirteenth Air Force in the Philippines. These commands maintained a high degree of vigilance. In spite of postwar strength reductions, these air forces in the Far East never lost their combat potential.

Most of the Army units occupied Japan and Okinawa. Another 45,000 soldiers were on occupation duty in South Korea. To cover all this territory the units were severely stretched. In Japan, Army occupation units were organized into four divisions under the Eighth Army. At full war strength an infantry division numbered 18,000 men. Budget restrictions authorized for Japan three divisions of 12,500 men and one division of 13,600 men. The larger authorization went to the 25th Division where two Afro-American units were kept at over combat strength. In order to keep all the other units at two-thirds strength, each infantry regiment and artillery battalion was reduced from three to two battalions and firing batteries respectively. Add to these reductions the normal shortages from transfers, sickness and other causes , and the final statistics for the troops of Eighth Army were about half strength for combat units and one fourth strength for service units.

Okinawa became a large base for bombers that could reach most targets in the Far East. Only one Army unit, the 29th Infantry Regiment, was stationed there. It consisted of three battalions on paper but like the Army units in Japan had been reduced to two-thirds strength. When the call came on 14 July, 1950 to go to Korea, the regiment was consolidated into only two battalions .

In Japan in the Spring of 1949 General MacArthur decided to relieve the Eighth Army of administrative duties and convert it into a combat-ready force. This decision was probably influenced by the rising threat of Communism in the Far East. MacArthur seemed to anticipate that it would be wise to have some combat trained Army units. Emphasis was placed on preparing for a defense of the beaches of Japan's northern island, Hokkaido, in the event of a possible invasion from the Soviet base on Sakhalin Island. The major deterrent would be atom bombs delivered to the Russians by U.S. Air Force bombers from Okinawa.

During the late 1940s little thought was given to a war on the Asian mainland or for that matter any limited war. Regular Army combat units were limited in their capabilities because they were not adequately armed. For example few American weapons in Japan were capable of knocking out the Soviet made North Korean T-34 tank. The American 3.5 rocket launcher, capable of knocking out any medium tank, was in very limited supply in the Far East. The supply of American medium tanks in the theatre was almost nonexistent. When the Korean War began and Russian -made T-34 tanks poured into South Korea and few means were available to stop them, a cry went up to get American medium tanks immediately. The Japanese at once rushed to the fought-over World War II Pacific islands to salvage American medium tank parts. Back at Japanese arsenals these parts were assembled into medium tanks and rushed to Korea. "Tankers" (soldiers to operate these tanks) were recruited from infantry units and by the first of August medium tanks were operating in most units in Korea.

In the overall strategic planning for the Far East after World War II no thought was given to any defense of Korea. The United States had never planned to occupy Korea. In September 1945 an American Army corps was rushed from Okinawa to occupy Korea south of the 38th Parallel. This line had been agreed upon as a demarcation line at the last minute by the Russians and Americans in the Summer of 1945 when Russian troops poured through Manchuria into Korea. By 1947 as this occupation mission of 45,000 men became a costly enterprise, Secretary of War, Robert P. Patterson, recommended that the American occupation end. Defense thinking at that time placed great stress on enemy neutralization by use of air power. The limiting of large ground operations would save the U.S. Government much money. A further study by the Joint Chiefs of Staff came to the conclusion that Korea was of little strategic value. The opportunity to withdraw American troops came in 1947 when the Russians proposed withdrawing their occupation forces from North Korea if the Americans would do the same in South Korea. Since South Korea was not part of the American strategic plan, the United States agreed to withdraw their occupation forces. By the Spring of 1949 most of these occupation forces on both sides of the 38th Parallel had been withdrawn.

By 1950 American strategic planning in the Far East was placing emphasis on the defense of Japan. Air power would be used to neutralize any invader who tried to land in Japan. Large strategic bases were built or enlarged throughout Japan and Okinawa; the Navy would defend the coastal waters, while the Eighth Army would act as a third defense force and halt any invader on the beaches of Japan.

In 1950 no thought was given by the Far East Command planners to the defense of any terri-tory outside Japan. The first line of defense was a vigilant Air Force whose mission was defense. In Japan the occupation troops of the Eighth Army were just being organized into combat units. At this time they were unprepared to wage any kind of war outside Japan. In all of the Far East only the Air Force had any capability of neutral-izing an enemy.

Chapter Three: Korea—Its History and Geography

Korea, a peninsula 575 miles long, averages only 150 miles in width except in the far north. For hundreds of years Korea was the stepping stone between the Asian continent and the islands of Japan. Separate in culture from China and Japan, Korea developed its own language and literature. Throughout history it was a battleground between the three great powers that surrounded her. Korea is mostly mountains. Two major ranges, the Taebacksan and the Nanqnimsan, run north to south and constitute the drainage divide between the eastern and western slopes. A spinal deviation from the central line makes the eastern slope steep, rockbound and devoid of plains and rivers. Smaller systems of mountains originating in the Taebaeksan and Nanqnimsan Ranges run parallel to each other in a northwest, southwest direction. Throughout history the mountain ranges have been a great barrier, particularly between the eastern and western sides of the peninsular as well as between the central and southern regions of the country. In the Korean War of 1950-1953 these mountains were of great importance in the strategy employed by the Communist forces.

The slopes of the mountains on the western side of the central line are more gentle and merge into fertile valleys. On the whole only 30 percent of Korea consists of gentle slopes, plains, and river basins. Similar slopes and plains are located also in parts of the southern region of the peninsula. Innumerable islands buffer the western and southern coasts in contrast to the east where the coast has few protective islands.

Five major rivers drain from the western and southern slopes of the mountains. The Amur (Amnokkang) in the north divides North Korea from China and flows into the Yellow sea. The Tuman River separates North Korea from Russia and flows into the Sea of Japan. The Naktong River, famous as the major defensive line of the American Army on the Pusan Perimeter in 1950, flows into the South China Sea. The Han and Kum Rivers, other defensive lines during the Korean War, flow into the Yellow Sea.

The fertile plains are distributed on the west coast along the rivers. These plains are Korea's major rice-producing regions and are Korea's most populated areas. The west coast is noted also for its extreme changes between high and low tide. These extreme changes became an important factor in the amphibious landing of American forces at Inchon in September of 1950.

The Korean climate is continental and runs to the extreme in cold and heat. Korea has an East Asian monsoon climate that in summer is very hot. The summer monsoon brings abundant moisture from the ocean and at times produces heavy rainfall. The summer humidity can become extreme and at times creates an environment that many American servicemen found difficult to overcome. In summer the numerous rice paddies and the use of human manure created breeding grounds for mosquitoes. Centuries of living in this environment made most Koreans immune to malaria, but to Americans it was a constant threat.

During the winter months continental high pressure air masses develop over inland Siberia from which strong, northwesterly winds bring dry, cold air into Korea. These winds cause much hardship. The Koreans, like the North Chinese, have learned to combat this extreme cold by developing radiant heating in their homes. In the average Korean house hot air is piped from the kitchen stove and passes under the floor of the major living space. Then it is vented up a chimney. For the Koreans a few arm fulls of rice straw is enough fuel to keep the clay floor warm at night. American servicemen, used to using wood for fuel, often substituted logs for straw in these stoves and sent whole houses up in flames.

From a military tactical point the cold, the rains, and the rice paddies greatly influenced the movement of modern mechanized armies. In summer the flooded rice paddies limited the movement of vehicles to roads only. When Korean dirt roads were weakened by rains, tanks and trucks often became mired in mud. On the other hand, once the paddies and roads became frozen, a mechanized force was able to maneuver. These physical characteristics greatly influenced the later campaign strategies of the warring armies between 1950 and 1953.

Koreans trace their history back many centuries and in many ways Korean history parallels Chinese history. The people of Ancient Chosen are recorded as "Eastern Barbarians" who spread north of the Yangtze River into Manchuria and the Korean Peninsula about 2300 B.C.

The dynasties of China greatly influenced Korea . When China was invaded by the Mongols in the 13th Century, Korea was also plagued by similar, consecutive Mongol invasions. When Mongol power declined from internal struggles in 1351 A.D., the state of Koryo in Korea succeeded in rising to power and eventually established the first state system. The establishment of institutions of Confucian learning was given a first priority, and in spite of power struggles, Confucianism influenced Korea for the next three centuries.

Japanese influence on Korea grew slowly. As early as the 12th Century, Japanese pirates made raids on Korea. Powerful feudal lords rose to power in Japan, and one, Hideyoshi, invaded Korea with his army in 1592. This incident marked the beginning of Japan's aggressive policy towards the peninsula.

During the 19th Century demands for commercial relations were made by Europeans on all three East Asian nations: China, Japan and Korea. After 1868 Japan joined the Europeans by trying to legitimize its aggression by demanding that Korea grant such privileges as extraterritoriality, exemption from customs duties, and legal recognition of Japanese currency.

After 1880 Korea was plagued by both China and Japan. China sent warships and landed 3000 soldiers. Japan consolidated its toeholds of privilege on the peninsula and landed troops of its own. Warfare between China and Japan ensued and was finally terminated with a peace treaty after the Sino-Japanese War in 1895. Despite Japanese brutality, the European powers in their apprehension over Russia's southward expansion from Siberia, welcomed overt Japanese aggression as a counter to the Russian threat. International recognition of Japan's aggressive policy gave the Japanese Army in Korea the burden of checking the Russian southward advance in the Far East. On February 8, 1904, Japan opened fire on the Russian Fleet

off Inchon, Korea and thus began the Russo-Japanese War (1904-1905).

By 1906 outright control of Korea by the Japanese began. Economic exploitation took place, and thousands of Japanese settled in Korea. Land expropriation was carried out, and Japanese farmers were settled on land seized from Koreans. Japan planned to meet her food deficit at home with increased rice production in Korea. This policy brought about a drastic decline in rice consumption by Koreans between 1912 and 1931.

Attempts to reestablish Korean independence failed, and most members of anti-Japanese movements were executed. A Japanese police state was established, and the police did their utmost to suppress spontaneous Korean activities. Judicial reforms were initiated that were designed to crack down on political offenses. In spite of these reforms secret Korean organizations took refuge in the mountains and from these bases attacked and destroyed many Japanese police stations and government buildings.

The beginning of Japan's war of aggression in Asia during the 1930s transformed Korea into a logistical base for continental warfare. In Korea emphasis gradually shifted from the manufacturing of food to the manufacturing of machines, chemicals and metals. As the war continued Korean manpower and materials were mobilized into the war effort. Korean labor was forcibly sent throughout the Japanese Empire. At the war's end 1.2 million Korean laborers worked in Japan and 4.1 million at home.

At the Potsdam Conference in July, 1945, after the defeat of Germany and several weeks before Japan's surrender, plans were made to have American troops occupy Korea. After the Russians entered the war against Japan in August, 1945 and moved against Manchuria and Korea, a hastily drawn, temporary, demarcation line at the 38th Parallel was established. Here the Russian and American forces would meet. Occupation of Korea by the Russian and American forces was supposed to be only temporary. In November, 1947 the United Nations voted to establish a temporary United Nations Commission on all of Korea to supervise elections for a representative National Assembly. The Russians, however, refused to accept this plan, effectively stopping free elections in North Korea.

In South Korea elections for the National Assembly were held in 1948. Syngman Rhee, who had been in exile in Hawaii, was elected Chairman. Shortly thereafter a constitution was adopted, and the Republic of Korea was proclaimed. In 1949 the United States recognized the Republic of Korea and withdrew most of its occupation troops.

North Korea formed the Democratic People's Republic of Korea which in reality was controlled by the Communist Party. Kim Il Sung, who had fought against the Japanese in Manchuria, became Premier. The Russians, who had agreed to withdraw their troops if the Americans did the same, had withdrawn their occupation forces by 25 December, 1948.

By July 1949 Russian and American troops had withdrawn, and now two Korean states existed. Much civil disorder occurred throughout South Korea. Many of the disturbances were instigated by North Korea in an attempt to overthrow the Rhee Government and replace it with a Communist one. Incidents occurred along the 38th Parallel, while much Communist inspired, guerrilla activity took place throughout South Korea.

The armed forces of the two Koreas were quite different. Americans, fearful that Rhee's army might attack North Korea, were reluctant to train and equip his forces beyond the role of a defense force. In North Korea, however, the Russians armed and equipped a large North Korean force. Over one-third of these North Koreans were combat veterans of the Chinese Communist Army who had returned from China after Mao's victory over the Chinese Nationalists in 1949.

Thus on the eve of the North Korean invasion two very different forces confronted each other. In 1950 the head of the American advisers to the South Korean Armed Forces was so uninformed about the true status of the North Korean Army, that he boasted that the South Korean Army was the best in Asia. The North Korean Forces, however, were not discouraged by this statement. On 30 June 1950 North Korean Forces shocked the world with their blatant invasion of South Korea.

Chapter Four: Outbreak—A Police Action

On Sunday 25 June, 1950, the world was shocked when 135,000 North Korean soldiers of the North Korean Peoples Army (NKPA) launched a cross-border invasion into South Korea. Was this deliberate, or had the North Koreans miscalculated America's intentions? Was Secretary of State Dean Acheson's statement concerning the exclusion of Korea from the U.S. defense perimeter in East Asia enough to have made the Soviet Union and China give their consent to this North Korean invasion? Whatever the misjudgments on both sides, on that date a brutal war began that lasted three years. More than 33,629 Americans were killed in action and 103,284 wounded.

The opposing sides were not evenly matched. The NKPA force consisted of seven assault infantry divisions, a tank brigade, an independent infantry regiment, a motorcycle regiment, three reserve divisions and five border constabulary brigades. The South Korean Armed Forces (ROKS) of 98,000 men were poorly equipped, un-deployed for combat and almost completely caught by surprise. Only one out of three regiments in each of the four ROK divisions defending the line on the 38th Parallel were prepared to fight, and they were easily overrun.

The main attack units of the NKPA came down the Ch'orwon Valley to the Uijongbu Corridor which led to Seoul. Leading the NKPA forces were Soviet -made T-34 medium tanks which found few obstacles to slow down their drive toward the South Korean capital.

The ROK defense varied in terms of leadership and location. Some units were quickly overrun and decimated. Other units, such as the

D. Randall Beirne, who served in six campaigns with K Company, 5th Infantry, from July 1950 through May 1951.

ROK 7th Division, aggressively counterattacked north of Uijongbu but could only slow the NKPA tanks. The ROK 2nd Division on the 7th Division's right tried to repulse the North Korean T-34 tanks with artillery and mortars. These tanks, however, crashed through the defending ROK infantry and moved on Uijongbu.

The first reports received by Washington on the 24th of June, 1950, from the American Ambassador, John J. Muccio, were sketchy. Muccio's cable to the State Department implied that he thought this was probably an all out attack by the North Koreans. As reports of the invasion started arriving from the United Nations Commission and newspapermen, a clearer picture of the NKPA attack appeared. Trygve Lie, the Secretary General of the United Nations, was furious because this invasion was a blatant attack against the United Nations. At 2 pm Sunday, June 25th, he called an emergency meeting of the U.N. Security Council.

At this Security Council meeting it was essential to adopt a resolution on the Korean crisis. Under the rules of the U.N. Charter a resolution could not pass if vetoed by one of the five great powers. At this meeting, however, the Soviet Deligate, Yakov Malik, who had veto power, was not in attendance. Six months earlier he had walked out of a Council meeting over the issue of seating Red China. He had not returned. Because there was no Soviet veto, the Security Council passed a resolution on the sudden North Korean invasion.

The resolution stated the following:
1. There should be an immediate end to hostilities.
2. The North Korean Army was to withdraw into North Korea.
3. Members were to support the U.N. in carrying out this resolution and refrain from helping North Korea.

On the evening of the same day President Harry Truman met with members of the State and Defense Departments. The U.N. Resolution on Korea was analyzed, and the American leaders agreed to support it. All agreed that the interests of the United States demanded such action.

The outbreak of hostilities took the United States Government completely by surprise. Soviet American relations had relaxed slightly after the Berlin Blockade in 1949. American strategists had felt that if Communist aggression was to take place, it would most likely take place in Europe. Engagement in Asia was not expected. Therefore American defenses worldwide had been predicated on the expectation of an all-

Members of the 1st Battalion of the Argyll and Sutherland Highlanders being oriented by a member of the 16th New Zealand Field Artillery, October 1950.

out attack by the Soviets that could be neutralized by American superiority in the delivery of nuclear weapons.

Suddenly American thinking had to change. American leadership felt that the loss of Korea to the Communists would be a definite threat to Japan. North Korean aggression was an overt action that was certain to arouse the American public. In addition the United Nations had reacted with resolution to save South Korea. In support of this resolution, any action taken by the United States would be sanctioned by the majority of other nations.

By 27 June the NKPA tank units had reached Seoul but were finding some ROK units putting up a stiff resistance. Leadership among top ROK officers, however, was inconsistent. Fear of the NKPA tanks spread panic among the South Korean soldiers and civilians who poured into Seoul from the north and attempted to leave the city over the Han River bridges. Confusion within the ROK Army set in. Orders came to blow the bridges. Most of the ROK Army with its heavy equipment was left north of the Han River. As a result, hundreds of soldiers and civilians died. This ill-advised decision destroyed the ROK Army. Of 98,000 men on the rolls of the ROK Army only 22,000 men were left to defend the area south of the Han River.

On the 26th of June General MacArthur sent a survey party under Brigadier General John H. Church to Suwon, south of Seoul, to determine what support could be given to the South Koreans. In Suwon Church talked with ROK military leaders and American officers in the Korean Military Advisory Group (KMAG). On the 28th he sent a message to General MacArthur that American ground troops would have to be committed in order to restore the boundary of the 38th Parallel.

A day later MacArthur flew to Suwon to talk to General Church and analyze the military situation himself. He was told that the ROK Army was badly disorganized and could only muster 25,000 men to fight south of the Han River. After driving up to the Han River and seeing thousands of refugees and disorganized ROK Army units, he concluded that the situation required the immediate commitment of American ground forces.

As the situation deteriorated, new directives to The Far East Command from the Joint Chiefs of Staff authorized MacArthur to send limited aid to Korea. The Air Force and Navy were ordered to support shipment of ammunition and other military supplies to Korea. They were also to help evacuate any American civilians from the peninsula. Combat and service troops were to protect the area around Pusan. The Navy and Air Force were authorized to attack military targets in North Korea.

Shortly after this directive went out, MacArthur returned to Japan. He immediately wired the Pentagon a report of his visit to Korea. He requested that an American regimental combat team be committed at once against the North Korean invaders. Two American divisions from Japan should be readied to counter attack and push back the NKPA forces. President Truman immediately approved sending one regiment to the combat zone After consulting with State and Defense Department officials, Truman authorized the sending of two divisions to Korea and the formation of a naval blockade of North Korea.

Task Force Smith

As soon as the decision was made by President Truman to send ground combat troops into Korea, General MacArthur went into action. The

24th Division under Maj. Gen. William F. Dean was the first division to go to Korea. Gen. Dean was to assume command of all United States Army Forces there. His mission was to delay the enemy advances as long as possible until other American Forces arrived in Korea. Dean immediately assigned a task force headed by Lt. Col. Charles B. Smith of two reinforced rifle companies and a field artillery battery to fly to Korea and move into a blocking position north of Osan. In the meantime the rest of the division was to be sent to Pusan by boat and to move to the front.

The concept violated all principals of military strategy. To slow the advance of a well trained NKPA force with a piecemeal attack invited disaster. American soldiers were being sacrificed to justify the bold political decision to stop the first major aggression by a communist force.

Smith's task force was made up of a mixed group of soldiers which reflected the Army as a whole. Many of the officers and noncommissioned officers were World War II veterans, and most had seen combat. A number of these officers were "career" Reserve Officers who had returned to military life after failure to adjust to the post World War II civilian world.

Among the enlisted men were a large number of underage enlistees who came from the poorest areas of the United States. In barracks life these soldiers had often been disciplinary problems. They were immature teenagers who often ended up in the stockade. When the war started, the stockades were emptied and these men joined their units. Ironically, once in combat, a number proved themselves good soldiers and even became noncommissioned officers.

Smith's force, composed of Company B and

Company C of the 21st Infantry Regiment, known later as Task Force Smith, was directed to dig into a position south of Suwon where the main highway to Seoul passed through a low saddle in a small ridge. About a mile to the rear Battery A of the 52nd Field Artillery Battalion under Lt. Col. Miller O. Perry placed their six 105 howitzers. Task Force Smith was soon to find out that they were not equipped with any real antitank devices such as antitank mines and 3.5 inch rocket launchers that could stop enemy medium tanks. In spite of rainy weather and inadequate supplies and preparation, however, the men felt confident that once the NKPA invaders knew that they had come up against Americans, they would slow down.

The NKPA in the meantime had been stopped at the Han River. In spite of the blown bridges, the North Korean troops rapidly repaired a railroad bridge and rushed their tanks across. ROK units put up only sporadic resistance. At Yongdungp'o the ROKs inflicted many casualties on the North Korean forces. Still by the 5th of July the main NKPA force led by tanks was heading south down the main highway to Osan.

The first contact that Task Force Smith had with this North Korean force was about 0745 on 5 July when a tank column approached. Through the gray sunrise Sgt. Loren Chambers yelled to 1st Lieutenant Philip Day, "Hey, look over there, Lieutenant. Can you believe?" Lt. Day made out a column of eight tanks. Sgt. Chambers said, "They are T-34 tanks that aren't going to be friendly."

When these North Korean tanks got within 700 yards of the dug-in American infantry, they were taken under fire by recoilless rifles and 2.36

23

Artillery during early stage of withdrawal, July 1950.

inch rocket launchers. These weapons were not effective in stopping the tanks. Only use of a 105 mm howitzer with HEAT ammunition stopped the two lead NKPA tanks. When the tank crews dismounted, a fire fight ensued and their crews were killed. Other tanks behind them kept on moving down the road to the American rear firing their 85mm cannon. In this very first ground skirmish with the enemy the American defense was penetrated.

After at least thirty-three North Korean tanks passed through the American defense and headed toward Osan, the defenders waited for almost an hour before a North Korean infantry truck convoy arrived. American mortar and machine gun fire immediately swept the column. The North Korean infantry dismounted and moved around the flanks of the defense position. By noon the enemy had reached high ground that dominated American defense positions on the west of the highway. At about the same time enemy infantry were enveloping the eastern flank of the American positions. Soon heavy

machine gun and mortar fire descended on the defenders.

By early afternoon the American defensive position became untenable. Colonel Smith, fearing being cut off, decided to withdraw. Although the method of withdrawing was the standard Army method of leapfrogging platoons, confusion in communication and coordination ensued, and Task Force Smith received its heaviest casualties. The dead and wounded were left behind along with many of the heavy weapons. All during the night of the 5th and morning of the 6th remnants from Task Force Smith began drifting into the 34th Regiment position north of P'yongt'aek. Since the North Koreans were slow to follow up this attack, some American stragglers were able days later to drift into Ch'onan, Taejon and points south. Overall Task Force Smith lost about 150 men killed, wounded, or missing.

The success of the North Korean units in their

first contact with the American Army made time even more important. Task Force Smith had started the delay. Other American units would now have to make sacrifices and continue to delay the NKPA until the American Army was able to build up forces to stop the North Korean drive. Geography acquired more importance. Rivers were excellent obstacles to slow down the NKPA tanks. Therefore General Dean and other American planners selected important terrain features where American units would fight.

Essential in carrying out a plan of defense in an area like Korea was good communication. Unfortunately communication systems in the American Army were poor. In use were radios of World War II vintage which could not maintain contact across the mountains. Telephone wires linking units were constantly cut by the thousands of refugees clogging the roads who used the wire to secure their luggage. In addition American tanks and trucks often cut the wire along the roads. These difficulties made communication a major problem in the American Army for most of the first year of the Korean War.

The failure of Task Force Smith to stop the North Korean Army sent a shock wave throughout America. Granting MacArthur's request for four more divisions would leave mainland America defenseless. Congress quickly added a one year extension to the recently expired Selective Service Act. In addition Congress authorized Secretary of Defense Louis Johnson to mobilize four divisions and two regimental combat teams from the National Guard. The Navy and Marine Corps called up an additional 86,000 men from the Reserve. Slowly America began to correct the military neglect of the preceding five years. The mobilization of manpower to stop the North Korean invasion was thus furnished by Congress. The failure of Task Force Smith had revealed the weakness of the post World War II Army. Now it was up to MacArthur to buy time until these additional forces arrived.

Delay

The big question was, "How could the Americans and ROKs delay the NKPA advance?" The key to slowing down the North Korean advance was to defend along the large rivers and key transportation hubs. If bridges were destroyed over large bodies of water, the enemy tanks could be slowed. In summer when the rice paddies were covered with water, tanks were limited to roads. At certain junctions where roads came together a good defense might stop the NKPA forces. The towns of Ch'onan and Taejon were key road junctions. The Kum River was the first large river south of the Han River, while at P'yongt'aek, a town 30 miles north of the Kum, an estuary of the Yellow Sea came up almost to the town and was an excellent barrier.

The next American unit in position to block the North Korean advance was the 34th Infantry Regiment of the 24th Division. The 1st Battalion moved to P'yongt'aek and the 3rd Battalion to Ansong, both north of the key road junction at Ch'onan. Somehow communications between these units and Regimental Headquarters broke down and confusion developed. At P'yongt'aek Lt. William Caldwell remembers trying to stop the lead North Korean T-34 tanks with 2.36 inch rockets. One tank lost its mobility and became a sitting target for his rocket launcher teams. This action was in vain. "The rockets were either duds or bounded harmlessly off the tank's armored sides," he said.

Enemy pressure on this defense position increased. While North Korean tanks were stopped at the blown bridge on the main highway, their infantry was able to cross a small

25

stream and spread out around the flanks of the American defensive position. When the Battalion Commander, Lt. Col. Harold B. Ayres, saw his unit being outflanked, he ordered a withdrawal. In the process disorganization set in among some units as they fell back to Ch'onan.

Confusion continued in the 34th Infantry Regiment. The 3rd Battalion at Ansong withdrew to Ch'onan to reinforce other units there. Immediately they were dispatched north towards P'yongt'aet from which the 1st Battalion had just withdrawn. The battalion had hardly moved three miles north of Ch'onan when they came under enemy fire. Disorder continued as men began to withdraw even when confronted by only a handful of enemy. Efforts were made by key officers to get these units back on position, but panic reigned as the battalion withdrew in ragged order to Ch'onan.

Col. Robert R. Martin relieved Col. Jay B. Lovless as Commander of the 34th Regiment. An experienced combat commander in Europe during World War II, Col. Martin was determined to defend Ch'onan. As NKPA tanks and infantry moved into town, Col. Martin moved up to be with his 3rd Battalion as they assumed the town's defense. In the process of trying to knock out a North Korean tank with a 2.36 inch rocket launcher, Col. Martin was killed. Infiltrating enemy soldiers soon caused more confusion among the defenders. In the process of withdrawing from the town many men of the 3rd Battalion became casualties.

During the early days of the war the weather had placed limits on the use of American air power. Not only did rain delay air strikes but early morning fog gave cover to the attacking North Koreans. On the ninth and tenth of July the sky cleared, and the Fifth Air Force struck

NKPA columns. A massive air strike of B-26s, F-80s and F-82s hit columns of tanks, half-tracks and trucks. This was possibly the greatest destruction in one day during the war of enemy armor and vehicles.

On July 13th General Walton H. Walker arrived from Japan as Commander of the Eighth Army and assumed control of all Korean operations. At this time the 25th Division was beginning to arrive from Japan and take up positions in central Korea. Pusan, with the best port facilities in Korea, became the main logistical base for all American forces in Korea.

After these first disastrous contacts with the enemy, Gen. Dean decided to use the Kum River as the 24th Divisions next line of defense. Successful defense of the Kum River and Taejon were essential to the American effort to delay the advance of the NKPA forces. The Kum was a natural defense against tanks, while Taejon was a central roadnet through which most North Korean tanks would have to pass. The river was from six to ten feet deep but had numerous sand bars across which attacking North Korean infantry could move. For the American defense the frontage to be defended was so great that enemy infiltration at night could not be prevented. For the first time the American Army was finding that the well trained North Korean soldiers could now resist American air strikes. The NKPA tanks and vehicles were concealed and camouflaged in the daytime and made most of their movements at night. The NKPA infantry had learned how to infiltrate American lines and establish roadblocks in the American rear. For the next year roadbound American units would find that the North Korean and later the Chinese were masters at infiltrating American defenses and establishing these roadblocks on their rear.

To defend the Kum River the 24th Division used two understrength regiments to cover an area that was almost impossible to defend. On the left was the 34th Regiment with its 3rd Battalion in defensive positions at Konju ,and its 1st Battalion placed approximately six miles south in a backup blocking position. Between them was the 63rd Field Artillery Battalion. Covering six miles west of Konju along the south bank of the Kum River was the 24th Reconnaissance Company. On the east was the newly arrived 19th Infantry Regiment under Col. Guy S. Meloy, a World War II combat veteran. Meloy placed his 1st Battalion along the Kum River at Taep'yong-ni and his 2nd Battalion to the rear of the 1st in a reserve position. Supported by two field artillery battalions, this regiment was placed so as to bear the brunt of the anticipated major North Korean attack on Taejon.

Disaster struck quickly. No communications existed between the line companies and headquarters in the 3rd Battalion, 34th Infantry. Sgt. Bill Menninger noted, "Communication was practically nil. Most radios didn't work, and the fact that the enemy was often between our headquarters and the rifle companies made it extremely hazardous to lay phone wires." Too many senior officers in the battalion had recently been evacuated for combat fatigue which limited the unit's experienced leadership. Rumors that North Koreans had crossed the Kum River two miles below, coupled with intensive enemy mortar fire caused panic among some of the units in the battalion. In the confusion Companies K and L had left their defensive positions while leaving only Company I remaining on position.

In the meantime the North Korean 16th Regiment made a night crossing through gaps in the defensive line of the 24th Reconnaissance

Company and swept over the positions of the surprised 63rd Field Artillery Battalion. Only the Service Battery of the Battalion survived this onslaught which destroyed ten guns and eighty vehicles and many men. The 1st Battalion in reserve tried to retake the artillery position, but by this time large numbers of the enemy had crossed the Kum River and quickly drove back this American unit. The 24th Division defensive position on the west was penetrated. NKPA forces were poised to attack Taejon from the west.

On the east the 19th Infantry was not faring well either. All day on the 14th enemy probing attacks were driven back. The enemy next tried attacks on the left flank and were driven back. Finally two days later under cover of darkness the North Korean 3rd Division found a gap on the battalion right flank. With heavy fire from artillery, tanks, mortars and small arms smashing into American defenses on the south shore, thousands of North Korean soldiers streamed across the river and established footholds . In spite of American gallantry, high casualties were suffered including the severe wounding of Col. Meloy. The battle to save Taejon was slowly drawing to a close.

General Walker needed two more days delay at Taejon to slow the NKPA forces in order to bring up on line two new American divisions which had just arrived in Korea, the 25th and 1st Cavalry. Dean decided to make a last stand in Taejon in hopes of delaying the NKPA. It was important to him also that he be there to keep up the morale of American soldiers as well as set an example for the leaders of the ROK Army to witness.

27

On the 20th of July the North Koreans assaulted Taejon by crashing into the defenders and then flanking them in the rear. Dean suddenly found himself as part of an antitank team. New 3.5 inch rocket launchers had just been airlifted from the United States. With this new weapon General Dean was able to knock out several NKPA tanks. As time went on, however, others just passed by him. "There was nothing we could do to stop it.— As that last tank passed I banged away at it with a .45, but even then I wasn't silly enough to think I could do anything with a pistol. It was plain rage and frustration— just Dean losing his temper."

In spite of a few local successes against this North Korean onslaught, by late afternoon on the 20th the overall situation in Taejon looked hopeless to Dean. He reluctantly initiated the withdrawal of his forces. The NKPA, however, had encircled the city, and withdrawing American units ran into a number of roadblocks. As the

North Korean forces tightened the noose around the city, many American units were forced to escape by abandoning the roads and climbing into the hills. According to Sgt. Daniel Cavanaugh, Medical Company 34th Regiment, "We were outmanned, outgunned, outtanked, and outflanked." Despite the mass confusion of the American withdrawal about seventy-five percent of the Taejon defenders managed to survive and eventually returned to American lines.

The capture of Taejon was a great victory for the North Koreans. Grudgingly, Americans were forced to respect NKPA forces and the fighting ability of its soldiers. By the end of the month the 34th Regiment had only 184 men remaining of the original 2,000 who had left Japan. Most of its men had been killed, wounded, or missing, and

Korean Refugees, Summer, 1950.

several weeks later the regiment was disbanded. The United States came to realize that in this war there would be no quick victory but a long brutal conflict.

Chapter Five: Enemy Pressure and Crisis Stand or Die

The last ten days in July and the first week in August 1950 were crucial in America's attempt to delay the NKPA long enough for the Eighth Army to establish a foothold in Korea. Both sides were racing against time. The North Koreans made an all out effort to complete their conquest before the American buildup. The Americans rushed in every available man to stem the North Korean tide.

For a period of seventeen days in July the 24th Division had been in constant contact with the NKPA. Finally on 22 July the division turned over the front line positions at Yongdong to the newly arrived American 1st Cavalry Division. To the right of this division was the newly arrived American 25th Division at Sangju. Both of these new divisions engaged in fierce struggles during their first few days of combat. Both were deployed west of the Naktong River, and over the next week would slowly withdraw to the east side of the river.

Time was on the side of the Eighth Army. American control of the air and sea allowed it to replenish its forces faster than the NKPA. Still the addition of two fresh American divisions could not stop the aggressive North Korean onslaught. Much of the American failure to stop this onslaught can be attributed to American dependence on roads and limited training of infantry in mountain warfare. In spite of American air superiority which destroyed many of the NKPA tanks and other vehicles, the North Korean soldier was an excellent mountain fighter.

At some points fresh American troops even attacked elements of the NKPA in order to slow them down. One of the first such attacks took place at Yechon on July 20th. The attackers were the 3rd Battalion, 24th Regiment of the newly arrived American 25th Division. The regiment was the only Afro-American unit in Korea at this time. It was looked upon with suspicion by most Americans who had biased attitudes toward Afro-Americans in general. This counter attack was successful and was instrumental in slowing down the pace of the NKPA offense in this area.

The Eighth Army, struggling to slow the NKPA, was hampered by the thousands of refugees who clogged the roads and railroads as they fled south. To Lieutenant Uzal Ent, "It seemed like everybody in the country was trying to go south. From one position we were on we overlooked a railroad, and we would see these trains coming through with the outside of the cars alive with people. They were hanging on the sides, on the roofs. They were jammed in over the couplings. And there were South Korean soldiers mixed in with the civilians." This confusion was beneficial to the enemy and often made the infiltration of the defensive positions of American soldiers possible.

Enemy aggressiveness continued to press the newly arrived American divisions. At Yongdong the NKPA 3rd Division penetrated the defensive positions of the 8th Cavalry Regiment of the 1st Cavalry Division. Attempts by the 5th Cavalry Regiment of this division to counterattack and help the 8th had limited results. On the morning of the 25th the enemy poured through gaps between units of the 1st Cavalry Division and infiltrated the columns of hundreds of Korean refugees. Although American troops were able to inflict enormous casualties on the enemy, the Ameri-

Members of a 3.5 Rocket Launcher Team, 24th Regiment, 25th Division Until the arrival of these launchers, few North Korean T-34 tanks were stopped.

can defense became untenable, and the 1st Cavalry Division was forced to withdraw.

To the east the 25th Division was having many of the same problems as the 1st Cavalry Division. At Sangju Division Headquarters sent one infantry regiment, the 27th, to the west to block the Poun-Hwanggan Road. As the 1st Battalion moved forward to make contact with the enemy, they met the forward elements of a North Korean division head on and became heavily engaged. With the help of air strikes American forces were able to knock out most of the attacking North Korean tanks. Despite heavy casualties the enemy was still able to infiltrate between the two roadbound American divisions. When the defensive positions of both divisions then became untenable, both units decided to withdraw. General Walker, an experienced combat commander under General Patton in Europe in World War II, was an aggressive, offense oriented soldier. When the two new divisions under his command both kept withdrawing steadily and not defending as aggressively as he had hoped, he was bitterly disappointed. On July 29th he issued his famous "stand or die" order. This order has been criticized because many men at the front attributed enemy success more to the paucity of numbers of the American defenders than to any weakness in

fighting ability. On receiving the command, an old sergeant in the 34th Infantry remarked, "Fight to the death? What does he think we've been doing for a month!" Often the enemy had merely bypassed American defenders and caused confusion with roadblocks to their rear. In any case Walker needed to build up the morale of the Eighth Army. As time goes on history may show that General Walker's greatest contribution to the war was his tenacious defense in the early days of the Korean War.

The Southern Threat to Pusan

While most of the Eighth Army was concentrated on the blockade of the NKPA forces north and northeast of Taegu, the 6th Division of the NKPA made a rapid wide swing south to the Strait of Korea and then east to outflank the Americans. The enemy understood the terrain well and knew a dash along the coast from the west would avoid the obstacle posed by the Naktong River until just outside Pusan. By July 25th the North Korean 6th Division was at Sunch'on, poised to take Chinju which was only 55 miles from Pusan. As guerrilla units in the mountains joined the advancing North Koreans, atrocities were committed on most South Korean officials and panic spread.

When the Eighth Army realized the enormity of the goal of the NKPA forces to capture Pusan and encirclement of the Allied forces, General Walker had to make a quick decision. His solution was to send the understrength, exhausted 24th Division posthaste to block this new enemy envelopment in the south. By July 26th the division minus the 21st Regiment, moved into a defensive area that covered a front of 30 miles from Koch'ang to Chinju.

The situation was critical. Newly arrived units were urgently needed to help the 24th

Division cover the front. Among those arriving were the 1st and 3rd Battalions of the 29th Infantry Regiment from Okinawa with 400 brand-new recruits. These recruits had just arrived in the Pacific and had never trained with the unit. They had been promised ten days of intensive field training before being committed to action, but the unit was immediately rushed to the front and attached to the 19th Infantry of the 24th Division.

Both battalions were almost immediately sent out from Chinju in different directions. The 3rd Battalion had orders to move to Hadong and block the Hadong-Chinju Road. The 1st Battalion had instructions to relieve the 1st Battalion, 19th Infantry, at Anui, 40 miles to the north, and block roads from the west.

Little did these battalions realize that they were the only forces in position to block the advances toward Pusan of the North Korean 4th and 6th Divisions in Southwest Korea. Nor did they know that in one day the two battalions would suffer 618 casualties.

The 3rd Battalion moved west from Chinju and by early 27 July were three miles east of Hadong. When the battalion was almost on top of Hadong Pass, they were surprised as they ran head-on into the advancing North Korean 6th Division. The North Koreans attacked this very green, inexperienced American unit with fury. Most of the experienced American commanders were killed or wounded as the unit suffered 50 percent casualties. All the battalion's heavy weapons and vehicles were lost. Later in September when American forces retook Hadong, the bodies of 313 Americans of this unit were recovered.

Men of the 5th RCT, 25th Infantry Division ready to be taken to the rear, August 1950.

Artillery withdrawal, Summer 1950.

The 1st Battalion moved north towards Anui and ran head-on into an attack by the NKPA 4th Division. Although Company B of the 29th Infantry was able to relieve Company A of the 19th Infantry, they both were cut off by elements of the North Korean division which had set up roadblocks around Anui. Company A was forced to abandon their trucks and withdraw on foot through the hills to the southeast. Company B with Company D of the 29th Infantry remained in Anui with some South Korean policemen as two columns of North Koreans, one 300 men strong , the other of 200 men, attacked the town from different directions. After constant street fighting and hand to hand combat throughout the burning town during the day, the Americans withdrew to the hills surrounding the town. After several days only half the men of these two companies had escaped through the enemy lines.

For the next two days pressure on the 24th

Division from the two North Korean Divisions caused a gradual withdrawal of American forces. The 19th infantry and the few remaining soldiers of the 34th Infantry withdrew back towards the Naktong River. The 1st Battalion, 29th Infantry when cut off near Chinju, was forced to withdraw on foot to safety by means of a mountain trail. Pfc. Leonard Korgie of L Company, 34th Infantry, describes how soldiers felt at that time:

"When we drove into the Pusan Perimeter, you never in your life saw a more beat -up bunch of soldiers. God, we were tired. We had no rest or letup anywhere on the road. The gooks had kept on our tails. The heat was atrocious. All I wanted to do now was drink water, any kind, anywhere I could find it. Rice-paddy water caused searing and bloody dysentery."

The situation for the next several days was fluid. The North Korean 6th Division pushed hard to reach Masan before enough American

pered by the terrain. The ROK units had limited firepower, so the conflict between the two Korean Armies became an infantry contest.

Initially the Pusan Perimeter gave the Eighth Army a continuous line of troops with few open flanks. However, the extreme unit frontages were to become a major tactical problem for most of the first year of the war. But this tenuous line was enough to detect any large breakthrough by the enemy. The dominance of the American Air Force prevented any major enemy buildup. Thus enemy attacks were piecemeal, and major breakthroughs were prevented during the forty-five days of the perimeter.

The wide frontages, however, did not preclude enemy units from infiltrating at night through American defensive positions. American air superiority dictated that most North Korean attacks would occur at night. Visibility by the defense was limited, and the wide frontages encouraged unit isolation. At this stage the enemy had a psychological advantage over the defenders. In spite of obstacles like the Naktong River, small units of the enemy would cross at fords under cover of darkness and infiltrate between American units.

Official statistics show that as fresh American units started arriving in Korea, the United Nations combat forces soon outnumbered the enemy, 92,000 to 70,000. These figures, however, can be misleading. Darkness had a tendency to equalize forces, because observation by the

Crew members of a 105mm howitzer, (L) Sgt. Wagner and Cpl. Briggs.

57th Recoiless Rifle Team, 1950.

defenders was limited. Americans were primarily daylight warriors who by August were dependent on observation and communication. At this time Allied air superiority had forced the NKPA to become an infiltrating, nighttime infantry force.

At night the American defenders were too often at the mercy of their North Korean attackers. American soldiers were green and had limited experience in night fighting. Lt. Harry Maihafer tells the story of one Sergeant DiHerrera who habitually checked his squad in its defensive position all night long. His method of forcing his men to stay awake was to creep up to a foxhole and try to grab a soldiers' weapon. One night a nervous, dozing, automatic rifleman saw this figure getting close and instinctively fired a burst at it. Unfortunately, he badly wounded Sergeant DiHerrera.

The Marines went through this same experience in night fighting during the early days of the war. Pfc. Fred Davidson, 5th Marines, remembers men forgetting the password, "That night the password was, "Mutton," the countersign, "Tallow." Over on my left Sergeant Ryder yelled, "Mutton!" No answer. He yelled again, "Mutton! Mutton, Goddamn you!" This was followed by the sound of a rifle stock hitting flesh and bone. Someone let out a long, loud moan, like he was really hurt. Silence again. Damn, I thought, the gooks are all around us and Ryder just got himself one. I was scared—I raised my carbine and squeezed the trigger. Over to my rear someone else pulled off a round. Next it was someone to my front. Then the firing pinballed from place to place all over the hill. The onesided firefight continued hot and heavy for a little while longer." Later he found out that Sergeant Ryder had hit a wandering young Marine who had forgotten the password. This example and others illustrate the problems that inexperienced American soldiers faced when fighting the enemy at night.

Task Force Kean

An old military maxim says, " The best

defense is an offense." Following this rule General Walker decided in early August to begin the first big offensive of the war in order to build up the confidence of the American soldier. Termed Task Force Kean after 25th Division Commander Maj. Gen. William B. Kean, this force consisted of the 25th Division plus the fresh 5th Regimental Combat Team and 1st Marine Brigade. (The 5th Marine Regiment reinforced)

The mission was assigned to four regiments. The 35th Infantry Regiment of the 25th Division would attack west along the north Masan Road to Much'on-ni. The 5th RCT would attack from the south road at Chindong-ni and link up with the 35th at Much'on-ni. The 5th Marines were to attack along the coast road from Chindong-ni to Kosong and Sachon. The 24th Regiment was to secure the area behind the attacking forces. In the last phase of the attack the 5th Marines from Sachon were to linkup in Chinju with the 5th RCT and the 35th Infantry attacking west from Much'on-ni.

As in most wars, actions often do not follow the original plan. In this case Task Force Kean met the North Korean 6th Division head-on as it was attacking toward Masan. In the ensuing confused struggle each side at times surprised the other and each inflicted heavy casualties.

The Eighth Army was unaware that several thousand members of the North Korean 6th Division had infiltrated the great hill mass of Sobuk-San between the north and south route to Masan Small enemy units were known to be in the area. These were to be eliminated by the 24th Regiment. This area, however, was honey-combed with old mines. The mine shafts made excellent bunkers for the defending North Koreans. In addition the approach roads to the

mines were from the west with few from the east. The mountains here were steep. It took units three to four hours just to climb the 60 degree slopes to the ridges.

The two armies fought each other under conditions of extreme heat. Korea that summer experienced a drought during July and August. Temperatures at times reached a scorching 120 degrees in the early days of this offensive. Americans suffered as much from the heat as from the enemy during the first days of this attack. Lt. John Cahill, Company G, 5th Marines, remembers clearly how they suffered from the heat. "The heat just baked us. Then the water ran out. At one point some people went down with canteens and came back with rice-paddy water. As a result we all ended up with worms. Hell, in that oven we were so thirsty we'd have drunk anything."

Initially the operation moved slowly because the enemy at Sobuk-san was at times able to impede American units massing along the coast road at Chindong-ni. On August 2nd units of the 2nd Battalion of the 5th RCT were rushed to Chindong-ni almost immediately after landing in Korea from Hawaii. While the 27th Regiment held the front line west of Chindong-ni, the 2nd Battalion of the 5th RCT moved in behind them onto a finger of Sobuk-san. For the next four days a constant fight ensued between the North Koreans on Sobuk-san and American units trying to keep open the main line of communication along the coast road to support Task Force Kean.

These conflicts were the first stages of the head-on collision between Task Force Kean and the attacking North Korean 6th Division. By August 7th the enemy had moved around Chindong-ni to the high ground east of the town and established a roadblock on the main road to Masan. With help from the 24th Infantry and a battalion of the 5th Marines the roadblock was cleared. Finally on August 9th the task force in the south believed that the main line of communication had been cleared and only a few enemy remained on the high ground around Sobuk-san. The 5th Marines and 5th RCT were now prepared to attack to the west.

On the northern route at the Notch between Chinju and Masan the 35th Regiment started the offensive on August 7th. The 2nd Battalion led the assault and after heavy fighting against stiff resistance they secured the high ground just east of Much'on-ni by nightfall. To the south the Sobuk-san area between the northern and southern roads to Masan were covered by the 24th Regiment. Here only a few small enemy forces were thought to exist. Intelligence had not determined the extent to which the Sobuk-san mass had been infiltrated by the enemy. The 24th Infantry, assigned to sweep the area, found themselves confronted by a very large enemy force.

The 5th Marines moved rapidly into the attack on the 9th of August and by the 11th had reached the town of Kosong. This American unit suffered more from the extreme heat than from the enemy. Just outside of Kosong, Marine Cosairs and Air Force F-51s destroyed a large convoy of North Korean vehicles. The enemy resistance was so weakened by this attack that fresh Marine units continued to push on unopposed until they were a few miles from Sach'on.

Just outside of Sach'on on August 12th, the North Koreans selected a narrow valley as a place to ambush the attacking Marines. This surprise was only a partial success. Alert Marines supported by Corsairs were able to control

the hills around the valley by late afternoon. Early the next morning the enemy counterattacked , inflicting heavy casualties on one company, but the Marines were able to retain their defensive positions. Subsequently the 5th Marines received orders to return to Chindong-ni to help extricate the 5th RCT which had been cut off by enemy units and needed assistance.

The central force of Task Force Kean encountered the most violent fighting and experienced the most casualties. On August 10th the 1st and 2nd Battalions of the 5th RCT had jumped off in the attack to link up with the 35th Infantry at Much'on-ni. The 1st Battalion, after some mix-up in directions, had eventually attacked along the main road leading to Much'on-ni and had encountered the enemy in Pongam-ni. The 2nd Battalion followed and by the end of the day both battalions controlled only part of the ridges that dominated the highway leading to Much'on-ni.

In spite of limited control of the highway that left Pongam-ni and went over a narrow pass to Much'on-ni, Col. Ordway, the Commanding Officer of the 5th RCT, decided to push his 3rd Battalion through the pass as quickly as possible. The entire battalion mounted vehicles and dashed through the pass. Enemy fire was light and other than having a few vehicle tires shot up, the entire battalion went through the pass unscathed.

Simultaneously artillery support for the force moved into the area around Pogam-ni. The 555 Field Artillery Battalion assumed positions on the east side of a flowing stream. The 90th Field Artillery Battalion of 155mm howitzers emplaced on the west side of the stream. A mile east of Pogam-ni elements of the 159th Field Artillery battalion took positions. By the evening of the 11th the entire valley around Pogam-ni was covered with artillery and regimental trains.

The 3rd Battalion moved forward to the railroad line near Song-dong. Here they linked up with the 35th Infantry. The battalion then followed the railroad tracks as they moved up Chinju Pass towards Chinju. The battalion moved in columns by companies with the battalion commander in the center of the column in a jeep bumping along over each tie. Suddenly the lead company encountered a railroad tunnel that was full of equipment of a North Korean battalion. Several guards, who had been left to guard the equipment while their unit was out attacking other American units, were caught by surprise. These guards refused to surrender and died defending this tunnel.

The battalion moved on up the railroad tracks through Chinju Pass to the highground overlooking Chinju. Here they dug in for the night. Early the next morning the men of K Company noticed what seemed to be leafy trees moving up toward the defensive positions of Company I. The men of K Company opened fire immediately on the attackers- men of a North Korean company who had tree branches strapped to their backs- who panicked and fled. One Lieutenant of K Company was reminded of Shakespeare's "MacBeth" where the prophecy of the play was about a castle assaulted by men who had tree branches attached to them (Birnam Wood).

While this unit of the 5th RCT was active close to its Chinju objective, more activity was taking place in the regiment's rear. On the night of August 10th the North Koreans attacked the 1st Battalion and artillery units in Pongam-ni. Enemy mortar and artillery fire landed all around them. Those units stationed to defend the river bed suffered excessive casualties because of the rock fragments thrown up by the detonation of this incoming artillery and mortar fire. At the height of this conflict the commanders of both the 1st Battalion, 5th RCT, and the 555FA Battalion were wounded. When daylight came American air strikes were able to drive the enemy back into the hills.

The Eighth Army began to pressure General Kean to speed up his attack. The Marines were having great success on their route, while the 5th RCT was moving too slowly. In response General Kean ordered Col. Ordway to send the 2nd Battalion and the 555FA Battalion through the pass northwest of Pongam-ni to join the 3rd Battalion outside Chinju.

In darkness the 2nd Battalion and one battery of the 555FA Battalion moved through the pass. This unit moved rapidly and lost communication with the regiment. The rest of the regiment at Pongam-ni lined up in a column and prepared to traverse the pass at daybreak.

Under cover of darkness before dawn on the morning of August 12th, the North Koreans attacked the unprotected artillery and trains of the 5th RCT from all sides. Lt. Bill Motley was one of the survivors of this attack. He remembers what happened as he crossed the highway bridge over a dry river bed. "I received heavy fire from the rice paddies. Several of us went over the side of our vehicle into the riverbed. I landed on my tailbone and was helped to cover at the river bank by a black 2nd Lieutenant." (This was Lt. Clarance Jackson, the only Afro-American Lieutenant on record at that time to command white troops. Jackson's assignment had been made a year and a half before President Truman integrated the Eighth Army in October 1951.)

At first light on August 12th the NKPA units noticed that they were receiving less small arms fire from Pongam-ni. Since all three of the infantry battalions were fully engaged a number of miles west of the artillery or through the pass, few infantry units were available to protect the artillery and trains. The resulting NKPA attack was almost a massacre. Enemy armor approached unopposed and fired at point blank range directly into the 555FA Battalion emplacements. Many artillerymen became infantrymen and gallantly defended their guns. In spite of this brave stand the 555FA Battalion lost eight of its 105mm howitzers and the 90th FA Battalion lost six 155mm howitzers. Together these two units had about 190 men killed and 140 wounded during this engagement.

On August 13th Task Force Kean received orders to return to their original lines. With the help of close air support from F-51s and Marine Corsairs, the task force withdrew. Most of the 5th RCT withdrew through the 35th Infantry on the northern route to Masan.

To the survivors of this conflict the name of the battle is known as "Bloody Gulch." Historians may argue over the losses and justify them in light of the success of an offense that stopped the enemy and hurled it back if only for a short time. Some of those who survived had other conclusions. To Master Sergeant Richard F. Lewis , a survivor of the 555FA Battalion and a thirty year professional soldier, "Nobody factored Murphy's Law into the equation. If it can go wrong, it will go wrong."

For the rest of August and early September the 25th Division withstood continuous assaults by the North Koreans. On August 17th the NKPA tried to sweep over the 35th Infantry positions but were driven back. Through an opening in an adjacent ROK unit several thousand North Korean soldiers infiltrated and hastily established roadblocks in the rear of the 35th. Quick action by the 27th Infantry Regiment in a savage counterattack in conjunction with a valiant defense by the 35th Infantry virtually destroyed the NKPA 6th and 7th Divisions.

For the rest of the month of August the 24th Regiment and 5th RCT resisted North Korean attacks along the Hamen-Chindong-ni line. From their highground fortresses on the heights of Sobok-san the North Koreans continued to attack the American defenders. The peaks fought over received names from the defenders such as Battle Mountain, Napalm Hill, Old Baldy and Bloody Knob. One survivor claimed that Battle Mountain changed sides nineteen times during August. Many heroes were involved in these battles. Msgt. Melvin Handrich, C Company 5th RCT, received the Congressional Medal of Honor for his valiant action in defending one of the peaks. A badly wounded acting Company Commander in B Company, 5th RCT refused to be evacuated on another defense of a peak. His men refused to withdraw and fought off enemy counterattacks.

According to David K. Carlisle, a former lieutenant in the Afro-American 24th RCT, "Without a doubt, the hardest fighting the 24th had to endure took place—in the remarkable defense of Battle Mountain, the key geographic feature of the Pusan Perimeter. The enemy threw wave after unrelenting wave in the effort to dislodge the US from the highest peak. The regiment took and retook the same ground 19 times in 30 days and nights. They suffered more than 500 casualties. Conditions were unimaginably harsh. — Published reports reveal that squads were often forced to share meals, consisting of a single large can of corned beef hash and a single large can of peaches per squad with little, if any drinking water."

Members of the 24th Division, Pusan Perimeter, having chow.

Several times the enemy almost broke through the 24th Infantry's defensive positions. Despite these hardships, the men of the 24th Regiment held on to their positions and the NKPA was never able to successfully hold Battle Mountain. At great cost these men and others of the 25th Division completed their mission: to block the fierce attacks of the NKPA force in the southern approaches to Pusan.

Forty-Five Days

The defense of the Pusan Perimeter lasted a total of forty-five days. During this period most of the fighting was at night. Days were quiet and few enemy were seen. Men lounged around and relaxed. Many of these daylight hours were used to build bunkers and lay barbed wire and antitank mines. Initially men dug foxholes on their defensive positions, but as time went on these holes became deeper and deeper. After several weeks they evolved into bunkers.

Patrolling is a key part of any defense. Most

Americans preferred day patrols that would go out far enough from the main line of resistance to try and find enemy positions. Night patrols were necessary but disliked. Americans prefer to be day fighters. Often American night patrols ran headfirst into North Korean attacks or patrols probing the American lines.

Americans learned rapidly how to conduct patrols. Initially their patrols would move down roads with men in columns on both sides and commanders in the middle. Robust lieutenants or sergeants with bars or stripes gleaming in the sunlight too often would walk down the center of the road. In the early days of the war these leaders became instant targets. An enemy soldier with a "burp" gun would suddenly rise up out of a rice paddy and blast the conspicuous leader.

Nighttime was dreaded by most American soldiers. Too often some outposts or front line units would be overrun by infiltrating North Koreans. Some American prisoners would be

41

killed without any mercy. A few might survive. One lucky prisoner was Pfc Jack Carter, C Company 23rd Regiment, who had a North Korean officer put a pistol to his head, jump on his back, and demand to be carried piggyback across a shallow river. Carter felt this was one of the most humiliating things he had ever done and was tempted to pitch the North Korean into the water. Fortunately his better judgment prevailed and he lived to be rescued several days later by American tanks on a patrol.

Historians have criticized the system of discipline in the American Army citing the lack of discipline in the family as a cause. Admittedly in the early stages of the war keeping men awake at night was a major task of squad and platoon leaders. Night after night lieutenants and sergeants constantly moved about to insure that no one was asleep. When an enemy attack suddenly came at night, the attackers were driven off because the American defenders were awake. Soldiers quickly realized the importance of self-discipline. Other areas where the soldiers learned self-discipline were in the prevention of malaria and dysentery. Soldiers soon learned to cover-up to guard against mosquitoes and to use Halizone tablets in their drinking water. By watching the examples set by experienced veterans, and developing self-discipline after observing the tragic results when proper procedures weren't followed, the young American recruits quickly turned into outstanding combat soldiers.

Most of the area in front of the defensive positions had been laid waste. The villages in front of the positions had all been abandoned. Often the stench of decaying cows permeated the American positions. Often decaying bodies of Korean civilians and North Korean soldiers lay along the roads and in the abandoned rice paddies. These Korean civilians were the victims

of the crossfire and air attacks that had taken place in the early days of the war.

In spite of the monotony that characterizes any war, soldiers found means to break the monotony. In August the left-most units on the Pusan Perimeter were from the 5th RCT who covered the area up to the coast. A most welcome sight to this unit was an American destroyer anchored offshore. The Navy wanted North Korean "burp guns" for souvenirs, and the Army wanted ice cream. Every evening a naval launch would come to shore and trading would take place.

During the early months on the Pusan Perimeter a number of South Koreans attached themselves to American units. Cutting hair was a service needed by most American units. Thus some Korean barbers found a new home in an American unit. When Eighth Army broke out of the Pusan Perimeter and moved into North Korea, many of these barbers went north with the unit. When cold weather arrived, however, along with the Chinese, many of these barbers found their fingers did not function in cold weather and returned to South Korea.

The abandoned villages in front of the defensive positions were daylight attractions for footloose bored soldiers. The lucky soldiers were those defending the low ground near these villages. Each village had deep wells full of cool water. During the hottest weather soldiers would sneak down to these villages. One would climb down into the well to cool off, while the others would keep guard. These soldiers had to be careful, however. Once in a while they would find that the North Koreans had stuffed a dead body down a well.

The defense of the Pusan Perimeter had its

problems. Every foot of the front could not be covered by small arms fire. Usually these fronts were covered only by artillery fire. Lt. Carl Schmidt, an artillery forward observer with the 1st Cavalry Division, remembers sitting with his team on top of a hill at the front during the night. He had no infantry in front of him. His mission was to call in artillery fires all night long to make the enemy think the area was defended by infantry. Lt. Ralph Hockley of the 37th Field Artillery was also on an FO mission similar to Schmidt. He was quietly sitting on a hill at night on the front with only four infantrymen to guard him and a phone connecting him to his battery. He remembers that "Suddenly, the phone rang. Riiiiiing! This infuriated the hell out of me. If the North Koreans didn't know where I was before, they knew now." He told the Lieutenant who called that he didn't have to ring the phone. The Lieutenant at the battery replied "Don't tell me you're afraid! This is your career. You're Army officers. Combat is what you're in the Army for."

History seldom tells about the boredom and monotony that go with every war. Soldiers count the days until they will go into reserve or the war will end. The defenders of the Pusan Perimeter were no different than soldiers in other American wars. When they had to fight, they fought bravely. The forty-five day pause gave the Eighth Army time to build a fighting team before it could begin a major offensive. The front line soldier was now protected by a smaller front to cover and an Air Force that put constant pressure on the remnants of the NKPA. This disciplined soldier who broke out of the perimeter in September to dash forward to link with the Marines was quite different from the recruit who first came on line in early August.

Naktong Bulge

All during the month of August the NKPA made aggressive piecemeal attacks hoping to penetrate the Eighth Army perimeter. Their first attack towards Masan failed. Their next big attack on August 8-18th was made by the North Korean 4th Division through the Naktong Bulge toward Miryang. In spite of surprise and local successes along the Perimeter, the NKPA never made a major penetration. One reason for their failure was their inability to concentrate large sustained forces because American air power was so effective. This forced the NKPA attacks to be piecemeal and limit the depth of any penetration of American defenses.

After Task Force Kean the next big challenge to the Eighth Army was the battle of the Naktong Bulge. Here the Naktong River makes a wide semicircular loop. The 24th Division was given the responsibility of defending the river front for thirty-four miles. The wide frontages plus shortages in unit strengths left many areas along the river unprotected by infantry fire. The defense of the river of eight and a half miles at the bulge was given to three companies of the 3rd Battalion, 34th Regiment.

The first successful river crossings by the North Korean 4th Division were made by lightly armed units on August 5th. They easily infiltrated and moved two miles to the rear. At this time the regimental reserve, the 1st Battalion, 34th Infantry, counterattacked. Company A under Capt. Al Alfonso with the help of Company B actually pushed the enemy back to the river.

The enemy continued to move reinforcements across the river to join up with the few units that had survived against the 1st Battalion counterattack. In spite of repeated counterattacks by the American forces on August 7th, the North Koreans still managed to get enough forces across the river to establish a salient. For the next three days both sides struggled for control of the dominant terrain , while North Korean reinforcements continued to pour across the river.

Both sides sped up their reinforcements during this conflict. The newly arrived 9th Infantry Regiment of the 2nd Division was rushed into the fray but could make little headway in its counterattack on the enemy salient. One of the reasons for failure of the counterattack was that the enemy had learned from the Russians how to build underwater bridges that could not be detected from the air. The NKPA was able to bring artillery and other heavy equipment across the Naktong River. By August 11th the enemy had penetrated the American lines and threatened the rear of the 9th Infantry. By the 12th they had created a roadblock to the east of Yongson. This last threat brought a quick response as troops from the headquarters units attacked this roadblock, while the 27th (Wolfhound) Regiment attacked the salient from the south. By August 15th the crisis was over, but neither side had the strength to dislodge the other.

The final action came when General Walker called on the Marine Brigade to reinforce a counterattack on the North Korean salient along with the 9th, 34th and 19th Infantry Regiments.

The attack began on August 17th. The enemy resisted every foot of the advance and caused many casualties among the American forces. The North Koreans even used tanks in their defense. But with help from Marine Cosairs and Air Force P-51s the attackers slowly moved forward. By the evening of August 18th enemy survivors were retreating back west across the Naktong. The enemy 4th Division suffered losses of about fifty-percent of its strength and most of its heavy equipment and weapons. For the Americans this

was their first real victory, and for the North Koreans their first real defeat.

Struggle for the Northern End of the Perimeter

The failure of the piecemeal attacks by the NKPA against the southern and western sides of the Pusan Perimeter changed the strategy of the NKPA. For the rest of August and early September the NKPA tried to cause a major breakthrough in the northern part of the perimeter. These forces attacked in two major areas. The first was a area of the northeast corridor along the coast where the four ROK Divisions, the 3rd, 6th, 8th and Capital were positioned. The second was the northwest sector leading into Taegu where the American 1st Cavalry and ROK 1st Divisions were deployed.

On August 27th the NKPA 5th and 12th Divisions attacked at Pohang and forced back the ROK 3rd and Capital Divisions. These two North Korean Divisions continued to push back the ROK forces and were helped by the aggressive attacks by the NKPA 8th and 15th Divisions to the west. As the crisis developed General Walker quickly rushed in the American 24th Division to support the withdrawing ROK Divisions. Finally a force consisting of the 19th and 21st Infantry Regiments plus the 3rd Battalion of the 9th Infantry under Brig. Gen. Gar Davidson drove back the NKPA forces and stabilized the front.

In the northwest sector the fighting was furious all during August and was to last until the Inchon invasion in the middle of September. Starting south of Waegwan on August 9th the NKPA forces met withering fire from the 1st Cavalry Division as they tried to cross the Naktong and were badly routed. North of Waegwan, however, the course of battle was different. Here the North Korean 3rd Division and the 105th Armored Division struck with fury. The 2nd Battalion, 5th Cavalry Regiment was cut off, and the enemy swarmed up the key hill, 303, that overlooked Waegwan. After a fierce air strike the 5th Cavalry counterattacked and retook the hill. The attacking Americans were shocked when they captured Hill 303 and found the bodies of twenty-six American soldiers who had been shot while being held prisoners. In this battle for Hill 303 one of those killed was Lt. Cecil Newman who had recently completed four years at West Point after surviving infantry combat in World War II.

On August 18th the NKPA 1st and 13th Divisions attacked towards Taegu from the north. During this engagement General Walker had time to rush in two of his best regiments, the 27th (Wolfhound) and the 23rd Infantry. Night after night enemy tanks and artillery surged forward firing down the road as they proceeded. Americans nicknamed this area the "Bowling Alley" because the rumbling tanks and the final crack of their guns sounded like bowling balls moving down an alley and hitting the pins. These continuing attacks against the steady defense of these two American regiments eventually exhausted the attackers. The North Korean offense had failed again.

Time was running against the NKPA as the Eighth Army slowly grew. The NKPA forces had been badly depleted by at least a third, and at this time their forces were being replenished with South Koreans. Some of these replacements were forced to serve. Others joined because they were South Korean Communists who were sympathetic with the North Korean cause.

As the Eighth Army grew in strength, the NKPA leaders realized that they had to make a final decisive blow and drive Eighth Army back to Pusan. Between September 3 through 13 the NKPA began its all out offensive to capture Taegu. The North Korean 1st, 3rd and 13th Divisions of 22,000 men prepared to make the attack. The 1st Cavalry Division anticipated this attack and decided to confuse the enemy by attacking first in what the military calls a spoiling attack. Instead everything went wrong with this plan.

The air strike and supporting artillery were ineffective , and the 1st Cavalry attack was strongly repulsed. The North Koreans then swarmed over the 1st Cavalry Division's defensive positions. Conditions were chaotic as the enemy pushed the division back to the high ground overlooking Taegu only ten miles away. The front line became fluid as each unit fought for its life. In the area of the 5th Cavalry Regiment the fighting never stopped. East of Waegwan Hill 174 changed hands seven times. Lt. Beecher Brian, one year out of West Point, fought with his platoon for almost a week in the struggle for Hill 174. He had started the battle with forty American and fifteen Korean soldiers and ended with only twelve American and five Korean soldiers.

The defense of Taegu became critical. Fighting became difficult compounded by heat and sudden torrential rains. In this struggle the American forces suffered many casualties. The high water mark of this NKPA offensive occurred on September 11th. The enemy took Hill 902 which was only seven miles from Taegu. At the same time every able-bodied man that the division could spare was rushed to the front. At this time Eighth Army had only one company in reserve for the entire perimeter. As he watched cooks, mechanics, truck drivers and staff rushed to the front, one soldier was reminded of other famous military last stand defenses in American history like the Texans in the siege of the Alamo in 1836.

Finally, by September 13th the enemy had exhausted its ability to attack any more. The Pusan Perimeter had held. The Air Force, along with the Naval and Marine air arms had been crucial in preventing the NKPA from concentrating forces for a major breakthrough. The Eighth Army under General Walker had made maximum use of American mobility and interior lines as it moved units about to plug gaps.

Under Walker's leadership and the excellent mobility of the American Army, units could be moved to meet each new enemy attack. The forty-five days of the Pusan Perimeter were an excellent training ground for the American soldier. He may have started on the perimeter as a green recruit, but after forty-five days on line he had turned into a brave, well disciplined fighting man.

Chapter Seven: Inchon Landing and Perimeter Breakout

By the middle of September 1950 American forces had built up in the Pusan Perimeter in such numbers that any enemy breakthrough to Pusan seemed unlikely. The NKPA had suffered many casualties from the superior firepower of the American air and ground forces. General MacArthur decided the time was at hand for the Allied Forces to take the offensive and end the war with one final devastating blow to the enemy.

Inchon Landing

The idea of making an amphibious landing behind the NKPA forces was not new. In early June 1950 Pentagon Plan SL-17 had been drawn up. General MacArthur and military planners had felt from the beginning that the impact on the enemy of an Allied amphibious landing was

Marines moving north of Seoul towards parallel, September 1950.

Marines landing on Inchon, September 1950.

both politically and militarily necessary. American armed forces still possessed the power of mobility and maneuver. As American and South Korean casualties mounted, however, the proposed amphibious landing kept being postponed.

But in mid-July MacArthur's staff was continuing to make plans for the amphibious operation. Several plans were drawn up for assaults on both the east and west coasts, in addition to Inchon. Finally MacArthur decided to make the amphibious landing at Inchon, while the Eighth Army was to break out of the Pusan Perimeter and link with them

The site chosen for the landing at Inchon was controversial. Opposed were the Chairman of the Joint Chiefs, General Omar Bradley, and the Army Chief of Staff, General J. Lawton Collins. They recommended sites closer to the Pusan Perimeter. MacArthur, however, would not change his views and emphasized that a landing at Inchon and a quick capture of Seoul would have great strategical, political and psychological importance. A successful landing at Inchon, MacArthur thought, would bolster the Western World's prestige throughout the Orient.

Inchon had many geographic hazards that

made an amphibious operation difficult. The oyster-shaped island of Wolmi lay in the channel off Inchon and had excellent command of the sea approaches from every direction. The 33 foot maximum tides here were among the greatest in the world. The channel approach to Inchon was so narrow that if a ship foundered in its final approach, the vessels ahead of it would be trapped. Finally, assault with LSTs (Landing Ship Tank) required of water depth at least 29 feet to reach the beaches, and on only four days each month did the tides reach this depth.

The force selected to spearhead the invasion was the newly activated X Corps. The commander of the force appointed by MacArthur was his own Chief of Staff, Far East Command, Maj. General Edward M. Almond. The major units of the command were the 1st Marine Division and the 7th Division of the US Army. The Navy commanders responsible for making the landing were outstanding, experienced leaders. The Commander of the Seventh Fleet, Vice-Admiral Arthur D. Struble, had participated in or commanded twenty-two amphibious operations in World War II. Under him was Rear Admiral James H. Doyle, Commander Amphibious Group One, who had had amphibious experience during the Solomon Islands Campaign and in other Pacific areas.

The plan of operations was first to make an initial landing by one Marine battalion on Wolmi Island outside Inchon harbor and secure it before the major landing at Incho. The principal landings would be made on three beaches at Inchon by the 1st Marine Division. The beachhead would be expanded rapidly to seize Kimpo, the major airfield in Korea. After they had secured this airfield, they would advance and seize Seoul. The 7th Infantry Division plus X Corps troops would make a normal landing at the Inchon docks and conduct operations as directed by the Corps Commander. Bombardment and fire support would be provided by Navy cruisers and destroyers. Air support would come from carrier based aircraft.

The first step in the invasion was the neutralization of Wolmi Island. On September 10th Marine aircraft of VMF-212 and 323 strafed the island with napalm. Other air strikes continued over the next two days. On September 13th the pre-invasion bombardment began from four cruisers and seven destroyers. According to Cdr. George H. Miller, Plans Officer for the Joint Task Force, " The destroyers were to draw the fire of the shore batteries so those batteries could be destroyed by the big cruisers and by air strikes." In addition these destroyers were to clear mine fields which were exposed at the low tide period. As the destroyers began to fire volley after volley directly at the island, they received return fire. The destroyers Jake and Collett each received minor hits while the destroyer Swenson took a near miss which killed one of its officers.

In the early morning of September 15th the 3rd Battalion, 5th Marines landed from 17 landing craft (LCVPs) and 3 landing ships (LSVs) on the shattered beach of Wolmi Island. They were met by light enemy resistance. Some of the enemy had fled back to Inchon by boat. Those who remained were mostly dazed into inaction by the three previous days of bombing. In less than an hour the Marines had scaled the hilly slopes and captured the island. Enemy casualties were 120 killed and 190 captured, while the Marines suffered only 20 men wounded.

The amphibious landing at Inchon was not so easy. Around Inchon harbor was a large heavy stone seawall. The assault on Wolmi Island had alerted the North Koreans who were now expecting the attack. Last but not least of the problems was that the landing had to take place just prior to darkness on a city with warehouses and other urban obstacles that could be utilized by a determined, defending enemy.

Using ladders, the first wave of the 5th Marines scaled the seawall on Red Beach in the center of Inchon at 1733 hours. On Blue Beach on the south side of Inchon the 1st Marines, commanded by the legendary Col. Lewis (Chesty) Puller, began landing at 1732 hours. They too had to scale a high seawall. On Red Beach some confusion occurred when Marines in the rear waves fired indiscriminately at the beach which caused twenty-four American casualties. Neither of these units, however, incurred much enemy resistance. Pfc. Doug Koch, Company D 5th Marines, remembers the biggest problem was trying to climb the seawall as his LCVP bounced up and down from wave action.

North of the Red Beach landing the enemy presented its only real resistance. Here A Company, 5th Marines, had an intense fight, and eight men were killed and twenty-two wounded before the company succeeded in seizing Cemetery Hill. Lt. Frank Muetzel was able to move his platoon up the rear of this hill in a skirmish line and catch the "Reds" in their holes looking forward.

Other waves of Marines with tanks and heavy equipment followed the first waves onto these beaches.

Within twenty-four hours the 1st Marine Division had secured a beachhead big enough for the rest of the X Corps to begin unloading. By September 18th the Marines had cleared Inchon, captured Kimpo Airfield and consolidated the beachhead. Their next step was the capture of Seoul.

Meanwhile the North Koreans had organized a substantial force to resist the Marines. On September 24th as the Marines initiated their final assault on Seoul, over 35,000 North Koreans had moved into defensive positions to protect the city.

Previously, on September 18th, the Army 7th Infantry Division had begun coming ashore. Their mission was to protect the right flank and rear of the Marines as they assaulted Seoul. The 73rd Tank Battalion and elements of the 31st Regiment had moved south to Suwon to secure the airfield. At Suwon this task force ran head-on into elements of the NKPA 105th Armored Division. After a vicious battle Suwon Airfield was secured on September 22nd and was opened to United Nations air traffic.

The plan devised for the capture of Seoul by the 1st Marine Division was for three regiments to attack Seoul in a pincers movement. The 1st Marine Regiment was to cross the Han River and attack Seoul from the south. The 5th Marines were to cross the Han west of Seoul and attack directly from the west. The 7th Marines were to make a wide sweep, attack Seoul from the northwest and try to block the roads running north out of the city.

On September 20th the 5th Marines crossed the Han River in LTVs and began their assault from the west. This area was strongly defended by the NKPA 25th Brigade. Most of the of officers and men in this North Korean unit were men who had had experience fighting with the Communists in China. During the 22nd and 23rd of September this unit put up a stiff resistance

against the 5th Marines. On September 24th the key terrain feature in the center of the enemy defense line, Hill 66, was assaulted during a heavy morning mist by D Company of the 5th Marines. Over 206 Marines started the assault but only 30 were alive when Hill 66 was finally taken. This last handful of men charged the top of the hill with such fury that the enemy panicked and fled down its rear slope. This action was the key to the collapse of the entire NKPA western defense and opened the way to Seoul. Enemy killed in this action were estimated at 1750 soldiers.

One of the lucky Marines in the assault was 1st Lt. Robert Bohn, Company G 5th Marines. A machine-gun bullet torn through his thigh just an inch below his private parts. The Navy corpsman (medic) pulled down his trousers and said, "Jeez, boss. Missed them by half an inch."

Since the Marine attack on Seoul was going slowly, General Almond decided to attack from the southeast with the 32nd Regiment, 7th Division and the ROK 17th Regiment. Helped by Marine amphibious tractors the 32nd Regiment crossed the Han on 25 September and took South Mountain. The enemy was taken by surprise and put up little resistance. The 3rd Battalion, 32nd Infantry and 17th ROKs moved rapidly to the northeast. In this move L Company surprised and overran a column of NKPA troops. In this fight over 500 enemy were killed and almost 50 enemy vehicles destroyed.

Other units of the 1st Marine Division attacked Seoul aggressively. The 1st Marines met stiff enemy resistance in Yongdungp'o south of Seoul and after a bloody struggle crossed the Han River on September 24th and attacked the city from the south. They fought a stubborn enemy block by block as they pushed into the city. The NKPA forces in the city would not give up easily and made violent counterattacks against the Marine forces. These fights, called "The Battle of the Barricades," lasted for several days. Enemy soldiers stretched barricades across streets and defended them with heavy anti-tank and machine gun fire. S/Sgt. Lee Bergee, E Company 1st Marines, noted "The enemy roadblocks were made from hunks of concrete, streetcar rails, steel beams, and large rocks. We destroyed many of the roadblocks with bulldozers. It seemed that every building in Seoul housed an enemy sniper. Inside some of the houses, we knocked holes in the walls and then tossed grenades through the openings." By the 28th the North Koreans became exhausted and withdrew, leaving Seoul to the victorious Marines.

Organized resistance by the NKPA forces in the Seoul area ceased after 3 October. X Corps pushed out from Seoul and reached Uijongbu to the north near the border with North Korea. To the south they established positions near Suwon and waited for the Eighth Army forces to break out of the Pusan Perimeter, push north and link up with them.

Amidst all this fighting the chaplains were kept busy. Chaplain Glyn Jones (USN) during this street fighting felt the Marines needed some prayers. In fatigues he celebrated Holy Communion on the back of a jeep. As the Marines began to gather around him, out of the holes of the buildings came Korean Christians. After receiving Holy Communion, these Koreans quietly disappeared.

In the city of Seoul as the NKPA forces withdrew, leaving devastation behind., most buildings had been destroyed in the fighting, and many innocent South Koreans had been slaughtered. On September 29th MacArthur victoriously entered with the President of South Korea, Syngman Rhee. In an emotional speech MacArthur returned the nation's capitol to Dr. Rhee.

The Breakout at Waegwan

The breakout of the Pusan Perimeter was a major offensive action of the Eighth Army. News of the Inchon landing was slow to reach the North Korean defenders on the Perimeter. For almost a week officers kept news of the Inchon landing from the lower echelons of the NKPA forces. The North Korean High Command probably did not decide to leave the Perimeter until almost four days after the landing. They did not collapse immediately as had been hoped, but continued to fight to the last man in many areas. Thus for almost a week some of the bitterest fighting in the war took place on the Perimeter.

The final breakout of the Pusan Perimeter took place on September 16th, one day after the Inchon landing. Its purpose was to fix and hold the NKPA's main combat strength and prevent movement of its units from the Pusan Perimeter to the Inchon-Seoul area. The plan called for the United States Ist Corps under Maj. Gen. Frank Milburn, which consisted of the 1st Cavalry Division, the 1st ROK Division, the 24th Division, the 27th British Brigade and the 5th RCT, to break out of the Perimeter at Waegwan. The main effort would be directed along the Taegu-Kumchon-Taejon-Suwon axis, the shortest distance to effect a junction with X Corps in the north.

Until the breakout the 1st Cavalry Division had been struggling just to hold their positions on the Perimeter. In this struggle just two days before the breakout, I Company 5th Cavalry recaptured Hill 174 which had changed hands eight times during the previous month. Capt. Norman Allen remembers that defending this hill two days before the breakout was "real hell". Company I repelled the first attack, but the second attack overran the Company Command Post. He remembers, "I was lying in a shelter when a gook stepped on my back and seemed unaware of what he was standing on. I was too afraid to move. He was silhouetted against the dark sky. I pulled the slide of my .45 slowly, slowly back and aimed over my left shoulder. The .45 exploded. The shot went true." This example is only one of many in which the men of the 1st Cavalry Division struggled prior to the breakout.

The plan of the 1st Cavalry Division was to attack north while the 5th Regimental Combat Team was to take Waegwan and the Naktong River crossings. The 5th Cavalry Regiment was assigned to the Division's west flank while the 8th Cavalry was on the division east flank and was to attack north. The 7th Cavalry was to shift from the division right to the division left and by a rapid encirclement over secondary roads link up with the 8th Cavalry at Tabu-dong. By this maneuver it was hoped that a large number of North Korean troops would be cut off.

The key point for breaking out of the Perimeter was the town of Waegwan. Here three major roads and a railroad met and crossed the Naktong River. There were two bridges which had been damaged but which eventually were used by I Corps to cross the river. This was the major axis for the I Corps movement to Seoul.

Two key hills guarded the approaches from the southwest toward Waegwan. These

Engineers build a road after the breakout of Pusan Perimeter, September 1950.

were Hills 303 and 268. From Hill 303 one looked directly down on the Naktong River, the Tabu-dong Road and the highway and railroad to Taegu. This hill had been fought over many times in the early days of the Korean War.

Hill 268 was the critical terrain feature in the breakout. This hill overlooked not only the Taegu highway and railroad but also the main highway running from Waegwan south along the east bank of the Naktong. Any attack by the Eighth Army toward Waegwan and the river crossings from the south had to take Hill 268.

Any attack north from Taegu along the highway running to Tabu-dong had to run a gauntlet between Hills 570, 351 and 902. These hills had also been fought over many times in August and loss of these hills had brought the NKPA to within eight miles of Eighth Army Headquarters in Taegu.

The NKPA forces in the area around Waegwan were three understrength infantry divisions reinforced by one armored regiment. Further to the east, covering the Taegu-Tabu-dong Highway, were the NKPA 1st and 13th Infantry Divisions. This area, known as "the Bowling Alley," was covered by high mountains and well fortified North Korean emplacements. Even when these NKPA forces received news of the Inchon landing through intercepted radio communications, they were commanded to "hold at all costs."

The 5th RCT started on its mission on 16 September, short by 1194 men because of casualties acquired during its forty-two day stay on the southwest flank of the Pusan Perimeter. On that date the 2nd Battalion ran into strong enemy resistance south of Waegwan. The next day the 1st Battalion joined it in an attack north along the Naktong River. The 3rd Battalion followed the other two battalions and branched off to the right. Rain was pouring down making quagmires of the dirt roads. The tanks accompanying the 3rd Battalion could not keep up. The weak shoulders of the road collapsed under the weight of the tanks and three tanks slid into a rice paddy.

Moving ahead without tanks, the 3rd Battalion infantry soon began to receive heavy enemy mortar and artillery fire. Companies K and L moved around a reservoir and attacked Hill 160 from which most of the enemy fire seemed to be coming. Company K, attacking on the right, was pinned down. Company L on the left met light resistance and had almost reached the top of the hill when it stopped. The Company Commander, Captain Hula, had been shot through the head and lay dying in front of his men. During this lull the 3rd Platoon of K Company made a flanking move, passed through L Company and captured the hill. When

the enemy withdrew, they left 16 dead on the top of the hill and several more in foxholes behind the hill.

That night the three rifle companies of the 3rd Battalion dug defensive positions on the hill as they were pounded by heavy enemy artillery and mortar fire. Some of the remaining wounded could not be evacuated until daylight the next day. Among these were Sgt. Hannikiavi with a serious stomach wound and Corp. Queja with a knee wound. Just at sunset a helicopter arrived to evacuate Capt. Hula, but he had died by that time and so there was space in the helicopter for one wounded soldier. Corp. Queja insisted that the helicopter take the more seriously wounded Sgt. Hannikiavi , and that he would wait to be evacuated in the morning. Unfortunately Queja's wound was more serious than he thought. He died of shock during the night.

The rest of the regiment was actively engaged. The 1st Battalion attacked Hill 178, fought all day long and by nightfall was 300 yards short of the objective. At the same time the 2nd Battalion attacked along the road parallel to the Naktong River. By 1850 hours it had seized Hill 121.3 near Waegwan and consolidated the position.

Hill 268 was really a long steep mountain with entrenchment at the south end and bunkers at the north end. This hill controlled most of the approaches into Waegwan and was heavily defended by at least a battalion of North Koreans. Again the 3rd Battalion , 5th RCT attacked with L Company on the left, K Company on the right and I Company in reserve. Both companies attacked the south end of Hill 268 from Hill 160 but had to descend into a draw and then attack uphill.. Farther to the left B Company, 1st Battalion assisted L Company.

Halfway up the south end of Hill 268 the 3rd Battalion came under intensive enemy rifle fire and were pinned down. M/Sgt. Kermit Jackson, a highly decorated veteran of World War II and a native of West Virginia, quickly assessed the situation and with three men from K Company fearlessly threw grenades into an enemy foxhole, charged over a barbwire emplacement and dashed into the enemy foxhole. Jackson and the three men then worked their way uphill to several unoccupied foxholes. From this position they were now behind the enemy defensive emplacements. Jackson was able to pick off eight enemy soldiers with his rifle. The rest of the enemy fled to the north end of Hill 268 as K Company charged up the hill. Thirty dead North Korean soldiers were found on the hill, but the assault cost K Company forty casualties.

Once the south end of Hill 268 was taken Company I moved through K and L Companies and attacked the heavily fortified end of the hill. Company I had ten men killed and many wounded and still could not take the fortified objective by the end of the day, so they withdrew for the night. Taking Hill 268 was tougher than anticipated. The enemy in this fortified position was estimated as 600 "die hards" who would not give up. Veterans were reminded of the bitter struggles in the mountains of Italy in World War II. The fighting resembled a shooting gallery. One could actually see the enemy shooting. When Americans shot, the enemy would duck down and then pop up and shoot back. During all this fire fight enemy mortar rounds landed every few minutes. By the end of the day American casualties were heavy. K Company had over 80 men killed or wounded.

Just before sunset as I Company pulled back, many dead and wounded were left in the open. Volunteers from K Company then rushed out under fire and dragged back the I Company

wounded. That night the heavy mortars and machine guns of M Company arrived. These men had been struggling all day to get these heavy weapons up on the mountain. That night all four companies of the 3rd Battalion dug in and awaited the morning when an air strike was to assist them in their final assault.

At dawn on the 19th three flights of P-51s dropped napalm on the enemy bunkers on the north end of Hill 268. After the air strikes I Company reinforced by K and L Companies assaulted the bunkers. Many of the enemy fought to the end. When the three companies finally took the enemy position, they counted over 250 enemy bodies. Among the enemy dead was a full colonel, a Regimental Commander of the NKPA.

Simultaneously the 2nd Battalion took Waegwan on the 19th and moved through what was left of the town to Hill 303. Two hours later the 1st Battalion moved to high ground north of town. These two battalions had killed over 300 North Koreans, taken twelve prisoners and taken much equipment including an unscathed T-34 tank. The 5th RCT's nine rifle companies had suffered many casualties, most of whom were in its 3rd Battalion. By the 21st, the 5th RCT had mopped up the area around Weagwan and moved across the Naktong River.

Meanwhile the rest of the 1st Cavalry Division was active. The 5th Cavalry Regiment attacked on the 17th of September along the Taegu-Waegwan Road. With help from the 7th Cavalry Regiment this regiment finally took Hills 253 and 300. Three rifle companies of the 1st Battalion were reduced to 165 men. Most of these casualties came from intense enemy mortar fire.

Two battalions 7th Cavalry aggressively

pushed up the Taegu-Waegwan Road . Once past the recently taken Hill 300, they turned off the main road and headed east toward Tabu-dong. By the 21st Tabu-dong was taken. While one battalion turned north into a blocking position, the other Battalion turned south and by late afternoon linked up with the 8th Cavalry which was attacking north from Taegu. Thus in three days the remnants of the NKPA 1st, 3rd and 13th Divisions had been encircled and many prisoners taken.

The Breakout on Other Fronts

On 16 September other units simultaneously broke out of the Pusan Perimeter. At the Naktong Bulge the 23rd Regiment, 2nd Division crossed the Naktong on the 16th of September and ran into stiff North Korean resistance. One of the first across the river in this unit was Lt. Bill Glasgow. He had just crossed when his company was nearly overrun by an enemy counterattack. An enemy round knocked his helmet off and grazed his skull. He remembers that "the enemy got in on us real close— and I was standing there holding my helmet with a hole in it in one hand and firing my machine gun with the other."

Some of the division units had trouble crossing the Naktong River. South of the 23rd Regiment crossing the 9th Infantry Regiment tried to cross on DUWKs. This crossing was a failure as they were driven back by strong enemy mortar and machine gun fire.

By September 21st the 23rd and 38th Infantry Regiments had established a bridgehead on the west side of the river and constructed a pontoon bridge for the rest of the division to use. After overcoming minor enemy resistance, they were able to push farther west. By the 26th they had reached Anui. Here the 3rd Battalion, 23rd Infantry encountered an enemy ambush. Heavy

enemy mortar fire suddenly fell all around them. The battalion staff was caught in the open and suffered heavy casualties. Killed were the battalion executive officer, the S-2, the assistant S-3, motor officer, the artillery liaison officer and an anti-aircraft officer. Badly wounded were the battalion commander and twenty-five enlisted men. Despite this surprise attack other enemy resistance was sporadic, and the division continued to keep pushing west.

On the right flank the ROK I and II Corps broke out of the Perimeter and drove north. The ROK I Corps at first ran into stiff resistance from the NKPA 12th Division, a unit originally made up of veterans of the Chinese Communist Army. Aided by American Naval support from the big guns of the battleship *Missouri* and other vessels, the North Koreans were slowly dislodge. By September 22nd the disorganized North Koreans was driven back.

The breakout on the left flank was initially slower than on the other fronts. The mountain mass of Battle-Mountain-Sobuk-San still served the enemy forces as a major defensive position. Before any offense could take place from this area, the 25th Division had to clear this mountain mass. From September 16th to 18th the division attacked this mountain fortress unceasingly but made little headway.

In spite of defeats in other areas along the Perimeter, the NKPA defensive forces on Sobuk-San refused to be defeated. For forty-five days these defenders had resisted all American attempts to take this fortress and still continued to hold this strategic position. All during August and early September efforts by the 24th 35th and 5th RCTs and later by the 27th RCT had made but limited gain. During this period life for the attacking American had been some of the most exacting that any soldier had to undergo during the war. The enemy attacked day and night. Even when American units acquired a small foothold, a soldier seldom left his defensive position. To maintain morale one hot meal a day was brought to each American platoon by Korean laborers who struggled each day to reach the American positions high on the mountain. Another morale factor was the daily ration of two cans of beer. In early September soldier morale fell when this beer ration was suddenly stopped after pressure was applied to the Army in the United States by the W.C.T.U (Women's Christian Temperance Union).

Failure to seize this North Korean stronghold during the early days of the breakout is shown by the futile efforts of Task Force Woolfolk. This battalion size force was made up of the 3rd Battalion, 35th Infantry and other smaller units under Major Robert Woolfolk. This offense was supposed to begin an all out effort to finally drive the NKPA forces from their citadel. Company A, 27th Infantry, attached to this task force, made it to the top of a ridge in one place on September 18th and set up a defensive position. The enemy counterattacked with vengeance. All day long Company A beat off enemy attacks and suffered fifty-seven casualties. When they ran low on ammunition and could not defend themselves, they were withdrawn. Fearing further high casualties in the task force, Major Woolfolk abandoned further attempts to dislodge the enemy from the mountain peak.

On the 20th of September, when word of the Inchon landing finally reached the enemy, NKPA forces slowly began to withdraw, and American units were finally able to occupy the mountain crests. By the 21st after hard fighting, the 35th Infantry was able to capture the Notch, an area north of Sobuk-San much fought over in

July and August. Even while withdrawing the NKPA 6th and 7th Divisions fought hard. One of the areas they defended was Chinju Pass where much fighting had taken place in early August.

The breakout of the Pusan Perimeter was the final blow to the NKPA. As an army the NKPA now ceased to exist. The immediate task of Eighth Army was to mop-up remaining pockets of resistance left by this defiant enemy and try to bring the war to a close.

Chapter Eight: Pursuit and Defeat of the NKPA

After the Eighth Army had broken out of the Pusan Perimeter, the next phase was to link up as quickly as possible with X Corps forces that had landed at Inchon. Time was a major factor as NKPA forces withdrew rapidly and blocked many key road junctions. The fighting in this pursuit phase was between exhausted understrength American units who had to overcome roadblocks and ambushes by fanatic North Koreans struggling to avoid the American pincers that was trying to cut off their escape to North Korea.

The 24th and the 1st Cavalry Divisions were assigned to make the major move northwest to link up with X Corps. The original plan was for the 1st Cavalry to follow the 24th after crossing the Naktong River and move east to Kumchon and Taejon. These plans were changed by I Corps however, when the American forces were met with determined resistance from the NKPA. The 1st Cavalry crossed the river north of Waegwan and established a course parallel to that of the 24th Division.

The reason for the change was that the 24th Division had run into a major delaying action at

Kumchon by the NKPA forces. Retreating North Koreans put up a stubborn fight here because Kumchon was a major road junction on their withdrawal route. This junction had to be controlled by the NKPA in order for their southern units to escape into North Korea.

The battle for Kumchon became a bitter struggle. As G Company of the 21st Infantry assaulted the fleeing enemy, Pfc. Leonard Korgie remembers the taste of revenge: "We had the enemy in a squeeze and intended to smash the hell out of him. All of a sudden we were winning the damned war! I began to feel like a normal human being again."

At this stage most American units were down to about half strength because of heavy losses in the final fight for Waegwan. One veteran of the 5th RCT remembers green replace-

ments beginning to arrive in the unit just prior to the assault on Kumchon. Three months of steady combat had trained the veterans to detect close enemy fire and learn when to take cover. The green replacements had not had time to learn about the sounds of combat. The sudden sound of an enemy rifle crack often sent a replacement headfirst into a stream amid roars of laughter from veterans.

South of Kumchon another battle was being fought by the first British troops to arrive in Korea. The 27th British Brigade fresh from Hong Kong consisted of two battalions, the Argyll and Sutherland Highlanders and the Middlesex Regiment. This unit which was attached to the 24th Division attacked toward Songju on the 23rd and met stiff enemy resis-

Fall, 1950. Soldiers of the 5th Regimental Combat Team crossing the 38th Parallel.

tance. During this attack the British called for air support. In spite of displayed white panels for aircraft recognition, confusion occurred. The American F-51 Mustangs mistakenly dropped napalm on the Argylls causing 89 casualties.

During this phase of the war both sides often became disoriented. Lt. Jim Carrozza of the 24th Division Artillery was in the vanguard of an artillery column in charge of security. He was in command of several armored half-tracks equipped with quad 50 cal. machine guns and 40mm anti-aircraft guns. On the move toward Taejon he rode in the lead vehicle and maintained radio contact with the part of his platoon bringing up the rear of the column. Suddenly he received a call from his platoon sergeant in the rear vehicle who informed him that a group of four trucks towing artillery pieces and with headlights blazing had fallen in behind his vehicle. On his instructions his sergeant, thinking these were ROK soldiers, yelled at them in Japanese to turn their lights off. (All Koreans understand Japanese.) He was answered with a burst of tommy-gun fire. The American soldiers immediately replied with their quad 50 cal. guns. Shortly thereafter they had captured a North Korean 76mm field gun battery.

Meanwhile other units of the 24th Division pushed on toward Taejon. On the 28th of September after constant air strikes against fleeing North Korean soldiers from remnants of seven different divisions, the 19th Infantry entered Taejon. To the 19th this was a memorable moment, particularly for the survivors of this same unit who had fought so bravely in the city's defense two and a half months earlier.

Elation turned to disgust as the 19th Infantry witnessed the result of atrocities committed by fleeing North Koreans. In their haste to leave the city the North Korean Security Police had speeded up their killing of American and ROK prisoners as well as South Korean civilians. Thousands were shot and dumped into a mass grave. Only six survived.

North of the 24th Division the 1st Cavalry Division led by the 7th Cavalry Regiment initiated an aggressive pursuit at Tabu-dong on 22 September. General Gay, who had been Chief of Staff for General George Patton in Europe during Patton's dash across France in 1944, wanted his 1st Cavalry Division to pursue the defeated North Koreans with the same aggressiveness. The spearhead of the force was Task Force Lynch, made up of the 3rd Battalion, 7th Cavalry and tanks of the 70th Tank Battalion. Task Force Lynch moved so rapidly that resistance was light. Racing into Naktong-ni at night the task force caught many North Korean soldiers in their vehicles trying to cross the Naktong River. This unit quickly crossed the river and continued its aggressive pursuit. In a period of thirty-six hours this task force had captured or destroyed almost 100 enemy vehicles and guns and had captured over 500 enemy soldiers. By the 24th the whole regiment had pushed as far forward as Prun.

After a slight delay the division was finally given the order to move on the 26th of September and link up with X Corps. All three regiments of the division quickly raced north. The 5th Cavalry dashed to Chochiwon on the main road between Taejon and Seoul and blocked all North Korean movement to the north. According to a letter written at the time by Pvt. James Cardinal of I Company, 5th Cavalry, "Korean prisoners were constantly streaming in, and some were horrible messes—one who had white phosphorus had maggots all over him. You can't imagine how terrible he looked.—I haven't seen too much fighting and probably won't now that the war is almost over."

The spearhead of Task Force Lynch was led by the 3rd Platoon of C Company, 70th Tank Battalion under Lt. Robert W. Baker. This small force of three tanks moved so rapidly that they overran and confused many units of the NKPA. North of Osan they dashed forward with headlights blazing until they made contact with the 31st Infantry, 7th Infantry Division. Miraculously, after traveling 106 miles from Prum through a number of retreating North Korean units, they had only one casualty.

Unknowingly, Lt. Baker had slipped his three tanks past an entire NKPA armored unit at Habone-ni. Task Force Lynch, following Baker, ran head-on into this enemy force. In the ensuing fight Captain James B. Webel and Sergeant Willard H. Hopkins distinguished themselves by personally mounting two enemy tanks. On one they poured gasoline into the engine hatch, and on the other they dropped grenades down the open commander's hatch. Of the ten enemy tanks who met this American force, seven were destroyed and three withdrew. Although Task Force Lynch was victorious in this fight, the cost was heavy. The force lost two killed and twenty-eight wounded. Two American tanks and fifteen vehicles were destroyed. Early the next morning the task force completed the link-up with the 31st Infantry. Over the next few days the linked forces fought small battles against cut off enemy forces trying to flee north.

In other parts of South Korea the pursuit was less spectacular and the terrain more difficult. The 25th Division on the Eighth Army's left flank had initially had difficulty dislodging the enemy from the Sobok San mountain mass and moving into the pursuit. Only by the 25th of

September did the 2nd Battalion of the 35th Infantry finally seize Chinju.

The next objectives of the 25th Division required it to attack through some of the most difficult terrain in Korea. Directly west of Chinju was the impenetrable 7000 foot high Chiri-san mountain mass. Before the war this area had been a haven for communists, as it now was for retreating North Korean stragglers and guerrillas. About 3000 North Korean soldiers of the retreating 6th and 7th Divisions had taken refuge here.

The 25th Division split into two forces with one going south of Chiri-san and the other north. The southern force made up of the 25th Reconnaissance Company, a company of tanks followed and part of the 24th Infantry by the 28th had reached Nawon. At the same time the northern spearhead of the 89th Tank Battalion, called Task Force Dolvin, overran many enemy forces. On the 28th at Hamyang they linked up with the 23rd Regiment and at Namwon with the 25th Division southern task force. In this short four day period the two 25th Division task forces in "Patton style fighting" had covered 220 miles and 138 miles respectively and had carried out one of the finest advances of the war.

The linking up of units from Eighth Army with X Corps was not the only objective of units from the Pusan Perimeter. Other units of the 25th Division were given the mission of cleaning up North Korean stragglers and guerrillas who had taken refuge in the mountains. The 3rd Battalion of the 35th Regiment moved into the mountains west of Hamchang and ran into resistance. Here they were trying to capture guerrillas and soldiers who had shed their uniforms. The mountains were rugged, and like the Chiri-san Mountains farther south in this same range, the area had been a haven for communist guerrillas prior to the war.

Distinguishing local civilians from ex-soldiers was difficult. Lt. Sam Holliday remembers using local police dressed in civilian clothes as agents to go into the mountain and entice hungry guerrillas to come down into the towns. "The Americans are crazy," they would say. "They are giving food to everyone. They even give the enemy rice and cigarettes. How can someone treat their enemies so well? They are crazy." Using this strategy the Americans, with Korean help, were able to coax a few guerrillas to surrender. On the whole, however, the enemy guerrillas remained in the mountains and attacked villages at night and continued to set up roadblocks. The fighting at times was vicious. Lt. Holliday remembers finding a dead South Korean with a rope around his neck swinging from a tree and with his big toe missing. Pinned to his chest was a message written in blood from his toe that said this was what the People's Party would do to anti-communists. Conflict with communist partisans remained a problem until later in the war when ROK and American units finally went into the mountainous areas and cleaned them out.

By October 1st the fighting in most parts of South Korea had ceased. Disorganized and demoralized remnants of the NKPA tried to infiltrate into North Korea. Out of 90,000 who had invaded South Korea in June approximately 25,000 disorganized NKPA soldiers returned to North Korea. By this date American and ROK units had reached the 38th Parallel and awaited further orders.

The Decision to Invade North Korea

The decision that the Eighth Army should invade North Korea was momentous. The landing at Inchon had been so controversial that other than linking forces with the Eighth Army in the Pusan Perimeter further plans for an advance after the link up had not been considered. The X Corps forces that had invaded Inchon were concentrated in the west around Seoul and did not complete the encirclement of NKPA forces by a swift drive to the east coast. Because MacArthur had placed the emphasis on the link-up of Allied forces only, many North Korean soldiers were able to escape through the mountains into North Korea.

The decision to invade North Korea involved a number of political issues. Syngman Rhee and his followers in South Korea wanted to invade North Korea in order to establish a united Korea under the leadership of South Korea. MacArthur wanted to destroy the NKPA so they would not rise again and resume their threat. A final factor was the issue of the reaction of the communist countries: the Soviet Union and the PRC.

In hindsight, a thorough understanding of Red China and her interests was lacking. American military leaders like Gen. Omar Bradley felt that the PRC was a Soviet satellite controlled by Moscow, and that the PRC's main interest was Taiwan. Others in Washington like Secretary of State Dean Acheson believed the CIA reports that "intervention by the PRC or Soviets would be confined to - covert assistance to the North Koreans." Little thought was given to Red China's fear of a foreign army on her border at the Yalu River within striking distance of the fertile North China Plain. Misreading this situation, and disregarding statements of the PRC, led the Allies into a tragic decision.

On October 7th the UN passed a resolution asking the North Korean communists to cooperate with the UN to ensure conditions of stability throughout Korea. This resolution was misleading as it asked the communists to hold elections. But this North Korean government had barred elections in 1948. In any case, the resolution, which was really an ultimatum, was interpreted by MacArthur as giving him the right to cross the 38th Parallel and invade North Korea.

This justification for crossing the 38th Parallel into North Korea can still be argued. At the time, however, the remnants of the NKPA were fleeing back into the sanctuary of North Korea. Unless North Korea was occupied, the NKPA could rebuilt and fight another day. History over the last forty-two years has shown that this is exactly what North Korea did after the armistice in 1953. Today the large armed forces of North Korea are still a threat to the neighboring countries of Asia.

Actual entrance into North Korea by Allied forces had occurred on September 30th when ROK troops crossed the 38th Parallel on the east coast on orders from President Syngman Rhee. Other ROK units followed and moved rapidly up the eastern side of the peninsula. American units waited, however, for a response from the North Koreans concerning the UN Resolution. This pause was a mere procedure to justify the later crossing of the 38th Parallel by Eighth Army.

Waiting

During this waiting period Eighth Army units rested. Most of these units were assembled around Seoul. The pause was a time of relaxation. For the first time the troops had camp fires at night. Some, for the first time, occupied Korean homes. The occupation of these homes had been minimal early in the war, because most houses were infested with fleas and flies. As the

weather turned colder these pests died, and the houses were more attractive. Americans were supposed to follow Korean custom and remove their boots before entering. Unfortunately few did, much to the distress of the Koreans. But Americans learned to adapt to the garlic smell of Kimche and the barn smell of family livestock, mainly pigs, that were sheltered near the houses.

Food and drink became a major morale factor. Units that had been stationed in Japan were sent alcoholic beverages by their clubs to replace the beer ration that had been stopped in September. To improve the army menu expeditions were sent out to procure chickens and eggs. Occasionally these were supplemented with native rabbits. These were welcome changes and did much to improve morale.

Units that could find cows were lucky. Many mess sergeants were from the west and had had experience slaughtering steers. When a cow was killed its throat was slit. The Korean villagers would rush up with containers to collect the blood.

One battery of the 77th Field Artillery Battalion had a comical experience with a stubborn cow. When the cow saw a six foot four battery commander and a five foot Chinese-American first sergeant lick their lips in anticipation of a forthcoming meal, she took off at full speed straight through the battery position. As the captain and sergeant chased the cow around the battery position trying to shoot it, the men whooped and hollered cheering the cow on. At last the cow was captured, quickly slaughtered and prepared for the evening meal. Unfortunately orders came for the unit to move out. The cow had to be left behind much to the delight of the local Korean villagers.

Many men in units near Seoul had recently been on occupation duty in Korea and had connections with some of the citizens. In some units as many as one-third of the soldiers were occupation veterans. As a result some units were temporarily depleted when veteran leaders sneaked into Seoul to renew old acquaintances.

At this time more South Koreans were attached to American units. On the Pusan Perimeter at least twenty carriers of the Korean Service Corps had been assigned to every company. These carriers had helped American units survive during the early days of the war by carrying food and ammunition up the steep and treacherous mountains and the badly wounded down the mountains. By September in addition as many as 100 ROK soldiers were assigned to each company. These were called KATUSAs (Korean Augmentation to the US Army). Some units had received them as early as 15 August, but most units did not receive them until late September. These Korean soldiers were paid and administered by the ROK Government but were fed and equipped by their host American unit. The intent of the program was to have each Korean soldier teamed with a UN soldier. Most American units kept them as separate squads or separate platoons. Americans of Japanese extraction (Nieci) were invaluable as squad leaders and platoon sergeants because they could communicate with Koreans in Japanese, a language known to all Koreans.

As the war progressed these KATUSA ROKs became very good soldiers. Their use of the Korean language in American units was their major handicap. Too often in night fighting they were mistaken in the dark for enemy soldiers by nervous American soldiers because of their chatter in a foreign tongue. Lt. Jim Carrozza tells of a rare case where one KATUSA went berserk, climbed up on a personal carrier with his rifle,

and shot at American soldiers. He was subdued by a sergeant who climbed up the back of the carrier and clubbed him with a monkeywrench. He was turned back to the ROK Army.

Another type of South Korean that was attached to each American company was a policeman. These police had joined units when the units first got to Korea. They had the mission of handling Korean civilians. At times they could be very brutal, especially when interrogating a civilian who might be a North Korean soldier in civilian clothes. ROK units used them to follow their own moving troops and catch stragglers. Sometimes Americans would witness straggler executions with horror, but the American Army had little control over actions taken by these police against their own people.

American food was too rich for most of these Koreans who had come from a rural environment. Rice had always been a major part of their diet. They would take American rice and throw in turnips, onions and peppers. Their favorite condiment was kimchi, a fermented cabbage laced with garlic. Also introduced was local Saki, a common alcoholic drink in Japan. Before long many American soldiers were eating the Korean food and enjoying it.

During this lull in the fighting American troops wondered what role the Chinese might play in this war. Savoring victory, the Americans didn't consider the Chinese a serious threat. The Americans considered themselves veterans who had survived and would soon be on their way home.

North to the Chongchon River

MacArthurs plan for the invasion of North Korea was to make a pincers move and attack from two directions. Eighth Army was to move north from Seoul to Pyongyang, the North Korean capital, while X Corps was to make an amphibious landing at Wonsan, attack northwest, and link-up with Eighth Army.

In hindsight this plan, which was approved at all command levels in Washington, had many weaknesses. As General Omar Bradley said later, "If a student at the Army Command and General Staff School had turned in this solution to the problem, he would have been laughed out of the classroom." The first obstacle to the successful completion of this plan was the terrain itself. A major range of rugged mountains split the forces and limited communication. Another problem was the delay which ensued when Eighth Army succeeded in capturing Pyongyang before X Corps had even landed at Wonsan. During all this period ports and rail lines were tied up transporting X Corps around to Wonsan instead of supplying Eighth Army for their final drive into North Korea. This supply problem still persisted when the Chinese entered the conflict.

It is difficult for many to understand why this plan was accepted. At the time General MacArthur had tremendous prestige. Against the advice of most military experts, he had had brilliant success in his amphibious invasion at Inchon. Who in the military had the nerve to challenge him on his latest plan?

The invasion of North Korea by the Eighth Army officially began on October 7th after General MacArthur's proclamation of the UN Resolution to the North Koreans which demanded their surrender had received no response. The major invasion force was I Corps led by the 1st Cavalry Division followed by the 24th Division. This force moved north from the Kaesong area towards the North Korean capital of Pyongyang.

In the east the ROK 3rd and Capitol Divisions captured Wonsan by the 10th of October. A week later they had moved on up the coast and captured Hamhung and the large port city of Hungnam. Meanwhile, in the center of the peninsula near Chunchon, the ROK 6th Division had crossed into North Korea by the 6th of October.

In the west the 1st Cavalry Division ran into a stubborn enemy defense on their way to Kumch'on. A strong enemy roadblock just north of Kaesong stopped the 1st and 2nd Battalions of the 5th Cavalry. Here in the process of driving back the enemy, Lt. Sam Coursen distinguished himself by conspicuous gallantry and received the nations highest award for bravery, The Congressional Medal of Honor. Lt. Coursen single-handedly saved the life of a wounded comrade by engaging the enemy in hand-to-hand combat until he (himself) was killed. In his struggle he killed seven enemy and eliminated the main position of the enemy roadblock.

The three regiments of the 1st Cavalry Division encircled an enemy pocket of resistance around Kumch'on. The 7th Cavalry made a wide sweep on the left, the 5th Cavalry on the right and the 8th Cavalry in the center. As the 7th Cavalry blocked the main highway north of Kumch'on to create a pocket, the 5th and 8th Regiments pushed the defending North Koreans slowly into the pocket. After five days Kumch'on fell and major enemy resistance had almost ceased.

As the North Korean forces weakened, they used more and more ambushes to try to slow down the advancing Eighth Army. Since these enemy forces were limited in size, they would concentrate on targeting headquarters and service units that would give them limited

American 24th Regiment (Afro-American until September 1951) helps a wounded soldier.

resistance. Mounted infantry units were avoided at all costs. The North Koreans would even allow the guns of an artillery battalion to pass by their roadblock in order to attack the sophisticated fire direction unit as they passed in their trucks and jeeps.

During this time two other divisions moved up on line with the 1st Cavalry Division. On the west the 24th Division moved toward Chinnapo. On the right the 1st ROK Division moved towards Pyongyang. In addition the 27th Commonwealth Brigade, now with the newly attached Australian 3rd Battalion, pushed through the 1st Cavalry Division in the center and took over the lead to Sariwon.

These attacking UN units were moving so fast that they overran many North Korean units. Different uniforms caused confusion on both sides. When the Argylls of the 27th Brigade took Sariwon and saw North Korean soldiers approaching them from the south, they mistook these enemy soldiers for ROKs. On the other hand, the approaching North Koreans thought that the Argylls in their strange Scot uniforms were Russians. Each greeted each other with open arms until they discovered their errors.

With the fall of Sariwon the race for the capture of Pyongyang began. From the south the US I Corps continued to push rapidly north. From the east four ROK divisions were racing each other to take the city in a wide envelopment from that direction. At 11a.m., 19 October, after sporadic enemy resistance, F Company, 5th Cavalry Regiment won the race and entered the North Korean capital.

The first Cavalry Division had become famous for putting up signs on almost every major road claiming that other units were using these thoroughfares, "Courtesy of the 1st Cavalry Division." In the attack on Chinnanpo, the port for Pyongyang,, which occurred after the fall of the North Korean capital, the 24th Divi-

63

187th Airborne RCT air drop into Sunchon, North Korea and Sukchon, October 1950.

sion finally got even. The 19th Infantry and supporting 24th Division artillery approached the city from the south, and placed artillery fire on the city across a wide body of water. The 1st Cavalry Division in the meantime had waited until the fall of Pyongyang to attack Chinnanpo from the east. When members of the 24th Division Artillery witnessed North Korean soldiers evacuating the city by boat, they quickly grabbed a boat themselves, crossed the body of water, and entered the city. When the 7th Cavalry arrived from the east at the gates of the city on October 22nd, they saw a hastily painted sign that said, "You are riding on Horseshit Street courtesy of the 24th Division Artillery."

Pyongyang was quickly evacuated by the enemy who feared being cut off by the enveloping ROK forces. Eighth Army quickly consolidated the city and gave responsibility for internal security to the 1st Cavalry Division. General MacArthur flew in from Tokyo and held a brief ceremony commemorating the capture of the enemy capital. Another national figure, Bob Hope, arrived soon after to perform his show for the troops. As he was making his congratulatory speech, the noise of machine gun fire was heard in the distance. Somewhat surprised, he quipped, "You did take this city, didn't you?"

The next step in the move north was for Eighth Army to push rapidly to the Chongchon River. On October 20th the 4000 man 187th Airborne RCT dropped twenty-six miles north of Pyongyang at Sukchon and Sunchon in hopes of capturing North Korean officials and troops fleeing from the capital. This drop was also to effect the rescue of American prisoners of war who were reported to be moving north by rail.

Unfortunately the 187th failed to catch any North Korean officials, or free any American prisoners. The 3rd Battalion, 187th drop at Sukchon, however, landed behind the 2500 man North Korean 239th Regiment which had been delaying Eighth Army forces in Pyongyang. On 21-22 October fierce fighting ensued between these two units. For a while the 3rd Battalion feared they might be overrun, but fortunately the NKPA 239th Regiment had to fend off the fierce attacks of the Australian 3rd Battalion which was hard on the heels of this enemy regiment. Hand-to-hand fighting took place. The Australians showed little mercy as they helped the 187th destroy this enemy unit. One American soldier following the Australians counted ninety-five North Korean soldiers in one area who had been killed while defending a sunken ditch along the road. Australian records show 270 enemy killed and 200 captured but only seven Australians wounded. The 3rd Battalion 187th reported 805 enemy killed and 681 captured. Overall this airborne drop cannot be considered a failure since the regiment as a whole captured 3,818 North Korean soldiers.

The attack north continued with little resistance. Northwest of Sunchon Americans discovered the result of an atrocity perpetrated by the fleeing North Koreans. Bodies of sixty-six American POWs were discovered in and around a railroad tunnel. Twenty-three American soldiers who had managed to escape were rescued. These Americans had been on two trains that had left Pyongyang several days earlier.

At this stage of the war morale was high. Every American soldier was anticipating getting home for Christmas. General MacArthur had promised that all troops would be home by Christmas. A feeling of victory and jubilation was at its height.

Eighth Army reached the Chonchon River by October 22nd. The ROK 1st and 6th Divisions pushed across the river and continued north into the high mountains of central North Korea. On the west the 24th Division crossed the Chonchon River and pushed on toward the Yalu River on the Chinese border. Spearheading this division was the attached 27th British Commonwealth Brigade. Enemy resistance stiffened at Paekchon as the Middlesex Battalion encountered a determined enemy with ten T-34 tanks. On 29-30 October the Australians ran into enemy resistance at Chongju. In this encounter during an enemy night attack the Australian Commander, Lt. Col. Charles H. Green, was mortally wounded by mortar fire.

At this stage the exhausted British Brigade was replaced by the 21st Regiment in Task Force Stevens. This force then pushed on to within seventeen miles of Sinuiju on the Yalu River. Simultaneously the 5th RCT moved on its right and by the 31st of October had reached a point ten miles beyond Kusong and only twenty-seven

Marine landings, Wonsan, Oct. 26, 1950.

Marine landings, Wonsan, Oct. 26, 1950.

Marine landings, Wosan, Oct. 26, 1950.

miles from the Yalu River. Suddenly an American plane flew over these units and dropped notes telling them to halt. At this time the lead company of the 5th RCT had captured two Chinese soldiers. (At the same time X Corps on the eastern side of Korea had captured sixteen Chinese soldiers.) News of both of these first Chinese captures was relayed all the way to Tokyo. In spite of speculation among front line soldiers about China's sudden role in the war, MacArthur's headquarters continued to report that these prisoners were not combat soldiers but only truck drivers delivering equipment to the North Koreans. The status of these captured Chinese was finally established on the evening of November 1st when the 24th Division was suddenly ordered to withdraw back to the Chongchon River. Chinese combat forces had struck the right flank of Eighth Army.

On the east coast meanwhile, X Corps had finally landed and units began to move north from the coast. The 1st Marine Division landed at Wonsan on the 26th of October and made plans to move north to the Chosin Reservoir, and the American 7th Infantry Division made plans to land at Iwon and move to the Yalu River. Meanwhile the ROK Capital Division had already moved past Hamhung on the coast and by the 28th had reached Songin.

From its inception the plan of using two main forces, Eighth Army and X Corps, was flawed. The rugged North Korean terrain created a large gap of at least fifty miles or more between these two units. Chinese intelligence was quick to spot the fallacy of this American plan. In addition control of these two forces remained under MacArthur in Tokyo, while communication between them was almost non-existant. The plan to use two forces controlled from Tokyo soon proved to be America's biggest strategic blunder.

Chapter Nine: Chinese Intervention into Western Korea

Unsan and Kunu-ri—Phase I of Chinese Intervention

A turning point in the war and an end to the defeat of North Korea came between 26 October and 1 November when the Chinese communist forces entered Korea and fell full fury on American and ROK forces in northwestern Korea. Some Chinese soldiers had been taken prisoner both by Eighth Army and X Corps. Simultaneously ROK units were beginning to meet and actually fight Chinese combat units. Through the 26th of October much fierce fighting ensued between these ROK units and "the Chinese volunteers." Eighth Army Intelligence still felt that these Chinese soldiers would "avoid any overt intervention." On 1 November the American Army was shocked to realize that they were being attacked by trained Chinese combat veterans.

From the beginning of the war North Korean and Chinese leaders had been confused over the policy and intentions of the US Government toward their countries. The North Korean Government had believed that the UN forces would stop at the 38th Parallel. A captured document of 14 October 1950 signed by the North Korean Premier, Kim Il Sung, implied that the 38th Parallel would be as far as the UN forces would attack. The UN crossing of the 38th Parallel on 9 October seems to have surprised not only the North Koreans but also the Chinese. Based on this American action lead units of the Chinese Peoples Volunteer Army (CCF) under Marshal Peng Dehuai on 18 October crossed the Yalu River into Korea. By the end of October six CCF Armies, eighteen divisions, were poised in the high mountains of central North Korea.

One of the best judges of the situation was

General Sun Yup Paik, the new Commander of the ROK II Corps, whose units were already engaged in fierce fighting with the Chinese by the 26th of October. He believed that the Allies were in a completely new war. He later realized that Marshal Deng's eighteen divisions had waited patiently as the momentum of the ROK units carried them deep into a Chinese mountain ambush. The Chinese cut off the ROK units routes of retreat and tried to annihilate them. Paik understood Chinese strategy well since he had served with the Japanese against the Chinese in World War II.

Reacting to the sudden Chinese entrance, General Walker ordered the 1st Cavalry Division which had been at Pyongyang to attack the Chinese forces at Unsan. Northeast of Unsan the ROK 6th Division had been destroyed, while the ROK 1st Division was still holding its position around Unsan. On November 1st the 8th Cavalry

Regiment replaced two regiments of the 1st ROK Division.

Hardly had the 1st and 2nd Battalions of the 8th Cavalry taken up their defensive positions north and west of Unsan when they were assaulted by two full Chinese divisions. The Chinese waves attacked in the evening supported only by mortars. The Chinese used bugles and signal flares as a means of control as their masses of infantry swarmed over the American positions.

The two American battalions fell apart and were driven back into Unsan. The 3rd Battalion, which had not been hit by the enemy, was

The Chinese Intervene in the West. (Source South to the Naktong, North to the Yalu, *office of the Chief of Military History, Department of the Army, 1961.)*

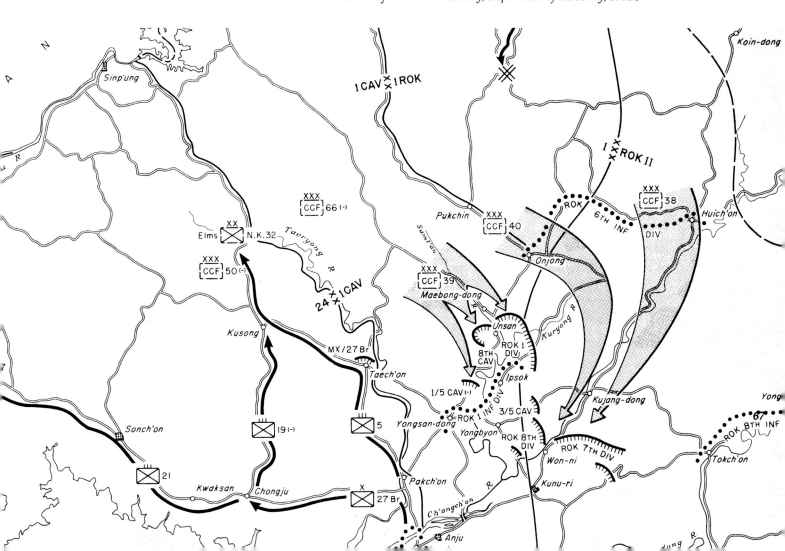

ordered to help the remnants of the other two battalions in a withdrawal. Unfortunately the Chinese attack was too rapid and by early morning of November 2nd the attackers overran the 3rd Battalion before they could begin their mission. Hand-to-hand fighting ensued. By mid-morning of November 2nd little was left of the 8th Cavalry Regiment whose survivors retreated on foot in small groups around Chinese road-blocks in the regiment's rear Efforts by the 5th Cavalry Regiment to break through these roadblocks caused tremendous American casualties, and the rescue of many survivors of the 8th Cavalry was in vain.

At this point in the hostilities the Chinese displayed one of their few humanitarian efforts. They allowed wounded Americans to return to their lines. Released walking wounded from the 5th Cavalry who had taken part in the effort to rescue the 8th Cavalry reported that the Chinese had placed captured American wounded along the road for Americans to pick up. A number of 5th Cavalry soldiers volunteered to risk rescuing these wounded men, and by dark the Chinese had allowed a number of jeep loads of wounded to be returned to American lines.

Other Allied units were quickly rushed to the Chongchon River line to back-up the 1st Cavalry Division. The Commonwealth Brigade at Pakchon came under severe attack by elements of the Chinese 39th Army. At that time the 24th Division withdrew around the British Brigade and took up positions to their right at Kunu-ri. Along with the 1st Cavalry Division these two divisions held a bridgehead that extended from Sinanju northeast to Kunu-ri. No sooner had the 24th Division units moved into defensive positions than the Chinese attacked them, and severe fighting ensued. The 19th Infantry was almost overrun as the 21st Infantry

rushed to their rescue on the north side of the Chongcong River.

Some members of the artillery support for the 19th Infantry were overrun and forced to swim across the Chongcong River to safety. Lt. Al Carozza of the 24th Division Artillery remembered from a training film that his heavy green field jacket and trousers were waterproof. When tightly buttoned, they could be filled with air and become life preservers. Using this technique, he and several others floated like corks with the current in the ice cold Chongcong River for half a mile, finally reaching the south shore and safety.

By November 6th all these American units and remnants of ROK units were desperately holding the line of the Chongchon River and expecting a renewed attack by the Chinese. Suddenly the enemy force to their front disappeared. To this day no clear answers have been given as to why the CCF suddenly withdrew. Some have speculated that this was a warning to the Allied forces to withdraw from North Korea.

A clear picture of the confusion during this battle can be given by comments of soldiers who were involved in this fight. They reported that all during the 3rd of November columns of retreating ROKs passed through the Allied forces. Not known at that time but supported by later evidence was that a number of Chinese soldiers dressed in American or ROK uniforms fell into the withdrawing ROK columns and passed through American lines. Once in the rear of the American positions they fired back at the unsuspecting American soldiers.

Company K 5th RCT, was one of the units rushed to the front to form a blocking position on the river's south side at Kunu-ri. While

19th Infantry, Winter, 1950-1951.

sloshing through mud in a downpour, carrying sleeping bags and feeling very dispirited, the men of this infantry company suddenly ran head-on into a mixed group of withdrawing ROKs and other soldiers in uniforms not familiar to the Americans. The advancing Americans with ponchos, pile caps and acquired Korean garments may have confused the approaching ROK column. Certainly the sergeant with the white fur hat that he had acquired with other Korean clothes because of the limited issue of Army winter clothing may have raised questions among the withdrawing ROKs. The confusion of identities on both sides led to a sudden fire-fight in which several men on each side became casualties.

In spite of such confusion credit should be given to veteran units that did not panic. Company K, 5th RCT, in spite of sudden casualties from a supposedly friendly unit, quickly adjusted to the situation and the men took cover. Suddenly more confusion occurred as American artillery began to land among the troops of Company K. This "friendly fire" caused injuries

to mount: Pfc. Rumery was hit in the foot, Corporals Prokovick, Rutledge and Bowling received stomach wounds. Pvt. German received a wound in his knee and Corporal Moran in his arm. In spite of this "friendly fire" Corporal Wixon rushed out through a hail of bursting shells and incoming rifle fire, picked up a wounded comrade and carried him to safety, During this time Sgt. Dorian, a platoon medic who had won the Silver Star on Hill 268 in Waegwan , unflinchingly continued to attend to the wounded . While he was bending over a wounded man, a bullet struck him in the arm. Disregarding his own wound, he fearlessly moved on to attend another wounded soldier. Suddenly a bullet hit him between the eyes, and he died instantly. The actions of most of these brave men remain unknown. For men like Sgt. Dorian the Korean War Memorial personifies the great sacrifices made by these servicemen.

Pause

The pause in the fighting caused by the withdrawal of the Chinese gave Eighth Army time to breathe. American leaders analyzed the

69

Chinese entry. At this stage in the war many discussions took place between MacArthur and the Joint Chiefs. Since China had entered the war should there be a policy change? MacArthur felt that it was important to complete the UN mission, which was to defeat North Korea and to institute a democratic system there. Both he and the leaders in Washington failed to understand the Chinese threat. Three weeks later this misunderstanding caused the UN forces to suffer dire consequences.

The Chinese soldiers were different from the North Korean. The Chinese Communist Force (CCF) was modeled on the communist guerrilla force that had been developed in the 1930s against the Japanese, and that had finally defeated the Nationalist forces of Chang Kai-shek. The NKPA was modeled on the Soviet Army. North Korean soldiers wore distinctive Russian uniforms that showed rank. These soldiers were supplied with heavy equipment such as artillery and tanks, and initially fought a modern style of war.

The soldiers of the CCF operated with simplicity and stressed egality between ranks. During the first year of the war this army was equipped with light weapons supported by mortars and machine guns. During the early attacks by hoards of Chinese infantry some men had no weapons at all. These soldiers were equipped with concussion grenades which were used to knock out Allied soldiers but not to damage their weapons. In the early fighting there were instances when Chinese soldiers tried to grab weapons away from American soldiers.

During the winter Chinese soldiers wore heavily quilted, brown cotton uniforms. They wore a quilted pile cap with ear flaps instead of helmets and wore canvas shoes. Because the cotton uniforms were not very warm, and the

caps and shoes were of poor quality, Chinese soldiers suffered from frostbite during the bitter Korean winter.

Chinese troops employed psychological warfare. Bugle calls and whistles were used extensively at night to frighten the enemy and as a means of control. Since daylight exposed the CCF to attacks from American air support, the Chinese fought mostly at night. Thus communication signals were essential. In the great CCF offensive of April 1951 suddenly armies of thousands of Chinese soldiers in green summer uniforms passed through defending armies of Chinese soldiers in quilted, brown uniforms. This was one of the few times in the war when the Chinese could be observed in bright sunlight assaulting Allied positions.

The major weakness of the CCF was in logistics. Throughout the war they appeared unable to sustain an offense beyond a six to eight day period. This limit was based on the amount of food an individual soldier could carry. The Chinese soldier carried a sock filled with flour or sorghum that would last him six to eight days. This diet was supplemented by any green vegetables and rice they could forage. One American theory was that once a Chinese offensive began, the Allies should withdraw to a defensive position at a point where the Chinese Army would run out of food and have to stop. During the winter of 1950-51 the Allies burned North Korean village stockpiles of rice and other food that might supplement the CCF diet in an attempt to slow down the movement of these large forces. In addition to individual soldiers the Chinese also used pack animals to haul supplies to forward areas. Such transport did not need roads. Consequently the Chinese could supply through the mountain trails and be undetected by American observers in the air.

The CCF had excellent training and became expert in tactics. Like the NKPA their method of attack was to work to the rear of a defending force and cut off escape routes. At night small units would approach Allied defense positions with the purpose of drawing fire in order to locate the positions. In assault the Chinese advanced in waves, and unlike most armies, they were willing to accept heavy casualties. One wave would come forward. In the event of heavy casualties another wave would replace the first wave. This would continue until the objective was taken. Any number of recorded instances can be cited by American veterans who remember Chinese bodies piling up in front of their machine guns.

The CCF were also well trained in strategy. In this they applied the same techniques used by Hannibal at the Battle of Cannae. There the attacking Romans moved into Hannibal's defending V formation whose sides then closed and trapped the Romans. The Chinese applied this same technique to the attacking Allied forces during the end of November-early December 1950. As MacArthur's offense moved slowly toward the Yalu for a second time, the CCF put up little resistance as they sucked the Allied forces deeper and deeper into the high northern mountains. In these mountains in the fifty mile gap between Eighth Army and X Corps they silently waited. On the night of November 25th they suddenly pounced on the over-extended Allies.

Chongchon River-Phase II Chinese Intervention against I US Corps

The brief withdrawal of the Chinese forces confused American Intelligence and caused them to believe that they had been fighting Chinese volunteers. The intelligence estimate of Chinese strength was only a third of actual strength. In addition to these faulty estimates, American Intelligence was not aware that new Chinese units were arriving across the Yalu River. East of the high Myomyang Mountains the Chinese Third Field Army, twelve divisions of 120,000 men, was assembling. In the west the eighteen division, 210,000 man Fourth Field Army withdrew from Unsan to the western side of this same range and also into the high Namgnim range just south of the Yalu River.

In the west the Allied Eighth Army waited for two weeks as it built up its strength to three corps. In the west was I Corps made up of the 24th Division, ROK 1st Division and the 27th British Commonwealth Brigade. In the center the 25th and Second US Divisions and the newly arrived 5,200 man Turkish Brigade formed IX Corps. On the east flank, extending to the western slopes of the Myomyang Mountains, was the ROK II Corps of the 6th, 7th and 8th Divisions. Other units arriving or in reserve were the 1st Cavalry Division, the 187th Airborne RCT, the British 29th Brigade and battalion size units from Belgium, Thailand and the Philippines.

An attack north with this force on 15 November had been planned, but logistics forced a delay until 24 November. It had been estimated that 4000 tons of supplies were needed for an offensive operation. This figure was not reached until the 24th. To reach this number 2000 tons had come by rail, 1000 tons by sea through the Port of Chinnampo and 1000 tons by air. However, the weather was turning cold and many units still did not have their full allotment of winter clothing.

The sudden appearance of the CCF at Unsan caused a precipitous drop in the morale of the fighting men in Eighth Army. No longer could they anticipate being home for Christmas.

To help boost morale General Walker insisted on giving every soldier a complete Thanksgiving meal. Cooks baked all night of the 22nd of November to prepare for the enormous feast the next day. In addition to turkey the men were given minced pie, fruit cake, nuts, candy and even shrimp salad. It was to be for most men their best meal in Korea. Most soldiers forgot the war for a moment. The enemy put up little resistance and remained concealed. For some the situation was too quiet. There was an ominous air. Men became suspicious.

The UN offensive jumped off along the Chongchon River on November 24th. On the first day of the attack American forces were successful and advanced slowly, but ROK units ran into stiff enemy resistance almost immediately. On the extreme right of Eighth Army the ROK II Corps were hit hard as the CCF 42nd Army pushed through them in a wide envelop-ment to get to the rear of Eighth Army. The Chinese applied a strategy that they continued to apply for much of the war. This strategy was to place the main thrust of their attacks initially against the South Koreans, because ROK units were not as heavily supported with heavy weapons as the American units.

On the left flank of US I Corps the 24th Division met scattered resistance. The ROK 1st Division on the right of the US 24th Division received almost immediately the full fury of the CCF Sixty-sixth Army. On the right flank of the 24th Division adjacent to the 1st ROK Division was the 5th RCT. Two Chinese Divisions pushed hard against the 1st ROK Division , while on their flank another Chinese Division struggled against the 5th RCT.

Members of the 24th Regiment, 25th Division receive incoming mortar fire, November 1950.

The story of the 5th RCT and its gradual contact with the CCF could be the same story told by other American units at that time. Initially 24th Division sent a company up alone into a blocking position to cover a gap on its flank next to the ROK 1st Division. When enemy activity began to build up in front of this company, the 2nd and 3rd Battalions 5th RCT were rushed up to strengthen the blocking position and protect the division right flank. The 3rd covered the right flank on a curved hill with L Company on the right facing east and K Company on its left facing north. Company I using tanks established a road block on the battalion left. The hill defended by the two companies was very steep and covered with dense foliage of scrub pine. Once the battalion positions had been established, patrols were sent out to find the exact enemy locations.

About 3 a.m. on 28 November an estimated two Chinese battalions attacked the 3rd Battalion 5th RCT position. The air suddenly filled with the sounds of battle of bugle notes, yells, machine gun clatter, and the thump of grenades, and these sounds ricocheted throughout the mountain valley. On that cold November night Corporal Arnett of K Company said to Corporal Bodie, "Do you hear anything or is that just the wind in the leaves?" Suddenly one of the attached KATUSAs opened fire. Immediately return fire came from down the hill. Concussion grenades began landing all over the American position. Enemy machine gun fire from the bottom of the hill started firing over the heads of the first wave of Chinese who were slowly crawling up the hill. The Americans quickly began throwing their own grenades down on the first wave of crawling Chinese. Several Chinese managed to crawl up between two American platoons. Lt. Jim Fife a platoon leader and World War II combat veteran, hit one over the head with his rifle and drove the others back down the hill. Corporal Raines, a machine gunner,

waited until the attacking Chinese were within 10 yards of his position before opening fire. He fired six full boxes of ammunition before his gun barrel burned out. At sunrise more than 50 Chinese bodies were counted in front of his machine gun position.

Although both companies were partially split by waves of Chinese, their defense was so strong that the enemy withdrew. Both companies suffered about 30 casualties each. The next day a liaison plane counted 300 Chinese bodies on the company positions. The greatest loss to the units was the great number of casualties who were well trained veterans, many of whom had just come back on line after being wounded in August and September.

Chongchon River-Phase II Chinese Intervention against US IX Corps

As the Chinese attacked along most of the Eighth Army front on the night of 25-26 November, the ROK IInd Corps and American IX Corps bore the brunt of the attack In the IX Corps the two divisions, the 25th on the left and 2nd on the right, had been progressing slowly toward the Yalu River in a northeast direction when they first came in contact with the Chinese. Leading the 25th Division was Task Force Dolvin made up of the 89th Tank Battalion and attachments On the right of this force was the 24th Infantry Regiment and on the left the 35th Infantry Regiment.

This force ran head-on into masses of attacking Chinese who struck between Task Force Dolvin and the 24th Regiment. All during the day of the 26th and into the evening fierce fighting ensued, and Task Force Dolvin was nearly overwhelmed by waves of Chinese. In this struggle Capt. Reginald Desiderio, commander of Company E, 27th Regiment, rushed

73

his company up to a key position to save the task force headquarters. He was accompanied by several tanks. Wave after wave of Chinese tried to assault his position. In spite of wounds Desiderio moved about the hilltop yelling, "Hold until daylight and you have it made." When another wave of Chinese overran a section of the position, the tanks and some of the men started to leave. Desiderio blocked the tanks from moving, and inspired his men to stand and fight, thus saving the position. During this last stand he was riddled by enemy bullets. The company took 60 casualties but held the position. Desiderio received the Congressional Medal of Honor, posthumously, for his staunch leadership.

On the task force right the 24th Regiment became heavily engaged and its three infantry battalions became widely separated. Communications between units, failed because the high mountains blocked radio communication between them. The 2nd Battalion was able to tie in with the 9th Infantry Regiment of the 2nd Division on its right. In the confusion the 27th (Wolfhound) Regiment was rushed in behind the 24th to cover the gaps between its battalions. The Chinese, however, managed to get around the 27th and establish a road block east of Yongbyon, cutting off the 27th. After severe fighting this roadblock was finally destroyed, and the 27th and part of the 24th Infantry were able to withdraw.

The 35th Infantry on the division left advanced northeast and by the 25th of November had reached a point overlooking Unsan where they had met limited resistance. At this time, fearing a trap, the division command stopped any further forward movement of the regiment. Not until two days later did the 35th Infantry begin to receive enemy pressure. On this date the whole 25th Division began to

withdraw, and the 35 Infantry was ordered to fall back towards the Chongchon River. Chinese forces somehow managed to block the main withdrawal route of the regiment at Yongsan-dong. To open the withdrawal route, elements of the 1st ROK Division counterattacked and retook the town. The 25th Division was then able to fall back to the Chongchon River bridges at Anju.

The Chinese Onslaught on the 2nd Infantry Division

The heaviest blows by the CCF on the American units in Eighth Army fell on the 2nd Infantry Division. It caught the full tide of three Chinese armies. Six Chinese divisions attacked the 2nd Division directly, while six more poured through the ROK II Corps and made a wide envelopment around the US IX Corps. The result of this conflict was one of the worst disasters incurred by any division size American unit in the war.

On the 25th of November the 2nd Division was northeast of Kujang-dong with the 9th Infantry on the left, the 38th Infantry on the right and the 23rd in reserve near Kunu-ri. The 9th Infantry was hit the hardest on both its flanks and rear. Two battalions of the 23rd Infantry along with the 2nd Engineer battalion were rushed up to cover both flanks of the 9th Infantry. Cpl. Don Thomas, K Company 23rd Infantry, was in a truck convoy that passed a convoy of 9th Infantry trucks that were stacked high with litters of dead American soldiers. The shock of this sight sobered up the men in his truck very quickly. In this move the 61st and 503rd Field Artillery Battalions moved up to positions in the Chongchon River bed to give close support to the infantry. The 1st Battalion, 23rd Infantry dug defensive positions along the river to protect the artillery. These two artillery units thought they were well secured.

At about 8 p.m. that evening, to the surprise of the Americans, an estimated 1000 Chinese soldiers suddenly appeared. These Chinese soldiers were naked from the waist down so they could ford this river even on this bitter cold night. Once across the river they paused to put on their trousers. This unexpected move by the Chinese so confused the American defenders that little resistance was put up before the Chinese soldiers were among the American positions. Hardest hit was the 61st FA Battalion which had positions on the river east of the infantrymen of the 23rd. Before A Battery could even get a defense organized, the commander was killed. Lt. Jack Kean took command and tried to rally his men as the Chinese swarmed over the FA battalion. Survivors withdrew into the 1st Battalion, 23rd Infantry positions to their south.. Luckily American tanks arrived on the position and rallied the 23rd infantrymen. Together they drove the Chinese back and secured the position. Driven off the American position on the river by the arrival of the American tanks, the Chinese veered to a ridge overlooking the camp called "Chinaman's Hat." Here they remained, a thorn in the 2nd Division's rear, until the division's withdrawal.

When the ROK II Corps collapsed on the right flank of Eighth Army and allowed six Chinese divisions to make a wide envelopment, the 2nd Division's escape route to Tokchon was blocked. The only route of withdrawal remaining for this division was along the Chongchon River from Kujang-dong to Kunu-ri. At Kunu-ri was a key road junction. Here the main route of withdrawal continued on south along the river to Anju. At Kunu-ri, however, a secondary road wound through a gap in the mountains to Sunchon. The river road was much longer than the eighteen mile mountain road, and if used ,would cause the 2nd Division to become involved with the traffic of withdrawing US I Corps and the 25th Division.

By the 27th the 23rd Infantry as well as the 38th Infantry on its right were fighting off more waves of Chinese attacks. The fighting was so fierce that the 23rd Command Post was overrun, but was recovered after a rallied counterattack. The enemy infiltrated through and around the 38th Infantry on the division right. By late on the 27th the division right flank was on the verge of collapse.

One American veteran who watched the confusion with horror was Capt. Sherman Pratt of Company B, 23rd Infantry whose company was in a blocking position. He remembers American soldiers retreating through his position who had no weapons, helmets, and packs, and sometimes no shoes. Pratt had captured about fifty Chinese prisoners who were in a rice paddy nearby. He tried to persuade one of the units passing through to take them with them to the rear. All declined. One passing officer even commented, "Just shoot the bastards." Pratt didn't follow that advice and somehow managed to get them to the rear.

To block the CCF envelopment against the 2nd Division right flank, IX Corps rushed in the newly arrived Turkish Brigade of 5000 men. Their mission was to push east on the Kunu-ri-Tokchon Road and slow down the Chinese advance. Eight miles outside of Kunu-ri the Turks ran head-on into advancing CCF forces. The Turks fought bravely and suffered many casualties but were forced to withdraw back towards Kunu-ri. Though greatly outnumbered, they refused to give up and continued to block the Chinese attempt to cut the 2nd Division rear. As a result of this fight they established an excellent reputation within Eighth Army as being a tough, fanatic fighting force. In fact when they reported casualties, they seldom reported wounded, and assumed all men were fit for duty if they could walk.

A weary soldier rests after a bitter fight.

On the 28th of November General Walker directed the withdrawal of the entire Eighth Army. He ordered the 1st Cavalry Division to cover the Eighth Army right flank to prevent the Chinese from severing the main lines of withdrawal. The 1st Cavalry Division which was in Eighth Army reserve, was moved to a blocking position at Sunchon. Only the 2nd Division and the Turkish Brigade were in a precarious position and found it difficult to withdraw.

The 2nd Division used basic withdrawing tactics: establishing blocking positions and having units leap-frog through each other. The reinforced 23rd Infantry withdrew to positions at Kujang-dong. The other Infantry regiments withdrew through these positions and moved southeast down the Chongchon River valley road and set up a blocking positions. Once most of the division vehicles had reached Kunu-ri, the 23rd Infantry moved back to Won-ni and established a blocking position to the right of the 9th Infantry.

At this point a major decision had to be made by the Division Commander, MG Lawrence Keiser. The enemy was reported to be blocking part of the mountain road through the gap between Kunu-ri and Sunchon. Keiser had sent small units to open this roadblock, but they had not been successful. He then ordered the 9th Infantry, with a strength by this time of only 400 men, to attempt to open the roadblock. Reports coming back to him from the 9th Infantry concerning success in overcoming this roadblock were conflicting. Should he try the route through the gap over the mountains to Sunchon and risk roadblocks, or should he take the longer route along the Chongchon River to Anju? He decided on the mountain road to Sunchon.

As the division moved out down the mountain road on November 30th, the infantry was dispersed throughout the column between the headquarters, artillery, and engineer units. No sooner had the lead units gone a mile when they ran into heavy enemy small arms and mortar fire. At this time they did not realize that this was not just a small enemy roadblock but an entire Chinese division stretched along both sides of the road for a distance of seven miles. It was an avenue of death.

Credit must be given to the US Air Force that the division was able to run this gauntlet. All day long aircraft flew up and down the road and strafed all suspicious enemy positions. When the planes were strafing, enemy fire stopped. When the planes stopped, the enemy fire would begin again. Aided by these air attacks and by fire from the artillery twin-40 mm guns, the division inched forward.

Disabled vehicles blocked the road and had to be pushed aside. Some, such as large artillery howitzers, could only be bypassed. Those vehicles that could move were loaded with the wounded. On this march no arms of the division suffered as much at this time as the engineers and artillery. The 2nd Division had been given the largest concentration of artillery support of any unit in Eighth Army. The division, overloaded with heavy equipment from these units, now had great difficulty in moving it through the narrow mountain road and over the mountain gap down to Sunchon.

No one in this division withdrawal was immune to the terrible enemy fire. MG Keiser and his Assistant Division Commander, MG Joseph Bradley, relinquished their vans to the wounded and rode in jeeps. Keiser's bodyguard was killed while manning the vehicle machine gun. At times Keiser dismounted and fired his rifle at the enemy while shouting encouragement to the men around him. No one could ever fault his division command and staff for not personally participating in the struggle common to all infantry riflemen.

Pfc. Kenneth Poss of the Heavy Mortar Company, 9th Infantry, remembers in detail the mass confusion on the road. It was clogged with every imaginable type of vehicle: jeeps, trucks of all sizes, tanks and artillery. At a U bend in the road a Chinese machine gun opened up on the truck he was riding in. He jumped out into a steep gully. Bodies of dead and wounded American soldiers were all around him. One soldier who was only slightly wounded was, "drunk as a skunk." With his rifle Poss picked off the three Chinese soldiers manning the machine gun. After this he followed a dry riverbed until he reached the lines of the newly-arrived, British 29th Brigade at Sunchon.

Other units trying to run through the fireblock at this gauntlet moved in spurts. Their

50 Caliber Machine Gunner, possibly anti-aircraft.

vehicles would dash forward until enemy fire stopped them. The men in these vehicles would jump into ditches along the road and return fire. After an American air strike there would be a lull, and the men would mount the vehicles and dash on until they came under fire again. At the large pass on the mountain route enemy mortar fire made passage almost impossible. The column was often held up for almost an hour. Eventually air strikes slowed down the Chinese mortar fire, and the column dashed on down the mountain towards Sunchon.

In the rear of the division column was the 23rd Infantry whose mission was to protect that part of the column and follow the division through the pass to Sunchon. As the day wore on Chinese pressure increased, and the Commander of the 23rd Infantry, Col. Paul L. Freeman, became concerned that his unit might be cut off. He felt that his best route of withdrawal was probably by way of the Chongchon River road to Anju. When he revealed his feeling that to comply with 2nd Division's order to go the mountain route was immediate suicide for his unit, the Assistant Division Commander, Maj.Gen. Joseph S.Bradley, gave him permission to use the Anju road.

With the 23rd Infantry no longer in the rear of the division column, the 503rd and 38th Field Artillery Battalions became the rear-guard. In the enemy roadblock at the gap, B Battery, 503rd Artillery was overrun, and the Battalion Commander, Lt. Col. Robert J. O'Donnell, was badly wounded. Three quad-50 and two dual-40 AAA guns were pushed to the front of the column and opened up on the Chinese. As the enemy fire slackened, part of the column dashed through the gap and sped toward Sunchon, surprising Chinese soldiers who had cut the mountain route at the burning village of Karhyon. The remainder of the battalion, about 200 men, walked out over the hills to safety.

Another unit in the rear of the division column that suffered when the 23rd Infantry withdrew to Anju was the 2nd Engineer Battalion. The battalion had defended two critical hills southwest of the former 2nd Division CP. With the withdrawal of the infantry they became wide open to attacks by Chinese from across the Chingchon River and from Chinese who had been attacking the 23rd Infantry from the east. In addition, the enemy at the fireblock at the gap attacked them from the south. On the evening of November 30th they found themselves alone and assaulted from all directions. Out of an authorized strength of 977 men only 266 remained when a final count was made. Over 95 percent of their t/o &e equipment was lost. They sustained one of the highest rates of battle casualties of any battalion in the Korean War.

Some soldiers who had successfully gotten through the pass decided to return and help others at the "Gauntlet." Sgt. Arthur Macedo, HQ 38th Regiment, grabbed several vehicles and returned to assist the battle-worn soldiers. He found men dazed with glazed eyes. They told stories of men too wounded to move from where they fell that were ground up like hamburger by escaping American tanks.

The 23rd Infantry withdrew south along the Chongchon River and passed through the 24th Division which was securing the Chongchon bridges at Anju. Few Americans have witnessed the withdrawal of their own defeated army as did the members of this division guarding the bridges. On that bitter cold November night the rag-tag survivors of the US. I Corps, ROK II Corps, 25th Division and 23rd Infantry poured across the bridges. All were heading south in a hurry. Trucks of all sizes, tanks, jeeps, howitzers and other wheeled vehicles , all crammed with frightened men, many without helmets or weapons, passed across the bridges and rushed south. These men, haggard and bearded, feared that they would be left behind in this big retreat.

The greatest tragedy, however, was the mass of North Korean refugees. They had to wait for completion of the Eighth Army withdrawal, before they were allowed to cross over the bridges. The stricken faces of these refugees revealed their dread of the conquest of their country by the Chinese. These refugees had an historical dislike of the Chinese, and they feared reprisals. Campfires flickered on the river bank as these refugees tried to repel the bitter cold. A few braved the frigid water and waded across the river. Finally, after the Eighth Army had completed passage over the bridges, they were blown by the engineers, and thousands of shivering refugees were left stranded on the north side of the river.

The Eighth Army survived the withdrawal

from the Chongchon River front, but many units suffered a terrible cost in casualties and equipment. The 2nd Division lost over 5000 men and most of its heavy equipment. The division had to be almost completely rebuilt to become combat effective again. The exhausted Eighth Army, now in a completely new war, was to continue the longest retreat in American history.

Chapter Ten: Chinese Intervention Chosen -Northeast

Chinese Intervention-Phase I

The activities of the "Chinese Volunteer Forces" against X Corps in northeast Korea in late October were a mirror image of their activities against Eighth Army. In spite of total destruction of the 7th ROK Regiment near Sudong and fierce fighting with the 7th Marines from 5 to 7 November near Chinhung, the Chinese forces suddenly melted away as they had at Unsan. Although this sudden withdrawal confused MacArthur and his staff in Japan, the Far East Command was still convinced that these Chinese soldiers were volunteers and limited in number.

The original plan, which was to have X Corps link up with Eighth Army and help take Pyongyang ,was changed when Eighth Army captured the North Korean capital before X Corps had landed in Northeastern Korea. On 24 October the mission for X Corps in the northeastern part of Korea was changed from attacking west to attacking north towards the Yalu River. Under this plan the 1st Marine Division was to push north toward the Chosen Reservoir, while the 17th Regiment of the 7th Division was to land at Iwon and advance north directly to the Yalu River.

The landing of X Corps began on 25 October when the first elements of the 1st Marine

American casualty of the 19th Inf. being carried to the aid station by Katusas.

Chosen, Marines, December 1950.

Chosen, Armored Personnel Carrier, December 1950.

Division landed at Wonsan. The 7th Marines led the drive north to Hamhung and the Chosen Reservoir. As the 7th Marines progressed north toward the Chosin Reservoir, they ran into an entire Chinese division which initially put up stiff resistance and then suddenly melted away.

On the 29th the 17th Infantry landed at Iwon, a port fifty miles northeast of Hungnam. During the next ten days over 25,000 men of the 7th Division and other units followed. By October 31st the 17th Infantry had pushed inland to the outskirts of Pungsan, an area which had recently been taken by the ROK Capital Division. Delays began to slow their northward movement. Fierce counterattacks by fanatical NKPA and limited bridging equipment slowed the regiment's progress. An additional contribution to the slowdown was the temperature, which was thirty-two degrees below zero. After surmounting several NKPA roadblocks, with one final push on November 21st the 17th Infantry covered the last thirty-one miles to the Yalu at Hyessanjin unopposed.

MacArthur believed this was a great political achievement and a public relations opportunity. Quickly generals arrived to have their pictures taken with the Yalu River in the background. The troops, however, faced a different reality. It was bitter cold, they were still eating canned rations, and they lacked proper winter clothing.

During this phase of the UN offensive individual units moved rapidly and often took great risks. Lieutenants Jack Madison and Joe Kingston of I Company, 32nd Infantry were ordered to secure a hydro-electric plant near the Fusan Reservoir. They crammed their company into boxcars on a North Korean rail line headed into the mountains. The train skidded and slipped often in the snow and ice. The train crew

frequently had to dismount to spread sand. As the train went deeper and deeper into enemy territory and passed through tunnel after tunnel, the Americans waited in suspense for the enemy to suddenly derail the train and have it tumbling down a mountainside.

Fortunately the company arrived safely at the power plant to find that many workers had fled into the mountains because they feared American atrocities. Madison, now Commander of the local village, persuaded the civilians to return to their homes and restored operations at the power plant He also gave the townspeople a lesson in democracy. He had them elect a new mayor.

The company next rejoined their regiment, traveling by trucks over hazardous icy mountain passes. They were then attached to Task Force Kingston for a dash to the Yalu River. Kingston's force, with limited resources, made a remarkably bold attack against very stiff enemy resistance. In bitter weather this small force finally reached the Yalu River on 28 November.

On November 24th Almond devised a new plan approved by MacArthur which was to be implemented on November 27th. The 1st Marine Division was to attack west from the Chosen Reservoir to Yudam and on the Yalu River. The 7th Division was now to move to the east side of the Chosen Reservoir, relieve the 5th Marine Regiment and advance to the Yalu. The newly arrived US 3rd Division would provide security for the Wonsan-Hamhung area.

This plan contained worrisome flaws. X Corps was overextended. There was a gap of eighty miles between the 1st Marine and 7th Infantry Divisions. The 7th Division redeployment was scattered, roadnets were jammed, and the weather slowed movement over the rugged mountains and isolated units,

MacArthur, however, had confounded the experts with his ingenious Inchon landing in September. Who was bold enough to challenge his risk taking in this latest plan? When the Chinese struck a few of his exposed forces individually between 28 October and 7 November and then disappeared, MacArthur's staff surmised that these were only token forces. Maj. Gen. Charles H. Willoughby, MacArthur's G-2, surmised that only volunteers had entered Korea and that probably only a few volunteers of each division identified were actually in Korea. Some commanders were unhappy with the dispersal of their units. Maj.Gen.Oliver P. Smith, Commander of the 1st Marine Division, was particularly worried and wanted his division consolidated. He was concerned about his exposed western flank. At the same time the 7th Infantry Division was scattered. The 17th Infantry was on the Yalu River, eighty miles from the other two division regiments, the 31st Infantry and 32nd Infantry. These two regiments were thirty miles east of the 1st Marine Division at the Chosen Reservoir. With the sudden change of plans, the three 7th Division regiments had to rush to the Chosen Reservoir in order to make a big attack with the Marines on November 27th.

The Chosen Reservoir is located in the middle of a 4000 foot high plateau. A very steep and difficult road stretches for sixty-four miles from Hungnam to the Chosen Reservoir. At the south end of the reservoir is the village of Hagaru, a junction where the main road south splits into two roads leading up both sides of the reservoir. This main road to Hungnam was the only road from the south into this rugged, mountainous plateau around the reservoir. It became a key feature in this campaign, because it

was the main supply route for X Corps. Hagaru became the major supply base for X Corps. Here a field hospital was constructed as well as an airstrip for evacuating the wounded.

It was necessary to supplement the truck route to Hungnam with an air route because the road up to the plateau from Chinhung to Koto was very treacherous. The airstrip at Hagaru that the engineers built was just long enough to permit the landing of C-47 two engine transport planes. The tiny valley had insufficient level ground and this factor, coupled with bad weather conditions, made the completion of this project. difficult. Fortunately the C-47 had incredible adaptability and somehow found a way to land and take off between the towering mountains that ringed the village of Hagaru.

Responsibility for work on the MSR from Hamhung to Hagaru was given to the X Corps Engineer, Lt. Col. Edward L. Rowny. The route became a narrow trail as it climbed from Chinhung to Kato. It had so many hairpin turns that heavy equipment was unable to negotiate much of this route. The escarpment was so steep that a narrow-gauge railroad that roughly followed the route became a cable car for the climb. On 16 November engineers began to improve the road. By 19 November large bulldozers finally were able to reach Hagaru to work on the airstrip. Still the Marine M-26 Pershing tank was too wide for most turns and further work was needed to get them up the pass.

Almond's order on the 25th of November gave the 1st Marine Division and the 7th Division only two days to get their troops into position for the attack. The 5th Marines were on the east side of the Chosen Reservoir and could not leave until replaced by a regiment of the 7th Division. To implement this order and attack on the 27th Maj. Gen. David G. Barr, Commander 7th Division, had to move his units piecemeal and rush in first his units nearest the Chosen Reservoir. He assembled a regimental task force under Col. Allan D. MacLean that consisted of the 2nd and 3rd Battalions, 31st Infantry, 1st Battalion 32nd Infantry, 31st Tank Company, 57th Field Artillery Battalion and D Battery, 15th AAA Battalion.

The closest unit of the task force which could relieve the 5th Marines was the 1st Battalion, 32nd Regiment commanded by Lt. Col. Don C. Faith, Jr.. This unit experienced several changes in orders and delays at the pass while climbing up the escarpment to the plateau, but late on the 25th the battalion closed in on the east side of the reservoir on Hill 1221 near Twiggae. A battalion perimeter was established for the evening. The weather was bitter and the men tended to over-relax when they got warm. Lt. James O. Mortrude, a World War II combat veteran and winner of the Distinguished Service Cross for heroism in the fight for Seoul, was critical of his men's laxness when he found most of his men asleep that night in their fox-holes.

On the 27th Col. MacLean arrived at Faith's location and took command. While there he received a report that a Chinese force of several hundred soldiers was in a village up the Pungnyuri River valley. The 31st Regiment I and R Platoon under Lt. Richard B. Coke Jr. was ordered to patrol the valley and investigate this report. This platoon vanished, and was never heard of again.

On the 27th Faith's battalion replaced the Marines and occupied most of the vacated Marine positions. Units of the 31st Infantry task force had arrived on the east side of the reservoir north of Hagaru, and were scattered in seven different locations over a distance of ten miles. This task force was far from concentrated and was vulnerable to any sizable enemy attack.

In the west the 1st Marine Division had been moving into position to start the attack north on the 27th. Two days earlier the 7th Marines pushed north from Toktong Pass and occupied Yudam. By the 27th the 5th Marines had moved from east of the reservoir through Hagaru and passed through the 7th Marines to continue the division attack from Yudam. While these two Marine regiments were concentrated, the third Marine regiment of the division, the 1st Marines, was spread out to secure the MSR from Hagaru as far south as Chinhung below the Funchllin Pass.

While X Corps was moving into position to attack north to the Yalu on the 27th, the Chinese Third Field Army of twelve divisions of 120,000 men was moving into position to destroy the American X Corps. General Almond believed there were no more than one or two CCF Divisions of about 20,000 Chinese soldiers on his Chosen Front. The ultimate clash between these two forces - The Battle of the Chosen Reservoir - is considered one of the major military mistakes in American history. Conversely it is one of the most brilliant and bravest withdrawals in American history.

Chinese Attack - Phase II - East of the Chosin Reservoir

At midnight on November 28th the CCF made their first big assault on the 7th Division forces east of the Chosin Reservoir. The 27th Chinese Army, an experienced army that had distinguished itself in the Chinese Civil War, sent its 80th Division to attack the dispersed units of Task Force MacLean.

The northern most unit of this task force was Faith's battalion. It was in a defensive perimeter with A Company facing north on the left side of the road, C Company was on the right side of the road and B Company was in reserve facing southeast. That night Company A was assaulted by the Chinese on both flanks in a double envelopment. At the same time part of C Company was overrun. Although Capt. Edward B. Scullion, the Company Commander, was killed in this struggle, the battalion managed to hold on to its position until sunrise. Carrier based Corsairs were able to hold back the Chinese during the day, so by nightfall the battalion perimeter was re-established.

Simultaneously on the evening of the 28th another perimeter at Sinhung made up of the 3rd Battalion, 31st Infantry and 57th Artillery Battalion was aggressively assaulted by the Chinese. By morning this perimeter was surrounded and had suffered many casualties. On the 29th Col. MacLean decided to move Faith's 1st Battalion, 32nd Infantry four miles south and unite with the perimeter at Sinhung. The CCF set up a roadblock to stop this move, but Faith moved his A Company out on the ice of the reservoir and destroyed this enemy force from behind. As Faith moved his battalion in to consolidate with the perimeter at Sinhung, he noticed that the 3rd Battalion area appeared to be a scene of total devastation. Chinese troops were observed moving about just outside the reduced perimeter.

In this early morning confusion MacLean moved about trying to restore some form of consolidation and establish a stronger perimeter. He was an aggressive commander and liked to command from the front. At this time he and Faith went on a reconnaissance around the perimeter. Through the early morning haze MacLean and his command party observed a column of troops approaching the perimeter. MacLean, thinking these were new arrivals from his own 31st Regiment and might receive fire from American troops in the perimeter, crossed an icy inlet towards them to prevent any confusion. When he got near the opposite side of the inlet, some of the troops in the column began shooting at him. Then MacLean's command group saw several Chinese come out on the ice and take him prisoner. He was never seen again. Col. Faith assumed command of the perimeter.

For two days the beleaguered battalions remained in the perimeter surrounded by thousands of Chinese. The Corsairs flew cover during the day and even by moonlight at night as they napalmed, rocketed and machine-gunned the enemy. During the day the perimeter received air drops of food and ammunition. With quiet desperation the defenders hoped that relief was coming. A division task force from Hagaru tried to break through the Chinese roadblocks and rescue them but was hurled back.

Capt. Edward Stamford was the Marine forward observer with Task Force Faith and controlled the Corsair attacks. According to pilots controlled by Stamford the sides of the perimeter were covered with communist troops, some of whom were so bold as to stand up in their foxholes and wave at the planes. S/Sgt. Chester Bair noted that the Chinese soldiers had white uniforms to blend with the snow. When the Corsair's attacked, most of the Chinese soldiers would fade into gullies where detection from the air became difficult.

Life inside the perimeter was a struggle. The cold caused most men, particularly the wounded, to suffer. A few warm up tents were erected, and mess halls tried to serve hot coffee and soup. Sleep was limited to two or three hours for most men. The dead and wounded began to mount up. The dead were stacked up in trucks. Medical supplies were sorely needed since only a few had been successfully air dropped. Col. Faith asked as many of the wounded as could possibly do so to come back on line and hold out until daylight when air support would arrive.

One of the survivors of Task Force Faith was Pfc. James Ransone Jr.: "I felt better when I saw Col. Faith in the middle of the perimeter. He was a Lieutenant Colonel in the middle of everything. More Chinese crawled along a ditch next to the railroad. My foxhole overlooked the ditch. There's no telling how many Chinese were killed right there. - They lay on top of each other, in some places ten deep. — They were everywhere. Only thing I can figure is they were hepped up with something, opium or whatever."

On December 1st Col. Faith made a fatal decision. The perimeter survivors were ordered to make a break for Hagaru. Only small supplies of ammunition, bandages and morphine were left. Continuing attacks by the CCF forces were slowly destroying the survivors, and any hope of being rescued by American forces from Hagaru had long since faded.

As the column broke out of the perimeter and moved south towards Hagaru, it maintained its organizational structure in spite of steady Chinese fire. US air support flew over and suddenly dropped napalm on the American column instead of on the Chinese. Panic set in, and all sense of organization was lost. The men that kept moving found that they were less apt to become targets for Chinese snipers. Those that stopped or delayed became Chinese victims. Chinese roadblocks were either assaulted or bypassed. It was during one of these roadblock

assaults that Col. Faith was mortally wounded. His loss was a shock to his men. Don Faith had been an inspiration to his men. For his outstanding gallantry and self-sacrifice he was awarded The Congressional Medal of Honor.

Now leaderless at the top, the American survivors scattered in all directions. Many who could still walk moved out on the ice of the reservoir. The Chinese refused to chase these survivors on the ice. By walking across the ice of the reservoir to Hagaru, some reached safety.

On December 2nd the Marines at Hagaru organized a task force of trucks, jeeps and sleds to try to rescue as many soldiers of Task Force Faith as they could find. The Marine task force rescued 319 soldiers, most of whom were suffering from wounds and frostbite. This rescue work continued and eventually 1900 men were saved. Of these only 385 were fit for duty. Of approximately 3000 men who had been in Task Force MacLean on November 27th about 1000 soldiers were killed, captured, or left in enemy held territory.

The sacrifice of Task Force MacLean may not have been in vain. Records indicate that during the five day delay this force almost destroyed the CCF 80th Division. This delay on the east side of the Chosen Reservoir prevented the CCF from taking Hagaru and allowed the 5th and 7th Marines to later withdraw south through Hagaru.

Chinese Attack - Phase II - West of the Chosin Reservoir

The engagement of the CCF forces and the Marines west of the Chosen Reservoir was in many ways similar to the engagement of the Chinese and Task Force MacLean east of the

Sgt. Pat Scully remembered with pride how Fox Company had defended for five days: "I saw Captain Barber go out onto the road and shake hands with Ray Davis, the officer who was leading the rescue force. And then Barber comes back and says, 'Sergeant Scully, Get this area squared away. We're getting out of here' We then walked six miles to the Marine positions at Haganu, frozen, dirty, starved and exhausted. Just before we got to the perimeter our platoon leader, Lt. Peterson said,' All right you guys, square yourselves away. We're gonna go in like Marines.' We straightened our helmets and gear and straightened our shoulders, somebody counted cadence, and we marched in like Marines."

On December 3rd the Marine "Ridgerunners" overcame the CCF defense positions at Toktong Pass with support from the spearhead of the main body as it moved through the MSR from Yudam. The 1st Battalion "Ridgerunners" then held the vital pass until the two regiments from Yudam had moved through. This was the last major obstacle on the way into Hagaru. On 4 December Lt. Col. Davis led his battalion into Hagaru. For his outstanding leadership and success on this very difficult mission, Lt. Col. Davis received our nation's highest award, The Congressional Medal of Honor.

Breakout to Hungnam

The first phase of the X Corps withdrawal was completed when Marine and Army units withdrew from both sides of the Chosin Reservoir into Hagaru. During this period CCF forces encircled the units at Hagaru and blocked the main MSR at a number of places between Hagaru and Chinhung. The 1st Marine Regiment who had been given the mission to keep this extensive route open ran into difficulties when confronted with the size of the Chinese forces.

On 29 November Task Force Drysdale at Koto, made up of British Marine Commandos, American Marines, and soldiers from the 7th Division, was given orders to fight up the MSR to Hagaru. Halfway to Hagaru the column came under severe attack in an open area later named "Hell Fire Valley." A Chinese mortar round set one of the trucks afire and prevented the column south of the vehicle from moving. Col. Drysdale, at the head of the column, not aware that the rear of the column couldn't move, advanced on toward Hagaru with Marine tanks and most of the Royal Marines. Outside Hagaru this advancing force ran into more Chinese resistance but fought their way into the Hagaru perimeter.

The cutoff American and British forces received fire from the Chinese on all sides of the column. A tank task force at Koto tried to break through the roadblock and rescue the column but was unsuccessful. During the day Corsairs kept the Chinese at bay, but in the evening hours of 30 November CCF soldiers made many probing attacks. In the confusion the Americans and British were overrun ,and a number were taken prisoner. Of the 922 men who started with the task force 321 became casualties.

During the Chosen engagement Hagaru had become a major supply base. The new airstrip allowed C-47 cargo planes to bring in supplies and evacuate the wounded. The town was full of supply, transportation, engineer, and headquarters units, but had only three companies of combat Marines to secure it. On 28 November the CCF attacked the supply base and at one point broke through the defense perimeter, but they did not follow up on their success. Hagaru was saved from a major CCF attack, because the main Chinese effort was concentrated south of Hagaru against the main MSR leading to Hungnam.

Lt. Tom Myer was one of a number of Marine replacements that were flown into Hagaru on December 1st and immediately "given instructions to help secure the hills above the MSR." He lasted three days. After holding off numerous attacks, he became a casualty and was evacuated by truck to Hungnam.

Phase II of the X Corps withdrawal began on December 6th as the Marines and Army broke out of Hagaru to fight south along the MSR to Chinhung. At Koto and Chinhung these forces were to join most of the 1st Marine Regiment. The first step in the withdrawal was to clear East Hill, an enemy salient that controlled the MSR leading out of Hagaru. The 2nd Battalion, 5th Marines took this objective and trapped many of the CCF defenders., killing almost 800 Chinese and capturing 220 of them.

The method used to open the MSR to Koto was to clear the hills and ridges on both sides of the road as they had done earlier when withdrawing from Yudam. The tank-infantry force would attack down the road at the same time. The 7th Marines were selected to lead the Corps column and clear the enemy from the road. The 1st Battalion moved on the ridges west of the MSR, while the 2nd Battalion moved with tanks down the main road or MSR. An Army battalion of survivors of the 7th US Infantry Division moved along the ridges on the east side of the MSR , while the 3rd Battalion, 7th Marines brought up the rear of this lead element of the Corps column. By moving at night and overcoming delays caused by blown bridges and scattered enemy resistance, the 7th Marines and other elements in the lead column reached Koto on the morning of December 7th.

The regimental train moving down the road to Koto-ri was not immune to sporadic enemy fire. Chaplain Cornelius Griffin (USN) was riding in a small ambulance when bullets smashed through the vehicle windshield. One struck him in the jaw. He asked Dr. Bob Wedemeyer whether he was bleeding to death. The doctor said to a Chief Pharmacist's Mate, "Don't let him exsanguinate. (Run out of blood.)" Chaplain Griffin replied, "I told him I'd forgotten more Latin than he ever learned."

The remainder of the 1st Marine Division and X Corps units did not move out of Hagaru until dark on December. All American units had cleared Hagaru by 10 AM on December 7th except for the rear guard, the 2nd Battalion, 5th Marines. As the entire column pulled into Koto, the rearguard followed closely after blowing up any equipment and supplies that had to be left behind at Hagaru.

Pfc. Doug Michaud, Headquarters and Service Company, 1st Battalion, 5th Marines was with this last group to leave. He remembers: "Hunger was a terrible problem. I came across four Marines huddled around a pathetic little fire trying to thaw a can of rations, four guys sharing one can. I said to Jerry Malone, ' You know, I shouldn't feel this way — I'm almost ready to shoot those guys to get that can.' 'You hungry?' he says, 'Ha, ha' and he starts laughing. Reaches down to the bottom of his parka and comes out with a can of C rations—chicken and vegetables, frozen like it had been in deep freeze. —We ripped the damn can open and put frozen pieces in our mouths and let them thaw there. When I asked Malone why he had saved this one can, he said, 'I was waiting for a special occasion."

Michaud also had strong memories of passing the carnage of former conflicts as his unit moved down the MSR to Koto. Stacks of

Wounded soldier, 32nd Regiment, 7th Division, October 1950.

89

frozen dead Chinese were piled along the road. Also he saw bodies of Americans who had been victims of earlier Chinese ambushes. He was reminded of American movies where western wagon trains were ambushed by Apaches. Dead drivers still sat behind the steering wheels of their trucks. "Footlockers had been pried open, mail satchels ripped apart, and the envelopes lay where the wind had blown them. Personal effects were thrown everywhere. All this, frozen in time—There was nothing but death."

The next phase in the withdrawal was the movement of 14,000 men, US Marines, British Royal Marines, and some soldiers from 7th Division and X Corps, to Chinhung. Here the MSR became precipitous and dangerous, because the route turned and twisted down the escarpment into the plain below. Funchilin Pass which led down the escarpment was a particularly dangerous spot, because it was a perfect location for Chinese roadblocks. At another point south of Koto a one lane bridge had been blown by the Chinese and had caused a sixteen foot gap in the winding road. The force from Koto had to move through all these obstacles.

This gap in the road was a sudden shock to many of the withdrawing Marines who had hoped that they had left all the major obstacles behind them. The reaction of 1st Lt. William Davis, A Company 7th Marines, was complete despair when he looked down from the high ground and saw a giant chasm. "Here was the great divide, this Korean mini-Grand Canyon that could cancel everything the Marines had achieved up to this point."

A major problem was to find six foot long, one ton, prefabricated treadway bridge sections for the sixteen foot gap and to find a way to get them to Koto. At this town were engineer

treadway bridge trucks that could move the sections to the bridge site. Since the CCF controlled much of the route south of Koto, the engineers decided that the only way to get the bridge sections to Koto was to drop them by parachute. After several trial attempts failed, large parachutes were flown in from Japan. On December 7th eight drops were made from C-119s on Koto, and six fell successfully into the hands of the engineers. Now the total force at Koto was prepared to attack south on the MSR and overcome the obstacles.

While the Koto force of 15,000 men began its push south down the MSR to Chinhung, a task force from the newly arrived US 3rd Infantry Division pushed north to meet them at Chinhung. The 3rd Division had landed earlier at Wonsan. Its 7th Regiment had moved west to Huksu to secure the west flank of X Corps. Task Force Dog, consisting of elements from the 65th and 15th Regiments plus the 64th Tank Battalion ,and two Field Artillery Battalions, moved north and reached Chinhung late on December 7th.

On the 8th a final drive was made in a pincers move from north and south to open Funchilin Pass and bridge the gap made by the destroyed bridge. The 1st Battalion, 1st Marine Regiment attacked from Chinhung north in a blinding snowstorm to capture Hill 1081, a key peak controlling Funchilin Pass. At the same time the 3rd Battalion, 7th Marines attacked south from Koto. By the 9th, after vicious fighting with the Chinese on the peak of Hill 1081, the 1st Battalion finally captured the mountain peak and gained control Funchilin Pass. On that same day the 3rd Battalion, 7th Marines, attacking against limited resistance, finally reached the site of the gap with the destroyed bridge.

The Engineers and treadway bridge trucks arrived intact from Koto and after several hours the bridge sections were in place. After the first few vehicles had crossed, a tractor almost broke through the new bridge. Fortunately the engineers found that by placing the treadways farther apart, tanks and jeeps could safely cross the span.

Sub-zero weather and malnutrition were seriously impeding Chinese Forces. The American rearguard was contested by the CCF all the way to the new bridge. In this rearguard force were 40 tanks. When they got to the new bridge, most of the tanks were able to ease across the bridge. Suddenly, near the end of the column, one tank's brakes froze, blocking the road and stranding the last nine tanks. A battle ensued as the Chinese tried to infiltrate among these tanks. Finally the lead tank's brakes unlocked and two more tanks made it across the bridge. In order to block the Chinese and get tank crews across the bridge to safety, the remaining seven tanks were abandoned, and the bridge blown. By December 10, the survivors of the Chosen Reservoir force had reached the safety of the 3rd Infantry Division at Chinhung.

The defense and withdrawal of the X Corps from the Chosen Reservoir is considered one of the great strategic withdrawals in military history. In spite of heavy losses by the US. forces, the losses sustained by the CCF in northeast Korea in November and December amounted to a disaster. The 3rd Field Army started with twelve CCF divisions of 120,000 men. Marine Corps studies estimate that CCF battle and non-battle casualties may have amounted to as many as 72,000. The CCF Twenty-Seventh Army reported 10,000 cases of incapacitating frostbite alone. The Marines, after landing at Wonsan, suffered 10,500 casualties: 4418 in battle and 6,174 non-battle. The Army figures are not clear , but it is estimated that they sustained 3000 casualties with over 1000 men killed or missing in action.

By 11 December 1950 X Corps had prevented a total disaster. The next mission was to withdraw successfully from northeast Korea and join Eighth Army in stopping the hordes of CCF that were about to invade South Korea.

Chapter 11 - From Bugout to Skillful Withdrawal

Withdrawal to the 38th Parallel

The entry of the Chinese into the war and their disastrous mauling of Eighth Army and X Corps sent shock waves throughout America. This was a new war in which the winner so far had been Communist China. What policy shift should the United States now make? Would the Chinese stop at the 38th Parallel or would they enter South Korea?

Early in December the British and Americans made a joint decision to end the war. They no longer retained a policy aimed at the unification of Korea. By the 8th of December Washington was giving support to this new policy that UN Forces would not invade North Korea again if the Chinese agreed to stop their forces at the 38th Parallel.

On December 14th the UN General Assembly passed a resolution calling for a cease-fire in Korea. On 21 December the Chinese Communist Government rejected this resolution because it was passed without their participation. They further stated that the 38th Parallel could no longer be considered in any UN resolution since the UN had already invaded North Korea. They further stated that no cease-fire would be considered until an agreement had been reached on the withdrawal from Korea of foreign troops, the withdrawal of American troops from Taiwan, and the seating of Communist China in the UN They also insisted that the Koreans be allowed to settle their own affairs.

A major influence on American decision making was the report by Army Chief of Staff, J. Lawton Collins, presented after his trip to Korea. On 8 December he reported that he believed that UN Forces would not be driven out of Korea. X Corps would evacuate northeast Korea and become part of Eighth Army. Once this corps joined the two American and two ROK Corps, Eighth Army would set up a perimeter around Pusan and would be almost impossible to dislodge.

General Walker had given up any idea of establishing a defensive line across North Korea. Many of his units were in disarray and needed time to re-organize. Supplying any army in North Korea, communist or UN, was difficult. His plan, therefore, was to establish a line, known as Line B, which extended from the Indian River east to the coast.

Since Eighth Army was leaving North Korea, Walker wanted to delay the Chinese as much as possible. Eighth Army needed time to reorganize. The best way to slow the Chinese advance was to limit their food supply. Thus the Chinese supply lines to Manchuria were constantly under air attack. At the same time a scorched earth policy was initiated whereby all supplies of food in North Korea which could supplement the CCF were destroyed.

A great problem was what to do with all the American equipment in North Korea that could not be transported back to South Korea. The Eighth Army solution was to destroy it rather than let it fall into the hands of the Chinese. Vast supply dumps in Pyongyang of food, ammunition and damaged vehicles were put to the torch. The sky was black from the fires of burning equipment. One withdrawing soldier remembers seeing much of the most luxurious accommoda-

tions of the Air Force going up in flames at Pyongyang Air Base.

The British military operating with the Americans were quite critical of the quick American exodus. Millions of dollars worth of valuable equipment had been destroyed without any attempt made to save it. The British felt that the Chinese were putting only limited pressure on Eighth Army, and that the Americans were leaving valuable equipment behind without firing a shot.

In a ten day period Eighth Army withdrew 120 miles. Much criticism of this rapid withdrawal can be leveled. To many Americans it was humiliating. Nevertheless, this rapid move to South Korea saved many units from destruction and gave them time to rebuild. Had the CCV caught American and ROK units, they would probably have defeated them and prevented them from fighting another day.

As Eighth Army withdrew south, the gap between them and the advancing CCV widened. In this gap Eighth Army units took turns establishing blocking positions along the major routes. While the CCV delayed in its movement south, thousands of North Korean refugees pushed in front of them heading for South Korea. Day after day these refugees as well as American and ROK units poured through the roadblocks. To the American soldier on these roadblocks there were always two basic questions. How many North Korean guerrillas are inter-mingled with these refugees? Will we be attacked from the rear?

Many Eighth Army units took part in this delaying phase. This action was illustrated during the second week in December 1950 by the experience of a battalion of the 24th Division near Yonchon.

The 3rd Battalion, 5 RCT, had the mission to cover the withdrawal of several ROK Divisions as well as to allow thousands of refugees to move south. Most of the units of the battalion were concentrated on the north side of town. On the south side of town in reserve were part of Company K, two tanks, and six howitzers of the 555 Field Artillery. Protecting the artillery were several half-tracks with 50 caliber machine guns.

That first evening of the battalion delaying action the local inhabitants and refugees mysteriously disappeared from the town. At 9:30 in the evening small arms and mortar fire were heard several miles to the rear of the roadblock. A little while later the air in the rear of the position was filled with hundreds of voices yelling, "Banzai!" The roar sounded almost like an American crowd at a football game. At the start of this sudden attack Company K's 4th Platoon mortars in the rear were quickly overrun, but the three mortar crews managed to join a rifle platoon on higher ground and shoot back at the enemy. Drivers, cooks, and headquarters personnel all joined the rifle platoon on the firing line to fight off the attack. The field artillery and tanks aimed their guns to the rear on the charging enemy and forced them back to high ground outside the American perimeter.

At one point several 60mm mortars were captured by the attacking enemy. The enemy force then tried to shoot them back at the American defenders on the higher ground, but they only knew how to fire Russian mortars. American mortar rounds had two safety pins, while Russian made mortars had only one.

The Americans could hear the thump as each

mortar round left the mortar tube, and then a swishing noise as these unexploded rounds passed overhead and landed around a kitchen fly in the company area.

When dawn came the mortar position was retaken, but the enemy had moved to high ground south of the position and cut off the battalion. American artillery and tanks continued to pound away all during the morning at enemy positions on the high ground south and east of town. At noon a ROK Regiment from the south attacked the rear of the enemy positions blocking the withdrawal, opened the route south and allowed the cutoff ROK units and 3rd Battalion to withdraw to safety.

During this deployment phase in the movement south the most unsung heroes of Eighth Army were military policemen. These soldiers were placed in isolated spots along highways to secure the movement of troops and supplies. They suffered from the bitter cold and also from enemy guerrillas. If they lighted fires at night to keep from freezing, they attracted the guerrillas. Often in isolated areas the bodies of M.P.s would be found near a fire that still had smoldering coals.

At the Imjin River refugees were not allowed to cross into South Korea until all UN units had passed over the bridges. As at Anju on the Chongchon River thousands of refugees in their white clothes huddled around fires and waited for an opportunity to move south. Most feared the Chinese and were struggling to keep ahead of the slow moving CCV force.

Slowly Walker built a new defensive line for Eighth Army named Line B. Emphasis was place on the defense of Seoul with concentration in a north-northeast semi-circle around the capital. On the west on the Imjin River was the U.S. 25th Division and the Turkish Brigade. To their right were the ROK 1st and 6th Divisions. On their right and directly north of Uijongbu was the U.S. 24th Division. Extending through the middle of Korea were five ROK Divisions. Later the line was completed when the ROK I Corps moved from Hungnam by boat and extended the line to the east coast.

On this line Eighth Army was determined to fight. American soldiers would now wait for the enemy. S/Sgt W. B. Woodruff of the 35th Infantry was one of those who waited in his deep foxhole for the Chinese. In front of him was strung barbed wire while next to it a mine field had been laid. He was determined and a little impatient. He would not, however, have long to wait.

Eighth Army concentrated its reserve in the western and central part of South Korea. The Commonwealth and British Brigades and the 187th Airborne RCT were all situated in the western half of Korea. The 2nd and 1st Cavalry Divisions which had suffered the most in North Korea were rebuilding. The 1st Cavalry was in the Seoul area,   while the 2nd was situated in central Korea behind the ROK Divisions.

On 23 December 1950 Eighth Army suffered the loss of its commander, Lt. Gen. Walton H. Walker. While driving north from Seoul to check his troops, his jeep was struck head-on by a truck from a ROK unit. Many historians feel that this marked a turning point in the war. Walker's replacement was Lt. Gen. Matthew B. Ridgway who had had a distinguished record in World War II. Ridgway's arrival brought a new spirit which built up the confidence of an army whose morale was low. It is easy in hindsight to criticize Walker for the first six months of combat, but most of the errors which occurred during that period can be attributed to forces and leaders over whom Walker had little control. In tribute one can say that he was like General George Patton: an aggressive fighter. Veterans of the Pusan Perimeter still give him credit for his tenacity and dedication in holding that perimeter for almost two months.

The last week in December was a period of calm. Intelligence reported the CCV forces moving slowly south toward South Korea. Eighth Army had had some time to rest and recover from the blows of early December. The men thought of Christmas and became homesick. Many men had been forced to leave in North Korea Christmas gifts from home that had arrived early. Despite the losses units nestled in South Korean villages and managed to create a Christmas spirit. Music was important , and somehow musical instruments appeared. In one unit Hispanic and Hawaiian soldiers put on a show and led in singing. Other music came by radio from Japan. As one soldier said, "It was wonderful to hear Japanese recordings of 'Silent Night' as a full moon shone down."

During this period the CO of the 5th Cavalry Regiment, Col. Marcel Crombez, initiated an early evening snack for his men. Every soldier would have a cup of bouillon soup at this time. This program lasted until the "Christmas holidays" were interrupted by the Chinese New Year's Eve offensive.

The military clubs in Japan supplied "Christmas cheer" to various units. Some of the young soldiers couldn't handle hard liquor. In one unit a soldier went raving mad and had to be given morphine. On the whole, however, the alcohol allowed the men to relax, and it was shared with our allies. In one village American liquor was offered to Korean adults. Many of them thought it was "soda." In one village the old "Papa-san" and Mayor enjoyed the "American cheer" and celebrated our friendship by becoming as high as a kite. One sourfaced old grandmother drank down much of a bottle of the "American cheer." She smiled and giggled and was full of praise for the U.S. Army.

Some units that manned the outposts were somewhat restricted in the celebration of Christmas. Company A, 35th Infantry made up of 149 American and 36 Korean soldiers under Capt. Sidney Berry was manning a long, thin regimental outpost of separated strong points that stretched three miles near the Imjin River. Two days before Christmas Chaplain Clayton Day conducted four services in Able Company— one service with each platoon outpost and one at the company command post. The service was simple

and moving. After singing Christmas carols and joining in the Lord's Prayer, the American and Korean soldiers were drawn together in a rare closeness. On Christmas Eve the CPA began their big attack in the east against Eighth Army but not against Company A, 35th Infantry.

On 29 December the Joint Chiefs sent a directive to MacArthur stating that Korea was not a place to fight a major war and that few additional forces would be sent there. They encouraged a successful resistance to the communist aggression as long an the UN did not incur heavy losses.

On 30 December MacArthur again sent proposals to Washington that would expand the war beyond Korea. He again stressed total

Christmas 1950, Eighth Army around Seoul.

victory. These proposals were in sharp contrast to the policy of the Truman Administration. Washington policy at that time stressed avoidance of becoming involved in a total war in Asia. The Korean War was to be limited to the carrying out of specific national aims.

Withdrawing X Corps

MacArthur decided to make an orderly evacuation of X Corps from Hungnam. On December 11th this evacuation began. It lasted until 24 December when the final serviceman of 105,000 men departed. The plan called for the evacuation not only of American soldiers, Marines and ROKs, but also their supplies and vehicles.

To protect this bridgehead while the evacuation took place, X Corps ordered the 3rd and 7th US Infantry Divisions to carry out this mission. On the left of the semi-circle perimeter around Hungnam was the 3rd Division while on the right was the 7th Division. Backing up these infantry divisions were AA half-tracks, tanks, and Division and Corps Artillery. Further protection was provided by Navy cruisers and destroyers plus aircraft from the Air Force, Navy and Marine Corps.

During the two week evacuation little resistance came from the Chinese. Had these CCF units attacked the bridgehead fiercely, they could have precipitated a possible catastrophe. A number of explanations have been given as to why they did not attack in any strength. The most logical explanation seems to be the weather. X Corps had inflicted terrible casualties on the Chinese, but the intense cold was even more terrible. It has been estimated that the cold weather may have caused almost 30,000 Chinese casualties. In any case the CCF did not attack this perimeter vigorously.

The Marines were the first unit to embark and by the 14th had been loaded on twenty-one Naval vessels and seven chartered merchant ships destined for Pusan. Next to embark was the ROK I Corps consisting of 25,000 men and 700 vehicles. On the 17th they landed near Mokho and became the right flank of Eighth Army's Line B on the east coast.

Loading ships seems easy on paper, but bad winter weather seriously hampered Naval operations. Westerly winds caused four LCMs to drift into minefields. This delayed loading for half a day. In addition, many sailors working in freezing cold, icy spray and relentless winds became casualties.

The key problem at Hungnam was the availability of ships. The turnaround time at Pusan was crucial. It was important for the unloading time at Pusan not to exceed the loading time at Hungnam. Diversion to Japan occasionally happened when Pusan became too congested. By the 18th, congestion had slowed as Pusan was operating at full force and unloading was taking place at the supplementary ports of Masan and Ulsan.

Slowly Army units began to embark and leave. First came the 7th Division which was going to Pusan for refitting before joining Eighth Army. On the 19th the perimeter was reduced as the 3rd Division under Maj. Gen. Robert Soule was responsible for the last defense. This last defense force of three infantry regiments was beefed up with six artillery battalions and three anti-aircraft battalions. As this last division began to load, the coverage missions of the artillery battalions was taken over by Naval gunfire.

From the 7th Division Lieutenants Jack Madison and Bob Kingston climbed on board the

USS *Billy Mitchell*. Both of these infantry officers were covered from head to foot with dirt and grime that had been accumulated from many days of front line fighting. As they passed the officer's mess they witnessed waiters in starched white jackets serving strawberry shortcake from silver trays. Both thought of what a contrast this was from the war they had just left.

Suddenly a new problem arose. Thousands of North Koreans descended on Hungnam as they fled from the Chinese. These North Koreans believed that a life in South Korea under an invader from overseas was preferable to living under the invading alien army from across the Yalu. It was originally estimated that there were 25,000 refugees to be evacuated. As more poured into Hungnam, the number rose to 50,000.

How could these refugees be evacuated? On some of the first ships the bodies of the refugees were squeezed on the ships like cattle. No LST ever carried less than 5,000 people. One LST actually carried 10,500 people , while the *Meridith Victory* squeezed on 14,000. Fortunately on the 23rd a temporary surplus of ships developed when three Victory ships and two LSTs arrived. Over 50,000 North Koreans were loaded on these last five ships for a record total of 91,000 civilians who left Hungnam. This is still remembered as one of the greatest evacuations of civilians in history.

On the 24th the 3rd Division had completed loading. A small force of several thousand remained to demolish everything left behind. Remaining stocks of shells and other military supplies that were left behind were fired. Anything in Hungnam that could have been of use to the enemy was destroyed. At noon on the 24th the remaining personnel embarked on LVTs and LSTs. At 1410 hours demolition charges

were setoff and "piers, cranes and walls of the inner harbor disappeared in an eruption of smoke and flame."

Full credit should be given to the U.S. Navy for the professional way they managed this evacuation. Over 105,000 US and Korean military personnel, 91,000 North Korean refugees, 350,000 tons of cargo and 17,500 vehicles had been rescued.

New Year's Eve Chinese Offensive

On New Year's Eve CCF forces assaulted Line B around Seoul and crossed the 38th Parallel into South Korea. The Chinese had been steadily moving south from the Chongchon River. The weight of their attack was directly north of Seoul. Seven CCF Armies and two North Korean Corps penetrated the UN forces. The attack centered on the ROK Divisions, survivors who had suffered much devastation in North Korea. The ROK 1st and 6th Divisions north of Seoul were hit hard, causing the Chinese to penetrate between the US 24th and 25th Divisions. The massive mortar barrages of the CCF were followed by thousands of foot soldiers blowing bugles and shooting flares. Fortunately the American divisions were able to maintain their tactical integrity by plugging gaps in their lines.

General Ridgway could not have arrived in Korea at a worse time. The new commander was taking over a defeated army. He moved about trying to calm the panic of many of his UN forces, but his pressure was of little avail. The weight of the CCF offensive was too great, and Ridgway now had to extricate his 24th and 25th Divisions to prevent a disaster.

Withdrawing while under constant attack by the Chinese was not easy. Sgt. F/C Warren Avery, G Company 21st Infantry, was north of

Uijongbu and was sent out with his platoon to an outpost. Around midnight the Chinese began moving into his area and so he notified his company by telephone. His platoon received no orders to withdraw and so remained in a hidden position. He remembers, "Shots near where the headquarters was set up. We whistled through the sound-power. A Chinaman answered and told us the rest of the unit had been captured and that we, too, should lay down our weapons and return to the headquarters area. I forget what our platoon sergeant told the Chinaman to do with himself, but we took off and moved south."

On the central front the CCF and two NKPA Corps forced back four ROK Divisions above Wonju. Fortunately the newly re-organized 2nd US. Division was backing up these ROK Divisions and immediately began attacking north. General Almond's new X Corps Headquarters was put into operation at Wonju, and he took direct command of the situation. A day later the 7th US Infantry Division arrived and quickly the central front began to stabilize.

In the west the fighting was not going well for the US I and IX Corps. The Commonwealth Brigade and the 24th Division on the right began to withdraw back to Uijongbu. On the left the 25th Division and the Turkish Brigade were not able to contain the advancing CCF and began withdrawing back on Seoul from Munsan. By January 2nd these two U.S. Corps had been squeezed into a bridgehead around Seoul. This made a formidable defense force capable of defending the capital of South Korea.

98   The collapse of the ROK Divisions northeast of Seoul opened the way for the CCF to outflank Seoul from the east and cut off the two U.S.

Corps defending the city. Ridgway's mission given to him by MacArthur was not to allow Eighth Army to be destroyed. He decided, therefore, that his best move was to give up Seoul on 3 January and evacuate his army to positions south of the Han River.

Extracting the army units from Seoul across Han River bridges while holding off the aggressive advancing CCF was not an easy undertaking. In addition to the CCF threat to the river crossings were the complications brought on by thousands of refugees clamoring to vacate the city over the same bridges.

Cpl. Leonard Korgie, 21st Infantry, remembers, "What a mess! Civilians—clothed, half-clothed, some barefooted; millions of them, all trying to get south with whatever they could carry or drag with them."

Another problem was whether the bridges over the Han would hold: three pontoon bridges and a railroad bridge. Engineers worried about the packed ice flows that could damage or destroy the bridges. Huge chunks of ice flowed down the Han and could strike a bridge with great impact. Another problem was caused by the weight of the heavy Centurion tanks crossing these weakened bridges.

But the movement out of Seoul proved to be easier than anticipated. Only the British Brigade became engaged in a vicious conflict and delayed its departure. At one time Eighth Army feared this unit might be left behind. Fortunately this unit was able to break contact with the enemy and made a timely withdrawal and successfully crossed the Han Bridges with other units. Other good fortune was that the four Han River bridges held.

Three bridges over the Han River.

As units in convoys of trucks on the way to the bridge crossings passed through Seoul and saw it burning, memories returned. Some of these soldiers could recall occupation duty in Korea. One lingering memory was of the "31st Circle" where many of them had gotten drunk and been rolled. As the men in trucks passed through this circle whose surrounding buildings were engulfed in flames, they broke out in loud cheers.

The last units crossed the bridges on January 4th. Since the pontoon bridges were frozen solid into the river ice, they could not be salvaged as had been hoped. Consequently all three pontoon bridges were blown up. The American engineers also blew up every other span of the railroad bridge so that individuals but not vehicles could still cross.

The saddest sight was continuing to watch thousands of Korean refugees trying to cross the river ice to safety. The weather was bitter and freezing winds whipped across the Han River.

Women with babies and men with the sick and old on their backs stumbled across the river. Bundles of household goods were piled high on oxen. Women as well as men carried huge A-frames on their backs that were loaded with every sort of cherished family item. Even family dogs trotted along. All these people were struggling to reach safety before the onslaught of the invaders from the north.

The next defense line of Eighth Army was supposed to be just south of the Han River. The CCF, however, after taking Seoul was in no hurry to attack Eighth Army from this location. Instead they concentrated in the vicinity of Yoju, about halfway between Suwon and Wonju., in hopes of cutting off X Corps from Eighth Army units in the west. To prevent this move Ridgway had to move Eighth Army farther south to a new defensive position.

This new defensive position about forty miles south of Seoul stretched from Pyongtaek to Changhowon to Checkon to a point on the east coast above Samchok. It was to be the farthest south Eighth Army would withdraw for the duration of the war. From this time in the war the communist enemy never ventured this far south again.

The new defense line began to form as new units began to fill gaps and build a strong solid front. The 187th Airborne RCT was put into the line as the 3rd U.S. Division slowly moved up from the south and joined I Corps on the west flank. New defensive formations were developed as company and battalion sized units were put out on outpost duty. Often company sized outposts were required to spend a day or two out five miles or more in front of their units. Sometimes these outposts were brought in at night. Most veterans will remember the bitter times in sub-zero weather, isolated many miles in front of their units, as they waited for a possible clash with a roving CCF patrol.

For most of January, in all but central Korea, a lull in fighting developed. The two army fronts, communist and allied, were from twenty to fifty miles apart. In between both armies the gap was filled with outposts and patrols. Probable cause for this lull was the intense cold. Experience by both armies at the Chosen Reservoir had taught them that they could not be careless with men's lives in this extreme weather.

At this time the Armed Forces started their policy of "Rest and Recreation," called R and R by the men. Japan became the favorite rest center. Men who had been in Korea the longest went to Japan first. Also priority in combat units went to those who had served on the front the longest. It was a wonderful respite for soldiers to have a bath again and see bright lights for the first time in months. Infantrymen who had been

fighting at twenty degrees below zero were delighted to relax in a Japanese bath and have beautiful female maiden attendants wash their backs with warm water. One Captain from the 24th Division actually spent an entire week in a hotel room, eating nothing but steaks, and being entertained by Hawaiian dancers.

Some soldiers on R and R went back to their home bases in Japan to the units from which they had come. Sometimes this was a difficult situation, because they had been in the front lines and knew what had happened to others in these units. They did not want to break bad news to wives and families, because sometimes notifications of tragedies had not yet arrived. For the most part, however, R and R became an essential morale builder. Returning to the fight and the bitter cold of Korea was depressing.

The new defensive line of Eighth Army initiated a new war. Eighth Army became cautious and moved slowly into attack. The preponderance of trained veterans and the superior fire power of the UN Forces never again allowed the CCV to devastate large American units as had happened in December 1950.

Withdrawal of X Corps from Hungnam December 1950.

Pershing M-4 Tank, 7th Division, Winter 1951.

Chapter 12: UN Winter Offensive 1951

Cautious Advance

The new Eighth Army was a different Eighth Army. The key to its new way of operating was caution. No longer would the Army operate recklessly as in the past. No longer would columns advance down roads with limited protection on their flanks. Eighth Army and X Corps had learned through attrition in December that the Chinese could easily challenge the roadbound UN Forces. Now the advancing forces of the new Eighth Army would have a solid front and each unit would maintain contact with a unit on its right and left flank

To provide more safety, large patrols were sent out to pin down specific enemy positions. These patrols were known as "Reconnaissance in Force." If the enemy put up a strong resistance, these patrols would try not to get into a violent conflict. Tanks, AA weapons and artillery would first attempt to flush out the enemy before the infantry advanced. Supporting the artillery would be aircraft using napalm, as they had before. When the infantry had swept the area clear, the aircraft would set upon the fleeing enemy. This style of advance differed from previous advances because the entire front moved forward at the same time. Early in January, strong regimental level patrols initiated

probing attacks. Ridgway ordered a strong armored attack on 15 January called Operation Wolfhound. This attack jumped off with seven infantry battalions, 150 tanks and three artillery battalions. All were from the 3rd US and 25th US Divisions. This task force drove the enemy back to Suwon, but the CCF began to consolidate in order to make a major counterattack. Fearing that the task force might be trapped, Ridgway ordered it to withdraw to Osan. Soon IX Corps initiated its own probing attack toward Ichon. Although little damage had been done to the CCF by these attacks, I and IX Corps became aware that the Chinese positions to their front were limited and that the Chinese were reluctant to fight against tanks in open country.

On January 25th, Ridgway ordered Operation Thunderbolt. In this operation I Corps was to advance to Yongdungpo opposite Seoul on the Han River. IX Corps was to advance to the Han River north of Ichon. Enemy resistance was limited as the two corps attacked slowly north By early February I Corps had taken Inchon and Kimpo Airfield and was on the south bank of the Han River across from Seoul. East of Seoul IX Corps made slower headway in more mountainous country as it advanced north against token enemy resistance.

Crisis on the Central Front

The Chinese strategy had changed by early February. Instead of making their major thrust into South Korea through the low ground south of Seoul where American tanks were dominant, the CCF shifted their main attack into mountainous central Korea. Chinese intelligence perceived the ROK III Corps as weak. The US X Corps was displacing from Hungnam and was not in a position to block a major CCF breakthrough toward Taegu and Pusan. But the hasty defense, quickly and brilliantly devised by the American units, was easily one of the turning points in the war. Their brave defense, coupled with extreme weather conditions, prevented any further advance of the CCF into South Korea.

The ROK III Corps was backed up by the newly organized US 2nd and 7th Divisions and the 187 Airborne RCT, a reserve regiment hastily shifted from the Seoul area. As the 2nd Division sent out probing attacks northwest of Chipyong-ni, they ran into stiff Chinese resistance. They realized that the CCF was building up massive forces on this central front.

On the night of 11-12 February elements of the 40th and 66th CCF Armies and the North Korean II and V Corps concentrated a massive attack on the ROK III Corps near Hongchon. These enemy units quickly penetrated the ROK units and created a salient in the UN front. The ROK 8th Division was overrun as the ROK 3rd and 5th Divisions withdrew to the X Corps perimeter around Hoengsong.

Two days later large CCF units attacked the US 2nd Division east of Chipyong-ni. The 23rd Infantry and the French Battalion attached to the division formed a defensive perimeter around Chipyong-ni and refused to give up this strategic road junction. Ridgway believed this was a key junction, and he ordered the 4000 defenders to hold this important position against the massive assault of about 25,000 Chinese. The enemy threw attack after attack against this position for two days, but the defenders refused to withdraw. During this stand the 23rd Infantry inflicted over 5000 Chinese casualties.

Many Eighth Army tanks had dragons painted on them during the Winter 1951 drive. Chinese were superstitious.

Lt. Lynn Freeman was on line with one of the rifle companies as the Chinese hit the first night: "Suddenly we heard this ungodly howl. Somebody among the French had cranked up a hand siren. It surprised the hell out of the Chinese. After the siren went off, the French troops jumped up out of their fox-holes and went at the Chinese with bayonets and grenades. Ran right at them. It was really extraordinary to see. That busted up the attack right away, and the Chinese quieted down rather quickly."

The 23rd became cut off and was completely surrounded by the Chinese. The morning of the second day after two night attacks the Chinese, according to Lt. Freeman: "Did not follow their usual practice and break off the attack. I'm sure they knew the Cav was coming (the armored task force from the 1st Cavalry Division), and they wanted to break our lines and finish us off. while they still had a chance."

Freeman's company fought most of the day trying to regain a key position on the perimeter that the Chinese had taken the night before. Finally, about four in the afternoon, tanks and infantry of the 5th Cavalry Regiment arrived to rescue the 23rd Regiment. As the lead tanks approached the perimeter, the Chinese withdrew. According to Freemen, "God, we were happy to see those guys. In fact we cheered like hell."

While the 23rd was struggling to survive at Chipyong-ni, the rest of the 2nd US Division and the 187th Airborne RCT were struggling to block the CCF penetration where the 8th ROK Division had collapsed. Elements of the 38th Infantry that were attached to the 8th ROK Division were trapped by CCF units who had established roadblocks on the Hoengsong-Hongschon highway. A small task force from the

187 Airborne RCT broke through the road block and helped rescue most of the cut off personnel, but much equipment including artillery howitzers was lost. The Dutch Battalion, which was attached to the 38th Infantry, put up a magnificent defense, took many casualties, and was instrumental in saving many of the men in the 38th Regiment. This unit was foremost in holding its ground as thousands of panic-stricken ROK soldiers poured to the rear. Mixed in among these fleeing ROKs were CCF soldiers dressed in South Korean uniforms. In the confusion the Dutch Battalion Commander was killed by such disguised Chinese.

On 14 February four full CCF Divisions assaulted Wonju. The 38th Infantry and 187th Airborne RCT received the attack head-on. Under normal circumstances they might have been overrun, but the superior American artillery was to much for the Chinese. The well concentrated artillery barrages of X Corps wrecked havoc on the masses of Chinese trying to swarm over the American positions. The slaughter continued hour after hour. Pilots reported that the river at Wonju was running red with the blood of massacred CCF. American artillery fire was so intense that the enemy assault divisions were shattered, and the CCF attack came to a halt.

The battle on the central front from February 11 to 13th was successful in stopping the Chinese drive but had been costly to UN Forces. A total of 11,800 UN soldiers were casualties of whom 9800 were ROKs, 1900 American and the rest other allies. Ridgway was angry, because he felt the loss of these soldiers and thirty-four howitzers was too great a price for this victory.

Eighth Army Continues to Slug Forward

By February 18th, reports came in to Ist and IXth Corps that the Chinese were pulling out south of the Han River. Evidence of this came from the 24th Division. One of its units had encountered 600 enemy dead in their fox-holes. These victims appeared to be the result of American massed artillery fire. At the same time reports were coming into X Corps that the CCF and North Koreans were withdrawing back across the Han. It was apparent that the communist forces had suffered a severe defeat. For the next two months the CCF would slowly withdraw behind the 38th Parallel to gain time to rebuild their divisions.

At this time it might be wise to explain the impact of American field artillery on the enemy. The success of the American forces at Wonju in February illustrated the power of artillery when controlled by a superior fire direction system. As the war progressed Eighth Army emphasized the build up of its field artillery. The various types of artillery was used not to support just American units, but also most of the other UN forces. Some of the heavy losses of artillery in the war occurred in units supporting ROK forces. Others losses came from units that took great risks to give close support to the infantry. Americans praise their air support, but do not give enough accolades to their field artillery. The defeated enemy in World War II, the Germans, called American field artillery the best in the world.

As the CCF, having sustained terrible losses at Wonju, pulled back across the Han River to begin withdrawing to the 38th Parallel, Ridgway insisted that Eighth Army continue to pressure them. The CCF needed time to reorganize. Ridgway believed pressure on them would give then neither rest nor a chance to restock supplies. Thus all during the rest of February and early March Eighth Army methodically moved northward against limited CCF resistance. Units were shifted to reinforce these drives. On 18 February the 1st Marine Division was attached to IX Corps to assist in Operation Killer, the first of several drives.

As Eighth Army moved slowly north, objectives were given names like Line Idaho and Line Kansas. Ridgway knew that the CCF was a long way from being beaten. American intelligence was aware that the Chinese were recoiling for a massive counterstrike sometime in the spring. The terrible weather with its mud and melting snow was an obstacle to both armies. But the Chinese were not in a hurry, and an offense begun in spring weather was preferable to the heavy rains and mud of March.

Eighth Army continued to push north. On March 7th Operation Ripper began. Its mission was to make a deep penetration into the high mountains of central Korea, creating an enormous salient that would force the enemy out of Seoul by enveloping it from the east. Ripper began with the U.S. 25th Division crossing the Han River. S/Sgt. W. B. Woodruff, Company L 35th Infantry, remembers the planning that went into the crossing. The crossing took place at night in boats supplied by the engineers. He recalls, "The boat scraped bottom on the north bank. The engineer at the bow leaped out with his rope, pulling the boat up as far as he could. We clambered ashore. -In the darkness, the current had carried us downstream, out of Love Company's zone." Fortunately resistance here was light and the operation was a success. Eighth Army continued to advance and in two weeks had reached Chunchon. The Chinese had seen the penetration coming and, fearful of being cut off in Seoul from the east, had vacated the capital a week earlier.

In this operation General Ridgway decided to use paratroopers to try to cut off fleeing Chinese. On 23 March the 1st and 3rd Battalions of the

Rain—the most miserable weather for infantry troops, March 1951.

187th RCT dropped near Munsan-ni. Some confusion ensued as the 1st Battalion missed its drop zone and landed on top of the 3rd Battalion. Little enemy opposition was encountered, however, as the regiment adjusted to the confusion and quickly began a foot march to assault Hill 228. In this conflict the toll was heavy. Company I alone had 84 casualties including all its platoon leaders. Among the casualties in this regimental assault was Lt. Doug Bush, an Air Force Forward Air Controller.

Doug Bush's story is unique. As a paratrooper, commander of an airborne pathfinder unit, he had jumped into Normandy with the 82nd Airborne Division in June 1944. Later he fought in the Battle of the Bulge. In July 1945 he gave up his commission to spend four years at West Point. While there he participated in six varsity sports and upon graduation was again commissioned in the infantry. Doug, however, had his eyes on becoming a fighter pilot. Not to be dismayed, he made a personal call on General Omar Bradley, Army Chief of Staff, and brashly asked to be transferred to the Air Force. One year later he was flying F-86 Sabre Jets over the Yalu River in Korea. While with his squadron in Japan he requested a thirty day leave to join the 187TH RCT and act as a Forward Air Controller in the attack on Hill 228. Here his luck ran out when a fragment from a Chinese mortar round ended his life.

As the Eighth Army crossed the 38th Parallel in early April enemy resistance became stiffer and stiffer. John Sonley, an infantryman in the 24th Division, remembers a rifle company attempting to take a small hill, and the Chinese throwing grenades down on the attacking infantrymen. Sgt. James Jackson, a nineteen year old farm boy from Indiana with three years service, grabbed a light machine gun and began firing the gun from his hip as he moved up the hill. Enemy mortar fire started to land, and one round landed at Jackson's feet. According to Sonley, "We all held him down as the medic gave him a dose of morphine. Jackson was trying to sit up and look at his feet. He mustered up some superhuman strength, threw off the men holding his arms and sat up. As he looked at where his feet had been, he said: 'Oh my God', and died."

The company hesitated and in a confusion of mortar bursts started to withdraw. Sgt. James Ackerly, the company supply sergeant who happened to be following the company in the attack, grabbed a rifle and yelled at the men around him, "What's the matter? Are you all cowards?" The men were suddenly so infuriated by his challenge that enmasse, with fixed bayonets, they charged up the hill and completely overran the Chinese defenders.

By the middle of April the Chinese were beginning to move into the Iron Triangle area near the Hwachon Reservoir. Fifty-seven CCF Divisions and eighteen NKPA Divisions were identified as building up in this area. On April 5th Operation Rugged was initiated to press hard against the Chinese buildup and try to reach Line Kansas on commanding ground north of the 38th Parallel. By 9 April this line had been reached. Further adjustments were made in order to gain key terrain in the Iron Triangle area, anticipating a Chinese spring offensive at any time.

Life on the Front

The life of the combat soldier during the winter drive from January to April was often brutal. Men spent hours preparing their defense positions, first digging through the frozen turf then laying wire and mines. They spent much time trying to devise ways to build comfortable

107

shelters which would withstand the 30 degrees below zero cold. The soldier on the front line in a fox-hole was envious of the local Korean villagers who were warm and snug in their thatched roof houses. After a soldier had worked for several days to make his fox-hole or bunker somewhat comfortable, the unit was inevitably told to move out. The company would move several miles ahead, and the building process would start again. It was always a nagging worry that the diagrams of the abandoned mine fields were inaccurate, and that the engineers, whose mission was to clear these fields, might suffer casualties.

Front line soldiers seldom got a chance to take a bath. Tours of duty at the front usually lasted several weeks, with three weeks on the front or in unit reserve and one week in division reserve or rest camp. The body in cold weather built up a protective oil that soldiers believed helped to keep out the bitter weather. When the company was in division reserve, bath units were usually available. Soldiers feared that washing off this protective oil was hazardous to their health in the cold weather, but few resisted the lure of hot water. Willard Schipper, 24th Division, looks back at how much he enjoyed the showers. "The nice part about it," he remarks, "was that I was able to wash my hair, what is left of it." He was given a new uniform, flu shots and another smallpox vaccination.

During the winter offensive infantry life was spent on the mountain ridges. The company command post (CP) was usually on the top of a mountain of 2000 feet or more with the men dug into a defensive perimeter surrounding it. Down in the valley the company rear controlled the vehicles, supply and kitchen. Often at two AM a company was told they would jump off at seven. At four AM a company executive officer or supply sergeant started up the mountain with

rations and hot breakfast carried by Korean laborers. At six AM the laborers reached the company, and hot breakfast was served. Usually this consisted of cool scrambled eggs, fresh fruit, army bread, jam and semi-hot coffee. Sometimes, depending on the enemy situation, a small fire was built to heat up the coffee. The men were given enough C-rations for a day. (In Korea many units gave their men a ration and a half in cold weather.)

When the first streaks of sunlight appeared across the sky the company would move into the attack. The objective would be in a general location perhaps eight miles away. When the sun rose, spotter planes would hover about and report enemy located on a specific mountain. The company would move along the ridges in a column with the lead squad or platoon rotating every few hours The Korean laborers with A-frames on their backs followed the column carrying extra ammunition, litters, and needed equipment normally carried by vehicles. The men carried not only weapons, ammunition and sleeping bags, but also a day's ration, a blanket, and extra socks. Most men had the new rubber combat boot. At the end of a hike the feet were soaking wet and men were supposed to change socks. Unfortunately sometimes circumstances didn't allow time for the men to change socks in the middle of battle. Wet feet in bitter cold weather was a hazard most men wished to avoid.

The column had to cross intervening mountains; so their route was constantly up and down and at times perpendicular. Men slipped and slid in the snow and slush. There would be an occasional crash as a helmet, rifle or mortar went sliding down a mountain side. At times the column would encounter snow drifts that came up to their knees. The Korean laborers would yelp as their sandaled feet, covered with old worn socks, stepped in icy slush. Occasionally a laborer would fall with his top heavy load on a stretch of ice. If he yelled with pain and was injured, he was given morphine and then, if he could walk, was left to find his way down the mountain. The company column moved on.

Before an assault by the company began, artillery fire was directed on the objective and then the Air Force dropped napalm on the targeted enemy. The narrow mountain ridges usually allowed only one squad or platoon to assault at a time. After all the artillery and air support, the infantry assaulted and usually found that the enemy had withdrawn. Americans often found an objective littered with charred enemy remains. Occasionally a few prisoners were taken.

Once a hill was occupied the long process of digging in began again. If company vehicles got near the foot of the mountain, the laborers would go down the mountain and bring up a hot meal. ROKs attached to American units were experts at scrounging wood and straw to give warmth to their fox-holes. Fires might be allowed during the day if enemy resistance had been limited, but at night they had to be extinguished. This process continued for weeks and only on occasion did the enemy put up any resistance that inflicted casualties on Americans. Then the laborers would be used to carry the dead and wounded down the mountain.

Sometimes a unit might have to occupy positions where the enemy had recently received devastating American air and artillery fire. Covering the positions were Chinese bodies or parts of bodies. American soldiers were too busy digging their own defensive positions to have time to bury the dead Chinese before night fell. Then during the long nights soldiers sat in

fox-holes surrounded by Chinese corpses. Such situations were not unknown in other wars. The memories of these situations, however, were ones that veterans would retain forever.

Long nightly vigils were the most dreaded aspect of fighting in Korea. Two soldiers usually shared a fox-hole or shelter and took turns sleeping in two hour shifts. The psychological fear of darkness and its mysteries was common to all Americans. As the night wore on soldiers on watch might hear more and more odd noises. The sound might be just a rustling tree branch or artillery across the valley. The soldiers were apprehensive and wondered if a mass of CCFs were crawling on their bellies up in front of their positions. Perhaps a soldier saw something moving. Quickly he grabbed a grenade, pulled the pin and tossed it into the gully below. There would be a muffled thump which was repeated dozens of times as the echo reverberated across the valley below.

Perhaps it began to rain. In March it often rained when the temperature was only thirty-five degrees, making the men cold and miserable. Soon the fox-holes would fill with water. A glimmer of hope for the cold, soaked soldier in the fox-hole was that possibly the enemy was just as miserable, and in no hurry to attack his position.

Finally the first rays of light appeared. Perhaps the company would stay in the same position for another day. Perhaps they would move out. Their only thoughts at this time were that they had survived the night and were anticipating the hot cup of coffee and soggy breakfast. Another grinding day awaited the front units as Eighth Army continued to push towards the 38th Parallel into North Korea.

Integration

The integration of Afro-Americans within the Armed Forces was incomplete in 1950. Only the Air Force had almost totally integrated before the Korean War. In the Army and Navy, however, very limited integration had taken place by the time the war began. The size of the Marine Corps had been badly cut after World War II and Afro-Americans were in limited numbers. During the rapid buildup of the 1st Marine Division in 1950 for the Inchon landing, a sizable number of Afro-American Marines on active duty were integrated into this unit. The Marine Corps Afro-American members grew from two officers and 1965 enlisted men in 1950 to nineteen officers and 24,468 men by 1953.

The integration of Eighth Army took place in 1951 after a proposal by Maj. Gen. William Kean of the 25th Division. On March 14th Ridgway wrote up a summary for MacArthur to review and approached the topic with Washington. The major Afro-American units in Eighth Army at that time were the 24th Regiment, the 3rd Battalions of the 9th and 15th Infantries, the 64th Tank Battalion and several all Afro-American artillery battalions.

Although the official integration policy did not start until the fall of 1951, units in Korea began integrating in early 1951. The shortage of manpower had units fighting to get replacements. One of the earliest units to begin accepting Afro-Americans was the 24th Division. In early 1951 the 21st Infantry and 5th RCT accepted a number of Afro-American replacements. The 5th RCT which had come from Hawaii had almost half its strength in Hawaiians who were descendants of natives of Japan, Korea, China, the Philippines and the Pacific Islands. These Hawaiians had adapted to a racially mixed environment. Those in the front line units were delighted to have English speak-

ing Afro-American replacements fill the foxholes beside them. Whatever prejudices they may have had were soon forgotten, when common suffering built a strong bond.

Ridgway had always wanted integration but was delayed in pressing this issue because of MacArthur's relief and his change in assignment. On 12 May Ridgway sent this classic cable to Washington saying: "It is my conviction that only in this way could we assure the sort of esprit a fighting man needs, where each soldier stands proudly on his own feet, knowing himself to be as good as the next fellow and better than the enemy. Besides it had always seemed to me both un-American and un-Christian for free citizens to be taught to downgrade themselves in this way, as if they were unfit to associate with their fellows or to accept leadership themselves."

Finally on October 1st, 1951 the 24th Infantry was disbanded and its personnel distributed throughout the Eighth Army. By July 1953 over ninety percent of the entire U.S. Army had been integrated.

The adjustment of Afro-American soldiers into white units was not always easy. Lt. Beverly Scott, who became the first Afro-American platoon leader in the 14th Regiment, is an instructive example. His relationships with his men were excellent, and he was accepted once they saw how competent he was. His relationship with the other officers, however, was cool. Some officers wouldn't talk to him. As time went on other officers warmed up to him. Still, by March 1952, he had earned enough points to go home, but the unit kept telling him, "We don't have a replacement for you." When the I. G. learned of his situation, Scott immediately received orders for home. In departing he said good-by only to the enlisted men of his unit. The men he commanded had developed great respect for him.

Another example of the slow adjustment to integration of Afro-Americans into white units is that of Lee Knight. Today Knight is active in veterans affairs and bonds closely with other veterans of his unit, the 5th RCT. When he got to Korea, he had had several years service and was quickly made a squad leader. While in this role he earned the Silver Star and was wounded by an enemy grenade during Operation Nomad in November 1951. As an E-7 he returned from the hospital in January 1952 and returned to his fifteen man squad. On an ambush patrol with his squad a rifle went off accidentally. This could have alerted the enemy. One frightened man said, "Nigger, you're going to get us killed." Knight paid no attention to this man and calmly moved his squad to a new position and later back to safety. After this incident he never heard a racial slur from his squad again. Slowly, but at times painfully, like the war itself, integration was succeeding.

MacArthur Relieved

The UN Force's drive to the 38th Parallel and the withdrawal of the CCV back into North Korea had given the UN an opportunity to negotiate a cease fire. The Truman Administration and the Joint Chiefs felt that a cease-fire might lead to a political settlement. Both Communist China and the UN had suffered in this war, and it was thought that a political solution for Korea could now be reached. On 19 March President Truman issued a public statement that the UN Command was willing to consider a cease-fire.

MacArthur on 24 March, after being notified of the Truman Policy, issued a statement on his own that defied the policy of the Administration.

While Truman wanted to restrict the war to Korea only, MacArthur wanted to expand it to all Asia. In his statement MacArthur said: "The enemy must now be painfully aware that a decision of the United Nations to depart from its tolerant effort to contain the war to the area of Korea through expansion of our military operations to his coastal areas and interior bases would doom Red China to risk of imminent military collapse."

By this statement MacArthur was making national policy on his own.

Not only did MacArthur challenge the President's directive, but he also made a fatal mistake that put him into the camp of Truman's political opponents. In a letter written on March 8th to Joseph W. Martin, House Minority Leader, MacArthur favored using Nationalist Chinese troops in this war. He also accused the Truman Administration of favoring Europe over Asia in their policies. On April 5th Martin, on reading the letter before the House of Representatives, made public MacArthur's opposition to the policy of the Truman Administration.

By these actions MacArthur was challenging the American political system. Under this political system foreign policy decisions are made by a political process initiated by democratically elected leaders. By making his own policy MacArthur was operating outside the American political system.

Truman had no choice but to relieve MacArthur. He felt, however, that he would listen first to leaders in his administration before he made his final decision. Truman asked Secretary of State Acheson, Secretary of Defense Marshall, Special Assistant W. Averell Harriman, and Chairman of the Joint Chiefs, Omar Bradley, to meet and reach a conclusion. On April 9th all four unanimously supported the Truman decision to relieve General MacArthur.

The next decision was to choose MacArthur's replacement. Bradley and Marshal recommended Ridgway. Truman approved this recommendation. At the same time Lieutenant General James A. Van Fleet, who had achieved success fighting Communists in Greece, was selected to replace Ridgway in Korea. The Far East Command and Eighth Army now had two experienced commanders who would work together closely to follow the Truman policy and restrict the war to the Korean peninsula.

Although a mix-up in communications caused MacArthur to find out about his relief from the public press, he remained composed and showed no trace of bitterness according to Ridgway. One great American leader was replacing another. The Korean War would go on. In a speech made before the joint houses of Congress, MacArthur made his famous flamboyant remark, "Old soldiers never die, they just fade away."

Chapter 13: Chinese Spring Offensive 22 April - 20 May 1951

The anticipated Chinese attack began at 10 PM on 22 April 1951 across a forty mile front. Over 250,000 soldiers in nine CCF Armies were concentrated in a two pronged attack in Western Korea. The biggest assault came from six CCF Armies that struck directly south toward Seoul. The other prong of the attack consisted of three Chinese Armies which attacked southwest through Kapyong. The objective of this attack was a double envelopment to pinch off Seoul.

The Chinese hoped that they would have the same success as they had had in the New Year's Eve offensive four months earlier. Since that date Eighth Army had built up its strength, particularly in artillery, and was now better able to withstand a major Chinese offensive.

When this Chinese attack failed to take Seoul by early May, the Chinese changed plans. A major shift of CCF units to the central Korean front took place. From 15-20 May a violent battle was fought on the central front , but the UN Forces held. Neither side could totally defeat the other. A stalemate developed, which prolonged the war for two more years.

CCF April Offensive - West Prong

On the west flank of Eighth Army was US I Corps made up of the ROK 1st Division, the British 29th Brigade, the US 3rd Division, the Turkish Brigade, the US 25th Division, and the US 24th Division. The British 29th Brigade defended the Imjin River on the historic main highway to Seoul. There the CPF Divisions concentrated and forced the brigade to withstand the main Chinese assault. The brigade was made up of three British Battalions and one attached Belgian Battalion and numbered about 5,000 men. This small force had to cover a front of nine miles.

The fighting between the CCF and the 29th Brigade was some of the most vicious in the war. The Belgium Battalion on the north side of the river was cut off soon after the Chinese attack, but was rescued by the Royal Ulster Rifle Battalion which was rushed up from its reserve position. Since the Imjin River was fordable at this location the Chinese crossed at a number of places and soon had infiltrated between the Gloucester and Northumberland Fusilier Battalions. The brigade held its position and fought off the massed CCF for two days.

On the left of the 29th Brigade was the ROK 1st Division. Unit after unit of the CCF attempted to break through this division, but initially it held its ground. Slowly it was forced to withdraw slightly. CCF troops were now able to encircle the left most 29th Brigade Battalion, the Gloucesters. Attempts by the Filipino Battalion to rescue the Gloucesters failed. The US 3rd Division was so hard pressed in plugging up gaps in the line that even their planned attempt to rescue the Gloucesters failed. Captain Anthony Farrar-Hockley of the Gloucesters described the defense of Hill 235, "Some one is throwing grenades; and they are throwing them at us. Here comes another one: a small dark object against the background of blue sky, its wooden handle turning over and over as it begins to descend on our positions." Farrar-Hockley continues in famous British understate-

ment his admiration for his commander, Lt. Col. James P. Carne: "He does not tell me that they have been under the most intense heavy machine-gun fire for the last fifty minutes; he does not admit to strolling about under fire along the whole front in order to visit and inspire the companies; he does not say that he has made another sortie to repel a group of would-be infiltrators. He puffs at his pipe for a moment, regards the smoke drifting up into the air, and taps some ash back into the pipe bowl. 'Not bad, really,' he says. 'Have you a match to spare?'"

Finally Col. Carne gave his Company Commanders permission to break out of the perimeter. He had just received word from his Brigade Commander that the artillery was no longer able to support them. He, himself, refused to leave.

A medic attending a wounded soldier, 3rd Division, Spring 1951.

113

The 3rd Division put up a strong defense north of Seoul in April 1951.

He felt it was his duty to remain with the wounded. Of 800 men in the Gloucestershire Battalion only about fifty managed to escape. When the entire 29th Brigade finally withdrew, they had suffered 25 percent casualties.

In the center of I Corps another battle was raging. The Puerto Rican US 65th Infantry of the 3rd Division with the Turkish Brigade to their right were fighting for their lives. The CCF hit the 65th and the Turks in full force with waves and waves of screaming soldiers and forced back the Turkish Brigade. To plug the gap the 3rd Division rushed in the reserve 7th Infantry to back up the Puerto Ricans. In this action part of the 7th Infantry was over-run. Pfc. James Cart of H Company was told by his platoon sergeant to pick up an 81 mm mortar base plate and head back into the hills in his rear. All that night and into the next morning he carried the heavy base plate for many miles until he ran into other members of his unit. His platoon first gunner asked him why he was carrying the base plate. "Hell," he said , "Sarge told me to." The gunner replied,

"Damn, we don't have no mortars - left everything behind."

At the same time the 35th Infantry of the 25th Division replaced the Turks. On their right the rest of the 25th Division was fighting 50,000 soldiers of two CCF Armies. Well disciplined troops like the 35th Infantry did not panic and were able to maintain an orderly withdrawal. Capt. Luther Weaver, L Company 35th Infantry, told his men, "Be ready to move on the trail toward where battalion was. We're probably gonna have to fight our way out, but we're going out as a company. Keep your squads intact. We're going out together."

On the division right the 27th Regiment (Wolfhound) was taking a terrific pounding from Chinese artillery. Behind the artillery came waves of infantry supported by a few T-34 tanks. These heavy weapons had rarely been used by the Chinese in the past. The 27th Regiment, however, was a disciplined, well led, outfit and held their position in close, hand-to-hand fighting. Supporting this defense was the fire-power of eight artillery batteries of the 8th, 90th and 176th Field Artillery Battalions. After thirty minutes the attacking Chinese had had enough and withdrew leaving almost a thousand dead and wounded behind.

Other UN units were moved about to block the Chinese penetrations and thus their front line was able to hold back the surging enemy masses. By orderly withdrawals coupled with tremendous artillery fire along the whole I Corps front, the CCF suffered thousands of casualties. In this method I Corps units north of Seoul moved back in leaps and bounds and caused the Chinese advance to slow almost to a halt.

CCF April Offensive - East Prong

The eastern prong of the Chinese offensive was launched from the west central mountains of the peninsula by three CCF Armies of 90,000 men. The objective of this attack was to concentrate on the ROK 6th Division, destroy it, and split the boundary between I and IX US Corps. Once the CCF attack started on the evening of 22 April the Chinese wasted no time in overpowering the ROK 6th Division and driving it back about ten miles. Little resistance was put up by these ROKs which left a huge breach, ten miles wide. The supporting 92nd and 987th Field Artillery Battalions were left in the breach and had to fend for themselves. The terrain was rugged and had few roads which made vehicular movement difficult. The 92nd which had twelve 155mm self-propelled howitzers and four eight-inch howitzers managed to extricate itself by fighting its way out with help from the 1st Battalion, 1st Marines. While the 987th was withdrawing, however, the weak road collapsed, and the battalion had to sacrifice fifteen self-propelled 105mm howitzers, sixty vehicles, and all its fire direction equipment.

This ten mile breach of the ROK 6th Division exposed both divisions on its flanks, the 24th Division on its left and the 1st Marine Division on its right. On the 24th Division front the 5th RCT was on the right, the 19th Infantry on the left and the 21st Infantry behind in reserve. By daylight of the 23rd the CCF 59th and 60th Divisions had penetrated three miles into the division's right rear. The 21st Infantry was rushed in to block the right rear flank of the division as the Chinese started pouring in. Still gaps appeared on the division's flank through which masses of the enemy were able to infiltrate. At one point a squad guarding a small road was suddenly confronted by 1000 Chinese soldiers coming down the road while marching four abreast.

On April 25th the 24th Division began to withdraw. The 5th RCT with the 8th Ranger Company was assigned to be the rear guard to cover the withdrawal of the 19th and 21st Regiments. One veteran remembers watching this withdrawal from a high hill on a beautiful spring day. Down in the valley on his left hundreds of 24th Division vehicles were slowly worming their way south. He then turned to his right and looked over to the next hill about a mile away. There he could see American soldiers defending a bunker by throwing hand grenades down on hundreds of Chinese who were crawling towards the bunker from all directions like ants. This was unusual since from early January few Chinese had been seen in the daylight. Now in bright sunlight they were swarming over the hills around American positions. These Chinese soldiers were in green summer uniforms which were quite different from the brown quilted ones worn by the Chinese all winter.

When it came time to withdraw, it was discovered that the 8th Ranger Company was cut off. Col. Harry Wilson, CO 5th RCT, rushed

Chinese dead after assault on American positions, April 1951.

back with tanks to rescue the company. He was able to break through the CCF perimeter, but could rescue only sixty-five rangers. This incident caused a delay in the withdrawal of the entire regiment and gave the CCF more time to advance deeper into the American rear.

When the regimental column finally withdrew, it led off with the 3rd Battalion. This unit had just cleared a steep mountain pass when the column was suddenly cut by a large Chinese force that established a major gauntlet. The attempt of the remainder of the 5th RCT to try to get through this gauntlet is known to survivors as "Death Valley." The result of this battle was a terrible slaughter as the RCT minus one infantry battalion was cut off by a Chinese force too large to dislodge. Over 100 artillerymen were killed or captured and thirteen 105mm howitzers and sixty vehicles were abandoned. Fortunately most of the regiment managed to escape because the Chinese were not aware of an uncharted road recently built by the regiment's own 72nd Engineers. Lt. Col. Clarence Steuart, the 555th

Artillery Battalion Commander, remembered the road and led the survivors of the regiment to safety.

Lt. Ed Crockett, a tank platoon leader in the regimental tank company commanding three M-4 medium tanks, was in the thick of the fighting: "By mid-day we could see the enemy moving past us along the high ridgeline running parallel to the withdrawal route. Small groups of Korean refugees had been passing through our position all morning. About 2 p.m. I was surprised to see one group headed in the wrong direction: north. I recognized some of the people as those who had passed our position headed south about an hour earlier. It was at that point that I realized that the Chinese were in our rear, probably blocking passage."

He moved his three tanks a short distance to the rear and encountered Chinese in the ditches along the road. One Chinese soldier with a wooden club jumped on his tank and assaulted him as he stood in the commander's hatch. Fortunately Crockett carried a .45 caliber pistol, which he used. As his three tanks approached the 555 FA Battalion at the gauntlet in the pass, he saw that the road was blocked with burning vehicles. Artillerymen behind their 105mm howitzers were engaging the enemy with direct fire. Wave after wave of Chinese attacked his tanks but were driven off by the firepower of his machine guns. At least 250 Chinese perished in front of his guns. Finally he was forced to abandon his tank when it was struck by a 3.5 inch rocket, one captured earlier from some American unit. His crew and a number of wounded American soldiers mounted his last two tanks and withdrew by way of the uncharted road.

An infantryman, Ivan Russell, remembers the orderly withdrawal as his unit was ordered to move out. "We weren't running, but we weren't walking either. One guy beside me was talkative, but I still don't know why. I guess he wanted to see if his mouth still worked. He had been shot through both cheeks and had to tell someone about it. He was so glad to have survived— he had a bloody grin on his face the whole time."

On the Eighth Army front east of the breach near Chuchon, the 1st Marine Division was attacked by three CCF Divisions. When the ROK 6th Division left the gap open, the 1st Marines who were the reserve regiment rushed in their 1st Battalion to plug the gap That night, while defending Horseshoe Ridge, they received the full impact of the CCF attack. One of the defenders remembers, "They were singing, humming and chanting 'Awake Marine'—After they knocked out our two machine-guns, we pulled back about fifty yards and set up a new line. All this was in pitch black night with Chinese cymbals crashing, horns blowing and those God-awful yells." Another Marine there, Pfc. Lyle Conaway, saw the attacking Chinese the next morning tie up bundles of straw, light them and follow behind the flames. They even tied burning straw to a donkey and chased it into the high grass. Despite this method of attack, the Chinese still failed to overrun the Marines.

Although the division received some pressure on its west flank and took some casualties, the Marines received only a glancing blow as the main Chinese drive was to the southwest toward Seoul.

The collapse of the ROK 6th Division opened a critical avenue southwest to Seoul. If the CCF controlled the highway route to Seoul, they would control the main MSR behind IX Corps. The key town in the area was Kapyong where the IX Corps reserve, the British Commonwealth Brigade, was positioned. On the 24th the CCF sent wave after wave against the Australian Battalion which was pushed back slightly. But with support from the Middlesex and Canadian Battalions, the Australians were able to hold their positions and stop the Chinese assault. The arrival of the 5th Cavalry reinforced the defense of Kapyong. This magnificent defense by the Commonwealth Brigade plugged the gap left by the ROK 6th Division and slowed the assault of the CCF.

Over the next few days both I and IX Corps slowly withdrew back into a tighter perimeter around Seoul. The new front line extended from north of Seoul eastward along the Han River to the junction with the Pukhan River. From here a new line called The No Name Line swung to the northeast all the way to a point above Yangyang on the east coast.

The withdrawal of these two American Corps was slow and methodical. Units withdrew through units as they moved south into the new perimeter. For those who defended the blocking positions on the withdrawal the situation was tense. An example of the moments of tension was when troops, pausing on a hill overlooking a bridge crossing of the Pukhan River, saw Army Engineers slowly dismantle the bridge. Would the Chinese attack before the bridge was dismantled? Once the bridge was dismantled how would this defending infantry unit get back across the river? These were questions that vexed the Americans as they waited above the bridge and listened to the clank of hammers as the bridge slowly came apart.

Chinese Spring Offensive - East 15-20 May 1951

The Chinese changed plans about May 10th after their terrible losses trying to break through the Eighth Army perimeter and take Seoul during early May. Eighth Army detected five CCF Armies moving east against the US X Corps and ROK III Corps. This move was similar to the one the CCF had made five months earlier in January. Van Fleet did not expect this move and had concentrated his forces around Seoul. Only the US 3rd Division was in a position to move rapidly to back up any possible CCF breakthrough.

On the night of 15 May the CCF struck X Corps and the ROK III Corps. On a thirty-two mile front the CCF hurled twenty-one Chinese Divisions at these corps. The heaviest Chinese force was concentrated against two ROK Divisions which fell back disorganized, causing an enemy salient in the UN front. The US 2nd Division to the west held its ground in spite of the salient. Air and artillery pounded the attacking CCF units which were densely concentrated in order to make a breakthrough. The US 2nd Division not only withstood the CCF attack but pushed into the flank of these attacking forces in the salient. Simultaneously the US 3rd Division was dispatched from the Seoul area and employed to block further movement of the CCF into the salient.

Since most of the No Name Line of Eighth Army held, most of the CCF and NKPA units could concentrate only in the salient. At the same time the US 2nd Division on the west side of the salient and the ROK I Corps on the east side, by holding their ground, formed a barrier on the two sides of the salient. These units were determined to hold. Cpl. Don Thomas, K Company 23rd Infantry remembers clearly the strong American determination to hold these defensive positions. Each squad in his platoon was assigned a tank, and they dug their defensive positions around the tank.

The tip of the salient was plugged up by the US 3rd Division and the 187 Airborne RCT

which completed the encirclement of the salient. The communist forces could go no further. This last attack had cost the CCF and NKPA 90,000 casualties. After four days the determined stand of the US 2nd Division and the ROK I Corps, coupled with the dominating deterrence displayed by the artillery, the air power, mines and barbwire, brought the communist second spring offensive to a standstill.

UN Counter-offensive 22 May - 23 June 1951

General Van Fleet realized that the Chinese had overextended themselves in this second attack. CCF strength in the west had shifted to the east leaving their remaining forces around Seoul vulnerable. On 22 May, Van Fleet ordered an immediate counteroffensive designed to exploit the Chinese defeat. The US IX Corps attacked vigorously to the northeast to Hwachon. US I Corps moved into the attack to protect IX Corps' left flank. After holding for two days, X Corps reinforced by the 187 Airborne RCT attacked northeast to Inje. General Almond pushed his corps hard in the hopes of cutting off a number of CCF units. Although Almond's defense of the salient was brilliant, he found it difficult to move swiftly through the mountainous terrain and destroy the rapidly fleeing Chinese.

Behind this X Corps offense was the driving force of General "Ned" Almond. He accepted no excuses. When forces were not moving fast enough, he would suddenly bring his helicopter down next to the spearhead of his attacking force. Boiling mad, he would accept no excuses from the spearhead commander and sternly say, "Get those tanks on the road and keep going until you hit a mine. I don't care about communications. I want you to keep going at twenty miles an hour."

During early June the UN Forces continued attacking north in limited operations to consolidate positions. After some strong enemy resistance, Eighth Army gained Chorwon and Kumwha at the Iron Triangle. When IX Corps units tried to push northeast from Kumwha, they found the enemy establishing a strong line, which this time the Chinese intended to hold.

At Inje X Corps reached the lower edge of a area known as the "Punchbowl." This was a depression three miles wide at one end, six miles wide at the other and six miles long. At the upper edge of the depression the CCF had dug in with intentions of staying. This depression was to become a contested area for the next two years.

The war of mobility had ended. The vast buildup in firepower and mobility by Eighth Army had made it impossible for the Communist Forces to break through her revitalized divisions. No longer could either side win a major victory without tremendous casualties. As in the First World War after the Battle of the Marne in 1914, the conflict turned into a stalemate that lasted to the war's end. Positional warfare had come to Korea. The political objectives of Communist China had changed between December 1950 and June 1951. Hopes of unifying Korea had died. The cost of the war to Communist China was staggering. The West was not going to leave Korea. It had shown China that it was willing to expend lives to save South Korea. The time for peace negotiations was now at hand.

Chapter 14: Stalemate 1951
Peace Talks

The military struggle between UN forces and combined forces of the CCF and the NKPA had reached a no-win situation. The war had

been costly to both sides, and both sides wanted peace Two major issues needed to be settled. How did each side interpret the term "cease-fire"? Should the peace talks be limited to military matters or should political and territorial matters be discussed? This last question caused disagreement between the two sides and delayed the peace talks for another five months.

On June 23rd 1951 Jacob Malik, Soviet Delegate to the United Nations, said that the Soviet Union believed the Korean War could be settled. Andre Gromyko, the Soviet Foreign Minister, supported Malik and proposed a military cease-fire. He added that the settlement should be limited to military matters only. Based on this proposal, Assistant Secretary of State, Dean Rusk, advised General Ridgway to invite the communist commanders to send representatives to meet in conference with UN representatives. Ridgway accordingly sent a message to the communist military commanders. On July 1st a joint notice from the commanders of the CCF and NKPA agreed to suspend military activities and hold peace negotations.

The suspension of military operations became a major issue. Ridgway and other American leaders were suspicious of the Chinese desire to suspend military operations before an armistace. Ridgway wanted military operations to continue while the peace talks went on. He feared that a cease-fire before peace negotiations would allow the Chinese time to build up their forces unmolested, leaving UN forces vulnerable to later attack. Ridgway took a tough position when dealing with the communists. In a letter to Washington he said, "To sit down with these men and deal with them as representatives of an enlightened and civilized people is to invite the disaster their treachery will bring upon us."

Searching for mines, 7th Division, Spring 1951.

On July 10th the peace talks began at Kaesong, a city still held by the communists. It became apparent to the UN representatives that the communists were not going to arbitrate an armistice. The communists were using the peace talks for propaganda purposes, implying that the UN had capitulated. The communists wanted to discuss political issues not military issues. By August 22nd the communist delegation broke off the talks, because their propaganda was not making the slightest impression on the UN delegation.

Both sides were suspicious of each other. The continued Chinese buildup with resupply of arms, ammunition, food and replacements could have been a defensive strategy, since the Chinese feared UN motives. On the other hand Ridgway did not trust the intentions of the communist command and feared the buildup might lead to another attack. The distrust on both sides caused violent fighting during the next five months over limited military objectives. The terrible casualties on both sides during this period eventually caused the two opponents to meet

again, and the communists to agree to limit the talks only to military aspects of the war.

The Battles of the Ridges August 1951

During the five weeks of talks the Eighth Army had held their positions which gave the communists useful breathing space. During this period the communists were able to reinforce their positions with deep fortifications, artillery, mines and barbwire. These new fortifications were reminiscent of those used by both sides in World War I. From this time on battles in Korea were fought for a few feet of terrain with heavy casualties on both sides. One has only to refer to the Battles of the Somme and Verdun in 1916 to see the similarities with Korea in 1951. From August to December 1951 UN forces suffered 60,000 casualties.

By the middle of August Ridgway was exasperated by the failure of the peace talks. He felt that it was time to exert more military pressure. At the same time General Van Fleet wanted to eliminate a sag in the UN front. A key piece of terrain was the Punch Bowl north of the Hwachon Reservoir. In order to control the reservoir, Eighth Army had to control the Punch Bowl. At this time the North Koreans controlled three sides of the Punch Bowl and could look down and direct artillery fire far into the rear of the American front. To prevent this dominant observation, the UN forces had to control both the eastern and western rim of the Punch Bowl.

The western rim of the Punch Bowl consisted of a ridge line with two major mountain masses, Bloody Ridge and Heartbreak Ridge. The southern most mass, Bloody Ridge, introduced Eighth Army to the new style of heavily fortified, deep trench and bunker warfare characteristic of World War I. Supplementing the machine guns and mortars of these enemy defensive fortifications were mine fields, barbwire and heavy artillery. Between August 17th and September 5th, 1951 the campaign to take Bloody Ridge proved to be one of the first of Eighth Army's costly endeavors.

The assault on Bloody Ridge began on 17 August. The initial mission was given to the ROK 36th Regiment of the ROK 7th Division. In spite of American artillery pounding, the hidden, well-constructed bunkers of the NKPA withstood the artillery assault. In the first ten days the ROK 36 th Regiment had taken over a thousand casualties just to reach the middle peak of the ridge, Hill 940. Control of 940 did not last long as a major NKPA counterattack drove the ROKs off the objective in panic and mass confusion.

On 27 August the US 9th Infantry was rushed in to continue the assault. The 2nd and 3rd Battalions of the 9th attacked towards Peaks 983 and 773 and were driven back from both by NKPA counterattacks.. Next, the 1st Battalion of

Infantry moving into an assault position, 7th Division, Spring 1951.

7th Division Patrol moving from their defensive positions, April 1952.

the 9th Infantry was thrown into the assault and it too was driven back with heavy losses. Replacements continued to pour into these units, but still more casualties were sustained.

One company in the 1st Battalion had over 100 percent casualties. The enemy was determined to hold at all costs. He pounded the attacking Americans with mortar and artillery fire while pouring heavy machine- gun fire across the barbwire emplacements and mine fields. When the US 23rd Infantry finally outflanked Bloody Ridge and threatened the NKPA positions there, the North Koreans withdrew to

121

positions on the next ridgeline, "Heartbreak" Ridge.

Among those on "Bloody Ridge" was Cpl. Ben Judd, F Company 23rd Infantry, Two men in his squad decided to take over a former enemy foxhole. Later one of them complained of the terrible smell in the foxhole. He said to Judd, "I'm sure there's a dead enemy soldier in our hole." Judd jokingly told the men to start digging and try to find him. Shortly thereafter they did find a corpse and decided "to move to a hole they dug themselves, one which had better ventilation."

Many questions may be asked concerning the high losses of UN troops. The defenses of the NKPA were able to withstand the tremendous pounding of American artillery and air strikes. This constant pounding had eliminated all the trees which had made detection of the enemy bunkers more difficult. These bunkers of heavy timbers were built into the hills in such a manner that UN artillery and air strikes had difficulty in reaching them. When these bunkers were not knocked out, the North Korean machine-gunners could pour heavy fire down on the attacking UN infantry as they tried to cross the barbwire and mine fields. Americans soon found that direct fire artillery was one of the best ways to eliminate an enemy bunker. The 155mm Long Tom direct fire gun was an excellent weapon to use on these bunkers if the gun could get into a direct fire position. Another device against bunkers that had been used against the Japanese in World War II was the flame thrower. Once infantrymen were trained to use flame throwers, a great many bunkers were destroyed.

Another reason for high American casualties might be attributed to the lack of training of the American replacements. Rotation started in the spring of 1951, and most veterans of the first year of the war went home. After they left, fighting was limited as the peace talks dragged on. Suddenly in late August fighting started again and green soldiers were thrown into the fray. As the casualties mounted, more green replacements were committed to the battle. Eighth Army had not had time to train these new replacements in how to fight the deeply entrenched Chinese and North Koreans.

Judd remembers the fatalism that soon developed among the men." We readied ourselves for an advance which we knew was to come. There was very little talk in the unit. I had never heard the men so silent. Someone remarked lightly that that I should stay behind, as I was to leave shortly. My answer was that I would not be leaving Korea on rotation or standing up. — I think others felt this way about themselves too; it would account for the moody silence that seemed to surround the company."

On the 31st of August the 1st Marine Division opened a drive to secure the high ground on the east rim of the Punch Bowl. On the first day enemy resistance was limited, but by the second day it stiffened. It took four days for the 7th Marines to secure their initial objectives. Every time a North Korean bunker was knocked out, it would be quickly rebuilt. Pfc. Troy Hamm remembers that one enemy bunker which his unit took was constructed of twelve layers of logs and ten feet of dirt. Artillery and air strikes had been unable to neutralize it. Marines with flame throwers finally destroyed the occupants. Hamm remembered that the mountain was so bare from artillery pounding that the soil had turned to silt. He walked only on trails the North Koreans had used because the rest of the mountain was covered with landmines and booby traps.

The enemy continued to contest every foot of ground. In the battle for Hill 749 on September 14th the 1st Marines advanced only 300 meters. According to Pfc. Floyd Baxter, "The enemy covered their foxholes with grass and leaves and whatever. Once we had run past their holes, they'd pop up and hit us from the rear. This is why we lost so many men."

Hill 749 was taken on 16 September, but the Marines had to defend against counterattacks for four more days before the hill was finally secure. The hill had cost the 1st Marines 90 killed and 714 wounded. A year earlier on the Nakong River on the Pusan Perimeter in a similar attack the 5th Marines had lost 66 men killed and 278 wounded against the same enemy. The difference in statistics reveals the changes that came about when the war became a stalemate and the enemy had time to construct strong defensive positions.

Heartbreak Ridge

The most famous and probably the most costly of all the ridge battles fought in the fall of 1951 was Heartbreak Ridge. Militarily the ridge pointed daggerlike into the NKVA front lines. Taking this ridge would allow Eighth Army to control a roadnet which at that time was in enemy hands.

X Corps selected the US 2nd Division to take the ridge. A single regiment, the 23rd, was to be the assault force and would approach the objective from the Satae-ri Valley on the east. Two battalions were to attack and take Hills 851, 931 and 894. As the mission began no one envisioned just how difficult a task it would be.

At dawn on 13 September the assault started with the 3rd Battalion coming under enemy fire

almost immediately. This unit moved slowly forward under constant attack. At noon the 2nd Battalion crossed the Line of Departure and immediately encountered fire from many automatic weapons. A North Korean regiment in concealed bunkers pinned down the two assaulting battalions as salvos of artillery and heavy mortar fire crashed among the Americans. Prospects for a quick victory vanished.

Major Sherman Pratt who had been with the 23rd Regiment at Kunu-ri, Chipyong-ni and the No Name Line watched the assaulting battalions and fully understood how the hill mass got the name Heartbreak Ridge. He watched enemy mortar and artillery rounds explode among the men of his regiment. He saw some men fall and not get up. Others would fall backward and roll down the slopes. "There would be little puffs of black smoke from the grenades the North Koreans would toss out at them." The withering fire of the NKPA continued to keep the Americans pinned down.

To relieve pressure on the 23rd Regiment, Brigadier General Thomas de Shazo, the Acting Division Commander, ordered the 9th Infantry Regiment to assault the southern peak of Hill 894. By the 15th of September the 2nd Battalion, 9th Infantry controlled Hill 894, but on the next two days they had to fight off NKPA counterattacks. In spite of this success, the maneuver failed to relieve pressure on the 23rd Regiment.

Companies were rapidly being reduced to a few men as casualties multiplied in the attacking battalions. Troops from Japan were brought in to replace the casualties. Among these troops were many recalled Reserve Officers who were combat veterans of World War II. These men were products of the Inactive Reserve. The Judge Advocate General had ruled that any man who

123

had once been commissioned could be recalled. Division policy was that these men must go to the front. Rear echelon jobs went to survivors of combat on the front line. These men, who had served before, were recalled from civilian lives. According to 2nd Lt. Marvin Muskat, who occupied Heartbreak Ridge later, "Korea was all carefully divided up into point zones so that each soldier would accumulate points for rotation according to the point rating of the zone in which he served. A four point was the highest rating there. Anyone lucky enough to last nine months in a four point zone automatically had enough points for rotation." Heartbreak Ridge had a rating of four.

Other units were thrown into the battle for Heartbreak Ridge. The 1st Battalion, 23rd Regiment briefly reached the top of Hill 931 but was driven off by a NKPA counterattack. The French Battalion then moved in to relieve the 2nd Battalion, 23rd Regiment. Major Sherman Pratt remembers watching them. "They fixed bayonets and charged into that awful fire, straight up one of the slopes, until they were stabbing the North Koreans to death in their foxholes." By September 26th the battle had become so costly that the new Division Commander, Maj. Gen. Robert Young, decided to call off further assaults.

A new plan, called Operation Touchdown, was devised to take Heartbreak Ridge by broadening the attack. A task force from the division moved up the Satae-ri Valley on the east side of Heartbreak Ridge as a decoy. At the same time a task force of the 38th and 9th Infantry Regiments with tanks moved up the Mundung-ni Valley on the west side of Heartbreak. Air and artillery supported this advance. At the same time the 23rd Regiment and French Battalion continued their attacks up on the ridge. With engineer support, mines were removed and the roadway

improved as the 38th Infantry supported by tanks pushed through Mundung-ni. This last move cut off NKPA reinforcements to Heartbreak Ridge. At the same time the 23rd Regiment finally secured the last peaks of Heartbreak.

At a terrible cost in lives Eighth Army had eliminated a slight bend in their line. The 2nd Division suffered more than 3700 casualties. Of these over half came during Operation Touchdown against three NKPA divisions and the one CCF division. No one knows the exact North Korean and Chinese casualties, but estimates put the number at 25,000. This battle influenced further conflicts along the front line. Van Fleet concluded it was, " Unprofitable to continue the bitter operation." He told his Corps Commander to, "Plan no further offensives."

Battle of the Ridges - September and October 1951

While the Marines and US 2nd Division were fighting fierce battles in August and early September, other units in Eighth Army were fighting in less publicized encounters. During most of September US I and IX Corps took part in a number of local attacks and counterattacks.

In the IX Corps movement called Operation Nomad were three divisions, the US 24th, ROK 2nd and ROK 6th. The objective was to gain high ground overlooking the Kumsong Valley. The two ROK divisions protected the flanks of the 24th Division. All three divisions had to overcome fierce and bloody resistance, but by 23 October they had taken their objectives. As difficult as these engagements were, none could compare to Heartbreak Ridge.

By 30 October the 1st Cavalry Division near Yonchon, in a seventeen day advance, had suffered 2900 casualties but had gained only five miles. In early October, in the Battle of Bloody Angle west of Chorwon, the US 3rd Div. took more than 500 casualties. That same month in the Iron Triangle the US 25th Div, trying to straighten out the front line, suffered a number of casualties from attacks on heavily defended Chinese positions. All these engagements are examples of the attrition caused by violent fighting for limited objectives.

To Sgt. Darrald Feaker, I Company 5th Cavalry, the fighting never stopped."The hills and fighting just went on and on and on — One hill we eventually bypassed - I don't know how many assaults were staged on that hill. Seemed like every time a unit went up only half its men came back. One company which had watched our futile attempts, refused when it became their turn. Some guys just decided they wouldn't go and refused the order —MPs were sent forward to put those guys under arrest."

The effectiveness of Chinese artillery was much greater in this statemate period than it was during the first year of the war. During that first year when the war was mostly mobile, their artillery was limited and support fires came mostly from mortars. Because of these heavy Chinese artillery and mortar concentrations during this phase of the war, Eighth Army soldiers learned to dig deep bunkers. One soldier survivor of this frontline warfare was Sgt. Feaker. At one time over 4000 enemy artillery and mortar rounds landed in his area . . ."The shelling," he says, "was so heavy we couldn't leave the bunker - couldn't get out to find food and water." One soldier always stood guard near the mouth of the bunker so that they could observe any attacking enemy soldier and prevent him from throwing a grenade into the bunker.

Eighth Army Infantry firing at the enemy, 1951.

By November 1st Eighth Army realized that any further attempt to adjust the front line would require a terrible cost in lives. From this time on offensive missions were limited. The communists likewise had suffered terrible casualties. By early November they were ready to meet again with the UN representatives and discuss peace talks.

Chapter 15: War in the Air

Histories of the Korean War have centered around the Army and the Marine Corps because they suffered the most casualties and their struggles are well documented. Contributions of the U.S. Air Force and Navy, and the roles they played in the war, have not been as well reported. Those on the ground who fought in Korea, however, developed a deep respect for the support and assistance of the Air Force and Navy which circumvented a total catastrophe.

The contribution of air support can be divided into four distinct roles. The role most well known is the support of UN ground operations. In this role the air war was most effective and very much influenced the final outcome of the war. The second role of air power was to gain air superiority over all Korea and allow ground forces freedom of movement. In Korea, as in World War II and Vietnam, U.S. air power quickly surpassed that of the enemy, and the ground forces rarely suffered any losses from enemy air power. The third role of the air forces was interdiction bombing along the Yalu River. The fourth role of the air forces covered a number of essential services. These were establishing organizations to work with other services, reconnaissance, combat cargo supply, search and rescue and medical evacuation.

The United States Air Force entered the Korean War believing that all future wars would be won almost entirely by superior air power. In spite of statistical data to the contrary, most Americans believed that the air war against Germany and Japan in World War II had brought about their surrender. In postwar America, Congress adopted this theory and created the separate Air Force. The priority given to the Air Force shaped the strategy newly in place in 1950. The Korean War proved that this theory did not work. North Korea was a relatively primitive country with few industrial targets. The CCF fought a non-mechanized war. Although strategic bombing had limited effect on North Korean morale, it did have some impact on the CCF efforts to supply its huge army in Korea. Overall the major contribution of the air forces was the close air support given to the UN forces.

Ground Support

In the first months of the war air support of the ground forces was essential to the survival of the UN force. The North Koreans fought a mechanized war initially, which allowed tanks and other vehicles to be targeted on roads. One need only to have driven in late September, 1950, from Taegu to Seoul to see along the roadside the number of North Korean tanks, trucks, and pieces of artillery destroyed by America's Air Force.

Some of the first action against the NKPA came from squadrons of F-80 Shooting Star jets based at Itazuke, Japan. These jets were instrumental in destroying most of the North Korean Air Force in the first few days of the war. Lts. Charles A. Wurster and John B. Thomas of the 36th Squadron downed two North Korean YAK-9s in one day.

During the battles of the Pusan Perimeter the NKPA shifted from fighting a mechanized war to an infantry war. This latter war allowed the enemy to move away from the roads and

American infantry interrogating a Chinese POW, Nov. 1950.

made them limited targets from the air. At the same time this enemy fought mostly at night , because the Allies controlled the air during the day. Even strategic bombers were at times called in by the Air Force to support the tactical air support. One veteran remembers the B-29 saturation bombing along the Pusan Perimeter at Waegwan. The entire river line east of the Naktong River received a carpet of bombs. Brown mist covered an area of about a square mile and rose slowly into the sky. It was a beautiful sight, but this bombing caused only some South Koreans civilians to be killed, while few North Korean soldiers were affected.

Night fighting esculated with the entry of the Chinese. Since the CCF was not mechanized, most of its movements were at night in tree covered country away from major roads. The Chinese became masters of concealment . In late 1950 their movements and concealment were so well performed that the UN Command was completely deceived as to the true size of their forces.

In the UN withdrawal in November-December 1950 when the Chinese masses were exposed in daylight, the Tactical Air Force in conjunction with the Naval and Marine Air Forces, was instrumental in saving Eighth Army and X Corps. In December 1950 the only way the U.S. 2nd Division could move through the pass between Kunu-ri and Sunchon in North Korea was when the Air Force pinned down the Chinese gunners controlling the pass. The effective close air support given by the Marine Corsairs to X Corps at the Chosen Reservoir has become a proud part of our history.

Close air support was outstanding not only defensively but also offensively. Beginning in January 1951 the slow movement north of Eighth Army was highly dependent on air support. Before an infantry assault on the ridges the targets were saturated with artillery fire and air strikes. In this type of operation the Air Force became expert in the use of napalm, frequently burning out the enemy before the infantry even attacked.

127

Marine Corsairs, and early fighter aircraft.

Not to be forgotten was the air support given by other UN forces. Australia provided a fighter squadron initially equipped with piston-engined F-51 Mustangs which were later converted to jet Gloster Meteors. South Africa furnished a squadron of Mustangs and later converted to F-86 Sabre jets. Even South Korea eventually developed fighter squadrons with Mustangs.

In order to break through the UN lines the enemy had to secretly mass large numbers of troops. Almost all the attacks by the NKPA against the Pusan Perimeter were piecemeal. One of the major reasons they had difficulty in massing for an attack was that the Air Force was constantly breaking up their attempts to mass. The Chinese, however, at times were able to mass and overrun UN lines, but at a terrible cost in casualties. Much of their success in massing can be attributed to their foot movements over rugged mountains at night and excellent use of camouflage. In the spring offensive in April 1951 the Chinese suddenly massed in broad daylight and became easy targets for artillery fire and air

strikes. In this instance the Chinese were willing to pay the cost in casualties to win the battle. As the war progressed, however, the CCF found this method of attack so costly that they were forced to go to the peace table in July 1953.

Interdiction

By the middle of July 1950 the small North Korean Air Force of 180 Soviet built planes had been cleared from the skies. In spite of its size compared to the U.S. Air Force, this propeller-driven air force was still far superior to the sixteen light planes of the ROK Air Force. The best of the North Korean planes were Soviet-built YAK fighters which destroyed most of the ROK Air Force in the first few days of the war.

During the first month of the war the North Korean Air Force had some success and was able to shoot down several US planes including one B-29 bomber. They were initially effective against forward elements of the US 24th Division. Once the US Fifth Air Force and Navy Task Force 77 started attacking North Korean airfields, North Korean Air Force attacks diminished. By 20 July the enemy force had been swept from the skies. For most of the remainder of the war the only enemy planes noted by Eighth Army were the nightly "Bedcheck Charlies" that made reconnaissance flights over the UN lines. Until the entry of the Chinese into the war the UN Air Forces maintained total air superiority over all of Korea.

On 1 November 1950 the total dominance of the UN Air Force ended. On that date Soviet - built Mig-15 jet fighters entered the Korean War. Because the Mig-15 had limited range, the Communist Chinese Air Force (CCAF) strategy was to use their air force over North Korea only as a defense against UN fighters and bombers. This CCAF, which grew from 650 aircraft in

November to 1,830 aircraft by June 1952, was never used to support Chinese ground troops.

The real air war started when the Fifth Air Force's B-26 light bombers and the FEAF Bomber Command's B-29 bombers began their deep interdiction bombing along the Yalu River. After 20 November 1950 the Mig-15 jet fighters of the CCAF seriously challenged these bombers from the political sanctuary of air bases in Manchuria. The struggle for air superiority in this area continued until the end of the war.

In the first stages of this conflict the American F-80 Shooting Stars were outclassed by the Mig-15 jets. Because UN aircraft were unable to battle over northwestern Korea on anything approaching equal terms, the FEAF intentionally avoided bombing in this area. As the UN Forces withdrew into South Korea, the fighter protection for the B-29s came out of range of the bomber targets. But by 1951 March, when Eighth Army had moved north again and opened up Suwon, Kimpo and Seoul airfields, the superfortresses again attempted to raid "Mig Alley." On a raid on March 1st 22 F-80s escorted 18 bombers, but unexpected head winds forced the fighters to turn back leaving the superfortresses unprotected. Nine Migs attacked them and badly damaged ten bombers.

Throughout March the US jet situation gradually improved. F-86 jets were slowly supplementing the F-80s at Suwon airfield. The air battles over Mig Alley continued into April, and only at certain times would the Migs attack. On 12 April on a mission to destroy the railroad bridge at Sinuiju, the 4th Wing Sabres flew high cover while the 27th Wing F-84 Thunderjets escorted 48 B-29s. Suddenly 70 Migs dove through the B-29 formations from above and denied the slower Thunderjets any opportunity

to retaliate. Since three superfortresses in this flight were lost, Lt.Gen. George E.Stratemeyer, Far East Air Force Commander, directed that B-29 attacks in this Mig Alley area be discontinued until some method was developed to protect them.

In late 1951 Captain R.O.Barton was on one of the F-86 missions flying cover for B-29s who were again given missions to bomb the Yalu bridges: "We could watch the Migs crank up, taxi out, take off, climb above us, cross the Yalu and shoot down many of our planes, and we couldn't do much of anything except watch the Migs break off, climb to altitude, cross the Yalu and land. The final daylight B-29 raid consisted of about 12 B-29s with P-51s above them, F-80s above them, F-84s above them, F-86s above them and ANZAC Meteors above us. A swarm of Migs came out and flew over all of us. One Mig dove through the entire Fifth Air Force and no one fired a shot. Far East Command decided that this kind of cover was not economically feasible, so the B-29s operated at night after that."

The Sabre jets were superior to the Migs and were able to dominate the skies over Korea. In their nose the Migs were armed with a cannon while the Sabres had only six .5 caliber machine guns. The American pilots were better, however, and could evade the Mig cannon, while getting maximum use out of their machine guns.

Much has been written about the higher quality of American pilots compared to Chinese pilots. Sometimes the Soviets trained their own pilots by testing them against the Americans. Sometimes US pilots would meet experienced pilots flying Migs who might have been mercenaries. Capt. R.O. Barton remembers flying wing on his Deputy Group Commander when the Group Commander hollered for help.

129

A Mig pilot, who Barton says was a German but called himself "Casey Jones," had cornered behind the Group Commander's plane. "Casey would shoot a few pieces off the C.O. and then pull alongside and motion him to bail out. The C.O, would shake his head and slowly continue to the south. We got into the fray and made 4 and 6 G turns until I was ready to roll out and surrender. Fortunately Casey ran low enough on fuel to force him to go home, and we three staggered into Suwon."

The basic rule that American pilots were supposed to follow was to never follow a MiG back across the Yalu into Manchuria. Doug Carter recalls following a MiG who, "flew across the Yalu into Manchuria, and we didn't hesitate to go after him— I moved in behind the MiG. By this time we were in the mountains, and he was twisting down through the valleys and over the hills and going around mountain tops like cops and robbers. I hit him with several good bursts— He lit up like a Christmas tree."

After the MiG burst into flames Carter turned south to cross back over the Yalu. Suddenly he discovered he didn't have any power. As he flew at five hundred feet, Chinese anticraft fire came at him, "like strings of little luminescent golf balls floating up and flattening to the size of baseballs as they went by the airplane." Fortunately, he discovered that in his excitement over the chase he had forgotten to retract his speed brakes, a device on the F-86 to slow down the plane. Once these brakes were retracted, he gained altitude quickly and sped safely south.

In August 1951 the Air Force began Operation Strangle which was an attempt to stop supplies from Manchuria from crossing the Yalu River and reaching CCF troops on the front line in Korea. Day after day roads, bridges, railroads and other communication net works were bombed. In spite of this constant bombing, the Chinese were still able to get over 1000 tons a day across the Yalu. The Chinese learned how to repair roads and rail networks rapidly. In addition they improved their antiaircraft defenses thus keeping UN bombers at high altitudes which affected bombing acuracy. UN bombing strategy was based on war with modern industrialized nations which required a huge consumption of supplies. The Chinese were able to fight a modern war and still consume only one twelfth of the supplies consumed by the American Forces. By the summer of 1952 Operation Strangle was given up.

Other Operations

Command and control of the air war became a major concern. The United States Armed Forces had three services with air arms whose operations had to be coordinated. They in turn had to be coordinated with UN air units. Each service took pride in its own arm and wanted to control its own units. Enemy targets had to be centrally controlled to prevent duplication. The Navy had always maintained control of the air combat connected with sea operations. For the Inchon landing control was theirs. For most of the war, however, the aircraft carriers were airports on the seas, and most missions given to Navy as well as Marine flyers were no different than those given to the Tactical Air Force.

Air reconnaissance became the most valuable means of determining the activities of the NKPA and the CCF. Air photography had been highly developed in World War II and continued to be of extreme importance in the Korean War. Targeting and bomb damage assessment photography were key missions carried out by the FEAF. Because U.S. air reconnaissance was so effective, the enemy developed elaborate means

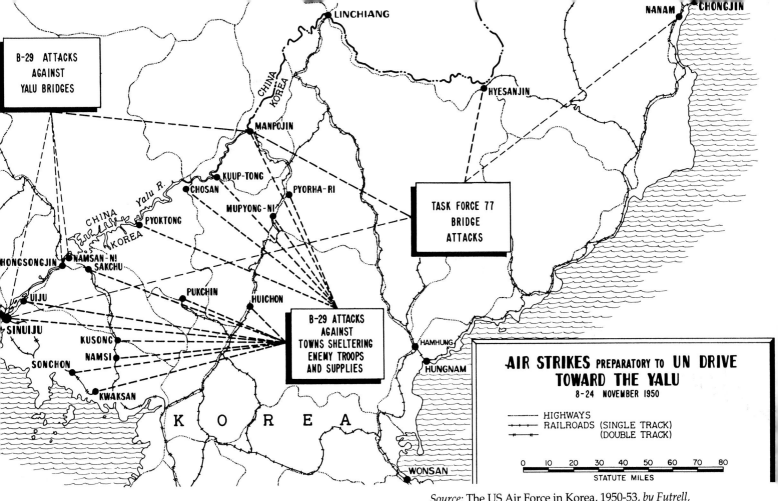

LINCHIANG

NANAM CHONGJIN

B-29 ATTACKS AGAINST YALU BRIDGES

CHINA KOREA

HYESANJIN

MANPOJIN

KUUP-TONG

CHOSAN

PYORHA-RI

MUPYONG-NI

TASK FORCE 77 BRIDGE ATTACKS

CHINA KOREA

PYOKTONG

HONGSONGJIN NAMSAN-NI SAKCHU

PUKCHIN

HUICHON

UIJU

B-29 ATTACKS AGAINST TOWNS SHELTERING ENEMY TROOPS AND SUPPLIES

SINUIJU

KUSONG

NAMSI

HAMHUNG

SONCHON

HUNGNAM

KWAKSAN

-AIR STRIKES PREPARATORY TO UN DRIVE TOWARD THE YALU
8-24 NOVEMBER 1950

K O R E A

HIGHWAYS
RAILROADS (SINGLE TRACK)
(DOUBLE TRACK)

0 10 20 30 40 50 60 70 80
STATUTE MILES

WONSAN

Yalu R.

Source: The US Air Force in Korea, 1950-53, *by Futrell, Robert, Office of the Chief of the Air Force.*

of camouflaging their activities. From the beginning the North Koreans used tree branches and other natural objects extensively to conceal their movements. In fact most of the early propaganda pictures from North Korea showed NKPA soldiers covered with camouflage materials.Along most highways both the NKPA and the CCF used hundreds of camouflaged ground enclosures where vehicles could be hidden from Air Force reconnaissance planes. Too often the Air Force reconnaissance had difficulty detecting communist movements in very high mountains where roads were few and trees plentiful, and where most movements were made at night.

A key arm of the Air Force was its 315th Air Division (Combat Cargo) under the direction of Major General William H. Tunner who had won international acclaim for his success in the CBI "hump" operation in World War II and later the Berlin Airlift. This unit moved 391,773 tons of air freight and evacuated 307,804 medical patients. It won distinction at Sukchon-Sunchon where it

dropped the 187 Airborne RCT. The unit also distinguished itself by helping X Corps in the battle at Chosen Reservoir.

Another mission of the air arm was search and rescue (SAR) whose duty was to rescue downed pilots on land and sea. Three services , the Air Force, Navy, and Marine Corps conducted these operations. Although most flyers whose planes went down were lost, these operations did rescue 170 Americans and 84 other UN airmen. This unit also assisted in evacuating critically wounded soldiers from front-line aid stations. Their work in this mission has been clearly illustrated in the famous T.V. series "Mash."

Many of these evacuation missions took place during critical battles. On 22 and 23 October 1950 five helicopters evacuated 47 injured paratroopers from the 187 Airborne RCT drop zones at Sunchon-Sukchon. When the 23rd Regiment of the US 2nd Division was cut off at Chipyong-ni

On some missions, especially over "Mig Alley,"
the enemy resisted.

in January, 1951, six H-5 helicopters delivered blankets, plasma and other medical supplies. Later these helicopters evacuated 30 wounded soldiers and the next day evacuated 22 more in a blinding snowstorm.

On 11 June 1951 Captain Kenneth Stewart bailed out of his damaged Mustang in the Taedong River in North Korea. His rescue is an example of the valiant missions of the SAR. Flights of Mustangs covered him and prevented North Korean soldiers from reaching him. Then Lt. John J. Najarian, piloting a SA-16 helicopter, landed in shallow water and successfully picked up Capt. Stewart. He was able to avoid low hanging high-tension wires because of the landing lights switched on by the covering Mustangs. It was a classic rescue.

The use of the three air arms was critical in

the war. In the early days the use of close air support was essential to the survival of the UN forces. Once air superiority had been established, the UN ground forces moved ahead. Much of the UN force's superiority in fire power which developed during the war can be attributed to the outstanding close support given by the air arms. Although the air forces through interdiction were only able to slow the flow of supplies to the communist forces in Korea, their close air support had such an impact that their operations played an important role in bringing the enemy to the peace table at Panmunjon in July 1953.

Chapter 16: The Naval War

When the decision was made to defend South Korea, a race was on in which the U.S. Armed Forces had to manipulate the variables of space, time and movement in order to check

Air fields were established to support infantry troops, 1950.

the invader and turn defeat into victory. Without the dedicated effort and efficiency of the United States Navy, especially from June through September 1950, the Korean War would have come to a sudden halt. The Navy's major role was getting the troops to Korea and keeping them supplied for three years. Six out of every seven UN personnel went to Korea by sea.

As the war progressed, other roles fell to the Navy. Naval Forces Far East (NAVFE) became the Naval component for the Far East Command (FECOM) and took over the the naval combat mission in Korea.

The first mission was the assault mission of the carrier strike force of Seventh Fleet called Task Force 77. Another combat mission was a blockading and escort force called Task Force 95. The final combat mission was to conduct an amphibious assault or an evacuation for which Task Force 90, the Amphibious Force Far East, was organized.

Air War

Naval support of the air war began early. Both the U.S. and British Navies supported the Fifth Air Force in the quick destruction of the North Korean Air Force. These Air Force strikes were supplemented by carrier strikes flown from the USS *Valley Forge* and the HMS *Triumph*. As time went on Great Britain committed other naval forces to supplement the Americans. The aircraft carriers HMS *Glory*, HMS *Ocean* and HMS *Thesus*, as well as the HMS *Triumph*, sent Seafire, Sea Fury, and Firefly piston-engined naval aircraft into combat.

By August 1950 the battle of the Pusan Perimeter was under way. The USS *Valley Forge* and USS *Philippine Sea* mounted close air support and interdiction missions from the offshore carriers of Task Force 77. In 1952 when the B-29 night bombers found that the communist night defenses had improved, they were escorted not only by USAF F-94 Starfires but also by Marine F3D Skyknights. When the communists used biplanes at low levels at night, radar equipped American night fighters had difficulty finding them. To combat this, piston-engined F4U Corsairs and F7F Tigercat Marine night fighters were called upon and helped to mitigate the problem.

Jim Service was a pilot flying from the USS *Valley Forge* in 1952. "Basically for pilots it was eat, sleep and fly. On a typical day the first flight would be up at three o'clock in the morning. You'd go to your briefing, get some breakfast, then man your airplane. At around five thirty you'd get launched."

He remembers the ground fire. He saw little white clouds and then big black ones. Each was an explosion. "Any single one could knock your airplane down, but you were simply too busy flying the aircraft to worry about getting hit," he said.

Bad landings on a carrier were a real threat. All pilots wanted to avoid overshooting and ending up in the ocean. According to Service, "That was a greater fear than being shot down. Going into the drink. We lost a couple of pilots that way. Neither one was in the water long, but they both froze to death before we could get them back aboard the ship."

Service's example of naval heroics is but one of many. The contributions of the Navy and Marine Strike Force throughout the war were a major supplement to that of the U.S. Air Force.

The Sea War - Blockade

The UN Navies controlled Korean waters completely around the Korean peninsula to the borders with China and the USSR. The only entrance into Korea by the communists was across the Yalu River. The Navy had the mission of blockading the entire peninsula and bombarding enemy instalations along the Korean coast.

At the beginning of the war a blockade had been established south of Chonjin on the east coast and south of the mouth of the Yalu River on the west coast. The main supply route from the USSR to Wonsan ran along the east coast. For most of the war this route was bombarded by some of America's largest warships: the battleships *Missouri*, *Iowa*, *New Jersey* and *Wisconsin*. The 16 inch guns could reach inland for 20 miles and played a major role in the interdiction strategy against the communists.

One aspect of the sea war was the denial of certain ports to the communists. Wonsan, a major port, was blockaded by the occupation of seven islands on the edge of the port by ROK Marines and U.S. Naval fire direction teams. These islands were excellent locations from which to direct the fires of offshore U.S. warships. One island, Hwangtu-do, was only 3000 yards from the shore and offered perfect observation of Wonsan and the main enemy supply route, as well railroad and highway bridges.The island was protected by nearby American destroyers, while communist mines between the island and Wonsan restricted the enemy's own movement.

From late July through September both ends of the Pusan Perimeter rested on water. At each of these locations the Army fire control parties were tied into the Navy communication network

Navy anti-aircraft gun crew.

and could select targets for the offshore cruisers and destroyers. On 27 July at Yongdok the 8-inch guns of the cruiser Toledo fired on troop concentrations of the invading NKPA. At night they fired star shells to illuminate the battlefield.

Veterans of the left most company on the Pusan Perimeter were from the US 25th Division and remember clearly their contacts with the Navy.Offshore to the company's left a destroyer rested for most of the month of August 1950. There was, however, no direct contact between the company and the destroyer. Only at regimental level was contact kept with the destroyer. This lack of communication eventually led to a major calamity. One day the destroyer spotted what they thought were North Korean soldiers on a distant hill and opened fire with their 5-inch guns. Unfortunately they fired on an American patrol and killed several men. Regrettably this was the type of problem with ensuing casualties has occurred from friendly fires in all wars.

Another major function of the Navy in any blockade or amphibious operation is mine sweeping. The Korean peninsula was ideally suited for the defensive use of mines by the enemy. In 1950 North Korean harbors provided the Soviet Navy an ideal way to test American methods of minesweeping. Knowing that the U.S. Naval Forces would control the seas and

135

could make amphibious landings at almost any point, the communists made full use of mines by planting minefields off every suitable beach. They also developed offshore moored minefields to make American coastal bombardment hazardous.

As early as July 1950 Soviet mines were coming southward from Vladivostok. Soviet naval personnel at Wonsan and Chinnampo were teaching North Koreans how to use mines. By 1 August Russian naval officers with shipments of mines had reached Inchon. Fortunately, when the American amphibious landing was made at Inchon, the harbor was only partially mined. The landing was made there at flood tide, and waiting mines were sighted and disposed of. The main attack then followed two cleared channels into Inchon harbor.

After September 1950 North Korea began an intense program of laying mines on both coast lines. This became a threat to ships engaged in fire-support missions. These ships had to operate either in mineswept channels or remain outside 100 fathom depth. On 26 September 1950 the destroyer Brush was the first casualty as it struck a mine off Korea's northeast coast. Thirteen men were killed and thirty-four seriously wounded. On 30 September the destroyer Mansfield hit a mine 60 miles north of the 38th Parallel and suffered twenty-eight casualties. On 1 October the minesweeper Magpie, 30 miles north of Pohang, nudged a floating mine and lost twenty-one of her thirty-three man crew. Minesweeping was one of the most hazardous of the Navy's missions.

By 1951 minesweeping began to change. The Naval crews became more experienced and haste in clearing the mine fields was not as urgent as in 1950 when Eighth Army and X Corps were invading North Korea. All during the blockade of Wonsan enemy mines were constantly being swept. A young Machinists Mate, Vincent Walsh, remembers his duty in November 1951 with a destroyer that protected minesweepers in Wonsan harbor: "One morning while we were up there dawn broke and here's this guy in a sampan out in the middle of the channel, putting down a mine. The North Koreans would go out in these little sampans at night, drop a couple of mines, and try to get back before it got light. But dawn broke and the ship caught this guy still out there."

The North Korean in the sampan didn't have a chance as the American sailors fired their main batteries at him. To the sailors on blockade and minesweeping duty there were few rewards and much anxiety.

Other Activities

The two major activities of the Navy during the Korean War which history books never stop praising were amphibious landings and evacuation of servicemen and refugees. The amphibious landing at Inchon in September 1950 and the quick defeat of the NKPA was one of the greatest feats by Americans in any modern war. Likewise the evacuation of X Corps and 90,000 North Korean refugees from Hungnam in December 1950 was another great naval operation. Both of these actions have been covered in detail previously in this book.

The Korean War showed the value of sea power. The need for a strong balanced Navy to maintain control of the seas was made clear. In the words of General Van Fleet: "We could not have existed without the Navy. The sea blockade was so complete that it was taken for granted. - Freedom from enemy air and naval attack left us free to operate in the open."

Without seapower UN soldiers and airmen and their equipment could never have gotten to the scene of conflict and have been kept supplied during the whole war.

Chapter 17: Allies

As the war progressed, UN allies took over more and more responsibility for the conduct of the war. The largest contribution came from the Republic of Korea which in June 1950 had a ground force of approximately 98,000 men. At wars' end it had grown to 590,911 men. Other countries contributed to the overall UN Armed Forces At the end of the war these forces numbered 39,145 men.

KMAG and the Growth of the ROK Armed Forces

After World War II the ROK military force had grown slowly and did not become the Republic of Korea Army until December 15th, 1948. The Republic of Korea Army gradually developed into eight poorly trained and equipped divisions. By June 1950 the ROK Armed Forces had reached a total of approximately 151,000 men of whom 98,000 were in the Army. Next in size to the Army were the 48,000 members of the National Police. There were 6100 men in the Coast Guard and 1800 in the Air Force.

At the end of 1945 Korea had been divided by a "de facto" frontier with Soviet advisors north of it and American advisors south of it. In the south, beginning in January 1946, a Bureau of Constabulary and a Bureau of Coast Guard were established. Provisional American advisors organized eight Korean Constabulary Regiments to support the National Police if internal condi-

Greek soldiers return from patrol, Winter 1951.

Lt. Winson, KMAG, Naktong River, August 1950.

tions got out of control. By March 1948 this Constabulary had grown to 50,000 men, and six months later it became the nucleus of South Korea's Army. In 1946 South Korea needed a coastal security force since smuggling and piracy were increasing. In the fall of that year eighteen new vessels arrived from Japan and with them fifteen American Coast Guard officers and enlisted advisors to organize a the new force. This marked the beginning of American influence on Korea's fledgling Coast Guard.

In June 1949 the occupation forces in both Koreas withdrew as both sides of the 38th Parallel became independent countries. Both sides retained their foreign military advisors. In the summer of 1949 in South Korea the Korean Military Advisory Group (KMAG) of American military advisors was established to train the military forces in the Republic of Korea. The new republic watched suspiciously as its communist rival in the north, with the help of Soviet advisors, rapidly built up its military forces.

The armed forces of the two Koreas were quite different. The ROKs were limited in heavy weapons to only light artillery, and they possessed no combat airplanes or tanks. The North Koreans brought back to Korea thousands of Korean veterans who had fought with the Chinese Communists. In addition the Soviet Union gave full

assistance to North Korea by training thousands of skilled pilots, mechanics, and tank drivers in its schools in the Soviet Union. At the same time arms shipments of tanks, heavy artillery and new combat airplanes flowed into North Korea from the Soviet Union. This was in stark contrast to the United States which at that time was giving only half-hearted support to the Army of the Republic of South Korea. The United States gave serious help only to the ROK Coast Guard. By June 1950 this service had grown to a force of 105 vessels.

Once the war began the American attitude toward training the ROKs changed. The United States gave full support to the "Koreanization" of the ROK military. In this mission the American KMAG played a very important part.

The development of the ROK Armed Forces varied by units and by time. Because the ROKs were poorly trained and equipped, resistance to the NKPA during the first weeks of the war was poor. By the 1st of July 1950 , of the initial ROK Force of 98,000 men, 44,000 had been killed, captured, or were missing.

Most surviving ROK units were disorganized and lacked equipment. Only the ROK 6th and 8th Divisions were able to withdraw into the Pusan Perimeter with their weapons and other equipment. During this period when the front finally stabilized, KMAG began a program to reconstitute these ROK forces. From the roughly 50,000 ROK survivors KMAG estimated there were enough men to reconstitute about three or four lightly supported divisions. The major weakness of this new force was its supply system which at this time was non-existent.

On 13 July 1950 KMAG was taken over by Eighth Army. At this time it consisted of 470 men. By August 1950 General Walker proposed creating a ROK Army of ten divisions. A year later KMAG had tripled in strength to 1308 men. By war's end in July 1953 the ROK Army had grown to sixteen divisions in addition to smaller supporting units totaling 570,911 men.

American veterans have tended to look down on the ROK Army because all they can remember was that ROK units were untrustworthy and quick to fold. Yet a close study shows that many ROK soldiers stood out in individual bravery and performed heroic acts. They suffered from poor leadership, limited training, and limited modern equipment. The better trained NKPA and CCF knew this and intentionally concentrated on fighting the ROK units whom they hoped to defeat easily.

A soldier, Blaine Friedlander, was assigned to KMAG and sent as a radio operator to the 11th ROK Division. There were forty American soldiers with the division at this time. Twenty were at troop level and twenty at Division Headquarters. Friedlander considered KMAG a very dangerous assignment. He remembers that other American soldiers used to say that, "KMAG really meant Kiss My Ass Goodby."

Friedlander felt that the South Koreans were excellent fighters once they had proper training and good leaders. They, like most Asians, had a very harsh disciplinary system that was quite different from that of the United States Army. He rembers that: "One soldier who was caught with a dirty rifle was made to stand all day in a barrel of water, in the dead of winter. Another who went AWOL (absent without leave) to see his family was caught and brought back in irons. He was ordered to dig a hole, with his entire battalion watching, and when he had finsihed he was ordered to kneel in front of it.The battalion commander walked up

behind him, shot him in the back of the head with a .45 and kicked him into the grave."

Friedlander developed great respect for the South Koreans: "They were not a bunch of faceless gooks, but people who cared very deeply about their country, who knew its history, and who also knew a surprising amount about our country, much more than the average American knew about Korea. They may have been brutalized, but they were not an army of dumb peasants. They were individuals."

As the ROK Army grew during the war, so did the ROK Air Force and Navy. By the end of the war the ROK Air Force had several squadrons of Mustangs that were integrated into the UN Air Force. When the war started the U.S.Navy took over the U.S.Coast Guard mission of training and operational control of the ROK Navy of 7000 men. The ROK Navy grew rapidly and received a number of vessels such as frigates, LSTs and minesweepers. By the end of the war it had become a major partner with the U.S.Navy in blockade operations.

By 1953 when the war ended, South Korea had developed a trained, equipped, dependable armed force with sixteen divisions in the field and four more in the planning stages. At this time much of the responsibility for defending the front of Eighth Army had been taken over by South Korea.

Other UN Forces

Although the United States offered the most assistance to the Republic of South Korea during the Korean War, forty-two other members of the UN furnished some form of assistance. Fifteen provided troop support and five provided medical units. Besides the United States and

Members of the Turkish Brigade interrogating a North Korean prisoner, winter 1951.

South Korea, the United Kingdom furnished the most troops followed by Canada and Turkey.

The greatest number of UN casualties was among the ground forces and therefore replacements for them was always a constant need. The largest contributions, about 5,000 men each, were infantry brigades furnished by Canada, Turkey and the United Kingdom. The next level were battalions of about 1000 men provided by Australia (2), Belgium, Columbia, Ethiopia, France, Greece, The Netherlands, the Philippines and Thailand. Ground support was provided by Canada, New Zealand and the United Kingdom. Together these UN units suffered a total of 17,260 casualties.

UN members provided over 30,000 naval and 1100 air force personnel. Air squadrons came from Australia, Canada, Greece, South Africa, Thailand and the United Kingdom. A total of twenty-two naval vessels were provided by Australia, Canada, Columbia, France, the Netherlands, New Zealand, Thailand and the

United Kingdom. Over 2168 medical personnel came from Denmark, India, Italy, Norway and Sweden. Overall these other UN forces supplied roughly 4 percent of the total UN force or 11 percent of the UN forces not counting South Korea.

These units performed heroic acts. History records the difficult struggle of the Turkish Brigade to help save the US 2nd Division at Kunu-ri in November 1950, and the last ditch stand of the Gloucester Battalion on Gloucester Hill near the Imjin River in April 1951. The French Battalion with the US 2nd Division at Chipyong-ni and Heartbreak Ridge in 1951 exemplified the best of any infantry combat unit. Another unit that stands out was the Greek battalion attached to the 7th Cavalry. At one time this unit was cut off and surrounded. When told to withdraw, the commander of the Battalion said, "We never withdraw. Normally we fire on a 180 degree front. When surrounded we can fire in all 360 degrees." Last but not least one should not forget the early days of the war and the struggles on the Pusan Perimeter of the newly arrived British 27th Brigade. Lt. Carl Schmidt from the 77th Field Artillery remembers discussing fire support with Brigadier Coad, the brigade commander, while in full view of the NKPA across the Naktong River. When Schmidt asked Coad where his unit was, Coad replied that they could hear them. Down the road in full view of the enemy and marching four abreast to the tune of bagpipes and drums came the Argyle and Sutherland Highlanders. When told that they would be exposed to the enemy, Coad replied, "I want the enemy to know that the British have arrived." The deeds of these units far exceed the number who participated.

The comradery of Americans with these units was outstanding. They all preferred American food and loved to tease American soldiers of being overpaid. A favorite pastime of US soldiers was to visit British units. American soldiers were always offered a drink of "grog," not an item of issue to the American soldier.

The largest contributor to the UN force next to South Korea and the United States was the British Commonwealth. In the summer of 1951 a Commonwealth Division was formed from units of the United Kingdom, Australia, Canada and New Zealand. It quickly distinguished itself under fire. The division consisted of two infantry brigades, an armored regiment and supporting artillery and engineers.

British soldiers are noted for their toughness when on defense. Trooper Victor Poole, a member of the 1st Royal Tank Regiment, remembers clearly how his unit defended a place called

Men of the 19th Inf. Regt., 24th Inf. Division with machine gun.

The Hook in May 1953. "The last battle of the Hook reached its climax on the night of the twenty-eighth of May. On that night all bloody hell broke loose. The Black Watch, a very famous British regiment, had already fought a terrific battle for the Hook back in November. They were relieved by the Duke of Wellingtons, and the Dukes ended up taking a horrible beating."

After much fighting, the infantry of the Dukes was overrun and a number of the men in the unit had been buried in deep trenches by the volume of artillery fire. He remembers that on the next day: "Our boys were still digging them out, many still alive, still holding tightly to their grenades and Bren guns because all night long there had been vicious close-quarter fighting going on in those tunnels and trenches. How could men take what they took? To stay in those trenches all night long, getting shot at and getting buried alive, and still fighting back. They were well led with officers and NCOs who had tremendous regimental pride. - I'm convinced they would have died to a man for that hill."

The attitude of trooper Victor Poole personifies the professional attitude of these other UN forces. The quality of these men was outstanding. The contributions to the war by these servicemen of the UN nations should not be forgotten.

Chapter 18: The Last Years

The struggles during the fall of 1951 had gained few military objectives and had inflicted tremendous casualties on both sides. Suddenly, on 7 November, the Communist Delegation proposed that the demarcation line become the line of contact between the opposing sides.

The Demarcation Line, July 27, 1953.

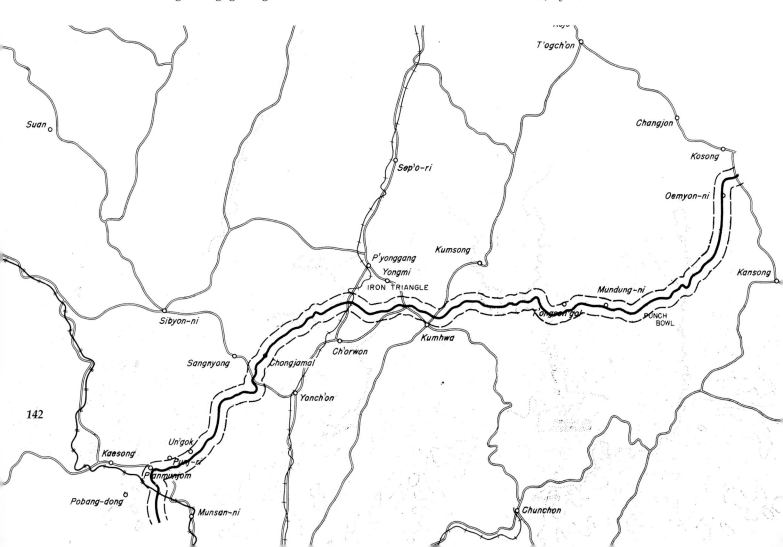

Ridgway at first refused and countered with his own proposal that said that the line of contact should be established after an armistice. Fearing that Ridgways' conccept of inspections might anger the communists and cause them to break off the talks, the Joint Chiefs in Washington turned down his proposal. Instead they proposed a "greater sanction" threat that were the Chinese to build up attacking forces in Korea after the demarcation line was established, America would widen the war in the Far East. Thus pressure from Washington forced Ridgway to concede to the existing line of contact as the demarcation line.

On some other issues each side compromised. On the subject of airfield rehabilitation the two sides could come to no agreement. The UN wanted to have airfields in South Korea but were opposed to allowing the North Koreans and Chinese to have their own airfields in North Korea. When a conclusion could not be reached, the issue was tabled for future discussions.

The issue that created the most conflict was the repatriation of POWs. Many historians feel that this issue extended the war for another year and a half. The issue concerned the right of North Korean and Chinese POWs to choose not to go back to communist rule. In December 1951 President Truman was behind the POW exchange plan of voluntary repatriation. On 2 January 1952 the UN proposal on POWs was resubmitted to the communists, but it still stressed voluntary repatriation. This proposal was bitterly rejected by the communists. The issue became a complicated moral issue, because Americans would die during the next year and a half over the right to freedom of choice for former enemy soldiers.

Stalemate - Trench Warfare 1952-1953

By the spring of 1952 the two sides were fairly evenly matched. The communists had 290,800 men on the front line and 617,300 in reserve in North Korea. Opposed to them on line were 247,554 men of a total UN Force of 700,000 soldiers. To strengthen South Korea the Eighth Army emphasized increasing the number of ROK units and overseeing their training. At this time UN Forces consisted of six US Army divisions, the 1st Marine Division, the Commonwealth Division and nine ROK Divisions. In December 1951 the US 45th Division, Oklahoma National Guard, had replaced the 1st Cavalry Division, and in January 1952 the US 40th Division, California National Guard, had replaced the US 24th Division. Both the 1st Cavalry and 24th Divisions returned to Japan.

For the next year and a half the fighting consisted of costly struggles for small pieces of terrain. Usually the UN forces fought to defend. Sometimes they were forced to counterattack. Well known are the battles of the Iron Triangle, Porkchop Hill and Old Baldy. Less well known are Bunker Hill, the Hook, and White Horse Mountain. Marine histories stress the battles over hills called Reno, Vegas and Carson. Little known are some of the most vicious fights, those over T-Bone Hill, Pike's Peak, Little Gibraltar, Outpost Harry, Outpost Kelly and Triangle Hill. To the men who struggled to survive during that year and a half, these names mean a great deal.

Some of the mountains along the demarcation line had been fought over since August 1951. One that was constantly fought over was Old Baldy, sixty miles north of Seoul. In the late fall of 1951 the 5th Cavalry Regiment had been responsible for its defense. Tom Clawson remembered what it was like at one time to live in a dugout on the hill. One thing that stuck in his mind was that the Army never gave up on morning police. Even on the front lines, as in basic training, men had to line up, bend over and police up just about everything from garbage to shell casings. In fact there is an old Army proverb that says, "Pick up everything you can. If it is too heavy, paint it. If it moves, salute it."

Life on Old Baldy for Clawson was lonely and boring. His daily high point was getting mail from home and a hot meal. The biggest nusiance was the rats in all the bunkers. One fell into his foxhole and wouldn't stop squeaking. He stopped the squeaking by dropping a grenade into his foxhole, but this annoyed his peers who thought the Chinese were coming.

The 1st Cavalry Division was replaced in the Old Baldy area by the US 45th Division. One order from division to the front line units was to capture some prisoners. These actions were unsuccessful as the enemy gave stiff resistance. By 21 July 1952 the 45th Division had suffered 39 killed, 234 wounded and 84 missing while causing only 1093 casualties on the Chinese. The high American losses from the raids convinced the higher commanders that the raids were not worthwhile.

Bunker Hill, a heavily fortified hill four miles east of Panmunjom, was fought over many times in the spring and summer of 1952. The superiority of American artillery and air power had forced the Chinese opposing Bunker Hill to build very elaborate positions with earth cover as high as 33 feet. Using the Chinese example American soldiers improved on their own fortifications, and by the summer of 1952 they had developed a prefabricated timber structure whose roof consisted of heavy timbers, sandbags, and earth.

The battles of the Marines for Bunker Hill and the outposts named for the Nevada cities of Vegas, Carson and Reno lasted all through the

summer of 1952 and into the spring of 1953. Chinese artillery had improved since 1951 and made life hell for the Marines. In addition to casualties from the intense CCF artillery, Chinese box mines were lethal against Marine night patrols. The Chinese used mines as a form of psychological warfare. One trick they had devised in 1951 was to place a number of mines on top of each other in one spot so that anyone steping on them would be blown to bits and totally vanish.

The one thing most combat veterans will always remember is the time when they were wounded. Cpl. James Prewitt of the 5th Marines was on Outpost Reno when an enemy grenade exploded six inches from his chest. His right forearm and elbow were badly damaged but his flak vest saved his life. He was carried by stretcher back to an evacuation point. Here he was moved by helicopter to another point behind the lines where a truck picked him up. He remembers, "That the driver did his best to miss the bumps, but considering the condition of the roads, it really wasn't possible. I got to ride in the truck cab, and that, combined with the effect of the painkiller, made the trip to Charlie Medical Company at least bearable." He was then evacuated to the Hospital ship USS *Repose* and then to the naval hospital in Yokosuka, Japan. Eventually he was transferred to the Great Lakes Naval Training Center for final recovery.

As the war progressed medical evacuation improved. One development in the Korean War that has become a symbol of the war to most Americans was the Army Surgical Hospital (MASH) which was made famous by television. These hospitals saved countless lives by their timely medical care. They were usually located near front-line infantry divisions where they could treat patients whose wounds needed immediate surigical care. Lt. Earl Owens of the

180th Infantry had a bad arm wound and remembers vividly being dropped off by truck at a MASH unit. He was put to sleep almost immediately and operated upon. Eventually he was sent to hospitals in the rear.

Later Battles

From the fall of 1952 until February 1953 the US 9th Infantry of the US 2nd Division occupied Hill 549 which was east of Old Baldy and looked down on Pork Chop Hill which was not occupied. Every night patrols would move out into no-man's-land. Capt. Eugene Forester, who led many of these patrols, explains the feelings of the men: "If you are in a full darkness mode, everyone moves slowly. You use your arms and feel where you are. You sense with your eyes and your nose, and have a tendency to think more clearly about what can happen to you. Now this in turn generates some uncertainty, and the uncertainty causes fear and from fear you find a reluctance to move and you find a reluctance to move rapidly."

He goes on to say that people got the impression that Americans abandoned the night to the Chinese and North Koreans.But in reality, after the first months in Korea, Americans built up their confidence and learned to cope with the night.

One of the more difficult missions in the 9th Infantry in November 1952 was given to Lt. Bill Miller, a recent ROTC graduate from Johns Hopkins University. Miller was to lead a platoon patrol over to a Chinese outpost bunker and take a prisoner. In bitter cold weather he crossed no-man's-land and assaulted a CCF bunker. However, the patrol was unable to take a prisoner. Miller would have returned to American lines, but his battalion commander radioed him to try again. On his second try the air was filled with grenades from both sides. In the process an enemy concussion grenade landed near him and knocked him unconscious. The patrol withdrew to American lines. Miller was carried back by one of the KATUSAs in his platoon. In spite of the violent response of the enemy, the patrol lost only one man.

The last big outpost battle in Korea was Pork Chop Hill in 1953. On April 16th the CCF assaulted Pork Chop which was defended by the 31st Infantry, US 7th Division. After getting a foothold, the Chinese were driven off by a counterattack of the 17th Infantry of the same division. Much credit for saving the hill should go to the artillery fire of nine battalions over a two day period. On 6 July the CCF again attacked and gained a foothold on part of the crest. At this time Eighth Army Commander, Lt. Gen Maxwell D. Taylor, made a decision to withdraw the US 7th Division units from Pork Chop because casualties suffered were not worth the tactical value of the hill.

Charles Brooks was in both the April and July fight for Pork Chop. In April he was part of the counterattack, while in July he was in a bunker that was overrun. For two days he remained in the bunker as he saw Chinese all over his hill. In his words: "What we tried to do was keep them away from the apertures so they couldn't throw grenades in on us, but they got a few in, and one guy had his feet blown off. - He sat on an old ammo box and just kept staring at his feet - I think if he'd of moved his legs, the feet would've fallen off."

At dawn two days later Brooks and most of the others in the bunker worked their way out and down the reverse slope of Pork Chop back to friendly lines. This was to be the last major conflict of the war. Only a short time later on 27 July an armistice was finally signed.

Koje-do

American policy which dealt with POWs changed during the war. Initial NKPA POWs were few and easily handled by the military police. After the Inchon landing in September 1950 and the rapid defeat of the NKPA, the number of enemy POWs began to escalate. By November 1950 the UNC had taken 130,000 prisoners. The sudden increase of prisoners was a problem as Eighth Army was not prepared to handle such numbers. In January 1951 the prisoners near Pusan were transported to Koje-do Island off the southern coast not far from Pusan. By January 31st over 50,000 POWs had been sent to the island. The rapid absorbtion of these POWs swamped the prison camp and UN control broke down.

When the peace talks began at Kaesong in June 1951 and the status of POWs was being discussed, the communist prisoners realized that their future was at stake. The issue of prisoner choice in repatriation was to be debated for the next two years. At this critical time North Korea infiltrated agents into the prison camps by positioning them to be captured. These agents kept in close touch with the progress of the armistice talks and used propaganda and intimidation to gain control of the compounds.

Stanley Weintraub was assigned to process the prisoners: "Processing the prisoners turned out to be one of our most naive episodes, because our knowledge of foreign languages was so lousy in this country. We were unprepared, totally, for being in Japan and then for being in Korea, and then for having the Chinese come in. We were incompetent in all three languages. So we needed to use POWs as our interpreters. We picked people who appeared smart, and who had some knowledge of English. But many of them were the most militant of the communists among the prisoners. Many of them were trained agents. North Korea was allowing trained agents to be captured as POWs. These people were under orders to organize the hardline communist prisoners and cause any kind of disturbance, with the aim of provoking a violent reaction from our side which could then be used for propaganda purposes. We found this out too late. We didn't realize that they were duping us, until the mutinies, when these people we had chosen to help us became the leaders of the various prison-camp insurrections."

The first major POW uprising began in February 1952 when the issue of voluntary repatriation was being hotly debated at Panmunjom. Over 1000 POWs attacked US soldiers with knives, spears and rocks. The Americans retaliated by killing 77 and wounding 140 POWs. One American was killed and 38 wounded.

According to Private Alan Maggio, a medical orderly in the camp, the POW camp at Koje-do was not managed well. No serious attempt was made by officers to impose leadership or discipline. He noted that, "The enlisted men ran the system. There were no officers who bothered to walk around or check what was going on. Anybody who couldn't make it on line was sent down to duty at Koje-do."

The high point of the conflict at Koje-do came on May 7th. Brigadier General Francis T.Dodd, the Camp Commandant, went to the gate of a compound to speak to NKPA POWs concerning grievances. He was seized, carried into the compound, and then used as a hostage to barter with the American camp command. On 9 May Brigadier Charles F.Colson, the newly assigned Commandant of the Camp, demanded Dodd's release. The prisoners refused to release him, and instead established a People's Court with Dodd on trial. According to historian Walter G. Hermes, "The spectacle of prisoners trying the kidnapped commanding officer of the prison camp on criminal counts and making him defend his record was without parallel in modern military history."

During the night of May 9th, tanks from the US 3rd Division arrived to support Colson's plan to assault the compound the next morning. When morning arrived , the POWs submitted a powerful propaganda document to Colson asking all kinds of impossible demands. The prisoners continued to argue with Colson who delayed action , while Dodd phoned him and presented the POWs side of the conflict. Then Colson replied in a document to the prisoner demands and gave them most of what they wanted in return for Dodd's release. In Hermes words, "Colson traded Dodd's life for a propaganda weapon."

As a result of this Dodd-Colson action, General Mark Clark, Commander of FECOM, was so angry that he ordered Brigadier Hayden L Boatner, Assistant Commander US 2nd Division, to bring the camp under control. Reinforced with combat experienced troops of the 187th Airborne RCT, and the 38th Infantry Regiment reinforced with tanks, the new Commandant took control of the POW compounds by force. On 10 June when prisoners in Compound 76 resisted Boatner's demands to be prepared to move out, crack paratroops using concussion grenades, tear gas and bayonets attacked and with only 15 American casualties, killed 31 and wounded 139 communists.

When other compounds witnessed this conflict, they quickly acquiesced. The communist POWs finally understood that Americans would use force to eliminate defiance.

Armistice

In 1953 world politics began to change. General Dwight Eisenhower replaced Harry Truman as President of the United States, promising to try to bring the Korean War to an end. In the Soviet Union Stalin died and political instability over his replacement encouraged a quick settlement of the war. Communist China was suffering from the cost of the three years of war. Now perhaps some agreement could be reached.

On March 28th the leaders of Communist China and North Korea accepted a prior proposal by the Red Cross for an exchange of sick and wounded prisoners. They also pushed for a settlement of the POW issue and a cease-fire. On 11 April the liason officers at Panmunjom reached an agreement on the exchange of sick and wounded POWs. Between April 20th and May 3rd in Operation Little Switch over 700 Chinese and 5100 North Koreans were exchanged for 450 South Koreans and 150 Allies.

Eisenhower was willing to compromise to end the war, but he confronted one major obstacle. This was President Rhee of South Korea who knew that Eisenhower was willing to accept a cease-fire based on the permanent division of Korea with a communist government still ruling in North Korea. Ree threatened to continue the war if the Chinese remained in North Korea. To the very end Rhee contested the decision of the UN for appeasement of the communists.

On 8 June terms for the reparation of prisoners were agreed upon. Under this agreement those who wished to go home would be exchanged immediately. Those who did not wish to return to North Korea or China such as ex-Nationalist Chinese and South Koreans who had been impressed by the NKPA, would be placed

147

under control of the Repatriation Commission for ninety days. During this time the governments of these POWs would have a chance to review each case.

On the night of 18 June 25,000 North Koreans who were unwilling to return home were suddenly released from their compounds by ROK guards and told to disappear into the country side. This order came directly from President Rhee. While the ROKs continued to help the escapees, American soldiers rushed to the compounds to try to enforce the terms of the POW agreement. By June 22nd only 9000 North Koreans remained in captivity.

Fear that the communists might break off the negotions spread to Washington. The South Korean action of President Rhee was publicy deplored by the UN. Days later the Chinese and North Korean Communists deplored the action but showed a willingness to understand the situation. Now the only obstacle to signing an armistice agreement was the approval of Syngman Rhee. To convince Rhee that the ROKs were not invincible, 100,000 communist soldiers struck five ROK Divisions and drove them back five miles. Fighting continued into July with both the UN and Communist Forces trying to prove they were invincible. Finally on 9 July Rhee agreed to accept the armistice but refused to sign it. He would, however, not obstruct the armistice. Thus on 27 July at Panmunjon the armistice went into effect. UNC Commander, General Mark Clark, signed for the UN minus South Korea, while Marshal Kim Il Sung of North Korea and Marshal Peng Teh-huai of the CCF signed for the Communists.

Big Switch, the exchange of prisoners, began on 5 August at Panmunjon. The communists released 7862 ROKs, 3597 Americans, 945 Britons, 229 Turks and 140 other UN soldiers. The UN released 70,183 North Koreans and 5640 Chinese who had volunteered to go home. A total of 14,704 Chinese and 7,900 North Koreans refused repatriation. Most of these remained in South Korea. A few on both sides refused repatriation to their native country but later changed their minds. The final exchanges were completed by 6 September 1953.

The war was costly. There were an estimated 2.4 million military casualties on both sides. The United States suffered a total of 33,629 military killed or missing on the battlefield and 103, 284 wounded. For the period of the three year war another 20,617 died from other causes. On the UN side South Korea suffered the most military casualties with 46,815 killed, 159,727 wounded and 66,436 missing. On the communist side North Korea had 620,264 military casualties and the Chinese 909,607.

For the unlucky few who were captured this was a brutal war. Only 3746 Americans were repatriated out of 7908 known or believed to have been in enemy hands. Most American captives came from the Army during the period June 1950 through February 1951. During this period the majority died in captivity. After June 1951 when the mobile war ended, fewer servicemen were captured and very few died in captivity. Although life as a POW was difficult, after June 1951 some medical supplies did reach the communist POW camps and chances of survival improved.

For American soldiers the military experience in Korea seemed like two different wars. The first year was a year of mobility. The last two years were a stalemate. The statistics are very revealing. The first year 52,384 men were wounded. In the next two years 50,900 were wounded. These figures are relatively equal. The statistics of those killed are quite different. Over 21,329 men were killed in the first year and 12,300 in the last two. Why the difference? The statistics seem to indicate an improvement in the American medical and evacuation system. Another possible difference is that the American military fought in more extreme weather conditions during the first year than the last two. In the later years of the war the U.S. Forces were better prepared to combat the elements. However, both periods were difficult for any soldier who had to serve on the front line

America learned important lessons. US firepower and air power could not be decisive against a well-led guerrilla force such as the CCF. The geography of the Korean peninsula favored the UN defenders because in this restricted peninsula UN firepower was able to neutralize massed Chinese armies.

For Korea the war was devastating. There were about two million civilian casualties. South Korea took almost 15 years to recover economically and eradicate the scars of war. North Korea was not overtaken economically by South Korea until 1965. Since then North Korea's economic growth has been very slow as most of its national wealth is used for military expansion. Today world powers are questioning her development of atomic weapons which are a threat to her neighbors. After 42 years the demarcation line still stands There are American and ROK soldiers on one side and North Korea soldiers on the other. Forty years of American and UN support have allowed South Korea to grow into a great economic power in the modern world. The fires between the two Koreas are banked, but they still smolder.

Epilogue
By D. Randall Beirne, Ph.D.

The Korean War represented a victory for the West, because collective security stopped the first major military conflict which tested the resolve of the UN. The UN was able to punish the aggressor, while keeping the war local. For the first time it convinced the communist nations that the UN was willing to fight.

Collective security against Soviet power led to cold-war driven competition in expenditures on defense. In retrospect it has become apparent that the arms race between the Soviet Union and the West helped to bring down the Soviet economic system in the 1990s.

The South Koreans have not forgotten this war. The preservation of South Korea and its capitalist system has led to the Korean economic miracle. Other East Asian nations who might have fallen under communist control have likewise performed economic miracles. After 40 years even Communist China has converted much of her economy to a capitalist system. The Korean War should not be forgotten but should be remembered as a catalyst that started the downfall of the communist economic system. The sacrifices of many were not in vain.

Korean War Unit Histories

First Marine Division

In early July 1950, when the call for help came from Korea, the Marines answered by sending the First Provisional Marine Brigade to the Far East within three weeks. The Brigade consisted of the 5th Marines, First Battalion- 11th Marines, and Marine Aircraft Group 33. The initial landing took place at Pusan on 2 August 1950. A few days later, the Brigade spearheaded the first 8th Army counter attack and captured Kosong. The 5th Marines continued to spearhead the American drive to maintain the Pusan perimeter until 11 September 1950, when they withdrew for further operations, in still another area.

Back in the United States, the rest of the 1st Marine Division embarked on a hurried program of rebuilding. Units form the 2d Marine Division were redesignated as the 1st, 7th, and 11th Marines and became the nucleus of the newly activated division. This force was soon bolstered to a full strength division by the transfer of regular Marines from various posts and stations and by reservists called to active duty. By late August, elements of the Division sailed for Japan.

On 15 September 1950, the First Marine Division which included the 5th Marines, assaulted the beaches of Inchon. By 27 September, the Division had swept inland to liberate Seoul. Shortly after taking the important rail and road junction at nearby Uijongbu, the Division was ordered back to Inchon. The division was to reembark and carry out a landing at Wonsan on the eastern coast of North Korea. Wonsan fell to the advancing South Koreans, which meant no amphibious assault was necessary. Once on land again; the division moved north to Hamhung.

With the Americans and South Koreans rapidly forging ahead toward the Yalu River, Communist China felt a major threat to their security. The Chinese acted by aiding their ally, North Korea. What followed has become one of the proudest chapters of the Marine Corps history. The 1st Marine Division contributed with its epic operation in the Chosin Reservoir area of North Korea. Some of the most bitter fighting of the Korean War followed as an estimated 9 Chinese Divisions appeared suddenly. The Chinese forces were trying to resist the advance of the U.S. forces. The Chinese attempted to encircle the division. In late November, with its advance halted the Marines began to withdraw to the sea. The breakthrough was a hard accomplished fight. The conclusion of a bitter, 15 day epic. The division came back with its wounded, some of its dead, and its combat equipment intact. Soon after completion of its withdrawal, the division embarked on board various Navy ships at the port of Hungnam. The division sailed to Pusan to wait for the next mission.

With the arrival of the new year, the 1st Marine Division engaged in various offensive operations. These operations included Operation Killer, which was to drive communist forces north of the Han River. Operation Ripper was developed to drive the enemy back to the 38th parallel. The 1st Marine Division also participated in Operation Detonate and the battle for the Punchbowl. The Marines continued to be locked in combat against the North Koreans and Chinese forces throughout the year. In September, the 5th Marines retook Hill 812 in what was the last offensive type action by Marines in Korea.

Truce talks caused changes in the way combat operations were conducted. The new phase in the Korean War for front-line units was termed position warfare. It was characterized by a strong defensive line from which patrols were sent out to maintain enemy contact. In March 1952, the 1st Marine Division moved from east to west Korea and took over a sector on the extreme left of the United Nations line, with responsibility of blocking the historic invasion route to Seoul.

Engagements that followed were aimed at either capturing enemy outposts or repelling enemy attacks. Major engagements of this nature include the battle for Bunker Hill, August 1952; battle of the Hook, October 1952; defense of the Nevada City outposts of Reno, Vegas, and Carson, March 1953; and the final Marine ground combat action at outposts Berlin and East Berlin, July 1953.

After months of negotiation, the cease-fire agreement went into effect on the evening of 27 July 1953. More than 4,000 Marines were killed in action as part of the price of freedom for South Korea, with more than 25,000 wounded in action in the 3 years and 1 month of bloody warfare on the Korean peninsula. Freedom is not free.

Fifth Cavalry

In the beginning of June 1950, the 5th Cavalry, a regiment of the 1st Cavalry Division, was on occupation duty on Honshu Island, Japan. On 1 July 1950, planning began for active duty in Korea to aid the Republic of Korea in its defense against the North Korean People's Army (NKPA). The NKPA had crossed the 38th parallel and invaded South Korea on 25 June 1950. The 5th Cavalry departed Yokosuku Naval Base on 15 July, and landed in Pohang-dong, Korea on 18 July.

On 19 July, the 5th Cavalry departed for Kwan-ni to relieve the 24th Infantry Division. Shortly after on 22 July, the regiment, upon

moving to Kumchon to secure Yongdong, made its first contact with the enemy, where they received heavy artillery fire. By 29 July, the regiment had withdrawn west of the Kochang-Kumchon road, and on 31 July moved to defend Kumchon.

On 2-3 August, the 5th Cavalry withdrew again near Waegwan in order to protect the withdrawl of the 24th Infantry Division. When the enemy crossed the Naktong River (south of Waegwan) and seized Hill 268, the regiment met them with heavy resistance, eventually destroying the enemy unit. As a result, the 5th Cavalry restored the lines and eliminated the enemy threat. As the Cavalry continued repulsing NKPA attacks, it was hit by strong tank-supported infantry attacks on 7 September. Heavy combat lasted until 15 September. On 16 September, the 5th Cavalry initiated its attempt at breaking out of the Pusan perimeter, but made only slight gains. On 19 September, with the help of the 8th Cavalry began successful enemy resistance.

Helping to relieve elements of the 7th Infantry Division on 2 October, the 5th Cavalry broke out of its bridgehead (near Haying-ni) and captured Kaesong. Then on 14 October, the regiment made contact with the 7th and 8th Cavalry, near Songnyon-ni, having crossed the 38th parallel.

On 19 October, the 5th Cavalry entered Pyongyang, the North Korean capitol, unopposed. Next it moved to the Yongsandong area, followed by an unsuccessful attempt to rescue the 8th Cavalry at Yongjung, which was surrounded by the NKPA on 1 November. The 5th Cavalry, joining the remaining 2d Division regiments, assumed defensive positions on the eastern flank of I Corps, near Unhung-ni. On 6

151

November, assumed the responsibility of patrolling the Kunu-ri area. The 5th Cavalry moved to Sunchon on 28 November, to cover the 8th Army's IX Corp's eastern sector.

By 11 December, the 5th Cavalry went into 8th Army reserve north of Seoul. The regiment was deployed behind the ROK III Corps. In January 1951, the 5th Cavalry moved south of the Han River, where it mopped up enemy troops.

On 25 January, the regiment participated in Operation Thunderbolt. They reached Khon unopposed, but on 30 January, it encountered heavy resistance which led to hand-to-hand combat in order to clear Benchmark 642. Fighting against increasing enemy resistance, the 5th Cavalry attacked northward to the Chipyong-ni line of defense, in order to break through to the 23d Infantry. The 5th Cavalry successfully broke through and secured the high ground around Koksu-ri.

Once again the regiment was detached form its Division and put into corps control on 1 April and attacked northward during Operation Rugged, the operation to secure the 38th parallel. On 8 April, the 5th Cavalry moved near Chunchon and rejoined its division, as enemy resistance dispersed. On 10 April, the 5th Cavalry, along with the rest of the division was relieved by the 1st Marine Division. The 5th Cavalry went into 8th Army reserve near Seoul.

By 18 May, the regiment advanced to Line Topeka. During the first part of June 1951, the regiment fought against strong enemy resistance along the Uijongbu-Chorwon road. During July, the 5th Cavalry patrolled Line Wyoming. The 5th relieved the 25th Infantry Division.

On the offensive again, the 5th attacked against heavy opposition towards Kwijon-ni on 5 August. Weather conditions restricted operations. One month later, while patrolling Line Wyoming, the 5th Cavalry was attacked by enemy forces. A fierce battle ensued and despite overwhelming odds, the regiment fought well. The regiment only retreated after inflicting heavy enemy casualties.

Taking part in Operation Commando, the 5th Cavalry helped take Line Jamestown on 3 October. By 18 October, the regiment had helped take Hill 346, which they were unable to take earlier. During November, the regiment started by guarding Line Commando, then went into corps reserve. By December, the 5th Cavalry had been relieved by the 45th Infantry Division. The 5th was then transferred to Japan. By 27 April 1952, the entire 5th Cavalry had arrived in Japan. After extended training exercises, the 5th Cavalry returned to Korea to relieve the 7th Cavalry. There, it was placed under operational control of the Korean Communications Zone until it returned to Japan. The 5th Cavalry was in Japan when the armistice, which ended the Korean War became effective on 27 July 1953.

Fifth Marines

On 2 July 1950, orders for the movement of a Regimental Combat Team (RCT) with a Marine Aircraft Group to the Far East were sent to Camp Pendleton, where on 7 July, the 1st Marine Provisional Brigade was activated. It consisted, in the main, of the 5th Marines and Marine Aircraft Group 33. The brigade sailed on 14 July and after an uneventful voyage reached Pusan on 2 August. The Marine air/ground team was the first land force sent from the United States to Korea.

Within a half day after arrival, the brigade

began a motor march to occupy Eighth Army reserve positions around Changwon, about 40 miles to the northwest. A few days later, the regiment spearheaded the first Eighth Army counterattack in Korea. Moving rapidly, the 5th Mrines attacked to the southwest and captured Kosong on the 11th. Immediately, the Marines turned to the northwest toward Sachon. While carrying out this attack the next day, the 5th received two orders: 1) dispatch a reinforced battalion back to Chindong-ni to assist the 25th Division in restoring its overrun lines 2) move to another trouble spot on the defensive line around Pusan.

In the First Battle of the Naktong, 17-19 August 1950, the regiment, in a series of assaults, secured the two objectives assigned it and drove the enemy into and across the river, thereby restoring the 24th Division lines. On 20 August the brigade moved back to an area, near Masan, called the "Bean Patch," where they received replacements, rested, and trained in a large bean field.

Next, the brigade returned to the Naktong River scene of its mid-August fighting for a second counteroffensive. En route to its line of departure on 3 September, the 5th had to clear out enemy troops that had smashed through the lines of the outnumbered 9th Infantry. Late on 14 September 1950, the 5th Marines began final preparations for landing at Inchon.

On 7 September, the brigade arrived in Pusan and late on 14 September 1950, began final preparations for landing at Inchon. On 15 September, at 1731, the balance of the 5th Marines' assault units commenced landing. Before midnight the regiment took Cemetery Hill and the larger Observatory Hill.

Just before the division landed at Wonsan, the United Nations Commander, General Douglas MacArthur, ordered a change in the X corps mission. Unexpected earlier successes caused him to void the 1st Division's movement to the west and direct instead a speedy northward thrust to the Manchurian border. The 5th Marines drew the task of relieving ROK troops at Fusen Reservoir, 100 air miles directly north of Wonsan, and denying enemy entrance into the Marines' zone.

On 17 November the division directed the regiment to advance up the east side of the Chosin Reservoir in order to seize the vital town of Kyomul-li. On the 27th, they were directed to pass through the 7th Marines and take up the advance. Although counterattacks early on the 28th by some elements of the 5th Marines restored some of the ground lost in their area, elsewhere the enemy's position and his overwhelming numerical superiority threatened to cut the division into several pieces. The enemy had applied particular pressure at Hagaru, the division's supporting base 14 miles south of Yudam-ni. On 29 and 30 November, the division issued the 5th and 7th Marines orders initiating a breakout from Yudam-ni and an attack to the south. While division units were fighting to save Hagaru and the perimeter 11 miles farther south at Koto-ri, units of the 5th and 7th Marines, in contact with the enemy northwest of Yudam-ni, began to disengage on 1 December. From Taktong pass to Hagaru the going was less difficult, at least when measured against the amount of enemy interference.

At Hagaru, the 5th Marines drew the mission of perimeter defense during the two-day stay. For the division, one of the major tasks at Hagaru was evacuation of wounded, and, in completing it, much credit went to the transport elements of Marine, Navy, and Air Force commands. In the division attack from Koto-ri to Hungnam, the 5th Marines' seized commanding terrain east of the MSR.

In mid-February 1951, the division was assigned to the IX Corps and were motored to the central front for the purpose of stemming a major Chinese conuterattack. This engagement was termed Operation KILLER. The 5th Marines also participated in Operation RIPPER and then continued its forward movement. By early April, they reached and crossed the Soyang River. The 5th Marines moved forward on 23 May to capture the vital road center of Yanggu, 17 miles east of Hwachon. In this advance, the regiment protected the division right flank. At the end of May, the 5th was 6,000 yards northeast of Yanguu.

After the Communists walked out of the truce talks on 22 August, the 1st Marine Division returned to the front to attack on 31 August 1951. During this advance, the 5th Marines assumed the Division frontline patrol and rear-area security missions. On 11 November, they participated in Operation SWITCH, the largest lift movement to date. While in the reserve area at Camp Tripoli, the 5th Marines joined with the rest of the division in executing Operation CLAM-UP, an Eighth Army-planned feigned withdrawal designed to get the enemy to move forward from his positions.

On 17 February, the 5th relieved the 1st in the first night relief conducted in Korea. On 26 March, after relief by ROK troops, the 5th departed on the East-Central front to occupy much more extensive positions on the Western front guarding the historic invasion corridor to Seoul. In western Korea, they defended the center of the division's sector on the

JAMESTOWN Line, north of Seoul in the vicinity of the 38th Parallel. After some time spent in reserve, the regiment returned to the lines on 12 October, relieving the 1st Marines. From this date until late March 1953, there was no significant enemy activity against the 5th Marines.

A final tour on the front lines for the regiment began on 7 July. The Communists penetrated the outpost trenches and were turned back only after reinforcements from the MLR countercharged in conjunction with effective supporting arms fire. Repulsing that attack was the last significant fight for the regiment. Three days later, on 27 July at 2200, the terms of the Korean cease-fire took effect.

Fifth Regimental Combat Team

Campaigns: North Korean aggression; Communist China aggression; 1st UN Counter-offensive; Communist China spring offensive, 1951; UN summer-fall offensive, 1951; 2nd Korean winter 1951-52; Korean defense, summer-fall, 1952; 3rd Korean winter, 1952-53; Korean, summer-fall, 1953.

Decorations: Republic of Korea Presidential Unit Citation

Commanders: Col. Godway Ordway, Jr. (July 50-Aug. 50); Col. John L. Throckmorton, Jr.(Aug. 50-Apr. 51); Col. Arthur H. Wilson, Jr. (Apr. 51-Sept. 51); Col. Alexander Surles, Jr. (Sept 51-Apr. 52); Col. Lee L. Alfred (Apr. 52-Jan. 53); Col. Harvey H. Fisher (Jan. 53-Apr. 53);Lt. Col. William H. Kasper (Apr. 53); Col. Lester L. Wheeler (Apr. 53-July 53).

The 5th Regimental Combat Team (5th) was located at Schofield Barracks, Hawaii, when it was alerted for combat duty in Korea on 13 July 1950. The regimental combat team was composed of three battalions of the 5th Infantry, the 555th Field Artillery Battalion, and the 72nd Engineer Combat Company. On 30 July, Eighth Army ordered the 5th, upon its arrival at Pusan, to assemble in the vicinity of Kumhae.

On 1 August 1950, the 5th was ordered to proceed to Masan for attachment to the 24th Infantry Division. The latter division was scattered in heavy fighting, and on 3 August the 5th was attached to the 25th Infantry Division. They were then committed to the front, southwest of Masan, along the Naktong River.

On 7 August, as part of Task Force Kean, the unit counterattacked west toward Chinju to secure Masan against hostile attack. The unit continued to advance against stubborn resistance at Kogan-Ni and Hogan-Ri reaching its objective in the vicinity of Sachon by 12 August. The 5th continued to engage in heavy fighting in late August and early September in the Sobuk-San area, then moving to Taegu, where on 13 September, it was transferred from Eighth Army reserve and attached to I Corps.

The 5th Regimental Combat Team was attached to the 24th Infantry Division on 18 September 1950, and served as its third regiment capturing Waegwan, and then crossed the Naktong river 20-21 September. It then advanced past Seoul and crossed the Imjin River in early October. On 16 October, it entered Yonan during the advance toward Pyongyang, the North Korean capital.

By 25 October, the 5th was assembled in the vicinity of the Chongchon River, preparatory to crossing the river and continuing its push northward to the Manchurian border. Three days later, it advanced to the south bank of the Chonbang River and captured Taechon on 29 October. The attack pressed on to the northeast against increasing enemy resistance, capturing Kuson and driving to within 30 miles of the Yalu River. Chinese Communist armies entered the Korean conflict in early November, forcing I Corps to withdraw its forward positions, pulling back to defensive positions along the Chongchon River line.

By late November, the Chinese Communist offensive forced the Corps to begin withdrawal and the 5th was ordered back to Pakchon. It screened the retreat of the ROK 1st and 24th Infantry Divisions by protecting the Chongchon crossings. The unit was forced to withdraw over the river itself on 30 November, and the withdrawal south continued until the UN counteroffensive in late January.

As part of Operation Thunderbolt, the 5th advanced on 25 January 1951, and attacked to the north, reaching Ichon without opposition. Fighting through enemy resistance, by 30 January, the 5th pushed northwest of Hyonbung-ni. The unit recrossed the Han River and fought to the juncture of the Han and Pukhan Rivers and by 5 April reached its objectives along Line Kansas.

The Chinese spring offensive was launched on 22 April 1951. On 23 April, elements of the 5th were subjected to ambush as they pulled back into blocking positions along the Han River. The 5th reconsolidated and reorganized its units and covered the retreat of other units in the area. By 3 May, the 5th occupied prepared defensive positions covering the ground above the Han River and covered the withdrawal of the 24th Infantry Division. Elements of the unit

155

engaged in continuous and extensive patrolling from these positions.

On 27 May 1951, elements of the 5th counter-attacked an enemy force attacking the command post of the 21st Infantry. This action ended in the capture of 1,141 Chinese prisoners. On 22 June, the 5th relieved the 32nd Infantry on Line Ermine and conducted aggressive patrolling from its defensive positions. On 2 August, a limited attack was launched which temporarily secured some commanding terrain, and then the 5th withdrew to Line Wyoming. On 8 August, the unit was relieved and placed in reserve.

The 5th, as part of the IX Corps offensive, attacked enemy positions on 13 October to gain Line Nomad. Following a series of limited attacks, it advanced to positions just south of Kumsong.

In February 1952, the 5th, less its 3rd Battalion, moved to Koje-do Island to guard the United Nations Prisoner of War Camp. The 3rd Battalion provided security in the sangdong Mining area. On 22 April, the 5th was relieved by the 38th Infantry on Koje-do.

Early in May, it was attached to the 25th Infantry Division and moved to positions on Line Minnesota on 18 June. The 5th remained on Line Minnesota in the Punchbowl sector under control of the 25th Infantry Division until 22 October, when the unit was transferred to the 40th Infantry Division in position. On 1 November, the 5th was relieved and placed in reserve just behind the front. A period on intensive training followed.

On 7 January 1953, the 5th was alerted to assume positions on the main line of resistance, and completed the relief of the 223rd Infantry the following day. This switch returned the 5th to its former positions on the norther rim of the Punchbowl occupied prior to its November relief. Throughout its stay on the front, the unit conducted numerous patrols and engaged in several small skirmishes. On 30 January, the 5th passed to the operational control of the 45th Infantry Division, but remained in the Punchbowl sector until relieved by the 224 Infantry on 16 April.

The 5th's 1st Battalion returned to the main line of resistance on 25 April in the central sector of the Iron Triangle while the remainder of the Team occupied blocking and reserve positions.

On 16 May, the 5th was relieved and moved to Chipo-ri to initiate a training and rehabilitation program. On 5 June, the 5th returned to the 3rd Infantry Division and deployed to forward assembly areas and blocking positions. From 11 June, the 1st Battalion was attached to the 15th Infantry. From 11 to 13 June, this battalion held Outpost Harry against sustained regimental-sized enemy attacks which were supported by concentrated mortar and artillery barrages. On 14 June, the battalion was detached from the 15th Infantry and relieved the 2nd Battalion, 15th Infantry on the main line of resistance in the Chorwon Valley, where it occupied Outpost Tom. The remainder of the 5th occupied blocking positions throughout this period.

On 20 June, the 5th was relieved by the 23rd Infantry and moved back to Chipo-ri. There it remained in Eighth Army reserve and was alerted for movement into the southern part of Korea, where it was needed to security duty by the Korean Communications Zone. On 1 July however, the 5th, less the 555th Field Artillery

Battalion and heavy mortar company, relocated to Inje and became part of X Corps reserve.

On 14 July, the 5th returned to the main line of resistance east of the Pukhan River in the Pleasant Valley sector and was attached to the 45th Infantry Division. During this period, the 5th repulsed several enemy attacks against its front line positions. The 5th was at this location when the armistice was signed on 27 July 1953, and shortly thereafter began withdrawing to newly mandated positions near Pol-mal.

Seventh Cavalry

On June 25 1950, while the North Korean People's Army crossed the 38th parallel to invade South Korea, the 7th Cavalry , part of the 1st Cavalry Division, was stationed on Honshu Island, Japan. The entire First Cavalry Division prepared for departure to Korea on 3 July 1950. The 7th Cavalry departed Yokoma for Pusan on 17 July, an arrived at Pohang-dong on 22 July. On 25 July, the 7th Cavalry replaced the 8th Cavalry in the Kumchon-Chinye area, immediately facing enemy attacks. Then during the night of 1-2 August the 7th Cavalry helped other friendly troops withdraw across the Naktong River. Next, the regiment also withdrew across the river and 0moved to the vicinity of Maegwan to Kaejin-Myon. On 14 August the NKPA crossed the river near Tuksong-dong and were repulsed by the 7th Cavalry along with the other 1st Cavalry Division Regiments. The 7th Cavalry also repulsed several enemy attacks on 4 September.

On September 13th 7th Cavalry was placed under I Corps, and attempted to break out from the Pusan perimeter against heavy resistance. By 22 September the attacks turned into delaying actions. On 26 September the regiment became part of Task Force Lynch, which was spearhead-

ing X Corps. After relieving elements of the 7th Infantry Division, the 7th Cavalry crossed the Imjin River on 5-6 October, and on the next day broke out of its bridgehead near Hajong-ni and captured Kaesong. Later that month on the sixteenth, almost 30 kilometers beyond Namchon, near Kit-Jan, the 7th Cavalry made contact with the ROK 1st Division. The next day it entered Hwangju against scattered resistance and by 21 October the Dregiment occupied Chinnampo. By the end of October the 7th Cavalry-moved to the Yongsondong area.

On 11 November the 7th Cavalry attacked across the Chongchon River and moved north of the confluence of the Chongchon and Kuryong Rivers. Then by 13 November the regiment had secured high ground and consolidated positions with the 5th Cavalry. The 7th Cavalry was relieved by the 24th and 25th Infantry and pulled back to Yongbyon on 22 November. Two days later the regiment was put in 8th Army reserves, securing the Sunchon and Kunu-ri areas. On 28 November the 7th Cavalry held positions near Sindhang-ni. By 7 December the 7th Cavalry had moved east of Sunchon on the first, fought past road blocks, then withdrew south and east of the Taedong River on to areas south of Koksan and finally north east of Sibyon-ni. Two days later the regiment made a limited attack toward Ichon. The 7th Cavalry went into 8th Army reserve north of Seoul on 11 December and patrolled as far as Chunchon, Hongchon, Wonju and Chupo-re without making enemy contact. The regiment was then deployed on 16 December behind the IX Corps to insure the security of the Seoul-Kapyong road. Next the 7th Cavalry was attached to the 24th Infantry Division to protect the right flank of the Seoul bridgehead on 2 January 1951, and on the following day pulled back south of the Han River. On 25 January the 7th Cavalry took part in Operation Thunderbolt, a counter offensive against the Chinese Communist Force, and reached Inchon without opposition. Three days later the regiment was hit hard by an enemy attack, but it prevailed with aid from air strikes and artillery fire. The 7th Cavalry also encountered heavy opposition on 30 January.

In the beginning of February the 7th Cavalry fought against enemy resistance, and on 21 February the regiment participated in Operation Killer, with the purpose of pushing the CCF north of the Han River. By the end of the month the 7th Cavalry had advanced to the Hongchon area. On 5 March the 7th Cavalry was shifted on the front of the 1st Division's line. Two days later it attacked in Operation Ripper intending to push the communists across the 38th parallel and retake Seoul. By 11 March the regiment has helped seize 3 fortified strong-points and on the 13th had reached line Albany.

On 3 April the offensive had been renamed Operation Rugged, with the same purpose of trying to secure the 38th parallel. After gains on all fronts, Task Force Caleway was formed on 9 April, including the 7th Cavalry, with the purpose of seizing the Hwachon Dam after the enemy had flooded the Han River. By 10 April the 7th Cavalry was relieved by the 1st Marine Division. On 26 April, the 7th Cavalry was attached to the 3d Infantry Division, but had to withdraw the next day. The regiment was immediately reverted to I Corps control and moved along the defensive line north of Seoul. On 28 April the 7th Cavalry was placed in division reserve.

On 4 May 1951, the 7th Cavalry established patrol bases behind Uijongbu to fire on enemy troops. Bu 18 May the regiment was forced to retreat due to enemy attacks which let up after the withdrawl. On 29 May, the 7th Cavalry was relieved from the front line. In the beginning of

June the regiment assaulted enemy troops on the Uijonbu-Chorwon road, followed by fortifying defenses along Line Kansas.

Throughout July and August the 7th Cavalry spent time patrolling Line Wyoming in the Yonchon area and in corps reserve along Line Kansas. On 6-7 September 1951, while patrolling Line Wyoming, the 7th Cavalry was assaulted on Hill 339, withdrawing despite strong resistance. On 3 October with the seizure of the Coursen Pocket.

On 6 November hill 200, held by elements of the 7th Cavalry was attacked and taken, but was restored the next day. On 12 November the Fregiment was relieved by the 3d Infantry Division and placed in corps reserve, and on 19 November began planning to transfer to Japan. Throughout the winter the 7th Cavalry was located at Camp Crawford and Hokkaido, assuming security responsibility. On 27 March the regiment was moved to Camp Chitose II, where it took part in training exercises throughout the summer and fall.

On 15 December 1952, the 7th Cavalry went back to Korea where it aided in securing the Pusan and Taegu areas along with the railways. It was relieved on 8 February by the 5th Cavalry and went back to Otaru, Japan, relocating to Camp Chitose II on 18 February 1953. There the regiment took part in training exercises and was stationed on security duty when the armistice became effective on 27 July 1953.

Seventh Infantry
On 25 June 1950 when the North Korean People's Army invaded the Republic of Korea, the 7th Infantry, part of the 3d Infantry Division was stationed at Fort Devens. After intensive

preparations the regiment left for Japan, arriving on 15 September. In Mori and Beppu, Japan, the regiment trained and in early October was alerted to sail for Korea. The 7th Infantry arrived in Wonsan, Korea and was split into Regimental Combat Teams, due to its large size.

The 7th Infantry's first assignment was to relieve elements of the 1st Marine Division, securing the Wonsan area and preparing for an offensive. From 22-30 November the regiment aided in successfully protecting the Wonsan area. The first major action the 7th Infantry saw was in the first part of December when it fought off enemy guerrilla groups. Then on 11-12 December, the 7th Infantry helped in a major resistance of enemy troops along the Hamhung-Hungnam defensive perimeter. Next morning to cover the withdrawl of the X Corps, through Hungnam, which had taken a beating up north. The withdrawl to Hungnam was completed on 24 December and the 7th Infantry headed form Pusan.

The 7th Infantry went into rehabilitation and intensive training on 31 December 1950, and by 6 January 1951 , was back on the front-line near Chonan, then moving onto Line Dog, near Suwon and Kumyangjang-ni ready for an offensive. The 7th Infantry began attacking on 6 February, gaining high ground near Benchmark 497, then pushing the communist forces across the Han RIver. The enemy counterattack came on 13-14 February. The next day the regiment participated in mopping-up operations, first, and then it aided in fortifing the south bank of the Han River, south and east of Seoul, called Line Boston.

From 1-15 March 1951, the 7th Infantry held Line Boston, aiding other troops and sending out patrols, then on 16 March, the regiment forged across the Han River, pushing toward Seoul. On 22 March, Operation Courageous was launched, bringing the 7th along with the rest of the 3d Division to Uijongbu by 22 March. Again, the 7th Infantry set out on an offensive, attacking north across the Sinchon River, reaching the Imjin River on 14 April. There, the I7th Infantry helped occupy and strengthen Line Utah. Then form 23 to 27 April, the enemy attacks in the east forced the regiment to withdraw to Line Golden, just north of Seoul. ON 12 May the regiment was situated in the Seoul-Inchon area, ready >to back up the corps zone, moving to Hoengsong to check enemy infiltration on 17 May. As part of Operation Piledriver, the 7th Infantry attacked across the Hantan River on 1 June and by 10 June was positioned south of Chorus. Then on 13 June the regiment attacked Pyonggang. By the end of June the 7th Infantry was finally occupying Line Wyoming, the base of the Iron Triangle.

On 1 July 1951, as part of Operation Doughnut, the regiment fought its way to the top of Hill 717 and 682, securing the positions by 5 July. Then spending the rest of the month strengthening positions on Line Wyoming and patrolling. During August 1951, the 7th Infantry only met scattered resistance, and maintained its positions.

Again meeting enemy attack on the night of 6-7 September, the 7th Infantry was struck by an enemy patrol 5 km north of Chorwon,which was repulsed. Following were one-day battles on 18 and 29 September. Then on 3 October the 7th Infantry took part in Operation Commando, securing Hills 477, 281 and 395, reaching Line Jamestown after three days of fighting on 6 October.

During December 1951, the 7th Infantry sent out patrols to gather information and capture prisoners. During January 1952, the regiment defended Line Jamestown until 19 January when it went into corps control for security assignments, returning to Jamestown on 27 February 1852.

The 7th Infantry moved to Field Training Command #1 on 26 April to participate in intensive training. Then on 1 July the regiment was deployed along the Kwigon-ni and Sinhyon-ni sector where it fortified its positions and conducted patrols through September. The 7th Infantry moved to reserve near Yongpyong, first on 1 October, next it moved to the Noltari-Sanggasan sector of Line Missouri on 25 October. All remained relatively quiet in the 7th Infantry's sector.

From 26 to 29 December the 7th Infantry was back in corps reserve to conduct training near Yongpyong until 27 January 1953, when the regiment relieved the 25th Division, then assumed positions on secondary defensive lines Wyoming and Wyoming Switch, joining the rest of the 3d Division on Line Missouri on 28 February. Throughout March the 7th Infantry aided in reconnaissance and ambush patrols, then in April enemy activity increased and in May there were battles on the outpost line.

During June the fighting escalated and front line positions came under attack, especially Outpost Harry, which was successfully held. From 13-14 July the 7th Infantry was placed in corps reserve, which was left to aid the Capitol ROK Division in the Pangtong-ni and Chuhtae-ri Line, and by 15 July was in command of the 3d Division. The 7th Infantry along with a Belgian battalion backed up the corps in the rear. From 16 to 17 July the 7th Infantry aided in conducting

raids and attacked enemy formations from 18-19 July. Then on 20 July a new line was established. On 27 July 1953, the 7th Infantry withdrew to new positions south of the 38th Parallel and the Demilitarized Zone in accordance with the Armistice.

Seventh Marines

The 7th Marines was reborn at Camp Pendleton on 17 August 1950 and Colonel Homer L. ("Litz the Blitz") Litzenber, Jr. was assigned as its commanding officer. All units of the regiment except the 3d Battalion were activated on the 17th with the largest proportion of reservists of any major unit in the 1st Marine Division-about 50 percent. The regiment was composed of: Headquarters and Service Company, 4-2-inch Mortar Company, Antitank Company, and three battalion each having a headquarters and service company, a weapons company, and three lettered companies.

The regiment along with the 3d Battalion, 11th Marines, an artillery unit, went ashore at Inchon on 21 September. The 7th Marines, assigned to capture the most important rail and road junction at nearby Uijongbu, succeeded in a smashing victory by causing enemy defenders to break and retreat into North Korea. Shortly after the taking of Uijongbu, the regiment moved to Inchon along with other units of the 1st Marine Division. The 7th Marines had been directed to go to Hamhung and then march north to relieve the 26th ROK Regiment which had reportedly been hit by Communist Chinese units. Relief of the South Koreans by the 7th Marines took place with little difficulty on the morning of 2 November.

The 7th Marines, which headed the 1st Marine Division's northward drive to the Chosin Reservoir, gained the distinction of being the first American military unit to defeat the Chinese Communists in battle. During efforts to seize Yudam-ni on the western side of the Chosin Reservoir, the Chinese launched a furious attack on both the 5th and 7th Marines. The savage blows that the Chinese hurled at the United Nations troops cut both the 5th and 7th Marines and their supporting units off from the rest of the division. This attack struck the 7th Marines with a viciousness that had not been seen before during the war.

Major General Oliver P. Smith, division commander, felt that the Marines' situation at Yudamni was precarious and ordered a withdrawal to Hagaru-ri and eventually to the sea. On December 1, 1950, Lt. Colonel Davis' 1st Battalion, 7th Marines lead the withdraw and its first objective was to relieve Company F and secure the vital pass. After contending with the snow, cold, rough terrain and enemy combat, the 1st Battalion completed its mission.

On 3 December, the 1st Battalion, 7th Marines received orders from Col. Litzenburg to asssault Chinese positions near Toktong Pass. The objective of this maneuver was to clear a path for the units from Yudam-ni. The 7th Marines successfully carried out a skillful attack that disrupted Chinese plans for an assault on the withdrawing column. The Chosin Reservoir campaign was a rugged, arduous military operation for the 7th Marines. This unit faced not only a determined foe but also the frightful hardships of a frigid climate. An unprecedented number of Medals of Honor-nine in all-were awarded to marines from the regiment for their valorous deeds during the campaign.

The 1st Marine Division soon after completion of its withdrawal embarked on board various Navy ships at Hungnam and sailed to the port of Pusan in South Korea. It then moved to Masan to regroup and replace its losses.

On 27 August, the 7th Marines and the Korean Marine Corps Regiment were ordered to relieve American and South Korean Army troops in the Punchbowl region of east-central Korea.

In October 1952, the Chinese stepped up their attacks on Marine outposts that guarded the division's right flank. These crucial positions were occupied by the 7th Marines. The enemy began by unleashing a mortar and artillery barrage on Outposts Seattle and Warsaw. Both fell but Warsaw was quickly reoccupied. Heavy shelling continued through October, but no new major Communist assault took place until the 26th when Outposts Ronson and Warsaw came under attack. Both were subsequently captured. The momentum of the attack carried the enemy into the main defenses. The men of the 7th Marines had to pull back and establish a new line. They initiated a counterattack on the 27th. Attacking through a veritable hail of small arms, artillery, and mortar fire, the company drove a wedge into Communist lines.

In early July the 1st Marine Division, led by the the 7th Marines, returned to the front. It relieved the Army's 14th Infantry Regiment and supporting Turkish troops. The Communists took advantage of the shifting forces and opened up with artillery and mortar fire before the Marines could complete their deployment. An infantry assault on UN lines came on the evening of 7 July. Waves of enemy soldiers with strong support from their artillery surged forth through the rain to strike at the Americans. The battle developed into a desperate hand-to-hand fight with the enemy literally being thrown down the slopes of the hill. The Americans had succeeded in driving out the enemy, but the 7th Marines sustained over 160 casualties in the action.

In July 1953 the Chinese assaulted and seized Outpost Berlin and East Berlin. By the 26th, the determined resistance of the 7th Marines stopped the Communists, and the whole Chinese effort ended with their forces being turned back. This engagement proved to be the last combat action for the regiment during the Korean War. Fighting for the month had taken a heavy toll - the regiment sustained over 800 casualties. The 7th Marines continued its deployment in Korea for over a year and a half after the 27 July 1953 armistice. To maintain its combat readiness so that it could meet its responsibility of repelling a potential attack from the north, the 7th Marines engaged in a number of training exercises and amphibious maneuvers. Redeployment to the United States eventually came in March 1955.

Eighth Cavalry

The 8th Cavalry was part of the 1st Cavalry Division. The 8th Cavalry was moved on 13 July and arrived in Korea on the following day. On the 21 July the division was moved to Kumchon to secure Yongdong and committed to action against the rapidly advancing North Korean Army. On that date, the 8th Cavalry made the first enemy contact near Yongdock.

From 22 July until early August the 5th and 8th Cavalry fought delaying actions in the Kumchon-Chirye area. Two days later, the 8th Cavalry reported the enemy had infiltrated behind its positions and established a road block. On the following day, a force of 3,000 enemy troops attacked the 8th Cavalry's left flank. The division withdrew five kilometers and units occupied new positions by nightfall.

By 29 July, strong enemy attacks on the division's front and flanks forced the 5th and 8th Cavalry to withdraw toward new defensive positions on the high ground west of the Kochang-Kumchon road. As enemy pressure continued, the division was ordered to move under cover of darkness to defend Kumchon.

During the first couple of days in September, 1950, enemy attacks gained ground in the 8th Cavalry sector. On the 4th of September, the 8th Cavalry repulsed several enemy assaults. The 8th Cav entered the walled city of Kazan before being forced to retreat south of Sonju. Due to continued pressure on the 8th Cavalry, the division was forced to withdraw to new defensive positions.

On 9 October, the 8th Cavalry attacked northward from Kaesong against stubborn resistance and crossed the 38th parallel. A few days later, the division completed a double envelopment of the enemy opposing the 8th Cavalry. On 21 October, Task Force Rogers (reinforced 1st Battalion, 8th Cavalry) advanced north and contacted the 187th Airborne Regimental Combat Team at Sunchon and Sukchon. By the end of the month, the division was in the Yongsandong area with the 8th Cavalry having just relieved the ROK 12th Regiment.

On 1 November 1950, the 8th Cavalry was surrounded at Yonghung-dong and suffered a sharp reverse, its 3d Battalion being practically destroyed. On 6 November, the division consolidated its forces and became responsible for patrolling the Kunu-ri area.

On 2 January 1951, the 1st Cavalry Division assumed control of the ROK 6th Division sector. The division pulled south of the Han River. A battalion of the 8th Cavalry covered blocking positions near Inchon during the retreat.

On 21 February, the 1st Cavalry Division participated in Operation Killer and attacked toward the ridge line south of Hagwaho with the 5th and 8th Cavalry in a column of regiments. By the end of the month, the division advanced to the Hongchon area. On 5 March 1951, the 1st Cavalry Division shifted its positions. The 8th Cavalry moved into division reserve. Two days later, the division attacked in Operation Ripper with the 7th and 8th Cavalry, and the attached Commonwealth 27th Brigade.

In August 1951, the 3d Battalion of the 8th Cavalry provided security guards for the Munsan-ni United Nations representative's tent camp. The division also strengthened defensive lines and bunker systems against the inclement weather.

On 19 November, the division was alerted to start planning for relief by the incoming 45th Infantry Division from Japan. On 16 December, the 8th Cavalry was relieved by the 108th Infantry. The division debarked from Korea (on the same ships used to bring increments of the 45th Infantry Division to Inchon) and sailed to Hokkaido, Japan.

On 8 October 1952, the 1st Cavalry Division sent the 8th Cavalry from Muroran port to Korea, where it was attached to the Korean Communications Zone on 16 October. The regiment assisted in the security of the Pusan and Taegu areas and the Korean railways. The 8th Cavalry was reinforced by the 99th Field Artillery Battalion, Battery C of the 29th Anti-Aircraft Artillery Battalion, and a detachment of the 510th Military Intelligence Service Platoon.

On 15 December, the 1st Cavalry Division conducted winter divisional field exercises in Japan. On 19 December, the regimental combat team based on the 8th Cavalry and the 99th Field Artillery Battalion, returned to Camp Crawford in Japan.

The 1st Cavalry Division was stationed in Japan on security duty. The regiment was busy performing advanced training exercises when the armistice became effective 27 July 1953.

Ninth Infantry

On 25 June 1950, as the North Korean People's Army crossed the 38th parallel, invading the Republic of Korea, the 9th Infantry, part of the 2d Infantry Division, was stationed at Fort Lewis, Washington. At Fort Lewis the 9th Infantry was supervising and training reservists and conducting the ROCT summer encampment when it was called for overseas duty on 9 July 1950. Elements of the 9th Infantry were the first among the division to sail from Tacoma, Washington from 17-19 July. The entire 9th Infantry moved immediately to Kyongsan in 8th Army reserve. From 6 to 22 August a battalion of the 9th Infantry participated in the 24th Infantry Division's offensive. On 8 August the regiment encountered its first combat near Suga-ri, then after repulsing enemy counterattacks near Kogana-re, advanced to Ogong-ni. At the same time the 3d Battalion of the 9th Infantry organized Task Force Bradley to secure the Pohang-dong airfield on the east coast. On 14 August the regiment joined Task Force Hill in the center of the 24th Infantry Division offensive. The regiment first captured Clover Leaf Hill and Maekok village, then on 16 August repulsed strong enemy counterattack and captured positions between Ikarikaku and Wokoku. On 18 August the 9th Infantry occupied the area from Kwandog to Sunto-ri, and finally on 19 August, was relieved, withdrawing near Yongson-Myon. On

163

22-24 August, the 9th Infantry was joined by the Second Infantry Division, taking over for the 24th Infantry Division along a 61-km stretch of the Naktong River and for the first time the whole division fought together. The 9th Infantry defended the strongpoints, getting involved in heavy fighting, but by 31 August it defeated a major enemy attack. Then on that same night the NKPA attacked across the Naktong and fighting broke out. The 9th Infantry finally forced the enemy in its sector to withdraw. On 15 September another enemy offensive hit the 9th Infantry which was repulsed, and on 19 September the regiment finally captured Hill 201. On 22 September the 9th Infantry along with the rest of the division was attached to IX Corps, advancing to capture Hyopchon on 25 September, and Kochang the following day. During October 1950 the 9th Infantry was involved in mopping-up operations. On 14 October the regiment arrived in areas between Seoul and Suwon, reverting to 8th Army reserve and becoming responsible for bridge security along the Han River on 17 October. On 19 October the 9th Infantry was attached to I Corps and secured Pyongyang and was back in 8th Army reserve on 29 October.

On 1 November the 9th Infantry moved to Sunchon and was attached to I Corps, then on 5 November was transferred to IX Corps. By 24 November the regiment opened an offensive on the Corp's right flank, and the next day crossed the Chongchon River. From 29 to 30 November, they fought through road blocks south of Kuni-ri, and as a result of its participation in the Ch'ongch'on battle, suffered heavy casualties. On 1 December 1950, the 9th Infantry went to Chungwha for rehabilitarion, then arrived near Munsan-ni from 3-4 December. By 9 December the regiment had withdrawn tothe Han River, securing floating bridges. On 23 December the regiment withdrew further to Chongju. Then moving northeast tothe Wondrously area on 2

January, the 9th Infantry occupied Line Y on 5 January, when it withdrew to a new line south west of Wonchon to Mosan-ni. After replacing ROK 8th Division, the 9th Infantry conducted reconnaissance patrols from Wonju to Hoengsong. During February the 9th Infantry was bombarded with heavy enemy pressure, but held part of their line from Wonju to the south west. Then, the regiment was relieved by the 1st Marine Division on 21 February and moved north west of Chechon, in time to assist in Operation Killer. It secured positions along the Wonju road area. Staying in the same area, the 9th Infantry helped lead Operation Ripper, securing Line Idaho, then Line Cairo on 26 March. On 5 April 1951 the 9th Infantry moved to Hongchon, and was placed in corps reserve 2 days later. In the beginning of May it conducted patrols until 17 may when the regiment was attacked, which sent it retreating to Line No Name, where defense positions were established south of Hangye. On 24 May the 9th Infantry counterattacked to the north east due to an attack on 20 May which had resulted in heavy casualties. Attacking towards Line Kansas, on 2 June, the 9th Infantry ended up at Inje, just north of the 38th parallel on 7 June. After moving north of the Soyang River on 16 July, the regiment began an offensive north of Yanggu. Next, on 18 August it fought in an intense battle for Hill 983 and surrounding areas. Similar battles continued through 23 October, when the regiment was relieved of front-line duty. By 18 December the 9th infantry returned to the front in the eastern point of the Kumhwa-Chorwon-Pyonggang area, the iron triangle, where patrols were conducted until January. Defensive positions were strengthened by the 9th Infantry on Line Missouri along with Operation Freeze-out, a series of raids on enemy bunkers. Patrols and Raids continued until February 1952 when the regiment participated in Operation Claim Up. Throughout March it remained along Line Missouri and Patrolled the area. In April the 9th Infantry was trained and sent to Koje-do Island to guard the POW compound until 15 July. Then on 15 July the 9th Infantry was attached to the Thai battalion and placed on the defensive line extending west of Sinhyon-ni to Noltari. On the defensive line the action occurred around Outpost Old Baldy, which was occupied by enemy troops on 17 July. On 21 September 1952, the 9th Infantry went into division reserves until 25 October when it went to defend Line Jamestown, experiencing heavy patrol clashes. Relieved by the 7th Infantry Division on 29 December, the 9th Infantry moved from the front to reserve, where it underwent training. In January the regiment went back to the front on Lime Jamestown, west of Chorwon, where it remained throughout February. All was relatively quiet except for 13 February 1953, when artilllery fire opened up on Outpost Hook. Receiving another attack on 17 March, east of the Bowling Alley, the 9th Infantry repulsed the communist forces.

During 5 to 9 April 1953, the 9th Infantry left the front and went into Field Training Command #1. The regiment continued training throughout April and May. After returning to combat the 9th Infantry engaged with enemy forces fron 17 to 19 July, which were all repulsed. On 27 July 1953, when the Armistice became effective, the 9th Infantry withdrew south of the Demilitarized Zone.

15th Infantry

On 25 June 1950, as the North Korean People's Army crossed the 38th Parallel and invaded the Republic of Korea, the 15th Infantry, part of the 3d Infantry Division was stationed at Fort Benning, Georgia. The 15th Infantry was alerted for shipment to the Far East on 10 August. From 21 August to 2 September, the regiment was at Camp Stoneman, California in preparation for their arrival in Moji, Japan on 15 September. Finally between 10 to 21 November 1950, the 15th arrived in Wonsan Korea, north of the 38th parallel.

The 15th Infantry's first assignment was to relieve elements of the 1st Marine Division, securing the Wonson area, and protecting the western flank of the X Corps. There orders were carried out until 5 November. Then in the beginning of December the regiment fought fierce groups of enemy guerrillas. Afterwards on 11 December, it fought through the 1st Marine Division to resist enemy advances along the Hamhung-Hungnam defense perimeter. The next day the regiment stopped advancing and aided in the withdrawl of the X Corps units through Hungnam. By 24 December there was a complete withdrawl from Hungnam and the 15th Infantry sailed for Pusan, debarking on 29 December and gathering near Toji-ri. After training in the 8th Army reserve beginning on 31 December, the 15th Infantry went to the front line near Chonan on 4 January, occupying Line Dog, near Suwon and Kumyanjanj-ni, from 6 to 27 January. Then on 6 February the 15th Infantry along with the rest of the 3d Division began an offensive, which led to an enemy counterattack on 13-14 HFebruary. By 15 February the 15th was involved in mop-up operations. Then on 16 February the regiment moved in the close vicinity of the Han River, followed by strengthening operations on the south bank of the river, known as Line Boston. The regiment stayed on the line from 1-15 March.

On15 March the 15th Infantry participated in an assault across the Han and towards Seoul, followed by Operation Courageous on 22 March. The Operation brought the regiment to Uijonbu the next day. Attacking across the Sinchon River, the 15th Infantry reached Line Utah on 14 April, where it fortified positions. After moving north from 15 to 22 April the regiment was pushed back to Line Golden, just north of Seoul from 23 to 27 April. Then went into reserve in the Seoul area.

Back on line in the Seoul-Inchon area, the 15th Infantry moved east to Hoensong on 17 May to check enemy penetration, which was completed by 28 May. On 10 June 1951, the regiment had moved near Chorwon, participating in attacks on Pyonggang on 13 June. At the end of the month the regiment occupied the base of the Iron Triangle along line Wyoming. Attacking Pyonggang again on 1 July, the 15th Infantry assisted in securing key positions by 5 July. Then securing Line Wyoming and patrolling throughout the rest of July and August, the 15th aided in Operation Cleanup on 18 September. The operation consisted of two, one-day battles on 18 and 29 September.

Operation Commando was launched on 3 October 1951 with the 15th assisting in securing Hills 477, 281 and 395, reaching Line Jamestown on 6 October. Once there, the regiment was involved in strengthening positions along the line and patrolling. The 15th Infantry went into corps reserve on 21 October conducted training until 20 November when it went back to Line Jamestown and resumed patrolling in the Kangso-ri and Omgogae sector.

On 26 April 1952, Part of the 15th Infantry went into Field Training Command #1 to conduct training operations, while the remainder of the regiment guarded the POW compound at Pusan from 29 April to 5 July. Then on 6 July the 15th went into division reserve at Camp Casey where it-took part in patrolling Kimpo.

Seeing action again the 15th Infantry was attacked on 28 July as the enemy seized Outpost Kelly, which it recaptured on 31 July, but remained under fire. August consisted of patrol engagements but no major offensives. On 10 September the regiment was sent back to reserves at Camp Casey.

The 15th Infantry moved to the Noltari-Sanggasan sector of the Line Missouri on 29 October, after leaving reserves. The regiment fought throughout the month in a see-saw-battle for Outpost Jackson, frequently coming in and out of reserves to stay in good condition. By 29 December the 15th Infantry was participating in training and security missions near Yonder.

The 15th Infantry was back on Line Missouri after relieving the 15th Division from 27 to 30 January. Throughout February and March 1953, the regiment participated in reconnaissance patrols and ambushes along with fortifing the line of resistance. The regiment was attacked on 3 and 24 April around Outpost Harry. The first attack was repulsed in hand-to-hand combat, the second by close-in defensive fore. The 15th Infantry fought Hoff attacks at Outpost Harry through May until 16 May when the regiment went into reserve.

In July the 15th Infantry assisted in replacing the devastated ROK Capitol Division in the Pangtong-ni and Chuktae-ri Zone. There the regiment conducted reads from 18 to 19 July and by the next day had established a line on the front. On 27 July 1953, when the armistice Dending the war became effective , the 15th Infantry withdrew to new positions south of the Demilitarized Zone (DMZ).

17th Infantry

At the outbreak of the Korean War on 25 June 1950, the 17th Infantry, a part of the 7th

Infantry Division was in Japan on Occupation duty. Throughout July the 17th Infantry occupied different camps in Japan. On 31 July, the regiment along with the rest of the 7th Division was ordered to prepare for commitment in Korea. Throughout August the 17th Infantry trained intensely and from 6-10 September it sailed to Pusan and was attacked to the 8th Army Reserve.

On 25 September, the 17th Infantry left Army reserve and engaged in its first combat at Inchon as it attacked east from Suwon. After its first engagement the 17th Infantry participated in mopping up activities along a 50 mile from on 30 September, then moved up to the Suwon area the same day. From 5 to 11 October, the regiment withdrew to Pusan by way of road and rail, encountering scattered attacks throughout the movement.

Departing Pusan on landing ship tanks, the 17th left Pusan on 27 October and debarked, unopposed at Iwon Harbor on 29 October. The regiment first went up to Pungsan, then on 12 November, was ordered to attack northward to take Kapsan and Hyensenju. On 21 November, after fighting through Pungsan and Kapsan, the 17th Infantry arrived at the Manchurian border at Hysenjin. On 28 November the regiment was attacked, but suffered better fate than other regiments in the area. The 17th Infantry participated in a fighting withdrawal to Hugnam, reaching its destination by 11 December. Then on 19 December, the regiment sailed for Pusan, beginning arrival on 16 December.

Moving from Pusan, the regiment moved 80 miles north and reorganized near Yongchon. On 4 January, the 17th Infantry was sent to the Chechon area and by the next day was fortifying blocking positions on Line Y, the supply route from Tanyang to Chechon. By 9 January 1951, the 17th Infantry came under attack and on 27 January participated in a counterattack toward Pyongchang.

On 6 February, the regiment aiding the ROK 5th Division moved to take Hungchon in Operation Roundup. Then the 17th Infantry was aided by the ROK Division to defend the Chechon area in mid-February. Operation Killer was the next offensive in which the 17th Infantry participated, attacking to the Wonju-Kangnung road on 21 February. The regiment came within 10 miles of the destination by 27 February.

Again on the offensive, the 17th Infantry attacked the enemy in the Hongchon-Hangye-Inge are, along Soyang-gang, from 1-20 March 1951. The regiment was also moved in rebuilding operations. Then on 5 April, it launched another offensive as part of Operation Rugged, crossing the 38th parallel and capturing Yanggu, by 16 April. Next, switching into a defensive mode, the 17th Infantry held the high ground near the Inge-Hamyang-ni corridor, repelling enemy attacks from 23-27 April.

ON 1 May, the 17th INfantry moved to Line No-Name, just south of the Hongchon River, beginning a counterattack towards line Topeka on 20 May. ON 27 May, the regiment took Hwachon, and in the process aided in breaking up thousands of enemy troops. As a part of Operation Pile Driver, the regiment fought along the Hwachon-Kumwha front until 23 June, when it was relieved and placed in reserve near Line Kansas, conducting training.

Moving back to the front on Line Wyoming from 9 August through September the 17th INfantry patrolled and participated in limited attacks to thin out the enemy in teh vicinity. Then on 5 October the entire 7th Division went into reserve first and next, went northeast of the Hwachon Reservoir, along Line Minnesota on 23 October. There the 17th Infantry patrolled the area.

The regiment went into division reserve on 7 January 1952, until February, when it went back to positions along Line Minnesota. Next, from 21-26 April, the regiment occupied blocking positions in Hwachon, moving to reserve areas near Taegong-ni on the 26th. Moving back to Line Missouri the 17th occupied the Kansan-ni-Kumhwa sector in the Iron Triangle from 15 to 28 April. There the regiment took part in raids and patrols until September.

On 3 July 1952, Operation Indicator was launched to destroy bunkers and capture prisoners near Hill 404. Then on 28 July, the regiment participated in a psychological warfare operation, called operation Heartbreak. On 16 October elements of the 17th Infantry were placed in the 32d Infantry. ON 14 October, the regiment participated in Operation Showdown, beginning by attacking Hill 598 and Jane Russell Hill, which were occupied after intense fighting by 16 October. The next several days were spent repelling enemy counterattacks.

Sent to guard the pow compound at Koje-do on 1 November 1952, the 17th Infantry was attached to the Korean Communication Zone on 9 November. By 29 December, the regiment went to reserve camp, Indianhead, and on 26 January 1953, was on the front, on Line Jamestown. The 17th Infantry stayed there, participating in reconnaissance and combat patrols, along with defending against scattered, sometimes strong, enemy attack. ON 15 May, the Communists attacked the regiment at

Outpost Snook. The attack was repulsed when reinforcements arrived.

During June 1953, it was relatively quiet in the 17th Infantry's sector. Heavy attacks on the front in the beginning of July were repulsed wit the help of the 17th Infantry. Then on 6 July, the Communist forces attacked outpost Pork Chop, which led to 5 days of heavy fighting, and ended with the withdrawal of the 17th Infantry and other UN troops. On 27 July 1953, the 17th Infantry withdrew further to positions south of the Demiliterized Zone, when the armistice became effective ending the Korean War.

21st Infantry

On 25 June 1950, when the North Korean People's Army crossed the 38th parallel to begin the Korean War, the 21st Infantry was stationed in Japan on occupation duty. It immediately prepared for duty in Korea. The first elements of the 21st Infantry arrived in Pusan on 1 July. The remainder of the regiment following on 4 July.

On 13 July the troops were already holding the western sector of the 8th Army 's front at Tumin. The next few days the 21st Infantry withdrew fighting from the south bank of the Kum River to the Taejon vicinity. Situated between Kong-ju and Taejon, the 21st Infantry aided in trying to stop the enemy's advance, By 20 July the regiment was engaged in combat in Taejon, quickly withdrawing south. Finally at Uongdong, the battered regiment was relieved, moving to Kumchon in the 8th Army reserve, where it was strengthened.

Due to a powerful enemy attack, which pushed the 24th Division line behind the Naktong River, the 21st Infantry left Pohang-dong to strengthen the line. After forging across the Naktong and regaining positions, the regiment was pushed behind the river. Moving east of the Naktong between 6 and 13 August. Unable to uproot the enemy, the 1st Provisional Marine Brigade was added to the 24th Division and helped destroy enemy bridgehead west of Yongsan. On 24 August, the 21st Infantry was relieved, moving into reserve near Kyongsan to be rehabilitated and set up blocking positions around Taegu.

Assuming defensive positions in Kuongju with recently attached elements of the 34th Infantry, the 31st Infantry joined Task Force Jackson on 5 September. The regiment then moved to Kyongsan on 16 September and crossed the Naktong on 19 September. Moving along the Kumchon-Taejon road, the 21st aided in an attack which resulted in the occupation of Kumchon on 25 September.

By 9 October, the 21st Infantry crossed the Imjin River and on 16 October, launched a major attack while pushing towards Hoegwangdong. The regiment was relieved near Pyongyang on 22 October, and headed towards the capital. On 27 October the 21st Infantry crossed the Chongchon River. Then on 31 October the regiment reached a point 10 km. west of Naechong Jong for 2 days before withdrawing to defensive positions near the Chongchon. There the 21st aided in securing a line from Sinanju to Unjung-ni, and by 16 November had secured the line.

By 22 November, the 21st Infantry was in reserve Pakchon. Leaving reserve the 1st Infantry pushed up to Chonhgju by 25 November, withdrawing on 28 November near Pakchon, then across the Chongchon River.

The regiment moved to Kangdong on the

eastern flank on 1 December. Then on 11 December the regiment occupied defensive positions near Chorwon, where it faced a major enemy attack on 31 December. The attack pushed the 21st Infantry beyond Sanbung-ni, then on 4 January 1951, to Suwon. Finally in the attack again the regiment took part in Operation Thunderbolt, a major counter offensive against the communist forces.

The 21st Infantry was attacked on 6 February 1951, repulsing most of the enemy troops the next day, but was under attack during its advance in Operation Roundup until 14 February. Pushing onward, the regiment reached positions near the Han River on 18 February and on 22 February began participation in Operation Killer.

Another operation (Ripper) was launched on 7 March, which sent the 21st Infantry attacking towards Yongmun Mountain and Line Albany. Following Operation Ripper, the regiment pushed onto Line Buffalo on 14 March and line Cairo on 22 March, which brought it to the Pukham River. By 3 April the 21st Infantry was relieved and ordered to Line Kansas.

After participating in Operation Dauntless, which pushed the 21st Infantry towards Line Utah, and Major enemy resistance, the regiment went into division reserve the next day on 20 April. Two days later the 21st Infantry was being driven back, withdrawing to Line Delta on 25 April.

The beginning of May was relatively quiet as the 21st Infantry patrolled the front line. Then on 17 May, the enemy attacked and the 21st Infantry aided in counter attacks, which were successful, but continued on 19 May when the enemy attacked again. Then the 21st Infantry participated in an offensive on 19 May which pushed it up to Line Topeka. Attacking again, the regiment reached Line Kentucky, west of Hwachon on 27 May.

Operation Pile driver was launched with the assistance of the 21st Infantry on 2 June 1951, which brought the regiment west of Hwachon. Next it went into division reserve to train from 5 to 21 June, when it made its way back to the front on Line Wyoming. There, the 21st Infantry was pushed off Hill 851 by enemy counterattack, but claimed the northeastern slope of Himbau San. Attacking in front of Lien Wyoming, the 21st Infantry helped secure Line Utah on 2-3 August. Then by 9 August the 21st Infantry was in reserve being rebuilt through August and September.

The 21st Infantry was back on Line Wyoming and engaged in patrolling on 5 October 1951. Then on 13 October the regiment attacked towards strategic positions north of Kumsong, occupying them by 17 October and pushing forward, securing Line Polar on 25 October. There it stayed through November and December on what was renamed Line Missouri.

In January 1952, the 21st Infantry began being replaced by the 41st Infantry Division. The regiment sailed out of Korea at Inchon by 4 February, and was assigned to Far East Command, debarking on Honshu Island, Japan on 9 February. There the 21st Infantry underwent extensive training until 5 July 1953, when the regiment went back to Korea to provide security. Then on 18 July, the 21st Infantry was sent to Koje-do, which was the location it was at when the war ended with an armistice on 27 July 1953.

23d Infantry

At the same time as the North Korean People's Army invaded the Republic of Korea on 25 June 1953, the 23d Infantry, part of the 2d Infantry Division was located at Fort Lewis, Washington. On 9 July 1950, the regiment was alerted for overseas duty in Korea. The 23d Infantry left the U.S. from 22 to 24 July, and arrived in Korea on 5 August and assembled near Won-dong.

Upon arrival in Korea, the regiment was immediately deployed north and west of Samnangjin ready for enemy crossing of the Naktong River. On 19 August the 23d Infantry was ordered to move North of Taegu, and was already repulsing a massive enemy attack on 22 August. After the attack the 23d Regiment, along with the rest of the 2d Division, established defensive position along a 60 mile stretch of the Naktong River. While in division reserve the 23d Infantry cleared the main Sangju-Taegu road, and reached Kumandong from 21 to 23 August.

Launching a major attack across the Naktong River on 31 August, the 23d was hit at three points in its line of defense, and next the NKPA established themselves on the east river bank. The regiment repulsed the attack on 5 to 6 September and continued defending its position until 13 September. By 16 September the 23d Infantry had advanced to the high ground next to the Naktong.

The tides turned again on 18 September when elements of the 23d Infantry were pushed back across the river, but by 20 September the 23d regiment had recrossed the river and was on high ground east of Sinban-ni on 21 September, making more gains on 25 and 26 September the 23d-aided by the capture of Hyopchon and Kochang.

By October 1950 the regiment was mopping-up in the rear of the 8th Army in the southwest. Next, it moved to the Suwon, Hansong and Yonju areas on 14 October, and on 17 October was placed in bridge security along the Han River. Finally at the end of October on the 29th, the 23d Infantry moved to secure the line from Chongdon to Singye, along with the main supply line from Pyongyang to the back of I Corps.

On 1 November the 23d Infantry gathered at Sunchon, moving from I Corps to IX Corps on 5 November. Next the regiment pushed up to Sinhung Dong and on 26 November was heavily attacked and lost its command post to the enemy. From 3-4 December the regiment arrived near Munsan-ni after one day of rehabilitation in Chunghwa. After moving southeast of Seoul to secure the floating bridges of the Han River on 9 December, the 23d moved on to Wonju, arriving on 29 December to secure Line Y.

Again meeting enemy attack, the 23d Infantry held the pass northwest of Chechon on 8 January 1951. Eventually the regiment repulsed the attack in spite of adverse weather conditions, and by 12 January along with the 38th Infantry, had seized Hill 247. Three days later the 23d Inf. with-drew to Mosan-ni to establish a new defensive line.

West of Sinchon on 1 February 1951, the 23d Infantry came under heavy attack and serious fighting ensued. On 12 February the enemy came at the regiment again around Wonju and in a matter of hours surrounded it at Chipyong-ni, where the 23d assumed heavy casualties. The regiment fought bitterly until the Division came to its aid. On 21 February the 23d helped secure positions along the Wonju and Pangnim-ni road network.

The 23d launched offensives across moun-

tains in the Wonju-Hoengsong area from 1-4 March. Then on 5 March the regiment was heavily attacked. Next it was relieved by the ROK 5th Division to prepare for Operation Ripper, which it would help spearhead on 7 March. By 26 March, Line Idaho and Cairo were secured. Again launching offensives the 23d Infantry successfully attacked northeast to the Hwachon Reservoir on 5 April 1951. Without any new incidents the regiment was ordered to Changbong-ni in reserve until 16 May.

On 17 May the 23d Infantry was partially surrounded and by the next day was totally surrounded by enemy troops. As a result the regiment was forced into a rout, abandoning most of their equipment, and by the end of the day were in reserve. After a few days of quiet the 23d Infantry forced its way along the Hongchon-Kansong highway, crossing the Soyang River south of Kwandae-ri on 26 May.

The next day, relieving the 23d Infantry from the front, Task Force Baker attacked through them on 27 May and on 31 May the regiment joined the Task Force. The 23d Infantry pressed on, attacking toward Line Kansas on 2 June. Assigned to a new zone the regiment headed south, assembling at Hongchon on 7 June. By 16 July the 23d was back at the front on Line Kansas north of Soyang River, beginning an offensive north of Yanggu. Then on 18 August the regiment saw more action in a major battle for Hill 983 which would be gained and lost many times before it was finally secured.

Facing heavy battle for 7 days, the 23d Infantry fought until 23 September the Hill 931, Heartbreak Ridge, which it won, then lost the next day. The Ridge was finally secured on 13 October in the 23d Infantry's attempt to gain defensive positions on high ground.

171

From 23 November to mid-December the regiment assisted in guarding the POW camp at Koje-do Island. After 16 December the 23d EInfantry was deployed in the middle of the eastern point of the Iron Triangle until February 10 1952. At that time the regiment aided in Operation Claimup, a series of enemy ambushes. Through March and April the regiment was on Line Missouri and participated in many of the same activities.

In May the 23d Infantry, under IX Corps' control, secured the Sangdong mines. On 9 July the regiment went to Line Jamestown first, then on 14-18 July moved to the left of a new defensive line from Sinhyon-Mni to Noltari. Seeing action again, the 23d Infantry recaptured Outpost Old Baldy, which had been in enemy hands since 17 July. Coming out of division reserve, the regiment's next defensive position was Line Jamestown, which it occupied on 21 September 1952.

From 29 December to 5 January the 23d infantry participated in intensive training. The regiment was then moved from Camp Casey to Koje-Bdo and Chiju-du to guard prison camps. On 24 March, the regiment rejoined its division, and was positioned in the middle of the front on Line Jamestown, moving to Camp Casey then Sintan-ni on line Holdback from 5 to 23 April. On 27 April the 23d was repositioned along secondary Line Kansas, where it strengthened defenses.

On 4 May 1953, the 23d Infantry was moved near Ussimjae to take part in training exercises. After training the regiment was relocated to the sector extending from Kangson-ni to Sanggasan from 21 June until 15 July when it occupied the right side of the defensive line in the Chorwon-JKumwa area. There it saw its last combat from

17 to 19 July. On 27 July 1953, when the Armistice became effective, the 23d moved to new positions south of the Demilitarized Zone (DMZ).

24th Infantry

When the Korean War began on 25 June 1950, the 24th Infantry, regiment in the 25th Division, was on occupation duty in Japan. On 13 July the 24th Infantry had arrived at Pusan, and was deployed in Task Force Able on 18 July.

The task force protected the 25th Division's left flank in the Sanhju and Hamchang region. In Sanhju the 24th Infantry occupied positions which were part of a defense line. By 26 July the regiment moved west and south of Hamchan as other 25th Division regiments were engaged in combat elsewhere. Then on 29 July, the 24th Infantry retreated again to a defensive line west of Sanhju. The next day the 1st battalion of the 35th regiment was attached to the 24th Infantry. Ordered within the Changnyong vicinity on 31 July, the regiment came under 24th Infantry Division control.

Back with the 25th Division, the 24th Infantry aided in stopping a major enemy drive. The regiment was hit again on 15 September, but by the next day had the enemy withdrawing across the Nam River after fierce battles.

Advancing forward, the 24th Infantry helped defeat strong enemy forces and capture Uiryong on 26 September. By 30 September the 24th Infantry helped take the port of Kunsan. Engaging in security mission through October, the regiment also conducted rehabilitation and training. After going into 8th Army reserve on 3 November the 24th Infantry moved to Tosong-ni by rail and road, gathering near Kaesong.

On the offensive the 24th Infantry attacked on 24 November, moving rapidly northwest of Yongsong-dong, where the communist forces counterattacked, pushing the regiment across the Chongchon River. Then on 28 November, the 24th Infantry moved to the division defensive line west of Sunchon. The communists launched a major offensive on 2 January 1951, forcing the 24th Infantry to withdraw to positions in the Seoul bridgehead. By 6 January the regiment went into reserve, half of which secured the Taejon-Chonan main supply route on 13 January.

On 25 January the 24th Infantry participated in Operation Thunderbolt. By 12 February Kimpo airfield was secured and on 16 February the regiment was advancing against resistance, reaching the Han River on 19-20 February. Operation Ripper was launched and the 24th Infantry crossed the Han River on 7 March and had reached the Seoul-Chunchon road west of the Pukchan River by 15 March.

By 29 March after attacking across rugged terrain in the northwest, the regiment occupied a new line form Sorum-ni to Pochon. The 24th Infantry attacked further in Operation Rugged, seizing Line Kansas by 5 April. Then after Operation Dauntless, the regiment had advanced to positions near the Chorwon Valley until 22 April when a major enemy counter-offensive pushed the regiment back to Line Golden, 10 km northeast of Seoul.

Advancing form Line Golden to Line Topeka on 20 May and reaching positions 50 miles north of the 38th parallel by the end of May the 24th Infantry resumed its advance in Operation Piledriver. Piledriver brought the regiment up to the Chorwon-Kumwha sector by 30 May. Then from 1 to 20 June 1951, the 24th Infantry

launched offensive operations in the Iron triangle. Finally going into reserve in the Uijongbu vicinity, the 24th Infantry fortified positions on Line Kansas.

Back on the front on Line Wyoming, southwest of Chonon, by 17 July, the 24th Infantry came under enemy attack on 20 July, pushing the regiment back to the Chorwon-Kumwha area. Throughout August and September the 24th Infantry participated in fortifying positions on Line Wyoming, conducting patrols and raids, and repulsing enemy attacks. During October, positions along Line Wyoming, south of Pyonggang were held, while the 24th Infantry was in light combat during November.

The 24th Infantry was relieved on 18 December and moved to positions along Line Missouri under the 2d Infantry Division's control until 29 January 1952. On 23 February, the regiment occupied the left sector of the 25th Division's defensive line on Line Minnesota. Through May and June the 24th Infantry resumed patrolling and repulsing attacks until 18 June when it was transfered to reserve positions at Inje.

By 19 July the regiment moved to reserve in Tokkol-li, and was back defending the front-line in August. Then in September, Hill 719, held by the 24th Infantry, was attacked, followed by hours of fighting, which ended in the successful repulsion of the enemy.

Continuing to defend its position through September and October, the 24th Infantry went into a training program on 24 October and on 12 November was on Line Missouri, on the sector from Kangsan-ni to Kumhwa. Spending December-January 28, 1953, participating in reconnaissance patrols and ambushes, the 24th Infantry was relieved and went into intensive training at Unchon-ni.

From 3 March to 24 April, the 24th Infantry came under 3d Division control and was positioned near Karogae. Then on 28 May it assisted the Turkish Brigade defending the outpost under enemy attack in the Nevada Complex until 29 May when the 5th Division regiments were ordered to retreat.

During June the 24th Infantry patrolled, and on 8 July went into corps reserve at Camp Casey. On 27 July 1953, the regiment withdrew to positions below the Demilitarized Zone as the armistice ending the war became effective.

27th Infantry

On 25 June 1950, the 27th Infantry was on occupation duty in Japan when the North Korean People's Army crossed the 38th parallel, beginning the Korean War. From 13 to 15 July the regiment departed from Japan and arrived in Pusan, Korea.

By 21 July the 27th Infantry moved into positions 17 km west of Sagju to secure a defensive line. Two days later the right flank of the 27th Infantry was in heavy conflict and needed the 1st battalion of the 35th Infantry to be attached for support. The next day the entire 27th Infantry was attacked by the enemy, and on the 25th the enemy continued attacking and gaining ground, but was successfully counterattacked.

ON 29 July, the 27th Infantry was pushed back west of Sangjuto a new defensive line, then moved to Waegwan in 8th Army reserve on 30 July. The next day the 27th Infantry was ordered to relocate to a line from Kumchon to Sabul-Myon to defend against enemy attack. Withdrawing through the first Cavalry Division at Waegwon, the regiment headed back south to Smnagjin form 1-3 August. There it gained responsibility for the southern sector of the Naktong River defensive line on 4 August.

On 7 August the 27th Infantry moved to reserve at Chirwon-ni, and by 18 August was ready for an offensive commencing in Kumwho-dong along the Sanju-Taegu road to wards Kazan. Despite enemy infiltration to the regiment's rear, the objectives were gained and the 27th Infantry went on to assist the 24th Infantry Division which was getting crushed. By 31 August the regiment returned to Masan. That night the enemy forces attacked in Haman which the 27th Infantry aided in containing.

Continuing to contain the enemy, the 27th Infantry helped halt a major enemy attack on the right of the defense line on 2 September, and two days later had repulsed the attack. Following the major attack, the regiment was involved in combat with further enemy attacks until 16 September whin the NKPA was pushed across the Nam River, south of Khayon-nii.

Finally able to advance, the 27th Infantry secured high ground near Sobuk-san and Paedun-ni from 17 to 10 September. Continuing its advance, the regiment aided in defeating strong enemy forces and capturing Uiryong on 26 September followed by occupying the port of Kunsan on 30 September. During October the 27th Infantry aided in mopping-up operations, rehabilitaion and extensive training, in the Suwon-Hansong-Jonju area.

On the advance again, the 27th Infantry

moved up to Tosongong-ni on 4 November and started assembling near Kaesong on 6 November, while an element of the 27th Infantry came under better attack at Togan-ni, which was immediately aided by the remainder of the regiment. Then after assembling near Anju on 19 November the 27th Infantry participated in an attack toward Yongsong-dong. Due to strong enemy counter attack the regiment withdrew across the Chongchon River.

On 28 November the 27th Infantry occupied positions on a defensive line west of Sunchon until 31 December, when an enemy offensive forced a withdrawal to the left side of the Seoul Bridgehead, occupied on 2 January 1951. The next day the 27th Infantry covered the withdrew of the 25th Infantry Division north of Suwon, assembling near Chonanon 6 January. On 7 January a reconnaissance-in-force mission was launched by the 27th Infantry toward Osan. Next the regiment attacked in Operation Wolf-hound, advancing toward Osan and Inchon through enemy resistance, and gained objective positions by 17 January. Finally on 19 January the 27th Infantry was relieved from the front.

Operation Thunderbolt was launched on 25 January with the 27th Infantry participating in the offensive. By 12 February the regiment aided in occupying Kimpo Airfield and on 15 February had taken over the corps' right flank. Then the next day the 27th Infantry attacked towards the Han River, reaching it by 19-20 February. Crossing the Han during Operation Ripper on 7 March, the 27th Infantry aided in taking part of the Seoul-Chunchon road by 15 March. Continuing to attack on 23 March over mountainous terrain, the 27th Infantry occupied the new front line running form Sorum-ni to Pochon by 29 March.

First in Operation Rugged beginning on 3 April 1951, then Operation Dauntless on 11 April the 27th Infantry advanced toward the Chorwon Valley until 22 April, when a major enemy counter-offensive lasting until 26 April pushed the regiment to Line Golden, 10 km northeast of Seoul. The 27th Infantry remained on Golden, patrolling until 20 May, when it aided in launching Operation Detonate, trying to take Line Topeka. Finally at he end of May the regiment was 50 km above the 38th parallel in the Kumwha area, launching Operation Piledriver through the Chorwon-Kumwha sector.

Through 1 to 20 June 1991, the 27th Infantry launched offensive operations in the Iron Triangle. Moving back to reserve positions on Line Kansas on 21 June, the regiment went on security missions, trained and fortified positions. While the 3d Battalion split off from the 27th Infantry to provide security for the UN armistice negotiations camp at Munsan-ni until 9 July.

The 27th Infantry was back on the front along Line Wyoming form 15-17 July, where it patrolled and conducted raids throughout August and September. In October the 27th Infantry helped hold the western portion of Line Wyoming also supporting the I Corps in Operation Commando form 3-9 October. Continuing to patrol and perform reconnaissance operations until 16-18 December when it gathered near Kanpyong on Line Kansas to conduct training until 29 January. Next the 27th Infantry relocated to Koje-do island to guard a POW compound until 27 February.

On 18 March 1952 the left sector of Line Minnesota was occupied by the 27th Infantry. There the regiment met scattered attacks and conducted patrols until 14 June when it went into division reserve at Tokkol-li. Leaving

Tokkol-li on 20 July, the 27th Infantry relieved the Turkish Brigade on the line. The regiment went in and out of reserve throughout the fall. Then on 10 November it relocated to Line Missouri, where it patrolled and ambushed.

In February 1953, the 27th Infantry went through an intensive training program at Yami-ri and stayed in corps reserve from February to April. Back on the front on Line Wyoming, along the sector form Kaikkyo-dong to Sokchuwon-ni on 5 May, the 27th Infantry repulsed attacks and aggressively patrolled until 8 July. Then the regiment relocated to Camp Casey, where it was when the armistice became effective on 27 July 1953, which sent the 27th Infantry to positions south of the Demilitarized Zone.

31st Infantry

On 25 June 1950, when the North Korean People's Army crossed the 38th parallel, invading the Republic of Korea, the 31st Infantry was on occupation duty in Japan with the entire 7th Division. On 31 July, the 31st Infantry was ordered to prepare for duty in Korea. The regiment began intensive training and by 10 September had left Japan for Korea. The regiment gathered at Inchon on 16 September, and participated in an amphibious landing on 20 September.

Upon arrival, the 31st Infantry gained responsibility for the Chansu-ri area and guarded the 7th Division's right flank. ON 25 September the regiment attacked toward Suwon, securing the Suwon airfield and defended against enemy elements trying to break through to Seoul. By 30 September the 31st Infantry was engaged in mopping-up activities. Finally the regiment left the Suwon area dn headed towards Pusan bu road and rail, while repulsing enemy

attacks the whole way down. It arrived on 11 October.

Delayed by rough seas, the regiment moved to Iwon, above the 38th parallel, debarking by 6 November. After patrolling the area the regiment was ordered to push up to the Korea-Manchuria border, est of the Fusen Reservoir. On 21 November, the 31st Infantry was patrolling the Fusen Reservoir area, then elements of the regiment advanced along the eastern shore of the Chosin Reservoir, accompanying the 1st Marine Division.

ON 28 November, the 31st Infantry was surrounded and crushed by the enemy as it was attempting to protect the flank o the 1st Marine Division. The remaining soldiers fought for 4 days and 5 nights in their withdrawal to Koto-ri. Finally by 11 December the remaining members of the regiment had retreated to Hungnam and were evacuated by 19 December.

By 26 December the regiment had debarked and was assembling 81 km north of Pusan near Yongchon to prepare for combat. On 4 January 1951, the regiment moved to the Chechon area. The next day the 31st Infantry was in blocking positions behind Line Y to protect the supply route from Tanyang to Chechon, beginning on 9 January. After destroying Communist forces in the area, the 31st Infantry attacked toward Pyongchang.

ON 6 February 1951, the 31st Infantry supported the ROK 5th Division, which was attacking toward Hongchon in Operation Roundup and on 21 February the regiment drove north towards the Wonju-Kangnung road in Operation Killer. Again on the offensive, the 31st Infantry took part in an attack in the

Hongchon-Hangye-Inje sector along Soyang-gang. The o 21 March, the regiment participated in patrolling and rebuilding the area.

Moving to a new sector along the Soyang-gang on 4 April, the regiment took part in Operation Rugged the next day. The regiment crossed the 38th parallel on 16 April and occupied Yanggu, Then the regiment defended the high ground overlooking the Inje-Hamyang-ni corridor from 23 to 27 April.

Occupying new positions along Line No-Name, south of the Hongchon River on 1 May 1951, the 31st Infantry counter attacked towards Line Topeka on 21 May. Then from 5 to 22 June, the regiment participated in Operation Piledriver, along the Hwachn-Kumwha line. Moving to positions on Line Kansas, the 31st Infantry went into reserve for intensive training on 23 June.

The 31st Infantry was back on the from by 9 August, but this time on Line Wyoming. On 26 August it began limited attacks to thin out enemy buildup near Hill 819 to the Pukhan River. During September the regiment patrolled and on 21 September, participated in Operation Cleaver, a raid on the eastern end of the Iron Triangle. by 23 October the 31st Infantry was in the Hwachon Reservoir sector along Line Minnesota, where it conducted patrolling.

During January 1952, the 31st Infantry switched to the left of the Paeon to Paktal sector on Line Minnesota. On 5 February, the regiment went into reserve. Then form 17 March to 23 April the regiment with an attached Colombian battalion performed security missions. Finally from 15 to 28 April it was back on Line Missouri, where it occupied positions in the Kansan-ni-

Kumhwa sector in the Iron Triangle. There the regiment participated in raids and patrols until 28 July, when it aided in launching Operation Heartbreak, a psychological warfare operation. After that it went into division reserve near Chipori.

On 16 October the 31st Infantry was back on Line Missouri. Throughout October and November activity increased. On 14 October after diversionary raids, the regiment took part in Operation Showdown, fighting for then defending Hill 598 and Jane Russell Hill until 25 October. On 29 December, the 31st Infantry moved to Line Jamestown in the area from Ojoksan-ni to Sonchyon. Next, the regiment moved into division reserve on 26 January at Camp Indianhead.

Elements of the 31st Infantry unsuccessfully raided T-Bone complex, then occupied Line Holdback, a division reserve defensive line. By 27 February the regiment was back on Line Missouri. Then on 24 March it counterattacked against enemy forces that had seized Outpost Old Baldy, but was unsuccessful. Another battle ensued in the 31st Infantry's sector at Outpost Pork Chop, which resulted in heavy hand-to hand combat, which finally repulsed the enemy troops.

Throughout May the 31st Infantry participated in patrol clashes and minor skirmishes. Then in June, the regiment helped defend the front-line. The on 6 July outpost Pork Chop was attacked again, which led to heavy fighting for five days, ending with the withdrawal of the 31st Infantry and the other 7th Division regiments. Finally on 27 July 1953, the regiment withdrew again to positions south of the Demilitarized Zone in accordance with the cease-fire agreement ending the Korean War.

32d Infantry

On 25 July 1950, the 32d Infantry, part of the 7th Infantry Division, was on occupation duty in Japan. On 31 July the regiment was ordered to full wartime strength and prepared for duty in Korea with intensive training. The 32d Infantry left Yohohama, Japan form 6 to 10 September, and arrived at Inchon on 17 September where it performed an amphibious landing.

By 19 September the 32d Infantry gained responsibility for the southern front below the Inchon-Seoul highway. Then the regiment moved eastward, taking objectives as it met enemy resistance. On 21 September, elements of the 32d Infantry departed Anyang-ni on the Seoul-Suwon highway, cutting off the capital from the south. Next, the regiment seized the south bank of the Han River on 24 September to prepare for and attack on Seoul. The next day the elements of the 32d Infantry forged the Han, repulsing enemy counter attacks to connect with the 1st Marine Division. By the 27th of September Seoul was liberated.

ON 5 October 1950, the 32d Infantry withdrew to Pusan by way of road and rail, meeting enemy attacks during the move. The regiment reached Pusan by 11 October. Then on 28 October the 32d Infantry departed for Iwon, arriving form 1-6 November, immediately commencing patrolling. The regiment was ordered to advance and destroy enemy forces on the Korean Manchurian border. It secured the southwest shore of the Fusen Reservoir and continued to provide security around Iwon.

The regiment also sent elements to the Chosin Reservoir through Hanhung. ON 28 November those elements were surrounded and crushed by communist forces. The remainder of the 32d Infantry who could not help the sur-

rounded troops withdrew fighting through to Hunganam, which was reached by 11 December. The entire 7th Division had evacuated, and was sailing toward s Pusan on 19 December.

ON 26 December, the 32d Infantry gathered north of Pusan, near Yongchon. Moving to Chechon on 4 January 1951, the 32d Infantry took blocking positions along LIne Y the following day. The regiment secured the supply route form Tayang to Chechon, fighting off attacks which began on 9 January. After the defensive operations the regiment aided in helping the ROK 5th Division secure Hongchon.

The 32d Infantry's next assignment was Operation Killer, which brought it north and west of Pangnim-ni by 26 February. Then in the Hongchon-Hangye-Inje area, along Sayang-gang, the 32d Infantry took part in offensive operations and on 21 March, began to patrol and rebuild the weathered infrastructure. ON 5 April the regiment participated in Operation Rugged, launching an attack which brought it north of the 38th Parallel on 9 April, next capturing Yanggu on 16 April. Finally the 32d Infantry spent the rest of April repulsing attacks.

The 32d Infantry moved to line No-Name, south of Hongchon on 1 May 1951. Then on 21 May a counterattack began along the Hongchon-Chunchon-Hwachon road toward Line Topeka. By 24 May the 32d Infantry, as a part of Task Force Able, attacked and and occupied Chunchon and aided in cutting off thousands of enemy troops. The regiment's next assignment was Operation Piledriver, which sent it on an advance along the Hwachon-Kumwha front. Then on 23 June 1951, the 32d Infantry went into reserve along Line Kansas, to conduct training.

ON 9 August, the 32d Infantry was back on the front along Line Wyoming, where it sent out patrols and on 26 August began limited attacks toward an enemy hill, Hill 819, to the Pukhan River. The patrols continued until 21 September when the regiment participated in Operation Cleaver, a raid on the eastern end of the Iron Triangle.

After brief reserve duty, the 32d Infantry was on the front, northeast of the Hwachon Reservoir along Line Minnesota on 23 October, continuing to patrol. Throughout December and January, the regiment stayed on LIne Minnesota for the most part. ON 5 February, the 32d Infantry was involved in Operation Clam-up, wit the intent of luring Chinese patrols into ambuscades. From 21-23 February the 32d Infantry was relieved and went into reserve and training until it relieved the 2d Infantry Division by 28 April 1952, moving into positions on Line Missouri with responsibility for the Kansan-ni-Kumhwa Sector in the Iron Triangle. There the regiment patrolled from May to August. Then it spent most of September in reserve, going back on Line Missouri on 2 October and gaining elements of the 17th Infantry on 16 October.

Throughout October and November the action on the line increased. The 2d Infantry participated in Operation Showdown. Beginning with diversionary raids, then on 14 October, the regiment attacked Hill 589 and Jane Russell Hill, which were secured 2 days later, and defended form counterattack until 25 October.

Moving to positions on Line Jamestown along the sector form Ojoksan-ni to east of Sunchyon, the 32d infantry relieved the 2d Division on 29 December. There the regiment stayed, involved in patrol clashes until 27 February 1953, when it went into division

reserve on Line Wyoming until 2 April. The the regiment went back to Line Jamestown. From 16 to 18 April the 32d Infantry came under attack at Outpost Arsenal, but quickly repulsed the enemy. During May the regiment participated in scattered offensives an defensives, then through April patrolled and defended the front line. Then on 4 June the 32d Infantry was attacked at Outpost Yoke and Uncle, but after intense artillery and tank fire the enemy was repulsed.

On 6 July the 32d Infantry fought its last major battle of the war at Outpost Porkchop, which lasted 5 days and ended with the withdrawal of the 32d Infantry alone with other regiments. The withdrawal continued on 27 July 1953, to positions south of the Demilitarized Zone, when the armistice became effective ending the Korean War.

34th Infantry

The 34th Infantry Regiment was on occupation duty in Japan on 25 June 1950, when the North Korean People's Army crossed the 38th parallel to invade the Republic of Korea. The 34th Infantry was immediately engaged and sent to Pusan, arriving by 3 July.

On 13 July 1959, the 34th Infantry occupied positions at Kongju. The regiment was immediately pushed back in a fighting withdrawal westward to the Taejon Area. Stopping on 15 July, the regiment helped in trying to stop the NKPA's advance. Two days later the regiment was uprooted and withdrew west of Taejon. In Taejon, the 34th Infantry met the enemy on 20 July in the battle of Taejon, resulting in a further withdrawal of the regiment 5 km. east of Kumchon.

The 34th Infantry was relocated to the 8th Army reserve near Kumchon to reorganize.

Then under fierce enemy attack the 34th Infantry was pushed back to the Naktong River and on 30 July withdrew further to positions behind the Naktong. There the regiment stayed, holding the sector between Kaejin and Myon, The enemy arrived at the 34th Infantry's positions from 6-13 August, forming a bridgehead which remained through successful counterattacks until 17-19 August, when the entire 24th Division along with eh 1st Marine Brigade destroyed it, forcing the KNPA to retreat.

The 34th Infantry was relieved and established blocking positions around Taegu on 24 August 1950. Then two days later the regiment was disbanded, its elements attaching to the 19th and 21st Infantry, along with the 13th and 52d Field Artillery Battalions. There they stayed until 20 March 1951, when the 34th Infantry completed a field exercise and reverted to division control.

From March 1952 to February 1953, the 34th Infantry went through intensive training. Then in April 1953 the regiment was sent to Koje-do in emergency reserve in case of POW disturbances. From 5 to 16 July, the regiment was joined by the remainder of the 24th Infantry Division to provide security in Korea. Then on 18 July 1953, the regiment was attached to the Korean Communication's Zone. On 19 July the 34th Infantry was sent to 8th Army control due to enemy breakthrough in the main line of resistance in Kumsong. Then on 27 July 1953, the Korean War ended with an armistice.

35th Infantry

The 35th Infantry was on occupation duty in Japan on 25 June 1950, when the north Korean People's Army crossed the 38th parallel, invading the Republic of Korea and beginning the war. The 35th Infantry arrived in Pusan, Korea from 13 to 15 July 1950.

By 21 July the regiment was in division reserve while one battalion combat team guarded Pohang-dong. The first assignment in which the 34th Infantry participated was guarding the division defense line west of Hamchang. At that time the 34th Infantry was only one battalion, so the other battalion was ordered to join the regiment, but on the way , the 27th Infantry came into desperate need for reinforcements, and the regiment's battalion was used. The reinforced battalion helped the 27th Infantry to repel the NKPA.

By 29 July the 35th Infantry occupied positions on a new defensive line west of Sangju after being forced to retreat two days later the regiment moved to a line from Kumcho to Sabul-Myon to cut off the enemy from eastward movement. Withdrawing again form 1-3 August, the 35th Infantry moved south to Samningjin. The following day the regiment was assigned to a sector of the Naktong River defense line, where it absorbed elements of the 29th Infantry's 3d Battalion.

On 18 August the 35th Infantry suffered from an enemy offensive across the whole 25th Division front. At first the enemy was successful, but by the end of the day all positions were regained. Another powerful enemy attack hit the 35th Infantry's sector on 31 August and this time pushed through the regiment to Haman but was contained the following day. Again containing an enemy drive on 2 September, the 25th Infantry continued to defend its sector until 16 September, when it aided in forcing the enemy to withdraw across the Naktong River.

Finally able to advance, the regiment joined Task Force Torman on 24 September east of Hotan-ni, and continued advancing north ward, fighting through enemy blockades. On 30

September the 35th Infantry aided in capturing the port of Kunsan. Through October security missions and mopping-up operations along with training exercises involved the 34th Infantry in the Suwon-Hansong-Yoju vicinity.

Heading north by rail and motor convoy, the 35th Infantry headed for Tosong-ni, reaching Kaesong beginning on 6 November. Then the regiment moved south of Anju, preparing for an attack which sent it rapidly towards Yongsong-dong met an enemy attack on 25 November which sent the regiment back across the Chongchon River. By 28 November the 35th Infantry occupied new defensive positions west of Sunchon until 31 December when a major communist offensive force the regiment to withdraw to Seoul. Starting on 3 January 1951, the 35th Infantry withdrew further to gather at Chonan on 6 January to go into corps reserve.

Relieving the 27th Infantry on 19 January the regiment entered Suwon the next day. On 1 February the 35th Infantry pushed north again and on 6 February had captured Hill 431 against strong resistance. By 12 February Kimpo Airfield was secured and on 19-20 February reached the Han River. Forging the Han River the 35th Infantry helped launch Operation Ripper, pushing up to the Pukchan River by 15 March. By 29 March the 35th Infantry had aided in moving the front-line from Sorum-ni to Pochon.

Operation Rugged was launched on 3 April which resulted in the seizure of positions on Line Kansas. Then on 11 April the 35th Infantry participated in Operation Dauntless, bringing the regiment to the Chorwon Valley. There the enemy counter attacked form 22 to 26 April, forcing the regiment to retreat to Line Golden, 10 km northeast of Seoul. The regiment patrolled on Golden until 20 May when it took Line

Topeka, moving 50 miles north of the 38th Parallel. On 30 May the 35th Infantry had made it to the Chorwon-Kumwha sector.

Engaging in offensive operations in the Iron Triangle area from 1 to 20 June. Then on 20 June the 35th Infantry went into reserve, fortifying positions on Line Kansas and performing security missions. By 17 July 1951, the 35th Infantry moved to Line Wyoming near Chorwon, on the front, meeting heavy enemy attacks on 24 July and sending the regiment back to previous positions on Line Wyoming. On Wyoming the 35th Infantry patrolled throughout August. The regiment saw heavy action on 6 to 7 September when the enemy attacked Hills 717 and 682, and was forced to withdraw, suffering major casualties. Through October and November 1951, the 35th Infantry maintained positions along Line Wyoming south of Pyonggang until 16 to 18 December, when it moved to Kapyong to conduct training, then went into reserve.

By 23 February 1952, the 35th Infantry moved to Line Minnesota, assuming responsibility for the Paeam-Satae-ri and Ihyon-ni sectors. The regiment stayed in that area from May through August, patrolling, raiding and defending its front-line. On 10 September the 35th Infantry moved to Koje-do to guard the pow compound, and was placed under Korean Communications Zone control on 14 September.

The 35th Infantry was repositioned to reserve positions near Chipo-ri on 20 November. By 18 December the regiment was finally back on the front on Line Missouri. Then on 1 February training began for the 35th Infantry at Chugni. Again on the front-line on Line Wyoming, the regiment gained responsibility for the Kaekkyo-dong to Sokchuwon-ni area. Then on 2 June, a patrol from the 35th Infantry was attacked. By 8 July the regiment moved to Camp Casey in corps reserve where it stayed until 27 July 1953. On that date the 35th Infantry moved south of the Demilitarized Zone in accordance with the armistice ending the war.

38th Infantry

Located at Fort Lewis, Washington, the 38th Infantry, part of the Second Division was supervising training and conducting summer camp when the North Korean People's Army crossed the 38th parallel and invaded the Republic of Korea. The 38th Infantry was alerted to overseas duty on 9 July 1950. Departing from Tocoma on 5 August, the regiment began arriving in Pusan, Korea on 19-20 August, and immediately was ordered to Miryang. The first duty of the 38th Infantry was defending a stretch of the Naktong River with the 2d Division beginning from 22-24 August. From 31 August to 1 September the 38th Infantry repulsed an attack, then counterattacked on 3 September against fierce enemy resistance near Yongson. After fighting off more enemy attacks the regiment took Hill G285 on 6 September, but by 10 September the regiment had lost Hill 208 and lost and regained Hill 115. Elements of the 38th Infantry forged the Naktong against scattered resistance and seized Hill 208, south of Tugong-ni on 18 September. The next day the regiment expanded its bridgehead across the river. Going to further successes. the 38th Infantry aided in the capture of Hyopchon and Kochang on 25 and 26 September, and captured Chonju on 28 September, leading to weakened enemy resistance.

The 38th Infantry became responsible for the Suwon-Hansong and Yonju areas on 8 October, assembling between Seoul and Suwon on 14 October. Then throughout the rest of October the regiment changed responsibilities from security along the Han River on 17 October to Task Force Indianhead, and finally security along the line from Chongdon to Singye, and the main supply line from Pyongyang to the rear of I Corps. Gathering at Suchon on 11 November, the 38th Infantry soon established bolcking positions at Yongdon-ni on 8 November to protect the 8th Army's eastern flank, where it aggressively patrolled. The regiment engaged in annoffensive on 26 Nvember, advancing west of Tongchang. By 30 November the 38th Infantry along with the rest of the 2d Division suffered severe casualties fighting through road blocks south of Kunu-ri. After escaping annihilation, the 38th Infantry moved to Chungwha for rehabilitation on 1 December. Two days later it moved to the Musan-ni area, beginning to secure floating bridges on the Han River south east of Seoul on 9 December. On 2 January 1951, the 38th Infantry moved from the Han River north east to the Hongchon-Wonju area, occupying line Y on 5 January. On 7 January the enemy troops launched an offensive and despite the heavy attacks and bad weather conditions, the regiment repulsed them. Then on 12 January the regiment aided in seizing Hill 247 to the east of Wonju, but then was ordered to withdraw southwest of Wonchon to Mosan on 15 January. The activities during the rest of the month consisted of reconnaissance patrols from Wonjy to Hoengsong. From 11-12 February the 38th Infantry was again engaged as the enemy launched heavy attacks. The regiment was able to keep a strong defense from Wonjy tothe southwest despite enemy pressure. The regiment was relieved from the front and went to a location northwest of Chechon on 21 February. The next day the regiment participated in Operation Killer, which was designed to push the Chinese Communist Force north of the Han River. The 38th Infantry accomplished securing positions along the Wonju and Pangnim-ni road network. During March the 38th Infantry participated in offensives in the Wonju-Hoengsong area, fighting through mountains and valleys to reach Line Arizona by 4 March.

As an element of Operation Ripper, which had the purpose of pushing the communists back to the 38th parallel, the 38th Infantry captured Pungan-nion 15 March. As the 2d Infantry Division attacked against the Hwachon Reservoir, the 38th Infantry protected the right flank on 5 April. Two days later the regiment had reached Songsamni, and went into reserve. Then in the beginning of May, the 38th Infantry participated in patrols until 17 Mary, when the 38th Infantry participated in patrols until 17 May, when the 38th Infantry and the enetire 2d Division was attacked and withdrew to Line No-Name. On 24 May the regiment along with the 9th Infantry counterattacked to the northeast. Then the 38th Infantry moved to the front on Lone Kansas, north of Yanggu. The regiment attacked and secured Taeu San (Hill 1179) along the rim of the Punchbowl, fighting through sever enemy resistance, gaining ideal strategic positions. The 38th Infantry was again involved in a battle for Hill 983 on 19 August, which was not secured until 6 September. The regiment aided the Netherlands battalion in a fight for another hill, Hill 1220, which was secured on 15 October 1951. The 38th Infantry was moved to Hwachon from 23-25 October, remaining until 16 December. Next it moved to the eastern point of the Iron Triangle, (the Kumhwa-Chorwon-Pyonggang area) where the regiment defended and patrolled the area until January. From January through march, the 38th Infantry helped to strengthen its defenses on Line Missouri and continued patrolling. On 15 April 1952, guarded the POW compound on Koje-do Island remaining there until 5 July. After being in reserve, the regiment moved to Line Jamestown, where they encountered many patrol clashes. On 21 September, the 38th Infantry counterattacked against the enemy who had seized Outpost Old Baldy on 18 September.

On 25 October 1952, the regiment was relieved by the 9th Infantry, but was back on

Line Jamestown by 25 November. The regiment went into division reserves at Camp Indianhead, on 29 December. Then on 17 January 1953, the regiment arrived at Camp Casey. At the end of January, the 38th Infantry moved back to Line Jamestown, but this time in the area from Korangpo-ri to Kangeso-ri. All was relatively quiet except for an attack on Outpost Hook in the 38th Infantry's sector of Line Jamestown, which occurred on 13 February.

The 38th Infantry was relocated to Fort George during the beginning of April. Near Pongsugol, the 38th relocated to participate in intensive training excercises. On 15 July 1953, the 38th Infantry was back on the line in the Chorwon-Kumhwan sector. The 38th Infantry saw its last action of the war from 17 July to 19 July, when the regiment was attacked by enemy forces. Hand-to-hand combat occurred, and finally the enemy was repulsed. Finally on 27 July 1953, the Armistice went into effect and the 38th Infantry withdrew to new positions south of the Demilitarized Zone.

65th Infantry

On 25 June 1950 the 65th Infantry, an all Puerto Rican regiment, was stationed in San Juan, Puerto Rico. In August the regiment became the 3d regiment of the 3d Infantry Division and sailed straight to Korea. The 65th Infantry met up with the 3d Division from 10-21 November. The 65th Infantry first went to Wonsan to secure the area and protect the western flank of the X Corps and prepare for an offensive to the west, which it did from 22 to 30 November. In the beginning of December 1950, the 65th Infantry fought aggressively guerilla groups. Then on 11 December, defended the front of the Hamhung-Hungham defensive perimeter form advancing enemy troops. The next day the 65th Infantry aided in covering the withdrawl of X Corps through Hungnam. By 24

December the withdrawl was complete and the regiment sailed to Pusan, where it finished debarking on 29 December, and moved up to Tojiri.

Beginning on 31 December, the 65th Infantry went into rehabilitation and participated in intensive training. Then on 4 January, the regiment was put back on the front line near Chonan, to move onto Line Dog, a sector near Suwon and Kumyangjong-ni, which it occupied form 6 to 27 January 1951. On 6 February the 65th Infantry participated in numerous enemy attacks until the enemy counterattacked on 13-14 February, which was mopped up by the next day. Then a line was fortified along the south bank of the Han, called Line Boston. A From 1 to 15 March 1951, the 65th Infantry occupied bunkers and trenches along Line Boston, conducting patrols across the Han River. Then on 16 March the 65th Infantry aided in an attack across the river, driving towards Seoul followed by Operation Courage, reaching Uijongbu by 23 March. Attacking again, the regiment forged across the Sinchon River, reaching objectives along the Imjin River by 14 April, called Line Utah. Due to enemy counter attacks form 23 to 27 April the regiment withdrew just north of Seoul to Line Golden. Finally on 28 April the regiment along with the rest of the 3d Infantry Division went into reserve near Seoul.

On 17 May the 65th Infantry was employed near Hoensong to check enemy infiltration until 28 May. By the end of June, the regiment occupied the base of the Iron Triangle from Chorwon to Kumwha along Line Wyoming. In an attempt to gain high ground south of Pyonggang, while the I7th Infantry fought up the slopes on 1 July. Pyonggang was taken in one day, but the high ground was not taken until July 4, which the 65th Infantry aided in capturing .

Throughout the rest of July through September the 65th Infantry helped strengthened on Line Wyoming, meeting both light and strong resistance. On 18 and 29 September the regiment took part in one-day battles near Chorwon, which were part of Operation Cleanup which was cancelled due to bad weather and strong enemy resistance.

The 65th Infantry participated in Operation Commando, beginning on I3 October. Aiding in attacking and securing Hills 477, 281 and 395, the Dregiment reached Line Jamestown on 6 October, 10 km forward of Line Wyoming. After establishing defensive positions and repulsing enemy attack on Line Wyoming, the 65th Infantry was relieved and put in reserve, where it went through intense training. Then the regiment went back to Line Jamestown on 20 November in the Kangso-ri and Omgogae sector, patrolling and repulsing enemy attacks until 27 February, when the regiment went into reserve to conduct training.

Moving with the entire 3d Division the 65th Infantry moved to Field Training Command #1 on 28 April to conduct intensive training. On 1 July 1952, the regiment was back on the line in the Kwijon-ni and Sinhyon-ni sector, attacked to the Belgian Battalion, conducting patrols until 10 September, when it was moved to the 15th Infantry's sector on the 3d Division's line. Then on 16 September in the new sector the 65th Infantry was hit by an enemy offensive which led to the loss of Outpost Kelly on 18 September and Outpost Norion on 25 September. The 65th Infantry along with the rest of the 3d Infantry Division was relieved on 30 September 1952 and went into reserve near Yongpyong. Then from 24 to 25 October 1952, the regiment took over the Noltari-Sanggasan sector from the ROK 9th Division on Line Missouri. The 65th Infantry came under fire on 27 October and the enemy took Outpost Jackson Heights which the regiment failed to regain before it switched positions along the line with the 15th Infantry. The 65th and 15th Infantries continued to switch from reserve to the front-line throughout November and December.

From 26 to 29 December 1952, the 65th Infantry along with the entire 3d Division moved into reserve near Yongpong for training and security missions. Moving back to Line Missouri from 27 to 30 January 1953, the regiment conducted reconnaissance patrols and ambushes until 28 February, when it went into reserve. On 4 March, the 65th Infantry moved to a training area and was integrated from an all-Puerto Rica status to a standard infantry regimental composition, and then reorganized and went into training. On 16 May the 65th Infantry relieved the 15th Infantry on Line Missouri and two days later was attached to the Greek Battalion. In June 1953, the regiment received attacks against Outpost Harry. From 13 to 14 July, the 65th Infantry went into corps reserve, moving to the Pangtong-ni and Chuktae-ri zone to replace the Capitol ROK Division. By 20 July, the 65th had helped establish a new line after attacks against the enemy on 18 to 19 July. Finally on 27 July 1953, the 65th Infantry moved to news positions established behind the Demilitarized Zone when the cease-fire came into effect.

65th Regimental Combat Team

In June 1950, the 65th Infantry was stationed at San Juan, Puerto Rico. In August, it was alerted for Far East service as the third regiment of the 3rd Infantry Division. the 65th embarked from Puerto Rico on 25 August and sailed directly to Korea. During 22 to 23 September, the 65th began arriving at Pusan, Korea. In the meantime, the following units were shipped from Japan and joined the unit to form the 65th Regimental Combat team: the 58th Field Artillery Battalion; Company C, 10th Engineer Combat Battalion; and Battery C, 3rd Anti-Aircraft Artillery Battalion.

The 65th Regimental Combat Team (65th) was ordered to an assembly area in the vicinity of Samnangin for two weeks of intensive training prior to deployment. On 25 September, the 65th was attached to IX Corps and moved to Chongnyoung by the end of the month. The 3rd Battalion, 65th Infantry, landed at Pusan on 1 October.

On 4 October 1950, the 65th relieved the British 27th Commonwealth Brigade and secured the Waegwan-Kumchon main supply route. The 65th's participation was primarily engaged in anti-partisan activities and blocking the escape routes of various isolated North Korean Army contingents. The 65th undertook extensive patrolling operations in conjunction with the ROK 11th Division against scattered resistance. At various times during this period the regimental combat team was attached to IX Corps, the 2nd Infantry Division, and the 25th Infantry Division and served as Eighth Army reserve.

The 65th was assigned to the 3rd Infantry Division on 6 October 1950. On 22 October, the Eighth Army issued orders attaching the organization to its direct control in preparation for its movement to join ints parent formation. In the meantime, patrolling continued. A 65th patrol clashed with enemy elements near Nupong-jang as late as 29 October. On 31 October, the 65th assembled from its widely scattered positions and moved to Pusan for shipment by sea to Wonsan, Korea, to join the 3rd Infantry Division.

On 5 November 1950, the personnel of the 65th departed Pusan for Suwon aboard six ships.

The team's vehicles, artillery, rations, ammunition, and equipment were delayed awaiting three Landing Ships, Tank (LST). On 6 November, the 65th completed landing at Wonsan and was attached to X Corps. The 1st Battalion was attached temporarily to 1st Marine Division. The 2nd and 3rd Battalions were assigned missions of guarding railroad bridges and construction sites in vicinity of Wonsan, operating directly under X Corps. The 65th Infantry then joined the 3rd Infantry Division as a component infantry regiment.

160th Infantry

On 25 June 1950, the 160th Infantry was a segment of a National Guard Division in California, called to Federal Service in September 1950. The regiment was alerted for over seas movement to For East Command on 24 February 1951, The 160th Infantry was alerted for duty in Korea to relieve the 24th Infantry Division on 22 December. The regiment landed at Inchon, Korea on 11 January 1952.

The 160th Infantry headed towards the Kumsong-Chawapae-ri vicinity on 19 January to relieve the 19th Infantry on the front-line. The operation was completed by 28 January 1952. Throughout the regiment's first full month it participated in combat and reconnaissance patrols and company raids. The regiment's first operation, Operation Clam-up, was launched on 10 February, lasting until 15 February with the purpose of luring out the Chinese Communist troops and setting up ambuscades.

Through March the 160th Infantry maintained the front-line and on 1 April was moved to a new sector on the front, along the segment form Kumwha-Kumsong where it patrolled all through April. In May defenses were tightened due to increased enemy fire. Moving to the

outpost line on 12 June, the 160th Infantry consolidated positions, obtaining better terrain. From 26 to 28 June the regiment went into corps reserve.

In reserve at Field Training Command #5, the 160th Infantry went through training and rehabilitation. Continuing training on 13 July near Kapyong, the regiment secured Line Kansas, a back up defensive line, and performed security missions until mid-October. On 16 October 1952, the regiment went back to the front in the Paeam-Ihyon-Ni area. Receiving heavy enemy fire on 26 October, the 160th Infantry engaged in combat in the Hertbreak Ridge area, but finally repulsed the enemy.

From November 1952 to January 1953, the regiment defended its positions and sent out reconnaissance and combat patrols. Then form 28 to 31 January, the regiment was relieved and went into reserve at Hwachon on 11 February. On 17 February elements of the 160th Infantry gained responsibly for the security in the Sangdong Mien area. After going into reserve on 19 April the regiment came out of reserve on 27 April and took a place on the front-line along the northern rim of the Punchbowl. Next it moved to the Ihyon-ni and Kalbakkumi sectors during May 1953.

By 11 July the 160th Infantry relieved positions along the Paeam to Ihyon-ni sector, shortly moving near Inje into reserve on 20 July. The regiment was in Inje when the armistice became effective on 27 July 1953, and it moved to positions south of the Demilitarized Zone.

179th Infantry

On 25 June 1950, when the North Koreans crossed the 38th parallel beginning the Korean

War, the 179th Infantry was part of a National Guard division from Oklahoma. It was ordered in active Federal service on 1 September 1950. The regiment carried out extensive training until 20 April 1951 when it arrived in Japan, and assumed security duty and continued to train. Then on 18 November 1951, the regiment was alerted for duty in Korea, where it arrived at Inchon on 7 December.

Upon arrival, the 179th Infantry occupied positions along Line Jamestown, which extended from Omgogae to Noltari. Through January the patrols and three major raids were carried out by the regiment. The raids were against the area around Hill 223 and 290, and were met with heavy resistance but succeeded in inflicting many enemy casualties.

From 10 to 16 February, participating in Operation Clam Up, the 179th Infantry aided in luring out Chinese forces for ambushes. During March patrolling continued and on 22 March and enemy attack against an outpost in the 179th Infantry's sector was met with heavy resistance which regained the partially overrun position. Line Jamestown continued to be occupied by the regiment through April and May.

The 179th Infantry was relieved on 2 June 1952, but was back on the front with an attached Philippine battalion on 17 June. In the beginning of July the 179th Infantry saw its heaviest fighting, receiving enemy attacks with increased patrols and raids. After heavy combat the regiment was relieved and went into reserve at Yanggu, where it remained conducting training, improving combat efficiency and maintaining equipment.

Back to the front line on Line Minnesota, the 179th Infantry occupied its positions between 21 and 25 September 1952. During the relief, the regiment was attacked, but regained positions. By 25 September the 179th Infantry went into division reserve at Inje until 27 October, when it relieved the 279th Infantry and reoccupied positions on Lie Minnesota. Patrols were conducted through November and December with the exception of a raid against Hill 812, guarded by the 179th Infantry on 25 December. By 30 December the regiment was in reserve at Inje until 21 February 1953.

Relieving the 279th Infantry o the main line of resistance between Paeam and Ihyon-ni on 20 February, the 179th Infantry gained positions and began patrolling throughout the remainder of February and March. Receiving enemy attack on 15 April, the 179th Infantry held its position with grenades and weapon fire, lasting 45 minutes. After skirmishes and patrols through June, the regiment went to a new area in the Tongsongol-Paeam sector on 19 July. Finally in accordance with the long awaited armistice, the 179th Infantry withdrew to positions south of the Demilitarized Zone.

180th Infantry

On 25 June 1950, the 180th Infantry was part of a National Guard division from Oklahoma. It was ordered in active Federal service on 1 September 1950, and carried out extensive training until 20 April 1951 when it arrived in Japan and assumed security duty and continued to train. Then on 18 November 1951, the regiment was alerted for duty in Korea, where it arrived on 5 December.

Upon arrival the 180th Infantry immediately was mobilized, moving up to Line Jamestown along the front to relieve the 8th Cavalry on 16 December. On Jamestown he regiment defended and strengthened positions throughout January. During the month, participating in 3 major raids, elements of the 180th Infantry met strong resistance in the Hill 223 and Hill 290 areas, ending up inflicting heavy casualties. Also participating in Operation Clam Up from 10 to 16 February, the regiment aided in luring the enemy into ambushes.

On 17 March, the 180th Infantry went into reserve, initiating Operation Rehearse, a movement from a secondary defensive zone on Line Wyoming, which became a requirement during relief missions. Exactly two months later, the regiment was back on Line Jamestown, initiating patrolling activities until 4 June. On that date the 180th Infantry participated in Operation Counter, aiding the 279th Infantry in taking 10 Enemy outposts by 12 June. The second phase of the offensive commenced on 12 June, and resulted in securing Outpost Eerie and objectives on Pokkae Ridge after bitter attacks and defense against counter attacks.

The 180th Infantry saw its heaviest fighting in the first two weeks of July 1952, with major enemy attacks on Jamestown, which resulted in increased patrolling. Finally by 18 July the 280th Infantry had been relieved, going into corps reserve at Hwachon. After training throughout August the 280th Infantry launched Operation Plan Eightbird on 21 through 25 September. The operation brought the regiment to positions on Line Minnesota where it experienced heavy combat on 26-27 September. After the positions on Minnesota were stabalized, patrols went out through October and November.

O 24 to 27 November, the 180th Infantry was relieved and went into division reserve, moving to reserve at Kowan-tong on 30 December. Then o 22 January 1953, the regiment relieved an element of the 40th Division on the front-line between Paeam and Ihyon-ni. From February through May the 180th Infantry was involved i several skirmishes, patrols and raids. Holding positions near Sandbag Castle, the 180th Infantry repulsed enemy attack o 1 June after five hours of fighting. During June and most of July the regiment switched positions with other regiment but stayed on the front-line until 19 July, when it went to reserve positions. Finally on 27 July 1953, the 180th Infantry withdrew to positions south of the Demilitarized Zone in accordance with the armistice.

187th Airborne Regimental Combat Team

Campaigns: North Korean aggression; Communist China aggression; First UN counteroffensive; Communist China spring offensive; Korea, summer-fall 1952; Korea, summer 1953. *Decorations*: Republic of Korea Presidential Unit Citation. *Commanders*: Col. Frank S. Bowen, Jr. (Aug. 50-Oct. 50), BG Frank S. Bowen, Jr. (Oct. 50)

During August, 1950, the 187th Airborne Regimental Combat Team (187th) was detached from the 11th Airborne Division at Fort Campbell, Kentucky, for service in Korea. The team's planning group arrived at Camp Drake, Japan, on 18 August and was immediately assigned to the Eighth Army.

On 6 September the 187th departed California and arrived in Japan on 20 September. It consisted of three battalions of the 187th Airborne Infantry, the 674th Airborne Field Artillery Battalion (reinforced), and Company A of 127th Airborne Engineer Battalion. Four days later, on 24 September, the 3rd Battalion was airlifted to Kimpo Airfield west of Seoul, Korea with the mission to secure the airfield prior to the arrival of the team. Initially, the 187th was attached to

Y Corps as a general reserve in the Inchon-Seoul area and cleared the Kimpo Peninsula west of Seoul. On 4 October, the unit was attached to I Corps and scheduled for deployment in a parachute spearhead capacity above the 38th parallel.

The first combat parachute jump of the war was executed on 20 October into the Sukchon and Sunchon areas north of Pyongyang, the North Korean capital. In the clearing operation that followed, 75 GIs were found executed at Sunchon. On 23 October the 187th went into I Corps Reserve at Pyongyang, providing security for the airfield and bridges across the Taedong River. This responsibility was expanded on 1 November to include security of the Eight Army's main supply routes connecting Pyongyand, Chinnampo Port, and Haeju.

The 187th fought in the vicinity of Singye from 18 to 27 November, when the Chinese Communist counteroffensive forced the Eight Army to commence a general withdrawal. at that time it was directed to safeguard the main supply route from Seoul to Pyongyang and to provide security and cover for withdrawing units. On 17 December the 187th moved to Suwon in Eighth Army Reserve. By 3 January 1951, it was ordered to move without delay to Ichon to block enemy movement west of the Corps boundary.

On 12 January the unit went into X Corps Reserve and moved its command post to Punggi. Three days later, on 15 January, elements of the 187th engaged an estimated 300 enemy soldiers one mile north of Andong as it screened the rear area in the Tanyang-Punggi sectors. The unit was on the move again by 2 February to positions in the vicinity of Wonju. This status was maintained until 21 February, when it went into

Reserve. On 27 February, the unit was relocated to K2 Airfield at Taegu for intensive training in parachute operations.

Operation Tomahawk, as the last wartime jump was called, took place on the morning of 23 March, with an air assault on Munsant-Ni, 20 miles northwest of Seoul. Relieved by advancing units on 29 March, the 187th returned to Taegu, where it engaged in training, preparing for various contingency operations. On 21 May, it was moved from reserve to front under X Corps command and prepared for offensive action.

Commencing on 25 May, the 187th spearheaded the attack on the Inje during the offensive stages of fighting in the Soyang river sector. By 2 June, it was relieved, then moved to Wonju as part of Eighth Army Reserve. Starting on 22 June, it moved to Pusan for transfer to Japan. Embarkation onto ships was completed by 26 June. The unit moved to Camp Chickamuaga, Japan, and was reassigned to General Headquarter, Far East Command.

Prisoner disturbances on Koje-do Island precipitated the return of the 187th to Korea. On 16 May 1952, the infantry units were alerted for security duty on Koje-Do. The first elements arrived at K9 Airfield from Japan at 8:20 PM on the same day. The entire personnel of the 187th were transported from Suyong to Koje-do in two landing ship tank (LST). With the island secured, on 17 July, the 187th was relieved from prison guard duty, shipped to Pusan and further transported by train to Taegu for training under Eighth Army control. The rest of the team, including the 674th Airborne Field Artillery Battalion and the 187th Anti-Aircraft Artillery Battery arrived by ship at Inchon on 14 July and were attached to I Corps for operational control.

By 7 August, the 187th had moved to Chongong-ni near the front line and passed to the operational control of I Corps. All organic elements being reassembled on 9 August, it moved to relieve the 17th Infantry on the mainline of resistance just west of Chorwon. It remained in this position until 3 October at which time it was withdrawn from the Eighth Army front line and moved to Yonchow. Eventually the unit was embarked for Japan by ship on 16 October 1952.

The 187th returned to Korea for the final time on 22 June 1953. In July, the enemy penetrated the Corps main line of resistance in the Kumsong salient and forced back the ROK Capital Division. In order to restore the situation in that sector, the 187th, under operational control of the 3rd Infantry Division, moved into position on the Division's left flank. By 20 July, the new line was organized and defensive positions were established. Shortly after the armistice agreement became effective on 27 July 1953, the 187th began withdrawing to newly mandated positions south of the demilitarized zone.

During the course of the war, 442 men of the 187th were killed in action and 1,656 were hospitalized from wounds received as a result of combat action.

223d Infantry

On 25 June 1950, the 223d Infantry was a segment of a National Guard division in California, activated to Federal service on 1 September 1950. The regiment was alerted for overseas movement to Far East Command on 24 February 1951. The 223d Infantry was alerted for duty in Korea to relieve the 24th Infantry Division on 22 December and landed in Korea on 24 January 1952.

Upon arrival in Korea the 223d Infantry moved to the Kumsong-Chawapae-ri area on the central front and relieved the 21st Infantry on 28 January. Throughout February 1952, the regiment took part in patrols and raids. Participating in Operation Clam up form 10-15 February, the 223d Infantry lured enemy Chinese forces into ambushes. March was characterized by patrols and fortifying positions on the front-line. Then in April the regiment moved to new positions on the line in the Kumwha-Kumsong sector.

Increased enemy fire was received in the 223d Infantry's sector during May, which led to reinforcement in defensive positions. While most of the regiment went into Field Training Command#5 in corps reserve, the 3d Battalion of the 223d Infantry went to secure the Sangdong Mines. Then by 19 July the regiment was still training, but near Kapyong, strengthening Line Kansas, and performing security missions until the end of October.

On 31 October 1952, the 223d Infantry was redeployed in the Paeam-Ihyon-Ni sector after coming out of reserve. Throughout November and December the 223d Infantry was involved in patrolling and improving defensive positions along the line. Then on 8 January 1953, the regiment went into division reserve, moving to corps reserve at Kowantong on 11 February.

Moving back to the front-line, this time along the northern rim of the Punchbowl on 27 April, the 223d Infantry stayed until May when it was deployed along the Ihyon-ni and Kalbakkumi sectors. Moving to its last front-line positions on 11 July, the regiment was on Heartbreak Ridge when the armistice became effective on 27 July 1953, when the regiment withdrew to new positions south of the Demilitarized Zone.

224th Infantry

On 25 June 1950, the 224th Infantry was part of a National Guard division in California. The regiment was alerted for overseas movement to Far East Command on 24 February 1951. The 224th Infantry alerted for duty in Korea n 22 December, to relieve the 24th Infantry Division. The regiment landed at Inchon, Korea on 3 February 1952.

The 224th Infantry's first assignment was in the central area of the front line along the Kumsong-Chawapae-ri sector, where the regiment relieved the 5th RCT on 10 February. During March the 224th Infantry fortified its positions. The regiment was then ordered to division reserve. Due to the 40th Division's changed boundary, the 224th Infantry moved to positions on the front to the left of the 223d Infantry. Engaged in combat on 16 April the regiment launched an operation which resulted in the occupation of favorable terrain for advanced patrol bases.

Strong enemy fire in May caused the 224th Infantry to strengthen defenses. Patrols and ambushes along with fortifying front-line positions continued through the end of June. On 5 July the regiment was attached to the 2d Logistical Command and guarded the pow compound at Koje-do until 10 September. Then on 16 October 1952, the left of the Paeam-Ihyon-Ni sector was taken over by the 224th Infantry. There the regiment remained until January 1953 and was involved in defending positions, limited combat and patrols.

On 8 January 1953, the 224th Infantry reverted to division reserve, then on 11 February the regiment went into corps reserve at Inje, where it trained and was rehabilitated. Transfering again to division reserve, this time

the 45th Infantry Division's, the 224th Infantry trained until 14 April 1953, when it relieved the 5th RCT on the front, along the Ihyon-ni and Kalbakkumi sectors, the 224th Infantry strengthened its new defensive positions.

Occupying positions in the new sector, the regiment conducted patrols and on 2 June saw heavy combat, but defeated the enemy, and remained in position. Transfering again to a sector along Heartbreak Ridge on 11 July, the 224th Infantry held its positions until 27 July 1953, when the armistice became effective and the regiment withdrew south of the 38th parallel.

279th Infantry

At the start of the Korean War, 25 June 1950, the 279th Infantry was part of a National Guard Division in Oklahoma, ordered into active Federal service on 1 September 1950. The regiment began intensive training in the states then moved to Otaru, Japan in April for further training and on 20 April 1951, assumed security responsibility. Departing Japan on 24 December 1951, and arriving at Inchon, Korea on 28 December.

Upon arrival in Korea, the 279th Infantry was put in division reserve until 15 January 1952, when it occupied positions on Line Jamestown. During the month ambush and reconnaissance patrols were prevalent. The regiment's first operation was Clam-up, a tactic to lure the Chinese forces into ambush situations. On 27 February, the 279th Infantry reverted to reserve, coming out to relieve the 18th Infantry on Line Jamestown on 17 March.

Conducting patrols and defending the front-line throughout April, the 279th Infantry was relieved on 28 April until 17 May when it relieved the 18th Infantry. Then it received minor attacks and aided in repulsing enemy attack on Hill 200. Activity increased in June with Operation Counter, beginning on 4 to 12 June, which led to the seizure of ten outpost positions.

Through July the 279th Infantry saw its heaviest fighting, with repeated enemy assaults on outpost positions on Line Jamestown. After serious combat, the regiment was relieved by the 2d Infantry Division from 14 to 18 July, going into corps reserve at Inje. In reserve it underwent major training through September.

Between 21 and 25 September 1952, the 179th Infantry moved to Line Minnesota, encountering enemy attack on the first night, but securing positions by 25 September. The next day, the regiment received scattered attacks along its sector. From October to December the 279th Infantry traded positions, but stayed on Line Minnesota, actively fortifying the defensive line and patrolling. Finally from 27 to 30 December, the regiment was relieved and reverted to reserve at Hwachon.

After a month of being in reserve, the 279th Infantry helped relieve the 40th Infantry Division between Paeam and Ihyon-ni on 28 to 31 January 1953. Throughout February and March the regiment participated in extensive but minor patrolling actions. Then on 17 March the regiment became responsible for guarding pow compounds at Koje-do, under the control of he Korea Communications Zone.

Reverting from Korean Communications Zone control to corps control on 4 June, then on 22 June relieved the 180th Infantry on Line Minnesota. The regiment saw its last combat on the nights of 14-15 July and 17-18 July. Finally

on 27 July 1953, the 279th Infantry moved to new positions behind the Demilitarized Zone in accordance with the armistice.

The Navy's Role in Limited War

by Adm. Arleigh A. Burke, USN, Chief of Naval Operations

When the Communists invaded Korea on June 25, 1950, the United States was neither expecting nor prepared to fight in that remote area. They apparently had analyzed United States willingness, readiness, and ability to fight and concluded that we would simply watch and complain, but not fight. The Communists apparently saw an opportunity to seize some additional free world territory with little risk and at little cost.

The United States Army had no troops in Korea, the United States Air Force had only a few wings in the Far East, and the United States Navy had only one cruiser, four destroyers, and a few minesweepers in the Sea of Japan.

With so few combat forces initially available, control of the seas (taken for granted as it is too often the case) was a prerequisite in implementing the United Nations decision to resist aggression against the Republic of Korea. Without the capability to use the seas, the decision to intervene on a rocky peninsula half-a-world away would have been meaningless and unenforceable. With control of the seas, the decision was sound and reasonable.

Once the decision was made, ships of the free world navies converged on Korea from every one of the seven seas—combatant ships, oilers, supply ships, ships loaded with troops, ammunition, guns, tanks, and aircraft; ships from the

South China Sea, the Indian Ocean, the Pacific, the Atlantic, and from the far-away Mediterranean.

Control of the seas gave the United Nations the advantage of mobility—the opportunity to consolidate and combine the free world's economic and military strength. Seapower brought American troops, first from Japan, later from the United States. Seapower defeated the initial aggression with the classic amphibious assault at Inchon. Seapower made it possible to redeploy the U.S. forces from Hungnam. Seapower helped to limit the conflict.

Use of the seas was denied to the Communists. This placed serious limitations on their ability to build up military power in Korea. It exposed the land flanks of the North Koreans (and later the Red Chinese). It denied them easy resupply by sea.

The Communists' attempt to seize Korea by military action was a failure. But this failure does not mean an abandonment of military adventures by the Communists. They will try again whenever other means fail or when they see a weakness they can exploit or find a vacuum they can fill.

The Communists have stated repeatedly that any means may be used to attain their goal of world domination, including war. The most important tenet of Communism—the one given most stress in their doctrine—is that Communism must continuously strive to possess all power, and conversely to destroy all rival power. This proposition is basic to Communism. It must be borne in mind constantly when dealing with Communists. Their tenet and their goal do not change.

There are many other explosive areas in the world. They are explosive because of this standing threat and this goal of Communism.

While the Korean War was unusual in many respects, it nevertheless has great meaning and significance for the future. In 1957 terminology, it would be called a "limited war." In the thermonuclear age, as major nations of the world improve their capability to wreck mutual destruction upon one another, the probability of all-out nuclear war is diminished. The probability of limited war is increased. It is important that the Korean War receive careful study. It is the first limited war the United Nations have fought against Communist totalitarianism.

The naval history of the Korean War is outlined in this book in great detail. The authors have distilled from it the lessons, results, and significance of the Korean War. This effort should be of great interest and benefit to every student of international or military affairs.

Of the many lessons of the Korean War, three stand out above all others: 1. The military forces of the United States must be vigilant and ready to defeat aggression in any area and in any form, whether it be large or small, atomic or conventional. Our hope, of course, is that our visible, vigilant strength will discourage Communist aggression. To do so, we must be capable of effective counteraction, ranging from the use of a squad of Marines to the use of atomic-tipped ballistic missiles. Our Navy must have many different arrows in its quiver. 2. Control of the sea is prerequisite to victory in modern war, whatever its size, type or scope. 3. The Korean War was a limited war. A limited war is the type of war most likely to occur in the thermonuclear age. (Quoted from "*The Sea War in Korea*," Malcolm W. Cagle, Commander, USN and Frank A. Manson, Commander, USN, U.S. Naval Institute, Annapolis, MD.)

Task Organization for Pohang, Inchon, Wonsan and Hungnam

Task Force Pohang Landing - 18 July 1950
Attack Force (TF-90)
91.0 Landing Force
90.1 Tactical Air Control
90.2 Transport Group
 Mt McKinley (AGC)
 Cavalier (APA)
 Union (AKA)
 Titania (AKA)
 Oglethorpe (AKA)
90.3 Tractor Group
611 (LST)
 Lipan (ATF)
 Conserver (ARS)
5 LSU (5 LSU)
 Cree (temporary)
96.5 Gunfire Support Group
 Juneau (CLAA)
 Kyes
 Higbee
 Collett
 HMAS *Bataan*
90.4 Protective Group
90.41 COMINRON
 Pledge (AM)
 Kite (AMS)
 Chatterer (AMS)
 Redhead (AMS)
90.42 COMINDIV
 Partridge (AM)
 Mockingbird (AM)
 Osprey (AM)
90.43
Higbee (DD)
Kyes (DD)
90.5 Close Air Support Group - Aircraft as assigned from 7th Fleet
90.6 Deep Air Support Group - Aircraft as assigned from 7th Fleet
90.7 Reconnaissance Group
 Diachenko (APD)
UDT 3 (DET)
90.8 Control Group
 Diachenko
 Lipan (ATF)
90.9 Beach Group
Beachmaster Unit One (DET)
UDT 3 (DET)
90.20 Administrative Element
 Conserver (ARS)
 Lipan (ATF)
 HMS *Main* (At Sasebo) (AH)
90.0 Follow-up Shipping Group
 USNS *Ainsworth* (AP)
 USNS *Shanks* (AP)
7 LST
96.2 Patrol Aircraft Group - Aircraft as assigned

Task Force Inchon Invasion - 15 Sept. 1950

Joint Task Force Seven
Task Force 90-Attack Force
(92.1) Landing Force 1st Marine Div. (Reinforced)
(90.00) Flagship Element
 Mt McKinley (AGC)
 Eldorado (AGC)
(90.01) Tactical Air Control Element

Tactical Air Squadron I
(90.02) Naval Beach Group Element
(90.02.1) Headquarters Unit
(90.02.2) Beachmaster Unit
(90.02.3) Boat Unit I
(90.02.4) Amphibious Construction Battalion
(90.02.5) Underwater Demolition Team Unit
(90.03) Control Element
 Diachenko (APD)
(90.03.1) Control Unit Red
 Horace A. Bass (APD)
(90.03.2) Control Unit Green
PCEC 896 (PCEC)
(90.03.3) Control Unit Blue
 Wantuck (APD)
(90.04) Administrative Element
(90.04.1) Service Unit
 Consolation (AH)
12 LSU
(90.04.2) Repair and Salvage Unit
 Lipan (ATF)
 Cree (ATF)
 Arikara (ATF)
 Conserver (ARS)
 Askari (ARL)
 YTB 405
 Gunston Hall (LSD)
 Fort Marion (LSD)
 Comstock (LSD)
(90.1) Advance Attack Group
(92.12.3) Advance Landing Force 3rd Battalion (RCT) 5th Marines
(90.11) Transport Element
 Fort Marion
3 LSU embarked
(90.11.1) Transport Unit
 Horace A. Bass
 Dianchenko
 Wantuck
(90.2) Transport Group
 G. Clymer (APA)
 Cavalier (APA)
 Pickaway (APA)
 Henrico (APA)
 Noble (APA)
 Union (AKA)
 Alshain (AKA)
 Achernar (AKA)
 Oglethorpe (AKA)
 Seminole (AKA)
 Thuban (AKA)
 Whiteside (AKA)
 Washburn (AKA)
 President Jackson (AP)
 Gunston Hall (LSD)
 Comstock (LSD)
3 LSU embarked
(90.3) Tractor Group
LST 611; 715; 742; 802; 845; 1048; 1123; 1134; 1138; 857; 859; 898; 914; 973; 799; 883; 975
SCAJAP LST
LST 419 (LSM)
(90.4) Transport Division 14
7th RCT U.S. Marines and MAG 33
 Bayfield (APA)
 Okanogan (APA)
 Bexar (APA)

Thomas Jefferson (APA)
Algol (AKA)
Winston (AKA)
Montague (AKA)
Catamount (LSD)
Colonial (LSD)
(90.5) Air Support Group
(90.51) CVE Element
 Badoeng Strait (CVE)
 Sicily (CVE)
(90.52) CVE Screen
 Hanson (DDR)
 Taussig (DD)
 George K. Mackenzie (DD)
 Ernest G. Small (DD)
(90.6) Gunfire Support Groups
(90.61) Cruiser Element
90.6.1 Fire Support Unit I
 Toledo (DA)
 Rochester (CA)
 HMS *Kenya* (CL)
 HMS *Jamaica* (CL)
(90.62) Destroyer Element
90.6.2 Fire Support Unit I
 Mansfield (DD)
 De Haven (DD)
 Lyman K. Swenson (DD)
(90.63) Fire Support Unit 3
 Collett (DD)
 Gurke (DD)
 Henderson (DD)
(90.63) LSMR Element
90.6.4 Fire Support Unit 4
LSMR 401; 403; 404
(90.7) Screening and Protective Group
 Rowan (DD)
 Southerland (DDR)
 Bayonne (PF)
 Newport (PF)
 Evansville (PF)
 HMS *Mounts Bay* (PF)
 HMS *Whitesand Bay* (PF)
 HMNZS *Tutira* (PF)
 HMNZS *Pukaki* (PF)
 RFS *La Grandiere*
 Pledge (AM)
 Partridge (AMS)
 Mocking Bird (AMS)
 Kite (AMS)
 Osprey (AMS)
 Redhead (AMS)
 Chatterer (AMS)
(90.8) Second Echelon Movement Group
92.2 7th Infantry Division - Reinforced
 USS *General G.M. Randall* (AP)
 USS *General F.C. Breckinridge* (AP)
 USS *General H.W. Butner* (AP)
 USNS *Fred C. Ainsworth* (T-AP)
 USNS *General Leroy Eltinge* (T-AP)
 USNS *Aiken Victory* (T-AP)
 USNS *Private Sadao S. Munemori* (T-AP)
 SS *African Rainbow*
 SS *African Pilot*

SS *Robin Kirk*
SS *Helen Lykes*
SS *Meredith Victory*
SS *Empire Marshall*
SS *Mormacport*
SS *Lawrence Victory*
SS *Southwind*
SS *Beaver Victory*
SS *Robin Goodfellow*
SS *California Bear*
(90.9) Third Echelon Movement Group
X Corps Troops
 USS *General William A. Mann* (AP)
 USNS *General William Weigel* (T-AP)
 USNS *Marine Phoenix* (T-AP)
 SS *Robin Trent*
 SS *Dolly Turman*
 SS *Charles Lykes*
 SS *Twin Falls Victory*
 SS *American Veteran*
 SS *American Attorney*
 SS *Empire Wallace*
 SS *Greenbay Victory*
 SS *P&T Navigator*
 SS *Luxembourg Victory*
 SS *Belgium Victory*
 SS *Bessemer Victory*
 SS *Cotton State*
(91) Blockade and Covering Force
 HMS *Triumph* (CVL)
 HMS *Ceylon* (CL)
 HMS *Cockade*
 HMS *Charity* (DD)
 HMCS *Cayuga* (DD)
 HMCS *Sioux* (DD)
 HMCS *Athabaskan* (DD)
 HMAS *Bataan* (DD)
 HMAS *Warramunga* (DD)
 HNethMS *Evertsen* (DD)
ROK Naval Forces
 Paik Doo San (PC 701)
 Kum Kang San (PC 702)
 Philippine Sea (PC 703)
 Chi Ri San (PC 704)
 YMS 302; 303; 306; 307; 501; 502; 503; 510; 512; 515; 518
Task Force 77-Fast Carrier Group
Carrier Division I
 Philippine Sea (CV)
Carrier Division 3
 Valley Forge (CV)
Carrier Division 5
 Boxer (CV)
(77.1) Support Group
 Worcester (CL)
 Manchester (CL)
(77.2) Screen Group
DesDiv 31
 Shelton (DD)
 James E. Kyes (DD)
 Eversole (DD)
 Higbee (DDR)
DesDiv 111
 Wiltsie (DD)
 Theodore E. Chandler (DD)
 Hamner (DD)
 Chevalier (DDR)
DesDiv 112

Ozbourn (DD)
McKean (DD)
Hollister (DD)
Frank Knox (DDR)
CortRon I
 Fletcher (DDE)
 Radford (DDE)
Task Force 79-Commander Service Squadron 3
(79.1) Mobile Logistic Service Group
 Cacapon (AO)
 Passumpsic (AO)
 Mount Katmai (AE)
 Graffias (AF)
(79.2) Objective Area Logistic Group
 Navasota (AO)
 Virgo (AKA)
 Grainger (AK)
 Hewell (AKL)
 Ryer (AKL)
 Estero (AKL)
(79.3) Logistic Support Group
 Piedmont
 Dixie
 Kermit Roosevelt
 Jason
 Cimarron (AO)
 Warrick (AKA)
 Uvalde (AKA)
 Nemasket (AOG)
 Karin (AF)
(79.4) Salvage and Maintenance Group
 Mataco (ATF)
 Bolster (ARS)
Task Force 99-Patrol and Reconnaisance Force
 USS *Curtiss* (AV)
 USS *Gardiners Bay* (AVP)
 USS *Salisbury Sound* (AV)

Task Force Wonsan - 25 June to 15 November 1950
Joint Task Force Seven
90 Attack Force
(92.1) Landing Force - 1st Marine Div. (Reinforced)
(90.00) Flagship Element
 Mount McKinley (AGC)
(90.01)'Tactical Air Control Element
(90.01.1) TacRon 1
(90.01.2) TacRon 3
(90.02) Naval Beach Group Element
(90.02.2) Beachmaster Unit
(90.02.3) Boat Unit One
(90.02.4) Amphibious Construction Battalion
(90.02.5) UDT Unit
(90.10) Flagship Element
 Eldorado (AGC)
(90.1.1) Medical Unit
 Consolation
LST 898; 975
(90.1.2) Repair and Salvage Unit
 Lipan (ATF)
 Cree (ATF)
 Arikara (ATF)
 Conserver (ARS)
 Askari (ARL)

Gunston Hall (LSD)
Fort Marion (LSD)
Comstock (LSD)
Catamount (LSD)
Colonial (LSD)
(90.1.3) Service Unit
LSU
(90.2) Transport Group
(90.21) Transport Division
Able
   Bayfield (APA)
   Noble (APA)
   Cavalier (APA)
   Okanogan (APA)
   Washburn (AKA)
   Seminole (AKA)
   Titania (AKA)
   Oglethorpe (AKA)
   Achernar (AKA)
   Marine Phoenix (TAP)
(90.22) Transport Division
Baker
   Henrico
   George Clymer
   Pickaway
   Bexar
   Union (AKA)
   Algol (AKA)
   Alshain (AKA)
   Winston (AKA)
   Montague (AKA)
   USNS Aiken Victory
   (TAP)
   SS Robin Goodfellow
   (AK)
(90.3) Tractor Group
LST 1123 (F), 715, 742, 799,
802, 845, 883, 898, 914, 973,
975, 1048
1138 (Assigned later to Iwon)
SCAJAP LST
LSM 419
   Gunston Hall (LSD)
   Fort Marion (LSD)
   Comstock (LSD)
   Catamount (LSD)
   Colonial (LSD)
3 LSU embarked
(90.4) Control Group
PCEC 896 (Central Control
Vessel)
(90.4.1) Control Unit Blue
   Wantuck (APD)
(90.4.2) Control Unit Yellow
   H.A. Bass (APD)
(90.6) Reconnaissance Group
   H.A. Bass (APD)
   Wantuck (APD)
(95.2) Gunfire Support Group
   Helena (CA)
   Rochester (CA)
   Toledo (CA)
   HMS Ceylon (CL)
   DESRON Nine (3DD)
   HMS Cockade (DD)
   HMCS Athabaskan (DD)
   HMAS Warramunga
   (DD)
LSR Div-11; 401; 403; 404
(95.6) Minesweeping and
Protective Group***
   Collett (DD)
   Diachenko (APD)
   Doyle (DMS)
   Endicott (DMS)
   Pledge (AM)
   Incredible (AM)
   Kite (AMS)
   Merganser (AMS)
   Mocking Bird (AMS)

Osprey (AMS)
Partridge (AMS)
Redhead (AMS)
Chatterer (AMS)
HMS Mounts Bay (PF)
HMSNZ Pukaki (PF)
HMSNZ Putira (PF)
FS La Grandiere (PF)
Curtiss (AV)
Gardiners Bay (AVP)
Patron Six
VP-42
VP-47
88th Sunderland Squadron
(96.8) Escort Carrier Group
   Badoeng Strait (CVE)
   Sicily (CVE)
   Taussig (DD)
   Hanson (DD)
   George K. Mackenzie
   (DD)
   Ernest G. Small (DD)
   Southerland (DD)
   Rowan (DD)
(70.1) Flagship Group
   Missouri (BB)
   Boxer
   Leyte
   Valley Forge
   Philippine Sea
   Manchester
DESRON-11, DESDIV-31
   Fletcher
   Gurke
   Henderson
DESDIV 92
79 Logistics Support Force

Hungnam Redevelopment
Task Force 90 - Commander
Amphibious Group I
(90.00) Flagship Element
   Mt McKinley (FF)
Mobile Surgical Team
No. 1 embarked (AGC)
(90.01) Tactical Air Control
Element
Tactical Squadron I
(90.02) Repair and Salvage
Unit
   Kermit Rooseevelet
   (ARG)
   Askari (ARL)
   Bolster (ARS)
   Conserver (ARS)
   Tawakoni (ATF)
(90.03) Control Element
   Diachendo (APD)
   Begor (APD)
   PCEC-882
90.2.1 Control Unit
   Dianchenko (APD)
(90.21) Transport Element
   Bayfield (APA)
   Henrico (APA)
   Noble (APA)
   Winston (AKA)
   Seminole (AKA)
   Montague (AKA)
   USS General F.C.
   Breckenridge (AP)
   USS General G.M.
   Randall (AP)
   USS General W.M.
   Mitchell (AP)
   USNS Fred C.
   Ainsworth (T-AP)
   USNS General A.W.
   Brewster (T-AP)
   USNS General D.I.

Sultan (T-AP)
USNS General E.T.
Collins (T-AP)
USNS General H.B.
Freeman (T-AP)
USNS General S.
Heintzelman (T-AP)
USNS Sergeant Andrew
Miller (T-AK)
SS Alamo Victory
SS Argovan
SS Bedford Victory
SS Belgium Victory
SS Bel Jeanne
SS Bel Ocean
SS California
SS Canada Mail
SS Carleton Victory
SS Choctaw
SS Citrus Packer
SS Clarksburg Victory
SS Cornell Victory
SS Del Alba
SS Denise
SS Elly SS
SS Empire Marshall
SS Empire Wallace
SS Enid Victory
SS Exmouth Victory
SS Gainesville Victory
SS Green Valley
SS Groton Trails
SS Helen Lykes
SS Hunter Victory
SS John Hanson
SS John Lyras
SS Kelso Victory
SS Denyon Victory
SS Lafayette Victory
SS Lane Victory
SS Letitia Lykes
SS Madaket
SS Manderson Victory
SS Meredith Victory
SS Morgantown Victory
SS Mormacmoon
SS Nathaniel Palmer
SS New Zealand Victory
SS Norcuba
SS Paducah Victory
SS Provo Victory
SS Rider Victory
SS Robin Gray
SS Robin Hood
SS Robin Kirk
SS Sea Spendor
SS Sea Wind
SS Southwind
SS St. Augustine Victory
SS Taineron
SS Towanda Victory
SS Twin Falls Victory
SS Union Victory
SS Virginia City Victory
SS Wacosta
SS Wesleyan Victory
Fentriss
Malay Maru #2
Senzan Maru (SKAJAP)
Shinano Maru (SKAJAP)
Tobato Maru (SKAJAP)
Yome Yama Maru
(SKAJAP)
USNS AKL 18
(SKAJAP)
27 SCAJAP LSTs
3 ROK LSTs
Fort Marion (LSD)
Colonial (LSD)
Catamount (LSD)

LST 715; 742; 799; 802; 845;
883; 898; 914; 973; 975; 1048;
1134; 419
(90.8) Gunfire Support Group
   Saint Paul (CA)
   Rochester (CA)
Destroyer Squadron 16
Destroyer Division 162
   Zellars (DD)
   Charles S. Sperry (DD)
   Massey (DD)
   Forrest Royal (DD)
LSMR Division II
LSMR 401; 403; 404
Destroyer Division 161
   English (DD)
   Hank (DD)
   Wallace L. Lind (DD)
   Borie (DD)
(95.2) Blockade, Escort and
Minesweeping Group
   Rochester (CA)
Destroyer Division 161
   English (DD)
   Hank (DD)
   Wallace L. Lind (DD)
   Borie (DD)
Escort Squadron 5
   Sausalito (PF)
   Hoquiam (PF)
   Gallup (PF)
   Goloucester (PF)
   Bisbee (PF)
   Glendale (PF)
(95.6) Minesweeping units
   Endicott (DMS)
   Doyle (DMS)
   Incredible (AM)
   Curlew (AMS)
   Heron (AMS)
Under TG 90 for Operational
Control
   Missouri (BB)
   Duncan (DDR)
   Consolation (AH)
   Foss (DE)
   Badoeng Strait (CVE)
Destroyer Division 71
   Lofberg (DD)
   John A. Bole (DD)
   Hanson (DDR)
(96.82) Carrier Element 2
   Sicily (CVE)
   VMF 214
Destroyer Division 72
   Mackenzie (DD)
   Taussig (DD)
   Ernest G. Small (DD)
(96.83) Carrier Element 3
   Bataan (CVL)
   VMF 212
   Brinkley Bass (DD)
   Arnold F. Isbell (DD)
(96.84) Screen Element
Destroyer Squadron 7
   Lofberg (DD)
   John A. Bole (DD)
   Mackenzie (DD)
   Taussig (DD)
   Ernest G. Small (DD)
   Brinkley Bass (DD)
   Arnold F. Isbell (DD)
Task Force 77 - Fast Carrier
Force
(77.1) Support Group
   Missouri (BB)
   Manchester (CL)
   Juneau (CL)
(77.2) Screen Group
Destroyer Squadron II

Destroyer Division III
   Wiltsie (DD)
   Theodore E. Chandler
   (DD)
   Hamner (DD)
   Chevalter (DDR)
Destroyer Division 112
   Ozbourn (DD)
   McKean (DD)
   Hollister (DD)
   Frank Knox (DDR)
Destroyer Squadron 3
Destroyer Division 31
   Shelton (DD)
   James E. Kyes (DD)
   Eversole (DD)
   Higbee (DDR)
Destroyer Squadron 5
Destroyer Division 51
   Rowan (DD)
   Gurke (DD)
   Henderson (DD)
   Southerland (DDR)
Destroyer Division 52
   Arnold F. Isbell (DD)
   Stickell (DD)
   Brinkley Bass (DD)
   Duncan (DDR)
Destroy Squadron 7
Destroyer Division 71
   John A. Bole (DD)
   Lofberg (DD)
Destroyer Division 72
   Taussig (DD)
   Ernest G. Small (DD)
Destroyer Division 92
   Maddox (DD)
   Brush (DD)
   Samuel N. Moore (DD)
   Herbert F. Thomas
   (DDR)
Escort Destroyer Division 61
   Fred T. Berry (DDE)
   Norris (DDE)
   Keppler (DDE)
   McCaffery (DDE)
(77.3) Carrier Group
   Leyte
Carrier Division 3 (CV)
   Valley Forge (CV)
(77.4) Carrier Group
Carrier Group
Carrier Division I
   Philippine Sea (CV)
   Leyte (CV)
Carrier Division 5
   Princeton (CV)
Air Group 19 embarked
(79.2) Hungnam Logistic
Support Group
   Dixie (AD)
   Mount Katmai (AE)
   Paricutin (AE)
   Graffias (AF)
   Merapi (AF)
   Chara (AKA)
   Diphda (AKA)
   Uvalde (AKA)
   Deal (AKL)
   Hewell (AKL)
   Ryer (AKL)
   Pollux (AKS)
   Ashtabula (AO)
   Cacapon (AO)
   Cimarron (AO)
   Kaskaskia (AO)
   Mispillion (AO)
   Passumpsic (AO)
   Kishwaukee (AOG)
   Jason (ARH)

United States Coast Guard

The United States Coast Guard supported the Allied effort during the Korean Conflict just as it had defended the nation during every conflict during the service's illustrious history. Indeed the Coast Guard's presence in Korea began prior to the outbreak of the Korean Conflict when a small Coast Guard advisory detachment assisted in the development and training of the Korean Coast Guard, which eventually became the Korean Navy. Although the Coast Guard advisory team departed Korea in 1948, the results of their effort were evident after the conflict was joined. Other Coast Guard units played an active role as well once the conflict commenced, carrying on the humanitarian tradition of the United States oldest sea-going service.

Coast Guard cutters served on open ocean weather stations commencing in the late 1930s to assist the burgeoning international air traffic industry. Cutters serving on two such ocean stations near Korean waters continued in this vital meteorological duty, providing Allied ground, naval, and air forces with direct information on weather patterns that affected their military actions. These cutters also served as communication support and as plane guards, ready to assist aircrews who were forced down at sea. They were in position to assist troop and supply transports on their way to Korea and back again as well in case of any emergencies. Twenty-four cutters served on these lonely outposts near Korean waters during the conflict. Their missions, in line with the Coast Guard's long history of saving life and property at sea, were a frequently unrecognized, yet important, contribution to Allied success.

Another Coast Guard mission that supported the Allied effort in Korea was the manning and operation of Long Range Aids to Navigation Stations, known as Loran stations, throughout the Pacific. There were nine stations that provided direct vital navigation support to Allied ships and aircraft engaged in the Korean Conflict, including one based on the Korean Peninsula itself. The headquarters section of the Coast Guard's Far Eastern Section and a Merchant Marine detachment providing logistical support to the Allied supply efforts also made a direct contribution to the war effort.

These missions, all extensions of the historic humanitarian duties of the Coast Guard, served to support the Allied war effort in Korea. On the home front Coast Guard expertise in captains of the port duties, cargo handling, and sabotage prevention also contributed to Allied success on the front and insured the uninterrupted flow of supplies to Korea, thereby permitting the Allies to carry on the war effort. As in every conflict in the nation's history, the Coast Guard is always ready to serve with the nation's other armed services to support the nation's efforts, anywhere around the globe.

U.S. Coast Guard Units Eligible For The Korean Service Medal

Cutters

1) USCGC *Bering Strait* (WAVP-382)
2) USCGC *Chautauqua* (WPG-41)
3) USCGC *Durant* (WDE-489)
4) USCGC *Escanaba* (WPG-64)
5) USCGC *Falgout* (WDE-424)
6) USCGC *Finch* (WDE-428)
7) USCGC *Forster* (WHE-434)
8) USCGC *Ironwood* (WAGL-297)
9) USCGC *Iroquois* (WPG-43)
10) USCGC *Klamath* (WPG-66)
11) USCGC *Koiner* (WDE-431)
12) USCGC *Kukui* (WAK-186)
13) USCGC *Lowe* (WDE-425)
14) USCGC *Minnetonka* (WPG-67)
15) USCGC *Newell* (WDE-422)
16) USCGC *Planetree* (WAGL-307)
17) USCGC *Pontchartrain* (WPG-70)
18) USCGC *Ramsden* (WDE-482)
19) USCGC *Richey* (WDE-485)
20) USCGC *Taney* (WPG-37)
21) USCGC *Wachusett* (WPG-44)
22) USCGC *Winnebago* (WPG-40)
23) USCGC *Winona* (WPG-64)

Shore Units:

1) Commander Far East Section, Tokyo
2) Loran Station (LORSTA) Bataan
3) LORSTA Elmo No. 4, Pusan
4) LORSTA Ichi Banare, Okinawa
5) LORSTA Iwo Jima
6) LORSTA Matsumae, Hokkaido, Japan
7) LORSTA Niigata, Honshu, Japan
8) LORSTA, Oshima, Honshu, Japan
9) LORSTA, Riyako Jima
10) LORSTA Tokyo, Honshu, Japan
11) MERMAR DET, Japan

The Making of the Korean War Veterans Memorial in Washington, DC
By Michael Richman, Ph.D.

Chapter One: Overview

The making of the Korean War Veterans Memorial, unveiled in Washington, DC, on July 27, 1995, is a story of vision, perseverance and passion. Many hands have played major roles in seeing the Memorial from first vision to hard-fought reality. Memorial-building is a deliberate, and often painstakingly, exhaustive process, baffling to many who are unaware of the scores of steps that must be traversed along the path from concept to completion. As the Nation's capital city, Washington endures many demands—one of which is the people's desire to remember and commemorate their heroes, causes and historical events.

To facilitate this process, four gatekeepers have been empowered to help advise, monitor and question. Congress is the first, where legislation is introduced that is required for any monument — from plaque to museum — to be placed on Federal land. The National Park Service (the National Capital Region is the branch in charge), part of the Department of the Interior, is oversight manager and has been since 1933. The third is the Commission of Fine Arts (CFA), created in 1910, as an advisory group of seven members who are: "well qualified judges of the fine arts to advise upon the location of statues, fountains, and monuments under the authority of the United States, . . . and the selection of models . . . and the selection of artist for the execution of same. "The last is the National Capital Planning Commission (NCPC), established in 1924 with statutory authority "to provide for the comprehensive, systematic, and continuous development of park, parkway and playground systems of the National Capital."

For many this may seem to be a bloated bureaucracy with overlapping jurisdictions. But

Grant Memorial, left face, US Capitol Grounds, example of multiple figure sculpture.

Grant Memorial, right face, US Capitol grounds.

in reality the process works, and the proof is visible all around monumental Washington. Yes, the building of a national memorial is a back-breaking undertaking, and in a climate where time is money, it may even contribute to increased costs. But it is a price worth paying for something that will be permanent, that is here for the present and the future.

The reality of this review-ladened process provides both the time and opportunity for all concerned to get it right. It is almost as if the length of time correlates to time-tested success. The *Ulysses S. Grant Memorial*, at the east end of the Mall at the foot of the United States Capitol, took 22 years to complete; the *Lincoln Memorial*, the near neighbor of the Korean War Veterans Memorial at the banks of the Potomac River, took 21 years from legislative idea to dedication, and its axial partner, the *Jefferson Memorial*, became a thirteen-year effort from Congressional start to the placement of the bronze portrait statue.

By the same measures, the Korean War Veterans Memorial, from its beginning in the spring of 1985, with the introduction of four bills in Congress to the summer celebration in 1995, marking on July 27th, the 42nd anniversary of the armistice, has proceeded with respectable promptness. And this ten-year Odyssean journey of determination, diligence and decorum, has been piloted by twelve dedicated Korean War veterans. Their role in this memorial project, which will enrich the visual and cultural landscape of Washington, was paramount. They have, at long last, honored their fellow veterans and served to raise the national conscience by paying tribute to the service and sacrifice of these brave men and women, too long forgotten.

Chapter Two: Legislative History

The American Battle Monuments Commission (ABMC) is a Presidentially appointed body that administers overseas cemeteries for American soldiery. Their charter also permits the erection of monuments in this country, and since 1967, they have been interested in seeking funding for a Korean War memorial. This government-sponsored effort fizzled by 1974, stymied by Vietnam-era budget priorities. When the National Committee of the Korean War

Memorial, Inc., announced its intention in 1981, ABMC was told by White House officials to let this private group seize the initiative.

The first bill introduced in Congress to create a Korean War memorial was offered on April 24, 1985, by James Florio of New Jersey (with original co-sponsors, G. V. "Sonny" Montgomery and John Paul Hammerschmidt, chair and ranking member of the House Committee on Veterans Affairs and later with 135 co-sponsors). That bill directed the Secretary of the Interior to be in charge of erecting a memorial to "honor members of the U. S. Armed Forces who served in the Korean War." It stated only two boilerplate conditions: approval by the Commission of Fine Arts and National Capital Planning Commission - and government funds could then be appropriated after October 1, 1985. This bill seemed to have garnered the proper attention and a solid head of legislative steam. A hearing was held before the Task Force on Libraries and Memorials, Committee on Administration on July 10, 1985. A second bill introduced by Stan Parris of Virginia (H. R. 2588), on May 25, 1985, called for the American Battle Monuments Commission to erect a memorial: "to honor members of the Armed Forces of the United States who served in the Korean War, particularly those who were killed in action, listed as missing in action, or were held as prisoners of war."

Meanwhile there was movement in the Senate Joint Resolution 184, offered by Senator Jeremiah Denton of Mississippi, on July 31, 1985, was ordered sent to the Subcommittee on Public Lands and the Committee on Energy and Natural Resources, chaired by Senator Malcolm Wallop of Wyoming. It authorized the National Committee for the Korean War Memorial, to build a memorial with private funding. Senator William Armstrong of Colorado introduced bill

S. 1223, the Korean War Memorial Act of 1985, which called for the ABMC to be in charge. The only legislative action that happened in the first session of the 99th Congress was for the House to pass (H. R. 2205) with a vote of 406-0 on November 6, 1985. The delay in the Senate was caused by Senator Wallop.

In the second session, sometime before April 2, 1986, Armstrong reintroduced a bill, now titled the "Korean War Veterans Memorial Act of 1986," that authorized the ABMC to build the Memorial but with several specific provisions. In fact, the language of this bill is virtually identical with the Public Law 99-572 that President Ronald Reagan signed on October 28, 1986.

It was Armstrong's willingness to work with Senator Wallop, who was actively protesting against the numerous memorial requests that flooded Congress and threatened the ultimate development of the Mall, that seemed to turn the corner. Wallop, instrumental in passing the Commemorative Works Act of 1986, supported Armstrong's bill over the Denton version. Future Board member Mike McKevitt, former one-term Congressman from Colorado, was instrumental in working for the bill's passage. Senator John Glenn of Ohio, who had spoken at the July 10th hearing, gave his support to the Armstrong bill,

Public law 99-572 being signed by President Reagan. (L to R) Sen. William Armstrong, Col. John Kennedy, Jr., USA (Ret) KWVMAB Exec. Dir., Edward Borcherdt*, Tom Dehne*, Gen. Ray Davis, USMC (Ret), Vice Chairman*, Gen. Richard Stilwell, USA (Ret), Chairman*, Gen. James Van Fleet, USA (Ret), Col. Konrad Hausman, USA (Ret)*, Col. Fred Cherry, USAF (Ret)*, Col. Rosemary McCarthy, USA (Ret)*, James D. "Mike" McKevitt*, Carlos Rodriguez*, Col. William Weber, USA (Ret)*, Col. Lloyd "Scooter" Burke, USMC (Ret) Medal of Honor, Korea, Richard Adams, Pres. of KWVA, William Norris, Founder of KWVA. Seated, President Ronald Reagan. *Korean War Veterans Memorial Advisory Board Member (KWVMBA)

which passed the Senate on October 9, 1986. It was returned to the House, where under suspension of the rules, Mary Rose Oakar of Ohio managed its passage on October 14, 1986. Many of those who testified at the first public hearing on July 10, 1985-Montgomery, Hammerschmidt, Florio and Stan Parris—participated in the floor debate and accepted the two Senate additions.

The legislation created a twelve-member advisory board of Korean War veterans, who were granted responsibilities in four areas — recommending a site; selecting a design for the Memorial (both with the concurrence of the ABMC and following the established design review process); promoting the establishment of the Memorial; and encouraging the donation of private funds for construction and maintenance. Congress also authorized $500,000 for site preparation, design and planning, and associated administrative costs, as well as $500,000 for the eventual construction.

A second round of legislative action would be needed in 1991. In creating the Commemorative Works Act of 1986, Congress gave groups interested in erecting a memorial in Washington five years from signing of the law to securing a permit - with all funds needed for construction in the "bank." This yardstick proved to be too restrictive, and a two-year extension, from five to seven, was proposed, providing a more realistic goal for completion. What first focused solely on the Korean War Veterans Memorial then became generic legislation for other in-progress and all future projects. Senator Glenn, a staunch supporter of the Memorial from the very beginning, introduced S. 855, on June 20, 1991. A House version (H. R. 3169) was offered by Congressman Montgomery on August 1st and passed on October 20th. A vote in the Senate occurred on November 25, 1991, and President George Bush signed Public Law 102-216 on December 11, 1991.

President George Bush.

Fortunately the provisions were again applied retroactively to October 1, 1991. Without this legislation, the work on completing the Memorial might have stopped. Now the ABMC and the Advisory Board, especially with the nearly $6 million dollars earned from the 38th-anniversary Korean commemorative silver dollar strike (May 6, 1991-November 15, 1991), had the time and the funding to meet the October 28, 1993 deadline for securing the construction permit.

Chapter Three: Forming the Korean War Veterans Memorial Advisory Board

As the legislation mandated, the Korean War Veterans Memorial Advisory Board (KWVMAB) members were appointed on July 20, 1987, by President Ronald Reagan. The American Battle Monuments Commission (ABMC) believed this group would be an active participant in the first phase of the project and a supporting player and cheerleader through the remainder of the five-year window mandated to complete the Memorial. The first meeting on September 23, 1987, began with a flourish; this would be a can-do, take-charge board, a fact confirmed by the first-day development of a concept paper intended to define the essence of the Memorial in words and symbolism.

This gathering, held at the Washington office of the Paralyzed Veterans of America, began with the formal introduction by General Andrew Goodpaster of the staff and three members of the Monuments Commission. The twelve veterans exchanged greetings, and to facilitate the morning session, General Richard G. Stilwell became the acting chair. A retired four-star general, former commander of the American Forces in Korea, 1973-76, and a widely respected soldier and diplomat, Stilwell seemed the logical leader.

From the project's inception in 1986 until his death on December 25, 1991, Stilwell, who was officially appointed Chairman at the November 24th meeting, worked tirelessly. The Vice-Chairman (and Stilwell's successor) was General Raymond Davis. One of the Korean War's 131 Congressional Medal of Honor recipients (a Marine Corps legend for his heroics at the Battle of the Chosin Reservoir during December, 1950),

Davis, reserved and quietly tenacious, was the perfect complement to Stilwell.

Of the original 12 Board members, seven served in the Army (Stilwell, Conrad K. Hausman, John B. Curcio, Carlos Rodriguez, William E. Weber, William F. McSweeney and Rosemary T. McCarthy), three were in the Marines (Davis, Thomas G. Dehne and Edward C. Borcherdt) and two served in the Air Force (Fred V. Cherry and James D. McKevitt).

Five members saw considerable front-line action during the war (Borcherdt, Davis, McSweeney, Rodriguez and Weber). Rodriguez

General Richard G. Stilwell, Chairman, KWVMAB, July 1987-December 1991). U.S. Mint, Philadelphia May 1991.

was paralyzed by wounds inflicted on his first day in combat. McSweeney "served as a Regular Army private, enlisting because I believed in the cause of fighting Chinese expansion/communism." As CEO of Occidental International Corporation, McSweeney "had some experience with cultural and design things in the city over the past two decades." Weber, who lost an arm and a leg in Korea, remained on active duty until 1980. Under his leadership, the RAKKASANS (the 187th Airborne Regimental Combat Team Association) raised $125,000 for the Memorial.

Three members were involved in national veterans groups: Rodriguez with the Eastern Paralyzed Veterans, Dehne with the Disabled American Veterans, and McCarthy with the Retired Army Nurse Corps Association. It would come to be important that seven Board members—Stilwell, Weber, McKevitt, Cherry, McCarthy, McSweeney and Hausman—were from the Washington, DC area. Interestingly, the appointment of Borcherdt, Hausman and Dehne, all members of the National Committee for the Korean War Memorial, Inc., caused no conflicts.

The selection of Board members was under the charge of the Executive Branch. ABMC, hoping to play a role in the Board's make-up, presented a blue-ribbon list to White House staffer Robert Tuttle on November 5, 1986. A list of 15 names included several members of Congress, three retired generals (neither Davis nor Stilwell), one private citizen (already an ABMC member) and five representatives of veterans groups (only Dehne and Rodriguez were appointed). An undated, hastily typed telephonic message from the White House (in the ABMC files) provides an interim list of only eight names: Cherry, Curcio, Davis, Dehne, Hausman, McKevitt, Rodriguez and Stilwell.

Gen. Stilwell, May 6, 1991. Luncheon after US Mint First Strike Ceremony in Philadelphia.

Gen. Ray Davis, USMC (Ret), Medal of Honor, Korea.

Why the remaining four were nominated cannot be documented precisely. Weber believes he was championed by Congressman Hamilton Fish of New York. McCarthy, former Army Nurse Corps Historian at the Center of Military History, was mentioned by a friend to Colonel Hausman, who had served as White House liaison at the Department of State. Borcherdt, owner of a small export business in southern California was married to a political appointee in Reagan's White House. McSweeney, a "life-long, Lyndon-Johnson Democrat, was well-known in West Wing circles."

It is interesting how many strangers and a few old friends rallied to the mission to build the Memorial, eager to define the objective and formulate a plan. As unpaid volunteers, their time, energy and commitment would be invaluable to the success of the project. Although the Board, by law, reported to the ABMC, they received little direct support either from the eleven-person staff (managed day-to-day by Colonels William E. Ryan, Jr. and Frederick C. Badger) or the eleven-member commission. What was troublesome to the Board, facing a massive fundraising campaign, was the meager success that the ABMC had in their corporate funding effort: a letter to 100 corporate heads netted only $700.00.

Stilwell, in a letter of November 23, 1987, stated the obvious to ABMC Chairman Goodpaster: "We shall be working in tandem for perhaps as long as five years to carry a noble project to completion. The Board has great respect for the super record of the Commission..., and for the professionalism of its leadership and staff. And for their part, my prestigious colleagues are prepared to donate whatever time and effort is required to bring the Memorial into being expeditiously. The Board considers that teamwork would be enhanced by early establishment of procedures for mutual coordination and by clear delineation of respective roles in carrying out a number of functions explicit in the overall memorial project."

This memorandum, finally signed on March 11, 1988, is a key document. It reflects the take-charge attitude of the Board. They were comfortable working within prescribed boundaries, recognizing there might be areas of overlap and points of potential dispute, but at least all were standing on a level playing field as the project commenced. The four-page document gave the Board major operating responsibilities (precisely those enumerated in the October 8, 1986 law—site selection, design selection, fundraising, publicity and promotion). It concluded in an optimistic tone: "While designation of specific focal points is essential to sound management, the importance of our common task requires the fullest possible contact and communication between the Commission members. This memorandum deals with an area that has been uncharted. On consultation of both parties, it is subject to update whenever experience or unforeseen issues so dictate."

Sooner rather than later, the Board considered the issue of money at its inaugural meeting. Although the ABMC received the first Memorial check in June, 1985, by this meeting date, 2,263 persons had given an amount totaling $1,583,896 (including $1 million from Hyundai Motor America). Unexplainably, the ABMC, with many friends on Capitol Hill, failed to request relief from regulations restricting the placement of donated funds into an interest bearing account. This tardy oversight was soon in the process of being corrected. With the support of Congressman Parris and Senators Armstrong and Glenn, bills (H.R. 1454 and S. 1525) were introduced on March 5, 1987 and on July 22, 1987, respectively, "authorizing the Treasurer of the United States to invest the contributions in public debt securities." By October 1, 1987, a shortcut had been found. The language of the FY1988 Supplemental Appropriation, stated that the KWVMAB account could now earn interest and the Advisory Board could, for its first year, spend up to $125,000 for administrative expenses. Board members would quickly learn all the special rules of the Memorial-making game, helped by those already comfortable in the halls of Congress.

The afternoon session found members reviewing the steps needed to find a site and better define what the Memorial should convey. Something in writing would serve two objectives, a first run-through for the design program as well as a document that could be distributed to the "6,800 fraternally and Federally chartered service organizations around America." Ideas were freely exchanged. Stilwell spoke of the "need to equally honor those who fought and survived and those who sacrificed their lives," and the need for "a physical representation of the four services." Davis stated that "we must not glorify war." McCarthy spoke about "the words and sayings ... rather than trying to have a nurse with a stethoscope around her neck." Weber stated for him "going to Korea was something that you were expected to do; if you're the one whose number is called, you go, you do it, and when you're done, you come back home to get on with your life." Borcherdt's idea was for a "functional working thing that people can participate in - not just stand and look at."

There is no better demonstration that the Board's creative juices were flowing than the first-day acceptance of the five-sentence Memorial concept statement. With but a few words changed and the deletion of the last three lines, the document was unanimously approved. From the beginning the Board knew where it wanted to go. The September 23, 1987 concept statement remained the linchpin of the January 30, 1989 competition. With the starting line nearby, the Board members were active, listening and learning, reflecting and pondering.

By the November 24th meeting, following the points outlined in an as-yet-to-be-signed ABMC/KWVMAB agreement, the Board created several committees: site and design, chaired by Davis with Rodriguez, Weber, McSweeney and McCarthy; fundraising, first headed by Curcio and then co-chaired by McSweeney, with Stilwell actively involved, and promotion, headed by McKevitt with Borcherdt. Weber, who lobbied strenuously that direct lines of communication be established with all veterans organization, large and small, agreed to chair this liaison group.

The Board's promotional efforts were considerable. Unexpected success came from the printing of two "Dear Abby" letters (on November 11, 1988 and January 2, 1989) that generated $332,000 from 27,838 contributors. Perhaps the finest coordination effort that focused early attention on the Memorial was provided in the 1988 anniversary remarks (possibly drafted by Board members McSweeney or Stilwell) delivered at Arlington National Cemetery on July 27th, by Secretary of Defense Frank C. Carlucci: "For America, the human legacy of the Korean War is the sterling performance of her uniformed sons and daughters who uncomplaining, took up arms to defend a nation they never knew and a people they never met. The courage and dedication of our Korean War veterans was as great as any American conflict. They endured bitter weather, inhospitable terrain and fanatical attackers. In that land so remote from America and America's consciousness, heroes came to the fore and the inner strength of our troops showed through."

Theirs is a remarkable, behind-the-scenes success story, not only for the prodigious fundraising efforts and the tireless promotional work they performed, but for their steadfast resolve during the tempestuous three years of design-development review. A propitious beginning for an ambitious undertaking, General Stilwell concluded the first meeting: "It's been quite a day. I think we've moved along and obviously you're a very compatible, flexible and dedicated group with a high capacity for innovation."

With a chorus of ayes, the first of what was to become more than sixty formal meetings, countless executive sessions, and scores of design reviews and site-inspections, adjourned.

The Board has continued its impressive work for eight years. Of the original twelve, one resigned in 1988 (Curcio, who was replaced by John Staum, past commander-in-chief of the Veterans of Foreign Wars in May, 1990) and two died, Hausman in 1988 and Stilwell in 1991. They were replaced, respectively by John R. "Jake" Comer, past national commander of the American Legion in May, 1990, and by John Phillips in January, 1995. When Davis succeeded Stilwell, Rosemary McCarthy became Vice-Chairman.

Ever mindful of the fragility of Presidentially appointed commissions, the Board was concerned, in the spring of 1989, that George Bush might exercise his prerogative and replace its members. The lobbying engine was started: "Pass on to the powers that be on commission selections that this unique, non-glamorous, but mission-oriented Board, will accomplish its completion of goals a lot more quickly if the turnover on the Board is kept to a minimum."

It was successful; there were no changes. And in late December, 1992, a letter from Congressman Sonny Montgomery to President-elect William J. Clinton, helped to avoid any disruptions.

All of the 15 KWVMAB members have contributed marvelously to this effort, and a few have earned special notice: Bill Weber and Rosemary McCarthy have toiled tirelessly and never in eight years has either missed a single meeting. Mike McKevitt and Bill McSweeney's

behind-the-scenes knowledge of the workings of Washington was invaluable. The second chairman Ray Davis, was a resourceful leader, indefatigable in his willingness to travel from his home in Stockbridge, GA to Washington. He steadfastly monitored every step of the project. The contribution by Richard G. Stilwell from September 23, 1987 to December 25, 1991, was, and still is, immeasurable. In the words of Colonel Weber: "Without his leadership these past five years, I truly believe the Memorial might have been cast aside. If any man should be credited with dedicating his life to this memorial, it is he!"

Chapter Four: The American Battle Monuments Commission

The American Battle Monuments Commission (ABMC), a Presidentially appointed group of eleven members, was originally created in 1923 to honor American servicemen who died in World War I either by creating shrines or maintaining markers previously erected. The legislation, updated in 1934, called for the oversight of eight European burial grounds and for future design, construction, operation and maintenance of additional cemeteries on foreign soil. After World War II, the ABMC became responsible for 18 national cemeteries and memorials honoring those who died in the European Theater of Operations and the Asiatic-Pacific Campaign as well as the *East Coast Memorial* in Battery Park, New York City and the *West Coast Memorial* in the Presidio, San Francisco (honoring those lost in American coastal waters).

Most of these projects were undertaken in concert with the U. S. Army Corps of Engineers with the ABMC exercising the direct appointment of architects, landscape designers and sculptors and maintaining oversight control of all implementing phases. The ABMC's first introduction into Washington memorial-making came in 1978 with the *American Expeditionary Forces Memorial* with its statue of General John Pershing, located on Pennsylvania Avenue, between 14th and 15th Streets, NW. In this case, the Commission secured the necessary legislation and formed a constructive partnership with the Pennsylvania Avenue Development Corporation.

Longtime ABMC staffers Ryan and Badger were eager to erect a national memorial to the veterans of the Korean Conflict. This interest (and support since 1987) was shared by the ABMC Chairmen: General Andrew J. Goodpaster (1985-90), General P. X. Kelley (1990-94) and General Frederick F. Woerner (1994-present). As early as 1971, seed monies were included in their annual operating budgets, only to be deleted in the higher-up reviews in the Office of Management and Budget. Ryan realized that the value of placing tax-deductible contributions in the Treasury would eliminate the fundraising mistakes that had plagued the Vietnam Veterans Memorial project.

A May 23, 1984 report of the Comptroller General of the United States on the Vietnam Veterans Memorial Fund's Financial Operations confirmed that the fundraising expenses and five-year administrative budget account were reasonable. But the fact that nearly 39% of the money raised was spent on behind-the-scenes administrative outlays, as well as for the services and costs of fundraising raised some eyebrows. Only 41% of the money collected was used for actual design and implementation. While those ratios might be technically defensible, they seem excessively wasteful. During the floor debate for the Korean War Veterans Memorial, Congressman "Sonny" Montgomery declared that the ABMC: "is a commission of the Federal Government and will watch and control what kind of memorial, what kind of monument we get. So

there is plenty of protection to see that the money is spent wisely. We thought it not a smart idea to spend $4 million or $5 million to raise $2 million or $3 million."

Chapter Five: Site Selection

The first "memorial" business that the Board addressed at its September 23, 1987 meeting was a briefing on site selection from the American Battle Monuments Commission representative. The ABMC had started the ball rolling by requesting, on March 31, 1987, that the Secretary of the Interior consider the placement of the Korean War Veterans Memorial in Area 1. Sites in this portion of the Federal city were to be reserved for prominent national memorials. Secretary Donald Hodel in turn, referred the request to the National Capital Memorial Commission (NCMC), recently created by Public Law 99-652. Even though the KWVM legislation predated the enactment of the Commemorative Works Act by a month, the project was retroactively covered.

The charge of this commission was profoundly simple: bring up-front procedural order to the chorus (which had occasionally reached the level of cacophonous chaos) of those wishing and hoping as well as those wanting (and capable) of erecting memorials in the Nation's Capital. Its membership was precisely defined: the heads of eight, city-wide agencies that include the Chairmen of the American Battle Monuments Commission, the National Capital Planning Commission and the Commission of Fine Arts, as well as the Secretary of Defense, the Commissioner of the Public Building Service of the General Services Administration, the Mayor of the District of Columbia and the Architect of the Capitol. The NCMC reports to the Secretary of the Interior, under whose charge are nearly all Federal open-space in the District of Columbia and under his direction, the National Park

Services maintains the City's impressive national treasures.

In practice this group was to be a clearinghouse for the prominent agencies with jurisdiction and precedent. These eight agencies have wisely delegated participation to staff members who have hands-on, day-to-day involvement. The NCMC, in the past eight years, has brought much needed discipline to memorial making in Washington as the prime sites and locations, in Areas I and II, have become increasingly scarce and sought after.

On April 23, 1987, the NCMC endorsed an Area I designation for the project, as it met "the criteria of preeminent historical and lasting significance to the Nation." It was not until weeks after the Board was formed that Secretary Hodel, on November 10, 1987, petitioned Congress to allow the Memorial to be placed in Area I. Phase one of the site selection process began officially with a House of Representatives hearing before the Subcommittee of the National Parks and Public Lands of the Committee on Interior and Insular Affairs on December 10, 1987. Board members Stilwell, Davis and McKevitt were aware of the need to get over this first hurdle and they lobbied for Joint Resolution 405. The ABMC reported that Representative Montgomery was always willing to circulate a "Dear Colleague" letter. The approval was granted by Congress and the bill was signed into law by President Reagan on March 28, 1988 (Public Law 100-267).

Before Area I status was actually confirmed, the search for sites began. During the luncheon recess of the first Board meeting, four locations, that Badger thought had potential, were visited: Constitution Gardens, near the corner of Constitution Avenue and 17th Street, NW; Ash Woods,

Constitution Gardens.

Ash Woods.

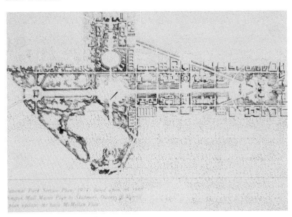

West Potomac Park.

near Daniel Chester French Drive and Independence Avenue, SW, south of the Reflecting Pool; a parcel north of the Tidal Basin, and a plot along the river in West Potomac Park, west of Ohio Drive.

By March 4, 1988, Site and Design Chair Davis was eager to get going. Badger said that although they were interviewing an architectural consulting company for analysis and evaluation, no contract could be let until Congress approved an Area 1 designation. Ryan was encouraged that the Korean War Veterans Memorial would be the first NCMC review.

207

At the May 3, 1988 meeting of the Board, Colonel Badger introduced Mary Ann Lasch, landscape architect in the Washington office of Hellmuth, Obata and Kassabaum (HOK). She presented a draft of the Site Selection Study (a final version was transmitted on August 12, 1988) that provided an unexpected ordering for the Board—lst rank—West Potomac; 2nd rank—Ash Woods, 3rd rank—Constitution Gardens, and 4th rank—Tidal Basin. She defended her first choice, saying "I think the greatest advantage of that site on the Potomac River is that it will be very easy to really focus on the message that you want to portray." After her presentation, McKevitt stated that the Board unanimously favored Constitution Gardens. Lasch countered that with this "more restrictive site, you will have more limited design options and more discussions (nitpicking reviews)."

Board members elaborated. Weber was strongly attached to the Constitution Gardens location because it was on "the main path of visitation." McKevitt stated that "we have to sell harder than ever why Korea needs to be on the Constitution Gardens site." Borcherdt said of the site "we are trying to resurrect a moment in the history of this country that has been forgotten." Lasch spoke about the practical problems of saving this area for future memorials. Badger, who apparently wished that the Board would let the NCMC react to each location and reach a decision without their input, hoped that the members were not offended that HOK did not come up with Site A as its first choice. To which Davis replied, "we are trying to enlist your enthusiastic support."

After lunch the Design Committee made its recommendation and the members present (with two proxies) voted: 1st rank—Constitution Gardens (9-0), 2nd rank—Ash Woods (9-0), 3rd rank—Tidal Basin (5-4) and 4th rank—West Potomac Park (5-4). Stilwell concluded that

Near Tidal Basin.

while: "the vote for the Constitution Gardens site reflected the strong view that the Board has had all throughout the intervening eight-month period. The Board recognizes that Ash Woods is a very, very good alternative, albeit an alternative to our preferred site and not our first selection."

The remainder of the meeting was focused on how to get the national veterans groups mobilized to support the Constitution Gardens campaign. The May 26th meeting of the National Capital Memorial Commission, the first of many public review exercises which KWVMAB members attended, headed down a different path. The NCMC members thought the 2-acre design contemplated for the Memorial would be too large for the northeast corner of Constitution Gardens and several recalled a long extant hope of the Park Service to erect a visitors pavilion there. They spoke positively about Ash Woods, citing the availability of the Tourmobile, balance with Vietnam Veterans Memorial and pedestrian movement from Lincoln Memorial. The vote was 6-1 (Badger dissented).

At the June 1, 1988 Executive Committee meeting, the Board mobilized hoping to have the NCMC reconsider this vote and requested a second review at the next scheduled (June 28th) meeting. Board members were assigned to speak directly to NCMC attendees. Weber talked with Elliott Carroll (Architect of Capitol representative) and reported he "will resist changing his vote but without rancor." McCarthy suggested that Gresham (NCPC) called Ash Woods the place for a "major memorial." She reflected that the NCMC judgment had been rendered carefully and stated that the Board had been misled by its advisers on the availability of sites that had been identifiable as possible locations for the Memorial." McSweeney spoke with both Jack Fish, head of the National Capital Region (unchangeable) and Carter Brown (persuadable).

While the Board may well have been angered by the vote, the personal discussion members had individually with NCMC members was productive. They were introduced to the reality of the Memorial review process, without expending energy. At this instance, the authorities backed the more exciting site.

With the vote (5-2 with Charles Atherton, Executive Director for the Commission of Fine Arts joining Col. Badger) for Ash Woods reaffirmed on June 28, 1988, Chairman Stilwell was given a personal inspection tour on the 29th by NCMC Chair John Parsons. In a letter of July 5, 1988, the Board outlined their concerns about the Park Police stables, the landscaping of Independence Avenue, the removal of food concessions and bus parking. With assurances provided in writing on August 8, 1988, the Ash Woods site was accepted. Soon, members would come to realize this to be a genuinely positive outcome, in spite of General Davis' plaintive memorandum of May 27th: "We met the enemy and were shot down in flames. I was surprised! My

hindsight says that we should have pursued our original, more aggressive plan, but the results would probably have been the same. Not one of them called it a 'veterans' memorial, even after I admonished them."

The Commemorative Works Act had been tested and the formal rhythm it sought to instill seems to have served each group well. The Board got to know the players who would be their jurors during the next several years. On September 8, 1988, the National Capital Planning Commission approved Ash Woods, requesting that they also receive a copy of the design competition program. On September 16th, the Commission of Fine Arts gave its endorsement. A formal ceremony at the site was held on September 26, 1988, with Secretary Hodel, members of the Board, and several veterans organizations, celebrating this event. The journey's first step had been taken. The national competition to secure a design for the Korean War Veterans Memorial could now begin.

Chapter Six: Defining the Competition Program

With the official approval by the Secretary of the Interior of the Ash Woods site on September 26, 1988, the ABMC authorized its agent, the Baltimore District of the United States Army Corps of Engineers, to begin the competition for the design of the Korean War Veterans Memorial. The genesis of this partnership began after the enabling legislation passed. ABMC Chairman Goodpaster wrote to General E. R. Heiberg, III, Commander, U. S. Army Corps of Engineers (COE), on November 13, 1986, requesting the Corps' and Commission's collaboration. Confirmation was sent on November 26th.

At the first staff-level meeting, held at the Pulaski Building in Washington, on December 4,

Ash Woods, Site Dedication, Sept. 26, 1988. (L to R): Col. William Weber, USA (Ret), Gen. Richard Stilwell, USA (Ret), Secretary of the Interior Don Hodel, Col. Rosemary McCarthy, USA (Ret).

1986, two items were addressed: an inter-agency agreement, and discussion of the design options. Colonel Badger and Paul Harbeson, consulting architect, presented the ABMC's views about the latter: the COE would hold a structured competition, limited to qualified professionals who learned of the Memorial project in the *Commerce Business Daily* (CBD) or other national media outlets. From those eligible, judged by reviewing the Standard Form 255, fifteen architects would be chosen to present designs, with Paul Harbeson serving on the pre-selection committee. With Badger, serving on the Phase II-final selection board, the COE would select six competent firms, give them each a $10,000 stipend, with the winner being chosen directly by the ABMC.

There was no mention of any role for the as-yet-to-be-named Korean War Veterans Memorial Advisory Board, even though the legislation specifically documented their primary participation in design selection. Whether this was an end-run before the whistle had sounded, or a

harmless first effort to get discussions started is not known. It is important to note that the selection scenario Badger was proposing was different than procedures previously practiced by the ABMC. In executing all of their major overseas memorial cemeteries, their precedent had always been to appoint architect and sculptor directly.

COE Engineering Division staff architect Alexandra M. S. Crawford proposed that the group consider an open national competition, following the guidelines of the American Institute of Architects. She thought the Corps' Baltimore office had the authority to conduct such an undertaking. The obvious impact of securing a brilliant design from an unexpected source was still fresh in the minds of America's architectural community. The discovery of Maya Lin's pencil rendering among the 1,451 entries reinforced the democratic openness—giving everyone the opportunity to compete. The discussion ended.

The other item on the agenda was the working agreement, defining roles, reporting methodologies and monitoring strategies. A draft was prepared by the Baltimore District staff early in 1987, revised by February 16th and readied for signatures after April 16, 1987. Unexplainably, formal execution of the document by the Corps and the Commission did not take place until January 10, 1989.

At the Advisory Board's first meeting, Badger presented another plan: "All interested designers will be invited to submit their past experiences on Standard Form 255 to the Baltimore District. Sculptors, artists and others may submit as long as they are associated with a competent architectural firm so that the final design can be made."

Next the AMBC and Corps staff would pre-screen 15 candidates; then a different panel would select six finalists, who would receive $15,000 each to develop a design concept for the Memorial. Only at this point would the Advisory Board be invited to review and recommend the winner, who would then enter into a contract with the Corps of Engineers for the full design of the Memorial.

This proposal made the Board little more than a rubber stamp. Perhaps, the ABMC staff thought they were reducing the work load for what might be a more-show-than-substance committee. Badger and Ryan underestimated the energy of this group. By March 4, talk focused on making sure that every submission would be seen by at least 7 of the Board members.

Design and Site Chairman Davis had been invited to an ABMC/COE meeting held on February 11, 1988, and reported in glowing

terms: "We found at the meeting that any idea that comes in can become ours to do something else with. So we don't want to limit them in any way. In that gigantic thing, there might be a gem of an idea we can use. And we pick it out and put it in something else. That's the thing that appeals to me to have a totally open input. Inviting all the ideas to come in."

He continued outlining the points of this latest proposal. From the 1500 entries, they would select 20 and learn from the Corps if each entrant was in technical compliance. Then an honorarium of $1,000 was to be paid. These, with more details, more conceptual guidance, would launch a second stage. They would then review the 20 submissions and pick three. These persons would each get $20,000 and receive further ideas, concepts and details. From the three, one would be selected and presented to the ABMC, awarded a $25,000 prize, and then, finally, taken to the different Washington review agencies for comment. With this program, the Board was reassured that they would be participating in securing a winning design.

But by May 4th, Badger outlined another variation, involving a protective shield—"on further consultation with experts in the field"— "One page announcement encouraging all to enter a project description, concept, and rules. An application form with $20.00 entry fee was proposed. After closing registration, develop project design program, with photos of the site, contour maps. After official start, thirty days to ask questions. All answers would be returned in two weeks. Entries submitted by May 1, A technical review will be undertaken on the 15 finalists, returned to the Board for first, second and third place awards."

The key for the Board was the Concept Paper—a document that had now been their beacon for over a year. In the September 1988 announcement flier, an excerpted version was printed: "The purpose of the Memorial is to express the enduring gratitude of the American people to all Americans who took part in that conflict and to project the spirit of service, the willingness to sacrifice and the dedication to the cause of freedom that characterized all participants."

By July 18, 1988, the ABMC and the Baltimore District jointly decided that time could be saved with a one-stage competition, with a pre-registration screening and the restriction that implementation of any design would be performed under a separate Architect-Engineer (A-E) services contract. An announcement flier "to enter a single-stage, open national design competition for a memorial honoring the veterans of the Korean war, to be located near the Lincoln Memorial in Washington, DC" was reviewed and accepted. The flier would be distributed nationally by September 16th; the due-date was December 30, 1988.

In the January, 1989 program announcement, it was fully promulgated: "The Korean War Veterans Memorial has two interrelated purposes which constitute primary consideration in its siting and design. The first and fundamental purpose is to express the enduring gratitude of the American people to all Americans who took part in that conflict; those who survived no less than those who gave their lives. The second purpose, which is of equal importance, is to project in the most positive fashion the spirit of service, the willingness to sacrifice, and the dedication to the cause of freedom that characterized all participants. These patriotic virtues have been common to those who served our country at other times of national crisis, and must not be lacking during future emergencies. The Memorial must radiate a message that is at once inspirational in content and timeless in meaning. Both purposes dictate that the Memorial be unique in concept, designed for public use, located on a prominent prospect, and present a renewable aspect of hope, honor and service."

As veterans and Presidentially appointed stewards of a long-awaited and unfairly-delayed memorial, this statement united the Board to march down an unswerving path—the 1.5 million soldiers who served on the Korean peninsula, as well as the 5.7 million men and women who were on active duty during these three years would be properly honored. A forgotten war would be remembered.

A far different instruction was transmitted in the November 1980 statement of purpose for an earlier competition: "The purpose of the Vietnam Veterans Memorial is to recognize and honor those who served and died. It will provide a symbol of acknowledgment of the courage, sacrifice and devotion to duty of those who were among the nation's finest youth. The Memorial will make no political statement regarding the war or its conduct. It will transcend those issues. The hope is that the creation of the Memorial will begin a healing process."

The promulgation of the competition was handled by the ABMC, and the announcement was placed in the *Commerce Business Daily* (no date recorded). Five hundred fliers were sent to the American Institute of Architects in Washington, and 1600 were mailed to art and architecture schools around the country. An advertisement appeared in the *USA Today* and *Stars And Stripes* and General Stilwell was interviewed on Good Morning America.

The design program document was also prepared in the fall by the Baltimore District, approved by the Board (and by request, reviewed by the National Capital Memorial Commission on December 13th) and printed. It was to be mailed on January 30, 1989 and returned by May 1, 1989, included a 15-page narrative, an aerial photograph of the western Mall from the Potomac River to the Washington Monument, two site-plan prints 1"=30' scale and 1"=200' scale, and sixteen photographs of the site, keyed directionally to a small scale orientation map. Pertinent highlights included:

1. The Ash Woods 7.5 acres site is located east of Daniel Chester French Drive and Independence Avenue, SW, and about two hundred feet south of the Reflecting Pool.

2. The Memorial was to be located on 2.2 acres in a 4.5-acre area with surrounding space for three acres of pathways and approaches.

3. The entries were limited to two, 20-inch by 30-inch panels.

4. A list of twenty-two design requirements and limitations, that helped to define the parameters of the competition, including:

-one 50-foot flag pole was required,

-arts forms that were contemplated could be figurative or abstract,

-water could be a design element,

-no roofed or domed structure, with 40-foot height limitation for any design element, and

-an area to accommodate several hundred participants.

Above: Design Competition Program Announcement. Below: Vietnam Veterans Memorial.

The eleven-page Design Competition and Rules was also included in the packet and it contained important facts:

A. $30.00 entry fee was required along with a February 27th notification of intent-to-participate.

B. Awards: $20,000 for first prize; $10,000 for second, $5,000 for the third and up to 15 honorable mentions ($1,000, each).

C. In the unlikely event the winning design is disapproved and cannot be altered to be acceptable and receive approval, then the second place design will be considered for approval and realization of the design. (Rule 3.6)

D. An Advisory Panel will provide professional support (in their disciplines of architecture, landscape architecture, sculpture, other fine arts) to the KWVMAB Jury, during the evaluation of design submissions, as may be necessary for it to make informed decisions. (Rule 5.2)

E. The ABMC shall review designs for the purpose intended. (Rule 9.2)

F. It is anticipated that the winner of the design competition will be retained in a consultant capacity under separate contract with the A/E firm selected by the Agent to realize the design. (Rule 10.2)

Architect Paul Harbeson, long-time consultant to the ABMC, would be the competition manager, and he was responsible for selecting the five-person panel of professional advisers—Frederick S. Osborne, Jr., Dean and Director of the Schools, The Pennsylvania Academy of the Fine Arts; Lauren Ewing, Mason Cross School of Art, Rutgers University; Ronald Lee Fleming, Townscape Institute (Cambridge, MA); Archie Mackenize, School of Architecture, Cornell University and Arthur Sullivan, Department of Landscape Architecture, North Carolina State University.

May 1989, Design Competition Jury. (L to R): Col. William Weber, USA (Ret), Gen. Richard Stilwell, USA (Ret), Col. Fred Cherry, USAF (Ret), Edward Borcherdt, Carlos Rodriguez, Gen. Ray Davis, USMC (Ret), William McSweeny, James D. "Mike" McKevitt. Photo by Col. Rosemary McCarthy, USA (Ret).

As early as January 23, 1989, the Design Committee prepared a six-page plan and guide for the two-week judging, scheduled for May 15th to 26th. It called for reviews, votes and discussions in four phases. Each juror, and by this time all Board Members had agreed to participate, could select 20 designs. This process would be completed twice more. There was an important stipulation agreed to: after each of the first three voting stages, a member could request that one design, not receiving three votes, be carried forward. At the end of each judging sequence, all rejected designs would be removed. The final vote (from the top twenty-five entries) would rank the top three finalists.

Things looked promising as the Board learned at a December 18, 1988 update: the COE Baltimore District had received over 1600 responses to the circular and anticipated 1200 entries. In fact only 1,019 registrations were submitted and 543 design submissions presented. This considerable reduction may well be attributed to the fact that thirty-five years after the end of this war, the passions of aged veterans were muted. The Vietnam War Memorial competition occurred only five years after the United States Embassy was surrendered. The design submissions were displayed in the Great Hall of the Pension Building, Washing-

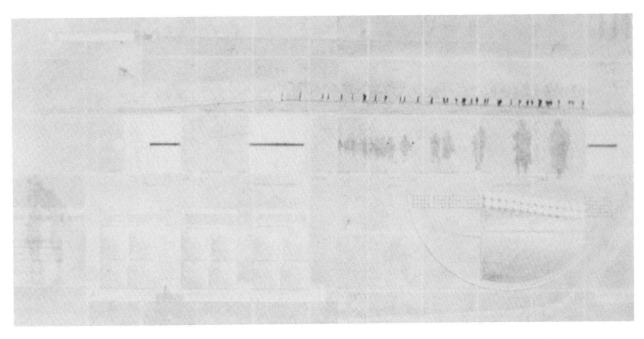

First Place winning design concept boards.

ton, DC, under the coordination of the Engineering Division of the Baltimore District. The designs were received in Baltimore, inventoried, photographed and sent to Washington by May 10. The installation was completed by May 15.

Ten members voted (Hausman was deceased and Curcio was absent), with some interesting procedural changes, two rather than three votes would be the cut-off, and the voting period of twelve days was reduced to six. In the first round, Board members also asked the five consultants to vote for twenty boards (not to influence the outcome, but as a comparison exercise). The first round was completed with 117 entries that received two or more votes brought forward. Interestingly, only one Board member voted for #247. By invoking the one vote design stipulation, this entry stayed alive. Two of the five consultants included this design in their top-twenty informal ranking. After the first vote, the Jury stated formally that "no entry submitted completely met the expectations of the concept statement developed by the Board."

A second vote was taken. This time only 22 entries received two votes or more, so three entries were forwarded to the next round by

the one vote design waiver. Now all of the entries were evaluated for potential cost by Paul Harbeson, who estimated that only one of the 25 finalists could be built for $5 million dollars. A third vote resulted in 23 entries. At this point, the ten members ranked the top eight designs: First prize (#247) to Burns-Lucas, Leon, Lucas and Pennypacker-Oberholtzer of State College, PA. (Leon was the designated team leader). Second prize (#27) to Ronald C. Nims of Las Cruces, NM. Third prize (#162) to Mark P. Fondersmith of Baltimore, MD. The prizes in the amount of $20,000, $10,000, and $5,000 were awarded to the three finalists. The fifteen honorable mentions (five were given special notice for merit) each received $1,000.

The final tally sheets were found in the KWVMAB archives and the voting breakdown survived: #247 got four first-place votes, two third-place votes and two 4th-place votes. Even though it did not receive a majority of votes, it became a "consensus" or "unanimous" choice, as a way to insure that everyone would actively support the winner. This action is in the tradition of military decision making, where after debate and argument, points are made and a decision reached, everyone rallies together to ensure a successful mission. It was also re-

215

corded that Consultant Ewing took several Board Members (McSweeney, Borcherdt and McCarthy actually recalled the importance of this visit) to inspect the Grant Memorial, eight blocks from their meeting place. This was done to show that a full-scale, multi-figured sculptural solution could be achieved. The record of the Board's vote was reported to the American Battle Monuments Commission on May 26th, the winners were personally notified and announced publicly on June 1, 1989.

Chapter Seven: The Design Concept

As the project was envisioned, the winning design would be implemented by a competent architectural firm. This safeguard was put in place by the Corps of Engineers because of the memories of complications of the Vietnam Veterans Memorial project: a second-year Yale University (School of Architecture) master's degree candidate won the competition. She had no practical training, and was not licensed as an architect in Washington. The client, the Vietnam Memorial Fund, had to advertise for an "Architect of Record" (a wonderful, inside-the-Beltway title) to develop, implement and build her design.

That the winners were themselves professionally credentialed and independently licensed was to become an issue. The four were faculty members in the College of Arts and Architecture, Penn State University, State College, PA: John Lucas (architect) and his wife Veronica Burns-Lucas (landscape architect) joined the faculty in 1988, having practiced before in Maryland; Don Alvaro Leon (architect) had left private practice in New York City and Philadelphia in 1979 to begin teaching, and Eliza Pennypacker Oberholtzer (landscape-architect), who came to the university as an instructor in 1982. Their collaboration only began in 1988, and this effort offered

a real test of their professional compatibility: "It was a matter of personalities seeming to match and our ideas on the design profession seeming to match. We had talked about doing some work together. This project was a low-riskway to find out if our ideas were truly compatible. It was really a surprise to all of us that the process went as smoothly and as productively as it did."

The four designers and the Board met for the first time in the basement of the Department of Interior building, on May 25, 1989, not only to get acquainted but to prepare a strategy for the McKevitt-McSweeney sponsored Rose Garden ceremony, scheduled for June 14th. The pressing matter was the need to build a model of the design as presented, a visual prop for the White House unveiling, little more than two weeks away. While there was much in the design to which Board members reacted individually: the red line—its reference to blood and its color association with Communism—was a detail that would go, the steepness of the ramp for wheelchair-bound Rodriguez, and an unrelenting interest in recognizing the contribution of women in the Korean War by McCarthy. Generals Stilwell and Davis, as the latter remembered, spoke about the need in the east plaza to tell more literally the story of the other soldiers, sailors, marines and airmen, who supported the ground troops, as well as a "sanctuary, an open chapel, a special place" to remember the dead, the missing in action and those that were held prisoner.

The positive kernel for these veterans was the line of soldiers, evoking a war fought on the ground, not unlike the trench fighting in World War I. A May 24, 1989 folder from the four designers, began by noting "the stunning news that we won the Design Competition,

216

marks a moment we will treasure forever." What must have appealed to the veterans was the explanation about sculptural development: "The proposed formation of the line of statues is inspired by documented Korean War photos (photocopies of 21 prints were included). This formation will be modeled in great detail, further based upon field-taken photos of specific individuals. An experienced Korean War veteran will function as technical advisor regarding outfitting and field practices."

The down-to-earth tone of the May 24th statement was next rudely balanced by a letter of May 30, 1989, sent to Colonel Badger, and unexplainably not to General Stilwell. The four now spoke in much more esoteric tones to the consternation of the Board: "From a distance, one sees the Memorial as an elusive dream-like presence of ghostly figures moving across a remote landscape. Walking with the thirty-eight figures . . ., the visitor is an observer, in the act of commemoration, and is simultaneously at one with the figures, the 39th presence . . . . Faintly the figures appear again . . . images recalled from the past to honor all acts of service in the war."

Burns-Lucas, Leon, Lucas and Pennypacker-Oberholtzer (BL3) had created their vision of a memorial to America's Korean War veterans; it was a four-month, intensive, well-researched effort. What was now needed, but apparently did not happen, was for the designers to begin to talk, interview and interact with the members of the Board to learn about their collective 36-year experiences, frames of references, remembrances. Most, if not all, of the great public monument projects in America are co-equal collaborations of client and creator. Daniel Chester French, sculptor of the nearby Abraham Lincoln statue, often called his patron's "co-creators," refer-

ring to his design as their concept. For some reason BL3 was unwilling to invest time in fact-finding with their new client. It seems, in retrospect, a common sense courtesy at best and a thoughtless oversight at worst.

In presenting their choice to the American Battle Monuments Commission, Stilwell carefully claimed: "The Board is of the unanimous view that its selection has captured the essence of the Korean War; will be applauded by the major veterans organizations, and in particular, by individuals who knew the conflict first hand, and above all, will constitute an uplifting experience for viewers of all ages, now and in the future."

From the very beginning BL3 misread Stilwell's word "unanimous." It did not reflect a perfect first-place vote from all KWVMAB members. In fact, among the ten, there were five different first-place finishers: #247 (4 votes), #27 (3), #243 (1), #210 (1) and #333 (1). No one was willing to change his/her vote.

Many members were still learning the ins-and-outs of their colleagues, some were a little defensive, others protective, almost territorial, of their favorite. A full day was spent talking, negotiating, lobbying; everyone listened, no vote was switched. But closure needed to be reached, as only one memorial was going to be built. As Stilwell later recalled: "It was the dialogue that convinced a majority of the jurors of the potential of #247 to achieve our goals. In short, the basis for selection of #247, and what has been heralded since, was the heroic-sized statues, mission bent, advancing on the American flag."

Advisory Board members saw a line of marching combat soldiers (albeit now one-inch figurines in the public-relations model) not an allegorical statement about war. Veronica Burns-Lucas felt that: "In our memorial the assignment was to commemorate all who served in Korea, the living and the dead, as well as the act of serving. In light of that, and with the difference in the public acceptance of the two wars (Vietnam and Korea), ours is a more positive representation, more of a celebration of human courage."

Board member McSweeney, writing in December, 1990, reacted differently to events he recalled from May of 1989: "I am sure that a soldierly formation can take the place of a line of march in some eyes, but the whole spiritual concept of the Memorial was that the line of soldiers could either be marching into contact or be returning from a mission well done."

The Board saw BL3's design as a point of departure. It was a line of soldiers, fellow combatants to these veterans—displayed on the presentation boards and suggested in an artisan's shorthand in the Rose Garden-generated model—that caught their collective eye.

At this point these soldiers were little more than make-believe sculptures. And BL3 would soon be entangled in a lose-it-all battle with the Board, which had every intention of winning. Why the Penn State professors failed to appreciate the nuances of Washington reviewer's pronouncements will always be a mystery. They were being bombarded with numerous go-slows.

Chapter Eight: Warning Signals and Troubled Times

BL3 seemed to believe the upcoming review presentation was to be a simple, rubber-stamping formality. Their focus for the Memorial was self-explanatory: the passage of a platoon-size military unit, moving from a zone of peace (a granite plaza with a grove of American dogwoods) through a zone of war (a central, 5-foot wide path, flanked by 38 granite soldiers walking over the rocky terrain of a shallow stream) to a plaza of reflection, peace, a metaphor for home.

While the Advisory Board liked the soldiers, they were less enamored of the metaphors and symbols. They were much more focused on the review process that would foretell the fate of their project.

The process, strengthened by the Commemorative Works Act of 1986, provided for a several-step procedural evaluation, that began with the "internal" examination by the National Capital Region of the Park Service at its several-agency working group—the National Capital Memorial Commission (NCMC), then moved to the "advisory" recommendation of the Commission of Fine Arts and to the "mandated" review of the National Capital Planning Commission. Each group could provide official commentary at any time. Follow-up discussions to address details at later stages of implementation were possible. All that was officially required was that all three agencies sign off on the first concept and the final design submission.

The National Park Service, in its submittal letter to the three review agencies, expressed detailed as well as thematic concerns. They questioned the wisdom of pruning the Linden

Model of winning design concept, June 1989.

Charles Atherton, Executive Secretary of the Commission of Fine Arts, countered, finding the design to be extraordinary: he was "incredibly relieved to view a conceptual design that offers great promise."

Plane trees to give the impression of battlefield devastation by artillery shelling, and identified a problem with the thorny barberry shrubs collecting trash and debris. They felt concern "that the unrelieved circulation embodied in the design concept would present real problems for the visitors." The shallow and gently flowing water areas under the soldiers' feet would have to be monitored to prevent the introduction of moss and algae that would make them "unattractive and potentially dangerous." They expressed concerns about the mature elms and red oaks in Ash Woods, and ordered that a tree inventory be included in future submissions identifying those that should be saved, if at all possible, and those that must be removed.

The clouds of doubt only darkened at the first NCMC review on June 20, 1989. The designers and the Board made their presentation and the eight commissioners reacted. Elliot Carroll (representing the Architect of the Capitol) spoke prophetically: "I respect the whole competition system as a way at arriving at design concepts of this nature. But I have also been a proponent of the idea that competitions are the way to select designers, not the design, because there is no opportunity in a competition for the designer to work closely with his clients—and that has to happen after the competition."

John Parsons, Chairman and a Park Service civil servant, representing the future custodian of the Memorial, talked in specifics: the narrow, 5-foot-wide pedestrian walkway, accessibility for the handicapped, railings along the ramp to the flag, moss and algae in the pools and water areas. He was particularly concerned about the dense southern-perimeter screen, intruding unacceptably into the openness of West Potomac Park.

Robert Gresham of NCPC also spoke, claiming that while he liked the theme, he struggled with approving a concept that is so closely dependent on a "fortress-like buffer of trees."

As this was the first major Area I project NCMC reviewed, their role became important. In the past the Park Service sent design-reviews directly to the Fine Arts and Planning Commissions; NCMC was a new cog in the wheel. An approval vote was ordered, it was a four-four tie—it must have sent shockwaves through the ranks of the four designers and four board members in the audience. A compromise was reached, the project with its boards, drawings and 1,000-pound model, would be returned without comment, with the stipulation that the design would be thoroughly restudied for resubmission. Four months of thinking by the Penn State University design-team and two

219

weeks of careful evaluation by KWVMAB, guided by five "knowledgeable" arts professionals, would not be lost.

The National Capital Planning Commission (NCPC) at a July 17, 1989 meeting gave what can only be regarded as bare-bones approval. While they responded favorably to the strong symbolism of the Memorial's theme, they questioned the containment landscaping—the bosque of trees on the north and the dense Arborvitae hedge on the south, feeling that it was an intrusive barrier to the openness in this area of the Mall. They indicated that the Memorial designers and the ABMC, in close coordination with the Park Service and the NCPC would be required to refine the concept.

In preparing preliminary design plans, nine specific reservations would need to be addressed, including a fundamental concern that "the single, one-way pedestrian circulation system . . . may not be practical to control in an open park environment." Also relief for the paved east plaza with planting materials or paving patterns was questioned as was the width and design of the central walkway. The prompt determination of the sculpture program as "they are the dominant feature in the design concept" was critical. The Commission's recommendation was followed by an eight-page single-spaced "Background and Staff Evaluation," which offered ample evidence of all areas of concern.

The Commission of Fine Arts raised fewer objections at its July 26, 1989 review, suggesting that holly trees, staggered in two rows might be employed at a southern end. They had no problem with the barberry and the pruned plane trees. The east plaza was acceptable but

the abundance of granite paving would leave this area "hot and glaring in the summer months." An optimistic tone was presented by Chairman J. Carter Brown, writing on August 9th, to Robert Stanton: "We viewed our meeting as the first of many occasions where we will be working with the design team in looking at the myriad details that evolve as the design itself further develops. We feel the concept design has great merit and holds out much promise for successfully taking its place with the major memorials in Washington."

But even this glowing sentence could not forestall the CFA's later decision (on June 26,1991), to reject the BL3 design, even as substantially modified by Cooper-Lecky, because the concept was too large and contained too many sculptures.

A fourth agency was permitted to comment about the design—the District of Columbia Historic Preservation Review Board of the DC-State Historic Preservation Office. Their involvement was requested by the National Park Service. On July 19, 1989, the Preservation Board reviewed the design concept and indicated that there was no adverse impact on its historically prominent national-landmark neighbors. But these seven, chaired by James Speight, Jr., offered their comments, questioning the monumental line of sculptures ending in an empty plaza, rejecting the high curving wall of trees as inappropriate, wondering if granite was the correct medium for the sculptures and encouraging the saving of all mature elms. They ended their report, "looking forward to reviewing the revised design and its details when developed." (On April 3, 1991, the Preservation Board noted the revised design had no adverse impact.)

From overall features to specific details, doubts and reservations, even objections were raised about the design whose only unconditional approval came from the American Battle Monuments Commission (as the model was being transported to the White House ceremony.) One might speculate from this present-day vantage point why the three Commissions and the National Park Service did not reject the proposed memorial scheme outright, given the abundance of their collective criticisms. That a terminal blow was not struck reflects the long established practices of the Planning and the Fine Arts commissions to work with prospective clients to bring out the best, even in the roughest of preliminary ideas.

Clearly there was much work to be undertaken. While the success of the June 14 Rose Garden reception was now severely tarnished by the official reviews, the clients and the designers should have regrouped, taking full measure of the "political" protection the White House ceremony provided. These sessions had provided, at best, lukewarm endorsement of the design. The June-July comments acknowledged that design development was going to be laborious, with many more opportunities for probing questions and hard-ball negotiations.

Rather than dismiss the considerable efforts already spent on this important national project by the Advisory Board and the ABMC members, these agencies gave a proceed-with-caution endorsement. It would take, given the first-round expressions of concern, even longer for the project to wend its way through the maze of Washington's art-review bureaucracies. But many other successful Washington landmarks had endured these commissions. Try as hard as one might, they could not be ignored, overlooked or dismissed.

The CFA and the NCPC have different mandates and, with the passage of the 1986 Commemorative Works Act, confusing spheres of jurisdiction and duplicate powers. But these nineteen individuals (seven with CFA and 12 with NCPC) usually get it right. They don't choose who is erecting a memorial; they only arbitrate with the messenger and the maker to deliver on what has been promised. The Nation's Capital deserves to have public art works of the highest order. No matter how deserving the cause or noble a purpose, the quest for quality should be paramount.

Why the designers and the Board did not immediately sit down for a series of frank discussions is not known. Their attention may have been focused on redefining its "designing" mission with the ABMC. In the original March 11, 1988 memorandum, there was the opportunity to renegotiate. Since the design selection was far from certain, the Board proposed an update, claiming that the "foreshortened single stage competition" had not produced a "fully developed, detailed concept."

The Board's involvement was still needed to deal with refinements—the wall of trees at the south, the layout of the East plaza and the new ideas—the content of the wall panels, the selection of quotations and the formation of the column of troops. This document was sent to General Goodpaster on August 3rd; Stilwell received an answer five days later: "Although there may be some disagreement as to the exact point of termination of the Board's responsibility for the selection of design, the Commission believes that the Board can make a significant contribution towards the complete definition of the concept."

The Board kept a foot in the door. The ABMC and the Corps were seeking the services of an Architect-Engineer firm. The Board turned its attention to fundraising as the ABMC's construction estimate for the design they had chosen grew from $5 million to $8.625 million.

Chapter Nine: Securing Architect-Engineering Services

Having successfully prepared the competition materials for the Board, the Corps of Engineers (Baltimore District) met with the ABMC in Washington on February 22, 1989, to begin the search for the Architect-Engineer (A-E). Since design development would take about one year, it was proposed that this phase be conducted concurrently with the competition. The ABMC said no; and the resulting postponement delayed project completion for many months.

The preparation of the Scope of Work statement was performed by the Baltimore District staff. The need for the services of an Architect-Engineer was announced in the Commerce Business Daily, the official Federal bulletin, only once, on June 22, 1989, under the heading— "Design and Related Studies in Connection with the Korean War Veterans Memorial, Washington, DC." Submittal deadline was July 20, 1989. Kent Cooper and William Lecky saw the CBD announcement. Having lived through the turmoil of the Vietnam Veterans Memorial, they initially wondered if the firm could survive a second memorial on the Mall. But having worked well with the Corps over the past 20 years, almost at the last minute, the principals decided to enter their credentials. In short order they submitted the required SF255 (project statement) and SF254 (professional credentials) forms, listing several collaborators - many from the design team who had worked with Cooper-Lecky years before on the Vietnam Veterans Memorial project.

Press conference on Ash Woods site announcing selection of Cooper-Lecky as the Architect of Record. (L to R): William Lecky, Kent Cooper, Gen. Richard Stilwell, USA (Ret).

The A-E Services review committee, that included 8 COE-Baltimore staff, landscape architect Murray Geyer (from Washington headquarters) and Colonel Badger (ABMC), met on August 9, 1989 to review just ten submissions. Four short-listed firms, Cooper-Lecky Architects, PC (CLA) of Washington, DC; Clarke Rapuano Inc. of New York, NY; Sasaki Associates, Inc. of Watertown, MA and EDAW, Inc. of Alexandria, VA, were invited to Baltimore to make a presentation and be interviewed, each for one hour, on September 13, 1989.

The Baltimore District selection group measured the four finalists in two areas, experience and understanding of the project: Cooper-Lecky ranked #1, because of their experience with the Vietnam Veterans Memorial, the inclusion on an art consultant, and for addressing the issue of circulation as CLA had "wrestled with the Vietnam Memorial's inability to handle large numbers of people." Third place was awarded to the Sasaki-BL3 group.

This was an unusual teaming. As the Penn State designers realized that their views and the Board's about the Memorial design were growing apart, they explored the option of working with a larger, more established firm. This would offer them a strong voice in design development. The Baltimore reviewers, quickly rejected this spur-of-the-moment arrangement, and questioned Sasaki's decision to place the BL3 firm in "a key management role in design rather than (serving) as a source of guidance, insuring the continuity of the competition winner in design implementation." They believed John Lucas sought out Sasaki, and noted, quite correctly, that BL3 "is a very small firm of professors, practicing architecture incidental to teaching." They felt that BL3 did not have "the expertise or the experience to manage a design of this magnitude and complexity."

The selection notification letter was sent to Cooper-Lecky, Architects, PC (CLA) on October 13, 1989. A draft of the Scope of Architect-Engineer (A-E) Services for Design and Related Studies document (developed by Murray Geyer, Alexandra Crawford and William Taylor with Fred Badger, beginning on September 15, 1989) was received by Cooper-Lecky on October 18th. In the spirit of renewed cooperation (captured in the revised memorandum of agreement of August 8, 1989), the ABMC sent a copy of the Scope of Work for review by the Board. The Baltimore District officials met with Kent Cooper and Bill Lecky on October 27th. (The KWVMAB was not invited to this meeting.) The architects were given until December 15, 1989, to submit their fee proposal along with written explanations of the work duties, for themselves and their sub-contractors, and estimates of work hours. The Scope of Work was returned for revisions; it was reworked by CLA and presented again on February 17, 1990. A third version was revised and resubmitted on March 14, 1990. Final

approval, as contained in Contract No. DACA31-90-C-0057, came on April 11, 1990.

Even though the Sasaki/BL3 joint venture failed to win Corps approval, the State College designers, as competition winners, were entitled to serve as project consultants to Cooper-Lecky. Meanwhile CLA was engrossed in defining how they would be reporting to the various clients and marshalling the design through the various review commissions. As the ABMC/KWVMAB timeclock was ticking, the architects were given permission by the Corps to undertake a specific task—secure the services of a sculptor or team of sculptors.

On October 31, 1989, John Lucas, his wife Veronica, Don Leon and Eliza Pennypacker-Oberholtzer came to Washington to meet with Bill Lecky and Kent Cooper to discuss how this relationship was to work. Any type of hierarchical arrangement among professionals poses difficulties; in this project, they would only be magnified. In an internal memorandum of November 8, 1989, CLA identified six areas of program analysis—the Central Hill, the Path, the Fountain, the Entrance Plaza, the Assembly Plaza and the Containment. At this time the architects had not met with the Board; they were receiving their marching orders from the ABMC. The often tumultuous experiences of the Vietnam project taught both Cooper and Lecky to be proactive and expansive.

John Lucas and his lawyer met with Bill Lecky on November 14, 1989 to negotiate both their role and fee. On December 4th, Lecky wrote to the Corps' project manager, William Taylor, seeking clarification: "The winning design team wanted to actively participate in the development of the design, i. e. lead in the working out of the details. CLA's interpretation of the Corps' directive is that CLA would develop design options and details, with BL3 playing an active consulting role in the reviewing process. Having lived through this process once before (Vietnam Veterans Memorial), and being contractually responsible to the Corps, CLA feels the second option is the only viable one. This issue can have tremendous impact on the hours and cost to be negotiated."

As contract negotiations began with the Corps of Engineers and Cooper-Lecky, that division would widen. BL3 proposed a consulting role for themselves amounting to $180,000; by the end of negotiations that figure was reduced, in large measure at the direction of the Corps, to about $50,000.

A March 26, 1990 letter from the Chief of the Engineering Division, Baltimore District, sealed the fate of BL3's active involvement: "Their proposed involvement should not create a redundancy of personnel or assigned tasks. Also our office selected your firm to perform subject design based on your team members. We in no way intend that you should substitute BL3 for any of your team members. In fact this would not be consistent with the basis for your being hired."

As directed by the Corps, BL3 would play a consulting role in the project; Cooper and Lecky would work directly with the clients. It was not a totally smooth arrangement. There were lots of letters exchanged; some never written. There were too few meetings held and too many postponed. The Corps provided the organizational cover for the ABMC. Although they had no experience building a memorial, they were not unfamiliar with the multi-tiered, only-in-Washington review process. The ABMC remained disappointed at being upstaged by the

Advisory Board. Ready to build the second of its three Washington memorials (the first was the Pershing, the third is the now-authorized World War II project), Ryan and Badger found the design phase of the Korean War memorial placed in the hands of 12 take-charge veterans.

The KWVMAB was aware that their wishes and BL3's desires for the Memorial were now widely divergent. After the December 20, 1989, gathering of the Board, Cooper/Lecky Architects and BL3, Lucas wrote to Cooper-Lecky: "Yesterday's meeting was not atypical of our discussions with them to date. The Board members seemed to have a vision of the project which is wholly literal, representational and, I am afraid in some ways, quite counter to the design."

These were confusing times, and things would only get worse in the coming months.

Chapter Ten: Behind-the-Scene Struggles and the Lawsuits

The June 14th ceremony in the Rose Garden meant different things to the various players. For some of the Advisory Board it was one of the first of many public-relations coups to stimulate their national fundraising efforts. This prestigious event demonstrated hands-on progress. For other Board members, cognizant of the mind-muddling review process that lay ahead, the event was a preemptive act, announcing to the governmental reviewers that this project had friends in high places.

To the competition design winners, John Lucas, Veronica Burns-Lucas, Don Leon, and Eliza Pennypacker-Oberholtzer, the Rose Garden ceremony provided an official stamp of approval for their design, a halo of executive respectability. As discussions about design intent and the ultimate message of the memorial continued with the Advisory Board, however, it was becoming clear that there was disagreement between the two parties.

As contract negotiations began in the fall of 1989 with the Corps of Engineers and Cooper-Lecky, that division would widen. BL3 proposed a consulting role for themselves amounting to $180,000; by the end of negotiations that figure was reduced, in large measure at the direction of the Corps, to about $50,000.

BL3 was not happy. In a December 18, 1990 press release, they claimed their design "had received unanimous approval" during the summer of 1989; though it clearly had, at best, received only a conditional go-ahead. From the outset, the Board believed they could accept and develop all, part, or any portion of the winning design. What caught the attention of the ten Board members was the line of sculpture soldiers, evocatively rendered by photographic images and tiny silhouetted figures on the two presentation panels. For the designers not to have assumed their sculptural program might be perceived differently by an engaged client—twelve veterans of the Korean War—seems, from today's vantage point, to be naively preposterous.

Cooper and Lecky listened hard to the Board's position and incorporated their changes—the open chapel, a narrative wall for honoring support troops and those who had fallen or been taken prisoner, and the need for the soldiers to be connected with Korean War combat. While there is no doubt that the elements of sculpture, architecture and landscape in the winning concept were evocative, BL3s reliance on symbolic messages was dropped. With the Board's blessing, the architects struggled with many troubling points in the

President George Bush unveiling winning memorial design model, June 1989.

Cooper-Lecky's first iteration of design concept.

design: the steep ramp, the barren plaza, the circular landscape screening and the 5-foot-wide, 320-foot-long path flanked by six pools. And as design alterations were developed by Cooper-Lecky, BL3 was furious. Despite the harsh criticism from the various reviewing agencies, BL3 thought that winning a national design competition was enough to justify making no changes to the design.

225

A new strategy began to emerge. Cooper and Lecky were working diligently to explore new directions that might gain approval from the CFA and the NCPC. BL3's isolation from the Board and their professional floundering in the world of memorial making in Washington would take its toll. As found in a September 4, 1990 letter to CFA Chairman Brown, BL3 lamented: "The design that the Commission of Fine Arts supported has been lost. The west-east axis representing the 38th parallel is gone; the white marble squares with their inscriptions invoking reflection upon war and peace are gone; the symbolic journey of the visitor from peace to war to peace is gone; the time line of the war is gone; the cruciform plan, relating the Memorial to archetypal sacred constructs, is gone."

It seems only natural that a client's ideas, views and desires about their memorial would evolve. Change seems to inevitably be at the heart of good memorial design. Work at it until it is right, or at least until some third-party referee gives its blessings. While some believe that these agencies give the designed-by-committee concept a bad name, the process works. These agencies pit their here-and-now expertise against the future's unknown standards of taste. That the *Lincoln*, *Jefferson* and *Vietnam* memorials were built under this stricture offers proof of its efficacy.

The ABMC had counted on the "design" work of the Advisory Board to be officially finished by June 14th. In fact just the opposite was of concern to the Advisory Board; the consultation, concern and commitment was needed all the more, as the design would have to change. The twenty-five objections raised by the NCMC, CFA and NCPC offered ample proof of the need for their continued participation.

226

Although lawyers were being threatened by September 17, 1990, BL3 hoped that the CFA

meeting on December 13, 1990, would settle the issue. After Cooper-Lecky and the Advisory Board presented their revised design, BL3 was, as a courtesy, provided an opportunity to speak. They presented the competition winning design with a few minor alterations. They apparently thought the CFA would see the wisdom of their design skills and recommend to the Advisory Board that they be reinstated. The CFA could only point out the impossibility of their request. Resolution in the courts, not in the drafting room was now to be their course of action. BL3 seemed convinced their design would be butchered without their counsel. They were now irrevocably out of the picture.

A law suit (90-3072) was subsequently filed against the Corps of Engineers, the ABMC, the Advisory Board and the architects, on December 19, 1990 in the United States Court of the District of Columbia, and it was given to Judge Charles R. Richey. After much back and forth, a hearing was set for September 20, 1991 and on October 24, 1991, the judge dismissed the charges against the ABMC, the Board and the Corps. Defendants Cooper-Lecky Architects had to wait; their case was dismissed on April 9, 1992.

The plaintiff then appealed to the United States Court of Appeals for the District of Columbia Circuit (Record No. 91-5396) on June 2, 1992, with oral arguments presented on March 8, 1993. The judgment of the District Court was reaffirmed on March 20, 1993, by Circuit Judges Silberman, Williams and D. H. Ginsburg.

A complaint (91-42C) was also filed in the United States Claims Court on January 16, 1991, asking $250,000 in damages. This case was dismissed on February 14, 1992, "for failure to state a claim on which relief can be awarded," with the comment: "Appellants read too much into the rules. Rather than guaranteeing the winners a role as consultants, the rules merely indicate that it is "anticipated" that the winners would be retained in that capacity. Far from giving the winners any right to protect the "integrity of their design," the rules state only that, as consultants, they will have "an opportunity to review and comment on the development of the design."

There was relief for the Board members that the legal wrangling was finally over. The legal shadow had caused everyone in official reviewing circles to go slow. These delays increased costs. Reactions from Board members ranged from headaches to roast-in-hell anger.

Chapter 11: Design Evolution 1990 - 1993

Although Cooper-Lecky had been permitted to begin work on the sculptor-selection phase, the firm was not officially hired by the AMBC (under contract with the Corps of Engineers) until April 11, 1990. The Baltimore District and the architects had now agreed to a set of tasks and a time schedule in which each would be performed.

After reviewing the competition winning design in some detail, and reading the various transcripts from the reviewing agencies, it was clear that some real problems existed. Some of the main issues were as follows:

A. Circulation through the memorial was one way. It was too narrow, and terribly confusing to the visitor.

B. The original design was surrounded by a high (20 ft.) hedge which blocked the view of the Lincoln Memorial from Independence Avenue.

C. Minimal tribute was made in the design to the support personnel - an important ingredient to the Advisory Board.

D. Minimal tribute was made to those who were killed, missing, or wounded.

E. The large plaza housing the flag was felt to be very unfriendly to the visitor - too hot, too sunny, too big.

F. The tortured landscape was criticized by the National Park Service.

G. The CFA warned that the entire composition was simply too big - too much of a statement for that location on the nation's Mall.

H. Many felt there was too much allegory, too much symbolism for the visitor to grasp.

As a result, for the next three months Cooper and Lecky had numerous discussions with BL3, trying to deepen their understanding of the most salient aspects of the design. It was clear to them that significant changes would need to be undertaken, but they hoped to preserve the essence of BL3's message. BL3, however, was unmoving on the issue of change. And, though Cooper-Lecky developed a series of optional alterations, BL3 asked that none of these be presented to the Advisory Board for their consideration.

So a meeting was arranged with the Advisory Board in early June of 1990. Out of respect for the original designers, Cooper-Lecky only presented very minor alterations to the original design - those approved by BL3. General Stilwell, Chairman of the Board, was not pleased. After the presentation, Cooper and Lecky privately explained that they had developed several other options, but had not presented them at the request of BL3. Stilwell asked for another meeting the next day to review those options. He asked that BL3 not be in attendance.

227

The next day, Cooper-Lecky presented a "Morphologies Drawing Book" that focused on the path, circulation, the east plaza and containment. This was subsequently developed into the "Circulation Design Workbook" of June, 1990, in which Cooper-Lecky laid out four solutions to the Memorial's circulation: (1) Bridge, (2) Overlook, (3) Delta and (4) Valley.

The Bridge scheme pulled the ramp away from the wall and permitted the visitor a second access to a northern "Chapel" area. The sloping ramp still divided the plaza, but the circulation was better.

The Overlook scheme, eliminated the ramp and direct access to the flag. Entrance to the plaza was along a slanting path tucked in behind the wall, or by pathways at the north and south. This scheme provided an uninterrupted wall surface of 250 feet.

The Delta scheme represented a major shift in the composition, breaking the design into three components - the column of ground troopers honoring the veterans who served in the field, a new element (the mural wall) which was there to honor all the support forces, and finally an area to honor those who were killed or missing. Circulation was arranged in a triangle (hence the Delta designation) with each leg devoted to one of the three areas of tribute.

The Valley scheme offered a flat, level path from west to east. The flag was visible through an opening in the wall. This eliminated the ramp. A diagonal walk under the plane trees at the north perimeter was introduced, providing two returns to the entrance plaza.

The Advisory Board was taken with the Delta scheme—clearly the most divergent option from the original BL3 design. It was clear that this would need further negotiation and discussion with the ABMC. After some behind-closed-doors, General-to-General negotiation, the matter was resolved; Cooper-Lecky was instructed to proceed with further development of the Delta scheme.

228

Bridge.

Overlook.

Delta.

Valley.

Cooper and Lecky were both concerned about BL3's reaction to this turn of events. The next day they both drove to Pennsylvania in an effort to ease the BL3 team through the recent changes. It didn't work. BL3 was outraged. It was their decision to withdraw from further design work.

The Board wholeheartedly supported CLA's rationale for the Delta traffic scheme exercises. On August 10, 1990, three iterations (3.2.1, 3.2.2, and 3.2.3) of this idea were presented. The schemes (several Board members thought one looked like an ice cream cone) brought further ideas into play. A United Nations flag plaza was introduced. A concave mural wall, a circular treatment of free-standing wall panels was introduced as a tribute to the support forces. In each study, some elements from the BL3's concept remained: a slanting walkway between the soldiers, flagpole, and landscaped areas of the barberry and plane trees, but the setting was radically different.

From these studies, Cooper-Lecky created an expanded design, which included the ever-consistent column of ground troopers going up a hill toward the American flag, a curvilinear mural wall, and a still, circular reflecting pool to honor the killed and missing. But the overall plan had moved away from the Delta plan geometry, and instead was configured along a series of curved pathways - similar in feeling to the recently developed "Constitution Gardens" on the north side of the Reflecting Pool. This scheme was enthusiastically supported by the Advisory Board and the ABMC. Through the review process, it received rave reviews from the Park Service and the Nat'l Capitol Memorial Commission.

The Commission of Fine Arts, however, was another story. They felt it was still too big, took up too much real estate, and was misguided in assuming that a curvalinear pathway system would ultimately be developed over time on the south side of the Reflecting Pool. It was not

Delta design plan, Scheme 3.2.1

Delta design plan, Scheme 3.2.2.

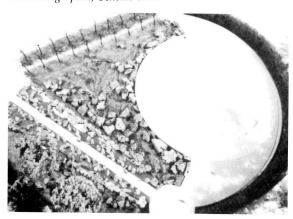
Delta design plan, Scheme 3.2.3.

rejected, but recommended that further study was in order. The Advisory Board was crushed. The design team was disheartened. It was "back to the boards one more time."

Lecky tried to sound an optimistic note to their consultants. General Stilwell reported to the ABMC that approval would surely be forthcoming in a few weeks. In fact, another year of design work lay ahead.

During the heartbreaking January 17, 1991 presentation to the Fine Arts Commission, J.

Carter Brown, the Commission's Chairman, commented that the scheme still had great potential, but needed to be simplified, the three strong components parts needed to be consolidated into a single, simple, elegant composition.

Design early, 1990.

Taking Carter Brown's comment to heart, the architects began to focus on a single, compact piece of geometry. The rethinking led to a new arrangement of the three elements that had now become essential ingredients both to the designers and to the Advisory Board. Referred to by the design team as the "dart in the target" scheme, the new composition picked up on the MacMillan Commissions's radial scheme for the west end of the Mall. The entrance walk would be a radial spoke flowing on a line from the center of the Lincoln Memorial to the Jefferson. The entrance walk would form one side of a narrow triangle, an exiting path would return to Daniel Chester French Drive. These two intersecting walks would come to a point in a circular pool. The column of ground troops would traverse the new triangle, moving uphill towards its apex. Along the south walk would be a straight, dark granite wall, etched with the faces of support forces. And at the top of the hill would be the pool of remembrance, honoring those who made the supreme sacrifice.

Design early summer, 1991.

Design mid summer, 1991.

Architect, sculptor, muralist and the Board were hard at work; the showdown was scheduled for June 26, 1991. An executive session of the CFA met first in the architect's display room at 1000 Potomac Street, NW, in Washington, with members of the Advisory Board. Frank Gaylord, the selected project sculptor, and Louis Nelson, the muralist, discussed their latest design evolutions which were favorably received. But when the meeting was formally reconvened later in the morning, there was consensus among CFA members that while the combination of the elements had promise, the

Design late summer, 1991.

design was still not working. The downsizing of the overall composition would require a reduction in the number of ground troopers. It was feared the new composition would create "a sea of bronze" on the Mall. Prudently and professionally, Chairman Brown delayed taking a vote; the new effort was laid to rest.

It was time to start over, from the beginning. Everyone was in a state of shock. Two years of struggling were wiped away. To the Board, perhaps the greatest blow was potentially losing the 38-soldier concept. They had struggled long and hard with each figure - how old, what rank, what ethnic origin, what branch of service. It was inconceivable to think of reducing that number.

On July 11, 1991, what was only bad, got worse. Executive Director Reginald Griffith responded for the NCPC, stating that its Commission members who attended a briefing at the architect's office also found that the major element of 38 sculptures overwhelmed the Lincoln Memorial. "A memorial to complement the pastoral setting south of the Reflecting Pool should be the objective." They urged all parties to take a fresh look at the design concept. But what was most upsetting to the Board was that this criticism of size and numbers had not been raised before. Why were such profoundly basic issues overlooked?

The design problem suddenly became political. It was clear that the current design would not be approved with 38 sculptures in the composition. Could the Board live with a smaller number? What would constitute an acceptable number - both in terms of a correct military unit, as well as a number capable of showing the diverse ages, ethnic backgrounds, ranks and branches of those in the battlefield. This was truly a bitter pill to those committed to honoring all the veterans.

Tired, but undaunted, the architects went back to work. Carter Brown had suggested, at

one point, looking at a bas-relief solution; this was examined. They looked at a variety of new settings; they examined a reduced number of sculptures. Five or six new schemes were proposed. But the triangle in the circle kept coming back as the best scheme. They would simply have to reduce the number of troops. Meetings began in earnest with the Board. With great reluctance on the Board's part, it was agreed to try the dart scheme with 19 figures. Some felt that the reflections in the polished granite wall would visually create 38 figures, allowing them to retain the symbolism of the 38th parallel and the 38 months of the war.

A series of informal progress meetings followed with Brown and other CFA members. This "when-all-else-fails" effort revitalized the project. Finally by August, 1991, a new concept was jelling. This sixth design would go through several refinements but the circle-triangle composition seemed to have won the day.

The ray of hope in this dark time was the newly secured support of Carter Brown. His door was open; he would hear any suggestion. He wrote General Kelley on July 12th: "This is one of the most important submissions to come before the Commission in some time. While we recognize that it is imperative that we proceed as rapidly as possible, the Commission must, to fulfill its Congressional mandate, take whatever steps and time necessary to achieve a simple, dignified and compelling design that will be a compatible element on the National Mall.

On September 5, 1991, Stilwell summarized the tumultuous past three months and hoped that: "The best memorial possible is one with the concept of the competition design, comprising a column of troops, outside of active battle, yet in a setting of potential danger, moving forward toward an objective, set against a Mural Wall commemorating support forces, with a still pool remembering the sacrifice of those who died, are still missing or were held as prisoners of war."

During this period, it was agreed that the visitors should not move between the column of soldiers, but instead the composition should be viewed from the perimeter of a broad triangle. By consensus, it was suggested to clad the sculptures in ponchos with the cold wind of Korea at their backs. The CFA and Frank Gaylord embraced the idea with enthusiasm. Louis Nelson's mural went through several iterations of oversized faces to life size to smaller than life size - finally settling on a fluid mix of small distant images to life size figures. Cooper, Lecky, and Rob Smedley, CLA'a Project Manager, were making multiple trips to Gaylord's studio in Vermont and Louis Nelson's offices in New York to prepare for the next round of presentations.

By December, 1991, the Board and architects were ready for yet another round of Commission testing. Informal meetings were held with the staff of the National Park Service and Planning Commission. On January 8, the Board got the formal sanction of the American Battle Monuments Commission. At the January 16, 1992 CFA meeting, Kent Cooper made what everyone hoped would be the final presentation.

Commissioner Adele Chatfield-Taylor responded: "That's an amazing accomplishment. What you always look for in a design is the feeling of inevitability. (While) I find the juxtaposition of these nationalistic figures and the geometric pattern contrived, I think the process has yielded the most positive result that it can."

Original composition of 19 statues after reduction from 38.

Second composition of 19 figures.

The meeting of the Planning Commission, on February 28, 1992, proved an unnecessary headache for the Board, as a few of its members, still opposed to any war memorial on the Mall, mounted a sustained drive to reject the design completely. Some felt that even the reduction to 19 figures was not enough. For some inexplicable reason, some felt that the potential symbolism of half the original 38 was inappropriate. In the end the NCPC agreed to a compromise of 16 figures as a requirement for approval.

It seemed a petty and insulting blow to the

Board who had played by the rules for three-and-a-half years. Everyone had swallowed hard to reach the parameter of 19, a 50% reduction. Distraught Board members reluctantly accepted the compromise. Plans were redrawn and submitted showing sixteen soldiers. Approval was granted on March 5, 1992. But the Commission had not heard the last of the three rejected figures.

At the official groundbreaking on Flag Day, June 14, 1992, President George Bush sounded the tone that promises would finally be realized in the final phases of the project, three years after the design model was displayed in the Rose Garden: "Let me salute the foot soldiers you see in this memorial, whose memory we take with us, whose nobility enriches us. I mean the men and women who braved the heat and cold, lack of sleep and food, and the human hell of fire. They were rich and poor, black and white and red and brown and yellow. The soldiers I speak of were young, I'm sure afraid, and far from home. And yet in their foxholes, in the foothills, across the rugged snow-capped ridges, they were selfless."

On June 23, 1993, the last act of the design development was passed. It was a year late, but worth the wait. The Commission of Fine Arts, gave its approval to the completion of 100% drawings and recommended the return of three soldiers. The following day the Planning Commission accepted the compromise and allowed the return to 19 sculptures as the Board had hoped. The quiet negotiation of Cooper and Lecky helped to right the wrong.

From June 20, 1989, to June 24, 1993, four years and four days, the Korean War Veterans Memorial Advisory Board and Cooper, Lecky,

Pres. George Bush turns first shovel at ground breaking.

Dignitaries, veterans, families and friends attending the ground-breaking ceremonies.

Gaylord and Nelson worked to get all of the approvals for their memorial. This dedication and perseverance paid dividends for the 15

Board members who worked so hard and so long to honor their Korean War colleagues.

Chapter 12: Selecting the Sculptor

What attracted many of those Board members who had not voted for this first-prize design on May 26th, was that it was the only entry that contained a sculpture grouping. As Board member Borcherdt recalled on July 21, 1990: "When I saw #247, I saw a column of advancing troops and vivid memories of the reality of war, and this is what the Memorial is about."

The State College architect/landscape architects planned for the 38 larger-than-life-size figures to be made of granite, a fact that would greatly limit the pool of qualified collaborators. The vast majority of America's figurative sculptors are modelers whose statues are cast in metal, usually bronze, occasionally iron, aluminum or steel - rather than carvers, whose works are cut in stone. Even though the designers did not have a sculptor as an original team member (relying instead on John Lucas's two years of undergraduate sculpture classes at the University of Maryland), they now wanted to be "comprehensively involved in all decision making regarding the execution of the statuary." They wrote Colonel Badger on August 15, 1989: "Sculptors prefer materials with which they are most accustomed, and today, the more common approach is casting. Yet, we are accumulating evidence that skilled stone carvers are available and that execution in granite is quite possible."

BL3 offered three stone and four metal casting estimates for the 38 figures, ranging in cost from $2 million to $6 million dollars for sculptures delivered. The work was to be performed under the direction of Charles Cropper Parks of Wilmington, DE, with BL3 asking for

Final design showing pool bisected by wall and curbstone.

View from west, showing column, mural wall flag pole and pool.

$304,000 ($8,000 per figure) for "document preparation."

Not only had the Corps of Engineers evaluators questioned the ability of these two men and two women, who had only been in practice together for less than two years, to complete a major project of this type, but they found a plus in Cooper-Lecky's August 13 presentation—the way to find a sculptor was to hold a national search. This task was to be assisted by Washington-based arts consultant John Beardsley. (Again, having lived through the addition of Frederick Hart's three sculptures to the Vietnam Veterans Memorial was ample precedent of CLA's management ability.)

BL3 was to be allowed to participate in the

selection process, but their request to control the effort was denied.

The announcement for "the sculpture commission of the century," as consultant Frederich Osborne had described it, was mailed on February 9, 1990. By March 12, 1990, 39 sculptors had submitted. On May 8 and 9, 1990, a jury of five—John Lucas of the design team, Bill Weber of the Advisory Board, Paul Harbeson of the ABMC and two arts professionals—Jack Cowart of the National Gallery of Art and Jane Livingston of the Corcoran Gallery, met in Washington and selected three finalists—Frank Gaylord, Rolf Kirken and Lawrence M. Ludtke. Each was given about two months and $3,000 to make a presentation.

They returned to Washington on May 31, 1990, for detailed discussions with Beardsley, Cooper and Lecky. Then, after a series of impressive presentations, on June 28, 1990, Frank Gaylord was announced the winner of the competition. On June 29, he signed a contract with CLA.

In most sculpture commissions, the design relationships and composition would normally be established with the sculptor before specifics and details were addressed. Not so with this project, as the deployment of the soldiers was determined months before. On September 1, 1989, the ABMC sent the Board a grid that detailed the exact position (distance from east wall and walkway-curb) of the 38 foot-soldiers on each side of the rocky creek-bed (based on a rendering taken from the BL3 model). It was requested that the layout (noting posture, ethnic origin and other characteristics) be returned by January 15, 1990, to be included in the sculptor-selection program. The Board, however, gave great attention to service, rank, duty as well as race—the ethnic distribution was 18 Caucasian, 6

First place sculptor winner Frank C. Gaylord.

Black, 6 Hispanic, 2 American Indian, 2 Oriental and 4 Korean (KATUSA's, South Koreans assigned to increase troop strength). The group would be made up of 23 Army, 9 Marines, 3 Navy, 2 Air Force and 1 KSC (Korean Service Corps).

Some Board members had originally wanted to convey a functioning platoon but compromise was reached—a combat-ready formation moving forward to contact on an undefined mission. They did, however, insist that: "the weaponry, gear and uniform on each statue must conform to the represented individual's normally assigned duties, in requisite detail so as to constitute an historically accurate record."

On that there would be no compromise. The racial make-up was equally important in this 38-trooper configuration (as it would be after July, 1991, in the 19-trooper grouping). As Bill McSweeney wrote to Stilwell: "I closely identify with those whom I lived with for so long, many from minority groups. And I have always been particularly proud that I commanded a unit made up of all races, and that they reciprocated my faith in them by following me."

Frank Gaylord, an experienced carver from Barre, Vermont, was trained at the Tyler School of Art, in Philadelphia and had been a life-long

235

fellow of the National Sculpture Society. While this specificity in a battlefield environment offended some, it did not bother Gaylord.

Gaylord gave three-dimensional life to BL3's line-drawn column. He appreciated and respected the Advisory Board's quest for accuracy. He was able to balance design and detail without sacrificing either. A 38-figure commission was an impressive undertaking, but the sculptor, working quickly in clay with 12-inch "sketches," modeled effortlessly. But, despite his facility with clay, he too was to become entrapped in controversy. The design team was suggesting an impressionistic styling of the figures - somewhat blurring the specificity of detail. The Board, on the other hand, was pressing for historic accuracy with every detail very clear to the visitor.

The January 17, 1991 comments of CFA member Robert Peck seemed to sum up the position the Commission would take on this issue: "One of the great traditions in military memorials is the heroic figure. You have crossed over the line . . . to the point of specifying the type of radio, the type of racial features. This sculpture will get to the point where the people will be looking at shoulder patches to make sure their unit is represented."

But Stilwell responded: "This is a unified column under direction, marching along. Korea was not a billiard table; any formation in the combat area traversed very irregular terrain. Gaylord had to have some guidance. We had to have a reasonable presentation of those who fought on foot, but we thought it extremely important to reflect the ethnic diversity of our nation on the battlefield in 1950 to '53."

First composition by sculptor depicting combat patrol being engaged by enemy, fall 1990.

Revised 38 figure column on tortured terrain, Spring 1991.

It appeared that Gaylord, a paratrooper in World War II, would have to grapple with the need for both sculptural vision and nuts-and bolts detail.

With the June, 1991, rejection, Gaylord turned his attention to a new 19-figure composition. A figure in prayer was the first to be seen, 17 followed, struggling with the realities of potential attack. The composition then ended with a celebtritory figure, signifying deliverance. Approval of the Board was quickly given, but the design team had real concern about the appropriateness of injecting two allegorical figures into the group. While some questioned Gaylord's unabashed flare, his understanding of the feelings of men who enter and endure combat was genuinely appreciated.

But the issue of specificity and detail still hovered. At the September 5, 1991, meeting at the Cooper/Lecky offices, a new wrinkle was introduced, ponchos would drape all 19 soldiers. While this detail had been suggested in earlier discussions, it had been dropped along the way. But now, after reconsideration, all agreed that the poncho cladding would help unify the composition, add the dimension of foul weather, but also obscure much of the realistic detail of weaponry so objected to by the CAF. Cooper-Lecky agreed to pursue the option again with the Board. In the end, even Board members, though interested in factual accuracy, saw the foul-weather gear as a way to recall the bleakness and misery of Korea's long winters.

At the October 24, 1991 meeting of the Commission, Chairman Brown spoke about the sculpture: "I find the figures very impressive. I love the metaphor of how they are being swept by an unseen wind and facing the adversity of environment. And I think it helps abstract them. I like the color that they will become (gray stainless steel), and the integration of all the colors is a great improvement."

But the composition demanded careful study. The nineteen figures formed a column of troops in hostile territory, out of contact. The only way to make sense out of the grouping was to drop the two allegorical figures and get back to a homogenized unit, all facing the same threat of potential combat. Somehow losing those two figures dampened Gaylord's enthusiasm. He elected to focus on the development of the 19 individual sculptures and let Cooper-Lecky deal with the overall issue of composition.

June 1991 version of lead figure in column.

Poncho depicting extreme weather conditions, fall 1991.

Depicting muted use of ponchos to convey less severe weather conditions.

237

In a January, 1992, CPA meeting, it was felt that Gaylord had carried the swirling ponchos too far. They were too pronounced; they were beginning to overtake the sculpture; a gale-force wind was suddenly blowing across the Mall. Gaylord, somewhat reluctantly, lowered the wind velocity as the series of two-foot models came to life in his studio. On February 28, 1992, NCPC reduced the number to 16, Gaylord still grumbled about the chance to tackle all 38 soldiers, let alone 19. When the NCPC finally reversed themselves in June, 1993, the sculptor felt a sigh of relief.

Foam board statue models to justify propriety of heroic scale sculpture in the memorial.

With the three soldiers restored, Gaylord was able to complete the maquettes within a month. But even Gaylord, working away in his remote studio in Vermont was to feel yet another bite from the approval system. Gaylord had a passion for heroic figures - not only in posture, but in size. He hoped all along that the size of the figures might reach to eight feet. But Cooper-Lecky, as well as Carter Brown, had a genuine concern about the figures becoming too big. Heroic scale was not the message of this memorial. To test the condition, CLA had a series of mockups developed at a variety of heights. It was immediately clear that 8 foot figures were too large. Cooper, Lecky and the Chairman of the Fine Arts Commission determined that the right size for the nineteen was in the range of 7 feet 3 inches. Gaylord acquiesced.

Pouring molten stainless steel at Tallix Art Foundry.

willingness to start, restart, and start over again, working and reworking, was a sustaining presence in the Memorial project's dark times.

One of the sustaining concepts of the Memorial has been to honor the personal sacrifice and heroic dedication of the front-line troops. The freeze-frame journey of 19 soldiers on patrol, in harm's way, brilliantly captures not only battlefield tensions but the harshness of Korea's winter cold. In all, Gaylord made over 100 sculptural models during a two-year period. It was a prodigious undertaking. His

In the one-foot sketches and two-foot maquettes, as well as the full-scale models made at the Tallix Foundry in Beacon, New York, Gaylord struggled with Cooper-Lecky's direction, worked with, listened to and debated with Board members. It is a tribute to his tenacity that the project ever came to fruition.

Chapter 13: Creating the Mural Wall

From the fall of 1989 through the spring of 1990, the Board pressed for a more meaningful tribute to all who served in Korea. Lessons had been learned from the Vietnam Memorial experience where a nurses memorial was recently added to the composition because they had not been included in Rick Hart's now famous sculpture of the three soldiers. The American Indians were not happy that they had not been included. Add to this Asian Americans, other ethnic groups, even the Canine Corps. The Board and the ABMC were determined that all would be included in this memorial. There would be no later additions in reflecting generic quotations about war and peace that was called for by BL3, the Board wanted to arrive at a storyline that referenced their many, many colleagues' contributions—the support troops behind the frontlines—the symbolic shaft that propels the spear.

In the September 23, 1989, memorandum from General Adams at the ABMC, the Board was asked to provide guidance for the mural section of the Memorial. At this point, they talked about depicting key phases in the Korean campaign—the Pusan Perimeter, the envelopment at Inchon, the advance north of the 38th parallel, the intervention of the Chinese, the precipitous withdrawal, the recapture of Seoul in the Spring of 1951, the two-year, politically constrained combat—generally stalemated with deaths and wounds no less real and painful - the long negotiations, and final signing of the Truce.

This episodic narrative would also include, but not be limited to, depictions of the rugged, brutal terrain and the "role of the land, sea and air support, medical support units including nurses and Chaplains - all must receive proper recognition."

Finishing area at Tallix Art Foundry.

Muralist Louis Nelson.

Comparing first wall design with sculpture to scale.

239

Photo depicting first wall design with faces 10x life size.

Initial design of mural wall treatment.

In creating the wall section of the Memorial, the Board carefully debated the inclusion of the dead, missing in action and imprisoned: "Individual names will not be listed. However, the impact of the dedicatory inscription should leave the reader with a solemn impact of the great sacrifice paid by those honored."

While the sculptor had been chosen by a limited competition, the wall designer was appointed from a preselected list of well known graphic designers. There was simply no time to go through the formal process undertaken for the sculptor selection. Cooper-Lecky interviewed several graphic designers before settling on Louis Nelson of New York City. A June 1990 meeting in Washington convinced everyone that there was much they could do together. Nelson was officially hired as a consultant on November 29, 1990. At the presentation before the Commission of Fine Arts in December, 1990, Nelson's idea for portraying the support forces with a series of faces etched into the stone may have been briefly discussed. But at that time there were more pressing concerns.

In the winter and spring of 1991, Nelson and chief designer Jennifer Stoller refined the concept of the large heads, developing these heroic images made famous by the David Douglas Duncan photographs. He suggested a novel scheme for the narrative theme, photographic images portraying the story of the behind-the-lines scenes would be etched in the pupils of the eyes. This compositional device would cause the visitor to interact both from a distance and at arm's length. The detail interested Board members, as much for its novelty as for the persuasive explanations the newest member of the design team offered.

With the rejection of the 38-figure grouping on June 26, 1991, the design program shifted

240

radically. Because the new schemes would place the wall and sculpture in close proximity, Nelson would now have to consider an array of smaller, less competitive heads and faces. The wall was now to be the southern terminus of the Memorial. And to sustain the grade shift, the bottom of the wall would be sloped with the grade. The top of the wall would remain level, causing the granite panels to increase in height as the visitor walked from east to west.

Artist Paul S. Ole's rendering in October 1991.

At a July 25, 1991, meeting, Chairman Brown stated that "the etched wall is a novel idea and represents a fresh concept for portraying the supporting soldiers." But by September 15, 1991, Nelson returned to 19 large heads, located at the end of the wide stripes — 19 soldiers and 19 portrait faces. So through the fall, Nelson focused on the large heads.

In the winter of 1991-92, the heads were rejected by Cooper-Lecky as being too overpowering. But undaunted, Nelson and Stoller were quick to recover. A greater number of heads would be used, arranged in a rhythmic pattern along the 164-foot expanse of the wall. Now designer Stoller and her colleagues searched the National Archives and the Air and Space Museum for portrait photographs, head-on views of soldiers, sailors, nurses, marines, chaplains, and airmen — all those who support the front-line combat. These images would be of real people, adding to the immediacy of the viewing public. Again, the Board, serving as the narrative coordinators, worked long and hard with Cooper-Lecky and Nelson to define the various elements in the wall.

Muralist Louis Nelson and assistant Jennifer Stoller by wall.

read from left to right - seemingly generated from the flag. And in the end the montage of more than 2400 faces balanced the heroic-sized soldiers with a subtle grace that invites inspection for a relative, family member, or friend. There are seemingly endless images to be searched out and found by even the most frequent repeat visitor to the Memorial.

So Nelson and Stoller set to work. Photographs were selected; the images scanned for computer manipulation; images were sharpened; sun angles added or adjusted so that the light

It was through Nelson's collaboration with Cooper-Lecky that the patterning sequences for the wall were refined—beginning with an undulating, Chinese scroll motif, then to force-lines, a series of diagonal patterns that suggest

241

mountainous terrain from a distance, but, on closer inspection, reveal a mixture of different sized heads. They create a geometric perspective that brings internal order to the composition. As an added feature, one debated extensively with the Board, it was finally agreed that some military equipment would be interspersed in the array as a way of defining the roles of the various groups.

Site surface and sub-surface preparation.

Chapter 14: Coming Together at Ash Woods

The years of planning, the meetings in the architects' offices, the endless presentations to the various reviewing agencies, the time-delaying lawsuits, the several lobbying efforts with Congress—the enabling legislation, the site designation, the extension of the Commemorative Works Act and the 38th anniversary silver coin strike, reached a watershed with the official approval of the Korean War Veterans Memorial design in January and February, 1992. The gestation period was over. The birthing process—a never-ending event where decisions were postponed, action delayed, views obfuscated, pronouncements interminably longwinded—was finally concluded. And the design, though enduring constant critique and change, had come together in a stirring composition. The concept was alive and well, the Memorial now needed to be reared.

Installation of granite wall panels.

The energy and vigilance of the designers, the ABMC, and the Advisory Board could now be turned to the sites and locations where the ideas that for so long had been reduced to paper in their drafting offices were ready to be fleshed out. There would be many trips to Gaylord's studios in Barre, VT; the Tallix Foundry in Beacon, NY; Nelson's offices in New York City; and the Cold Spring Granite Co. in Cold Spring, MN. All work was directed to the 4.5 acres on the Mall—Ash Woods. It would now become a hands-on adventure, a patrolling of the flanks to be sure that no group would try to undo, redo, or undercut what had been so painstakingly nurtured.

By the winter of 1990, the Board had coalesced into a unified body. With a myriad of tasks to perform, hearings to monitor, fundraising to encourage, designs to review, everyone participated. Delegated assignments would be completed. There was unity and trust. Progress was palatable. The artists were brought under contract. The entire team quickly became old friends.

The endless discussions about content details of the Memorial - getting it right so that the story of the warriors on the ground and the soldiers behind the lines could be told - were now to be translated into architectural, sculptural and mural life. Making sure that all parties understood the message, and that the Board in turn grasped the intricacies of the creative process, produced a strong, symbiotic joining of forces.

The awarding of the construction contract on March 31, 1993, launched the final chapter of the Korean War Veterans Memorial. During the summer and fall of 1993, the Faith Construction Company, led by the on-site monitoring of Jay Fisher and Harry Helwig (a Korean War veteran), began Phase I - Site Stabilization. Millions of pounds of earth were brought to the site to squeeze out underground water. Like its monumental neighbors—the Lincoln and Vietnam memorials, the Korean War Veterans Memorial sits on what was, in the late 19th century, Potomac River tidal flats. The earth is soft, unstable, and highly saturated.

The R. J. Crowley Company, with on-site direction provided by Donald Sansing and Jerry Bell, signed its contract for Phase II-Construction on September 29, 1993. Over 125 steel pilings were driven to bedrock forty feet below the surface. From the fall of 1993 to the summer of 1994, a massive, underground, reinforced concrete skeleton was poured to create the supporting structure for the Memorial. The principal triangle element measured 162' x 215' x 270'. The stability of these underpinnings should insure the timelessness of this memorial.

Again visits to the site became pilgrimages of reassurance for Board members, at long last

Panorama view of site prior to installation of sculpture.

Delivery and installation of sculptures on site.

secure in the knowledge that their memorial was being built. The years of work were coming to fruition - becoming a reality under the dedicated guidance of the United States Army Corps of Engineers, Baltimore District, supported by William Taylor, Engineering Division and John R. Sadler, Programs and Projects Management Division. On site management was provided by Major Peter Taylor and Richard W. Dean, II.

Their management has been thoughtful, permitting Board members regular access to see first-hand the day-to-day growth of the Memorial. It is in these moments of quiet contempla-

243

tion that memories of fallen comrades well up, rewarding their commitment to bring this Memorial to the country. At this point, the project finds it's perspective. The process of design has undergone numerous changes and reviews. Details, near and dear to Board members (the soldier hit by a bullet was a poignant detail for Colonel Weber, himself thrice wounded in battle), were lost, but the artistic whole had been strengthened. For those people only exposed to the pretended violence of television, this Memorial tells the truth about the horrors of war. The commitment of men and machinery, against great odds in the harsh terrain and inhuman weather of Korea, was a monumental demonstration of courage and strength.

While there is no way to recreate the raw bleakness of Korean terrain or the misery of a 40-below zero blizzard, the black granite risers and the wind-twisted ponchos are the architect and sculptor's best effort. This Memorial must tell the story of the soldier in combat. Weber opined: "For me the total symbolism of the Memorial occurs as the line of troopers emerges form the dark shadows of the woods into the open field; their reflections off the polished wall meeting the faces that emerge from the depth of the black granite. At this transition of images, a spatial time-line is crossed. The soldiers of the Korean War are freed from the oblivion of a forgotten war. They are accepted back, taking their rightful place in the ranks of America's soldiery from other wars, who have been honored previously by their countrymen."

This is the message that will greet the American people as this Memorial is presented to the Nation on July 27, 1995. The dedicated members of the Korean War Veterans Memorial Advisory Board have completed their

Augustus Saint-Gauden's Shaw Memorial, Boston Common, Boston, MA.

mission - a job well done for the Korean War veteran and for America.

Chapter 15: A Great American Memorial

Since the end of the Civil War, the American people have asked their architects and artists to commemorate military triumphs, celebrate the service of veterans, and remember the supreme sacrifice of those who died defending their country's flag in an array of memorials and monuments. At first there was great uncertainty as to how (or even whether) to honor the Korean War veterans. This country's first-ever participation in a United Nations police action occurred as political leaders struggled to define and implement a policy of containment while World War II allies (Russia and China) became cold-war adversaries.

The Vietnam Veterans Memorial paid tribute to the soldiers who died in an unpopular war. Erected in 1982, with Maya Lin's brilliant concept and Cooper-Lecky's fastidious development of the design, this Memorial helped a divided country come to terms with America's unpopular military adventurism. Seizing upon the acceptance and success of that achievement, many Korean War veterans called for a memorial to mark their service, and began to organize a national effort to focus debate on how America's forgotten war should be remembered. Veterans in their sixties, seventies and eighties were ready at long last to be honored.

But the three-year fight in Korea became a ten-year struggle in Washington, to design, develop and execute a memorial decades overdue. The first concept of Burns-Lucas, Leon, Lucas and Pennypacker-Oberholtzer provides, even today, a faint historical starting line. The dedication of architects Kent Cooper, William Lecky, Rob Smedley, and their many associates and consultants, sculptor Frank Gaylord and his assistant John Triano, and muralist Louis Nelson and his chief designer Jennifer Stoller have brought this vision to life.

Their resolve to think and plan, then to rethink and replan, only to restart and reinvent, has paid worthy dividends. The co-equal, never wavering presence of the Korean War Veterans Memorial Advisory Board—the Memorial's stewards, its intellectual and emotional visionaries—guided, sustained and energized this memorial project, at every crossroads. General Stilwell, General Davis, Colonel Weber, Rosemary McCarthy, Mike McKevitt, and all the other Board members were a constant source of energy and inspiration to the design team. Theirs has truly been a triumph of mind and heart. Successful public artists are good storytellers, but they must have clients to provide the message, the will, the character and the charisma to see the task through to completion. Their message must be personal, pragmatic and panoramic.

In the countenance of steel statues, etched faces, still water, war is not glorified - battles are not heralded - victories are not trumpeted.

The veterans who fought in Korea are reborn on the symbolic center of America, the National Mall in Washington, at a sylvan setting, known as Ash Woods. This column marches over a small section of this site—if you will, a symbolic rendering (aided by the black granite lines) of the tortured terrain of Korea. The citizen soldiery—whether volunteer or career professional—who answered their country's call are recreated here with compelling mastery. These men and women, in numbers that suggest the magnitude of their commitment, are rightfully honored for their valor, their service and their sacrifice.

The dedication of the Korean War Veterans Memorial on July 27, 1995 (42nd anniversary of the Armistice signing) celebrates the placement of the last of the great 20th-century Mall monuments in Washington, —the *Grant* (1922), the *Lincoln* (1922), the *Jefferson* (1943) and the *Vietnam Veterans* (1982). The Korean War stalemate has now become the Korean War Veterans Memorial's victory.

There are a few great narrative war memorials in America. Most sculptures are single-episode portraits—generals on horseback, soldiers charging forward or standing smartly at parade-rest. The best of the thematic memorials are: the *Colonel Robert Gould Shaw Memorial* in Boston Common, designed by sculptor Augustus Saint Gaudens and architect Charles F. McKim and erected in 1897 (with sixteen soldiers of the 54th Massachusetts Infantry— the first black regiment to fight in the Civil War); the *Grant Memorial* at the eastern end of the Mall, executed by sculptor Henry Merwin Shrady and architect Edward Pearce Casey and erected in 1922, after the thirty-one-year-old sculptor won a national competition; and the *All Wars Memorial To The Colored Soldiers And Sailors,* in West Fairmount Park, Philadelphia, designed by J. Otto Schweizer and erected in 1934.

The *Korean War Veterans Memorial* rightly deserved its ranking among these great American treasures.

The Memorials, that are the principal attractions at the western terminus of the Mall, form a serendipitous union, that honors the nation's three most contentious wars in a time-honored pyramid construct.

The *Lincoln* pays tribute to one man's vigilant determination to wage a principled war at all costs.

The Vietnam Veterans Memorial mirrors the stridency of engaging in, enduring and ending an unwinable war. There is a riveting emptiness to that Memorial that rarely recedes. Names are read and lost lives remembered.

The Korean War Veterans Memorial promises metaphorically, and with special poignancy for those who fought there, to tell about the service of those who went and returned as well as those who fell in battle. The soldiers on the front lines, as well as the legions who sustained those in combat, deserve their moment of recognition and national acclaim.

The sanctity of the open space that joins Lincoln and Washington, the Vietnam Veterans and the Korean War Veterans together, is our great National Mall. It has become an impressive American shrine. Linked at the shaft of the cross, are memorials to two great American Presidents, and at its arm, we remember two American wars, fought thousands of miles from our shores, that tested the courage and patriotism of those who answered our nation's call. The final element of that great composition will be dedicated on July 27, 1995. We will, at last, herald the courage and steadfast devotion to country of our Korean War veterans.

247

Photo courtesy of Ray Donnelly.
Copyright Frank Gaylord.

The Korean War Veterans Memorial
Some Thoughts from the Designers
By Kent Cooper and William Lecky

Charles Moore, an early Chairman of The Commission of Fine Arts, observed that in the monuments of the Capital, one can read the country's history. The National Mall, at the heart of the Capital's Monumental Core, is where much of that "reading" happens. To be worthy of a place on the Mall, a memorial must present a message of such significance that it often surpasses the particular event or person commemorated.

The design problem in every memorial is establishing that appropriate message, and then expressing it in a simple, powerful form. The task becomes even more complex when the point of departure is a concept which is the product of a national competition. In the two national memorial projects which Cooper•Lecky has completed, the Vietnam Veterans Memorial and the Korean War Veterans Memorial, both located on the National Mall, the extreme difficulty inherent in achieving this goal is evident.

In 1981, a jury of internationally established artists and architects selected a fascinating abstract, lyrical and somewhat ambiguous, pastel drawing as the winner of a mammoth competition to memorialize the veterans of the conflict in Vietnam. Each juror reportedly saw something different in that design concept, and the veterans themselves were divided from the start as to the intent of its message. Conceived as a "Book of the Dead," it infuriated many survivors.

The ultimate success of the Vietnam Veterans Memorial, we believe, lies in the fact that the final design remained abstract and thus continued to afford a profound opportunity for individual interpretation. The expression of personal grief overwhelmed the need for specifically honoring the survivors. The addition of the flag and sculpture, mandated by a political compromise with those who could not understand the abstract concept and which allowed the wall to be built, in no way altered the essential simplicity of the basic concept. The flag, sculpture, and later the nurses' memorial, well executed as they may be, however, are superfluous to the basic message content.

In 1989, when Congress authorized the Korean War Veterans Memorial, its purpose was clearly articulated to honor all those who served, were captured, wounded or remain missing., as well as those who fell. Hoping to avoid the controversy which surrounded the Vietnam Memorial, the competition program reflected this mandate.

There was another critical difference in this second competition. The jury that selected a winner from among over five hundred entries, was composed of a group of Presidentially-appointed, former military personnel, rather than a group of artists and architects. This group was highly dedicated but also attracted to far more conventional and realistic designs than the Vietnam jury had settled on. Abstraction was not on their agenda.

The Korean War Veterans Memorial competition winning design submission was a montage of images that left much to the imagination. The jury, however, was reported to be of a single mind as to the image and message they were selecting: a column of battle-clad soldiers, resolutely moving up a hill toward an American flag. Yet shortly after selection, the competition winners presented a far more allegorical interpretation for their design, elaborating many symbolic messages for the visitor to interpret. Their view of the memorial's message was very different from those who had selected it. This laid the groundwork for a deepening dispute between the Presidentially-appointed Advisory Board (the design jurors) and the competition winners. This difference in design intent ultimately led to a lawsuit and eventually their unceremonious withdrawal from the design process.

As a result of this sequence of events, when Cooper Lecky began its work, there was a design idea but not an agreement as to the specifics of the message content. For us, this was different than the Vietnam experience in that the Korean competition design itself was basically flawed, but it was similar to Vietnam in that the message content was controversial. While this memorial needed to address that war's place in our nation's history, more importantly, it needed to focus on the veterans' experience.

For many decades the pivotal success of the Korean War was eclipsed by the later conflict in Vietnam, an event which so occupied our attention during a period when our nation might otherwise have been sorting out the significance of those critical years from 1950 to 1953. It is ironic that the memorial erected in memory of the veterans of the unpopular war in Vietnam has been so wildly successful with the general public, while a similar attempt to honor the veterans of the Korean War languished in the halls of Congress and had such difficulty finding support.

The reason for this difficulty may be embedded in the profound cultural shift which has taken place in our concept of citizenship. For the first two centuries of our nation's history, when our well being was challenged by threat from other countries, our young men answered the call to service not only with a sense of duty but with pride. The war in South Korea was to be the last in a long line of such conflicts. When the next major war came in Vietnam, many answered our nation's call to duty, many did not. The compact between our government and our youth seemed to fracture. And since Vietnam, every military action - even humanitarian efforts involving our troops - has come under question, frequently challenged by both the general public as well as right or left wing political factions.

The Korean War Veterans Memorial is, therefore, in some ways, a tribute to simpler times. As the Vietnam Memorial is a statement about sacrifice and loss, the Korean War Veterans Memorial is a tribute to a classic concept of service to our country. It was the last true foot soldier's war; it was during this conflict that our branches of service became fully racially integrated; it was our nation's first action to thwart the spread of Communism; it was the world's first conflict to be undertaken under the banner of the United Nations. But most importantly, it was a time when our sons and daughters again were asked to go to a country they did not know to defend a people they had never met - and they did so without question. There was, no doubt, fear in their hearts when confronted with the face of battle, but there was never a doubt about the rightness of their actions.

Thus, the challenge for the designers of the Korean Memorial was how best to incorporate the realistic narrative theme, the column of troopers marching toward an American flag, into a form which projected this willing attitude to serve, without, at the same time, glorifying war itself.

249

Whenever designers attempt to rework a design, the result is chancy to say the least, and so it was for us - as well as time consuming. Our early efforts were directed toward utilizing the original competition geometry, correcting circulation deficiencies and responding to the numerous criticisms offered by the four major review agencies. These studies moved gradually toward a three part scheme similar in sequential concept to the FDR Memorial presently under construction near the Jefferson Memorial. This concept was rejected by The Commission of Fine Arts as being overblown in size and too complex in message content.

One of the most controversial planning concepts embodied in the rejected scheme was an attempt to fit the memorial into its site more harmoniously than the original competition. The site, like the entire west end of the Mall, is reclaimed land, a product of a landfill/dredging program by the Army Corps of Engineers undertaken late in the 19th century to fill in the tidal flats of the Potomac. The McMillan Plan of 1901 assigned this new area south of the Reflecting Pool the name "Potomac Park" and left it as a wooded grove (Ash Woods). It has remained unchanged, except for the wartime temporary office structures, throughout the many plans developed during this century. Today, there still is no master development plan for this area and little guidance as to what the ultimate character of the area should be.

In our first proposal to The Commission of Fine Arts, we attempted to place the new memorial in a curvilinear system of pedestrian paths extending from Lincoln Circle to 17th Street. This circulation concept mimicked that of Constitution Gardens which is located north of the Reflecting Pool. We thought that maintaining a similar concept of park planning on both sides of the reflecting pool was a well conceived, logical approach. This idea in particular was rejected as misguided. No commitment to an

Model of curvilinear path scheme.

overall plan could be agreed upon at this point in time. Thereafter we focused our attention on creating a memorial which tied directly to Lincoln Circle and thus would balance the Vietnam Veterans Memorial, which we had completed a decade earlier, which also has an entrance sequence leading directly from the Lincoln Memorial.

This decision allowed the Lincoln Memorial, the great anchor in the McMillan Plan, to remain the focus of that now completed west end of the Mall. That Memorial was always conceived as a stand-alone piece of architecture, honoring both the national compact of union among the states as well as Lincoln the man. The two subsequent veteran's memorials, almost hidden in the surrounding landscape, respect this original intention, unfolding radially at Lincoln's feet - the Korean Memorial on the right, proclaiming the spirit of military service to country, the Vietnam Memorial to the left, embodying the tragedy and loss of war.

As already mentioned, when Congress appropriated the land for the Korean War Veterans Memorial, the legislation stipulated that the design must recognize the contribution of all those Americans who participated in the Korean conflict - the veterans who fought in the war and returned, those who gave their lives, and those who were taken prisoner or remain missing. The emphasis on all Americans led the American Battle Monuments Commission and the Korean War Veterans Memorial Advisory Board to include clear recognition of the personnel who, perhaps did not serve on the front lines, but provided the necessary support for our ground troops to be successful. Since no women served in the ground troopers this decision also provided for their appropriate inclusion. Many are not aware that for every soldier in the field, eight to ten support personnel are needed. And added to these considerations was the desire to recognize that this was action undertaken under the auspices of the United Nations.

A new design was developed which attempted to tie together the program requirements by compressing the earlier composition into a single, unified concept embodying two overlapping geometric components. A "field of service" which honors all who served and returned, is a triangular plane, slightly tilted up hill. At the top is a circular "pool of remembrance" which honors all who died, were captured or wounded, or who remain missing. This concept immediately won strong approval from all review agencies and served as the foundation for the memorial which has now been constructed on the Mall. But developing this concept was not as noncontroversial as it first appeared.

The Field of Service

The powerful triangular field which honors all who served in the Korean conflict, lies at the entrance to the Memorial and contains four major areas of tribute. While they were all developed more or less simultaneously, each has an interesting and unique story to tell. Cooper Lecky served as both Architects and Art Coordinators for each element during the entire development process which lasted over two years.

Study model of first "Dart-in-Target" scheme.

The Statues

It was clear from the start that the thirty-eight figurative sculptures were the heart of the competition concept. As a result we were surprised to find that there was not a sculptor on the competition winning team. The sculptural imagery shown in the competition entry had been derived from David Douglas Duncan's masterful documentary photographs of the Korean War. It was clear that we needed to bring a competent sculptor on-board the design team as early as possible. The selection program to accomplish this end proceeded concurrent with the early planning studies.

Author/historian John Beardsley was retained by Cooper Lecky to lead in this undertaking. An open invitation was published nationally, announcing the search for a sculptor capable of producing thirty-eight figurative sculptures for the Memorial, in either metal or stone. Thirty-nine sculptors responded, submitting credentials and photographs of their work. On May 8 and 9, 1990, a five person review panel, chaired by John Beardsley, reviewed the submissions and selected four finalists who were each offered a stipend of $3,000 to develop an approach to the design. It is interesting to note that at the start of the review session, John Lucas of BL3, who had not yet withdrawn from the design team, made an extended statement as to the message content of

251

the competition winning concept and the role the sculpture would play in it. Later that same day, Jack Cowart, Curator of Contemporary Art at the National Gallery, observed that "this design is so freighted with allegory that it is apt to turn over and sink before it is ever completed." Both Cowart and Jane Livingston, of the Corcoran Gallery, the two "outside-professionals" on the selection committee ended the second day of jurying with a less than enthusiastic feeling about the ultimate success of the project. Within the week, Jane Livingston resigned from further participation.

The panel selected the finalists: Frank Gaylord, Vermont, Rolf Kirken of California and Lawrence Ludtke of Texas. A fourth sculptor, Manuel Neri of California was also designated, but he withdrew from consideration immediately upon learning of his selection, as he misunderstood that this was to be a realistic, figurative

commission. On May 31, 1990 the three remaining finalists came to Washington to receive an orientation, and visit the site. On June 28, 1990 they returned to present their ideas to the selection panel. George Gurney, Curator of Sculpture at the Museum of American Art, had replaced Jane Livingston on the panel which otherwise remained the same under John Beardsley's leadership. The panel utilized three criteria as the basis for their selection: the artistic merit of the approach, the ability of the artist to function as a member of the design team, and the ability of the sculptor to produce the work within the projected time.

Gaylord, a WWII combat veteran, made a riveting oral presentation and his emotion-packed, three dimensional studies captured everyone's attention. He was clearly the winner.

The design team and Advisory Board at Gaylord's studios.

The expert representational work of the other finalists seemed somewhat bland by comparison. In response to the unanimous recommendation of the selection panel, Cooper Lecky brought Gaylord onto the team.

As Gaylord started his work, the project was in increasing disarray. The competition winners had envisioned a set of impressionistic granite figures arranged along a time line with each figure allegorically expressing a different stage of the conflict. In contrast, the Memorial's Design Advisory Board which was also the original jury, had seen the line of figures as a combat ready unit on patrol proceeding on an unidentified mission, a "moment-in-time" lifted from the Korean War, in which each figure was assigned a specific branch of the service, rank, ethnicity and military function. And Gaylord soon injected a third element of strong emotional content, proposing a lead figure throwing down his weapons in relief and joy at achieving the "objective," and another figure further back in the column falling wounded from enemy fire. The establishment of message content became a task of first-order importance.

As the overall design matured during the sequence of alterations and reviews described previously, so did the sculpture. The first step was the development of an appropriate setting. The concept of thirty-eight statues in the competition was based on the symbolism of the thirty-eighth parallel, the line dividing North and South Korea, rather than any artistic or compositional need. When the project was reduced in scale and complexity during the development process, it became clear that thirty-eight figures were too many, and a reduction in numbers was necessary. Ultimately, the use of the mirrored granite wall, paralleling the line of statues, established this setting and allowed a reduction in the number of figures to nineteen, with

William Lecky discussing finishing techniques for sculpture at Tallix Art Foundary.

reflections of the statues on the Wall restoring the symbolic number. At the same time, the triangular field was opened in width and the ground surface simplified. These changes reduced the visual complexity of the design significantly and finally opened the way for approval by the design review agencies.

The second problem was one of composition. Military realism dictated that the figures be separated by ten to fifteen feet, a spacing which safety demands on a military mission. The development of a visual connection between figures separated by a distance twice their height presented a particularly difficult design problem.

Frank Gaylord is endowed with the ability to work quickly with clay models and maquettes, and this proved to be an invaluable tool in helping the team understand the problems inherent in the composition. First In his studio in Barre, Vermont, and later in a special studio in Washington, known as "The Cave," the minia- 253 ture sculptures were arrayed, moved, twisted and manipulated until a final composition which projected the theme and message of the Memorial was achieved.

In this process, it became clear that we needed some means of visually unifying the figures. After an extended debate between the designers, sculptor and the Advisory Board, we agreed to try cladding all the figures in wind - blown ponchos. This was intended to bring the figures together artistically as well as inject a sense of adverse weather, a persistent condition in Korean. The use of the poncho in a single stroke also solved a variety of other problems. By covering the figures, they provided a means for suppressing much of the military equipment which each ground trooper carried in this, the last foot-soldiers' war, while at the same time maintaining military accuracy. This change was viewed quite positively by some members of The

Commission of Fine Arts who worried about adding so many battle-clad statues on the Mall. The ponchos also allowed a natural means of accenting a single weapon, or communication device as a way of heightening the story line of each figure. Gaylord's style allowed for the impressionistic depiction of age and ethnicity while maintaining the larger message of willingness to serve in a time and place of extreme danger.

Finally as the composition developed, the figures began to establish a collective life, to communicate with each other, to "chatter"with voice and gesture, a manner well known to those who have experienced combat. At each stage during the enlargement process, which started at one-seventh full scale, we found it necessary to

J. Carter Brown and William Lecky at Tallix Art Foundry examining sculptures, Fall 1994.

254

array and review the entire composition and make adjustments in order to maintain this critical sense of collective life. As a result, major compositional changes were still being made a week before the shipment of the finished sculptures to Washington for installation.

While the process of bringing the sculptural composition to life evolved, it became increasingly clear that the use of granite as the material of choice would be too restricting. White bronze, aluminum and stainless steel were each, in turn, considered. The color, strength, and permanence of stainless steel finally led to its selection, and the choice of the Tallix Art Foundry in Beacon, New York provided the unique technical capability to bring the design into reality.

But before Tallix could begin the enlarging and casting, one final decision was required: exactly how tall the statues should be. Cooper Lecky prepared photographic blow-ups of the small clay studies at three different sizes - six, seven and eight feet in height. These were taken to the site and arrayed in a composition similar to that which was ultimately intended. Aided by Carter Brown, Chairman of The Commission of Fine Arts, a decision was made to establish slightly over seven feet as the average height. At six feet high, the static figures seemed smaller than life. At eight feet high they seemed to be giants. Only at around seven feet did it seem possible to identify with the individual figures, a quality which is critical to communicating the Memorial's message.

In order to test the overall size and composition, a mock field of service was erected on a large open field adjacent to the foundry. Each figure was placed, after casting, in its designated position. The precaution proved essential as figures were moved, turned and adjusted up to the day of shipment.

While the column of troopers, moving toward an American flag, remains the central theme, they are not alone. The development of the new setting led to a dramatic enrichment of the original concept in the form of the polished granite wall in which the troopers are reflected.

The Wall

As the Memorial Wall became a major contributor to establishing the setting, as well as the means for acknowledging the services of the vast military support forces, the need for an accomplished muralist became evident. Again with John Beardsley's expert assistance, a search for the right artist began. A more limited approach seemed appropriate and five graphic designers were finally interviewed in depth.

Louis Nelson, a designer with offices in New York City came forward with a design approach based on the use of faces, the faces of the veterans who served in the support services during the Korean War: quartermasters, nurses, artillerymen, airmen, etc. This straightforward, powerful approach immediately attracted the design team, and Louis Nelson became the next major addition to the design team.

As with the sculpture, the mural matured along with the overall design. In the beginning we examined the use of superscale faces, eight feet high, the eyes of which would be inlaid with scenes depicting the work of each support category. But this concept failed to receive The Commission of Fine Arts' approval. It became increasingly apparent that a key problem was making the wall and sculpture work together without creating visual "static." This seemed to call for a reversal in the scale strategy. Instead of utilizing nineteen superscale faces as the backbone of the composition, with small scale inlays for detail and specificity, Nelson suggested a

255

concept of nineteen constellations comprised of perhaps a hundred faces each, organized by branch of service or military function. From a distance this appeared as a landscape of mountains and valleys, but at closer inspection, constituted an exciting tribute to the intense, youthful servicemen and women who gave of their time and energy, and sometimes their lives, to support the ground troopers in the field. With this concept, the Memorial began to come together as a unified whole.

While he might easily have elected to treat the mural as a hand drawn composition, Nelson chose to undertake a far more difficult task ,constructing the design out of photographic images taken from archival photographs of the war period. This was a monumental task, requiring close to 2500 images. Each face had to be digitized, taken out of photographic context, stripped of insignia, mustaches and other markings, lit from the left side and then arranged in this enormous composition. After yet another extensive debate, it was decided that items of equipment would be added into the composition, to make the function of the groupings more intelligible to the viewer, but without allowing the Mural to become a "military hardware display."

An over-all geometry, referred to by the design team as the "constellation map," organized the Mural composition which measures 164 feet in length and varies in height from eleven feet at the west end to four and a half feet at the east. It began as a computer generated pattern of "stars" of various sizes and intensities which were manipulated until a harmonious abstract composition was brought into being. One by one, each dot was replaced by a face as archival research provided the images needed to bring each cluster to life. When the translation was complete, the composition was tested in

"The Cave" together with the composition of clay maquettes which Frank Gaylord had prepared. Subtle changes in scale were again made to bring the sculpture and mural compositions into visual balance.

The design called for etching the composition into a polished granite wall surface. In the early 1980's when the Vietnam Veterans Memorial wall was under design, the process of etching images onto a granite surface was not a developed art. The only firm we could find which would undertake the task of etching 57,000 names onto large polished granite panels was the Binswanger Glass Company in Memphis, Tennessee. A young inventor, Larry Century, had developed a process of utilizing a photosensitive rubberized coating to provide a blasting shield that allowed images of the names to be etched deeply with aluminum oxide grit. The Cooper Lecky and Binswanger team developed this prototype into a production process, and managed the precise, close to flawless, etching which is so important where the straight lines of names seem to extend endlessly into the horizon.

During the decade between the Vietnam and Korean Memorials, the etching process has developed great versatility. A new patented process, developed by Cooper Graphics of North Carolina, now affords a designer the capability of etching detailed photographic images onto polished stone. This is the process which was used by Cold Spring Granite Company in the etching of the Mural Wall.

It was important to the overall design concept that the mural not appear to be an applied design, a painted image, but that the faces seem to emerge from the grain of the Academy Black granite. After many trials, Nelson overlaid a course mezzotint screen on the composition of faces and the combination of that screen and grain of the granite began to work together to produce the haunting, emerging, quality which the Mural now possesses. These faces seem to have been called back to life from the deep recesses of memory to tell their story of service from another era.

Similar to the sculpture mock-up, the entire granite wall was assembled in Minnesota before shipment to Washington. In that location we were able to examine and correct details in the mural, but the overall impression was somewhat disappointing. Set in the snowy fields of Minnesota where the wall reflected only the vast panorama of the prairie sky, it seemed a bit lonely. Only in its present location on the Mall, where the statues and nearby memorial icons fill the reflected surfaces, does the composition come fully to life.

Opposite the mural, on a low curb which edges the entrance pathway, the names of the twenty-two nations which came together in Korea under a unified United Nations command are engraved, arranged alphabetically. This tribute reminds the visitor that the United States did not fight alone in this the first successful United Nations intervention.

The Inscriptions

Perhaps because the competition design was so burdened with allegorical quotations, the design team was reluctant to utilize words to establish the message of the Memorial. But gradually, almost inevitably, two inscriptions emerged as simple defining statements. The first seemed to capture a message of service to country which was particularly relevant to the Field of Service; the other to the Memorial Pool.

Secretary of Defense Frank Carlucci, marking the thirty-fifth anniversary of the cease-fire

Reviewing the few panels in the mural wall mock-up in Cold Spring, Minnesota.

Mural wall in place on the Mall.

ending the Korean War, spoke movingly of the willingness of America's "uniformed sons and daughters who took up arms to defend a nation they never knew and a people they never met." This phrase haunted us throughout the development process and finally served as the basis for the development of the thematic, dedicatory statement for the Field of Service: *"Our Nation honors her uniformed sons and daughters who answered their Country's call to defend a country they did not know and a people they had never met."*

We first considered engraving this message on a large boulder to be located beside the pathway at the entrance to the Memorial. But our inability to find an appropriate form for this idea began to suggest to us that perhaps that setting was wrong. We wanted the visitor to experience the Memorial, not read about it. Recalling that the dedication of the Vietnam Memorial was located at its mid-point, the apex, offered a clue. The visitors would not find any inscription until they had first experienced passing through the Field of Service. Then at the

257

base of the flag pole, the point of intersection between the two geometric components of the design, they would find a huge triangular slab of polished granite, the largest granite slab Cold Spring had ever quarried and finished, and set on its surface, the inscription would define the message of this Memorial.

Architect/designer Jeff Howard, while a member of the Cooper Lecky design team for the Vietnam Memorial, had played an important role in the development of the graphic design of that memorial. Now a principal of Howard-Revis Design, he returned as the graphic consultant for the Korean Memorial, charged with designing the graphic messages.

The choice of typeface was critical. In order to maintain the kinetic quality of the Memorial's design, Howard chose a relatively unknown typeface, "Syntax-Antiqua." This sans-serif design blends a formal Roman face with a more humanistic calligraphic edged-pen style and is therefore well adapted for the variety of applications: carving, inlaying and etching which are each used in the Memorial. Howard proposed inlaying the inscription on the large triangular slab with polished stainless steel letters that would reflect the sky and seem to float on the polished dark surface.

After several trial designs, the design team came to the realization that this dedication message needed to read backwards from the entry pattern so that the visitor would stop and look back, to the west, viewing the composition of statues, mural, and curb together while reading the statement.

Determining the second inscription took longer.

Dan Rea with huge triangular dedication stone.

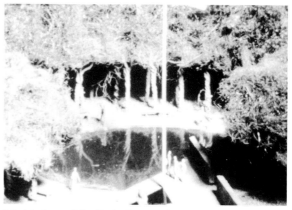

Model photo of the Pool of Remembrance

The Pool of Remembrance

Early in the project, when we first visited The Commission of Fine Arts, one of the comments made was "why don't you forget the statues and bring us back just the pool?" This was the final element in the tripartite design we first presented, and was an idea to which everyone responded. It is interesting that during the development of the design, this element changed the least of all.

The concept of the Memorial Pool was quite simple: a circular reflection pool surrounded by a bosque of trees, trimmed to branch above ten feet in height. Landscape Architect Henry Arnold designed a densely planted ring of pleached linden trees, thirty feet in height, to contain the space and reinforce the precise geometry of the circular pool. Under this shady bower, benches were located affording visitors a place to pause and reflect, to remember the enormous sacrifice of the Korean War. At the perimeter of the pool, the still water cascades down a stepped incline, creating a rushing sound that blocks out noises from the city beyond, then finally disappears into the ground.

The pathways that edge the Field of Service extend into this still pool as a peninsula. Along one side, the Mural Wall, now less than five feet in height, also penetrates the water. It is here, on this wall, that the second inscription is located.

Originally we had settled on an inscription: "In memory of those who made the supreme sacrifice." This thought seemed quite appropriate as a tribute to the fifty-four thousand who died. But gradually, we began to feel that a bolder, more universal thought would be more appropriate as the second focal point of this Memorial. We selected: *"Freedom is not free."*

This brief statement seemed more inclusive of all the sacrifice that stemmed from military service to country during the Korean War. It was hand carved into the granite by Ann Hawkins, and lined with platinum which causes it to glimmer against the dark polished stone. This tribute is deepened by the engraving of the curb which flanks the Wall on the north side of the peninsula. There the numbers of casualties for both the United States and the United Nations armed forces are listed: the dead, the missing, the captured and the wounded.

The Honor Roll

From the start of our involvement in the design of the Korean War Veterans Memorial, we have been acutely aware that this memorial to the veterans of a conflict over 40 years old, would not have the emotional immediacy, the poignancy, that the Vietnam Veterans Memorial had when it was dedicated. Therefore it seemed quite appropriate to focus on the somewhat abstract concept of service to country as the central message here rather than creating a second "book of names." Yet, the success of the Vietnam Memorial has brought a great cry from many veterans to list the names of those killed in

battle. Here an interactive computer Honor Roll fills this need.

In a National Park Service kiosk, located at the head of the walkway that leads into the Memorial, a bank of computer screens flashes endless images of those who died in Korea, often in the prime of their youth. The visitor is stunned by the seemingly endless sea of faces. To watch this panorama of men and women pass across the computer screens is to confront the grave implication of service to our country, and to be reminded of the importance of that sacred trust between government and citizen which when violated, is so difficult to restore.

Visitors to the Kiosk may seek out service information about any of those who died using an interactive computer program designed by Greg Blair of Blair Dubilier and Associates. This program will allow snapshots and portraits, supplied by families and friends, to be added to each individual's service record over the coming years, which will make this a living, growing tribute to those who made the supreme sacrifice in Korea.

The willingness to serve in a citizens army lies at the heart of our democracy.

The Korean Memorial reminds us of the critical importance of that compact we sometimes call Patriotism, sometimes Duty. It is a message for all time.

A Postscript

As we conclude our thoughts about a process which has consumed much of five years of our lives, we also want to acknowledge the role played by the Korean War Veterans Memorial

259

Advisory Board. Presidentially appointed, all volunteers, the members of this group were unfailing in their dedication to make this memorial worthy of its place on the National Mall.

Without the leadership of General Richard Stilwell, the project might not have survived its controversial beginnings, and when he left us, General Raymond Davis stepped forward to continue his task. Colonel Rosemary McCarthy continually reminded us all of the place of women in service. But in many ways, we owe our greatest debt of gratitude to Colonel William Weber, whose critical eye goaded us

William Weber and and John Staun at the Mural mock-up.

to ever greater heights, and to whom we could always turn for a keen analysis of how our ideas might be viewed by the critically important veteran. *(Cooper Lecky Architects,1 June 1995)*

Kent Cooper, William Lecky, Col. Rosemary McCarthy at the Ash Woods Site.

Korean War

Medal of Honor Recipients

*ABRELL, CHARLES G.

Rank and organization: Corporal, U.S. Marine Corps, Company E, 2d Battalion, 1st Marines, 1st Marine Division (Rein)

Place and date: Hangnyong, Korea, 10 June 1951

Entered service at: Terre Haute, Ind.

Born: 12 August 1931, Terre Haute, Ind.

Citation: For conspicuous gallantry and intrepidity at the risk of his life above and beyond the call of duty while serving as a fire team leader in Company E, in action against enemy aggressor forces. While advancing with his platoon in an attack against well concealed and heavily fortified enemy hill positions, Cpl. Abrell voluntarily rushed forward through the assaulting squad which was pinned down by a hail of intense and accurate automatic-weapons fire from a hostile bunker situated on commanding ground. Although previously wounded by enemy handgrenade fragments, he proceeded to carry out a bold, single-handed attack against the bunker, exhorting his comrades to follow him. Sustaining 2 additional wounds as he stormed toward the emplacement, he resolutely pulled the pin from a grenade clutched in his hand and hurled himself bodily into the bunker with the live missile still in his grasp. Fatally wounded in the resulting explosion which killed the entire enemy guncrew within the stronghold, Cpl. Abrell, by his valiant spirit of self-sacrifice in the face of certain death, served to inspire all his comrades and contributed directly to the success of his platoon in attaining its objective. His superb courage and heroic initiative sustain and enhance the highest traditions of the US Naval Service. He gallantly gave his life for country.

ADAMS, STANLEY T.

Rank and organization: Master Sergeant (then Sfc.), U.S. Army, Company A, 19th Infantry Regiment

Place and date: Near Sesim-ni, Korea, 4 February 1951

Entered service at: Olathe, Kansas

Born: 9 May 1922, DeSoto, Kansas

G.O. No.: 66, 2 August 1951

Citation: M/Sgt Adams, Company A, distinguished himself by conspicuous gallantry and intrepidity above and beyond the call of duty in action against an enemy. At approximately 0100 hours, M/Sgt Adams platoon, holding an outpost some 200 yards ahead of his company, came under a determined attack by an estimated 250 enemy troops. Intense small-arms, machine-gun and mortar fire from 3 sides pressed the platoon back against the main line of resistance. Observing approximately 150 hostile troops silhouetted against the skyline advancing against his platoon, M/Sgt Adams leaped to his feet, urged his men to fix bayonets, and he, with 13 members of his platoon, charged this hostile force with indomitable courage. Within 50 yards of the enemy, M/Sgt Adams was knocked to the ground when pierced in the leg by an enemy bullet. He jumped to his feet and, ignoring his wound, continued on to close with the enemy when he was knocked down 4 times from the concussion of grenades which had bounced off his body. Shouting orders he charged the enemy positions and engaged them in hand-to-hand combat where man after man fell before his terrific onslaught with bayonet and rifle butt. After nearly an hour of vicious action M/Sgt Adams and his comrades routed the fanatical foe, killing over 50 and forcing the remainder to withdraw. Upon receiving orders that his battalion was moving back he provided cover fire while his men withdrew. M/Sgt Adams superb leadership, incredible courage, and consummated devotion to duty so inspired his comrades that the enemy attack was completely thwarted, saving his battalion from possible disaster. His sustained personal bravery and indomitable fighting spirit against overwhelming odds reflect the utmost glory upon himself and uphold the finest traditions of the infantry and the military service.

BARBER, WILLIAM E.

Rank and organization: Captain, U.S. Marine Corps, commanding officer, Company F, 2d Battalion, 7th Marines, 1st Marine Division (Rein)

Place and date: Chosin Reservoir area, Korea, 28 November to 2 December 1950

Entered service at: West Liberty, Kentucky

Born: 30 November 1919, Dehart, Kentucky

Citation: For conspicuous gallantry and intrepidity at the risk of his life above and beyond the call of duty as commanding officer of Company F in action against enemy aggressor forces. Assigned to defend a 3-mile mountain pass along the divisions march from Yudam-ni to Hagaru-ri, Capt. Barber took position with his battle-weary troops and, before nightfall, had dug in and set up a defense along the frozen, snow covered hillside. When a force of estimated regimental strength savagely attacked during the night, inflicting heavy casualties and finally surrounding his position following a bitterly fought 7-hour conflict, Capt. Barber, after repulsing the enemy, gave assurance that he could hold if supplied by airdrops and requested permission to stand fast when orders were received by radio to fight his back to a relieving force after 2 reinforcing units had been driven back under fierce resistance in their attempts to reach the isolated troops. Aware that leaving the position would sever contact with the 8,000 Marines trapped at Yudam-ni and jeopardize their chances of joining the 3,000 more awaiting their arrival at Hagaru-ri for the continued drive to the sea, he chose to risk loss of his command rather than sacrifice more men if the enemy seized control and forced a renewed battle to regain the position, or abandon his many wounded who were unable to walk. Although severely wounded in the leg in the early morning of the 29th, Capt Barber continued to maintain personal control, often moving up and down the lines on a stretcher to direct the defense and consistently encouraging and inspiring his men to supreme efforts despite the staggering opposition. Waging desperate battle throughout 5 days and 6 nights of repeated onslaughts launched by the fanatical aggressors, he and his heroic command accounted for approximately 1,000 enemy dead in this epic stand in bitter subzero weather, and when the company was relieved, only 82 of his original 220 men were able to walk away from the position so valiantly defended against insuperable odds. His profound faith and courage, great personal valor and unwavering fortitude were decisive factors in the successful withdrawal of the division form the deathtrap in the Chosin Reservoir sector and reflect the highest credit upon Capt Barber, his intrepid officers and men and the U.S. Naval Service.

*BARKER, CHARLES H.

Rank and organization: Private First Class (then Pvt.), U.S. Army, Company K, 17th Infantry Regiment, 7th Infantry Division
>*Place and date:* Near Sokkogae, Korea, 4 June 1953
>*Entered service at:* Pickens County, South Carolina
>*Born:* 12 April 1935, Pickens County, South Carolina
>*G.O. No.:* 37, 7 June 1955
>*Citation:* Pfc. Barker, a member of Company K, distinguished himself by conspicuous gallantry and indomitable courage above and beyond the call of duty in action against the enemy. While participating in a combat patrol engaged in screening and approach to Pork-Chop Outpost, Pfc. Barker and his companions surprised and engaged an enemy group digging emplacements on the slope. Totally unprepared, the hostile troops sought cover. After ordering Pfc. Barker and a comrade to lay down a base of fire, the patrol leader maneuvered the remainder of the platoon to a vantage point on higher ground. Pfc. Barker moved to an open area firing his rifle and hurling grenades on the hostile positions. As enemy action increased in volume and intensity, mortar bursts fell on friendly positions, ammunition was in critical supply, and the platoon was ordered to withdraw into a perimeter defense preparatory to moving back to the outpost. Voluntarily electing to cover the retrograde movement, he gallantly maintained a defense and was last seen in close hand-to-hand combat with the enemy. Pfc. Barkers unflinching courage, consummate devotion to duty and supreme sacrifice enabled the patrol to complete the mission and effect and orderly withdrawal to friendly lines, reflecting lasting glory upon himself and upholding the highest traditions of the military service.

*BAUGH, WILLIAM B.

Rank and organization: Private First Class, U.S. Marine Corps, Company G, 3d Battalion, 1st Marine, 1st Marine Division (Rein)
>*Place and date:* Along road from Koto-ri to Hagaru-ri, Korea, 29 November 1950
>*Entered service at:* Harrison, Ohio
>*Born:* 7 July 1930, McKinney, Kentucky
>*Citation:* For conspicuous gallantry and intrepidity at the risk of his life above and beyond the call of duty while serving as a member of an antitank assault squad attached to Company G, during nighttime enemy attack against a motorized column. Acting instantly when a hostile handgrenade landed in his truck as he and his squad prepared to alight and assist in the repulse of an enemy force delivering intense automatic-weapons and grenade fire from deeply entrenched and well-concealed roadside positions, Pfc. Baugh quickly shouted a warning to the other men in the vehicle and, unmindful of his personal safety, hurled himself upon the deadly missile, there saving his comrades from serious injury or possible death. Sustaining severe wounds from which he died a short time afterward, Pfc. Baugh, by his superb courage and

valiant spirit of self-sacrifice, upheld the highest traditions of the U.S. Naval Service. He gallantly gave his life for his country.

*BENFORD, EDWARD C.

Rank and organization: Hospital Corpsman Third Class, U.S. Navy attached to a company in the 1st Marine Division
>*Place and date:* Korea, 5 September 1952
>*Entered service at:* Philadelphia, Pennsylvania
>*Born:* 15 January 1931, Staten Island, New York
>*Citation:* For gallantry and intrepidity at the risk of his life above and beyond the call of duty while serving in operations against enemy aggressor forces. When his company was subjected to heavy artillery and mortar barrages, followed by a determined assault during the hours of darkness by and enemy force estimated at battalion strength, HC3c. Benford resolutely moved from position to position in the face of intense hostile fire, treating the wounded and lending words of encouragement. Leaving the protection of his sheltered position to treat the wounded when the platoon area in which he was working was attacked from both the front and rear, he moved forward to an exposed ridge line where he observed 2 marines in a large crater. As he approached the 2 men to determine their condition, and enemy soldier threw 2 grenades into the crater while 2 other enemy charged the position. Picking up a grenade in each hand, HC3c. Benford leaped out of the crater and hurled himself against the onrushing hostile soldiers, pushing the grenades against their chests and killing both the attackers. Mortally wounded while carrying out this heroic act, HC3c. Benford, by his great personal valor and resolute spirit of self-sacrifice in the face of almost certain death, was directly responsible for saving the lives of his 2 comrades. His exceptional courage reflects the highest credit upon himself and enhances the finest traditions of the U.S. Naval Service. He gallantly gave his life for others.

*BENNETT, EMORY L.

Rank and organization: Private First Class, U.S. Army, Company B, 15th Infantry Regiment, 3d. Infantry Division
>*Place and date:* Near Sobangsan, Korea, 24 June 1951
>*Entered service at:* Cocoa, Florida
>*Born:* 20 December 1929, New Smyrna Beach, Florida
>*G.O. No.:* 11, 1 February 1952
>*Citation:* Pfc. Bennett a member of Company B, distinguished himself by conspicuous gallantry and intrepidity at the risk of his life above and beyond the call of duty in action against an armed enemy of the United Nations. At approximately 0200 hours, 2 enemy battalions swarmed up the ridge line in a ferocious banzai charge in an attempt to dislodge Pfc. Bennetts company from its defensive positions. Meeting the challenge, the gallant defenders delivered destructive retaliation, but the enemy pressed the assault with fanatical determination and the integrity of the perimeter was imperiled. Fully aware of the odds against him, Pfc. Bennett unhesitatingly left his foxhole, moved through withering fire, stood within full view of the enemy, and, employing his automatic rifle, poured crippling fire into the ranks of the onrushing

assailants, inflicting numerous casualties. Although wounded, Pfc. Bennett gallantly maintained his 1-man defense and the attack was momentarily halted. During this lull in battle, the company regrouped for counterattack, but the numerically superior foe soon infiltrated into the position. Upon orders to move back, Pfc. Bennett voluntarily remained to provide covering fire for the withdrawing elements, and, defying the enemy, continued to sweep the charging foe with devastating fire until mortally wounded. His willing self-sacrifice and intrepid actions saved the position from being overrun and enabled the company to effect and orderly withdrawal. Pfc. Bennetts unflinching courage and consummate devotion to duty reflect lasting glory on himself and the military service.

BLEAK, DAVID B.

Rank and organization: Sergeant, U.S. Army, Medical Company, 223d Infantry Regiment, 40th Infantry Division
Place and date: Vicinity of Minari-gol, Korea, 14 June 1952
Entered service at: Shelley, Idaho
Born: 27 February 1932, Idaho Falls, Idaho
G.O. No.: 83, 2 November 1953
Citation: Sgt. Bleak, a member of the medical company, distinguished himself by conspicuous gallantry and indomitable courage above and beyond the call of duty in action against the enemy. As a medical aidman, he volunteered to accompany a reconnaissance patrol committed to engage the enemy and capture a prisoner for interrogation. Forging up the rugged slope of the key terrain, the group was subjected to intense automatic weapons and small arms fire and suffered several casualties. After administering to the wounded he continued to advance with the patrol. Nearing the military crest of the hill, while attempting to cross the fire-swept area to attend the wounded, he came under hostile fire from a small group of the enemy concealed in a trench. Entering the trench he closed with the enemy, killed 2 with bare hands and a third with his trench knife. Moving from the emplacement, he saw a concussion grenade fall in front of a companion and, quickly shifting his position, shielded the man from the impact of the blast. Later, while ministering to the wounded, he was struck by a hostile bullet but, despite the wound, he undertook to evacuate a wounded comrade. As he moved down the hill with his heavy burden, he was attacked by 2 enemy soldiers with fixed bayonets. Closing with the aggressors, he grabbed them and smacked their heads together, then carried his helpless comrade down the hill to safety. Sgt. Bleaks dauntless courage and intrepid actions reflect utmost credit upon himself and are in keeping with the honored traditions of the military service.

*BRITTIN, NELSON V.

Rank and organization: Sergeant First Class, U.S. Army, Company I, 19th Infantry Regiment
Place and date: Vicinity of Yonggong-ni, Korea, 7 March 1951
Entered service at: Audubon, New Jersey
Born: Audubon, New Jersey
G.O. No.: 12, 1 February 1952

Citation: Sfc. Brittin, a member of Company I, distinguished himself by conspicuous gallantry and intrepidity above and beyond the call of duty in action. Volunteering to lead his squad up a hill, with meager cover against murderous fire from the enemy, he ordered his squad to give him support and, in the face of withering fire and bursting shells, he tossed a grenade at the nearest enemy position. On returning to his squad, he was knocked down and wounded by an enemy grenade. Refusing medical attention, he replenished his supply of grenades and returned, hurling grenades into hostile positions and shooting the enemy as they fled. When his weapon jammed, he leaped without hesitation into a foxhole and killed the occupants with his bayonet and the butt of his rifle. He continued to wipe out foxholes and, noting that his squad had been pinned down, he rushed to the rear of a machine-gun position, threw a grenade into the nest, and ran around to its front, where he killed all 3 occupants with his rifle. Less than 100 yards up the hill, his squad again came under vicious fire from another camouflaged, sandbagged, machine-gun nest well-flanked by supporting riflemen. Sfc. Brittin again charged this new position in an aggressive endeavor to silence this remaining obstacle and ran direct into a burst of automatic fire which killed him instantly. In his sustained and driving action, he had killed 20 enemy soldiers and destroyed 4 automatic weapons. The conspicuous courage, consummate valor, and noble self-sacrifice displayed by Sfc. Brittin enable his inspired company to attain its objective and reflect the highest glory on himself and the heroic traditions of the military service.

*BROWN, MELVIN L.

Rank and organization: Private First Class, U.S. Army, Company D, 8th Engineer Combat Battalion
Place and date: Near Kasan, Korea, 4 September 1950
Entered service at: Erie, Pennsylvania
Born: Mahaffey, Pennsylvania
G.O. No.: 11, 16 February 1951
Citation: Pfc. Brown, Company D, distinguished himself by conspicuous gallantry and intrepidity above and beyond the call of duty against the enemy. While his platoon was securing Hill 755 (the walled city), the enemy, using heavy automatic weapons and small arms, counterattacked. Taking a position on a 50-foot-high wall he delivered heavy rifle fire on the enemy. His ammunition was soon expended and although wounded, he remained at his post and threw his few grenades into the attackers causing many casualties. When his supply of grenades was exhausted his comrades from nearby foxholes tossed others to him and he left his position, braving a hail of fire, to retrieve and throw them at the enemy. The attackers continued to assault his position and Pfc. Brown weaponless, drew his entrenching tool from his pack and calmly waited until they 1 by 1 peered over the wall, delivering each a crushing blow upon the head. Knocking 10 or 12 enemy from the wall, his daring action so inspired his platoon that they repelled the attack and held their position. Pfc. Browns extraordinary heroism, gallantry, and intrepidity reflect the highest credit upon himself and was in keeping with the honored traditions of the military service. Reportedly missing in action and officially killed in action, September 5, 1950.

BURKE, LLOYD L.

Rank and organization: First Lieutenant, U.S. Army, Company G, 5th Cavalry Regiment, 1st Cavalry Division

Place and date: Near Chong-dong, Korea, 28 October 1951

Entered service at: Stuttgart, Arkansas

Born: 29 September 1924, Ticknor, Arkansas

G.O. No.: 43

Citation: 1st Lt. Burke, distinguished himself by conspicuous gallantry and outstanding courage above and beyond the call of duty in action against the enemy. Intense enemy fire had pinned down leading elements of his company committed to secure commanding ground when 1st Lt. Burke left the command post to rally and urge the men to follow him toward 3 bunkers impeding the advance. Dashing to an exposed vantage point he threw several grenades at the bunkers, then returning for an M1 rifle and adapter, he made a lone assault, wiping out the position and killing the crew. Closing on the center bunker he lobbed grenades through the opening and, with his pistol, killed 3 of its occupants attempting to surround him. Ordering his men forward he charged the third emplacement, catching several grenades in midair and hurling them back at the enemy. Inspired by his display of valor his men stormed forward, overran the hostile position, but were again pinned down by increased fire. Securing a light machine-gun and 3 boxes of ammunition, 1st Lt. Burke dashed through the impact area to an open knoll, set up his gun and poured a crippling fire into the ranks of the enemy, killing approximately 75. Although wounded, he ordered more ammunition, reloading and destroying 2 mortar emplacements and a machine-gun position with his accurate fire. Cradling the weapon in his arms he then led his men forward, killing some 25 more of the retreating enemy and securing the objective. 1st Lt. Burkes heroic action and daring exploits inspired his small force of 35 troops. His unflinching courage and outstanding leadership reflect the highest credit upon himself, the infantry, and the U.S. Army.

*BURRIS, TONY K.

Rank and organization: Sergeant First Class, U.S. Army, Company L, 38th Infantry Regiment, 2d Infantry Division

Place and date: Vicinity of Mundung-ni, Korea 8 and 9 October 1951

Entered Service at: Blanchard, Oklahoma

Birth: Blanchard, Oklahoma

G.O. No.: 84, 5 September 1952

Citation: Sfc. Burris, a member of Company L, distinguished himself by conspicuous gallantry and outstanding courage above and beyond the call of duty. On 8 October, when his company encountered intense fire form an entrenched hostile force, Sfc. Burris charged forward alone, throwing grenades into the position and destroying approximately 15 of the enemy. On the following day, spearheading a renewed assault on enemy positions on the next ridge, he was wounded by machine-gun fire but continued the assault, reaching the crest of the ridge ahead of his unit and sustaining a second wound. Calling for a 57mm. recoilless rifle team, he deliberately exposed himself to draw hostile fire and reveal the enemy position. The enemy machine-gun emplacement was destroyed.

The company then moved forward and prepared to assault other positions on the ridge line. Sfc. Burris, refusing evacuation and submitting only to emergency treatment, joined the unit in its renewed attack but fire from hostile emplacement halted the advance. Sfc. Burris rose to his feet, charged forward and destroyed the first emplacement with its heavy machine-gun and crew of 6 men. Moving out to the next emplacement, and throwing his last grenade which destroyed this position, he fell mortally wounded by enemy fire. Inspired by his consummate gallantry, his comrades renewed a spirited assault which overran enemy positions and secured Hill 605, a strategic position in the battle for Heartbreak Ridge, Sfc. Burris indomitable fighting spirit, outstanding heroism, and gallant self-sacrifice reflect the highest glory upon himself, the infantry and the U.S. Army.

CAFFARATA, HECTOR A., Jr.

Rank and organization: Private, U.S. Marine Corps Reserve, Company F, 2d Battalion, 7th Marines, 1st Marine Division (Rein)

Place and date: Korea, 28 November 1950

Entered Service at: Dover, N.J.

Birth: 4 November 1929, New York, N.Y.

Citation: For conspicuous gallantry and intrepidity at the risk of his life above and beyond the call of duty while serving as a rifleman with Company F, in action against enemy aggressor forces. When all the other members of his fire team became casualties, creating a gap in the lines, during the initial phase of a vicious attack launched by a fanatical enemy of regimental strength against his companys hill position, Pvt. Cafferata waged a lone battle with grenades and rifle fire as the attack gained momentum and the enemy threatened penetration through the gap and endangered the integrity of the entire defensive perimeter. Making a target of himself under devastating fire from automatic weapons, rifles, grenades and mortars, he maneuvered up and down the line and delivered accurate and effective fire against the onrushing force, killing 15, wounding many more, and forcing the others to withdraw so that reinforcements could move up and consolidate the position. Again fighting desperately against a renewed onslaught alter that same morning when a hostile grenade landed in a shallow entrenchment occupied by wounded marines, Pvt. Cafferata rushed into the gully under heavy fire, seized the deadly missile in his right hand and hurled it free of his comrades before it detonated, severing part of 1 finger and seriously wounding him in the right hand and arm. Courageously ignoring the intense pain, he staunchly fought on until he was struck by a snipers bullet and forced to submit to evacuation for medical treatment. Stouthearted and indomitable, Pvt. Cafferata, by his fortitude, great personal valor and dauntless perseverance in the face of almost certain death, saved the lives of several of his fellow marines and contributed essentially to the success achieved by his company in maintaining its defensive position against tremendous odds. His extraordinary heroism throughout was in keeping with the highest traditions of the U.S. Naval Service.

*CHAMPAGNE, DAVID B.

Rank and organization: Corporal, U.S. Marine Corps,

Company A, 1st Battalion, 7th Marines, 1st Marine Division (Rein)

Place and date: Korea, 28 May 1952
Entered Service at: Wakefield, Rhode Island
Birth: 13 November 1932, Waterville, Maryland
Citation: For conspicuous gallantry and intrepidity at the risk of his life above and beyond the call of duty while serving as fire team leader of Company A, in action against enemy aggressor forces. Advancing with his platoon in the initial assault of his company against a strongly fortified and heavily defended hill position, Cpl. Champagne skillfully led his fire team through a veritable hail of intense enemy machine-gun, small-arms and grenade fire, overrunning trenches and a series of almost impregnable bunker positions before reaching the crest of the hill and placing his men in defensive positions. Suffering a painful leg wound while assisting in repelling the ensuing hostile counterattack, which was launched under cover of a murderous hail of mortar and artillery fire, he steadfastly refused evacuation and fearlessly continued to control his fire team. When the enemy counterattack increased in intensity, and a hostile grenade landed in the midst of the fire team, Cpl. Champagne unhesitatingly seized the deadly missile and hurled it in the direction of the approaching enemy. As the grenade left his hand, it exploded, blowing off his hand and throwing him out of the trench. Mortally wounded by enemy mortar fire while in this exposed position, Cpl. Champagne, by his valiant leadership, fortitude, and gallant spirit of self-sacrifice in the face of almost certain death, undoubtedly saved the lives of several of his fellow marines. His heroic actions served to inspire all who observed him and reflect the highest credit upon himself and the U.S. Naval Service. He gallantly gave his life for his country.

CHARETTE, WILLIAM R.

Rank and organization: Hospital Corpsman Third Class, U.S. Navy, Medical Corpsman serving with a marine rifle company

Place and date: Korea, 27 March 1953
Entered Service at: Ludington, Michigan
Birth: Ludington, Michigan
Citation: For conspicuous gallantry and intrepidity at the risk of his life above and beyond the call of duty in action against enemy aggressor forces during the early morning hours. Participating in a fierce encounter with a cleverly concealed and well entrenched enemy force occupying positions on a vital and bitterly contested outpost far in advance of the main line of resistance, HC3c, Charette repeatedly and unhesitatingly moved about through a murderous barrage of hostile small-arms and mortar fire to render assistance to his wounded comrades. When an enemy grenade landed within a few feet of a marine he was attending, he immediately threw himself upon the stricken man and absorbed the entire concussion of the deadly missile with his body. Although sustaining painful facial wounds, and undergoing shock from the intensity of the blast which ripped the helmet and medical aid kit from his person, HC3c. Charette resourcefully improvised emergency bandages by tearing off part of his clothing, and gallantly continued to admin-

ister medical aid to the wounded in his own unit and to those in adjacent platoon areas as well. Observing a seriously wounded comrade whose armored vest had been torn from his body by the blast from an exploding shell, he selflessly removed his own battle vest and placed it upon the helpless man although fully aware of the added jeopardy to himself. Moving to the side of another casualty who was suffering excruciating pain from a serious leg wound, HC3c. Charette stood upright in the trench line and exposed himself to a deadly hail of enemy fire in order to lend more effective aid to the victim and alleviate his anguish while being removed to a position of safety. By his indomitable courage and inspiring efforts in behalf of his wounded comrades, HC3c. Charette was directly responsible for saving many lives. His great personal valor reflects the highest credit upon himself and enhances the finest traditions of the U.S. Naval Service.

*CHARLTON, CORNELIUS H.

Rank and organization: Sergeant, U.S. Army, Company C, 24th Infantry Regiment, 25th Infantry Division
Place and date: Near Chipo-ri, Korea, 2 June 1951
Entered Service at: Bronx, New York
Birth: 24 July 1929, East Gulf, West Virginia
G.O. No.: 30, 19 March 1952
Citation: Sgt. Charlton, a member of Company C, distinguished himself by conspicuous gallantry and intrepidity above and beyond the call of duty in action against the enemy. His platoon was attacking heavily defended hostile positions on commanding ground when the leader was wounded and evacuated. Sgt. Charlton assumed command, rallied the men, and spearheaded the assault against the hill. Personally eliminating 2 hostile positions and killing 6 of the enemy with his rifle fire and grenades, he continued up the slope until the unit suffered heavy casualties and became pinned down. Regrouping the men he led them forward only to be again hurled back by a shower of grenades. Despite a severe chest wound, Sgt. Charlton refused medical attention and led a third daring charge to the crest of the ridge. Observing that the remaining emplacement which had retarded the advance was situated on the reverse slope, he charged it alone, was again hit by a grenade but raked the position with a devastating fire which eliminated it and routed the defenders. The wounds received during his daring exploits resulted in his death but his indomitable courage, superb leadership, and gallant self-sacrifice reflect the highest credit upon himself, the infantry and the military service.

COLLIER, GILBERT G.

Rank and organization: Sergeant (then Cpl.), U.S. Army, Company F, 223d Infantry Regiment, 40th Infantry Division.
Place and date: Near Tutayon, Korea, 19-20 July 1953.
Entered service at: Tichnor, Ark.
Born: 30 December 1930, Hunter, Ark.
G.O. No.: 3,12 January 1955.
Citation: Sgt. Collier, a member of Company F, distinguished himself by conspicuous gallantry and indomitable courage above and beyond the call of duty in action against the enemy. Sgt. Collier was pointman and

assistant leader of a combat patrol committed to make contact with the enemy. As the patrol moved forward through the darkness, he and his commanding officer slipped and fell from a steep, 60-foot cliff and were injured. Incapacitated by a badly sprained ankle which prevented immediate movement, the officer ordered the patrol to return to the safety of friendly lines. Although suffering from a painful back injury, Sgt. Collier elected to remain with his leader, and before daylight they managed to crawl back up and over the mountainous terrain to the opposite valley where they concealed themselves in the brush until nightfall, then edged toward their company positions. Shortly after leaving the daylight retreat they were ambushed and, in the ensuing fire fight, Sgt. Collier killed 2 hostile soldiers, received painful wounds, and was separated from his companion. Then, ammunition expended, he closed in hand-to-hand combat with 4 attacking hostile infantrymen, killing, wounding, and routing the foe with his bayonet. He was mortally wounded during this action, but made a valiant attempt to reach and assist his leader in a desperate effort to save his comrade's life without regard for his own personal safety. Sgt. Collier's unflinching courage, consummate devotion to duty, and gallant self-sacrifice reflect lasting glory upon himself and uphold the noble traditions of the military service.

COLLIER, JOHN W.

Rank and organization: Corporal, U.S. Army, Company C, 27th Infantry Regiment.

Place and date: Near Chindong-ni, Korea, 19 September 1950.

Entered service at: Worthington, Ky.

Born: 3 April 1929, Worthington, Ky.

G.O. No.: 86, 2 August 1951.

Citation: Cpl. Collier, Company C, distinguished himself by conspicuous gallantry and intrepidity above and beyond the call of duty in action. While engaged in an assault on a strategic ridge strongly defended by a fanatical enemy, the leading elements of his company encountered intense automatic weapons and grenade fire. Cpl. Collier and 3 comrades volunteered and moved forward to neutralize an enemy machine-gun position which was hampering the company's advance, but they were twice repulsed. On the third attempt, Cpl. Collier, despite heavy enemy fire and grenade barrages, moved to an exposed position ahead of his comrades, assaulted and destroyed the machine-gun nest, killing at least 4 enemy soldiers. As he returned down the rocky, fire-swept hill and joined his squad, an enemy grenade landed in their midst. Shouting a warning to his comrades, he, selflessly and unhesitatingly, threw himself upon the grenade and smothered its explosion with his body. This supreme, personal bravery, consummate gallantry, and noble self-sacrifice reflect untold glory upon himself and uphold the honored traditions of the military service.

COMMISKEY, HENRY A., SR.

Rank and organization: First Lieutenant (then 2d Lt.), U.S. Marine Corps, Company C, 1st Battalion, 1st Marines, 1st Marine Division (Rein).

Place and date: Near Yongdungp'o, Korea, 20 September 1950.

Entered service at: Hattiesburg, Miss.

Birth: 10 January 1927, Hattiesburg, Miss.

Citation: For conspicuous gallantry and intrepidity at the risk of his life above and beyond the call of duty while serving as a platoon leader in Company C, in action against enemy aggressor forces. Directed to attack hostile forces well dug in on Hill 85, 1st Lt. Commiskey, spearheaded the assault, charging up the steep slopes on the run. Coolly disregarding the heavy enemy machine-gun and smallarms fire, he plunged on well forward of the rest of his platoon and was the first man to reach the crest of the objective. Armed only with a pistol, he jumped into a hostile machine-gun emplacement occupied by 5 enemy troops and quickly disposed of 4 of the soldiers with his automatic pistol. Grappling with the fifth, 1st Lt. Commiskey knocked him to the ground and held him until he could obtain a weapon from another member of his platoon and killed the last of the enemy guncrew. Continuing his bold assault, he moved to the next emplacement, killed 2 more of the enemy and then led his platoon toward the rear nose of the hill to rout the remainder of the hostile troops and destroy them as they fled from their positions. His valiant leadership and courageous fighting spirit served to inspire the men of his company to heroic endeavor in seizing the objective and reflect the highest credit upon 1st Lt. Commiskey and the U.S. Naval Service.

COURSEN, SAMUEL S.

Rank and organization: First Lieutenant, U.S. Army, Company C, 5th Cavalry Regiment.

Place and date: Near Kaesong, Korea, 12 October 1950.

Entered service at: Madison, N.J.

Birth: 4 August 1926, Madison, N.J.

G.O. No.: 57, 2 August 1951.

Citation: 1st Lt. Coursen distinguished himself by conspicuous gallantry and intrepidity above and beyond the call of duty in action. While Company C was attacking Hill 174 under heavy enemy small-arms fire, his platoon received enemy fire from close range. The platoon returned the fire and continued to advance. During this phase 1 of his men moved into a well-camouflaged emplacement, which was thought to be unoccupied, and was wounded by the enemy who were hidden within the emplacement. Seeing the soldier in difficulty he rushed to the man's aid and, without regard for his personal safety, engaged the enemy in hand-to-hand combat in an effort to protect his wounded comrade until he himself was killed. When his body was recovered after the battle 7 enemy dead were found in the emplacement. As the result of 1st Lt. Coursen's violent struggle several of the enemies' heads had been crushed with his rifle. His aggressive and intrepid actions saved the life of the wounded man, eliminated the main position of the enemy roadblock, and greatly inspired the men in his command. 1st Lt. Coursen's extraordinary heroism and intrepidity reflect the highest credit on himself and are in keeping with the honored traditions of the military service.

CRAIG, GORDON M.

Rank and organization: Corporal, U.S. Army, Reconnaissance Company, 1st Cavalry Division.

Place and date: Near Kasan, Korea, 10 September 1950.
Entered service at: Brockton, Mass.
Birth: 3 August 1929, Brockton, Mass.
G.O. No.: 23,25 April 1951.
Citation: Cpl. Craig, 16th Reconnaissance Company, distinguished himself by conspicuous gallantry and intrepidity above and beyond the call of duty in action against the enemy. During the attack on a strategic enemy-held hill his company's advance was subjected to intense hostile grenade, mortar, and small-arms fire. Cpl. Craig and 4 comrades moved forward to eliminate an enemy machine-gun nest that was hampering the company's advance. At that instance an enemy machine gunner hurled a handgrenade at the advancing men. Without hesitating or attempting to seek cover for himself, Cpl. Craig threw himself on the grenade and smothered its burst with his body. His intrepid and selfless act, in which he unhesitantly gave his life for his comrades, inspired them to attack with such ferocity that they annihilated the enemy machine-gun crew, enabling the company to continue its attack. Cpl. Craig's noble self-sacrifice reflects the highest credit upon himself and upholds the esteemed traditions of the military service.

CRUMP, JERRY K.

Rank and organization: Corporal, U.S. Army, Company L, 7th Infantry Regiment, 3d Infantry Division.
Place and date: Near Chorwon, Korea, 6 and 7 September 1951.
Entered service at: Forest City, N.C.
Birth: 18 February 1933, Charlotte, N.C.
G.O. No.: 68, 11 July 1952.
Citation: Cpl. Crump, a member of Company L, distinguished himself by conspicuous gallantry and outstanding courage above and beyond the call of duty in action against the enemy. During the night a numerically superior hostile force launched an assault against his platoon on Hill 284, overrunning friendly positions and swarming into the sector. Cpl. Crump repeatedly exposed himself to deliver effective fire into enemy soldiers endeavoring to capture a friendly regaining control of the weapon. Returning to his position, now occupied by 4 of his wounded comrades, he continued his accurate fire into enemy troops surrounding his emplacement. When a hostile soldier hurled a grenade into the position, Cpl. Crump immediately flung himself over the missile, absorbing the blast with his body and saving his comrades from death or serious injury. His aggressive actions had so inspired his comrades that a spirited counterattack drove the enemy from the perimeter. Cpl. Crump's heroic devotion to duty, indomitable fighting spirit, and willingness to sacrifice himself to save his comrades reflect the highest credit upon himself, the infantry and the U.S. Army.

DAVENPORT, JACK A.

Rank and organization: Corporal, U.S. Marine Corps, Company G, 3d Battalion, 5th Marines, 1st Marine Division (Rein).
Place and date: Vicinity of Songnae-Dong, Korea, 21 September 1931, Kansas City, Mo.
Entered service at: Mission, Kansas

Birth: 7 September 1931, Kansas City, Mo.
Citation: For conspicuous gallantry and intrepidity at the risk of his life above and beyond the call of duty while serving as a squad leader in Company G, in action against enemy aggressor forces, early in the morning. While expertly directing the defense of his position during a probing attack by hostile forces attempting to infiltrate the area, Cpl. Davenport, acting quickly when an enemy grenade fell into the foxhole which he was occupying with another marine, skillfully located the deadly projectile in the dark and, undeterred by the personal risk involved, heroically threw himself over the live missile, thereby saving his companion from serious injury or possible death. His cool and resourceful leadership were contributing factors in the successful spirit of self-sacrifice in the face of almost certain death enhance and sustain the highest traditions of the U.S. Naval Service. Cpl. Davenport gallantly gave his life for his country.

DAVIS, GEORGE ANDREW, JR.

Rank and organization: Major, U.S. Air Force, CO, 334th Fighter Squadron, 4th Fighter Group, 5th Air Force.
Place and date: Near Sinuiju-Yalu River area, Korea, 10 February 1952.
Entered service at: Lubbock, Texas.
Birth: 1 December 1920, Dublin, Texas.
Citation: Maj. Davis distinguished himself by conspicuous gallantry and intrepidity at the risk of his life above and beyond the call of duty. While leading a flight of 4 F-86 Saberjets on a combat aerial patrol mission near the Manchurian border, Maj. Davis' element leader ran out of oxygen and was forced to retire from the flight with his wingman accompanying him. Maj. Davis and the remaining F-86's continued the mission and sighted a formation of approximately 12 enemy MIG-15 aircraft speeding southward toward an area where friendly fighter-bombers were conducting low level operations against the Communist lines of communications. With selfless disregard for the numerical superiority of the enemy, Maj. Davis positioned his 2 aircraft, then dove at the MIG formation. While speeding through the formation from the rear, he singled out a MIG-15 and destroyed it with a concentrated burst of fire. Although he was now under continuous fire from the enemy fighters to his rear, Maj. Davis sustained his attack. He fired at another MIG-15 which, bursting into smoke and flames, went into a vertical dive. Rather than maintain his superior speed and evade the enemy fire being concentrated on him, he elected to reduce his speed and sought out still a third MIG-15. During this latest attack his aircraft sustained a direct hit, went out of control, then crashed into a mountain 30 miles south of the Yalu River. Maj. Davis' bold attack completely disrupted the enemy formation, permitting the friendly fighter-bombers to successfully complete their interdiction mission. Davis, by his indomitable fighting spirit, heroic aggressiveness, and superb courage in engaging the enemy against formidable odds exemplified valor at its highest.

DAVIS, RAYMOND G.

Rank and organization: Lieutenant Colonel, U.S. Marine Corps, commanding officer, 1st Battalion, 7th Marines, 1st Marine Division (Rein).

Place and date: Vicinity Hagaru-ri, Korea, 1 through 4 December 1950.

Entered service at: Atlanta, Ga.

Born: 13 January 1915, Fitzgerald, Ga.

Citation: For conspicuous gallantry and intrepidity at the risk of his life above and beyond the call of duty as commanding officer of the 1st Battalion, in action against enemy aggressor forces. Although keenly aware that the operation involved breaking through a surrounding enemy and advancing 8 miles along primitive icy trails in the bitter cold with every passage disputed by a savage and determined foe, Lt. Col. Davis boldly led his battalion into the attack in a daring attempt to relieve a beleaguered rifle company and to seize, hold, and defend a vital mountain pass controlling the only route available for 2 marine regiments in danger of being cut off by numerically superior hostile forces during their redeployment to the port of Hungnam. When the battalion immediately encountered strong opposition from entrenched enemy forces commanding high ground in the path of the advance, he promptly spearheaded his unit in a fierce attack upon the steep, ice-covered slopes in the face of withering fire and, personally leading the assault groups in a hand-to-hand encounter, drove the hostile troops from their positions, rested his men, and reconnoitered the area under enemy fire to determine the best route for continuing the mission. Always in the thick of the fighting Lt. Col. Davis led his battalion over 3 successive ridges in the deep snow in continuous attacks against the enemy and, constantly inspiring and encouraging his men throughout the night, brought his unit to a point within 1,500 yards of the surrounded rifle company by daybreak. Although knocked to the ground when a shell fragment struck his helmet and 2 bullets pierced his clothing, he arose and fought his way forward at the head of his men until he reached the isolated marines. On the following morning, he bravely led his battalion in securing the vital mountain pass from a strongly entrenched and numerically superior hostile force, carrying all his wounded with him, including 22 litter cases and numerous ambulatory patients. Despite repeated savage and heavy assaults by the enemy, he stubbornly held the vital terrain until the 2 regiments of the division had deployed through the pass and, on the morning of 4 December, led his battalion into Hagaru-ri intact. By his superb leadership, outstanding courage, and brilliant tactical ability, Lt. Col. Davis was directly instrumental in saving the beleaguered rifle company from complete annihilation and enabled the 2 marine regiments to escape possible destruction. His valiant devotion to duty and unyielding fighting spirit in the face of almost insurmountable odds enhance and sustain the highest traditions of the U.S. Naval Service.

DEAN, WILLIAM F.

Rank and organization: Major General, U.S. Army, commanding general, 24th Infantry Division.

Place and date: Taejon, Korea, 20 and 21 July 1950.

Entered service at: California

Born: 1 August 1899, Carlyle, Ill.

G.O. No.: 7,16 February 1951.

Citation: Maj. Gen. Dean distinguished himself by conspicuous gallantry and intrepidity at the repeated risk of his life above and beyond the call of duty. In command of a unit suddenly relieved from occupation duties in Japan and as yet untried in combat, faced with a ruthless and determined enemy, highly trained and overwhelmingly superior in numbers, he felt it his duty to take action which to a man of his military experience and knowledge was clearly apt to result in his death. He personally and alone attacked an enemy tank while armed only with a handgrenade. He also directed the fire of his tanks from an exposed position with neither cover nor concealment while under observed artillery and small-armed fire. When the town of Taejon was finally overrun he refused to insure his own safety by leaving with the leading elements but remained behind organizing his retreating forces, directing stragglers, and was last seen assisting the wounded to a place of safety. These actions indicate that Maj. Gen. Dean felt it necessary to sustain the courage and resolution of his troops by examples of excessive gallantry committed always at the threatened portions of his frontlines. The magnificent response of his unit to this willing and cheerful sacrifice, made with full knowledge of its certain cost, is history. The success of this phase of the campaign is in large measure due to Maj. Gen. Dean's heroic leadership, courageous and loyal devotion to his men, and his complete disregard for personal safety.

DESIDERIO, REGINALD B.

Rank and organization: Captain, U.S. Army, commanding officer, Company E, 27th Infantry Regiment, 25th Infantry Division.

Place and date: Near Ipsok, Korea, 27 November 1950.

Entered service at: Gilroy, Calif.

Born: 12 September 1918, Clairton, Pa.

G.O. No.: 58,2 August 1951.

Citation: Capt. Desiderio distinguished himself by conspicuous gallantry and intrepidity at the repeated risk of his life above and beyond the call of duty. His company was given the mission of defending the command post of a task force against an enemy breakthrough. After personal reconnaissance during darkness and under intense enemy fire, he placed his men in defensive positions to repel an attack. Early in the action he was wounded, but refused evacuation and despite enemy fire continued to move among his men checking their positions and making sure that each element was prepared to receive the next attack. Again wounded, he continued to direct his men. By his inspiring leadership he encouraged them to hold their position. In the subsequent fighting when the fanatical enemy succeeded in penetrating the position, he personally charged them with carbine, rifle, and grenades, inflicting many casualties until he himself was mortally wounded. His men, spurred on by his intrepid example, repelled this final attack. Capt. Desiderio's heroic leadership, courageous and loyal devotion to duty, and his complete disregard for personal safety reflect the highest honor on him and are in keeping with the esteemed traditions of the U.S. Army.

DEWERT, RICHARD DAVID

Rank and organization: Hospital Corpsman, U.S. Navy. Hospital Corpsman attached to Marine infantry company, 1st Marine Division.

Place and date: Korea, 5 April 1951
Entered service at: Taunton, Mass.
Born: Taunton, Mass.
Citation: For conspicuous gallantry and intrepidity at the risk of his life above and beyond the call of duty as a platoon cammander in Company H, in action against enemy aggressor forces. Grimly dertermined to dislodge a group of heavy enemy infantry units occupying well-concealed and strongly fortified positions on commanding ground overlooking unprotected terrain dashed back through the fire swept area to carry a second wounded man out of the line of fire. Undaunted by the mounting hail of devastating enemy fire, he bravely moved forward a third time and received another serious wound in the shoulder after discovering that a wounded marine had already died. Still persistent in his refusal to submit to first aid, he resolutely answered the call of a fourth stricken comrade and, while rendering medical assistance, was himself mortally wounded by a burst of enemy fire. His courageous initiative, great personal valor, and heroic spirit of self-sacrifice in the face of overwhelming odds reflect the highest credit upon HC Dewert and enhance the finest traditions of the U.S. Naval Service. He gallantly gave his life for his country.

DEWEY, DUANE E.

Rank and organization: Corporal, U.S. Marine Corps Reserve, Company E, 2d Battalion, 5th Marines, 1st Marine Division (Rein).
Place and date: Near Panmunjon, Korea, 16 April 1952.
Entered service at: Muskegon, Mich.
Born: 16 November 1931, Grand Rapids, Mich.
Citation: For conspicuous gallantry and intrepidity at the risk of his life above and beyond the call of duty while serving as a gunner in a machinegun platoon of Company E, in action against enemy aggressor forces. When an enemy grenade landed close to his position while he and his assistant gunner were receiving medical attention for their wounds during a fierce night attack by numerically superior hostile forces, Cpl. Dewey, although suffering intense pain, immediately pulled the corpsman to the ground and, shouting a warning to the other marines around him, bravely smothered the deadly missile with his body, personally absorbing the full force of the explosion to save his comrades from possible injury or death. His indomitable courage, outstanding initiative, and valiant efforts in behalf of others in the face of almost certain death reflect the highest credit upon Cpl. Dewey and enhance the finest traditions of the U.S. Naval Service.

DODD, CARL H.

Rank and organization: First Lieutenant (then 2d Lt.), U.S. Army, Company E, 5th Infantry Regiment, 24th Infantry Division.
Place and date: Near Subuk, Korea, 30 and 31 January 1951.
Entered service at: Kenvir, Ky.
Born: 21 April 1925, Evarts, Ky
G.O. No.: 37, 4 June 1951.
Citation: 1st Lt. Dodd, Company E, distinguished himself by conspicuous gallantry and intrepidity above and beyond the call of duty in action against the enemy.

First Lt. Dodd, given the responsibility of spearheading an attack to capture Hill 256, a key terrain feature defended by a well-armed, crafty foe who had withstood several previous assaults, led his platoon forward over hazardous terrain under hostile small-arms, mortar, and artillery fire from well-camouflaged enemy emplacements which reached such intensity that his men faltered. With utter disregard for his safety, 1st Lt. Dodd moved among his men, reorganized and encouraged them, and then single-handedly charged the first hostile machinegun nest, killing or wounding all its occupants. Inspired by his incredible courage, his platoon responded magnificently and, fixing bayonets and throwing grenades, closed on the enemy and wiped out every hostile position as it moved relentlessly onward to its initial objective. Securing the first series of enemy positions, 1st Lt. Dodd again reorganized his platoon and led them across a narrow ridge and onto Hill 256. Firing his rifle and throwing grenades, he advanced at the head of his platoon despite the intense concentrated hostile fire which was brought to bear on their narrow avenue of approach. When his platoon was still 200 yards from the objective he moved ahead and with his last grenade destroyed an enemy mortar killing the crew. Darkness then halted the advance but at daybreak 1st Lt. Dodd, again boldly advancing ahead of his unit, led the platoon through a dense fog against the remaining hostile positions. With bayonet and grenades he continued to set pace without regard for the danger to his life, until he and his troops had eliminated the last of the defenders and had secured the final objective. First Lt. Dodd's superb leadership and extraordinary heroism inspired his men to overcome this strong enemy defense reflecting the highest credit upon himself and upholding the esteemed traditions of the military service.

DUKE, RAY E.

Rank and organization: Sergeant First Class, U.S. Army, Company C, 21st Infantry Regiment, 24th Infantry Division.
Place and date: Near Mugok, Korea, 26 April 1951.
Entered service at: Whitwell (Marion County), Tenn.
Born: 9 May 1923, Whitwell, Tenn.
G.O. No.: 20, 19 March 1954.
Citation: Sfc. Duke, a member of Company C, distinguished himself by conspicuous gallantry and outstanding courage above and beyond the call of duty in action against the enemy. Upon learning that several of his men were isolated and heavily engaged in an area yielded by his platoon when ordered to withdraw he led a small force in a daring assault which recovered the position and the beleaguered men. Another enemy attack in strength resulted in numerous casualties but Sfc. Duke, although wounded by mortar fragments, calmly moved along his platoon line to coordinate fields of fire and to urge his men to hold firm in the bitter encounter. Wounded a second time he received first aid and returned to his position. When the enemy again attacked shortly after dawn, despite his wounds, Sfc. Duke repeatedly braved withering fire to insure maximum defense of each position. Threatened with annihilation and with mounting casualties, the platoon was again ordered to withdraw when Sfc. Duke was wounded a third time in both legs

and was unable to walk. Realizing that he was impeding the progress of 2 comrades who were carrying him from the hill, he urged them to leave him and seek safety. He was last seen during devastating fire into the ranks of the onrushing assailants. The consummate courage, superb leadership, and heroic actions of Sfc. Duke, displayed during intensive action against overwhelming odds, reflect the highest credit upon himself, the infantry, and the U.S. Army.

EDWARDS, JUNIOR D.

Rank and organization: Sergeant First Class, U.S. Army, Company E, 23d Infantry Regiment, 2d Infantry Division.

Place and date: Near Changbong-ni, Korea, 2 January 1951.

Entered service at: Indianola, Iowa

Born: 7 October 1926, Indianola, Iowa.

G.O. No.: 13,1 February 1952

Citation: Sfc. Edwards, Company E, distinguished himself by conspicuous gallantry and intrepidity above and beyond the call of duty in action against the enemy. When his platoon, while assisting in the defense of a strategic hill, was forced out of its position and came under vicious raking fire from an enemy machinegun set up on adjacent high ground, Sfc. Edwards individually charged the hostile emplacement, throwing grenades as he advanced. The enemy withdrew but returned to deliver devastating fire when he had expended his ammunition. Securing a fresh supply of grenades, he again charged the emplacement, neutralized the weapon and killed the crew, but was forced back by hostile small-arms fire. When the enemy emplaced another machinegun and resumed fire, Sfc. Edwards again renewed his supply of grenades, rushed a third time through a vicious hail of fire, silenced this second gun and annihilated its crew. In this third daring assault he was mortally wounded but his indomitable courage and successful action enabled his platoon to regain and hold the vital strongpoint. Sfc. Edwards' consummate valor and gallant self-sacrifice reflect the utmost glory upon himself and are in keeping with the esteemed traditions of the infantry and military service.

ESSEBAGGER, JOHN, JR.

Rank and organization: Corporal, U.S. Army, Company A, 7th Infantry Regiment, 3d Infantry Division.

Place and date: Near Popsudong, Korea, 25 April 1951.

Entered service at: Holland, Mich.

Born: 29 October 1928, Holland, Mich.

G.O. No.: 61, 24 April 1952.

Citation: Cpl. Essebagger, a member of Company A, distinguished himself by conspicuous gallantry and outstanding courage above and beyond the call of duty in action against the enemy. Committed to effect a delaying action to cover the 3d Battalion's withdrawal through Company A, Cpl. Essebagger, a member of 1 of 2 squads maintaining defensive positions in key terrain and defending the company's right flank, had participated in repulsing numerous attacks. In a frenzied banzai charge the numerically superior enemy seriously threatened the security of the planned route of withdrawal and isolation of the small force. Badly shaken, the grossly outnumbered detachment started to fall back and Cpl. Essebagger,

realizing the impending danger, voluntarily remained to provide security for the withdrawal. Gallantly maintaining a 1-man stand, Cpl. Essebagger raked the menacing hordes with crippling fire and, with the foe closing on the position, left the comparative safety of his shelter and advanced in the face of overwhelming odds, firing his weapon and hurling grenades to disconcert the enemy and afford time for displacement of friendly elements to more tenable positions. Scorning the withering fire and bursting shells, Cpl. Essebagger continued to move forward, inflicting destruction upon the fanatical foe until he was mortally wounded. Cpl. Essebagger's intrepid action and supreme sacrifice exacted a heavy toll in retiring squads to reach safety. His valorous conduct and devotion to duty reflected lasting glory upon himself and was in keeping with the noblest traditions of the infantry and the U.S. Army.

FAITH, DON C., JR.

Rank and organization: Lieutenant Colonel, U.S. Army, commanding officer, 1st Battalion, 32d Infantry Regiment, 7th Infantry Division.

Place and date: Vicinity Hagaru-ri, Northern Korea, 27 November to 1 December 1950.

Entered service at: Washington, Ind.

Born: 26 August 1918, Washington, Ind.

G.O. No.: 59, 2 August 1951.

Citation: Lt. Col. Faith, commanding 1st Battalion, distinguished himself conspicuously by gallantry and intrepidity in action above and beyond the call of duty in the area of the Chosin Reservoir. When the enemy launched a fanatical attack against his battalion, Lt. Col. Faith unhesitatingly exposed himself to heavy enemy fire as he moved about directing the action. When the enemy penetrated the positions, Lt. Col. Faith personally led counterattacks to restore the position. During an attack by his battalion to effect a junction with another U.S. unit, Lt. Col. Faith reconnoitered the route for, and personally directed, the first elements of his command across the ice-covered reservoir and then directed the movement of his vehicles which were loaded with wounded until all of his command had passed through the enemy fire. Having completed this he crossed the reservoir himself. Assuming command of the force his unit had joined he was given the mission of attacking to join friendly elements to the south. Lt. Col. Faith, although physically exhausted in the bitter cold, organized and launched an attack which was soon stopped by enemy fire, got his men on their feet and personally led the fire attack as it blasted its was through the enemy ring. As they came to a hairpin curve, enemy fire from a roadblock again pinned the column down. Lt. Col. Faith organized a group of men and directed their attack on the enemy positions on the right flank. He then placed himself at the head of another group of men and in the face of direct enemy fire led an attack on the enemy roadblock, firing his pistol and throwing grenades. When he had reached a position approximately 30 yards from the roadblock he was mortally wounded, but continued to direct the attack until the roadblock was overrun. Throughout the 5 days of action Lt. Col. Faith gave no thought to his safety and did not spare himself. His presence each time in the position of greatest danger was an inspiration to his men. Also, the damage he personally inflicted firing from his position at the head of his men was of material assistance on several occasions. Lt. Col. Faith's outstanding gallantry and noble self-sacrifice above and beyond the call of duty reflect the highest honor on him and are in keeping with the highest traditions of the U.S. Army. (This award supersedes the prior award of the Silver Star (First Oak Leaf Cluster) as announced in G.O. No. 32, Headquarters X Corps, dated 23 February 1951, for gallantry in action on 27 November 1950.)

GARCIA, FERNANDO LUIS

Rank and organization: Private First Class, U.S. Marine Corps, Company I, 3d Battalion, 5th Marines, 1st Marine Division (Rein).

Place and date: Korea, 55 September 1952.

Entered service at: San Juan, P.R.

Born: 14 October 1929, Utuado, P.R.

Citation: For conspicuous gallantry and intrepidity at the risk of his life above and beyond the call of duty while serving as a member of Company I, in action against enemy aggressor forces. While participating in the defense of a combat outpost located more than 1 mile forward of the main line of resistance during a savage night attack by a fanatical enemy force employing grenades, mortars, and artillery, Pfc. Garcia, although suffering painful wounds, moved through the intense hail of hostile fire to a supply point to secure more handgrenades. Quick to act when a hostile grenade landed nearby, endangering the life of another marine, as well as his own, he unhesitatingly chose to sacrifice himself and immediately threw his body upon the deadly missile, receiving the full impact of the explosion. His great personal valor and cool decision in the face of almost certain death sustain and enhance the finest traditions of the U.S. Naval Service. He gallantly gave his life for his country.

GEORGE, CHARLES

Rank and organization: Private First Class, U.S. Army, Company C, 179th Infantry Regiment, 45th Infantry Division.

Place and date: Near Songnae-dong, Korea, 30 November 1952.

Entered service at: Whittier, N.C.

Born: 23 August 1932, Cherokee, N.C.

G.O. No.: 19,18 March 1954.

Citation: Pfc. George, a member of Company C, distinguished himself by conspicuous gallantry and outstanding courage above and beyond the call of duty in action against the enemy on the night of 30 November 1952. He was a member of a raiding party committed to engage the enemy and capture a prisoner for interrogation. Forging up the rugged slope of the key terrain feature, the group was subjected to intense mortar and machinegun fire and suffered several casualties. Throughout the advance, he fought valiantly and, upon reaching the crest of the hill, leaped into the trenches and closed with the enemy in hand- to-hand combat. When friendly troops were ordered to move back upon completion of the assignment, he and 2 comrades remained to cover the withdrawal. While in the process of leaving the trenches a hostile soldier hurled a grenade into their midst. Pfc. George shouted a warning to 1 comrade, pushed the other soldier out of danger, and, with full knowledge of the consequences, unhesitatingly threw himself upon the grenade, absorbing the full blast of the explosion. Although seriously wounded in this display of valor, he refrained from any outcry which would divulge the position of his companions. The 2 soldiers evacuated him to the forward aid station and shortly thereafter he succumbed to his wound. Pfc. George's indomitable courage, consummate devotion to duty, and willing self-sacrifice reflect the highest credit upon himself and uphold the finest traditions of the military service.

GILLIAND, CHARLES L.

Rank and organization: Corporal (then Pfc.), U.S. Army, Company I, 7th Infantry Regiment, 3d Infantry Division.

Place and date: Near Tongmang-ni, Korea, 25 April 1951.

Entered service at: Yelklville (Marion county), Ark.

Born: 24 May 1933, Mountain Home, Ark.

G.O. No.: 2,11 January 1955.

Citation: Cpl. Gilliland, a member of Company I, distinguished himself by conspicuous gallantry and outstanding courage above and beyond the call of duty in action against the enemy. A numerically superior hostile force launched a coordinated assault against his company perimeter, the brunt of which was directed up a defile covered by his automatic rifle. His assistant was killed by enemy fire but Cpl. Gilliland, facing the full force of the assault, poured a steady fire into the foe which stemmed the onslaught. When 2 enemy soldiers escaped his raking fire and infiltrated the sector, he leaped from his foxhole, overtook and killed them both with his pistol. Sustaining a serious head wound in this daring exploit, he refused medical attention and returned to his emplacement to continue his defense of the vital defile. His unit was ordered back to new defensive positions but Cpl. Gilliland volunteered to remain to cover the withdrawal and hold the enemy at bay. His heroic actions and indomitable devotion to duty prevented the enemy from completely overrunning his company positions. Cpl. Gilliland's incredible valor and supreme sacrifice reflect lasting glory upon himself and are in keeping with the honored traditions of the military service.

GOMEZ, EDWARD

Rank and organization: Private First Class, U.S. Marine Corps, Reserve, Company E, 2d Battalion, 1st Marines, 1st Marine Division (Rein).

Place and date: Korea, Hill 749, 14 September 1951.

Entered service at: Omaha, Nebr.

Born: 10 August 1932, Omaha, Nebr.

Citation: For conspicuous gallantry and intrepidity at the risk of his life above and beyond the call of duty while serving as an ammunition bearer in company E, in action against enemy aggressor forces. Boldly advancing with his squad in support of a group of riflemen assaulting a series of strongly fortified and bitterly defended hostile positions on Hill 749, Pfc. Gomez consistently exposed himself to the withering barrage to keep his machinegun supplied with ammunition during the drive forward to seize the objective. As his squad deployed to meet an imminent counterattack, he voluntarily moved down an abandoned trench to search for a new location for the gun and, when a hostile grenade landed between himself and his weapon, shouted a warning to those around him as he grasped the activated charge in his hand. Determined to save his comrades, he unhesitatingly chose to sacrifice himself and, diving into the ditch with the deadly missile, absorbed the shattering violence of the explosion in his body. By his stouthearted courage, incomparable valor, and decisive spirit of self-sacrifice, Pfc. Gomez inspired the others to heroic efforts in subsequently repelling the outnumbering foe, and his valiant conduct throughout sustained and enhanced the finest traditions of the U.S. Naval Service. He gallantly gave his life for his country.

GOODBLOOD, CLAIR

Rank and organization: Corporal, U.S. Army, Company D, 7th Infantry Regiment.

Place and date: Near Popsu-dong, Korea, 24 and 25 April 1951.

Entered service at: Burnham, Maine.

Born: 18 September 1929, Fort Kent, Maine.

G.O. No.: 14, 1 February 1952.

Citation: Cpl. Goodblood, a member of Company D, distinguished himself by conspicuous gallantry and intrepidity at the risk of his life above and beyond the call of duty in action against an armed enemy of the United Nations. Cpl. Goodblood, a machine gunner, was attached to Company B in defensive positions on thickly wooded key terrain under attack by a ruthless foe. In bitter fighting which ensued, the numerically superior enemy infiltrated the perimeter, rendering the friendly positions untenable. Upon order to move back, Cpl. Goodblood voluntarily remained to cover the withdrawal and, constantly vulnerable to heavy fire, inflicted withering destruction on the assaulting force. Seeing a grenade lobbed at his position, he shoved his assistant to the ground and flinging himself upon the soldier attempted to shield him. Despite his valorous act both men were wounded. Rejecting aid for himself, he ordered the ammunition bearer to evacuate the injured man for medical treatment. He fearlessly maintained his 1-man defense, sweeping the onrushing assailants with fire until an enemy banzai charge carried the hill and silenced his gun. When friendly elements regained the commanding ground, Cpl. Goodblood's body was found lying beside his gun and approximately 100 hostile dead lay in the wake of his field of fire. Through his unflinching courage and willing self-sacrifice the onslaught was retarded, enabling his unit to withdraw, regroup, and resecure the strongpoint. Cpl. Goodblood's inspirational conduct and devotion to duty reflect lasting glory on himself and are in keeping with the noble traditions of the military service.

GUILLEN, AMBROSIO

Rank and organization: Staff Sergeant, U.S. Marine Corps, Company F, 2d Battalion, 7th Marines, 1st Marine Division (Rein).

Place and date: Near Songuch-on, Korea, 25 July 1953.

Entered service at: El Paso, Tex.

Born: 7 December 1929, La Junta, Colo.

Citation: For conspicuous gallantry and intrepidity at the risk of his life above and beyond the call of duty while serving as a platoon sergeant of Company F in action against enemy aggressor forces. Participating in the defense of an outpost forward of the main line of resistance, S/Sgt. Guillen maneuvered his platoon over unfamiliar terrain in the face of hostile fire and placed his men in fighting positions. With his unit pinned down when the outpost was attacked under cover of darkness by an estimated force of 2 enemy battalions supported by mortar and artillery fire, he deliberately exposed himself to the heavy barrage and attacks to direct his men in defending their positions and personally supervise the treatment and evacuation of the wounded. Inspired by his leadership, the platoon quickly rallied and engaged the enemy in fierce hand-to-hand combat. Although critically wounded during the course of the battle, S/Sgt. Guillen refused medical aid and continued to direct his men throughout the remainder of the engagement until the enemy was defeated and thrown into disorderly retreat. Succumbing to his wounds within a few hours, S/Sgt. Guillen, by his outstanding courage and indomitable fighting spirit, was directly responsible for the success of his platoon in repelling a numerically superior enemy force His personal valor reflects the highest credit upon himself and enhances the finest traditions of the U.S. Naval Service. He gallantly gave his life for his country.

HAMMOND, FRANCIS C.

Rank and organization: Hospital Corpsman, U.S. Navy, attached as a medical corpsman to 1st Marine Division.

Place and date: Korea, 26-27 March 1953.

Entered service at: Alexandria, Va.

Birth: Alexandria, Va.

Citation: For conspicuous gallantry and intrepidity at the risk of his life above and beyond the call of duty as a HC serving with the 1st Marine Division in action against enemy aggressor forces on the night of 26-27 March 1953. After reaching an intermediate objective during a counterattack against a heavily entrenched and numerically superior hostile force occupying ground on a bitterly contested outpost far in advance of the main line of resistance, HC Hammond's platoon was subjected to a murderous barrage of hostile mortar and artillery fire, followed by a vicious assault by onrushing enemy troops. Resolutely advancing through the veritable curtain of fire to aid his stricken comrades, HC Hammond moved among the stalwart garrison of marines and, although critically wounded himself, valiantly continued to administer aid to the other wounded throughout an exhausting 4-hour period. When the unit was ordered to withdraw, he skillfully directed the evacuation of casualties and remained in the fire-swept area to assist the corpsmen of the relieving unit until he was struck by a round of enemy mortar fire and fell, mortally wounded. By his exceptional fortitude, inspiring initiative and self-sacrificing efforts, HC Hammond undoubtedly saved the lives of many marines. His great personal valor in the face of overwhelming odds enhances and sustains the finest traditions of the U.S. Naval Service. He gallantly gave his life for his country.

HAMMOND, LESTER, JR.

Rank and organization: Corporal, U.S. Army, Company A, 187th Airborne Regimental Cobat Team
   Place and date: Near Kumwha, Korea, 14 August 1952.
   Entered service at: Quincy, Ill.
   Born: 25 March 1931, Wayland, Mo.
   G.O. No.: 63, 17 August 1953.
   Citation: Cpl. Hammond, a radio operator with Company A, distinguished himself by conspicuous gallantry and outstanding courage above and beyond the call of duty in action against the enemy. Cpl. Hammond was a member of a 6 man reconnaissance patrol which had penetrated approximately 3,500 yards into enemy-held territory. Ambushed and partially surrounded by a large hostile force, the small group opened fire, then quickly withdrew up a narrow ravine in search of protective cover. Despite a wound sustained in the initial exchange of fire and imminent danger of being overrun by the numerically superior foe, he refused to seek shelter and, remaining in an exposed place, called for artillery fire to support a defensive action. Constantly vulnerable to enemy observation and action, he coordinated and directed crippling fire on the assailants, inflicting heavy casualties and repulsing several attempts to overrun friendly positions. Although wounded a second time, he remained steadfast and maintained his stand until mortally wounded. His indomitable fighting spirit set an inspiring example of valor to his comrades and, through his actions, the onslaught was stemmed, enabling a friendly platoon to reach the beleaguered patrol, evacuate the wounded, and effect a safe withdrawal to friendly lines. Cpl. Hammond's unflinching courage and consummate devotion to duty reflect lasting glory on himself and uphold the finest traditions of the military service.

HANDRICH, MELVIN O.

Rank and organization: Master Sergeant, U.S. Army, Company C, 5th Infantry Regiment.
   Place and date: Near Sobuk San Mountain, Korea, 25 and 26 August 1950.
   Entered service at: Manawa, Wis.
   Born: 26 January 1919, Manawa, Wis.
   G.O. No.: 60, 2 August 1951.
   Citation: M/Sgt. Handrich, Company C, distinguished himself by conspicuous gallantry and intrepidity above and beyond the call of duty in action. His company was engaged in repulsing an estimated 150 enemy who were threatening to overrun its position. Near midnight on 25 August, a hostile group over 100 strong attempted to infiltrate the company perimeter. M/Sgt. Handrich, despite the heavy enemy fire, voluntarily left the comparative safety of the defensive area and moved to a forward position where he could direct mortar and artillery fire upon the advancing enemy. He remained at this post for 8 hours directing fire against the enemy who often approached to within 50 feet of his position. Again, on the morning of 26 August, another strong hostile force made an attempt to overrun the company's position. With complete disregard for his safety, M/Sgt. Handrich

rose to his feet and from this exposed position fired his rifle and directed mortar and artillery fire on the attackers. At the peak of this action he observed elements of his company preparing to withdraw. He perilously made his way across fire-swept terrain to the defense area where, by example and forceful leadership, he reorganized the men to continue the fight. During the action M/Sgt. Handrich was severely wounded. Refusing to take cover or be evacuated, he returned to his forward position and continued to direct the company's fire. Later a determined enemy attack overran M/Sgt. Handrich's position and he was mortally wounded. When the position was retaken, over 70 enemy dead were counted in the area he had so intrepidly defended. M/Sgt. Handrich's sustained personal bravery, consummate courage, and gallant self-sacrifice reflect untold glory upon himself and the heroic traditions of the military service.

HANSON, JACK G.

Rank and organization: Private First Class, U.S. Army, Company F, 31st Infantry Regiment
   Place and date: Near Pachi-dong, Korea, 7 June 1951.
   Entered service at: Galveston, Tex.
   Born: 18 September 1930, Escaptawpa, Miss.
   G.O.No.: 15, 1 February 1952.
   Citation: Pfc. Hanson, a machine gunner with the 1st Platoon, Company F, distinguished himself by conspicuous gallantry and intrepidity at the risk of his life above and beyond the call of duty in action against an armed enemy of the United Nations. The company, in defensive positions on two strategic hills separated by a wide saddle, was ruthlessly attacked at approximately 0300 hours, the brunt of which centered on the approach to the divide within range of Pfc. Hanson's machinegun. In the initial phase of the action, 4 riflemen were wounded and evacuated and the numerically superior enemy, advancing under cover of darkness, infiltrated and posed an imminent threat to the security of the command post and weapons platoon. Upon orders to move to key terrain above and to the right of Pfc. Hanson's position, he voluntarily remained to provide protective fire for the withdrawal. Subsequent to the retiring elements fighting a rearguard action to the new location, it was learned that Pfc. Hanson's assistant gunner and 3 riflemen had been wounded and had crawled to safety, and that he was maintainig a lone-man defense. After the 1st Platoon reorganized, counterattacked, and resecured its original positions at approximately 0530 hours, Pfc. Hanson's body was found lying in front of his emplacement, his machinegun ammunition expended, his empty piston in his right hand, and a machete with blood on the blade in his left hand, and approximately 22 enemy dead lay in the wake of his action. Pfc. Hanson's consummate valor, inspirational conduct, and willing self-sacrifice enabled the company to contain the enemy and regain the commanding ground, and reflect lasting glory on himself and the noble traditions of the military service.

HARTELL, LEE R.

Rank and organization: First Lieutenant, U.S. Army, Battery A, 15th Field Artillery Battalion, 2d Infantry Division.

Place and date: Near Kobangsan-ni, Korea, 27 August 1951.

Entered service at: Danbury, Conn.

Birth: Philadelphia, Pa.

G.O. No.: 16, 1 February 1952.

Citation: 1st. Lt. Hartell, a member of Battery A, distinguished himself by conspicuous gallantry and intrepidity at the risk of his life above and beyond the call of duty in action against an armed enemy of the United Nations. During the darkness of early morning, the enemy launched a ruthless attack against friendly positions on a rugged mountainous ridge. 1st Lt. Hartell, attached to Company B, 9th Infantry Regiment, as forward observer, quickly moved his radio to an exposed vantage on the ridge line to adjust defensive fires. Realizing the tactical advantage of illuminating the area of approach, he called for flares and then directed crippling fire into the onrushing assailants. At this juncture a large force of hostile troops swarmed up the slope in a banzai charge and came within 10 yards of 1st Lt. Hartell's position. 1st Lt. Hartell sustained a severe hand wound in the ensuing encounter, but grasped the microphone with his other hand and maintained his magnificent stand until the front and left flank of the company were protected by a close-in wall of withering fire, causing the fanatical foe to disperse and fall back momentarily. After the numerically superior enemy overran an outpost and was closing on his position, 1st Lt. Hartell, in a final radio call, urged the friendly elements to fire both batteries continuously. Although mortally wounded, 1st Lt. Hartell's intrepid actions contributed significantly to stemming the onslaught and enabled his company to maintain the strategic strongpoint. His consummate valor and unwavering devotion to duty reflect lasting glory on himself and uphold the noble traditions of the military service.

HARVEY, RAYMOND

Rank and organization: Captain, U.S. Army, Company C, 17th Infantry Regiment.

Place and date: Vicinity of Taemi-Dong, Korea, 9 March 1951.

Entered service at: Pasadena, Calif.

Born: 1 March 1920, Ford City, Pa.

G.O. No.: 67, 2 August 1951.

Citation: Capt. Harvey, Company C, distinguished himself by conspicuous gallantry and intrepidity above and beyond the call of duty in action. When his company was pinned down by a barrage of automatic weapons from numerous well-entrenched emplacements, imperiling accomplishment of its mission, Capt. Harvey braved a hail of fire and exploding grenades to advance to the first enemy machinegun nest, killing its crew with grenades. Rushing to the edge of the next emplacement, he killed its crew with carbine fire. He then moved the 1st Platoon forward until it was again halted by a curtain of automatic fire from will-fortified hostile positions. Disregarding the hail of fire, he personally charged and neutralized a third emplacement. Miraculously escaping death from intense crossfire, Capt. Harvey continued to lead the assault. Spotting an enemy pillbox well camouflaged by logs, he moved close enough to sweep the emplacement with carbine fire and throw grenades through the openings, annihilating its 5 occupants. Though wounded he then turned to order the company forward, and, suffering agonizing pain, he continued to direct the reduction of the remaining hostile positions, refusing evacuation until assured that the mission would be accomplished. Capt. Harvey's valorous and intrepid actions served as an inspiration to his company, reflecting the utmost glory upon himself and upholding the heroic traditions of the military service.

HENRY, FREDERICK F.

Rank and organization: First Lieutenant, U.S. Army, Company F, 28th Infantry Regiment.

Place and date: Vicinity of Am-Dong, Korea, 1 September 1950.

Entered service at: Clinton, Okla.

Birth: Vian, Okla.

G.O. No.: 8, 16 February 1951.

Citation: 1st Lt. Henry, Company F, distinguished himself by conspicuous gallantry and intrepidity above and beyond the call of duty in action. His platoon was holding a strategic ridge near the town when they were attacked by a superior enemy force, supported by heavy mortar and artillery fire. Seeing his platoon disorganized by this fanatical assault, he left his foxhole and moving along the line ordered his men to stay in place and keep firing. Encouraged by this heroic action the platoon reformed a defensive line and rained devastating fire on the enemy, checking its advance. Enemy fire had knocked out all communications and 1st Lt. Henry was unable to determine whether or not the main line of resistance was altered to this heavy attack. On his own initiative, although severely wounded, he decided to hold his position as long as possible and ordered the wounded evacuated and their weapons and ammunition brought to him. Establishing a 1-man defensive position, he ordered the platoon's withdrawal and despite his wound and with complete disregard for himself remained behind to cover the movement. When last seen he was single-handedly firing all available weapons so effectively that he caused an estimated 50 enemy casualties. His ammunition was soon expended and his position overrun, but this intrepid action saved the platoon and halted the enemy's advance until the main line of resistance was prepared to throw back the attack. 1st Lt. Henry's outstanding gallantry and noble self-sacrifice above and beyond the call of duty reflect the highest honor on him and are in keeping with the esteemed traditions of the U.S. Army.

HERNANDEZ, RODOLFO P.

Rank and organization: Corporal, U.S. Army, Company G, 187th Airborne Regimental Combat Team.

Place and date: Near Wontong-ni, Korea, 31 May 1951.

Entered service at: Fowler, Calif.

Born: 14 April 1931, Colton, Calif.

G.O. No.: 40, 21 April 1962.

Citation: Cpl. Hernandez, a member of Company G, distinguished himself by conspicuous gallantry and intrepidity above and beyond the call of duty in action against the enemy. His platoon, in defensive positions on Hill 420, came under ruthless attack by a numerically superior and fanatical hostile force, accompanied by heavy artillery, mortar, and machinegun fire which inflicted numerous casualties on the platoon. His comrades were forced to withdraw due to lack of ammunition but Cpl. Hernandez, although wounded in an exchange of grenades, continued to deliver deadly fire into the ranks of the onrushing assailants until ruptured cartridge rendered his rifle inoperative. Immediately leaving his position, Cpl. Hernandez rushed the enemy armed only with rifle and bayonet. Fearlessly engaging the foe, he killed 6 of the enemy before falling unconscious from grenade, bayonet, and bullet wounds but his heroic action momentarily halted the enemy advance and enabled his unit to counterattack and retake the lost ground. The indomitable fighting spirit, outstanding courage, and tenacious devotion to duty clearly demonstrated by Cpl. Hernandez reflect the highest credit upon himself, the infantry, and the U.S. Army.

HUDNER, THOMAS JERONE, JR.

Rank and organization: Lieutenant (jg.) U.S. Navy, pilot in Fighter Squadron 32, attached to U.S.S. *Leyte*.

Place and date: Chosin Reservoir area of Korea, 4 December 1950.

Entered service at: Fall River, Mass.

Born: 31 August 1924, Fall River, Mass.

Citation: For conspicuous gallantry and intrepidity at the risk of his life above and beyond the call of duty as a pilot in Fighter Squadron 32, while attempting to rescue a squadron mate whose plane struck by antiaircraft fire and trailing smoke, was forced down behind enemy lines. Quickly maneuvering to circle the downed pilot and protect him from enemy troops infesting the area, Lt. (jg.) Hudner risked his life to save the injured flier who was trapped alive in the burning wreckage. Fully aware of the extreme danger in landing on the rough mountainous terrain, and the scant hope of escape of survival in subzero temperature, he put his plane down skillfully in a deliberate wheels-up landing in the presence of enemy troops. With his bare hands, he packed the fuselage with snow to keep the flames away from the pilot and struggled to pull him free. Unsuccessful in this, he returned to his crashed aircraft and radioed other airborne planes, requesting that a helicopter be dispatched with an ax and fire extinguisher. He then remained on the spot despite the continuing danger from enemy action and, with the assistance of the rescue pilot, renewed a desperate but unavailing battle against time, cold, and flames. Lt. (jg.) Hudner's exceptionally valiant action and selfless devotion to a shipmate sustain and enhance the highest traditions of the U.S. Naval Service.

INGMAN, EINAR H., JR.

Rank and organization: Sergeant (then Cpl.), U.S. Army, Company E, 17th Infantry Regiment, 7th Infantry Division.

Place and date: Near Maltari, Korea, 26 February 1951.

Entered service at: Tomahawk, Wis.

Born: 6 October 1929, Milwaukee, Wis.

G.O. No.: 68, 2 August 1951.

Citation: Sgt. Ingman, a member of Company E, distinguished himself by conspicuous gallantry and intrepidity above and beyond the call of duty in action

against the enemy. The 2 leading squads of the assault platoon of his company, while attacking a strongly fortified ridge held by the enemy, were pinned down by withering fire and both squad leaders and several men were wounded. Cpl. Ingman assumed command, reorganized and combined the 2 squads, then moved from 1 position to another, designating fields of fire he charged it alone, threw a grenade into the position, and killed the remaining crew with rifle fire. Another enemy machinegun opened fire approximately 15 yards away and inflicted additional causalities to the group and stopped the attack. When Cpl. Ingman charged the second position he was hit by grenade fragments and a hail of fire which seriously wounded him about the face and neck and knocked him to the ground. With incredible courage and stamina, he arose instantly and, using only his rifle, killed the entire gun crew before falling unconscious from his wounds. As a result of the singular action by Cpl. Ingman the defense of the enemy wax broken, his squad secured its objective, and more than 100 hostile troops abandoned their weapons and fled in disorganized retreat. Cpl. Ingman's indomitable courage, extraordinary heroism, and superb leadership reflect the highest credit on himself and are in keeping with the esteemed traditions of the infantry and the U.S. Army.

JECELIN, WILLIAM R.

Rank and organization: Sergeant, U.S. Army, Company C, 35th Infantry Regiment, 25th Infantry Division.

Place and date: Near Saga, Korea, 19 September 1950.

Entered service at: Baltimore, Md.

Birth: Baltimore, Md.

G.O. No.: 24, 25 April 1951.

Citation: Sgt. Jecelin, Company C, distinguished himself by conspicuous gallantry and intrepidity above and beyond the call of duty in action against the enemy. His company was ordered to secure a prominent, sawtoothed ridge from a well-entrenched and heavily armed enemy. Unable to capture the objective in the first attempt, a frontal and flanking assault was launched. He led his platoon through heavy enemy fire and bursting shells, across rice fields and rocky terrain, in direct frontal attack on the ridge in order to draw fire away from the flanks. The unit advanced to the base of the cliff, where intense, accurate hostile fire stopped the attack. Realizing that an assault was the only solution, Sgt. Jecelin rose from his position firing his rifle and throwing grenades as he called on his men to follow him. Despite the intense enemy fire this attack carried to the crest of the ridge where the men were forced to take cover. Again he rallied his men and stormed the enemy strongpoint. With fixed bayonets they charged into the face of antitank fire and engaged the enemy in hand-to-hand combat. After clubbing and slashing this force into submission the platoon was forced to take cover from direct frontal fire of a self-propelled gun. Refusing to be stopped he leaped to his feet and through sheer personal courage and fierce determination led his men in a new attack. At this instant a well-camouflaged enemy soldier threw a grenade at the remaining members of the platoon. He immediately lunged and covered the grenade with his body, absorbing the full force of the explosion to save those around him.

This incredible courage and willingness to sacrifice himself for his comrades so imbued them with fury that they completely eliminated the enemy force. Sgt. Jecelin's heroic leadership and outstanding gallantry reflect the highest credit upon himself and uphold the esteemed traditions of the military service.

JOHNSON, JAMES E.

Rank and organization: Sergeant, U.S. Marine Corps, Company J, 3d Battalion, 7th Marines, 1st Marine Division (Rein.)

Place and date: Yudam-ni, Korea, 2 December 1950 (declared missing in action on 2 December 1950, and killed in action as of 2 November 1953).

Entered service at: Washington, D.C.

Born: 1 January 1926, Pocatello, Idaho.

Citation: For conspicuous gallantry and intrepidity at the risk of his life above and beyond the call of duty while serving as a squad leader in a provisional rifle platoon composed of artillerymen and attached to Company J, in action against enemy aggressor forces. Vastly outnumbered by a well-entrenched and cleverly concealed enemy force wearing the uniforms of friendly troops and attacking his platoon's open and unconcealed positions, Sgt. Johnson unhesitatingly took charge of his platoon in the absence of the leader and, exhibiting great personal valor in the face of a heavy barrage of hostile fire, coolly proceeded to move about among his men, shouting words of encouragement and inspiration and skillfully directing their fire. Ordered to displace his platoon during the fire fight, he immediately placed himself in an extremely hazardous position from which he could provide covering fire for his men. Fully aware that his voluntary action meant either certain death or capture to himself, he courageously continued to provide effective cover for his men and was last observed in a wounded condition single handedly engaging enemy troops in close handgrenade and hand-to-hand fighting. By his valiant and inspiring leadership, Sgt. Johnson was directly responsible for the successful completion of the platoon's displacement and the saving of many lives. His dauntless fighting spirit and unfaltering devotion to duty in the face of terrific odds reflect the highest credit upon himself and the U.S. Naval Service.

JORDAN, MACK A.

Rank and organization: Private First Class, U.S. Army, Company K, 21st Infantry Regiment, 24th Infantry Division.

Place and date: Near Kumsong, Korea, 15 November 1951.

Entered service at: Collins, Miss.

Born: 8 December 1928, Collins, Miss.

G.O. No.: 3, 8 January 1953.

Citation: Pfc. Jordan, a member of Company K, distinguished himself by conspicuous gallantry and indomitable courage above and beyond the call of duty in action against the enemy. As a squad leader of the 3d Platoon, he was participating in a night attack on key terrain against a fanatical hostile force when the advance was halted by intense small-arms and automatic-weapons fire and a vicious barrage of handgrenades. Upon orders

for the platoon to withdraw and reorganize, Pfc. Jordan voluntarily remained behind to provide covering fire. Crawling toward an enemy machinegun emplacement, he threw 3 grenades and neutralized the gun. He then rushed the position delivering a devastating hail of fire, killing several of the enemy and forcing the remainder to fall back to new positions. He courageously attempted to move forward to silence another machinegun but, before he could leave his position, the ruthless foe hurled explosives down the hill and in the ensuing blast both legs were severed. Despite mortal wounds, he continued to deliver deadly fire and held off the assailants until the platoon returned. Pfc. Jordan's unflinching courage and gallant self-sacrifice reflect lasting glory upon himself and uphold the noble traditions of the infantry and the military service.

KANELL, BILLIE G.

Rank and organization: Private, U.S. Army, Company I, 35th Infantry Regiment, 25th Infantry Division.

Place and date: Near Pyongyang, Korea, 7 September 1951.

Entered service at: Poplar Bluff, Mo.

Born: 26 June 1931, Poplar Bluff, Mo.

G.O. No.: 57, 13 June 1952.

Citation: Pvt. Kanell, a member of Company I, distinguished himself by conspicuous gallantry and outstanding courage above and beyond the call of duty in action against the enemy. A numerically superior hostile force had launched a fanatical assault against friendly positions, supported by mortar and artillery fire, when Pvt. Kanell stood in his emplacement exposed to enemy observation and action and delivered accurate fire into the emplacement and, although seriously wounded by the first missile, he summoned his waning strength to roll toward the second grenade and used his body as a shield to again protect his comrades. He was mortally wounded as a result of his heroic actions. His indomitable courage, sustained fortitude against overwhelming odds, and gallant self-sacrifice reflect the highest credit upon himself, the infantry, and the U.S. Army.

KAUFMAN, LOREN R.

Rank and organization: Sergeant First Class, U.S. Army, Company G, 9th Infantry Regiment.

Place and date: Near Yongsan, Korea, 4 and 5 September 1950.

Entered service at: The Dalles, Oreg.

Born: 27 July 1923, The Dalles, Oreg.

G.O. No.: 61, 2 August 1951.

Citation: Sfc. Kaufman distinguished himself by conspicuous gallantry and intrepidity above and beyond the call of duty in action. On the night of 4 September the company was in a defensive position on 2 adjoining hills. His platoon was occupying a strong point 2 miles away protecting the battalion flank. Early on 5 September the company was attacked by an enemy battalion and his platoon was ordered to reinforce the company. As his unit moved along a ridge it encountered a hostile encircling force. Sfc. Kaufman, running forward, bayoneted the lead scout and engaged the column in a rifle and grenade assault. His quick vicious attack so surprised the enemy that they retreated in confusion. When his platoon joined the company he discovered that the enemy had taken commanding ground and pinned the company down in a draw. Without hesitation Sfc. Kaufman charged the enemy lines firing his rifle and throwing grenades. During the action, he bayoneted 2 enemy and seizing an unmanned machinegun, delivered deadly fire on the defenders. Following this encounter the company regrouped and resumed the attack. Leading the assault he reached the ridge, destroyed a hostile machinegun position, and routed the remaining enemy. Pursuing the hostile troops he bayoneted 2 more and then fled to a village and Sfc. Kaufman led a patrol into the town, dispersed them, and burned the buildings. The dauntless courage and resolute intrepid leadership of Sfc. Kaufman were directly responsible for the success of his company in regaining its positions, reflecting distance credit upon himself and upholding the esteemed traditions of the military service.

KELLY, JOHN D.

Rank and organization: Private First Class, U.S. Marine Corps, Company C, 1st Battalion, 7th Marines, 1st Marine Division (Rein).
Place and date: Korea, 28 May 1952.
Entered service at: Homestead, Pa.
Born: 8 July 1928, Youngstown, Ohio.
Citation: For conspicuous gallantry and intrepidity at the risk of his life above and beyond the call of duty while serving as a radio operator of Company C, in action against enemy aggressor forces. With his platoon pinned down by a numerically superior enemy force employing intense mortar, artillery, small-arms and grenade fire, Pfc. Kelly requested permission to leave his radio in the care of another man and to participate in an assault on enemy key positions. Fearlessly charging forward in the face of a murderous hail of machinegun fire and handgrenades, he initiated a daring attack against a hostile strongpoint and personally neutralized the position, killing 2 of the enemy. Unyielding in the fact of heavy odds, he continued forward and singlehandedly assaulted a machinegun bunker. Although painfully wounded, he bravely charged the bunker and destroyed it, killing 3 of the enemy. Courageously continuing his 1-man assault, he again stormed forward in a valiant attempt to swipe out a third bunker and boldly delivered pointblank fire into the aperture of the hostile emplacement. Mortally wounded by enemy fire while carrying out this heroic action, Pfc. Kelly, by his great personal valor and aggressive fighting spirit, inspired his comrades to sweep on, overrun and secure the objective. His extraordinary heroism in the face of almost certain death reflects the highest credit upon himself and enhances the finest traditions of the U.S. Naval Service. He gallantly gave his life for his country.

KENNEMORE, ROBERT S.

Rank and organization: Staff Sergeant, U.S. Marine Corps, Company E, 2d Battalion, 7th Marines, 1st Marine Division (Rein.)
Place and date: North of Yudam-ni, Korea, 27 and 28 November 1950

Entered service at: Greenville, S.C.
Born: 21 June 1920, Greenville, S.C.
Citation: For conspicuous gallantry and intrepidity at the risk of his life above and beyond the call of duty as leader of a machinegun section in Company E, in action against enemy aggressor forces. With the company's defensive perimeter overrun by a numerically superior hostile force during a savage night attack north of Yudam-ni and his platoon commander seriously wounded, S/Sgt. Kennemore unhesitatingly assumed command, quickly reorganized the unit and directed the men in consolidating the position. When an enemy grenade landed in the midst of a machinegun squad, he bravely placed his foot on the missile and, in the face of almost certain death, personally absorbed the full force of the explosion to prevent injury to his fellow marines. By his indomitable courage, outstanding leadership and selfless efforts in behalf of his comrades, S/Sgt. Kennemore was greatly instrumental in driving the enemy from the area and upheld the highest traditions of the U.S. Naval Service.

KILMER, JOHN E.

Rank and organization: Hospital Corpsman, U.S. Navy, attached to duty as a medical corpsman with a Marine rifle company in the 1st Marine Division.
Place and date: Korea, 13 August 1952.
Entered service at: Houston, Texas
Born: 15 August 1930, Highland Park, Ill.
Citation: For conspicuous gallantry and intrepidity at the risk of his life above and beyond the call of duty in action against enemy aggressor forces. With his company engaged in defending a vitally important hill position well forward of the main line of resistance during an assault by large concentrations of hostile troops, HC Kilmer repeatedly braved intense enemy mortar, artillery, and sniper fire to move from 1 position to another, administering aid to the wounded and expediting their evacuation. Painfully wounded himself when struck by mortar fragments while moving to the aid of a casualty, he persisted in his efforts and inched his way to the side of the stricken marine through a hail of fire, he skillfully administered first aid to his comrade and, as another mounting barrage of enemy fire shattered the immediate area, unhesitatingly shielded the wounded man with his body. Mortally wounded by flying shrapnel while carrying out this heroic action, HC Kilmer, by his great personal valor and gallant spirit of self-sacrifice in saving the life of a comrade, served to inspire all who observed him. His unyielding devotion to duty in the face of heavy odds reflects the highest credit upon himself and enhances the finest traditions of the U.S. Naval Service. He gallantly gave his life for another.

KNIGHT, NOAH O.

Rank and organization: Private First Class, U.S. Army, Company F, 7th Infantry Regiment, 3d Infantry Division.
Place and date: Near Kowang-San, Korea, 23 and 24 November 1951
Entered service at: Jefferson, S.C.
Born: 27 October 1929, Chesterfield County, S.C.
G.O. No.: 2, 7 January 1953.

Citation: Pfc. Knight, a member of Company F, distinguished himself by conspicuous gallantry and indomitable courage above and beyond the call of duty in action against the enemy. He occupied a key position in the defense perimeter when waves of enemy troops passed through their own artillery and mortar concentrations and charged the company position. Two direct hits from an enemy emplacement demolished his bunker and wounded him. Disregarding personal safety, he moved to a shallow depression for a better firing vantage. Unable to deliver effective fire from his defilade position, he left his shelter, moved through heavy fire in full view of the enemy and, firing into the ranks of the relentless assailants, inflicted numerous casualties, momentarily stemming the attack. Later during another vicious onslaught, he observed an enemy squad infiltrating the position and, counterattacking, killed or wounded the entire group. Expending the last of his ammunition, he discovered 3 enemy soldiers entering the friendly position with demolition charges. Realizing the explosives would enable the enemy to exploit the breach, he fearlessly rushed forward and disabled 2 assailants with the butt of his rifle when the third exploded a demolition charge killing the 3 enemy soldiers and mortally wounding Pfc. Knight. Pfc. Knight's supreme sacrifice and consummate devotion to duty reflect lasting glory on himself and uphold the noble traditions of the military service.

KOELSCH, JOHN KELVIN

Rank and organization: Lieutenant (jg.), U.S. Navy, Navy helicopter rescue unit.

Place and date: North Korea, 3 July 1951.

Entered service at: Los Angeles, Calif.

Birth: London, England

Citation: For conspicuous gallantry and intrepidity at the risk of his life above and beyond the call of duty while serving with a Navy helicopter rescue unit. Although darkness was rapidly approaching when information was received that a marine aviator had been shot down and was trapped by the enemy in mountainous terrain deep in hostile territory, Lt. (jg.) Koelsch voluntarily flew a helicopter to the reported position of the downed airman in an attempt to effect a rescue. With an almost solid overcast concealing everything below the mountain peaks, he descended in his unarmed and vulnerable aircraft without the accompanying fighter escort to an extremely low altitude beneath the cloud level and began a systematic search. Despite the increasingly intense enemy fire, which struck his helicopter on 1 occasion, he persisted in his mission until he succeeded in locating the downed pilot, who was suffering from serious burns on the arms and legs. While the victim was being hoisted into the aircraft, it was struck again by an accurate burst of hostile fire and crashed on the side of the mountain. Quickly Koelsch led them from the vicinity in an effort to escape from hostile troops, evading the enemy forces for 9 days and rendering such medical attention as possible to his severely burned companion until all were captured. Up to the time of his death while still a captive of the enemy, Lt. (jg.) Koelsch steadfastly refused to aid his captors in any manner and served to inspire his fellow

prisoners by his fortitude and consideration for otheres. His great personal valor and heroic spirit of self-sacrifice throughout sustain and enhance the finest traditions of the U.S. Naval Service.

KOUMA, ERNEST R.

Rank and organizatin: Master Sergeant (then Sfc.) U.S. Army, Company A, 72d Tank Battalion.

Place and date: Vicinity of Agok, Korea, 31 August and 1 September 1950.

Entered service at: Dwight, Nebr.

Born: 23 November 1919, Dwight, Nebr.

G.O. No.: 38, 4 June 1951.

Citation: M/Sgt. Kouma, a tank commander in Company A, distinguished himself by conspicuous gallantry and intrepidity at the risk of his life above and beyond the call of duty in action against the enemy. His unit was engaged in supporting infantry elements on the Naktong River front. Near midnight on 31 August, a hostile force estimated at 500 crossed the river and launched a fierce attack against the infantry positions, inflicting heavy casualties. A withdrawal was ordered and his armored unit was given the mission of covering the movement until a secondary position could be established. The enemy assault overran 2 tanks, destroyed 1 and forced another to withdraw. Suddenly M/Sgt. Kouma discovered that his tank was the only obstacle in the path of the hostile onslaught. Holding his ground, he gave fire orders to his crew and remained in position throughout the night, fighting off repeated enemy attacks. During 1 fierce assault, the enemy surrounded his tank and he leaped from the armored turret, exposing himself to a hail of hostile fire, manned the .50 caliber machinegun mounted on the rear deck, and delivered pointblank fire into the fanatical foe. His machinegun emptied, he fired his pistol and threw grenades to keep the enemy from his tank. After more than 9 hours of constant combat and close-in fighting, he withdrew his vehicle to friendly lines. During the withdrawal through 8 miles of hostile territory, M/Sgt. Kouma continued to inflict casualties upon the enemy and exhausted his ammunition in destroying 3 hostile machinegun positions. During this action, M/Sgt. Kouma killed an estimated 250 enemy soldiers. His magnificent stand allowed the infantry sufficient time to reestablish defensive positions. Rejoining his company, although suffering intensely from his wounds, he attempted to resupply his tank and return to the battle area. While being evacuated for medical treatment, his courage was again displayed when he requested to return to the front. M/Sgt. Kouma's superb leadership, heroism, and intense devotion to duty reflect the highest credit on himself and uphold the esteemed traditions of the U.S. Army.

KRZYZOWSKI, EDWARD C.

Rank and organization: Captain, U.S. Army, Company B, 9th Infantry Regiment, 2d Infantry Division.

Place and date: Near Tondul, Korea, from 31 August to 3 September 1951.

Entered service at: Cicero, Ill.

Born: 16 January 1914, Chicago, Ill.

G.O. No.: 56, 12 June 1952.

Citation: Capt. Krzyzowski, distinguished himself by conspicuous gallantry and indomitable courage above and beyond the call of duty in action against the enemy as commanding officer of Company B. Spearheading an assault against strongly defended Hill 700, his company came under vicious crossfire and grenade attack from enemy bunkers. Creeping up the fire-swept hill, he personally eliminated 1 bunker with his grenades and wiped out a second with carbine fire. Forced to retire to more tenable positions for the night, the company, led by Capt. Krzyzowski, resumed the attack the following day, gaining several hundred yards and inflicting numerous casualties. Overwhelmed by the numerically superior hostile force, he ordered his men to evacuate the wounded and move back. Providing protective fire for their safe withdrawal, he was wounded again by grenade fragments, but refused evacuation and continued to direct the defense. On 3 September, he led his valiant unit in another assault which overran several hostile positions, but again the company was pinned down by murderous fire. Courageously advancing alone to an open knoll to plot mortar concentrations against the hill, he was killed instantly by an enemy sniper's fire. Capt. Krzyzowski's consummate fortitude, heroic leadership, and gallant self-sacrifice, so clearly demonstrated throughout 3 days of bitter combat, reflect the highest credit and lasting glory on himself, the infantry, and the U.S. Army.

KYLE, DARWIN K.

Rank and organization: Second Leiutenant, U.S. Army, Company K, 7th Infantry Regiment, 3d Infantry Division.
Place and date: Near Kamil-ni, Korea, 16 February 1951.
Entered service at: Racine, W. Va.
Born: 1 June 1918, Jenkins, Ky.
G.O. No.: 17, 1 February 1952.
Citation: 2d Lt. Kyle, distinguished himself by conspicuous gallantry and intrepidity above and beyond the call of duty in action against the enemy. When his platoon had been pinned down by intense fire, he completely exposed himself to move among and encourage his men to continue the advance against enemy forces strongly entrenched on Hill 185. Inspired by his courageous leadership, the platoon resumed the advance but was again pinned down when an enemy machinegun opened fire, wounding 6 of the men. 2d Lt. Kyle immediately charged the hostile emplacement alone, engaged the crew in hand-to-hand combat, killing all 3. Continuing on toward the objective, his platoon suddenly received an intense automatic-weapons fire from a well-concealed hostile position on its right flank. Again leading his men in a daring bayonet charge against this position, firing his carbine and throwing grenades, 2d Lt. Kyle personally destroyed 4 of the enemy before he was killed by a burst from an enemy submachinegun. The extraordinary heroism and outstanding leadership of 2d Lt. Kyle, and his gallant self-sacrifice, reflect the highest credit upon himself and are in keeping with the esteemed tradition of the military service.

LEE, HUBERT L.

Rank and organization: Master Sergeant, U.S. Army, Company I, 23d Infantry Regiment, 2d Infantry Division.
Place and date: Near Ip-o-ri, Korea, 1 February 1951.
Entered service at: Leland, Miss.
Born: 2 February 1915, Arburg, Mo.
G.O. No.: 21, 5 February 1952.
Citation: M/Sgt. Lee, a member of Company I, distinguished himself by conspicuous gallantry and intrepidity above and beyond the call of duty in action against the enemy. When his platoon was forced from its position by a numerically superior enemy force, and his platoon leader wounded, M/Sgt. Lee assumed command, regrouped the remnants of his unit, and led them in repeated assaults to regain the position. Within 25 yards of his objective he received a leg wound from grenade fragments, but refused assistance and continued the attack. Although forced to withdraw 5 times, each time he regrouped his remaining men and renewed the assault. Moving forward at the head of his small group in the fifth attempt, he was struck by an exploding grenade, knocked to the ground, and seriously wounded in both legs. Still refusing assistance, he advanced by crawling, rising to his knees to fire, and urging his men to follow. While thus directing the final assault he was wounded a third time, by small-arms fire. Persistently continuing to crawl forward, he directed his men in a final and successful attack which regained the vital objective. His intrepid leadership and determination led to the destruction of 83 of the enemy and withdrawal of the remainder, and was a vital factor in stopping the enemy attack. M/Sgt. Lee's indomitable courage, consummate valor, and outstanding leadership reflect the highest credit upon himself and are in keeping with the finest traditions of the infantry and the U.S. Army.

LIBBY, GEORGE D.

Rank and organization: Sergeant, U.S. Army, Company C, 3d Engineer Combat Battalion, 24th Infantry Division.
Place and date: Near Taejon, Korea, 20 July 1950.
Entered service at: Waterbury, Conn.
Birth: Bridgton, Maine.
G.O. No.: 62, 2 August 1951.
Citation: Sgt. Libby distinguished himself by conspicuous gallantry and intrepidity above and beyond the call of duty in action. While breaking through an enemy encirclement, the vehicle in which he was riding approached an enemy roadblock and encountered devastating fire which disabled the truck, killing or wounding all the passengers except Sgt. Libby. Taking cover in a ditch Sgt. Libby engaged the enemy and despite the heavy fire crossed the road twice to administer aid to his wounded comrades. He then hailed a passing M-5 artillery tractor and helped the wounded aboard. The enemy directed intense small-arms fire at the driver, and Sgt. Libby, realizing that no one else could operate the vehicle, placed himself between the driver and the enemy thereby shielding him while he returned the fire. During this action he received several wounds in the arms and body. Continuing through the town the tractor made frequent stops and Sgt. Libby helped more wounded aboard. Refusing first aid, he continued to shield the driver and return the fire of the enemy when another roadblock was encountered. Sgt. Libby received additional wounds but held his position until he lost consciousness. Sgt. Libby's

sustained, heroic actions enabled his comrades to reach friendly lines. His dauntless courage and gallant self-sacrifice reflect the highest credit upon himself and uphold the esteemed traditions of the U.S. Army.

LITTLETON, HERBERT A.

Rank and organization: Private First Class, U.S. Marine Corps Reserve, Company C, 1st Battalion, 7th Marines, 1st Marine Division (Rein).

Place and date: Chungchon, Korea, 22 April 1951.

Entered service at: Blackhawk, S. Dak.

Born: 1 July 1930, Mena, Ark.

Citation: For conspicuous gallantry and intrepidity at the risk of his life above and beyond the call of duty while serving as a radio operator with an artillery forward observation team of Company C, in action against enemy aggressor forces. Standing watch when a well-concealed and numerically superior enemy force launched a violent night attack from nearby positions against his company, Pfc. Littleton quickly alerted the forward observation team and immediately moved into an advantageous position to assist in calling down artillery fire on the hostile force. When an enemy handgrenade was thrown into his vantage point shortly after the arrival of the remainder of them, he unhesitatingly hurled himself on the deadly missile, absorbing its full, shattering impact in his body. By his prompt action and heroic spirit of self-sacrifice, he saved the other members of his team from serious injury or death and enabled them to carry on the vital mission which culminated in the repulse of the hostile attack. His indomitable valor in the face of almost certain death reflects the highest credit upon Pfc. Littleton and the U.S. Naval Service. He gallantly gave his life for his country.

LONG, CHARLES R.

Rank and organization: Sergeant, U.S. Army, Company M, 38th Infantry Regiment, 2d Infantry Division.

Place and date: Near Hoengsong, Korea, 12 February 1951.

Entered service at: Kansas City, Mo.

Born: 10 December 1923, Kansas City, Mo.

G.O. No.: 18, 1 February 1952.

Citation: Sgt. Long, a member of Company M, distinguished himself by conspicuous gallantry and intrepidity above and beyond the call of duty in action against an armed enemy of the United Nations. When Company M, in a defensive perimeter on Hill 300, was viciously attacked by a numerically superior hostile force at approximately 0300 hours and ordered to withdraw, Sgt. Long, a forward observer for the mortar platoon, voluntarily remained at his post to provide cover by directing mortar fire on the enemy. Maintaining radio contact with his platoon, Sgt. Long coolly directed accurate mortar fire on the advancing foe. He continued firing his carbine and throwing handgrenades until his position was surrounded and he was mortally wounded. Sgt. Long's inspirational, valorous action halted the onslaught, exacted a heavy toll of enemy casualties, and enabled his company to withdraw, reorganize, counterattack, and regain the hill strongpoint. His unflinching courage and noble self-sacrifice reflect the highest credit on himself

and are in keeping with the honored traditions of the military service.

LOPEZ, BALDOMERO

Rank and organization: First Lieutenant, U.S. Marine Corps, Company A, 1st Battalion, 5th Marines, 1st Marine Division (Rein).

Place and date: During Inchon invasion in Korea, 15 September 1950.

Entered service at: Tampa, Fla.

Born: 23 August 1925, Tampa, Fla

Citation: For conspicuous gallantry and intrepidity at the risk of his life above and beyond the call of duty as a rifle platoon commander of Company A, in action against enemy aggressor forces. With his platoon 1st Lt. Lopez was engaged in the reduction of immediate enemy beach defenses after landing with the assault waves. Exposing himself to hostile fire, he moved forward alongside a bunker and prepared to throw a handgrenade into the next pillbox whose fire was pinning down that sector of the beach. Taken under fire by an enemy automatic weapon and hit in the right shoulder and chest as he lifted his arm to throw, he fell backward and dropped the deadly missile. After a moment, he turned and dragged his body forward in an effort to retrieve the grenade and throw it. In critical condition from pain and loss of blood, and unable to grasp the handgrenade firmly enough to hurl it, he chose to sacrifice himself rather than endanger the lives of his men and, with a sweeping motion of his wounded right arm, cradled the grenade under him and absorbed the full impact of the explosion. His exceptional courage, fortitude, and devotion to duty reflect the highest credit upon 1st Lt. Lopez and U.S. Naval Service. He gallantly gave his life for his country.

LORING, CHARLES J., JR.

Rank and organization: Major, U.S. Air Force, 80th Fighter-Bomber Squadron, 8th Fighter-Bomber Wing.

Place and date: Near Sniper Ridge, North Korea, 22 November 1952.

Entered service at: Portland, Maine.

Born: 2 October 1918, Portland, Maine.

Citation: Maj. Loring distinguished himself by conspicuous gallantry and intrepidity at the risk of his life above and beyond the call of duty. While leading a flight of 4 F-80 type aircraft on a close support mission, Maj. Loring was briefed by a controller to dive-bomb enemy gun positions which were harassing friendly ground troops. After verifying the location of the target, Maj. Loring rolled into his dive bomb run. Throughout the run, extremely accurate ground fire was directed on his aircraft. Disregarding the accuracy and intensity of the ground fire, Maj. Loring aggressively continued to press the attack until his aircraft was hit. At approximately 4,000 feet, he deliberately altered his course and aimed his diving aircraft at active gun emplacements concentrated on a ridge northwest of the briefed target, turned his aircraft 45 degrees to the left, pulled up in a deliberate, controlled maneuver, and elected to sacrifice his life by diving his aircraft directly into the midst of the enemy emplacements. His selfless and heroic action completely destroyed the enemy gun emplacement and eliminated a dangerous threat to United Nations ground forces. Maj. Loring's noble spirit, superlative courage, and conspicuous self-sacrifice in inflicting maximum damage on the enemy exemplified valor of the highest degree and his actions were in keeping with the finest traditions of the U.S. Air Force.

LYELL, WILLIAM F.

Rank and organization: Corporal, U.S. Army, Company F, 17th Infantry Regiment, 7th Infantry Division.
Place and date: Near Chup'a-ri, Korea, 31 August 1951.
Entered service at: Old Hickory, Tenn.
Birth: Hickman County, Tenn.
G.O. No.: 4, 9 January 1953.
Citation: Cpl. Lyell, a member of Company F, distinguished himself by conspicuous gallantry and outstanding courage above and beyond the call of duty in action against the enemy. When his platoon leader was killed, Cpl. Lyell assumed command and led his unit in an assault on strongly fortified enemy positions located on commanding terrain. When his platoon came under vicious, raking fire which halted the forward movement, Cpl. Lyell seized a 57 mm. recoilless rifle and unhesitatingly moved ahead to a suitable firing position from which he delivered deadly accurate fire completely destroying an enemy bunker, killing its occupants. He then returned to his platoon and was resuming the assault when the unit was again subjected to intense hostile fire from 2 other bunkers. Disregarding his personal safety, armed with grenades he charged forward hurling grenades into 1 of the enemy emplacements, and although painfully wounded in this action he pressed on destroying the bunker and killing 6 of the foe. He then continued his attack against a third enemy position, throwing grenades as he ran forward, annihilating 4 enemy soldiers. He then led his platoon to the north slope of the hill where positions were occupied from which effective fire was delivered against the enemy in support of friendly troops moving up. Fearlessly exposing himself to enemy fire, he continuously moved about directing and encouraging his men until he was mortally wounded by enemy mortar fire. Cpl. Lyell's extraordinary heroism, indomitable courage, and aggressive leadership reflect great credit on himself and are in keeping with the highest traditions of the military service.

MARTINEZ, BENITO

Rank and organization: Corporal, U.S. Army, Company A, 27th Infantry Regiment, 25th Infantry Division.
Place and date: Near Satae-ri, Korea, 6 September 1952.
Entered service at: Fort Hancock, Tex.
Born: 21 March 1931, Fort Hancock, Tex.
G.O. No.: 96, 29 December 1953.
Citation: Cpl. Martinez, a machine gunner with Company A, distinguished himself by conspicuous gallantry and outstanding courage above and beyond the call of duty in action against the enemy. While manning a listening post forward of the main line of resistance, his position was attacked by a hostile force of reinforced company strength. In the bitter fighting which ensued, the enemy infiltrated the defense perimeter and, realizing that encirclement was imminent, Cpl. Martinez elected to remain at his post in an attempt to stem the onslaught. In

a daring defense, he raked the attacking troops with crippling fire, inflicting numerous casualties. Although contacted by sound power phone several times, he insisted that no attempt be made to rescue him because of the danger involved. Soon thereafter, the hostile forces rushed the emplacement, forcing him to make a limited withdrawal with only an automatic rifle and pistol to defend himself. After a courageous 6-hour stand and shortly before dawn, he called in for the last time, stating that the enemy was converging on his position. His magnificent stand enabled friendly elements to reorganize, attack, and regain the key terrain. Cpl. Martinez' incredible valor and supreme sacrifice reflect lasting glory upon himself and are in keeping with the honored traditions of the military service.

MATTHEWS, DANIEL P.

Rank and organization: Sergeant, U.S. Marine Corps, Company F, 2d Battalion, 7th Marines, 1st Marine Division (Rein).
Place and date: Vegas Hill, Korea, 28 March 1953.
Entered service at: Van Nuys, Calif.
Born: 31 December 1931, Van Nuys, Calif.
Award presented: 29 March 1954.
Citation: For conspicuous gallantry and intrepidity at the risk of his life above and beyond the call of duty while serving as a squad leader of Company F, in action against enemy aggressor forces. Participating in a counterattack against a firmly entrenched and well-concealed hostile force which had repelled 6 previous assaults on a vital enemy-held outpost far forward of the main line of resistance, Sgt. Matthews fearlessly advanced in the attack until his squad was pinned down by a murderous sweep of fire from an enemy machinegun located on the peak of the outpost. Observing that the deadly fire prevented a corpsman from removing a wounded man lying in an open area fully exposed to the brunt of the devastating gunfire, he worked his way to the base of the hostile machinegun emplacement, leaped onto the rock fortification surrounding the gun and, taking the enemy by complete surprise, singlehandedly charged the hostile emplacement with his rifle. Although severely wounded when the enemy brought a withering hail of fire to bear upon him, he gallantly continued his valiant 1-man assault and, firing his rifle with deadly effectiveness, succeeded in killing 2 of the enemy, routing a third, and completely silencing the enemy weapon, thereby enabling his comrades to evacuate the stricken marine to a safe position. Succumbing to his wounds before aid could reach him, Sgt. Matthews, by his indomitable fighting spirit, courageous initiative, and resolute determination in the face of almost certain death, served to inspire all who observed him and was directly instrumental in saving the life of his wounded comrade. His great personal valor reflects the highest credit upon himself and enhances the finest traditions of the U.S. Naval Service. He gallantly gave his life for his country.

MAUSERT, FREDERICK W., III

Rank and organization: Sergeant, U.S. Marine Corps, Company B, 1st Battalion, 7th Marines, 1st Marine Division (Rein.)

Place and date: Songnap-yong, Korea, 12 September 1951.

Entered service at: Dresher, Pa.

Born: 2 May 1930, Cambridge, N.Y.

Citation: For conspicuous gallantry and intrepidity at the risk of his life above and beyond the call of duty while serving as a squad leader in Company B, in action against enemy aggressor forces. With his company pinned down and suffering heavy casualties under murderous machinegun, rifle, artillery, and mortar fire laid down from heavily fortified, deeply entrenched hostile strongholds on Hill 673, Sgt. Mausert unhesitatingly left his covered position and ran through a heavily mined and fire-swept area to bring back 2 critically wounded men to the comparative safety of the mines. Staunchly refusing evacuation despite a painful head wound sustained during his voluntary act, he insisted on remaining with his squad and, with his platoon ordered into the assault moments later, took the point position and led his men in a furious bayonet charge against the first of a literally impregnable series of bunkers. Stunned and knocked to the ground when another bullet struck his helmet, he regained his feet and resumed his drive, personally silencing the machinegun and leading his men in eliminating several other emplacements in the area. Promptly reorganizing his unit for a renewed fight to the final objective on top of the ridge, Sgt. Mausert boldly left his position when the enemy's fire gained momentum and, making a target of himself, boldly advanced alone into the face of the machinegun, drawing the fire away from his men and enabling them to move into position to assault. Again severely wounded when the enemy's fire found its mark, he still refused aid and continued spearheading the assault to the topmost machinegun fire. Stouthearted and indomitable, Sgt. Mausert, by his fortitude, great personal valor, and extraordinary heroism in the face of almost certain death, had inspired his men to sweep on, overrun and finally secure the objective. His unyielding courage throughout reflects the highest credit upon himself and the U.S. Naval Service. He gallantly gave his life for his country.

MCGOVERN, ROBERT M.

Rank and organization: First Lieutenant, U.S. Army, Company A, 5th Cavalry Regient, 1st Cavalry Division.

Place and date: Near Kamyangjan-ni, Korea, 30 January 1951.

Entered service at: Washington, D.C.

Birth: Washington, D.C.

G.O. No.: 2,8 January 1952.

Citation: 1st Lt. McGovern, a member of Company A, distinguished himself by conspicuous gallantry and intrepidity at the risk of life above and beyond the call of duty in action against an armed enemy of the United Nations. As 1st Lt. McGovern led his platoon up a slope to engage hostile troops emplaced in bunker-type pillboxes with connecting trenches, the unit came under heavy machinegun and rifle fire from the crest of the hill, approximately 75 yards distant. Despite a wound sustained in this initial burst of withering fire, 1st Lt. McGovern, assured the men of his ability to continue on and urged them forward. Forging up the rocky incline,

he fearlessly led the platoon to within several yards of its objective when the ruthless foe threw and rolled a vicious barrage of handgrenades on the group and halted the advance. Enemy fire increased in volume and intensity and 1st Lt. McGovern, realizing that casualties were rapidly increasing and the morale of his men badly shaken, hurled back several grenades before they exploded. Then, disregarding his painful wound and weakened condition, he charged a machinegun emplacement which was raking his position with flanking fire. When he was within 10 yards of the position a burst of fire ripped the carbine from his hands, but, undaunted, he continued his lone-man assault and, firing his pistol and throwing grenades, killed 7 hostile soldiers before falling mortally wounded in front of the gun he had silenced. 1st Lt. McGovern's incredible display of valor imbued his men with indomitable resolution to avenge his death. Fixing bayonets and throwing grenades, they charged with such ferocity that hostile positions were overrun and enemy routed from the hill. The inspirational leadership, unflinching courage, and intrepid actions of 1st Lt. McGovern reflected utmost glory on himself and the honored tradition of the military services.

MCLAUGHLIN, ALFORD L.

Rank and organization: Private First Class, U.S. Marine Corps, Company L, 3d Battalion, 5th Marines, 1st Marine Division (Rein.)

Place and date: Korea, 4 and 5 September 1952.

Entered service at: Leeds, Ala.

Born: 18 March 1928, Leeds, Ala.

Citation: For conspicuous galantry and intrepidity at the risk of his life above and beyond the call of duty while serving as a machine gunner of Company L, in action of duty while serving as a machine gunner of Company L, in action against enemy aggressor forces on the night of 4-5 September 1952. Volunteering for his second continuous tour of duty on a strategic combat outpost far in advance of the main line of resistance, Pfc. McLaughlin, although operating under a barrage of enemy artillery and mortar fire, set up plans for the defense of his position which proved decisive in the successful defense of the outpost. When hostile forces attacked in battalion strength during the night, he maintained a constant flow of devastating fire upon the enemy, alternately employing 2 machineguns, a carbine, and handgrenades. Although painfully wounded, he bravely fired the machineguns from the hip until his hands became blistered by the extreme heat from the weapons and, placing the guns on the ground to allow them to cool, continued to defend the position with his carbine and grenades. Standing up in full view, he shouted words of encouragement to his comrades above the din of battle and, throughout a series of fanatical enemy attacks, sprayed the surrounding area with deadly fire, accounting for an estimated 150 enemy dead and 50 wounded. By his indomitable courage, superb leadership, and valiant fighting spirit in the face of overwhelming odds, Pfc. McLaughlin served to inspire his fellow marines in their gallant stand against the enemy and was directly instrumental in preventing the vital outpost from falling into the hands of a determined and numerically superior hostile force. His outstanding heroism and unwavering devotion to duty reflect the highest credit upon himself and enhance the finest traditions of the U.S. Naval Service.

MENDONCA, LEROY A.

Rank and organization: Sergeant, U.S. Army, Company B, 7th Infantry Regiment, 3d Infantry Division.
Place and date: Near Chich-on, Korea, 4 July 1951.
Entered service at: Honolulu, T.H.
Birth: Honolulu, T.H.
G.O. No.: 83, 3 September 1952.
Citatation: Sgt. LeRoy A. Mendonca, distinguished himself by conspicuous gallantry above and beyond the call of duty in action against the enemy. After his platoon, in an exhaustive fight, had captured Hill 586, the newly won positions were assaulted during the night by a numerically superior enemy force. When the 1st Platoon positions were outflanked and under great pressure and the platoon was ordered to withdraw to a secondary line of defense, Sgt. Mendonca voluntarily remained in an exposed position and covered the platoon's withdrawal. Although under murderous enemy fire, he fired his weapon and hurled grenades at the onrushing enemy until his supply of ammunition was exhausted. He fought on, clubbing with his rifle and using his bayonet until he was mortally accounted for 37 enemy casualties. His daring actions stalled the crushing assault, protecting the platoon's withdrawal to secondary positions, and enabled the entire unit to repel the enemy attack and retain possession of the vital hilltop position. Sgt. Mendonca's extraordinary gallantry and exemplary valor are in keeping with the highest traditions of the U.S. Army.

MILLET, LEWIS L.

Rank and organization: Captain, U.S. Army, Company E, 27th Infantry Regiment.
Place and date: Vicinity of Soam-Ni, Korea, 7 February 1951.
Entered service at: Mechanic Falls, Maine.
Born: 15 December 1920, Mechanic Falls, Maine.
G.O. No.: 69, 2 August 1951.
Citation: Capt. Millett, Company E, distinguished himself by conspicuous gallantry and intrepidity above and beyond the call of duty in action. While personally leading his company in an attack against a strongly held position he noted that the 1st Platoon was pinned down by small-arms, automatic, and antitank fire. Capt. Millett ordered the 3d Platoon forward, placed himself at the head of the 2 platoons, and, with fixed bayonet, led the assault up the fire-swept hill. In the fierce charge Capt. Millett bayoneted 2 enemy soldiers and boldly continued on, throwing grenades, clubbing and bayoneting the enemy, while urging his men forward by shouting encouragement. Despite vicious opposing fire, the whirlwind hand-to-hand assault carried to the crest of the hill. His dauntless leadership and personal courage so inspired his men that they stormed into the hostile position and used their bayonets with such lethal effect that the enemy fled in wild disorder. During this fierce onslaught Capt. Millett was wounded by grenade fragments but refused evacuation until the objective was

taken and firmly secured. The superb leadership, conspicuous courage, and consummate devotion to duty demonstrated by Capt. Millett were directly responsible for the successful accomplishment of a hazardous mission and reflect the highest credit on himself and the heroic traditions of the military service.

MITCHELL, FRANK N.

Rank and organization: First Lieutenant, U.S. Marine Corps, Company A, 1st Battalion, 7th Marines, 1st Marine Division (Rein).
Place and date: Near Hansan-ni, Korea, 26 November 1950.
Entered service at: Roaring Springs, Tex.
Born: 18 August 1921, Indian Gap, Tex.
Citation: For conspicuous gallantry and intrepidity at the risk of his life above and beyond the call of duty as leader of a rifle platoon of Company A, in action against enemy aggressor forces. Leading his platoon in point position during a patrol by his company through a thickly wooded and snow-covered area in the vicinity of Hansan-ni, 1st lt. Mitchell acted immediately when the enemy suddenly opened fire at pointblank range, pinning down his forward elements and inflicting numerous casualties in his ranks. Boldly dashing to the front under blistering fire from automatic weapons and small arms, he seized an automatic rifle from one of the wounded men and effectively trained it against the attackers and, when his ammunition was expended, picked up and hurled grenades with deadly accuracy, at the same time directing and encouraging his men in driving the outnumbering enemy from his position. Maneuvering to set up a defense when the enemy furiously counterattacked to the front and left flank, 1st Lt. Mitchell, despite wounds sustained early in the action, reorganized his platoon under the devastating fire, and spearheaded a fierce hand-to-hand struggle to repulse the onslaught. Asking for volunteers to assist in searching for and evacuating the wounded, he personally led a party of litter bearers through the hostile lines in growing darkness and, although suffering intense pain from multiple wounds, stormed ahead and waged a singlehanded battle against the enemy, successfully covering the withdrawal of his men before he was fatally struck down by a burst of small-arms fire. Stouthearted and indomitable in the face of tremendous odds, 1st Lt. Mitchell, by his fortitude, great personal valor and extraordinary heroism, saved the lives of several marines and inflicted heavy casualties among the aggressors. His unyielding courage through-out reflects the highest credit upon himself and the U.S. Naval Service. He gallantly gave his life for his country.

MIYAMURA, HIROSHI H.

Rank and organization: Corporal, U.S. Army, Company H, 7th Infantry Regiment, 3rd Infantry Division.
Place and date: Near Taejon-ni, Korea, 24 and 25 April 1951.
Entered service at: Gallup, N. Mexico
Birth: Gallup, N.Mex.
G.O. No.: 85, 4 November 1953.
Citation: Cpl. Miyamura, a member of Company H, distinguished himself by conspicuous gallantry and

intrepidity above and beyond the call of duty in action against the enemy. On the night of 24 April, Company H was occupying a defensive position when the enemy fanatically attacked threatening to overrun the position. Cpl. Miyamura, a machinegun squad leader, aware of the imminent danger to his men unhesitatingly jumped from his shelter wielding his bayonet in close hand-to-hand combat killing approximately 10 of the enemy. Returning to his position, he administered first aid to the wounded and directed their evacuation. As another savage assault hit the line, he manned his machinegun and delivered withering fire until his ammunition was expended. He ordered the squad to withdraw while he stayed behind to render the gun inoperative. He then bayoneted his way through infiltrated enemy soldiers to a second gun emplacement and assisted in its operation. When the intensity of the attack necessitated the withdrawal of the company Cpl. Miyamura ordered his men to fall back while he remained to cover their movement. He killed more than 50 of the enemy before his ammunition was depleted and he was severely wounded. He maintained his magnificent stand despite his painful wounds, continuing to repel the attack until his position was overrun. When last seen he was fighting ferociously against an overwhelming number of enemy soldiers. Cpl. Miyamura's indomitable heroism and consummate devotion to duty reflect the utmost glory on himself and uphold the illustrious traditions on the military service.

MIZE, OLA L.

Rank and organization: Master Sergeant (then Sgt.), U.S. Army, Company K, 15th Infantry Regiment, 3d Infantry Division.

Place and date: Near Surang-ni, Korea, 10 to 11 June 1953.

Entered service at: Gadsden, Ala.

Born: 28 August 1931, Marshall County, Ala.

G.O. No.: 70, 24 September 1954.

Citation: M/Sgt. Mize, a member of Company K, distinguished himself by conspicuous gallantry and outstanding courage above and beyond the call of duty in action against the enemy. Company K was committed to the defense of "Outpost Harry", a strategically valuable position, when the enemy launched a heavy attack. Learning that a comrade on a friendly listening post had been wounded he moved through the intense barrage, accompanied by a medical aid man, and rescued the wounded soldier. On returning to the main position he established an effective defense system and inflicted heavy casualties against attacks from determined enemy assault forces which had penetrated into trenches within the outpost area. During his fearless actions he was blown down by artillery and grenade blasts 3 times but each time he dauntlessly returned to his position, tenaciously fighting and successfully repelling hostile attacks. When enemy onslaughts ceased he took his few men and moved from bunker to bunker, firing through apertures and throwing grenades at the foe, neutralizing their positions. When an enemy soldier stepped out behind a comrade, prepared to fire, M/Sgt. Mize killed him, saving the life of his fellow soldier. After rejoining the platoon, moving from man to man, distributing ammunition, and

shouting words of encouragement he observed a friendly machinegun position overrun. He immediately fought his way to the position, killing 10 of the enemy and dispersing the remainder. Fighting back to the command post, and finding several friendly wounded there, he took a position to protect them. Later, securing a radio, he directed friendly artillery fire upon the attacking enemy's routes of approach. At dawn he helped regroup for a counterattack which successfully drove the enemy from the outpost. M/Sgt. Mize's valorous conduct and unflinching courage reflect lasting glory upon himself and uphold the noble traditions of the military service.

MONEGAN, WALTER C., JR.

Rank and organization: Private First Class, U.S. Marine Corps, Company F, 2d Battalion, 1st Marines, 1st Marine Division (Rein).

Place and date: Near Sosa-ri, Korea, 17 and 20 September 1950.

Entered service at: Seattle, Wash.

Born: 25 December 1930, Melrose, Mass.

Citation: For conspicuous gallantry and intrepidity at the risk of his life above and beyond the call of duty while serving as a rocket gunner attached to Company F, and in action against enemy aggressor forces. Dug in on a hill overlooking the main Seoul highway when 6 enemy tanks threatened to break through the battalion position during a predawn attack on 17 September, Pfc. Monegan promptly moved forward with his bazooka, under heavy hostile automatic weapons fire and engaged the lead tank at a range of less than 50 yards. After scoring a direct hit and killing the sole surviving tankman with his carbine as he came through the escape hatch, he boldly fired 2 more rounds of ammunition at the oncoming tanks, disorganizing the attack and enabling our tank crews to continue blasting with their 90-mm guns. With his own and an adjacent company's position threatened by annihilation when an overwhelming enemy tank-infantry force bypassed the area and proceeded toward the battalion command post during the early morning of September 20, he seized his rocket launcher and, in total darkness, charged down the sloe of the hill where the tanks had broken through. Quick to act when an illuminating shell lit the area, he scored a direct hit on one of the tanks as hostile rifle and automatic-weapons fire raked the area at close range. Again exposing himself, he fired another round to destroy a second tank and, as the rear tank turned to retreat, stood upright to fire and was fatally struck down by hostile machinegun fire when another illuminating shell silhouetted him against the sky. Pfc. Monegan's daring initiative, gallant fighting spirit and courageous devotion to duty were contributing factors n the success of his company in repelling the enemy, and his self-sacrificing efforts throughout sustain and enhance the highest traditions of the U.S. Naval Service. He gallantly gave his life for his country.

MORELAND, WHITT L.

Rank and organization: Private First Class, U.S. Marine Corps Reserve, Company C, 1st Battalion, 5th Marines, 1st Marine Division (Rein).

Place and date: Kwagch'i-Dong, Korea, 29 May 1951.
Entered service at: Austin, Tex.
Born: 7 March 1930, Waco, Tex.
Citation: For conspicuous gallantry and intrepidity at the risk of his life above and beyond the call of duty while serving as an intelligence scout attached to Company C, in action against enemy aggressor forces. Voluntarily accompanying a rifle platoon in a daring assault against a strongly defended enemy hill position, Pfc. Moreland delivered accurate rifle fire on the hostile emplacement and thereby aided materially in seizing the objective. After the position had been secured, he unhesitatingly led a party forward to neutralize an enemy bunker which he had observed some 400 meters beyond, and moving through a fire-swept area, almost reached the hostile emplacement when the enemy launched a volley of handgrenades on his group. Quick to act despite the personal danger involved, he kicked several of the grenades off the ridge line where they exploded harmlessly and, while attempting to kick away another, slipped and fell near the deadly missile. Aware that the sputtering grenade would explode before he could regain his feet and dispose of it, he shouted a warning to his comrades, covered the missile with his body and absorbed the full blast of the explosion, but in saving his companions from possible injury or death, was mortally wounded. His heroic initiative and valiant spirit of self-sacrifice in the face of certain death reflect the highest credit upon Pfc. Moreland and the U.S. Naval Service. He gallantly gave his life for his country.

MOYER, DONALD R.

Rank and organization: Sergeant First Class, U.S. Army, Company E, 35th Infantry Regiment.
Place and date: Near Seoul, Korea, 20 May 1951.
Entered service at: Keego Harbor, Oakland, Mich.
Born: 15 April 1930, Pontiac, Mich.
G.O. No.: 19, 1 February 1952.
Citation: Sfc. Moyer assistant platoon leader, Company E, distinguished himself by conspicuous gallantry and intrepidity at the risk of his life above and beyond the call of duty in action against an armed enemy of the United Nations. Sfc. Moyer's platoon was committed to attack and secure commanding terrain stubbornly defended by a numerically superior hostile force emplaced in well-fortified positions. Advancing up the rocky hill, the leading elements came under intense automatic-weapons, small-arms, and grenade fire, wounding the platoon leader and platoon sergeant. Sfc. Moyer, realizing the success of the mission was imperiled, rushed to the head of the faltering column, assumed command and urged the men forward. Inspired by Sfc. Moyer's unflinching courage, the troops responded magnificently, but as they reached the final approaches to the rugged crest of the hill, enemy fire increased in volume and intensity and the fanatical foe showered the platoon with grenades. Undaunted, the valiant group forged ahead, and as they neared the top of the hill, the enemy hurled a grenade into their midst. Sfc. Moyer, fully aware of the odds against him, unhesitatingly threw himself on the grenade, absorbing the full blast of the explosion with his body. Although mortally wounded in this fearless display of

valor, Sfc. Moyer's intrepid act saved several of his comrades from death or serious injury, and his inspirational leadership and consummate devotion to duty contributed significantly to the subsequent seizure of the enemy stronghold and reflect lasting glory on himself and the noble traditions of the military service.

MURPHY, RAYMOND G.

Rank and organization: Second Lieutenant, U.S. Marine Corps Reserve, Company A, 1st Battalion, 5th Marines, 1st Marine Division (Rein).
Place and date: Korea, 3 February 1953.
Entered service at: Pueblo, Colo.
Born: 14 January 1930, Pueblo, Colo.
Citation: For conspicuous gallantry and intrepidity at the risk of his life above and beyond the call of duty as a platoon commander of Company A, in action against enemy aggressor forces. Although painfully wounded by fragments from an enemy mortar shell while leading his evacuation platoon in support of assault units attacking a cleverly concealed and well-entrenched hostile force occupying commanding ground, 2d Lt. Murphy steadfastly refused medical aid and continued to lead his men up a hill through a withering barrage of hostile mortar and small-arms fire, skillfully maneuvering his force from one position to the next and shouting words of encouragement. Undeterred by the increasing intense enemy fire, he immediately located casualties as they fell and made several trips up and down the fire-swept hill to direct evacuation teams to the wounded, personally carrying many of the stricken elements, 2d Lt. Murphy employed part of his unit as support and, during the ensuing battle, personally killed 2 of the enemy with his pistol. With all the wounded evacuated and the assaulting units beginning to disengage, he remained behind with a carbine to cove the movement of friendly forces off the hill and, though suffering intense pain from his previous wounds, seized an automatic rifle to provide more firepower when the enemy reappeared in the trenches. After reaching the base of the hill, he organized a search party and again ascended the slope for a final check on missing marines, locating and carrying the bodies of a machinegun crew back down the hill. Wounded a second time while conducting the entire force to the line of departure through a continuing barrage of enemy small-arms, artillery, and mortar fire, he again refused medical assistance until assured that every one of his men, including all casualties, has preceded him to the main lines. His resolute and inspiring leadership, exceptional fortitude, and great personal valor reflect the highest credit upon 2d Lt. Murphy and enhance the finest traditions of the U.S. Naval Service.

MYERS, REGINALD R.

Rank and organization: Major, U.S. Marine Corps, 3d Battalion, 1st Marines, 1st Marine Division, (Rein).
Place and date: Near Hagaru-ri, Korea, 29 November 1950.
Entered service at: Boise, Idaho.
Born: 26 November 1919, Boise, Idaho.
Citation: For conspicuous gallantry and intrepidity at the risk of his life above and beyond the call of duty as

executive officer of the 3d Battalion, in action against enemy aggressor forces. Assuming command of a composite unit of Army and Marine service and headquarters elements totaling approximately 250 men, during a critical stage in the vital defense of the strategically important military base at Hagaru-ri, Maj. Myers immediately initiated a determined and aggressive counterattack against a well-entrenched and cleverly concealed enemy force numbering an estimated 4,000. Severely handicapped by a lack of trained personnel and experienced leaders in his valiant efforts to regain maximum ground prior to daylight, he persisted in constantly exposing himself to intense, accurate, and sustained hostile fire in order to direct and supervise the employment of his men and to encourage and spur them on in pressing the attack. Inexorably moving forward up the steep, snow-covered slope with his depleted group in the face of apparently insurmountable odds, he concurrently directed artillery and mortar fire with superb skill and although losing 170 of his men during 14 hours of raging combat in subzero temperatures, continued to reorganize his unit and spearhead the attack which resulted in 600 enemy killed and 500 wounded. By his exceptional and valorous leadership throughout, Maj. Myers contributed directly to the success of his unit in restoring the perimeter. His resolute spirit of self-sacrifice and unfaltering devotion to duty enhance and sustain the highest traditions of the U.S. Naval Service.

OBREGON, EUGENE ARNOLD

Rank and organization: Private First Class, U.S. Marine Corps, Company G, 3d Battalion, 5th Marines, 1st Marine Division (Rein).
Place and date: Seoul, Korea, 26 September 1950.
Entered service at: Los Angeles, Calif.
Born: 12 November 1930, Los Angeles Calif.
Citation: For conspicuous gallantry and intrepidity at the risk of his life above and beyond the call of duty while serving with Company G, in action against enemy aggressor forces. While serving as an ammunition carrier of a machinegun squad in a marine rifle company which was temporarily pinned down by hostile fire, Pfc. Obregon observed a fellow marine fall wounded in the line of fire. Armed only with a pistol, he unhesitatingly dashed from his covered position to the side of the casualty. Firing his pistol with 1 hand and, despite the great peril to himself dragged him to the side of the road. Still under enemy fire, he was bandaging the man's wounds when hostile troops of approximately platoon strength began advancing toward his position. Quickly seizing the wounded marine's carbine, he placed his own body as a shield in front of him and lay there firing accurately and effectively into the hostile group until he himself was fatally wounded by enemy machinegun fire. By his courageous fighting spirit, fortitude, and loyal devotion to duty, Pfc. Obregon enabled his fellow marines to rescue the wounded man and aided essentially in repelling the attack, thereby sustaining and enhancing the highest traditions of the U.S. Naval Service. He gallantly gave his life for his country.

O'BRIEN, GEORGE H., JR.

Rank and organization: Second Lieutenant, U.S. Marine Corps Reserve, Company H, 3d Battalion, 7th Marines, 1st Marine Division (Rein).

Place and date: Korea, 27 October, 1952.
Entered service at: Big Spring, Tex.
Born: 10 September 1926, Fort Worth, Tex.
Citation: For conspicuous gallantry and intrepidity at the risk of his life above and beyond the call of duty as a rifle platoon commander of Company H, in action against enemy aggressor forces. With his platoon subjected to an intense mortar and artillery bombardment while preparing to assault a vitally important hill position on the main line of resistance which had been overrun by a numerically superior enemy force on the preceding night, 2d Lt. O'Brien leaped from his trench when the attack signal was given and, shouting for his men to follow, raced across an exposed saddle and up the enemy-held hill through a virtual hail of deadly small-arms, artillery, and mortar fire. Although shot through the arm and thrown to the ground by hostile automatic- weapons fire as he neared the well-entrenched enemy position, he bravely regained his feet, waved his men onward, and continued to spearhead the assault, pausing only long enough to go to the aid of a wounded marine. Encountering the enemy at close range, he proceeded to hurl handgrenades into the bunkers and, utilizing his carbine to best advantage in savage hand-to-hand combat, succeeded in killing at least 3 of the enemy. Struck down by the concussion of grenades 3 occasions during the subsequent action, he steadfastly refused to be evacuated for medical treatment and continued to lead his platoon in the assault for a period of nearly 4 hours, repeatedly encouraging his men and maintaining superb direction of the unit. With the attack halted, he set up a defense with his remaining forces to prepare for a counterattack, personally checking each position, attending to the wounded and expediting their evacuation. When a relief of the position was effected by another unit, he remained to cover the withdrawal and to assure that no wounded were left behind. By his exceptionally daring and forceful leadership in the face of overwhelming odds, 2d Lt. O'Brien served as a constant source of inspiration to all who observed him and was greatly instrumental in the recapture of a strategic position on the main line of resistance. His indomitable determination and valiant fighting spirit reflect the highest credit upon himself and enhance the finest traditions of the U.S. Naval Service.

OUELLETTE, JOSEPH R.

Rank and organization: Private First Class, U.S. Army, Company H, 9th infantry Regiment, 2d Infantry Division.
Place and date: Near Yongsan, Korea, from 31 August to 3 September 1950.
Entered service at: Lowell, Mass.
Birth: Lowell, Mass.
G.O. No.: 25, 25 April 1951.
Citation: Pfc. Ouellette distinguished himself by conspicuous gallantry and intrepidity in action against the enemy in the Makioug-Chang River salient. When an enemy assault cut off and surrounded his unit, he voluntarily made a reconnaissance of a nearby hill under intense enemy fire to locate friendly troop positions and obtain information of the enemy's strength and location. Finding that friendly troops were not on the hill, he worked his way back to his unit under heavy fire. Later,

when an airdrop of water was made outside the perimeter, he again braved enemy fire in an attempt to retrieve water for his unit. Finding the dropped cans broken and devoid of water, he returned to his unit. His heroic attempt greatly increased his comrades' morale. When ammunition and grenades ran low, Pfc. Ouellette again slipped out of the perimeter to collect these from the enemy dead. After collecting grenades he was attacked by a enemy soldier. He killed this enemy in hand-to-hand combat, gathered up the ammunition, and returned to his unit. When the enemy attacked on 3 September, they assaulted his position with grenades. On 6 occasions Pfc. Ouellette leaped from his foxhole to escape exploding grenades. In doing so, he had to face enemy small-arms fire. He continued his resistance, despite a severe wound, until he lost his life. The extraordinary heroism and intrepidity displayed by Pfc. Ouellette reflect the highest credit on himself and are in keeping with the esteemed traditions of the military service.

PAGE, JOHN U.D.

Rank and organization: Lieutenant Colonel, U.S. Army, X Corps Artillery, while attached to the 52d Transportation Truck Battalion.

Place and date: Near Chosin Reservoir, Korea, 29 November to 10 December 1950.

Entered service at: St. Paul, Minn.

Born: 8 February 1904, Malahi Island, Luzon, Philippine Islands.

G.O. No.: 21, 25 April 1957

Citation: Lt. Col. Page, a member of X Corps Artillery, distinguished himself by conspicuous gallantry and intrepidity in action above and beyond the call of duty in a series of exploits. On 29 November, Lt. Col. Page left X Corps Headquarters at Hamhung with the mission of establishing traffic control on the main supply route to 1st Marine Division positions and those of some Army elements on the Chosin Reservoir plateau. Having completed his mission Lt. Col. Page was free to return to the safety of Hamhung but chose to remain on the plateau to aid an isolated signal station, thus being cut off with elements of the marine division. After rescuing his jeep driver by breading up an ambush near a destroyed bridge Lt. Col. Page reached the lines of a surrounded marine garrison at Koto-ri. He then voluntarily developed and trained a reserve force of assorted army troops trapped with the marines. By exemplary leadership and tireless devotion he made an effective tactical unit available. In order that casualties might be evacuated, an airstrip was impoverished on frozen ground partly outside of the Koto-ri defense perimeter which was continually under enemy attack. During 2 such attacks, Lt. Col. Page exposed himself on the airstrip to direct fire on the enemy, and twice mounted the rear deck of a tank, manning the machinegun on the turret to drive the enemy back into a no man's land. On 3 December while being flown low over enemy lines in a light observation plane, Lt. Col. Page dropped handgrenades on Chinese positions and sprayed foxholes with automatic fire from his carbine. After 10 days of constant fighting the marine and army units in the vicinity of the Chosin Reservoir had succeeded in gathering at the edge of the plateau and Lt.

Col. Page was flown to Hamhung to arrange for artillery support of the beleaguered troops attempting to break out. Again Lt. Col. Page refused an opportunity to remain in safety and returned to give every assistance to his comrades. As the column slowly moved south Lt. Col. Page joined the rear guard. When it neared the entrance to a narrow pass it came under frequent attacks on both flanks. Mounting an abandoned tank Lt. Col. Page manned the machinegun, braved heavy return fire, and another attack threatened his section of the convoy, then in the middle of the pass, Lt. Col. Page took a machinegun to the hillside and delivered effective counterfire, remaining exposed while men and vehicles passed through the ambuscade. On the night of 10 December the convoy reached the bottom of the pass but was halted by a strong enemy force at ehe front and on both flanks. Deadly small-arms fire poured into the column. Realizing the danger to the column as it lay and plunged forward into the heart of the hostile position. His intrepid action so surprised the enemy that their ranks became disordered and suffered heavy casualties. Heedless of his safety, as he had been throughout the preceding 10 days, Lt. Col. page remained forward, fiercely engaging the enemy singlehandedly until mortally wounded. By his valiant and aggressive spirit Lt. Col. Page enabled friendly forces to stand off the enemy. His outstanding courage, unswerving devotion to duty, and supreme self-sacrifice reflect great credit upon Lt. Col. Page and are in the highest tradition of the military service.

PENDLETON, CHARLES F.

Rank and organization: Corporal. U.S. Army, Company D, 15th Infantry Regiment, 3d infantry Division.

Place and date: Near Choo Gung-Dong, Korea, 16 and 17 July 1953.

Entered service at: Fort Worth, Tex.

Born: 26 September 1931, Camden, Tenn.

Citation: Cpl. Pendleton, a machine gunner with Company D, distinguished himself by conspicuous gallantry and indomitable courage above and beyond the call of duty in action against the enemy. After consolidating and establishing a defensive perimeter on a key terrain feature, friendly elements were attacked by a large hostile force. Cpl. Pendleton delivered deadly accurate fire into the approaching troops, killing approximately 15 and disorganizaing the remainder with grenades. Unable to protect the flanks because of the narrow confines of the trench, he removed the machinegun from the tripod and, exposed to enemy observation, positioned it on his knee to improve his firing vantage. Observing a hostile infantryman jumping into the position, intent on throwing a grenade at his comrades, he whirled about and killed the attacker, then inflicted such heavy casualties on the enemy force that they retreated to regroup. After reorganizing, a second wave of hostile soldiers moved forward in an attempt to overrun the position and, later, when a hostile grenade landed nearby, Cpl. Pendleton quickly retrieved and hurled it back at the foe. Although he was burned by the hot shells ejecting from his weapon, and he was wounded by a grenade, he refused evacuation and continued to fire on the assaulting force. As enemy action increased in tempo, his machinegun was destroyed by a grenade but, undaunted, he grabbed a carbine and continued his heroic defense until mortally wounded by a mortar burst. Cpl. Pendleton's unflinching courage, gallant self-sacrifice, and consummate devotion to duty reflect lasting golry upon himself and uphold the finest traditions of the military service.

PHILLIPS, LEE H.
Rank and organization: Corporal, U.S. Marine Corps, Company E, 2d Battalion, 7 Marines, 1st Marine Division (Rein).
Place and date: Korea, 4 November 1950.
Entered service at: Ben Hill, Ga.
Born: 3 February 1930, Stockbridge, Ga. Cpl. Phillips was killed in action 27 November 1950.
Citation: For conspicuous gallantry and intrepidity at the risk of his life above and beyond the call of duty while serving as a squad leader of Company E, in action against enemy aggressor forces. Assuming the point position in the attack against a strongly defended and well-entrenched numerically superior enemy force occupying a vital hill position which had been unsuccessfully assaulted on 5 separate occasions by units of the Marine Corps and other friendly forces, Cpl. Phillips fearlessly led his men in a bayonet charge up the precipitous slope under a deadly hail of hostile mortar, small-arms, and machinegun fire. Quickly rallying his squad when it was pinned down by a heavy and accurate mortar barrage, he continued to lead his men through the bombarded area and, although only 5 members were left in the casualty ridden unit, gained the military crest of the hill where he was immediately subjected to an enemy counterattack. Although greatly outnumbered by an estimated enemy squad, Cpl. Phillips boldly engaged the hostile force with handgrenades and rifle fire and, exhorting his gallant group of marines to follow him, stormed forward to completely overwhelm the enemy. With only 3 men now left in his squad, he proceeded to spearhead an assault on the last remaining strongpoint which was defended by 4 of the enemy on a rocky and almost inaccessible portion of the hill position. Using 1 hand to climb up the extremely hazardous precipice, he hurled grenades with the other and, with 2 remaining comrades, succeeded in annihilating the pocket of resistance and in consolidating the position. Immediately subjected to a sharp counterattack by an estimated enemy squad, he skillfully directed the fire of his men and employed his own weapon with deadly effectiveness to repulse the numerically superior hostile force. By his valiant leadership, indomitable fighting spirit and resolute determination in the face of heavy odds, Cpl. Phillips served to inspire all who observed him and was directly responsible for the destruction of the enemy stronghold. His great personal valor reflects the highest credit upon himself and enhances and sustains the finest traditions of the U.S. Naval Service.

PILILAAU, HERBERT K.
Rank and organization: Private First Class, U.S. Army, Company C, 23d Infantry Regiment, 2nd Infantry Division.

Place and date: Near Pia-ri, Korea, 17 September 1951.
Entered service at: Oahu, T.H.
Born: 10 October 1928, Waianae, Oahu, T.H.
G.O. No.: 58, 18 June 1952.
Citation: Pfc. Pililaau, a member of Company C, distinguished himself by conspicuous gallantry and outstanding courage above and beyond the call of duty in action against the enemy. The enemy sent wave after wave of fanatical troops against his platoon which held a key terrain feature on "Heartbreak Ridge." Valiantly defending its position, the unit repulsed each attack until ammunition became practically exhausted and it was ordered to withdraw to a new position. Voluntarily remaining behind to cover the withdrawal, Pfc. Pililaau fired his automatic weapon into the ranks of the assailants, threw all his grenades and, with ammunition exhausted, closed with the foe in hand-to-hand combat, courageously fighting with his trench knife and bare fists until finally overcome and mortally wounded. When the position was subsequently retaken, more than 40 enemy dead were counted in the area he had so valiantly defended. His heroic devotion to duty, indomitable fighting spirit, and gallant self-sacrifice reflect the highest credit upon himself, the infantry, and the U.S. Army.

PITTMAN, JOHN A.
Rank and organization: Sergeant, U.S. Army, Company C, 23d Infantry Regiment, 2d Infantry Division.
Place and date: Near Kujangdong, Korea, 26 November 1950.
Entered service at: Carrolton, Miss.
Born: 15 October 1928, Carrolton, Miss.
G.O. No.: 39, 4 June 1951.
Citation: Sgt. Pittman, distinguished himself by conspicuous gallantry and intrepidity above and beyond the call of duty in action against the enemy. He volunteered to lead his squad in a counterattack to regain commanding terrain lost in an earlier engagement. Moving aggressively forward in the face of intense artillery, mortar, and small-arms fire he was wounded by mortar fragments. Disregarding his wounds he continued to lead and direct his men in a bold advance against the hostile standpoint. During this daring action, an enemy grenade was thrown in the midst of his squad endangering the lives of his comrades. Without hesitation, Sgt. Pittman threw himself on the grenade and absorbed its burst with his body. When a medical aid man reached him, his first request was to be informed as to how many of his men were hurt. This intrepid and selfless act saved several of his men from death or serious injury and was an inspiration to the entire command. Sgt. Pittman's extraordinary heroism reflects the highest credit upon himself and is in keeping with the esteemed traditions of the military service.

POMEROY, RALPH E.
Rank and organization: Private First Class, U.S. Army, Company E, 31st Infantry Regiment, 7th Infantry Division.
Place and date: Near Kumhwa, Korea, 15 October 1952.
Entered service at: Quinwood, W. Va.
Born: 26 March 1930, Quinwood, Va.

G.O. No.: 97, 30 December 1953.

Citation: Pfc. Pomeroy, a machine gunner with Company E, distinguished himself by conspicuous gallantry and indomitable courage above and beyond the call of duty in action against the enemy. While his comrades were consolidating on a key terrain feature, he manned a machinegun at the end of a communication trench on the forward slope to protect the platoon flank and prevent a surprise attack. When the enemy attacked through a ravine leading directly to his firing position, he immediately opened fire on the advancing troops inflicting a heavy toll in casualties and blunting the assault. At this juncture the enemy directed intense concentrations of artillery and mortar fire on his position in an attempt to neutralize his gun. Despite withering fire and bursting shells, he maintained his heroic stand and poured crippling fire into the ranks of the hostile force until a mortar burst severely wounded him and rendered the gun mount inoperable. Quickly removing the hot, heavy weapon, he cradled it in his arms and, moving forward with grim determination, raked the attacking forces with a hail of fire. Although wounded a second time he pursued his relentless course until his ammunition was expended within 10 feet of the foe and then, using the machinegun as a club, he courageously closed with the enemy in hand-to-hand combat until mortally wounded. Pfc. Pomeroy's consummate valor, inspirational actions and supreme sacrifice enabled the platoon to contain the attack and maintain the integrity of the perimeter, reflecting lasting glory upon himself and upholding the noble traditions of the military service.

PORTER, DONN F.

Rank and organization: Sergeant, U.S. Army, Company G, 14th Infantry Regiment, 25th Infantry Division.

Place and date: Near Mundung-ni Korea, 7 September 1952.

Entered service at: Baltimore, Md.

Born: 1 March 1931, Sewickley, Pa.

G.O. No.: 64, 18 August 1953.

Citation: Sgt. Porter, a member of Company G, distinguished himself by conspicuous gallantry and outstanding courage above and beyond the call of duty in action against the enemy. Advancing under cover of intense mortar and artillery fire, 2 hostile platoons attacked a combat outpost commanded by Sgt. Porter, destroyed communications, and killed 2 of his 3-man crew. Gallantly maintaining his position, he poured deadly accurate fire into the ranks of the enemy, killing 15 and dispersing the remainder. After falling back under a hail of fire, the determined foe reorganized and stormed forward in an attempt to overrun the outpost. Without hesitation, Sgt. Porter jumped from his position with bayonet fixed and, meeting the onslaught and in close combat, killed 6 hostile soldiers and routed the attack. While returning to the outpost, he was killed by an artillery burst, but his courageous actions forced the enemy to break off the engagement and thwarted a surprise attack on the main line of resistance. Sgt. Porter's incredible display of valor, gallant self-sacrifice, and consummate devotion to duty reflect the highest credit upon himself and uphold the noble traditions of the military service.

RAMER, GEORGE H.

Rank and organization: Second Lieutenant, U.S. Marine Corps Reserve, Company I, 3d Battalion, 7th Marines, 1st Marine Division (Rein).

Place and date: Korea, 12 September 1951.

Entered service at: Lewisburg, Pa.

Born: 27 March 1927, Meyersdale, Pa.

Citation: For conspicuous gallantry and intrepidity at the risk of his life above and beyond the call of duty as leader of the 3d Platoon in Company I, in action against enemy aggressor forces. Ordered to attack and seize hostile positions atop a hall, vigorously defended by well-entrenched enemy forces delivering massed small-arms mortar, and machinegun fire, 2d Lt. Ramer fearlessly led his men up the steep slopes and, although he and the majority of his unit were wounded during the ascent, boldly continued to spearhead the assault. With the terrain becoming more precipitous near the summit and the climb more perilous as the hostile forces added grenades to the devastating hail of fire, he staunchly carried the attack to the top, personally annihilated 1 enemy bunker with grenade and carbine fire and captured the objective with his remaining 8 men. Unable to hold the position against an immediate, overwhelming hostile counterattack, he ordered his group to withdraw and single-handedly fought the enemy to furnish cover for his men and for the evacuation of 3 fatally wounded marines. Severely wounded a second time, 2d Lt. Ramer refused aid when his men returned to help him and, after ordering them to seek shelter, courageously manned his post until the hostile troops overran his position and he fell mortally wounded. His indomitable fighting spirit, inspiring leadership and unselfish concern for others in the face of death, reflect the highest credit upon 2d Lt. Ramer and the U.S. Naval Service. He gallantly gave his life for his country.

RED CLOUD, MITCHELL, JR.

Rank and organization: Corporal, U.S. Army, Company E, 19th Infantry Regiment, 24th Infantry Division.

Place and date: Near Chonghyon, Korea, 5 November 1950.

Entered service at: Merrilan, Wis.

Born: 2 July 1924, Hatfield, Wis.

G.O. No.: 26, 25 April 1951.

Citation: Cpl. Red Cloud, Company E, distinguished himself by conspicuous gallantry and intrepidity above and beyond the call of duty in action against the enemy. From his position on the point of a ridge immediately in front of the company command post he was the first to detect the approach of the Chinese Communist forces and give the alarm as the enemy charged from a brush-covered area less than 100 feet from him. Springing up he delivered devastating pointblank automatic rifle fire into the advancing enemy. His accurate and intense fire checked this assault and gained time for the company to consolidate its defense. With utter fearlessness he maintained his firing position until severely wounded by enemy fire. Refusing assistance he pulled himself to his feet and wrapping his arm around a tree continued his deadly fire again, until he was fatally wounded. This heroic act stopped the enemy from overrunning his company's position and gained time for reorganization and evacuation of the wounded. Cpl. Red Cloud's dauntless courage and gallant self-sacrifice reflects the highest credit upon himself and upholds the esteemed traditions of the U.S. Army.

REEM, ROBERT DALE

Rank and organization: Second Lieutenant, U.S. Marine Corps, Company H, 3d Battalion, 7th Marines, 1st Marine Division (Rein).

Place and date: Vicinity Chinhung-ni, Korea, 6 November 1950.

Entered service at: Elizabethtown, Pa.

Born: 20 October 1925, Lancaster, Pa.

Citation: For conspicuous gallantry and intrepidity at the risk of his life above and beyond the call of duty as a platoon commander in Company H, in action against enemy aggressor forces. Grimly determined to dislodge a group of heavy enemy infantry units occupying well-concealed and strongly fortified positions on commanding ground overlooking unprotected terrain, 2d Lt. Reem moved slowly forward up the side of the ridge with his platoon in the face of a veritable hail of shattering hostile machinegun, grenade, and rifle fire. Three times repulsed by a resolute enemy force in achieving his objective, and pinned down by the continuing fury of hostile fire, he rallied and regrouped the heroic men in his depleted and disorganized platoon in preparation for a fourth attack. Issuing last-minute orders to his noncommissioned officers when an enemy grenade landed in a depression of the rocky ground in which the group was standing, 2d Lt. Reem unhesitatingly chose to sacrifice himself and, springing upon the deadly missile, absorbed the full impact of the explosion in his body, thus protecting others from serious injury and possible death. Stouthearted and indomitable, he readily yielded his own chance of survival that his subordinate leaders might live to carry on the fight against a fanatic enemy. His superb courage, cool decisiveness, and valiant spirit of self-sacrifice in the face of certain death reflect the highest credit upon 2d Lt. Reem and the U.S. Naval Service. He gallantly gave his life for his country.

RODRIGUEZ, JOSEPH C.

Rank and organization: Sergeant (then Pfc.), U.S. Army, Company F, 17th Infantry Regiment, 7th Infantry Division.

Place and date: Near Munye-ri, Korea, 21 May 1951.

Entered service at: California.

Born: 14 November 1928, San Bernardino, Calif.

G.O. No.: 22, 5 February 1952.

Citation: Sgt. Rodriguez, distinguished himself by conspicuous gallantry and intrepidity at the risk of his life above and beyond the call of duty in action against an armed enemy of the United Nations. Sgt. Rodriguez, an assistant squad leader of the 2d Platoon, was participating in an attack against a fanatical hostile force occupying well-fortified positions on rugged commanding terrain, when his squad's advance was halted within approximately 60 yards by a withering barrage of automatic weapons and small-arms fire from 5 emplacements directly to the front and right and left flanks, together with grenades which the enemy rolled down the hill toward the advancing troops. Fully aware of the odds against him, Sgt. Rodriguez leaped to his feet, dashed 60 yards up the fire-swept slope, and, after lobbing grenades into the first foxhole with deadly accuracy, ran around the left flank, silenced an automatic weapon with 2 grenades and continued his whirlwind assault to the top of the peak, wiping out 2 more foxholes and then, reaching the right flank, he tossed grenades into the remaining emplacement, destroying the gun and annihilating its crew. Sgt. Rodriguez' intrepid actions exacted a toll of 15 enemy dead and, as a result of his incredible display of valor, the defense of the opposition was broken, and the enemy routed, and the strategic strongpoint secured. His unflinching courage under fire and inspirational devotion to duty reflect highest credit on himself and uphold the honored traditions of the military service.

ROSSER, RONALD E.

Rank and organization: Corporal, U.S. Army, Heavy Mortar Company, 38th Infantry Regiment, 2d Infantry Division.

Place and date: Vicinity of Ponggilli, Korea, 12 January 1952.

Entered service at: Crooksville, Ohio.

Born: 24 October 1929, Columbus, Ohio.

G.O. No.: 67, 7 July 1952.

Citation: Cpl. Rosser, distinguished himself by conspicuous gallantry above and beyond the call of duty. While assaulting heavily fortified enemy hill positions, Company L, 38th Infantry Regiment, was stopped by fierce automatic-weapons, small- arms, artillery, and mortar fire. Cpl. Rosser, a forward observer was with the lead platoon of Company L, when it came under fire from 2 directions. Cpl. Rosser turned his radio over to his assistant and, disregarding the enemy fire, charged the enemy positions armed with only carbine and a grenade. At the first bunker, he silenced its occupants with a burst from his weapon. Gaining the top of the hill, he killed 2 enemy soldiers, and then went down the trench, killing 5 more as he advanced. He then hurled his grenade into a bunker and shot 2 other soldiers as they emerged. Having exhausted his ammunition, he returned through the enemy fire to obtain more ammunition and grenades and charged the hill once more. Calling on others to follow him, he assaulted 2 more enemy bunkers. Although those who attempted to join him became casualties, Cpl. Rosser once again exhausted his ammunition, obtained a new supply, and returning to the hilltop a third time hurled grenades into the enemy positions. During this heroic action Cpl. Rosser singlehandedly killed at least 13 of the enemy. After exhausting his ammunition he accompanied the withdrawing platoon, and though himself wounded, made several trips across open terrain still under enemy fire to help remove other men injured more seriously than himself. This outstanding soldier's courageous and selfless devotion to duty is worthy of emulation by all men. He has contributed magnificently to the high traditions of the military service.

SCHOONOVER, DAN D.

Rank and organization: Corporal, U.S. Army, Company A, 13th Engineer Combat Battalion, 7th Infantry Division.

Place and date: Near Sokkogae, Korea, 8 to 10 July 1953.
Entered service at: Boise, Idaho.
Born: 8 October 1933, Boise, Idaho.
G.O. No.: 5, 14 January 1955.
Citation: Cpl. Schoonover, distinguished himself by conspicuous gallantry and outstanding courage above and beyond the call of duty in action against the enemy. He was in charge of an engineer demolition squad attached to an infantry company which was committed to dislodge the enemy from a vital hill. Realizing that the heavy fighting and intense enemy fire made it impossible to carry out his mission, he voluntarily employed his unit as a rifle squad and, forging up the steep barren slope, participated in the assault on hostile positions. When an artillery round exploded on the roof of an enemy bunker, he courageously ran forward and leaped into the position, killing 1 hostile infantryman and taking another prisoner. Later in the action, when friendly forces were pinned down by vicious fire from another enemy bunker, he dashed through the hail of fire, hurled grenades in the nearest aperture, then ran to the doorway and emptied his pistol, killing the remainder of the enemy. His brave action neutralized the position and enabled friendly troops to continue their advance to the crest of the hill. When the enemy counterattacked he constantly exposed himself to the heavy bombardment to direct the fire of his men and to call in an effective artillery barrage on hostile forces. Although the company was relieved early the following morning, he voluntarily remained in the area, manned a machinegun for several hours, and subsequently joined another assault on enemy emplacements. When last seen he was operating an automatic rifle with devastating effect until mortally wounded by artillery fire. Cpl. Schoonover's heroic and willing self-sacrifice inspired his comrades and saved many lives, reflecting lasting glory upon himself and upholding the honored traditions of the military service.

SCHOWALTER, EDWARD R., JR.

Rank and organization: First Lieutenant, U.S. Army, Company A, 31st Infantry Regiment, 7th Infantry Division.
Place and date: Near Kumhwa, Korea, 14 October 1952.
Entered service at: Metairie, La.
Born: 24 December 1927, New Orleans, La.
G.O. No.: 6, 28 January 1954.
Citation: 1st Lt. Schowalter, commanding, Company A, distinguished himself by conspicuous gallantry and indomitable courage above and beyond the call of duty in action against the enemy. Committed to attack and occupy a key approach to the primary objective, the 1st Platoon of his company came under heavy vicious small-arms, grenade, and mortar fire within 50 yards of the enemy-held strongpoint, halting the advance and inflicting several casualties. The 2d Platoon moved up in support at this juncture, and although wounded, 1st Lt. Schowalter continued to spearhead the assault. Nearing the objective he was severely wounded by a grenade fragment but, refusing medical aid, he led his men into the trenches and began routing the enemy from the bunkers with grenades. Suddenly from a burst of fire from a hidden cove off the trench he was again wounded.

Although suffering from his wounds, he refused to relinquish command and continued issuing orders and encouraging his men until the commanding ground was secured and then he was evacuated. 1st Lt. Schowalter's unflinching courage, extraordinary heroism, and inspirational leadership reflect the highest credit upon himself and are in keeping with the highest traditions of the military service.

SEBILLE, LOUIS J.

Rank and organization: Major, U.S. Air Force, 67th Fighter-Bomber Squadron, 18th Fighter-Bomber Group, 5th Air Force.
Place and date: Near Hanchang, Korea, 5 August 1950.
Entered service at: Chicago, Ill.
Born: 21 November 1915, Harbor Beach, Mich.
Citation: Maj. Sebille, distinguished himself by conspicuous gallantry and intrepidity at the risk of his life above and beyond the call of duty. During an attack on a camouflaged area containing a concentration of enemy troops, artillery, and armored vehicles, Maj. Sebille's F-51 aircraft was severely damaged by antiaircraft fire. Although fully cognizant of the short period he could remain airborne, he deliberately ignored the possibility of survival by abandoning the aircraft or by crash landing, and continued his attack against the enemy forces threatening the security of friendly ground troops. In his determination to inflict maximum damage upon the enemy, Maj. Sebille again exposed himself to the intense fire of enemy gun batteries and dived on the target to his death. The superior leadership, daring, and selfless devotion to duty which he displayed in the execution of an extremely dangerous mission were an inspiration to both his subordinates and superiors and reflect the highest credit upon himself, the U.S. Air Force, and the armed forces of the United Nations.

SHEA, RICHARD T., JR.

Rank and organization: First Lieutenant, U.S. Army, Company A, 17th Infantry Regiment, 7th Infantry Division.
Place and date: Near Sokkogae, Korea, 6 to 8 July 1953.
Entered service at: Portsmouth, Va.
Born: 3 January 1927, Portsmouth, Va.
G.O. No.: 38, 8 June 1955.
Citation: 1st Lt. Shea, executive officer, Company A, distinguished himself by conspicuous gallantry and indomitable courage above and beyond the call of duty in action against the enemy. On the night of 6 July, he was supervising the reinforcement of defensive positions when the enemy attacked with great numerical superiority. Voluntarily proceeding to the area most threatened, he organized and led a counterattack and, in the bitter fighting which ensued, closed with and killed 2 hostile soldiers with his trench knife. Calmly moving among the men, checking positions, steadying and urging the troops to hold firm, he fought side by side with them throughout the night. Despite heavy losses, the hostile force pressed the assault with determination, and at dawn made an all-out attempt to overrun friendly elements. Charging forward to meet the challenge, 1st Lt. Shea and his gallant men drove back the hostile troops. Elements of Company

G joined the defense on the afternoon of 7 July, having lost key personnel through casualties. Immediately integrating these troops into his unit, 1st Lt. Shea rallied a group of 20 men and again charged the enemy. Although wounded in this action, he refused evacuation and continued to lead the counterattack. When the assaulting element was pinned down by heavy machinegun fire, he personally rushed the emplacement and, firing his carbine and lobbing grenades with deadly accuracy, neutralized the weapon and killed 3 of the enemy. With forceful leadership and by his heroic example, 1st Lt. Shea coordinated and directed a holding action throughout the night and the following morning. On 8 July, the enemy attacked again. Despite additional wounds, he launched a determined counterattack and was last seen in close hand-to-hand combat with the enemy. 1st Lt. Shea's inspirational leadership and unflinching courage set an illustrious example of valor to the men of his regiment, reflecting lasting glory upon himself and upholding the noble traditions of the military service.

SHUCK, WILLIAM E., JR.

Rank and organization: Staff Sergeant, U.S. Marine Corps, Company G, 3d Battalion, 7th Marines, 1st Marine Division (Rein).

Place and date: Korea, 3 July 1952.

Entered service at: Cumberland, Md.

Born: 16 August 1926, Cumberland, Md.

Citation: For conspicuous gallantry and intrepidity at the risk of his life above and beyond the call of duty while serving as a squad leader of Company G, in action against enemy aggressor forces. When his platoon was subjected to a devastating barrage of enemy small-arms, grenade, artillery, and mortar fire during an assault against strongly fortified hill positions well forward of the main line of resistance, S/Sgt. Shuck, although painfully wounded, refused medical attention and continued to lead his machinegun squad in the attack. Unhesitatingly assuming command of a rifle squad when the leader became a casualty, he skillfully organized the 2 squads into an attacking force and led 2 more daring assaults upon the hostile positions. Wounded a second time, he steadfastly refused evacuation and remained in the foremost position under heavy fire until assured that all dead and wounded were evacuated. Mortally wounded by an enemy sniper bullet while voluntarily assisting in the removal of the last casualty, S/Sgt. Shuck, by his fortitude and great personal valor in the face of overwhelming odds, served to inspire all who observed him. His unyielding courage throughout reflects the highest credit upon himself and the U.S. Naval Service. He gallantly gave his life for his country.

SIMANEK, ROBERT E.

Rank and organization: Private First Class, U.S. Marine Corps, Company F, 2d Battalion, 5th Marines, 1st Marine Division (Rein).

Place and date: Korea, 17 August 1952.

Entered service at: Detroit, Mich.

Born: 26 April 1930, Detroit, Mich.

Citation: For conspicuous gallantry and intrepidity at the risk of his life above and beyond the call of duty while serving with Company F, in action against enemy aggressor forces. While accompanying a patrol en route to occupy a combat outpost forward of friendly lines, Pfc. Simanek exhibited a high degree of courage and a resolute spirit of self-sacrifice in protecting the lives of his fellow marines. With his unit ambushed by an intense concentration of enemy mortar and small-arms, fire, and suffering heavy casualties, he was forces to seek cover with the remaining members of the patrol in a nearby trench line. Determined to save his comrades when a hostile grenade was hurled into their midst, he unhesitatingly threw himself on the deadly missile absorbing the shattering violence of the exploding charge in his body and shielding his fellow marines from serious injury or death. Gravely wounded as a result of his heroic action, Pfc. Simanek, by his daring initiative and great personal valor in the face of almost certain death, served to inspire all who observed him and upheld the highest traditions of the U.S. Naval Service.

SITMAN, WILLIAM S.

Rank and organization: Sergeant First Class, U.S. Army, Company M, 23d Infantry Regiment, 2d Infantry Division.

Place and date: Near Chipyong-ni, Korea, 14 February 1951.

Entered service at: Bellwood, Pa.

Birth: Bellwood, Pa.

G.O. No.: 20, 1 February 1952.

Citation: Sfc. Sitman distinguished himself by conspicuous gallantry and intrepidity above and beyond the call of duty in action against an armed enemy of the United Nations. Sfc. Sitman, a machinegun section leader of Company M, was attached to Company I, under attack by a numerically superior hostile force. During the encounter when an enemy grenade knocked out his machinegun, a squad from Company I, immediately emplaced a light machinegun and Sfc. Sitman and his men remained to provide security for the crew. In the ensuing action, the enemy lobbed a grenade into the position and Sfc. Sitman, fully aware of the odds against him, selflessly threw himself on it, absorbing the full force of the explosion with his body. Although mortally wounded in this fearless display of valor, his intrepid act saved 5 men from death or serious injury, and enabled them to continue inflicting withering fire on the ruthless foe throughout the attack. Sfc. Sitman's noble self-sacrifice and consummate devotion to duty reflect lasting glory on himself and uphold the honored traditions of the miitary service.

SITTER, CARL L.

Rank and organization: Captain, U.S. Marine Corps, Company G, 3d Battalion, 1st Marines, 1st Marine Division (Rein).

Place and date: Hagaru-ri, Korea, 29 and 30 November 1950.

Entered service at: Pueblo, Colo.

Born: 2 December 1921, Syracuse, Mo.

Citation: For conspicuous gallantry and intrepidity at the risk of his life above and beyond the call of duty as commanding officer of Company G, in action against enemy aggressor forces. Ordered to break through enemy-infested territory to reinforce his battalion the morning of 29 November, Capt. Sitter continuously exposed himself to enemy fire as he led his company forward and, despite 25 percent casualties suffered in the furious action, succeeded in driving through to his objective. Assuming the responsibility of attempting to seize and occupy a strategic area occupied by a hostile force of regiment strength deeply entrenched on a snow-covered hill commanding the entire valley southeast of the town, as well as the line of march of friendly troops withdrawing to the south, he reorganized his depleted units the following morning and boldly led them up the steep, frozen hillside under blistering fire, encouraging and redeploying his troops as casualties occurred and directing forward platoons as they continued the drive to the top of the ridge. During the night when a vastly outnumbering enemy launched a sudden, vicious counterattack, setting the hill ablaze with mortar, machinegun, and automatic-weapons fire and taking a heavy toll in troops, Capt. Sitter visited each foxhole and gun position, coolly deploying and integrating reinforcing units consisting of service personnel unfamiliar with infantry tactics into a coordinated combat team and instilling in every man the will and determination to hold his position at all costs. With the enemy penetrating his lines in repeated counterattacks which often required hand-to-hand combat, and, on one occasion infiltrating to the command post with handgrenades, he fought gallantly with his men in repulsing and killing the fanatic attackers in each encounter. Painfully wounded in the face, arms, and chest by bursting grenades, he staunchly refused to be evacuated and continued to fight on until a successful defense of the area was assured with a loss to the enemy of more than 50 percent dead, wounded, and captured. His valiant leadership, superb tactics, and great personal valor throughout 36 hours of bitter combat reflect the highest credit upon Capt. Sitter and the U.S. Naval Service.

SKINNER, SHERROD E., JR.

Rank and organizaiton: Second Lieutenant, U.S. Marine Corps Reserve, Battery F, 2d Battalion, 11th Marines, 1st Marine Division (Rein).

Place and date: Korea, 26 October 1952.

Entered service at: East Lansing, Mich.

Born: 29 October 1929, Hartford, Conn.

Citation: For conspicuous gallantry and intrepidity at the risk of his life above and beyond the call of duty as an artillery forward observer of Battery F, in action against enemy aggressor forces on the night of 26 October 1952. When his observation post in an extremely critical and vital sector of the main line of resistance was subjected to a sudden and fanatical attack by hostile forces, supported by a devastating barrage of artillery and mortar fire which completely severed communication lines connecting the outpost with friendly firing batteries, 2d Lt. Skinner, in a determined effort to hold his position, immediately organized and directed the surviving personnel in the defense of the outpost, continuing to call down fire on the enemy by means of radio alone until his equipment became damaged beyond repair. Undaunted

by the intense hostile barrage and the rapidly-closing attackers, he twice left the protection of his bunker in order to direct accurate machinegun fire and to replenish the depleted supply of ammunition and grenades. Although painfully wounded on each occasion, he steadfastly refused medical aid until the rest of the men received treatment. As the ground attack reached its climax, he gallantly directed the final defense until the meager supply of ammunition was exhausted and the position overrun. During the 3 hours that the outpost was occupied by the enemy, several grenades were thrown into the bunker which served as protection for 2d Lt. Skinner and his remaining comrades. Realizing that there was no chance for other than passive resistance, he directed his men to feign death even though the hostile troops entered the bunker and searched their persons. Later, when an enemy grenade was thrown between him and 2 other survivors, he immediately threw himself on the deadly missile in an effort to protect the others, absorbing the full force of the explosion and sacrificing his life for his comrades. By his indomitable fighting spirit, superb leadership, and great personal valor in the face of tremendous odds, 2d Lt. Skinner served to inspire his fellow marines in their heroic stand against the enemy and upheld the highest traditions of the U.S. Naval Service. He gallantly gave his life for his country.

SMITH, DAVID M.

Rank and organization: Private First Class, U.S. Army, Company E, 9th Infantry Regiment, 2d Infantry Division.

Place and date: Near Yongsan, Korea, 1 September 1940.

Entered service at: Livingston, Ky.

Born: 10 November 1926, Livingston, Ky.

G.O. No.: 78, 21 August 1952.

Citation: Pfc. Smith, distinguished himself by conspicuous gallantry and outstanding courage above and beyond the call of duty in action. Pfc. Smith was a gunner in the mortar section of Company E, emplaced in rugged mountainous terrain and under attack by a numerically superior hostile force. Bitter fighting ensued and the enemy overran forward elements, infiltrated the perimeter, and rendered friendly positions untenable. The mortar section was ordered to withdraw, but the enemy had encircled and closed in on the position. Observing a grenade lobbed at his emplacement, Pfc. Smith shouted a warning to his comrades and, fully aware of the odds against him, flung himself upon it and smothered the explosion with his body. Although mortally wounded in this display of valor, his intrepid act saved 5 men from death or serious injury. Pfc. Smith's inspirational conduct and supreme sacrifice reflect lasting glory on himself and are in keeping with the noble traditions of the infantry of the U.S. Army.

SPEICHER, CLIFTON T.

Rank and organization: Corporal, U.S. Army, Company F, 223d Infantry Regiment, 40th Infantry Division.

Place and date: Near Minarigol, Korea, 14 June 1952.

Entered service at: Gray, Pa.

Born : 25 March 1931, Gray, Pa.

G.O. No.: 65, 19 August 1953.

Citation: Cpl. Speicher distinguished himself by

conspicuous gallantry and indomitable courage above and beyond the call of duty in action against the enemy. While participating in an assault to secure a key terrain feature, Cpl. Speicher's squad was pinned down by withering small-arms, mortar, and machinegun fire. Although already wounded he left the comparative safety of his position, and made a daring charge against the machinegun emplacement. Within 10 yards of the goal, he was again wounded by small-arms fire but continued on, entered the bunker, killed 2 hostile soldiers with his rifle, a third with his bayonet, and silenced the machinegun. Inspired by this incredible display of valor, the men quickly moved up and completed the mission. Dazed and shaken, he walked to the foot of the hill where he collapsed and died. Cpl. Speicher's consummate sacrifice and unflinching devotion to duty reflect lasting glory upon himself and uphold the noble traditions of the military service.

STONE, JAMES S.

Rank and organization: First Lieutenant, U.S. Army, Company E, 8th Cavalry Regiment, 1st Cavalry Division.
Place and date: Near Sokkogae, Korea, 21 and 22 November 1951.
Entered service at: Houston, Tex.
Born: 27 December 1922, Pine Bluff, Ark.
G.O. No.: 82, 20 October 1953.
Citation: 1st Lt. Stone, distinguished himself by conspicuous gallantry and indomitable courage above and beyond the call of duty in action against the enemy. When his platoon, holding a vital outpost position, was attacked by overwhelming Chinese forces, 1st Lt. Stone stood erect and exposed to the terrific enemy fire calmly directed his men in the defense. A defensive flame-thrower failing to function, he personally moved to its location, further exposing himself, and personally repaired the weapon. Throughout a second attack, 1st Lt. Stone; though painfully wounded, personally carried the only remaining light machinegun from place to place in the position in order to bring fire upon the Chinese advancing from 2 directions. Throughout he continued to encourage and direct his depleted platoon in its hopeless defense. Although again wounded, he continued the fight with his carbine, still exposing himself as an example to his men. When this final overwhelming assault swept over the platoon's position his voice could still be heard faintly urging his men to carry on, until he lost consciousness. Only because of this officer's driving spirit and heroic action was the platoon emboldened to make its brave but hopeless last ditch stand.

STORY, LUTHER H.

Rank and organization: Private First Class, U.S. Army, Company 9th Infantry Regiment, 2d Infantry Division.
Place and date: Near Agok, Korea, 1 September 1950.
Entered service at: Georgia.
Born: 20 July 1931, Buena Vista, Ga.
G.O. No.: 70, 2 August 1951.
Citation: Pfc. Story, distinguished himself by conspicuous gallantry and intrepidity above and beyond the call of duty in action. A savage daylight attack by elements of 3 enemy divisions penetrated the thinly held lines of the 9th Infantry. Company A beat off several banzai attacks but was bypassed and in danger of being cut off and surrounded. Pfc. Story, a weapons squad leader, was heavily engaged in stopping the early attacks and had just moved his squad to a position overlooking the Naktong River when he observed a large group of the enemy crossing the river to attack Company A. Seizing a machinegun from his wounded gunner he placed deadly fire on the hostile column killing or wounding an estimated 100 enemy soldiers. Facing certain encirclement the company commander ordered a withdrawal. During the move Pfc. Story noticed the approach of an enemy truck loaded with troops and towing an ammunition trailer. Alerting his comrades to take cover he fearlessly stood in the middle of the road, throwing grenades into the truck. Out of grenades he crawled to his squad, gathered up additional grenades and again attacked the vehicle. During the withdrawal the company was attacked by such superior numbers that it was forced to deploy in a ricefield. Pfc. Story was wounded in this action, but, disregarding his wounds, rallied the men about him and repelled the attack. Realizing that his wounds would hamper his comrades he refused to retire to the next position but remained to cover the company's withdrawal. When last seen he was firing every weapon available and fighting off another hostile assault. Private Story's extraordinary heroism, aggressive leadership, and supreme devotion to duty reflect the highest credit upon himself and were in keeping with the esteemed traditions of the military service.

SUDUT, JEROME A.

Rank and organization: Second Lieutenant, U.S. Army, Company B, 27th Infantry Regiment, 25th Infantry Division.
Place and date: Near Kumhwa, Korea, 12 September 1951.
Entered service at: Wisconsin.
Birth: Wausau, Wis.
G.O. No.: 31, 21 March 1952.
Citation: 2d Lt. Sudut distinguished himself by conspicuous gallantry above and beyond the call of duty in action against the enemy. His platoon, attacking heavily fortified and strategically located hostile emplacements, had been stopped by intense fire from a large bunker containing several firing posts. Armed with submachinegun, pistol, and grenades, 2d Lt. Sudut charged the emplacement alone through vicious hostile fire, killing 3 of the occupants and dispersing the remainder. Painfully wounded, he returned to reorganize his platoon, refused evacuation and led his men in a renewed attack. The enemy had returned to the bunker by means of connecting trenches from other emplacements and the platoon was again halted by devastating fire. Accompanied by an automatic-rifleman, 2d Lt. Sudut again charged into close-range fire to eliminate the position. When the rifleman was wounded, 2d Lt. Sudut seized his weapon and continued alone, killing 3 of the 4 remaining occupants. Though mortally wounded and his ammunition exhausted, he jumped into the emplacement and killed the remaining enemy soldier with his trench knife. His single-handed assaults so inspired his comrades that

they continued the attack and drove the enemy from the hill, securing the objective. 2d Lt. Sudut's consummate fighting spirit, outstanding leadership, and gallant self-sacrifice are in keeping with the finest traditions of the infantry and the U.S. Army.

THOMPSON, WILLIAM

Rank and organization: Private First Class, U.S. Army, 24th Company M, 24th Infantry Regiment, 25th Infantry Division.

Place and date: Near Haman, Korea, 6 August 1950.

Entered service at: Bronx, N.Y.

Birth: New York, N.Y.

G.O. No.: 63, 2 August 1951

Citation: Pfc. Thompson, distinguished himself by conspicuous gallantry and intrepidity above and beyond the call of duty in action against the enemy. While his platoon was reorganizing under cover of darkness, fanatical enemy forces in overwhelming strength launched a surprise attack on the unit. Pfc. Thompson set up his machinegun in the path of the onslaught and swept the enemy with withering fire, pinning them down momentarily thus permitting the remainder of his platoon to withdraw to a more tenable position. Although hit repeatedly by grenade fragments and small-arms fire, he resisted all efforts of his machinegun and continued to deliver deadly, accurate fire until mortally wounded by an enemy grenade. Pfc. Thompson's dauntless courage and gallant self-sacrifice reflect the highest credit on himself and uphold the esteemed traditions of military service.

TURNER, CHARLES W.

Rank and organization: Sergeant First Class, U.S. Army, 2d Reconnaissance Company, 2d Infantry Division.

Place and date: Near Yongsan, Korea, 1 September 1950.

Entered service at: Massachusetts.

Birth: Boston, Mass.

G.O. No.: 10, 16 February 1951.

Citation: Sfc. Turner distinguished himself by conspicuous gallantry and intrepiditiy above and beyond the call of duty in action against the enemy. A large enemy force launched a mortar and automatic weapon supported assault against his platoon. Sfc. Turner, a section leader, quickly organized his unit for defense and then observed that the attack was directed at the tank section 100 yards away. Leaving his secured section he dashed through a hail of fire to the threatened position and, mounting a tank, manned the exposed turret machinegun. Disregarding the intense enemy fire he calmly held this position delivering deadly accurate fire and pointing out targets for the tank's 75mm. gun. His action resulted in the destruction of 7 enemy machinegun nests. Although severely wounded he remained at the gun shouting encouragemet to his comrades. During the action the tank received over 50 direct hits; the periscopes and antenna were shot away and 3 rounds hit the machinegun mount. Despite this fire he remained at his post until a burst of enemy fire cost him his life. This intrepid and heroic performance enabled the platoon to withdraw and later launch an attack which routed the enemy. Sfc. Turner's valor and example reflect the highest credit upon

himself and are in keeping with the esteemed traditions of the U.S. Army.

VAN WINKLE, ARCHIE

Rank and organization: Staff Sergeant, U.S. Marine Corps Reserve, Company B, 1st Battalion, 7th Marines, 1st Marine Division (Rein).

Place and date: Vicinity of Sudong, Korea, 2 November 1950.

Entered service at: Arlington, Wash.

Born: 17 March 1925, Juneau, Alaska.

Citation: For conspicuous gallantry and intrepidity at the risk of his life above and beyond the call of duty while serving as a platoon sergeant in Company B, in action against enemy aggressor forces. Immediately rallying the men in his area after a fanatical and numerically superior enemy force penetrated the center of the line under cover of darkness and pinned down the platoon with a devastating barrage of deadly automatic weapons and grenade fire, S/Sgt. Van Winkle boldly spearheaded a determined attack through withering fire against hostile frontal positions and, though he and all the others who charged with him were wounded, succeeded in enabling his platoon to gain the fire superiority and the opportunity to reorganize. Realizing that the left- flank squad was isolated from the rest of the unit, he rushed through 40 yards of fierce enemy fire to reunite his troops despite an elbow wound which rendered 1 of his arms totally useless. Severely wounded a second time when a direct hit in the chest from a hostile handgrenade caused serious and painful wounds, he staunchly refused evacuation and continued to shout orders and words of encouragement to his depleted and battered platoon. Finally carried from his position unconscious from shock and from loss of blood, S/Sgt. Van Winkle served to inspire all who observed him to heroic efforts in successfully repulsing the enemy attack. His superb leadership, valiant fighting spirit, and unfaltering devotion to duty in the face of heavy odds reflect the highest credit upon himself and the U.S. Naval Service.

VITTORI, JOSEPH

Rank and organization: Corporal, U.S. Marine Corps Reserve, Company F, 2d Battalion, 1st Marines, 1st Marine Division (Rein).

Place and date: Hill 749, Korea, 15 and 16 September 1951.

Entered service at: Beverly, Mass.

Born: 1 August 1929, Beverly Mass.

Citation: For conspicuous gallantry and intrepidity at the risk of his life above and beyond the call of duty while serving as an automatic-rifleman in Company F, in action against enemy aggressor forces. With a forward platoon suffering heavy casualties and forced to withdraw under a vicious enemy counterattack as his company assaulted strong hostile forces entrenched on Hill 749, Cpl. Vittori boldly rushed through the withdrawing troops with 2 other volunteers from his reserve platoon and plunged directly into the midst of the enemy. Overwhelming them in a fierce hand-to-hand struggle, he enabled his company to consolidate its positions to meet further imminent onslaughts. Quick to respond to an urgent call for a rifleman to defend a heavy machinegun positioned on the extreme point of the northern flank and virtually isolated from the remainder of the unit when the enemy again struck in force during the night, he assumed position under the devastating barrage and, fighting a single- handed battle, leaped from 1 flank to the other, covering each foxhole in turn as casualties continued to mount, manning a machinegun when the gunner was struck down and making repeated trips through the heaviest shellfire to replenish ammunition. With the situation becoming extremely critical, reinforcing units to the rear pinned down under the blistering attack and foxholes left practically void by dead and wounded for a distance of 100 yards, Cpl. Vittori continued his valiant stand, refusing to give ground as the enemy penetrated to within feet of his position, simulating strength in the line and denying the foe physical occupation of the ground. mortally wounded by the enemy machinegun and rifle bullets while persisting in his magnificent defense of the sector where a pproximately 200 enemy dead were found the following morning, Cpl. Vittori, by his fortitude, stouthearted courage, and great personal valor, had kept the point position intact despite the tremendous odds and undoubtedly prevented the entire battalion position from collapsing. His extraordinary heroism throughout the furious nightlong battle reflects the highest credit upon himself and the U.S. Naval Service. He gallantly gave his life for his country.

WALMSLEY, JOHN S., JR.

Rank and organization: Captain, U.S. Air Force, 8th Bombardment Squardron, 3d Bomb Group.

Place and date: Near Yangdok, Korea, 14 September 1951.

Entered serrvice at: Baltimore, Md.

Born: 7 January 1920, Baltimore, Md.

Citation: Capt. Walmsley, distinguished himself by conspicuous gallantry and intrepidity at the risk of his life above and beyond the call of duty. While flying a B-26 aircraft on a night combat mission with the objective of developing new tactics, Capt. Walmsley sighted an enemy supply train which had been assigned top priority as a target of opportunity. He

immediately attacked, producing a strike which disabled the train, and, when his ammunition was expended, radioed for friendly aircraft in the area to complete destruction of the target. Employing the searchlight mounted on his aircraft, he guided another B-26 aircraft to the target area, meanwhile constantly exposing himself to enemy fire. Directing an incoming B-26 pilot, he twice boldly aligned himself with the target, his searchlight illuminating the area, in a determined effort to give the attacking aircraft full visibility. As the friendly aircraft prepared for the attack, Capt. Walmsley descended into the valley in a low level run over the target with searchlight blazing, selflessly exposing himself to vicious enemy antiaircraft fire. In his determination to inflict maximum damage on the enemy, he refused to employ evasive tactics and valiantly pressed forward straight through an intense barrage, thus insuring complete destruction of the enemy's vitally needed war cargo. While he courageously pressed his attack Capt.

Walmsley's plane was hit and crashed into the surrounding mountains, exploding upon impact. His heroic initiative and daring aggressiveness in completing this important mission in the face of overwhelming opposition and at the risk of his life, reflects the highest credit upon himself and the U.S. Air Force.

WATKINS, LEWIS G.

Rank and organization: Staff Sergeant, U.S. Marine Corps, Company I, 3d Battalion, 7th Marines, 1st Marine Division (Rein).

Place and date: Korea, 7 October 1952.

Entered service at: Seneca, S.C.

Born: June 1925, Seneca, S.C.

Citation: For conspicuous gallantry and intrepidity at the risk of his life above and beyond the call of duty while serving as a guide of a rifle platoon of Company I, in action against enemy aggressor forces during the hours of darkness on the morning of 7 October 1952. With his platoon assigned the mission of retaking an outpost which had been overrun by the enemy earlier in the night S/Sgt. Watkins skillfully led his unit in the assault up the designated hill. Although painfully wounded when a well-entrenched hostile force at the crest of the hill engaged the platoon with intense small- arms and grenade fire, he gallantly continued to lead his men. Obtaining an automatic rifle from 1 of the wounded men, he assisted in pinning down an enemy machinegun holding up the assault. When an enemy grenade landed among S/Sgt. Watkins and several other marines while they were moving forward through a trench on the hill crest, he immediately pushed his companions aside, placed himself in a position to shield them and picked up the deadly mile in an attempt to throw it outside the trench. Mortally wounded when the grenade exploded in his hand, S/Sgt. Watkins, by his great personal valor in the face of almost certain death, saved the lives of several of his comrades and contributed materially to the success of the mission. His extraordinary heroism, inspiring leadership, and resolute spirit of self- sacrifice reflect the highest credit upon himself and enhance the finest traditions of the U.S. Naval Service. He gallantly gave his life for his country.

WATKINS, TRAVIS E.

Rank and organization: Master Sergeant, U.S. Army, Company H., 9th Infantry Regiment, 2d Infantry Division.

Place and date: Near Yongsan, Korea, 31 August through 3 September 1950.

Entered service at: Texas.

Birth: Waldo, Ark.

G.O. No.: 9, 16 February 1951.

Citation: M/Sgt. Watkins distinguished himself by conspicuous gallantry and intrepidity above and beyond the call of duty in action against the enemy. When an overwhelming enemy force broke through and isolated 30 men of his unit, he took command, established a perimeter defense and directed action which repelled continuous, fanatical enemy assaults. With his group completely surrounded and cut off, he moved from foxhole to foxhole exposing himself to enemy fire, giving instructions and offering encouragement to his men. Later when the need for ammunition and grenades became critical he shot 2 enemy soldiers 50 yards outside the perimeter and went out alone for their ammunition and weapons. As he picked up their weapons he was attacked by 3 others and wounded. Returning their fire he killed all 3 and gathering up the weapons of the 5 enemy dead returned to his amazed comrades. During a later assault, 6 enemy soldiers gained a defiladed spot and began to throw grenades into the perimeter making it untenable. Realizing the desperate situation and disregarding his wound he rose from his foxhole to engage them with rifle fire. Although immediately hit by a burst from an enemy machinegun he continued to fire until he had killed the grenade throwers. With this threat eliminated he collapsed and despite being paralyzed from the waist down, encouraged his men to hold on. He refused all food, saving it for his comrades, and when it became apparent that help would not arrive in time to hold the position ordered his men to escape to friendly lines. Refusing evacuation as his hopeless condition would burden his comrades, he remained in his position and cheerfully wished them luck. Through his aggressive leadership and intrepid actions, this small force destroyed nearly 500 of the enemy before abandoning their position. position. M/Sgt. Watkins' sustained personal bravery and noble self-sacrifice reflect the highest glory upon himself and is in keeping with the esteemed traditions of the U.S. Army.

WEST, ERNEST E.

Rank and organization: Private First Class, U.S. Army, Company L, 14th Infantry Regiment, 25th Infantry Division.
Place and date: Near Sataeri, Korea, 12 October 1952.
Entered service at: Wurtland, Ky.
Born: 2 September 1931, Russell, Ky.
G.O. No.: 7, 29 January 1954.
Citation: Pfc. West distinguished himself by conspicuous gallantry above and beyond the call of duty in action against the enemy. He voluntarily accompanied a contingent to locate and destroy a reported enemy outpost. Nearing the objective, the patrol was ambushed and suffered numerous casualties. Observing his wounded leader lying in an exposed position, Pfc. West ordered the troops to withdraw, then braved intense fire to reach and assist him. While attempting evacuation, he was attacked by 3 hostile soldiers employing grenades and small-arms fire. Quickly shifting his body to shelter the officer, he killed the assailants with his rifle, then carried the helpless man to safety. He was critically wounded and lost an eye in this action, but courageously returned through withering fire and bursting shells to assist the wounded. While evacuating 2 comrades, he closed with and killed 3 more of the foe. Pfc. West's indomitable spirit, consummate valor, and intrepid actions inspired all who observed him, reflect the highest credit on himself, and uphold the honored traditions of the military service.

WILSON, BENJAMIN F.

Rank and organization: First Lieutenant (then M/Sgt.), U.S. Army, Company I, 31st Infantry Division.
Place and date: Near Hwach'on-Myon, Korea, 5 June 1951.

Entered service at: Vashon, Wash.
Birth: Vashon, Wash.
G.O. No.: 69, 23 September 1954.
Citation: 1st Lt. Wilson distinguished himself by conspicuous gallantry and indomitable courage above and beyond the call of duty in action against the enemy. Company I was committed to attack and secure commanding terrain stubbornly defended by a numerically superior hostile force emplaced in well-fortified positions. When the spearheading element was pinned down by withering hostile fire, he dashed forward and, firing his rifle and throwing grenades, neutralized the position denying the advance and killed 4 enemy soldiers manning submachineguns. After the assault platoon moved up, occupied the position, and a base of fire was established, he led a bayonet attack which reduced the objective and killed approximately 27 hostile soldiers. While friendly forces were consolidating the newly won gain, the enemy launched a counterattack and 1st Lt. Wilson, realizing the imminent threat of being overrun, made a determined lone-man charge, killing 7 and wounding 2 of the enemy, and routing the remainder in disorder. After the position was organized, he led an assault carrying to approximately 15 yards of the final objective, when enemy fire halted the advance. He ordered the platoon to withdraw and, although painfully wounded in this action, remained to provide covering fire. During an ensuing counterattack, the commanding officer and 1st Platoon leader became casualties. Unhesitatingly, 1st Lt. Wilson charged the enemy ranks and fought valiantly, killing 3 enemy soldiers with his rifle before it was wrested from his hands, and annihilating others with his entrenching tool. His courageous delaying action enabled his comrades to reorganize and effect an orderly withdrawal. While directing evacuation of the wounded, he suffered a second wound, but elected to remain on the position until assured that all of the men had reached safety. 1st Lt. Wilson's sustained valor and intrepid actions reflect utmost credit upon himself and uphold the honored traditions of the military service.

WILSON, HAROLD E.

Rank and organization: Technical Sergeant, U.S. Marine Corps Reserve, Company G, 3d Battalion, 1st Marines, 1st Marine Division (Rein).
Place and date: Korea, 23-24 April 1951.
Entered service at: Birmingham, Ala.
Born: 5 December 1921, Birmingham, Ala.
Citation: For gallantry and intrepidity at the risk of his life above and beyond the call of duty while serving as platoon sergeant of a rifle platoon attached to Company G, in action against enemy aggressor forces on the night of 23-24 April 1951. When the company outpost was overrun by the enemy while his platoon, firing from hastily constructed foxholes, was engaged in resisting the brunt of a fierce mortar, machinegun, grenade, and small-arms attack launched by hostile forces from high ground under cover of darkness, T/Sgt. Wilson braved intense fire to assist the survivors back into the line and to direct the treatment of casualties. Although twice wounded by gunfire, in the right arm and the left leg, he refused medical aid for himself and continued to move about

among his men, shouting words of encouragement. After receiving further wounds in the head and shoulder as the attack increased in intensity, he again insisted upon remaining with his unit. Unable to use either arm to fire, and with mounting casualties among our forces, he resupplied his men with rifles and ammunition taken from the wounded. Personally reporting to his company commander on several occasions, he requested and received additional assistance when the enemy attack became even more fierce and, after placing the reinforcements in strategic positions in the line, directed effective fire until blown off his feet by the bursting of a hostile mortar round in his face. Dazed and suffering from concussion, he still refused medical aid and, despite weakness from loss of blood, moved from foxhole to foxhole, directing fire, resupplying ammunition, rendering first aid, and encouraging his men. By his heroic actions in the face of almost certain death, when the unit's ability to hold the disadvantageous position was doubtful, he instilled confidence in his troops, inspiring them to rally repeatedly and turn back the furious assaults. At dawn, after the final attack had been repulsed, he personally accounted for each man in his platoon before walking unassisted 1/2 mile to the aid station where he submitted to treatment. His outstanding courage, initiative, and skilled leadership in the face of overwhelming odds were contributing factors in the success of his company's mission and reflect the highest credit upon T/Sgt. Wilson and the U.S. Naval Service.

WILSON, RICHARD G.

Rank and organization: Private First Class, U.S. Army, Col., Medical Company, 187th Airborne Infantry Regiment.
Place and date: Opari, Korea, 21 October 1950.
Entered service at: Cape Girardeau, Mo.
Born: 19 August 1931, Marion, Ill.
G.O. No.: 64, 2 August 1951.
Citation: Pfc. Wilson distinguished himself by conspicuous gallantry and intrepidity above and beyond the call of duty in action. As medical aid man attached to Company I, he accompanied the unit during a reconnaissance in force through the hilly country near Opari. The main body of the company was passing through a narrow valley flanked on 3 sides by high hills when the enemy laid down a barrage of mortar, automatic-weapons and small-arms fire. The company suffered a large number of casualties from the intense hostile fire while fighting its way out of the ambush. Pfc. Wilson proceeded at once to move among the wounded and administered aid to them oblivious of the danger to himself, constantly exposing himself to hostile fire. The company commander ordered a withdrawal as the enemy threatened to encircle and isolate the company. As his unit withdrew Private Wilson assisted wounded men to safety and assured himself that none were left behind. After the company had pulled back he learned that a comrade previously throught dead had been seen to be moving and attempting to crawl to safety. Despite the protests of his comrades, unarmed and facing a merciless enemy, Pfc. Wilson returned to the dangerous position in search of his comrade. Two days later a patrol found him lying beside the man he returned to aid. He had been shot several times while trying to shield and administer aid to the wounded man. Pfc. Wilson's superb personal bravery, consummate courage and willing self-sacrifice for his comrades reflect untold glory upon himself and uphold the esteemed traditions of the military service.

WINDRICH, WILLIAM G.

Rank and organization: Staff Sergeant, U.S. Marine Corps, Company I, 3d Battalion, 5th Marines, 1st Marine Division (Rein).
Place and date: Vicinity of Yudam-ni, Korea, 1 December 1950.
Entered service at: Hammond, Ind.
Born: 14 May 1921, Chicago, Ill.
Citation: For conspicuous gallantry and intrepidity at the risk of his life above and beyond the call of duty as a platoon sergeant of Company I, in action against enemy aggressor forces the night of 1 December 1950. Promptly organizing a squad of men when the enemy launched a sudden, vicious counterattack against the forward elements of his company's position, rendering it untenable, S/Sgt. Windrich, armed with a carbine, spearheaded the assault to the top of the knoll immediately confronting the overwhelming forces and, under shattering hostile automatic-weapons, mortar, and grenade fire, directed effective fire to hold back the attackers and cover the withdrawal of our troops to commanding ground. With 7 of his men struck down during the furious action and himself wounded in the head by a bursting grenade, he made his way to his company's position and, organizing a small group of volunteers, returned with them to evacuate the wounded and dying from the frozen hillside, staunchly refusing medical attention himself. Immediately redeploying the remainder of his troops, S/Sgt. Windrich placed them on the left flank of the defensive sector before the enemy again attacked in force. Wounded in the leg during the bitter fight that followed, he bravely fought on with his men, shouting words of encouragement and directing their fire until the attack was repelled. Refusing evacuation although unable to stand, he still continued to direct his platoon in setting up defensive positions until weakened by the bitter cold, excessive loss of blood, and severe pain, he lapsed into unconsciousness and died. His valiant leadership, fortitude, and courageous fighting spirit against tremendous odds served to inspire others to heroic endeavor in holding the objective and reflect the highest credit upon S/Sgt. Windrich and the U.S. Naval Service. He gallantly gave his life for his country.

WOMACK, BRYANT E.

Rank and organization: Private First Class, U.S. Army, medical Company, 14th Infantry Regiment, 25th Infantry Division.
Place and date: Near Sokso-ri, Korea, 12 March 1952.
Entered service at: Mill Springs, N.C.
Birth: Mill Springs, N.C.
G.O. No.: 5, 12 January 1953.
Citation: Pfc. Womack distinguished himself by conspicuous gallantry above and beyond the call of duty in action against the enemy. Pfc. Womack was the only

medical aid man attached to a night combat patrol when sudden contact with a numerically superior enemy produced numerous casualties. Pfc. Womack went immediately to their aid, although this necessitated exposing himself to a devastating hail of enemy fire, during which he was seriously wounded. Refusing medical aid for himself, he continued moving among his comrades to administer aid. While he was aiding 1 man, he was again struck by enemy mortar fire, this time suffering the loss of his right arm. Although he knew the consequences should immediate aid not be administered, he still refused aid and insisted that all efforts be made for the benefit of others that were wounded. Although unable to perform the task himself, he remained on the scene and directed others in first-aid techniques. The last man to withdraw, he walked until he collapsed from loss of blood, and died a few minutes later while being carried by his comrades. The extraordinary heroism, outstanding courage, and unswerving devotion to his duties displayed by Pfc. Womack reflect the utmost distinction upon himself and uphold the esteemed traditions of the U.S. Army.

YOUNG, ROBERT H.

Rank and organization: Private First Class, U.S. Army, Company E, 8th Cavalry Regiment, 1st Cavalry Division.
Place and date: North of Kaesong, Korea, 9 October 1950.
Entered service at: Vallejo, Calif.
Born: 4 March 1929, Oroville, Calif.

G.O. No.: 65, 2 August 1951.
Citation: Pfc. Young distinguished himself by conspicuous gallantry and intrepidity above and beyond the call of duty in action. His company, spearheading a battalion drive deep in enemy territory, suddenly came under a devastating barrage of enemy mortar and automatic weapons crossfire which inflicted heavy casualties among his comrades and wounded him in the face and shoulder. Refusing to be evacuated, Pfc. Young remained in position and continued to fire at the enemy until wounded a second time. As he awaited first aid near the company command post the enemy attempted an enveloping movement. Disregarding medical treatment he took an exposed position and firing with deadly accuracy killed 5 of the enemy. During this action he was again hit by hostile fire which knocked him to the ground and destroyed his helmet. Later when supporting tanks moved forward, Pfc. Young, his wounds still unattended, directed tank fire which destroyed 3 enemy gun positions and enabled the company to advance. Wounded again by an enemy mortar burst, and while aiding several of his injured comrades, he demanded that all others be evacuated first. Throughout the course of this action the leadership and combative instinct displayed by Pfc. Young exerted a profound influence on the conduct of the company. His aggressive example affected the whole course of the action and was responsible for its success. Pfc. Young's dauntless courage and intrepidity reflect the highest credit upon himself and uphold the esteemed traditions of the U.S. Army.

Those Who Worked On The Memorial In Some Way Over The Years

The Korean War Veterans Memorial Advisory Board

General Raymond G. Davis, USMC (Ret)
Medal of Honor, Korea, Chairman
Colonel Rosemary T. McCarthy, USA (Ret)
Vice Chairman

The Honorable Edward R. Borcherdt, Jr., USMC
Colonel Fred V. Cherry, USAF (Ret)
The Honorable John P. "Jake" Comer, USA
The Honorable Jack B. Curcio, USA
The Honorable Thomas G. Dehne, USMC
The Honorable James D. "Mike" McKevitt, USAF
The Honorable William F. McSweeny, USA
The Honorable John C. Phillips, USA
The Honorable Carlos Rodriguez, USA
The Honorable John S. Staum, USA
Colonel William E. Weber, USA (Ret)

General Richard G. Stilwell, USA (Ret), deceased
Colonel Conrad Hausman, USA (Ret), deceased
Colonel John Kenney, USA (Ret)
Executive Director 1987-1989
Robert L. Hansen, USN
Executive Director 1989-1995

Staff

Bennett, Melanie
Byington, Sally
Donnelly, Ray
Fiffe, Brian
Kenney, Katie
Russell, Bill

American Battle Monuments Commission

Commissioners

General Fred F. Woerner, USA (Ret)
Chairman
The Honorable Hugh L. Carey
Vice Chairman
Colonel Ken Pond, USA (Ret)
Executive Director/Acting Secretary
Brigadier General Evelyn P. Foote, USA (Ret)
The Honorable Rolland E. Kidder
Brigadier General Douglas Kinnard, USA (Ret)
The Honorable Alfred S. LosBanos
The Honorable Thomas F. Lyons
The Honorable Brenda L. Moore
Brigadier General Gail M. Reals, USMC (Ret)

The Honorable F. Haydn Williams

Past Commissioners

General Paul X. Kelley, USMC (Ret)
The Honorable Francis J. Bagnell
The Honorable William P. Campbell
The Honorable Aubrey O. Cookman
The Honorable Jack O. Guy
The Honorable Robert C. Laughter
The Honorable John C. McDonald
The Honorable Ronald D. Ray
The Honorable Peter W. Senopoulos
The Honorable Mark V. Rosenker
Brigadier General David H. Sudderth, USA (Ret)
The Honorable William E. Hickey
The Honorable Rexford C. Early
The Honorable Armistead J. Maupin
The Honorable Freda J. Poundstone
The Honorable Kitty D. Bradley
The Honorable Joseph W. Canzeri
The Honorable Preston H. Long
General Andrew J. Goodpaster, USA (Ret)

Staff

Major General A. J. Adams
Lieutenant General Joseph S. Laposata
Colonel William E. Ryan, Jr.
Colonel Kevin C. Kelley
Colonel Kenneth S. Pond
Lieutenant Colonel Ernest R. Morgan, III
Colonel Frederick C. Badger
Colonel Clayton L. Moran, USA (Ret)

Friends of ABMC

The Honorable Pete Wheeler
The Honorable Sarah McClendon
The Honorable Bill Mauldin
Rear Admiral Ming Chang, USN (Ret)
The Honorable Jon Mangis
Major General Robert Moorhead, USARNG (Ret)
The Honorable Dr. Miguel Encinias
The Honorable Dr. Helen Fagin
The Honorable Jess Hay
The Honorable J. William Murphy
The Honorable Melissa Durbin
The Honorable William Ferguson, Sr.
John Schuhart
Mico M. Schmidt
The Honorable Joseph Greene

Friends Not Listed Elsewhere

Aleksandrowicz, Frank
Anderson, Clifton

Andrews, Leo
Antippas, Andrew
Arndt, Edward
Bair, Chester
Ballington, H.M.
Barnum, Barney
Barr, Andy
Bates, Hugh
Beck, Lois
Belil, Eli
Benshoof, Jake
Bentley, Bill
Berling, Raymond
Beyers, Don
Boatwright, Scott
Booker, Ken
Bosma, Bob
Brady, James
Broughan, John
Brown, Ernest
Brown, Hugh
Brown, Robert
Buddo, Louis
Byrne, Frank
Campbell, Joe
Chung, Donald
Cloman, Jack
Clooney, Rosemary
Cobb, Calvin
Colley, Ralph
Cooke, Harry
Cooper, Charles
Corley, Arthur
Creech, Bill
Currieo, James
Curto, Tony
Dagley, Hugh
Dantzler, Earl
Dauberman, Bart
Davis, Wilbur
Dean, James
Dear Abby
Derwinski, Edward
Desfor, Max
Devine, Danny
Diamond, Tony
Donaldson, Hale
Donnelly, Ray
Duffey, Dennis
Dunn, Roy
Edwards, John
Ennis, Robert
Farris, Tyson
Fazakerley, Dick
Fiffe, Brian
Flanagan, Richard
Fleischman, Norma

Fox, Jack
Friedman, Philip
Gardner, John
Garvey, Joe
Gill, Bill
Grau, Jim
Gloppel, Thomas
Graupman, Dwight
Guthrie, John
Haas, Pete
Harris, Dave
Harris, Sherman
Hems, Joseph
Heying, Lisa
Hockley, Ralph
Hogan, Bob
Holland, John
Holley, Jim
Holt, Cooper
Hope, Bob
Horwat, Michael
Hoyt, Michele
Humphreys, Dick
Humphreys, Ned
Jackson, Jan
Johnson, Gloriana
Johnson, Karl
Jordan, Cleveland
Junot, Arthur
Kolb, Richard
Krejci, John
LaSpada, Carmella
Leathers, Gene
Levick, Robert
Lindeneau, Wulf
Lisi, Joe
Lively, C. Judson Jr.
Lyke, Thomas
Maines, Thomas
Malin, Don
Mangler, William
Martin, Ronald
Masters, Rex
McAnaw, John
McCoy, Victor
McDonnell, James Jr.
McGahn, Paddy
McMahon, Ed
Monkman, Bruce
Moore, Taylor III
Murray, Jack
Murray, Mark
Nelson, Stuart
Nickelson, Howard
Norris, Bill
Pace, James
Palmer, Perry

Parks, Don
Parris, Stan
Patterson, Arthur
Penman, Ralph
Peters, James
Pittaway, Jim
Posata, Joe
Powell, Colin
Powell, R. Jack
Pratt, Sherman
Queen, Jim
Quinn, Daniel
Reeves, Maurice
Reiner, Norb
Repass, Don
Rivers, Larry
Rock, Michael
Rodda, Charlie
Rosenbleeth, Herb
Ross, Kenwood
Rudman, Warren
Satterlee, Francis
Sazardia, Emilio
Schaumberg, Ken
Schoch, Frank
Sease, Joe
Segarra, Joseph
Schultz, Richard
Shortell, Tom
Sincock, Morgan
Skypeck, George
Smith, Dan
Smith, Stanley
Smith, William
Sommer, John Jr.
Spanogle, Robert
Spilotro, Joe
Springer, June
St. Laurant, Larry
Stilwell, Richard Jr.
Stilwell, Alice
Strongnin, David
Temple, Hebert Jr.
Turner, David
Vollmer, Douglas
Walker, Jack
Walker, Richard
Watts, Joe
Wheeler, Daniel
Wiedhahn, Warren
Williams, Charles
Williams, Donald
Wilson, Carroll
Wolf, Duke
Wycoff, Odessa
Yawn, Thomas
Zimmerman, Doug

Architects

KWVM Competition-Winning Design Concept By:

Don Alvaro Leon
Veronica Burns-Lucas
John Paul Lucas
Eliza Pennypacker

Army Corps of Engineers

Programs and Project Management Division

Military Project Mgmt. Section

Adams, Frances
Anderson, Lisa
Argentieri, Linda
Armstrong, Mike
Bandera, John
Benner, Marilyn
Butler, John Jr.
Callander, Bruce
Campbell, Mary
Ciesla, Joseph
Crawford, Alexandra
Dean, Richard
Delgrosso, Brian
Dey, Donald
Egolf, Ken
Elgohary, Ayad
Faulkner, Doris
Faulkner, Jesse
Frantz, Robert
Gantt, David Jr.
Gembicki, Stan
Glock, Brian
Graves, LTC
Hanle, Susan
Helmbold, William
Inouye, Col.
Jirsa, Kim
Jobe, Clyde Jr.
Kiersarsky, Raymond
Klosterman, Dennis
Leketa, Anthony
Mardaga, Ronald
Merski, Rhonda
Morsey, Glenn
Musial, Ed

Nine, Marylin
Pope, Patricia
Riche, Mary
Robertson, Mary
Sadler, Jon
Stello, Mike
Taylor, Peter Maj.
Taylor, William
Vogel, Jon
Wallace, Ella
Webb, Dennis
White, Richard
Wilson, William
Zimmerman, Margaret

Cooper-Lecky, architect of record

Larry Cooper, president
Martha Collins, comptroller
W. Kent Cooper, principal in charge
William P. Lecky, principal in charge
Robert R. Smedley, project architect
James P. Clark
Louise Cook
James Cummings
Nesli Dogrusoz
Karen Murray
Dan Redman
Rick Schneider
Katherine Stifel

CLA Subcontractors

John J. Christie & Associates

John J. Christie
Elio Lopez
Massoud Nadjmabadi
Said Nadjmabadi

Claude R. Engle Lighting

Claude Engle
John Wood

Scharf-Godfrey, Buck Young

John B. Avery
Ed Condolon
Diane Cooney
Eugene Dershimer
Mike Flannick
Robin Godfrey
Joe Jiacinto
Jim Miller
Mike Pons
Howard Thomas
Bruce Van Hart
Buck Young

Wiles Dailey Pronske

Keith A. Lawson
Joseph P. Mensch
Kurt N. Pronske
Mary Sweeney
Mohammed Zaki

WM. Hobbs, LTD

William Hobbs, CEO/designer
Jim Snyder, designer
Roger Graham, designer/engineer
David Saylor, designer/engineer
Carlos Bascas, engineer/detailer
Doug Graf, head shop craftsman/welder
Carlton Oglesby, shop craftsman/assembler
Mike Benton, machinist/assembler

James Madison Cutts

James Madison Cutts
Steven Colby
Tina Bernhardt
Thomas McElwain

Arnold Associates

Henry Arnold
Stephen Lederach

Howard-Revis Design Services

Dru Colbert
Ann Hawkins
Buddy Harris

Jeff Howard

Blair, Dubilier & Associates

Greg Blair
Dale Alward
Robert Julia
Jennifer Meehan

Frank C. Gaylord, Sculptor

Buzzi, Victoria
Carr, David
Cattelona, Dick
Erdman, John & Caroline
Fredenberg, Mark
Free, Ed
Frum, Austin
Garfinkle, Ann
Gaylord, Charles
Gaylord, John Richard (son) in memory of
Gaylord, Mary (wife)
Hall, Willard
Hanna, John
Kelly, Bill
Kelly, Jack
Kendrick, Butch
Keropian, Michael
Kurjanowicz, George
Lindsay, Jay
Martinez, Adolf
Mason, William (Red)
McGrath, Chris
Oberg, Eric
Polich, Dick
Quade, Joe
Smith, William
Strikwerda, Dirk
Tenney, Paul
Thompson, Robert
Triano, John N. Sr.
Triano, Leanne
Turner, Stansfield
Vitale, Joseph
Wagner, Bill
Williams, Jerry

Louis Nelson Associates Team

Muralist

Louis Nelson, artist and creative director
Jennifer Stoller, senior project designer
Andrea Green
Nicholas Musco
Giovanni Pellone
Jean Koeppel
Molly Hayden
Louis Plummer
Mort Sheinman
Paul and Mary Beyer
National Archives
National Air & Space Museum, photo source
Linda Christenson

Faith Construction, Inc.

Alvarez, Fredy
Brown, Henry
Earl, Leon
Edgardo, Mejia
Fisher, Jay
Green, Harold
Harcum, Maurice
Hardy, William
Helwig, Harry
Hughes, Persel
Majano, Pastor
Pierce, Prince
Reid, George
Swickert, Steve
Thomas, Ollie
Tyger, Floyd
Wallace, Robert J.
Zeiders, Jacob W.

R.J. Crowley

Becky Crowley
Brent Bowman
Brian Wese
Bryan Mueller
Carlos Abraham
Carlos Hernandez
Charlie Beam
Chris Soto
Dean Harting
Dennis Frampton
Don Sansing
George Dunaway
Hector Sormiento
Jerry Bell
Joe Ailstock

302

John Bunting
Jorge Orellana
Jorle Escobar
Linda Dolan Crowley
Martin Garcia
Pete Crowley
Salvadore Bonilla

Goldin & Stafford

Herbert Moore
Mark Trujillo
Melvin Johnson
Gerard Couture, Jr.
Jon Rothfolk

Coastal Piling

Richard Hill
Doug Lee
Tony Ferraro
Bobby Meisner

Jrg Contractors

Bill Cowger
Bob Shinn
David Ventura
Jose Vanegas
Carson Miller
Partick Butler
Steve Ward
J. Robert Wass

Mekco

Rick Flinn
Dave Barbee
Warren Smith
Lonnie Smith
James D. Richardson
Roy D. Colvin
William G. Cole
William Mcmillian
Andrew Juggins
Sonny Mcdaniel
Donny Slack
Fred Kakascik
Ed Sullivan
Albert Murphy
Willie Pope
John Legrand
Phillip Hewit
Jerret Wes
Dave Mcdaniel
Herman Hooper

Carl Lee

Jett Mechanical

Mell Parker
Bill Sweetman
Jim Martinson
Michael Fletcher
Jay Yager
Eric Meese
Jimmy Yager
Mike Jett
Robert Hall
Silbio Parrales
David Miller
Espectacion Ventura
Felix Medrano
Bobby Cole
J.C. Grosnickle
Don Wolfe

Union Electric

Nolan Glasby
Keith Williams
Doug Schemmel
Khan Nguyen
Rich Murphy
Maurice Baker
Mike Skipper
Chris Potkay
Shawn Stringfield
Derwin Bell

CEINC—Certified Environments, Inc.

Zoran Dragacevac
John Carver
Suri Suhrendhi

Schiller Assoc.

John F. Schiller
James L. Myers

Greenthumb

Mike Wheeler
Chris Kokoskie
Joe Swoboda
Rafeal Valvez
Pedro Abila
Ruben Castro
Rony Alarcon
Cenobio Marquel

Juan Alarcon
Donaldo Martinec
Nickolas Sandoval
Ruben Abelar
Ezequiel Avelar
Jose Avelar

Superior Foundations

Ron Dansiz
Tarkino Alverez
Jerimiah Jimenez
Benito Cervantes
Qurntero
Macedonio Topia
Rivera
Gregorio Maldonado
Sixto Castillo
Lucio Alvarez
Richard Corbett

Eastern Waterproofing

Jeff Gray
Willis Fouts
Kevin Grey
Mike Jarboe
Rick Buzard
Clifton Johnson
David Scot
Bobby Jordan

Superior Iron Works

Clifton Green
Barney Morse
Mike Finamore
Scot Mcnair
Bob Sparrough, Jr.
Jerry Palmer
David Lucks
Mike Kennedy
Don Kaetzel
Robert L. Murphy
John Morris
James Brown
Daniel Mcgraw

PRI-Professional Restorations, Inc.

Reinaldo Lopez
Scott Price

Paul Monesi
Jose Tagoada
Andy Gerez
Cipriano Vidal
Juan Portello
Feliciano Villatoro
Jose Rivas
Luis Cano
Timothy Nojaim
Manuel Rivas

Cold Spring Granite Company USA

Daniel J. Rea
Patrick D. Alexander
Patrick J. Mitchell
John W. Maile
George J. Schnepf
Michael Lizarraga
Scott S. Barthel
Brad R. Barthelemy
James M. Cota
Kenneth Schindele
Richard Knapp
John Packer
Joseph Theis
Lee Person
Walt Thomas

Tallix

Aviles, Alberto
Bachmann, Harry
Behl, Kuldip
Beyer, Patricia
Boisvert, Patsy
Brewer, Robert
Burger, Hamilton
Cafarelli, Insun
Calabrese, Louis
Colburn, David
Conklin, Andrew
Cornett, Joan
Dailey, Michael
Decaprio, Chris
Deguise, Leander
Delaney, William Jr.
Donohue, Elizabeth
Donohue, Laura
Donohue, Morgan
Dwan, Lawrence
Fautz, Mary
Fern, Catherine
Fonseca, Manuel

303

Fordham, Tammie
Garnot, Mark
Garrett, Darren
Garrett, Dolores
Glasson, Gregory
Greer, Rodney
Gunsch, Laura
Gunter, Gerhard
Haley, Maureen
Hammond, Henry
Hammond, Michael
Hockler, Elizabeth
Hof, Carisa
Holmes, Denis
Holowiak, Robert
Hughes, Fredrick
Jeter, Tina
Jimenez, Beatriz
Johansen, Richard
Jolly, James
Jones, Todd
Karales, Joseph
Keropian, Michael
Knapp, Jesse
Kniffin, Nancy
Koury, Richard
Lagares, Antonio
Lalonde, Edson
Lalonde, Jay
Langley, Robert
Lewis, Darren
Lindsay, Melvin Jay
List, Michael
Lucy, Naomi
Magagnos, Thomas
Malouf, Gary
Malouf, Melissa
Malouf, Steven
Manetta, John
McCarty, Jacqueline
McGrath, Christine
McNeill, Michael
Mee, Soo Kim
Megna, Melissa
Montegari, Amy
Montegari, Raymond
Mortensen, Charles
Murray, Irene
Nardin, Mario
Nardone, Vincent
Ngo, Meng
Peterson, Robert
Pilon, Michael
Pivarnik, Margery
Plass, Wallace
Polich, Richard
Pomarico, Cathy

Powers, Christopher
Quercia, Raymond
Rednour, Rosemary
Rhoten, Charles
Ross, Peter
Rutter, Kurt
Sarlin, Debra
Sarvis, Patricia
Sauter, Eric
Sjoholm, Thor
Smith, J. Raymond
Solomon, Vanessa
St. George, Anne
Stewart, Kevin
Sylvester, James
Sylvester, Peter
Szilaski, Ferenc
Szilaski, Joseph
Tobin, Jerry
Van Amburgh, Samuel
Van Winkle, Robert
Wood, Leonard
Wood, Nina

The Commission of Fine Arts

J. Carter Brown, Chrm.
Carolyn J. Deaver
Roy M. Goodman
Frederick E. Hart
Neil H. Porterfield
Pascal Regan
Diane Wolf
Joan Abrahamson
Adele Chatfield-Taylor
George E. Hartman
Jeannine Smith Clark
Robert A. Peck
Susan Porter Rose
Rex Ball
Carolyn Brody
Eden Rafshoon
Harry G. Robinson III
Charles Atherton

National Capital Planning Commission
Korean War Veterans Memorial Planning

Presidential Appointees

Melvyn J. Estrin

Dr. Thaddeus Garrett Jr.
Margaret G. Vanderhye

Mayoral Appointees

Dr. Patricia Elwood
Edward S. Grandis

Ex-Officio Members (Alternates)

John G. Parsons, Vice Chairman
Jerry R. Shiplett
Jack Finberg
David Colby
Robert E. Miller

Ex-Officio Members

Roland Gunn
Mark Eichler
Charlene Drew Jarvis
Albert G. Dobbins, III

Past Commission Members

Glen T. Urquhart
William E. Baumgaertner
W. Don MacGillivray
Robert J. Nash
John Belferman
Linda L. Eastman
Judith Friedman Binder
Dietra L. Ford
Fred L. Greene
Richard M. Hadsell
James C. Handley
Eric Jones
David S. Julyan
Steven N. Kleiman
Alvin R. McNeal
James Whittaker

Commission Staff

Robert H. Cosby
Maurice Foushee
Robert E. Gresham
Reginald W. Griffith
David L. Hamilton
Ronald E. Wilson

Former Staff

Linda Dodd-Major
Katherine Soffer

United States Department of the Interior

National Park Service, National Capital Region
Robert Stanton
John G. Parsons
Sally Blumenthal
Nancy Young
Gary Scott
Robert DeFeo
Sean McCabe
Arnold Goldstein
William I. Newman
Darwina Neal
Mark Clapp
Vicky McGraw
Glenn DeMarr
David Sherman
Sandra Alley
Richard Merryman
Earl Kittleman
Norbert Erickson

General Services Administration

James N. Barnard
Claude G. Bernier
William B. Owenby
Jeffrey M. Hysen

Special Events Staff

James Arthur, director
William White, deputy director
William Dodson
Jim Dodson
George Kemp
Randy Matthews
John Reid
Reginald Word

Arlington National Cemetery

Raymond J. Costanzo
John C. Metzler Jr.

Thurman Higginbotham

State Department Officials

United States Ambassadors to the ROK

1986-Present

James Lilley,1986-1989
Donald P. Gregg, 1989-1993
James T. Laney, 1993-Present

Assistant Secretaries of State For East Asia/Pacific

1986-Present

Gaston J. Sigur, 1986-1989
Richard H. Solomon, 1989-1992
William Clark, Jr., 1992-1993
Winston Lord, 1993-Present

Deputy Assistant Secretaries of State For East Asia/Pacific

1986-Present

William C. Sherman, 1985-1987
William Clark, Jr., 1987-1989
Desaix Anderson, 1989-1992
Lynn Pascoe, 1992-1993
Thomas P. Hubbard, 1993-Present

Directors, Office of Korean Affairs

1986-Present

David Blakemore, 1986-1987
Thomas P.H. Dunlop,

1987-1989
Spence Richardson, 1989-1991
Charles R. Kartman, 1991-1993
David E. Brown, 1993-Present

Deputy Directors, Office of Korean Affairs

1986-Present

Jack Gosnell, 1986-1988
Neil Silver, 1988-1990
Margaret McMillion, 1990-1991
Eugene Schmeil, 1991-1993
Lynn Turk, 1993-1994
Richard A. Christenson, 1994-Present

Korean War Veterans Association

Adams, Dick
Alexander, Richie
Avery, Warren
Benjamin, Emmett
Bradley, Bill
Bronfenbrenner, Michael
Burke, Scooter
Camp, Amos
Caulfield, Joe
Chilcott, Tom
Clark, Vernon
Coate, Richard
Coe, Bill
Comley, Guy
Coons, Harley
Dawson, Charles
Donnelly, Ray
Dube, Leonard
Edwards, John
Fletcher, Paul
Friedlander, Blaine
Gerst, Victor
Grygier, Ed
Hadden, Stan
Jett, Ira
Kenney, John
Maines, Tom

Melchor, Tim
Murphy, Jeff
Murray, Marci
Norris, William
Pappas, Nicholas
Patterson, Art
Pratt, Sherman
Reiner, Norbert
Roberts, Nole (dec.)
Scalf, Roger
Selmi, Lou
Smith, Billy
Smyers, Bill
Wainwright, Dick
Wallace, Harry
Worsham, Wes
Wyosnick, Kathleen

The Sentry Post

Nannos, J. Craig, GS PAARNG
Beauregard, Gary

Washington, Inc.

Gretchen Posten
J. Michael O'Connell III
Suzanne Orndorff
Jo Izzagurrie
John Paul Hansen
Mary Becker

World Travel Partners

Alexander, Jack
Caputo, Al
Cawley, Carolyn
Chisolm, Bruce
Fineken, Heide
Hartzer, Jonathan
Jones, Jerilyn
Learst, Brian
Mui, Juliana
Montgomery, Elizabeth
Steimart, Susan
Russo, Chris
Schumacher, Gary
Smith, Cary
Tambone, Victor
Tierney, Brian
Tutwiler, Margaret
Wang, Sherri
Winston, Chris
Yarosh, Mark

Veteran Organizations

100th Infantry Division Assoc.
101 Abn Div. Assoc. Upstate Council
101st Abn Div.
11th Airborne Division Assoc.
11th Ranger Co R.I.C.A.
129th Inf 44th Div Hqd Co. G
129th Inf Reg 44th Inf Div
13th Bomb Sq (Korea)
182nd Infantry Assn
187th Arct Assn Rakkasans
196th Lt Inf Bde
1st Cav Div 8th Cav Reg Med Comp
1st Cavalry Division Assoc.
1st F.O.B. Reunion
1st Marine Div Korea G-3-1
1st Marine Division Assoc.
23rd Infantry Regiment Korean War
24th Infantry Division Assoc.
24th Infantry Regiment Assoc.
25th Inf Div Assn
2nd (Indian Head) Div Assoc.
307th Infantry Vets Society Inc.
307th Replacement Depot Assoc.
3320 Correction & Rehab Squadron
3440th Participating Patriots
399th Ord Bn Lewis Viviani
3rd Marine Division Assoc.
40 & 8 Voiture
40th Div 223rd Regt Reunion Assoc.
44th Inf Div 129 Inf Rgt
45th Infantry Division Assoc.

4th Inf (Ivy) Div Assoc Florida Ch
505 Airborne Assoc. Of NJ, Inc.
532nd Eb And Sr
5th Comm Group Reunion Committee
6170th Sec. Police Br.
620 AAA Assoc.
C/O Louis Brown
720th Military Police Battalion
720th Mp Bn Reunion Assoc.
724th T.R.O.B. Veterans Korea
78th Div Leader
7th Cav, 1st Cav Div
7th Cavalry Korea
7th Cavalry Regiment
7th Infantry Division Assoc.
82d Airborne Div Assoc.
85th Gm Reunion Assoc.
883rd Maint, Co Ft Derussy
899th Association, Battery C
98th Bomb Group Veterans Assoc
A.F.A. Association
Air Force Sergeant's Assoc.
Allied Airborne Assoc
Alsaf Post No 167
Austin Hanscom
American Defense Preparedness Assoc
American Ex Prisoners Of War
American Gi Skyline Chapter
American Gold Star Mothers
American Legion
American Portuguese War Veterans A
American War Dads Aux Ch 1
American War Mothers
American Wheelchair Vets Assoc.
Army And Navy Union
Army Installation Detention Flty.

Assoc Of Ranger Inf Co's
Assoc Of Retired Members Of Armed
Assoc Of Sergeant Majors Usa
Assoc., Of U.S. Army
Assoc Women Marines
Auxilary To The Battle Born
Aviation Reconnaissance Assoc Inc.
C.C.R.O.A.
CA Division United Daughters of the Confederacy Cahokia
Cape Canaveral Ladies Aux 10131
Cape Cod Chapter Cpoa, Inc.
Catholic Chaplain Fund
Catholic War Veterans
Charging Charlie
Civil Affairs Association
Colorado Veterans Service Officers Assoc
D.A.R.
D.A.V.
Dads Of Foreign Service
Eastern P.V.A., Inc. Vets No 49
Delaware Veterans Inc Emblem Club
Ex-Pow Of Korean War Assoc
Fleet Reserve Association
Friendly Valley Veterans Club
Friends Of Veterans
Gold Star Wives Of America, Inc.
Italian American War Vets.
Jewish War Veterans
Korean Service Veterans Assoc.
Korean War Awareness Project
Korean War Veterans Assoc., Inc
Korean Women's Association Of

America
Korean-American Women's Club Of Sar
Korean-Vietnam War Mem, Onondaga C
Marine Corps League
Marine Korvets
Marlboro Veterans Council
Mil Order Of The Carabao
Mil Order Of The Cootie
Mil Order Of The Purple Heart
Mil Order Of The World Wars
Mothers And Wives Service Club
Mothers Of WWII Unit No. 7
Navy Club-Ship #1
Navy Mothers Club 700 La Puente
Navy Wives Clubs Of America #130
NCO Assoc Ch 646
NCO Basic Academy Augsburg
NCO Military Wives Club
Officers Wives Club
P.V.A. Assoc, Inc.
Polish Legion #13 Of Am, Vets
Polish Legion Of American Vet, Usa
Portland Group E 7-8-9 Club
Pow Committee Of Michigan
Pow/Mia Minnesota Won't Forget
Red Badge Of Courage, Inc.
Reserve Officer Assoc. Of The USA
Retired Officers Assoc.
Snet Vets
Society Of The 3rd Inf Div
Sons Of Italy Lodge No. 2054
St Leo Veterans
St Mary's Council No 2228
Third Marine Div

Assoc
Ties Of Honor
United Allied Veteran's & Aux Coun
United Daughter Of The Confed 2126
United Daughters Of The Confederacy
United Veterans Council
US Coast Guard Cpo Assoc Aux
USA Arrowhead Post 420 Ladies
USA Warrant Officer Asso., Berlin
USS *Arizona* Chapter #78
Vet Of The Vietnam War
Veteran Of Korean War
Veterans Action Committee
Veterans C.A.R.E.
Veterans Day Parade Assoc.
Veterans Helping Veterans, Inc
Veterans Home Minnesota
Veterans Home Missions
Veterans Insight Group
Veterans Interiors
Veterans Leadership Program Georgia
Veterans Of Lansingburgh
Veterans Reserve Operating Fund
Veterans Service Officers Assoc
Veterans, Delaware Inc.
VFW
Vietnam Combat Veterans Association
Vietnam Era Veterans Assoc Mass
Vietnam Vet Of Marquette County
Vietnam Veterans & Friends
Vietnam Veterans Delaware
Vietnam Veterans For

America
Vietnam Veterans
Greater Attleboro
Vietnam Veterans
Nevada
Vietnam Veterans Of
America
Vietnam Vets Nebraska Reunion
Vietnow
West Point Class Of
1948 USMA
Westerfield, Gordon
Western Spgs Mem
Post No 10778
Woman's Overseas
Service League
XII Corps Association
Yongsan, E9 Assoc

Contributions by Corporations

A. M. Pickus, Inc.
A.V. Lake Steel Co.,
Inc.
ABC Delivery, Inc.
Abell-Baker Electric,
Inc.
Abrams Foundation,
Inc.
Abrams Mercantile
Co/Florine Abrams
Abruzzi's Cafe 422,
Inc.
Accurate Screw
Machine Products
Ace Rubber Stamp &
Engraving, Inc.
Ace Service
Acorn Gas Co.
Addario & Associates
ADF Construction
Corp.
Adolph Coors Foundation
Advance Exploration
Co., Inc.
Advanced Laboratory
Associates, Inc.
Advanced Tech Sys/
Robert Hamilton
Advertising Partners,
Inc.
Air Line Pilots Assoc.
Int'l.
Air Renew Co. (FLA),

Inc.
Aircontrol Industries,
Inc.
Al Ames & Associates
Aladdin's Beauty Salon
Alameda Electric
Motors
Alco Metal & Supply,
Inc.
Alcon Leasing Corp.
Alex's Electric Service
Alexander &
Alexander
All American Sport
Shop
All Heads West
All Star Realty Corp.
All the Best Nutrition,
Anton, B.
Allegany Nursing
Home
Allen's Masonry
Allied Airborne Assoc.
Allied Business Brokers, Inc.
Allied-Signal Foundation, Inc.
Almasian Associates,
Inc.
Alpha 1, Inc.
Alpine Garage-The
Tackle Shop
Amavisca Jewelry
Repair, Inc.
Amelang Investment
Builders
American Chamber of
Commerce/Korea
American Cleaners of
Ill, Inc.
American Culinary
Supply Co.
American Defense
Prepredness Assoc.
American Engineer
Model Co.
American Historical
Foundation
American International
Group, Inc.
American Medical
Assoc.
American Refrigeration
American Travel
Center
Americares Foundation, Inc.

Amoco Corporation
Anco Tool and MFG
Co.
Ancom Industries, Inc.
Andrew Square Auto
Glass, Inc.
Andy's Short Shop
Anheuser-Busch, Inc.
Antrac Construction
Co.
Archer Daniele Midland Co.
Arden Communications
Armand's Beauty
Salon
Armed Forces Comm
& Elec Assoc.
Armed Forces Insurance
Armstrong
Chiropractic Clinic
Arnold & Porter/Mrs.
Sweenie
Arnold, J & J Co.
Arnolds Beauty
College
Arrow Advertising Co.
Arrow Marking
Service
Art's Auto Service
Associated Chemicals
Co.
Astro-Lite, Inc. D/B/A
Astrogold
ATA Travel Consultants, Inc.
Atlantic Coast Alarm,
Inc.
Atlantic Recording
Corp.
Atlantic Recruiters, Inc.
Atlantic Steel Works
Atlas Products, Inc.
Attorney Administrative Services
Atwood Security
Services, Inc.
Auto Vac, Inc.
Automation Aids, Inc.
Aux. Serv. and Hardware Supply Co.
Axios Foundation for
Worthiness
B & B Aviation
B & K Properties
B & W Oil Co.

B and A Enterprises
B & B Roofing &
Waterproofing Co.
B & D Construction
Back in '55, Inc.
Backer Spielvogel
Bates, Inc.
Bagwell's Office
Products
Baker's Auto Service
Bald Hill Nurseries,
Inc.
Baldwin, Porter &
Wheelock, Inc.
Bank of America/A.W.
Clausen
Barbara's Beauty Salon
Barken, Norman and
Assoc.
Barkleys Service Nova
Ent., Inc.
Barmazel Construction
Co.
Barr, Geoffrey/C/O A
Morgan & Assoc.
Barrel Drive-in
Barrett Assoc., Inc.
Barto Associates
Basf Corp., Chemicals
Div.
Bass River Rod & Gun
Club, Inc.
Bastian Adj. Co.
Battery C 899th Assoc.
Bauer, F C Company
Bay Area Services
Bay West Supply, Inc.
Bayouland Party Sales
Bayside Nursing
Center
Bear's Restaurant
Corp.
Beards' Timeshare
Rentals, Inc.
Beaufort Memorial
Hosp./Mrs. William
Beech Builders
Belford & Belford
Bell Industries, Inc.
Bell Advertising
Belles Lettres Club
Beltone Hearing Aid
Center
Beltone Hearing Aid
Service
Ben Franklin Coin
Club

Ben Mac Motors
Bender & Sons School Supply, Inc.
Benjamin Moore & Co.
Bensons Auto Machine Service
Ber Lou Associates
Bergen Brunswig Corp.
Bergen Passaic R.O.A.L. Club
Berkowitz, S & Associates
Bernard, Paul Associates
Bert Nelson's Tip Top Realty
Bessemer Property
Best & Bedvorek
Betac Corp.
Betac Corp./Earl F. Lockwood
Bethlehem Steel/ Walter F. Williams
Betsy Ross 4-H Club
Beverly Charitable Trust
Bewell Industries, Inc.
Bi-Rite Salvage Co.
Bicket Special Acct.
Big B Importing Co.
Bikoff, William C/O Wm. Bikoff Assoc.
Bill Beckus Towing Service
Bill Mader Co.
Bill McCracken Motors
Black Diamond Navy Club
Black Rock Restorations
Blackmer Mower Service, Inc.
Blackstone Valley Chapter #284
Blake Farms (Wayne Blake)
Blake Sheet Metal, Inc./B. Hetterich
Blakely Construction Co.
Blakely Excavating
Blish-Mize Co.
Bloomington Emblem Club #432
Blue Mountain Waves
Bob & John's Body Shop

Bob Levine Shoes, Inc.
Bob Marine's Crest Cleaners
Bob Petkin Land Co.
Bob's Custom Builders, Inc.
Bob's Cycle Sales, Inc.
Bobs Glass Shop
Boettcher & Co.
Bogart-Bullock Corporation
Bollinger & Co., Inc.
Bondsville Dairy Bar
Booker Associates, Inc.
Boris Insurance Agency
Boston Chem. Industries, Inc.
Braun Advertising, Inc.
Brennan Computer Systems, Inc.
Brewsaugh Dental Lab
Bridgeport Junior High Teachers Fund
Bridges Sportswear Terry Bridge
Broadbent's Scrap Metal
Broadview Active Disposal Ser., Inc.
Brock Candy Co.
Brock, Investments/ Stan Brock
Brooks, Lawrence A, Inc./Karl H. Brooks
Broward Medical Supply, Inc.
Brown Psychological Services
Brownsboro Center Animal Clinic
Bruce's Mower Service/Nolf, Bruce
Brunswick Foundation, Inc.
Bryda Day Realty
Bryla Construction
Bucci Furniture Co., Inc.
Buck Board Sales, Inc.
Buckeye Aero Supply
Buckeye Chapter
Bucks County Fur Products, Inc.
Buddys Hardware and General Merchadise
Bullick County Ins.

Burch Metal Fabricating
Burdick's Hatboro News Agency
Burge Publishing
Burger Consultants LTD, Inc.
Burle Industries, Inc., Co-workers
Burroughs Wellcome Co.
Bushman & Perras
Bushman, H R & Son Corp.
Butcher Van Gourmet Meats
Butler Associates
Butler Funeral Home
BWH Enterprises
C & B Enterprises, Inc.
C & L Sweeper Service
C & N Construction Co.
C & P Telephone
C & R Copr (DBA Joey Mac's)
C.H. Briggs Hardware Co.
C.L. Press Engineering
CMS Trucking Co.
C R Engineering, Inc.
CSL Assoc., Inc.
C T Systems
C.A.S. Maintenance
Cabanatuan POW Mem. Foundation, Inc.
Cal. West MGMT Group, Inc.
California Construction Co.
California Korea Bank
Calistra, Cal Corp.
Calvary Apostolic Church
Campbell Construction (Stephen O.)
Camperdown Company, Inc.
Capital City Enterprises
Capital Financial Planning
Capitol Polishing Co.
Capri Sales and Consulting, Inc.
Carey Ramsey
Carl F. Schmoyer

Funeral Home
Carlin Contracting Co., Inc.
Carlson Consultants & Photography
Carol Powers
Carole's Beauty Salon
Carolyn Oautreaux Insurance Co.
Carson, McBeath and Boswell, Inc.
Carter Drug Store, Inc.
Carters Used Cars
Casey's Automotive
Cassis Management Corp.
Catholic Chaplain Fund, Suwon Air
Cauble-Stone Tile
CBI Industries, Inc.
CDB Enterprises, Inc.
Centennial Sales
Center Advertising Agency
Center Apartments
Central City Trailer Park
Central Electric Co.
Central War Surplus, Inc.
Century Appraisal Bureau
Century Ford of Middletown, Inc.
Ceres Group
Chandler Ace Hardware
Charging Charlie Company Fund
Charles Auto Repair
Charles Fabricare Center
Charlie Cheddar, Inc.
Charlie's Siding
Cherry-Stone & Construction Co.
Chester Mental Health Center
Chesterfield Roofing & Siding Co.
Chestnut Log Store-Von Matthews
Chevron USA, Inc.
Chicks Auto Service
Childers Drilling, Inc.
Childs & Bishop Law Offices, Inc.

Chlorination Equipment Co.
Chris Posey Chevrolet Nissan, Inc.
Chrysler Corporation Fund
Chucks Television Engineers
Ciminelli Development Co., Inc.
Circle K Corporation
Citizens for Gold
Citywide Investment Co.
C.J. Hash & Assoc. KIA Ins. Assoc.
Clark Equipment Co.
Clark Tire & Auto Supply Co.
Clark, Clark & Clark Assoc., Inc.
Classic Accessories
Coast Hematology-Oncology Assoc.
Coastal Orthopaedics Assoc., PA
Cocoa Interstate Exxon
Cog Railway, Inc.
Cohassett Police Assoc.
Colfry Material Supply Co.
Collateral Loans, Inc.
Colonial Dames 17th Century Gibbs
Color, Etc., By Ellie
Columbus Foundation
Columbus Reproduction & Supply
Combined Federal Campaign-OA NVOCC
Community Foundation Eastern Shore, Inc.
Community Mental Health
Community Shopping Center #11
Conagra Charitable Foundation, Inc.
Connomac Corp.
Consolidated Graphic Foundation
Consolidated Supply Co.
Construction Midwest, Inc.
Construction Special-

ties, Inc.
Contractors Bookkeeping Service IC
Control Consultants & Assoc.
Control Data
Cooper, Lecky Architects, PC
Coopers & Lybrand
Coosa Valley Retired Officers Assoc.
Copeland Fastener Co.
Corey Charitable Foundation
Corning, Inc. Foundation
Corp. ERC International
Corp. VSE
CPO Wives Club of Port Hueneme
CRA Realty, Inc.
Cream City Lodge 1061
Crestar Bank
Crocker Lions Club
Croddy Machine & Engineering, Inc.
Croft, Inc.
Cromwell Logging Co.
Cross Nurseries, Inc.
Crown Coatings Company, Inc.
Cubic Corp.
Culligan Lincoln Mercury, Inc.
Custom Hearing Aid Systems, Jordan
Cypress International
D & S Janitorial Service
D A Construction Co.
D and R Distributers
D.L. Collins Insurance Agency
D & M Welding & Industrial Supplies
D.M. Auto Body
D.H. Johnson Co. Mason Contractors
D.S.A. Services
Daelim America, Inc.
Daewoo International (America) Corp.
Daily Monument Co.
Dale Sorensen Co., Inc.
Daly, C U JFK Library Foundation
Daubert Rentals

Daugherty & Associates
Dave Sawyer Associates
Daves Repair Service
Davis Construction
DBA Classic Wood Floors
D.C. Lang & Associates
De Lears Success Through Humaneeri
Dealers TV Service
Dean Automotive/Sawitskas Richard
Dee Pet Clinic
Deer Springs Water Co.
Del Grande Realty, Inc.
Delane's Beauty Corner/Reynolds L.
Delmarva Phone Co., Inc.
Deltons, Chocolates, Inc.
Deluxe Business Machines Co.
Denuzze CO Realtoro
Dept. of Corrections-Clements
Derochers Market
Desanty Sign Service
Design Service
Designs by Patricia/Kissell Pat
Devco Envelope Corp.
Devries and Associates
Diamond Development, Inc.
Dibello Landscapte Svc.
Dibert Valve & Fitting Co., Inc.
Dick Goplin Ins.
Dick-Mack Paving/Asphalt
Dickerson Motors
Diffee, Jim & Assoc.
Difilippo, Inc.
Dilgard Frozen Foods, Inc.
Dobro Dentures
Dodd Mini Storage (Mike Dodd)
Don Comer Ford, Inc.
Don Teffer Const. Corp.
Don-Lyn, Inc.

Donaldson Dental Service
Dong-A-Book Plaza
Dons Appliance Service
Doosan America Corporation
Dorel Steel Erection Corp.
Dorsey Insurance
Double L. Welding Service
Double T. Corporation
Doug Marcum Insurance Agency
Dover Jewelry & Broker, Inc.
Dowell Insurance Agency
Doylestown Podiatry Assoc.
Draeger Langendorf Funeral Home
Dramco/Nicholas D. Dramis
DSR, Inc.
Dun Well Services, Inc.
Duncan Farms
Duncan Ranch Mgmt. Co.
Duracell, Inc.
Duraclean Fabric Specialists
Duty & Duty
E M D & Associates
E.I. DuPont De Nemours & Co.
Eagle Scaffolding, Inc.
East Bay Roal Club
East Coast Lumber Company
East Haven Stoners Club
East Side Clinical Lab
Eastern Engineering Co.
Eastwind Management Corp.
ECI Employees Federal Credit Union
Ed Bertholet & Associates
Eddy Current International, Inc.
Eds Radio-TV Service
Educational & Indus, Communication

Edward F. McElroy
and Associates
Edward J. Ford Associates
Edwards Builders, Inc.
Edwards, A.G. & Sons,
Inc.
Edward D. Berger
Realty, Inc.
Elsenberg, Leo & Co.
Elderidge Enterprises,
Inc.
Electrologics, Inc./
Quinlin, Maggie
Eli Lilly & Co.
Elizabeth S Hooper
Foundation
Empire Machinery &
Supply Corp
Empire Office Equipment, Inc.
Empol Electric Service
Enkay Engineering &
Equipment Co.
Ergonomic Mgmt.
Systems, Inc.
Erin Communications/
Joe Garvey
Esch Construction
Supply, Inc.
Esma Chemicals, Inc.
Evans Publications
F & F Installations, Inc.
F & R Refrigeration
F.O.E. Lodge No. 376
Fabian Waterprofing,
Inc.
Factor's Walk Historical Comm, Inc.
Fairbanks N. Star Boro
Sch. Dist.
Fairfax Cty. Retired
Police Assoc.
Farrell Sales Assoc.
Farren Fuel Co., Inc.
Fairview Foods Co.
FDNY Retirees, Inc., SI
Div.
FEIP, Inc.
Federal Express
Fessenden Construction Co.
Fifth Third Bank
Fillman Insurance
Agency
Findalay Electric
Supply, Inc.

Fireside Forum Fund
First Federal Savings
First Financial Fiduciary Corp.
First National Bank of
St. Marys
First National Bank
Fisher Adjustment
Service
Fleury Funeral Homes,
Inc.
Floorcoverers Apprentice Fund
Florida Lubricants, Inc.
Florida Rock Industries, Inc.
Food Circus Super
Markets, Inc.
Forbes Foundation
Ford Motor Company
Fund
Forstner Fire Apparatus
Fort Mountain Carpets
Fort Rucker National
Bank
Foster, Larry Senior
NCO
Four Seasons Florist
Four Seasons Pool
Service
Fralic Fabricators, Inc.
Frank's Big & Tall
Men's Shop, Inc.
Frankie's Towing &
Storage
Franklin Mens Shop
Franklin Motel
Franklin Printing Co.,
Inc.
Franklin Tool & Die
Co.
Frederick Hotel,
Limited Partnership
Freund Tax Services,
Inc.
Friendly of Hudson
Valley, Inc.
Friends of Barbara
Haynes
Friends of Sheriff Tom
Higgins
Friends of Veterans
Frontier Mechanical,
Inc.
Frontier National
Corp.

Frydman Properties
Furrer Enterprises/
Turner, Larry D.
G A M Industries
G.O.S., Inc.
G.P.G. Advertising,
Photography
G.W. Longserre No. 7
GA Dept. of Corrections
Gage Real Estate
Gainesville Community Foundation
Gardner Funeral Home
Garners Associates
Gary Wilson Office
Supply
Gary's Yesteryears
Shop
Gasparini, Jim - Civic
Assoc.
Gateway Tele Communications, Inc.
Gavin and Associates
Geary Welding, Inc.
GELB Enterprises
General Business
Services
General Dynamics
General Electric
General Motors Corp/
Jim Johnston
Genesco, Inc.
Geneva Auto Body
Co., Inc.
Gentleman Jerry's Belle
Shoppe
George Stovall Agency
Gerard Enterprises
Gerrard Tire Co., Inc.
Gerweck Associates
LTD
Gift Market Assoc.
Gilford Builders &
Contractors
Ginn, Edington, Moore
& Wade
GJR Investments, Inc.
Gloria Merrill Enterprises, Inc.
Golden Bell USA Co,
Inc.
Golden Gate Services
Golden West Adjusting
Service
Goldstar Electronics
International

Goodrich Gas, Inc.
Goodyear Tire &
Rubber Corp.
Gould, Inc., Circuit
Protection Div.
Goyette Funeral Home
Granbury Bookkeeping
Service
Grand Voiture De New
York
Grande Voiture
D'Illinois
Granite State Detachment Marine Co.
Grants Pass High
School
Graph-ITTI Sportswear
& Spec C
Graphic Equipment
Co.
Great Dane Fanciers of
the North
Great Delicatessen
Extravaganza
Great Lakes Carbon
Corp.
Greene River Foundation, Inc.
Griffith Machinery and
Supply Co.
Grim Reaper Assoc.
Grim Reaper Assoc.
Vets
Group Enterprises LTD
Grumman Corp.
GSA Insurance Agency
Guarantee Auto Sales
Guardsman TV Radio
Service
Gurtner Metal & Build
Specialties
Guthrie Foundation
H&L Super Market,
Inc.
H & N Crafts and
Collectibles
H & N Packaging, Inc.
H & R Auto Radio
Service, Inc.
H and C Service Co.
Hahn Kook Center
(USA), Inc.
Hai Tai America, Inc.
Hal West Real Estate
Hallmark Mortgage
Co.
Hamilton Thrift Shop/

R. Thompson
Hanil Trading Corp.
Hanson Management Co.
Hanson Management Corp.
Har-Les Tool, Inc.
Harco Chemical Coatings, Inc.
Harmony Hall Chapter NSDAR
Harrison Public Relations
Hartman, Construction Co/J Hartman
Hawaii-Marina Investment Co.
Hawk Crest Farms, Inc.
Haywood Foundation, Inc.
Heath Crysler, Assoc.
Hellender Realty
Hellenic Club of North Shore
Heller, Morris (Able Heller Corp.)
Hempstead Lincoln-Mercury Motors
Hendricks, Harold Contracting Co.
Henry Bireline Co., Inc.
Henry Elden & Associates
Herb Gordon Nissan
Heritage Bank Tinley Park
Heritage Furniture Discount
Herman Pharmacy, Inc.
Hewitt Enterprised
Hexcel Chemical Products
Hi Desert Trophies
Hi-Tek Electronics, Inc.
Hiawatha Repair Service
Highlands Portage Dairy Queen
Hills Surplus
Hocking Correction Facility
Hogan Land Title Co.
Hohner Funeral Home
Hollywood Nursery
Holmes Transportation
Holt Products Co., Inc.

Home Federal Savings Bank
Home Health Care Co.
Home Interiors & Gifts, Inc.
Homes Consulting LTD
Hon Company
Hooyman Surveying Associates
Horiba Instruments, Inc.
Hotel & Theatre Contractors, Inc.
Houk Consulting Co., Inc.
House of Treasures, Inc.
Houston Aeronautics, Inc.
Hub Construction Specialties, Inc.
Hughes Aircraft Co/M D Merritt
Hughes, Jay E Real Estate
Humboldt Republican Women
Hunter Chiropractic Offices
Hutchinson Corporation
Hyosung (America), Inc.
Hyundai Arrow, Inc.
Hyundai Auto West, Inc.
Hyundai Bailey
Hyundai Bill Watson, Inc.
Hyundai Blume, W.B.
Hyundai Bob Frink Mgmt., Inc.
Hyundai Bob Lee
Hyundai Bower Buick/Peugeot, Inc.
Hyundai Buena Park
Hyundai Burns, John
Hyundai Caldrello, Joseph M.
Hyundai Case, Rita
Hyundai Cavalier
Hyundai Center
Hyundai Central
Hyundai Cerritos
Hyundai Checkered Flag

Hyundai Chuhinko, John F.
Hyundai Coggin Jr., Luther
Hyundai Cormier
Hyundai Courtesy, Inc.
Hyundai Crabtree, Inc.
Hyundai Difeo, Inc.
Hyundai Drew
Hyundai Duval
Hyundai East
Hyundai Ed Voyles
Hyundai Eleazer Jr., L.E.
Hyundai Escondido
Hyundai Fairfax
Hyundai Forsyth
Hyundai Fox
Hyundai Frank
Hyundai Gaillard, George E.
Hyundai Globe Auto Imports
Hyundai Goldenberg, James Mr.
Hyundai Harbour
Hyundai Henry Buth
Hyundai Henry Butts, Inc.
Hyundai Herb Chambers
Hyundai Holmes Tuttle
Hyundai Huntington, Inc.
Hyundai Jimmy Bryan Hyundai, Inc.
Hyundai Joe Bullard
Hyundai Key
Hyundai Kim-Hankey (Richard Kim)
Hyundai King, Inc.
Hyundai Lane LTD
Hyundai Lange
Hyundai Lapointe
Hyundai Larry H. Miller
Hyundai Lee, Inc.
Hyundai Lehman Dealership Entrp.
Hyundai Levis, Robert
Hyundai Loren Buick, Inc.
Hyundai Lou Grubb
Hyundai Manhattan
Hyundai McDermott
Hyundai McDonald,

James F.
Hyundai Menard
Hyundai Mesquite
Hyundai Metro
Hyundai Mid-Atlantic Cars, Inc.
Hyundai Modern Motors
Hyundai Motor America
Hyundai Naversen, Robert H.
Hyundai Neesen, Dennis R.
Hyundai Nison Oldsmobile
Hyundai North Park
Hyundai Northstar Auto, Inc.
Hyundai Norwood, Inc.
Hyundai Olympic Oldsmobile G.M.C.
Hyundai One More
Hyundai-Little Rock
Hyundai Osborn, Gene
Hyundai Palm, Inc.
Hyundai Parkway, Inc.
Hyundai Pierre, James P.
Hyundai Pohanka, Inc.
Hyundai Potamkin, Inc.
Hyundai R.C. Hill's of Daytona
Hyundai Reed IV, James H.
Hyundai Rice-Marko
Hyundai Ridge Motors
Hyundai Ristuccia, Joel M.
Hyundai Riverdale
Hyundai Santa Monica
Hyundai Savage, Inc.
Hyundai Schlanger, Harold
Hyundai Scottsdale
Hyundai Serra, Anthony F.
Hyundai Sewell
Hyundai Silver City, Inc.
Hyundai Singer, Paul
Hyundai Smyly, Inc.
Hyundai Snider, Blake
Hyundai South Blvd.
Hyundai Steen, Tho-

mas
Hyundai Stevens
Creek
Hyundai Stillman, W.
Robert
Hyundai Sun Valley
Ford
Hyundai Tate, Inc.
Hyundai Torrance
Hyundai Twin City,
Inc.
Hyundai Vann York,
Inc.
I L Special Activity
Fund Committee
I.M. Jarrett & Son, Inc.
IBM Corp.
Impey's Sewing
Machine Service
Independent Industries
& Supply
Indiana Bell
Industrial Glove
Cleaning Co.
Infotax, Inc.
Inland Industrial Elec.
Suc. Co.
Inland Packaging, Inc.
Inn Towner Motel
Insulation Supply
Industries
Int. Brotherhood of
Boiler Makers
Inter State Services
Interactive Business
Systems Inc.
International Assoc. of
Machinsts
International Business
Machines
International Direct
Response, Inc.
International Mgmt.
Systems, Inc.
Interstate Realty and
Investment
Intl. Business Machines
Corp.
Intuitive Intelligence
Application
Irwin Fischman & Co/
CPA
ISAT Inc.
Istivan and Michelini
Attnys.
Italian Food Shoppe
Inc.

J & L Special
J & J Metals
J. Chew and Company
J.F. Cronin and Sons
J.J. Shea Associates,
Inc.
J. Orbel Investments
J.S. Perlman & Co.
J. Stuart Brand Co.
J. Sullivan, Associates
J&R Glaziers, Glass
and Mirrors
J.B. Cart Return
Service, Inc.
J.R. Tree Company,
Inc.
J.A.W.D. Associates,
Inc.
Jack Brauer Excavating
Co.
Jack's Pour House, Inc.
Jaeck, W.C.
James D. Flood Assoc.
James Photo Art/
RHACO Advertising
James Robinson Co.
Japan International P O
Jay Silverman, Inc.
Jay-Rae Enterprises
JDG Financial Services
Inc.
JEONG-EUM Book
Center
Jersey Hose Fire Co.
Jim Thomas Motors,
Inc.
Joe Goldsmith Con-
struction, Inc.
Joe Helzer Construc-
tion
Joe Shafran Enter-
prises, LTD
John Croft Lumber
Inspection
John G. Reutter Assoc.
John McKittrick
Contracting, Inc.
John's Auto Sales, Inc.
Johnson & Higgins
Johnstown Junior High
School
Johnstown Regional
Central Labor C.
Johson & Higgins of
Michigan, Inc.
Jolly 050 Club C/O M.
Stevens

Jonathan Ross Search
Consultants
Jonowika Realty Corp.
Joseph E. Seagram &
Sons, Inc.
Judd Chiropractic
Corp.
Jung-Parks Ent., Inc.
JV Bookkeeping and
Tax Service
K & E Associates
K and L Associates
K.C. Jones Insurance
Agency
K.A.C.C.
K.A.G.W.
Kamrath, Richard H.
Kauszler's Do-it Center
Kazsu Wire Stitcher
Service, Inc.
Keller, Paul
Kelley's Circle
Kelln, Albert Alkcon,
Inc.
Kelly Refinishing, Inc.
Ken Dor Enterprises,
Inc.
Ken Self & Assoc., LTD
Ken-Way Corp./Keith
Kenyon
Kenner, J.D. and
Associates
Kerlin Enterprises, Inc.
Kerr Mac's Inc. (DBA
Roslindale)
Key, Kendreck W.
KIH Investment Group
Kihekah Steh Club
Killarney Estates
Kims Chesapeake
Motel Corp.
King Construction
King Copeland Co.
Kinsinger, Dorothy
Kirby Co. of Denver,
Inc.
Klamath Cold Storage,
Inc.
Klebba, Joseph A.
Kless Construction
Klotz Agency, Inc.
Knollcroft Social &
Athletic Club
Kobara, S & Sons
Koissian Ins. Agency
Kollman, K.R. Capt.
Koram Insurance

Center
Kruske's Floor Ser-
vice/Richard T.
Kuehnert, Donald
Kumnam Corp.
Kumpf & Associates
Kuppinger, John R.
Kurth, Bob & Assoc.
Kwik Kopy Corp.
Kwik-Kopy Printing
No. 980
Kyser III, James G.
Assn. Mgr.
L B & M Associates,
Inc.
L.B. Foster Co.
L.E. Walz & Assoc.,
Inc./Walz, Louis
L&L Camera, Inc.
L.A. Music Co., Inc.
Lakeport Resort/
Watkins, Goldie
Lakeside Distributing
Corp.
Lakeville Wines &
Liquors, Inc.
Lakewood Pediatrics
Laser Surgical Systems
Laurentian Athletic
Club
Lawson, Robert M.,
Inc.
Lazar, Jacob No. 418
Leadership Training
Svcs., Inc.
League of Korean
Americans - LOKA
Leavens, R.J. Medical
Corps USA RET
Lebanon Dairy Queen
Lebanon Paint and
Wallpaper Co.
Lee-Fran Painting
Contractors
Lekas & Associates,
Inc.
Leo Burnett Co., Inc.
Leroy's Flowers &
Gifts, Inc.
Lestan Inc. DBA
Foremost Liquor
Letlow & Associates
Liberty Parlor No. 213
N.D.G.W.
Liberty Printing
Liberty Trophies
Lindenbaum Reality

Co.
List Excavating, Inc.
Lite Trol Service Co., Inc.
Little Transfer & Storage Inc.
Litton Industries/ Orion L. Hoch
Local No. 2210 UAW
Longshoremen's Memorial Assoc.
Longwood Buick Co., Inc.
Loose Change Investments, Inc.
Lou Nathan & Assoc.
Love Universal Sales
Lucy Mcniece Bull Agency, Inc.
Luzerne Assoc. of Senior Citizens
Lydig Construction, Inc.
M & M Investigations
M.J. Kelly Sales/ Marketing Co.
M K Engineering
M. Schepps Co.
M V & Son Masonry MacDonald, Inc.
MacGregor Assoc. Corp.
MacKeown & Assoc.
MaClennan, J.A.
Magee Enterprises
Maggiacomo Pharmacy, Inc.
Maggies, Pub., Inc.
Magyar Savings Bank SLA
Mahrco Industries, LTD
Mahwah BPO Elks No. 1941
Maine, John
Majestic Carpets, Inc.
Major Realty Inc.
Mallard Medical Bridgeview House
Mallinckrodt
Manley Company Realtors
Manning Truck Modification, Inc.
Manpower Temporary Services
Manton Trading Corp.

Maple Park Properties, Inc.
Mar Dek Realty
Mardian Development Co.
Marietta Automotive Warehouse, Inc.
Marker, Patrick C.
Marketin Resource Concepts, Inc.
Marketing Management Assoc.
Marlboro Veterans Council
Marshall Electronics Services, Inc.
Marshall, Properties, Inc.
Martin Marietta
Martin, Eunice Beauty Shop
Mason, Marton I.
Maxwell D. Taylor Chapter
May's Frederick Hardware Inc.
May, Evelyn
Mayer's Citgo Service
McCurry, Ann M.
McDonnell & McDonnell
McGinnis Oil
McKee Central Agency
McBride & Son Home Services
McCaffrey Insurance Agency
McCaleb Tool Supply, Inc/McCaleb
McCrosky Brotherly Service
McDonnell Douglas Doug Jacobsen
McDowell & Son's Excavating, Inc.
McGahn/Friss/Miller/ Pat McGahn
McGloin Buick, Inc.
McKelvie, C. Ross Ins. Agency
McLeod County Voiture 414 (40 & 8)
McNally Supply, Inc.
McNamee International Services
McNulty, Patrick J.
MDM Financial

Services
MEAD Corp/Sydney Hawkes
Medical Center Pharmacy
Memorial OBS & GYN Medical Group
Merced Central Labor Council
Merchants Park KWIK Kopy, Inc.
Michigan Trenching Service, Inc.
Middle Pennsylvania Chapter
Midway Packaging, Inc.
Miles Rankin Realtor, Inc.
Miller, Ferree & Assoc.
Miller, John E.
Miller-Norris Company, Inc.
Minchey's Shell Service Station
Mine Safety Appliances Company
Minuteman Press
Minuteman Press of Countryside
Mission Helpers of the Sacred Heart
Mitchell, Jim Honorable
MNTNCE, & Erection Machinists #166
Mobil Administrative Services Comp.
Modern Clerical Management
Modern Graphics, Inc.
Modern Sales
Mollo, Salvatore
Monforton, Edward E. Mrs.
Mongello Assoc.
Morales, Antonio Berrios
Morgan, Frederick L. CDR USN (RET)
Morgan, Paul E.
Morita, Claude G. USAPSC-H Unit 2
Morollo-Brown Assoc.
Mortie's Electric Service
Mother Nature Garden

Center
Mothers and Wives Service Club
Mothers of WWII Unit #7
Mountain View Realty, Inc.
Mr. Floppy Discount Computers, Inc.
MRC Computer Corp. (Morton Crandall)
Mulkerin Milk Distributors
Munce Motor Works
Muraik, Peter
Murkey, M. F. Maj. USMCR (RET)
Murray Conveyor Service Wm. Murray
Musslewhite Co.
Mutual of Omaha
Myerson, David J.
N. American Philips Corp/T. Patton
N.A.C.
N.A.L.C., Branch 1152
N/A
Namkung Promotions
National Assoc. of Senior Travel, Inc.
National Assoc. Civil. Conservation
National Data Mart
National Fitness Council, TX Dist.
National Home Products, Inc.
National Labor Services, Inc.
National Soft Drink Assoc. Foundation
National Starch & Chemcial Foundation
Nationwide Credit Corp. of VA
Navy Club-Ship #1
Navy Mothers Club 700 La Puente
NCO Basic Acadamy Augsburg
Nebraska Vietnam Vets Reunion
Nelson Drug and Photo, Inc.
Nelson, Bert Assoc.
New Providence Development Corp.

New York Times
Newport Heights
Memorial
Newport Lodge No.
2155
Newport News
Shipbldg./E.J.
Campbell
Newsletter Services,
Inc.
Niagara Printing Corp.
Nicholas Communica-
tions Inc.
Nick Tile Co.
NJ State Corrections
CTL #215
NKT Travel
No, Phillip "Scheffler's
Liquor St.
Nokomis Shoe Shop
Inc.
Nolan & Co.
Nor Tex Environmen-
tal Systems
Norco Container, Inc.
Norcross Medical
Clinic PC
Norgus Silk Screen Co.,
Inc.
Norman P. Rappaport
Foundation, Inc.
North American
Manufacturing Co.
North End Cafe &
Restaurant In
North End Plumbing
Inc.
Northside Improve-
ment League, Inc.
Northeast GA Adjust-
ment Service, Inc.
Northrop Corp.
Matthews, Bobby
Northville Rotary Club
Northwest Nursery &
Garden Ctr.
Nova Techno Corp.
Novak Realty, Inc.
Novak's Inc.
NYNEX/Peter C.
Czekanski
NYS Higher Education
Services Corp.
O'Rourke & Associ-
ates, Inc.
OBC, Inc.
Ocean Palms Condo-

minium Assoc., Inc.
Ocean Realty Co.
Odenton 55+ Club
Officers Wives Club Ft.
Snelling
Officers Wives Club of
Ft. Benning
Olsen Insurance
Agency
Olympic Luggage Co.
Onyx Packaging Corp.
Opthamology Consult-
ants, P.A.
Oriental Building
Maintenance
Original Boosters Club
ORO Construction, Inc.
Oste Auto Wholesale,
Inc.
OTRA, Inc.
Overman & Son Crane
Service
P & R Auto Supply,
Inc.
PA Collection & Adjust
Service, Inc.
Pacific International
Packaging Corporation
of America
Packard Electric
Employees Dept.
Pagano Service Station
Palmer Apts.
(McDermott Flea Mkt.)
Palmetto Investment
Club
Pamplin Foundation
PAR, Inc.
Paramount Guns Disc.
County
Park & Associates, S.C.
Park Propterty
Parkville Texaco
Parsons Tudor Engi-
neering Co.
Partee IOL Co.
Patony's Pizza, Inc.
Patrick and Watson,
Attorneys at Law
Paul Construction Co.
Pauls Deli, Inc.
PEF Division #190
Pennco Mortgage
Services Corp.
Pennsylvania Book
Center, Inc.
Pennsylvania Supply &

Mfg. Co.
Pennzoil Company
Peoria Plaza Tire, Inc.
Peoria Rug & Carpet
Cleaners
Peoria Savings & Loan
Pepco
Perillo & Sons, Candy
Distr. Inc.
Perry Personnel Plus,
Inc.
Pharmacy, Inc.
Philip Morris, Inc.
Phillips, James S/USG
Corp.
Photocopier Distribu-
tors, Inc.
Physical Therapy
Service/Palmer, B.
Pickwick Tree Service
Pilot Club of
Booneville, Inc.
Pilot Metal Fabricators,
Inc.
Pimco, Inc.
Pinellas Adjustment
Bureau
Pittsburgh Accounting
Services
Plantations Seed &
Supply Co.
Pleasure Ridge Park
Office Supply
Pohang Steel America,
Inc.
Pohang Steel America,
Inc./Mr. Park
Polish National Union
of America
Polk Bros. Foundation
Porterville Bookkeep-
ing Service
Portland Group E 7-8-9
Club
Power Transmission
Specialties, Inc.
Preferred Electric, Inc.
Premier Lighting &
Electric Supply
Prestige Capital Corp.
Princopol Consulting
Privac, Inc.
Pro-Specs American
Corp.
Professional Billing &
Mailing Ser.
Professional Courier

Network
Professional Manage-
ment Consulting
Professional Services
International
Programs Unlimited,
Inc.
Progressive Packaging
Sales
Protestant Chaplain
Funds Korea
Pub Bar & Liquor, Inc.
Public Employees Fed.
AFL-CIO
Pugliese, R. & Co., Inc.
Pullin's Custom
Processing
Quality Fuel and
Transportation
Quality Products Mfg.
Co.
Quality Sprayers, Inc.
Quantum Chemical
Corp.
Queensbury Faculty
Assoc.
Questech, Inc.
Quiet Ones
Qunicy Raceways, Inc.
R & H Cycle Sales &
Service
R & J Exterminating
Co.
R.E. Mann General
Agency
R.G. Brown Properties,
Inc.
R.J. Russell Insurance
Agency
R.R.B. Enterprises
R.W. Joyce Co., Inc.
R.W. Kehn Assoc., Inc.
R&B Liquors II, Inc.
R&R Visual Produc-
tions
R.E.O. Services
R.O. Smith Assoc.
R.J.B. Management
Corp.
R.V. Storage Co/Jones,
Norman E.
RAIA Enterprises Inc.
Raleigh Durham ROAL
Club
Ram Appliance Service
(Buckley)
Randel Lock Service

Raymond Keyes Assoc.
Readers Digest Assoc/
Skip McCarthy
Readers Digest Assoc.,
Inc.
Reagan, Ronald C/L
Roy D. Miller
Red Badge of Courage,
Inc.
Reda Pharmacy LTD
Redmon, B.G. & Assoc.
Redwood Ampire
Chap Ret. Ofc. Assoc.
Reed, John M. Consult-
ants in Pub. Re.
Reese Associates, Inc.
Regional Chem. Labs,
Inc.
Reliable Networking,
Inc.
Rem Office Systems,
Inc.
Renneker, Tichansky &
Assoc., Inc.
Republic Realty Co.
Research and Consult-
ants Intl.
Retail Systems Con-
sulting
Retired Servicemen's
Club
Rhee, Jhoon
Rheuban, Robert &
Assoc.
Rhodes & Gardner, Inc.
Rich's Lawn Service
North
Richardson & Com-
pany
Richwood Food
Market
Ridgeview Homes, Inc.
Ridgewood Council
#1814
Rinehimer Bus Lines,
Inc.
Rival Automotive
Products, Inc.
Robert, Norman &
Associates
Robinson Printing
Service
Rockwell Inter/Evelyn
Labriola
Rockwell International
Rockwell, Bebe
Rogers, F.A. Invest-

ment Account
Roland's Appliance
Service
Roll Flex Label Co.
Roman Gardens Cafe
Corp.
Ron Wolfe Sales
Agency
Ronald, Reagan C/O
Roy Miller
Roofers Union Local 33
Roseau Deputy Regis-
trar, Inc.
Ross, AL Inc. Sales
Mfg. Agents
Ross, George S. Enter-
prises, Inc.
Roswell Mills, Inc.
Rotary Club of
Marysville
Rotary Club of
Watchung
Roth-Paris Marketing,
Inc.
Rowland, Specialty/
R.E.G. Porter
Royalties Unlimited,
Inc.
RRF Industries, Inc.
Rubber Workers Local
307 Fed. Cred.
Russell's 5th Avenue,
Inc.
Ryan Advertising Co.
S. Boston Liquor Mart,
Inc.
S&K/Air Power Tool
& Supply Corp.
S. Jacoby & Associates
Sabella's Pool Service
Sadka Realty Co.
SAES Student Activity
(Elem. School)
Saginaw Maintenance
Co. Inc.
Saint Dismas Founda-
tion
Salyers Insurance
Agency
Sammi-Al Tech, Inc.
Samsung America, Inc.
San-Mar Laboratories,
Inc.
Sanders, A. Lockheed
Co.
Santa Paula Little
League

Sartain Law Offices
Sauk Trail Gun Collec-
tors Assoc.
Sauter, John C.
Agency, Inc.
SBS Associates, Inc.
Schamu, Machowski,
DOO & Associate
Scott Paper Co. Foun-
dation
Se Jong Corp.
Sea Lane Seafood Sales
Seal Products
Seaside Ventures, Inc.
Sebring Professional
Second Stage Enter-
prises
Security Electric, Inc.
Security Plastics, Inc.
Seitz, Peter & Assoc.,
Inc.
Sellers-Sexton, Inc.
Seminole Post #111
Service & Reliability
Industrial
Service Employees
International
Severson Oil Company
Shane Security Service,
Inc.
Shannon Equipment &
Supply Co., Inc.
Sharon Womens Club
Shaughnessy-Kniep-
Hawe Paper Co.
Shepard and Associ-
ates
Shepherd Foundation,
Inc.
Sherman Media Co.,
Inc.
Shindong California
Corp.
Shinn Business Forms,
Inc.
Show America Inc.
Showcase Signs, Inc.
Sidney Baritz Founda-
tion, Inc.
Siegel Properties
Management
Sikes Tile Distributors,
Inc.
Sil-Med Corp.
Silver Spur Realty
Silvey Corp.
Simmons Industries,

Inc.
Simpson Electric
Simpsons Indian
Room, Inc.
Singleton, Inc.
Ski Carpentry Con-
tracting
Skip's Service Station,
Wilson
Smith and Ogle
Funeral Home, Inc.
Smith Steel Workers
Smyrna Surf Shack,
Inc.
Snively, Harold H.
Foundation, Inc.
So. Harriman Middle
School Service Club
Society of Jesus C/O
McBride, John
Solid State Electronics
Somerset County
Executive Committee
Sone Star Brush Co.
South Auburn Grange
#1188
South Farmingdale
Fire Dept.
Southside Trust &
Savings Bank
Southwest, Poultry
Supply
Space Sales, Inc.
Spacer Connection
Sparks Insurance, Inc.
Speck, Wilbur & Senn
Co., LPA
Spreckelmeyer, Kent F.
Assoc. Prof.
Springbrook Fire Co.,
Inc.
Sprock, Richard M.
Agency
Square Club of Dela-
ware Valley
SSangyong (USA), Inc.
St. Lawrence Council
#2458
St. Leo Veterans
St. Mary's Council
#2228
Staff Directories
Stagecoach Antiques
Stan Young Television
Services
Standex International
Foundation

Stanley C. Miller Ins.
Star Market Co.
State Correctional Institution
State of AZ Dept. of Corrections
State of California
Stateline Pipeline Corp.
Stauffer Sales & Service
Steel Exchange, Inc.
Stockton Insurance Agency
Story Engineering Co.
STS
Sudi-Bee Enterprises
Suffolk Management Group
Summit County Tool Rental, Inc.
Sun Company Inc./ Thomas L. Wylie
Sunbelt Advertising Services
Sunyong America, Inc.
Sunrise Detachment Marine Corps
Sure-Fine Foods, Inc.
Surovec and Associates
Sussen Foundation, Inc.
SW Industries, Inc.
SY Prevulsky Assoc.
Systems Repair Service Co., Inc.
Systems Research and Applications
T&S Welding and Fabricating
T&T Enterprises
T-Lee Enterprises
T.A.K. Inc.
T.R.W. Foundation
Tactical & Estate Security
Tadlock Realtors
Taylor Insurance Agency
Telemark, Inc.
Temperature Control, Inc.
Terry, David T. Development Co.
Thaler Engineering Co.
The Alabama Gun Collectors Assoc.
The Associates
The Boeing Company/

Jim Kanouse
The Buchanan Co.
The Buffalo News
The Buyer's Connection, Inc.
The Circle K Corp.
The Coca-Cola Co.
The Committee to Elect Jack Wagner
The Donalen Group, Inc.
The Equitable Foundation
The F.D. Lawrence Electric Co.
The Gavin Group
The Henley League
The Higley Co.
The Irwin Agency 22
The Korean Federal Credit Union
The Krasnow Foundation
The Land Service Co.
The Lerner Organization, Inc.
The Minner Co.
The Morris Plan Co. of California
The National Bank of Washington
The Norman Enterprises
The Ohrstrom Foundation, Inc.
The Overlooked Cartridge Co.
The Ponagansett Foundation, Inc.
The Swig Foundation
The Times Journal Co.
The W.R. Wynkoop Co.
Thirteenth Bomb Sq. (Korea) Reunion
Thompson Service Agency/Henry, D.M.
Thompson Tank and Mfg. Co., Inc.
Thompson, Ray Trucking Co., Inc.
Three Score Club
Thurmond, Strom Senator
Tibbs Bros. Inc.
Ticor Title Ins./Paulus, Edward

Tidewater Realty, Inc.
Tieger Realty Co., Inc.
Ties of Honor
Tinley Automotive, Inc.
TMC Escrow Co.
Tobiason, Inc.
Tom Smith Plumbing Co.
Tom's Aircraft Service
Tommy Mackall Post 5647
Tomorrow's Talent Today, Inc.
Toomey Insurance Agency
Topham Management Services, Inc.
Topp Foundation, Inc.
Town & Country Women's Club
Town of East Hartford
Transwestern Services
Travel, Insurance Programs Corp.
Travelers Delivery Service
Treasure Coast
Trebesch & Associates, Inc.
Tri-Angle Sheet Metal Co.
Triborough Cleaning Industries, Inc.
Trieschmann Foundation
Tristate Industrial Lubricant
Trojan Chemical Equipment Co.
Tropic Oil Co.
Tropicana Club
Tru-Pals Pet Supplies, Inc.
Tryon Uniforms, Inc.
Tsakonas, POH and Co.
Tunnel Electric Construction Co.
U.S. Treasury
U.S. West Foundation
UFCW, Local 1445
Undercar, Inc.
Uniglobe The Travel Connection, Inc.
Union County Church Fed Bowling

Unisys Corp./Bobby Trent
Unisys Corp.
United Daughter of the Confed 2126
United Daughters of the Confederacy
United Jersey Bank
United Parcel Service
United Services Life Ins. Co.
United States Automobile Assoc.
United Technolgies
United Vets Council of Greater ALB
Univar Corp.
Universal Leaf Foundation
Universal Life Church Rev. Wm. Parr
Urologic Medical Group of Long Beach
U.S. Beet Sugar Assoc.
U.S. Cane Sugar Refiners Assoc.
U.S. Coast Guard CPO Assoc. Aux.
USS Arizona Chapter #78
V V Data, Inc.
Vac RO & Ins.
Vajentic Flooring Co., Inc.
Valis Assoc.
Valley Accounting Service
Valley Distributors, Inc.
Valley Springs Mobile Home Area
Valley Veterinary Service
Van Den Eng. Realty, Inc.
Variety Knit Corp.
Vartkess Tarbassian
Venango Machine Products, Inc.
Vererans Cable Service, Inc.
Veterans Assoc. Inc.
Vets Living & Health, Inc.
Victor Knitwear Co., Inc.
Viking Machinery

Sales
Viking Machinery Sales, Inc.
Virginia Beach Detachment
Vogel Insurance Agency
W.H. Daniel Supply Co.
W.J. Enterprises
W.J. Lougheed and Associates
Wagner, Phyllis Deluxe Corp.
Waikiki Resort Hotel
Walgreen Co.
Walker Co.'s
Walker Enterprises, Inc.
Walnut Street Cafe
Walsenburg Club
Walsh, John P., R & Jarvis Co.
Walter Burger Building Contractor
Warner, Volney F. & Associates
Washington Golf Center/C. Chay
Washington Seoul Women's Club
Washington Soldiers

Home
Watauga Hospital, Inc.
Watervliet Arsenal Directorate
Watkins Insurance Agency
Wayne Bolt & Nut Co.
Wearly Monument Co./Daniel
Weatherford Co., Inc.
Weems Produce Co.
Welcome Corp.
Welcome Lodge No. 829 F&AM
Weldon C. Harris & Assoc.
Wells Fargo Bank
Welty Enterprises
West Point Class of 1948 USMA
West Productions
West Side Beer Distributing
West Virginia Postal Employees
Western Auto Clearance
Western Corridor District
Western Insulation
Western Leasystems
Western Spgs. Mem.

Post No. 10778
Westport Glass & Paint Co.
Whats Your Sign, Inc.
Whelply's Real Estate
Whisler Construction Co./Lillian E.
White Hills Vol. Fire Co. #5
Whitford Construction Co.
Wholesale Auto Brokers, Inc.
Wig and Variety Hong Kong
Wilkinson Leasing, Inc.
William J. Beal Post No. 466
William J. Cole Real Estate, Inc.
William S. Frank and Assoc.
Williams Brothers Grocery Co.
Williston Park Day Chapter
Willoughby EXXon (Wyung K. Lee)
Wilson Supply
Wilson's Home Center
Windows Perfect
Witmer & Assoc.

Wm. Wright Investment Account
Women's Overseas Service League
Wood Engineering, Inc.
Wood, John E. Enterprises
Woodlawn Memorium
Woodlie Assoc.
Woodline Inc.
World Employment Service
Worrel Exploration Inc.
Worthy Co.
Wright Assoc.
Wynett Resumes, Inc.
Wyoming Militia Historical Society
XII Corps Assoc.
Yellow Cab Co. of Sacramento
Youngsan, E9 Assoc.
Yorkshire Management Co.
Younghwa Co. Inc.
Youngstrom Electrical Co.
Zehfuss, William R. & Assoc.
Zel Realty, Inc.

Epilogue
by Col. William E. Weber, USA (Ret)

So it is that "The Forgotten War" has come full circle! No longer is it destined to remain in the back pages of history, buried in the subconscious of a people, or to be denied full credit for that which is the legacy given to the cause of world peace.

A war we did not seek and yet one it is well we did not avoid. A war fought not to preserve our nation but rather a nation then lying outside the periphery of our sphere of interest. A war that changed the course of history of the world. A war, not to end all wars, but instead, a precursor of what the future would bring if the message of our resolve was not demonstrated and understood.

Still, it is within the bounds of logic to accept why, at the time, the war was deemed insignificant, worthy of being forgotten. No definitive victory was discernible. No grand purpose seemed apparent and, no concrete results obtained.

Absent the crusade mentality of previous wars, it was ordained that Korea would be shunted to a sidetrack of awareness. So too were those who sacrificed in, succumbed to, or survived the war that was neither declared nor remembered.

In his closing of "All Quiet on the Western Front," Erich Maria Remarque said, "And men will not understand us- for the generation that grew up before us, though it has passed these years with us here, already had a home and a calling: now it will return to its old occupations, and the war will be forgotten- and the generation that has grown up after us will be strange to us and push us aside."

So it was! But, so it is not now! The generation that followed us suffered a too well remembered war, no less bravely fought, but to the same extent that Korea was ignored, Vietnam was vilified. The Korean veteran returned and found a nation displaying apathy over what they had attempted; the Vietnam veteran returned to a nation appalled at what they had attempted.

A decade passed before the nation recognized that the Vietnam veterans had, and continued, to honor the code of American soldiery, and a further decade to realize that Korean veterans also had, and continued to honor that code! That passage of time dimmed, but could not erase, the need for the Nation to acknowledge that these veterans were as all other veterans of America's wars. Deserving of honor for what they did and the way they did their duty. The "why" of that service is no longer a bar to honor or a burden they must bear.

And so the cycle is now complete! The Korean War Veterans Memorial joins the Vietnam Memorial on the hallowed ground of our Nation's Grand Mall. They are two dissimilar Memorials, yet with a common purpose. They honor, not war, but those the nation sent to war! In perfect symmetry, they unite with the Lincoln Memorial and the Washington Monument in a cruciform signifying that a people and Nation remembers and reveres.

The Korean War . . .
The Forgotten War, A Remembered Victory

Bibliography

Alexander, Bevin Korea, *The First War We Lost*, Hippocrene Books, 1986.

Appleman, Roy E., *South to the Naktong North to the Yalu*, U.S.Army in the Korean War, Office of the Chief of Military History, US Army 1961.

Appleman, Roy E., *East of Chosin, Entrapment and Breakout in Korea 1950*, Texas A & M University Press, 1987.

Appleman, Roy E., *Disaster in Korea- The Chinese Confront MacArthur*, Texas A & M University Press 1989 .

Biderman, Albert D, March to Calumny, *The Story of American POWs in the Korean War*, The Macmillan Company, 1963.

Blair, Clay *The Forgotten War, America in Korea 1950-53*, Times Books, 1987.

Bradley, Omar and Blair, Clay *A General's Life, An Autobiography*, Simon and Schuster, 1983.

Cagle, Malcolm W. and Manson, Frank A. *The Sea War in Korea*, US Naval Institute, 1957.

Churchill, Winston *The Second World War*, 6 Vols. Houghton Mifflin, 1948-1953.

Dell Publishing Company, Inc. The Congressional Medal of Honor Library- Korea, the Names, the Deeds, 1987.

Farrar-Hockley, Anthony *The Edge of the Sword*, Buchan and Enright, 1985.

Fehrenbach, T.R. *This Kind of War- A Study in Unpreparedness*, MacMillan 1963.

Ferrell, Robert H. Edit. *The Eisenhower Diaries*, W.W.Norton, 1981.

Field, James A. Jr. *Korea - A History of United States Naval Operations*, US Government Printing Office,1962.

Forty, George *At War in Korea*, Crown Publishers, Inc. 1985.

Futrell, Robert F.*The United States Air Force in Korea 1950-1953*, Office of Air Force History, US Air Force, 1983

Goulden, Joseph Korea, *The Untold Story of the War*, Times Books, 1982.

Hastings, Max *The Korean War*, Simon and Schuster, 1987.

Hermes, Walter G. *The US Army in the Korean War-Truce Tent and Fighting Front*, Office of the Chief of Military History, US Army 1966.

Huston, James A. *Guns and Butter- Powder and Rice - US Logistics in the Korean War*, Sesquehanna University Press, 1989.

Kinkead, Eugene *In Every War But One*, W.W.Norton & Co., 1959

Knox, Donald ,The Korean War-An Oral History Vol 1 Pusan to Chosin, Harcourt, Brace, Jovanovich 1985

Knox, Donald with Coppel, Alfred Vol II *Uncertain Victory*, Harcourt, Brace, Jovanovich 1988

MacDonald, Callum A. *Korea,-The War Before Vietnam*, The Free Press, 1986

Maihafer, Harry J. *From the Hudson to the Yalu*. West Point 49 in the Korean War, Texas A & M University Press, 1993.

Marshall, S.L.A. *Pork Chop Hill*, William Morrow & Co. , 1956.

Marshall, S.L.A. *The River and the Gauntlet*, William Morrow & Co 1953

Meid, Pat Lt.Col & Yingling, James Major, *US Marine Operations in Korea 1950-1953*, Vol V *Operations in West Korea*, Historical Division, Hq US Marine Corps, 1972. 1953 The East Central Front,Historical Division, Hq US Marine Corps 1962

Miller, John Jr., Carroll, Owen J. and Tackley, Margaret E. *Korea 1951-1953*, Office of the Chief of Military History, Department of the Army, 1982.

Paik, Gen. Sun Yup, *From Pusan to Panmun-jon*, Brassey's Inc, 1992.

Rees, David , Consultant and Editor, *The Korean War- History and Tactics*, Cresent Books, 1984

Ridgway, Matthew Montross, Lynn, Kuokka, Hubard D. & Hicks, Norman W. *US Marine Operations in Korea 1950- B. The Korean War*, Doubleday & Co. 1967.

Sawyer, Robert K. *Military Advisors in Korea: KMAG in Peace and War*, Office of the Chief of Military History, Department of the Army, 1962.

Schnabel, James F. and Watson, Robert J. *The History of the Joint Chiefs of Staff*, The Joint Chiefs of Staff National Policy, Vol 3 *The Korean War Part 1 (1978)*, Part 2 (1979), Historical Division, JCS.

Toland, John, *In Mortal Combat- Korea, 1950-1953*, William Morrow & Co. Inc. 1991.

Tomedi, Rudy, *No Bugles, No Drum- An Oral History of the Korean War*, John Wiley, 1993.

Turner Publishing Company, (Barry Craig writer), *The Chosen Few*, North Korea November-December 1950. 1989 & 1993.

Von Luck, Hans, *Panzer Commander: The Memoirs of Col. Hans Von Luck*, Praeger, 1989.

Whelan, Richard *Drawing the Line*, The Korean War, 1950-1953, Little Brown & Co. 1990.

Articles and Manuscripts

Carlisle, David K., "The Last of the Black Regulars," *Assembly*, November 1994, U.S.Military Academy.

The Forrestal Diaries, Viking Press, 1951

Mandelbaum, Michael, "The Day the Kremlin Called it Quits," *Baltimore Sun*, 20 August 1993.

Marshall, George Testimony," *N.Y. Times*, 12 May 1951.

Interviews and Personal Records

Barton, Raymond O. 335th Squadron, 4th Fighter Group, Fifth Air Force, -Notes

Beirne, D. Randall, 3rd Bn., 5RCT - Letters, notes, personal films.

Berry, Sidney B. 35th Infantry Regiment, Interview and notes.

Carozza, Albert, 24th Division Artillery, Interview and notes.

Crockett,Edward, The Newsletter of the 5RCT in Korea, April 1991.

Holliday, Sam C., 29th RCT and 35th Regiment,25th Division, "Up and Down Korea 24 July 1950 to 24 July 1951," Notes About My Combat Experiences in Korea, 1953.

Forester, Eugene, 9th Infantry Regiment, 2nd Division, Notes on his activities in Korea.

Knight, Lee, 2nd Bn. 5th RCT- Interview.

McAdoo Albert J. 2nd Bn. 5th RCT, The First Fifty Days - The 5RCT in Korea, Pamplet 1990.

Miller, William, 9th Infantry, 2nd Division, - Interview.

Myer, Thomas, 2nd Battalion, 7th Marines - Interview and notes.

Russell, Ivan The Newsletter of the 5th RCT in Korea, April 1991.

Korean War Veterans Killed in Action/Missing in Action Roster

(official list from National Archives)

— A —

George Aaron
John Aaron, Jr.
Marion V. Aaron
William E. Aaron, Jr.
Leonard S. Aarons
Mylo S. Aaser
Dirk Robert Abbas
Vincent G. Abbate
Augustus A. Abbey
Richard E. Abbey, Jr.
Charles L. Abbott
Francis Ralph Abbott
J. C. Abbott
John D. Abbott
Leroy Abbott
Richard F. Abbott
Wilbur E. Abbott
William R. Abderhalden
James Abdon
Charles L. Abel, Jr.
Donald R. Abel
James A. Abel
Francis H. Abele
Robert P. Abele
George E. Abeles
Aaron R. Abercrombie
Charlie Abercrombie
Wherry Abercrombie
David Herbert Abernathy
W. B. Abernethy, Jr.
Billy R. Ables
James Lathem Ables
Bruno F. Ablondi
Artis Abney, Jr.
Donald Lee Abney
Homer Ray Abney
Jack W. Abney
Norbert J. Abraham
Harald Abrahamsen
Ronald C. Abrahamson
Albert Stanley Abram
Charles Gene Abrell
Manuel Abreu, Jr.
Roberto Abreu-Garcia
Lester W. Abshire
Rurie Tyree Abshire, Jr.
Edward F. Accarizzi
Vincente G. Acedo
Isaac Acevedo
Louis V. Acevedo
Salvador Acevedo
Nicolas Acevedo-Cruz
Juan A. Acevedo-Tirado
Henry L. Aceves
Bill J. Acinelli
Marion A. Acitelli
Delano H. Acker
Albert A. Ackerman
Jack M. Ackerman
William C. Ackermann
Edwin F. Ackley
Philip W. Ackley
Preston E. Acock
David Acosta
Francisco Acosta
Ismael A. Acosta
Lupe P. Acosta
Pablo Acosta
Raymond J. Acosta
Ruben Acosta
Jaime Acosta-Garcia
Jo Acosta-Martinez
Lu Acosta-Martinez
Marvin D. Actkinson
Floyd N. Acton
Henry Acuna
Angel L. Acuna-Otero
Billie J. Adair
Hugh Donald Adair, Jr.
Clyde E. Adam
Leroy H. Adam
Robert C. Adam
Ruben Sanchez Adame
George E. Adamec
Wilbert V. Adamick
Joseph J. Adamo
Walter J. Adamowicz
Alfred B. Adams
Ambros R. Adams
Angus Buck Adams
Arthur L. Adams
Aubrey Glenn Adams
Bernard B. Adams

Billie F. Adams
Bosie Arnold Adams
Calvin Porter Adams
Charles W. Adams
Clarence Adams
Clayton D. Adams
Clifford L. Adams
Daryl Tine Adams
Dennis L. J. Adams
Donald Edwin Adams
Donald Lester Adams
Edwin E. Adams
Elbern T. Adams
Elno Adams, Jr.
Francis V. Adams
Garnett J. Adams, Jr.
George R. Adams
Harold L. Adams
Harry Leo Adams
Hollis J. Adams
Isaac F. Adams
J. B. Adams, Jr.
J. D. Adams
Jackie L. Adams
James C. Adams
James D. Adams
James H. Adams
James O. Adams
John Amos Adams
John D. Adams
John Edwin Adams
John Gordon Adams
John H. Adams
John Howard Adams
John Q. Adams
John R. Adams
Lewis C. Adams, Jr.
Lewis E. Adams
Lloyd C. Adams
Loren V. Adams
Loyd E. Adams
Marvin E. Adams
Melville E. Adams
Melvin R. Adams
Oliver Adams
R. A. Adams
Raymond A. Adams
Raymond J. Adams
Richard L. Adams
Robert Adams
Robert Adams
Robert C. Adams
Robert E. Adams
Robert E. Adams
Robert Earl Adams
Robert Henry Adams
Robert Irving Adams
Robert Wayne Adams
Roger K. Adams
Ronald Hunter Adams
Rufus Adams
Thessalonians Adams
Thomas Adams
Troulius Adams
Warren Edward Adams
Wilbur J. Adams
William A. Adams
William H. Adams
William Hill Adams
William Robert Adams
Willie Guy Adams, Jr.
Harry G. Adamson, Jr.
Robert E. Addcox
Harold L. Addington
Alphonso Addison
Robert E. Addison
Samuel Addison
Harold Adelman
Robert A. Adelman
Sylvan W. Adelsgruber
Clifford Adkins
Colie J. Adkins, Jr.
Fletcher Adkins
Hatten Adkins
Hillrey B. Adkins
James H. Adkins
Vernon A. Adkins
Virgil Boyd Adkins
Harold F. Adkinson
Forrest D. Adkisson
Willard J. Adkisson
George H. Adlam
Ernest Max Adler
Junior Merle Adler
Maxwell Adler

Joseph L. Adlesic
Seymour R. Adsem
Frederick J. Aeschliman
Litisoni Aetonu
Robert E. Afflerbach
Alfred Hiram Agan
Robert Allen Agar
Charles L. Agard
Robert C. Agard, Jr.
Junius B. Agnelli, Jr.
Henry P. Agnew
Jorge L. Agostini
Ralph J. Agostini
Berrios A. Agosto
Ricardo A. Agrait
Carleton V. Agrell
Manuel N. Aguayo
Perez Jose M. Aguayo
Richard Aguayo
James Girald Aguda
Henry Nicholas Aguel
Enrique Aguiar-Marquez
Jesus T. Aguigui
Gilberto Aguilar
Lucio R. Aguilar
Richard Aguilar
Saul Aguilar
Florencio C. Aguilera
Luciano Aguilera
Benito R. Aguinaldo
Jose M. Aguirre
Richard C. Aguirre
Santiago Aguirre
Pedro L. Aguon
Let Louis Ah
Frank B. Ahern
John Paul Ahlers
Howard J. Ahles
Louis Ahlet
Eric L. Ahlstrom, Jr.
Lusio Castanoz Ahumada
Edward J. Aiken
James R. Aiken
John P. Aiksnoras
John A. Aimer
James E. Ainscough
Albert Ainsworth, Jr.
Homer Ray Ainsworth
Donnie J. Airington
Howard G. Airington
Virgil F. Aitkens
Leroy J. Aitkin
Raymond J. Aizen
Howard D. Akard
Kazuaki Akazawa
Bobby Ellis Akers
Donald W. Akers
Herbert Dale Akers
James Francis Akers
Richard Allen Akers
Victor Akers, Jr.
William R. Akers
John E. Akey
Clarence H. Aki
Rolan Maurice Akin
Frederick K. Akina
Joe W. Akins
Larry B. Akins
Lloyd E. Akins
Teddy B. Akins
W. T. Akins
Willis L. Akins
Willis T. Akins
Walter R. Akridge, Jr.
Charles Aksamit
Frank T. Alaniz
Robert G. Alaniz
Daniel Alarcon
Ramon Alba
Abraham Albaladejo
David Albanese
Paul Albaugh
Billie D. Albers
Robert H. Albers
Winston L. Albers
Donald Alberson
Dewillis Lee Albert
Donald O. Albert
Durham O. Albert
Gilbert W. Albert
Henry John Albert, Jr.
John Stewart Albert
Joseph R. Albert
Ray Albert
Richard Schaeffer Albert

John William Alberts
Verle S. Albertson
Estell C. Alberty
James D. Albey
Carlo L. Albi
Elmer J. Albrecht
Eugene D. Albrecht
John A. Albrecht
Barry E. Albright
Charles R. Albright
Elzia R. Albright
Richard Louis Albright
Richard V. Albright
John Edgar Albring
Charles Lyndell Albritton
Gilbert R. Alcantar
Frank Alcaraz
A. Alcazar-Lugo
Alejandro A. Alcencio
John T. Alcock
Phillip F. Alcorn
Gerardo R. Aldana
Boyd K. Alderdice
James A. Alderdice
Lloyd H. Alderfer
Ellsworth L. Alderman
Marvin B. Alderman
Joseph A. Aldo
Joseph Aldrete
Malcolm E. Aldrich
Alphonse Aldridge
Ben R. Aldridge
Edward F. Aldridge
Ellis L. Aldridge
Eugene Gilbert Aldridge
Harry H. Aldridge
James R. Aldridge, Jr.
Robert Lewis Aldridge
Harry L. Alecock
Leonel Aleman
Marion Louis Ales
Anthony C. Alexa, Jr.
Alfred L. Alexander
Billy B. Alexander
Charles B. Alexander
Charles E. Alexander
Colbert J. Alexander, Jr.
Dennis Alexander
Durward F. Alexander
Earl Alexander
Floyd N. Alexander
George R. Alexander
Howard E. Alexander
Hypolite A. Alexander
Jack Duane Alexander
James T. Alexander
James T. Alexander
James W. Alexander, Jr.
John Bennett Alexander
Johnnie C. Alexander, Jr.
Joseph S. Alexander
L. W. Alexander, Jr.
Leroy B. Alexander
Lonnie V. Alexander
Lucius Alexander
Marvin I. Alexander
Robert Ellis Alexander
Summey R. Alexander
Thomas R. Alexander
Wallace Alexander
Eddie Carvalho Alfaro
Hector Alfaro-Alfaro
Clifford W. Alford
Horace Alford, Jr.
Larry E. Alford
Ottis F. Alford
Raymond K. Alford
Dan Oliver Alfred
Rodriguez F. Algarin
Teodoro Alicea
Luis Alicea-Coto
Ramon Alicea-Reyes
Thomas Raymond Aliff
Robert Thomas Alilovich
James H. Aliston
Charlie R. Alitz
Jimmie Harold Alkire
Donald Noble Allan
Donald P. Allan
Arthur S. Allard
Raymond A. Allard
Jack Allbritton
James Allbritton
Raymond L. Allbritton
Roger H. Alle

Angelo Allegretto
Larry C. Alleman
Percy Allemand
Hilary F. Allemeier
Ace Allen
Alden D. Allen
Alfonzia D. Allen
Alonzo Allen
Arthur B. Allen
Arthur W. Allen
Baker Allen
Billy James Allen
Charles Allen
Charles Allen
Charles C. Allen
Charles E. Allen, Jr.
Charles Roy Allen
Charles S. Allen
Charles W. Allen
Charlie E. Allen
Chelcia A. Allen
Claude E. Allen
Clyde J. Allen
Commer E. Allen
Dave Allen, Jr.
David Allen
David Faxon Allen
Donald E. Allen
Douglas A. Allen
Earnest Allen
Ellery D. Allen
Elmer G. Allen
English W. Allen
Eric G. Allen
Ernest R. Allen
Fred Milburn Allen
George Allen, Jr.
George W. Allen
Glen Allen
Gordon R. Allen
Harold E. Allen
Henry L. Allen
Herbert Lee Allen
Hubert Odell Allen
Jack Leon Allen
Jack Victor Allen
Jackie D. Allen
James Allen
James Edward Allen
James L. Allen
James R. Allen
James Robert Allen
James Rogers Allen
Jean R. Allen
Jimmie Allen
John A. Allen, Jr.
John P. Allen
Johnny Lee Allen
Joseph N. Allen
Kenneth N. Allen
Kenneth R. Allen
Leo Allen
Marcellous Allen
Max Allen
Neil E. Allen
Oreall L. Allen
Paul A. Allen
Paul L. Allen
Paul T. Allen
Phillip P. Allen
Raymond Charles Allen
Raymond L. Allen
Richard L. Allen
Richard Lee Allen
Robert F. Allen
Robert H. Allen
Robert N. Allen
Roy L. Allen
Thomas E. Allen
Van Allen
Walter Edmond Allen
Walter Henry Allen
Warren E. Allen
William Allen
Willie Allen, Jr.
Charles J. Allend
G. Allende-Cepeda
Howard Allen Allender
Robert Lee Allender
James Lee Alley
John C. Alley
Ray Carles Alley
Wilmer L. Alley
Julius E. Allgood, Jr.
Richard O. Allie

John Wesley Alling, Jr.
Buddy Eugene Allison
James E. Allison
James Leonard Allison
John Williams Allison, Jr.
Joseph R. Allison, Jr.
Richard J. Allison
William J. Allison
Winfred L. Allison
Jacob W. Allmaras
Donald R. Allmon
John W. Allmond
Robert Ervin Allred
James Hartford Allston
Morris Allums
Robert W. Allyn
Daniel R. Almanza
Armando Almaraz
Donaciano B. Almazan
Bernard Almeida
Joseph Almeida
Segarra S. Almodovar
Clifton Leon Almonrode
Maximino Alomar-Ruiz
Alfred H. Sr Alonzo
Francisco Alonzo, Jr.
Edward Norman Alpern
Donald Alpers
Clarence E. Alspaugh
Foster L. Alston
George A. Alston
James M. Alston
Herman Alsup
Dwain K. Alt
Francis R. Altavilla
Robert J. Altemus
Helmut Altergott
Ruffus B. Althiser
Louis D. Altieri
Comer L. Altland
William E. Altomare
Elmer Vance Alton, Jr.
Gordon H. Alton
John Skinner Alton
Robert Edward Altosino
James E. Altum
Lloyd A. Alumbaugh
Macaril Q. Alva
Roberto Alva
Eilalio Alvarado
Hector Luis Alvarado
John Alvarado
Manuel G. Alvarado
Richard Luna Alvarado
Santos V. Alvarado, Jr.
William I. Alvarado
Miguel T. Alvarenga
Adalberto Alvarez
Agustin Alvarez
Armando Alvarez
Daniel Montez Alvarez
Ernest Alvarez
Gilbert Alvarez
Higinio Alvarez
Hugo Alvarez
A. Alvarez-Mercado
Hermogenes Alverio
Alfred J. Alverson
R. C. Alverson
Louis A. Alves
Arthur L. Alveshere
Anthony P. Alvis
John C. Alvis
Dennis W. Alward
John J. Alyanakian
Richard G. Amadon
William P. Amaker
Leslie R. Amann
Richard Joseph Amann
Yutaka Amano
Luis Amaro-Garcia
Joseph D. Amato
Donald F. Ambeau
Karl A. Amberg
William D. Amberger
Humbert J. Ambriz
Clement A. Ambrose
Thomas Ambrose
Dominick M.I Ambrosino
Hertzel J. Amdur
Wayne R. Amelung
Ralph E. Amend
Andrew J. Amendola
Joseph J. Amendola
Norman Richard Amendt

321

Lorenza Amerson
Richard C. Ames
Roger D. Ames
William Harold Ames
Amous Leroy Amey
Robert B. Amezcua
Robert L. Amick
Donald Prentice Amidon
Harry L. Amigh
Marvin B. Amiot
Alfredo Amis
Bob T. Amis
James D. Ammons
John C. Ammons
Mondal Rayburn Ammons
Otto Ammons
Thurman R. Ammons, Jr.
Charles G. Amos
Gaylord Amos
General P. Amos
Morris Amos
Joseph Obonon Ampon
Norman E. Amsden
Ferdinand V. Amthor
Harold L. Amundson
Ray M. Amuro
Oris W. Amy
Santiago Jose A. Amy
Jack K. Amyx
Robert M. Ancel
Christopher C. Ancelet
Gerald R. Anctil
Laurence Edward Anctil
Jack Duane Anderberg
James John Anderle, Jr.
Fred Anders
Aage E. Andersen
Charles A. Andersen
Harry D. Andersen
A. C. Anderson
Alfred J. Anderson
Alfred Anderson, Jr.
Allen G. Anderson
Austin J. Anderson
Beriger A. Anderson
Billy D. Anderson
Billy G. Anderson
Billy G. Anderson
Billy Wayne Anderson
Bobby G. Anderson
Carl E. Anderson, Jr.
Charles E. Anderson
Charles E. Anderson
Charlie M. Anderson
Clarence D. Anderson
Clinton L. Anderson
Clyde E. Anderson
Clyde Earl Anderson
Clyde T. Anderson
Dale William Anderson
Dewey Rex Anderson
Donald E. Anderson
Donald T. Anderson
Douglas R. Anderson
Duane W. Anderson
Dwain Anderson
Edward C. Anderson
Ellis L. Anderson
Ellsworth L. Anderson
Eric W. Anderson
Eugene A. Anderson
Eugene C. Anderson
Francis C. Anderson
Fred Lee Anderson
Gale C. Anderson
Gene Everett Anderson
George F. Anderson
Gerald Phillips Anderson
Glenn M. Anderson
Gordon E. Anderson
Harold E. Anderson
Harry W. Anderson
Hebert A. Anderson
Herbert Monroe Anderson
Herman E. Anderson, Jr.
Homer V. H. Anderson
Jacob G. Anderson
James Anderson
James A. Anderson
James E. Anderson
James F. Anderson
James T. Anderson
James T. Anderson
James V. Anderson
Jesse K. Anderson
John Anderson
John H. Anderson
John W. Anderson
John W. Anderson

Keith Anderson
Kendall G. Anderson
Larry Joe Anderson
Leonard W. Anderson
Linford R. Anderson
Lloyd G. Anderson, Jr.
Lloyd P. Anderson
Loren Eugene Anderson
Loris W. Anderson
Louis D. Anderson
M. C. Anderson
Melvin F. Anderson
Merwyn D. Anderson
Milton A. Anderson
Morris Allen Anderson
Nalton J. Anderson
Norbert O. Anderson
Omer Lee Anderson
Oscar Rutger Anderson
Perry A. Anderson
Pleze Anderson
Port A. Anderson, Jr.
Raymond G. Anderson
Raymond O. Anderson
Raymond W. Anderson
Richard A. Anderson
Richard E. Anderson
Richard Neal Anderson
Richard P. Anderson
Robert A. Anderson
Robert D. Anderson
Robert E. Anderson
Robert E. Anderson
Robert Eugene Anderson
Robert H. Anderson
Roy Gilbert Anderson
Roy H. Anderson, Jr.
Russel E. Anderson
Stanley A. Anderson
Terrell Anderson
Thomas E. Anderson
Tommy J. Anderson
Walter C. Anderson
Warren L. Anderson
Wesley A. Anderson
William Anderson
William C. Anderson
William C. Anderson
William G. Anderson
William H. Anderson
William P. Anderson
William P. Anderson, Jr.
Willie L. Anderson
Horace B. Anderton
Lope A. Andino-Fonseca
Emiliano Andino-Perez
John P. Andonian
Raymond Andrade, Jr.
Roberto Alvarez Andrade
Herbert C. Andreas
Edward C. Andres
Charles A. Andresen
James R. Andresen
John S. Andresen
Roy J. Andresen
Joseph J. Andrew
Albert S. Andrews
Charles L. Andrews
Charles Melvin Andrews
Earl R. Andrews
Earnest M. Andrews
Edward R. Andrews
Gary G. Andrews
George A. Andrews
Harold Q. Andrews
Howard Andrews
Howard D. Andrews
Isaac Andrews
Joseph Andrews
Kenyon E. Andrews
Leo Dwaine Andrews
Leon E. Andrews
Robert Andrews
Robert Basil Andrews
Shirley B. Andrews, Jr.
Herbert W. Andridge, Jr.
Arnold V. Andring
Thomas E. Andrzejewski
William D. Aney
Tito Angarano
Luther M. Ange
Jack E. Angel
Nick W. Angelakos
Joseph Angeli, Jr.
Victorio E. Angeline
Eugene Leroy Angell
George Angelus
Robert H. Angevine
Maurice Angland

Donald E. Angle
Artemus F. Angles
George J. Angles
Vito L. Angona
Forrest Bernard Angstman
Ernest M. Angus
James R. Angus
Henry C. Aniszewski
Okey M. Ankrom
Russell Annis
Gabriel Carl Anselmo
George Anspaugh
Hubert Earl Antes, Jr.
Louis L. Anthis
Charles W. Anthony
Ernest L. Anthony
Herman Anthony
Joseph W. Anthony
Roy Anthony
Stanley H. Anthony
James L. Antle
Lindy R. Antonio
Vittorio M. Antonio
Anthony J. Antonoff
William Louis Antonucci
Harold B. Antrim
Joseph Antrom
Jose Antonio Antuna
Baldomero Anzaldua
Samuel Anzellotti, Jr.
George Apao
Arthur M. Apmann, Jr.
August L. Apo
Abie L. Apodaca
Delgado Roberto Aponte
Francisco J. Aponte
Hector L. Aponte
Juan P. Aponte
Herbert G. Appel
William J. Append
Joseph F. Appenfelder
Francis E. Appis
Herbert L. Apple
Billy Roy Appleby
Robert L. Applin
David G. Apt
Michael J. Aquilino
Arthur L. Aragon
James Aragon, Jr.
Gregorio N. Aragones
Tatsuo Arai
James Seifuku Arakai
Seichi Arakaki
Wilfred H. Arakawa
Mitchell G. Araman
Frank Araujo
Eugene E. Arbogast
Julian S. Arbonies
Ricardo T. Arca
Eugene J. Arcand
Charles Arce
Harry A. Arceneaux, Jr.
Charles E. Arch
John Arch
Donald E. Archambault
Gilbert A. Archambeault
Richard J. Archambeault
Walter G. Archambo
Francesco Archangeli
Alexander G. Archer
B. R. Archer
David Melton Archer
George W. Archer, Jr.
John D. Archer
John F. Archer
Robert Gene Archer
Ronald Royce Archer
James O. Archerd
Vallellanes Archilla
Jose A. Archuleta
Jose L. Archuleta
Juan Archuleta
Juan B. Archuleta
David O. Archuletta
Pangra A. Arcidiacono
Nicholas Michael Arcuri
Theodore M. Ard, Jr.
Herbert Ardis
Joseph R. Arel
Ernest Arellano
Nicholas G. Aremia
Peter G. Arend
Hugh H. Arendale
Doyle R. Arendall
Stanley P. Arendt
Alfred A. Arenobina
Anthony E. Arezzo
Joseph S. Argenziano, Jr.
James Argetis

Florencio Arias
Frank V. Arias
Lawrence L. Arias
Milton Arias, Jr.
Alexander D. Arick
Peter Emilio Arioli, Jr.
Lyman Henry Arionus
Walter J. Arkenberg
Bob L. Arley
Henry Armada
Juarbe Luis F. Armada
John R. Arman
Joe T. Armas
Clarence E. Armbrister
Herbert Armbruster
Conrad James Armel
Joaquin A. Armenta
James S. Armentrout
Lewis H. Armentrout
Richard E. Armentrout
James R. Armer
Donald W. Armeson
James Louis Armour
John H. Armour
Thomas J. Armour
Ernest H. Arms, Jr.
John Walter Arms
Billy J. Armstrong
Byron K. Armstrong
Clarence D. Armstrong
David W. Armstrong
Dennis R. Armstrong
James A. Armstrong
James H. Armstrong
Jerry W. Armstrong
John D. Armstrong
Kenton W. Armstrong
Louis W. Armstrong
Raymond F. Armstrong
Richard Armstrong
Robert W. Armstrong
Thurman N. Armstrong
Walter G. Armstrong
Wayne F. Armstrong
William Joseph Armstrong
William N. Armstrong
Wilson C. Armstrong
John Robert Arnall
Elmer L. Arndt
Richard William Arndt
Donald W. Arneson
John Grey Arnett
Beverly I. Arnold
Billy A. Arnold
Bloyce C. Arnold
Clyde B. Arnold
Donald D. Arnold, Jr.
Drexel E. Arnold
Ervin L. Arnold
Frederick B. Arnold
George C. Arnold
Harry Arnold, Jr.
James A. Arnold
James Edward Arnold
James J. Arnold
Lincoln C. Arnold
Wallace M. Arnold
William M. Arnold, Jr.
David Arnott, Jr.
Walter T. Arose, Jr.
Ray Louis Arpke
Isidore C. Arredondo
Mariano Arredondo
Stanley C. Arredondo
John Arreola, Jr.
Raymond C. Arriaga
Gomez E. Arrigoitia
Alfred Walter Arrington
Andrew B. Arrington
Elbert Arrington, Jr.
James F. Arrington
Ralph Elgin Arrington
Fernado L. Arriola
David Arthur Arrivee
Clayton Arrowwood
Miguel A. Arroyo
Ruben Arroyo-Abreu
Francisco Arteaga
John Horace Arter
Bobbie R. Arthur
Leonard L. Arthur
Melvin Arthur
Melvin C. Arthur
Patrick James Arthur
William R. Arthur
John Artis, Jr.
William O. Artrip
Will Arvangle, Jr.
Arthur A. Arveson

Keith L. Arvidson
Recil P. Arwood
Hiroshi Asada
Albert H. Asau
James W. Asbury
William W. Asbury
Henry H. Ascencio
A. Aschenbrenner
Leroy E. Aschenbrenner
Guzman C. Asencio
Alfred H. Ash
Billy Edmond Ash
Dean M. Ash
Orville E. Ashbaker
James V. Ashbaugh
Robert W. Ashbaugh
James L. Ashbrook
Billie Joe Ashby
John E. Ashby
Augustus Ashe
Robert J. Ashe
Russel S. Ashenfelder
Henry L. Ashenfelter
Bobby L. Asher
Jack D. Asher
Ollie Ray Asher
Ralph S. Asher
Francis A. Ashey
James Joseph Ashford
Paul J. Ashford, Jr.
Louis W. Ashforth
Alfred B. Ashley
Billy J. Ashley
Charles Ashley
Donald J. Ashley
Eugene Leroy Ashley
Floyd J. Ashley
Gilbert Lamour Ashley, Jr.
Thomas R. Ashley
Vernon R. Ashley
Ronald Edward Ashline
George Ashton
Alton M. Ashworth
Huey Ashworth
Theron Clark Askew
Felix Asla, Jr.
John J. Aspden
William Aspell
David Aspili
Philip J. Aspinwall
Nick Aspromigos
Kenneth W. Asquith
Michael Astary, Jr.
Manford W. Astill
Charles Arthur Astley, Jr.
Frank V. Aston
Wilford Astor
Julian Asuncion
Ralph E. Atchison
Oren C. Atchley
Fred William Aten
John R. Atencio
Robert H. Atha
Donald B. Atherton
Harold J. Atherton
Kenneth E. Atherton
Charles Robert Athey
Walter M. Atkin
Albert E. Atkins
Elroy J. Atkins
Irvin L. Atkins
Leonard H. Atkins
Benny C. Atkinson
Carson J. Atkinson
Enrique M. Atkinson
Fred Franklin Atkinson, Jr.
George J. Atkinson
Howard C. Atkinson, Jr.
Stanley J. Atkinson
William W. Atkinson
Douglas Earl Attinger
Walter Attwood
Willie J. Atwater
Victor William Atwell
Clyde B. Atwood
Rowan Duane Atwood
Virgil M. Atwood
Monroe Joseph Aubain
Alexander Aubrey
Alfred E. Aubuchon
Joseph P. Aucoin
Monte M. Auer
Norman A. Auer
Ira A. Augenblick
Alfred H. Auger
Chester E. August
Thomas W. August
Robert J. Aukerman
Opal D. Aulds

Arte Aulet-Mercado
Cruz Auli-Osorio
Leo R. Ault
Edward J. Aumack
Eddie D. Auman
John A. Aumon
Clarence M. Aunchman
Cosmo F. Aurigemma
Henry G. Ausburn, Jr.
Clarence N. Aust
Edward Charles Aust
Arthur Myles Austin
C. J. Austin
Delbert Frederick Austin
Don L. Austin
Earl E. Austin
Leon Austin, Jr.
Monroe Austin, Jr.
Raymond S. Austin, Jr.
Wayne D. Austin
Ralph Edward Auten
Samson Authement, Jr.
Bob D. Autrey
Albert G. Autry
Clarence K. F. Auyong
Joe T. Avant
Laverle Avant
Eugene Avants
Allen O. Avara
Charles Avarello
Charles Russell Avary
Domino T. Avelino
Billy R. Aven
Clarence R. Avent
David Avent
Robert Warren Averill
Charles Tillman Avery
Clifton F. Avery
Harold S. Avery, Jr.
Herbert Avery
Jack A. Avery
James L. Avery
Joseph Preston Avery
Arturo D. Avila
Clarence T. Avila
Peter R. Avila
Ruben Guadalupe Avila
Stanley L. Avila
William D. Aviles
Jerry Avina
Billy W. Awtrey
Burton C. Awtrey
Harold R. Axelson
Everett J. Axtell
Thomas E. Axtell
Roy D. Axton
Bernardo Ramos Ayala
Angel Ayala-Esquilin
Enrique Ayala-Ferrer
Donald James Ayen
Elliott Dean Ayer
George F. Ayers
Harmon H. Ayers
Merle Truman Ayers
James Francis Aylward
Ramon Luis Aymerich-Gonzalez
Albert James Ayo
Earl C. Ayotte
Hector H. Ayotte
Ronald W. Ayotte

— B —

Henry R. Baas
Joseph M. Babasa, Jr.
Raul B. Babasa
John L. Babbick, Jr.
George H. Babcock
James Marlin Baber
Alfred R. Babicz
Joseph Philip Babin, Jr.
Paul E. Babin
Robert A. Babin
Philip Andrew Babine
John Low Babson, Jr.
Edward J. Bac
Abel Baca
Alexander A. Baca
Antonio L. Baca
Frank S. Baca
Lorenzo Baca
Russell L. Baca
Florentino Bacarro
Libby H. Bacaylan
Hugo Victor Baccari
Ivy O. Baccus
Richard B. Bach
Virgil Bach

Ernest H. Bachmann
Thomas M. Bachop
Solomon A. Bachrach
Claude E. Bachtell
Richard E. Bachus
Arthur D. Back
Raymond W. Backhaus
Richard Irving Backoff
John H. Backstrom
John G. Bacon, Jr.
Kenneth R. Bacon
Raymond Randolph Bacon
Richard L. Bacon
Roger A. Bacon
John Stephen Baczewski
William F. Baden
Gene M. Badgley
Harold Edward Badgley
James B. Badon, Jr.
Daniel Baduria, Jr.
James L. Baechle
Paul Gerald Baenen
Donald L. Baer
Harry W. Baer
Jack W. Baer
Ronald C. Baer
David J. Baermann
Robert C. Baetz
De Jesus Pedro Baez
Neftal Baez-Canino
John Donald Bagale
Reuben S. Baggett
John R. Baggi, Jr.
Felix P. Baginski
Albert G. Bagley
Harry B. Bagnell
Cecil R. Bagwell
John Frederick Bagwell, III
Joseph E. Bahleda
James Baido
Eugene Baidy
Edwin H. Bailer
Joe D. Bailes
Ralph L. Bailets
Arthur G. Bailey
Bert G. Bailey
Charler Bailey
Charles M. Bailey
Charles V. Bailey
Clair E. Bailey
Clarence M. Bailey
Donald Bailey
Earl Thomas Bailey
Edward J. Bailey
Elmer C. Bailey, Jr.
Glen A. Bailey
Haroldene Bailey
Henry M. Bailey
Herbert Alvin Bailey
Hugh H. Bailey
James A. Bailey
James J. Bailey
James M. Bailey
Lawrence Austin Bailey
Max L. Bailey
Milton W. Bailey
Otis Clyde Bailey
Paul R. Bailey
R. V. Bailey
Ralph E. Bailey
Ray C. Bailey
Raymond E. Bailey
Renfrew D. Bailey
Robert Franklin Bailey
Ross Bailey
Sesco L. Bailey
Stanley Warren Bailey
Troy W. Bailey
Walter Edmundson Bailey
Walter J. Bailey
Willard E. Bailey
William C. Bailey
William J. Bailey
Wilmer Bailey
Allan R. Bain
George Bain
John J. Bain
Odom Carl Bain
Edmon S. Bainbridge
James R. Bair
Charles W. Baird
Leon Baird
Vernon Baird
Bobby G. Baize
Anthony Bajkiwski
Joseph Bak
Albert M. Baker
Allen Baker
Alvin D. Baker

Arthur L. Baker
Baxter L. Baker, Jr.
Billy Wayne Baker
Boris Baker
Brownell E. Baker, Jr.
Burton E. Baker
Charles A. Baker
Charles B. Baker
Charles E. Baker
Charlie C. Baker
Claude F. Baker
Clifford E. Baker
Clifton G. Baker
Cornelius J. Baker, Jr.
David Baker
Dennis Lewis Baker
Donald H. Baker
Donald Lewis Baker
Donnie E. Baker
Eddie C. Baker
Ernie L. Baker
Eugene James Baker
Floyd K. Baker
Francis L. Baker
Frank Alton Baker
Fred Baker
Fred E. Baker
Ganes L. Baker
George A. Baker
George Lorin Baker, Jr.
George R. Baker
Henry Baker
Herbert E. Baker
Isaac E. Baker
Jack B. Baker
James A. Baker
James Darnell Baker
James K. Baker
James L. Baker
James M. Baker
Jimmy A. Baker
John D. Baker
John Edward Baker
June M. Baker
K. W. Baker
Kellis B. Baker
Kenneth C. Baker
Lawrence M. Baker
Lee D. Baker
Leonard A. Baker
Leroy Baker
Leroy Linwood Baker
Melvin E. Baker
Nathaniel Baker
Paul E. Baker
Paul E. Baker
Paul Tipton Baker
Ralph E. Baker
Ralph V. Baker
Ralph W. Baker
Raymond L. Baker
Richard M. Baker
Robert L. Baker
Robert L. Baker
Robert W. Baker
Roland Baker
Russell Arthur Baker
Samuel D. Baker
Sidney Baker
Stanley L. Baker
Stewart M. Baker, Jr.
Thomas Charles Baker
Thomas L. Baker
Victor Baker
Virgil K. Baker
Wade Baker
Walter C. Baker, Jr.
Walter R. Baker
Webster R. Baker
William D. Baker
William H. Baker
William Kenneth Baker
William M. Baker
William R. Baker
Michael A. Bakich
Donald Linwood Bakie
Elroy H. Bakker
Theodore W. Bakker
James Emery Baksa
Joseph V. Baksa
George A. Baksankas
Jose Balalong
Marcelo A. Balanag
Pastor Balanon, Jr.
Stanley J. Balasa
Joseph A. Balbi
Herbert Walter Balboni
Joseph W. Balboni
Phillip Kendall Balch

Rufus Balch
Bear F. Bald-Eagle
Elmer E. Baldock
John Baldock
Joe R. Baldonado
William H. Baldree
James J. Balduzzi, Jr.
Benjamin B. Baldwin
Harold M. Baldwin
Jack Leon Baldwin
Lawrence Baldwin
Louis W. Baldwin
Thomas A. Baldwin, Jr.
Watson A. Baldwin
William C. Baldwin
Woodrow W. Baldwin
Walter Baleja
Ralph B. Balentine
Donald J. Bales
Philip E. Balfe
George F. Balfour
Marvin G. Balhorn
Cecil R. Ball
Clarence H. Ball
Dale E. Ball
Edward Ball
Hayward C. Ball
James B. Ball
James H. Ball
John W. Ball
Kenneth Ball
Mathis O. Ball, Jr.
Oliver Ball, Jr.
Ralph Edward Ball
Raymond Orval Ball
Walter J. Ball
Willam Robert Ball, Jr.
James L. Ballantyne
Clarence C. Ballard
Dale R. Ballard
George F. Ballard
Guy A. Ballard
Harlan G. Ballard
Harvel L. Ballard
Joseph John Ballard, Jr.
Robert Ballard, Jr.
Roger Ballard
William J. Ballard
Daniel Joseph Ballem
Jay T. Ballenger
Frederick D. Ballentine
Howard E. Ballentine
Ricardo Ballestero
Frederick L. Balling
Kenneth M. Ballinger
Gus George Ballis
Jack Morton Ballmer
Howard L. Ballou
Homer R. Ballow
James Howard Balls
Keith Duane Ballwahn
Henry R. Balmer
James Leslie Balog
John Balog
Richard J. Balog
Richard C. Balogh
Durrell M. Balthazor
Jose A. Baltomei
Robert L. Baltz
Edward J. Baluta
Rafael E. Balzac
Francis M. Bambino
Arnold L. Bamburg
Charles M. Bamford
Stanley Adam Banach
Robert K. Bancker
Arthur Richard Bancroft
Edward B. Bancroft
Wayne Eugene Bancroft
James J. Banczak
William E. Bane
Billie B. Banes
Gerald O. Bangert
Loyd K. Bangs
John J. Banish
Florenz Michael Banjavcic
Charles J. Banks
Charles M. Banks
Daniel E. Banks
Earl Banks
Earl Banks
George Ralph Banks
Joseph Banks
Ray L. Banks
Samuel Banks
Starl L. Banks
Thomas J. Banks
Travis L. Banks
Wilbur S. Banks

William P. Banks
William R. Banks
Albert Bankston
Bobbie Ray Bankston
Frank W. Bankston
James Wade Bannantine
Coy E. Banner
Malcolm G. Bannerman
George C. Banning
Bob R. Bannister
Norman L. Bannister, Jr.
Rudolph P. Baquet
Rubin G. Bara
Robert Rodriquez Barajas
Andrew Barakoskie
Robert A. Baranek
Slvato Barbagallo, Jr.
Lawrence E. Barbarin
Franklin D. Barbe
Wilbur T. Barbeau
John P. Barbee
Albert L. Barber
Anthony J. Barber
Clifford A. Barber
Franklin M. Barber
Jack Eugene Barber
Leroy R. Barber
Lodean A. Barber, Jr.
Loyd E. Barber
Marvin W. Barber
Raymond H. Barber
William A. Barber
Worth H. Barber
John C. Barbery
George M. Barbiere
Henry Jasper Barbieri
Pasquale E. Barbiero
Ceferino I. Barbosa-Marrero
Diego Barbosa-Velez
Robert L. Barbour
Charles D. Barcak
Daniel Clarence Barcak
Lester V. Barchesky
Baldwin B. Barclay, Jr.
Jimmie E. Barcom
Ward Oliver Bard
Billy L. Barder
John B. Bardwell
Donald A. Bare
Jay T. Bare
Elmer G. Barefoot
Juan M. Barela
Alex Bareski
David D. Barfield
Wade Hilton Barfield
William J. Barfield
William Vinson Barfield
Joe E. Bargas
Calvin K. Barger
William B. Barger
Edward W. Bargfrede
Fred Bargo, Jr.
Phillip Perrin Barham
Charles H. Barker
Donald L. Barker
Earl R. Barker
Edgar N. Barker
Jesse J. Barker
John G. Barker
Malen W. Barker
Norbert L. Barker
Robert W. Barker
Ronald Rhodes Barker
Vernon R. Barker
William A. Barker
William C. Barker
William G. Barker
William Moran Barker
William R. Barker
William T. Barker
Leonard H. Barklage
Elmer L. Barkley
Francis B. Barks
Thomas E. Barksdale
Thomas J. Barksdale
Roy A. Barlettani
Carlton L. Barley
Salvatore J. Barlotta
Arthur L. Barlow
Carl F. Barlow
Duane L. Barlow
Edmund J. P. Barlow
George T. Barlow
Kenneth W. Barlow
Edwin Jerome Barman
Joseph M. Barna
Edward J. Barnak
Gilbert E. Barnard

William M. Barnard
John Barnello, Jr.
Albert Prentiss Barnes, Jr.
Bernard Eugene Barnes
Carl M. Barnes
Daniel Webster Barnes
David Porter Barnes
Donald E. Barnes
Donald L. Barnes
Ellis Barnes
Ernest Wayne Barnes
Francis J. Barnes
George E. Barnes
George Barnes, Jr.
Glenn E. Barnes
Herbert R. Barnes
Howard James Barnes
Joe E. Barnes
Keith W. Barnes
Kenneth Lynn Barnes
Kenneth N. Barnes
Kenneth W. Barnes
Lee R. Barnes
Len Barnes
Mack R. Barnes
Raymond C. Barnes
Robert A. Barnes
Samuel Barnes
Ted U. Barnes
Thomas J. Barnes
William F. Barnes
William M. Barnes, Jr.
William O. Barnes
Billy E. Barnett
Calvin Paul Barnett
Carl George Barnett, Jr.
Cecil A. Barnett
Charles Robert Barnett
Deane Moser Barnett
Donald Norman Barnett
Earl J. Barnett
Frankie L. Barnett
George J. Barnett
Ivey G. Barnett
James J. Barnett, Jr.
Jerry W. Barnett
John R. Barnett
Joseph L. Barnett
Lewis A. Barnett, Jr.
Melvin H. Barnett
Murray W. Barnett
Raymond E. Barnett
Richard C. Barnett
Robert A. Barnett
Robert N. Barnett
Wilburn H. Barnett
George D. Barnette
Homer E. Barnette
David E. Barney
Freddie Barney
Joseph J. Barney
William Barney, Jr.
Carl Lee Barnhart
Dale G. Barnhart
Dale K. Barnhart
Robert C. Barnhart
Kenneth R. Barnhill
Paul C. Barnhouse
Jim Bob Barns
Jerome F. Barnwell
Charles J. Baron, Jr.
Frank R. Baron
John Baron
Ronald P. Baron
Charles E. Barr
Clifford J. Barr, Jr.
Joseph Lindsey Barr
Norman F. Barr
Wallace E. Barr
William Charles Barr
Michael J. Barra
Ora Earl Barratt, Jr.
Robert F. Barratt
Manuel A. Barraza
George Barrell
Ignacio D. Barrera
Jaime Barreto
Alvin James Barrett
Andrew H. Barrett
Arlie P. Barrett
Courtenay L. Barrett, Jr.
David M. Barrett
Frank Robert Barrett
J. B. Barrett
James Joseph Barrett
Jesse Barrett
John J. Barrett, Jr.
John Michael Barrett
John Patrick Barrett, Jr.

Rush W. Barrett
Silas F. Barrett
Thomas G. Barrett
Thomas J. Barrett
Eugene A. Barrica
George M. Barrick, Jr.
James F. Barrier
Charles H. Barringer
Edgar Foy Barrington
Edward Paul Barrios
Bennie T. Barron
Edward M. Barron
George L. Barron
Lawrence H. Barron
Ruben Barron
Jack L. Barrons
Edward E. Barrow
Edwin S. Barrow
George C. Barrow
Henry G. Barrow
Roy E. Barrow
Arthur Agustus Barry
Edward M. Barry
Eugene C. Barry
Jerry Barry
Richard H. Barry
Richard J. Barry
Edward J. Barskitas
Valentine N. Barsoukoff
Davey Harley Bart
John L. Bartberger
Charles Tracy Barter
Frederick W. Barth
Harry James Barth
Cyril B. Bartholdi
Roger Post Bartholf
George H. Bartholomew
Lindsay S. Bartholomew
Gerald H. Bartholow
Joseph E. Bartle
Ernest P. Bartlett
Horace B. Bartlett, Jr.
Donald D. Bartley
Lawrence H. Bartley
Lynn E. Bartley
Raymond J. Bartley
Richard D. Bartley
Wayne J. Bartley
Matthew P. Bartnick
Louis E. Bartning
Theodore J. Bartol
Mickeal F. Bartola
Donald K. Bartoli
Leo R. Bartolo, Jr.
Jose A. Bartolomei
Bruce O. Barton
Charles W. Barton
Donald J. Barton
Dwayne W. Barton
Eldon L. Barton
Franklin D. Barton
Gene E. Barton
Howard R. Barton
James M. Barton
John E. Barton
John L. Barton
Raleigh Edward Barton, Jr.
Thomas A. Barton
James C. Bartram
John P. Bartueck
Horace J. Barwick
Elias G. Basa
Earl D. Basco
Hiram L. Basco
Roosevelt Basco
Roger W. Bascom
Charles Russell Bash
Freddie Basha
Edwin R. Basham
Ernest E. Basham
John H. Basham
Kenneth R. Basham
Donald B. Bashaw
Gilbert Bashem
Ernest E. Bashem
Marlin F. Basina
Kenneth Baskerville
Curtis D. Baskin
Herbert Lester Baslee, Jr.
Lester W. Bason
Gerald D. Basquin
Charlie O. Bass
James J. Bass
James W. Bass
Joseph T. Bass
Lonza Z. Bass
Nova L. Bass
Philip J. Bass
Robert L. Bass

Roy C. Bass
William T. Bass, Jr.
Daniel J. Bassarab
Henry D. Bassett
Weldon L. Bassett
William S. Bassett
Dwino J. Bassignani
William F. Bastie, Jr.
Marion F. Batchelor
Clyde H. Bateman
James Albert Bateman
Leroy Raymond Bateman
Marlyn Bateman, Jr.
Richard Alan Bateman
Lawrence H. Bater
Elmore C. Bates
Francis N. Bates
Harold H. Bates
John O. Bates, Jr.
Lonzo Bates
Thomas W. Bates
William A. Bates
Ronald D. Bateson
Luther R. Batey, Jr.
Joseph Batiste
Joseph Jack Batluck
Stanley R. Bator
Harold L. Batrez
James M. Batson
Roland Russell Batson, Jr.
Bobbie L. Batte
Lloyd Batten
Reginald James Batten
Charles R. Battershell
Amos Battle
Mike Battle, Jr.
Porter Wilson Batts
Claude Albert Batty, Jr.
George E. Baty
Willie J. Baty
Erwin G. Bauer
George F. Bauer, Jr.
Gerald Allen Bauer
Gerald W. Bauer
Harold B. Bauer
Jessie E. Bauer
John William Bauer
Lester W. Bauer
Louis A. Bauer
Philip F. Bauer, Jr.
Willie Bauer
George C. Bauerfeind
Melvin A. Bauerfield
Howard H. Bauernfiend
William Bernard Baugh
William Mayo Baugh, Jr.
Phillip J. Baughans
Allen E. Baugher
Allen A. Baughman
Donald E. Baughman
Richard Earl Baulk
Edgar D. Bauman
Gerald L. Bauman
George A. Baumer
Robert Black Baumer
Edward W. Baumgard, Jr.
Raymon Baumgardner
William M. Baumgardner
Robert Joel Baumgart
Gerald F. Baumgartner
Richard C. Baumgartner
Robert A. Baur
Harold J. Baus
Philip C. Baus
Eugene Edward Bauwin
Charles R. Bawden
Ralph J. Bax
George V. Baxley
Buddy H. Baxter
Donald Thomas Baxter
Douglas Baxter
Earl R. Baxter
Elfred Eugene Baxter
Jack Eugene Baxter
Lawrence Baxter
Louis M. Baxter
Neil B. Baxter
Samuel Castner Baxter
Thurston Richard Baxter
Walter J. Baxter, Jr.
William Thomas Baxter
Frank Daniel Bay
William A. Bay
Mark E. Baylark
Willard E. Bayles
Keith Robert Bayley
Charlie F. Baylor
Stanley E. Baylor
Billie C. Bayne

Bob L. Bayne
Jimmie D. Bays
Jesus C. Bazan
Willard A. Bazemore
Herbert L. Bazley
Benjamin R. Bazzell
Archie C. Beach, Jr.
Charles Beach, Jr.
Charles Robert Beach
Floyd T. Beach
Merl A. Beach
Rex J. Beach
Thomas Henry Beacham
John S. Beacher
Robert J. Beachy
John David Beagles
Thomas J. Beahm
Edward N. Beal
Lawrence Beal
Robert L. Beale
Judson Harmon Beall
James B. Beals
Donald Beam
Gordon R. Beam
Harry Raymond Beam
Richard M. Beam
Charles L. Beams
Frederick B. Bean
Harry R. Bean
Henry H. Bean
Jackson Ray Bean
John Larkin Bean
Walter Donald Bean
Billy Bear
Elmer Bear
Huville E. Bear
Stanely W. Bear
Beverly Rhea Beard
Bonnie D. Beard
David Beard
David L. Beard
Harold E. Beard, Jr.
Howard Beard, Jr.
Richard R. Beard
Robert A. Beard
Robert D. Beard
Robert N. Beard
Harold Martyn Beardall
Daniel E. Beardsless
Ramon C. Bearse, Jr.
Clyde Bearstail
Carrie L. Beasley
Clifford D. Beasley
Clifford L. Beasley
Henry E. Beasley
John A. Beasley
Kenneth Lee Beasley
Morris F. Beasley
Wilbur E. Beasley
Willard G. Beasley
Gerald G. Beason
Howard Eugene Beason
Franklin E. Beattie
David W. Beatty
Glen I. Beatty
Thomas W. Beatty
Benjamin L. Beaty
Charles E. Beaty
Sherman Randolph Beaty
Hubert W. Beaubien
Ernest R. Beaubier
Victor P. Beauchamp, Jr.
Joseph C. Beauchemin
Alfred Beauchesne, Jr.
Robert A. Beaudette
William G. Beaudoin
Joseph Beaulieu
Richard J. Beaulieu
James W. Beaumont
Gerard E. Beaupre
Clarence C. Beaver, Jr.
Jefferson Beaver
Bandy Beavers, Jr.
Harold R. Beavers
James I. Beavers
Thomas L. Beavers
Billy W. Beaverson
Wayne E. Bebb
Evert H. Bebee
Lavern Harold Becher
Donald K. Bechtel
John Harold Bechtel
Richard L. Bechtel
Bruce Beck
Jack A. Beck
Jay Eugene Beck
Joseph S. Beck
Leo D. Beck
Lewis O. Beck

Robert Augustus Beck
Robert C. Beck
Roy W. F. Beck
William E. Beck
William G. Beck
Clarence R. Becker
Clarence W. Becker
Donald R. Becker
Ferrill A. Becker
Francis Eugene Becker
Grover Becker
James Lee Becker
James M. Becker
Joseph L. Becker
Joseph Martin Becker
Melvin H. Becker
Richard R. Becker
Robert C. Becker
Robert Reed Becker
Roger Paul Becker
Russell R. Becker
William F. Becker
Harold L. Beckert
Clyde N. Beckett, Jr.
Robert H. Beckett
William Moore Beckett
Henry L. Beckham
Larry E. Beckham
Kenneth Eugene Beckley
Willie Beckley
Carl F. Becklin
Charles W. Becklin
Charles L. Beckman
Darwin P. Beckwith
J. D. Beckwith
Melvin C. Beckwith
Arthur Edward Becton
Fred Beddingfield
Jasper W. Beddingfield
Norman C. Bedell
Frank J. Bednara, Jr.
Charles J. Bedore
Raymond J. Bedore
Vincent V. Bedoya
John H. Beebe
John Ward Beebe
Wilbert C. Beecher
Carl Beechwood
Milton M. Beed
Robert E. Beede
Eldert J. Beek
Joseph L. Beel
Charles P. Beeler
James Dayton Beeler
Thomas L. Beelman
Roger Baron Beem
James L. Beeman
Bernard A. Beemon
Norman L. Been
Wilson J. Beene, Jr.
George Edward Beer
Leroy Julian Beer
Alan Beers
Frank N. Beerwa
Albert W. Beerwinkle
Jack Melvin Beeson
Austin Wescott Beetle, Jr.
James E. Beever
Frank W. Begasse
Gerald Lester Beggs
John E. Beggs
Frank Earl Begley
James E. Begley
Julius Begley
Clyde J. Behney
Christian A. Behr, Jr.
Raymond J. Behringer
Russell Behringer
Floyd J. Beichner
Josiah S. Beiler, Jr.
Dale L. Beishir
Charles Beisswanger
William E. Beitel
Ruben Bejarano
Arthur N. Belanger
Edward Robert Belardi, Jr.
Wedro C. Belarmino
Samuel L. Belasky
John A. Belavic
Claude Hicks Belcher
Donald N. Belcher
James H. Belcher, Jr.
Howard R. Belden
Carroll E. Belenski
Andrew Beley
Bernard J. Belfe
Joseph A. Belfiore
John L. Belhumeur
Robert L. Belille

Arthur J. Beliveau
Robert E. Beliveau
Earl L. Belk
Augustine A. Belko
George P. Belkom
Alton R. Bell
Alvin D. Bell
Beaumont B. Bell, Jr.
Bonnie Bell
Bulo Bell, Jr.
Charlie Bell
Charlie D. Bell
Delbert C. Bell
Donald Edwin Bell
Donald I. Bell
Donnie E. Bell
Edmond V. Bell
Floyd K. Bell
Gary A. Bell
Herbert D. Bell
James D. Bell
James H. Bell
James Harold Bell
James Lloyd Bell
James Marcella Bell
Jessie S. Bell
John Clayton Bell
Johnnie C. Bell
Johnnie G. Bell, Jr.
Joseph T. Bell
Lawrence Bell
Melvin R. Bell
Peter C. Bell
Ralph Bell
Richard A. Bell
Robert A. Bell
Robert E. Bell
Robert G. Bell
Thomas F. Bell
Thomas L. Bell
Timothy Bell
Vernard G. Bell
Vesteen Bell, Jr.
Wardell A. Bell
William D. Bell
William E. Bell
William G. Bell
William John Bell
William Bell, Jr.
Morgan V. Bellah
Clyde Hughes Bellamy
Freeling W. Bellamy
Howard Dale Bellamy
Roy K. Bellamy, Jr.
James Bellan
Bennie E. Bellar
Lowell W. Bellar
Francis A. Bellasino
Salvatore T. Bellavia
Alfred M. Bellavigna
Robert P. Belle
Edgar Lucian Bellefleur
Nicolai Bellegarde
James E. Beller
Dan Freas Belles
Elza L. Bellew
Edward M. Bellflower
William H. Bellinger
Rosario J. Bellio
Donald P. Bellis
Archie K. Bellon
Charles O. Bellon, Jr.
Richard R. Bellon, Jr.
J. E. Bellon-Rodriguez
Glen E. Bellow
James Mayo Bellows, Jr.
Albert Bellucci
Robert Bellus
Harold D. Bellville
George A. Belmar
Frank J. Belskie
Vincent P. Belstle
Arthur L. Belt
Claude C. Belt
Milford C. Belt
Ollie James Belt
Robert J. Belt
Garold E. Belton
Wyatt H. Belton
Enrique Beltran
David Leroy Beltz
Frankey D. Beltz
Lloyd E. Beltz
William B. Beltz
Thomas La V. Belyea
George E. Bemis
Juan D. Benavente
Paul Benavides
Edward Benavidez

Robert Herbert Benck
Donald J. Bender
Earl E. Bender
Harold V. Bender
Ralph Bender
Robert L. Bender
Victor V. Bender
William Bender, Jr.
Leonard J. Bendinsky
John D. Bendix
William C. Bendorf
Fred W. Benedict
Landon E. Benedict
Joseph A. Benedino
James W. Benefiel
Torney R. Benefiel
Denson H. Benefield
William M. Benefield, Jr.
Robert F. Beneke
Walter Charles Beneke, Jr.
Frank Joseph Benenati
James H. Benfield
Edward Clyde Benfold
Martin Benge
James A. Benger
Claude F. Bengtson
William L. Bengtson
Robert W. Benington
Richard C. Benitez
N. Benjamin, Jr.
Otis P. Benjamin
Robert Kendall Benjamin
William M. Benn
Joseph A. Benner
Warren W. Benner
Bennie Bennett, Jr.
Bert A. Bennett
Billy G. Bennett
Bobby L. Bennett
Boyd J. Bennett
Calvin Bennett
Chauncey A. Bennett, Jr.
Clemmett Bennett, Jr.
Clyde L. Bennett
Clyde W. Bennett
Earl Bennett
Emory L. Bennett
George G. Bennett
Granvil L. Bennett
Harry M. Bennett
Hayden Bennett
Henry A. Bennett
Hoyt J. Bennett
Hughes Bennett
John R. Bennett
Keith E. Bennett
Kenneth F. Bennett
Kenneth L. Bennett
Leo F. Bennett
Leonard H. Bennett
Marshall Edward Bennett
Percy L. Bennett
Raymond Bennett, Jr.
Raymond Rodney Bennett
Richard W. Bennett
Robert C. Bennett
Russell M. Bennett, Jr.
Snowden Bennett, Jr.
Stanley K. Bennett
Vanderbilt Bennett
William A. Bennett
William D. Bennett
William M. Bennett
Clyde Joseph Benney
Robert W. Bennington
Andrew Benoit
Joseph Pierre Benoit
Lionel V. Benoit
Marcel P. Benoit
Alfred G. Bensinger, Jr.
Norman E. Bensinger
David Benson
Gerald B. Benson
Kenneth L. Benson
Laverne G. Benson
Maurice Benson, Jr.
Thomas W. Benson
William Benson
William A. Benthien
Leo M. Bentkowski
Billy J. Bentley
Clarence Lyle Bentley
Francis H. Bentley
Jerry D. Bentley
Robert Carl Bentley
Russell D. Bentley
Corydon W. Benton
Daniel F. Benton
George M. Benton

John E. Benton
Obbie M. Benton
Paul A. Benton
William Benton, Jr.
Harold G. Bentz
Xavier J. Benziger, Jr.
Cesar Ignacio Benzoni
Karl J. Bera
Thomas Henry Berardi
Ignacio M. Berasis
Jennings H. Berdine
Henry Berendowski
Alfred M. Beres
Charles Wilmer Berg
John Anthony Berg
Marvin Leland Berg
Richard William Berg
Stanley M. Berg
Walter E. Berg
William Berg, Jr.
Ralph O. Berge
Donald E. Berger
Francis C. Berger
Gerard P. Berger
Lloyd M. Berger
Stanley L. Berger
Charles Francis Bergeron
Dwight M. Bergeron
Joseph E. Bergeron
Paul Bergeron
Stanley E. Bergeron
Leon Jay Berghouse
Richard D. Bergland
Louis H. Bergman
Robert Arnold Bergman
William J. Bergman
Louis Henry Bergmann
Robert O. Bergmann
William D. Bergmann
Orle Sidney Bergner
Harold E. Bergquist
Gordon Floyd Bergren
Clarence O. Bergstraesser
Edmund J. Bergum
Walter Peter Berhing
Milo Allen Berke
Bromley E. Berkeley
Patrick J. Berkley
Robert H. Berlemann
Earl J. Berling
Anthony C. Berlinghiere
Bernard Berman
Sully I. Berman, Jr.
Antonio Bermudez
Joseph S. Berna
Joe M. Bernal
Leo J. Bernal
Leon John Bernal, Jr.
Natibidad Bernal
Jorge Bernal-Medina
Alfred P. Bernard
Elton J. Bernard
Alfred J. Bernardy
Fred W. Berneburg, Jr.
William N. Bernet
Ralph L. Bernhardt
Gerald N. Bernhart
Robert W. Bernier
Stephen L. Bernier
Wilfred Joseph Bernier
William A. Bernier
Maurice J. Berning
James A. Berninger
Robert L. Bernloehr
Anthony Bernosky
Matthew R. Berres
Clarence R. Berreth
Henry L. Berrien
Jackie G. Berrier
Diaz Victor M. Berrios
Gilberto A. Berrios
Pedro M. Berrios
Velazquez L. Berrios
Candido Berrios-Ortiz
Jorge Berrios-Santiago
Antonio Berrios-Suarez
A. D. Berry
Arthur Berry, Jr.
Benny Berry
Billy Berry
Billy A. Berry
Dennis Joseph Berry
Edmund William Berry
Floyd E. Berry
Fred C. Berry, Jr.
George W. Berry
Henry W. Berry
James Berry
Jerome G. Berry, Jr.

L. J. Berry
Leonard Berry
Raymond H. Berry
Richard W. Berry
Robert H. Berry
Robert Mc Thies Berry
Jerald J. Berryessa
Richard D. Berryhill
Bennie Joe Berryman
Bryan Dugles Berryman
Thomas Richard Berryman
Robert Eugene Bertain
Joseph P. Bertani
Robert L. Bertolio
Charles E. Bertram
Robert L. Bertram
Thomas E. Bertram, Jr.
Gerald J. Bertrand
Leo B. Bertrand
Frederick W. Bertrang
Joseph P. Berube
Herbert Besch, Jr.
Robert L. Besemer
Alva L. Beshears
John Beskid, Jr.
John Beskon
William H. Bess
Arnold L. Best
Billy J. Best
Carl H. Best
James L. Best
John I. Best
Leonard J. Best
Robert A. Best, Jr.
John J. Betancourt
Autrey J. Betar
Robert Charles Beth
Horace Bethea
Charles A. Betsworth
John S. Bettem
Ernest D. Bettencourt
Michael Duane Betthauser
Allan Shields Bettis
Guy L. Bettis, Jr.
Baxter H. Betts, Jr.
Charles C. Sr Betts
George L. Betts
James R. Betts
Clifford Allyn Betz
Dewitt Betz
Henry J. Betz, Jr.
Irvin N. Betz
Robert Joseph Betz
Grover R. Betzer
Michael J. Bevacqua
Robert Warren Bevans
Charles M. Bevels
Perry Mcphail Bevens
Leo E. Bever
Felix R. Beveraggi
Bruce Beveridge, Jr.
James A. Beveridge
John H. Beverley, Jr.
Arthur Q. Beverly
Otis E. Beverly
Fred George Bevfoden
Vincent James Bevilacqua
James Elmer Beville
Roger Allen Beville
Ersel Bevilock
Bruno D. Bevivino
Floyd Traylor Bey
Dean H. Beyer
Harold Arthur Beyer
Romero E. Bezares
Arthur Gaston Bezart
Robert R. Bianchi
Daniel C. Bianco
Vito J. Bianco
Kennith L. Biard
Donald G. Bias
Donnie L. Bias
Robert P. Bibb
Wayne C. Bibeau
Robert O. Bichard
Carl J. Bichler
Robert Sterling Bick
Oval O. Bickel
Robert T. Bickel
Glenn W. Bickell
Leroy Bickers
Gerald R. Bickham
David Ray Bickley
Marvin Bickley, Jr.
Robert A. Bicknell
Glen Earl Biddle
Nelson A. Biddle
Carlos R. Bidopia
William R. Biedenkapp

Matthew John Biedka
Thomas Bienaszewski
Aloysis C. Bienkowski
Paul Henry Bienvenu
Robert E. Bienz
James C. Bierer
Jimmie B. Bierner
James E. Bierwirth
Ronald S. Bies
Leon D. Biesheuvel
Thomas C. Biesterveld
Jack Beverly Bigden
Lyman W. Iii Bigelow
Richard E. Bigelow
Charles L. Bigger
Guy K. Biggerstaff
Elmer Tee Biggs
Glynn R. Biggs
Lester W. Biggs
Samuel W. Biggs
Donald Gaile Bigham
Robert George Bigley
Eugene J. Bigness
Joseph E. Bilby
Petro Bileckyj
Dwayne Leroy Biles
Hubert L. Bill
Clarence A. Billheimer
Joseph C. Billick
Walter H. Billiel
Milton P. Billigmeier
Richard J. Billinger
Frank Bond Billings, Jr.
Charles Le Billingslea, Jr.
Billy C. Billington
Donald Sydney Bills, Jr.
Farel R. Bills
Marion D. Bills
Adrian L. Bilodeau
Joseph B. Bilohlavek
James C. Bilty
Michael G. Bilyeu
Herman Binam
William Binaxas
Clarence E. Bindt
Donald Harold Binek
Morgan Edward Binet
Theodore F. Binette
George L. Bing
Jerry Douglas Bingaman
Wilson Lee Bingaman
Charles F. Binge
Marvin H. Binggeli
Holman B. Bingham
Jimmie D. Bingham
James F. Binkley
John R. Binnicker
Charles C. Binnion
James E. Bionaz
Alfred Duncan Birch, Jr.
David K. Birch
James A. Birch
Edward E. Birchfield
Silas Birchmore, Jr.
Charles F. Bird
Delbert W. Bird
James P. Bird
John O. Bird
Louis Henry Bird
Milo W. Bird
Robert James Bird
Rosado Enrique Bird
Leo R. Birdsall
Peter A. Birkel
Galen S. Birkeland
Gary A. Birkhimer
Melvin A. Birkholz
Paul E. Birmingham
John Birochak
Leo Anthony Biross
Frank Leon Birrell
Walter Lester Birt
Frank Biselis
Arthur L. Bishop
Avery G. Bishop
Billy Rhea Bishop
David Earl Bishop
Donald L. Bishop
Eulis Edwin Bishop
James D. Bishop
James E. Bishop
James W. Bishop
John K. Bishop
Joseph H. Bishop
Lester E. Bishop
Pink W. Bishop
Robert A. Bishop
Robert G. Bishop
Theodore C. Bishop

Travis A. Bishop
Wesley W. Bishop, Jr.
Charles H. Bissell
George T. Bissell
James R. Bissell
John Jackson Bissell, Jr.
Stephen Anthony Bitner
Gordon R. Bittell
Alfred Allen Bitter
Douglas R. Bitterle
John Lewin Bitters
Gordon R. Bittle
Franklin E. Bittner
Medon Armin Bitzer
Bennie M. Bivens
William F. Bivens
Bennie M. Bivins
Lloyd J. Bixby
Thomas M. Bixler
Dominic F. Bizzarro
Lawrence L. Bjelland
Orville C. Bjerkebek
Robert Bjorge
William Wesley Bjork
Abner S. Black
Adrain Black
Alfred D. Black
Clement L. Black
Clyde Edward Black
Darwin M. Black
Fritz F. Black
Huey G. Black
James Edward Black
James Marvin Black
James W. Black
James W. H. Black
John L. Black
Junior Black
Norman S. Black
Paul A. Black
Paul Eugene Black
Robert A. Black
Robert H. Black
Robert J. Black
Robert Raymond Black
Shuman Harlan Black
Stanley D. Black
Stephen Black
Vance Eugene Black
Wayne Forrest Black
William H. Black
William M. Black
Winfield M. Black
Arthur I. Black-Hawk
Harold E. Blackburn
Roger Blackburn
Thomas J. Blackburn
Neldon E. Blackett
Forest W. Blackford
William C. Blackford, Jr.
Charles E. Blackley
Vinner E. Blackley
Jack Warren Blacklidge
Mack J. Blackmon
Thomas W. Blackmon, Jr.
Tilmer H. Blacksmith
Paul Blackstock
Eugene O. Blackston
Benjamin R. Blackwell
Thomas L. Blackwell
Turner F. Blackwell
James R. Blackwood
Remus M. Blackwood
Russell E. Blade
Kenneth E. Blades
Wendell E. Blagg
Laurent R. Blain
William C. Blain
Bobby R. Blair
Charles J. Blair
Elzie L. Blair
Eugene S. Blair
George W. Blair
James A. Blair
James R. Blair
Larry L. Blair
Merviol W. Blair
Paul Leverne Blair
Raymond Joseph Blair
Robert E. Blair
Robert R. Blair
Roy T. Blair, Jr.
Samual B. Blair
Warren Daniel Blair
Theodore W. Blaisdell
Norman M. Blake
Reynolds G. Blake
Robert E. Blake
Robert L. Blake
Ronald Blake

Ted Blake
Warren Blake, Jr.
Virgil A. Blakeley
David R. Blakelock
George W. Blakely
Robert E. Blakely
Willis Blakely
John E. Blakemore
Richard J. Blakeney
Gerald E. Blakeslee
Leland F. Blakeslee
James C. Blakesley
Robert T. Blakey
Glen Blakley
Max H. Blalock
Walter M. Blalock
Adrian G. Blanchard, Jr.
Donald Roy Blanchard
Edward B. Blanchard
Harlan D. Blanchard
Joseph L. Blanchard
Thomas W. Blanchard
Archie L. Blanchett
Charles C. Blanchette
Omer R. Blanchette
Robert W. Blanchfield
Bennie Bland
David P. Bland
Douglas K. Bland
Ellie B. Bland
W. C. Bland
Don G. Blandford
Jack S. Blankenbaker
John Andrew Blankenburg
Charles D. Blankenship
Charles L. Blankenship
Clinton L. Blankenship
Donald Keith Blankenship
Herman W. Blankenship
Randolph M. Blankenship
Roy B. Blankenship
Willie F. Blanks
Douglas W. Blankschen
Alonzo Gene Blanton
Emory M. Blanton
Howard Henry Blanton
Paul J. Blasczyk
William S. Blasdel
Stanley P. Blase
Edward Blasejewski
Hubert F. Blashill
Joseph Blasiole
Edward Francis Blasko
Thomas J. Blataric
Joseph Everett Blattman
Edward F. Blazejewski
Stuart M. Blazer
Stanley A. Blazewicz
Alva Leslie Bleau
Ferdinand T. Blechinger
Jerry C. Bleen
Bruce A. Blegen
George H. Bleicher
John R. Blenkinsop
Chester Blevins
Curtis J. Blevins
Galliehue Blevins
Herene Kline Blevins
Joe I. Blevins
John D. Blevins, Jr.
Johnny H. Blevins
Lonie Karnes Blevins
Paul Blevins
William H. Blevins
Paul R. Blew
Erich W. Bley
William E. Blickenstaff
John Dorland Blinn
Clyde A. Blisard
Clarence B. Bliss
Joseph A. Blissenbach
Arnold L. Block
Gerald V. Block
Kenneth R. Block
Robert S. Block
Wilbert G. Block
Harold G. Blodgett
Russell R. Blodgett
Fred Ernest Bloesch
Robert F. Blohowiak
Charles Herbert Blomberg
Deloy Blood
Clarence E. Bloodsworth
Charles Bloom
Frederick J. Bloom
Raymond U. Bloom
Robert F. Bloom
Frank E. Bloomenshine
David F. Blosser

Guy Blosser, Jr.
Jackey D. Blosser
Alfred M. Blotz
Clyde D. Blount
Evans G. Blount
James R. Blount
John C. Blount, Jr.
Rex P. Blow
Ormar G. Blowers
Daniel Lee Blubaugh
Adelbert Blue
Billie S. Blue
Clois M. Sr Blue
Emerson R. Blue
George J. Blue
Henry Blue
Samuel T. Blue
Willie E. Blue
Adolph D. Bluedog
Shirley K. Bluhm
Lee Bluit
Nelson F. Blum
John T. Blume
Andrew G. Blumhoefer
Howard Bluttman
Richard Lee Bly
Stanley A. Blye, Jr.
Milton Blythe
Roy S. Boach
Stuart A. Boardman
Clarence E. Boatwright
Hoyt B. Boatwright
Herbert L. Boaz, Jr.
Swanson Lee Bobbitt
John William Bobbs
Howard T. Bobo
James E. Bobovnyk
Thaddeus S. Bobowiec
Michael Bochnovic
Robert C. Bockey
Theodore J. Bockhoff
Eugene Bockhorn
Fred B. Bockleman
Henry W. Bode, Jr.
Kenneth A. Bodeker
Thomas Richard Bodell
Harry E. Bodenhamer, Jr.
John A. Bodewig
Melvin J. Bodily
Ernest L. Bodison
Peter B. Bodnarik
William V. Boehler, Jr.
Henry C. Boehling
John Anton Boehm
Richard F. Boehme
Richard F. J. Boehme, Jr.
Vincent Carl Boehnert
Richard W. Boer, Jr.
Lester W. Boerner
Eldean E. Boese
Fred Walter Boesiger
Bruce Duane Boettcher
Henry F. Boetticher
Donald E. Bogan
Clifford R. Bogard
Glen D. Bogard
Clayton L. Bogart, Jr.
Martin Bogart, Jr.
William T. Bogart
Howard J. Bogenschild
Leonard J. Boger
John Bogert, Jr.
Robert A. Bogert
Dixie F. Boggess, Jr.
Earnest H. Boggess
Maurice Ivan Boggess
Bish Boggs
Charles W. Boggs
Elmo D. Boggs
James V. Boggs
Virgil Boggs
Edward J. Boglin
Leonard G. Bogusz
Thomas Bohatch
Raymond N. Boheler
Robert H. Bohl
Neil H. Bohm
Edward James Bohnas
Howard L. Bohner
Herman C. Bohnke, Jr.
Rosario D. Boisse
Elmer M. Boisseau, Jr.
Jacques A. Boissonneault
John P. Boisvenue
Eugene R. Boisvert
Joseph R. Boitano
Charlie Boitnoitt, Jr.
Albert W. Boland
Arthur A. Boland

Frederick Boland
Robert J. Boland
William H. Bolander
C. G. Bolden
Charles E. Bolden
Francis J. Bolden
George E. Bolden
Raymond M. Bolden
Freddie R. Bolds
William Frederick Bolduc
Vladimir Boldyrev
German O. Bolen
James E. Bolen
Robert A. Bolen
Robert J. Bolen
Darwin E. Boler
Louis Carter Boles
Richard G. Boles
Herbert E. Boley
Alvin J. Bolf
James John Bolicek, Jr.
Billy R. Bolin
James H. Bolin
Philip L. Bolin
Denver Henry Boling
Howard Gerald Boling
Loyd D. Boling
Roy Lee Boling
Ross L. Bolinger, Jr.
Duane Lee Boll
John Frederick Boll
Lloyd Bolles, Jr.
Jesse B. Bolling
Thomas E. Bolling
Charles R. Bollinger
Raymond E. Bollman, Jr.
Joseph M. Bologna
Richard L. Bolognani
George Chris Bolotas
John L. Bolster
James T. Bolsum
Donald David Bolt
Frank J. Bolt
George D. Bolton
James J. Bolton
Marshall D. Bolton
Richard T. Bolton
Robert E. Bolton
William M. Bolton
Elmer Bolus
Richard Leslie Bolyard
Earnest H. Boman
Donald Bombardier
John D. Bomer
De Jesus A. Bonano
Frank L. Bonar
Wetzel Z. Bonar
Herbert F. Bonas
William E. Bonawitz
Ted Bonchek
Leonard J. Bonczkowski
Charles E. Bond
Dathron Bond
Elihue Bond, Jr.
Guy E. Bond
John H. Bond
Lee W. Bond
Malcolm D. Bond
Ralph A. Bond
Raymond I. Bond
Robert D. Bond
Wilbur L. Bond
Isaac Bondar
Harve Bonds, Jr.
Charles E. Bone
Jessie C. P. Bone
Leroy Bone
Zack A. Bone
Ted Ralph Bones
Carl Bonet-Morales
John W. Bonetti
Robert W. Boney
Frank J. Bonfiglio
Warner T. Bonfoey, Jr.
Marcus H. Bongard
Almedina D. Bonilla
Gonzalo Bonilla-Arce
D. Bonilla-Davila
Julio Bonilla-Vega
Roger Rapheal Bonin
Rudolph Bonincontri
John Carnevale Bonino
Richard J. Bonkowski
Clarence Bonner
Gerald P. Bonner
James W. Bonner
Robert L. Bonner
William N. Bonner
Robert F. Bonnett

Edwin A. Bonnette
Buddy Joe Bonney
Frank V. Bonomo
John F. Bonser
Jacob H. Bonshire
Arthur Milton Bonwell, Jr.
John R. Bonzo
Clem R. Boody
Bobby R. Booher
George W. Booher
James E. Booher
Andrew G. Book
Gerald R. Book
Gerald Richard Bookamire
Alexander Booker
Dorsie Henry Booker, Jr.
George Glen Booker
Joseph Booker
Oscar L. Booker
Robert L. Booker
Walter G. Booker
Walter M. Booker
Joe J. Bookout
Arthur Howard Books
Boyce J. Boone
Charles H. Boone
Charles X. Boone
James L. Boone
Leroy Boone
Willie Boone
Harry W. Boord
George O. Boos
Carnell Edward Booth
Euell C. Booth, Jr.
Gilbert H. Booth
Guy R. Booth
Herbert H. Booth
Izea Booth
Robert E. Booth
Robert W. Booth
Truman E. Booth
William Edward Booth, Jr.
Glen E. Boothe
Kenneth Jordan Boothe
Albert E. Boothroyd
Denman G. Booton
Frank J. Bopp
Felix V. Bor
John Manley Borah
Robert S. Boras
Anthony Simon Boraski
Walter Carl Borawski
Salvador G. Borbon
Alfred C. Bordeau
Donald L. Borden
Charles H. Borders
Edward Lee Borders
Roscoe Borders, Jr.
Edward F. Borell
Emanuel Borg
Harry W. Borgia
William C. Borgman
Clifford J. Boring
Paul E. Boring
William R. Boring
Alfred G. Borkland, Jr.
Henry Adalbert Borkowski
Maxmillian J. Borkowski
Joseph Borla
William J. Borland, Jr.
Everett H. Borley
Donald M. Born
Frederick William J. Born
Ralph E. Bornes
Edward J. Borowski, Jr.
Marvin L. Borror
Walter O. Borror
Richard West Borschel
John Peter Borseti
Arthur W. Borst
Charles L. Bortner, Jr.
Donald J. Bortner
William J. Bortolotti
Loren C. Bortz
Donald Lee Boruff
Charles Borum
James Borum
Ralph L. Borum
Carlos P. Borunda
George E. Borus
Merlin W. Borwick
Lloyd J. Bosben
Edward Ronald Bosch
Marvin Boschee
Albert C. Bosford
Merlyn Earl Boshaw
Robert E. Boshears
Marvin L. Bosher
Nick E. Bosko

Jack Bosselli
Frederick W. Bossert
Adolph M. Bosshardt
Charles P. Bost
William A. Bost
David Bostic, Jr.
Frank Bostic
Charles L. Bostick
John Bostick
Harry F. Bostrom
John Stewart Bostwick
Elvin L. Boswell
George Leo Boswell
Anton Botek, Jr.
Alfred M. Botelho
Glenn R. Bothwell
Robert H. Botkin
Philip A. Botsford
Fred J. Bott, Jr.
Henry Bott
William Joseph Botter
Earl Edward Bottoms
William G. Bottorff
Sidney J. Botts
Arthur A. Bouchard
Lawrence J. Bouchard
Lucien J. Bouchard, Jr.
Rolland Bouchard
John G. Boucher
Joseph Hector Boucher
Jules T. Bouckhuyt
Amos Jules Boudreaux
Felix Boudreaux
Leonard R. Boughan
Ralph S. Boughman
James M. Boughter
James H. Boughton
Ludwest J. Bouillion
Christos S. Boukedes
Earl C. Bouldin
Joseph W. Boulware
Norman L. Bounds
Robert L. Bounds
Travis O. Bounds
Allan John Bouquin
William Arthur Bouquin
Ernest H. Bourassa
George L. Bourdeau
Harry J. Bourdeau
Robert L. Bourdeau
George D. Bourdieu
Thomas Joseph Bourg
Alvin Roland Bourgeois
Joseph R. Bourgeois
George D. Bourieu
William C. Bourke
A. D. Bourland
Lucien J. Bourque
Norman A. Bourque
G. W. Bourrage
Gerard Arthur Bourret
James Henry Bove
Richard R. Bove
Paul Hugo Bovensiepen
Edwin A. Bowden
Eugene Whitney Bowden
Gerald B. Bowden
Peter H. Bowden
William Everett Bowden
William L. Bowden
Ben R. Bowen
Charles E. Bowen
Charles L. Bowen
Edward Marion Bowen
Elzie R. Bowen
Frederick William Bowen
Glenn L. Bowen
Jack L. Bowen
James R. Bowen
Joseph A. Bowen
Murray Malone Bowen
Norman Edgar Bowen
Richard Bowen
Robert A. Bowen
Arthur John Bower, Jr.
Richard Langdon Bower
Robert C. Bowerman
William J. Bowerman
Harold C. Bowers
Harry L. Sr Bowers
Horace N. Bowers, Jr.
James Elmore Bowers
Jefferson A. Bowers
John R. Bowers
Lester J. Bowers
Paul B. Bowers
Raymond T. Bowers
Robert Lyman Bowers, Jr.
Russell H. Bowers, Jr.

Thomas N. Bowers
W. F. Bowers
Frank Bowie
Phom Bowie
Richard A. Bowler
Larry A. Bowles
Milas E. Bowlin
Archie J. Bowling
Charles F. Bowling
Darrell R. Bowling
Jerry C. Bowling
Karl F. Bowling
Lawrence Bowling
Morris A. Bowling
Warren Bowling
Allen Milford Bowman
Curtis L. Bowman
Herbert L. Bowman
James C. Bowman
Joseph Wisler Bowman
Lloyd Pugmire Bowman
Mason J. Bowman
Richard E. Bowman
Richard Murrill Bowman
Jack T. Bowser
Lemuel R. Bowser
Roland L. Bowser
Stanley B. Bowsher
Ronald C. Bowshier
Benny Bowstring
John David Bowyer
Bobby S. Box
William S. Boxer
Alvin A. Boxler
George W. Boyce
James A. Boyce
James L. Boyce
Marvin L. Boyce
Ronald L. Boyce
Willie C. Boyce
Alton C. Boyd
Barney J. Boyd
Charles E. Boyd
Charles W. Boyd
Donald W. Boyd
Edward Joseph Boyd
Harold R. Boyd
Hugh Walter Boyd
James E. Boyd
John Douglas Boyd
John Gilbert Boyd
Joseph Edward Boyd
Lonzo Boyd, Jr.
Mose Boyd, Jr.
Richard A. Boyd
Robert J. Boyd
Sammy J. Boyd
Simon Boyd
William O. Boyd
William Q. Boyd
William T. Boyd
Melvin Boyden
Stewart S. Boyden
James L. Boydston
Thomas W. Boydston
Alfred N. Boyer, Jr.
Andrew P. Boyer
Charles Edwin Boyer
Donald Frederick Boyer
Gerald F. Boyer
Glennon J. Boyer
Howard E. Boyer
Joseph G. Boyer
Robert M. Boyer
Virgil W. Boyer, Jr.
William H. Boyer
William S. Boyer
Silas W. Boyiddle
Wayne J. Boyk
Edward P. Boykin
Freeman E. Boykin
Hugh J. Boylan
Thomas Joseph Boylan
Albert Boyle
Clarence Edward Boyle, Jr.
Douglas R. Boyle
Earl B. Boyle
John Joseph Boyle
Terrance F. Boyle
Thomas D. Boyle
Ralph L. Boyles
Wayne Eugene Boyles
Joseph Bozza, Jr.
Palmer Sylvester Braaten
John F. Brabant
Ferdinand O. Braboy
Alfredo Bracamonte
Calvin Howard Brace
William Bracewell

James W. Bracken, Jr.
Jimmie Bracken
Russell Bracken
Billie E. Brackenbury
Norman C. Brackett
Arthur Bracknell
Isaac M. Bradburn, Jr.
Harold F. Braddock
James Braddock
Linsey Braden
Perry O. Braden
Robert D. Braden
Clark M. Bradford
David Bradford
Dennis B. Bradford
Edward F. Bradford, Jr.
Herbert L. Bradford
Leonard G. Bradford
Paul G. Bradford
Reginald O. Bradford
Ulysses H. Bradford
Walter J. Bradicich
Donald R. Bradish
Douglas H. T. Bradlee
Alford L. Bradley
Bobby L. Bradley
Charles W. Bradley
Donald Joseph Bradley
Earl L. Bradley
Edgar N. Bradley
Eldon R. Bradley
Floyd Bradley, Jr.
Frederick T. Bradley
George C. Bradley, Jr.
George W. Bradley
Gerald Paul Bradley
Harry C. Bradley, Jr.
James Bradley
Jerry D. Bradley
Kenneth E. Bradley
Lewis Bradley, Jr.
Napoleon Bradley
Oscar Samuel Bradley
Paul R. Bradley
Peter J. Bradley
Ralph Porter Bradley
Raymond G. Bradley
Ronald G. Bradley
Thomas B. Bradley
William C. Bradley
William J. Bradley
Wallace B. Bradly
George D. Brado
Alfred Paul Bradshaw
Billie Frank Bradshaw
Charles W. Bradshaw
Clarence Bradshaw, Jr.
David F. Bradshaw
Freddie Lee Bradshaw
Robert Henry Bradshaw
Verlan R. Bradshaw
George Ervine Bradway
Judson Jack Bradway
Dennis H. Brady
Eldridge Brady
John T. Brady
Kenneth Earl Brady
Robert C. Brady
Anthony Braga
Charles T. Bragg
Charles W. Bragg
Clifton C. Bragg
Nicholas M. Bragg
Orval Richmond Bragg
Raymond F. Bragg
Reuben R. Bragg
William P. Bragg, Jr.
Robert E. Brailey
George H. Brainard
George Spencer Brainard
Philip F. Braithwaite
Robert E. Braithwaite
James W. Brake
Edward F. Brakes
James R. Braly
Richard Quinlan Braman
Francis Bramande
James S. Bramblett, Jr.
James L. Brambo
Ray G. Bramhill
James T. Brammer
Ross Kay Bramwell
Bobby P. Branch
Charles S. Branch
Elmer J. Branch
John E. Branch
Melvin Branch
Nathan L. Branch, Jr.
Samuel A. Branch, Jr.

Manuel Branco
Joe Lycurgus Brand, Jr.
Elmer H. Brandanger
Chrle A. Brandenburg
Clifton Brandenburg
Kenneth Brandenburg
Ralph Brandenburg
Ralph D. Brandenburg
Charles N. Brander
Donald S. Brander
Robert D. Brandes
Bernard Lee Brandfass
Charles Nelson Brandner
Delbert Brandon
Ewing A. Brandon
N. Y. Brandon
Sterling Brandon, Jr.
Theodore A. Brandow
Cecil William Brandsted
Arnold N. Brandt
Carroll G. Brandt
Edward D. Brandt
Lyle H. Brandt
Walter John Brandt
William Eugene Brandt
Albert C. Brandvold
Benny L. Brandvold
Clyde Branham
Earl Fonzy Branham
Harold D. Branham
Oliver Branham
Jack Branhan
Paul A. Brannock
Charles E. Brannon
Donald J. Brannon
James E. Brannon, Jr.
Wilmer Brannon
Edwin L. Branscome
Clythell Branson
Samuel R. Bransteitter
Albert W. Brant, Jr.
Duane F. Brant
Floyd P. Brant
George J. Brant
James E. Brant
Melvin L. Brant
Marvin E. Branting
Marshall K. Brantley
J. W. Branton
William E. Brashear
Melvin A. Brashears
Louie D. Brashere
Harry Brassfield
Billie L. Braswell
Carl William Braswell
Robert C. Braswell
Vernon L. Braswell
Earl Bennett Bratback
Thomas E. Bratcher
Julian N. Brathwaite
Charles E. Bratton
Lewis Wilson Bratton
Robert A. Bratton
Claude Braud
Victor Braud
Eldred L. Brauer
Joseph J. Braun
Sylvester A. Braun
Wayne F. Braun
Robert F. Brauns
Eugene B. Braunsdorf
Henry J. Brautigam
Harold R. Bravard
John Charles Bravo
Charles W. Braxton
Edmond R. Braxton, Jr.
Gordon L. Braxton
Harold L. Braxton
Gerald Bray
Glen L. Sr Bray
Joseph Albert Bray
Robert L. Bray
George Brazell, Jr.
Paul R. Brazell
James Brazil
Walter Campbell Brazill
Ferman T. Breaker
Raymond J. Brech
Ervin E. Breckenridge
James E. Breckenridge
John Cabell Breckinridge
Willis M. Brede
Arlin S. Bredeson
Charles Breeden
Harry B. Breeden
Joseph N. Breeden
Roy G. Breedlove
Virgil L. Breedlove
William M. Breedlove

Morris W. Breezee
Ralph F. Breitfeld
John J. Breitkreutz
Roy F. Breitsprecher
Ernest J. Brendel
Dillman Lawrence Brendle
Furman T. Brendle
Frederick W. Brendley, Jr.
Valentin F. E. Brenes
Maurice N. Brengard
Odell C. Brenna
John C. Brennan
John Richard Brennan
Murray J. Brennan
William Randolph Brennan
Austin E. E Brenneman
Fred Arthur Brenner
Daniel A. Brennie
Irvin L. Brent
Roger E. Brent
Sterling M. Brent
George C. Brents
Lloyd H. Bresett
Kenneth J. Breslin
Charles F. Bressler
Ryan A. Bressler
Lyle A. Brest
James R. Brett
Jessie J. Bretz
Edward W. Breutzmann
Henry E. Brew
Anton E. Brewer
Carl D. Brewer
Clyde Ira Brewer
Coy Marcus Brewer
Donald Edward Brewer
Ellis M. Brewer
Howard G. Brewer
Hugh H. Brewer
Lowell Ray Brewer
Morris D. Brewer
Nicodemus Brewer
Paul M. Brewer, Jr.
Pinckney A. Brewer
William E. Brewer
Carl Brewington
Howard Brewington
Billy B. Brewster
Robert L. Brewster
Thomas Brewster
Elwood Earl Brey
Joseph W. Briand
James L. Brice
Victor A. Brice
Lewis G. Brickell
George Bricker
James Adrian Bricker
Joe F. Bricker
Berley C. Brickey
Edward F. Bridenhagen
Charles E. Bridge
James R. Bridger
Kenneth L. Bridger
Anice D. Bridges
Elmo R. Bridges, Jr.
John R. Bridges
Lindy L. Bridges
Lolan O. Bridges
M. Jay Bridges
James N. Bridgett
Donald L. Bridgewater
Milton H. Bridwell
William J. Briere
Charlie Briers
Allan F. Briggs
Charles Ronald Briggs
Eugene A. Briggs, Jr.
Harry K. Briggs
James H. Briggs
Merton Elmer Briggs
Norman E. Briggs
Ray Allen Briggs
Raymond I. Briggs
Robert L. Briggs
Rodney M. Briggs
Leslie Brigham
Carlton R. Bright
J. W. Bright
James L. Bright
Robert Bright
William H. Bright
James T. Brigman
William F. Brigman
Ray A. Briley
Mac Brillantes
Daniel L. Brim
Zephry Brim
Darrel R. Brimberry
Larry C. Brimhall

Berthier W. Brimm, Jr.
Derick F. Brinckerhoff
Clyde W. Brindel, Jr.
Jacob S. Brindle
Jack Elton Brindley
Donald E. Brine
Donald P. Bringe
Harry Martin Bringes
Robert L. Bringhurst
Dale E. Bringle
Newton W. Bringle
John Richard Brinkley
A. S. Brinksmeyer
John C. Brinsmead
Earl T. Brinson
Ephrian L. Brinson
Gilbert D. Brinson
Grover Brinson, Jr.
Paul Brinson
Charles E. Brintle
James V. Briody
Leo P. Briones
Henry Brisco, Jr.
Albert Aloysius Briscoe
Kenneth J. Briscoe
William R. Briscoe, Jr.
Leo R. Briseno, Jr.
Harvey B. Brisson
Richard G. Bristol
Robert O. Bristol
Benjamin F. Bristow
Ivan P. Bristow
James Ray Bristow
John B. Bristow
Melvin L. Bristow
Max Brito
Lawrence Britt, Jr.
Robert E. Britt
Seth E. Britt
Thomas J. Britt
Carl F. Brittian
Nelson Vogel Brittin
Paul L. Brittingham
Bernie B. Britton
James L. Britton
Jolly Wilburn Britton
Peter Jack Britton
Ralph Arthur Britton
Martin Craig Brizius
Steve N. Brklich
Wendell I. Broad
Walter T. Broaddus
Michael J. Broaderick, Jr.
Claude M. Broadhurst, Jr.
George R. Broadhurst
Charles H. Broadnax
Merle D. Broadston
Thomas G. Broadwater
J. D. Broadway
Keith O. Broadway
Robert G. Brobst, Jr.
Sam Brocato, Jr.
Dennis Brock
Donald L. Brock
Hubert J. Brock
Jack M. Brock
James B. Brock
Joseph H. Brock
Kenneth Wilbur Brock
Lee D. Brock
Wilborn W. Brock
Harvey L. Brocker
Norvin D. Brockett
Clarence Brockman
Gordon Brockman
John Joseph Brockman
John Thomas Brockman
William Brockmire
Edward G. Brockway
Ronald Francis Brodeur
Richard R. Brodhead
John William Brodie
Louis Brodur
Leroy J. Broeders
Elwyn G. Broege
Donald C. Broemeling
Carl H. Broers
Lewis Brogens
Robert L. Brogna
Philip R. Brohen
Vernon Lloyd Brokke
Donald C. Bromeling
Mervin G. Bromfield, Jr.
Bruce Bromley, Jr.
Dominic A. Bronele
Robert J. Bronson
Bill M. Brookin
Arnel J. Brooks
Bruce E. Brooks

Carl P. Brooks
Charles E. Brooks
Charles H. Brooks
Clarence M. Brooks
Clifton Elmer Brooks
Dale H. Brooks
David C. Brooks
Donald Brooks
Dories William Brooks, Jr.
Earl G. Brooks
Edward W. Brooks
Gilbert B. Brooks
Herman Brooks
Iauno Oliver Brooks
J. L. Brooks
Jack E. Brooks
Jack E. Brooks
James E. Brooks
Jerome J. Brooks
Jewell Brooks
John H. Brooks
John W. Brooks, Jr.
Julian T. Brooks
Lawrence C. Brooks
Leotis Brooks
Lewis F. Brooks
Lloyd K. Brooks
Lloyd K. Brooks
Louis P. Brooks
Marvin R. Brooks
Melvin Duaine Brooks
Raymond Brooks
Richard Alfred Brooks
Richard H. Brooks
Robert Franklin Brooks
Robert Gene Brooks
Roy E. Brooks
Tauno Oliver Brooks
Thomas Boggs Brooks
Wiley B. Brooks
William P. Brooks
William T. Brooks
Charles L. Broome
Laney Bruce Broome
Otis L. Broome
Eugene T. Brophy
Patrick R. Brophy
Gerald Leroy Brose
John Calvin Brossard
Herman L. Brothers
Richard D. Brothers
Paul W. Brouchet
Woodrow H. Broughman
Buford E. Broughton
Neilson W. Brouillette
Edger B. Brouse
Victor E. Brousek
Edward Broussard, Jr.
George C. Broussard
Reed O. Broussard
Simon W. Broussard
Woodrow W. Broussard
E. A. Brousseau, Jr.
Philip F. Brousseau
Edward J. Brouwer
George T. Brower
Richard Eugene Brower
Samuel E. Brower
William J. Brower
Albert L. Brown
Alfred R. Brown
Allen R. Brown
Almo Brown
Alonzo W. Brown
Alvin H. Brown
Alvin L. Brown
Andrew B. Brown
Anthony Eugene Brown
Arthur L. Brown
Arthur Leroy Brown
Ben L. Brown
Benner B. Brown
Bill E. Brown
Billy C. Brown
Bobby C. Brown
Bobby Leland Brown
Bruce F. Brown
Buford M. Brown
Calvin D. Brown
Carlton Henry Brown
Charles Brown
Charles A. Brown
Charles E. Brown
Charles J. Brown
Charles J. A. Brown
Charles J. Brown, Jr.
Charles Joseph Brown
Charles L. Brown
Charles L. Brown

Charles O. Brown
Charles P. Brown
Charles R. Brown
Charles W. Brown
Charles W. Brown
Charles W. Brown
Clarence G. Brown
Clarence J. Brown
Cleo Arthur Brown
Clyde U. Brown
Curtis Waymon Brown
Dale Eugene Brown
Damon Kirk Brown
Daniel K. Brown
David L. Brown
David O. Brown
Delmar H. Brown
Donald C. Brown
Donald D. Brown
Donald Richard Brown
Donald W. Brown
Doris Frances Brown
Doyl G. Brown
Doyle R. Brown
Duane D. Brown
Earl Brown
Earl A. Brown
Earl J. Brown
Earl W. Brown
Eddie D. Brown
Edward L. Brown
Edward O. Brown
Edward R. Brown
Edwin E. Brown
Elgie D. Brown
Emory L. Brown
Era H. Brown
Eugene D. Brown
Eugene F. Brown
Ferris Brown
Floyd E. Brown
Floyd M. Brown
Frank L. Brown
Frank M. Brown
Franklin D. Brown
Franklin W. Brown
Fred G. Brown
Frederick O. Brown
Garland S. Brown
George Brown
George A. Brown
George Clayton Brown, Jr.
George Elwood Brown
George Brown, Jr.
Gerald Rodney Brown
Gilbert H. Brown
Glenn C. Brown
Harold B. Brown
Harold G. Brown
Harold M. Brown
Harry L. Brown
Henry Brown
Herbert F. Brown
Herbert W. Brown
Howard G. Brown
Hugh M. Brown
Inda Brown
Isaac Brown
Jacob Brown, Jr.
James A. Brown
James B. Brown
James B. Brown
James C. Brown
James Caviness Brown
James Drake Brown
James F. Brown
James Fred Brown
James G. Brown
James Howard Brown
James Brown, Jr.
James Montgomery Brown
James Walter Brown
Jesse Leroy Brown
Jessie Brown
Jimmie L. Brown
Jimmie L. Brown
Joe L. Brown
John Brown
John C. Brown
John E. Brown
John H. Brown, Jr.
John L. Brown
John Robert Brown
Joseph C. Brown
Joseph S. Brown
Joshua E. Brown
Juelynn O. Brown
Keith E. Brown

Kenneth Brown
Kenneth E. Brown
Kenneth L. Brown
Kenneth O. Brown
Lawrence L. Brown
Lawrence R. Brown
Leland Gray Brown
Leonard Charles Brown
Leroy L. Brown
Leslie Brown, Jr.
Loyd O. Brown
Malcolm J. Brown
Marion A. Brown
Marvin G. Brown
Mckinley Brown
Meade M. Brown
Melvin Louis Brown
Michael J. Brown
Morris E. Brown
Muriel G. Brown
Nelson Marion Brown
Orville R. Brown
Oscar M. Brown
Otto V. Brown
Palmer H. Brown, Jr.
Paul E. Brown
Paul M. Brown
Paul M. Brown
Phillip E. Brown
Ralph G. Brown
Ralph Junious Brown
Raymond H. Brown
Raymond R. Brown
Richard A. Brown
Richard E. Brown
Richard H. Brown
Robert A. Brown
Robert A. Brown
Robert B. Brown
Robert C. Brown
Robert E. Brown
Robert E. Brown
Robert Elmo Brown
Robert N. Brown
Rufus Brown, Jr.
Samuel Brown
Samuel C. Brown
Samuel D. Brown
Samuel Brown, Jr.
Samuel Brown, Jr.
Shelby B. Brown, Jr.
Solomon M. Brown
Stanley Brown
Stanley Brown
Thomas Brown
Thomas G. Brown
Thomas J. Brown
Turnace H. Brown
Vernon L. Brown
Wallace Brown
Walter B. Brown, Jr.
Walter E. Brown
Walter Brown, Jr.
Warren R. Brown, Jr.
William A. Brown
William C. Brown
William E. Brown
William E. Brown
William E. Brown, Jr.
William Edmund Brown
William F. Brown
William F. Brown
William L. Brown
William L. Brown, Jr.
William Perry Brown, Jr.
William R. Brown
William R. Brown
Willie Brown
Willie L. Brown
Willis Ray Brown
Donald L. Brownawell
William W. Brownback, Jr.
Dexter W. Browne
Donald Carroll Browne
Earl A. Browne
John J. Browne
Kenneth A. Browne
Richard A. Browne
Billy J. Browning
Charlie M. Browning
J. W. Browning
James E. Browning
Joseph D. Browning
Paul J. Browning
Perry H. Browning
Philip Wells Browning
Robert L. Browning, Jr.
Robert R. Browning
William J. Browning

Clifford G. Brownson
Severy B. Broxholme
Bruce M. Broyles
Carrol Broyles, Jr.
Edwin Nash Broyles, Jr.
Albert M. Brozell
Kenneth C. Brubaker
Dewey F. Bruce
Donald D. Bruce
Guy Bruce, Jr.
Jackson Bruce
James O. Bruce
Jewell Clyde Bruce
John Frank Bruce
Kenneth C. Bruce
Ralph T. Bruce
Richard Worth Bruce
Sam R. Bruce
Thomas Charles Bruce
William K. Bruce
Richard C. Brucker
John A. Iv Bruckner
Rudolph L. Bruckner, Jr.
Henry Lee Bruder
Donald G. Brudy
Willard J. Bruette
Carl Henry II Bruggemeier
Rudolph T. Bruggner
Eugene O. Bruhn
David C. Bruin
Russell Bruin
Homer Bruington
Marinus Bruinooge
Arthur Bruinsma
Clifford J. Bruinsma
Daniel T. Brumagen
Wesley Brumbles
Aubry L. Brumfield
James D. Brumley
Paul W. Brumley
Dallas R. Brummett
Walter L. Brummett
Walter R. Brummett
Paul Brunda
Herbert S. Bruner
Oscar E. Bruner
Walter T. Bruner
Floyd L. Brunette
Robert F. Brunke
Leroy C. Brunner
Lawrence F. Brunnert
George B. Brunnhuber
Alan L. Bruno
Edward J. Bruno
Gaeton Anthony Bruno
Giovanni M. Bruno
John F. Bruno
Lawrence A. Bruno
Nicholas M. Bruno, Jr.
Robert P. Bruno
Pedro Bruno-Vidal
John Richard Bruns
Jerome Brunson
Thomas Wilbur Brunson
Cletus F. Brunswick
James R. Brunt
Thonas F. Brusaw
Raymond E. Brush
Jack Lambert Brushert
Jean W. Bruso
Louis B. Brusse
John L. Bruster
Jackie M. Bruton
Thad Bruton, Jr.
Robert W. Bruveleit
David Bruzelius, Jr.
Bobbie L. Bryan
Clifford W. Bryan
Fred Vincent Bryan
James C. Bryan
John Charles Bryan
John Dwayne Bryan
John P. Bryan
Richard Alvin Bryan
William J. Bryan
Booker T. Bryant, Jr.
Cecil Bryant, Jr.
Charles J. Bryant
David Bryant
Don W. Bryant
Emmitt R. Bryant
Floyd Glenn Bryant
Frederick F. Bryant
Gilbert Bryant, Jr.
Gladen B. Bryant
Harold F. Bryant
James C. Bryant
James E. Bryant
Jerry Richard Bryant

Joe Henry Bryant
Junior R. Bryant
Kinney Bryant
Leroy W. Bryant
Morris N. Bryant
Paul C. Bryant
Robert Bryant
Rollins Mason Bryant
Roy L. Bryant
Russel Bryant
Vernon L. Bryant
Vivian D. Bryant
William Arnold Bryant, Jr.
William E. Bryant
William F. Bryant
William J. Bryant
William J. Bryant
William L. Bryant
Willie N. Bryant, Jr.
Oscar H. Bryce
Roger C. Bryce
Walter James Brydon
Bernard F. Bryk
Norbert A. Brzycki
Mirko Bubalo
Romolo Anthony Bucci
William R. Bucey
Edward R. Buchan
Eldon Rex Buchan
Don Ray Buchanan
Edgar Le Roy Buchanan
Elson Buchanan
Ernest L. Buchanan
Joel H. Buchanan
John E. Buchanan
Thomas M. Buchanan
Willard Buchanan
Robert C. Bucheit
Robert L. Bucher
Edward John Bucherich
Harold C. Buchholz
Jack Joseph Buchl
Robert Everett Buchmann
Willard L. Buchols
Edward J. Bucholtz
Bill E. Buck
Eugene Buckalew
Glenford Buckalew
Lawrence K. Buckhorn
Richard I. Buckingham
Clarence V. Buckland
Arthur D. Buckley, Jr.
Dennis D. Buckley
George J. Buckley, Jr.
James W. Buckley
John Harrison Buckley
Oliver E. Buckley, Jr.
Paul F. Buckley
William Henry Buckley
Jerry G. Buckman
Buddy E. Buckmaster
Buddy E. Buckmaster
Joseph G. Bucknavage
Franklin Edison Buckner
John Lennon Buckner
Mc Kinley G. Buckner
Robert M. Buckner
Tommy Buckner
Wilburn Dee Buckner
Andrew P. Bucko, Jr.
George Buckson
Theodore J. Bucolo
Martin E. Budack
James E. Budd
Malcolm Lloyd Budd
Robert E. Budd
James Walter Buddenburg
Joseph Martin Budesky
Eldon O. Budke
John Frederick Budke, Jr.
James Budlow
Irving C. Budnick
John T. Budny
Stanley Budzinski
Leroy M. Buechel
Maurice A. Bueck
Leo T. Buehler
Roy E. Buell
Thomas M. Buell
Frank S. Bueno
Joseph R. Bueno
Bernard C. Buettner
Jack Y. Buff
Peter Buffa, Jr.
Charles S. Buffalano
Lee A. Sr Buffington
Ralph M. Buffington
Gregory E. Buford
John R. Bugg

Philemon S. Buhisan
Edwin L. Buhler
Richard Dale Buhs
Alfred R. Buie
Herbert Edward Buik
Melvin G. Buist
Carlos S. Buitron
Earl J. Buku
George Bulkowski
Albert H. Bull
Clifford G. Bull
Richard G. Bull
Basil B. Bullard
Benjamin F. Bullard
Jeral H. Bullard
Jerry Ellis Bullard
Floyd D. Buller
Ambrose Bullerman
William A. Bullinger
Harry L. Bullington, Jr.
Milton T. Bullis
Wayne F. Bullis
Robert E. Bullman
Elmer Trombly Bullock
Elmo Bullock
Frank W. Bullock
Johnie B. Bullock
Johnnie R. Bullock
Stanley E. Bullock
Mark B. Bulluck
Morgan L. Bulman
Fred C. Bumgardner
Earl Gerald Bumpas
Carl E. Bumpus
Gerald F. Bumstead
Alvin G. Bunch
Arthur Bunch
Charley C. Bunch
Curtis E. Bunch
Elbert Bunch
Paul T. Bunch
Frank Bunchuk
Dean C. Bundschuh
Walter W. Bundy
Edgar A. Bunker
Claude F. Bunn
George William Bunn
Hubert Bunn
Isaac Bunn, Jr.
Richard E. Bunn
Willie G. Bunn
Hubert K. Sr Bunnell
Jack Edward Bunnell
Robert J. Bunnell
Donald A. Buntenbach
Charles Warner Buntin
Raymond James Buntin
Worth L. Bunting
Hansel Bunton, Jr.
Carrol E. Bunyard
William Buraczewski
Charles E. Burba
Gerard R. Burbach
Byron Mcquady Burbage
Pete Burbage, Jr.
Billie Burch
George E. Burch
Hershel B. Burch
Hugh Maynard Burch
Isaac W. Burch
Joseph D. Burch
Louie F. Burch
Naman Burch
Robert G. Burch
William John Burch
Jesse L. Burcham
Travis Burchan
Water C. Burchell
Bobby G. Burchett
John G. Burchett
Donald V. Burchette
Clifford E. Burchfield
Riley Burchfield
Robert G. Burciaga
Joseph Coleman Burd
Charlie Burden, Jr.
Obie R. Burden
Donald Burdette
Richard G. Burdette
Robert M. Burdette
Herbert H. Burdick
Sterling M. Burdick
Stewart C. Burdick
Wayne Henry Burdue
Bobby L. Burford
Jack R. Burford
William Burford
Elmer Valence Burger, Jr.
Lawrence Edward Burger

Burton E. Burgess
Charles E. Burgess
Damon Burgess
Earl J. Burgess
Howard P. Burgess
John A. Burgess
John D. Burgess
John P. Burgess
Preston M. Burgess
Ted Columbus Burgess
Alfred T. Burgett
Elroy F. Burgett
Joseph Burgin, Jr.
Anthony R. Burgio
John K. Burgio
Loreto Burgos
Velazquez M. Burgos
Robert James Burgwinkle
Raymond F. Burhorst
Donald L. Burk
William A. Burk
Arlynn C. Burke
Billy R. Burke
Carl Milton Burke
Crawford W. Burke, Jr.
David S. Burke
Douglas A. Burke
Doyle J. Burke
Ermon Rogers Burke
Francis William Burke
Harvey Willis Burke
James E. Burke
James Peter Burke
John Edwin Burke
John H. Burke
John Sherman Burke
Lawrence E. Burke
Lawrence V. Burke
Raymond Burle Burke
Raymond L. Burke
Robert H. Burke
Robert L. Burke
Roland L. Burke
Rothwell W. Burke
Sharman K. Burke
Thomas J. Burke
William J. Burke
William J. Burke, Jr.
William Roderick Burke
Billie R. Burkeen
Clarence Burkes
Daniel W. Burkes, Jr.
Eugene B. Burkett
John J. Burkett
Merritt R. Burkett
Sidney J. Burkett
Louis V. Burkhalter
Rodney F. Burkham
Carl J. Burkhardt
Billie R. Burkhart
Floyd K. Burkhart
Glenn E. Burkhart
Howard Burkhart
Edward M. Burkhead
Donald M. Burkholder
Raymond R. Burkholder
William C. Burkit
Gene Rowland Burkman
Donald W. Burks
Fred E. Burks
Jack D. Burks
Joseph Harlow Burks
Silas Burks
Lawrence L. Burleigh
Charles E. Burley
Alvin C. Burman
Duane J. Burmeister
Donald J. Burmingham
William R. Burn
Aaron Sylvester Burnan
Wadus H. Burnanam
Thomas Gene Burnaugh
Robert E. Burner
Ernest Burnet
Anthony L. Burnett
Avery E. Burnett
Fount V. Burnett
Ira Emmett Burnett
Jack E. Burnett
Raymond M. Burnett
Robert Gray Burnett
Robert R. Burnett
Snowden D. Burnett
Gibson Burnette
Henry W. Burnette
James I. Burnette
Robert M. Burnette
Ralston L. Burney, Jr.
Raymond E. Burnheimer

Bernard J. Burnott
Benjamin Burns, Jr.
Buford Lee Burns
Chadwick Otis Burns
Charles E. Burns
Charles P. Burns
Charles P. Burns
Donald P. Burns
Forrest Steele Burns
Francis Bernard Burns
Francis P. Burns
Francis T. Burns
Fred Burns, Jr.
James A. Burns
James L. Burns
Jere E. Burns
John J. Burns
John J. Burns
Julian W. Burns
Paul J. Burns, Jr.
Peter J. Burns
Ralph W. Burns
Raymond Burns
Richard N. Burns
Robert D. Burns
Robert L. Burns
Vernon Burns
Walter G. Burns
William T. Burns
Forrest Edwin Burnsed
Willie H. Burnside, Jr.
Jackson E. Burnsworth
Donald K. Burr
J. C. Burr
James Burr
Jackson Alexander Burrell
Matthew Burrell
Melvin J. Burrell
Guenther A. Burrer
William Jerome Burrey
Buddy B. Burris
Earl Franklin Burris
Gerald R. Burris
Jesse C. Burris
Tony K. Burris
Rudy L. Burrola
Bobby B. Burroughs
Kendall Burroughs
Kenneth Claire Burroughs
William Burroughs
Buford Burrow, Jr.
John K. Burrows
Lester M. Burrows, Jr.
Ernest E. Burruel
Paul Conrad Burrus
Levi Burs
Jose F. Burset-Melendez
Billy B. Burson
Homer L. Burt
James Bryan Burt, Jr.
John E. Burt
Kemper H. Burt
Myron H. Burt
John Robert Burtis
Charles Burton
Donald K. Burton
Eddie Burton
Fred Burton
George Riley Burton
John F. Burton, Jr.
Leonard L. Burton
Lloyd L. Burton
Melvin David Burton
Ray Burton
Robert C. Burton
Robert E. Burton
Samuel L. Burton
Samuel M. Burton
Thomas H. Burton
Walter A. Burton
Walter R. Burton, Jr.
Willie G. Burton
Woodrow Burton
William Thomas Burtyk
David L. Burwell
Frank H. Burwell, Jr.
George Benjamin Burzota
Joseph S. Burzynski
James E. Busby
Charles R. Busch
George Walter Busch
Louis G. Busch
Herman J. Buschschulte
Billy J. Bush
Clarence M. Bush
Harold C. Bush
James Arthur Bush
John F. Bush, Jr.
John R. Bush

Joseph C. Bush
Leon Ross Bush
Lester Bush
Marshall Lindley Bush
Reuben H. Bush
Robert Arthur Bush
Robert E. Bush
Robert G. Bush, Jr.
William D. Bush, Jr.
Herschel Lee Bushman
Warren M. Bushman
Bruce E. Bushre
William C. Bushrod
Sterling Joseph Bushroe
William J. Bushway
Charles D. Busic
Ernest Busico
George E. Buskirk
Odell Busler
Donald Henry Buss
Thomas Buss
William H. Bussey
Ervin J. Bussian
Paul J. F. Bussiere
Frank J. Bustamante
Jesus F. Bustamante
Johnnie J. Buster
Richard E. Bustle
James T. Butcher
John P. Butcher
Kenneth Butcher
Lewis A. Buterakos
Arthur B. Butler
Billy J. Butler
Charles C. Butler
Eldon D. Butler
Gene P. Butler
Gerald G. Butler
Gilbert J. Butler
Glen D. Butler
Howard A. Butler
John R. Butler
Joseph W. Butler
Kenneth E. Butler
Nehemiah E. Butler
Paul Leigh Butler
Paul Martin Butler
Robert C. Butler
Virgil E. Butler
Wallace S. Butler, Jr.
Wallace V. Butler
William E. Butler
Richard Alfred Buttery
Ronald E. Buttery
Anthony Buttinsky
Leland L. Buttler
Charles Dale Button
Landis L. Button
Leonard W. Button
Owen G. Buttress
William V. Buttrey
Lemon Butts, Jr.
Oscar H. Butts, Jr.
William H. Butts
Raymond W. Butynsky
William R. Butz
Roger F. Buxman
Edwin R. Buxton
James Emmett Buxton
George F. Buyense
Joseph S. Buzyniski
Billie J. Byard
Bobby L. Byars
Edward Walter Byczkowski
Melvin Floyd Bydalek
Robert L. Byerly
Charles E. Byers
Harold E. Byers
Stanley F. Bykowski
Jackie B. Bynum
Joseph Bynum
Kenneth G. Bynum
Billy R. Byrd
Carl Byrd
Clayton J. W. Byrd
Conley E. Byrd
Curtis P. Byrd
Ervin A. Byrd
Frank Byrd, Jr.
Glenn H. Byrd
Hubert F. Byrd
Jack Byrd
James W. Byrd
Milton C. Byrd
Orvil W. Byrd
Owen Cecil Byrd
Richard Edward Byrd
Tommy Byrd
Wendell F. Byrd

William Eugene Byrd
William H. Byrd
James T. Byrne
Thomas J. Byrne
William P. Byrne
Delbert A. Byrom
William Byron
Clarence H. Byrum
Elmer E. Byrum, Jr.
Edward L. Bytnar
William D. Bywater

— C —

Eduardo M. Caballero
James D. Caballero
Pedro Caballero
Rosario J. A. Caballero
Aramis Caballero-Moreno
Theodore S. Cabanbam
Jimmie Cabe
Lloyd R. Cabe
Sidney G. Cabell
Joseph B. Cabiness
Donald Oren Cable
John L. Cable
David Eugene Cabral
John J. Cabral
Richard J. Cabral
Isaac S. Cabrera
Johnnie R. Cabrera
Froilan Cabrera-Gonzalez
Nicholas C. Caccese
Charles C. Cackowski
Donald Caddell
James Dickinson Caddell
Arturo Cadena
Daniel Cadena, Jr.
Leberato B. Cadiz
Roy J. Cady
Nicola Cafaro
Robert Paul Caffrey
Vincent R. Cage
Charlie F. Cagle
Euzell E. Cagle
George W. Cagle
Milton L. Cagle
Daniel E. Cahalan
Chester Cahill
Francis X. Cahill
John A. Cahill
Samuel C. Cahow
James Benedict Caillouet
Edmund H. Cain
Frank P. Cain
James Edward Cain
Jim C. Cain
John M. Cain
Mabry E. Cain
Sidney Gershwin Cain
Tommy J. Cain
Edward H. Caine
Bernard J. Caione
Carlos M. Cajero
Orlando J. Calabrese
Robert R. Calahan
Joe J. Calaman
Antonio Calaustro
William E. Calaway
Ortiz Jacinto Calcano
Roscoe M. Calcote
Franklin D. Calcutt
Dominick P. Caldarella
Daniel Caldeira
Jenaro R. Calderon
Tomas Calderon-Cosme
Juan Calderon-Osorio
Alvin O. Caldwell
Berlin Caldwell, Jr.
Crayton Lowell Caldwell
Donald D. Caldwell
Ernest Truman Caldwell
Gerald Kenneth Caldwell
Howard O. Caldwell
James C. Caldwell
James L. Caldwell
John B. Caldwell, Jr.
John W. Caldwell, Jr.
Odell Caldwell
Richard Bruce Caldwell
Sherman H. Caldwell
Theartis Caldwell
Thomas T. Caldwell
Veodis E. Caldwell
William S. Caldwell
Ralph L. Cale
Otto B. Calegari
William L. Calfee
Ernest M. Calhau

Cecil O. Calhoon
Chester J. Calhoun
Harold Calhoun
Lee R. Calhoun
Sammie D. Calhoun
Stanley Louis Calhoun, Jr.
Frank M. Cali
M. Calimano-Texidor
Harold D. Calkins
James L. Calkins
James R. Callaghan
Robert Monroe Callaghan
Carl Callahan, Jr.
Carlis J. Callahan
Edward J. Callahan
Francis E. Callahan
Francis J. Callahan
Jack W. Callahan
James D. Callahan
Lewis Ray Callahan
William F. Callahan
Arthur Delbert Callan
James I Callan
Harold A. Callaway
James Edward Callaway
Vernon A. Callaway
Henry O. Callis
Tommie Lavere Callison
Albert Callon
Adolph C. Calloway
John Callum
Constan Calogianes
Vincent William Calvanico
Thomas J. Calvelage
George E. Calvert
James O. Calvert
Robert R. Calvert
Supremo Calves
Harvey E. Calvin
Jesus A. Camacho
Louis C. Camacho, Jr.
Raul O. Camacho
Roman M. A. Camacho
Rubertino P. Camacho
Bobby L. Cameron
David Cameron, Jr.
Donald B. Cameron
Edgar Cameron
Floyd D. Cameron
George G. Cameron
James H. Cameron
Joseph A. Cameron
Lewis Hine Cameron
Owen Joseph Cameron
Porter S. Cameron
Anastacio Camillo
Henry Victor Camire
Onesimu Camiscioli
Fred C. Cammack, Jr.
Thomas A. Cammarano
Philip D. Cammarota
Gerald M. Camp
Henry Clay Camp, Jr.
Jack Camp
Felipe F. Campa
Alexander Campbell
Alton R. Campbell
Alvin B. Campbell
Booker T. Campbell, Jr.
Charles C. Campbell
Charlie A. Campbell
Clark G. Campbell
David L. Campbell
Dewitt Campbell, Jr.
Donald Eugene Campbell
Duncan A. Campbell, Jr.
Earl A. Campbell
Edward Everett Campbell
Forrest R. Campbell
George G. Campbell
George H. Campbell
Howard D. Campbell, Jr.
Howard L. Campbell
Howard V. Campbell
Jackie A. Campbell
James E. Campbell
James F. Campbell
James L. Campbell
Jimmie Rae Campbell
John B. Campbell
Joseph Campbell
Joseph F. Campbell
Joseph L. Campbell
Joseph Lawler Campbell
Laverne H. Campbell
Lloyd C. Campbell
Louis L. Campbell
Omar P. Campbell
Raymond B. Campbell

Razor J. Campbell
Reynold George Campbell
Richard F. Campbell
Robert D. Campbell
Robert G. Campbell
Roscoe C. Campbell
Vernon L. Campbell
Warren R. Campbell
William J. Campion
Leonard R. Campisi
Angelo Campo
Joseph Salvatore Campo
Arthur E. Campomizzi
Carlos C. Campos
Gilbert Campos
Jose C. Campos, Jr.
Richard A. Campos
Cecil H. Canady
Robert C. Canales
Rudolph M. Canales
Gregory O. Canan
Roy C. Canby
Jonathan Johnny Cancel
Paul Candelaria
L. Candia-Francisco
Claudie B. Candler
Donald L. Canfield
Gordon A. Canfield
Lee L. Canfield
Robert D. Canfield, Jr.
Ronald A. Canfield
Lewis E. Canie
Kenneth James Cann
John Joseph Canney, Jr.
William Alfred Canning
Thomas Cannizzaro
Bob Pearce Cannon
Clyde E. Cannon
Donald R. Cannon
Hugh L. Cannon
Jack E. Cannon
Leroy Cannon
Robert T. Cannon, Jr.
Salvato Cantarella
Nicholas Cantella
Robert Cantelmo
Doran L. Canter
Bobby C. Canterberry
Franklin M. Canterbury
Frederick P. Canterbury
Roy W. Canterbury
Luther E. Cantley
Milton Cantor
Glenn W. Cantrall
Cecil D. Cantrell
Earl E. Cantrell
Howard W. Cantrell, Jr.
Neal P. Cantrell
Odes I. Cantrell
Paul Eugene Cantrell
Rode C. Cantrell
Joseph M. Cantrelle, Jr.
Arturo Cantu
Jesus R. Cantu
Raymond D. Cantu
John Canty
Robert H. Canupp
James E. Canyock
Milton L. Caouette
Frederick Capallia
Joseph A. Capano
Joe B. Capehart
Erwin A. Capen
Samie Capers
Herbert Caperton
Max L. Caperton
Salvator L. Capitelli
John Nunzio Capizzi
Dayton L. Caplinger
Albert C. Capozzi
Anthony Michael Cappucci
John Philip Caprio
Donald Vincent Capron
Ronald L. Captain
Louis Caputo
Louis Michael Caputo
Gerald B. Capwell
Benigno R. Caraballo
Vincent Caramadre
Juan Carambot-Ortiz
Cody E. Caraway
Fred Caraway
Raymond V. Caraway
Jesse Carbajal
William J. Carbaugh
Oswald E. Carbonneau
Robert N. Carbray
David W. Card
Vincent C. Cardarella

Edward C. Cardenas
Marcel M. Cardenas
Willie R. Cardenas
Clyde Dailey Carder
nLeland A. Carder
Paul V. Carder
Lorimer P. Cardiel
James R. Cardillo, Jr.
Mario Joseph Cardillo
Edward Joseph Cardin
Edward A. Cardinal
Marrero A. Cardona
Orlando Cardona
Joseph M. Cardone
Joseph Cardoza
Robert R. Cardoza
Hugh T. Cardwell
Joel L. Cardwell
John M. Cardwell
Rosendo P. Careara
Larry A. Carella
Kenneth J. Carew
Edwin A. Carey, Jr.
Gale Carey
Gerald D. Carey
Henry R. Carey
James Desmond Carey
James L. Carey
Joseph J. Carey, Jr.
Matthew Carey
Maurice F. Carey
Stanley G. Carey, Jr.
Walter Francis Carey
William Carey
Joseph C. Carfield
Brice G. Cargin
Santo A. Cargola
Louis J. Sr Cariati
Douglas Bishop Carico
Edward M. Carico
Rocco Caridi
William Joseph Carine
Marvin W. Carius
James A. Carl
Peter P. Carlino
John J. Carlisle
Osborne Tommee Carlisle
William S. Carlisle
Vicente Carlo-Perez
James L. Carlock
Arthur P. Carlsen
Harold D. Carlsen
Albert Bertie Carlson
Charles E. Carlson
Donald C. Carlson
Frances T. Carlson
Harold J. Carlson
Henry B. Carlson
James John Carlson
John A. Carlson, Jr.
John H. Carlson
Leonard D. Carlson
Norman G. Carlson
Ralph W. Carlson
Raymond J. Carlson
Robert E. Carlson
Robert Erwin Carlson
Robert Lee Carlson
Sigurd L. Carlson
Henry Frank Carlton
James T. Carlton
Lyle Harvey Carman
Royal G. Carman
Joseph Carmello
Cyril E. Carmichael
Donald Carmichael
Gerald Joseph Carmichael
Glenn Frye Carmichael
John Davis Carmicheal
Francis Carmody
Archie L. Carmon, Jr.
Primo C. Carnabuci
Harold L. Carnahan
William J. Carnahan
Donald E. Carnes
Gerald D. Carnes
Harry Zane Carnes
John M. Carnes
Norman R. Carnes
Roscoe Carnes, Jr.
Bill Carnett
James Charles Carney
James R. Carney
Robert W. Carney
John W. Carol
John E. Carolan
Clayton Wilfred Caron
James N. Caron, Jr.
Carmen A. Carosella

Billie Carl Carothers
C. S. Carothers, Jr.
Jerry F. Carothers
Benny Carpenter
Charles Franklin Carpenter
Douglas D. Carpenter
Douglas R. Carpenter
Gerald W. Carpenter
Harold L. Carpenter
Harvey E. Carpenter
John Adrian Carpenter
Otis C. Carpenter
Robert E. Carpenter
Robert E. Carpenter
Robert John Carpenter
Robert W. Carpenter
Sam Jasper Carpenter
Wesley B. Carpenter
William E. Carpenter
Xavier O. Carpenter
Aorise W. Carr
Baldwin Ronald Carr
Benjamin F. Carr
Bernard E. Carr
Charles Carr
Clifford L. Carr
Clifton M. Carr, Jr.
Duane E. Carr
George D. Carr
George G. D. Carr
Harold Carr, Jr.
Harry L. Carr
Howard L. Carr
Isaac Carr, Jr.
James T. Carr
Johnnie Carr
Leroy F. Carr
Luther E. Carr
Marvin Dexter Carr
Patrick F. Carr
Paul E. Carr
Ralph Rodney Carr
Thomas F. Carr
Thomas Gerard Carr
William H. Carr
Winston A. Carr
Thomas M. Carraher
Jack Carrara
Jesus Rodriquis Carrasco
Jose U. Carrasco
Leandro C. Carrasco
Ricardo Carrasco
Lee C. Carraway
Marion Carreathers
Richard J. Carrell
Curtis E. Carrere
Charles L. Carrier
Lawrence E. Carrier
Oscar G. Carriere
James A. Carrigan
Zinn Carrigan, Jr.
Richard C. Carrigo
Alejandro Carrillo, Jr.
Alexander A. Carrillo
Carmen Carrillo
Leopold M. Carrillo
Nieves Carrillo
Raul Carrillo
Bruce Lynn Carrington
James A. Carrington
Michael P. Carrington
Robert R. Carrington
Frederick Carrino
Contreras M. Carrion
Jorge L. Carrion
Martino Luis Carrion
Miguel A. Carrion
Alfredo Carrizales
Charles F. Carrol
Aubrey D. Carroll
Billy W. Carroll
Charles F. Carroll
Charles L. Carroll, Jr.
Charlie Paten Carroll, Jr.
Cornie E. Carroll
Daniel Joseph Carroll
Edwin E. Carroll
Frank Bassett Carroll
Garland R. Carroll
George Carroll
James Carroll
James A. Carroll
James R. Carroll
James W. Carroll
John E. Carroll
John J. Carroll
Joseph S. Carroll
Patrick Joseph Carroll
Percy C. Carroll

Peter J. Carroll
Raymond B. Carroll
Raymond E. Carroll
Robert C. Carroll
Robert Joseph Carroll
Robert L. Carroll
Roland S. Carroll
William G. Carroll
John Zaphyr Carros
Ralph N. Carrouth
Murray B. Carrow
Peter Michael Carrozo
Royce Carruth
Donavon R. Carson
John Spencer Carson
Maynard E. Carson
Vernon C. Carson
Gordon B. Carsrud
William O. Carstarphen
Robert L. Carstensen
Miguel R. Cartagena-Colon
Thomas Cartalino
Albert Carter
Albert R. Carter
Andrew Carter
Andrew Carter
Bennie Gerald Carter
Bobby Ray Carter
Bryant W. Carter
Carl E. Carter
Clarence O. Carter
Clyde M. Carter
Cornelius Carter, Jr.
Daniel J. Carter
David W. Carter
Donald E. Carter
Donovan E. Carter
Douglas E. Carter
Doyle Carter
Dudley Carter
Edward A. Carter
Edward R. Carter
Eldridge Carter
Emmett J. Carter
Fred C. Carter
George Carter
George E. Carter
Grant Dee Carter, Jr.
Hampton Curtis Carter
Harold Carter
Harold B. Carter
Harry Frederick Carter
Henry L. Carter
Horace Judson Carter
J. B. Carter
James B. Carter
James E. Carter
James Carter, Jr.
James M. Carter
James R. Carter
Joe D. Carter
John W. Carter
Joseph C. Carter
Joseph F. Carter
Joseph R. Carter
Leo Carter
Leonard Penrose Carter
Lloyd L. Carter
Louis Alfred Carter
Owen M. Carter
Ray Carter
Raymond Carter
Robert L. Carter
Robert X. Carter
Samuel R. Carter
Sidney C. Carter, Jr.
Theodore Carter
Thomas Carter
Thomas F. Carter
William H. Carter
William J. Carter
William L. Carter
William M. Carter
Willie E. Carter
Robert O. Cartier
William A. Cartier
Daniel L. Cartwright
Paul K. Carty
Carmen F. Caruso
Frank P. Caruso, Jr.
Herman R. Caruso
Joseph Eugene Caruso
Mathew Caruso
Frank B. Carver
John E. Carver
Willie L. Carver
Charles C. Cary
Daniel A. Cary
Libero P. Casaccia

Robert Edward Casagrand
Alex Casanova
Herbert V. Casanova, Jr.
Alfred P. Casares
Fernando Casas, Jr.
Gilberto Casas
William Lee Cascell
Carl Seab Case
Charles E. Case
Jack W. Case
Lloyd A. Case
Thomas Harry Case
Charles L. Casey
Frank L. Casey
Hugh B. Casey
Jeremiah Casey
John J. Casey, Jr.
Joseph Francis Casey
Kenneth C. Casey
Neil Francis Casey
Peter Francis Casey
Raymond Joseph Casey
Robert M. Casey
Russell M. Casey
William Alfred Casey
William D. Casey
Floyd Cash
Hoyt B. Cash
Jack M. Cash
James Russell Cash
Bobby R. Cashion
David J. Cashion
William W. Cashour, Jr.
Joe Cashwell
Daniel Casillas
Manuel G. Casillas
Roberto L. Casillas
Billy Glen Casker
James E. Cason
Prince A. Cason
Charles D. Casper
Clyde H. Casper
Richard Casper
Vincent A. Cassano
Patrick T. Cassatt
Harry L. Cassell
Thomas H. Cassens
Thomas Francis Casserly
Frank M. Cassetta
Vincent A. Cassiano
Boyd W. Cassidy
Lonnie Nathan Cassle
Gerald E. Castagnetto
Calude Camille Castaing
Pete Castana
Agapito R. Castaneda
Arthur C. Castaneda
Barney P. Casteel, Jr.
Donald E. Casteel
John A. Casteel
Mark J. Castellano
Edmund L. Castello
Eugene Castellone
Richard Stephen Caster
Anthony J. Castiglia
Paul Castiglione
Ernesto Paiz Castilla
Felix Alfred Castille
Melvin M. Castille
Augustine Castillo
Leopoldo V. Castillo
Martin Castillo
Pablo A. Castillo
Quinones R. Castillo
Ramon Castillo
Leon Leonard Castino
Clifford C. Castle
Fred Castle
Herman Castle, Jr.
Ralph A. Castle
Robert E. Castle
William B. Castle
William Castleberry
William J. Castleman, Jr.
Taylor K. Castlen
Donald Castonguay
Romeo J. Castonguay
Ricardo Castor, Jr.
Charles Castorena
Frederick Castrataro
Louis Castrataro
Antonio Castrellon
Armando Castro
Arthuro C. Castro
Hectotr L. Castro
Ignacio C. Castro
Jesus B. Castro
Joseph M. Castro
Luis G. Castro

Pedro O. Castro
Ruben Castro
Victor E. Castro
J. Castro-Henriquez
Dominik Cataldo, Jr.
Frank Nick Cataldo
Dominador G. Catalon
Clifton Catchings
Monroe Cater, Jr.
James G. Cates
Robert S. Cathcart
Charles V. Cathey
Alfred Fabula Catimon
Fred S. Catlett
David L. Catlin
Edward W. Catlos
Robert E. Catlow
Charlie L. Cato
Wilbert W. Cato
Carlton R. Caton
Wayne R. Caton
Alva E. Catt
Merlin Lee Cattell
Roy M. Caudell
James A. Caudill
James C. Caudill
Ralph K. Caudill
Walton M. Caudill
Gilbert N. Caudle, Jr.
Robert Louis Caudle
William J. Caughey
Wilbur O. Caul
Carson B. Caulder
George W. Cauley
Alton M. Causey
Billy J. Causey
Lewis Paul Causey
Paul O. Causey
Brenice Cauthen
Marion F. Cauthen
Winifred Cauthen, Jr.
Robert E. Cauthers
William E. Caution
John S. Cavagnaro
Nick J. Cavaliero
James H. Cavanaugh
Charles L. Cave
James Albert Cave
James Edward Cave
Willard S. Cave
John J. Cavender
John Lester Cavender
Mack D. Cavender
William E. Cavender
John C. Cavil
Lee R. Cawley
James R. Cawthon
Norman G. Cawthorn
Donald C. Cayan
Robert J. Caye
Edward C. Cayemberg
Donald C. Cazel
Edward Cearlock
James Ceasor
Jose A. Ceballos
Edward J. Cebula
George A. Cecchel
Charles L. Cecil
George T. Cecil
Jesse L. Cecil, Jr.
Raymond Cecil
William A. Cecil
Benito Antonio Cecilia
William Ceckowski, Jr.
Robert Adam Cecot
Richard J. Ceculski
Howard F. Cedars
Martin Louis Cedeno
Ramos Armando Cedeno
Richard E. Ceglorek
Raul M. Ceniseroz
Bernardo D. Centeno
Isreal Centeno
Manuel C. Centeno
Linden Centers
Americo D. Cerasuolo
Vincent Spino Ceritello
Joe V. Cerri, Jr.
Joseph Certa
Wayne L. Cervenka
John R. Cervi
Reynaldo Cesena
Marvin Cessna, Jr.
Selby F. Chabot
Soto Nilton Chacon
Earbie Chaddrick
John G. Chadek
George R. Chadwell
Fred David Chadwick

James R. Chadwick
Kenneth L. Chadwick
Richard E. Chadwick
Alden R. Chaffin
Clifford R. Chaffin
James A. Chaffin
Robert E. Chaffin
Roy O. Chaffin, Jr.
Leo Chaffins
Edward G. Chairess
Henry Chaisson
Dale E. Chalfant
Alfred M. Chalfin
Lawrence F. Chalifoux
George J. Challender
Francis E. Chamberlain
John L. Chamberlain
John M. Chamberlain
Alvernon A. Chambers
Andrew Chambers
Bennie E. Chambers
Clarence Chambers
Earl F. Chambers
Grady L. Chambers
Harvey Chambers
Henry L. Chambers
Horace Chambers
Hugh Strong Chambers
Leslie D. Chambers
Lewis W. Chambers
Osric E. Chambers
Richard J. Chambers
William J. Chambers
William J. Chambers
Willis M. Chambers
Harvey L. Chambles
Denver Isaah Chambliss
Samuel A. Chami
David B. Champagne
John T. Champagne
Morris J. Champagne
Aubry W. Champion
Felipe A. Champion
John Champion
Merrill A. Champion
Clarence Chan
Donald W. Chan
John B. Chan
David Chance
Thomas L. Chancellor
Joseph D. Chancery
Guy Chancey
Howard Harrell Chancey
Bobby Joe Chandler
Carl H. Chandler
Charles G. Chandler
Elmer M. Chandler
Gordon Harwood Chandler
Herbert W. Chandler
James O. Chandler
John W. Chandler, Jr.
Kenneth H. Chandler
Prentice S. Chandler
Robert C. Chandler
Teddy R. Chandler
Charles R. Chaney
Dean D. Chaney
Donald L. Chaney
Jack A. Chaney
James G. Chaney
Wilson Chaney, Jr.
Albert Sa Kin Chang
Robert E. Channon
Delbert Chansler, Jr.
Harry Leddy Ii Chant
Melvin H. Chantre
Juoquin M. Chapa
Jacob W. Chapin
Ross H. Chapin
Charles F. Chaplin
R. B. Chaplin
Alfred E. Chapman
Charles David Chapman
Charles W. Chapman
Curtis Earl Chapman
Dewey Lyle Chapman
George Logan Chapman
Harold S. Chapman
Herman Chapman
James Virgil Chapman
Melvin C. Chapman
Neil A. Chapman
Raymond B. Chapman
Raymond Curtis Chapman
Raymond L. Chapman
Richard A. Chapman
Sam Chapman
Samuel A. Chapman
Theodore Willie Chapman

William M. Chapman
Kenneth E. Chapp
Cyril G. Chappel
Richard A. Chappel
Bartley S. Chappell
Billie F. Chappell
Everett F. Chappell
Gene A. Chappell
James R. Chappelle
Donald Meredith Chapple
Diaz B. Charbonier
Frank C. Charcas
Robert J. Charette
Richard B. Charland
Frank J. Charldo
Alfredo Paredes Charles
Anthony J. Charles
Dean Donald Charles
James O. Charles
Joseph Charles, Jr.
Madison F. Charles
Marvin Ray Charles
Raymond M. Charles
William H. Charles
Arthur Charleston
Sam Charleston, Jr.
Gerald E. Charlesworth
Leo Edwin Charley
Paul J. Charlier
Cornelius H. Charlton
Peter F. Charnetski
Andrew Charnichko
George P. Charnock
Fred Charnow
Howard Charte, Jr.
Gerald L. Chartrand
James C. Charves
Dupree Charvis
Byron Harold Chase
George I. Chase
Howard Francis Chase, Jr.
John L. Chase
Lester Thomas Chase
Lewis E. Chase
Robinson Chase
Rene P. Chasez
George E. Chastain
John Hilmon Chastain
John W. Chastain
R. E. Chastain
Thurman J. Chastain
Vaskel T. Chasteen
Wade J. Chataignier
Dennis Leroy Chatellier
Fred T. Chatfield
Thomas J. Chatigny
Leroy Chatman
Louis Chatman
Joe Chatmon, Jr.
Raymon Chatmon
John J. Chauvin
Elma Isaac Chavers
Albert J. Chavez
Alfredo Guerrero Chavez
Arnold F. Chavez
Benny R. Chavez
Bernard R. Chavez
Celestino Chavez, Jr.
Charles Chavez, Jr.
Daniel Chavez
Daniel V. Chavez
Don Chavez
Edward J. Chavez
Eloy A. Chavez
Gilbert E. Chavez
Jose Maria Chavez
Miguel S. Chavez
Ralph G. Chavez
Ruben Chavez
Silas E. Chavez
Vincent J. Chavez
George E. Chavira
Herman Chavira
Burnice Chavis
Narcisco Chavis, Jr.
Edwin D. Chavous
John B. Cheatam, Jr.
George L. Cheatem
James Cheatham, Jr.
Robert E. Cheatun
Stanley Joseph Checki
Daniel E. Checola
Joseph Chee
Robert V. Cheek
Robert H. Iii Cheeks
James L. Cheers
John Cheeves, Jr.
Louis Cheff
George Chegay

James E. Chenault
Victor Alger Cheney
Martin M. Chepke
Michael Cheppa
Lawrence Cheramie
A. J. Cherconis, Jr.
Thomas J. Cherf
George Lee Cherrington
Augustus W. Cherry
Clarence Martin Cherry
R. B. Cherry
Richard F. Cherry
Robert Lionel Cherry
Walter W. Cherry
John Sam Cherskov
Harold J. Chesbro, Jr.
Leonard Ray Cheshire
Darrol C. Chesley
Guy O. Chesley
George J. Chesmore
George R. Chesney
Frank J. Chesnowsky
Fred D. Chesnut
Joseph G. Chess
George R. Chesser
Donald H. Chestnut
Roland B. Chestnut
Ronald Willis Cheston
Joseph L. Chettle
Gumersindo Chevre
Charles A. Chew
Harry John Chewning
James F. Chezek
Antonino Chiarello
Joseph F. Chiavetta
Roy Chichenoff
Grover C. Chick, Jr.
Arthur Adolph Chidester
Gilbert L. Chidester
Gerald Chieppo
Robert N. Chilcote
Bonnie Chilcutt
Edward S. Child
Harold D. Childers
Bennie F. Childree
Willard Childres
Charles L. Childress
Ernest A. Childress
James N. Childress
John L. Childress
Raymond A. Childs
Robert L. Childs
Russell H. Childs
Owen D. Chilton
Harry M. Chinen
Candido Chini
Leonard K. Chinn
Louis O. Chinn
Herbert W. Chipman
Gibbs Chisholm
Dennis J. Chism
Cain Chisolm
James L. Chitty
Floyd Vernon Chitwood
John Vernon Chitwood
Howard E. Chivvis
Edward J. Chmelka
Alban Chmielewski
Loyd L. Choat
Francis N. Choate
Gerlad A. Choate
John E. Choate
Joseph D. Choate
Stanley Anthony Chocian
Victor J. Choiniere
C. N. Chojnacki, Jr.
Frank Chojnowski, Jr.
Alphonsus Cholewsky
Ellis A. Choma
Marchmont T. F. Chong
Bernard A. Chopek
Arthur George Choquette
Havy O. Chorn
Edward G. Chotkey
Leo J. Chouinard
Martin Chovanec, Jr.
Kenneth Chrisenbery
Cyril M. Chrisjohn
Fitzhugh L. Chrisman, Jr.
Pierre C. Chrissis
Boris Robert Christ
Earl A. Christensen
Frank P. Christensen, Jr.
George K. Christensen
Jack W. Christensen
Jerry C. Christensen
Louis Norgall Christensen
Thomas A. Christensen, Jr.
Val D. Christensen

Adrian L. Christenson
Loyal E. Christenson
Richard J. Christenson
Andrew J. Christian
Berthold Butler Christian
Claiborn Christian
Earl E. Christian
James W. Christian
Jimmy L. Christian
Roland E. Christian
Stuart B. Christian
Warren Eugene Christian
William Christian
John B. Christiana
Donald R. Christiansen
Warren C. Christiansen
John P. Christianson
Leonard Christianson
Stanley R. Christianson
Alton Christie
William K. Christie
Rosario J. Christina
Jerome B. Christine
John R. Christle
Harry A. Christman
Lloyd E. Christmas
Michael Christodulou
W. R. Christoffersen
Curtis W. Christopher
Lawrence W. Christopher
Philip J. Christopher
Ronald N. Christopher
Donald G. Christophersen
Alvin J. Christy
John F. Christy
Wilbur R. Christy
John C. Chronister
David Burnell Chrystie
John Chudo
Stanley J. Chudobski
Dan D. Chulibrk
Edward Chumak
Wilfred Y. W. Chun
Raymond C. S. Chung
Alphonso Church
Freddie E. Church
Harold C. Church
Lorin D. Church
Mack Church
Merle E. Church
Ray Church, Jr.
Vernon J. Church
John W. Churchill
Robert Arnold Churchill
Ralph Edward Chute
Peter P. Ciaccio
Vincent Ciaramitaro
Anthony J. Cicalese
John Ciccarelli
Michael V. Cicchella
Joseph Elwood Cicchino
Orlando A. Ciccone
William E. Cicon
John T. Cicur, Jr.
Joseph P. Cidade
Rudy Cienega
Mitchell John Cieplak
Edwin W. Ciesielski
Joseph K. Cieslak
John Anthony Cima
Larry Raymond Cimino
Bert F. Cinkovich
Herminio Cintron
Miguel A. Cintron
Teodulo Cintron
Modesta Cintron-Pagan
Vincent Cipolla
George Cipriano
Jack J. Cirimele
Rivera Arthur D. Cirino
G. Cirino-Pizarro
Samuel J. Cirulli
Dominic Anthony Cisco
Thomas Ciskitti
Robert A. Cisler
Arthur Cisneros
Rudolph Cisneros
Joseph John Citera
August D. Citrone
George L. Ciucci
Charles V. Claeys
Van E. Clagg
Donald J. Clairmont
James O. Clamp
William H. Clampitt
James W. Clance
Edwin L. Clancy
Everell V. Clanin
John N. Clanton

Robert W. Clanton
Wilbert W. Clanton
Loyd Valentine Clapp, Jr.
Richard E. Clapp
Francis I. Clapper
Norman H. Clapper
Eugene E. Clardy
Thomas C. Clare
George B. Claridy
James R. Clarin
Albert Clark
Alexander Sr Clark
Alvin L. Clark
Andrew Clark
Arthur Leroy Clark
Bartholomew N. Clark
Basil L. Clark
Bob Edward Clark
Bobby J. Clark
Boyers Morgan Clark, Jr.
Bruce Leroy Clark
Charles L. Clark
Charles W. Clark
Charles W. Clark
Claude E. Clark
Clifford E. Clark
Clinton Clark
Curtis W. Clark
Donald Holland Clark
Donald J. Clark
Donald J. Clark
Dow Jay Clark
Edward Clark
Edward Leon Clark
Eldred B. Clark
Frederick T. Clark
Gene F. Clark
George A. Clark
George E. Clark
George F. Clark
Glen J. Clark
Glenn M. Clark
Hallie A. Clark, Jr.
Harold Robert Clark
Henry D. Clark
Herbert F. Clark, Jr.
Howard Franklin Clark
Howard Lee Clark
James H. Clark
James Clark, Jr.
James R. Clark
James V. Clark
Jesse F. Sr Clark
Jewel Clark
John J. Clark
John M. Clark
John Powell Clark
John Thomas Clark, Jr.
Joseph E. Clark
Keith K. Clark
Larry L. Clark
Leonard W. Clark
Lewis C. Clark, Jr.
Luther N. Clark
Meachem W. Clark
O. C. Clark, Jr.
Odell Clark
Raymond Lewis Clark
Richard Douglas Clark
Richard N. Clark
Robert E. Clark
Robert L. Clark
Robert Leroy Clark
Robert M. Clark
Roosevelt Clark
Samuel G. Clark
Stuart G. Clark
Thomas Leroy Clark
Vern R. Clark
Virgil D. Clark
Walter B. Clark
Walter H. Clark
Walter L. Clark
Warren M. Clark
Wesley H. Clark
William Copeland Clark
William D. Clark
William E. Clark
William J. Clark
William J. Clark
Willie Clark
Harry Bernard Clarke
Robert J. Clarke
Wilson D. Clarke
Russell W. Clarkson, Jr.
Thomas Clarkson, Jr.
Thomas S. Clarkson
Troy Clarkson, Jr.
Edward W. Clarno

Marion L. Clary
Ralph Raymond Clary
Raymond L. Sr Clary
Walter E. Class, Jr.
Robert Odis Clatter
Roland W. Clatterbuck
Robert G. Clatworthy, Jr.
Carl J. Claus
Walter R. Claussen
Dominique Claverie
Paul E. Clawson
Alex C. Clay
Arthur Clay
Carleton B. Clay
George Tolbert Clay
James E. Clay
Olin S. Clay
Richard F. Clay
Robert E. Clay
Willie Lee Clay
James George Clayberg
James S. Clayborne
Owen L. Claycomb
Russell E. Claymon
Floyd M. Claypool
Charles L. Clayton
Claud Albert Clayton
Dallas E. Clayton
Denver R. Clayton
Donald James Clayton
Earl F. Clayton
Howard E. Clayton
James W. Clayton, Jr.
Phillip A. Clayton
Raymond H. Clayton
Raymond L. Clayton
Robert J. Clayton
Russell Clayton
Theodore C. Clayton
Edward O. Cleaborn
David F. Clear
Patrick J. Cleary
Delmon Cleaver
Robert D. Cleckner
Edward L. Clegg
Charles M. Clem
Kenneth A. Clem
Anthony J. Clemens, Jr.
John J. Clemens
Raymond T. Clement
David C. Clements
Elzie G. Clements
Louis C. Clements
Robert D. Clements
Terrell C. Clements
Arden M. Clemmer
Anderson M. Clemmons, Jr.
Kenneth D. Clemmons
Teddy V. Clemmons
Charles E. Clemons
Clifford J. Clemons
Fred C. Clemons
Robert N. Clendenin
Frank E. Clendening
John Clendinning
Dominick Clesceri
Giovanni Cleva
Clifton Cleveland
Euclid L. Cleveland
Frank J. Cleveland
Hereford W. Cleveland
John Rufus Cleveland
Ned J. Cleveland
Paul A. Cleveland
Stanley K. Cleveland
Bruce W. Clevenger
Clariel M. Clevenger
James N. Clevenger
Leon E. Clevenger
Leslie D. Click
Wayne K. Click
George W. Clickner
Clyde R. Clifford
Arthur A. Clifton
Arthur Z. Clifton
Milo F. Clifton
Obie Clifton
Ralph D. Clifton
Robert L. Clifton
Roy M. Clifton
Sammie L. Clifton
William L. Clifton
Nathan O. Climer
Willard L. Clinch
Charles Jarden Cline
George Hay Cline
Harold C. Cline
Harold H. Cline
James E. Cline

Otis H. Cline
Parker L. Cline
Robert L. Cline
William H. Cline
William J. Cline
Richard Cedric Clinite
Harold Clinkscale
Walter Andrew Clinnin, Jr.
Bob G. Clinton
Socrates J. Cliotes
James V. Clodfelter
Walter Henry Cloe
Jack B. Cloin
James F. Clopton
Archie J. Closson
Evans Cloud, Jr.
George Grady Cloud
Charles W. Clough
Kenneth H. Clough, Jr.
Jimmy R. Cloughly
Bernard Cleo Clouse
Earl S. Clouser
Robert E. Clouser
Robert J. Cloutier
Rodney F. Cloutman
Lawrence Clover
Melvin Elijah Clover
Algernon S. Clowe
Alfred W. Clowers
Alvis Clowers
Anthony David Cluff
William R. Cluff
Robert J. Clukey
Norman E. Clupe
Dale Eugene Clutter
Lesley W. Clyburn
Merle Delmar Clymer
Cecil Harrison Clyott, Jr.
Cyrus Cnossen
James Coachman, Jr.
Ernest L. Coakley
William E. Coale
Barton Coalson
Edward Joseph Coalson
Clyde Philip Coates, Jr.
Frederick D. Coates
Robert Coates
Roman W. Coates
Willard H. Coates
Jessie Coats, Jr.
Terrill O. Coats
Charles A. Cobb
Donald Stanley Cobb
Harlan Paige Cobb
James O. Cobb
Orlan G. Cobb
Robert L. Cobb
William L. Cobb
Arthur C. Cobbs
Leslie K. Cober
Franklin E. Coble
Walter R. Coble
Ernest Arthur Coblentz
Frank A. Coburn
Howard Coburn
Valentin Coca
Anthony L. Cocchi
James M. Cochenour
Billy Edward Cochran
Billy G. Cochran
Coonfield Cochran
Donald R. Cochran
Hubert F. Cochran
Jack D. Cochran
Jack W. Cochran
James L. Cochran
John W. Cochran
Joseph A. Cochran, Jr.
L. G. Cochran
Lawrence R. Cochran, Jr.
Thomas John Cochran
William L. Cochran
Roberto Cocio
Harlan R. Cockerham
Elmer M. Cockrell
John E. Cockrell
Hayden D. Cockrum
John P. Coco
Francis A. Codd
Gilbert Coddington
Carlos P. Codina
George G. Cody
William F. Cody
James F. Coe
Allan A. Coelho
Joe P. Coelho
Walter L. Coen
Burt N. Coers
Charles L. Coffee

Robert George Coffee
William W. Coffee
Arthur G. Coffey
Clifford V. Coffey
Gordon R. Coffey
J. C. Coffey
Jack D. Coffey
John E. Coffie
James Warren Coffin
Paul C. Coffin
Charles G. Coffman
Emory Ronald Coffman
Melvin S. Coffman
Robert M. Coffman
Ronal W. Coffman
Willie F. Cofield
Charles D. Cogar
Kenneth C. Cogdill
Denver Clyde Coger
Carl L. Coggin
Earl Coggin
Robert H. Coghan
Purl Leon Coghill
Thomas E. Coghlan
Frank Joseph Cogings
Cecil K. Coglan
Carmelo A. Cognata
Robert Whitney Cogswell
Frank Cohan
Bernard Cohen
David J. Cohen
Norman Cohen
Richard W. Cohenour
Floyd E. Cohick
Herbert Cohn
Max H. Cohoe
William S. Cohowitz
Phillip L. Coiner
Randall E. Coiner
James R. Cointment
Jonas Coit, Jr.
Edward F. Coiteux
Richard B. Coke, Jr.
Cecil A. Coker
Clyde Coker
Floyd T. Coker
Martin A. Coker
Richard D. Coker
Louis A. Colageo
Richard A. Colaluca
Domenic Colameta
George T. Colangelo
Salvatore Colao
James L. Colarusso, Jr.
James A. Colasanti
Mussenden S. Colberg
Charles Norman Colbert
James A. Colbert
James C. Colbert
Donald C. Colburn
Albert C. Colby
David L. Colby
Edward L. Colby
William Colby
Bobby Joe Cole
Burrell B. Cole
Charles H. Cole
Charles M. Cole
David L. Cole
Delmar P. Cole
Donald B. Cole
Donald P. Cole
Edward L. Cole, Jr.
Frank N. Cole
George William Cole
Henly P. Cole, Jr.
Jackie L. Cole
James C. Cole
John M. Cole, Jr.
Johnnie B. Cole
Lee R. Cole
Mathey G. Cole
Merle L. Cole, Jr.
Phillip M. Cole
Ralph R. Cole
Randolph J. Cole
Richard V. Cole
Schuyler B. Cole
Shirley W. Cole
Thomas E. Cole
Walter E. Cole
William H. Cole
David Thomas Colegate
Oliver Colegrove
Russell Lee Colegrove
Daniel Colello
Alan R. Coleman
Alfred L. Coleman
Alfred Lewis Coleman

Blaine M. Coleman
Charles Coleman
Charles L. Coleman
Chauncey E. Coleman
Dennis W. Coleman, Jr.
Donald Lamar Coleman
Elmer L. Coleman
Elmer Louis Coleman
Francis W. Coleman
Gilbert T. Coleman
Glynn A. Coleman
Grover W. Coleman
Herbert Coleman
Jack Coleman
James Allen Coleman
John B. Coleman, Jr.
John C. Coleman
John Joseph Coleman
Joseph L. Coleman
Lawrence Q. Coleman
Leroy R. Coleman
Norris L. Coleman
Richard Allyn Coleman
Richard F. Coleman
Richard R. Coleman
Robert Coleman
Robert B. Coleman
Wilfred E. Coleman, Jr.
William N. Coleman
Buford Coleson
Grover Coley
Lee Edward Coley
Raymond W. Colflesh
Wilbur B. Colford
Donald Richard Colgett
Donald E. Colgrove
Raymond Francis Colin
Richard Dean Collage
Either M. Collazo
Raymond H. Coller
James Robert Colleran
John Andrew Collett
Walter Collett
Joseph P. Collette
Joseph R. Collette
Ernest J. Colletti, Jr.
William Colletti
Eugene J. Colley
Charles E. Colley
Donald Ray Collier
Edward L. Collier
Gilbert G. Collier
John A. Collier
John W. Collier
Rogers B. Collier, Jr.
Roy D. Collier
Toland J. Collier
Willie L. Collier
Charles L. Collings
Albert Harvey Collins
Calvin Robert Collins
Charles E. Collins
Charles H. Collins
Clairence H. Collins
Clarence H. Collins
Claude E. Collins
David Collins
Dennis J. Collins
Doyle Collins
Edmond Collins, Jr.
Edward E. Collins
Edward H. Collins
Edward J. Collins
Edward R. Collins
Edwin Wesley Collins
Estle L. Collins
Frank Collins
Frederick Collins
Galvis Collins
Gerald J. Collins
Glenn E. Collins
Harry Loran Collins, Jr.
Harry P. Collins
Harvey N. Collins
Henry Collins, Jr.
Jack L. Collins
James E. Collins
James Lawrence Collins
James R. Collins
James R. Collins
James Robert Collins
Jewel W. Collins
John Collins
John E. Collins
John M. Collins
John Soulard Collins
John W. Collins
John W. Collins
Joseph Collins

Joseph E. Collins
Joseph Stephen Collins
Junior Rasie Collins
Louis E. Collins
Marvin R. Collins
Max Harvey Collins
Oliver Collins, Jr.
Paul Douglas Collins
Paul M. Collins
Raymond J. Collins
Robert E. Collins
Roy J. Collins
Scoop O. Collins
Sidney L. Collins
Thomas B. Collins
Thomas C. Collins
William Collins
William E. Collins, Jr.
William H. Collins
William K. Collins
William L. Collins
William R. Collins
Woodrow Collins
Mario L. Collinsworth
John C. Collonia
August E. Colmenares
Rexford L. Colombel
Alicea Joaquin Colon
Concepcion Colon
Euripides A. Colon
Fantauzzi I. Colon
Flores Antonio Colon
Martinez M. Colon
Perez Jose S. Colon
Reyes Felix Colon
Rodriguez A. Colon
Rodriguez F. A. Colon
Manuel Colon-Aponte
Pedro Colon-Burgos
C. Colon-Fonseca
Rafael Colon-Marquez
Luis Colon-Negron
Wilfrido Colon-Ramos
F. Colon-Velazquez
Francis Colonna
Gaetano A. Colonna
John Camillo Colonna
Josephs Colonna
Michael V. Colonnello
David Paul Colopy
Richard Joseph Colpaert
Allen W. Colsden
Harry Lee Colson
Hurder F. Colson
Joseph R. Colson
Charles Ragon Colt
Edward A. Colton
Roy P. Colvard, Jr.
Clyde R. Colvin
Robert Charles Colvin
Thomas L. Colvin
Juan A. Coma
Anthony Combs
Bobby Van Combs
Carl B. Combs
Carl Edsel Combs
Ferrice G. Combs
Forrest G. Combs
Horace G. Combs, Jr.
Robert L. Combs
Joseph W. Comeau
Rayford J. Comeaux
Cloral L. Comer
Eugene C. Comer
Samuel W. Comer
Joe C. Comier
Donald W. Comins
Louis S. Comis
Charlie L. Comolli
Albert K. Comp
Rudy Comparin
Charles R. Compton
Charles T. Compton
Floyd E. Compton
John Telmage Compton
Johnny H. Compton
Edward W. Comstock
Donald R. Comtois
John J. Conahan, Jr.
Robert E. Conant
Lester Conard
Frank W. Conarro
Charles W. Conarroe
Perry J. Conaway
Joseph F. Concannon
Pabon R. Concepcion
Heriberto Concepcion-Diaz
Jose J. Concepcion-Lopez
Quilin C. Conceptiones

Louis B. Conde
Boyd E. Conder
Robert Conder
Elishie M. Condict
John L. Condit
Elbert A. Condley
Richard G. Condon
Stephen A. Condon
Herbert W. Condor
Thomas John Condron
Victor J. Condroski
Robert E. Condy
Harvel L. Cone
Ulysses Conely
Clyde L. Confer, Jr.
Herbert R. Confer
John L. Confer
Richard A. Confer
Jack G. Conger
James M. Conger
George T. Congleton, Jr.
Henry E. Congleton
Stanley J. Conhartoski
Marvin G. Conica
Alva Britton Conine
Eugene J. Conis
John D. Conkerton, Jr.
Charles W. Conklin
George W. Conklin, Jr.
John E. Conklin, Jr.
Paul F. Conklin
Charles G. Conley
Clayton Conley
Clifton W. Conley
James T. Conley
James W. Conley
Pete Conley
Robert H. Conley
Paul D. Conlin
John Joseph Conlon
Owen H. Conlon
William Joseph Conlon
Clinton De Waine Conn
James J. Connally
George W. Connaughton
Henry D. Connell
John M. Connell
Robert Thomas Connell, Jr.
Charles K. Connelly
Edward J. Connelly
James P. Connelly
Louis B. Connelly
Ronald T. Connelly
Connie M. Conner
Delmar E. Conner
Donald E. Conner
George W. Conner
Gerald W. Conner
James W. Conner
Raymond E. Conner
Robert J. Conner, Jr.
Robert K. Conner
Robert W. Conner
Donald C. Connett
Karl F. Connick
David W. Connolly
Gerald John Connolly
James Joseph Connolly
Mark Connolly
Patrick E. Connolly
Paul Martin Connolly
Robert C. Connolly
Andrew E. Connor, Jr.
Billy J. Connor
Jefferson L. Connor
Normand Page Connor
Archibald H. J. Connors
Harry Robert Connors
Howard Joseph Connors
Robert Edward Connors
Thomas J. Connors
Delbert Conover
Christian L. Conover
Ralph James Conover
David R. Conrad
Jack D. Conrad
Merrill S. Conrad
Norman P. Conrad
Paul R. Conrad
Richard L. Conrad
Robert D. Conrad
Wilbur L. Conrad
John K. Conroy
Joseph P. Conroy
Joseph P. Conroy
Michael F. Conroy
Patrick J. Conroy
Thomas E. Conroy, Jr.
Bernard J. Considine

Robert F. Considine
Henry Consigli, Jr.
Melvin E. Constable
James L. Constant
Gerlando Constantino
Edward L. Consylman
Johnnie E. Contario
Frederick A. Conti
Joseph P. Conti
Mario Contiliano
Espectac Contreras, Jr.
Hermino V. Contreras
Liandro Contreras, Jr.
Lupe Contreras
Rudolph R. Contreras
Brooks E. Conway
Dehaven L. Conway
James A. Conway
Robert Walter Conway
Thomas P. Conway
Edward L. Conyers
Jean R. Conyers
John R. Coogan
Alfred Cook
Baxter Hughes Cook
Bernard D. Cook
Campbell D. Cook
Carl W. Cook
Charles A. Cook
Charles F. Cook
Charles J. Cook
Charles R. Cook
Charles W. Cook
Charlie C. Cook
David L. Cook
Edward H. Cook
Eli William Cook
Emil E. Cook, Jr.
Gerald V. Cook
Harold D. Cook
Harry W. Cook, Jr.
Henry W. Cook, Jr.
Howard D. Cook
Irvin H. Cook, Jr.
J. C. Cook
Jack L. Cook
James D. Cook
James L. Cook
John E. Cook
John M. Cook
John T. Cook
Joseph J. Cook
Kermit E. Cook
Lamonte B. Cook
Lewis Dale Cook
Maurice E. Cook
Mc Kinley C. Cook
Orville Melvin Cook
Osborn H. Cook
Paul K. Cook
Richard K. Cook
Roscoe Cook, Jr.
Roy R. Cook
Theodore Amos Cook
Thomas H. Cook
Thomas Ray Cook
Wilford Theodore Cook
William R. Cook
William W. Cook
Albert B. Cooke
Bobby G. Cooke
Glen L. Cooke
Jackson Cooke
John M. Cooke
John P. Cooke
Leon O. Cooke
Leroy D. Cooke
Leroy Moore Cooke
Vincent M. Cooke
William A. Cooke, Jr.
Jesse R. Cooksey
Ocie W. Cooksie
Fred E. Cookson, Jr.
John Cooley, Jr.
Leslie L. Cooley
Michael Everett Cooley
Paul R. Cooley
William Cooley, Jr.
Ellis Coon
Elmer Clark Coon, Jr.
Marvin Harold Coon
Edward J. Cooney
Edward T. Cooney
John J. Cooney
Thomas Edward Cooney
Earl R. Coonrod
Charles E. Coons
Frederick E. Coons
Virgil Coontz

331

Arthur Cooper
Billie J. Cooper
Billy Gene Cooper
Boyd L. Cooper
Burl L. Cooper
Charles R. Cooper
Clarence A. Cooper
David Quint Cooper
David R. Cooper
Denis V. Cooper
Donald D. Cooper
Floyd Cooper, Jr.
George Cooper
Gilbert R. Cooper
Harold R. Cooper
Jack R. Cooper
James M. Cooper
James P. Cooper
James R. Cooper
James W. Cooper
Jimmie R. Cooper
John J. Cooper
John W. Cooper
Joseph Cooper
Lawrence E. Cooper
Leroy Cooper
Melvin C. Cooper
Norwood C. Cooper
Oren S. Cooper
Paul D. Cooper
Paul R. Cooper, Jr.
Ralph L. Cooper
Richard J. Cooper
Richard R. Cooper
Robert Cooper
Robert E. Cooper
Roland E. Cooper
Russell A. Cooper
Sammy Buck Cooper
Spencer R. Cooper, Jr.
Stephen P. Cooper
Utah Noah Cooper
William E. Cooper
Winston Rasey Cooper
George W. Copas
Richard A. Cope
Robert H. Cope
Robert L. Cope
Troy Gordon Cope
Walter G. Cope
Dale R. Copeland
Ellis H. Copeland, Jr.
Everett L. Copeland
James H. Copeland
Jiles P. Copeland
Melvin C. Copeland
William B. Copeland
Walter W. Copenhaver
Arnold Leroy Copitzky
Kearney E. Copley
William E. Copley
Grady Coplin
Robert C. Coppage
Francis X. Coppens
Thomas E. Coppinger
Earl L. Copple
Robert T. Copple
Vincent A. Coppola
Jewel Dwain Coquat
Thomas J. Coraci
Junior K. Coram
Earnest J. Corbett
Hiliary E. Corbett
John Edward Corbett
John Miles Corbett
Kenneth L. Corbett
Robert Leroy Corbett
George A. Corbin
James W. Corbin
Mccrary Corbin
Frederick A. Corbine
Clarence Corby, Jr.
Donald R. Corby
John Corcoran
John Joseph Corcoran
William E. Corcoran
Charles P. Cordani
Thomas E. Cordell
Charles Corder, Jr.
Doyle Edward Corder
Lewis K. Sr Corder
De La Rosa A. Cordero
Ernesto J. Cordero
S. Cordero-Barreto
Zenon Cordero-Cajigas
Felipe Cordero-Cantino
Gilbert Marsh Cordes
Victor Cordes
Philip H. Cordier

Charles O. Cordle
Carmelo Cordone
Joseph J. Cordone
Andrew Cordova
James Henry Cordova
Joe D. Cordova
Juan Benito Cordova
Richard E. Corey
Ernest James Corin
Thomas R. Cork
Roberto Corkill
Raymond F. Corl
Don Leroy Corley
Freddie C. Corley
Johnny M. Corley
Ralph B. Corley
Howard Thomson Corliss
Martin N. Corman, Jr.
La Moine V. Cormican
Ferman Cormier
Martin V. Corn
John J. Cornacchia
Louis E. Cornelia
Lloyd E. Cornelious
Arnold Cornelius
Jack William Cornelius
Patrick E. Cornelius
Edward S. Cornell, Jr.
Frederick R. Cornell
Homer John Cornell
James H. Cornell
Paul D. Cornell
Roy G. Cornell
Stanford O. Corner
Crowden Cornett
Troy Cornett
Jesse B. Cornette
Samuel Corney
Robert L. Cornibe
Henry Cornies, Jr.
Conrad Lee Cornman
Wilmer Cornn
Donald F. Cornwall
Jaime Corona
Victor Galvan Corona
Vincent Corona
David Corrales
Dan Corralez
Benjamin M. Correa
Jesus D. Correa
John Trappe Correa
Daniel Correia
Joe L. Correia
Bobby Doster Correll
Daniel A. Correll
Chester Lloyd Corrello
Francis D. Corrette
Frank Corrigan
Herbert Leo Corrigan, Jr.
Donald F. Corriveau
Lorne W. Corrow
Joshua Corruth
Robert W. Corsetti
Richard Attilio Corsiglia
Guido James Corsini
Bruce Haines Corson
Harold G. Corson
Concepcion J. Cortes
Juan F. Cortes
Rodriguez F. Cortes
J. Cortes-Boijoli
Angel L. Cortes-Ostolaza
Rivera Rufino Cortez
Rudolph Cortez
Raymond W. Cortwright, Jr.
William H. Cortwright
Felipe Corujo
Mac Rockwell Corwin
Matthew R. Cory
Robert R. Cory
Folton Cosby
Richard Cosh
John H. Coskey
R. Cosme-Almeztica
Francisco Cosme-Baez
Frank J. Cosnahan
Delbert L. Cosner
Donald C. Coss
Charles W. Cossaboon
L. T. Cossey
Ted W. Cossin
Anthony E. Costa
George Costa
John Costa, Jr.
John L. Costa
Pasquelino J. Costantino
Charles A. Costello
Charles W. Costello
Henry G. Costello

James C. Costello, Jr.
James E. Costello
John T. Costello
Joseph P. Costello
Raymond V. Costello
William J. Costello
Elmer K. Costigan
Rupert J. Costlow
Homer R. Costner
Marvin Costner
John Coston, Jr.
Metro Coston
Roland E. Coston
Joseph J. Costroff
Clarence S. Cota, Jr.
Eugene Cota
Francis H. Cote
Maurice Philip Cote
Roger B. Cote
Wayne K. Cothren
Comer D. Cotney
Anthony Joseph Cotroneo
Lawrence Edward Cotten
Albert H. Cotter
Gerard F. Cotter
Cyrenus E. Cottier
Darrell Ralph Cottier
Donald Franklin Cottle
Luyanda Calixto Cotto
Sierra Francis Cotto
A. Cotto-Hernandez
William Eugene Cottom
Clifton Clyde Cotton
Elijah Cotton
Melvin L. Cotton
Donald Cottrell
Raymond A. Cottrell
Arthur R. Cottrill
Robert E. Cottrill
Clifton Z. Couch, Jr.
James B. Crane Couch
Samuel H. Couch
Walter R. Couch
Robert A. Couey
Ralph L. Coufal
Frank J. Coughlin
Paul R. Couillard
Delbert Coulam
Joseph M. Coulombe
Calvin Coulon, Jr.
Douglas B. Coulter
John Robert Coulter
Julius C. Coulter
Leon Stanley Coulter
Phillip W. Coulter
Richard C. Coulter
John A. Coulton
Darrel D. Council
William E. Council
William W. Council
Michael T. Counihan
Billy E. Counts
Charles M. Counts
Ernest Counts
George W. Counts
Woodrow W. Counts
John H. Courchaine
Samuel S. Coursen
Thomas H. Court
Francis J. Courtney
Similian Courville
Calvin C. Cousins
Charles M. Cousins
Reginald J. Coutant
Willard Albert Coutant
Rogerio Lewis Couto
George Coutts, Jr.
Joseph A. W. Couture
Jose R. Couvertier
James J. Couvillier
Bobby G. Cover
William R. Coverstone
Edward Covington
Elvin Ray Covlin
Don A. Cowan
John E. Cowan
Moses Cowan, Jr.
Vestal R. Cowan
William D. Cowan
William Norton Cowan
William W. Cowan
Carey S. Cowart, Jr.
Charles C. Cowart
Garey Shaw Cowart, Jr.
Linton J. Cowart
Bruce P. Cowden
Loyd Cowden, Jr.
Richard Merlin Cowden
Ray P. Cowdin

Clare E. Cowee
Reginald L. Cowen
Donald C. Cowger
John Harold Cowger
Ray Walter Cowles
Roy A. Cowles
Al Bert Cox
Arthur W. Cox
Billie W. Cox
Boyd E. Cox
Calvin M. Cox
Charles W. Cox
Clarence V. Cox, Jr.
Clayborn L. Cox
Donald G. Cox
Donald W. Cox
Durwin Jessie Cox
Edward Cox
Ernest W. Cox
Eugene M. Cox
Everle Cox
Floyd Sampson Cox
George Manson Cox, Jr.
Glenn Leroy Cox
Harold E. Cox
James A. Cox
James Coolley Cox
James G. Cox
Jansen Calvin Cox
Joseph D. Cox
Joseph E. Cox
Kenneth Ray Cox
Larry T. Cox
Lester A. Cox
Mack Cox, Jr.
Malcolm R. Cox, Jr.
Marshall L. Cox
Mortimer W. Cox, Jr.
Norman D. Cox
O. Dean T. Cox
Paul D. Cox
Richard G. Cox
Robert C. Cox
Robert F. Cox
Robert L. Cox
Thomas F. Cox
Ulysses M. Cox, Jr.
Walter J. Cox
Wesley G. Cox
William A. Cox
William C. Cox
William Otow Cox
Adrian G. Coyle
Roger T. Coyle
Garrett Coyne
Ronald B. Coyne
Allen B. Coyner
Donald Edward Cozad
Kenneth L. Cozad
Albert Cozart, Jr.
Robert James Cozzalio
Dean E. Crabb
Billie R. Crabtree
David E. Crabtree
Ivan E. Crabtree
Morgan L. Crabtree
Paul C. Crabtree
Porter F. Crabtree
Clifford P. Craddock
Lonnie E. Craddock
William G. Craddock
Wilson Craddock, Jr.
Chester J. Craft
Donald D. Craft
Donald F. Craft
Henry Craft, Jr.
Howard D. Craft
Noah Webster Craft
Raymond Craft
William E. Crago
Armand Craig, Jr.
Carl E. Craig
Gordon M. Craig
Harry E. Craig
James Samuel Craig
Jerry P. Craig
John E. Craig
John F. Craig
John J. Craig
John R. Craig
Joseph L. Craig, Jr.
Leo P. Craig
Luther O. Craig
Paul E. Craig
Robert C. Craig
Robert P. Craig
William Evert Craig
Willie Craig
Rufus P. Craighead

Billy Crail
David R. Crain
Oliver Beecher Crain, Jr.
Billy W. Craine
Earl H. Cram
Glen Roy Cramer
Harry F. Cramer
Richard E. Cramer
Winford R. Cramer
Don E. Crammer
Russell L. Crampton
Chester H. Cramton, Jr.
Franklin Lavon Crandall
Jack A. Crandell
Alvin Earl Crane, Jr.
James B. Crane
Lebanon Crane
Robert L. Crane
Robert M. Crane
John W. Cranfield
Matthew Crankovich
Lyman Thomas Crannell
George E. Cranor
William B. Crary
Francis Crater, Jr.
Joseph E. Crater
Willie Crater
Richard Cratic
Chester Craven
Clifford H. Craw
John H. Crawbuck
Linden G. Crawfoot
Bobby G. Crawford
Charles A. Crawford
Charles E. Crawford
Charles F. Crawford
Claude I. Crawford
Cline S. Crawford
David A. Crawford, Jr.
Dewitt Crawford
Edward G. Crawford
Ellis Crawford, Jr.
Elmer E. Crawford
Garland D. Crawford
George C. Crawford
Grady Jack Crawford
Harold E. Crawford
Hoover Crawford
James A. Crawford
James T. Crawford
Jesse M. Crawford
John E. Crawford
Joseph Crawford
Kenneth E. Crawford
Lawrence Crawford
Marion J. Crawford
Mckinley Crawford
Noble L. Crawford
Noland F. Crawford
Norman E. Crawford
Paul D. Crawford
Ralph W. Crawford
Raymond A. Crawford
Robert L. Crawford
Roy W. Crawford
Samuel L. Crawford
Stanley C. Crawford
Thomas Crawford
Thomas A. Crawford
Vernon J. Crawford
William F. Crawford
William L. Crawford
Benjamin R. Crawley
Francis E. Crawley
Jimmie M. Crawley
Edward M. Crays
James H. Crayton
Thomas Crayton
Thomas V. Craze
Patrick H. Creagan
Thomas A. Creamer, Jr.
Wallace Creamer
William H. Creamer
Hollis M. Creasy
James A. Creazzo
Ronald Ross Cree
Clayton F. Creech
Dewey W. Creech, Jr.
James B. Creech
Leonard O. Creech
Robert R. Creech
William T. Creel
Dale F. Creger
William D. Cregger
Frank Edward Crego
Lloyd R. Creller
Dean W. Cremeens
Jeff Crenshaw
Roy N. Crenshaw

Frank J. Creshine
Allen Ray Cressey
Barry Hall Cressman
Eugene R. Creuziger
Myron G. Crevelling
Alphonso Crew
Bryant Crews
Charles J. Crews
Elwood Stone Crews, Jr.
Irvin T. Crews
James Crews
Mancie L. Crews
Herbert Ernest Cribb
James J. Cribben
George A. Cribbie
James R. Crider
Arnold L. Cridland
Charles R. Criger
Arthur E. Crim
Asa J. Crimin, Jr.
Raymond J. Crimmins
Peter P. Crisona
Charles S. Crisp
George S. Crisp
Charles E. Criss
Theodore D. Criss
Everett Lloyd Crist
William W. Crist
Reed A. Criswell
Paul P. Crittenden
Matthew Crnkovich
Charles W. Crocker, Jr.
Frank William Crocker, Jr.
George A. Crocker
Jerone C. Crocker
Robert Otis Crocker
Charles R. Crockett
John O. Crockett
Johnny Sr Crockett
Owen Everett Crockett, Jr.
Albert L. Croft, Jr.
George Croft, Jr.
James A. Croft
Johnny Croft, Jr.
Charles B. Crofts
Varnold Gene Croghan
William V. Croke
John R. Croley, Jr.
Fred W. Cromer
Clarence Cromier
Eugene Cron
Richard E. Cronan, Jr.
George Leo Cronauer
Frank H. Cronce
William Delbert Crone
Maynard A. Cronin
Richard F. Cronin
Clifford J. Cronk
Avon H. Crook, Jr.
Harold R. Crook
John B. Crook
Joseph Walter Crook, Jr.
Richard R. Crook
Stanley W. Crook
William C. Crookham
Floyd D. Crooks
Archie T. Croom, Jr.
Donald W. Cropper
Frank M. Cropper
Robert D. Cropper
Charles M. Cropsey
Cecil Crosby
Harry H. Crosby
James Z. Crosby
Lloyd B. Crosby
Louis Nelson Crosby
Lynnward T. Crosby
Stanley W. Crosby, Jr.
Howard Lamont Croshaw
Richard G. Croskrey
Powell IV Crosley
Robert Marion Crosley
August B. Cross, Jr.
Frederick D. Cross
George R. Duane Cross
Harold R. Cross
Howard M. Cross
James H. Cross
John Coles Cross
Ralph Cross
Raymond Lee Cross
Robert H. Cross
Roy Edward Cross
Thomas E. Cross
Will Tom Cross
Jimmie C. Crossland
Franklin W. Crossman
James Theador Crossman
Jack R. Crosta

Robert E. Croteau
Richard E. Crotty
Jack Dean Crouch
Milton Vernon Crouch
Donald E. Crouse
James Clarence Crouse
John B. Crouse
Paul Crouse
William F. Crouse, Jr.
Dale Duane Crow
David F. Crow
Harold Morris Crow
William H. Crow
Wilton P. Crow, Jr.
Donald Gene Crowder
Lorenzo D. Crowder
Paul E. Crowder
Marshall Crowe, Jr.
Richard E. Crowe
Sanford D. Crowe
William Clark Crowe, Jr.
William H. Crowe
Allen B. Crowell
Dean G. Crowell
Donald E. Crowell
Leroy Crowell
Willard W. Crowell, Jr.
William N. Crowell
James E. Crowl
Charles Stewart Crowley
Frank T. Crowley
John Joseph Crowley, Jr.
Neil J. Crowley
Willie B. Crowley
Raymond F. Crown
Ewell D. Crozier
James W. Cruce
Marvin V. Cruce
G. Cruhigger-Rodriguez
Charles Parker Cruikshank
James O. Cruise
Charles M. Crum
Charles R. Crum
Rush F. Crum
Y. J. Crum
Clinton D. Crumley
Marion N. Crump
Floyd T. Crumpton
Chester A. Cruse
Herbert H. Cruse
James V. Cruse
Roy K. Cruse
Robert Joseph Cruser
Charles H. Crutcher
Graves B. Crutchfield
James Frank Crutchfield
James Henry Crutchfield
Roy S. Crutchman
Sherman P. Cruts, Jr.
Alicea Juan Cruz
Amadeo A. Cruz
Earnest P. Cruz
Esequiel E. Cruz
Freddy Cruz
Leonal M. Cruz
Martin Cruz, Jr.
Ramon Cruz
Richard Sanchez Cruz
Rosas Pablo Cruz
Ruben Ceireco Cruz
Santos Cruz
Santos Tomas E. Cruz
Velez Ismael Cruz
Ernesto Cruz-Alicea
Jesus Cruz-Beltran
Jose A. Cruz-Carrero
Roberto Cruz-Espinoza
Rafael Cruz-Marrero
Juan A. Cruz-Martinez
Pedro A. Cruz-Otero
Nicolas Cruz-Perez
Jesus Cruz-Ramos
Angel L. Cruz-Sanchez
William R. Cruzan, Jr.
William Rudolph Csapo
N. Cuadrado-Rivera
David E. Cubby
Donald James Cubranich
Ernest P. Cuddeford
David L. Cudger, Jr.
Johnny H. Cuellar
Jose Alejandro Cueto
Alfredo Cuevaf
Edward F. Cuevas
Gene Alan Culbertson
John J. Culbertson, Jr.
Cecil W. Culdice
John A. Culhane
William D. Culhane

Donald F. Cullen
Donald P. Cullen
George T. Cullen, Jr.
James Victor Cullen
John J. Cullen
Paul Francis Cullen
Robert Edward Cullen
Eugene Culler, Jr.
Robert G. Cullers
Joseph C. Culligan, Jr.
William Francis Cullinane
Roland W. Cullins
Ralleigh D. Cullison
Thomas W. Culliton
Freddie L. Culmer
Arnold D. Culp
Clayton J. Culp
James R. Culp
Bobby R. T. Culpepper
Lonnie Culpepper, Jr.
Roy K. Culpepper
Turner F. Culpepper, Jr.
Charles L. Culver
Clifton M. Culver
John P. Cumbelich
Jack B. Cumbie
Lawrence C. Cumbo
Barnard Cummings, Jr.
Charlie W. Cummings
Chester Ellis Cummings
Edward Patrick Cummings
Francis J. Cummings
Herbert C. Cummings
Jacob C. Cummings
James L. Cummings
James T. Cummings
John P. Cummings
Kennie Cummings
Paul D. Cummings
Robert L. Cummings
Robert R. Cummings
Roger D. Cummings
Ronald C. Cummings
Thompson Cummings
Carl E. Cummins
Elza M. Cummins
Richard F. Cummins
Robert L. Cummins
Zolton Cummins
Donald John Cunha
Elidio A. Cunha
Donald Joseph Cunniffe
Alfred Hugh Cunningham
Augustus V. Cunningham
Carse J. Cunningham
Charles B. Cunningham
Conzaad E. Cunningham
Daniel D. Cunningham
Daniel E. Cunningham
Eddie G. Cunningham
Ernest J. Cunningham
Eugene M. Cunningham
Frank Cunningham, Jr.
Jack J. Cunningham
James L. Cunningham
James O. Cunningham, Jr.
Jimmie D. Cunningham
John F. Cunningham
Kenneth Cunningham
Kenneth E. Cunningham
Luther Cunningham
Odell Cunningham
Raymond L. Cunningham
Richard D. Cunningham
Robert A. Cunningham
William R. Cunningham
William S. Cunningham
William T. Cunningham
Paul A. Cuozzo
William H. Cupples
Thomas W. Cuprak
John Cupryna
Dominik Cupryniak
James C. Curcio, Jr.
Carl S. Curl
Daniel Vincent Curley
George A. Curley, Jr.
James Harold Curneal
Donald J. Curran
Patrick J. Curran
Richard P. Curran
Robert G. Curran
William H. Curran
William K. Curran, Jr.
Calvin Kenneth Currens
John W. Currie, Jr.
Norman R. Currie
Owen J. Currie, Jr.
Willie L. Currin

Charles Marvin Curry
Derril G. Curry
Edward R. Curry
Ernest L. D. Curry
Glenn David Curry
Henry L. Curry
Maurice L. Curry
Paul F. Curry
William Frierson Curry
Edward L. Curtin
Frank W. Curtin
Albert Noal Curtis
Dana A. Curtis
Harold L. Curtis
Jack Curtis
John C. Curtis
Lloyd L. Curtis
Lloyd N. Curtis
Lloyd W. Curtis
Ralph E. Curtis
Robert L. Curtis
Virgil M. Curtis
William R. Curtis
Woodrow W. Curtis
Stanley Debolt Curyea
Jess M. Cushing
Ronald D. Cushing
Donald Aidan Cushman
Richard G. Cushman
William J. Cusick
Jerome E. Cusimano
Donald Mccrary Custard
Robert Murray Custer
Vernon Cecil Custer
William King Custer, Jr.
Peter J. Cusumano
Donald J. Cutler
Myron L. Cutler
Robert G. Cutler
Harold Cutlip
Ray A. Cutsforth
Hughie Cutshall
Fred Cutter
Charles W. Cutts
Thomas A. Cuva
Edward C. Cwikla
Raymond J. Cyborski
Joseph E. Cybulski
Gerard Peter Cyr
Joseph E. Cyr
Michael J. Czarniewsky
Leo P. Czubak

— D —

Robert P. D'Alessandro
Anthony V. D'orazio, Jr.
Fonseca Rui M. Da
Daniel J. Dabkiewicz
Willie L. Dabney
Bernard Z. Dabrowski
Chester L. Dabrowski
Laurence J. Dacasto
William Dacek
Wade Lee Dade
Frederick H. Daehnke
Byron B. Daer
Rui Matos Dafonseca
Joseph Dagastine
De Loren D. Dage
Norman Stewart Dagenais
Manville E. Dagenhart
Calvin A. Daggett
Harlan R. Daggett
Harold J. Dagnon
Thomas J. Dagon
Howard Winston Dahart
Arlen C. Dahl
Dennis Dahl
Gayle Howard Dahl
Raymond F. Dahlgren
Goodrich I. Dahlin
Roy E. Dahlka
Donald E. Dahms
Elmer C. Dahn
Earl W. Dahnke, Jr.
Joseph R. Daigle
Lifford J. Daigle
Richard C. Daigle
Roy W. Daigle
Wilbert P. Daigle
Robert G. Daignault
Phillippe Daigneault
John D. Dail
Francis J. Dailey, Jr.
Fred J. Dailey
Maurice Leroy Dailey
Murlie Dailey
Ralph Dailey, Jr.

Richard L. Dailey
James F. Dairda
Raymond G. Dake
Russell E. Dake
Robert C. Dakin
Collo Angelo Dal
Delford M. Dalberg
Allen R. Dale
Buford Larkin Dale
Curtis L. Dale
Douglas Dale
Edward B. Dale
Harold E. Dale
James V. Dale
John N. Dale
Oliver Dale
Robert L. Dalen
Daniel E. Daley
James M. Daley
Richard A. Daley
Daniel John Dalier
Jack E. Dallas
Wilfred S. Dallas
Carmen J. Dallesandro
Benito Dalleva
Arthur Dallison
Kenneth Horton Dally
Joseph Louis Dalmon
Robert A. G. Daloisio
John R. Dalola, Jr.
Joseph A. Dalszys
Edmund F. Dalton
Emanuel L. Dalton
Howard D. Dalton
Lloyd Dalton
Thomas W. Dalton
Charles S. Daly
Gene D. Daly
Jerome M. Daly
Joseph F. Daly, Jr.
Wallace James Daly
Bernard A. Damato
James H. Dame
Anthony Damelia
Charles W. Dameron
Louis Ashby Damewood
Charles Damiano
George A. Damico
George G. Damico
John C. Damico
Louis T. Damitz
James Kelly Damon
Robert Vincent Damon
Robert S. Dampier
Aaron W. Damron
William S. Damron
Donald W. Dana
Louis Joseph Dana
James Oscar Dance, Jr.
John Dancik
Charles Dandrea
Pasquale C. Dandrea
Richard L. Danel
Asher Daniel
James E. Daniel
Melvin B. Daniel
Ray Thomas Daniel
Richard A. Daniel
Robert A. Daniell
Bobbie R. Daniels
Buster L. Daniels
Charles C. Daniels
Claude H. Daniels, Jr.
Conrad R. Daniels
Curtis Lee Daniels
Donald Ray Daniels
George T. Daniels
Grady Gail Daniels
Gus J. Daniels, Jr.
Hansel Daniels
Isom J. Daniels
James R. Daniels
John Daniels, Jr.
Joseph P. Daniels
Judge Daniels
Norman Daniels
Paul E. Daniels
Paul L. Daniels
Paul M. Daniels, Jr.
Theotis Daniels
Thomas W. Daniels
William J. Daniels
Willis L. Daniels
Carl J. Danielson
Otis Daniely
Ralph E. Danilson
Stanley R. Dankowski
Kenneth L. Danks
Daniel D. Dann

Edward L. Dann
Luther B. Dannel
Ervin Dannemiller
Oscar F. Danner, Jr.
Roscoe E. Danner
Philip F. Dannolfo
Anthony Dannucci
John Dannunzio
Alex Danowski
Earl L. Dansberry
Richard Dansberry
William E. Danta, Jr.
Arthur Lee Danzer
William P. Darah
Peter Manuel Darakis
Harry P. Darby
Wilbur Smith Darby
William E. Darby
Edward Dale Darchuck
James P. Darcy
Ray John Darcy
Thomas P. Darcy
Alvin Dardar
Glen Darden
Kenneth P. Darden
Roy Darden, Jr.
Robert E. Dare
William L. Dark
Arthur M. Darling
Norman O. Darling
Laurence L. Darmstadt
Kenneth Darnall
John Henry Darnell, Jr.
W. D. Darnell
Charles W. Darr
Hubert Edward Darr
Roy E. Darrell
Garland E. Darter
Lesley W. Darting
Allen D. Dashiell
Robert Dashkovitz
Little N. Dates
Norman E. Daub
Clair C. Dauberman
Wayne R. Daubert
Duncan N. Daugherty
Henry F. Daugherty
J. C. Daugherty, Jr.
James F. Daugherty
Lloyd W. Daugherty
William Burton Daugherty
Allen J. Daughtery
Charles E. Daughtry
Roosevelt M. Daughtry
Walter H. Daughtry
William G. Daulton
Jack R. Dauphin
Elton Dauphiney
Daniel Davalos
Melvin R. Dave
Bethel Davenport
Billy R. Davenport
Curtis J. Davenport
Curtis Davenport, Jr.
Glynn Edward Davenport
Hayden H. Davenport
Henry Davenport
Howard M. Davenport, Jr.
Jack A. Davenport
Kenneth E. Davenport
Marvin J. Davenport
Warren Davenport, Jr.
Wellington Davenport
William E. Davenport
Vanderbilt Daves
Edward S. Davey, Jr.
Gerald James Davey
William S. Davey
Clophas J. David
Edward David
Mike S. David
Richard L. David
Robert L. David
E. David-Pedrogo
Joseph Davidoski
John Davidovic
Chester Davidowski
Archibald Davidson
Donald E. Davidson
Douglas Edward Davidson
Edward E. Davidson
Frank T. Davidson
Gerald E. Davidson
Harold J. Davidson
James G. Davidson
Leslie H. Davidson
Richard C. Davidson
Robert J. Davidson
Thomas L. Davidson

Ralph H. Davidter
Clair L. Davie
Herbert E. Davie
Esau E. Davies, Jr.
Everett E. Davies
Howard Joseph Davies
Howard M. Davies
Lewis J. Davies
Ned E. Davies
Robert L. Davies
Angel R. Davila
Carlos M. Davila-Rivera
Ralph H. Davioter
Alfred D. Davis
Alfred L. Davis
Arnold G. Sr Davis
Austin Davis
Banard R. Davis
Bellinger Davis, Jr.
Bernard N. Davis
Billie Dean Davis
Billie Howard Davis
Billy G. Davis
Bobby Davis
Byron S. Davis
Charles E. Davis
Charles Eugene Davis
Charles F. Davis
Charles Jonies Davis
Clark M. Davis
Claude L. Davis
Courteney C. Davis, Jr.
Curtis Davis
Dan Ruben Davis
Daniel Hill Davis
Dariel Lane Davis
David L. Davis
Donald Dean Davis
Donald H. Davis
Donald L. Davis
Donald Leon Davis
Earl Arthur Davis
Earl G. Davis
Eddie Davis, Jr.
Edgar E. Davis, Jr.
Edward Davis
Edward H. Davis
Edward J. Davis
Elton Raymond Davis
Ezekiel A. Davis
Finley James Davis
Frank Allen Davis
Frankie L. Davis
Frederick F. Davis
George A. Davis, Jr.
George Andrew Davis, Jr.
George H. Davis, Jr.
George J. Davis
George Parker Davis
Gerald O. Davis, Jr.
Gordon E. Davis
Harold James Davis
Harold W. Davis
Harris N. Davis
Harry P. Davis, Jr.
Harvey Davis, Jr.
Hayward Davis
Henry Lee Davis
Henry W. Davis
Herbert H. Davis, Jr.
Herbert L. Davis
Herschel D. Davis
Howard Davis
Isaac S. Davis
Isaiah Davis
J. D. Davis, Jr.
Jack A. Davis
Jack E. Davis
Jack R. Davis
Jack Sherman Davis
James B. Davis
James Carroll Davis
James E. Davis, Jr.
James Franklin Davis
James J. Davis
James Leo Davis, Jr.
James R. Davis
Jefferson Frank Davis
Jerry Davis
Jimmie L. Davis
John Davis
John Gerald Davis
John J. Davis
John Lyman Davis
John Robert Davis
Joseph L. Davis
Kenneth R. Davis
Leo Clifford Davis
Leroy Davis

Leslie Davis
Louis H. Davis
M. L. Davis
Madison L. Davis
Marvin L. Davis
Max O. Davis
Mervin H. Davis
Morton C. Davis
Murrit Herman Davis
Nicholas Davis
Norman Glen Davis
Norman Ray Davis
Nubern Delbert Davis
Onley T. Davis, Jr.
Ralph Allen Davis
Ramon Roderick Davis
Raymond Slate Davis
Richard Davis
Richard Calvin Davis
Richard E. Davis
Richard F. Davis
Robert Davis
Robert A. Davis
Robert C. Davis
Robert Eugene Davis
Robert L. Davis
Robert M. Davis
Robert Thomas Davis
Roger Riblet Davis
Ronald W. Davis
Roscoe Maurice Davis
Ross Hamilton Davis
Roy Anderson Davis
Russell G. Davis
Sam H. Davis
Samuel Davis
Samuel L. Davis
Sanford J. B. Davis
Stanley J. Davis
Thomas L. Davis
Timothy Davis
Troy C. Davis
Walter E. Davis
Walter E. Davis
Walter V. Davis
Weldon Alonzo Davis
William Davis
William D. Davis, Jr.
William E. Davis
William E. Davis
William E. Davis
William E. Davis, Jr.
William T. Davis
William T. Davis, Jr.
Willie Davis
Willie D. Davis
Willie M. Davis
Leslie E. Davison
Reuben J. Davison
Robert Dwight Davison
Thomas R. Davison
Jimmy Lee Davisworth
Willie D. Daw
John Lawrence Dawber
Melnie H. Dawes
Francis M. Dawkins
Willie L. Dawkins
Bobbie Dawson
James G. Dawson
Jurel O. Dawson
Laverne Dawson
Norman F. Dawson
Perry Agustus Dawson
Richard Dale Dawson
Thomas E. Dawson
W. N. Dawson, Jr.
Wallace James Dawson
Winfred N. Dawson, Jr.
Billie W. Day
Charles M. Day
Charles N. Day
Claron O. Day
Dave H. Day, Jr.
Donald Day
Earlie Day
Gerald F. Day
Gerald Joseph Day
Glen R. Day
Harold D. Day
Horace William Day
James A. Day
James E. Day
John W. Day
Lamon M. Day
Maynard N. Day
Morris N. Day
Nathan O. Day
Robert H. Day, Jr.
Robert J. Day

Robert W. Day
Warren C. Day
Wayne H. Day
William A. Day
William F. Day
Robert M. Dayton
Charles Elmer Dazey
Rodriguez De Alba
Daniel De Anda
Gennaro S. De Angelis
Guy Joseph De Angelis
Homer G. De Angelis
Charles R.De Armon, Jr.
Arturo De Avia
Michael De Benedictus
Arend De Boer
Billy A. De Bord
Jimmie De Bord
William L. De Bruyn
Wilbur H. De Busk
Raymond D. De Buske
James M. De Camp
Francis R. De Capot
Attilliom De Carli
Leo N. De Cicco
Elbert C. De Cook
Floyd De Correvont
Richard Anthony De Costa
Salvatore De Costa
Thomas W. De Coste
Gerald J. De Flora
Benjamin C. De Forest
John R. De Forest
George Louis De Forge
James E. De Frain
Charles M. De France
John Andre De Franchesi
Samuel W. De Freese
Richard J. De Freitas
Robert L. De Frier
James De George
David Elmer De Golyer
Charles W. De Graff
Gilbert L. De Grant
Frank De Gregorio
Roland E. De Groat
Jerome S. De Groot
John De Groot, Jr.
Kenneth L. De Groot
Joseph N. De Haan
Robert F. De Haan
Billy D. De Hart
Melvin Leroy De Hart
Oliver Powell De Hart, Jr.
Willie D. De Herrera
Adorno T. De Jesus
Feliciano De Jesus
Figueroa R. De Jesus
Medina R. De Jesus
Nieves E. A. De Jesus
William De John
Cruz Lorenzo De La
Fuente Trini De La
Pena Tommy De La
Rocha Daniel De La
Rosa Antonio De La
John Glendale De Lancy
Ernest Aldrete De Leon
Lloyd M. De Leon
Phillips D. De Leon
Petro J. De Leonardo
Clayton C. De Long
Denton Kieth De Long
Guy W. De Long, Jr.
Harold T. De Long
Norman John De Long
Zane Ellis De Long
Santos Modesto P. De Los
Ellie E. De Lozier
Joseph J. De Luca, Jr.
Leslie J. De Luca
Leonard Owen De Luna
Joseph De Mase
Anthony Frank De Meo
Raymond Earl De Mers
Wilfred K. De Meule
James J. De Mieri
Casimire S. De Moll
Antonio V. De Nigris
Roy J. De Nike, Jr.
Harry R. De Nofio
Ernest De Ochoa
Fred P. De Palma
Frank De Pasquale
Robert P. De Petro
Joseph De Pietro
Angelo De Politi, Jr.
Carmine F. De Prisco, Jr.
Howard L. De Pue

Eugene C. De Rose
Adam J. De Rouen
James D. De Roule
Robert F. De Rousse
Joseph Anthony De Santi
Mario Anthony De Santis
Lawrence K. De Sau
Eugene A. De Sautel
Anthony John De Scisciolo
Nicholas De Simone, Jr.
Gerald J. De Sousa
Alfred De Vanno
William C. De Vaul
Milton H. De Vault
John Nicholas De Virgilio
Michael L. De Vita
Anthony R. De Vito
Patrick A. De Vivo, Jr.
Richard K. De Voe
Billy R. De Voll
Paul Nolan De Vries
Wesley E. De Vries
Charles E. De Wees
Donald L. De Wees
Donald B. De Witt
Jack L. De Witt
John Franklin De Witt
Robert C. De Witt
Robert E. De Witt
Stanley L. De Witt
Grover C. De Wolfe
Gene M. De Young
Reginald B. De Young
Juan De-Hoyos-lopez
George A. Deacon
Rolland G. Deacon
Frank L. Deaderick
Clarence W. Deal
Clyde C. Deal
Frazier Deal
Fredrico F. Dealba
Glen R. Deale
Alvin Clinton Dean
Bobby Lee Dean
Boyden M. Dean
Charles Albert Dean
Ercel Wayne Dean
George Dean
Glenn R. Dean
John R. Dean
Lewis D. Dean
Marion V. Dean
Martin R. Dean, Jr.
Paul Delmar Dean
Robert Dean
Robert E. Dean
Tulon V. Dean
William Harold Dean
Marcelo C. Deanda
Alexander Deans
Arthur B. Dearing
James D. Dearman
Clarence E. Dearth
Reginald M. Deas
George B. Dease
Charles Leo Deason
George Deason, Jr.
Willie Ray Deason
Robert M. Deavor
George Debaun, Jr.
Willis R. Deberry
Charles A. Deblasi
Henry C. Deboer
David J. Debolt
Walter Dec
Richard J. Decandio
John Decerno
Anaclethe P. Decesare
Paul Deceukeleire
Alfred H. Dechant
Paul W. Deckard
Clayton E. Decker
Clellan H. Decker
Delmas G. Decker
Ernest Floyd Decker
Forest D. Decker
Frank E. Decker, Jr.
Hobart Decker
Lee D. Decker
Lloyd M. Decker
Raymond Alfred Decker
Robert W. Decker
Ronald R. Decker, Jr.
William T. Decker
William P. Decoto
Daniel D. Decrease
Eugene Dedman
Harold D. Dedmon
John Dedon

Robert C. Deel
Robert F. Deem
George R. Deemer
Wm. P. Deer-With-Horns
Ernest E. Deering
Robert Franklin Dees
Roy A. Dees
Alex Deese
Edward W. Deeter, Jr.
Robert Andrew Deeter, Jr.
David N. Defibaugh
Carl E. Deford
Lloyd D. Degler
Thomas E. Dehm
Robert Leonard Dehn
William W. Dehner, Jr.
Thomas L. Deignan, Jr.
Ellis L. Deihl
George J. Deinhardt
Andrew F. Deisenroth
Henry Deiss, Jr.
Gene A. Del Percio
Joseph A. Del Pizzo
Angelo J. Del Pozzo
Frederick D. Del Priore
Raymond Del Toro
Cancel F. Del Valle
D. Joseph Del Vecchio
Romeo J. Del Villano
Rosa A. Dela, Jr.
Toba Loreto Dela
Lorenzo Delacruz
Arthur Donald Delacy
Charles Kenneth Delafield
Charles L. Delafield
Trinadad Delafuenye
Rufus Delancy
Edward E. Deland, Jr.
Francisco T. Delaney
James D. Delaney
James G. Delaney
Francis N. Delano
Lawrence H. Delany
Loreto Delatoba
Roy Charles Delauter
Cyril E. Delay
Lionel J. Delcambre, Jr.
Calixte J. Delesha
Acosta Rene Delgado
Alfred Delgado
Gilbert J. Delgado
Nicholas Delgado
Nieves Pedro Delgado
Pablo E. Delgado
Pacheco L. Delgado
Pedro A. Delgado
Raymundo Delgado
Rivera C. Delgado
Rudolfo Delgado, Jr.
Miguel A. Delgado-Colon
Francisco Delgado-Diaz
Ramon Delgado-Gonzalez
Sabin Delgado-Resto
M. Delgado-Rodriguez
Wenceslao Delgado-Ubiles
Gilbert M. Deliz
David Pryor Dell
Olio Nicholas S. Dell
Patsy M. Dellacio
Joseph W. Deller
Richard P. Delligatti
Dana A. Dellinger
Nicholas Dellolio
Thomas J. Delohery
Howard E. Delon
Charlie E. Deloney
Harry F. Delosh
Robert Lee Delp
Hubert A. Delph
Clifford A. Delphin
Theodore R. Delplain
Emil W. Delu
Alfred L. Demain
Ralph J. Demaio
Anthony P. Demanno
Herbert Elwood Demarest
Joseph Demase
Justin M. Demello
Stanley C. Demello
Billy E. Dement
Onzel Charles Dement
Joseph A. Marc Demers
Richard L. Demers
Steven Demeter, Jr.
Kenneth E. Demiere
Charles R. Demilte
Dale Allen Demmin
Rolland W. Demo
General Demonbreun

Paul L. Demorest
Edward Demoski
Frederick J. Dempcy
George Earl Dempsey
Robert Dempsey
Bernard A. Demski
John Henry Demundo
Willie L. Denard
Frederic C. Denbigh
Cecil M. Denby
Raymond Denchfield
Ernest D. Denham
Anthony M. Denicola
Pedro A. Deniza
J. B. Denkins
Jimmy R. Denmon
Willard Martin Denn
Ray Allen Dennard
Frederick W. Denne
James R. Dennehy, Jr.
Richard W. Denner
Clifford R. Denney
Norman W. Denney
Thomas D. Denney, Jr.
William E. Denney
Henry P. Denning
James V. Denning
Charles M. Dennis
Frank S. Dennis
Gene Alton Dennis
Harry C. Dennis
Henry W. Dennis
Jerry L. Dennis
Johnny C. Dennis
Marvin John Dennis
Stanley Ray Dennis
Vivan Dennis
William H. Dennis
Ralph E. Dennison
Russell L. Dennison
Paul Edward Denny
Roger L. Denny
Harry R. Denofio
Lynwood L. Denson
William C. Denson
William M. Denson
Albert Frank Dent
Daniel W. Dent
William A. Dent, Jr.
Leonard Denti
Louie B. Denton
Robert Denton
James Leslie Dentz
George Denyse
Clarence E. Deon
Ferdinand N. Depappa, Jr.
Roger E. Depatie
Leona J. Depermentier
David E. Depew
Stanley T. Depki
Salvatore Deponti
G. A. Depperschmidt
Oscar Lee Depriest
George Dequire
Philip V. Deragon
Robert Karl Derby
Benedik M. Derek
Carlo F. Derivi
Frank Dominick Dermilio
Edgar R. Dern, Jr.
Robert Dorman Dern
Rocco William Derose
Albert Paul Derosier
Max L. Derossett
Pearl G. Derossett
Robert E. Derr
Thee O. Derrick
Wesley G. Derrick
Anthony J. Derrico
Earnest E. Derringer
Elzeard John Des Champs
John Arthur Des Rosier
Richard G. Desautels
William James Desbro
Harold E. Descamp
Kenneth W. Descheneaux
Armand R. Deschenes
Roger Louis Desclos
Phillip E. Deshaw
George T. Deshields
Vernon L. Deshields
Grover W. Deshotel
Reginald B. Desiderio
Louis Joseph Desimone
Norman E. Desjarlais
Joseph A. R. Desloges
Richard L. Desmond
Gerald G. Desmul
Roy C. Despain

Jean A. Desroberts
Robert Gail Detamore
Donald J. Dettling
Alan A. Dettloff
Harry B. Dettmering
Charles H. Detweiler
Robert W. Deutsch
Robert Elwood Devans
Thomas H. Devault
Edward P. Deveau
Jack B. Deveny
Frank S. Devers, Jr.
Edward G. Devery
Leroy L. Devilbiss
Leon Fabian Devillier
Richard Edward Devilliers
Aaron W. Devine
Robert M. Devine
William Lester Devinney
James J. Devlin
John F. Devlin
George Dewey Devone
Stuart A. Dewalt, Jr.
John W. Dewerff
Richard David Dewert
Delbert Frank Dewey
James David Dewey
John F. Dewey
Lee Andrew Dewey
Rodger B. Dewey
Joseph Garrett Dews
Gilbert L. Dexter
John Luzerne Dexter
John D. Deyoe
Gene Ai Di Battista
Louis R. Di Camillo
Anthony J. Di Carlo
Louis A. Di Carlo
Louis A. Di Croce
Mark R. Di Domenico
John Di Donna
Fiore J. Di Giorgio
Louis J. Di Gregorio
Nicholas P. Di Leo
Raymond L. Di Maleo
Joseph S. Di Maria
Peter P. Di Martino
Michael F. Di Napoli
Joseph N. Di Nardo
Vincent Joseph Di Palermo
Ralph Di Palma
Frank E. Di Pasquale
Daniel Di Pasquo
Joseph F. Di Pietro
Joseph V. Di Pietro
Frank J. Di Pino
Agostino Di Rienzo
Edward Allen Di Ruscio
Angelo Eugene Di Stefano
Daniel J. Di Sylvester
Charles R. Di Ulio
Homer F. Dial
Hugh D. Dials
Alfred P. Dianda
Asbert L. Diaz
Blaz Diaz
Charbonier A. Diaz
Donald Diego Diaz
Lebron Alfonso Diaz
Manuel Diaz, Jr.
Nieves Clemente I. Diaz
Phillip R. Diaz
Ramos Fernando Diaz
Rodriguez F. Diaz
Victoriano Diaz
Vincent V. Diaz, Jr.
Luis Diaz-Acevedo
Demetrio Diaz-Algarin
Fernando L. Diaz-Colon
Rafael Diaz-Coto
Eduardo Diaz-Jimenez
Jose F. Diaz-Jimenez
Ricardo Diaz-Martinez
Emilio Diaz-Sanchez
Clarence M. Dibble, Jr.
Dale L. Dibble
Donald Edward Dibble
Ronald W. Dibble
Donald L. Dick
Hobert C. Dick
James Blanding Dick
Louis R. Dick
Myron Gracian Dick
William B. Dick
William L. Dick, Jr.
James A. Dickens
John N. Dickens, Jr.
Lynburg Dickens
Brister Dickerson

Calvin S. Dickerson
Clarence D. Dickerson
Dallas W. Dickerson
Donald R. Dickerson
Grover T. Dickerson
Martin L. Dickerson
Norman E. Dickerson
Paul Dickerson
Paul L. Dickerson
Robert H. Dickerson
Roger W. Dickerson
William H. Dickerson
Ephram L. Dickey
Thomas M. Dickey
Donald R. Dickinson
George H. Dickinson, Jr.
Matthew L. Dickinson
Percy E. Dickinson
Charles R. Dickison
Charles A. Dickman
Jack L. Dickman
Mark W. Dickman
Ronald J. Dicks
Ben H. Dickson
Donald A. Dickson
Franklin P. Dickson
Paul H. Dickson
Richard B. Dickson
Serafino S. Dicrispino
Miles H. Didd
Donald Joseph Didier
Robert J. Didier
Alexander Didur
Woodrow L. Diebold
John W. P. Diedeman
Harold Michael Diederich
Robert Diedrich
Robert J. Diegel
Harold F. Diekman
Lester H. Diekmann
Jerold W. Diemer
John William Diemer
William Frederick Diemler
James H. Dier
Thomas Gerald Dier
Norman Herman Dierks
Paul A. Dieterle
Gordon A. Dietrich
Kenneth W. Dietz
Patrick Michael Differ
James L. Diggs, Jr.
Frederick Digilio
Arvle Dill
Carl Dill
Dugald Allen Dill
Glenn I. Dill, Jr.
Michael William Dill, Jr.
Paul N. Dill
Donald W. Dillard
Floyd N. Dillard
George H. Dillard
Ray G. Dillard
Robert E. Dillard
John Adams Dille, Jr.
Gerald D. Diller
Clifford A. Dilley
Charles L. Dillion
Earl E. Dillion
Lahue B. Dillion
Carlton E. Dillon
Edward Vincent Dillon
Everett E. Dillon
Frank A. Dillon, Jr.
George A. Dillon
John F. Dillon
John J. Dillon
John L. Dillon
Tennis Dillon
Winfred Dillon
Wallace J. Dillwood
James A. Dilver
John T. Dilworth
Charles W. Dinan
Milton Dinerboiler, Jr.
Allen Charles Dinger
Glenn F. Dinger
Bernie Dingess
Harry Waldo Dingle
Wilbert I. Dingman
Giles C. Dingus
Waldo M. Dingus
Jack L. Dinkel
William J. Dinsdale, Jr.
John W. Dinsmore
Frank D. Dinwiddie
Henry J. Dionne
James K. Dionne
Tony Dirk
Dale D. Dirks

Leon D. Dirks
Abraham Dirksen, Jr.
Loyd Vernon Dirst
Peter A. Disabella
Domenico S. Disalvo
Edwin Richard Dischinger
Mario A. Disenso
Leonard J. Dishman
William J. Diskin
Charles E. Dismukes
Elwood Lewis Ditmer
John C. Ditner
Gene M. Dittbenner
Robert W. Dittbenner
Robert Dittler
George E. Dittmer
Horace J. Divens
Winfield Divine
Frank J. Divis, Jr.
Marvin Dix
Arthur Dixon
Charles R. Dixon
Clyde G. Dixon
Darl D. Dixon
Derryl Dean Dixon
Donald C. Dixon
Henry Trimble Dixon
James E. Dixon
James W. Dixon
Johnnie E. Dixon
Kenneth R. Dixon
Melvin L. Dixon
Osborne J. Dixon
Paul A. Dixon
Robert E. Dixon
Roger J. E. Dixon
Rooselvelt Dixon, Jr.
Wayne E. Dixon
William M. Dixon
William R. Dixon
Willie Floyd Dixon
Willie H. Dixon
Ralph William Doaty
Robert B. Dobbie
Albert D. Dobbins
Enoch A. Dobbins
Harry R. Dobbins
Raymond A. Dobbins
Robert J. Dobbins
Gilbert Mosher Dobbs
J. B. Dobbs
James A. Dobbs
Robert Lee Dobbs
Edmund F. Dobek
King D. Dobie
Richard D. Dobie
Teddy Arthur Dobrenz
Ward A. Dobson
Alfonzo Doby
John A. Doby
Volney Faye Dobyns
Joseph V. Docchio
Lawrence D. Dockerty
Earl Dockery
Aubrey W. Dockins
Donald E. Dockstader
Leland D. Dockum, Jr.
Dennis R. Dodd
Howard H. Dodd
John E. Dodd
Peter J. Dodd
Robert R. Dodd
Eugene E. Dodge
Laverne H. Dodge
Richard Allen Dodge
Furman A. Dodgens, Jr.
Richard F. Dodmead
Carl Dodro
Billy J. Dodson
David I. Dodson, Jr.
George W. Dodson
Kenneth Dodson
Kenneth Leroy Dodson
Marvin M. Dodson
Rance H. Dodson
Thomas A. Dodson
Thomas V. Dodson
Ernest C. Doepner
Charles William Doerr
Frank R. Doerr
Cornelius H. Doherty
Curtis W. Doherty
John C. Doherty
John H. Doherty
Joseph Edward Doherty
Robert T. Doherty
Frank H. Dohoney
James F. Dolan
James Melvin Dolan

Michael James Dolan
Raymond Edmund Dolan
William J. Dolan
Bobby Joe Dolen
Ernest L. Dolezal
Albert J. Dolge
Robert A. Doll
Jack Dollahan
William A. H. Dollar
Dale A. Dollenbacher
James A. Dollings
Burleigh V. Dolph
Robert P. Domaleski
Robert P. Doman
Stephen Dombrowski
Joseph Dometrovich, Jr.
David Dominguez
Jesse Phillip Domingue
Buddy Dominguez
David Dominguez
Henry R. Dominguez
Luis R. Dominguez
Richard Dominguez
Robert Henry Dominick, Jr.
Edward Dominquez
Mortimer Domroe
James Wallace Donaghe
Vicenzo G. Donaglia
Horace E. Donaho
Billy G. Donahoe
Floyd W. Donahoo
Harold D. Donahoo
Daniel D. Donahue
James Henry Donahue
Joseph P. Donahue
C. Franklin Donaldson
Daniel Donaldson
Tellis W. Donaldson
Weldon C. Donaldson
Christopher P. Donall
Anthony J. Donatelli
James Clarence Donham
Remo Donini
Harry Winfield Donkers
Johnie Donkers
John F. Donlin
Paul K. Donlon
Wardell Donlow
Donald Warren Donnell
Lionell Donnell, Jr.
Bearl Donnelly
Eugene J. Donnelly
William F. Donnelly
Alfonso Donofrio
Denis J. Donoghue
Ray S. Donohew
Samuel J. Donohoe, Jr.
Alfred W. Donohue
James J. Donohue
Derrick F. Donovan
Francis Xavier Donovan
George T. Donovan
John F. Donovan
John H. Donovan
Maurice P. S. Donovan
James Thomas Doody
Francis C. Doogan
James A. Dooley, Jr.
Johnnie K. Dooley
William N. Dooley
Kenneth Leon Doolittle
Norrie C. Doolittle
John Joseph Dopazo
Bernard Doran
Edward J. Doran
James Kenneth Doran
Michael J. Doran
Robert G. Doran
Thomas Peter Doran
William Doran
William F. Dorand
N. J. Dorch
Don J. Doremus
Harvey E. Dorff
James N. Dorland
Edward Neil Dorman, Jr.
George Dorman
Conrad Edwin Dorn
Donald Walker Dorn
William A. Dorn
James Lee Dorrance
Thomas A. Dorrell
Hugh C. Dorrien, Jr.
Neil K. Dorrion
Fred A. Dorris
Harold D. Dorris
Leonard H. Dorsch
Jimmie L. Dorser
Carl J. Dorsey

Harold R. Dorsey
Harold W. Dorsey
Joyce Merlin Dorsey
Ural Dorsey
Gilbert Dortch
Edward G. Dosch
Herman C. Doss
Theodore R. Doss
William H. Doss, Jr.
Edward W. Dossie
Charles J. Dostart
Roland J. Dostie
Cecil F. Dotson
Dallas M. Dotson
Lawrence Dotson
Robert F. Dotson
William H. Dotson
George Wesely Doty, Jr.
Gerald Edward Doty
Glenn F. Doty
Marion R. Doty
Thomas Sherlock Doty
Joseph Doucet
Preston G. Doucet
Anthony C. Doucette
Lawrence J. Doucette
Vernon John Doucette
Marvin N. Doud, Jr.
Thomas L. Doufexis
John B. Dougan
William M. Dougan
Bernard P. Dougherty
Donald P. Dougherty
Edward M. Dougherty
Joseph S. Dougherty
Paul Dougherty
Vincent P. Dougherty, Jr.
William Joseph Dougherty
Herbert J. Doughty
William H. Doughty
Allen D. Douglas
Amos Douglas, Jr.
Carl E. Douglas
Charles G. Douglas
Dewain Douglas
Donald A. Douglas
Harold Douglas
Harold F. Douglas
Leo Douglas
Robert Douglas
Robert Douglas
Tony W. Douglas
William Douglas
William S. Douglas
Woody L. Douglas
Thad Douglass
William E. Douglass
Rupert L. Dougless, Jr.
Henry L. Dove
Horace M. Dove
Le Roy J. Dove
Robert F. Dovenbarger
Ernest J. Dover
Paul W. Doverspike
Charles Alexander Dow
Earl G. Dow
George R. Dow
James Arthur Dowd
William J. Dowd, Jr.
Glynn A. Dowdy
James H. Dowdy
Charles D. Dowell
Clarence M. Dowell
Donald D. Dowell
Edward G. Dowell
Guy Dowell
James Clayborn Dowell
Richard L. Dowell
James A. Dower
Don D. Dowler, Jr.
Ray Edward Dowler
Alvin Dowleyne
Donald Francis Dowling
Henry E. Dowling
James Robert Dowling
Lacy Dowling
Paul Eugene Dowling, Jr.
Richard L. Dowling
Robert V. Dowling
Thomas E. Dowling, Jr.
Earle S. Downes
Harold Webb Downes, Jr.
Charles E. Downey
Thomas R. Downie
Clarence C. Downing, Jr.
Walter W. Downing
James T. Downs
Matthew R. Downs
Morgan L. Downs

Robert I. Downs, Jr.
William John Downs
William R. Downs
Paul Doxie
Charles C. Doyle
Clyde G. Doyle
Eldon F. Doyle
Frank A. Doyle
Jackie Deane Doyle
James M. Doyle
John A. Doyle
John J. Doyle
John W. Doyle
Lawrence A. Doyle
Thomas Joseph Doyle
Walter J. Doyle
Lawrence D. Doyon
Barto H. Dozier
Glenn D. Dozier
Andrew G. Drabant
Marion Thomas Dragastin
Robert V. Dragoo
Michael J. Drahos
John Donald Drainer
Charles E. Drake
Curtis T. Drake
Darrel E. Drake
Delbert R. Drake
John M. Drake, Jr.
Robert Edmond Drake
Theron W. Drake, Jr.
Willie J. Drake
Donald Milan Drakulich
Allen E. Drallmeier
Donald John Drama
Albert W. Draper
Glen Roy Draper
James A. Draper
Leroy M. Draper
Robert J. Draugelis
David B. Drawdy
Dale E. Drayer
Louis Dale Drazey
John Longcoy Dreese
Edward Franklin Dreher
George W. Dreisbach
John Dreith
Charles Drengberg
Robert Emmet Drennan
Hugh J. Drennen
James L. Drenth
Albert Shannon Dreon, Jr.
Andrew F. Dreske
Albert S. Dress
Elmer E. Dress
Carl W. Dressler
William E. Dressler
Charles F. Drew
Donald D. Drew
Kenneth H. Drew
Richard R. Drew
Harold F. Drews
Jack Drexler
Howard L. Dreyer
Richard S. Drezen, Jr.
William B. Driesbaugh
James Driggers, Jr.
Douglas L. Drinkard
Dale B. Drinko
Charles D. Drinkwater
Donald D. Drinnen
Charles D. Driscoll
Donald L. Driscoll
Harold J. Driscoll
Herman L. Driskell
William Chris Driskill
Billie C. Driver
Cleve Driver
Fred F. Driver
James Driver
Stephen W. Drochowski, Jr.
Chancey E. Droney
Arthur W. Dronse
Bernard J. Drouillard
Arthur E. Drouin
Harold E. Drown
Richard F. Drown
Robert Lyle Droysen
Saul A. Droz-Cartegena
John J. Drozdowicz
Stanley J. Drozdowski
George A. Drum
Albert E. Drummond, Jr.
Henley D. Drummond
Leonard W. Drummond
Woodrow W. Drummond
Raymond C. Drury, Jr.
Donald John Drust

John G. Druzianich, Jr.
Kenneth E. Dryden
Archibald B. Drysdale
Loren G. Du Bois
Clyatt R. Du Bose
Isreal C. Du Bose, Jr.
Rafael Anthony Du Breuil
Robert H. Du Chemin
Norman P. Du Fresne
James R. Du Puis
Bernardino O. Duarte
Donaciano Duarte
Miguel T. Duarte
Phillip M. Duarte
Rodolfo V. Duarte
William R. Duarte
Gregor Dubas, Jr.
Gerard L. J. Dubay
Robert Peter Dubay
Adelard D. Dube
Stephen Dubinsky
Timothy J. Dublin
Mcclellan A. Dubois
Stevie J. Duboise
Leo E. Dubos
Frank J. Ducharme
Richard E. Ducharme
Edward S. Duchnevich
Choy J. Duck
Howard A. Duck
Johnnie R. Duck
James H. Duckworth
Ernest H. Duderstadt, Jr.
Henry A. Dudleson
Charles B. Dudley
David H. Dudley
Jack Dudley
John Crawford Dudley
Carl Lee Due
Victor Leroy Duer
William J. Duerr
Johnnie J. Dues
Paul E. Duez
Darrell M. Duff
Donald L. Duff
George A. Duff
Russell C. Duffer
John J. Duffey
Thomas A. Duffey
James Robert Duffin
Clifford G. Duffner
Alfred P. Duffy
Thomas J. Duffy
Thomas W. Duffy
Vernon Velmore Duffy
William T. Duffy
Gerald L. Dufrane
Robert Elmer Dufrene
Norman P. Dufresne
Francis Xavier Dugan
John J. Dugan
Ralph Edwin Dugan
Daniel Joseph Duggan
David J. Duggan
James Cornelius Duggan
Fred Dugger
Lindy M. Dugger
Thomas Adrian Dugger
Paul Anson Dugle
Thomas Anthony Dugo, Jr.
Herman A. Duhaime
Louis S. Duhaime, Jr.
Alvin L. Duhon
Kibbie Duhon
Kenneth Ronald Duhr
John Dukarm
Arthur J. Duke
Earl C. Duke
James D. Duke
Joseph J. Duke
Kenneth Lee Duke
Ray Eugene Duke
Roy E. Duke
Frank Dukes
Robert L. Dukes
Donald J. Dulac
Charles L. Dulaney
Robert Duld
Daniel Dulin
James R. Dulin
Harold B. Dulyea
Gilbert David Dumais
Roger A. Dumas
Albert John Dumbeck
Robert E. Dummermuth
Gilman Dumond
Stanley Dumpman
Hershel D. Dunagan
William A. Dunavant

335

Ralph W. Dunbar
Franklin P. Dunbaugh
Alvin D. Duncan
Charles J. Duncan
Charles W. Duncan
Cleo L. Duncan
Donald Marion Duncan
E. W. Duncan
Earl W. Duncan
Edward R. Duncan
Herman C. Duncan
James Harold Duncan
Lester A. Duncan
Phillip Duncan
Raymond E. Duncan
Raymond Eugene Duncan
Richard E. Duncan
Robert W. Duncan
Roy E. Duncan
William E. Duncan
William E. Duncan
William J. Duncan
Wyatt G. Duncan, Jr.
Donald I. Dundore
Herman Dungen
Byron R. Dunham
David Joe Dunham
Donald E. Dunham
James W. Dunham
Leland D. Dunham
Robert B. Dunham
Ronald B. Dunham, Jr.
Benjamin F. Dunkle, Jr.
Donald Clinton Dunkle
Harold L. Dunkle
Albert Howard Dunlap, Jr.
Alva F. Dunlap
Bernard A. Dunlap
Charles H. Dunlap
Delcher F. Dunlap
Duane V. Dunlap
George W. Dunlap
Gerald P. Dunlap
John Guy Dunlap
Johnny E. Dunlap
Kenneth Wayne Dunlap
Raymond E. Dunlap
Daniel U. Dunn
Everett D. Dunn, Jr.
Francis Dunn
George W. Dunn, Jr.
Gifford Eugene Dunn
Harold Uhland Dunn
J. T. Dunn
Jack Dunn
James J. Dunn
James L. Dunn
James Millard Dunn
James R. Dunn
James W. Dunn
John H. Dunn
Larry D. Dunn
Larry M. Dunn
Marce Presnell Dunn
Paul L. Dunn
Ralph Raymond Dunn
Richard T. Dunn
Robert A. Dunn
Robert C. Dunn
Ronald L. Dunn
Samuel V. Dunn
Sylvester Dunn
Donald L. Dunnaway
Kenneth L. Dunnaway
Charles Shelby Dunne
John Michael Dunne
Robert Len Dunne
Thomas Joseph Dunne
Ramon H. Dunnigan
John A. Dunning
Edward D. Dunphy
Alva L. Dunsworth
Arthur W. Dunton, Jr.
Joseph W. Dupart
John C. Dupeey
Robert H. Duperre
Henry F. Duplease
Louis J. Duplessis
Alfred A. Duplissis
Donald A. Dupont
Lyle R. Dupont
Richard Dupont
John L. Dupre, Jr.
Dewey Joseph Dupuis
Joseph N. Dupuis
Raymond J. Dupuis
Wayne Lewis Dupuis
Glen Merrill Dupuy
Junius Dupuy

Laverne Duquenne
Roger L. R. Duquesne
Leo J. Duquette
Stanley G. Durachta
Joseph Durakovich
Anthony Domingo Duram
Ernest Duran
Harold D. Duran
Horace Duran
Joshua R. Duran
Pedro Duran
Tony G. Duran
William C. Durand
Joseph R. Durant
Rudy F. Durazo
Andrew L. Durbin
Gerald D. Durbin
Harold L. Durbin
Edward F. Durborow, Jr.
Richard H. Durborow, Jr.
Leon Dureiko
David Glenn Duren
Donald C. Durfee
Lamont J. Durfee
Charles H. Durham
George B. Durham
James R. Durham
Jesse Durham
Richard Warren Durham
Vergil Durham
Wade Lester Durham
William Durham
Seth Dean Durkee
Edward M. Durkin
John P. Durkin, Jr.
Alfonzo A. Durnell
Edward J. Durney, Jr.
Robert G. Durochin
Joseph A. Durovec
Gerald O. Durrett
Donald G. Durst
John Duschane
Ronald D. Dusek
J. D. Dushane
Edward Dushaw, Jr.
Walter D. Dusoblom
Arthur Dussault
William A. Duster
Harry Max Dusterhoff
Douglas Truman Dustin
Edward W. Duston
Mike W. Dutchak
Lee Edward Dutcher
Lynn Francis Dutemple
Eugene J. Dutra
John L. Dutra
Fay J. Dutson
Billie J. Dutton
Adgie Duvall, Jr.
Alfred E. Duvernay
Cornelius C. Duyf
Kenneth Edward Dvorak
Milton F. Dvorak
Billy Dwier
Ernest F. Dwight
Craig S. Dwinnell
Michael A. Dworshak
Charles K. Dwyer
Francis W. Dwyer
James Dwyer
Leonard Joseph Dwyer
Richard Thomas Dwyer
Stanley T. Dybol
Arnold G. Dye
Cecil G. Dye
Dailey Francis Dye
Doyle J. Dye
Karl L. Dye
Richard Dye
Robert L. Dye
Robert Lee Dye
Archie W. Dyer
Bobby L. Dyer
Donald C. Dyer
Horace G. Dyer
Thomas G. Dyer
Raymond R. Dykes
Wayne Arthur Dykes
Marlin Dyment
Michael Dyondya
Harold Dyson
Michael L. Dzielski
John J. Dzienis
Albert W. Dzinkowski
Edward M. Dziura

— E —

William T. Eade, Jr.

Charles Lee Eades
Andrew E. Eads
Avon Edward Eads
Creed Lea Eads
Donald W. Eads
Ernest Leroy Eads
Jerry J. Eads
Lloyd M. Eads, Jr.
James Keyser Eagan
Ben Eagle
Wilbur C. Eagle
Elburne O. Earby
Paul Earhart
Leonard Earheart
James E. Earl
Robert J. Earl, Jr.
James Samuel Earles
John J. Earley
Joseph P. Earls, Jr.
Milo G. Earls
William B. Earls
Elbyrne O. Early
George R. Early
James E. Early
Laurence P. Early
Rutherford Early, Jr.
Donel F. Earnest
William Sydney Earns
Arthur H. Earnshaw
Joseph F. Eartbawey
Conley C. Earwood
Wendell Easley
Charles D. Eason
James Loyd Eason
Theon O. Eason
Wildon C. East
William C. Easte
Charles W. Easterday
Roscoe W. Easterling
Robert Eastlack
Carroll M. Eastman
Charles J. Eastman
Donald V. Eastman
Eugene G. Eastman
Arthur T. Eastwood
Archie L. Eaton
Edward Drew Eaton
Frederic N. Eaton
George R. Eaton
Glennon W. Eaton
Jack Richmond Eaton
John Omer Eaton
Robert Eaton
Ronald Dow Eaton
William N. Eaton
Bobby W. Eaves
Joseph D. Ebarb
Clarence W. Ebensperger
Clarence A. Eberly
Lewis W. Ebernikle, Jr.
Donald W. Ebersole
Donald F. Ebert
John W. Ebert
Melvin H. Ebert
Robert D. Ebert
John O. Eberwein
Gerald D. Ebner
Wayne E. Ebright
Colin C. Eccles
Edward Elisha Eccleston
Keith W. Echelberger
Calvin C. Echoles
Tommie L. Echols
Marion M. Eck
Charles K. Eckard
Lester R. Eckard
Carl F. Eckardt
Herron M. Eckels, Jr.
Albert Eckerdt
Harry Eckert
Roger F. Eckert
Thomas R. Eckert
Theodore Eckhardt
Joseph H. Eckhart, Jr.
John W. Eddins, Jr.
Homer R. Eddy
John F. Eddy
F. William J. Edelman
Charles Eden
Malcolm Brodie Edens
Melvin Edens
William H. Eder, Jr.
Kenneth R. Edgar
Noel J. Edgar
William Thomas Edgar
Edward C. Edge
Ernest E. Edge
Percy W. Edge
Francis M. Edgemon, Jr.

Carl W. Edgemond
Delbert V. Edgette
Alvin Lee Edgington
Harold M. Edgington
James Edmonds, Jr.
James Louis Edmonds
James S. Edmonds, Jr.
Lester E. Edmonds, Jr.
Marvin M. Edmonds
Henry F. Edmonson
Jesse W. Edmonson
Clifton Edmonston
Patrick J. Edmunds
Walter L. Ednie
Edward A. Ednie
J. C. Edson
Roy H. Edstrom
Carrol Edvalson
Leroy Edward
Albert Edwards
Carl W. Edwards
Cecil C. Edwards
Charles P. Edwards
Charles W. Edwards
Clarence Edwards, Jr.
Cleveland Edwards, Jr.
Coleman Edwards
Donald A. Edwards
Donald E. Edwards
Donald Eugene Edwards
Dwight W. Edwards
Elijah Edwards
Elzia M. Edwards
Eugene Edwards
Gary Richard Edwards
George Neil Edwards
Harold R. Edwards
Herbert R. Edwards
James A. Edwards
James E. Edwards
James J. Edwards
James S. Edwards
John L. Edwards
Junior D. Edwards
Kenneth J. Edwards
Morton G. Edwards
Odis W. Edwards
Paul Kenneth Edwards
Ray Edwards
Robert Bruce Edwards
Robert E. Edwards
Robert L. Edwards
Stacy Edwards
Thomas Arthur Edwards
Thomas D. Edwards
Thomas Leroy Edwards
Ty C. Edwards
Victor M. Edwards
Willard H. Edwards
William H. Edwards
William T. Edwards
Willie J. Edwards
Willis L. Edwards
Floyd Eells, Jr.
Gerald H. Effa
Kenneth A. Effenbeck
Donald C. Efland
Patrick J. Egan
Raul G. Egan
Thomas E. Egan
Thomas Joseph Egan
Duane E. Ege
Robert C. Egelkraut
Henry C. Eggenberger
Vernon A. Eggenburg
Carl Eggers, Jr.
Herbert P. Eggers
Irwin L. Eggert
Lowell J. Eggert
Arnold E. Eggleston
Marvin L. Eggleston
Robert D. Egley
James John Egresitz
Donald L. Eheler
Ben J. Ehle
Myrle W. Ehle
Kenneth F. Ehlers
Rudolph Ehlers, Jr.
Donald A. Ehlert
Edgar A. Ehrlich
Leland Ernest Ehrlich
George B. Eichelberger, Jr.
Walter R. Eichholz
Carl Eichhorn, Jr.
Vincent J. Eicholtz
Donald Earl Eichschlag
Richard Henry Eidam
John Eide
Harold H. Eidemiller

Jan Robert Eike
Lewis C. Eikner
Durward S. Eiland
Harrold John Eiland
Richard O. Eiler
James W. Eilers
John F. Eilers
Bernard J. Einum
Kenneth C. Eirich
Daryl K. Eiseman
Kenneth R. Eisenhardt
Leonard Daniel Eismin
Edwin G. Eklund, Jr.
Eyvind A. Ekset
Boyd W. Elam
Ivan O. Elam
David N. Elander
Matthew J. Elberth, Jr.
Delbert G. Elder
Glen R. Elder
Howard G. Elder
Harry F. Eldredge
Donald E. Eldridge
Melburn H. Eldridge
Ronald T. Eldridge
Kenneth G. Eley
Samuel Eley, Jr.
Raymond W. Elgland
Daniel A. Elias
Vernon C. Eliason
Fritz P. Eliassen
Dick J. Eliot
Clyde W. Elkins
George Daniel Elkins
Paul E. Elkins
Tellus H. Elkins
Robert Marvin Ellars
Junior E. Ellefson
Fred D. Ellen
Richard H. Ellenberger
Roger Roscoe Ellerd
William G. Ellerington
Vernon Ellifritz
Ralph J. Ellingsen
Chevlyn M. Ellingson
Eugene M. Ellingson
John Edward Ellington
Carl W. Elliot
Bill Elliott
Jackson C. Elliott
James Alvert Elliott
James C. Elliott, Jr.
James H. Elliott
John Martin Elliott
Junnie L. Elliott
Louis T. Elliott
Orin B. Elliott
Ova E. Elliott
R. J. Elliott
Roy Edward Elliott
Shelby F. Elliott
Wayne F. Elliott
Andrew Jackson Ellis
Charles R. Ellis
Chester L. Ellis
David F. Ellis
David M. Ellis
Delton Ellis
Donald D. Ellis
Donald R. Ellis
Emanuel Ellis
Fred M. Ellis
Grady W. Ellis
Grant Ridgway Ellis
Henry Edward Ellis
James E. Ellis
James H. Ellis
James I. Ellis
James R. Ellis
John Francis Ellis
Julius L. Ellis
Martin R. Ellis
Ralph Alan Ellis, Jr.
Raymond C. Ellis
Richard Dee Ellis
Theodore Clarence E. Ellis
Walter L. Ellis
Wandal R. Ellis
Bobby L. Ellison
Coleman C. Ellison
Conwell G. Ellison
Emmett P. Ellison
Harold Edward Ellison
J. C. Ellison
James H. Ellison
John Y. Ellison
Kenneth Lloyd Ellison
Rex Donald Ellison
Virgil J. Ellison

Charles V. Ellsworth
R. M. Ellsworth, Jr.
Robert R. Elmer
Howard C. Elmes
Charles E. Elmore
Everitt L. Elmore
George William Elmore
Joe S. Elmore
John D. Elmore
Johnnie Elmore, Jr.
Lincoln Elmore
William True Elrod
Richard W. Elsass
Walter Else
Ralph Elsman, Jr.
Donald L. Elsner
Bill Elsom
Earl P. Elswick
George I. Elsworth
Walter S. Eltringham
Edward H. Eltzroth
Glen G. Elus
John Bob Elwell
Sherman L. Elwood
Boris A. Ely
Jacob A. Ely
Lowell E. Ely
Robert Louis Elze
Frank Emanuel, Jr.
Solomon Emanuel
John Henry Embach
Paul T. Embrey
Forest Embry
Delbert D. Emehiser
Paul D. Emeola
Robert K. Emerick
Amos Emerson, Jr.
Bertram F. Emerson
Bob J. Emerson
James Louis Emerson
Philip Emerson
Willie Bruce Emerson
Thomas T. Emerton
Donald L. Emery
James R. Emery
Robert Lee Emery
George Richard Emhoff
Roy W. Emhoff
Lawerence F. Emigholz, Jr.
Gerald R. Emmans
Fidel Emmanuelli
Vincent N. Emmett
Clifford O. Emmons
Robert P. Emmott
Stanley Howard Emond
Paul Emory, Jr.
James Roy Empfield
Howard W. Emrick
Richard Enaena
William E. Enas
Benjamin R. Encinas
Richard C. Encinas
Edward R. Enders
Paymond A. Enderson
Milton Charles Endicott
Hachiro B. Endo
Wendall Charles Endsley
Edgar Enfinger
Daniel Julius Eng
James W. Engdahl
Stanley Engeholm
Joseph James Engelbreit
James N. Engelhardt
Leo F. Engelhart
Harvey G. Engelman
Albert H. Enger
Myron J. Enger
Donald C. Engh
Donald Ernest Engh
Russell J. Englade
Cary Juan England
David E. England, Jr.
Emery J. England
Horace Smith England
Donald Englehart
Robert M. Englehart
Walter S. Englehart
Kenneth R. Engleman
Claude M. Engler, Jr.
Alvin English
James English
Lemuel L. English
Leonard English, Jr.
Robert B. English
Ted English
Vernon R. English
Ralph Merle Engstrom
Dale Thomas Enlow
Fred L. Enlow

336

Fred Asher Ennis
William C. Ennis
Joseph William Ennist
Paul A. Eno
Henry P. Enoka
George W. Enos
Gordon Francis Enos
Ormell L. Enos
Joseph E. Enrico
James P. Enright, Jr.
Lawrence John Enright
Marvin C. Enright
Robert Eugene Enright
William Chester Enright
Mario M. Enriquez
William Enriquez
Llewellyn J. Enstrom
Marcelo O. Enzinger
William George Epp
Charles R. Eppelman
Glen E. Epperson
Robert Lee Epperson
Martin Eppinger
Russell C. Eppinger
Charles R. Eppleman
Albert M. Eppley
Franklin Herbert Eppley
Richard Levi Eppley
Louis W. Epstein
Noel Epstein
Homer A. Erb
Vernon J. Erby
Richard W. Erdenberger
Lawrence W. Erdman
William Kenneth Erdman
James Erdos
Harold E. Erhardt
Albert C. Erickson
Dean J. Erickson
Donald M. Erickson
Edwin O. Erickson, Jr.
Eugene L. Erickson
Harold L. Erickson
Herbert L. Erickson
Lee Eldon Erickson
Reuben C. Erickson
Richard D. Erickson
Robert L. Erickson
Roger L. Erickson
Walter H. Erickson
Jack Ericson
Raymond C. Ericson
Knute O. Eriksen
Dominic Eritano
Gregory F. Erlach
Theodore Russell Erler
Andrew Ernandis
John A. Erndt
Clarence J. Ernest, Jr.
William Charles Ernst
James D. Eroddy
Wesley E. Erola
Joseph Rease Errgang
Joseph A. Errigo
John Harrison Errington
Daniel G. Erste
Charles Dennis Ertle
Burt Ervin
Charles G. Ervin
Eldon W. Ervin
Robert Harold Ervin
Granville C. D. Erving, Jr.
Charles Ervins
Joseph L. Erwin
William C. Escalante
Teofilo Escalera
Jimmy Louis Escalle
Lyle E. Eschenbrenner
Erasmo Escobar
George J. Escobar
Pablo A. Escobar, Jr.
Gerardo Escontrias
Francis William Escott
Joseph Escourido
Robert E. Eshenbaugh
John S. Eshima 30
Martin S. Eskin
Malcolm J. Eskine
Benny L. Esparza
Oscar Emil Espelin
Dougall Harry Espey, Jr.
Robert G. Espey
Jose E. Espinoza
Joseph Espinoza
Richard D. Espinoza
James Espita
Anthony D. Esposito
Frank J. Esposito, Jr.
John A. Esposito

Louis T. Esposito
Victor Esposito
Enzo Esposti
Paul Austin Esque
Gabriel V. Esqueda
Librado E. Esquer
Cruz G. Esquibel
Jesus Esquibel
David Essberg, Jr.
John Essebagger, Jr.
Robert Laurence Essig
Elwood R. Essler
William Essmeier
Carl K. Estell
Eugene Estep
Othar E. Estep
Wayne Estep
Cleston B. Estes
Edward Eugene Estes
Felix J. Estes
Raymond E. Estes
Richard L. Estes
Robert C. Estes
Robert V. Estes
Roy Lee Estes
Thomas C. Estes
William T. Estes
A. J. Esteves-Rivera
Milton L. Estill
Albert J. Estrada
Alfonso A. Estrada
Armand Ernest Estrada
Cecil Estrada
Johnnie P. Estrada
Willie N. Estrada
Benjamin B. Estrella, Jr.
Thomas Carl Estwick
Donald H. Esway
Clifford Etheridge
Herbert J. Etie, Jr.
Herbert G. Ettel
Ray W. Etter
Guy T. Eubanks, Jr.
Randolph Eubanks
Robert R. Eubanks
John V. Eudy, Jr.
Raymond R. Eufimia
Timothy Tai S. Eum
James A. Euman
George E. Eustis
Stowell Eustis
Thomas James Euston
Leo Edward Eutsler
Andrew Evanich
Alexander Evans
Arthur J. Evans, Jr.
B. J. Evans
Bryant Evans, Jr.
Carl Julius Evans
Charles H. Evans
Charles Jerry Evans
Charles O. Evans
Clifford G. Evans
Corbit Evans
Curtis D. Evans
Daniel John Evans, Jr.
David Burton Evans
Donald Evans
Donald E. Evans
Donald L. Evans
Dudley Lewis Evans
Earl Evans
Earl Evans
Edward J. Evans
Edward R. Evans
Edwin L. Evans
Emmett O. Neal Evans
Eugene L. Evans
Everette R. Evans
Floyd Robert Evans
Gene E. Evans
George Conley Evans
George J. Evans
Halbert Knapp Evans
Harold A. Evans
Harold L. Evans
Henry E. Evans
Herbert W. Evans
Hosea L. Evans
Howard H. Evans
Hubert T. Evans
J. C. Evans
James H. Evans
James L. Evans
James Mackie Evans
James R. Evans
James Richard Evans
Jess Eldridge Evans
Jimmie R. Evans

John Addison Evans, Jr.
John H. Evans
John Lee Evans
Johnny B. Evans
Joseph Kenneth Evans
Joseph Wayne Evans
Junior C. Evans
Kenneth Ormand Evans
Murl R. Evans
Owen M. Evans
Owens B. Evans
Phillip J. Evans
Robert E. Evans
Robert Joseph Evans, Jr.
Robert Lee Evans
Robert Lee Evans
Robert M. Evans
Roy B. Evans
Thomas B. Evans, Jr.
Thomas L. Evans
Vernon Lee Evans
Virgle J. Evans
Wallace Evans, Jr.
Wallis J. Evans
Walter D. Evans
Walter R. Evans
Ward Evans, Jr.
William E. Evans
William F. Evans
William J. Evans
William L. Evans
William V. Evans
Willie G. Evans
Bobbie Evants
Harford C. Eve, Jr.
Charles W. Everatt
Coleman L. Everett
Fred E. Everett
Harry S. Everett, Jr.
William L. Everett
Clarence A. Everetts
Elmer Everhart, Jr.
Leonard V. Everhart
Usrey H. Everhart
John B. Evering
James R. Everling
Donald E. Everly
Leonard Evers
Walter F. Everson
William B. Everson
Loyd W. Everts
Thomas D. Eveslage
Albert T. Evonska
Jack F. Ewart
Edward F. Ewens
Grant Harry Ewing
Harry W. Ewing
John D. Ewing
John M. Ewing, Jr.
Neal Richard Ewing
William G. Ewing
James F. Exley
Billie J. Exline
William J. Exum
Melvin Leroy Eye
Gordon L. Eyer
Daniel J. Eyler
Albert R. Eytchison
Clarence E. Ezell
William D. Ezell
Deroyce H. Ezzell

— F —

Ernest Fabbi
Alfred J. Faber
Gerald A. Faber
Donald A. Fabrize
Lewis Fabrizio
Alexander Facchini
Kenneth Jenky Factor
Willard F. Faddis
William Patrick Faeth
Willie J. Fagain
Frederick R. Fagan
Joseph P. Fagan, Jr.
Cecil W. Fagg
Lawrence Fahey
John B. Fahl
Donald R. Fahrenholz
Kermit C. Fahrmeyer
Charles W. Faidley
Billie Randolph Faile
Bill Gray Fain
J. C. Fain
James E. Fain
John W. Fain, Jr.
Curtis A. Fair
Robert C. Fair

Willie Fair
Richard M. Fairbanks
Kenneth R. Fairchild
Leslie L. Fairchild
Lofton B. Fairchild
Ray Palmer Fairchild
Alfred L. Fairfield
Jesse H. Fairless
Theron Fairley
Joseph J. Fairo
Clarence E. Fairrow
Ray Lebarry Faison
Don C. Faith, Jr.
Robert G. Faith
Felix Raymond Fajkus
Matagisa S. Falanai
Anthony Julius Falatach
Robert F. Falco
Eugene H. Falcon
Roberto Falcon
Donald P. Faldet
Michael J. Faleshock
Jno E. Falin
Charles Albert Falk
Henry J. Falk
Herman Louis Falk, Jr.
Harry J. Falkenburg
Alexander C. Falkowski
Fortunato C. Fallanca
John Fallat
Walter Fallesching
Daniel Fallind, Jr.
Orson D. Fallis
Richard Lee Fallon
Pivo Fallorina
Eino Erland Falls
George A. Falls
George N. Falvey
Leo F. Falvey
Charles L. Falwell
Charles Michael Familia
Pasquale Famularo
Harold S. Fancher
Maxie Fancher
Glenn W. Fannin
Clyde Anson Fanning
Jack R. Fannon
William J. Fano
Albert Hall Fant
William J. Fantozzi
Charles K. Farabaugh
William L. Farabee
John W. Farber
Joseph Louis Farber
Kenneth Wayne Fare
Lawrence Bob Farfan
Joseph G. Faria, Jr.
Harold D. Farias
Lino Farias
Andrew Liddell III Farie
Marion D. Faries
Nicolo D. Farina
Paul L. Farinacci
Henry B. Farinholt
Robert W. Faris
Isaac Fariss
Hugh Phillip Farler
Earl J. Farley
Homer C. Farley
Jack Farley, Jr.
John Devereux Farley
Louis George Farley
Ronald J. Farley
Clarence L. Farmer
George R. Farmer
Harvey L. Farmer
James W. Farmer
John N. Farmer
Joseph F. Farmer
Kenneth L. Farmer
Kenneth W. Farmer
Melvin E. Farmer
Norman L. Farmer
Paul C. Farmer
Robert P. Farmer
Robert W. Farmer
Rudolph Farmer
William G. Farmer
William L. Farmer
Robert E. Farnesi
Donald H. Farnham
Glenn W. Farnham
Philip C. Farnham
William M. Farone
Charles E. Farr
Guss R. Farr
Joe Ray Farr
Jimaye Keigh Farrar
John W. Farrar

Clarence C. Farrell, Jr.
Edward Joseph C. Farrell
George J. Farrell, Jr.
James F. Farrell
Joseph E. Farrell
Michael J. Farrell
Thomas F. Farrell, Jr.
William F. Farrell
William Henry Farrell
William T. Farrell
Felix D. Farrelly
John A. Iii Farren
Alvin R. Farris
Charles L. Farris
Clofus O. Farris
Gerald A. Farris
Stephen J. Farris
Thurman Lee Farris
William M. Farris
Ernest Farrow
Robert Farthing
Robert Jess Farthing
Charles R. Farus
Frank Faruzzi
Raymond A. Fashone
William F. Fasick
Lyle E. Fassett
Michael C. Fastner
Donald Anthony Fatica
Warren Henry Faubel
John J. Faughman
Floyd N. Faulconer
Paul Douglas Faulconer
Frank R. Faulhaber
Vernon O. Faulkenberry
Alfred B. Faulkner
Charles C. Faulkner
Lynn Reed Faulkner
Prince E. Faulkner
Robert A. Faulkner
Robert C. Faulkner
Arthur Brooks Faunce
Louis P. Fausone
Albert H. Faust
Thomas Owen Faust
Leo Simon Fautsch
Thomas Christopher Fava
James F. Favaloro
Daniel V. Favella
Lloyd Morgan Faver
Lionel R. Favreau
Harold M. Fawcett
Richard R. Fawley
Frank G. Fay
Harold O. Fay
Preston Stackpole J. Fay
John Francis Fayman
Dominick J. Fazio
Carroll R. Feagans
Harley A. Feagin
T. J. Feagins
Edward Livingston Feakes
Victor Eugene Feany
Richard J. Fecko
Milton Fedchisin
Rosario Fede
Walter Carl Feder
Stephen Federiniec
Michael Fedikovich, Jr.
Charles J. Fedorka
Denver Fee
Donald George Feeney
Edmond G. Feeney
Joseph L. Feeney, Jr.
Patrick J. Feeney
Raymond Feenstra, Jr.
Edmond G. Feeny
Berkley S. Feese
William J. Fehring
Gerald Feinstein
Myron H. Feinstein
Donald F. Feist
Vincente Q. Fejaran
Juan C. Fejerang
Harmon C. Felder
Willie J. Felder
Warren J. Feldges
David E. Feldmeth
Herman G. Felhoelter
Raul R. Felician
Carlos D. Feliciano
Jose A. Feliciano
Lino Feliciano
Julio Feliciano-Nieves
B. Feliciano-Otero
S. Feliciano-Quinones
Miguel Angel V. Felix
Robert Lewis Felix
P. Felix-Rodriguez

Sterling F. Feliz
Earl W. Felker
George L. Felkon
Theodore Fellis
Charles H. Fellows
Marshall G. Fellows
Willie Fellows, Jr.
Leo D. Fels
Harlon C. Feltner
John Albert Felton
Thomas Edward Felton
Oscar M. Felts
Raymond R. Felts
Stephen J. Femino
Luther Fendley, Jr.
Thomas Fendya
Gordon O. Fengstad
Isaac Fennell, Jr.
Donald Melvin Fenner
James H. Fenner
Richard F. Fennessey
Marvin J. Fenske
Ellery A. Fenstamaker, Jr.
Robert G. Fenstermaker
John R. Fenton
Ralph Emerson Fenton
Nelson E. Fenwick
William D. Fenwick
Henry Ferazzoli
Joseph Ference
Anthony M. Ferentine
Andrew A. Ferguson, Jr.
Bobby H. Ferguson
Carlos E. Ferguson
Charles C. Ferguson
Charles G. Ferguson
Charley Ferguson
Clyde J. Ferguson
David L. Ferguson
George D. Ferguson
Hugh W. Ferguson, Jr.
Jake L. Ferguson
James T. Ferguson
Joseph R. Ferguson
Lawrence R. Ferguson
Marvin D. Ferguson
Ottie K. Ferguson
Raymond A. Ferguson
Ronald P. Ferguson
Sam W. Ferguson
Theodore Gregg Ferguson
Thomas D. Ferguson
Vincent A. Ferguson
Wendell E. Ferguson
Jose A. Feria-Vilanova
David A. Feriend
Leonard James Ferko
Lawrence J. Ferkovich
James E. Fern
Anthony K. Fernandes
John A. Fernandes
Casiano J. R. Fernandez
Eleodoro R. Fernandez
Emil F. Fernandez
Joe D. Fernandez
Calvin D. Fernau
August R. Ferracane
Alers Vin Ferrante
Albert S. Ferrara
Albert J. Ferrari
David J. Ferrari
Albert A. Ferraris
Alfred G. Ferraro
Nolan Herbert Ferree
Gerald J. Ferreira
Raymond Ferreira
Harry Elmer Ferrell
James L. Ferrell
John W. Ferrell
Kermit Mcgee Ferrell
Robert S. Ferrell
Carl M. Ferrer
George Ferri
Edward R. Ferris
Fred G. Ferris
Ronald R. Ferris
Vernon G. Ferris
Elwood Ferry, Jr.
Richard Paul Ferry
Nicholas Ferzetti, Jr.
Raymond A. Fessler
Steve Joseph Festini
Grant R. Fetrow
Fred D. Fetter
Leo E. Fetzer
William J. Feury
Eugene L. Fey
Robert F. Feyereisen
Walter K. Fialkowski

337

Mayer D. Fiance
Chester P. Fibich
Mojmir Peter Ficek
Salvatore Fichera
Erich R. Fichter
Robert J. Fick
William Robert Ficke
Fred Burno Fickel
William J. Ficker
Warren Myers Ficklen
William C. Ficor
Charles E. Fiddler
Ernest Charles Fiebelkorn
James Thomas Fiedler
Joseph F. Field
Paul E. Field
Paul G. Field
Robert L. Field
Donald L. Fielder
Wilson Fielder, Jr.
Clifford E. Fielding
Bert L. Fields
Billy Gene Fields
Buddy R. Fields
Chester A. Fields
Curtis L. Fields
Dwaine Edward Fields
George D. Fields
Gerald Fields
Gerald J. Fields
John H. Fields
Kennith G. Fields
Lonnie Fields
Oliver M. Fields
Rodger E. Fields
Ruebin Fields
Saint Elmore Fields
Stanley A. Fields
Jesse F. Fierro
Roger L. Fife
Walter Marshall Fife
Joseph G. Figaro
Ronald A. Figel
Dennard Merrill Figg
Francisco Figueroa
Frank R. Figueroa
Julio Figueroa
Luis A. Figueroa
Massas S. Figueroa
Medina Luis Figueroa
Muniz F. Figueroa
Otero A. L. Figueroa
Otero Luis R. Figueroa
Seda German Figueroa
Luis Figueroa-Barbosa
J. Figueroa-Rodriguez
Ronald Figureid
James A. Fike
Michael J. Fila
Edward J. Filarecki
Robert T. Filbin
John A. Filener
Walter F. Filkins
Clemond W. Filler
Donald Lavern Filler
Cecil W. Fillingame
Phillip J. Fillion
Richard Don Filloon
Alex Garcia Filomeno
Lawrence Filosena
Oscar Filyaw
James Francis Finau
Edward A. Finch
Frank O. Finch
Jack R. Finch
Robert A. Finch
Robert Clarence Finch
Stanton E. Finch
William Paul Finch
Deltis Herman Fincher
Roy L. Fincher
Gerald K. Findel
Edward H. Findlay
Harry J. Findley
Richard O. Findley
Darrell Eugene Fine
Richard Melvin Fine
Donald E. Fingers
James Walter Fink
Robert E. Fink
Roy C. Fink
William P. Finlan
Leonard E. Finlay
Kenneth C. Finlayson
Douglas Shirley Finley, Jr.
Edward Finley
Green Finley, Jr.
Jerry L. Finley
Richard H. Finley

William J. Finley
Clifford C. Finn, Jr.
Erskine Donald Finn
Howard W. Finn
John B. Finn
John Edward Finn
Patrick Thomas Finn
Paul E. Finn
Robert Joseph Finnegan
Thomas J. Finnegan, Jr.
William W. Finner
Lawrence Finneran
Glen Dwayne Finney
Robert A. Finney, Jr.
David L. Finnie
Richard T. Finnigan
Wilho O. Finnila
George H. Finstad
Coy F. Firestone
Lewis M. Firey, Jr.
George Firment
Eugene H. Firnges
Clyne C. Fischer
Edward Dennis Fischer
George Jay Fischer
Horace Ray Fischer
Jack Stewart Fischer
James F. Fischer
James F. Fischer
Ralph Rupert Fischer
Virgil Lesley Fischer
William R. Fischer, Jr.
June H. Fiscus
Donald Leroy Fish
John M. Fish
Warren A. Fish
William Fish
Wilmer R. Fish
Alva Rudolph Fisher
Amos Fisher
Arlis H. Fisher
Bernard J. Fisher
Charles V. B. Fisher
Clarence R. Fisher
Dale L. Fisher
David L. Fisher
Donald E. Fisher
Donavan L. Fisher
Edward R. Fisher
George Lester Fisher
George T. Fisher
Jack Alvin Fisher
James Elton Fisher
James R. Fisher
Jewell R. Fisher
Joe H. Fisher
John A. Fisher
John Theodore Fisher
John W. Fisher
Kenneth C. Fisher
Levin F. Fisher
Norman R. Fisher
Pervis Fisher
Ralph G. Fisher
Richard L. Fisher
Robert James Fisher
Robert John Fisher, Jr.
Robert W. Fisher, Jr.
Ronald J. Fisher
Thomas F. Fisher
Virgil L. Fisher
Walter F. Fisher
Wayne Floyd Fisher
William H. Fisher
William M. Fisher
William Royal Fisher
Willie Henry Fisher, Jr.
Donald D. Fislar
Conrad G. Fislul
Edward Patrick Fitch
Francis L. Fitch
Robert Stuart Fitch
John M. Fitt
Leslie J. Fitts
Robert Cameron Fitts
Freeman O. Fitz
Harold Lewis Fitz
Robert G. Fitzer
Charles E. Fitzgerald
Edward F. Fitzgerald
Ernest Fitzgerald, Jr.
John J. Fitzgerald
John Timothy Fitzgerald
Lawrence E. Fitzgerald
Major W. Fitzgerald
Richard M. Fitzgerald
Richard M. Fitzgerald
Robert J. Fitzgerald
Robert J. Fitzgerald, Jr.

Thomas Joseph Fitzgerald
Laurie Fitzgibbon, Jr.
Harry B. Fitzgibbons
Thomas J. Fitzgibbons
Howard Fitzhugh
James E. Fitzhugh
Francis J. Fitzpatrick
George Francis Fitzpatrick
Michael Fitzpatrick
Michael J. Fitzpatrick
T. R. Fitzpatrick
Thomas A. Fitzpatrick
William E. Fitzpatrick
Carl J. Fitzwater
Robert L. Fitzwater
Billy J. Fixico
Charles Arthur Fjaer
Alan D. Flack
Cameron M. Flack
Jack Edward Flack
Lawrence E. Flack
Eric N. Flackman, Jr.
Donald Edward Flagg
Francis L. Flagg
Russel William Flaglore
Coleman J. Flaherty
Edmund R. Flaherty
John Francis Flaherty
John W. Flaherty
Joseph L. Flaherty
Michael W. Flaherty
Thomas L. Flaherty
Peter F. Flaime
Raymond R. Flair
Paul Henry Flamand
Kenneth Flamer
Roy Flaming
Donald F. Flanagan
Edward G. Flanagan
Edward James Flanagan
James Edward Flanagan
Jimmy G. Flanagan
Richard Arthur Flanagan
Thomas E. Flanagan
Samuel H. Flanary
Henry C. Flanders
John D. Flanders
James M. Flanigan
Douglas L. Flannery
Wayne V. Flannigan
Harold James Flarty
Morris E. Flater
Ervin Joe Flauger
Howard C. Flavell, Jr.
Robert D. Flear
Richard A. Fleck
Fred Fleener, Jr.
Stanley Merwin Fleenor
Richard E. Fleischer
Richard L. Fleischmann
Antonio J. Fleitas
Cecil Leon Fleming
Charles H. Fleming
Charles J. Fleming
Claude B. Fleming
Edward D. Fleming
Edward John Fleming
Frederick E. Fleming
Gearold Deloss Fleming
Isaac Fleming
James William Fleming, Jr.
John Fleming
John M. Fleming
Oranzel Fleming
Richard E. Fleming
Robert P. Fleming
Ronald R. Fleming
Sam Fleming, Jr.
Thomas H. Fleming
William J. Flemming
Charles C. Flener
Oscar Flenory
Donald L. Flentke
George J. Flerx
Charles F. Fletcher
Clyde W. Fletcher
Fred C. Fletcher
James A. Fletcher
James Harold Fletcher
John E. Fletcher
Marshall E. Fletcher
Morris W. Fletcher
Robert S. Fletcher
Roy L. Fletcher
Terrence W. Fletcher
William L. Fletcher
Kenneth C. Fletke
Leonard J. Flett
Wilmer G. Fleury

Jesse L. Flickinger
David H. Flight
James H. Fling, Jr.
Bobby D. Flinn
Robert L. Flinner
Cornelius H. Flint
Merton V. Floe
Robert Floeck
Edward A. Flom
David Roger Flood
Richard Augustine Flood
Robert F. Flood
Arnold R. Flook
Grady Harold Flook
Charles Kenneth Flora
John C. Flora
Paul E. Flora
Edward S. Florczyk
John A. Florek
Alfred S. Flores
Andres Flores
Braulio Flores
Ernesto M. Flores
Fidel Guzman Flores
Florencio Gomez Flores
Frank G. Flores, Jr.
Frank R. Flores
Froelan Flores
Henry Victor Flores
Jesus C. Flores
Manuel Flores
Manuel H. Flores, Jr.
Polito Flores
Roque Ike Flores
Will F. Flores
William Billy Flores
Willie S. Flores
Julio Flores-Baez
G. Flores-Maldonado
Juan R. Flores-Navarro
Edward G. Floreskul
Daniel Wilburn Florey
John Frank Florez
Raymond E. Flortard
James A. Flory
Rene Joseph Flory, Jr.
Wayne K. Floto
John James Flournoy
Arthur S. Flower
Paul Cahall Flower
Alflorance Flowers
Clyde Flowers
Henry E. Flowers
Horrie Flowers, Jr.
Joe Flowers
Kenneth R. Flowers
Lonnie B. Flowers
Obert B. Flowers
Odis B. Flowers
Ronald W. Flowers
Albert Sidney Floyd
Andrew J. Floyd, Jr.
Cecil R. Floyd
Ernest L. Floyd
Jack Floyd
James E. Floyd
James E. Floyd
John C. Floyd
Lawrence Blake Floyd
Newt H. Floyd
Thomas Floyd
Arthur L. Flucker
James D. Flud
Martin C. Fluegel
Elmer Fluellen
Mozell Fluellin
Jerry Flug
Julius Cleveland Fluhr, Jr.
Peter P. Fluhr, Jr.
Robert Stanley Fluhr
Robert W. Fluke
Arthur L. Fluker
Robert N. Fluno
Clifford A. Fly
Charles Leo Flynn
Jerry P. Flynn
John A. Flynn
Norman E. Flynn
Patrick J. Flynn
Philip D. Flynn
Roy S. Flynn, Jr.
Walter Matthew Flynn
William J. Flynn
Donald G. Fochler
Irvin E. Focht
James B. Foggin
Billy Gene Fogle
Leonard A. Fogle
Robert D. Fogle

Warnell A. Fogle
Weldon S. Fogleman
Roma Carl Foglesong, Jr.
Ronald Joseph Foglietta
Edward Thomas Fogo
Lloyd O. Fogt
Wilbur W. Folck
Arthur A. Foley, Jr.
Charles Thomas Foley
Duane L. Foley
Earl W. Foley
James J. Foley
Michael E. Foley
Paul Foley
Raymond P. Foley
Robert J. Foley
Dallas Lee Folkner
Charles C. Follese
Erwin J. Folmar
James H. Fomond
Walter A. Fonder
Gerald E. Fondry
Hong Fong
Oliver Fong
William C. Fonner
Miguel A. Fonseca
M. E. Fonseca-Acevedo
Rafael Font-Guzman
Benjamin Fontaine
Ernest J. Fontaine
Norman R. Fontaine
Robert L. Fontana
Alvin Fontenot
Burkeman Fontenot
Joseph C. Fontenot
Joseph W. Fontenot
Samuel Fonville
Howard Osborn Foor
John Foot
Victor Gene Foote
James W. Foran
Albert P. Forand
Billie J. Forbes
Charles M. Forbes
Dewey A. Forbes
Donald Wayne Forbes
John J. Forbes, Jr.
John M. Forbes
Wesley O. Forbord
Alvis L. Ford
Arthur F. Ford
Ben E. Ford
Charles W. Ford
Clyde S. Ford
Donald R. Ford
Douglas Ford
Emmitt M. Ford
Ernest C. Ford
Eugene W. Ford
Francis Edward Ford
Frank D. Ford
Frankie J. Ford
Henry L. Ford
Hershel Ford
Isaac D. Ford
James E. Ford
James L. Ford
James Rudolph Ford
Joe L. Ford
John L. Ford
John W. Ford
Kenneth E. Ford
Leonard Ford
Lornel Ford
Marlyn Carr Ford, Jr.
Maurice E. Ford
Nolan Earl Ford
Norman Richard Ford
Patrick H. Ford, Jr.
Paul Leon Ford
Paul R. Ford
Robert E. Ford
Robert M. Ford
Russell Hinton Ford
Stephen T. Ford
Wilbert Smiley Ford
Wilfred S. Ford
Leroy S. Fordahl
Norman H. Forder
Ralph W. Fordyce
John E. Fore
Charles E. Forehand
Thomas A. Forehand
Doyle Foreman
Ira Lee Foreman
Jack C. Foreman
Kenneth R. Foreman
Russell John Foreman
Wiliam J. Foreman

Charles R. Foren
James L. Forenza
Norman D. Forget
Russell S. Forgrave, Jr.
Henry A. Foris
John C. Forkel
Kenneth R. Forman
Conrad F. Formica
George G. Fornelius, Jr.
Frank H. Forney
Andrew H. Fornica
Charles G. Fornuff
Charles D. Forrest
David Alan Forrest
Edsel Grady Forrester
Emmett E. Forrester
Jack Forrester
Kenneth B. Forrester
Eugene R. Forsgren, Jr.
Thomas L. Forshay
Frederick P. Forste
Harold S. Forster
Carl L. Forsyth, Jr.
Robert N. Forsythe
Robert W. Forsythe
Walter Corlett Fort
James Forte
Jessie L. Forte
Peter R. Forte, Jr.
William H. Fortenberry
William Edgar Fortin
Roger D. Fortinberry
Juan C. Fortis
Donald Fortner
Gilbert H. Fortner
William H. Fortner
Francis W. Fortney
George A. Foshee
Delbert J. Fosnaugh
Beverley H. Foss
Eugene A. Foss
George H. Foss
Glen E. Foss
Kenneth C. Foss
Oliver R. Foss, Jr.
Benny G. Foster
Bobbie Foster
Carl F. Foster
Cearvest Foster
Charles E. Foster
Charlie Foster
Clyde N. Foster
David W. Foster
Delmar L. Foster
Donald K. Foster
Donald Sylvester Foster
Elmer E. Foster
Garfield Foster
George E. Foster
Harold E. Foster
Harry S. Foster
Henry Myers Foster
James H. Foster
Joseph M. Foster
Kimble H. Foster
Larry F. Foster
Lewis C. Foster
Milton Foster
Paul Riley Foster
Richard K. Foster
Robert A. Foster
Robert B. Foster
Robert G. Foster
Robert H. Foster
Robert J. Foster
Robert Richard Foster
Sidney E. Foster
Spurge Foster
Thomas E. Foster, Jr.
Thomas H. Foster
Virgil L. Foster, Jr.
Wilber N. Foster
Wilson P. Foster
Robert E. Fostie
Burl Foston
Chris Fotinos
Bernard E. Fouchey
James Arch Foulks, Jr.
Andrew F. Fountai
Edward J. Fountain
Robert O. Fountain
Robert Steven Fountain
Henry J. Fouracres
Donald R. Fourman
Kenneth L. Fouse
Alfred Dell Foust, Jr.
Arthur J. Foust
Clarence D. Foust
Frank Andrew Foust

Noel Leonard Fouts
Sanford W. Fouty
Alvie L. Fowler, Jr.
Alwyn F. Fowler
Charlie H. Fowler
Darrell L. Fowler
Dorsey R. Fowler
George F. Fowler
Harry T. Fowler
Keith B. Fowler
Murry Neil Fowler
Norman Clyde Fowler
Samuel R. Fowler
Sherman E. B. Fowler
Thomas O. Fowler
Walter W. Fowler
William C. Fowler
William T. Fowler
Alfred W. Fox
Colby G. Fox
Eldon Eugene Fox
F. C. Fox
Frank W. Fox
Gordon R. Fox
Henry Robert Fox
James L. Fox
Jared W. Fox
John E. Fox
John F. Fox
Louis David Fox, Jr.
Orrin Russell Fox
Richard Fox
Richard A. Fox
Richard A. Fox
Robert F. Fox
Robert J. Fox
Robert L. Fox
Robert Leroy Fox
Topel C. Fox
William C. Fox
Grover J. Foy
Sam Foy
David D. Frack
Peter K. Fraenkel
Joseph P. Fragosa
Melvin P. Frahm
Gilbert S. Fraize
Edward Leo Frakes
Robert J. Fralich
Donald Paul Frame
Lanty R. Frame
Donald Richard France
Earnest France
John Franchino
James Wilson Franchow
Anthony P. Francis, Jr.
Charles Henry Francis
Eddie L. Francis
Edward Rolland Francis
Gilbert D. Francis
Kaye D. Francis
Richard E. Francis
William Francis
William R. Francis
George Francischelli
Eliazar Franco
Julio E. Franco
Noe Franco
Benoit R. Francoeur
Joseph L. Francomano
Eugene B. Francovich
Joseph F. Franczak
James C. Frangello
Dewayne N. Frank
Elmer N. Frank
Larry A. Frank 26
Louis M. Frank
Robert F. Frank
William A. Frank
Ned Charles Frankart
Howard M. Frankel
Vernon F. Frankenberg
Wilfred G. Frankenberg
Francis Frankey
Allen Franklin
Anthony Emlen Franklin
Benjamin A. Franklin
Donald E. Franklin
Ernest Newton Franklin
Harold Franklin
Hiram Franklin
James B. Franklin
James L. Franklin
James L. Franklin
James L. Franklin
Jeff Franklin
John D. Franklin, Jr.
John Franklin, Jr.
Julius C. Franklin

Paul Allan Franklin
Preston Franklin
Rayfus Franklin
Richard L. Franklin
Teddy L. Franklin
Thomas S. Franklin
William D. Franklin
Winburn B. Franklin
William Mark Frankovich
Alfonso Franks
Charles Joseph Franks
Henry A. Franks
Norman Franks, Jr.
Jack M. Frans
George Arthur Frantz
Albert G. Frantzich
Edwin Fred Franz
Eugene Leo Franz
Orvill E. Franzen
Gary Everett Frase
Harrison M. Fraser
William H. Fraser
Donald M. Frasher
Adam D. Frasure
Jack L. Frater
James J. Frattaroli
Alfred L. Fratto
Arthur J. Fratus, Jr.
George E. Fray
C. L. Fraze
John David Frazer
Carlton Frazier
Charlie Frazier, Jr.
David W. Frazier
Donnie L. Frazier
Edward M. Frazier
Elam L. Frazier
Glen Elsworth Frazier
Herbert W. Frazier
Hugh Robert Frazier
James C. Frazier
James Lowman Frazier
Joe P. Frazier
John A. Frazier
John W. Frazier
Junior E. Frazier
Reginald E. Frazier
Robert Frazier
Vance N. Frazier
William H. Frazier, Jr.
William Roy Frazier
Richard Parman Frazure
Norman Peter Frazzini
Wilson A. Frease
John Frech, Jr.
Charles J. Frechette 28
Donald L. Fredenburg
Johnny J. Frederic
Autrey W. Frederick
Howard B. Frederick
Nicholas J. Frederick
Willard Novia Frederick
William H. Frederick
Dean Edward Fredericks
Joyce E. Fredericksen
Ralph T. Frederiksen
Willie Lee Fredrick
Ralph L. Fredrickson
William T. Fredrickson, Jr.
Marvin E. Freed
Arthur N. Freeman
Bill Henry Freeman
Billy E. Freeman
Billy L. Freeman
Bobby Eugene Freeman
Calvin R. Freeman
Charles F. Freeman
Dariel J. Freeman
Donald R. Freeman
Elmer Freeman
George Allen Freeman
Grady L. Freeman
Harold W. Freeman
Harry W. Freeman
James A. Freeman
James W. Freeman
James W. Freeman
Jean Freeman
Jim C. Freeman
John Freeman
John H. Freeman
John Nance Freeman
John W. Freeman
Leonard Freeman, Jr.
Niel M. Freeman
Oswald B. Freeman
Robert A. Freeman
Stacy H. Freeman
Theron H. Freeman

Walter H. Freeman
William F. Freeman, Jr.
Anton Joseph Freer
Arthur W. Fregeau
Lyle A. Frego
Rudolph C. Fregoso
Joe L. Freitas
Leo Thomas Freitas
Arthur R. French
Cecil W. French
Charlie French
David J. French
Earl R. French, Jr.
Elvin E. French
Hartwick T. French
Huey P. French
Jennings French
Othar C. French
William L. French
Jimmie Earl Frenchman
Ramon M. Frescas
Richard D. Fresen
Arthur D. Freshour, Jr.
Cecil T. Fretwell
Aloysius J. Freund
Edward Ivan Frey, Jr.
Frank Theodore Frey
Harvey L. Frey
Hugh G. Frey
Kenneth J. Frey
Stanley W. Frey
John W. Freymiller
Harold J. Freymuth
Reuben W. Freytag
Louis B. Frezzo
Tedward E. Friar
Harry D. Frick
Leroy Arnold Frick
Ervin A. Fricke
Billie J. Fricker
Dewey M. Friday
James Francis Friday
Robert E. Friday
Richard L. Friedlund
Donald A. Friedly
Frederick A. Friedman
Richard Melvin Friedman
Ernest D. Friel
James B. Friel
John P. Friel, Jr.
Harvey Jessie Friend
James Emerson Friend
William B. Friend, Jr.
Cleo Bernard Friess
Armand Alfred Frigon
William Paul Friley
Ralph G. Fringeli
Jay W. Frisbey
James Nelson Frisbie
Samuel E. Frisco
Robert D. Frisk
Herman R. Friske
Edward Fristock
Charles D. Frisz
Clarence H. Fritsche
Billy E. Fritts
Dawsey H. Fritts
Charles P. Fritz, Jr.
Clarence J. Fritz
Don E. Fritz
Joseph E. Fritz
Marland E. Fritz
Gerald Kenneth Frizzell
Amadio J. Frizzi
Junior F. Frock
Ernest A. Froeb
Emil Froehlich
William Arthur Froelich
Van Jack Froenfield
Theodore C. Frois
Gordon N. Froisness
Wayne Fromback, Jr.
Joseph B. Fromhold
Van J. Fronefield
Jerrold Fronzowiak
Peter Charles Froslev
Carl D. Frost
Donald W. Frost
John S. Frost
Lewis B. Frost
Paul A. Frost
Roger Alan Frost
William B. Frost
William R. Frost, Jr.
Alan D. Fry
Jesse Lewis Fry, Jr.
Lyman Fry
William Lloyd Fry
Harold E. Fryar

David Frye
Jack L. Frye
James H. Frye
Samuel O. Frye
Vernon F. Frye
Arby A. Fryer, Jr.
Thomas J. Fryer, Jr.
Kyrle S. Fryling, Jr.
Norbert W. Fryman, Jr.
Clement D. Frymark
Marvin C. Frysinger
John J. Fucito
Clarence Fudge, Jr.
Donald E. Fueglein
Alois Anton Fuehrer
Dale L. Fugate
Hobart Fugate, Jr.
Joseph J. Fugate
Leonard Fugate
Norris Fugate
Richard Fugate
James B. Fugett
William Don Fugit
Donald A. Fuhrman
Edward F. Fuhrman, Jr.
Frederick E. Fuhrman
Samuel A. Fujii
Junichi Fujimoto
Hitoshi Fujita
Takeshi Fujita
Richard Otto Fuka
Haruo Fukamizu
Ralph T. Fukumoto
Yoshimi Fukumoto
Albert W. Fulk, Jr.
Lester E. Fulk
Vernon E. Fulkerson
Daniel W. Fulks
Ira J. Fulks
Orlan J. Fulks
Francis J. Fullam
Gerald W. Fullbright
Robert L. Fullen
Donald A. Fuller
Henry A. Fuller
Kemper Fuller
Noah D. Fuller
Richard Carrell Fuller
Robert L. Fuller
Terrell J. Fuller
Vern Harris Fuller
William E. Fuller
Willie C. Fuller
Wirt C. Fuller, Jr.
Donald V. Fullerton
Harold O. Fullerton
Marvin C. Fulton
William Fulton, Jr.
Everett E. Fultz
John Fultz
John Francis Funa
Thomas Y. Funakoshi
James G. Funderburk
Joseph R. Funes
Robert Milton Funk
Robert R. Funke
Eugene L. Funkhouser
Marvin C. Funkhouser
Vernon B. Funkhouser
Wayne L. Funkhouser
John M. Fuore
Ernest V. Fuqua, Jr.
Fred Fuqua
Leonard L. Furbee
Francis N. Furey
Robert Daniel Furlow
Cecil A. Furman
Norman J. Furman
Walter F. Furman
Robert E. Furr
Lester J. Furseth
John Allen Furst
Walter C. Furtado
Isaac Furukawa
Daniel Gabriel Fury
Charles M. Fuson
Herschel E. Fuson
Palmer G. Fuson
William G. Fuss
Norman Fussell
Arvous Futch
James T. Futch
Harold E. Fye
Luke Cole Fyffe
Sherwood D. Fyler

— G —

Christian Peter Gaael, Jr.

Harold R. Gaberdiel
Benny G. Gable, Jr.
John W. Gable
James S. Gablehouse
William C. Gabos
Charles R. Gabriel
Murphy J. Gabriel
Carl L. Gabrielson
Peter J. Gabrish
James M. Gaby
Louis R. Gaccione
Rudolph V. Gacobelli
Andrew J. Gaddis
Robert H. Gaedeke
William R. Gaeuman
Patrick J. Gaffey
Kenneth Leroy Gage
Martin H. Gage
Edward R. Gagenah
Gordon W. Gager
Sydney A. Gager
Daniel F. Gagliardi
Anthony H. Gagliormella
Gerald Joseph Gagne
Joseph E. Gagne
Antonio T. J. Gagnon
Arnold Gene Gagnon
Jesse B. Gagnon
John William Gahan
Charles N. Gahm
Robert George Gailey
Billie H. Gainer
Jack C. Gainer
Fletcher Gaines
Jack Dee Gaines
Lawrence W. Gaines
Melvin Albert Gaines
Obie Mack Gaines
Van Edward Gaines
Gary P. Gainey
Marvin Lee Gainey
Thomas L. Gainey
W. J. Gainey
Charles Gains
James Edward Gaisford
Jesse M. Gaitan
Jimmie J. Gaitan
Willie Gaither, Jr.
Alfredo Gajeton
Alicea Angel Galan
Edwin L. Galarneau
Thomas P. Galberth, Jr.
Presiliano Galbon
Orville J. Gale
Stewart J. Gale
George M. Gales
Michael Galetie
Hugh E. Galigher
Capiel Raf Galindo
Manuel J. Galindo, Jr.
Roberto R. Galindo
George A. Galion
Rosalio Galius
William J. Galivan
Francis Charles Gall
Paul S. Galla
Donald J. Gallacher
Donald W. Gallagher
Jack J. Gallagher
Jerome E. Gallagher
Lawrence W. Gallagher
Patrick J. Gallagher
Patrick J. Gallagher
Patrick J. Gallagher
Raymond X. Gallagher
Robert J. Gallagher
Herman David Gallant
James Alvin Gallant
Marcel A. Gallant
Morris Leo Gallant
Raymond Henry Gallant
Charles P. Gallardo
Guadalupe Gallart
Ernest E. Gallatin
Gilbert G. Gallego
Albert Gallegos
Frank R. Gallegos
Jose Gallegos, Jr.
Polito G. Gallegos
Victor I. Gallerani
Kenneth Eugene Galley
Armand J. Galli
John A. Galligan
Joseph E. Gallitz
Angelo Benjamin Gallo
George Gallo
Nickolas R. Gallo
Arnold C. Galloway
David L. Galloway

Gordon Ray Galloway
Harold J. Galloway
Irven Galloway
Paul E. Galloway
C. Galloza-Mendoza
Cyril A. Gallup
William E. Gallup
Justus P. Gallus
Jose M. Galnares, Jr.
Richard Galpin
Robert L. Galt, Jr.
Manuel G. Galvan
Osvaldo R. Galvan
Willie V. Galvan
Bartholomew Galvin
Peter Galvin
Albert R. Gamache
Ames J. Gamache
Leo A. Gamache
Melvin Paul Gamache
Roy F. Gamache
Raymond A. Gamba
James D. Gambill
James L. Gambill
Calvin D. Gamble
David T. Gamble
Eldridge M. Gamble
Gilbert Gamble
Hence Gamble
Henry C. Gamble
Lawrence C. Gamble
Selestino M. Gambol
Harry P. H. Gambrel, Jr.
William Gambrell
Harry C. Gammage
James E. Gammans
Gordon C. Gammon
Wayne Gammon
Alfredo M. Gampon
James R. Gamwells
Pedro A. Ganal
Albert Ganchuk
David Gandin
Ike Gandy
John E. Gandy
Seiken Ganeku
Charles Gangl
Edward J. Ganis
Albert E. Gann
Clay W. Gann
Robert R. Gann
Michael Gannon
Valentine R. Gannon
William J. Gannon
Jay M. Gano
Ronald Arlo Ganoung
Walter J. Gant
Billie S. Gantt
Joseph Enoch Gantt
William W. Gantt
Lawrence J. Gapinski
Robert C. Gapinski
Richard C. Garabedian
Rufino Garalde
Dale T. Garber
Ralph E. Garbisch
Abel Garcia
Alfonso Garcia
Arthur D. Garcia
Arthur S. Garcia
Ayala Irene Garcia
Bartolome Garcia
Bennie Garcia
Carlos Garcia
Charles M. Garcia
Cresenciano Garcia, Jr.
Domingo Garcia
Domingo Garcia
Eddie M. Garcia
Edward L. Garcia
Emilio Garcia
Ernesto Garcia, Jr.
Fernando Luis Garcia
Frank Donald Garcia
Fred N. Garcia
Fredie Garcia
Guadalupe Garcia
Guillermo G. Garcia
Hiliberto Garcia
Ismael Garcia
Jack Garcia
John J. Garcia
John R. Garcia
Jose A. P. Garcia
Jose E. Garcia
Jose M. Garcia, Jr.
Joseph G. Garcia
Leon Athony Garcia
Leonard P. Garcia, Jr.

Luis G. Garcia
Manuel L. Garcia
Mose Garcia, Jr.
Oscar Garcia
Paul Garcia
Perfecto Garcia
Porfirio H. Garcia
Ralph Garcia
Ramiro Garcia
Raul G. Garcia
Raynaldo C. Garcia
Reginald J. Garcia
Richard Dickie Garcia
Roberto Garcia
Roger B. Garcia
Rosado Cand Garcia
Serafin R. Garcia
Steven M. Garcia
Tony Garcia
Victor Garcia
Ismael Garcia-Clara
Jose M. Garcia-Cruz
Jose Garcia-Marrero
Rafae Garcia-Ojeda
Isa Garcia-Oquendo
Garcia-Orlando
Carlos Garcia-Rivera
D. Garcia-Rodriguez
F. Garcia-Rodriguez
George B. Garden, Jr.
Monton L. Garder
Randall G. Gardien
Curtis C. Gardiner
Donald F. Gardiner
Murvee D. Gardiner
Beverly A. Gardner
Channing Gardner
Charles E. Gardner
Charles T. Gardner
Elmer D. Gardner
Frederick G. Gardner
Glenn Gardner
Henery L. Gardner
James D. Gardner
James D. Gardner
James O. Gardner
Koeling B. Gardner
Ladon A. Gardner
Lawrence B. Gardner
Lawrence N. Gardner
Maurice P. Gardner
Merritt H. Gardner
Ralph Henry Gardner
Tennie Gardner
Weldon Danforth Gardner
William Gardner
William B. Gardner
John F. Gargan
Joseph J. Gargiulo
Richard Joseph Garguillo
Robert Gariel
Albert W. Garland
Felix Garland
Fletcher R. Garland
James L. Garland
Rudolph C. Garland
Melvin R. Garlets
Donald Eugene Garman
George D. Garman
Harry G. Garman, Jr.
Paul P. Garman
William Knox Garmany
Wilton E. Garmon
Arvil R. Garner
Austin L. Garner
Charles D. Garner
Gordon Garner
Herman C. Garner
Hubert L. Garner
James W. Garner
Lester R. Garner
Maurice M. Garner
Max F. Garner
Patrick J. Garner
Ted Garner
Theo Levi Garner, Jr.
Charles E. Garnett
Charles J. Garnett
Stanley C. Garnett
William Earl Garnett
Gregorio Garnica
Ernest Joseph Garnier
Louis P. Garrell
Richard F. Garrels
Roger W. Garrepy
Ben Garrett
Bobby R. Garrett
Franklin Delano Garrett
George R. Garrett

Harry A. Garrett
Herbert J. Garrett
James Paul Garrett
John Holder Garrett
Lee M. Garrett
Lonnie O. Garrett
Nathaniel Garrett
Ralph E. Garrett
William F. Garrett
William L. Garrett
William M. Garrett
Lloyd G. Garrette, Jr.
Charles Garrigus
Gerald D. Garris
Charles Garrison
Dale R. Garrison
Fred Herren Garrison
Glenn T. Garrison
James Louis Garrison, Jr.
Jerry M. Garrison
Otis L. Garrison
Vernon T. Garrison
Leslie Lee Garrow
Billy E. Gartin
John L. Gartrell
Charles E. Garver
Richard Eugene Garver
Stanley F. Garvey
John H. Garvin, Jr.
Murrel Garvin
Robert M. Garvin
Theodore E. Garvin
George Garvis
Anthony Gary
George E. Gary
Louis Austinea Gary
Alberto B. Garza
Armando Moreno Garza
Gilberto Garza
Humberto Garza
John H. Garza
M. M. Garza
Mauro Garza, Jr.
Mike M. Garza
Nicolas C. Garza
Osbaldo Garza
Ricardo Garza
Richard Castillo Garza
Rubin F. Garza
Billie L. Gaskins
Charlie P. Gaskins
Clarence L. Gaskins
Webber J. Gaskins
Leroy P. Gaspard
Bert John Gaspord
Andrew J. Gasquet, Jr.
Bill Bruce Gass
Charles Gass
Clarence E. Gassman
Henry A. Gastelo
William K. Gaston
James E. Gatchel
Donald W. Gately
Donald L. Gates
Doyt K. Gates
Havert Luther Gates
Huston E. Gates
Roland L. Gates
Thomas V. Gates
William C. Gates, Jr.
Tommy Gatewood
Edward E. Gath
Eugene Gathers
Dale Gatten, Jr.
Robert Phillip Gaude, Jr.
Bernard J. Gaudet
Gilbert Raymond Gaudet
George A. Gaudette, Jr.
Wallace Gaudinier
William Marshall Gaul
William R. Gaul
Curtis C. Gauldin
Gilbert F. Gauldin
Thomas F. Gaule
Arthur G. Gault
Charles E. Gaumer
James Charles Gaun
James D. Gausnell
Franklin Dale Gaut
Gerald P. Gauthier
Normand Gautreau
Brockhart E. Gave
Robert A. Gavin
Martin J. Gavio
Andrew C. Gavurnik
Eugene A. Gawlik
Billy E. Gay
Charles L. Gay
Herbert L. Gay

James H. Gay
John S. Gay
Richard E. Gay
Romie R. Gay
Ramon Gaya-Arce
James D. Gayhart
John L. Gayhart
William L. Gayhart
Harold Gayle
Ulysses Gayle, Jr.
Alvin Gayles
William A. Gaylord
Joseph G. Gazaille, Jr.
William H. Gazaway, Jr.
Riley C. Gazzaway
Michael A. Gbur
Louis Orville Ge Rue
Peter L. Geannopulos
James H. Gearhart
William R. Gearhart
Billy Lewis Geary
Sterling Geary, Jr.
William L. Geary
Edgar N. Geater
Arthur William Gebaur, Jr.
Anthony Gebbia, Jr.
Ervin A. Gebhardt
James William Gebhardt
James E. Gebhart
William S. Gebou
Albert F. Geckle
Nelson Raymond Geddes
Kendall Courtney Gedney
Robert Earl Gedney
Clarence W. Gee
Richard Price Geer
William R. Geer, Jr.
James D. Geeslin
Robert Allen Gehman
Gilbert R. Gehrke
Marvin C. Geiger
Robert E. Geiger
Robert F. Geiger
Jack H. Geis
Joseph H. III Geis
Ronald J. Geis
Robert L. Geise
Donald Bruce Geisler
Richard J. Geissler
C. R. Geiszler
Willard F. Geivett
James F. Gendilo
Armand J. Gendreau
Frank J. Gendusa
Robert M. Genereux
Harold A. Gengler
Paul E. Genino
Thomas J. Genis
Anthony Genovese
Victor James Genre
Morris C. Gensch
Charles M. Gentle, Jr.
Archie C. Gentry
Arglister A. Gentry
Charles C. Gentry
Edwin Gentry
James D. Gentry
John Samuel Gentry
Ray Gentry
Robert E. Gentry
Troy L. Gentry
Willie G. Gentry
William D. Genung
Harold W. Geoit
Burton J. George
Carl B. George
Charles George
Chriss George, Jr.
Earl W. George
Edward George
Hogal M. George
Larson George
Nicholas J. George
Ralph F. A. George
Thomas C. George
Walter Wilfred George
Wilbur G. George
Winifred Robert George
Harold O. Georgeson
Frank M. Geraghty
James J. Geraghty
William R. Geraghty
William D. Gerald
Donald Conrad Gerber
Edward J. Gerber
Joseph Gerchman
Rosario Gerena
John George Gergely
Francis Gene Gergen

Kenneth G. Gerhard
Robert L. Gerhart
John L. Gerheart
George J. Gerig
John L. Gerig, Jr.
Robert A. Gerlach
Richard E. Gerrish, Jr.
Donald L. Gerrits
Daniel W. Gerrity
Robert M. Gerron
Arthur Joseph Gersebeck
John P. Gershewski, Jr.
Anthony Gersoskey
John H. Gerstner
Richard F. Gerstner
Robert Gerstner
Albert R. Gerth
Harley G. Gerth
Robert H. Gertsen
Norman Arthur Gertzen
Louis Orville Gerue
Reginald E. Gervais
Robert J. Gervais
Richard M. Gessaman
Alvin B. Gessner
Maurice S. Getchell
Eugene L. Gettig
Charles E. Gettings
Gordon J. Gettman
Ernest E. Getts
Charles Samuel Getz
Meyer Louis Getz
M. C. Geurin, Jr.
Albert Jose Gevara
Lennard E. Gewin
Basil William Gewvellis
Robert F. Geyer
Bernard J. Geygan, Jr.
George R. Gfeller
Frank Gfroerer
George Gherghescu, Jr.
Donald Charles Ghezzi
Mario R. Ghinazzi
Anthony J. Ghiozzi
George Gia
Joseph Giacopelli
Dominic Gianchetta, Jr.
Felix Giangrande
Fred J. Giangrasso
Frank J. Gianitelli
Charles Giannetto
Ralph Giannotta
Frank J. Giantitelli
Robert Duncan Gibb
William H. Gibbens
Carl R. Gibbons
Carl William Gibbons
James Gibbons
Richard P. Gibbons
Billy H. Gibbs
Clifford L. Gibbs
Joe P. Gibbs
Malcolm A. Gibbs
Walter H. Gibbs
Eddie Gibby
George W. Gibeaut, Jr.
George G. G Giblin
Owen J. Giblin
Aubrey L. Gibson
Carl A. Gibson
Charles E. Gibson
Charles G. Gibson
Charles L. Gibson
Charles V. Gibson
Clarence E. Gibson, Jr.
Clifton E. Gibson
Dallas W. Gibson
David W. Gibson
Denny J. Gibson
Don E. Gibson
Donald D. Gibson
Donald W. Gibson
Edbridge C. Gibson
Edward Gibson
Edward B. Gibson
Elbridge C. Gibson
Frank W. Gibson
Garrett F. Gibson
George D. Gibson
George Oliver Gibson
Grady W. Gibson
Guy T. Gibson
Hal Thomas Gibson
Hayward L. Gibson
Henry Edward Gibson
Howard J. Gibson
John O. Gibson
John R. Gibson
Johnny W. Gibson

Karl H. Gibson
Lewis C. Gibson
Lonnie E. Gibson
Luther E. Gibson
Maxie Leverne Gibson
Rex D. Gibson
Robert L. Gibson
Royce C. Gibson
Willard M. Gibson
William A. Gibson
Zollie Gibson
Kimbough Giddens
Albert E. Giddings
Joseph A. Giddings, Jr.
William James Giddings
Herbert L. Gideon
James Gidron
George Giedosh
Scott George Gier
Richard F. Giese
John Gieseking
William E. Giffen
Clyde Marvin Gifford
Jack Brennan Gifford
Merle C. Gifford
Miles R. Gifford, Jr.
Troy H. Gifford
Quillie S. Gigger
Thomas E. Giglio
Albert P. Giguere
Robert D. Gilardi
Robert Wesley Gilardi
Arthur J. Gilbert
Billy M. Gilbert
Charles M. Gilbert
Chesley George Gilbert
Clarence J. Gilbert
Daniel N. Gilbert
David O. Gilbert
Dennis A. Gilbert
Foster Gilbert, Jr.
Francis Gilbert, Jr.
Frank Joseph Gilbert
Garland Gilbert
James H. Gilbert
John M. Gilbert
Marvin L. Gilbert
Nathan Gilbert
Raymond B. Gilbert
Robert G. Gilbert
Robert Henry Gilbert
Russell J. Gilbert
Sylvester E. Gilbert
William E. Gilbert
Francis R. Gilbertson
William F. Gilboe
Michael J. Gilbride
George E. Gilchrist
James C. Gilchrist
Tom Allen Gilchrist
Willie Arthur Gilchrist
Elbert E. Gilder, Jr.
Hume Anderson Giles, Jr.
Ralph Regis Giles
Robert J. Gilford, Jr.
Richard C. Gilkey
Robert L. Gilkison
Bobby D. Gill
Bobby R. Gill
Charles L. Gill
Eugene C. Gill
Gerald S. Gill
Harles Gill
Howard L. Gill
Irving L. Gill
John H. Gill
Leo G. Gill
Louis Marvin Gill
Samuel F. Gill, Jr.
Wayne B. Gill, Jr.
James Letcher Gillam
J. W. Gilland
James W. Gillaspy
Paul J. Gillaspy
Durston Dwain Gillean
Charles W. Gilles, Jr.
John H. Gilles
Walter Peter Gilles
Champ G. Gillespie
David Ray Gillespie
Evan L. Gillespie
George D. Gillespie, Jr.
Lawrence T. Gillespie
Robert Gillespie
Robert Wheeler Gillespie
Rubin W. Gillespie
Ray Gillett
Richard Gillett
Claude S. Gillette

John F. Gillette
Robert Lee Gillette
Billy J. Gilley
Darrell G. Gilley
Edward L. Gilley
Homer B. Gilley
Melvin James Gilley
Claude Gilliam
Patteson Gilliam
Thomas E. Gilliam
Volney H. Gilliam
W. M. Gilliland, Jr.
Buford C. Gilliard
Edmund B. Gilligan
Delmas W. Gillikin
Charles L. Gilliland
Edward L. Gilliland
William L. Gilliland
Charles E. Gillingham, Jr.
Daniel E. Gillis
Richard A. Gillis
Leroy Gillispie
Willie J. Gills
Thomas F. Gilmartin
Donald L. Gilmore
Edward Eugene Gilmore
John R. Gilmore
Knots Gilmore
Lawrence J. Gilmore
Melvin G. Gilmore
Timothy J. Gilmore
Bernard J. Gilroy
Hiram E. Gilroy
William A. Gilson
Clifford T. Gilstad
Robert Mardin Giltner
Marvin C. Gilvin
Edmund G. Gincley
Wilbur G. Gincley
Wayne E. Ging
Robert L. Ginger
Rex D. Gingles
Leon Robert Ginglewood
Alver H. Ginn
Floyd A. Ginn
Dominic J. Giordano
William V. Giovanniello
Joseph L. Giovenco, Jr.
Dallas L. Gipson
Glenn H. Gipson
Jim Gipson
Ralph James Gipson
Oscar P. Girany
Andrew Girard
Vernon E. Girdley, Jr.
Edwin Giron
Emil Joseph Girona
Frederick J. Giroux
William H. Gish
Harry C. Gittelson
James W. Gittings, Jr.
Conrad M. Gitzen
Charles J. Gitzlaff
Vincenzo Giuffrida
Peter R. Giulioni
Salvatore Giusto, Jr.
Donald Fountain Givens
Thomas F. Givens
Martin Lionel Givot
Wilbur E. Glace
Elmer T. Gladden
James W. Gladden
Alphons F. Gladkowski
Benjamin F. Gladney
Leroy Gladney
Louis A. Gladney
Charles R. Gladstone
Peter Gladwell, Jr.
Edgar S. Glaise
Robert T. Glakeler
Harold B. Glancy
Michael W. Glaser
Francis T. Glasgow
Frank E. Glasgow
James Edward Glasgow
Ralph N. Glasgow
Henry H. Glashoff, Jr.
August J. Glasmeier
Morris Glasper
Alfred B. Glass
Arthur W. Glass
Cecil Robert Glass
Heath Thurman Glass, Jr.
Herman Glass
John R. Glass
Raymond Glass
Fletcher Glasscox, Jr.
Gerald W. Glasser
Martin J. Glasser

340

Jonas W. Glassgow
Harold S. Glauder
Joseph M. Glavina
Kenneth H. Glawf
Claude Glaze
Robert L. Glaze
Bruno Glazers
Edward J. Gleason
John J. Gleason
Norman L. Gleaton
James Albert Gleaves, Jr.
Charles F. Glenn
Jack D. Glenn
Lester E. Glenn
Philip K. Glenn
Robert L. Glenn
Patrick R. Glennon
Billy F. Glessner
Milton Glessner, Jr.
Leonard G. Glica
William A. Glick
Donald E. Glidden
Vernon H. Glidden
Vernon R. Glidden
James L. Glidewell
Joseph Stanley Gliniak
Morgan G. Glinkerman
Charles Olan Glisson, Jr.
Paul H. Gloria
Alphonso L. Glover
Carnese Glover
Charles C. Glover
Charles H. Glover
Clell C. Glover
Doyle E. Glover
Joseph E. Glover, Jr.
Joseph R. Glover
Paul R. Glover
Ralph L. Glover
Richard H. Glover
Robert T. Glover
Thomas Glover, Jr.
Alpho A. Glowaczewski
Leroy M. Gluckman
William J. Glunz
John G. Gnall
Eual Goad
Homer J. Goad
William E. Goan
Samuel H. Goats
Pryor Gobble
Arvle G. Gober
Bernard J. Goble
Julius R. Goc
Ralph J. Godbout
Charles A. Godchaux
Jack M. Goddard
Lionel Godeaux
Earl J. Godfrey
Edgar R. Godfrey
Leland Clair Godfrey
Raymond D. Godfrey, Jr.
Robert E. Godfrey
Wilford G. Godfrey
Carl L. Goding
Aubrey Godwin
Charles W. Godwin
Eli Godwin
Howard Godwin, Jr.
John M. Godwin
Robert E. Godwin
Clyde Goe
Donald Edward Goebel
Duane E. Goebel
Edwin Goede, Jr.
John F. Goeken
Gilbert George Goepel
Theodore J. Goerge
Carl George Goering
Reuben J. Goerl
Richard H. Goerlich
Robert G. Goerlich
John Baptist Goery
Charles C. Goetschius
Harry Goetting
George R. Goetz
Herbert Herman Goetz
Marvin Goetz
William C. Goetz
William O. Goetz
Charles Curtis Goff
Kenneth E. Goff
Kennetth Wilber Goff
Wallace E. Goff
Willie Kelton Goff
Dean R. Goforth
Donald A. Goggins
Joseph N. Goggleye
Stanley A. Gogoj

Lavern P. Gohl
Paul R. Gohlke
Ronald W. Goik
Martin L. Goins
William R. Goins
Donald C. Gokel
Alfred Gold
Lawrence M. Gold
Murray Gold
Mathew John Golda, Jr.
Arnold Jay Goldberg
Bailey H. Goldberg
Irwin Louis Goldberg
Leonard S. Goldberg
Alphonce Golden
Billy R. Golden
Donal L. Golden
Donald E. Golden
Herbert Golden
Newman Camay Golden
Peter T. Golden
Richard Mead Golden
Robert L. Golden
Walter T. Golden
William E. Golden
Bernard Golding
Herbert Louis Golding
Elmer E. Goldman
Johnny W. Goldman
Mister Goldman
Hilliard Mayer Goldorf
Thomas O. Goldsberry
Paul D. Goldsborough
Harold B. Goldsmith
Leonard W. Goldsmith
Melvin Eugene Goldsmith
Raymond J. Goldsmith
Fred Goldstein
Lawrence Goldstein
Leroy Goldstein
Max D. Goldstein
Jack L. Goldston
Leroy Goldston, Jr.
James E. Goldsworthy
Albert Elijah Goldy
Charles P. Golisano
William Robert Goll
Joseph Henry Gollner
Benjamin J. Golston
Arlyn R. Golter
Nicholas N. Gombos
Antone Gomes
John Henry Gomes, Jr.
Robert Gomes
Benjamin Gomez
Edward Gomez
Enrique G. Gomez
Felipe C. Gomez
Felipe C. Gomez
Gustavo K. Gomez
Jaime Ovidio Gomez
Joseph Gomez
Luis Gomez
Moreno Benjamin Gomez
Pete Gomez, Jr.
Richard Z. Gomez
Roy Gomez
Ruben J. Gomez
Vincente G. Gomez
William C. Gomez
William M. Gomez
Donald H. Gonano
Harry J. Gonia
Harold L. Gonsalves
Chester H. Gonse
Richard F. Gonsiorowski
Henry P. Gonsouland
John Stanley Gonteski
Alejandro A. Gonzales
Alex L. Gonzales
Alfonso Gonzales
Alvin J. Gonzales
Andrew L. Gonzales
Armando Gonzales
Conrad Gonzales
Domingo J. Gonzales
Donald P. Gonzales
George C. Gonzales
Gilberto Gonzales
Henry C. Gonzales
Joe Gonzales
Joe F. Gonzales
Jose Gonzales
Leo Robert Gonzales
Pedro Velasco Gonzales
Roger Gonzales
Roosevelt Gonzales
Rudolph V. Gonzales
Servando Gonzales

Toribio M. Gonzales
Eusebio Gonzales-Osorio
Anastacio Gonzalez, Jr.
Armando Pedro Gonzalez
Arnold Gonzalez
Garcia Pe Gonzalez
George L. Gonzalez
Hernandez L. R. Gonzalez
Ignacio Salazar Gonzalez
Jose Gonzalez
Juan A. Gonzalez
Juan E. Gonzalez
Luis Gonzalez
Manuel E. Gonzalez
Manuel Y. Gonzalez
Oscar Gonzalez
Osoria E. Gonzalez
Pierluissi W. Gonzalez
Roberto G. Gonzalez
Santos Gonzalez
Victor Gonzalez
E. Gonzalez-Abreu
Manuel Gonzalez-Bernard
J. Gonzalez-Calzada
D. Gonzalez-Cardona
Pablo Gonzalez-Colon
C. Gonzalez-Cordero
Ramon A. Gonzalez-Cruz
P. Gonzalez-Encarnacio
L. Gonzalez-Martinez
Israel Gonzalez-Nazario
Juan E. Gonzalez-Ortiz
Justo E. Gonzalez-Ortiz
V. R. Gonzalez-Perez
I. Gonzalez-Pizarro
J. A. Gonzalez-Ramirez
Porfirio Gonzalez-Renta
Juan Gonzalez-Rivera
Angel Gonzalez-Rosario
Israel Gonzalez-Saez
A. Gonzalez-Santiago
W. Gonzalez-Soto
David Gooch
Dinsmore T. Gooch, Jr.
John A. Gooch
Roscoe Fletcher Good, Jr.
Thomas E. Good
William H. Good
John E. Goodall
Robert Goodall
William Roberts Iii Goodall
Clair Goodblood
Mowrey Goodbread
Allen R. Goode
John Goode
David Theodore Gooden
Nelson B. Goodenough
John W. Goodheart
James Lemuel Goodin
Hershel B. Gooding
Luther O. Gooding, Jr.
William Ernest Gooding
Glenn Harold Goodlander
John S. Goodlive, Jr.
Thomas Goodloe
Dale Edmund Goodman
Donald R. Goodman
Donald S. Goodman
Edward Herbert Goodman
George Morris Goodman
Grover D. Goodman
James C. Goodman
Richard L. Goodman, Jr.
Wendell R. Goodman
Wilburn M. J. Goodman
William L. Goodman
Gerald W. Goodner
Floyd Vaughn Goodrich
Donald J. Goodridge
Harlan Gay Goodroad
William E. Goodrum
Carl B. Goodsell
Paul R. Goodson
Andrew J. Goodwin
Bert L. Goodwin
Bobbie Alfred Goodwin
Claude Reginald Goodwin
Elmore B. Goodwin
Frank Goodwin, Jr.
George Goodwin, Jr.
Howard C. Goodwin
Martin H. Goodwin
Robert J. Goodwin
Robert L. Goodwin
William D. Goodwin
William J. Goodwin
James E. Goody
William P. Goodyear
Connie Goosby

Leroy Goosen
Robert J. Gora
Edwin S. Goraj
Delbert B. Gorby
Wilfred F. Gordanier
James Edward Gordley
Alfred N. Gordon
Alfred Nelson Gordon
Charles J. Gordon
Clarence J. Gordon, Jr.
Clyde O. Gordon
David C. Gordon
David M. Gordon
Edward J. Gordon
Ernest J. Gordon
George L. Gordon
George T. Gordon
Homer G. Gordon
John Robert Gordon
Paul M. Gordon
Richard James Gordon
Robert H. Gordon
Will H. Gordon, Jr.
William Clark Gordon
William Lloyd Gordon
Gerald King Gordy
Dionicio Juan Gorena, Jr.
Arthur C. Gorman
Frank G. Gorman, Jr.
Harold L. Gorman
John R. Gorman
Kenneth J. Gorman
Norbert J. Gorman
Raymond D. Gorman
Robert F. Gorman
James W. Gormley
William C. Gormley
James B. Gorral, Jr.
Louis Paul Gorrell
Albion J. Gorris
William Harrison Gorsuch
Wesley H. Gorton
Thomas B. Gorup
James V. Gorzynski
Ray V. Gose
Earl D. Goshorn
Albert A. Gosnell
Eugene E. Gosney
Dwight M. Goss
Frederick Charles Goss
George C. Goss
Harold L. Goss
Harvey Ashley Goss
Patrick J. Goss
Richard Herbert Goss
Theodore L. Goss
William H. Goss, Jr.
Edward Gossar
Richard C. Gosselin
John Louis Gossett
William Bennett Gossett
Benjamin J. Gossman
Frank J. Gossmann
Aubrey P. Gosvener
M. Gotay-Maldonado
Clifford E. Gothard
Gerald G. Gothe
Ervin P. Gothier
Louis P. Gothman
Paul J. Gotney
Mitsuro Goto
Raymond T. Goto
Satoshi Goto
Felix W. Goudelock, Jr.
Samuel Goudelock, Jr.
David J. Goudlock
Gene Wilton Gould
Nelson S. Gould
William T. Gould
Marvin P. Goulding
Alfred V. Gouldman
Wilfred J. L. Goulet
Edward J. Gourinski
Donald J. Gouveia
Joseph G. Govan
Marion E. Gower
Sterling C. Gower
George E. Gowin
David William Gowman
Masao Goya
Joseph T. Goyette
Paul A. Graber
William S. Grable
Alfred E. Grablewski
Richard A. Grablin
John Eugene Grabosky
John J. Gracan
Edward Grace
Eulis G. Grace

Luther Grace
Robert B. Iii Grace
Robert M. Grace
Robert W. Grace
Burton A. Gracey
Eddie Gracia-Sanchez
Alexander W. Gracki
Frederick Graczyk
William J. Graddy
Reginald F. Gradias
Albert W. Grady
Joe Buell Grady
John H. Grady, Jr.
Alton Elmer Graf
Robert E. Graf
Russel John Graf
Rene Grafals-Rivera
Herman L. Graff, Jr.
Robert L. Graff
Rodney F. Graff
Philip G. Graffeo
James H. Gragg
Leslie O. Gragg
Riley J. Gragg
Alexander Graham, Jr.
Alfred L. Graham
Arnold W. Graham
Arthur L. Graham
Billy J. Graham
Billy J. Graham
Charles W. Graham
David Leroy Graham
Floyd E. Graham
Glenn W. Graham
Isadore R. Graham, Jr.
James J. Graham
James W. Graham
Jarrell D. Graham
John H. Graham
Johnny C. Graham
Joseph Graham, Jr.
Leonard F. Graham
Orville E. Graham
Paul Kirker Graham
Robert Bruce Graham
Robert L. Graham
Robert L. Graham
Robert P. Graham
Ronald T. Graham, Jr.
Walter R. Graham
Wiley Graham, Jr.
William L. Graham
William M. Graham
William M. Graham
William Wayne Graham
Hans Walter Grahl
Ernest W. Grainger
P. R. Grajales-Nieves
J. Grajales-Rosario
James W. Gram
Bernard M. Gramberg, Jr.
Herman H. Grammer
Wilbert W. Grammer
James W. Grams
Ronald Richard Grams
Kenneth Joseph Granberg
Carl J. Granberry
Martin Leon Granillo
Calvin C. Grant
Charles Grant
Duffie C. Grant
Dwyer Davis Grant
Earlon Virgil Grant
Frederick Edward Grant
George H. Grant, Jr.
Johnny W. Grant
Michael J. III Grant
Paul Grant
Robert L. Grant
Virgil Grant
Wilbur M. Grant
Lawrence D. Grantham
Victor Bernard Graper
Don Juan W. Graphenreed
Lawrence R. Graske
Dave Grass, Jr.
Garland Anthony Grass
Wilbur L. Grass
Ronald J. Grassold
Richard E. Grauman
William Karl Grauman
Joseph W. Grause, Jr.
Gerald Clifford Graveen
Charles L. Gravel
Joseph M. Gravel
Ernest L. Graveline, Jr.
James Gravely
Ben H. Graves
Frederick H. Graves, Jr.

Frederick W. Graves
Jack N. Graves
Lee A. Graves
Marion Graves
Nelson L. Graves
Paul A. Graves
Paul E. Graves
Riley W. Graves
Robert E. Graves
Wilbur J. Graves
William E. Graves
Winston Graves
Lorenzo L. Gravina, Jr.
Jack W. Gravley
Albert N. Gray
Alfred W. B. Gray
Billie J. Gray
Ceircell Gray
Dale Phoenix Gray
Edgar B. Gray
Emory Bertrand Gray
Ernest Gray
Frederick M. Gray
George Elbert Gray
Glen L. Gray
Golden L. Gray
Harold Gray, Jr.
Harry N. Gray, Jr.
Howard G. Gray
Ira A. Gray
John S. Gray
Lawrence Gray
Lemuel T. Gray
Leo H. Gray
Marion D. Gray
Merrett G. Gray
Richard E. Gray
Richard J. Gray
Robert A. Gray
Robert H. Gray
Robert L. Gray
Roy R. Gray, Jr.
Walter L. Gray
Wilbur Bennett Gray
William C. Gray
William Harry Gray
Woodrow Gray
David A. Graybeal
Donald R. Graybeal
B. L. Grayson
Clyde B. Grayson
David J. Grayson
Roy A. Grayson
Thomas J. Grayson
Jack R. Grazier
Howard J. Greaver
Robert E. L. Greaver
Robert Greaves, Jr.
Edward L. Greco
Joseph P. Greco
Ralph Greco
Rosario Greco
Thomas Guy Greco
Ronald William Greeb
Anthony Joseph Greeley
Al Green, Jr.
Allen R. Green
Arther W. Green
Avery J. Green
Billy F. Green
Carey Green
Charles A. Green
Charles M. Green
Crystal M. Green
David E. Green
Demon C. Green
Edgar L. Green
Edwin L. Green
Elmer D. Green
Elwood Green
Fred W. Green
George W. Green
Gilbert A. Green
Grover G. Green
Harold E. Green
Harold Leroy Green
Herbert W. Green
Herschel D. Green
Homer Green
Hueston M. Green
James D. Green
James E. Green
James L. Green
James La Verne Green
James Thurston Green
Jim Green
Joe C. Green
John H. Green
John L. Green

John M. Green
Johnnie Green
Joseph Thomas Green
Kenneth L. Green
Lowell Green, Jr.
Nolan Aldaine Green
Norman Green
Rastus E. Green
Richard B. Green
Robert A. Green
Robert B. Green
Robert E. Green
Robert G. Green
Robert K. Green
Robert L. Green
Robert R. Green
Tom W. Green
Tomas A. Green
Walter William Green
Ward M. Green
Wendell H. Green
Wilba Green
William Edward Green
William G. Green
William S. Green, Jr.
Willie J. Green
Jose Green-Rodriguez
Jerome E. Greenberg
Paul Greenberg
A. C. Greene
Claud Greene, Jr.
David Clark Greene
Earl Greene
Edward Henry Greene
Edwin A. Greene, Jr.
Gordon A. Greene
Howard Bart Greene
James H. Greene
John F. Greene
John T. Greene
John W. Greene
Joseph P. Greene
Ralph H. Greene
Richard D. Greene
Robert H. Greene
Thomas P. Greene
William E. Greene
William James Greene
William James Greene, Jr.
Larry Ory Greenfield
Leland L. Greenhagen
Bruce Jay Greenhill
Bernard A. Greenleaf
James E. Greenleaf
Robert L. Greenup
Cecil L. R. Greenwall
J. Ray Greenway, Jr.
Rudolph V. Greenway
George Griffin Greenwell
Carroll D. Greenwood
Donald Ray Greenwood
Francis C. Greenwood
Ivan J. Greenwood
Melvin T. Greenwood
Andrew L. Greer
Euzziah Greer
Frederic W. Greer
John A. Greer
Leslie F. Greer
Lester R. Greer
Pressgrove Greer
Robert Lamar Greer
Roby H. Greer
Thomas W. Greer
Walter M. Greer
William J. Greer
William Raymond Greer
Frank Gregg
Glen Finley Gregg, Jr.
Ivan E. Gregg
John L. Gregg
Levern Gregg
William T. Gregg
Robert L. Greggs
Edward J. Gregorczyk
Joseph Gregori
Alfred R. Gregory
Charles W. Gregory
Donald V. Gregory
Earl L. Gregory
Fred A. Gregory
James Allen Gregory
Joe B. Gregory, Jr.
Leslie Gregory
Marvin Clarence Gregory
Otis C. Gregory
Raymond Gregory
Richard J. Gregory
Robert E. Gregory

Robert S. Gregory
Raymond C. Greis
Tyrel J. Gremillion
Eugene W. Grendell
Donald T. Grenier
Eugene H. Grenier
Rosslyn E. Gresens
James A. Gresham
Frank S. Gress
Norman J. Gressens
Arnold G. Gresser
Carl H. Gressman
Claudius J. R. Grey
Donald G. Grey
Robert E. Grey
Henry O. Greybuffalo
Homer F. Gribbins
Clark Wales Gribble
Arthur O. Grice
Charles G. Grice
Henry Grice
Jack T. Grider
Kenneth G. Grider
John Gridley
William H. F. Griechen
Anthony J. Grieco
Edward H. Griefenstine
Milton Ray Grieff
Juan A. Griego
Louis Fernandez Griego
Simon Griego
Edwin Eddie Grienke
Alonzo Grier
Cecil Scott Grier, Jr.
Ralph Henry Gries
Robert R. Griese
Alfred August Griess
John Dale Grieve
Lee L. Grife
Charlie L. Griffeth
Bradley J. Griffey
Charles W. Griffin
Dower L. Griffin, Jr.
Francis J. Griffin, Jr.
Frank M. Griffin
Glen W. Griffin
Harry H. Griffin
Horace A. Griffin
Howard J. Griffin
James E. Griffin
John T. Griffin
Julian Floyd Griffin
Loy Griffin
Nelson H. Griffin
Richard John Griffin
Roy Leo Griffin
Silas E. Griffin
Verbel J. Griffin
Walter C. Griffin, Jr.
Walter L. Griffin
William J. Griffin
Charles E. Griffis
Willie D. Griffis
Bobby E. Griffith
George H. Griffith, Jr.
Harold W. Griffith
Jack Walter Griffith
Jacob T. Griffith
Joseph Marvin Griffith
Randolph F. Griffith
Robert S. Griffith
Ronald R. Griffith
Samuel C. Griffith
Walter L. Griffith
William G. Griffith
William S. Griffith
Jack D. Griffiths
Stanley Griffiths
George P. Grifford
Jerome H. Grigal
Charles Grigelis
Benjamin W. Griggs, Jr.
Clifford B. Griggs
Harry Griggs
Robert J. Griggs, Jr.
Virgil L. Griggs
Clifford J. Grignon
Eugene C. Grigsby
Wiley Julian Grigsby, Sr.
Finley Grills
Boyd F. Grim
Carl D. Grimes
Eugene Grimes
George T. Grimes
Joseph E. Grimes, Jr.
Keith H. Grimes
Paul K. Grimes, Jr.
Raymond Grimes
Allen E. Grimm

Norman A. Grimm
William D. Grimm
Willis Francis Grimm
Oliver E. Grimmett
William O. Grimmig
Charles E. Grimpe
Everett V. Grimsley
Robert L. Grimsley
Lawrence David Grine
Thomas D. Grinnell, Jr.
Robert H. Grinstead
Thomas E. Grisard
Leonard J. Griscones
Charles Edward Grise
Lowell R. Griser
David H. Grisham
David Howard Grisham
Freddie C. Grission
Delmer Ray Grissom
Robert W. Grissom
James R. Grist
Harry Ellsworth Griswold
James Theodore Griswold
James Franklin Grizzard
Johnnie A. Grizzle
Frank A. Groach
Richard H. Grob
Raymond A. Grodhaus
Eugene L. Grodzki
Arnold E. Groeneveld
Theodore Groeneveld
Clarence R. Grogan
William J. Grogan
Willis Devon Grogg
Edmund Phillips Groh, Jr.
Robert B. Grohmann
Robert G. Groleau
Charles J. Groll
George R. Groll
Cecil Wayne Groom
Ivan W. Groom
Marvin L. Groom
Arthur Grooms
Billy S. Grooms
Rollie D. Grooms
Willie L. Grooms
John J. Groot
Morgan K. Groover, Jr.
Eno J. Gros, Jr.
Herbert B. Grosche
William E. Grose
Billy L. Gross
Carl A. Gross
Donald Robert Gross
George P. Gross
James T. Gross
John E. Gross
Kenneth B. Gross
Lawrence Leo Gross
Malvin L. Gross
Myron E. Gross
Robert Franklin Gross
Walter F. Gross
John Frank Grossman, Jr.
William C. Grossman
Richard F. Groth
Bernard Grotkowski
John O. Grotte
Nelson T. A. Groulx
Melvin R. Grounds
George W. Grove
James A. Grove, Jr.
James R. Grove
William Clyde Grove
John S. Grover
William H. Grover
Alva C. Groves
Robert Groves, Jr.
John F. Grovier
John E. Grow
Kenneth H. Grow
Carl Ray Grubb
Charles H. Grubb
David Morrell Grubb
Frank Clark Grubb
Robert L. Grubb
Eugene M. Grubbs
Victor A. Gruben
Clarence E. Gruber
Laverne A. Gruber
Michael Carl Grubisich
Stanley A. Grudzinski
Walter H. Gruebbeling
Brock D. Gruetzner
Raymond Frank Gruhot
Henry T. Gruna
Richard A. Grundman
Richard Lamar Gruneberg
Oswald Grunig

Alexander T. Grunow
Angel V. Gruttadauria
Anthony C. Gruzinski
Frank S. Grykiewicz
Edwin C. Grzeca
Jesus Guajardo
Joe R. Guajardo
Daniel P. Gualtiere
Anastacio Guardian
Edward A. Gude
Joseph D. Gudger
George H. Guenther
Jose A. Guerra
Roberto Guerra
Hector Guerrero
Julian A. Guerrero
Moses G. Guerrero
Thomas G. Guerrero
Juan Guerrero-Orona
Girolamo J. Guerrise
John E. Guerue
Ray M. Guess
George E. Guest
Fred E. Guffey
Herbert E. Guffey
Henry Gugliciello, Jr.
Alfred Guglielmone
Sergio P. Guiang
Albert D. Guidelly
Joseph Guido
Joseph Guidry
Thomas R. Guiheen
John Ninian Guild
Lewis A. Guilds
Charles J. Guile
Richard Floyd Guiles
Howarth I. Guilford
Cornelius Patrick Guilfoyle
Ambrosio Guilien
Leslie Guill, Jr.
Paul E. Guill
R. Guillet-Lorenzo
Charles C. Guinn
Lisbon Guinn, Jr.
Mortimer G. Guinn
Anthony Guinta
Harry J. Guinther
Wych Eugene Guion
Jorge L. Guiot
Cecil H. Guiter
Jay Leslie Guiver
John Max Guldhorn
Benjamin Gulizia
James E. Gullage, Jr.
Charles Henry Gulledge
Joe Gulley
William K. Gum
Fred E. Gummow
Raymond B. Gunderson
Leonard Arlo Gundert
Stanley J. Gundlach
Orvis J. Gunhus
James R. Gunion
George P. Gunkel
Arthur S. Gunnell
Rex C. Gunnell
James T. Gunnels
Marvin L. Gunns
Donald E. Gunstrom
David Lemuel Gunter
Ossie Mayo Gunter
William Howard Gunter
Charles William Gunther
Joseph W. Gupko
Willard H. Gupton
Matthew F. Gura
Frank Gurchik
Edwin M. Gurecky
Leon Gurfein
Walter H. Gurley
Jimmie Gurr
A. Gurule, Jr.
James F. Guscott
Richard J. Gusek
Gilbert M. Gushiken
Louis G. Gussine
Dale R. Gustafson
Harold W. Gustafson
Henry L. Gustafson
Orville E. Gustafson
Roger W. Gustafson
Ralph S. Gustin
Yoshinobu Gusukuma
Sylvester L. Guszregen
Charles Gutgesell, Jr.
Edward S. Guthrie, Jr.
Marvin Lee Guthrie
Patrick W. Guthrie
Robert H. Guthrie

Adolfo Moreno Gutierrez
Fidencio Gutierrez
Gilbert Gutierrez
Isador Gutierrez
Jose R. Gutierrez
Lucio R. Gutierrez
Melisendeo Gutierrez
Rudolph R. Gutierrez
A. Gutierrez-Jimenez
A. Gutierrez-Suarez
Harry J. Gutteridge
Charles Bernie Guy
Virgel Guy
Edward S. Guyer, Jr.
Garfield William Guyer, Jr.
Jesse V. Guyer
John M. Guyer, Jr.
Thomas Howard Guyn
John E. Guynn
William L. Guyton
Rodrigo Q. Guzman
Salbador Guzman
Salvador M. Guzman
J. D. Guzman-Rodriguez
Leo Guzman-Rosario
James S. Guzzi, Jr.
Francis J. Gwaltney
Julius J. Gwazdacz
Boyd Bernard Gwin
Vance W. Gwinn
Harold E. Gwynn
Derry Gyden, Jr.
Richard Stanley Gzik

— H —

Robert E. Haack
Douglas H. Haag
Walter C. Haag
Richard Allan Haagensen
Russell N. Haakenson
Buster Haas
James Lee Haas
John L. Haas
Richard W. Haas
Elvin Wallace Haase
Herman C. Haase
Wilbert E. Habakangas
William C. Habbard
Orville Reinholdt Haber
Robert E. Haberern
William Joseph Haberle
Ray A. Habourne
Donald E. Habul
Darreld D. Hackbarth
Walter C. Hackenberg
James E. Hackengurg
Allan P. Hackett
Thomas J. Hackett
Adrian A. Hackney
Willaim L. Hackney
John T. Hadding, Jr.
Ernest H. Haddock
John H. Haddock, Jr.
Harry J. Haden
Milton D. Hadges
Billy A. Hadley
Donald Frederick Hadley
George Allen Hadley
George J. Hadley
Leo J. Hadley
Thomas Erle Ii Hadley
W. B. Hadley
William C. Hadley
Charles D. Hadnot
Albert John Haebe
Lewis Gene Haefele
Steven P. Haeg
Gerald Leon Haerr
Rudy H. Haferkamp
Neal W. Haferman
James Anthony Haffey
Burt Hafkin
Harry N. Hagadorn
Claudius F. Hagan
Frank D. Hagan
James E. Hagan, Jr.
Malcom Charles Hagan
John Hagar
Charles H. Hagemier
Darwyn L. Hagen
David R. Hagen
Orlin K. Hagen
Ronald Wayne Hagen
Roy Arthur Hagen
Edward R. Hagenah
Joseph Henry Hageney
Hallie E. Hager
Harvey R. Hager

John Hager
Russell D. Hager
William A. Hager, Jr.
Charles Hagerich
Edward D. Hagerty
Joseph F. Hagerty
Raymond W. Hagerty
Billy M. Haggard
Donald Hugo Hagge
George C. Hagie
Hiroshi Hagino
Yoshio Hagiwara
Carl Junior Hagle
R. V. Hagle, Jr.
Bernie Hagler, Jr.
Carter B. Hagler
Allan E. Haglund
Carl M. Hagman
Alexander R. III Hagner
Eddie Hagood, Jr.
James Joseph Hague
Wayne G. Hagy
Edwin E. Hahn
Harry E. Hahn
Howard John Hahn
George Edward Haigh
Harley Eugene Haigh
Raymond C. Haigh, Jr.
Dwain Leroy Haigwood
Raymond A. Haili
Charles F. Haines
George E. Haines
Harry G. Haines
William T. Haines, Jr.
William T. Hair, Jr.
Ova L. Haire
Robert L. Haire, Jr.
Louis C. Hairsine
Irvin D. Hairston
Wilbur C. Hairston
Charles G. Haitz
Albert W. Hajduk
Gerald Joseph Haker
Stanley Bernard Haladyna
John J. Halamuda
Robert G. Halay
George R. Halbert, Jr.
Douglas I. Halcomb
John T. Halcum
Carl V. Halcumb
Thomas R. Haldeman
Raymond Haldenwang
Alfred B. Hale
Ernest Hale
Eugene Brewer Hale
Herman F. Hale
Isaac K. Hale
James T. Hale
Jay L. Hale
Paul Hale
Shirley Dee Hale
Charles A. Haley
Leonard C. Haley
Louis R. Haley, Jr.
Morris E. Haley
Richard A. Haley
Donald L. Halferty
Van Lee Halferty
Abner C. Hall
Adam H. Hall
Allen L. Hall
Andrew Hall
Arthur James Hall
Arthur Paul Hall
Carlton E. Hall
Charles H. Hall, Jr.
Chester I. Hall
Clinton J. Hall
Cooper K. Hall
Darrell G. Hall
Dwaine Hall
Fred C. Hall
Fred G. Hall
Gale Hall
Garland R. Hall
Gene T. Hall
George Alfred Hall
George Leo Hall
George W. Hall
Glenn M. Hall
Harlan Porter Hall
Harold L. Sr Hall
Harold Tomas Hall
Harrison E. Hall
Harry R. Hall
Hedrey D. Hall
Howard Wesley Hall
Jerry Hall, Jr.
John Bryon Hall

John C. Hall
John F. Hall
John Hall, Jr.
John W. Hall
Joseph H. Hall, Jr.
Joseph Spence Hall
Julius E. Hall
Lendell Hall
Leroy Hall
Leroy S. Hall
Lester J. Hall, Jr.
Marvin Hall
Quinton V. Hall
Ralph Harlen Hall
Raymon F. Hall
Raymond D. Hall
Raymond Earl Hall
Richard Lee Hall
Richard W. Hall
Robert B. Hall
Robert D. Hall
Robert K. Hall
Robert R. Hall, Jr.
Roger Clifford Sr Hall
Ronald Glynn Hall
Ronald L. Hall
Russell L. Hall
Samuel A. Hall
Samuel S. Iii Hall
Stanley F. Hall
Stephen Cowles Hall
Theodore K. Hall
Thomas Burns Hall
Tommie L. Hall
Vincent R. Hall
Wallace L. Hall
Wilfred Eugene Hall
William E. Hall
William H. Hall
William Hall, Jr.
Willie Hall
David J. Hallahan
Walter Hallam
Robert Hugh Hallawell
Frederick W. Hallett
Frank Warren Halley
W. T. Hallford
Clarence T. Halliday, Jr.
Roscoe E. Halliday
Darrow T. Halligan
Ronald E. Halliman
Robert Allie Hallman
Robert D. Hallmark
Thomas J. Hallmark
Wesley Ivan Hallock
Bernard W. Halloran
Robert E. Halloran
Robert E. Hallowell
Allen Lynwood Hallum
Leonard David Hallum
Herbert J. Halm
Kenneth L. Halm
Kenneth N. Halsor
Bobby J. Halstead
F. B. Halter
Clarence V. Halton
William Timothy Halton
David Emil Halverson
Donald E. Halverson
Lawrence H. Halverson
Verlyn S. Halverson
Harold R. Halvorson
Leroy K. Halvorson
Russell Burton Ham, Jr.
Mitsuo Hamada
Patrick K. Hamada, Jr.
Kenichi Hamaguchi
Rodney N. Hamaguchi
David V. Haman
Philippe Emilien Hamann
Francis D. Hamblin, Jr.
Robert Warren Hamblin
William Hugh Hamblin
S. R. Hambrick
Shelly D. Hambrick
Garnett K. Hambright
Cleo D. Hamby
Larry P. Hamby
Marvin G. Hamelin
Charles E. Hamerquist
Russell G. Hamershy
Herman Hames
Edward T. Hamill
Bennie Wilson Hamilton
Bobbie S. Hamilton
Clyde Hamilton
David Lester Hamilton
Donald E. Hamilton

Donald S. Hamilton
Edward J. Hamilton, Jr.
Eugene E. Hamilton
Freddie L. Hamilton
Gene E. Hamilton
George B. Hamilton
George F. Hamilton
Glenn E. Hamilton
Howard B. Hamilton
James H. Hamilton
James Thomas Hamilton
Jeff L. Hamilton, Jr.
Joseph W. Hamilton
Kenneth Carroll Hamilton
Leon D. Hamilton
Merlin Jack Hamilton
Paul W. Hamilton
Percy D. Hamilton
Raymond W. Hamilton
Robert Hamilton
Robert E. Hamilton
Robert S. Hamilton
Robert T. Hamilton
Ronald W. Hamilton
Thomas A. Hamilton
Thomas Ray Hamilton
William J. Hamilton
William W. Hamilton
Willie Hamilton
Billy R. Hamlin
Charles James Hamlin
Elmer R. Hamlin
Fred Hamlin
Robert J. Hamlin
Samuel C. Hamlin
Albert E. Hamm
Donald L. Hamm
James F. Hamm
Robert H. Hamm
Jesse T. Hammack, Jr.
Raymond D. Hammel
William J. Hammel, Jr.
Carl A. Hammer
Carl P. Hammer
Gerald E. Hammer
Ambrose B. Hammerel
William G. Hammerle
Ronald Ray Hammett
Warren Rod Hammett
Alonzo R. Hammock
Glynn R. Hammock, Jr.
Tommie Hammock
Keith Edward Hammon
Clifford Hammond
Donald J. Hammond
Emmett T. Hammond
Francis Colton Hammond
Frank E. Hammond
George W. Hammond
Hugo Hammond
James D. Hammond
Lester Hammond, Jr.
Lyman Hammond
Phillip O. Hammond
Robert L. Hammond
Robert T. Hammond
Roger Clark Hammond
Roger W. Hammond, Jr.
Homer M. Hammonds
James L. Hammonds
Rene Hammonds
Fred F. Hammontree
Lloyd Wesley Hamon
Alfred Hampton
Charlie D. Hampton
David L. Hampton
Emile Hampton, Jr.
Henry J. Hampton
Herman Hampton
Kendrick Hampton
Leo Hampton
Leroy Hampton, Jr.
Aurel G. Hampu
Flavy G. Hamrick
Hayward J. Hamrick
John Forrest Hamrick
Alvan M. Hanaver
Billie Hance
Norman W. Hance
Rome H. Hance
Beltron R. Hancey
Russell Hancharyk
Carlos L. Hanchett
Charles L. Hancock, Jr.
George R. Hancock, Jr.
Harold Eugene Hancock
Jack Hancock
Jack Hancock
John Richard Hancock

Milton Hancock, Jr.
Richard Everett Hancock
Richard L. Hancock
William J. Hancock
George Edward Hand
Manley R. Hand
Norman C. Hand
Wallace D. Hande
Richard John Handing
Joseph E. Handl
Irwin Handler
Danny J. Handley
Mac A. Handley
Bobby L. Handlin
Melvin O. Handrich
Kenneth N. Handy
Melvin L. Handy
Raymond T. Handy
Robert M. Handy
Lloyd L. Hane
James F. Haner, Jr.
Don Gene Hanes
Walter J. Hanes
Alvin Clair Haney
Alvin Richard Haney
Andrew J. Haney, Jr.
Elven Newman Haney
Jack Haney, Jr.
Joseph B. Haney
Leroy Alvin Haney
Marvin A. Haney
Marvin L. Haney
Guy J. Hanford
Darrell G. Hanger
John Robert Hanigan
Irvin E. Hank
Fred A. Hankamer
Robert H. Hanke
Irvin E. Hankel
Jerald J. Hankins
Arthur P. Hanks
Thomas E. Hanks
Tommie T. Hanks
Woodrow Irvin Hanks
Jack Hanley
Robert Hanley
Ernest M. Hanlin
Frank Hanlon
John W. Hanlon
John T. Hanna
Robert D. Hanna
Gordon L. Hannah
Jack Leonard Hannah
Jerry B. Hannah
Morgan H. Hannah
William H. Hannah
George E. Hannan
Thomas F. Hannan
William T. Hannan
Clarence E. Hannen
Milton L. Hanner
Billy D. Hannig
Robert W. Hannigan
Arthur Thomas Hannon
Paul Joseph Hannon
Richard M. Hannon
Arnold Gust Hannuksela
William T. Hannum
Gilbert P. Hannweeka
Edward John Hanrahan
John W. Hansard
Earl Henry Hansel
Morgan B. Hansel
Andrew G. Hansen, Jr.
Arthur Hansen, Jr.
Bernard N. Hansen
Carl E. Hansen
Dan H. Hansen
Darrel D. Hansen
Darrell J. Hansen
Eugene Ralph Hansen
Floyd M. Hansen
George Herman Hansen
John J. Hansen
John L. Hansen
Kenneth R. Hansen
Lawrence Dale Hansen
Leonard Harold Hansen
Macca P. Hansen
Martin A. Hansen
Meidel Hansen
Olaf R. Hansen
Oscar E. Hansen, Jr.
Reed H. Hansen
Robert Gordon Hansen
Robert M. Hansen
Robert T. Hansen
Wayne C. Hansen
Harold C. Hanshaw

William H. Hanshaw
Nicholas J. Hansinger
Robert Eugean Hansler
William R. Hansman
Carl Harry Hanson
Edward C. Hanson
Ellwood F. Hanson
Harlan B. Hanson
Harlan T. Hanson
Jack G. Hanson
Leland Hanson
Leroy E. Hanson
Leroy R. Hanson
Luther D. Hanson
Lyle E. Hanson
Melvin F. Hanson
Milnor D. Hanson
Raymond W. Hanson
Richard Bennett Hanson
Robert James Hanson
Thomas Clay Hanson
William W. Hanson
Arthur Wesly Hanton
Daniel W. Hanus
Gene O. Hanzer
Frederick J. Hapgood
Carl George Happ, Jr.
Anthony T. Haralson
William D. Haralson
William Rudolph Haralson
Richard C. Harang
Edward E. Harber
Howard M. Harbin
Earl H. Harbour
Ronald E. Harbour
Howard R. Harbridge
James J. Harchenhorn
Carl Craig Harcourt
Gordon W. Harcourt
Thomas G. Hardaway
Edward C. Hardcastle
Julius F. Hardeman
John A. Harden, Jr.
Norwood Henry Harder
Booker T. Hardeway
Howell W. Hardgrave
Kenneth Alan Hardigan
Michael P. Hardiman
Horace Hardimon
George E. Hardin
George R. Hardin
Ivon Herbert Hardin
John D. Hardin
Kermit M. Hardin
Uncas B. Hardin
Vernon C. Hardin
Weldon Edgar Hardin
William Gordon Hardin
Horace C. Harding
Joseph W. Harding, Jr.
Remer L. Harding
Richard D. Harding
Thomas Harding, Jr.
Warren G. Harding
Donald P. Hardinger
Thurmond C. Hardison
Clifford F. Hardman
Guy G. Hardman, Jr.
Kester B. Hardman
Henneth L. Hardwick
Richard L. Hardwick
David E. Hardy
Edgar Warren Hardy
Elmer E. Hardy
Isac Hardy
James S. Hardy
James W. Hardy
James William Hardy
Leon Hardy, Jr.
Lester R. Hardy
Ray Lee Hardy
Robert Francis Hardy
Robert J. Hardy
Thomas R. Hardy
William R. Hardy
Clement J. Hare
James R. Hare
William H. Hare
Tommie Harges, Jr.
James Harget
James William Hargis
Maynard L. Hargo
Alan Hargrave
David J. Hargrave
Obie E. Hargrove
Oscar H. Hargrove
Richard C. Hargus
Wilson B. Harjo
Charles Abbott Harker, Jr.

Ernest B. Harkey
Floyd Homer Harkins
Ervin Estes Harkness
Grant D. Harkness
Harry E. Harkness
Richard F. Harla
Gary L. Harlan
Harold W. Harland
Richard G. Harless
Walter R. Harless
William A. Harless
Earl M. Harley
Harold E. Harley
Jesse Harlow, Jr.
Richard Lee Harlow
William Henry Harlow
Edgar Franklin Harman
Howard Henry Harman
Richard C. Harman
Charlie Harmon
Donald R. Harmon
Francis Milton Harmon
Gilbert L. Harmon
Hubert Harmon
James Harmon
James E. Harmon
John Harmon
John A. Harmon
John William Harmon
Marcus L. Harmon
Norman Cline Harmon
Paul H. Harmon
Robert Duane Harmon
Roy B. Harmon
Stanley W. Harmor
Garriet A. Harms, Jr.
Warner H. Harms
Lawrence A. Harnage
Charles K. Harned
George N. Harner
Clay Harness
Cornelius Francis Harney
Clode Marvin Harold
Donald G. Harold
Mearl L. Harp
Ralph A. Harp
James Linward Harpe
Arthur L. Harpel
Alton E. Harper
Bill F. Harper
Claude L. Harper, Jr.
Edward Harper
Edward W. Harper
Everette C. Harper
Harry James Harper
Howard R. Harper
Joseph M. Harper
Joseph T. Harper
Lee A. Harper
Max H. Harper
Merlin L. Harper
Mitchell Harper, Jr.
Rayford H. Harper
Richard S. Harper
Robert M. Harper
Robert R. Harper
Thomas M. Harper
Wilbert R. Harper
Fred W. Harpster
Donald F. Harr
Charles Lamar Harrell
Douglas D. Harrell
Guy Buchanan Harrell, Jr.
James A. Harrell
James V. Harrell
Jeffery W. Harrell
Lucious L. Harrell
Virgil Bryan Harrell, Jr.
William M. Harrell
John P. Harrich
Clifford R. Harries
William E. Harrigan
Sheldon L. Harriman
Daniel Harrington
Eldridge Harrington
George W. Harrington
Henry J. Harrington
James A. Harrington
James F. Harrington
Jon G. Harrington
Julius Gene Harrington
Robert F. Harrington
Robert J. Harrington
Russell D. M. Harrington
Forrest D. Harriott
Alan Maurice Harris
Albert M. Harris
Arnold Harris
Artheria M. Harris

Arvid J. Harris
Austin L. Harris
Bobby R. Harris
Buster Harris
Charles Ames Harris
Charles E. Harris
Charles M. Harris
Charles William Harris
Clarence A. Harris
Clarence Harris, Jr.
Donald W. Harris
Dugan Harris
Eddie V. Harris
Edgar H. Harris
Edward P. Harris
Ellis Harris
Elmer Harris, Jr.
Eugene S. Harris
Evan Charles Harris
Floyd Harris
Frank Harris
George Harris
Harley Stafford Harris, Jr.
Harold W. Harris
Henry C. Harris
Herman G. Harris
Houston Harris
Howard K. Harris
Isadore Harris
Jack D. Harris
Jack E. Harris
James Harris
James Harris
James A. Harris
James A. Harris, Jr.
James C. Harris
James C. Harris
James C. Harris
James Milton Harris
Jasper L. Harris
Jewel Winfred Harris
John E. Harris
John T. Harris
Johnson S. Harris
Lawrence Harris, Jr.
Lenvil D. Harris
Lewis A. Harris
Loviel S. Harris
Lyle B. Harris
Major M. Harris
Manuel Harris
Max E. Harris
Montgomery Harris
Odis M. Harris
Parrion R. Harris
Paul Harris
Rachell Harris
Ralph Lionel Harris
Rastine Harris
Richard E. Harris
Richard Edward Harris
Richard Gilbert Harris
Richard J. Harris
Richard L. Harris
Robert C. Harris
Robert G. Harris
Robert Harris, Jr.
Robert L. Harris
Robert L. Harris
Robert S. Harris
Roosevelt Harris
Rudolph Harris
Sam C. Harris, Jr.
Sylvester Harris
Theodore J. Harris
Thomas R. Harris
Thomas W. Harris
Virgil Lee Harris, Jr.
Walter Harris
Walter L. C. Harris
Wayne E. Harris
Weldon Darwood Harris
Wilbur F. Harris
Wilkie Harris, Jr.
William D. Harris
William Frederick Harris
William L. Harris
William L. Harris
William R. Harris
Willie L. Harris
Arthur Harrison
Bannie Harrison, Jr.
Benjamin F. Harrison, Jr.
Charles Harrison
Dick Harrison
Elbert D. Harrison
Francis E. Harrison
Fred Harrison
Glen O. Harrison

343

Henry G. Harrison
Hubert C. Harrison
Jack Ray Harrison
James Harrison, Jr.
James M. Harrison
Jimmie Marvin Harrison
Lewis T. Harrison, Jr.
Louis Harrison
Lowell G. Harrison
Marshal L. Harrison
Maxie G. Harrison
Oren B. Harrison, Jr.
Philip T. Harrison
Ralph L. Harrison
Richard E. Harrison
Robert L. Harrison
Roy Ernest Harrison
Shirlie D. Harrison
J. D. Harrower
Edward S. Harry, Jr.
Donald Ray Harryman
Dale L. Harshbarger
Lewis S. Harsher
Leonard G. Harsy
Albert L. Hart
Alvin Dale Hart, Jr.
Clayton D. Hart
Donald Lee Hart
Ellis Collins Hart
Eugene Francis Hart
Everett W. Hart
George Walter Hart, Jr.
Howard F. Hart
James Hart, Jr.
John T. Hart
Kenneth S. Hart
Melbourne Carol Hart
Michael J. Hart, Jr.
Paul C. Hart
Rex R. Hart
Richard H. Hart
Robert H. Hart
Russell C. Hart
William Hart
Lee R. Hartell
Joseph L. Harter, Jr.
Robert E. Harthun
Loren D. Hartjen
Edwin E. Hartlaub
Jessie M. Hartle, Jr.
Arthur G. Hartley, Jr.
Charles W. Hartley
Charlie Hartley, Jr.
Clarence G. Hartley
George W. Hartley
James E. Hartley, Jr.
Kenneth Dwight Hartley
Lawrence J. Hartlieb
Alfred B. Hartman
Charles W. Hartman
David R. Hartman
George E. Hartman
John R. Hartman
Myron A. Hartman
Richard M. Hartman
Roger W. Hartman
Woodrow P. Hartman
Harry J. Hartmann
Clifford J. Hartneck
Warren P. Hartney
John J. Hartong
Charles W. Hartsfield
Arthur L. Hartshorn
Robert E. Hartsock
Harold L. Hartson
George E. Hartwell
Gerald L. Hartwick
Ross Alvin Hartwig
Vernon G. Hartwig
James Hartzer
Edward J. Hartzold
Baxter R. Harvel, Jr.
Amon Frank Harvey, Jr.
Arthur E. Harvey
Artie A. Harvey
Carthel E. Harvey
Charles G. Harvey
Charles V. H. Harvey
Clyde M. Harvey
Daniel Albert Harvey
Earl D. Harvey
Frankie Harvey
George W. Harvey
Joe W. Harvey
John C. Harvey
Lawrence T. Harvey
Norman Fay Harvey
Robert Gordon Harvey
Roscoe L. Harvey

William R. Harvey
Wilson H. Harvey
Keith J. Harview
Leland E. Harville
Joe H. Harvison
Elton J. Harwell
Otis Merle Harwell
Chester L. Harwood
Billie J. Hash
Donald F. Hash
Eldon E. Hash
Beverly T. Haskell
Gordon Edward Haskell
George Norman Haskett
William T. Haskett, Jr.
Morris D. Haskins
Warren F. Haskins
Charles T. Haslet
George R. Haslett
Harold L. Hasley
Andrew Hassage
Isiah Hassel
John T. Hassel
La Mar F. Hassel
George J. Hassell
Charles A. Haste
John C. Hastie
Charles Hastings
Charles J. Hastings
Donald D. Hastings
Donald W. Hastings
Robert A. Hastings
Ross E. Hastings
Thomas J. Hastings
Wilbur D. Hastings
Donald Glynn Hasty
Roy Hataway
William R. Hataway
Gene N. Hatch
Kenneth G. Hatch
Robert E. Hatch
Embree H. Hatcher
Gordon M. Hatcher
J. P. Hatcher
James E. Hatcher
Louis J. Hatcher
James A. Hatchett
John Willis Hatchitt
Cecil Hatfield
Curtis Adrian Hatfield
Douglas Hampton Hatfield
Henry F. Hatfield, Jr.
Jerome D. Hatfield
Raymond D. Hatfield
Raymond L. Hatfield
Robert L. Hatfield
Theodore Leroy Hatfield
Andrew E. Hathaway
Gordon E. Hathaway
William A. J. Hathcox
Kermit Keith Hathorn
Billy Doyle Hatley
Harold W. Hatley
Robert C. Hatley
William H. Hatley, Jr.
Ellsworth J. Hatt
John A. Hatt
Allan Perry Hatton
George C. Hatton
Sydney Hatton
William B. Hatton, Jr.
Fred L. Hatzold
Carl F. Hauer, Jr.
Arnold E. Haugen
Donn Herbert Haugen
Richard Dean Haugen
Robert O. Haugen
Leroy G. Hauger
Alonzo J. Haugh, Jr.
Otho L. Haughn
Haakon M. Haugland
Harold P. Haugland
Orvis A. Haugtvedt
John Henry Haun
Raymond Haun
John Myron Hausemann
Christian W. Hauser
Robert G. Hauser
Woodrow R. Hauserman, Jr.
Ernest Erich Haussler
Jules Hauterman, Jr.
Arnold Haveika
Edwin Bowne Havens, Jr.
Junior L. Havens
Tate M. Havnaer
Erwin A. Havranek
Michael Havrilla, Jr.
Charles R. Hawes
Richard Elliott Hawes

Dan Bruno Hawke
Richard Hawkes
Billy C. Hawkins
Carlis Darryl Hawkins
Eddie V. Hawkins
Edward Hawkins
George Everett Hawkins
Henry M. Hawkins
Horace Melvin Hawkins
James L. Hawkins
Julius Wiley Hawkins
Luther Reid Hawkins, Jr.
Ralph E. Hawkins
Robert C. Hawkins
Robert W. Hawkins
Russell Hawkins, Jr.
William M. Hawkins
Wilson Hawkins, Jr.
Verpo L. Hawks
Clifford B. Hawley
George L. Hawley
Jesse Vick Hawley
Richard Everett Hawley
Robert Schuler Hawn
Roscoe L. Hawn
Perry R. Haworth
Wilbur A. Haworth, Jr.
Howard V. Hawse
Charles R. Hawsey
Clarence E. Hawthorne
Earl C. Hawthorne
Vernon A. Hawthorne
Kenneth V. Hay
Richard Y. Hayakawa
Charles B. Hayden
Edward B. Hayden
James Austin Hayden
John Beal Hayden
Orville L. Hayden
Ryland E. Hayden
Albert R. Haydock
Kenneth D. Hayen
Alfred G. Hayes
Billy A. Hayes
Cecil W. Hayes
Cornelius E. Hayes
Donald Alger Hayes
Dover D. Hayes
Dulaney R. Hayes
George W. Hayes
Harry G. Hayes
Horace Hayes
Howard Anthony Hayes
Jack B. Hayes
James Hayes
James E. Hayes
James O. Hayes
James P. Hayes
James W. Hayes
John Curtis Hayes
John Edward Hayes
John Joseph Hayes
Keith M. Hayes
Laddie Lee Hayes
Louie R. Hayes
Peter S. Hayes
Ralph H. Hayes
Randolph Hayes
Richard Verne Hayes
Richard W. Hayes
Robert David Hayes
Roland Hayes
Sylvester R. Hayes
Walter R. Hayes, Jr.
Freddye L. Haygood
James R. Hayman
Thomas O. Haymore
James F. Haynam
Bobby L. Haynes
Donald A. Haynes
Earnest Haynes
Elwood W. Haynes
Ethyl B. Haynes
James L. Haynes
John E. Haynes
John L. Haynes
Lawrence Edward Haynes
Marvin H. Haynes, Jr.
Nathan C. Haynes, Jr.
Otis Shelton Haynes, Jr.
Paul Haynes
Richard C. Haynes
Robert F. Haynes
Robert L. Haynes
Roy C. Haynes
William C. Haynes
Harold Haynesworth
Robert E. Haynie
Curtis G. Hays

Frederick S. Hays, Jr.
Lewis Edward Hays
Melvin Blaine Hays
Ray E. Hays
Robert A. Hays
Robert Charles Hays
Sandy Hays
James B. Hayslett
Wallace A. Hayslip
Justice K. Haythorne
Laverne Hayton
Doyle E. Hayward
Carmon C. Haywood
Mineford Lee Haywood
Leonard E. Hayworth
Mason Carl Hazard
Caleb W. Hazel
Albert W. Hazelton, Jr.
Harkness W. Hazelwood
Jim T. Hazelwood
Charles W. Hazlett
Clifford Hazwood
Cerl V. Head
James E. Head
Richard G. Head
Roy Earl Head
Charles T. Headley
Clarence M. Headley
Verdun E. Headley
Gerald J. Heagney
Arthur D. Heald
Howard F. Heald
Paul E. Heald
Owen F. Healey
Daniel Edward Healy
Daniel M. Healy
John William Healy
Robert Carlton Healy
Thomas J. Healy
Booker T. Heard
Delbert E. Heard
Elbert E. Heard
James L. Heard
Marvin W. Heard
Richard L. Heard
Sam Heard, Jr.
Ollie L. Hearell
Charles J. Hearn
Craig H. Hearn
David C. Hearn
Edwin F. Hearn
John E. Hearn
Robert L. Hearn
George E. Hearnsberger
Raymond L. Hearren
Richard M. Heaser
Howard Wakely Heater
Robert S. Heater
Edward F. Heath, Jr.
James Darrell Heath
Leslie Ray Heath
Mayo S. Heath
Ralph Roosevelt Heath
Richard C. Heath
Robert E. Heath
Thomas H. Heath
Vincent F. Heath
Wayne D. Heath
William E. Heath
Edsel Heathcock
Willie S. Heatherly
Clarence M. Heaton
Herman F. Heaton
James L. Heaton
Raymond E. Heaton
Robert R. Heaton
John A. Heavener
John J. Heavey, Jr.
Leonard Hebb
Charles K. Hebert
Robert J. Hebert
Robert R. Hebert
Sylvio L. Hebert
Henry A. Hecht
Robert A. Hecht
Frederic H. Heck
Kenneth R. Heck
Maurice Alin Heck
Ray Heck
Lester A. Hecker
Charles William Heckman
Robert W. Heckman
Howard D. Hector
Benjamin L. Hedden
John Brown Heddons
Jack Holly Hederstrom
Bennie J. Hedgcoth
James R. Hedgcoth
Clifton E. Hedgepeth

Dollie Hedgepeth
Ralph J. Hedger
Edwin G. Hedges
Clifton Hedgespeth
Louis M. Hedin
Robert S. Hedman
Herman Hedrick
Howard E. Hedrick
Leonard A. Hedrick
Ralph Hedrick
Roy W. Hedrick
Earl W. Hedrington, Jr.
Walter Lau Hee
David Thames Heer
Donald O. Heesen
Edgar S. Heffley
Bobbie D. Heffner
Robert M. Heffner
James H. Heffron
Joseph L. Heflin
Robert P. Heflin
Everette R. Hefner
Ivan F. Hefner
Kenneth Hefta
John Joseph III Hegarty
Arnold M. Hegg
Herbert Heggar
George D. Heichel
Homer A. Heichel
Arthur V. Heide
Willie M. Heidelberg
Joseph J. Heider
Wilbert M. Heider
Carl John Heigl
James R. Heiligh
Ernest L. R. Heilman
John L. Heilman
Warren E. Heim
Richard H. Heimbigner
Joseph H. Heinbach
John E. Heinchon
Merlin A. Heinecke
Harry S. Heinke, Jr.
Frederick Heinlein
Henry T. Heins
Richard H. Heins
Rolland C. Heintzelman
Erwin Gustav Heinz, Jr.
Eugene L. Heinz
Thomas Warren Heinzen
Rayman G. Heiple
Arthur Heise
Dale A. Heise
Adolf F. Heissler
Henry W. Heit, Jr.
Gerald G. Heither
Donald R. Heitkamp
Clarence M. Heitman
Raymond F. Hejny
Merlin J. Helbach
Harold J. Helbing
Stewart Gordon Held
Arthur W. Helderman
Fred Dale Helems
Charles R. Helgerson
Donald R. Helgeson
Russell L. Helie
Orline W. Heling
Joseph Helke
James Wornlee Hellem
Irving Hellman
J. B. Helm
John Francis Helm
Carl F. Helman
Glenwood C. Helman
Edward A. Helmes
Theodore H. Helmich
Harry R. Helmick
James E. Helmondollar
Eugene Helms
Euriah Helms
Henry L. Helms
Jack Ross Helms
Wallace W. Helms
W. L. Helnarski
Chester R. Helsel
Joseph E. Helsel
Donald C. Helt
Je Mickey Helt
Henry Edgar Helton, Jr.
Orvil Helton
Robert E. Helton
Thomas Luke Helton
Wilburn Helton
Richard R. Heltsley
Thomas F. Hema
Frank R. Hembree
John Hembree, Jr.
William C. Hembree

John J. Hemenway
Robert W. Hemenway
Milton F. Hemmingsen
Charles J. Hemphill
Dearl Leon Hemphill, Jr.
Theodore Hemphill
William C. Hemsher
William J. Hemskey
Warren B. Hemstrought
Harold R. Hendershaw
Roland A. Hendershot
Albert W. Henderson
Alexander C. Henderson
Arthur R. Henderson
Charles L. Henderson
Clifford M. Henderson
Delbert E. Henderson
Donald James Henderson
Edwin R. Henderson
Ernest W. Henderson
Harold L. Henderson, Jr.
Herbert Henderson
Howard Henderson
Jack H. Henderson
James A. Henderson
James E. Henderson
Joseph Francis Henderson
Lester V. Henderson
Martin Henderson
Merle Allan Henderson
Morris Henderson
Norman R. Henderson
Ralph Henderson
Richard Earl Henderson
Richard L. Henderson, Jr.
Richard Ray Henderson
Roy A. Henderson
Travis E. Henderson
William K. Henderson
William P. Henderson
Willie M. Henderson
Louis B. Hendren
Gerald R. Hendrick
Hazen C. Hendrick
Charles H. Hendricks
Darrell T. Hendricks
Donald E. Hendricks
Edward L. Hendricks
Frank B. Hendricks, Jr.
George H. Hendricks, Jr.
James H. Hendricks
John T. Hendricks
Joseph L. Hendricks
Owen W. Hendricks
William Hendricks
Bertra Hendrickson
Donald R. Hendrickson
Harvey Hendrickson
Jack K. Hendrickson
Charles R. Hendrix
Donald Jerry Hendrix
Raymond L. Hendrix
Thomas Calvin Hendrix
Astor Ray Hendry
Robert C. Hendry
Lawrence James Hengy
Francis B. Henig
Bruno R. Henke
Leo Joseph Henkenius
Clifford D. Henkle
Hamilton C. Henley
Julius Henley, Jr.
Lloyd J. Henley
Louis F. Henn
Jimmy E. Henness
Vernon R. Hennigan
Kenneth S. Henning
Luvern O. Henning
James K. Hennington
Donald N. Hennricks
Gerard M. Henrich
Norman R. Henricksen
Augustus J. Henry
Clifton D. L. Henry
Dewey Roseswall Henry
Donald E. Henry
Elton Thomas Henry
Ernest A. Henry
Fred S. Henry
Frederick F. Henry
Jerald W. Henry
John Franklin Henry
John J. Henry
Joseph P. Henry
Kenneth Henry, Jr.
Lee D. Henry, Jr.
Leo Henry, Jr.
Maurice I. Henry
Michael P. Henry

344

Otis Henry, Jr.
Paul J. Henry
Ray F. Henry
Richard A. Henry
Robert C. Henry
Robert Elmer Henry
Robert L. Henry
Robert L. Henry
Robert M. Henry
Roper Henry
Wilbert R. Henry
William F. Henry
William F. Henry
Allan M. Henslee
Robert M. Hensler
Bird Hensley, Jr.
Brown Hensley
C. B. Hensley
Darold D. Hensley
Eldred J. Hensley
Jasper N. Hensley
Lee Hensley
Alfred Henson, Jr.
Bennie Henson
Charles R. Henson
Collie Henson
Ernest H. Henson
Freddie L. Henson
George Henson
Glenn E. Henson
Harry L. Henson
J. D. Henson
Richard C. Henson
Robert E. Henson
Shields Taylor Henson
Walter L. Hentz
Clayton F. Hephner
Raymond L. Hepler
Herbert George Her
Paul G. Herald
Peter M. Herardo
Edward D. Herb, Jr.
James D. Herb
Andrew John Herbenick
Hershel F. J. Herbert
Valentine W. Herbert
Harley K. Herbster
John F. Herdlick
David A. Herendeen
Edward W. Hereth
Raymond Lee Hergert
Willard F. Heritage
Eugene H. Herkless
Michael Herko, Jr.
Michael Herlihy
Robert G. Herlihy
J. W. Herlston
Alfred H. Ii Herman
Marcel Herman, Jr.
Paul O. Herman
Theodore J. Herman
Wallace B. Hermann
Walter Hermansen
Charles R. Hermes
Carlos Hermosillo
Jessie E. Hermosillo
Neal R. Hern
Paulino E. Hernaez
Pedro E. Hernaez
Edwin James Hernan, Jr.
Alberto Hernandez
Andres Hernandez
Anthony Hernandez
Antonio P. Hernandez
Carlos M. Hernandez
Domingo Hernandez
Ernesto G. Hernandez
Florentino G. Hernandez
Francisco A. Hernandez
George Hernandez
Gustavo Hernandez
Henry S. Hernandez
Jesus Hernandez
Jesus Hernandez
Jesus S. Hernandez
John Hernandez
Jose Hernandez
Juan C. Hernandez
Juan G. Hernandez
Luis Hernandez
Manuel B. Hernandez
Max F. Hernandez
Pedro Hernandez
Raul A. Hernandez
Roberto P. Hernandez
Rodolfo L. Hernandez
Ruben Hernandez
Trinidad Hernandez
A. Hernandez-Concepcio

Isidro Hernandez-Dones
E. Hernandez-Gonzalez
P.A. Hernandez-Hernandez
E. Hernandez-Jimenez
H. Hernandez-Rodriguez
L. Hernandez-Rodriguez
B. Hernandez-Torres
James Wesley Hernden
Joseph M. Herndon
Albert E. Herold
James M. Herold
Jesse E. Herpeche
George Herr
Thomas D. Herr
Walter C. Herr
Edward L. Herrera
Eloy Herrera
Guilberto Herrera
Julian Herrera
Lorenzo Herrera
Pablo Herrera
Basil H. Herrholz
Lyle E. Herrick
Virgil B. Herrick
James F. Herriman
Darwin E. Herrin
Donald Ray Herrin
Eugene Herring
Grant J. Herring
John O. Herring
Ralph D. Herring
Garland Herrington
Robert N. Herrington
William F. Herrington
William J. Herrington
Eugene H. Herrmann
John P. Herrmann
Wesley H. Herrmann
Richard L. Herrold
Curtis W. Herron, Jr.
Jessie E. Herron
Paul E. Herron
Raymond J. Herron
Roxy A. Herron
Wayne M. Herron
Murray G. Hershkowitz
Ronald Arthur Herson
Christian Frederick Hertel
Donald H. Hertrick
Thomas A. Hertzler
Andrew Heryla
Jack A. Herzet
Claude R. Hess
Edward J. Hess
Edward J. Hess, Jr.
Irvin Woodrow Hess
Kenneth Leland Hess
Merle A. Hess
Herbert A. Hesseltine, Jr.
Robert E. Hessenflow
Ross Dean Hesser
Eugene H. Hessig
John F. Hessler
Charles G. Hester
Harrison L. Hester
James Clifford Hester
Joseph C. Hester
Will H. Hester
Loren Heston
Laverne M. Hettenbach
Thurman B. Hetzler
Herbert Fah Yen Heu
William M. S. Heu
Don Peter Heubel
William F. Heuer
Eugene J. Heumiller
Paul F. Heuss
Francis L. Hewett
Isham C. Hewgley, Jr.
Donald C. Hewins
Allen S. Hewitt
Bernard R. Hewitt
Charles V. Hewitt
Clyde Lee Hewitt
Dwight M. Hewitt
Joseph R. Hewitt
Robert A. Hewitt
Robert Lee Hewitt
William Glen Hewitt
Richard D. Hewlen
Douglas Leroy Hewlett
Irving W. Hey
Howard Francis Heyliger
Edward Heynoski, Jr.
William H. Hiatt
Earl J. Hibbard
James C. Hibben
Charles Marland Hibbert
Donald R. Hibbs

James W. Hibbs
Rollo D. Hibbs
Peter T. Hibma
D. F. Hickenbottom, Jr.
Damon W. Hickerson
James G. Hickerson
Orman L. Hickerson
James L. Hickey
John Edward Hickey, Jr.
John M. Hickey
John Murray Hickey
Richard D. Hickey
Sterling C. Hickey, Jr.
Ernest F. Hickling
Delbert D. Hickman
Emery M. Hickman
Evans Hickman
Gerald E. Hickman
Harold Lee Hickman
Henry E. Hickman
Homer Hickman
Robert R. Hickman
William G. Hickman
William H. Hickman
William H. Hickman, Jr.
Charles E. Hickox
Arb Hicks, Jr.
Arewood W. Hicks
Arvil Hicks
Buel G. Hicks
Charles Hicks
Chester S. Hicks
Dale David Hicks
Ellis Hicks
Francis P. Hicks
Henry L. Hicks
James E. Hicks
James E. Hicks
John Daniel Hicks
John E. Hicks
Kenneth A. Sr Hicks
Luther Hicks
Martin L. Hicks
Newgames Hicks
Norval L. Hicks
Oscar A. Hicks, Jr.
Paul James Hicks
Richard C. Hicks
Thomas Hicks
Tommy V. Hicks
Vester Hicks, Jr.
Jack R. Hiday
Bernard P. Hiegert
Ansel C. Hiers
Johnnie Morris Hiers
Sadayasu Higa
Yutaka Higa
Walter W. Higashida
Kenneth J. Higbee
Charles H. Higdon
Billy R. Higginbotham
Charles Higgins, Jr.
Edward D. Higgins
Edward J. Higgins
Elijah J. Higgins
Elijah T. Higgins
Frederick A. Higgins
George Carlton Higgins
George W. Higgins
James E. Higgins
James T. Higgins
John A. Higgins
John H. Higgins
John Joseph Higgins
John S. Higgins, Jr.
Paul Daniel Higgins
Robert Higgins
Thomas Robert Higgins
Walter N. Higgins
William Augustus Higgins
William K. Higgins
Allen Higgs, Jr.
Carl Higgs
Garland R. Higgs
John Frederick Higgs, Jr.
Kenneth W. Higgs
William O. Higgs, Jr.
Benjamin F. High
Carlis E. High
Charles High
Lewis W. High
George D. Highberger
Joseph Henry Highley
Maynard Lee Highley
Charles C. Highsmith, Jr.
Cecil O. Hightower
Ernest James Hightower
Ural W. Hightower
Gilbert R. Higuera

Ronald J. Higuera
Willard F. Hilbert
Harry S. Hilburger
Odis Hilburn
Harold S. Hildebrand
Roscoe Hildebrand
William H. Hildebrand
Warren L. Hildebrandt
Ray W. Hildeman
Clarence Francis Hile, Jr.
Thurle L. Hileman
John Hilemon
Carter D. Hilgard
Kenneth C. Hilgart
Earl E. Hilgenberg
Robert Henry Hilgenberg
John J. Hilgerson, Jr.
A. V. Hill
Billy C. Hill
Carl L. Hill
Charles Cleveland Hill
Charles H. Hill, Jr.
Charlie H. Hill
Clarence H. Hill
Dale C. Hill
Daniel G. Hill
Donald G. Hill
Earl Robert Hill
Edward O. Hill
Edwin E. Hill
Frank L. Hill
Fred G. Hill
George E. Hill
George Edward Hill
George N. Hill
George Thomas Hill
George W. Hill
Griswold M. Hill, Jr.
Harold E. Hill
Herman E. Hill
James C. Hill
James F. Hill
James Howard Hill
James Hill, Jr.
James L. Hill
James Martin Hill
James Mitchell Hill
James O. Hill
Jesse D. Hill
Jesse E. Hill
John A. C. Hill
John William Hill, Jr.
Kenneth Jack Hill
Leroy A. Hill
Lewis W. Hill
Lloyd Evan Hill
Melvin Jalmer Hill
Melvin R. Hill
Nathan L. Hill
Norman F. Hill
Owen T. Hill
Philip C. Hill
Philip J. Hill
Raymond Frederick Hill
Richard D. Hill
Richard E. Hill
Robert E. Hill
Robert H. Hill
Robert J. Hill
Robert Hill, Jr.
Robert L. Hill
Robert L. Hill
Robert L. Hill
Robert Livingston Hill
Robert Lloyd Hill
Samuel B. Hill
Shermont M. Hill
Thomas H. Hill
Thomas L. Hill
Thomas W. Hill
Wayne R. Hill
Wayne W. Hill
William A. Hill
William Francis Hill
William Francis Hill
William G. Hill
Willie D. Hill
Xavier W. Hill
Charles Sr Hillanbrand
Joseph F. Hillard
James D. Hille
James W. Hillen
Harry Hillenbrand
Fred D. Hilliard
Gerald G. Hilliard
Virgil C. Hilliard
Delbert J. Hillman
Chester E. Hills

Hunter Hills
Leslie B. Hills
Faine L. L Hillsman
Robert R. Hillyer
Carl G. Hilt
Charles E. Hiltibran
Bill G. Hilton
Clyde R. Hilton
George W. Hilton
Leo E. Hilton
Robert Warren Hilton
Selven Hilton
Richard E. Himelhan
Henry Himmel, Jr.
Paul J. Himmels
Homer Clair Hinckley
David C. Hindman
Robert Lee Hinds
Charles Henry Hines
Charles W. Hines
Edward F. Hines
Frank D. Hines
George H. Hines
Kenneth E. Hines
Leonard Hines
Milton Hines, Jr.
Richard Ellis Hines
Rollie W. Hines
Sam Hines
Wendell D. Hines
Robert F. Hiney
Lester C. Hingsbergen
Robert N. Hinkel
Floyd Everett Hinkle
William B. Hinkle
Weston Hinkley
David Hinkson
William H. Hinkson
Ned Hinnant, Jr.
August Henry Hinrichs, Jr.
Charles B. Hinson
Davey Lee Hinson
Grady Loyd Hinson
Henry E. Hinson
John R. Hinson
Talmage A. Hinson
Charles E. Hinte
Bobbie Jean Hinton
Lee R. Hinton
William Joseph Hinton
Harold Hintz
Lee P. Hintz
Henry G. Hiott
Robert J. Hipkins
Harold G. Hippie
Aranari Hiraga
Edward K. Hirakawa
Rin Hiraoka
Louis M. Hirata
Donald C. Hirn
Jiro Hirokane
Gerald M. Hironimus
Theodore B. Hirsch
Darrel Blaine Hirschbach
Axel Hirschberger
George O. Hiser
Paul L. Hitch
Velmon Hitchcock
Omar T. Hitchner
Clyde J. Hite
Eugene Taylor Hite
Thomas L. Hitt
William H. Hitt
Roger E. Hittle
George B. Hittner
Donald L. Hitz
Edmond Hitziger
Jack A. Hiwatashi
Raymond Hixenbaugh, Jr.
Woodrow W. Hixon
Shigeo Hiyane
Edward V. Hladik, Jr.
James F. Hlavac
Albert S. Hlousek
Edward L. Hluboky
Everett Ah Fong Ho
Arnold A. Hoag
Allan Bennett Hoagland
Charles R. Hoak
Moses K. Hoapili, Jr.
James M. Sr Hobar
Richard H. Hobart
William Otis Hobba
Jack Melvin Hobbie
Bill F. Hobbs
Carol H. Hobbs
Elven J. Hobbs
Howard L. Hobbs
Hoy E. Hobbs

Jack Donald Hobbs
Kenneth W. Hobbs
Robert L. Hobbs
Jimmie Rowland Hobday
Donald E. Hobin
Carlton L. Hobson
Lester E. Hobson
Philip Noyes Hobson, Jr.
Robert W. Hobson
William R. Hobson
Howard Robert Hoce
Marti F. Hochenberger
Bruce A. Hochstetler
Andrew D. Hockaday
Lonnie Hockaday
Charles W. Hockman
Arthur Leon A. Hodapp
Henry Charles Hodde, Jr.
Calvin Edgar Hodel
Charles Joseph Hodge
Elmer Hodge
Floyd L. Hodge
Harold L. Hodge
Herman H. Hodge
Lester L. Hodge
Odell A. Hodge
Tommie L. Hodge
Virgil L. Hodge
Wilbur L. Hodge
Willard P. Hodge
William M. Hodge
Arthur A. Hodges, Jr.
Charles E. Hodges
Emory E. Hodges
James L. Hodges
Kenneth Sherrill Hodges
Milton D. Hodges
Otmer F. Hodges, Jr.
Ralph Arnold Hodges
Theodore R. Hodges
William E. Hodges
Judd C. Hodgson
Thomas Salkald Hodgson
James R. Hodsdon, Jr.
Ralph L. Hodson
Verne E. Hodson
George M. Hoefeler
Irvin D. Hoeflich
Herbert G. Hoehn
Richard E. Hoehn
Douglas C. Hoekstra
James A. Hoelscher
Walter W. Hoeltje
Howard Frederick Hoelzel
John Thomas Hoenes
Raymond T. Hoeppner
Gabriel R. Hoerner
Dale A. Hoerr
Frank K. Hoesch
Kenneth G. Hoeschen
John L. Hoey
Robert E. Hoey
Weston Wesley Hoey
Alan Hoff
Herbert W. Hoff, Jr.
Stanford I. Hoff
Warren Mervin Hoff
Frank S. Hoffecker, Jr.
Donald L. Hoffenkamp
Donald Edward Hoffman
Earl L. Hoffman
Ernest Hoffman
Eugene G. Hoffman
Frank Carl Hoffman, Jr.
Frank V. Hoffman
Franklin R. Hoffman
Howard B. Hoffman, Jr.
Jerold C. Hoffman
Jo Hoffman
John A. Hoffman, Jr.
Kyle Arnold Hoffman
Lawrence E. Hoffman
Martin J. Hoffman
Marvin R. Hoffman
Patrick M. Hoffman
Ralph R. Hoffman, Jr.
Richard E. Hoffman
Ronald A. Hoffman
Samuel E. Hoffman
Theodore J. Hoffman
William B. Hoffman
William R. Hoffman
Lynn G. Hoffmaster
James G. Hofius
Warren J. Hofman
Kurk Hofmann
Henry Hofmeister, Jr.
Gerald D. Hofmeyer
David Duane Hofrichter

345

Ralph L. Hofstetter
Ashton S. Hogan
Billy R. Hogan
Charles L. Hogan
James F. Hogan
John R. Hogan
Kenneth A. Hogan
Mark L. Hogan
Paul E. Hogan
Richard Dudley Hogan
Richard Norman Hogan
Robert W. Hogan
Sylvester J. Hogan
Pearlie Hogans
Raymond H. Hogarth
Frederick W. Hogert
James Dean Hoggatt
Ishmael D. Hogston
Charles Donald Hogue
Clarence S. Hogue
James W. Hogue
Thomas E. Hogue
Joseph G. Hoh
Marvin J. Hoheimer
Karl Hoher, Jr.
Jack Hohman
Francis J. Hohn
James J. Hohn
Henry E. Hohne
William Harold III Hoiles
Freddie G. Hoit
Zane Moses Hoit
Walter M. Hojara
John David Hoke
Paul H. Hokoana
Bobby B. Holbrook
George H. Holbrook
Robert James Holbrook
William Holbrook, Jr.
Julius J. Holbrooks
John K. Holburn
William Lee Holcom
Elmer E. Holcomb
Francis A. Holcomb
Lester A. Holcomb
Donald J. Holcombe
Alford L. Holden
John J. Holden
Carl Henry Holder
J. P. Holder
Johnnie R. Holder
Ralph S. Holder
Ray E. Holder
Billy E. Holdman
Franklin J. Holdridge, Jr.
Donald F. Holdway
Preston Holeman, Jr.
Glenn P. Holenbeck
Joseph P. Holencik
Raymundo E. Holguin
Earl Holiday
Ebner C. Holke
William A. Holladay
Arlie Holland
Arthur J. Holland
Bill Jerome Holland
Carl C. Holland, Jr.
Dean M. Holland
Earl L. Holland
Everette Holland
Francis Eugene Holland
Frank E. Holland
Frank J. Holland
Gerald L. Holland
James R. Holland, Jr.
John D. Holland
Leland L. Holland
Louis Dearve Holland
Robert E. Holland
Wayne R. Holland
William M. Holland
Willie L. Holland
Ivan Lowell Hollar
Owen Hollar
Jack A. Hollars
Joseph F. Holle
Roy W. Hollenbaugh
Richard W. Hollenbeck
Charles J. Holleran
Frank R. Holley
J. T. Holley
James Lavell Holley
James M. Holley
John Cyril Holley
John F. Holley
Richard R. Holley
Thomas E. Holley
Billy E. Holliday
Delbert J. Holliday

Raymond F. Holliday
Raymond L. Holliday
Roy L. Hollifield
James N. Hollimon
Curtis Hollinger
Glenn E. Hollingshead
Dale G. Hollingsworth
Will H. Hollingsworth
G. D. Hollins
Paul A. Hollinshead
Edwin Hollis
Monroe J. Hollis
Robert L. Hollis
Edgar Allen Hollister
Paul H. Hollman
Arthur A. Holloway
Arthur W. Holloway
Frank Orville Holloway
Herschel E. Holloway
Jack Sinclair Holloway
James A. Holloway
Jimmie Holloway
Paul G. Holloway
Sherlyn Holloway
William G. Holloway
Clifford A. Holly
Ralph R. Holly
James R. Hollyfield
Richard G. Hollyoak
Alfred L. Holm
Albert C. Holman, Jr.
Charles R. Holman
Clark L. Holman
John Harvey Holman
John W. Holman
Charles W. Holmes
Clyde Thadeus Holmes, Jr.
Daniel L. Holmes
Earl Holmes
Edward E. Holmes
Freddie W. Holmes
Gilbert E. Holmes
Harold Ray Holmes
James R. Holmes
John E. Holmes
John Herbert Holmes
John Ray S. Holmes
L. C. Holmes, Jr.
Lawson Holmes
Oliver W. Holmes
Pervis S. Holmes
Richard D. Holmes
Richard L. Holmes
Ronald W. Holmes
Sonnie L. Holmes
Wallace Holmes, Jr.
Willard B. Holmes
William C. Holmes
Nathan Holmon, Jr.
Pentti J. Holmroos
Raymond H. Holsch
Norman R. Holsinger
Claude D. Holt
Crenshaw A. Holt
Henry E. Holt
Jack H. Holt
Kirby Howlett Holt
Max S. Holt
Melbourne Girard Holt
Oliver Holt
Norbert Francis Holter
Carl Henry Holtham
Raymond A. Holthaus
Charles E. Holticlaw
Robert F. Holtman
Robert F. Holtman
C. B. Holtzclaw, Jr.
Charles E. Holtzclaw
Charlie Holtzclaw
John M. Holtzclaw
Paul S. Holtzclaw
Walter Holynskyj
Scott Andersen Holz
Wayne M. Holzer
Wilfred J. Holzman
James W. Homan
Alfredo C. Homawan
Lawrence Homen
Clyde E. Homesley
Paul E. Homier
John Homola
Edward A. Homsey
Everette T. Honaker
John William Honaker
Tomio Honda
William R. Hone
Charles H. Honea
Eugene R. Honel
Dallas Honeycutt

J. W. Honeycutt
James B. Honeycutt
Roy J. Honeycutt
Louis C. Honeyman, Jr.
Jack Honixfelt
Harry Albert Honza
Charles E. Hood
George C. Hood
Haskel H. Hood
James J. Hood
James L. Hood
Lawrence C. Hood
Leonard Hood
Walter B. Hood
Walter L. Hood
Wilberforce Hood
Philip T. Hoogacker
Bruce A. Hook
Russell E. Hook
William K. Hook
Peter M. Hookano
Vernard K. Hookano
Charles H. Hooker
Joe E. Hooker
Alfonso E. Hooks
Charles E. Hooks
Leo H. Hooks
Patrick William Hoolahan
William J. Hoolihan
Alonza L. Hooper
Floyd E. Hooper
Gerald Duane Hooper
Joe Hooper
Maynard A. Hooper
Robert M. Hooper, Jr.
William Lee Hooper
Richard G. Hooten
Nils V. Hootman
Paul E. Hoots
Dale Lloyd Hoover
Marion D. Hoover
Robert E. Hoover
Robert G. Hoover
John G. Hope, Jr.
O. B. Hope, Jr.
Elbert L. Hopes
Daniel D. J. Hopfenperger
Arthur W. Hopfensperger
Donald L. Hopke
Robert Hopke, Jr.
Theodore H. Hopke
Albert Hopkins
Andrew L. Hopkins
Charles G. Hopkins
Donald W. Hopkins
Earl Goodman Hopkins
Francis J. Hopkins
Frank S. Hopkins
Gene L. Hopkins
Howard A. Hopkins
James R. Hopkins
James Rockne Hopkins
Jimmie L. Hopkins
Robert J. Hopkins
Robert Q. Hopkins
Russell C. Hopkins
Willard H. Hopkins
William E. Hopkins
Billy E. Hopper
Charles T. Hopper
George Hopper, Jr.
James Howard Hopper
Joseph J. Hopper
Roy J. Hopper
William P. Hopper
Byrd W. Hoppes
Daniel H. Hopping
Robert C. Hopping
Charles W. Hopson
John Rockne Horan
Robert M. Horan
Leonard M. Horender
William C. Horensky
Charles Ernest Horn
Harrold Kent Horn
Herman James Horn
Hubert F. Horn
Jack Horn
John Lucius Horn
Merwin K. Horn
Roland E. J. Horn
Samuel J. Horn
Willard Boyden Horn
James H. Hornback
Walter Barry Hornbeak
Arvel C. Horne, Jr.
Billie D. Horne
Robert J. Horne
Russell T. Horne

Waymond Leon Horne
Hamilton P. Horner
Herbert M. Horner
Jack A. Horner
John Joseph Horner
Joseph H. Horner
Walter C. Horner
William D. Horner
Floyd J. Horning
James W. Horning, Jr.
William J. Horning
Glenn W. Hornsby
Frederick L. Iii Hornung
John A. Horony
Robert A. Horowitz
William R. Horrigan, Jr.
Doyle C. Horst
Bill Horton
Charles Thomas Horton
Duane F. Horton
Harold E. Horton
Herman Leon Horton
Hubert Horton, Jr.
Isaac Horton
John B. Horton
Leroy S. Horton, Jr.
Leroy William Horton
Lonnie Edward Horton
Lovie L. Horton
Roosevelt Horton
Thomas Lyle Horton
Wallace R. Horton
Henry G. Horwath
Clarence G. Hosch
Stephen Vincent Hoschler
Clarence E. Hoskins
Clyde R. Hoskins
Dale O. Hoskins
Howard Hoskins
William R. Hoskins, Jr.
Robert E. Hosler
Robert J. Hossler
Samuel Hoster, Jr.
Edward Hostler, Jr.
William H. Hotchkiss
William H. Hott
Thomas A. Hotte
Oliver W. Hottenstein
Frederick Hottin
William Francis Hottinger
Joseph A. Houchens
Robert E. Houchin
Jack Allen Houck
Norvel Floyd Houck
Arnold J. Houdek
Ronald L. Houdek
Billy Elvis Hough
James D. Houghton
Rodney H. Houghton
Eugene O. Houle
Patrick J. Houlihan
Arthur William Hoult
Robert B. Hounchell
Adelbert R. House
Douglas V. House
Elon Lewis House
Eugene T. House
Harvey J. House
Henry W. House, Jr.
Russel Junior House
Winfield Scott House
George Housekeeper
John C. Houser
Marlyn F. Houser
Robert D. Houser
Wayne E. Houser
Eldon E. Housh
Bernard Houston
Bobby L. Houston
Calvin C. Houston
James L. Houston
James M. Houston
Lonzo Houston
Raymond Burl Houston
Ronald B. Houston
Rufus Houston
Donald James Hovatter
Sanford Hovda
Alfred O. Hove
John Hovel
John I. Hoven
Glenn A. Hovey
Howard C. Hovey
Kenneth B. Hovis, Jr.
Albert Howard
Arnold L. Howard
Arnold S. Howard
Brison Howard
Charles H. Howard

Cordell Howard
Daniel B. Howard
David Wayne Howard
Eddie Howard, Jr.
Edward M. Howard
Everett J. Howard
Frank R. Howard
Henry C. Howard
James L. Howard
James W. Howard
Joe W. Howard
John C. Howard
Lewis P. Howard
Lloyd Leslie Howard
Melvin John Howard
Olin Howard
Oliver M. Howard
Philip J. Howard
Ralph A. Howard
Robert C. Howard
Robert W. Howard
Solomon C. Howard
Walter R. Howard
William G. Howard, Jr.
William T. Howard
Zebulon Howard
James A. Howard, Jr.
Raymond Howard, Jr.
David Kenyon Howcroft
James H. Howdyshell
Bernard L. Howe
Edwin Yates Howe
Jack D. Howe
James R. Howe
James W. Howe
Louis W. Howe
Robert G. Howe
Robert N. Howe
Robert L. Howe
Claude C. Howell, Jr.
Clifton O. Howell
Edward D. Howell
Elmer Howell
Gilbert L. Howell
Harley D. Howell
Harold Howell
Harold J. Howell
Howard Dempsey Howell
James Howell
James Hoff Howell, Jr.
John Theodore Howell
Joseph A. Howell
Lloyd B. Howell
Luther Ray Howell
Martin Fredrick Howell, Jr.
Martin L. Howell
Robert N. Howell
Roy L. Howell
Virgil L. Howell
William Howell, Jr.
William L. Howell
Ruel L. Howell
Dale R. Howell
Benjamin B. Hower
Wayne E. Howerton
Bruce D. Howes
Ross L. Howey
Roy Franklin Howington
Edward F. Howley
Gary B. Howse
Edward D. Howser
Frank B. Howze
Orville C. Howze
John Alfred Hoy, Jr.
Thomas Samuel Hoy
Russell S. Hoyer
William C. Hoyes
Duane A. Hoyle
Donald C. Hoysradt
Donald L. Hoyt
Lester G. Hoyt
Vernon N. Hoyt
Jurij B. Hrab
Michael Hrabcsak
George J. Hric
Emil J. Hrisko
Clayton Hristopulos
Milan Hrnciar
John F. Hronek
John R. Hronek
Glen M. Huback
Ralph E. Hubartt, Jr.
Lester Hubbard
Raymond C. Hubbard
Raymond E. Hubbard
Thomas Amory Hubbard
Walter C. Hubbard
William Hubbard, Jr.
Ralph O. Hubbell

Sammie Hubbell
Harry A. Hubbs
Paul Edward Hubbs
Robert D. Hubbs
Gene Huber
Henry L. Huber
Ramon L. Huber
William J. Huber, Jr.
Charles J. Huber
William Augusta Hubert
William F. Hubert
Raymond E. Huck
Billy R. Huckabee
John B. Huckin
Clayton M. Huckins
Leland C. Hucks
Robert J. Hudak
George Huddleston
James L. Huddleston
Leonard G. Huddleston, Jr.
Marion E. Hudecek
James Robert Hudgens
Winston H. Hudgins, Jr.
Con Doffie Hudnall
Belvin Hudson
Benjamin R. Hudson
Billie R. Hudson
Carl H. Hudson
Carroll W. Hudson
Dover C. Hudson
Earl Gene Hudson
Frank C. Hudson
Frederick G. Iii Hudson
George Marvin Hudson
Harold L. Hudson
Harry C. Hudson, Jr.
James A. Hudson
James Hudson, Jr.
John E. Hudson
Lamar G. Hudson
Laurence Harold Hudson
Leslie D. Hudson
Raymond F. Hudson
Robert Edward Hudson
Robert L. Hudson
Robert W. Hudson
Rufus F. Hudson, Jr.
William J. Hudson
Jack G. Hudspeth
Ronald D. Huebner
George F. Huetger
Carl Huey, Jr.
Alfred A. Hufendick
Clarence Henry Huff, Jr.
Earl J. Huff, Jr.
Emerson P. Huff, Jr.
Glenn Huff
Grange W. Huff
Kenneth L. Huff
Eugene Huff
Acy Huffman
Gerald L. Huffman
Glenn E. Huffman
Herbert D. Huffman
Ronald C. Huffman
Roy L. Huffman
William R. Huffman
Rufus G. Huffstickler
Joe A. Huffstutler
John O. Hugg
Horace W. Huggins
Kennon A. Huggins, Jr.
Leland V. Huggins
Albert J. Hughes
Arthur L. Hughes
Bobby F. Hughes
Charles C. Hughes
Claude E. Hughes
Clifford Hughes
Dorman D. Hughes
Elzie F. Hughes
Ernest D. Hughes
Floyd W. Hughes
Frankie B. Hughes
Fred Hughes
Fred Curtis Hughes
Fred L. Hughes
George L. Hughes
Gordon Matthew Hughes
Harold Donald Hughes
Jack W. Hughes
James C. Hughes, Jr.
James L. Hughes
Jesse M. Hughes
John Allen Hughes, Jr.
John E. Hughes
John Joseph Hughes, Jr.
John P. Hughes
Joseph L. Hughes

Leonard Harold Hughes
Leroy Hughes
Lloyd Edgar Hughes
Lucius W. Hughes
Michael J. Hughes
Morris E. Hughes
Norman R. Hughes
Philip T. Hughes
Phillip C. Hughes
Ray T. Hughes
Richard K. Hughes
Robert E. Hughes
Robert J. Hughes
Roy T. Hughes
Walter L. Hughes
Walter N. Hughes
Wayne G. Hughes
William L. G. Hughes
Gerard Hughes
Kenneth W. Hughes
Barney W. Hughes, Jr.
Bruce J. Hughes
Dalton R. Hughey
Harry R. Hughes
Barney M. Huguley
Kenneth P. Huhn
Paul F. Hukill
Frank E. Hula
John Hula
Gary F. Hulburt
Ervin Hulett
Harold L. Hulett
Arlton C. Hull
Homer Wylie Hull
Leonard C. Hull
Richard Barnett Hull
Charles O. Hull
Jackie Lee Hulse
Benjamin William Hulsey
Ray Dean Hulsey
Thomas J. Hulsey, Jr.
William H. Hulska
Miles N. Hultberg
Jans H. Hulzebos
Max R. Humbarger
Ralph H. Humboldt
Thomas A. Hume
James E. Humerick
Melvin J. Humes
Robert A. Humes
Barnum Ray Humiston
Donald L. Humiston
Leslie R. T. Humiston
Jerome V. Hummel
Joseph Hummel
Ralph M. Hummel, Jr.
William E. Hummel
William John Hummer
Joseph Humphery
Sam Humphfus
Douglas E. Humphrey
Harold W. Humphrey
Robert Jay Humphrey
Thomas H. Humphrey
Veloy Gene Humphrey
Wilfred H. Humphrey
Richard D. Humphreys
Gordon P. Humphries
James W. Humphries
Eugene H. Hums
Coleman C. Hundley
Elrin M. Hundley
Leonard J. Hundshamer
Herbert D. T. Hung
Edward W. Hunn
James A. Hunnicutt
Matthew Hunnicutt
John Davis Hunsberger
Kenneth P. Hunsicker
Robert K. Hunsinger
Alexander Hunt
Allan Parker Hunt, Jr.
Arnold M. Hunt
Byron J. Hunt
Carl V. Hunt
Charles E. Hunt, Jr.
Charles Onyx Hunt
Charlie J. Hunt
Daniel Hunt
David J. Hunt
Duane M. Hunt
Frederic L. Hunt, Jr.
Frederick Stoughton Hunt
Gwyn R. Hunt
Lawrence E. Hunt
Melvin Joseph Hunt
Ora Hunt, Jr.
Ray D. Hunt
Richard Hunt

Robert D. Hunt
Robert Griffith Hunt
Robert Joseph Hunt
Robert R. Hunt
Ronald Jackson Hunt
Thomas A. Hunt
William Clifton Hunt
William E. Hunt
William J. Hunt
William P. Hunt, Jr.
Willie R. Hunt
Dallas W. Hunt
Allen Edward Hunter
Carson Hunter
Charles O. Hunter
David F. Hunter
Donald B. Hunter
Donald E. Hunter
Edward D. Hunter
Forrest L. Hunter
Francis J. Hunter
Gerald J. Hunter
Herbert Frederick Hunter
James E. Hunter
James L. Hunter
James W. Hunter
Joe Hunter
John L. Hunter
Joseph Hunter, Jr.
Marrion L. Hunter
Millard Harold Hunter
Robert E. Hunter
William Hunter
William Bryant Hunter
William C. Hunter
William Ralph Hunter
Mackabee Hunter, Jr.
Henry H. Hunter
George Hunter, Jr.
James B. Huntley
James E. Huntley
Robert L. Hupel
Austin West Hurd
Charles W. Hurd, Jr.
Judson P. Hurd
Joseph A. Hurd
Warren O. Hurdle
Robert G. Hurley
William Hurley
David A. Hurr
Elijah P. Hursey
Jans Fredrick Hursey
Franklin Deland Hursh
Charles M. Hurst
Charley L. Hurst
Donald L. Hurst
Elmer B. Hurst
Francis J. Hurst
Franklin D. Hurst
Henry D. Hurst
Irwin M. Hurst
James Hurst
Roy L. Hurst
Charles Wayne Hurst
Billie Hurst
Clarence A. Hurt, Sr.
Donald J. Hurt
Garrison G. Hurt
Norbert G. Hurt
Thomas E. Hurt
Albert F. Hurtt
Donald J. Hushelpeck
William C. Hushion
Spencer V. Huskey
Robert Francis Huss
Wilfred K. Hussey, Jr.
Willie J. Huston
Louis B. Huston
Andrew Huszar
Ernest Hutchens, Jr.
Lawrence W. Hutchens
Harold E. Hutchens
Phares I. Hutcherson
Thomas E. Hutcherson
Amos R. Hutchins
Earl T. Hutchins
Fletcher Marion Hutchins
James C. Hutchins
Johnnie R. Hutchins
Arthur Earl Hutchinson
Donald L. Hutchinson
Gerald W. Hutchinson
Hardy James Hutchinson
Lorenzer Hutchinson
Richard D. Hutchinson
William P. Hutchinson
Ross E. Hutchinson
Alfred O. Hutchison
Barney E. Hutchison

David C. Hutchison
Jack W. Hutchison
Otis E. Hutchison
Raymond E. Hutchison
Robert N. Hutchison
Robert W. Hutchison
William Paul Huth
William Hutnick, Jr.
Spencer W. Hutsenpiller
Robert D. Hutson
Thomas Joseph Hutson
Clyde Cecil Hutson
Daniel H. Huttner, Jr.
Albert C. Hutto
George H. Hutto
Donald J. Hutton
Herbert H. Hutton
James A. Hutton
Louie E. Hutton
Richard E. Hutton
William F. Hutton, Jr.
William Hutzel
Aubrey E. Hux
Charlie E. Hux
Billy C. Huxhold
Donald George Huyck
William L. Huyette
Benab Hyatt
Don Hyatt
Edward Hyatt
Lester T. Hyatt
Raymond G. Hyatt
S. A. Hyatt, Jr.
Richard K. Hybarger
Lee Roy Hyche
Charles Russell Hyde
Daniel T. Hyde
David Lee Hyde
Robert J. Hyde
Vernon D. Hyde
James H. Hyde
Brendan P. Hyland
Billy E. Hylton
Emory E. Hylton
Lonnie B. Hylton, Jr.
Rufus J. Hyman
Benjamin A. Hymel, Jr.
Martin A. Hynek
James Harris Hynes
Joseph W. Hynes
Robert E. Hynes
Jack R. Hyre
Kenneth C. Hyslop
Theodore A. Hyson

— I —

Alvin H. Iaea
Elia J. Iannelli
Joe D. Ibanez
Luis Joe Ibarra
Joe W. Ibay
Clayton G. Ibbotson
Colin C. Iccles
Harold William Icett, Jr.
David W. Icho
Claudio Icmat
Paul J. Iddings, Jr.
Wilbert R. Idle
Herbert K. Idol
Miguel Igartua, Jr.
Chares Ludwig Igel
Victor M. Iglesias
Antonio H. Ignacio
William C. Igo
Tamiya Ikeda
Yoshio Ikeda
Arthur R. Ikkala
Thomas Michael Ilic
James Alfred Illa
John P. Imber
John J. Imbert
David W. Imel
Charles Henry Imhof
James Paul Immel
Peter Immordino
Robert K. Imrie
Roy H. Inboden
Nicholas C. Incontrera
Walter S. Ingalls
James F. Ingelsby
Gordon Ray Ingersoll
Rolland Ingersoll
Samuel D. Inghram
Warren A. Ingland
Clarence B. Ingle
Kenneth Russell Ingman
Martin V. Ingoglia
William Randolh Ingold

Gerald Ellis Ingraham
Burnett H. Ingram
Edward Ingram
Eugene B. Ingram, Jr.
Gene M. Ingram
George Ingram
Glenn R. Ingram, Jr.
Harold G. Ingram
Hubert D. Ingram
James L. Ingram
John Edward Ingram
Van Conrade Ingram
Lloyd Wendell Ingrim
William S. Inloes
Anderson F. Inman
Richard George Inman
Mark Inokuchi
John R. Inyard
Harold J. Iott
Frank Ippolito
Charley B. Ireland
Malcolm D. Ireland
Rodriguez Irizarry
Obdulio Irizarry-Gerena
Juan R. Irizarry-Oliver
Theodore R. Irvin
Richard D. Irvine
Dennis Irving
Leon C. Irving, Jr.
Gerald Irwin
Tedrick G. Irwin
William J. Irwin
Thomas Isaac, Jr.
Bernard A. Isaacs
Elmer C. Isaacs
Wilbur A. Isaacs
Billy J. Isbell
Richard Isbell
William H. Isbell
Robert Campbell Isbester
Eugene J. Isbrandt
Raymond E. Iserman
Ortiz Raymon Isern
Harry Ishem
Edward M. Ishibashi
Hidemro Saito Ishida
Mitsuyoshi Ishida
Wallace K. Ishikawa
Albert A. Ishimoto
Robert S. Ishimoto
Anthony T. Iskierka
Raul R. Islas
Richard Martin Islas
Rollin J. Isler
Dayton F. Isley
Guiseppe Isolano
Joseph M. Isom
Richard Isovitsch
Paul E. Israel
Yukinobu Ito
Yeikichi B. Itokazu
Ralph M. Iuliano
Lester G. Ivancich
David Darwin Ivens
James Eugene Iverson
William M. Ives
Charles Edward Ivey
John Ray Ivey
Lacy C. Ivey
Theodore A. Ivey
Marvin L. Ivie
John E. Ivins
Robert D. Ivison
Emmit M. Ivy
Woodson L. Ivy
Osamu Iwami
Frank J. Iwanczyk
Shogo Iwatsuru
Philip James Iyotte
Paul Izor
Francisco A. Izquierdo
Isamu Izu
Franklin Narwaki Izuo

— J —

Daniel Jack
James Hamilton Jack
Kenneth J. Jack
Nick Sam Jack
Amel C. Jackl
Jackie D. Jackman
William Edwin Jackman
David Jackmon
Albert Jackson
Amos J. Jackson
Archie C. Jackson
Arnold R. Jackson
Arthur Jackson

Bailey Jackson, Jr.
Billy J. Jackson
Bobby J. Jackson
Bruce D. Jackson
Calvin Jackson
Carol J. Jackson
Charles Perry Jackson
Charlie L. Jackson
Chester A. Jackson
Clinton H. Jackson, Jr.
Comer Jackson, Jr.
Dan Jackson, Jr.
David Jackson, Jr.
Donald Joe Jackson
Donald L. Jackson
Donald Ray Jackson
Donovan J. Jackson
Douglas G. Jackson
Earl K. Jackson
Edward M. Jackson
Elman Jackson
Elwood L. Jackson
Eugene A. Jackson
Eugene L. Jackson
Floyd J. R. Jackson
General E. Jackson
George Jackson
George W. Jackson
Harold S. Jackson
Harold S. Jackson
Henry A. Jackson
Herbert Jackson
Herbert H. Jackson
Howard Leon Jackson
Howard T. Jackson
Irby L. Jackson
Irvin L. Jackson
Irvin L. Jackson
J. C. Jackson
James A. Jackson
James Douglas Jackson
James E. Jackson, Jr.
James H. Jackson
James Harvey Jackson
James Henry Jackson
James L. Jackson
James R. Jackson
Jeff D. Jackson
Jeremiah Jackson
Jerry Jackson, Jr.
Jesse C. Jackson
Jim H. Jackson
John E. Jackson
John J. Jackson
John W. Jackson
Kenneth R. Jackson
Knausberry Jackson
Laurence Bell Jackson
Lawrence Jackson
Leonard L. Jackson
Levi Jackson, Jr.
Marion E. Jackson
Melvin R. Jackson
Newton C. Jackson
Oliver Jackson
Otis L. Jackson
R. A. Jackson
R. D. Jackson
Ralph V. Jackson
Richard D. Jackson
Richard Loran Jackson
Robert E. Jackson
Robert E. Jackson
Robert G. Jackson
Robert H. Jackson
Ronald C. Jackson
Ronald C. Jackson
Ronald M. Jackson
Roy R. Jackson
Virgil Andrew Jackson, Jr.
Walter Jackson
William Jackson
William D. Jackson
William L. Jackson
William R. Jackson
William R. Jackson
William T. Jackson
William T. Jackson
Willie Jackson
Willie L. Jackson
Arthur F. Jacob
Walter G. Jacob
Carl A. Jacobs
Christopher Keith Jacobs
Fleming B. Jacobs
George J. Jacobs
George L. Jacobs
Harrison Chase Jacobs
Herbert J. Jacobs

Herman L. Jacobs
James E. Jacobs
Joseph Thomas Jacobs
Lloyd W. Jacobs
Michael Lester Jacobs
Norval C. Jacobs
Ralph E. Jacobs
Robert H. Jacobs
Robert T. Jacobs
Ronald D. Jacobs
Harry Reichert Jacobsen
Robert Jacobsen
Norman W. Jacobson
Paul Joseph Jacobson
Vernelle Jacobson
Ernest J. Jacques
Leo W. Jacques
Leon J. Jacques, Jr.
Mariano Jacques, Jr.
Robert D. Jacques
Ronald R. Jacques
John Thomas Jageacks
Edward J. Jager
Joseph Anthony Jagielio
Arthur C. Jagnow
Erich W. Jahn
Richard Jahnke
Antonio Jaime
Frank J. Jakabosky
Eugene Jakielek
Edward Jakubowski
Andrew Ralph Jakusz
John R. Jalas
Felton L. Jamerson
Frank O. Jamerson
Albert James, Jr.
Alex Daniel James
Carroll L. James
Charles E. James
Charles J. James
Clarence A. James
Davis E. James
Elwood F. James
George T. James
Gerald Jerry James
Henry P. James
Howard E. James
Howard F. James
Jesse Edward James
Jesse J. James
John Alvin James
John Clell James
John W. James
Joseph H. James
Larry P. James
Lawrence B. James
Leo J. James
Luther Jesse James
Robert H. James
Roy F. James
William R. James
William R. James
William Reid James
Allan E. Jamieson
Joseph Charles Jamieson
Hugh D. Jamison
James R. Jamison
James Ray Janca
Paul Janco
Joseph A. Janczak, Jr.
Walter P. Janeczko
Harlan S. Janeksela
Thomas Arthur Janelle
Howard W. Janes
Robert L. Janes
Peter M. Janettas
George Jangula
Leonard D. Janicki
Adrian D. Janiszewski
Richard Jankowski
Richard J. Jankowski
Rudy Jann
Otto Carl Jannusch
Frank P. Janowitz
Paul Joseph Janowsky
Edward W. Jansen
Stanley W. Jansen
Marvin T. Janssen
James January
Joseph Januszewski
Dominick Januzzi
Ananias Janvrin
Richard J. Jaques
Louis Naranjo Jaramillo
Roselio Jaramillo
Ray F. Jardine
Robert V. Jardine
Harold Jarmon
Ervin R. Jarmusek

347

J. D. Jarnagin
Spencer Hewitt Jarnagin
Walter S. Jarosik
Thomas R. Jarrard
Calvin C. Jarrell
Charles E. Jarrell
Cleveland Jarrell
Lonnie Ray Jarrell
Mont Jarrell
Carl E. Jarrett
Charles Edward Jarrett
John Jarrett
John W. Jarrett
Roland J. Jarvey
Donald R. Jarvis
Frederick C. Jarvis
Raymond F. Jarvis
John Jasinski
Donald C. Jaskulske
Laurence R. Jasmer
Joe Jaso
Charles Jasperson
Harold D. Jasperson
Alan R. Jastram
Joseph Jaszemski
Carter W. Jaudon, Jr.
Francisco G. Javier
Albert H. Jay, Jr.
James Frederick Jay
Edward R. Jaynes
Eugene C. Jaynes
John W. Jeal
Henry Jeanjacques, Jr.
Paul A. Jeanplong
William R. Jecelin
John S. Jeffcoat
Martin Luther Jeffcoat, Jr.
Donald J. Jeffers
Darwin I. Jefferson
Edward V. Jefferson
Harry F. Jefferson
James Jefferson
James H. Jefferson
James Jefferson, Jr.
John D. Jefferson
Loyd Jefferson
Robert L. Jefferson
Sam H. Jefferson, Jr.
Thomas E. Jefferson
James H. Jefferys
Wayne O. Jeffords
Alford Jeffrey
Howard R. Jeffrey
Robert L. Jeffrey
Paul E. Jeffries
Victor L. Jeffries
Frank Joseph Jeffs
Stuart Raymond Jelly
Raymond J. Jelniker
Jose D. Jemente
Charles Jemison
Gerald J. Jendraszek
James Craig Jenkel
Albin R. Jenkins
Benjamin W. Jenkins
Calvin Jenkins
Carl August Jenkins
Clifford L. Jenkins
Donald C. Jenkins
Donald Russell Jenkins
Edward Jenkins
Floyd B. Jenkins, Jr.
Francis R. Jenkins
George W. Jenkins
Grover G. Jenkins
Harland D. Jenkins
Howard L. Jenkins
Hugh Jenkins
Jessie R. Jenkins
Kermit E. Jenkins
Paul L. Jenkins
Thomas K. Jenkins
Vernon D. Jenkins
William C. Jenkins
William H. Jenkins
William L. Jenkins
Dalton M. Jenks
Raymond P. Jenner
Delbert G. Jennette
Alfred S. Jennings
David B. Jennings
Elijah L. Jennings
Frank P. Jennings
Harold L. Jennings
John E. Jennings, Jr.
Joseph F. Jennings
Payne Jennings, Jr.
Ralph Jennings, Jr.
Ray L. Jennings

Robert Elmer Jennings
Robert L. Jennings
Carl C. Jensen
Dale Ellsworth Jensen
David G. Jensen
George R. Jensen
Gordon W. Jensen
John Robert Jensen
Keith A. Jensen
Kenneth Lyle Jensen
Morton Henry Jensen
Paul T. Jensen
Richard A. Jensen
Richard Delbert Jensen
Roy L. Jensen
Sylvester L. Jensen
Walter V. Jensen
Wayne Frederick Jensen
Wilbur Dean Jensen
William L. Jensen
Austin Clifford Jenson
Henry Dillon Jenson
Stanley C. Jenson
Donald P. Jentzsch
Harlan L. Jeppson
Billy Jerkins
Donald W. Jerman
Carl Odell Jernigan
Vernon Jernigan
Richard Jerome
John M. Jerred
Lawrence E. Jerrell
Thaddeus J. Jerz
Paul S. Jerzak
Raymond Earl Jesko
Marvin D. Jessen
Howard L. Jessup
William T. Jessup
William F. Jester
William R. Jester
Donald E. Jeter
James L. C. Jeter
Robert M. Jeter
Zee A. Jeter, Jr.
Joseph S. Jett
Karl R. Jetter
Charles L. Jetton
Daniel B. Jewell
William Clark Jewell, Jr.
Donald T. Jewels
Arthur F. Jewett
Richard G. Jewett
Pete Jimenes
Amador Jimenez
Candido Jimenez
Hernandez Jimenez
Joe V. Jimenez
Manuel J. Jimenez
Merced Ang Jimenez
Nieves Ism Jimenez
Victor P. Jimenez
Antonio Jimenez-Olivencia
Miguel Jimenez-Tosado
Billie Joe Jimerson
Elvis J. Jimes
Marvin H. Jines
Leonard W. E. Jinks
Williard Gene Jiricek
Edward H. Joachinson, Jr.
Jose Joaquim
Lewis Earl Jobe
Vernon D. Jobe
Kenneth J. Jobin
Cornelius A. Jochim
Lawrence O. Jock
James L. Joe
Joseph B. Joe
John Edward Joens
Richard Arnold Johannsen
Edward C. Johansen
Martin P. Johmann
David Murdock John, Jr.
Leroy John
Robert L. John
Caleb Johnkins, Jr.
Frank R. Johns
Johnnie E. Johns
Morris W. Johns
Philip E. Johns
Ronald L. Johns
Willie Lee Johns
T. T Johnsbury
Norman Dale Johnsen
Adrian R. Johnson
Adrian Warren Johnson
Alex Johnson
Alfred Johnson
Alfred L. Johnson
Alton T. Johnson

Andrew Johnson, Jr.
Andy C. Johnson
Arthur Johnson
Arthur Edward Johnson
Arthur Jack Johnson
Arthur O. Johnson
Arthur R. Johnson
Arthur W. Johnson
Benjamin Johnson
Bill Ed Johnson
Billy Edward Johnson
Bobbie J. Johnson
Bobby Johnson
Bobby L. Johnson
Carl J. Johnson
Carl W. Johnson
Carlis E. Johnson
Cassius E. Johnson
Cecil E. Johnson
Charles B. Johnson
Charles E. Johnson
Charles E. Johnson
Charles F. Johnson
Charles L. Johnson
Charles L. Johnson
Charles Lee Johnson
Charles R. Johnson
Clarence A. Johnson
Claude L. Johnson
Clifford R. Johnson
Clifford S. Johnson
Curtis Lee Johnson
Darrel V. Johnson
David A. Johnson
David H. Johnson
David Lee Johnson
De Witt W. Johnson
Dean B. Johnson
Donald H. Johnson
Donald J. Johnson
Donald M. Johnson
Donald R. Johnson
Donald R. Johnson
Donald T. Johnson
Earl N. Johnson
Edgar Johnson
Edgar E. Johnson
Edmund R. Johnson
Edward A. Johnson
Eldride Johnson
Elijah G. Johnson
Elma H. Johnson
Eric Johnson, Jr.
Ervin M. Johnson
Eugene Johnson
Eugene A. Johnson
Eugene Fred Johnson
Eugene P. Johnson
Eugene V. Johnson
Everett E. Johnson
Francis E. Johnson
Francis M. Johnson
Frank Johnson
Frank H. Johnson
Franklin D. Johnson
Fred A. Johnson
Fred R. Johnson
Fred S. Johnson
Frederick Johnson
Gaynor T. Johnson
George A. Johnson
George B. Johnson
George J. Johnson
George W. Johnson
George Walter Johnson
Gerald D. Johnson
Gerald Emmett Johnson
Gordon Eugene Johnson
Gordon R. Johnson
Granville Johnson
Gudmund C. Johnson
Harold A. Johnson
Harry Johnson
Harry C. Johnson
Harry W. Johnson, Jr.
Henry F. Johnson
Herbert Johnson
Herbert Johnson
Herbert C. Johnson
Herbert C. Johnson
Herbert W. Johnson
Irl O. Johnson, Jr.
Irving D. Johnson
Jack Weldon Johnson
James Johnson
James A. Johnson
James A. Johnson
James A. Johnson
James B. Johnson

James E. Johnson
James E. Johnson
James J. Johnson
James N. Johnson
James V. Johnson
James W. Johnson
James W. Johnson
Jay D. Johnson
Jefferson Johnson
Jesse Johnson
Jessie Johnson
Joe E. Johnson
Joe Lanfort Johnson
John B. Johnson
John E. Johnson
John E. Johnson
John E. Johnson
John H. Johnson
John H. Johnson
John H. Johnson
John Laverne Johnson
John N. Johnson
John P. Johnson
John P. Johnson
John R. Johnson
John Ross Johnson
John W. Johnson
John William Johnson
Johnny Menlo Johnson
Jose Johnson
Joseph Johnson
Joseph E. Johnson
Joseph E. Johnson
Kenneth C. Johnson
Kenneth J. Johnson
Kenneth M. Johnson
Kenneth M. Johnson
Lawrence D. Johnson
Lee G. Johnson
Leon Johnson
Leonard Le Roy Johnson
Leroy Johnson
Leroy Johnson
Leroy Johnson
Lewis Harry Johnson
Louis C. Johnson
Lowell W. Johnson
Lyle E. Johnson
Mack D. N. Johnson
Major A. Johnson
Marvin J. Johnson
Maurice Johnson
Maynard B. Johnson
Mckinley Johnson
Mearl E. Johnson
Melfred Johnson
Melvin E. Johnson
Melvin J. Johnson
Melvin Leroy Johnson
Melvin M. Johnson
Merlin E. Johnson
Merlyn Johnson
Merton R. Johnson
Milton Johnson
Milton E. Johnson
Myron Johnson
Nathaniel Johnson
Nathaniel Johnson
Neil R. Johnson
Norman H. Johnson
Norman John Johnson
Norman Riley Johnson
Olin Lyle Johnson
Olin W. Johnson
Orvel J. Johnson
Otis S. Johnson
Ottis D. Johnson
Paul L. Johnson
Phillip B. Johnson
Randle Johnson
Randolph A. Johnson
Ray Johnson
Raymond Lloyd Johnson
Raymond R. Johnson
Reginald Varnell Johnson
Rex G. Johnson
Richard Johnson
Richard A. Johnson
Richard B. Johnson
Richard Gustav Johnson
Richard L. Johnson
Richard M. Johnson
Robert F. Johnson
Robert F. Johnson
Robert Johnson, Jr.
Robert L. Johnson
Robert M. Johnson
Robert William Johnson
Ronald H. Johnson

Ronald J. Johnson
Ronald M. Johnson
Rosamond Johnson
Roy C. Johnson
Roy L. Johnson
Roy L. Johnson
Samuel Johnson
Samuel W. Johnson
Seldon T. Johnson
Theodore R. Johnson
Thomas C. Johnson
Thomas M. Johnson
Thomas M. Johnson
Thurman Russell Johnson
Tom Henry Johnson
Tommy Johnson
Tommy J. Johnson
Travis M. Johnson
Truman E. Johnson
Varnell Johnson
Vernon Glen Johnson
Vernon V. Johnson
Victor E. Johnson
Walter C. Johnson
Walter H. Johnson
Walter Martin Johnson
Warren E. Johnson
Warren G. Johnson
Wesley Johnson
Wesley H. Johnson
Wilford Johnson
William Johnson
William Binkley Johnson
William C. Johnson
William D. Johnson
William D. Johnson
William D. Johnson
William E. Johnson, Jr.
William F. Johnson
William H. Johnson
William H. Johnson
William J. Johnson
William O. Johnson
William W. Johnson
William Z. Johnson
Carl F. Johnston, Jr.
Edward P. Johnston
Edwin E. Johnston
Frank Staley Johnston, Jr.
George Johnston
George E. Johnston
Harold D. Johnston
Harold Monroe Johnston
James F. Johnston
James F. III Johnston
Jimmie Curtis Johnston
Joseph E. Johnston
Richard E. Johnston
Robert F. Johnston
Robert L. Johnston
Thomas Henry Johnston
Waldo J. Johnston
William R. Johnston
Roy T. Johr
Paul J. Joiner
Joseph E. Jolley
Jack A. Jolliff
Marvin H. Jolliff
Lovell P. Jollymore
Robert R. Joly
Bernard Charles Jonas
Adolph Jones
Albert T. Jones
Allie C. Jones
Andrew W. Jones
Anthony J. Jones
Arthur Macon Jones
Arthur O. Jones
Ashley C. Jones
Aston Jones
Baskil Jones
Bertram E. Jones
Billy B. Jones
Bobby J. Jones
Bobby J. Jones
Buster Brown Jones
Calvin Solmon Jones
Carl R. Jones
Carl R. Jones
Carol Joseph Jones
Charles Jones
Charles C. Jones
Charles Moye Jones
Charles W. Jones
Charlie Jones
Charlie F. Jones
Clanton C. Jones, Jr.
Clarence E. Jones
Clarence G. Jones

Clifford L. Jones
Clifford M. Jones
Clyde Jones
Connie W. Jones
Dale Royce Jones
David Jones
David R. Jones
Davis W. Jones
Delman J. Jones
Dennis Jones
Dennis M. Jones
Donald Jones
Donald Earnest Jones
Donald J. Jones
Donald L. Jones
Doyle T. Jones
Dwight D. Jones
Earl E. Jones
Edgar D. Jones
Edward Jones, Jr.
Edward M. Jones
Emerson L. Jones
Ensley Jones
Eugene Jones
Eugene N. Jones
Eugene Vester Jones
Everett M. Jones
Floyd L. Jones
Frank L. Jones
Frank L. Jones
Franklin L. Jones
George Jones
George Jones
George Dewey Jones, Jr.
George J. Jones
George J. Jones, Jr.
George K. Jones
George L. Jones
George M. Jones
George W. Jones
Gerald Jones
Gilbert V. Jones
Glen D. Jones
Glenn Irving Jones
Henry Jones
Herbert E. Jones
Herbert H. Jones
Isaac Jones
Jack E. Jones
Jack O. Jones
James D. Jones
James E. Jones
James E. Jones
James Emmett Jones
James L. Jones
James Lewis Jones
James Wesley Jones
Jesse D. Jones
Jessie L. Jones
Joe D. Jones
Joe Jones, Jr.
John E. Jones
John H. Jones
John Lawrence Jones
John P. Jones
John R. Iv Jones
John W. Jones
John W. Jones
John W. Jones
John Willie Jones
Johnny C. Jones
Joseph Jones
Joseph Jones
Joseph H. H Jones
Joseph N. Jones, Jr.
Kassidy K. Jones
Kenneth L. Jones
Kenneth R. Jones
Le Roy Jones
Leo S. Jones
Leslie J. Jones
Leslie M. Jones
Lester O. Jones
Linwood G. Jones
Lisburn H. Jones
Lotchie J. R. Jones
Lucian Mccustian Jones
Lucius Jones
Mack D. Jones
Marion M. Jones
Marvin W. Jones
Melber J. Jones
Melvin Harvey Jones
Merrill A. Jones
Miles H. Jones
Millard Jones
Moise Jones, Jr.
Moses Jones, Jr.
Nathaniel G. Jones

Odell Jones
Odis F. Jones
Oliver Eugene Jones
Oliver R. Jones
Osborn Jones
Ralph Dale Jones
Ralph G. Jones
Ray M. Jones
Raymond L. Jones
Raymond L. Jones
Reeves S. Jones
Richard A. Jones
Richard L. Jones
Robert Jones
Robert A. Jones
Robert C. Jones
Robert C. Jones
Robert Calvin Jones
Robert J. Jones
Robert L. Jones
Robert N. Jones
Robert S. Jones
Robert Wilson Jones
Ronniemore A. Jones
Roy V. Jones
Rufus J. Jones
Russell A. Jones
Sam Jones
Samuel L. Jones
Samuel R. Jones
Thomas C. Jones
Thomas Dale Jones
Thomas E. Jones
Thomas Edward Jones
Thomas Leo Jones
Tilford R. Jones, Jr.
W. R. Jones
Waldo Benn Jones
Walter L. Jones
Walter L. Jones
Wilber G. Jones, Jr.
William Jones
William C. Jones, Jr.
William D. Jones
William Edward Jones
William Estill Jones
William Gardner Jones
William Glenn Jones
William H. Jones
William H. Jones
William Herbert Jones
William J. Jones
William J. Jones
William Lewelleyn Jones
William N. O. Jones
William P. Jones
William T. Jones
William T. Jones
Willie D. Jones
Willie M. Jones
Woodrow D. Jones, Jr.
Nicholas W. Jonquil
Neil E. Joppie
Ace Jordan
Alfred S. Jordan
Archie A. Jordan
Arthur Jordan
Barney H. Jordan
Benjamin F. Jordan
Cecil F. Jordan
Charles E. Jordan
Charles T. Jordan
Eugene Jordan
Fred O. Jordan
George A. Jordan, Jr.
Harold R. Jordan
Herbert L. Jordan
Jack M. Jordan
James Jordan
John Duncan Jordan, Jr.
Lambert Aaron Jordan, Jr.
Lester L. Jordan
Lewis P. Jordan
Lonnie Van Jordan, Jr.
Louis J. Jordan
Mack A. Jordan
Martin J. Jordan
Richard W. Jordan
Robie L. Jordan
Thomas M. Jordan
Warren H. Jordan
Willie E. Jordan
Luther B. Jordon
Paul Herbert Jordon
Dale E. Jorgensen
Edward V. Jorgensen
George A. Jorgensen
John Henry Jorgensen, Jr.
Jodie A. Jorgenson

Thomas J. Jorgenson
Raymond E. Jose
Adolph Joseph
Arthur Joseph
Clayton W. Joseph
David J. Joseph
Francis R. Joseph
Gerard Joseph
Johnnie Joseph, Jr.
Morris E. Joseph
Ralph A. Joseph
William Joseph
William Samuel Joseph
James L. Joshua
Dale E. Joslin
Boyd La Verne Jothen
Richard M. Journey
William G. Joy
David Alton Joyce
James O. Joyce, Jr.
Thomas Joyce, Jr.
William H. Joyce, Jr.
Barnabas Joyner
Edwin A. Joyner
Lloyd V. Joyner
Raymond C. Joyner
Theodore Joyner
William L. Joyner
Esteban Juarez
Porfirio Juarez, Jr.
Victoriano Juarez
James I. Jubb
Ray A. Juday
John C. Judd
Morris R. Judd
Vernon R. Judd
Daniel S. Judge
Bryant Escar Judson, Jr.
Stephen Henry Judson
Denzil L. Judy
Robert Arthur Juhl
Scott M. Julian
Virgil R. Julian
John Mcleod Jullien, Jr.
Jimmie Jumbo
Raymond A. Jump
Joseph Jumper
Paul Howard June
Wilson L. Juneau
Vito John Junevicus
Raymond C. Jung
Walter Jung
J. D. Floyd Junior
Carl F. Junker
Bronislaw M. Juras
Leo Jurasz
Sylvester J. Jurek
Doran L. Jurgensen
Paul Gus Juric
Edward P. Juristy
Bohdan Jurkiw
Francis R. Jurkovic
Robert J. Jurkowski
John J. Jurmu
Robert Alfred Jursch
Francie J. Jury
James W. Just
Gerald W. Justen
Lawrence A. Justi
Alvis Justice
Edwin Glen Justice
Herbert Justice
James W. Justice
Kelly Justice
Marion W. Justice
Thomas McMaster Justice
Wallace Justice
William A. Justice
Leon P. Justin
Hilary W. Justman
Bert W. Justus, Jr.
Elden C. Justus

— K —

Michael C. Kaaihue
John K. Kaakimaka
Basil K. Kaapana
Rollin J. Kaat
James Kabalen
Stanley J. Kacar
Charles J. Kachele
Byron Kacheris
Joe Kaczmarczyk
Robert J. Kaczmarek
Casimer P. Kaczor
Emil L. Kaczrowski
Richard A. Kadlec
Robert C. Kadlec

Edward D. Kafara
Paul M. Kafer
Vincent P. Kafton
Jimmie L. Kahanek
Gordon King Kahl
Herman C. Kahl, Jr.
Leonard J. Kahl
Frederick C. Kahnt
Anth Kahoohanohano
William F. Kahrhoff
Arthur Cecil Kahue
John Frederick Kail
Robert W. Kailianu
Denver A. Kain
Joseph C. Kainz
Kenneth Kaiser, Jr.
Raymond Roy Kaiser
Theodore E. Kaiser
Howard W. Kaiuwailani
Haskell Kaizerman
Carlos S. Kakar
Clarence L. Kalama
Herbert Kalama
Albert Kalawe
William K. Kaleo
Lewellyn K. Kalepa
Eugene M. Kalin
Herbert K. Kalino
Carl A. Kalmar
Elmer John Kallmeyer
Ralph N. Kallock
Herman B. Kamai
W. M. Kamakaokalani, Jr.
Joseph R. Kambic
William W. Kamekona
Harold D. Kamholz
Wasil M. Kamierzia
Norman L. Kaminga
Ernest Kaminski
Albert Kaminsky
Alfred R. Kaminsky
Oliver W. Kamm
Deroy F. Kammerer
Benjamin S. Kamoku
Henry Kamowski
David B. Kampa
Delbert R. Kamphaug
Daniel F. Kamps
John Kampschneider
Buford E. Kane
Harold J. Kane
James Joseph Kane
John J. Kane
John R. Kane
Kenneth Kane
Fred T. Kanekura
Billie G. Kanell
David T. Kaneshiro
Harry Y. Kaneshiro
Hayato Kaneshiro
Jack S. Kaneshiro
Charles G. Kaniatobe
Joseph M. Kanney
Richard S. Kanoski
Richard A. Kanski
Gordon W. Kanter
Ira Wilson Kantner
Emil Joseph Kapaun
Anth Kapfensteiner
Steven C. Kapitan
Manfred Kapp
Ernest Kappelmann
R. Louis Sr Kappelmann
Robert L. Kappenman
Gerald D. Kappler
Clyde W. Kappus
Thomas Karadeema
Vasilio Karagiozis
Raymond Karaiseky
Francis A. Karalewicz
Charles H. Karcher
William C. Karin
William G. Karinen
Robert D. Karkalik
Arnold William Karlin
Richard J. Karnos
Michael Karpinecz
Robert C. Karpinen
Jerome Karpowicz
Alvis E. Karr
Everett M. Karr
Robert R. Karr
Adolph R. Kartes
Dennis K. Karty
Milton J. Kasarda
Amel O. Kasinger
James H. Kasinger
Jerome J. Kasiulin
Benjam Kasmerovitz

James K. Kasprzak
Leo L. Kasselman
Conrad W. Kasselmann
William A. Kast
Walter Francis Kasterko
Charles Richard Kastor
Stanley J. Kasza
Clarence S. Kates
John H. Katilius
Robert N. Katlarek
Theodore A. Katsoolias
Donal Katzenberger
Ross William Katzman
Alexander K. Kauahi
Ernest C. Kauer
Clarence J. Kauffman
Edgar H. Kauffman
Alfred L. Kaufman
Edward Karl Kaufman
Frank E. Kaufman
Loren R. Kaufman
Luther W. Kaufman
Robert P. Kaufman
Samuel K. Kauhane
Leroy St John Kauhini
Sidney K. Kaui
David W. Kaul
Lloyd Dawson Kaul
Frank M. Kautman
John James Kavanagh
Masayoshi Kawahara
Suyeo Kawahara
Masami Kawamura
William Kawashima
Harold L. Kay
Minoru Kaya
Billy J. Kays
Arthur R. Kazmierczak
Edward Kazmierczak
Hiram L. Ke
Robert W. Ke
Floyd A. Keacher
Richard A. Keagle
Daniel Kealalio
Edward L. Keally, Jr.
Richard E. Keane
Clyde D. Kear
Clarence Kearney
Donald J. Kearney
Harry Lee Kearney
James A. Kearney
Carl L. Kearns
Paul J. Kearns
Robert G. Kearns
William H. Kearns
James C. Keathley
Charles E. Keating, Jr.
Frank L. Keck, Jr.
Gerald Pete Keck
Willie F. Kee
Loras Joseph Keegan
Charles J. Keel
Clyde W. Keel
David L. Keel
Edward J. Keeler
Charles E. Keeley
Furman Keeley
John W. P. Keeley
Ronald O. Keeley
Bobby W. Keen
Junior D. Keen
James F. Keenan
Joseph Francis Keenan
William R. Keenan
Frederick Keene, Jr.
Kassel Monford Keene
Leon L. Keene
Robert G. Keene
Demar D. Keener
Fletcher M. Keener
Floyd C. Keeney
George P. Keeney
William Patrick Keery
Jimmie Keese
Elmer W. Keesee, Jr.
Roland T. Keesee
Paul Ottis Keeth
Bailey Keeton, Jr.
Walter L. Keeton
Francis W. Keever
Orren R. Keever
Ralph Edward Kegley
John J. Keglovitz
Billy A. Kehoe
Thomas F. Kehoe
Dean Deloss Kehr, Jr.
Francis M. J. Keifer
Robert D. Keim
Harold A. Keiran

Meredith Frank Keirn
Cornelius Keirnan
Charles C. Keiser
John Carl Keiser
Robert L. Keish
Daniel J. Keister
Harold O. Keister
Charles M. Keith
Cloyce Keith
Curtis A. Keith
Danny R. Keith
Donald G. Keith
Edward L. Keith
Euel J. Keith
Isiah H. Keith
James W. Keith
John W. Keith, Jr.
Lester R. Keith
Page L. Keith
Gus Kekis
Nelson Kekiwi
Basil Keklak
Joseph K. Kekoa
Robert B. Kelder
Patrick M. Keliher
Matthew K. Kelii
David K. Keliikuli
Fay N. Kell
Richard D. Kellam
Jack E. Kellams
Francis Kelleher
James E. Kelleher
John D. Kelleher
John F. Kelleher
John J. Kelleher
Robert Patrick Kelleher
Edward B. Keller
Ernest R. Keller
Francis W. Keller
Gerald J. Keller
Harold Wade Keller
James H. Keller
John Charles Keller
John F. Keller
John Kemp Keller
Lawrence B. Keller
Paul L. Keller
Richard D. Keller
Robert W. Keller
Rodney V. Keller
Ronald Lee Keller
Russell R. Keller
Clement Kellerman
George S. Kellett
Harold D. Kellett
Billie F. Kelley
Cecil D. Kelley
Charles A. Kelley
Charles Kelley, Jr.
David J. Kelley
Delbert Francis Kelley
Frank H. Kelley
Frederic Stanley Kelley
George A. Kelley
Hobert G. Kelley
Homer L. Kelley
Irvin Russell Kelley
John M. Kelley
Kenneth E. Kelley
Leslie L. Kelley
Marvin O. Kelley
Patrick H. Kelley
Raymond E. Kelley
Robert G. Kelley
Russell E. Kelley
Tommy R. Kelley
Vernon L. Kelley
Wesley R. Kelley
William A. Kelley
Charles W. Kellison
Bernard L. Kellogg
Paul Kenneth Kellstrom
Raymond F. Kellum
William H. Kellum
Aubrey H. Kelly
Bernard L. Kelly
Carl L. Kelly
Charles Kelly, Jr.
Curtis C. Kelly
Daniel Francis Kelly
Donald E. Kelly
Douglas F. Kelly
Edward J. Kelly, Jr.
Ernest M. Kelly
Francis Bernard Kelly
George A. Kelly
George E. Kelly
George Richard Kelly
Guy B. Kelly, Jr.

Henry Bradford Kelly
Herbert Kelly
Homer Lee Kelly
James C. Kelly
James William Kelly
Joe Kelly
John Doren Kelly
John H. Kelly
John L. Kelly, Jr.
Lawrence Bertrand Kelly
Louis C. Kelly
Obie L. Kelly
Raymond Gene Kelly
Robert N. Kelly
Robert Thomas Kelly
Thomas Kelly
Thomas J. Kelly
Virlen E. Kelly
Walter J. Kelly
Warren Andrew Kelly
Warren F. Kelly
William C. Kelly
William W. Kelly
Willis E. Kelly
Robert J. Kelp
Donald Lorane Kelsch
Joseph Kelsey
Billy E. Kelso
Gene B. Kelso
Jack William Kelso
Glen G. Kemery
Raymond Kemick
Robert Gene Kemmerer
Gilbert A. Kemnitz
Chester L. Kemp
Don L. Kemp
Harvey Dupree Kemp
William S. Kempen, Jr.
David R. Kemper
Claude J. Kenan
John W. Kenawell
Elmer Blaine Kendall
Randolph L. Kendall
Richard Kendall
Ronald E. Kendall
Warren O. Kendall
John Philip Kendig
George J. Kendle
David O. Kendrick
Jesse R. Kendrick
Kelly K. Kendrick
James R. Kenealy
Gaylord W. Kenfield
William J. Kenigseder
Charles R. Kenley
Edward D. Kenneally
Michael J. Kenneally
Arthur M. Kennedy
Carl Ray Kennedy, Jr.
Carlon F. Kennedy
Clyde S. Kennedy
Donald J. Kennedy
Donald P. Kennedy
Edward L. Kennedy
Ellis D. Kennedy
Franklin P. Kennedy
George B. Kennedy
George Quinton Kennedy
Gilbert C. Kennedy
Jack E. Kennedy
Jack Spencer Kennedy
James E. Kennedy
John E. Kennedy
Larry Kennedy
Leonard M. Kennedy
Michael L. Kennedy
Richard Michael Kennedy
Richard T. Kennedy
Robert E. L. Kennedy
Robert G. Kennedy
Robert L. Kennedy
Robert L. Kennedy
Theodore Kennedy
William C. Kennedy
Joseph R. Kennel, Jr.
Llewellyn Kenneson
Richard Kenney
Robert Elwood Kenney
William Richard Kenney
Frank Henry Kennon, Jr.
James Roger Kenny
Kenneth E. Kenny
Arthur Kenolio
Kenneth W. Kenslow
Duane E. Kent
Morris H. Kent
Paul B. Kenton
Wayne Kenton
Arthur Max Kenty

Donald Aston Kenworthy
Robert W. Kenzel
Danny J. Keogh
Samuel K. Keomaka
Elva Lewis Keopke
Billy J. Keough
Joseph Clarence Kepford
Jack L. Kephart
John W. Kephart
Wilbert B. Kephart
Robert L. Kepley
Walter Maurice Kepley
William J. Keppel
Albert John Keppler
Charles F. Kerber
John J. Kerby
Febres Max Kercado
Walter H. Kerce
John T. Kerchinsky
Joseph J. Kerekes
John Robert Kerivan
James H. Kerklin
Curtis P. Kern
Donald A. Kern
Douglas Bruce Kern
Leo P. Kern
James P. Kerney
Jerry Joe Kerns
John A. Kerns, Jr.
Thomas F. Kerns
Charles K. Kerr
Jack Kerr
Lee O. Kerr
Lester P. Kerr
Ray Dale Kerr
William R. Kerr
Donald Kenneth Kerrigan
John E. Kerry
Billy M. Kershner
John C. Kerska
John Kerwin
Robert L. Keshick
Vernon L. Kesler
Lawrence H. Kessick
George E. Kessler
James L. Kessler
Jessie Junior Kestner
Glenn M. Ketchersid
Robert Ketchingman
Elvin L. Ketchum
Pinkney R. Ketchum
Rufus Lloyd Ketchum
Samuel L. Ketchum
Andre J. Ketele
Harold L. Ketner
Andrew R. Ketterman
Robert Kettlewell
William Charles Kettrick
Arthur V. Key
Robert E. Key
Wilber J. Key
David N. Keyes
Edward M. Keys
George D. Keys
Orbin Keys
Carl R. Keyser
Gerald E. Keyser
Jacob M. Keyser
Richard D. Keysor
Paul D. Khula
John R. Kibbe
Earl E. Kibbey
Linn E. Kibler
Russell Kiblinger
Charle Kicklighter
Eugene B. Kiczek
Billy L. Kidd
Charles A. Kidd
Elmer C. Kidd
Genine Kidd
Miles H. Kidd
Jesse L. Kiddy
James M. Kidwell
Edward Kiedrowski
Harry D. Kiefer
Yale Sheldon Kiefer
Donald J. Kiefling
Herbert M. Kiek
David Anthony Kiene
Joseph Harrison Kienholz
Hugh Lewis Kienitz
Harold Kiepke
Daniel J. Kiernan
Edward Kiernan
James J. Kiernan, Jr.
Curtis James Kiesling
Edmund Kiezanowski
Virgil Junior Kigar
John J. Kiggins

Amos L. Kight
Jack Carl Kightlinger
Masayuki Kihara
Robert James Kikta
Robert Kilar
Johnny Kilburn
Thomas E. III Kilby
John Edward Kilduff
George D. Kile
Richard A. Kile
Frank W. Kilgore
Hugh C. Killam
Merlon Leonard Killam
Paul M. Killar
Edward M. Killeen
Charles O. Killian
Clarence A. Killian
Edward M. Killian
Leo Killingsworth
Myrt Killingsworth
Robert Killingsworth
William Killingsworth
Charles J. Killoran
John Edward Kilmer
Richard W. Kilmer
Ralph Harold Kilner
Kenneth Kilpatrick
Robert J. Kilpatrick
John H. Kilroy
Albert W. Kim
Chan J. P. Kim, Jr.
Charles C. S. Kim
John Chung-june Kim
Richard Bok Kell Kim
David A. Kimball
Donald J. Kimball
Hunter H. Kimball
James E. Kimball
Roger E. Kimball
Timothy E. Kimball
John W. Kimberlin
Kenneth Kimberlin
Ernest W. Kimble
Fred V. Kimbrell, Jr.
William R. Kimbro
Colonel J. Kimbrough
David Kimbrough, Jr.
Jack Holt Kimbrough
James Robert Kimbrough
Willard A. Kimle
Arthur W. Kimmel
John Dague Kimmins
Seiki Kimura
Floyd Kinard
Wesley Kinard
Gayle C. Kincade
Charles B. Kincaid
James E. Kincaid
Lonnie Harrison Kincaid
Richard H. Kincaid
Robert Kincaid, Jr.
Ronald E. Kinch
Willard Kinchelow
Arthur S. Kinder, Jr.
Robert Blair Kinder
Tommy Kinder, Jr.
William L. Kinder
Donald A. Kindseth
Albert King, Jr.
Alfred Holowell King
Allen D. King
Andrew W. Iv King
Armstead King
Billy L. King
Blaine D. King
Bobby R. King
Charles E. King
Charles Eugene King
Charles J. King, Jr.
Charley L. King
Charlie R. King
Clarence B. King
Clifford B. King
Darrell L. King
David M. King
Denver King
Donald R. King
Dorel E. King
Dunbar A. King
Earl L. King
Edmund King
Edward J. King
Eldred H. King
Elster R. King
Frank H. King, Jr.
Frank King, Jr.
Franklin D. King
George F. King
George R. King

George Ray King
Harold O. King
Harvey King
Herbert King
Herbert King
Homer G. King
Hubert R. King
Jack E. King
Jack R. King
James Albert King
James Daniel King
James E. King
James Earl King
James Earl King
James Hubert King
James Patrick King
James Paul King
James Vinton King
Jason R. King
Jimmy E. King
John E. King, Jr.
John N. King, Jr.
John W. King
Joseph R. King
Keith Duane King
Leroy F. King
Lionel King
Lonnie King
Loyd King, Jr.
Marion Ray King
Martin Allen King
Michael T. King
Morris O. King
Ralph King
Ralph E. King
Ralph Edwin King
Ralph K. King
Ray R. King
Raymond F. King
Reginald W. King
Richard M. King
Richard W. King
Robert King
Robert C. King
Robert D. King
Robert V. King
Robert W. King
Roland L. King
Theodus George King
Thomas R. King
Thomas W. King
Vernon R. King
Walter S. King
Welton B. King
Wilbur A. King
Willard G. King
William A. King
William Atwell King
William Don King
William J. King
William J. King, Jr.
Willis G. King
Deloraine M. Kingsbury
John E. Kingsley
Willie L. Kingsley
Gene D. Kingston
John David Kington
Larry P. Kinler
Richard L. Kinloch
William L. Kinman
Francis L. Kinney
Frank E. Kinney
George H. Kinney
Grover D. Kinney
Howard C. Kinney
James Robert Kinney
John A. Kinney
John S. Kinney
Ralph L. Kinney
Salvadore D. Kinney
Raymond D. Kinnunen
Richard Kinoshita
Don F. Kinsey
Kenneth Wayne Kinsey
Harold A. Kinzer
Kenneth Rumberger Kipp
Robert Paul Kipp
Jerome J. Kippley
Carlie P. Kirby
Charles Kirby, Jr.
Fred S. Kirby, Jr.
Jesse L. Kirby
Paul Kirby
Robert D. Kirby
Robert E. Kirby
Bruce Cedric Kircher
Kenneth Kirchhefer
Leo J. Kirchner
Roger B. Kirchofer

Hiroshi Kiriu
Albert Kirk, Jr.
Charles Frank Kirk
Dwight Allan Kirk
Harold E. Kirk
William Kirk, Jr.
Paul R. Kirkbride
Hubert Kirkconnell
William Kirkendall
Daniel W. Kirkland
James Kirkland
Oland H. Kirkland
Lawrence E. Kirkley
Robert R. Kirklin
Clarence E. Kirkner
Ardell Kirkpatrick
Charle Kirkpatrick
Edward Lewis Kirkpatrick
Junior Kirkpatrick
Leslie Kirkpatrick
Roy L. Kirkpatrick
John E. Kirksey
Jonathan Kirksey
Paul W. Kirschmann
Robert S. Kirschner
William Kirshfield
Rein Kirsimagi
Darell D. Kirstine
Warren E. Kirtland
De Maret M. Kirtley
Roy R. Kirton
John William Kirwin
Thomas W. Kirwin
Joseph Gerald Kisela
Bill Kiser, Jr.
Henry Gaines Kiser
Roy G. Kiser
Travis N. Kiser
George J. Kish
Geza Kish
Robert J. Kishbaugh
James E. Kisor
Richard E. Kissick
Robert A. Kistler
Maxwell D. Kitchen
George T. Kitchens
Ruben W. Kitchens
William M. Kitchens, Jr.
Matthew Kitt
Peter Kitt
James Junior Kittle
William Kittle
David R. Kittleson
James Lee Kittrell
Calvin H. Kitzmiller
Carl D. Kitzmiller
Peter Harry Kivalos
Allan F. Kivlehan
Tetsuo Kiyohiro
Herbert R. Klaeren
Marinus Klarenbeck
Norman L. Klaris
Richard H. Klase
Fred P. Klassen
Andrew Klatko, Jr.
Charles R. Klatt
Robert N. Klaus
William Clarence Klaus
Merten G. Klawitter
Clifford John Kleber
Harry A. Klebo, Jr.
Leslie F. Klees, Jr.
Gerald J. Kleimeyer
Charles M. Klein
George D. Klein
George R. Klein
John A. Klein
Louis J. Klein
Melvin R. Klein
Robert Charles Klein
Roy D. Klein
Sidney R. Klein
William L. Klein
Harold Kleinfeldt
Howard F. Kleinkauf
Erwin W. Kleinschmidt
Albertus T. Kleintop, Jr.
John W. Kleist
John Klemiatof
Richard Klenz
Edward A. Klepajda
Arthur W. Kleppe
Burton Kleppinger
Laverne R. Klevgard
George Carl Klieser
Richard E. Klimback
William Klimitchek
Stanisla Klimowicz
Joseph W. Klimsey, Jr.

Edgar H. Klindworth
Billie F. Kline
Charles W. Kline
Earl E. Kline
Harry W. Kline
John F. Kline
Palmer Kline
Joe T. Klinefelter
Austin L. Klinekole
Charles J. Kling
Eugene H. Kling
Harry J. Kling
Edwin John Klinger
James F. Klinger
John Wendell Klinkerman
George Klinkhammer
Henry Frederick Klinzing
Ronald J. Kloeckner
Robert T. Klogy
Raymond L. Klopp
Arthur Fred Kloppenburg
Gene F. Klos
Walter B. Klose
Roger E. Klouser
Karl Vernon Kludt
Kenneth W. Klug
Paul Adam Klug
Warren E. Klug
Charles Kluge
John Klunk
Edward Daniel Klusky
Bobby B. Klusmeyer
Joe Kluss
Raymond Klussmann
Carl F. Klutts
Lewis C. Kluttz
Clyde E. Knaggs
Anthony L. Knapke
Donald W. Knapp
Edward G. Knapp
Kingdon Roger Knapp
Robert L. Knapp
William C. Knapp
Othello C. Knapper
William George Knauf
Robert P. Knaus
Edward Dewey Knecht, Jr.
George N. Knecht
Albert J. Knechtel
Russell L. Kneisley
Harry F. Knepp
Forrest N. Knich
Harr Knickerbocker
Melvin T. Knickerbocker
Howard H. Knieriem
John H. Knigge, Jr.
Burl Knight
David C. Knight
Donald E. Knight
Earle O. Knight
Franklin J. Knight
George J. Knight
Harold Knight
Harold K. Knight
Jack Arthur Knight
Jake Knight, Jr.
James H. Knight
John F. Knight
L. C. Knight
Neal M. Knight
Noah O. Knight
Richard James Knight
Robert L. Knight
Robert M. Knight, Jr.
Roscoe Knight
Walter E. Knight
William C. Knight
Jimmy Knighton, Jr.
Roy J. Knipe
Oley B. Knipp
Bernard Kniznick
Francis D. Knobel
Carl F. Knobloch
Harry A. Knoke
Jerome R. Knolle
Erwin H. Knope
Roy E. Knopp
Jerome W. Knorr
Regis R. Knorr
Gerald Wesley Knott
Leo Knott, Jr.
Walter Dean Knott
Harry H. Knotts
Rudolph S. Knotts
Frank H. Knowles
Gerald T. Knowles
Virgil L. Knowles
Herbert Knowlton
Albert Knox, Jr.

Allan L. Knox
Boyd Dale Knox
James E. Knox
Joseph Jude Knox
Merrill Irven Knox
William R. Knox
Jack L. Knudson
Lamar Arnold Knudson
Raymond John Knueppel
Ralph E. Knuth
Edwin H. Knutson
Floyd V. Knutson
Jerome Francis Knutson
Paul C. Knutson
Andrew J. Kobage
Robert Kobashigawa
Dale L. Kobbeman
Donald Shields Kobey
Arthur R. Kobie
Anthony A. Koch
Clarence Koch
Felix H. Koch
Fred Leslie Koch
Jack H. Koch
Kermit K. Koch
Thomas Koch
Karl J. Kochanowicy
Paul E. Kochanski
Victor M. Kocher
Takashi Kochi
Thaddeus Kociencki
Buddy Norman Koehler
Frank J. Koehler, Jr.
Leonard C. Koehler
Robert H. Koehler
Victor August Koehler
Walter T. Koehler
Bob J. Koehn
Douglas Joseph Koehnen
Harry W. Koelmel
John Kelvin Koelsh
Frederick C. Koenig
Jack M. Koenig
Karl G. Koenig, Jr.
Roy Eugene Koenig
Sammy G. Koenig
Edward C. Koenke, Jr.
Floyd W. Koepka
Clifford L. Koeppel
George E. Koestler
Frederick J. Kogel
Bernard R. Koger
Eugene C. Kohfield
Kenneth John Kohlbeck
Glenn E. Kohn
Joshua K. Kohn
Edward L. Kohout
John L. Kohut
Satoru Kojiri
William J. Kok
Clarence W. Koke
Edward Kokott
Richard A. Kolar
Robert Kolasinski
Donald Francis Kolb
Gary B. Kolb
William O. Kolb
Delos G. Kolbe
Harvey A. Kolberg
William V. Kolberg
Arnold R. Kolden
Carl W. Kolhagen
Robert E. Koller
William S. Koller
Edward L. Kollessar
Donald Eugene Kolling
Robert E. Kolling
Lorenzo Kollock
Charles Kolody
Frank Kolonich, Jr.
Michael Kolson
Raymond H. Kolthoff
Ken K. Kondo
Richard Yasuyuki Kono
Donald M. Konrad
Andrew Kontrik
Anthony Konze
Young C. Koo
George W. Koon
Charles E. Koonce
Don Wyandotte Koontz
Eugene Koontz
Frederick Russell Koontz
John Lawrence Koop
Leroy D. Kooper
Joseph A. Kopczak, Jr.
Frank J. Koperdak
Richard R. Koperski
James J. Kopf

Leonard J. Kopicki
Robert E. Kopp
George Kopscick, Jr.
George Kopta
Jack Korakian
Russell E. Korb
George Korbe
Arthur Korbmacher
Charles E. Korcz
John Edward Kordelski
George R. Korem
James L. Kornegay
Gerald Kornreich
Mike M. Korolia
John Koroly
Richard R. Koroser
Joseph L. Korstjens
Donald D. Korte
Joie Korte
John Kortyna, Jr.
Milton John Kosar
Leonard J. Koscielak
George J. Koscik
Paul Kosco
Donald Raymond Kosel
Muneo Koshimizu
Frederick John Koshko
Edward S. Kosieniak
Arnie V. S. Koski
Toivo W. Koski
William J. Koski
George T. Koskinas
Donald Kosmecki
Stanley Kost
Edward Joseph Koster
Julius H. Koster
Melferd L. Kostoff
Nicholas L. Kostoff
Joseph J. Kostuch
Anthony E. Kostura
Fabian Tom Kotara
John Kotora, Jr.
Chester F. Kotowicz
Daniel Benjamin Kott
Jerome W. Kottmer
Branko Kotur
Willia Kotwasinski
Joseph James Kotwica
Robert M. Kouns
Stanely F. Kountney
Richard William Kountz
Delbert D. Kovalcheck
John Kovaleski, Jr.
Michael P. Kovalish
Fred R. Kovalyak
Leo F. Kovar
Edward M. Kowalko
Edward R. Kowalski
Joseph Edward Kowalski
Leonard P. Kowalski
Stanley M. Kowalski
Sueo Koyanagi
Grant W. Koyle
Roman V. Kozak
Michael P. Kozer, Jr.
Donald L. Kozlik
Aloysius Kozlowski
Stephen Kozlowski
Thadeus Kozlowski
Arthur Masaru Kozuki
Leo J. Kraft
Robert E. Kraft
Roger John Kraft
Martin Joseph Krager
Joseph P. Krahel
Richard W. Krahl
Milan Krainovich
Ralph E. Kralicek
Andrew P. Kralick
Cornelius W. Kramer
Eugene B. Kramer
Fredrick H. Kramer
Ronald L. Kramer
Marshall Edward Krantz
Elmer H. Kranz
Morrlyn Dwight Kranzler
Raymond Krasinski
Henry Kraszewski
James H. Kratz
Edward C. Kratzer, Jr.
Adolph J. Kraus
Bernard C. Kraus
Louis Casper Kraus
Don G. Krause
Francis J. Krause
Veer M. Krause
Harry A. Krauss
Edward Kravetz
Leonard M. Kravitz

Nick Krawcion
Raymond A. Krawczyk
James John Krcil
David W. Krebs
George J. Krebs
John G. Krebs
Clarence E. Krei
Lester K. Kreibich
Leighton G. Kreider
Bernard J. Kreidermacher
Peter Kreiter, Jr.
William P. Krell
Daniel L. Kremer
Joseph C. Kreminski, Jr.
Richard G. Kreml
Paul E. Kremser
Raymond Sylvester Krenek
Mason H. Krenzel
Richard W. Krepps
Earl B. Kresen
Joe C. Kresno, Jr.
George Kressich
Eugene Kressin
Walter B. Kretlow
Graham H. Kreunen
Edward Oliver Kreutz, Jr.
Harry J. Krey
Robert Orville Krider
Jason D. Kriedler
Richard Krieg
Gunther H. Krieger
Lyle Henry Krienke
Floyd Therman Krigbaum
Lester E. Kriha
John Krimsky
John A. Kripoton
Stephen Krischak
Joseph F. Krishefski
George W. Kristanoff
Glen E. Kritzwiser
Joseph Kriwchuk
George A. Krizan
Jered Krohn
Edmund A. Krol
Chester Andrew Krolak, Jr.
Alex E. Kroll
Steve J. Kroll
William C. Kroll
Eugene A. Kronbeck
Earl Victor Charles Krone
Gene Kent Krongard
Eugene A. Kropp
David T. Krouse
Eugene Paul Krouskoupf
Ernest R. Krout
Edward A. Krucek
Edwin James Kruciak
Donald D. Krueger
Robert Carl Krueger
Wayne Allen Krueger
Regis Edward Krug
Donald A. Kruger
James V. Kruger
Alex Kruk
Paul J. Kruk
Stanley Krukowski
Norman J. Krull
Janis Krumins
Robert Mitchell Krumm
Martin M. Krump
Anthony P. Krumpach
Jerome M. Krumpos
Joseph Krupa
Laddie Krupa
Adolph A. Krupicka
Mitchel Kruszewski
Wallace Kruszewski
Michael Krutty
Francis J. Krygowski
Raymond Krzyzaniaki
Edward Krzyzowski
Edward Kubes, Jr.
Leo John Kubiak
Peter Kubic
Henry Kubicki
Charles W. Kubicsko
Sumner J. Kubinak
Roland W. Kubinek
Robert Louis Kubisty
Alex H. Kubovich
Nickolas Kubovich
Theodore H. Kuch, Jr.
Henry J. Kucharczyk
Anton J. Kucsera
Harvey Earl Kudick
Douglas S. Kuechler
Melvin L. Kuehl
Wayne A. Kuehn
Gordon V. Kuehner, Jr.

Adrian A. Kuenle
Robert Albert Kueny
Marylyn Darrell Kuester
Edward L. Kuhar
Arnold O. Kuhlman
Roger R. Kuhlman
William F. Kuhlman
Donald W. Kuhn
Edward Dean Kuhn
Herman Kuhn
Raymond J. Kuhn
Richard Clyde Kuhn
Charles E. Kuhns
Homer K. Kuhns
Raymond E. Kuhr
David A. Kuikahi
David H. Kuiper
Robert M. Kula
Stephan F. Kuldanek
Franceszek J. Kulik
Walter J. Kulik
William Howard Kuller
Adam Kulovich
George M. Kumakura
Masaru Kumashiro
Dan C. Kuna
George H. Kunc
Harlan E. Kunde
John Kundratik
Joseph Harold Kuney, Jr.
Moses E. Kuni
Minoru Kunieda
William M. Kunkel
Charles Henry Kunsch, Jr.
Aden H. Kuntz
Nickolaus Kuntz
Thomas Richard Kuntz
William F. Kunz
James F. Kunzmann
Lawrence Jay Kunzweiler
Leonard Kupau
Richard Kupau
Oliver B. Kupferle
Clarence P. Kupp
Joseph J. Kupraites
Joseph Richard Kurcaba
Stanislau Kurdziel
Walter Kures
Billie Kurgan
Susumu Kurosawa
Adrian Kurowski
Arthur R. Kurts
Arthur R. Kurtz
Dennis Cottrell Kurtz
Donald N. Kurtz
Marvin W. Kurtz
Samuel L. Kurtz
Walter E. Kurtz
Joseph Frank Kurzawski
Harold L. Kusel
Joseph P. Kushnir
Adrian J. Kusiolek
Walter J. Kusper
Shigetoshi Kusuda
Jack H. Kutchey
Kiyomitsu Kutsunai
William Kutters
Harold O. Kuuttila
Shoso Kuwahara
Roy M. Kuykendall
Benjamin Kuzminski
Edward J. Kuzniar
Richard T. Kuzniar
Freddie Alvin Kvale
Harold Kvam
Louis Paul Kwader
Richard Kwiatkowski
George A. N. Kwock
Dale L. Kyle
Darwin K. Kyle
Francis Lee Kyle
James Archibald Kyle
John Kyle
Kenneth W. Kyle
William S. Kyles
Albert L. Kymer
Robert L. Kyser
George L. Kyzer

— L —

Donald E. La Barge
Francis J. La Barge
Paul La Barr
Roger F. La Beau
Americo M. La Bella
Edmond P. La Breck, Jr.
Clarence Ronald La Brie
Charlie M. La Caze

Raymond H. La Coste
Robert F. La Cout
Howard D. La Dieu
Robert L. La Fave
Merton V. La Favor
Carl Robert La Fleur
Roland E. La Fleur
Paul E. La Fond
Leroy La Fontaine
Don M. La Forest
James W. La Forge
Salvator La Franca
Dale Elden La France
Delmar J. La France
Roderick Henry La France
James J. La Grange
Robert M. La Gruth
Phillipp La Londe
Robert N. La Mastus
Anthony Daniel La Monica
Vernon A. La More
Wilbrod La Plante
Leo H. La Pointe
Walter B. La Pointe
Eugene R. La Preese
Santo J. La Quatra
Salvatore T. La Rocca
Wilfred Olin La Rochelle
Robert J. La Rose
Anthony R. La Rossa
Billy J. La Roue
Earl M. La Salle
Robert A. La Shier
Will C. La Suer
Edward La Tourneau
Raymond La Valley
Lester Charles La Voie
Peter Paul La Voie
Robert W. Labar
Roland L. Labelle
Paul Labergne
Jimmie Dancel Labogen
Arthur Raymond Labonte
John Ellis Laborg
Edward Labossiere
Collazo Atnory Laboy
Martinez Raf Laboy
Robert C. Labree
Raymond Lacavera
Haden R. Lacey
Robert L. Lacey
Robert Oliver Lacey
Ivan Marcian Lachnit
James C. Lacke
Arnold B. Lackie
Booker T. Lackland
Vincent F. Lackman
Joseph C. Lackner
Harry D. Lacour
Gerard F. Lacourse
George Lacro
Maximiano T. Lacsamana
Allen Brandon Lacy
Ivan E. Lacy
James R. Lacy
Robert C. Lacy
Peter J. Lada, Jr.
Edward Ladao
James T. Ladd
William H. Ladd
Simon Ladell
Robert E. Laden
Hobert Prentis Ladner
Moise J. Ladner
Eugene J. Ladson
Kenneth F. Laessig
Arthur J. Lafevers
Dale M. Lafferty
Thomas C. Lafferty
Huey Pierce Laffoon
Charles S. Lafleur
Reginald P. Lafleur
Allen J. Laflin
William J. Lafrance
Teofilo Lagansua
Robert E. Lagess
John A. Laghner
Ditlef J. Lagoni
Fernando Lagrimas
Robert Laguardia
Robert J. Lahey
Leonard E. Lahm
Jerome Lahood
William F. Lahrmer
William A. Lahti
Robert Holmes Laier
Dan B. Lail
Guy Lee Laine
Carroll F. Laing

Robert H. Lair
Donald E. Laird
Harold L. Laird
Rob R. Laird
John Joseph Laiveling, Jr.
John Lajuannessee
Austin K. Lake
Frank N. Lake
Harold J. Lake
Jesse F. Lake
Elmer Clinton Lakin
John G. Lakin
Paul Lalatovich
David W. Lam
Kenneth C. Lam
William W. Lam
Michael Lamagna
Raymond C. Lamance
Guerra Rafae Lamar
Thomas C. Lamar
Arnett Lamb
Charles M. Lamb
Donald E. Lamb
Joseph M. Lamb, Jr.
Melvin Howard Lamb, Jr.
Raymond Lamb
William E. Lamb
John Toivo Lamberg
Charles Arnold Lambert
Charles R. Lambert
Daniel R. Lambert
Delbert M. Lambert
Donald Francis Lambert
Elmer H. Lambert
Gerald G. Lambert
James O. Lambert
John Norris Lambert
Joseph A. Lambert
Marvin Robert Lambert
Richard L. Lambert
Robert R. Lambert
Roland Lambert
Rudolph J. Lambert
Frank A. Lamberti
Chauncey V. Lambeth
Otis H. Lambeth
Harry Lambing, Jr.
Peter Donald Lambrecht
Edward Francis Lamers
George H. Lamitie
Clyde E. Lamkins
John W. Lamm
John Eugene Lammers
Leroy A. Lamont
Alcide H. Lamoureux
Abraham E. Lamoutte
Douglas H. W. Lamp
Donald Lampenfeld
Frederick Lamport
Harold L. Lampson
Edward James Lanahan
Edward J. Lanau
Benjamin S. Lancaster
Leon E. Lancaster
Roy A. Lancaster
Thomas W. Lancaster
Herman Lance
Jean A. Lanctot
Edwin Land
John F. Land
John Harvey Land
William G. Land
Joseph Landa
Arthur Lee Landacre
Lawrence E. Lander
Deloy J. Landers
Homer James Landers
Jerry T. Landers
Lloyd Wayne Landers
Robert B. Landers
Robert E. Landes
Robert Landmesser
Charles R. Landon
Nelson James Landon
Robert E. Landreth
Avery M. Landry
Edmund Landry
Howard J. Landry
James E. Landry
Jules Herman Landry
Robert Landry
Theodore Paul Landry, Jr.
Rolland P. Landwehr
Theodore Landy
Brink E. Lane
Clarence E. Lane
Donald R. Lane
Elmer L. Lane
George A. Lane

Horace Lane
Howard Lee Lane
James E. Lane, Jr.
James K. Lane
James P. Lane
John Francis Lane
John Lane, Jr.
Lawrence A. Lane
Leroy Lane
Melvin H. Lane
Monty Jack Lane
Otis O. Lane
Robert C. Lane
Robert V. Lane
Robin L. Lane
Thomas D. Lane
Thomas M. Lane, Jr.
Tyler E. Lane
Homer V. Lanehart
Irvin E. Lanehart
Guy Floyd Laney
Robert T. Laney
Roosevelt Lanfair
Charles R. Lanford
Arthur G. Lang
Edward A. Lang
Fred M. Lang, Jr.
John R. Lang
Leslie Earl Lang
Lloyd L. Lang
Melford H. Lang
Milton F. Lang
Raymond J. Lang
Richard Lang
Robert David Lang
Charles Augustus Langdale
Elmer R. Lang
Johnny D. Lange
Lee W. Langeberg
Eugene Langenfeld
Francis Langenfeld
Bruce B. Langfitt
Joseph D. Langford
Ervin William Langlas, Jr.
Robert G. Langley
Lyle M. Langlitz
Wallace J. Langlitz
Anthony L. Langone
Richard Langowski
Roy E. Langrell
Alfred L. Langston
Jack Clarence Langston
Charles Sumter Langtry, Jr.
John Paul Langwell
Robert Warren Langwell
George Langwiser
Claude Lanier
Jack D. Lanier
Orlin N. Lanier
Robert L. Lanier
Shelton Lanier
Walter J. Lanken
L. P. Lankford
John J. Lannon
George B. Lansberry
Charles Lee Lansdell
Clifford Lansdell
Jerry D. Lansford
James M. Lansing
Melvin E. Lansing
John H. Lantry
Marvin Edgar Lantz
Roy D. Lapham
Harry F. Lapich, Jr.
Faustino Laping
John F. Lapinski
Joseph E. Lapinski
George R. Laplante
Jean P. Laplante
Normand L. Laplante
John N. Lapointe
Edwin Lapp
Tony Lappas
William J. Laprade
Luis P. Lara
Richard Roca Lara
Rudolph Lara
James Moss Laramore
Frank F. Lardino
Donald Francis Lare
Jose F. M. Large
Bonifacio Largusa
Frederick N. Larivee, Jr.
Frederick E. Larkin
Hugh Francis Larkin
James N. Larkin
Lorin H. Larkin
Martin J. Larkin
Ralph W. Larkins, Jr.

William A. Larkins
Vernon G. Larman
Floyd R. Larney
Clayton J. Larose
David A. Larrabee
William B. Larry
Charles Hans Larsen
Emil A. Larsen, Jr.
James M. T. Larsen
Lawrence E. Larsen
Lawrence Oliver Larsen
Bertil S. Larson
Damon Juan Larson
Duane Warren Larson
Durfee Larson
Edgar J. Larson
Gerald R. Larson
Jason C. Larson
Orvall P. Larson
Paul A. Larson
Richard E. Larson
Robert V. Larson
Stanley S. Larson
Wayne L. Larson
Wendell L. Larson
Alvin A. Lartigue
Paul M. Larue
Alonzo L. Larwood
Laurent J. Lasante
George A. Lasasso
John C. Lasater
Marvin J. Lashley
Edward R. Lashok
John Lasiuk, Jr.
John Hubert Laskey
Joseph J. Laskowski
Franklin Laskowsky
David R. Lasky
Paul E. Lasley
Dean W. Lass
Velez Ism Lassalle
Paul A. Lassan
Robert J. Lassen
Donald T. Lassiter
John H. Lassiter
William H. Lassiter
Winifred Lassiter
Loyal Gene Lassley
Antonio V. Lastella
William C. Lastinger
Lawrence P. Lasua
Luther L. Laswell
Mike Latanation
Billy J. Latham
Bobbie J. Latham
Glenn D. Latham
Leslie B. Latham
Paul Walker Latham, Jr.
Sheldon W. Latham
Beondred K. Lathan
Climon N. Lathan, Jr.
Robert T. Latta
George Gerald Lattin
Charles Lauderdale
Robert M. Lauer
John W. Lauf
De Forrest August V. Laufer
Robert Laufer
Donald E. Laughlin
Jack K. Laughlin
William Laughlin
William R. Laughlin, Jr.
Donald L. Laughran
James Patric Laughy
Jaime Laugier
Joseph Laukaitis
William Roland Laundry
Ruben Laureano
George E. Laurence
Harry J. Laurence
Douglas J. Laurent
Othello Laury, Jr.
John William Lausberg, Jr.
Louis Lautenbacher
Bob Alfred Lauterbach
Dona Lautzenheiser
Joseph R. Lauzon
Harold Lavala
Alfred Lavallie, Jr.
Louis J. Lavasseur
Geoffrey Lavell
John G. Lavelle, Jr.
Mark D. Lavelle
Roy C. Lavia
Arnold J. Lavin
Patrick J. Lavin
George A. Lavoie
Frank C. Lavora
William Lavorgna

Asa Lawrence Law
John A. Law
Richard Law
Theodore Law, Jr.
Tommy K. Law
Wayne E. Law
George H. Lawall
Milton Ray Lawhorn
Donald C. Lawhorne
Martin A. Lawing
Charles S. Lawler
Robert F. Lawler
Donald F. Lawlis
Alfred Edwin Lawrence, Jr.
Charles Lawrence
Donald E. Lawrence
Emory T. Lawrence
Francis A. Lawrence
George W. Lawrence, Jr.
Irving G. Lawrence
Jack Lee Lawrence
James W. Lawrence
John Patrick Lawrence
John R. Lawrence
Robert Lawrence
Robert T. Lawrence
Theodore Lawrence
Willard Earl Lawrence
William B. Lawrence
William C. Lawrence
William L. Lawrence
William W. Lawrence
Robertson Gene A. Laws
Aaron Augustus Lawson
Alvis D. Lawson
Bobby E. Lawson
Carl B. Lawson
David R. Lawson, Jr.
Elmer L. Lawson
Eugene Lawrence Lawson
Frank Joe Lawson
Fred A. Lawson
Harvey Lawson
John E. Lawson
Milton Eugene Lawson
Richard A. Lawson
Robert C. Lawson
Robert E. Lawson
Robert Rex Lawson
Venson Lawson
Walter Keith Lawson
Wesley C. Lawson
William H. Lawson
William S. Lawson
Ellison J. Lawton
John Donald Lawton, Jr.
Jack D. Lawver
James L. Laxton
Thomas A. Laxton
Carl S. Lay
Jack E. Lay
Esidro A. Laycock
Robert P. Laydon
John C. Layfield
Elmer L. Laymon
Julian Laymon
James T. Layne
Roy L. Layne
Gene R. Layton
Howard J. Layton
Laurence Coe Layton
Robert Hollace Layton
Robert V. Layton
William M. Layton
John Cobos Lazalde
John Lazar
Lazaros Lazarou
Stanley Lazarus
William C. Lazenby
James Robert Le Baron
Gerald C. Le Blanc
Henry Thomas D. Le Blanc
Hubert Joseph Le Blanc
Oreste I. Le Blanc
Rawford E. Le Blanc
Roland L. Le Blanc
Meus Le Bleu
Bruce P. Le Clair
Billy J. Le Compte
William Le Fevers
Arnold L. Le Fevre
Luke D. Le Fevre
Charles R. Le Force
Warren Le Jeune
John C. Le Master
Donald Gene Le Matty
Adolphus M. Leach
Charles L. Leach
Charles R. Leach

Cloyd E. Leach
Edward Thomas Leach
Carlton Leadbetter
Maple L. Leader
Ralph E. Leaf
Charles Leak
Daniel B. Leake, Jr.
William M. Leake, Jr.
Antonio A. Leal
Victor C. Leal
Robert W. Leaman
Joe Z. Leamon
Leslie Wayne Lear
Max L. Lear
Russell Jackson Lear
Edwin J. Leary
John N. Leary
Robert B. Leary
Gene Henry Lease
Kenneth C. Lease, Jr.
Harry F. Leathers
Thomas Jack Leaver
Thomas J. Leavey
James M. Leavins
Bernard Sheridan Leavitt
James Robert Lebaron
Willis C. Lebarron
Adrien Lebel
Joseph Lebiedz
Richard S. Lebioda
Rawford E. Leblanc
Reginald L. Leblanc
Roland L. Leblanc
Robert Wilson Lebo
Lawrence J. Leboeuf
Joseph F. Lebow
Jose J. Lebron
Lebron Davi Lebron
Mendez Jose Lebron
Nelson G. Lebron
Alfred B. Ledbetter
Hugh G. Ledbetter
Jack W. Ledbetter
John B. Ledbetter
Staffard Ledbetter
Arnold Lederer, Jr.
Alberto Ledesma
Gilbert Ledesma
Aubrey Ledford
Howard R. Ledford
J. T. Ledford
Thomas Franklin Ledford
Vernon S. Ledford
William H. Ledford
Ernest W. Ledger, Jr.
William Ledington
Theodore W. Ledoux
Wilton C. Ledoux
Abraham Lee
Alfred C. Lee
Arnold T. Lee
Arthur Lee
Benjamin G. Lee
Billy Sam Lee
Byron D. Lee
Carson Lee, Jr.
Charles E. Lee
Charles E. Lee
Charles S. A. Lee
Clarence O. Lee
Cordell Lee, Jr.
Donald Lee
Donald D. Lee
Donald Walter Lee, Jr.
Doyle Lionel Lee
Elvin M. Lee
Emil E. Lee
Ernest A. Lee
Felix S. Lee
George Cabot Lee, Jr.
George W. Lee
Harold Lee
Harry F. Lee
Hayward R. Lee
Henry A. Lee
Herbert Y. Lee
Isaac Lee, Jr.
Jack Lee
James C. Lee
James D. Lee
James Franklyn Lee
Jasper W. Lee
Kenneth Roland Lee
Lawrence Jerimiah Lee
Leon Lee
Leonard G. Lee
Rayburn D. Lee
Raymond H. Lee
Richard J. Lee

Robert Lee
Robert A. Lee
Robert E. Lee
Robert M. Lee
Robert P. Lee
Roland Edward Lee
Sunnie Say Mun Lee
Wilford Homer Lee
William C. Lee
Mc Dowell, WV
William T. Lee
Willie Lee
Willie E. Lee
Willie Lee, Jr.
Yuk Kay D. Lee
James Robert Leech
Joseph Robert Leeds
David H. Leedy
Delman E. Leedy
Henry Leenstra
Gene N. Leeper
Offie L. Leeper, Jr.
William R. Lees
Gordon D. Leesch
Edward Raymond Leeson
Tony R. Leet
Jack D. Lefever
Everett W. Leffler
Richard C. Leffler
Robert G. Leffler
Harry E. Lefler
Frank E. Lefort
Albert Leftwich
Marion Legare
Joseph H. Legee
Alfred J. Leger, Jr.
John H. Legette
Frank R. Legg
John Wesley Legg
Mancel N. Legg
Paul W. Legg
Allen K. Legge
Raymond Leggett
Benjamin Leggette
Thomas Leggs
Charles Francis Lehman
Jacob C. Lehman
Meredith L. Lehman, Jr.
Kenneth Oliver Lehnus
George S. Leibrand
Dewey Leiby, Jr.
Homer Leichliter, Jr.
Willis Leichliter
Eugene G. Leider
Roy S. Leidy
Clifford Leighton
Edmond G. Leighton
Santa Clara, CA
Robert W. Leighton
Matt P. Leinen
Vance R. Leinen
Warren H. Leining
John E. Leist
Harry O. Leisure
Jesse L. Leisure
Eugene L. Leitch
Phillip L. Leitch
Dennis Leite
Ralph L. Leitner
Arthur W. Leiviska
Eloie D. Lejeune
Kermit J. Lejeune
Adam A. Lell
Loyd O. Lemarr
Ervin Lemaster, Jr.
James E. Lemaster
Lester E. Lemaster
Ernest L. Lemay
George R. Lemay
Leland P. Lemay
Clifford E. Lemere
John J. Lemes
Joseph J. A. Lemieux
Joseph A. Lemme
John R. Lemmen
Ray Franklin Lemmons
Anthony R. Lemoine
Earl J. Lemoine
Edward M. Lemon
Sherwin A. Lemon
Arvil Lemons
Bennie Z. Lemons
Louis B. Lemons
Stanley L. Lencicki
Charles W. Lender
William E. Lender
Grant W. Leneaux
Edward Cozed Leneve
John Lenko

George J. Lennon
Richard Neal Lennox
Kenneth E. Lennox
John H. Leno
John J. Leno
Edward Archie Lenoir
Guss Ronald Lenon
Edward Allen Lent
Frank J. Lente
Eugene C. Lentz
Gerald Lee Lentz
Arden J. Lenz
Philip Immanuel Lenz
Robert G. Lenz
Philip Carl Leo
Angel Leon
Clarence B. Leon
Guerrero Jose Leon
Robert V. Leon
Albert N. Leonard
Charles W. Leonard
Baltimore City, MD
David A. Leonard
Dwight F. Leonard
Earnest W. Leonard
Edward J. Leonard
Edwin R. Leonard
Herbert A. Leonard
James J. Leonard, Jr.
Jearold D. Leonard
Owen L. Leonard, Jr.
Reuben Leonard
Robert A. Leonberger
Jacob P. Leonello
Donald M. Leonhard
John J. Leonhard
Harlan A. Leos
Francis P. Lepage
Carlo Lepizzera
John J. Lepp
Barney Lerner
William Ernest Lesage
John W. Lescallett
Jerome Leshaw
John Francis Lesko
James R. Lesley
Albert Floyd Leslie
Frank Lesniewski
Thomas Lesperance
Armando D. Lespron
Clarence A. Lester
Earl William Lester
George E. Lester
Melton Lester
Richard Colbert Lester
Walter T. Lester
William A. Lester
John Leszczynski
Joseph John Leszczynski
Roger N. Letendre
Russell Alfred Lethbridge
Lawrence Everette Lett
Gordon J. Levahn
Edmond D. Levasseur
Ronald Norman Levasseur
Burton Hessel Levenson
Michael E. Levercom
Welcome Leverett
Lee G. Levering
Joseph A. Levesque
Joseph H. Levesque
Norman R. Levesque
James Levi, Jr.
William J. Levi
Albert Dale Levie
Harvey N. Levin
Arthur I. Levine
Harvey Franklin Levine
Louis Hyman Levine
Marion Levine
Rubin Levine
Lawrence J. Levis
Walter J. Levitski
David D. Levleit
Harold Levy
Leo Levy
Edward Lewandowski
Ernest Lewandowski
Frank Lewandowski
John Adam Lewchuk
Robert J. Lewelling
Elmer E. Lewellyn
A. D. Lewis
Abe Lewis
Albert A. Lewis
Albert E. Lewis
Alfred J. Lewis
Arthur E. Lewis
Atlas E. Lewis

Billie E. Lewis
Blair Lewis, Jr.
Charles A. Lewis
Charlie L. Lewis
Conrade E. Lewis
Daniel H. Lewis
David W. Lewis
Davis Lewis
Donald Rex Lewis, Jr.
Duant E. Lewis
Earl Lewis
Earl C. Lewis
Edward Leonard Lewis
Edward W. Lewis, Jr.
Elwood Lewis
Emmett E. Lewis
Eugene D. Lewis
George W. Lewis
Gordon P. Lewis
Guy Lewis
Harold Lewis
Harold W. Lewis
Harry A. Lewis
Henry P. Lewis
Herman O. Lewis
Isaac Lewis, Jr.
Jack Lewis
Jack Hunter Lewis
Jack T. Lewis
Jack W. Lewis
James A. Lewis
James E. Lewis
James M. Lewis
James M. Lewis, Jr.
James W. Lewis
Johnnie L. Lewis
Joseph E. Lewis
Joseph Lewis, Jr.
Lawrence Lee Lewis
Lloyd B. Lewis
Lyman Eugene Lewis
O. C. Lewis
Olen Lewis
Pete H. Lewis
Phillip G. Lewis
Richard Hammond Lewis
Richard Stanley Lewis
Robert C. Lewis
Robert I. Sr Lewis
Robert N. Lewis
Robert O. Lewis
Samuel B. Lewis
Stewart C. Lewis, Jr.
Walter B. Lewis, Jr.
Warren Gunn Lewis
Wayne Edwin Lewis
Wilbur Eugene Lewis
William Lewis
William Glenn Lewis, Jr.
William N. Lewis, Jr.
William T. Lewis, Jr.
William Wellington Lewis
Willie Lewis
Willie Encil Lewis
Willie N. Lewis
Richard Mitchell Lewry
Freddie Reid Lewter
Conrad J. Lexvold
Frederick Adrian Ley
Richard J. Leyden
David Edmond Leyshon
Lupe Leyva, Jr.
Raymond Lhommedieu
Vincent Libassi
Loran K. Libbert
George D. Libby
Samuel A. Libertz
Garcia Samu Libran
Salvatore Libretti
Elroy C. Lichey
Norval L. Liddicoat
Harry H. Liddle, Jr.
Raymond J. Lieb
Earl F. Liebal
Robert W. Liebeg
Ralph O. Lien
Ronald L. Lien
Walter D. Lien
Virgil Bernard Lienemann
Rudolfs Liepa
Phillip Andre Lierse
Cletus R. Lies
John P. Lieuwen
Charles E. Liford
Amos Lige
Ernest A. Liggett
James M. Liggett
Alvin R. Liggins, Jr.
James E. Light

352

Johnny D. Light
Jack A. Lighter
Richard E. Lightner
Roger W. Lightner
Arthur Ligon
Gerald G. Lile
Joseph Edward Lile, Jr.
Donald J. Lilek
Harold R. Liles
Herbert Lilientha
Robert Lilienthal
Gene Edward Lillard
Ralph G. Lillard
Ronald David Lilledahl
Max W. Liller
Donald E. Lilley
Jack E. Lilley
Meritt Truman M. Lilley
Charles R. Lillie
Darwin Arthur Lillie
Arthur Henry Lilly
Edmund B. Lilly
Edmund J. III Lilly
Evand Lilly
Gene Frank Lilly
James Alfred Lilly
Ray Kirby Lilly
Kermit K. Lilyroth
Ernest C. K. Lim
Miguel S. Lima, Jr.
Herman L. Limberg
Jose M. Linares-Ortiz
Sabana Grande, PR
Joseph Aaron Lincoln
Dale E. Lind
Henry A. Lind
John G. Lind
John J. Lindahl
Rune Lindahl
Stuart R. Lindahl
Arland Duane Lindberg
Charles A. Lindberg
Walter E. Lindberg
Lindor H. Lindblade
Willard T. Lindborg
Earl Otto Lindemann
Erwin A. Lindemans
David E. Lindenau
Joseph L. Linder
William C. Linder
Quinton E. Lindler
Alfred B. Lindley
Carl E. Lindquist, Jr.
Carl H. Lindquist
Donald C. Lindquist
Francis E. Lindsay
Homer F. Lindsay
James J. Lindsay
Max A. Lindsay
R. L. Lindsay
Raymond L. Lindsay
John Marlin Lindseth
Edward W. Lindsey
Freeman Lindsey
James A. Lindsey
John Madison Lindsey, Jr.
John R. Lindsey
Nathan L. Lindsey
Ray Edward Lindsey
Richard Mckay Lindsey
Robert T. Lindsey
Walter G. Lindsey
Carlo A. Lindstrom
Floyd A. Lindstrom
Vernon A. Lindvig
Charles T. Lindwall
Philip G. Lindwurm
Edgar L. Line
George L. Line
Orvill F. Linebaugh
William R. Liner
John W. Ling
William Lingerman
Keith Le Velle Lingle
William J. Lingle
Edgar M. Lininger
Charles P. Link
Haviland J. Link
Leonard Link
Robert Lawrence Linke
Adam Linkewicz, Jr.
Basil C. Linkinogger
Richard Linkletter
Golden W. Linkous
John G. Linkowski
Frank Milton Linn
Roy W. Linne
Harry Linneman, Jr.
Floyd Paul Linnemeier

Giles C. Linthicum
William Linthicum
Robert J. Linton
Robert S. Linton
Billy Liolin
George Lionberger
Billy Dean Lipe
William Stanhope Lipe
Henry L. Lipes
Richard Ray Lipes
Herbert C. Lippert
Kenneth W. Lippert
Charles Lipphardt
Eugene B. Lipps
Charles D. Lipscomb
Herbert E. Lipscomb
Melvin E. Lipscomb
Orville Jack Lipscomb
William Lipscomb, Jr.
William T. Lipscomb
Frank I. Lipscombe
Henry Lipshay
Kenneth C. Lipshitz
Lawrence Liscano
Walter Ernest Lischeid
John H. Lisenby
Johnnie B. Lisenby
John P. Liskowski
James R. Lister
John W. Liston, Jr.
Lawrence Miller Liston
John K. Litch, Jr.
Gilbert Litchauer
Billie G. Litchfield
William J. Litman
Henry Litmanowitz
Thomas E. Littell
Blaine L. Little
Donald A. Little
Earl Little
Ernest Sr Little
Henry Dean Little
Herman H. Little
John P. Little
John Q. Little
Keith J. Little
Oscar L. Little
Paul E. Little
Robert H. Little
Wallace R. Little
Melvin J. Little-Bear
Gary E. Littlefield
Gordon Ackly Littlefield
Warren Littlefield
John Littlehawk, Jr.
Charles Littlejohn
Frankli Littlejohn
Harold Littlejohn
Ralph Littler, Jr.
Santos Livas
Jack Lively
James O. Livesay
Joseph Michael Livich
Charles W. Living
Archie Livingston
Jimmie B. Livingston
John A. Livingston
Lawrence Livingston
Odyce Watson Livingston
Raymond Livingston
Thomas Livingston
Cora Fidel Llanot
Alvin S. Lloyd, Jr.
Bruce Bowen Lloyd
Carl Hubert Lloyd
James J. Lloyd
Miles D. Lloyd
Thomas R. Lloyd
Frank Lo Dolce
John Lo Schiavo
Arnold F. Lobo
Sammie Locash
Thomas J. Lochrane
Donald E. Lockard
Holice Lockard
Kennis E. Lockard
William C. Lockard
Lloyd M. Locke
Roscoe Hubbard Locke
Frank V. Lockefer
Lewis A. Lockerson
Eddie Lockett, Jr.
Isaac W. Lockett, Jr.
Johnny B. Lockett
Lindsey C. Lockett
Jack Netta Lockhart
Jimmie Ermia Lockhart
John A. Lockhart
Ross Moore Lockhart

Spencer L. Lockhart
James R. Locklar
Vernon H. Locklar
Junior Locklear
James P. Lockman
Earl M. Lockwood, Jr.
John B. Lockwood
William A. Lockwood
James N. Locus
Joseph B. Lodder
Bradford Lodge
Sal Lodolce
Donald A. Loeffler
Robert D. Loeh
Vernon R. Loescher
Laverne J. Loether
Harold Loewenkamp
Julius H. Lofgren
Preston Loftin
Clifford A. Loftis
Arthur F. Loftus
David Loga
Carl D. Logan
Carter B. Logan, Jr.
Charles E. Logan
Clarence J. Logan
Earl W. Logan
Edward N. Logan
Herbert H. Logan
Joe Adams Logan
John Logan
John J. Logan
Robert C. Logan
Robert E. Logan
Samuel Porter Logan, Jr.
William F. Logan
Mildon H. Loge
Floyd B. Loggins
John Logoyda
Earl R. Logston
Edward Royce Logston
Lloyd A. Logue
Silvester Logwood
Henry E. J. Lohmer
Robert F. Lohr
Frank Loiacono
Linn F. Loida
Donald E. Loire
Norman J. Loiselle
Alfred A. Loken
Melvin E. Lokken
Leslie V. Lokker
Jasper Clyde Lomax, Jr.
John A. Lombardi
Joseph J. Lombardi
Thomas A. Lombardo
Vincent Francis Lombardo
Luca J. Lomurno
William S. Loncar
Cecil Loncasesion
Donald Earl London
Robert Patrick Loney
Aubery C. Long
Carl R. Long
Cecil C. Long
Charles H. Long
Charles Maurice Long
Charles R. Long
Clinton Long
Donald G. Long
Edward Long
Emmett Napoleon Long
Fred H. Long
Hansford Dee Long
Jac E. Long
Jackie D. Long
Jacob W. Long
James E. Long
James W. Long
John B. Long
John W. Long
Johnnie R. Long
Joseph Sheldon Long, Jr.
Junior Long
Junior E. Long
Kenneth J. Long
Martie Denson Long
Melvin I. Long
Owen C. Long
Robert Ralph Long
Stewart W. Long
Thomas A. Long
Tommie L. Long
Tyson R. Long
Van W. Long
Vincent T. Long
Warren G. Long
William C. Long
William F. Long

William M. Long
Paul F. Longale
Stephen Longamore
Duane Eugene Longbrake
Norman L. Longdon
George Longenecker
Chester Longmire
Ralph A. Longo
Vincent Longo
Juan M. Longoria
Leopoldo Longoria
Horace J. Longshore
Lamar B. Longshore
Robert Alan Longstaff
William O. Longway
John W. Longwitz
Norman Paul Looker
Charle Lookingbill
Richard Charles Loomer
Charles W. Loomis
Otis Wayne Loomis
Thomas H. Loomis
Harold W. Looney
Lawrence E. Loos
Anthony J. Lopa
Alfred Lopes, Jr.
Frank M. Lopes
Joseph W. Lopes, Jr.
Adalberto Villareal Lopez
Alfonso E. Lopez
Almodovar Pa Lopez
Angel L. Lopez
Arnoldo V. Lopez
Arturo Lopez
Baldomero Lopez
Batiz Jose A. Lopez
Carlos Lopez
Cristobal Lopez
Cronoz Luis Lopez
Edward E. Lopez
Eloy E. Lopez
Esmeal Lopez
Evangelio Lopez
Feliciano F. Lopez
Fernado L. Lopez
Frank Lopez, Jr.
Gerald Alvin Lopez
Guillermo P. Lopez
Jimenez Robe Lopez
Joe M. Lopez
John A. Lopez
John L. Lopez
Jose M. Lopez
Joseph B. Lopez
Larry C. Lopez
Manuel A. Lopez
Mario G. Lopez
Mike R. Lopez
Milton Lopez
Pedro Antonio Lopez, Jr.
Peter R. Lopez
Ray W. Lopez
Raymond Lopez
Raymond G. Lopez
Raymond P. Lopez
Richard E. Lopez
Richard S. Lopez
Sanchez Feli Lopez
Tony Lopez
Victor M. Lopez
William J. Lopez
Luis Lopez-Oronoz
Joseph Lopiccolo
Salvadore L. Lopiccolo
Francis J. Lopreta
Andrew Lopuhovsky
Roy Lynn Lorah
Charles A. Lord
Charles H. Lord, Jr.
Edward L. Lord
Ira F. Lord, Jr.
Joseph L. Lord
Roy Byron Lord, Jr.
William A. Lord
Ralph E. Lorenz
Robert Edward Lorenz
William Henry N. Lorenz
Elmer M. Lorenzo
George H. Lorimer
Charles Joseph Loring, Jr.
Joseph Lorio
David C. Lorrey
Arthur G. Losh
John L. Losh
Mannie L. Loshaw
James N. Lossett
Joseph Philip Lostetter
Arthur E. Losure
Cosimo S. Lotempio

Thomas D. Lotis
Daniel Vito Lotrecchaiano
George W. Lott
Kenneth H. Lott
Paul J. Lotti
Harley J. Lottman
James E. Lotz
Ernest Hayes Louden
Arnold E. Loudermilk
Gibson Loudin, Jr.
Donald H. Loudon
Freeman W. Loudon
Frank Thomas Loughery
Philip J. Loughman
Edward D. Louis
William Brian Lourim
James H. Loury
Jack E. Loutzenhiser
Ray V. Louviere
Gilbert Lovato
Bruce I. Lovdokken
Arthur Love, Jr.
Charles A. Love
Edwin N. Love
Emmett L. Love
Fred Love, Jr.
Guy R. Love, Jr.
Herbert G. Love
Matthew Love
Robert James Love
Roosevelt Love
Rudolph Love
William Murdock Love
Willie Love, Jr.
Robert V. Loveday
Vaun A. Loveday
Edward G. Lovejoy
Wallace Ray Lovelady
Emery E. Loveland
Niles S. Loveland
Edward Glenn Loveless
Larry Loveless
Richard L. Loveless
John Raymond Lovell
Robert W. Lovell
Thomas D. Lovell
Rex Lovely
Donald W. Lovern
Charles E. Lovett
Frank E. Lovett, Jr.
John Mercer Lovett
Leroy Lovett
William J. Lovill
Charles R. Loving
William N. Loving
Arthur Ray Lovins
Edward Lovins
Anthony J. Lovolo
Michael Lovra
Charles R. Low
Alfred N. Lowder
George William Lowder
Billy J. Lowe
Gerald A. Lowe
Jack C. Lowe
James Alfred Lowe, Jr.
James Edward Lowe
James F. Lowe
James G. Lowe
John L. Lowe, Jr.
Johnson Lowe, Jr.
Junior B. Lowe
Lawrence C. Lowe
Merlin Roy Lowe
Milford G. Lowe
Ray J. Lowe
Stanley R. Lowe
Thomas Lowe
Thurman J. Lowe
William R. Lowe
Ralph Eugene Lower
James E. Lowery
Paul Arthur Lowery
Robert L. Lowery
Theodore E. Lowery
Thomas E. Lowery
Lyle L. Lowman
Roy G. Lowman
James H. Lowrance
William T. Lowrey
Ellsworth J. Lowry
Harry G. Loy
Frank R. Loyd, Jr.
Roy Loyd
Wallace B. Loyd
Fermin P. Lozoya
George S. Lublinski
Theodore A. Lubobanski
Harvey E. Luby

Irvin M. Luby
Edward Stanley Lucarz
Bobby Dean Lucas
Carl Lucas
Charles R. Lucas
Duane Grouse Lucas
Earl B. Lucas
George Lucas
Harry R. Lucas
Herbert Lucas
James Franklin Lucas
James R. Lucas
Jimmy Lucas
Marshall R. Lucas
Richard A. Lucas
Richard Fred Lucas
Robert J. Lucas
Roy Lucas, Jr.
Russell K. Lucas
Steven Lucas
Torres Jose Lucca
Earland Leroy Luce
Howard J. Luce
Alfred G. Lucero
Elias W. Lucero
Louis Lucero
Manuel Lucero
Seferino Lucero
Harvey J. Luchies
Gerald P. Lucht
Rodriguez Luciano
Edward Lucid
Paul Lucik
Jose B. Lucio
Pablo Lucio
Warren A. Lucio
Henry Lucke
Ray Frank Luckenbill
Andrew J. Luckett
John B. Luckett
William James Ludes
James H. Ludlow
Frank L. Ludwig
James E. Ludwig
Schrader E. Ludwig
William F. Ludwig
Daniel E. Luebbers
Gordon Willys Luedke
Robert C. Luedtke
Santiago B. Luera
Walter L. Luft
Harold E. Lugenbeel
Carbrera Rube Lugo
Inez G. Lugo
Rafael Lugo, Jr.
Will Lugo
Paul Vincent Luhrs
Carlo A. Luhta
Harvard Eldon Luick
Louie M. Luisi
Edward F. Luisser
Blas W. A. Lujan
Eutiquio J. Lujan
George Lujan
Herman J. Lujan
Juan Lujan
George M. Lukakis
Mike Lukas
John Edward Luke
Lee F. Luke
Orville D. Luke
Richard L. Luke
Horace Luker
John Joseph Lukitsch
Chew W. Lum
King Alfred Lum
Milton S. F. Lum
Norman J. Lumb
Edward G. Luna
Fred Ernest Luna
Gilbert F. Luna
Librado Luna
Richard S. Luna
Charles E. Lunbeck
Elbert R. Lunce
Daryl Delane Lund
Edward A. Lund
Harold Jack Lund
Harold S. Lund
James W. Lund
David Lee Lundberg
Earl E. Lundberg
Kenneth Lundberg
Warren Arthur Lundberg
John Lundelius
Winston Lundervold
Charles Lundquist
William E. Lundquist
John F. Lunduski

Arthur C. Lundy
Clifton D. Lundy, Jr.
Virgil E. Lundy
Frank A. Lunedi
Richard M. Lunn
James E. Lunsford
James E. Lunsford
Ronald D. L. Lunsford
Lowell D. Lunt, Jr.
Allan Eugene Luoma
Attilio Michele Lupacchini
Carmine Lupinacci
Donald Joseph Lupo
Leo Lupton
John S. Lush
Lloyd Raymond Lusher
Arthur E. Lusignan
Billy J. Lusk
Jesse M. Lusk
Tom Edward Lusk
Wallace R. Lusk
Remi G. Lussier
Eugene V. Luszewicz
Raymond E. Lutes
Charles W. Luther
Anthony Luti
Samuel A. Lutterloh
Clarence P. Luttrall, Jr.
Edward J. Luty
Billy J. Lutz
Frank Lutz
John W. Lutz
Robert G. Lutz
William Hubert Lutz
Mortimer E. Lux
William P. Luyendyk
William E. Luzadder
Robert B. Lyall
John Smith Lycan, Jr.
William Robert Lyden
Robert M. Lydolph
Edward T. Lydon
Eugene M. Lydon
William F. Lyell
Byron K. Lykins
Clarence B. Lykins
William A. Lyle
Dean Lyles
Paul E. Lyles
Willie L. Lyles
William J. Lyman, Jr.
Ozzie Lynah
Dan G. Lynch
Elwin R. Lynch
Fredrick Charles Lynch
Harold M. Lynch
Harold P. Lynch
James Harold Lynch
James Robert Lynch
John A. Lynch
John F. Lynch
Joseph H. Lynch
J. Lynch
Philip C. Lynch
Robert Eugene Lynch
Robert Fowler Lynch
Thomas J. Lynch
William C. Lynch
William T. Lynch
Don O. Lynd
Elmer L. Lynn
Frank W. Lynn
James L. Lynn
Edward A. Lyon
Galen L. Lyon
Leonard G. Lyon
Trenton R. Lyon
Elvin H. Lyons
Gordon E. Lyons
J. C. Lyons
James H. Lyons
James R. Lyons
Jesse D. Lyons
John Francis Lyons, Jr.
Marshall F. Lyons
Patrick Arnold Lyons
Vernon Lyons
Jack Wayne Lytle
James W. Lytle
Leslie Donald Lytle

354

— M —

Melvin D. Maas
Robert A. Maas
Wayne B. Maas
Frederick Maasberg
Albert C. Maass
Pacifico Mabanag

Issac S. Mabe
Firminio Mabenis
Frank E. Mabey
George J. Mabin
Arnett C. Mabry
James Mabry
John R. Mabry
Richard W. Mac Adam
Howard T. Mac Arthur
Malcolm Angus Mac Askill
Dewey Mac Clintock
James H. Mac Donald
James R. Mac Donald
Robert Mac Donald
Robert Mac Donald
Roderic Mac Donald
William R. Mac Donald
Bernard A. Mac Dougall
Archibald S. Mac Farlane
Willia Mac Farlane
Henry T. Mac Gill
George L. Mac Isaac
William A. Mac Kean
Guy Allan Mac Laury
Allan D. Mac Lean
Donald V. Mac Lean
Kenneth C. Mac Lean
Kenneth N. Mac Lean
Billy M. Mac Leod
Duncan A. Mac Leod
Lloyd S. Mac Leod
Alexander Mac Millan
James A. Mac Millan
William Arthur Mac Millan
Hector Mac Nair-Raga
Charles E. Mac Neil
Edward W. Mac Neill
Allen Hugh Mac Quarrie
Douglas Jay Macarthur
Buhl J. Mace
Delbert Ulysses Mace
Jackie M. Mace
Rolette Mace
William B. Mace
Arthur S. Macedo, Jr.
Frank J. Macek
Gilbert V. Machado
Henry Borges Machado, Jr.
Edward P. Machala
Joseph A. Machann, Jr.
Daniel Machcinski
William A. Machen
Lawrence K. Machida
Alfred Lloyd Machmer
Harry Machnicki
John A. Maciag
Michelo A. Macino
Walter A. Maciorowski
Alvin Leroy Mack
Artemus A. Mack
Fred Ernest Mack, Jr.
Herbert U. Mack
Lenton L. Mack
Leroy F. Mack
Louis I. Mack
Paul Mack, Jr.
Gabriel M. Mackall
William A. Mackean
Ernest Mackey
Robert D. Mackey
Robert K. Mackey
Richard B. Mackin
Robert James Mackinson
Glenn R. Mackley
Clinton Bernard Macklin
Joseph E. Macklin
William A. Macklin
Donald V. Maclean
Malcolm D. Macleod
James L. Maclin
Harold P. Macmunn
Wayne B. Macomber
Robert J. Macon
Leo J. Maczuga
David E. Madden
Oscar B. Madden
Robert F. Madden
Walter J. Madden
William H. Madden
William T. Maddix
Donald Maddox
James W. Maddox
Pleasant M. Maddox
Robert L. Maddox
William E. Maddox
Allen T. Maddy
Walter E. Maddy
Richard Madej
Gerald D. Madel

Garland E. Madison
Reginald Madison
Hubert A. Madosh
George Edward Madress
Leonard I. Madrid
Luciano Ernest Madrid
Robert Banuelos Madrid
Benjamin G. Madrigal
Frank T. Madrigal
Joe L. Madril
Frank J. Madsen, Jr.
Grant W. Madsen
John Eizear Madsen
John Madsen, Jr.
Kenneth E. Madsen
Marlin O. Madsen
John Lloyd Madvig
Eugene A. Maeckel
Hanford K. Maeda
Haruo Maeda
Stanley William Maedke
Robert F. Maenhout
Hilario A. Maes
Pellegrino J. J. Maffeo
Thomas M. Maffett
Pete G. Magallanez
Edwardo Magana
John Joseph Magda
Byron D. Magee
John Vincent Magee
William T. Magee
Albert J. Magers
Dale L. Magers
John H. Maggard
Marvin V. Maggett
Anthony J. Maggi
Morris R. Magnan
Cecil L. Magner
Donald F. Magnus
Lawrence G. Magnus
Henry Joseph Magolan
Robert L. Magoon
Lawrence Magouirk
Fernando Magri
Munro Magruder
Frances P. Maguire
James L. Maguire
John J. Maguire
Joseph E. Maguire
Leo W. Maguire
William R. Magyar
Charles E. Mahaffey
Rufus H. Mahaffey, Jr.
Joseph Mahalak
Robert D. Mahan
Vernon Mahan
Elden E. Mahannah
John F. Mahar
Melvin E. Mahar
Frank X. Maher
John B. Maher
Thomas A. M. Maher
Norman J. Mahler
Duane E. Mahnesmith
Andrew W. Mahon
James R. Mahon
Kenneth Roland Mahon
Eddie R. Mahone
Edwin F. Mahoney
Francis B. Mahoney
James J. Mahoney
John T. Mahoney
Kenneth R. Mahoney
Michael Joseph Mahoney
Thomas R. Mahoney
Walter A. Mahoney
Richard Wayne Mahr
Louis Charles Maid
Clarence F. Maiden
Thomas J. Maidens
Donald A. Maier
Harold L. Main
John W. Maines
James T. Mainhart
Billy Mainous
Mark W. Mairich
William Wylie Maisch
Santiago Maisonet
George A. Maitland
Arthur Majeske, Jr.
Leroy E. Majeske
Milton L. Majette
Edward A. Majewski
Albert A. Majomut
Charlie Leon Major
George Major
Jay E. Major
Richard F. Majszak
Charles K. Makaena

Joseph J. Makara
Charles D. Makela
Bernard E. Maki
Lawrence S. L. Maki
Anthony J. Makosky
Antonio M. Malacara
Victor Malacara
Allen B. Malachi
Merel R. Malak
Morgan J. Malaney
Angelo S. Malanga
Israel Malaret-Juarbe
Cecil A. Malcolm
Howard G. Malcolm
William J. Malcolm
Frank M. Malczewski
Lalo S. Maldonado
Ayala Jo Maldonado
Cortada Rafael Maldonado
Garcia J. Maldonado
Jimenez Maldonado
Luciano M. Maldonado
Morales Maldonado
Pedro Maldonado
Rudolph Maldonado
Torres A. Maldonado
Victor S. Maldonado
Robert L. Male
Daniel D. Maletta
Jerry L. Maley
James William Maliff, Jr.
Geno J. Malise
Franklin C. Malkemes, Jr.
Robert Malkiewicz
Harry E. Mallery
Thomas O. Mallery
Robert Alfred Mallett
Donald J. Mallette
Richard L. Mallette
William Mallick, Jr.
James Joseph Malloy
Robert Hugh Malloy
Robert J. Malloy
William H. Malloy
J. B. Malmay
Francis P. Malone
Joe W. Malone, Jr.
Robert J. Malone
Sherman W. Malone
Thomas Malone
Francis M. Maloney
James F. Maloney
Ronald Ray Maloney
Candido Malonzo
George J. Malool
Charles P. Maloy
Arthur W. Maltais
Rubin R. Maltbie
Donald F. Maltesen
James A. Maly
Manuel D. Mamaril, Jr.
George H. Mammes
Thomas V. Manahan
John W. Manasco
Richard R. Mancebo
Guy G. Manchester
Thomas Manchester
Ronald J. Mancini
Tony L. Mancuso
Abraham Issac Mandel
David Mandell
Gerardo R. Mandia
Robert Sylvester Mandich
Eugene T. Mandick
Tony Mandino
Philip Vincent Mandra
James Lazar Mandrean, Jr.
Donald A. Mandrier
John David Mandt
Leo J. Manegre
Horace M. Maner
Patrick J. Mangan
Richard A. Mangan
Charles Howard Mangin
Albert J. Mangini
Jerome M. Mangner
Billy C. Mangrum
Lenzie H. Mangrum
Selman D. Mangrum
Roby L. Mangum
Charles Manhollan
John Steven Maniatty
John L. Manier
Robert S. Manier
Everett D. Manion
Herbert L. Manion
Jack C. Manis
Philip F. Manis
Mario J. Maniscalco

Alphons Manitowabi
Bob R. Mankin
Robert W. Manley
William J. Manley
Donald Livingston Mann
Donald W. Mann
Harold R. Mann
J. W. Mann
Jackie N. Mann
James E. Mann
Jay Mann
Nathaniel Floyd Mann, Jr.
Otto Mann
Richard H. Mann
Robert A. Mann
Robert Hawkins Mann, Jr.
Robert M. Mann
Robert V. Mann
William Cornett Mann
Walter E. Manninen
Albert Manning, Jr.
Arthur E. Manning
Bill D. Manning
Elija Keith Manning
Ira Manning
James E. Manning
Lee H. Manning
Norman S. Manning
William Roland Manning
James S. Mannino
William Andrew Manns
Nicholas Manos
Billy E. Manring
George C. Manring
Thomas M. Manross
James E. Mansell
Frederick Manship
Ray Wosley Mansholt
Lowell D. Manson
Peter Mansueto
Gilbert Paul Mantey
Beverly S. Manton
Philip W. Mantor
Delmer R. Manuel
Franklin Manuel
John R. Manuel
Robert J. Manuel
William D. Manuel
William G. Manuello
Pastor B. Manzano
Richard J. Manzel
Lavern E. Maple
Percy Jerome Maples
Warren R. Mar
Yandal H. Marable
Benny Maragioglio
Joseph Maranche
Frank M. Marassa
Howard Lyle Marble
Myron P. Marble
Charles E. Marburger
Anthony Marcatante
Donald E. Marcelli
David Thomas Marchant
Glen V. Marchant
Melvin Marchbanks
Fred John Marchert, Jr.
Alexander J. Marchese
John Marchese
John Albert Marchese
Anthony J. Marchino
Martin Marchowsky
Nicholas James Marciano
Armando R. Marcias
Mike Marcin, Jr.
Henry Marcinkowski
Leonar Marcinowski
George I. Marcks
Charles E. Marco
Paul Nicholas Marco
Allen Marcotte
Adrian T. Marcus
Martin Marcus
Marcus, Jr.
Salvatore Marcuzzo
Alfred Raymond Marek
Lee Roy J. Marek
Raymond W. Marek
Thomas D. Marek
Bennie Z. Mares
Charlie J. Mares
Edward F. Mares
Paul F. Maret
Natherene C. Marett
Peralta He Mariani
John Mariano
Salvatore Mariano
David Charles J. Marier
Joe W. Marigna

De La Rosa J. Marin
Ignatius Marinello
Charles Marino
Frank Marino
William John Marino
Christopher C. Marion, Jr.
Robert G. Marion
Roy L. Marjama
Hubert David Mark
Oscar Haslup Mark, Jr.
Ottis P. Mark
Wayne Allen Marker
Harold Arnold Markey
Leo Patrick Markey, Jr.
Elbert O. Markham
Wallace K. Markland
Earl H. Markle
Floyd A. Markle
Robert A. Markle, Jr.
Wilbur L. Markos
Amar Dudley Marks
Don D. Marks
Eugene L. Marks
Harry T. Marks
Harvey L. Marks
James I. Marks, Jr.
Kent M. Marks
Robert A. Marks
George Joe Markus
James F. Marlar
Donald L. Marlatt
Bobby G. Marler
James E. Marler
Walter L. Marler
Fred James Marley
Raymond John Marlier
Charles Marlow, Jr.
Frankie D. Marlow
Charles S. Marlowe
Fred E. Marlowe
Henry A. Marney
William E. Marold
John Maroni
Bernard Marquardt
Cruz Carme Marquez
Gilbert Marquez
Hernandez Marquez
Jasper V. Marquez
John Marquez, Jr.
Martin Marquez
Quinones M. Marquez
Rudolph Marquez
Leon Ramon Marquez-De
  Auburn Mar
Charles L. Marr
John T. Marr
Alexander P. Marra
Joseph Marrelli
John A. Marren
Buccheciam Marrero
Darius M. Marrero
Negron Ism Marrero
Rivera Jos Marrero
Alfredo Marrero-Rivera
Dominic F. Marrocco
George A. Marrocco
John I. Marruso
Joseph Marryott
Louis A. Marryott
Frank O. Mars
Otto E. Marschke
Douglas R. Marsh
Elija Marsh
French E. Marsh
George W. Marsh
Harold L. Marsh
Howard Mcclelland Marsh
James Howard Marsh, Jr.
Robert Lee Marsh
Teddy C. Marsh
Albert Marshall, Jr.
Alfred Marshall
Calvin C. Marshall
Clarence Marshall
Cloma Marshall
Donald M. Marshall
Ellis Marshall
Eugene D. Marshall
Forrest M. Marshall
George G. Marshall
Harry A. Marshall
Isreal Marshall, Jr.
Jack E. Marshall
James D. Marshall
James E. Marshall
James T. Marshall
Melvin E. Marshall
Merlin E. Marshall
Norman F. Marshall

Paul J. Marshall
Richard L. Marshall
Ronald D. Marshall
Wendell W. Marshall
William B. Marshall
Willie F. Marshall
Herbert E. Marshburn, Jr.
Richard E. Marsland
Richard William Marson
Francis Julian Marstiller
Bobby R. Marston
Robert Clifford Martell
Ronald W. Martens
Wayne N. Martens
Albert F. Martin
Albert J. Martin
Albert L. Martin
Alfred J. Martin
Arthur F. Martin
Bobbie G. Martin
Carl D. Martin
Carl E. Martin
Cecil G. Martin
Charles Martin
Charles C. Martin
Charles R. Martin
Claire Martin
Clarence A. Martin, Jr.
Clarence F. Martin
Claude E. Martin
Clyde B. Martin
Clyde H. Martin, Jr.
David J. Martin
Dickie C. Martin
Dominique K. Martin
Donald W. Martin
Earl Martin
Edward F. Martin
Edward J. Martin
Edward L. Martin
Edward R. Martin
Edward W. Martin
Edwin C. Martin
Elmer E. Martin
Elwin C. Martin, Jr.
Ernest K. Martin
Eugene R. Martin
Eugene W. Martin
Floyd W. Martin, Jr.
Frank Iii Martin
George Alan Martin
George Martin, Jr.
Gerald F. Martin
Gilbert L. Martin
Glen R. Martin
Harvey J. Martin
Henry Charles Martin
Herbert O. Martin
Horace Edmund Martin, Jr.
J. D. Martin
James Martin
James A. Martin
James E. Martin
James F. Martin
James F. Martin
James F. Martin, Jr.
James H. Martin
James M. Martin
James R. Martin
James W. Martin
James W. Martin
Jewel R. Martin
Jimmie G. Martin
Joel R. Martin
John Martin
John A. Martin
John A. Martin, Jr.
John G. Martin
John P. Martin, Jr.
John R. Martin
John W. Martin
Joseph J. Martin
Karl L. Martin
Kenneth E. Martin
Ladson K. Martin
Leander Martin
Leland M. Martin
Leon E. Martin
Nicholas Martin
Nicholas P. Martin
Orley C. Martin
Oscar D. Martin
Paul Edward Martin
Rex C. Martin
Robert A. Martin
Robert C. Martin
Robert G. Martin
Robert Martin, Jr.
Robert L. Martin

Robert Lee Martin
Robert R. Martin
Robert V. Martin
Silton J. Martin, Jr.
Vernelle T. Martin
William B. Martin
William H. Martin
William M. Martin
William R. Martin
George Percy Martineau
Lavon Martineau
Louis Martinex
Alex Vidal Martinez
Alfredo L. Martinez
Ambrosio Martinez
Antero Martinez
Arnulfo Martinez
Arturo B. Martinez
Basilio Martinez
Benito Martinez
Carlos M. Martinez
Claude Dionsic Martinez
Colon Cri Martinez
Delores Martinez
Dennis D. Martinez
Dionisio Martinez
Efrem G. Martinez
Ernest Martinez
Ernest L. Martinez
Ernest R. Martinez
Felix Martinez
Gonzalez Martinez
Gualberto Martinez
Henry Martinez
Hernandez Martinez
Jacabo Luis Martinez
Jesus C. Martinez
Jesus P. Martinez
John A. Martinez
Jose E. Martinez
Jose Martinez, Jr.
Joseph A. Martinez
Joseph A. Martinez
Juan J. Martinez
Lee R. Martinez
Louis Martinez
Luis Martinez
Luis B. Martinez
Luis P. Martinez, Jr.
Manuel Martinez
Manuel H. Martinez
Manuel J. Martinez
Manuel Martinez, Jr.
Nicolas Martinez
Oliver Martinez
Oquendo A. Martinez
Otero And Martinez
Paul Martinez
Primero R. Martinez
Raymond R. Martinez
Richard J. Martinez
Rosado Ju Martinez
Rosario R. Martinez
Sergio Mercado Martinez
Trinidad Martinez
Wenceslao Martinez
Xavier P. Martinez
Tomas Martinez-Candelario
Luis Martinez-Hernandez
Ramon L. Martinez-Landron
Pedro J. Martinez-Otero
John Martinko
John Martins
Odvin A. Martinson
William J. Martis
Edward G. Martone
Albert E. Marty
Raymond R. Marty
Zigmund M. Maruk
William Walter Marwood
Donald M. Marx
John Edward Marzec
Muniz Manuel R. Mas
Silva Ivan Mas
Ralph S. Masatusugu
Michael Mascara
John M. Masch
Jason Maschist
Robert Raymond Mase
Lawrence A. Masesie
Domenick J. Mash
Nick J. Masiello
Nathan Masin
Edward Richard Masiulis
John E. Masko
John William Maslin
John L. Masnari
Alwin L. Mason
Billie F. Mason

Burke J. Mason
Charles Mason
Charles D. Mason
Charles W. Mason
Earl H. Mason
Earon L. Mason
Edward M. Mason
George H. Mason
James L. Mason
Jim H. Mason
Joseph E. Mason
Kenneth C. Mason
Kenneth K. Mason
Paul Mason
Ralph E. Mason
Ray S. Mason
Richard Mason
Robert G. Mason
Robert L. Mason
Thomas E. Mason
Walter Edward Mason
Walter J. Mason
Raymond P. Masperi
Almodovar Massanet
Robles Heri Massas
Robert Massengale
Anthony Massey, Jr.
Bobby J. Massey
Edward D. Massey
George C. Massey, Jr.
Elmore Massie
James Clifford Massie
Marcos A. Massini
Figueroa Jor Masso
Homer E. Masson
Clifford Henry Mast
Steve A. Mastabayvo
Alva R. Masters
Emmet P. Masters
Laurence Edward Masters
Louis R. Masters
William J. Masters
Harold A. Masterson
Robert O. Masterson
Tommy E. Masterson
Robert L. Mastin
Verlin Dean Maston
Willia Mastroianni
Giovann Mastroinni
Daniel N. Mata, Jr.
Frank C. Mata
Francis John Matasovsky
Edward W. Matchett
Stephen Mate, Jr.
Donald V. Mateer
Joseph T. Matej
John D. Matejovich
Aurelio Mateo
Lafe Henry Materne
Daniel D. Mathena
Jack D. Matheny
Clavis C. Mather
David J. Mather
Randolph E. Mather
James P. Mathers
Leonard J. Mathers
Douglas N. Matheson
Roy C. Mathess
Howard W. Mathew
George A. Mathews
Kenneth J. Flood Mathews
Lionel Eric Mathews
Norman C. Mathews
Richard J. Mathews
Roy E. Mathews
Bruce Mathewson, Jr.
Ward F. Mathewson
Grayson L. Mathis
Howard J. Mathis, Jr.
J. L. Mathis
James I. Mathis
Joseph M. Mathis
Lawrence Edward Mathis
Melvin G. Mathis
Robert K. Mathis
Roy L. Mathis
Raymond Charles Mathony
Albert K. Mathre
Henry D. Mathus
Remigio Mar Matias
Charles A. Matlach
Howard K. Matlack
Melvin J. Matlock
Rufus W. Matlock
Donald E. Matney
Joseph Matonis
Michael J. Matonis
Irizarry Ram Matos
Rivera Anton Matos

Santiago Cri Matos
Torres Ismae Matos
F. A. Matos-Gonzalez
Gabrie Matrisciano
Le Roy Matsen
Peter T. Matsikas
Arthur A. Matson, Jr.
Charles F. Matson
Charles R. Matson
Edward Matson
Gary E. Matson
Howard L. Matson
Heishin Matsuda
Kumaji Matsuda
Joseph J. Matsunaga
Jun Matsushige
Elmy L. Matta
John Ralph Mattei
Frederick Henry Mattheis
Richard R. Matthess
Donald F. Matthew
Arnold B. Matthews
Clarence Matthews
Daniel P. Matthews
George M. Matthews
Glenn Matthews
Henry T. Matthews
Irving P. Matthews
Jack H. Matthews
James A. Matthews
James F. Matthews
James L. Matthews
Lexie D. Matthews
Oliver W. Matthews
Richard F. Matthews
Richard L. Matthews
Robert Matthews
Roy W. Matthews
Willie J. Matthews
John B. Matthys
Stanley R. Mattier
Charles E. Mattingly
Donald L. Mattingly
Gerald J. Mattingly
Harry E. Mattis, Jr.
Herbert H. Mattocks
Alfred W. Matton
Andre J. Matton
Henry E. Matton, Jr.
James H. Mattoon
Charles Henry Mattox
Willie E. Mattox
Clarence A. Mattson
Dale I. Mattson
Henry J. Mattson
John Albert Mattson
Walter A. Mattson
Anthony M. Mattucci
Joseph Sam Matulich
Michael S. Matusik
Robert James Matusowski
William Stephen Matusz
Marian Matuszewski
Gregorio E. Matutino
Melvin R. Matzen
Clarence B. Mauer
Graham W. Maughmer
Charles R. Mauldin
Earl L. Mauldin, Jr.
Gene Remus Mauldin
Sydney R. Mauldin
William Kennedy Mauldin
Billie T. Maupin
Clifton W. Maupin
Robert C. Maupin
Robert C. Maurer
Ovide L. Maurice
James P. Mauricio
Paul F. Mauricio
Robert S. Mauro
Edmund R. Maury
Edward O. Maury
Donald J. Maus
Donald V. Maus
William F. Maus
Joseph R. Mauser
Frederick W. III Mausert
Ervin E. Mautz
Wesley M. Mawson
George A. Max
Ira A. Maxam
Frankie L. Maxey
Joseph S. Maxson
Billy J. Maxwell
Glenn E. Maxwell
Henry C. Maxwell
Herbert Ray Maxwell
James Maxwell
Joseph Maxwell

Joseph T. Maxwell
Raymond B. Maxwell
Roy Lee Maxwell
Albert Charles May
Alfred May
Charles William May
Delmar Eugene May
Donald A. May
Donald Lee May
Donald R. May
Elton L. May
Gus May
Harley D. May
Henry D. May
Homer I. May
Irvin W. May
Levert May
Lincoln C. May
Melvin C. May
Raymond F. May
Robert L. May
Russell D. May
Rodolfo A. Maybe
George M. Mayberry
James Patrick Mayberry
Johnny H. Mayberry
Warren E. Mayberry
Wilbur Maycox
Clinton G. Maye
Thomas E. Maye
Larry J. Mayeaux
Jimmie Mayemura
Roy E. Mayer
Thomas C. Mayer
Donald Mayerhofer
John J. Mayerhofer
Donald F. Mayerle
Charles F. Mayes
Eugene M. Mayes
Gordon E. Mayes
Hershel B. Mayes
James D. Mayes
Marshall M. Mayes
Robert A. Mayes
Robert C. Mayes
Lannis J. Mayeux
Charlie Mayfield
James E. Mayfield, Jr.
James Harold Mayfield
Weldon E. Mayfield
Robert Leland Mayhew
William K. Mayhugh
George E. Mayle
Donald R. Maynard
Edward Wiley Maynard
Elbert J. Maynard
Jerry K. Maynard
Max E. Maynard
Norman K. Maynard
Ray L. Maynard
William D. Maynard
Donald L. Mayo
Earney Alfred Mayo, Jr.
Gene R. Mayo
Green B. Mayo
James Joseph Mayo
John M. Mayo
Joseph Haynes Mayo
Marvin Mayo
Melvin J. Mayo
Figueroa Mayol
Charles E. Mayrand
Andrew G. Mays
Edwin D. Mays
John Mays, Jr.
Thomas C. Mays
Paul W. Maze
Walter J. Maziarz
Mortimer Mazur
Josep Mazurkiewicz
Frank J. Mazzarella
Ralph J. Mazzaufo
James W. Mazzu
Anthony R. Mazzulla
Thomas F. Mazzulla
Billy L. Mc Abee
James E. Mc Abee
Ernest G. Mc Adams
Michael L. Mc Adams
Ronald L. Mc Adams
George U. Mc Aden
Ernest Robert Mc Adoo
David E. Mc Afee
Henry L. Mc Afee
James T. Mc Afee
Johnson Mc Afee, Jr.
Raymond D. Mc Afee
Alvie Mc Alexander
Emmett Mc Alister

Harold Mc Alister
John Albert Mc Allaster, Jr.
Jack E. Mc Allister
John F. Mc Allister
Kennet Mc Allister
Robert E. Mc Allister
William Mc Allister
William J. Mc Allister
Michael J. Mc Alpin
John M. Mc Alpine
John Matheson Mc Alpine
Johnny L. Mc Alpine
Charles A. Mc Andrews
Felix J. Mc Andrews
Robert Winfred Mc Anelly
Alfonso Mc Arthur
Charles H. Mc Atee
Madison B. Mc Atee
James A. Mc Ateer
Philip D. Mc Aughan
Corneli Mc Auliffe
Donald J. Mc Avoy
Harold E. Mc Avoy
John Francis Mc Avoy
George Mc Bath
James R. Mc Bee
Donald Mc Beth
Lee R. Mc Brayer
Charles Mc Brian, Jr.
Charles Howard Mc Briar
Aaron H. Mc Bride
Bobby Gene Mc Bride
Charles Leroy Mc Bride
George M. Mc Bride
James F. Mc Bride
James Lloyd Mc Bride, Jr.
James W. Mc Bride
Joe D. Mc Bride
John Joseph III Mc Bride
Robert Mc Bride
Robert L. Mc Bride
William M. Mc Bride
Hugh G. Mc Bryde
David L. Mc Burney
Donald J. Mc Cabe
John E. Mc Cabe
John W. Mc Cabe
Joseph Mc Cabe
Sherman Mc Caffery
William Mc Caffery
Bernard Mc Caffrey
James D. Mc Cain
John W. Mc Cain
Robert L. Mc Cain
Douglas F. Mc Caine
Neely T. Mc Caleb, Jr.
Clarence A. Mc Call
Edward L. Mc Call
Franklin L. Mc Call
John Henry Mc Call
Julius J. Mc Call
Leston R. Mc Call
Marvin E. Mc Call
Rufus Arthur Mc Call
Terry S. Mc Call
Willi Mc Callister
Kenneth Eugene Mc Camie
Robert Mc Cammack
Ernest Mc Campbell
Cecil D. Mc Can
James J. Mc Cann
John J. Mc Cann
John L. Iii Mc Cann
Russell J. Mc Cann
Charles Mc Carney
Billie Jack Mc Carrell
Raymond Mc Carrell
William S. Mc Carson
Kenneth Mc Cartan
Albert A. Mc Carthy
Edward F. Mc Carthy
Edward J. Mc Carthy
Frank L. Mc Carthy
Gordon D. Mc Carthy
Homer C. Mc Carthy
Leonard J. Mc Carthy
Philip A. Mc Carthy
Thomas F. Mc Carthy
Wilbur C. Mc Carthy
Charles Mc Cartney
Harold Mc Cartney
William Mc Cartney
Claude J. Mc Carty, Jr.
Donald Earl Mc Carty
Frank W. Mc Carty
Troy D. Mc Carty
William Logan Mc Carver
Stuart Mc Cash
Wayne W. Mc Casland

Keith V. Mc Caslin
Robert J. Mc Caul
Ernest G. Mc Cauley
Corne Mc Clafferty
Carl E. Mc Claflin
Earl E. Mc Clain
Frederick F. Mc Clain
Richard Mc Clain
Gaylon L. Mc Claine
Alton L. Mc Clanahan
Ray Allen Mc Claskey
Herman L. Mc Clatchey
Robert Mc Claverty
Le Roy Mc Cleain
Donald E. Mc Clellan
Harlan E. Mc Clellan
Maurice N. Mc Clellan
Thomas P. Mc Clellan, Jr.
Cleon K. Mc Clelland
Herbert Hoover Mc Clelland
Arthur W. Mc Clenaghan
James Mc Clenathan
Herbert Mc Clendon
Horace Mc Clennon
Alfred Mc Clintock
John R. Mc Clintock
Michael W. Mc Clone
Steve Mc Cloud
James E. Mc Cloy
Willia Mc Cluggage
Aubrey C. Mc Clung
William John Iii Mc Clung
Charles E. Mc Clure
Clarence Mc Clure, Jr.
Cleo L. Mc Clure
Ferdinand Mc Clure
Fred H. Mc Clure
Gilbert N. Mc Clure
Herman C. Mc Clure
James L. Mc Clure
Jerome E. Mc Clure
Jessie D. Mc Clure
Jim Mc Clure
John S. Mc Clure
Kenneth C. Mc Clure
Leroy S. Mc Clure
Sam Mc Clure
Tom N. Mc Clure
Virginia May Mc Clure
Ronald Mc Cluskey
Luther E. Mc Clusky
Lee F. Mc Coats
Robert L. Mc Cole
Chester Mc Colley
Lawrence Mc Collim
Francis N. Mc Collom
Herman L. Mc Collum
John J. Mc Collum
Leon B. Mc Collum
William J. Mc Collum
Beuford Mc Comas
Ronald J. Mc Comb
Raymond Roy Mc Comber
Cloyd M. Mc Combie
Aaron James Mc Combs
James C. Mc Comic
Gerald J. Mc Conkey
Will Mc Connaughey
Paul Mc Connel
Albert Mc Connell
Charlie Mc Connell
James R. Mc Connell
James W. Mc Connell
Ronnie Mc Connell
Stanley Mc Connell
Marshall Mc Cook
James A. Mc Cool
Cordis B. Mc Cord
Donald William Mc Cord
Irvin M. Mc Cord
Robert C. Mc Cord
Roy D. Mc Cord
James Felder Mc Corkle
Edward Mc Cormack
Harold Mc Cormack
Terence F. Mc Cormack
Arthur Mc Cormick
Billy Gene Mc Cormick
Charles Mc Cormick
Fred G. Mc Cormick
Howard Mc Cormick
James Mc Cormick
James J. Mc Cormick
John J. Mc Cormick
Lafayet Mc Cormick
Oran Mc Cormick
Robert Mc Cormick
Robert E. Mc Cormick, Jr.
Robert G. Mc Cormick

Sherman T. Mc Cormick
Theodore E. Mc Cormick
Thomas J. Mc Cormick
Wade L. Mc Cormick
William Mc Cormick
Charles A. Mc Coskey, Jr.
David Allen Mc Coskrie
James A. Mc Cotter
Raymond J. Mc Coun
Richard C. Mc Cowan
John B. Mc Cowen
Carl R. Mc Coy
Charles Alden Mc Coy
Charles E. Mc Coy
Charles W. Mc Coy
Conly Mc Coy
Floyd Mc Coy
Gerald V. Mc Coy
Glen B. Mc Coy
Glenn Mc Coy
Grady L. Mc Coy
James R. Mc Coy
Joe Mc Coy
John E. Mc Coy
John J. Mc Coy, Jr.
John R. Mc Coy
Lloyd Mc Coy
Lonnie Mc Coy, Jr.
Paul E. T. Mc Coy
Raymond H. Mc Coy
Richard Thomas Mc Coy
Robert H. Mc Coy
Shafter Mc Coy, Jr.
Ulyess E. Mc Coy
K. W. Mc Cracken, Jr.
Paul T. Mc Cracken
William Mc Cracken
Curtis C. Mc Crary
Bufford E. Mc Craw
James W. Mc Craw
Miles E. Mc Craw
Clinton H. Mc Cray
Wade A. Mc Cray
Verne L. Mc Crea
William E. Mc Crea
Addison Mc Creary
Cecil J. Mc Creary
James Z. Mc Creary
Mark F. Mc Creary
Ralph Noah Mc Cuan
Louis A. Mc Cullar
Thomas Charles Mc Cullen
Charles Mc Cullers
John G. Mc Cullin
Edmund Mc Cullough
James Mc Cullough
Joel F. Mc Cullough
John Mc Cullough
Joseph Mc Cullough
Richar Mc Cullough
Robert Mc Cullough
Willie Mc Cullough
Richard Eugene Mc Cune
Robert R. Mc Cune
Richard Mc Curley
Gilbert L. Mc Curry
Buster Mc Curtain
Wayne Homer Mc Cuskey
James Mc Cutcheon
William George Mc Dade
Billy Jean Mc Daniel
Charles Mc Daniel
Charles Mc Daniel
Charles H. Mc Daniel
Claude Clark Mc Daniel
Delmar T. Mc Daniel
Homer M. Mc Daniel
Howard H. Mc Daniel
Hughlon Mc Daniel
Jay D. Mc Daniel
Lamar Howard Mc Daniel
Marion Edward Mc Daniel
Merle A. Mc Daniel
Ray E. Mc Daniel
Raymond Mc Daniel
Wendell Mc Daniel
William Mc Daniel
William F. Mc Daniel
Henry Mc Daniels
Emmett Mc David, Jr.
Patrick Mc Dearmon
Robert P. Mc Dermond
Michael A. Mc Dermont
Eugene Mc Dermott
John W. Mc Dermott
Joseph Mc Dermott
Martin Mc Dermott, Jr.
Thomas Mc Dermott
George W. Mc Divitt

Richard C. Mc Dole
Alton Gore Mc Donald
Billy D. Mc Donald
Bobby W. Mc Donald
Charles L. Mc Donald, Jr.
David N. Mc Donald
Donald D. Mc Donald
Edward J. Mc Donald
Floyd J. Mc Donald
George J. Mc Donald
Jack Mc Donald
Jack E. Mc Donald
John D. Mc Donald
John J. Mc Donald
Kenneth Mc Donald
Nathan U. Mc Donald
Norbert Mc Donald
Ralph G. Mc Donald
Roger G. Mc Donald
Velton R. Mc Donald
Warren B. Mc Donald
William Mc Donald
William Clifford Mc Donald
Raymond J. Mc Doniel
John M. Mc Donnel
Francis Mc Donnell
John James Mc Donnell
John M. Mc Donnell
Jackie Mc Donnough
Charles E. Mc Donough
Howard A. Mc Donough, Jr.
John C. Mc Donough
Paul J. Mc Donough
Phillip Mc Donough
Richard E. Mc Donough
Robert Mc Donough
Thomas Mc Donough
Charles C. Mc Dougal
Garnet W. Mc Dougal
Leslie D. Mc Dougal
Albert R. Mc Dowell
Charles Mc Dowell
Clyamon George Mc Dowell
Clyde R. Mc Dowell
Dale W. Mc Dowell
Donald P. Mc Dowell
Edmond M. Mc Dowell
George C. Mc Dowell
John Franklin Mc Dowell
Junior R. Mc Dowell
Leonard Mc Dowell
Reed C. Mc Dowell
William C. Mc Dowell
John R. Mc Duffee
Clem D. Mc Duffie
Bob D. Mc Elhaney
Powell Hope Mc Elhenney
Patrick Mc Elholm
John P. Mc Elmurry
Pat A. Mc Elmurry
Augustus Mc Elroy
Benjamin Mc Elroy
Clyde E. Mc Elroy
Edward R. Mc Elroy
Forest E. Mc Elroy
Joseph A. Mc Elroy
Elmer C. Mc Elvain
Joseph E. Mc Elvain
Stanley Dennis Mc Elwee
Patrick Mc Enery
Bernard Frederick Mc Evoy
James Charles Mc Evoy
James L. Mc Evoy
Stanley J. Mc Evoy
Larry C. Mc Ewen
Curtis R. Mc Fadden
Kendrick Mc Fadden
William Mc Fadden
Billie E. Mc Fall
David L. Mc Farland
Dennis Mc Farland
Walter Mc Farland
Donn A. Mc Farlane
Edward Q. Mc Farren
Claude Douglas Mc Fee
Robert J. Mc Fee
Edward N. Mc Gaffic
Hallett E. Mc Gaffigan
James F. Mc Garity
Frederick Mc Gaugh
Henry R. Mc Gauley
Charles F. Mc Gee
Dave Mc Gee
David F. Mc Gee
Floyd D. Mc Gee
Marshall H. Mc Gee
Robert Lee Mc Gee
William R. Mc Gee
Thomas P. Mc Geever

Dewey E. Mc Gehee
Leo F. Mc Geough
Walter Mc Gettigan
Maurice Mc Ghee
Richard D. Mc Ghee
William T. Mc Ghee
Willie F. Mc Ghee
Ladell Mc Gill
William F. Mc Gill
John M. Mc Ginithen
Charles Mc Ginnis
Donald Mc Ginnis
John Crysostom Mc Ginnis
Thomas Leslie Mc Ginnis
William Albert Mc Ginnis
John J. Mc Ginty
George F. Mc Givney
William R. Mc Glennon
Frank J. Mc Glinchey
Harold Mc Glothin
Brian D. S. Mc Glynn
Charles R. Mc Glynn
James J. Franci Mc Goey
Patrick T. Mc Gonagle
Harry T. Mc Gonigle
John P. Mc Gonigle
John R. Mc Gonigle
Eugene H. Mc Govern
James J. Mc Govern
James Vincent Mc Govern
Jerome F. Mc Govern
John F. Mc Govern
John P. Mc Govern
Robert M. Mc Govern
Ronald F. Mc Govern
Clarence A. Mc Gowan
Clifton J. Mc Gowan
Donald C. Mc Gowan
Donald Mc Gowan, Jr.
Douglas H. Mc Gowan
Eugene Mc Gowan
Philip T. Mc Gowan
Robert Francis Mc Gowan
William G. Mc Gowan
Kenneth Edward Mc Grady
Edmund J. Mc Grath
Edward J. Mc Grath, Jr.
Edward R. Mc Grath
James J. Mc Grath
Orville B. Mc Grath
Ronald George Mc Grath
Ross Robert Mc Grath
Daniel E. Mc Graw
Lloyd James Mc Graw
Richard P. Mc Graw
Robert L. Mc Graw
Thomas Leo Mc Graw, Jr.
Dale Alvin Mc Gregor
Robert Carson Mc Gregor
James Richard Mc Grew
Grover J. Mc Griff
James L. Mc Guffin
Clarence E. Mc Guiness
Edward J. Mc Guinness
John Bernard Mc Guinness
Bobby A. Mc Guire
Charles Frederick Mc Guire
Charles L. Mc Guire
Clyde A. Mc Guire
Edward J. Mc Guire
Grover Gene Mc Guire
James C. Mc Guire
James P. Mc Guire
John N. Mc Guire
Oliver Mc Guire
Patrick W. Mc Guire
Stanley R. Mc Guire
Thomas J. Mc Guire
William M. Mc Guire
Paul A. Mc Hale
Robert Vincent Mc Hale
Leslie Edward Mc Haney
Richard Mc Hargue
Everett E. Mc Henry
Lorn D. Mc Henry
Paul H. Mc Henry
Robert W. Mc Henry
W. L. Mc Horney
John Joseph Mc Hugh
Delton Mc Innis
John R. Mc Innis
Norman Mc Innis
Thomas A. Mc Innis
Harry H. Mc Intire
Millard E. Mc Intire
Richard Mc Intire
Alfred Mc Intosh, Jr.
Brownlow Mc Intosh
Charles F. Mc Intosh

Curlie Mc Intosh
Henry Mc Intosh, Jr.
Lamar M. Mc Intosh
Kenneth Edwin Mc Intush
Billy M. Mc Intyre
Charles Mc Intyre
Charles Henry Mc Intyre
Claude L. Mc Intyre
Clifton Mc Intyre
Dean I. Mc Intyre
James T. Mc Intyre
Richard A. Mc Intyre
Robert E. Mc Intyre
Robert H. Mc Intyre
Warren H. Mc Intyre
Clarence Mc Junkin
William Mc Junkin
James M. Mc Junkins
Marshall F. Mc Kain
Max E. Mc Kamey
Connie C. Mc Kay
James Martin Mc Kay
Joseph R. Mc Kay
Lewis Mc Kay
Murdock Mc Kay
James H. Mc Kechnie
Harry H. Mc Kee
Henry L. Mc Kee
John M. Mc Kee
Louis F. Mc Kee
Paul L. Mc Kee
Robert Edgar Mc Kee
Herbert V. Mc Keehan
Joe P. Mc Keehan
Donald Francis Mc Keever
Merlin Martin Mc Keever
Jack D. Mc Keighen
Esque Mc Keithan
Dan I. Mc Keithen
Robert D. Mc Kell
William Mc Kellar
Richard Mc Kelvey
Daniel Mc Kenna
Edward J. Mc Kenna
Gilbert W. Mc Kenna
Harold Michael Mc Kenna
Hugh Patrick Mc Kenna
James E. Mc Kenna
John J. Mc Kenna
John Patrick Mc Kenna
Joseph Andre Mc Kenna
Richard J. Mc Kenna
Robert James Mc Kenna
Herbert Mc Kenzie
Hubert Mc Kenzie
James E. Mc Kenzie
John L. Mc Kenzie
John W. Mc Kenzie
Marion D. Mc Kenzie
Neil S. Mc Kenzie
Norman M. Mc Kenzie
Ronald W. Mc Kenzie
Donald L. Mc Keon
Joseph T. Mc Keon
Robert E. Mc Keon
Joseph T. A. Mc Keown
William M. Mc Key
John F. Mc Kibbin
Harry A. Mc Kie
Robert J. Mc Kie
Gerard J. Mc Kiernan
Robert B. Mc Kim
Andrew J. Mc Kinley
Gordon L. Mc Kinley
John Mc Kinley, Jr.
Konrad J. Mc Kinley
Ralph H. Mc Kinley
Thomas H. Mc Kinley
Arnold E. Mc Kinney
Billy R. Mc Kinney
Bratton Mc Kinney, Jr.
Charles Mc Kinney
Daniel Worth Mc Kinney
Edward Mc Kinney
Eugene L. Mc Kinney
Henry C. Mc Kinney
Jack M. Mc Kinney
John V. Mc Kinney
Julius E. Mc Kinney
Kenneth Mc Kinney
Lance L. Mc Kinney
Richard H. Mc Kinney
Ronald E. Mc Kinney
Mackey D. Mc Kinnon
Vanderberg Mc Kinnon
Richard E. Mc Kinstry
Paul L. Mc Kittrick
Frank D. Mc Klusky
Arthur Lee Mc Knight

Harold J. Mc Knight
Preston Mc Knight
William J. Mc Knight
Edward T. Mc Kotch
Bruce C. Mc Kown
Billy J. Mc Lain
Frances E. Mc Lain
James William Mc Lain
Mcdoyle Mc Lane
James T. Mc Laren
Terence Mc Larnon
Andrew Mc Laughlin
Clinto Mc Laughlin
Edward Mc Laughlin
Edwin Mc Laughlin
Franci Mc Laughlin
Jack E. Mc Laughlin
John Mc Laughlin
John J. Mc Laughlin
John Patrick Mc Laughlin
Joseph Mc Laughlin
Loran Mc Laughlin
Paul J. Mc Laughlin
Raymon Mc Laughlin
Robert Mc Laughlin
Harold James Mc Laurin
Artis Mc Lean
Gerald W. Mc Lean
Henderson Doty Mc Lean
Kenneth Mc Leister
Alexande Mc Lellan
John W. Mc Lellan
Billy E. Mc Lemore
David J. Mc Lendon
Willie P. Mc Lendon
Andrew G. Mc Leod
Frank H. Mc Leod
John J. Mc Leod
Richard N. Mc Leod
Robert Edward Mc Leod
Walter L. Mc Leod
William Mc Leod
James E. Mc Leroy
William F. Mc Levis
Peter J. Mc Linko
Robert John Mc Loughlin
Wynard C. Mc Mahan
Dwight D. Mc Mahon
George T. Mc Mahon
James P. Mc Mahon
John E. Mc Mahon, Jr.
John J. Mc Mahon
Raymond F. Mc Mahon
Paul Joseph Mc Makin
Bernard L. Mc Manaman
John Gerald Mc Mann
Billy E. Mc Manus
George H. Mc Manus
Paul D. Mc Manus
Richard B. Mc Manus
Robert A. Mc Manus
Robert L. Mc Manus
Joseph W. Mc Master
Kenneth Mc Meekin
Michael Mc Menamin
Richard C. Mc Michael
Charles Mc Millan
Arthur Mc Millian
Raymond K. Mc Millian
Reveren Mc Millian
Jerry M. Mc Million
Harold D. Mc Million
Robert R. Mc Millon
Victor E. Mc Minn
William Mc Morran
Patrick James Mc Mullan
James J. Mc Mullen
Donald E. Mc Murray
Leroy Mc Murray
Joseph L. Mc Murry
William Fletcher Mc Murry
William Mc Murtrie
Joseph L. Mc Nally
George W. Mc Namara
Martin J. Mc Namara
Raymond Mc Namara
Robert E. Mc Namara
Clarence Mc Names
Walter David Mc Nary
Alonzo J. Mc Natt
Burton Mc Naughton
Donald Mc Naughton
John R. Mc Naughton
Melvin Gerald Mc Nea
Delmas Mc Neal
M. Mc Neal
Robert D. Mc Neal
Albert Mc Neeley
Charles R. Mc Neely, Jr.

Guy W. Mc Neely
Morgan B. Mc Neely
Richard A. Mc Nees
Charles M. Mc Neil
Richard G. Mc Neil
Robert W. Mc Neil
Stewart Mc Neil, Jr.
Willis F. Mc Neil
Curtis Mc Neill
Lewis O. Mc Neill
James Robert Mc Neilley
George A. Mc Nerney
Dean R. Mc New
Willis F. Mc Nirl
Richard O. Mc Nitt
Fred R. Mc Nulty
John William Mc Nulty
Patrick J. Mc Nulty
Richard Lee Mc Nulty
Russell Fabian Mc Nulty
Terence John Mc Nulty
Billie W. Mc Nutt
G. W. Mc Nutt
William H. Mc Nutt
William H. Mc Nutt
Prestiss Mc Phate
Willia Mc Pheeters
Carl E. Mc Pherson
Charles W. Mc Pherson
Ellis G. Mc Pherson
Frankli Mc Pherson
Anne Arundel, MD
Gerald W. Mc Pherson
Patrick J. C. Mc Pherson
William Mc Pherson
John P. Mc Quade
Russell H. Mc Quain
Gilbert D. Mc Queen
Norman Mc Queen
Gerald J. Mc Querry
William E. Mc Quien
Kennet Mc Quilliam
Billy M. Mc Quinn
John M. Mc Quinn
Vance R. Mc Quiston
Clinton Mc Rae
Kenneth Mc Ritchie
James H. Mc Roberts
Roy Mc Roberts
Edward P. Mc Shane
Robert L. Mc Shaw
William Mc Spadden
Leon Mc Swain
John L. Mc Taggart, Jr.
Franklin W. Mc Vay
James Herbert Mc Veen
Thomas Lyons Mc Veigh
Thomas Mc Vicker
Carl R. Mc Voy
Patrick James Mc Waide
Charles Earnest Mc Whirk
Alfred C. Mc Whirter
Vance B. Mc Whorter
Irvin Robert Mcdaniel
Alfred K. Mcilquham
William H. Mclellan
Marion G. Meacham, Jr.
John L. Mead
William C. Mead
Freeman R. Meade
John J. Meade
Marvin D. Meade
Ruby L. Meade
Billie W. Meadors
Andrew J. Meadows
Carl J. Meadows
Charles R. Meadows
Cleveland Meadows
Emmette S. Meadows
Ernest C. Meadows
Hobert E. Meadows
Jesse C. Meadows
Kenneth W. Meadows
Merle L. Meadows
Robert H. Meadows
Vernon Meadows
Neil W. Meagher
Roger F. Meagher
Samuel K. Meagher
Emmett Lloyd Meaghers
Shannon Lord Meany, Jr.
Charles Vernon Mears
Homer G. Mears
Roy C. Meathenia
Douglas F. Mebane
Wallace Allen Mebane
Richard Lee Mechanic
Wilson Mark Meche
Jerome D. Mechler

William L. Meckley
Wilson Meckley, Jr.
Paul Gregory Meckstroth
Albert Medas, Jr.
Edmund B. Medeiros
Joseph Medeiros
Ramon Medero
James T. Medford
Robert Donald Medford
Edward Medina
Frank Raul Medina
Guzman Efra Medina
Joe S. Medina
Loy L. Medina
Luis Padilla Har Medina
Ramirez Flo Medina
Raul C. Medina
Thomas A. Medinger
Fred Medley, Jr.
Billie Joe Medlin
Bobby J. Medlin
Frederick Medrano
Peter Medunic
Walter R. Medved
Orvis Roger Mee
James J. Meehan
Joseph J. Meehan, Jr.
Owen J. Meehan
Alfred C. Meek
Frank Meek, Jr.
Selia M. Meek
William E. Meeker
John W. Meekins, Jr.
Charles E. Meeks
Raymond D. Meeks
Virgil Scott Meenach
Glenn D. Meffert
Jake Mefford, Jr.
Duane B. Megard
Raymond L. Megerle
Richard E. Megin
James J. Meglan
Earl R. Mehaffey
Joseph L. Meher, Jr.
Paul J. Mehle
Leo M. Mehler
Dale Burton Mehlhorn
Fredrick Mehlhorn
Edward Henry Mehmen
Nick A. Meick
Arnold Meier
George H. Meier, Jr.
Jacob J. Meier
Otto A. Meier
David H. Meiers
Richard W. Meiggs
Alfred E. Meikle
John D. Meikle
Homer L. Meinen
John H. Meiners
August W. Meinhardt
Kenneth W. Meints
Richard Joseph Meinz
Charles F. Meisner
John L. Meiss
Paul Emil Meister, Jr.
Robert P. Meister
Richard M. Meiswinkel
David T. Mejia
Gerardo Mejias
Martinez La Mejias
Edmund Mekhitarian
Edward Mekilo
Moise Melancon, Jr.
Norman A. Melander
Roland John Melbye
Ervin S. Melcher, Jr.
Huey P. Melcher
John J. Melchior
Joseph D. Melchiorre
Edward Meldonian
John H. Meldrum, Jr.
Spencer Carl
Hernandez Melecio
Lopez Leop Melecio
Cintron E. Melendez
Gilbert Melendez
Jose M. Melendez
Sanchez R. Melendez
A. Melendez-Meldendez
Marcial Melendez-Negron
Daniel Gilbert Melendrez
Nicholas Melillo
Claude Stanley Melioris
Kennet Mellenthien
Walter Anthony Meller
Kenneth N. Mellick
Cecil George Mellinger
James R. Mellinger

Enrique Hector Mello
Francis J. Mello
Russell D. Melser
Earl W. Melsness
Billie G. Melton
Burl Dwight Melton
Charles W. Melton
George D. Melton
J. P. Melton
James A. Melton
John T. Melton
Richard D. Melton
Roy Gene Melton
William Robert Melton
William S. Melton
Alfred W. Melvin, Jr.
Charles Melvin
Clifford E. Melvin
Ralph L. Melvin
Richard C. Melvin
Charles Wesley Melvold
Gaylard D. Melvold
Ernest J. Melzer
Donald J. Memmer
Fernando Mena
Johnnie V. Mena
Edward Menard
Nelson John Menard
Walter C. Menard
James L. Menatola
Arturo Menchaca
Clarenc Menclewicz
John C. Mendel
David C. Mendelsohn
Alfred Mendendorp
Jimmie Lee Mendenhall
Robert Mendenhall
Alvin R. Mendes
Baron Iii Mendez
Luis A. Mendez-Hernandez
Joe C. Mendibles
Jesus Mendiola
Ferdinand Mendonca
Joseph R. Mendonca
Leroy A. Mendonca
Alfonso L. Mendoza
Daniel Paul Mendoza
James J. Mendoza
Jerry J. Mendoza
Joseph Mendoza
Julian L. Mendoza
Manuel Trujillo Mendoza
Phillip C. Mendoza
Raymond Mendoza
Ellsworth Meneeley
Middlesex, NJ
Juan B. Menendez
George Meneses
Clarence Stanley Mengler
William H. Menke, Jr.
Donald L. Menken
George H. Mennig, Jr.
Robert R. Mensch
Cloyd L. Menser
Paul Gust Mentzos
Donald H. Menz
Hugh Menzies, Jr.
Atanacio Mercado
Elias Mercado
Gomboa Jos Mercado
Gonzalez J. Mercado
Hernandez S. Mercado
Humberto Mercado
Jose Heriberto Mercado
Louie Mercado
Rafael V. Mercado
Torres Sam Mercado
Rafael Mercado-Andino
Martys Paul Merced
Earl S. Mercer
Ed F. Mercer
Foster M. Mercer
John A. Mercer, Jr.
Perry Junior Mercer
Robert A. Mercer
William N. Mercer
Stanley Bruce Merchant
Jos H. R. Mercier
Edward A. Mercurio
Frank Mercurio
Hubert A. Meredieth
David Meredith
Lawrence A. Meredith
Albert Mergendahl
Emanuel R. Merida
Louis A. Merino
Charles Merjanian
Howard P. Merkle
Nathan Merling

Jay J. Mermilliod
Marcus Paul Merner
William Henry Mero
Vincent J. Merola
Clifford Stanley Meronk
Richard Charles Merrick
Anthony G. Merriett
Donald L. Merrill
Gerald F. Merrill
John N. Merrill, Jr.
Kenneth W. Merrill
Larry O. Merrill
Ralph C. Merrill, Jr.
Ralph T. Merrill
Earl W. Merriman
Ralph E. Merriman
Roy T. Merriman
Donald R. Merrithew
Henry C. Merritt
James Merritt
Max H. Merritt
William Merritt
William J. Merritt
Charles R. Merrow
Alonda L. Merry
Robert B. Merryman
David F. Mershon
John H. Mertens, Jr.
Allen C. Mertes
Philip F. Merth
Charles W. Mertz
Robert L. Mervicker
Richard H. Mervin
Milan Mervosh
Edgar Merz, Jr.
Norberto Noriega Mesa
Rudy V. Mesa
Kenneth M. Mesel
Donald Earl Meshaw
Morris Meshulam
Felix A. Mesiavech
William Michael Meskowski
Philip James III Mess
John H. Messer
Owenne Messersmith
Charles G. Messick
Orace J. Mestas
Joseph Balint Meszaros
Donald D. Metcalf
Edward M. Metcalf
James H. Metcalf, Jr.
William G. Metcalf
Daniel Gordon Metiva
Alphege M. Metivier
Edward Metkowski
Edgar A. Metler
Raymond E. Mettert
Allen Lyle Mettler
Laurence Lee Mettlin
Gene A. Metz
James H. Metz
Richard Clare Metz
Thomas C. Metz
Wallace Ray Metz
Maurice Metzcar
Earl Sanford Metzger
Edwin Irving Metzger
Gilbert Metzger
Kenneth Eugene Metzger
William Charles Metzger
George P. Metzker
Earl Chandler Metzler
Joseph D. Metzo
Lavern Meuffels
Norman O. Meunier
Charles Albert Meuse
Clarence T. Meuse
Edward J. Meuse, Jr.
Ralph Nelson Mew
Raymond K. W. Mew
Albert W. Meyer
Francis Joseph Meyer
Frederick R. Meyer
Harry Meyer, Jr.
Jake Raymond Meyer
James E. Meyer
Joseph Meyer
Joseph John Meyer
Joseph K. Meyer
Raymond J. Meyer
Wayne O. Meyer
William Meyer
William Samuel Meyer
Allen Dean Meyers
Charles E. Meyers
Glenn D. Meyers
Harold Meyers
J. B. Meyers
Joseph Donald Meyers

Robert E. Meyers
Wayne A. Meyers
William A. Meyers
Henry Mezzatesta
Armand Mezzopera
Joseph Micel, Jr.
Raymond A. Micele
James P. Miceli
Edward Micenhammer
Junior E. Michael
William F. Michael
Al Michaelis
Frederick Michaelis, Jr.
Felix Michaeliski
Melvin J. Michaels
Raymond Michaels
Leland P. Michalak
Edgar E. Michalek
Joseph E. G. Michaud
Wilfred S. Michaud
Gordon G. Micheau
John Carl Micheel
Alvin J. Michel
James D. Michel
Richard Thomas Michel
Henry Martinez Michell
Max R. Michiel
Donald L. Michoff
Joseph W. Mick
Lewis V. Mick
Jacob E. Mickael
Morris S. Mickelsen
Leon E. Mickelson
Robert Mickelson
Robert D. Mickle
Robert Frederick Miconi
Lindbergh Mictcham
Donald Middendorf
George Middlebrook
Henry Middlebrooks
Rober Middlesworth
Harry Richard Middleton
James E. Middleton
Joshua Middleton
Ralph Middleton
Rex B. Middleton
Alexander J. Midgett
William Anthony Midyett
Joseph V. Miele
Robert C. Mielke
Roger E. Miels
Ernest Mier
Joseph Miezejewski
Jerome Peter Migala
Thomas Migliaccio
Harry Miguel
Leonard Miguel
Lloyd L. Miguel
Andrew P.
Kenneth E. Mikalauskas
Carnell J. Mikell
Floyd M. Mikell
James C. Mikell
Harold E. Mikesell
Hugh J. Mikkelsen
Leonard Miklovich
Joseph C. Mikronis
Arthur A. Mikula
Arthur K. Mikulik
Frank S. Mikulski
Charles N. Milam
Charles W. Milam
James T. Milam
Lin Milam
Otis Eugene Milam
Samuel Henry Milander
David B. Milano
Wilhelm Milbrandt
Ronald F. Milbrath
Gilbert D. Milburn
Theodo Milczarczyk
Lloyd O. Milender
Charles A. Miles
Claud Miles
Clifton F. Miles
David Edward Miles
Dewitt C. Miles
Earl Clarence Miles
Frank Miles
Gerald Donald Miles
Harry Robert Miles
Herbert A. Miles
James W. Miles
John G. Miles
Levon Miles
Rex H. Miles
Theodore Miles
William T. Miles, Jr.
George R. Miley

Robert T. Miley
Vernon J. Milgate
Frederick H. Milhaupt, Jr.
Brunko R. Miljus
George H. Milk
Gustavo A. Millan
Charles P. Millar
William M. Millar
Albert H. Miller, Jr.
Alfred L. Miller
Allen I. Miller
Andrew L. Miller
Arther L. Miller
Arthur L. Miller
Arthur R. Miller
Augustus Miller
Billy F. Miller
Bobby Miller
Carleton A. Miller
Cecil Miller
Charles Anthony Miller
Charles D. Miller
Charles E. Miller
Charles H. Miller
Charles R. Miller
Charles Robert Miller
Chester Miller
Clifford J. Miller
Darden D. Miller
Donald C. Miller
Donald G. Miller
Donald M. Miller
Donald N. Miller
Donald R. Miller
Duane A. Miller
Earl K. Miller
Eddie M. Miller, Jr.
Edison W. Miller
Edmund H. Miller, Jr.
Edward J. J Miller
Edwin E. Miller
Elbert Miller
Elden L. Miller
Elwyn John Miller
Ervin A. Miller
Eugene E. Miller
Eugene N. Miller
Eugene R. Miller
Everett H. Miller
Everett L. Miller
Floyd Gay Miller
Floyd Miller, Jr.
Foster C. Miller
Frank Edward Miller, Jr.
Gene P. Miller
George D. Miller
George J. Miller
George Steven Miller
George W. Miller
George W. Miller, Jr.
Gerald E. Miller
Gerald Eugene Miller
Gerold M. Miller
Gordon Arthur Miller
Grady H. Miller
Grant S. Miller
Gus E. Miller
Harlan H. Miller
Harold J. Miller
Harry Miller
Harry L. Miller
Harry V. Miller
Henry A. Miller
Henry David Miller
Herman W. Miller
Howard A. Miller
Howard Preston Miller, Jr.
Ira L. Miller, Jr.
Jack H. Miller
Jackie E. Miller
James B. Miller
James E. Miller
James H. Miller
James L. Miller
James N. Miller
Jerry Elmer Albro Miller
Jesse L. Miller
Joe R. Miller
John A. Miller
John B. Miller
John G. Miller
John L. Miller
John M. Miller
John R. Miller
John Richard Miller
John T. Miller
John W. Miller
Johnnie E. Miller
Johnny J. Miller

Joseph C. Miller
Joseph E. Miller
Joseph Edward Miller
Joseph J. Miller, Jr.
Joseph Roth Miller
Kenneth R. Miller
Kenneth S. Miller
L. C. Miller
Larry Eugene Miller
Linuis D. Miller
Lloyd E. Miller
Lloyd E. Miller
Lloyd J. Miller
Lloyd K. Miller
Lowell E. Miller
Marvin L. Miller
Max H. Miller
Merle W. Miller
Mike A. Miller, Jr.
Milan E. Miller
Norman B. Miller, Jr.
Norman Miller, Jr.
Orville D. Miller
Oscar W. Miller
Paul Burnell Miller
Paul E. Miller
Paul Luther Miller
Posey L. Miller
Quinton E. Miller
Ralph Bernard Miller, Jr.
Raymond Miller
Raymond E. Miller
Raymond H. Miller
Raymond L. Miller
Raymond Mortimer Miller
Raymond Thomas Miller
Reuben Miller
Richard E. Miller
Richard K. Miller
Richard P. Miller
Robert A. Miller
Robert B. Miller
Robert C. Miller
Robert D. Miller
Robert E. Miller
Robert E. Miller
Robert F. Miller
Robert F. Miller
Robert F. Miller
Robert G. Miller
Robert J. Miller
Robert L. Miller
Robert S. Miller
Roger G. Miller
Roger L. Miller
Rolly G. Miller
Ronald R. Miller
Rothell Miller
Roy W. Miller
Ruby L. Miller
Russell R. Miller
Sam Questell Miller
Seth S. Miller
Theodore R. Miller
Thomas C. Miller
Thomas Dawayne Miller
Thomas Edward Miller
Thomas F. Miller
Thomas M. Miller
Thomas W. Miller
Trenton S. Miller
Verdis L. Miller
Vernon Eugene Miller
Vernon R. Miller
Waldemar Willie Miller
Wallace A. Miller
Walter C. Miller
Wesley Dale Miller
Willard E. Miller
Willard J. Miller
William F. Miller
William Jennings Miller
Willie Miller
Wilmar R. Miller
Hugh P. Milleson
Gerard G. Millette
Archie Clark Milligan
Kenneth J. Milligan, Jr.
Richard Milligan
Benjamin Milliken
James Bendler Millington
Richard E. Millis
Robert M. Millner
Jerry Milloff
Johnny A. Millon
Albert D. Mills
Albert E. Mills
Alvin F. Mills
Bruce R. Mills

Carroll E. Mills
Crawford Mills
Donald F. Mills
Doyle Mills
Eddie L. Mills
Edward F. Mills
Edward Leon Mills
Eugene O. Mills
Ezekiel C. Mills
Frederick E. Mills
George C. Mills
Hilery W. Mills
Hubert Mills
Jerry E. Mills
John W. Mills
Laird C. Mills
Laster Mills
Lawrence W. Mills
Marvin L. Mills
Mosco Mills
Robert John Mills
Therlous Mills
Walter B. Mills
Walter T. Mills, Jr.
William E. Mills
William J. Mills
William Paul Mills, Jr.
Judson Millspaugh
Monroe Mason Millwood
Wallace D. Milner
Willard H. Milner
Edward R. Milos
Kenneth Lee Milstead
Charles W. Milton
Nick Milus
Vincent A. Mimm
James R. Mims
Jesse L. Mims
William W. Mims
George Y. Minakata
Charles W. Minard
Wayne Minard
Robert W. Minch
Leonard E. Mineer
Andrew J. Miner
Asa B. Miner
Donald Dale Miner
Donald W. Miner
Frederick Wales Miner
John F. Miner
James W. Minerd
Ronald S. Miniard
Matthew Minichillo
Edward W. Minikus
Joseph Minjack
Jack Robert Minkin
Donald T. Minkler
Robert W. Minkler
Wallace T. Minnich
Earl G. Minnick
Robert G. Minniear
Gilbert J. Minning
Charles M. Minor
James Henry Minor
John Minor
Marcus Lajoie Minor, Jr.
T. L. Minor, Jr.
Travis E. Minor
Robert Allington Minser
Lloyd S. Minter, Jr.
Richard M. Minton
Albert Mintz
Charles L. Minyard
Harold C. Minyard
James R. Minyard
Alexander Miranda
Erasto Miranda
Gonzalez H. Miranda
Vazquez An Miranda
Victor M. Miranda
Carlos J. Miranda-Cotto
Macario Mireles
Crescencio Mirelez
Kenneth A. Misaki
George Misaras
Luke T. Misciagno
Victor Misekow
Donald D. Misemer
Harvey John Misener
James E. Mishler
Russell Gordon Mishler
Louis F. Miskavage
Joseph J. Misko
James J. Mislosky
Gerald L. Misner
Harley Mason Misner
Norbert Joseph Misorski
Michael Misovic, Jr.
Albert L. Miss

Ira Victor Miss, Jr.
Michael Missentzis
Francisco Misseri
Robert A. Missman
Conrad P. Mistle
Victor C. Mistretta
Jerome A. Misuraco
Donald George Mitch
Robert F. Mitcham
Rudus Mitchel, Jr.
Alfred D. Mitchell
Alfred E. Mitchell
Alvin C. Mitchell
Ancil Abner Mitchell, Jr.
Archie F. Mitchell
Bernard Mitchell
Bobby A. Mitchell
Carlton E. Mitchell
Coy F. Mitchell
Donald K. Mitchell
Edwin L. Mitchell
Everett L. Mitchell
Finnie C. Mitchell
Francis L. Mitchell
Frank Nicias Mitchell
Frank R. Mitchell
Franklin Mitchell
Frederick Mitchell
Frederick W. Mitchell
Grady Purden Mitchell, Jr.
Guy E. Mitchell, Jr.
Harry D. Mitchell
Hilton L. Mitchell
Howard L. Mitchell
James L. Mitchell
Jesse Leroy Mitchell
John H. Mitchell
John Mitchell, Jr.
John W. Mitchell
Johnnie Mitchell
Lawrence Terril Mitchell
Lindsay W. Mitchell
Linus D. Mitchell
Michael V. Mitchell
Philip C. Mitchell
Raymond E. Mitchell
Richard W. Mitchell
Robert Mitchell
Robert A. Mitchell
Robert E. Mitchell
Rudus Mitchell, Jr.
Russell Y. Mitchell
Tommy F. Mitchell
Verdo Andrew Mitchell
Willard G. Mitchell
William A. Mitchell
William B. Mitchell, Jr.
William C. Mitchell
William D. Mitchell
William L. Mitchell
William L. Mitchell
William M. Mitchell
William P. Mitchell
Thomas P. Mitchelson
Kermit Mitcheltree
Arnold S. Mitchem
Paul Mitchem
Raymond L. Mitchem
Ralph R. Mitola
Sebastian Mitrano, Jr.
Gerald J. Mitten
James Miuccio
Herman L. Mixon
Alan T. Miyahira
Samuel S. Miyahira
Donald S. Miyajima
Robert K. Miyamoto
Ichiro R. Miyasaki
Wilbert Y. Miyasato
Daniel T. Miyashiro
Tamotsu Miyashiro
Tomoyosh Miyashiro
Harry Y. Miyata
Shigeo Miyazaki
Aubrey W. Mize
Howard R. Mizell
Tsunemats Mizusawa
Milton J. Mlaskac
Joseph A. Mlynarski
William J. Moak
Eugene Moats
Herbert A. Moats
Melvin L. Moats
Peppino N. Mobilio
Alexander Mobley
Rufus D. Mobley
Willis W. Mobley
Raymond D. Moccio
Bobbie Frank Mock

David H. Mock
Robert Chalice Mock, Jr.
Earl Joseph Mocklin
Richard Mocksfield
Willie E. Modena
George L. Modglin
Emery L. Modos
Arne O. Moe
Arthur A. Moeller
Albert D. Moen
Frank Robert Moen
Howard M. Moen
Truman O. Moen
Clarence R. Moening
Richard L. Moesch
Leroy J. Moffett
Robert V. Moffett
Floyd W. Moffitt
James Richard Moffitt
Samuel D. Mogg
Wesley K. Mohagen
William A. Mohlman
Gene A. Mohney
Richard Mohowitsch
Cecil Rhodes Mohr, Jr.
Harry A. Mohr
Louis W. Mohr
Richard D. Mohr
Eugene F. Mohs
Bruce O. Moilanen
Ralph Moisa
Raymond T. Mokiao
Loue J. Molar
Irwin Moldafsky
George Molenaar
Wendel R. Moles
Jack Harry Molin
August A. Molina
Benjamin Molina
Epiphanio G. Molina
Rivera Vict Molina
Serrano San Molina
Roberto Molina-Garcia
Maximino Molina-Gerena
Anthony Molinaro
Anthony J. Molinaro
De Sanche Molinary
Louis N. Molino
Rolv Moll
Leland P. Molland
Earl Purdon Mollerud
Chester Eugene Mollnow
Louis Molnar
Edward J. Moloney
Marvin L. Molter
James E. Molton
William E. Moment
David P. Mompher
Arnold L. Mon
Paul Monaco
Peter Monaco, Jr.
Eugene J. Monaghan
Thomas James Monaghan
William W. Monaghan
William J. Monahan
George Edward Moncrief
Jessie Monday
John Mondello
Vincent H. Mondragon, Jr.
Walter C. Monegan, Jr.
Roosevelt Monette
Thurmon Wayne Money
Francis C. Monfette
Peter H. Monfore
Eugene P. Monforton
Jeremiah F. Mongan
Rodriguez An Monge
Walter J. Mongeon
Angelo Mongiardo
Francis Frederick Mongone
Albert V. Monk
Billy J. Monks
Stanley T. Monkut
Jerome Noah Monney
Jack D. Monnot
Billy J. Monroe
Emery L. Monroe
Forrest A. Monroe
Fred B. Monroe
James H. Monroe
Napoleon Monroe
Paul Monroe
Rondo J. Monroe
Shelton Wilson Monroe
Tracy William Monroe, Jr.
Donald L. Monson
Fred W. Monson, Jr.
Alfred J. Montagna
Charles J. Montagna

Francis Montagnolo
Earle E. Montague
Guy E. Montague, Jr.
John W. Montague, Jr.
Manuel V. Montana
Ernesto Montanez
Rios Eras Montanez
Sixto E. Montanez-Franco
John Montano, Jr.
Tony A. Montano
Adolfo Monteberde
Robert James Monteith
Donald Monteleone
Andrew J. Montello
Gilbert Montenegro
Jose Montero
Albino C. Montes
Jose A. Montesinos
Horacio Nevarez Montez
Houston E. Montfort
C. W. Montgomery
C. T. Montgomery, Jr.
Daniel Montgomery
Emery Montgomery
Floyd W. Montgomery
Gerald E. Montgomery
Gerald E. Montgomery
Gifford Montgomery
Harold W. Montgomery
Herman Montgomery
James C. Montgomery
James E. Montgomery
James R. Montgomery
Percy L. Montgomery
Ray Mckinley Montgomery
Raymond Montgomery
Robert Montgomery
Sherlin Montgomery
Melvin M. Montie
Rene R. Montigny
James R. Montlouis
Bernie Montoya
Enoch P. Montoya
Ernest Montoya
Feles Montoya
Gilberto Montoya
James Anthony Montoya
Joe E. Montoya
Jose P. Montoya
Louis Montoya
Paul Montoya
Stephen Montoya
Thomas Montoya
Ronald E. Montross
Anthony Monze
Henry A. Monzo
Charles R. Moody
Charles V. Moody
Edward Moody
Horace A. Moody
J. R. Moody
James A. Moody
Joey Moody
John I. Moody
John Peter Moody, Jr.
Robert J. Moody
Samuel M. Moody
Troy E. Moody, Jr.
George Mooiki
Kenneth L. Moomey
Thomas C. Moon
Allen E. Mooney
Custer E. Mooney
Francis J. Mooney
Gordon Wayne Mooney
James William Mooney, Jr.
John Mooney
Martin F. Mooney
Robert Perry Mooney
Arthur A. Mooneyham
Calvin L. Mooneyham
Ara Mooradian
Albert Moore
Alfred H. Moore, Jr.
Arthur L. Moore
Benny A. Moore
Bert Moore
Bobby M. Moore
Booker Moore
Braddy III Moore
Bryant E. Moore
Carl C. Moore
Charles E. Moore
Charles G. Moore
Charles I. Moore
Charles J. Moore
Charles S. Moore
Chester H. Moore
Clarence N. Moore

Claude Augustus Moore, Jr.
Claude F. Moore, Jr.
Clell Moore
Curtis Moore
David Alexander Moore
David L. Moore
David N. Moore
Dexter Moore
Doris T. Moore
Earl J. Moore
Edgar Eugene Moore
Edward J. Moore, Jr.
Ernest L. Moore
Eugene K. Moore
Floyd E. Moore
Frank Moore
Frank Moore, Jr.
Gene S. Moore
George J. Moore
Harold B. Moore
Harry Cecil Moore
Henry F. Moore
Henry M. Moore
Hercules Moore
Howard E. Moore
Irvine W. Moore
Isadore O. Moore
Jack Moore
Jack D. Moore
Jack S. Moore
James E. Moore
James E. Moore
James L. Moore
James R. Moore
John Charles Moore
John D. Moore
John D. Moore, Jr.
John George Moore
John H. Moore
John M. Moore
John T. Moore
John U. Moore
John W. Moore
John Wallace Moore
Johnnie E. Moore
Joseph F. Moore
Laymon Moore, Jr.
Lenzey Moore
Leon Moore
Leon M. Moore
Leonard Moore, Jr.
Leroy Moore
Leroy L. Moore
Lesley A. Moore
Leslie D. Moore
Louis A. Moore
Louis Brandt Moore, Jr.
Lucien S. Moore
Lyle Earl Moore, Jr.
Merle M. Moore
Milford J. Moore
Miller E. Moore
Moris G. Moore
Myral N. Moore
Norman E. Moore
Oren Richard Moore
Paul J. Moore
Philip Treffle Moore
Rex D. Moore
Richard D. Moore
Richard L. Moore
Robert B. Moore
Robert F. Moore, Jr.
Robert L. Moore
Robert M. Moore, Jr.
Roland A. Moore
Roosevelt J. Moore
Roy E. Moore
Samuel Eugene Moore
T. S. Moore
Thomas E. Moore
Thomas F. Moore, Jr.
Thomas O. Moore, Jr.
Thomas P. Moore
Tommy D. Moore
W. C. Moore
Walter L. Moore
Wayne T. Moore
Wilbur D. Moore
William C. Moore
William David Moore
William E. Moore
William Lee Moore
William R. Moore
William Russell Moore
William T. Moore
Willie L. Moore
Brooks Eugene Moorhead
Robert E. Moorman

Paul Moose
Angel R. Mora
Jack J. Morack
Alamo Vict Morales
Ben R. Morales
Carlos Y. Morales
Carmelo O. Morales
David O. Morales
Frank M. Morales
Gilbert Morales
John A. Morales
Jose D. C. Morales
Joseph S. Morales
Lozada Cri Morales
Oscar M. Morales
Rivera Dio Morales
William Morales
Alfredo Morales-Reyes
Charles Barthell Moran
Donald S. Moran
Jack H. Moran
William G. Moran
Leon F. Morand, Jr.
James E. Morany
Melvin W. Morden
Marvin Dale More
Melvin W. More
Carol J. Moreau
Lloyd W. Moreau
Russell Morecraft
Alvaro Joseph Moreira
Harry D. Moreland, Jr.
Weldon J. Moreland
Whitt Lloyd Moreland
Eugene M. Morelli
Andrew J. Moren
Adelorde Gene Morency
James R. Morency
Albert Moreno
Albert G. Moreno
Alexander M. Moreno
Benigno Moreno
Gilbert T. Moreno
Isaac Padilla Moreno
Joe G. Moreno
Manuel H. Moreno
Pedro Moreno
Ramon R. Moreno
Raymond M. Moreno
Rudolph Moreno
Tirado Adol Moreno
Nelson Moreno-Rosa
Leon C. Morey
Raymond E. Morford
Aaron Morgan
Albert Morgan
Andrew J. Morgan, Jr.
Arlen Jackson Morgan
Arnold L. Morgan
Arthur W. Morgan
Austin Morgan
Charles C. Morgan
Charles F. Morgan
Clarence E. Morgan
Cyrus L. Morgan
Dale C. Morgan, Jr.
Dannie C. Morgan
David L. Morgan
Dennis R. Morgan
Donald Morgan
Edwin L. Morgan
Elbert L. Morgan, Jr.
Enoch E. Morgan
Frankie K. Morgan
Herbert Frederick Morgan
Howard A. Morgan
Howard J. Morgan
Jack W. Morgan
James A. Morgan
James P. Morgan
James P. Morgan
John A. Morgan
John David Morgan
Lawrence D. Morgan
Leroy Albert Morgan, Jr.
Lloyd E. Morgan
Melvin H. Morgan
Paul E. Morgan
Ralph C. Morgan
Ralph Edgar Morgan
Roger L. Morgan
Roy Elliotte Morgan
Thomas D. Morgan
Tommie Lee Morgan
Vern A. Morgan
Warren L. Morgan
Winfred D. Morgan
Paul E. Morgenstern
Donald F. Moriarty

Henry I. Moriarty
Jenro Morillo
Arthur Robert Morin
Fernand A. Morin
Joseph R. Morin
Peter J. Morin, Jr.
Theodore E. Morin
Carmel Morina
Akeji Morinaga
Richard Moring
Eiji Morishige
Donald E. Morissett
Tetsue Moriuchi
Kiochi Moriwaki
Fumio Moriyama
Haruo Moriyasu
Edgar Benedict Mork
Pearl H. Morman
Rolland Morneault
David Morningstar
John M. Moronski
Julius L. Moroz
James E. Morphew
George J. Morreale
Martin G. Morrill, Jr.
Albert E. Morris
Albert H. Morris
Alpha L. Morris
Alvin E. Morris
Billy G. Morris
Burtis L. Morris, Jr.
Chalmis L. Morris
Charles G. Morris
Clarence A. Morris
Clarence Taylor Morris
David Henry Morris
David Wesley Morris
Forrest P. Morris
George A. Morris
George Frank Morris
George J. Morris
Harry R. Morris
Hugh J. Morris
James Glendell Morris
James Morris, Jr.
James R. Morris
Jesse Elmo Morris
John C. III Morris
John P. Morris
John W. Morris
Marion E. Morris
Max A. Morris
Milton Morris, Jr.
Neal M. Morris
Nicholas Morris
Norman F. Morris
Norman M. Morris
Prince H. Morris
Ray M. Morris
Rayford C. Morris
Robert Eugene Morris
Roland W. Morris
Ronald G. Morris
Ronald R. Morris
Rufus R. Morris
Russell A. Morris
Russell F. Morris
Stafford L. Morris
Tom J. Morris
William A. Morris
William Duffy Morris
Wilmer W. Morris
Richard W. Morrisey
Thomas O. Morrish
Anthony George Morrison
Buster E. Morrison
Clarence Morrison
Clyde C. Morrison
Edward M. Morrison
Elbert Morrison
Harry S. Morrison
J. A. Morrison
Jack A. Morrison
James F. Morrison
James F. Morrison
James K. Morrison
James L. Morrison
Jessie Morrison
Lane Morrison
Lloyd V. Morrison
Norman F. Morrison
Norman W. Morrison
Raymond H. Morrison
Robert C. Morrison
Thomas C. Morrison
William F. Morrison
William R. Morrison
Charles L. Morriss
Edmund V. Morrissey

John A. Morrissey
Raymond Morrissey
Richard Eugene Morrissey
Paul L. Morristell
Peter P. Morrone
George Morrosis
Billy J. Morrow
Carl N. Morrow
Douglas E. Morrow
Henry Morrow
Jack L. Morrow
James W. Morrow
Jared W. Morrow
John J. Morrow
John W. Morrow
Joyce R. Morrow
Robert Leroy Morrow
Robert S. Morrow
Arthur J. Morse
Dale B. Morse
Durlin J. Morse
Edward J. Morse, Jr.
Herman E. Morse
John Morse, Jr.
Robert A. Morse
Robert C. Morse
Sims Fay Morse
Wilbur G. Morse
John Christian Mortensen
William C. Mortesen
Duwayne C. Mortimer
Benjamin J. Mortner
Albert Joseph Morton
Donald R. Morton
Edward W. Morton
Floyd Morton
George E. Morton, Jr.
Henry S. Morton
James Amil Morton
James W. Morton
Raeford L. Morton
Ralph Frankline Morton
Robert W. Morton
Victor Morton
Philip Moscatelli
Archie J. Moschella, Jr.
Eugene Martin Moscicki
John A. Moseley
Marvin Euberto Moseley
Samuel L. Moseley
Earnest Moser
Max H. Moser
Robert H. Moser
William Harold Moser
Louis R. Moses
Robert L. Moses
Vivian Mordaunt Moses
Walter Moses, Jr.
Norman F. Mosher
Billy Mosier
Leonard L. Mosier
William C. Sr Moskosky
Edward Moskowitz
Charles Moslander
W. M. Mosley
Willard L. Mosley
Alonza Moss
Daniel W. Moss
Emmett D. Moss
Henry Moss, Jr.
John Moss, Jr.
Joseph Donald Moss
Lawrence Dale Moss
William H. Moss
William R. Moss
Wynn Thomas Moss, Jr.
Vernon David Mossberg
Thomas A. Mosso
Carl R. Mosson
Senator Moten, Jr.
James B. Motherway
Claude B. Motley, Jr.
John D. Motley
Shizuo Motoyama
Murel R. Mott
Manuel Motta
Gordon C. Motz
Harold V. Motzko
Forest E. Mougey
Robert J. Moulaison
Collins Moulden, Jr.
Francis C. Moultane
Lewis C. Moulton
Charles H. Mounce
Rufus Lloyd Mounce
French Mounts, Jr.
Carl E. Mourer
James O. Mouser
Robert W. Mouser

August Wilson Mouton
Joseph F. Mouzer
Jackie L. Mowery
Lewis D. Mowery
Walter L. Mowrer
Harve C. Mowry
Lewis G. Moxley
William C. Moxley
Isidore A. Moy
Carlos B. Moya
James A. Moya
Tony Moya, Jr.
Hobert C. Moye
Manuel R. Moyeda
Donald L. Moyer
Donald R. Moyer
Glyndon E. Moyer
James A. Moyer
Sylvian A. Moyers
Dudley G. Moyle
John T. Moynihan
Thomas J. Moynihan
Ralph C. Mozee
Robert Ardell Mozer
Leonard F. Mrazek
William J. Mroseske
Donald E. Mrotek
Lawrence M. Mrotek
Leo Walter Mryncza
Anthony John Mucci
Elmo R. Mudge
Kenneth Arthur Mudge
Anthony J. Mudicka
Alvin F. Mueck
David Dwain Mueller
Edward J. Mueller
Edwin H. Mueller
Gerald J. Mueller
Harold Ervin Mueller
Herman B. Mueller
Jack C. Mueller
Lawrence C. Mueller
Lester C. Mueller
Morton D. Mueller
Wilbur John Mueller
Frederick Mac Monni Muer
Allen C. Muhlbach
Lester J. Muhle
Charles E. Muhleback
William G. Muirhead
Merlin M. Mulcahy
William R. Mulcrone
Delano B. Mulder
Ervin L. Muldoon
Norbert J. Mulgrew
Gerald Mulholland
Robert Mulholland
Wayne E. Mulholland
Jack R. Mulhollen
Ralph Donald Mulhollen
George Mulik
Delbert E. Mulinex
Bill T. Mulkey
William Derral Mulkins
Thomas L. Mull
Donald Mullane
John W. Mullaney
James E. Mullarkey
William Mullarkey
Alfred E. Mullen
Bernard Mullen
Jim G. Mullen
John J. Mullen
John L. Mullen, Jr.
Kenneth James Mullen
Roland B. Mullen
Adam Muller, Jr.
Carl H. Muller
Gunther T. Muller
Arlie D. Mullet
Richard Everett Mullett
Paul F. Mullicane
Robert A. Mulligan
Vernon G. Mulligan
Sidney Redd Mullikin, Jr.
Carl H. Mullin, Jr.
Edward Joseph Mullin, Jr.
Stacy A. Mullinax
Verlon L. Mullinax
Burl Mullins
Cebert W. Mullins
Charlie Mullins, Jr.
Elmer Mullins
Emil Wayne Mullins
James C. Mullins
Joe S. Mullins
Kenneth Mullins
Malcum Mullins
Myles L. Mullins

Patrick A. Mullins
Paul S. Mullins
Preston Mullins, Jr.
Thomas Gene Mullins
Thomas Hays Mullins
James D. Mulloy
Arthur F. Mulock
Edward L. Mulrooney
John W. Mulvenna
Erwin R. Mumford
Jesse Muncy
William A. Muncy
Joseph F. Munda
James D. Munday
Robert Thomas Munday
Mike H. Mundy
Graham B. Munger
Luman Eliott Munger
Uvaldo M. Munguia
Joseph Francis Munier, Jr.
George Muniz
Torres Alber Muniz
Peter Munjian
John N. Munkres
Oliver B. Munn
John S. Munos
Jose E. Munoz
Moises Munoz
Rafael Munoz
Valente V. Munoz
Irving Munroe
Davis S. Muns
Frederick Munsell
Roy L. Munsey
Arvid O. Munson
Dave Lewis Munson
Merle C. Munson
Warren Lee Munson
Donald L. Munster
Edward Arthur Muntz
Joseph F. Mura
Tadao Murakami
Tsukasa Muraoka
Yukio Murata
Joseph A. Murchison
Thomas J. Murchison
Orlin T. Murchland
John T. Murdich
Charles D. Murdock
Dale Murdock
Herold F. Murdock
Jackie Lee Murdock
Lonnie Murdock
Joseph H. Murga
Ramon Murga-Amador
George J. Murillo
Harry E. Murnighan
Calvin B. Murphree
Charles P. Murphy
Christopher M. Murphy, Jr.
Daniel P. Murphy
David Lee Murphy
Donald L. Murphy
Edmund J. Murphy
Eugene Thomas Murphy
Francis Phillip Murphy
Fred Murphy, Jr.
Glen W. Murphy
Harry T. Murphy
Henry G. Murphy, Jr.
Jack Murphy
James David Murphy
James P. Murphy
Joe L. Murphy
John B. Murphy, Jr.
John D. Murphy
John F. Murphy
John M. Murphy
John Michael Murphy
Joseph Edward Murphy
Kenneth D. Murphy
Kenneth H. Murphy
Kenneth J. Murphy
Leonard A. Murphy
Leslie O. Murphy
Marvin S. Murphy
Michael D. Murphy
Monroe P. Murphy
Ralph Joseph Murphy
Raymond B. Murphy
Raymond William Murphy
Richard H. Murphy
Richard J. Murphy
Robert Elbridge Murphy
Robert J. M. Murphy
Robert M. Murphy
Robert Mervin Murphy
Robert W. Murphy
Ronald B. Murphy

Ronald D. Murphy
Ronald L. Murphy
Thomas C. Murphy, Jr.
Thomas F. Murphy
Thomas J. Murphy
Walter L. Murphy
Wayne A. Murphy
William Murphy
William F. Murphy
William H. Murphy
William J. Murphy
William Joseph III Murphy
Willie B. Murphy
Winfred R. Murphy
Arnold L. Murray
Bernard M. Murray
Bobby Lee Murray
Carl D. Murray
Duane L. Murray
Floyd A. Murray
Fred W. Murray
Frederick Murray
Harold B. Murray
Harold L. Murray
Howard William Murray
Izei Murray
Jack Lewis Murray
James Murray
James E. Murray, Jr.
James H. Murray
James S. Murray
John F. Murray
Joseph John Murray
Luther E. Murray
Neil A. Murray, Jr.
Norval L. Murray
Ray Eugene Murray
Raymond M. Murray
Robert J. Murray
Victor R. Murray
William L. Murray
Mike Murrieta
Harold D. Mursch
Eugene E. Murtaugh
Earl L. Muse
Daniel Lorenz Musetti
Arthur R. Musgrave
Melvin R. Musgrave
Arthur E. Musgrove
Charles M. Musgrove
Richard Dearl Musgrove
Joseph Mushko
Edward D. Mushrush
Edward M. Musich
George Musick
Lee R. Musick
Orville D. Musick
Angelo A. Musone
Michael Ernest Mussatto
Virgil D. Musselman
Willie Musselwhite
Alvin D. Musser
John Adam Muszynski
Frank A. Muth
Robert Arthur Muth
Forrest Martin Mutschler
Louis P. Mutta
Gene Mutter
Rapherd C. Muxlow
Calvin A. Myatt
Bobby G. Myer
George D. Myer
William H. Myer, Jr.
Allie E. Myers
Bryan Myers, Jr.
Carol R. Myers
Charles A. Myers
Donald E. Myers
Donald William Myers
Ellis E. Myers
Fred H. Myers
Fred K. Myers
Fred Lawrence Myers
George W. Myers
Guy K. Myers
Harry F. Myers
Horace Herman Myers, Jr.
James W. Myers
Jesse Leon Myers
John C. Myers
John R. Myers
Max L. Myers
Olen Franklin Myers
Paul E. Myers
Paul H. Myers
Raymond Myers, Jr.
Robert H. Myers
Robert J. Myers

Robert W. Myers
Ronald D. Myers
Samuel J. Myers
Stephen A. Myers
Thomas Myers
Thomas Ellis Myers
Marvin J. Myhre
Harvey A. Mykrantz
Thomas Myles
Edgar L. Mynatt
Horace E. Myrick
Edwin J. Myslinski
Vernon Mzhickteno

— N —

Robert G. Naatz
Milton W. Naber
Vincent L. Nabholz
Dixon H. Nabors
John H. Nabors
Eugene L. Nabozony
Julius Caesar Nacci
Irvin E. Nachman
Sam L. Nadai
Kenneth D. Nadeau
John Daniel Nadelhoffer
Fadallah N. G. Nader
Edward Nadir
John E. Naetzker
Ernest A. Nagai
Hiroshi Nagamine
Edward J. Nagel
William E. Nagel
Dale B. Nagle
Ferris J. Nahas
Adam L. Nahodil
Hideo Nakama
Seiso Nakama
Noboru Nakamura
Wataru Nakamura
Satoshi Nakasato
Yeichi Nakasato
Roy T. Nakashima
Shinichi Nakata
Seinojo R. Nakatani
Joseph J. Nalepka
1Raymond E. Nall
Willie C. Nall
Arnold Nalley
Raymond J. Namba
Charles F. Nance
Gerald Nance
Jimmie P. Nance
Paul R. Nance
Robert Calvin Nance
Wallace R. Nance
Tom William Naney
John J. Nannery, Jr.
Philip R. Naone
James Albert Naour
Alfred W. Napier
Charles Napier
Golden Napier
John E. Napier
Walter Gilbert Napier
J. A. Napoleon-Escudero
Frank J. Napolitano
Agapito D. Naranjo
Raymond Naranjo
Norman C. Nardick
Martin R. Narey
Montalvo M. Narvaez
Reinaldo Narvaez
George R. Naset
Charles Nash
James Terrell Nash
Richard L. Nash
W. E. Iii Nash
William L. Nash
William R. Nash
Irvine M. Nason
Rex E. Nason
Harold C. Nass
Peter Michael Nassetta
Walter Stanley Nastawa
Louis F. Natale
Napoleon Nathan
Ronald A. Naugle
Walter E. Naugle
Robert E. Nault
Alfred Edward Nauman, Jr.
Adolphus Nava
Manuel Navarra
Vincent C. Navarra
Adolfo Navarro
Bernard Jo Navarro
Julio Q. Navarro
Matos Aure Navarro

Ralph O. Navarro
Roberto Navarro
Rodriguez Navarro
Herley E. Nave, Jr.
Robert Stanley Navin
Stanley R. Nawrocki
Clifford M. Naylor
John E. Naylor
John L. Naylor
Lewis J. Naylor
Earl C. Nazelrod
Charlie Neace, Jr.
Alfred L. Neal
Ardell M. Neal
Clarence J. Neal
Duane B. Neal
Emmett Neal
Frank A. Neal
Frank A. Neal
Houston A. Neal
Jessie P. Neal
John E. Neal
Robert B. Neal
Silas Neal, Jr.
Wilma R. Neal
Paul A. Neale
Arthur J. Nealon
Odell W. Nealy
Harry Neanover
John J. Nearey
John W. Nearhood
Sanford C. Nearhoof
Charles E. Neary
Philip Patrick Neary
Richard A. Neary
James J. Neaton
Philip E. Neavil
Edwin J. Neckers
George R. Nedley, Jr.
Frederick E. Nedved
Eugene A. Neeb
Al G. Needham
Douglas M. Neel
Walter Philip Neel
Tony A. Neeley
Joe Edward Neely
Loyd R. Neely
Robert Neely, Jr.
Ronald Eugene Nees
R. Bentley Neese
Kenneth E. Neff
Manuel H. Neff
Richard E. Neff
Robert E. Neff
Ted C. Neff
William Howard Neff
Stanley Neffendorf
Michael T. Negrich
Angel L. Negron
Carlos M. Negron
Jorge Negron-Martinez
Jose A. Negron-Ortiz
Pedro J. Negron-Rodriguez
James B. Nehowig
Richard Neidinger
Earl Kenneth Neifer
James H. Neighbors
Percy W. Neighbors
Richard Neighbors
Robert Otis Neighbors
Norman L. Neiheisel
George G. Neil
William L. Neil
Richard E. Neillands
Edmund W. Neilson
Paul H. Neilson
Ralph Andrew Neis
Thomas W. Neiswinger
Mike E. Neisz, Jr.
Joseph J. Neitzer
Charles V. Nejedly
John J. Nejman
Woodrow Nellons
James Nelms
Tendell R. Nelms, Jr.
Charles W. Nelsen
Alvin H. Nelson
Antone Nelson
Benjamin F. Nelson
Carl Thomas Nelson
Charles L. Nelson
Charles T. Nelson
Clayburn E. Nelson
David J. Nelson
Edwin George Nelson
Eli Malachi Nelson
Ernest E. Nelson
Forest A. Nelson
George W. Nelson

Gilbert Nelson, Jr.
Gordon C. Nelson
Herbert C. Nelson
James A. Nelson
James H. Nelson
James L. Nelson
James W. Nelson
Jerome S. Nelson
John H. Nelson
John H. Nelson
John Nelson, Jr.
John L. Nelson
John M. Nelson
Laurence H. Nelson
Laurin R. Nelson
Lawrence Archie Nelson
Oscar R. Nelson
Paul R. Nelson
Paul W. Nelson
Richard P. Nelson, Jr.
Robert A. Nelson
Robert C. Nelson
Robert John Nelson
Rolf W. Nelson
Roy R. Nelson
Rupert H. Nelson
Sam Nelson, Jr.
Thomas Edward Nelson
Thurman E. Nelson
Walter Lewis Nelson
William A. Nelson
William B. Nelson
William E. Nelson
William F. Nelson
Wilmont A. Nelson
Woodrow W. Nelson
Dion L. Neman
Stephen P. Nemec
Ben S. Nemeth
Alvin M. Nemitz
Marvin D. Nemitz
Eneas John Nenema
Anthony G. Nero
Cecil E. Nesbit
Lyle L. Nesbit
Thomas J. Nesis
Dunnick N. Ness
Gordon P. Ness
John H. Ness
Ralph Dean Ness
William Harold Ness, Jr.
Albert Oscer Nessi, Jr.
Paul M. Nestler
David L. Nestor
Leonard D. Nestor
Edward D. Nethery
John W. Netka, Jr.
Vernon Netolicky
Rudy T. Netry
John M. Netterblad
Major J. Nettles
Oscar H. Nettles
Eugene Q. Neubauer
Harold L. Neubold
Curtis T. Neumann
Gary J. Neumann
Rhinold Neumiller
Alvin Neustadt
Diaz Candi Nevarez
Sam E. Nevarez
Harlan R. Nevel
John Nevers, Jr.
Tommy Jack Neves
Conrad Leroy Neville
Fred G. Neville
Lawrence W. Neville
Robert B. Neville
Shelby Vaughn Neville
Ward O. Neville
Willie I. New, Jr.
Charles W. Newberry
Dallas L. Newberry
James R. Newberry
Joel C. Newberry
Charles E. Newcomb
Charles E. Newel
Calvin C. Newell
Charles Newell
Earl W. Newell
Hershell E. Newell
Hugh Franklin Newell
James Carl Newell
Jerome E. Newell
Johnnie C. Newell
Tommy Newell
Leo Alexander Newhouse
Bobby R. Newland
John E. Newland, Jr.
Billy G. Newman

Cecil A. Newman
Cecil E. Newman, Jr.
Cecil G. Newman
Charles A. Newman
George R. Newman
Gerald L. Newman
Harold D. Newman
Ira Newman
Jack D. Newman
James A. Newman
Lamar E. Newman
Leonard H. Newman
Marvin L. Newman
Myron E. Newman
Robert Lee Newman
Sylvester Newman
Thomas H. Newman
Charles J. Newport
Kenneth O. Newsom
Robert H. Newsom
Johnnie R. Newsome
Robert E. Newsome
Quentin L. Newswanger
Charles L. Newton
Charles W. Newton
Charlie G. Newton
Earle C. Newton, Jr.
Foster E. Newton, Jr.
Gilmer G. Newton
James A. Newton
James Elbert Newton
John Eugene Newton
Richard C. Newton
Robert Roy Newton
William A. Newton
Charles H. Ney
Felix R. Nez
George K. S. Ng
Charles L. Nibert
James L. Niblick
Leo John Nicaise, Jr.
Wayne Nicewanner
Louis B. Nichol
Ira Forrest Nicholas, Jr.
Robert L. Nicholas
William Nicholoson
Charles E. Nichols
Claude Yeomen Nichols, Jr.
Dale L. Nichols
David H. Nichols
Donald Nelson Nichols
Donald S. Nichols
Edmund H. Nichols
Everet C. Nichols
Herman R. Nichols
James D. Nichols
James Lorence Nichols
Joe H. Nichols
Louis Frank Nichols
Milton E. Nichols
Rice M. Nichols
Robert A. Nichols
Sylvester Nichols
Willis J. J Nichols
David L. Nicholson
Donald G. Nicholson
Franklin Nicholson
James Andrew Nicholson
Joe B. Nicholson
Memminge Nicholson
Richard L. Nicholson
William Nicholson
William H. Nicholson
Donald E. Nickel
Melvin H. Nickel
Ronald Louis Nickel
Corbett Nickell
Willard E. Nickens
Donald Walter Nickerson
James Elliot Nickerson
Donald John Nickey
Lonnie Nickles
Richard Lee Nickles
Ronald Clyde Nicklos
Milton E. Nicks
Robert Lee Nickson
James R. Nicodemus
William E. Nicol
August M. Nicolai
Christian Ball Nicolaisen
Herbert A. Nicolaus
David Montgomery Nicoll
Robert A. Nicoll
Robert Jelio Nicora, Jr.
Anthony J. Nicowski
Harold B. Nidiffer
William C. Nidiffer
Kenneth W. Nieb
Harry L. Niebel, Jr.

Joseph Nieberlein
Clarence R. Nieboer
Melvin E. Niedens
Henry Niederriter
Arild Christian Nielsen
David Leon Nielsen
Harry S. Nielsen, Jr.
Howard C. Nielsen
John E. Nielsen
Paul Elvin Nielsen
Russel H. Nielsen
Robert C. Niemann
Robert Frank Niemann
Howard W. Niemeyer
Charles R. Niemi
Chester Niemic
James Edward Nieporte
Roy M. Nier
Carl W. Niestadt
Castro Juan Nieves
Morales Dav Nieves
Pedro Nieves, Jr.
Arcadio Nieves-Larry
Carlos M. Nieves-Lopez
Daniel Nieves-Morales
Arnold E. Niewald
Martin Nigerville
Francis Nigra
Lawrence Y. Nihei
Rudolf Nikles
Bruce Kelly Nims
Richard K. Nirei
Gerard M. Niscia
Richard K. Nishida
Warren T. Nishihara
Charles Nishimura
Ernest B. Nitsche
Frederick M. Nitta
Donald G. Nitz
Daniel J. Niwa
Carl Francis Nix
Charles L. Nix
Forrest C. Nix
Victor H. Nix, Jr.
Daniel W. Nixdorf
Calvin K. Nixon
Charles L. Nixon
Edwin Allen Nixon, Jr.
Frederick R. Nixon
Junior Joseph Nixon
Richard A. Nixon
William H. Nixon
Donald A. Noble
William Noble, Jr.
Jay T. Nobles
Wayne O. Nobles
Roy V. Noceti
Ernest W. Nockeman
James L. Noe
Donald D. Noehren
James B. Noel
Robert Leo Noel
Roberto V. Nogales, Jr.
Joseph J. Nokes
Alfred E. Nolan
Donald F. Nolan
John Nolan
Lawrence T. Nolan
Marlin T. Nolan
William D. Nolan
Wilbur W. Nolda
Arthur P. Nolen
Richard Nolen, Jr.
Robert A. Nolen
Robert Howell Nolen
Virgil Nolen
Willie E. Nolen
Jake R. Noll
William E. Noll
William W. Nolze
Robert N. Nonella
Richard Nonemaker
Robert P. Noneman
William Donald Noonan
Gerald M. Noone
Grayson Gail Norbom
Ralph J. Nord
Robert I. Nordell
Gerald D. Norder
David T. Nordin, Jr.
Vern H. Nordquist
Elwyn D. Nordyke
Harold K. Norfleet
Irvin Norfleet
Clarence Norice, Jr.
Deane Wilfred Noringseth
John A. Norlander
Raleigh T. Norlien
Ray G. Norling

Vincent P. Norling
Carl L. Norman
Carl R. Norman
Clyde L. Norman
Conrad W. Norman
Harley Norman
James W. Norman
John F. Norman
John T. Norman
Richard P. Norman
Charles Rivers Norment
Ross L. Normington
Adin C. Norris, Jr.
Billy B. Norris
Cecil C. Norris
Clifford E. Norris
George D. Norris
Howard G. Norris
John A. Norris
Joseph C. Norris
Llewellyn F. Norris
Merle E. Norris
Mervin G. Norris
Thurkese Norris
Walter Michael Norris, Jr.
William Thomas Norris
Philip Norseworthy
Norman Perry North
Charles Northcutt, Jr.
Emery B. Northcutt
Virgil L. Northcutt
William Northcutt
Charles Duane Norton
Elmer R. Norton
Harold Verne Norton
Herbert M. Norton
Johnnie Norton
Joseph F. Norton
Larry Eugene Norton
Leon Norton
Milton A. Norton, Jr.
Owen Anderton Norton
Paul R. Norton
Robert D. Norton
Robert L. Norton
Elmer E. Norvell
Willard V. Norwick
Tommie L. Norwood
Kenneth L. Nosk
Earl R. Notbohm
Henry C. Notbusch
Marvin Eugene Nothstein
Harold Nels Notsund
William J. Notter
William Paul Noud
Reino Nousiainen
Donald W. Novacek
Daniel Novack
Jerry O. Novak
Mike R. Novak
Paul J. Novick
Edward D. Nowaczyk
Bert L. Nowak
John F. Nowak
Martin Joseph Nowak
Stanley Nowak, Jr.
Bert J. Nowakowski
Joseph M. Nowicki
Kasmir E. Nowicki
Leo Peter Nowicki
Richard R. Nowicki
Ernest G. Nowlin
Lee R. Nowlin
Carl A. Nowoczynski
Richard A. Noyes
Francis J. Nuce
Donald Gilbert Nuckel
Donald R. Nullmeyer
Lawrence Numkena
Thomas F. Nunes
Juarez Ramon Nunez
Raymond Nunez, Jr.
Ronald Joseph Nungesser
Lester J. Nunley
Reginald Nunn
Henry C. Nunnery
Erwin R. Nussbaumer
Harry David Nutt
James E. Nutt
Lewis N. Nutter
William Joseph Nutter
John M. Nutting
Louis G. Nuxoll
George Nwranski
Aaron Nydick
Alan Reed Nye
Glenn Carlyle Nye
Walter R. Nye
Dennis J. Nyhan

Stanley Nyhlen
John Henry Nyhuis
Robert Nykvist
William N. Nykytuk
Kenneth R. Nylander
Orville J. Nyquist
John W. Nystrom

— O —

Eric Franklin O'Briant
Charles R. O'Brien
Donald P. O'Brien
Edward J. O'Brien
James D. O'Brien
James P. O'Brien
John Patrick O'Brien
Larrie Dennis O'Brien
Paul T. O'Brien
Raymond J. O'Brien
Robert J. O'Brien
Robert J. O'Brien
Robert W. O'Brien
Thomas J. O'Brien
Warren Edward O'Brien
William J. O'Brien
Richard P. O'Connel
Alphonsus O'Connell
Bernard R. O'Connell
Edmund D. O'Connell
James E. O'Connell
Paul Harold O'Connell
Richard P. O'Connell
Thomas E. O'Connell
William T. O'Connell, Jr.
Edward M. O'Conner
Donald G. O'Connor
James William O'Connor
John D. O'Connor, Jr.
John J. O'Connor
Michael Joseph O'Connor
Patrick Frank O'Connor
Raymond R. O'Connor
Richard Joseph O'Connor
Timothy Patrick O'Connor
William J. O'Connor
Walter George O'Day
Laurence O'Dea
Ernest R. O'Dell
Fenton M. O'Dell
Howard Elliott O'Dell
Jimmie Leon O'Dell
Robert L. O'Dell
Thomas J. O'Donnel
Daniel T. O'Donnell
Edward F. O'Donnell
Joseph Steven O'Donnell
Joseph T. O'Donnell
Terrence W. O'Donnell
Thomas J. O'Donnell
William J. O'Donnell
Cordell O'Hara
Edwin C. O'Hara
Paul F. O'Hara
Thomas J. O'Hara
William T. O'Hara
John Joseph O'Kane
Eugene W. O'Keefe
John F. O'Keefe
John R. O'Keefe
Haword Donald O'Kelley
James Paul O'Leary
Jerome L. O'Leary
James E. O'Malley
Theodore O'Malley
William T. O'Malley
Arthur John O'Mara, Jr.
James J. O'Meara, Jr.
Walter J. O'Meara, Jr.
George E. O'Neal
Henry Roland O'Neal
Julius Elliott O'Neal
Raymond G. O'Neal
Clayton L. O'Neil
Edward F. O'Neil
Edward O'Neill
Eugene F. O'Neill
Fred C. O'Neill
John O'Neill
John H. O'Neill
Luther D. O'Neill
Morris A. O'Neill
Owen R. O'Neill
Philip J. O'Neill
Vincent W. O'Neill
Alfred Joseph O'Shea
Damian Fidelis O'Toole
James William O'Toole
Walter R. Oak

Aubrey N. Oakes
Ronald E. Oakes
Arthur Appel Oakley
Delbert W. Oakley
James Oakley
Ronald R. Oakley
Joseph Stephen Oaks
Paul N. Oaks
Alwin D. Oar
Nelson I. Oatsvall
Tadashi Obana
Stanley Thurmond Obanion
Melvin Dale Obee
Charles A. Oberdorf
Elmer Oberlander
Ray W. Oberlin
Arthur Leonard Oberman
William E. Oberry
Edward Joseph Obershaw
Donald C. Obert
Irwin J. Oborn
James M. Oboyle
Eugene Arnold Obregon
Carl Obringer, Jr.
Nicholas Obrovac
Frank Obzina
Angel L. Ocasio
Alberto Ochoa
Arnold Ochoa
Clifford Patrick Ochoa
Heradio Ochoa
Marcos M. Ochoa
William Edward Ockert
Russell M. Odberg
Jimmie L. Oden
Willie E. Oden
Thomas C. Odenbaugh
Thomas D. Odenbaugh
Kirkland Odes
Clarence B. Odle
Kelly Clayton Odneal
Billy J. Odom
Elijah Odom
Jessie Odom
Lloyd Benjamin Odom
Newman R. Odom
Oren M. Odum
Luther Odums
Paul A. M. Oechsle
Carl Henry Oelschig, Jr.
Robert H. Oesterwind
John H. Oetjen
Edward G. Offerdahl
Leonard M. Officer
Robert Stephen Ofsonka
Neil N. Ogasawara
Suetoshi Ogata
Joe H. Ogburn
Richard Floyd Ogburn
Charles A. Ogden
Frank Samuel Ogden
Henry Ogden, Jr.
Howard W. Ogden
James Wallington Ogden
Richard Ogier
John R. Ogilvie
Michael J. Oginski
L. G. Ogle
Le Roy Ogle
James A. Oglesbee
Alfred D. Oglesby
James N. Oglesby
Leo Dale Oglesby
James A. Oglethorpe
James Larry Ogletree
Edwin Peter Ogrodnik
Takeo Ogusuku
Thomas R. Ohanlon
David James Ohl
Robert G. Ohler
Otto A. Ohme
William R. Oiler
Maurice F. Okain
Arthur I. Okamura
Togo Okamura
Richard C. Okeefe
Hisao Okimoto
Clifford H. Okinaga
Hiroshi Oku
Hubert E. Olach
Antonio M. Olachea
Esequiel A. Olachia
Joe Rodriguez Olague
Richard N. Olague
Freddy J. Olaker
Ray William Olcott
Richard L. Olcott
Edward J. Oldenburg
Robert E. Oldenburg

Edward M. Oldfield
Kenneth H. Oldham
Darrell Olds
Joseph Thaddeus Olejarka
Stephen J. Oleksiuk
Paul Eugene Olenick
Peter Oles
Michael F. Oleshko
Robert D. Olesinski
Allen K. Oleson
Frank J. Oleyar
Alfredo B. Olguin
Louis D. Olguin
Elmer B. Olinger, Jr.
Joe A. Olinger
Roman A. Olinger
Ernest Cornelius Oliphant
Victor Olish
Luis A. Oliva
Secundino V. Olivares
Albert R. Olivas
Albert S. Olivas
Enriques Jeronimo Olivas
Lorenzo Olivas
James G. Olive
John A. Oliveira
Arlanza Oliver
Carl Duane Oliver
Dempsey R. Oliver
Edward L. Oliver
Harold E. Oliver
Jack A. Oliver
Jack Grimes Oliver
James C. Oliver
Jesse Harold Oliver
Joe B. Oliver, Jr.
Kenneth E. Oliver
Robert Nelson Oliver
Samuel R. Oliver, Jr.
Walter H. Oliver
William J. Oliver
Llantin V. Oliveras
Francis Joseph Olivigni
Luciano F. Ollero
Charles L. Ollom
Edward Charles Olman
Don E. Olmstead
Augustin I. Olnagan
Arthur Robert Olsen
Carl C. Olsen
Eugene Page Olsen
Hugh A. Olsen
Ludvig E. Olsen
William E. Olsen
Albert S. Olson
Allan James Olson
Arnold Eugene Olson
Charles M. Olson
Charles R. Olson
Donald L. Olson
George H. Olson
Harold B. Olson
John E. Olson
Kenneth L. Olson
Lelon A. Olson
Leonard Stanley Olson
Maurice Arthur Olson
Norman E. Olson
Paul Olson
Ralph M. Olson
Richard L. Olson
Richard O. Olson
Robert A. Olson
Sigurd Carl Olson
Stanley R. Olson
Vernon D. Olson
William Thomas Olson
Bernard J. Olsovsky
Clarence Olszewska
Donald W. Olszewski
Leonard Olszewski
Robert L. Olt
Charles R. L. Oltman
Louis Oluich
Robert Olvera
Leonard K. Olvis
Marvin E. Omans
Frank Ernest Omeis
James M. Omelveny
Robert Ondish
Paul Ondrey
Vernon J. Onion
John S. Oniszczak
Kenneth W. Onka
Milton T. Onomura
Howard L. Onstott
Timothy Ontayabbi
Edward Joseph Ontko
Edward J. Onze

Roland C. Opel
Nels Opheim
Bascomb M. Oppert
Clarence E. Opperud
William K. Opulauoho, Jr.
George F. Oquinn
Jessie W. Oquinn
Marquis H. Oracion
Moreno Anto Oramas
James A. Orback
Allen L. Ord
Roger Hull Ore
Arthur P. Orear
Richard B. Oreilly
Steve Oreson, Jr.
Henry R. Oretta
Bruno P. Orig
Anthony G. Orlandi
Villafane Orlandi
Robert L. Orman
Richard J. Ormiston
Robert John Ormond
Edward D. Orndorff
Alex Ornelas
Pedro Ornelas
Richard L. Oroark
Ishmael Orozco
Rudolph R. Orozco
Charles Denton Orr
Clifton C. Orr
Clyde Orr
Donald A. Orr
Ernest L. Orr
Jack F. Orr
Joseph M. Orr
Loyde Ray Orr
Richard T. Orr
Charles V. Orrie
Robert C. Orris
Eladio M. Ortega
Eppie J. Ortega
Harry Ortega
Jesus Moralez Ortega
John E. Ortega
Jose H. Ortega
Perez Manue Ortega
Juan P. Ortegas
Edward J. Ortego
James D. Ortego
Carlo Joseph Ortenzi
Abalardo Ortiz
Angel L. Ortiz
Cosme Juan Ortiz
Earl Ortiz
Edmund E. Ortiz
Eriverto Ortiz
Esteban Ortiz
Franco J. Ortiz
Fred G. Ortiz
Gomez Jose R. Ortiz
Hernandez Mi Ortiz
Isabel A. Ortiz
Ismael Ortiz
Luis A. Ortiz
Manuel A. Ortiz
Moreno Marce Ortiz
Negron Ciril Ortiz
Ocasio Guillermo Ortiz
Ortega Rafae Ortiz
Ortiz Rafael Ortiz
Rodriguez Jo Ortiz
Rodriguez Ru Ortiz
Rosa Luis Ortiz
Ruben M. Ortiz
Rufus M. Ortiz
Ysabel A. Ortiz
Ramon Ortiz-Duran
Robert H. Ortloff
Claude W. Ortman
Antonio Ortogero
Lewis Russell Orvis
John G. Orzechowski
Andrew Orzehowski
Charles Roland Osborn
Donald G. Osborn
Edison M. Osborn
James W. Osborn, Jr.
William T. Osborn
Charles E. Osborne
Dick E. Osborne
Harold H. Osborne
Jess Alex Osborne, Jr.
John H. Osborne
John R. Osborne
Owen H. Osborne
Richard A. Osborne
Richard Gardner Osborne
Robert W. Osborne
Stanley D. Osborne

Donald C. Osbourn
Lovender C. Osburn
Robert Osby
Kenneth A. Oshinski
Paul H. Oshiro
Wesley Booth Osler
Curtis G. Osmer
Martinez Fe Osorio
Edmund J. Ososki
Joseph F. Osovick
Arnold J. Ostendorf
Robert H. Ostendorf
Gerald Allen Osterberg
Neil Roger Osterberg
Joseph B. Ostergaard
Donald E. Osterkamp
John F. Ostick
Robert D. Ostler
Charles M. Ostrander
Alva C. Ostrom
Albert Ostrowski
Chester Ostrowski
Theodore Ostrowski
Michael Osullivan
David Osuna
Jackie T. Oswald
Richard Bruce Oswald
Eugene J. Osweiler
Mitsuyuki Ota
Thomas N. Otaguro
Colon Alejan Otero
Louis Otero
Clifford L. Otis
Harold A. Otis
William E. Otis, Jr.
Bill M. Otomo
John E. Ott
Kenneth J. Ott
Robert T. Ott
Gerome E. Otterson
Rawland Otterstrom
Eugene L. Ottesen
William E. Ottmann
Amen P. Otto
Bruce Watson Otto
Charles F. Otto
George R. Otto
George W. Otto
Robert F. Otto
William E. Otto
Byron M. Otwell, Jr.
Wendell H. Otwell
Albert J. Ouellet
George W. Ouellet
Joseph G. P. Ouellette
Joseph R. Ouellette
Eduardo Ouslan
James A. Ousley
Bernard J. Ousnamer
Charles M. Outland
George M. Outlaw
Howard Outley
Richard Frederick Outtrim
Ted Ovbey, Jr.
Forrest Lee Overall
Walter Howard Overback
Charles M. Overbay
Jacob K. Overbay
Clayton Overbee
Harvin J. Overbeek
James E. Overend
George N. Overfield
Elwood E. Overgard
Lawrence Wayne Overman
William Rudolph Overman
Charles Overstreet
James Douglas Overstreet
James R. Overstreet, Jr.
Donald Raymond Overton
Donald Wesley Overton
Harold F. Overton
Lawrence S. Overton
Robert E. Overton
Robert Edward Overton
Albert C. Owen
Billy Owen
Billy A. Owen
Claud Owen
Donald Leland Owen
Edward V. Owen
Glen R. Owen
Herbert R. Owen
Jack C. Owen
James B. Owen
Marvin P. Owen, Jr.
Paul C. Owen
Reuben D. Owen
George E. Owenby
Andrew Owens

Bernard A. Owens
Billy E. Owens
Carl Hubert Owens
Charles B. Owens
Charles H. Owens
Edison F. Owens
Erwin P. Owens
Eugene Riley Owens
Frank Owens, Jr.
Franklin A. Owens
Jasper Newton Owens
John Joseph Owens, Jr.
John Richard Owens
Lawrence J. Owens
Leonard Grady Owens
Norris Owens
Perry D. Owens
Raymond E. Owens
Richard K. Owens
Robert Allen Owens
Robert L. Owens, Jr.
Vola J. Owens
William H. Owens
Ralph D. Owings
Harvey Owner
Bill F. Owsley
Richard Colin Oxborough
John D. Oxford
Irad Blair Oxley
Bert Oya
Ernest Renwick Oyler
German Oyola
Ralph M. Ozbun
Robert J. Ozelas
Walter E. Ozias

— P —

Edsel Paavola
Gonzalo M. Pablo
John Alcides Pabon
Charlie J. Pace
Ford E. Pace
Horace Pace
James O. Pace
William L. Pace
Louis Michael Pacelle
Vincent D. Pacelli
Edward P. Pacewicz
Casimiro Pacheco
James F. Pacheco
Lespier Lu Pacheco
Narcisso Pacheco
Roman Pasc Pacheco
Tapia Juan Pacheco
Y. Pacheco-Bartolomei
Gonzalo Trejo Pachuca
Thomas R. Pacini
Ransom Pack
Szentfulopi Z. Pack
William R. A. Packard
Leo M. Packer
Irvin H. Packo
Pantolion M. Pacleb
Michael H. Paczocha, Jr.
Jerome J. Paden
Raymond E. Paden
Richard M. Paden
Clyde P. Padgett, Jr.
Eulia Padgett
Freddie E. Padgett
Heber R. Padgett
Paul Padgett
William Boyd Padgett
Alexander Beck Padilla
Gilberto J. Padilla
James Padilla
Raul Padilla
Lupe R. Padron
Maurice Anthony Padwa
Albert W. Paepke, Jr.
Harry E. Paetz
Albert William Paffenroth
Anthony E. Pagano
Frank Ambrose Pagano
Cecil F. Page
Henry Page
James A. Page
James W. Page
Jerry J. Page
John U. D. Page
Lester Frank Page
Mark G. Page
Robert E. Page
Roosevelt Page
Ruffus D. Page
Thomas A. Page, Jr.
William E. Page
Charles T. Pagel

Albert Joseph Paglione
Sergio Paguia
Joseph T. Pahle
Billy Joe Paige
Herman T. Paige
James E. Paige
Ray S. Paige
Thomas Paige
George H. Paine
Jack G. Paine
John Miller Paine
Alvin Earl Painter
Francis Edward Painter
Harry Richard Painter
Kenneth E. Painter
Lincoln R. Painter
Norman E. Painter
Sterling G. Painter
Joseph Paiva, Jr.
Paul Pakidis, Jr.
Alfredo Palad
Bernard M. Paladino
Gino Palamara
Elpedio P. Palcat
James Palenapa
Emil Leopold Palenik
Robert W. Palitti
John Pallagi, Jr.
August P. Pallasia
Edmund C. Pallesen
Robert Gene Pallesen
Rollyn E. Palm
Bud T. Palmatier
Alford Cleve Palmer
Allen L. Palmer
Bob R. Palmer
Donald W. Palmer
Forest M. Palmer
Harold E. Palmer
Henry P. Palmer
James O. Palmer
James R. Palmer
John W. Palmer
Milburn H. Palmer
Richard Eugene Palmer
Ronald J. Palmer
Thomas F. Palmer
Thomas L. Palmer
Warren E. Palmer
William H. Palmer
Nicholas Michael Palmiotti
Amado Palomares, Jr.
Martin Palomo
Andrew S. Palsa
Clarence Palsgrove
Steve Paluski
Zino M. Pampanin
Louis J. Panacek
Angelo A. Panaro
Joe M. Panaro
Joseph William Pancamo
Esmenio Panela
Andrew Vincent Panella
Peter J. Panetski
Anthony F. Panetta
Hoover T. H. Pang
Richard E. Pann
Francis Panno
James A. Panosh
John J. Panosso
Jimmy Pantozopulos
Pasquale B. Panzini
Saverio Panzitta
Dominic C. Paolucci
Ralph Joseph Papa
John Papademetriou
Raphael J. Paparillo, Jr.
Thomas O. Pape
Milton M. Papenfuss
John M. Papich
Chester J. Papineau
William Pappapetru
George Pappas
James T. Pappas
Sam W. Pappas
Richard C. Pappin
Albert C. Paquette, Jr.
Charles N. Paradeis
John R. Paradise
Harvey M. Pardee
Billy Jewel Pardue
Glendon J. Parenti
John H. Parezo
Charles Easton Parham, Jr.
Edward Parham
Jas E. Parham
Virgil Howard Parham, Jr.
Arthur R. Paris
Chester Earl Paris

Ronald Eugene Paris
Angelo C. Parise
Charles G. Parish
Edmond G. Parish
George W. Parish
James Parish
John F. Parish, Jr.
Robert A. Parish
David Humbert Park
Howard G. Park
John D. Park
Marmer J. Park
Raymond Park
Wilson Park
David D. Parke
Robert E. Parke
Alfred P. Parker
Andrew Parker
Arthur G. Parker
Billy L. Parker
Charles D. Parker
Charles E. Parker
Charles R. Parker
Charles Walter Parker
Chester L. Parker
Clifford A. Parker
Clinton W. Parker
Dixie S. Parker
Edward S. Parker
Ernest G. Parker
F. D. Parker
Floyd B. Parker
Gary Newton Parker
Harold Lloyd Parker
Harry J. Parker
Henry L. Parker
Herbert F. Parker
Jack D. Parker
James E. Parker
James E. Parker
James N. Parker
Jerry W. Parker
John T. Parker
John W. Parker
Kenneth W. Parker
Leroy Parker
Lonnie Lavern Parker
Medford O. Parker
Melvin Bryan Parker
Milton Le Roy Parker
Morris R. Parker
Olen Parker
Oscar B. Parker
Patsey C. Parker
Richard Alvin Parker
Richard T. Parker
Richard Vernon Parker
Robert B. Parker
Robert H. Parker
Ronald E. Parker
Stanley Parker
Thomas L. Parker
Vincent Parker
Charles Rupert Parkerson
Patrick E. Parkes
John W. Parkey
David O. Parkhurst
Paul O. Parkhurst
Charles F. Parkinson
Alfred Parks
Charles W. Parks
David L. Parks
Donald L. Parks
Donald Lawrence Parks
Douglas Allen Parks
Edward C. Parks
Harold P. Parks
Jack F. Parks
James H. Parks
John L. Parks
John O. Parks
Laurel E. Parks
Ralph Lee Parks
Ralph Loenard Parks
Ray E. Parks
Raymond F. Parks
Richard W. Parks
Robert F. Sr Parks
Robert Lee Parks
Ronald R. Parks
Roy Parks
Harold J. Parksion
Charles L. Parle
Martin H. Parlet
Charles E. Parlier
Harold W. Parlier
Arthur J. Parmenter
Larry L. Parmentier
David L. Parmer

William E. Parmer
Robert E. Parnow
Gustave Parr, Jr.
Jesus C. Parra
Jose M. Parra
Torres Rafae Parra
William E. Parra
James D. Parrent
Carl C. Parrick
Earnest B. Parris
Harold G. Parris
Arkie Basil Parrish
Bill Eiland Parrish
Charles Weslie Parrish
Claude Thomas Parrish
Leroy Parrish
Patrick Obrien Parrish
Raymond Shirley Parrish
Thomas E. Parrish
Watson F. Parrish
Willie P. Parrish
Willie P. Parrish
Henry A. Parron
Ray Parrott
John Charles Parry
Joseph Buford Parse, Jr.
Levant S. Parsell
Richard S. Parsell
Max B. Parson
Carl B. Parsons
Carl E. Parsons
Carson L. Parsons
Charles W. Parsons
Clent E. Parsons
Darrell J. Parsons
Earl J. Parsons
Harry F. Parsons
Jackie Edwin Parsons
James Parsons
Julian K. Parsons
Dean W. Partin
General H. Partin
William D. Partin
Willie Parton
Kenneth Angus Partlow
Farrell Parton
Eddy G. Partridge
Frederick Ray Partridge
Walter R. Partridge
Tom Parungao
James V. Parziale
Louis Pascarella
Richard B. Paschall
Rudolph W. Paschbeck, Jr.
Alfred Paschelke
Edward A. Pascoe
Marvin E. Pascoe
Peter J. Paserk, Jr.
James S. Pashnee
Harry L. Pask, Jr.
Robert W. Paske
William E. Paskett
Bruce Monroe Pass
Wayne F. Pass
Rosario Passarelli
Herbert J. Passer
Guerino Passero, Jr.
Thomas L. Pastorius
Walter J. Pastuszek
Donald L. Patch
Leon Ernest Patchen
Billy C. Pate
Henry N. Pate
Jack K. Pate
Leland M. Pate
William Harold Pate
Armand A. Patenaude
William Paternoster
Peter A. Patete
Raymond Joseph Patin
Elmiro Patitucci
Felix P. Patovski
Frank Patrick, Jr.
George J. Patrick
James Patrick
James J. Patrick
Joseph Patrick
Lewis D. Patrick
Preston C. Patrick
Willie Patrick
Leighton H. Patriquen
Charles R. Patten
Edwin E. Patten
Roy M. Patten
Arthur J. Patterson
Billy J. Patterson
Billy Louis Patterson
Bobbie J. Patterson
Bruce Robert Patterson

Clarence Patterson
Clarence E. Patterson
George Patterson
Harold F. Patterson
Ithal T. Patterson
James E. Patterson
James S. Patterson
James W. Patterson
Jerome E. Patterson
Jesse W. Patterson
Joe N. Patterson, Jr.
Joseph A. Patterson
Lindle E. Patterson
Mason N. Patterson
Oliver J. Patterson
Reginald Patterson
Richard Patterson
Wallace Irwin Patterson, Jr.
Richard William Pattillo
Albert Patton
Billy R. Patton
Delmar Patton
Edwin Mccoy Patton
George Vernon Patton
Jack D. Patton
James Alma Patton
James Rudy Patton
James W. Patton
Johnny L. Patton
Marvin S. Patton
Robert E. Patton
Wallace D. Patton
William Ernest Patton
Andre A. Pattyn
Igmedio Patubo
Daniel Richard Paul
Kenneth D. Paul
Lawrence E. Paul
Oliver Paul
Robert L. Paul
Teddy L. Paul
Luther R. Pauling
Joseph W. Paull
Robert L. Paulley
Charles R. Paulsen
Wayne H. Paulsen
Gotfried Paulson, Jr.
Robert John Paulson, Jr.
Herman E. Pauly
Lawrence A. Pauly
Robert J. Paun
Heinz Pautke
Eugene Joseph Paveglio
Leo S. Pavilcek
Edward Pavlak
John C. Pavlak
Joseph Pavlak
Dalko D. Pavletich
Robert S. Pavlick
Jacob Louis Pawer, Jr.
Antoni M. Pawlik
George H. Paxton
Jesse J. Paxton
Lawrence D. Paxton
Irving Arthur Paylor
Baltimore Payne
Billie Payne
Billy J. Payne
Calvin F. L. Payne
Carl W. Payne, Jr.
Carroll W. Payne
Charles D. Payne
Charles E. Payne
Charles R. Payne
Charlie W. Payne
Cleo O. Payne
D. F. Payne
Douglas W. Payne
Eddie L. Payne
Ernest E. Payne
Eugene E. Payne
Frank D. Payne
Glenn Payne
Harold B. Payne
J. F. Payne
Jake Payne
John Payne
John A. Payne
Murray L. Payne
Oliver E. Payne
Robert L. Payne
Thomas L. Payne
Wilbert Payne
Willard Dennis Payne
William Floyd Payne
William George Payne
Milo G. Paynovich
John L. Paytes
Bruce Walter Payton

Eunis Osben Payton
Alvaro Paz-Lansot
John T. Peace
Donald A. Peach
Earl Francis Peach
Billy Eugene Peacock
Broughton Peacock
Shellie Peak, Jr.
Willie L. Peak
Thomas Peake
Aaron Pearce
Harold Pearce
John D. Pearce
Richard A. Pearce
Thomas P. Pearce, Jr.
Andrew D. Pearish
Carl W. Pearl
Louis G. Pearl
Gerald P. Pearo
Gilbert B. Pearsall
Bernard Lee Pearson
Charles Albert Pearson
Helge E. Pearson
Henry C. Pearson
James R. Pearson
Jimmy F. Pearson
Lawson Pearson
Merle D. Pearson
Raymond D. Pearson
Raymond E. Pearson
Raymond E. Pearson
Raymond T. Pearson
William Arnold Pearson, Jr.
Edwin A. Peart, Jr.
Duane N. Peaschek
Richard E. Pease
Darrell D. Peasley
William E. Peavers
Billy R. Peavey
Albert Pecha
Alfred James Pechin
James Kenneth Peck
Kesley S. Peck
Robert L. Iii Peck
John F. Peckham
William H. Peckham
David D. Pecor
Domenick Pecoraro
Ralph A. Pecot, Jr.
Harvey L. Pedersen
Richard L. Pedersen
Delbert J. Pederson
Le Roy O. Pederson
Marvin W. Pederson
William A. Pedigo
Florencio Pedraza
Edward M. Pedregon
George A. Pedrizet
Antionio A. Pedro
Angel O. Pedroza
James E. Peek
Ernest K. Peeler
John A. Peeples
Eugene P. Peery
Thomas A. Peet
Marcel C. Peeters
Grover C. Pegg, Jr.
Walter G. Pehling
William J. Peifer
Alfred G. Peiffer
Richard F. Peinado
Frank George Peiritsch
John H. Pekkala
Maika Pele
John E. Pelfrey
Lewis J. Pelfrey
Rudolph Pellegrini
Leland R. Pellerin
Claude Pelletier
Joseph N. Pelletier
Robert L. Pelletier
John Pels
William H. Pelton
Thomas R. Pemble
Albino Suares Pena
Fernando S. Pena
Louie Pena
Mike C. Pena
Rodriguez Raf Pena
Urbano Pena
Juan Pena-Andujar
Calvin K. Penberthy
Charles G. Pence
George Allen Pence
Everett Pendarvis
Vance L. Pendarvis
Benjamin E. Pendell
Sylvester Pender
Glenn Ray Pendergast

Willis Pendergraf
Leon B. Pendergrass
Charles Pendleton
Roy G. Pendleton
Billy Pendley
Michael Pengrin
William Penington
Raymond D. Penland
Troy Penland
Arnold Penn
Edward Lovey Penn
Robert J. Penn
Nicholas Penna
Aldee H. Penner
Chester O. Penney, Jr.
Roger William Penninger
Bartie Pennington
Eugene Pennington
James H. Pennington
Louis A. Pennington
Wilgus Pennington
Salvatore Pennisi
Billy Dean Penniston
Alvah J. Pennock
Robert A. Penny
Percy L. Penrose
Paul P. Pensak
John Riley Pentecost, Jr.
Paul M. Pentecost
Robert W. Pentland
Frank L. Penwell
Claude Peoples
Harry T. Peoples, Jr.
Louis Charles Pepera
Edward J. Pepin
Aloysius Pepion, Jr.
John B. Peppard
Bernard M. Pepper
Norton Peppmuller
Fidel Peralta
Joseph C. Peralta
James B. Percival
George Alfred Perdrizet, Jr.
Camerino Perea
Joseph W. Pereira
Richard J. Pereira
Pedro Jose Pereles
Roland M. Perell
Ernest H. Peres
Aaron Perez
Alejandro G. Perez
Alfred Perez
Alonzo Perez
Arthur J. Perez
Aviles Juan Perez
Baez Serafin Perez
Crespo Georg Perez
Cruz Isidro Perez
Frank M. Perez
Isamel U. Perez
Jaime R. Perez
Jesse G. Perez
Jesus Jose Perez
Joe C. Perez
Joffrey Perez
Jose G. Perez
Jose Santos Perez
Loubriel Mig Perez
Manuel G. Perez
Marcos H. Sr Perez
Miguel Perez
Pizarro Manuel Perez
Rene Perez
Roman Ismael Perez
Simon Mendoza Perez
Torres Arcad Perez
Tranquilino Perez
Pedro Perez-Perez
Efrain Perez-Rodriguez
Luis D. Perez-Villegas
Jack Ray Perigo
Daniel B. Perio
Charles R. Perkey
Algie Perkins
Alva J. Perkins
Arthur L. Perkins
Donald J. Perkins
Frank Perkins
James C. Perkins
Jesse B. Perkins
Jesse L. Perkins
Jessie R. Perkins
John Lavigne Perkins
Lloyd R. Perkins
Malcolm D. Perkins
Otto T. Perkins
Robert E. Perkins
Thomas Albert Perkins
William G. Perkins

Robert Jelene Perkinson
Ervin A. Permann
Ronald J. Pernack
James P. Pernell
James F. Peronto
Marvin Perper
Kenneth Allen Perraut
George A. Perreault
Henry J. Perreault
Silvio T. Perrella
William P. Perrella
Albert C. Perrera
Clarence D. Perrin
Donald B. Perrin
Ralph L. Perrin
Julio I. Perrone
Frederick Perrotta
Edward E. Perrotti
Albert A. Perry
Alfred Ogle Perry
Alfred Patrick Perry
Augustine Perry
Bradley Gaylon Perry
Charles R. Perry
Clarence A. Perry
Cleveland Perry
Clyde A. Perry
Edward F. Perry
Fletcher F. Perry
Frank J. Perry
Frank W. Perry
Franklin R. Perry
Gerald L. Perry
Harold Perry
Jack L. Perry
John Clarence Perry
Kenneth Owens Perry
London L. Perry
Margaret Fae Perry
Norman C. Perry
Raymond Jackson Perry
Roscoe E. Perry
Russell L. Perry
Thomas O. Perry, Jr.
Trevor J. Perry
William Perry
William C. Perry
William R. Perry
William S. Perry, Jr.
Willie E. Perry
C. Perryjohn, Jr.
James Persianni
William Persinger
Alfred M. Person, Jr.
Warren Roy Person
Zelmar Person
William Personett
Clifford A. Persons
James L. Perts
Thomas L. Perugini
Harvey E. Perusse
Edward Peska
Frederick N. Pestana
Nickolas Petcosky
Gray P. Pete
George W. Peterburs
Herbert D. Peterman
Paul Peterman
Daniel G. Peters
Delbert O. Peters
Earl K. Peters
Forrest L. Peters
Frank W. Peters
Fred H. Peters
Gerald T. Peters
Jack Dempsey Peters
James M. E. Peters
Leonard L. Peters
Loyd Maxwell Peters
Marvin V. Peters
Ralph E. Peters
Raymond D. Peters
Richard E. Peters
Robert K. Peters
Russell F. Peters
Spiro Joseph Peters
Tillman O. Peters
Travis L. Peters
William F. Peters, Jr.
Armand A. Petersen
Carl D. Petersen
Clarence A. Petersen
Dean H. Petersen
Fred A. Petersen, Jr.
Fred N. Petersen, Jr.
Marvin H. Petersen
Maun T. Petersen
Robert Willard Petersen
Arnold E. Peterson

Bruce A. Peterson
Charles E. Peterson
Clarence Peterson
Clifford Sidney Peterson
Dean V. Peterson
Donwin Ross Peterson
Earl W. Peterson
Edward J. Peterson
Gerald B. Peterson
Gordon Alfred Peterson
Jack D. Peterson
Jerry H. Peterson
John H. Peterson
Larry Lee Peterson
Leland G. Peterson
Lyle E. Peterson
Lynn R. Peterson
Myron D. Peterson
Norman Wayne Peterson
Orville P. Peterson
Parodis P. Peterson
Peter E. Ii Peterson
Philip O. Peterson
Robert D. Peterson
Ronald D. Peterson
Russell D. Peterson
Stanley F. Peterson
Udell Lee Peterson
David J. Pethel
Andrew F. Petho
Wheeler E. Pethtel
Nicholas A. Petluk
Neil P. Petraglia
John S. Petras
Harold Lester Petree
Ralph J. Petrell
James E. Petress
James H. Petrey
Clyde E. Petri
Vernon E. Petri
Earl Frederick Petrick
Edmund F. Petrie
Adelchi A. Petrillo
Louis A. Petrillo
Louie J. Petro
Michael J. Petro
John Petroff, Jr.
Frank H. Petrone
Delmar Lee Petrowske
Edward H. Petrunyak
Michael C. Petruska
Philip M. Petry
Charles W. Petsche
George E. Pett
James Petteress, Jr.
Philip Nels Petterson
Harold J. Petticord
John Bob Pettigrew
Vernon L. Pettigrew
David E. Pettis
Gilbert L. Pettis
John W. Pettit
Raymond C. Pettit
Thomas Junior Pettit
Thomas P. Pettit
Edwin C. Petts
Firman E. Pettus, Jr.
Alvin R. Petty
George Petty, Jr.
Howard A. Petty
James H. Petty
John W. Petway
James Vincent Peuter
Ray T. Pevehouse
Oscar P. Peveler
James Ansel Peveto
Malcolm Bruce Peveto
Welford B. Peyton
William F. Pfann
Eugene Alexander Pfeifer
Ralph R. Pfeiffer
Wilmer R. Pfeifle
William F. Pfleegor
Nicholas A. Pfliger
Robert F. Phalen
Wilbur W. Phares
William A. Pharris
Robert James Phelan
William T. Phelan
Bayard G. Phelps
Bobbie D. Phelps
Donald R. Phelps
Harry E. Phelps
Harry L. Phelps, Jr.
John M. Phelps
Lowell E. Phelps
Ralph Lawrence Phelps
Richard Phelps
Woodrow W. Phelps

Glendon Philbrick
Robert J. Philippen
Don L. Philipps
George W. Phillippe
Allen Lee Phillips
Benjamin Phillips
Billy A. Phillips
Billy L. Phillips
Billy M. Phillips
Bruce K. Phillips
Carson Phillips
Charles A. Phillips
Charles Albert Phillips
Charles F. Phillips
Charles Joseph Phillips
Charles L. Phillips
Charlie A. Phillips
Denny Powell Phillips
Donald E. Phillips
Duane Martin Phillips
Elda Phillips, Jr.
Francis M. Phillips
Frank Frederick Phillips
Gerald J. Phillips
Henry Lewis Phillips
Howard D. Phillips
Hugh B. Phillips
Hyde Phillips
Jackie L. Phillips
James D. Phillips
James Edmund Phillips
James K. Phillips
James W. Phillips
John A. Phillips
John E. Phillips
John E. Phillips
John J. Phillips
John P. Phillips
Joseph F. Phillips
Lee Hugh Phillips
Marvin Earl Phillips
Orville P. Phillips
Peter Gordon Phillips
Raymond E. Phillips
Richard E. Phillips
Richard Henry Phillips
Richard L. Phillips
Robert Phillips
Robert A. Phillips
Robert L. Phillips
Robert L. Phillips
Virgil L. Phillips
Walter Dixon Phillips, Jr.
William D. Phillips
William Richardson Phillips
William Kay Phillis
Loy Allen Philpot
Hugh W. Philpott
Alvin Phipps
Harry C. Phipps
Jeirl B. Phipps
Herman R. Phy
Ralph Irwin Phy
Paul Robert Piana
Joe D. Piasse
Vincent Piattelli
William A. Picard
Alton H. Pickard
Maxie L. Pickard
Clarence D. Pickens
Ernest M. Pickens
Freddie F. Pickens
Russell B. Pickens
William H. Pickens
Fred D. Pickering
Robert P. Pickering
Clayton H. Pickett
George Pickett, Jr.
James E. Pickett
James L. Pickett
James Truman Pickett
Robert Edward Pickett
James B. Pickworth, Jr.
Alexander Joseph Picone
William R. Pictun
James Jerome Picucci
Gene L. Piela
Rolly Lafond Pieper
James E. Pier
Albert C. Pierce
Arthur J. Pierce
Clayton M. Pierce
Desmond Pierce
Donald L. Pierce
Edward E. Pierce, Jr.
Frederick E. Pierce
George Pierce, Jr.
James R. Pierce, Jr.
James T. Pierce

Joseph William Pierce
Leonard L. Pierce, Jr.
Luther S. Pierce
Orville W. Pierce
Raymond Pierce
Raymond O. Pierce
Richard O. Pierce
Richard P. Pierce
Robert D. Pierce
Robert E. Pierce
Robert F. Pierce
Thomas C. Pierce, Jr.
Walter Pierce
Walter J. Pierce
William M. Pierce
Zachary T. Il Piercy
Paul Mario Pieri
Everett F. Pieron
Robert Emil Pierroux
Howard E. Piersee
Robert W. Piersee
Jack D. Pierson
Robert Leach Pierson
Taylor O. Pierson
Harold Leonard Piesik
Clement L. Pietrasiewicz
Herman Pietrowski
Eugene H. Pietrus
Raymond E. Pietrzak
Charlie F. Pigford
Marlin L. Pigott
Donald L. Pike
Emerald W. Pike
Odie T. Pike
Raymond S. Pike
Ted Pike
Robert E. Pilch
Salvatore Anthony Pileri
Floyd A. Pilgrim
Herbert K. Pililaau
John A. Pillar
Frank J. Pillon
Wade Maxwell Pillow
William T. Pilmer
Alphonse Richard Pilosi
Caliz Fernand Pina
Conroy T. Pina
David F. Pina
Donald A. Pina
Frank J. Pina
Bobbie N. Pinckney
Herbert Pincus
Joseph F. Pindel
James W. Pineda
William E. Piner
Clifton F. Pines
Carter N. Ping
Leon A. Pingenot
Otis E. Pingleton
Joseph L. Pinkham
Clyde M. Pinkston
James L. Pinkston
Virgil F. Pinkston
Harold L. Pinnell
Russell C. Pinnell
Arlin J. Pinneo
Frederick D. Pinner
Lloyd A. Pinner
Bernard S. Pinter
James Pinto
Edmundo Pintor
Leonard Piorunski
Foley D. Piper
Ransom D. Piper, Jr.
Richard D. Piper
Wallace R. Piper
Walter F. Piper
Wesley Leonard Piper
Thomas Pipic
Paris J. Pipkin
John F. Pippin
Victor M. Pirowski
Clifford A. Pirtle
John P. Pisani
Albert Piskolti
Joseph Pistonetti
Leonard E. Pisula
Donald L. Pitchford
Arnold Pitman
Frank Pitman
William E. Pitman
Charles D. Pitre, Jr.
Ernest J. Pitre
Frank Anthony Pitre
John A. Pitterson
Clyde B. Pittillo
Patrick D. Pittillo
Charles Pittman, Jr.
Clark Joe Pittman

Gerald E. Pittman
Irvin W. Pittman
Norman E. Pittman
Ray J. Pittman
Russell G. Pittman
Walter Everett Pittman
Carl W. Pitts
Cleo Pitts
Clyde Thomas Pitts
John W. Pitts
Louis Pitts, Jr.
Wayford Byron Pitts
Robert L. Pitzinger
Walter F. Piver
Leon Piwoni
George Pixley
Gilberto Pizana
Nicolas Pizarro-Matos
Samuel P. Pizzo
Duane Clinton Place
Duane K. Place
Camillo Placencia
Louis Peter Plagakis
Camille Plaisance
Daniel W. Plank
Charles R. Plantz
Juan Z. Plata
Benjamin S. Plater
Robert Dixon Plato
Hamilton C. Platt
Kay Sherill Platt
Wesley Mccoy Platt
Joseph A. Platzkoester
Robert W. Plaunt
Billy N. Player
Claude Playforth
Joseph G. Pleasants
Albert Edward Plecha
Lewis Peifer Pleiss
Roger W. Pleshek
Raymond T. Plevyak
Norman C. Plinske
Edward V. Pliska
Frank L. Plocha
Roy Henry Ploeger, Jr.
Alphonso H. Plonk
Alexander Plotkin
Gerald R. Plotner
William Plotnik
William Plott, Jr.
Raphael Plotzki
Marvin S. Sr Plue
Albert W. Plumb
Reed Edwin Plumb
Harold R. Plumley
Alan F. Plummer
Harry R. Plummer
James R. Plummer
Max L. Plummer
Paul W. Plummer
James Plump
Harry E. Plunkett
Waitcell Plunkett
Justyn Cynan Pluta
Robert F. Plzak
Bobby Ray Poare
Kenneth D. Pockey
Edward F. Poczekaj, Jr.
Robert J. Poczekaj
Richard D. Podesta
Edward Podmajersky
Harold Roosevelt Podorson
Norman Iver Podos
Steve A. Podplesky
Chester Poe, Jr.
George Joseph Poe
Robert H. Poe
Marcel C. Poelker
Anthony J. Poffahl
James A. Pogue
James F. Pogue
Marion B. Pogue
Otis H. Pogue
Donald J. Pohlman
William R. Pohlman
Paul O. Pohlson
Rufus C. Poindexter
Ray Point
John Pointeck, Jr.
Max Owen Pointer, Jr.
Bernard A. Poirier
Gerard J. Poirier
Herman Aloysius Poisson
Rene G. Poitras
Edward Pojatina
Charles L. Pokojski
Lawrence Elmer Polan
Gilbert K. Poland
J. B. Poland

Shirley M. Poland
Howard L. Polarie
George J. Polcer, Jr.
Richard Alan Polen
Kenneth Otto Polenske
Angelo G. Poletis
Karl Lewis Polifka
David E. Poling
Edward M. Poling
Forest J. Poling
Forrest C. Poling
Philmore Polk
Robert P. Polk
Warren Franklin Polk
Francis Polka
Aubrey W. Pollard
Clyde D. Pollard
Glen D. Pollard
Leon W. Pollard, Jr.
Richard J. Pollard
Walter M. Pollard
William Bock Pollard
Everett E. Pollen
Clay H. Polley, Jr.
James A. Pollock
Robert F. Pollock
Anthony Polotto, Jr.
Robert Ervine Polzine
Pedro Pomales-Pomales
Epifanio Pomales-Santiago
Robert L. Pomerene
Ralph E. Pomeroy
William A. Pomeroy
Wyatt H. Pomeroy
Benjamin Ponciano
Burnell C. Pond
Stanl Poniewierski
Robert D. Pontius
Donald Edward Ponto
Edward Pool
Jack A. Pool
Benjamin Poole
Billy R. Poole
Dale Herbert Poole
Harold J. Poole
Jack E. Poole
Lovell Poole
Major E. Poole
William Poole
William J. Poole
John E. Poolman
John W. Poor
Elvis J. Poore
Fred C. Poore
John H. Poore
Lowell T. Poore
John W. Poors
Crisanto N. Popa
Charles Edward Pope
James Dean Pope
Joseph Pope
Ray Pope
Leonard T. Popham
Michael Popovich
John Frederick Popp, Jr.
Robert L. Poppe
Fred L. Poppell
Homer L. Port
Santiag Portalatin
John Portas
Sierra Jua Portela
Alec W. Porter
Alvin Porter
Ben C. Porter
Bill J. Porter
Carter S. Porter
Cecil L. Porter, Jr.
Charles A. Porter
Donn F. Porter
Earl G. Porter
Elmo Porter
Enoch S. Porter
Franklin D. Porter
George A. Porter
Harold B. Porter
Henry A. Porter
Henry N. Porter
Homer Lee Porter
Horace Hill Porter, Jr.
James B. Porter
James Howard Porter
Jasper M. Porter
Jimmy T. Porter
John K. Porter
Keith Maynard Porter
Mose Porter
Oliver Porter
Oscar Porter, Jr.
Perry W. Porter, Jr.

Raymond S. Porter
Richard E. Porter
Rogers Porter
Ronald John Porter
Thomas R. Porter
William Bradley Porter
James T. Porterfield, Jr.
John D. Porterfield
Henry Bustamente Portillo
Eldon G. Portschi
Frank Portugal
Richard Portwood
Sylvester Porubsky
Karnig A. Poryazian
Harold T. Posey
Jonathan Reed Posey, Jr.
Lawrence W. Posey
Noland D. Posey
Thomas A. Posey
Michael J. Posivak, Jr.
Dale A. Pospyhalla
Arthur H. Post
Dale Robert Post
David E. Post
Jack K. Post
Jack Leroy Post
Ronald A. Postance
William Peter Posten
Joseph Postick
Clarence E. Postlethwait
William Postlewait
Andrew G. Postma
Clifford E. Poston
Edmund D. Poston
Freeman Poston, Jr.
Ronald L. Poston
Bobby Lee Pothast
John S. Potorski
Donald B. Potratz
Calvin R. Potter
Charles Potter
Harry E. Potter
Leroy W. Potter
Morris L. Potter
Myron L. Potter
Robert Potter
Thomas Lee Potter
William R. Potter
Bernace F. Potts
Charlie M. Potts
Hubert W. Potts
James E. Potts
James W. Potts, Jr.
Lawrence W. Potts
Richard A. Potts
Robert Joseph Potts
Roy H. Potts
William B. Potts
Joseph E. Potvin
Alvin E. Potz
Andrew P. Pouk
Thomas J. Poulin
Edward M. Poulsen
George Poulsen, Jr.
George A. Poulson
Gerald J. Poulson
John Eugene Pound
Lester M. Pounds, Jr.
Richard C. Poupard
Bruce A. Pourciau
Clayton L. Poust
James D. Pow
John Belton Powe, Jr.
Arthur Duane Powell
Arthur Walter Powell, Jr.
Brook Powell
Buford B. Powell
Charles E. Powell
David Allen Powell
Donald W. Powell
Earnest T. Powell
Forrest E. Powell
George Powell
Harold L. Powell
Harry Albert Powell
Hollis Powell
Jackie L. Powell
James L. Powell
James M. Powell
James R. Powell
Joe B. Powell
John Phillip Powell
Joseph C. Powell
Joseph C. Powell
Marion Jackson Powell
Railey L. Powell
Rex W. Powell
Richard M. Powell
Robert L. Powell

Roy L. Powell
Samuel B. Powell
Sidney Powell
W. D. Powell
Waldo A. Powell
Wayne E. Powell
William Powell
William Neal Powell
William S. Powell
Willie Powell
Charles W. Power
Bernard M. Powers
Burnice D. Powers
Earl L. Powers
Edwin E. Powers
Elbert D. Powers, Jr.
Frank L. Powers
Jairus E. Powers
Jerry B. Powers
Joe H. Powers, Jr.
John E. Powers
John K. Powers
Kenneth W. Powers
Kenneth W. Powers
Matthew G. Powers, Jr.
Richard C. Powley
Con Foly Poynor
James Irsley Poynter
Miguel Pozos
Alvin J. Pradat
Pacheco Pedr Prado
Carl C. Prange
Eugene J. Praska
James Clarence Prasnikar
Joseph F. Prast
James A. Prater
Robert F. Prater
Kermit Q. Prather
Lawrence H. Prather
Paul E. Prather
Robert L. Prather
Charles H. Pratt
Charles William Pratt
Clifford F. Pratt
Clifford F. Pratt
Edward J. Pratt
Elmer Pratt
Glen Leroy Pratt
John L. Pratt
Merritt L. Pratt
Parker H. Pratt
Robert D. Pratt
John E. Pratter
William C. Preacher
Curlous M. Preas
John E. Pree
James T. Preece
Leslie E. Preece
Carol Chester Prejean
Albert C. Prendergast
Maurice W. Prendergast
Herbert W. Prentice
Robert H. Prentice
Coleman L. Prescott
Delbert F. Prescott
Luverne C. Prescott
Sidney T. Prescott
Noah Presley, Jr.
Irving A. Press
James L. Pressey
Robert H. Pressler
Prince Georges, MD
William R. Pressley
Vernon D. Presswood
Douglas W. Prestage
Charles Prestiss
Chester Preston
Daniel E. Preston
David R. Preston
Don R. Preston
Jesse L. Preston
Ronald L. Preston
Victor M. Prestwood
Virgil W. Prestwood
Robert J. Prettner
Cloyse A. Prible
Albert L. Price
Charles F. Price
Charles H. Price, Jr.
Commie Eugene Price
Coy W. Price
Duane Freeman Price
Forrest L. Price
Frederick C. Price
Harold L. Price
Herbert L. Price
Hughey D. Price
James E. Price
John F. Price

John Wayne Price
Kenneth D. Price
Richard L. Price
Richard M. Price
Robert Edward Price
Robert Guy Price
Talmadge Price, Jr.
Thomas J. Price
Thomas R. Price
William D. Price
William P. Price
William T. Price
Dale P. Prickett
Laurence Parker Priddy, Jr.
Marvin Bruce Priddy
Howard Clifford Pride
Earnest Pridemore
Miner W. Pridemore
Coley Grey Pridgen
Barnard V. Priest
Edward N. Priest
James W. Priest
Merlin G. Priest
James R. Priester
Raymond Rivera Prieto
Charles W. M. Prince
Duward H. Prince
Ernest Ray Prince
Floyd Prince
Gene C. Prince
Harry John Prince
Marvin Eugene Prince
Wade Prince, Jr.
Wesley Prince, Jr.
William F. Prindle
Theodore B. Pringle, Jr.
James Jordan Prior
Richard E. Prior
Harold E. Prisk
Prence Alvin Prisock
Donald E. Pritchard
George R. Pritchard
Milford Harry Pritchard
Walter C. Pritchard
Walter Oswald Pritchard
Arnie R. Pritchett
August Pritchett, Jr.
Chester Pritchett
Dixie C. Pritchett
Eugene Pritchett
Irby L. Pritchett
Ronald D. Pritchett
Willie G. Pritchett
Thomas E. Privett
William W. Privett
Roy D. Probst
Theodore G. Procter, Jr.
Calvin E. Proctor
Donald Wayne Proctor
Gene F. Proctor
William E. Proctor
Donald J. Proffitt
Homer Proffitt
Preston J. Proffitt
Richard E. Prohl, Jr.
Robert Lee Proud, Jr.
Armand H. Proulx
William J. Proulx
Frank Provenzano
Leonard E. Provost
Robert Provost
Robert F. Prue
James T. Prueitt
Clarence P. Pruett
J. D. Pruitt
Newman C. Pruitt, Jr.
Oliver L. Pruitt
Harry C. Prunier
Vaughn Dale Prunier
Gerald Pryhoda
Harvey E. Pryne
Floyd W. Pryor
George T. Pryor
Dennis A. Pryzgoda, Jr.
Thaddeus Przeslica
Billy Przyborski
Alexander Przybysz
Raymond Kauinohea Pua
Alfred A. Pucci
Nicholas S. Pucci
Virgil L. Puck
Charles C. Puckett
Clinton S. Puckett
Dewey Robert Puckett
Ernest E. Puckett
James Daniel Puckett
Carl R. Puetz
Joseph Louis Puffer
James J. Pugel

Rudolf Pugel
Thomas Pugh
Clyde Pugh
David L. Pugh
Donald O. Pugh
Gaston Pugh
Henry Pugh, Jr.
Jack Pugh, Jr.
Joe L. Pugh
John Pugh
Kenneth A. Pugh
William Pugh
Joseph F. Pugliese
Vito R. Pugliese
Richard G. Puhl
Robert E. Puhl
George Stephen Puhr, Jr.
Joseph P. Pulak
John Vincent Puleo
Charles E. Pulido
Louis D. Pullano
Willard C. Pullen
Jack C. Pulley
Jessie E. Pulley
Thomas M. Pulley
Ben O. Pulliam
George E. Pulliam
John J. Pulliam
William Ellis II Pulliam
Odren R. Pullin
Glen Kenneth Pullins
Olaf P. Pulver
Thomas L. Pulver
Benny L. Pummell
Melvin J. Pumper
Edward J. Punch
Joseph J. Puopolo
Charles W. Purcell
Joseph S. Purcell
Loyd E. Purcell
William Penn Purcell
Charles Purdon, Jr.
Bobby Lee Purdy
Donald E. Purdy
Willis H. Purdy
Ervin H. Pure
Leandro L. Purganan
Michael A. Purgaric
Leonard V. Purkapile
Amos Purnell, Jr.
Jerome A. Purnell
Willie B. Purnell
John E. Purple, Jr.
Robert Pursifull
David E. Pursley
Joseph R. Pursley
Richard L. Pursley
Mariani Purugganan
John H. Purvey
Theodore A. Pushnig
Fred R. Putman
Linzy L. Putman
James Eugene Putnam
Eugene H. Putney
Elwood C. Putt
Raymond E. Puttin
Herbert Putzek
Gene A. Putzier
Walter Puzach
Richard E. Puzio
George H. V. Pyatt
Lowell H. Pyatt
James H. Pyke
James H. Pylate
Walter P. Pytak
Leon J. Pytel

— Q —

Donald Quackenbush
Edwin John Quade
Joseph Michael Quagley
William H. Quale
Curtis W. Qualls
David H. Quam
Joseph R. Quaresma
Charles D. Quarles
Charles H. Quasius
Robert D. Quatier
Louis G. Queary
Bobby L. Queen
Gilmer D. Queen
Ralph H. Queen
Ruff G. Queen
Winston R. Queen
Edward A. Queja
Joseph G. Quellette
Billy Quesenberry
John E. Quick

Chester Darwin Quider
Lawrence Laverne Quiel
John F. Quigg
James P. Quigley
Richard B. Quigley
James E. Quillen, Jr.
Marion A. Quillen
Robert H. Quillman
Jose A. Quinata
John Patrick Quinlan, Jr.
William Malcolm Quinley
Glenn F. Quinlivan
Charles D. Quinn
Charles P. Quinn
Claude J. Quinn
Donald Raymond Quinn
Jerome William Quinn
Lloyd Byron Quinn, Jr.
Thomas S. Quinn
William A. Quinn
William L. Quinn, Jr.
John M. Quinnan
Davila Ro Quinones
Natal Ant Quinones
Pedro A. Quinones
William H. Quint
Anastacio Quintana, Jr.
Charlie D. Quintana
Juan Quintana
Manuel M. Quintana
Mike J. Quintana
Albert E. Quintero
Augustin Quintero
Frederick Quinton
Marino Quirindongo
John A. Quiroz
Robert Quiroz
Santiago Quiroz
Bruno C. Quitilen
James L. Quong
Niels Iver Qvistgaard

— R —

Robert L. Rabb
Rains, TX
Rudolph Raber
Green Rabon, Jr.
Ronald Raboye
Wayne J. Rabun
Cleon Raburn
Frank P. Rachou
John Racich
Earnest E. Rackley
Irvin A. Rackley
Myron F. E. Radank
Stevan Radanovic
Harry J. Radanovich
James E. Radcliff
Charles Radcliffe
David V. Radcliffe
Dorrance Sielaff Radcliffe
Wayne S. Radebaugh
Marion W. Radecke
Philip T. Radecker
Kenneth C. Radeke
Eugene Rademacher
Edward R. Raden
Lazel Raden
Benjamin Neale Rader
Lester Doyle Rader
Lyle L. Rader
Charley L. Radford
Johnnie E. Radford
John J. Robert Radsewitz
Chester R. Radziszewski
George William Rae
Robert P. Raess
Gerald B. Raeymacker
James W. Rafferty
Lloyd I. Ragar
James C. Rager
Carl W. Ragin
John Ragland, Jr.
Leslie D. Ragland
Robert Wayne Ragland
Virgil F. Ragland
Erwin Doyle Raglin
Frank P. Ragone
John J. Ragucci
James V. Ragusa
Russell L. Rahn
Frank A. Raihl
Joseph W. Railey, Jr.
Thomas Earl Railling
William John Rainalter
Claude R. Rainer, Jr.
Sebastian Raineri
Alford B. Raines

Alton B. Rainey
Herbert Rainey
William J. Rainey
William L. Rainey
Sterling Raisbeck
Richard F. Rake
Harold P. Rakke
Kenneth S. Ralph
James Dorman Ralston
John H. Ramaekers
Marion A. Ramage
Robert Clayton Ramaker
James D. Ramel
George Henry Ramer
Homer F. Ramey
James N. Ramey
Lloyd C. Ramey
Alberto S. Ramirez
Alvaro Ramirez, Jr.
Antulio Ramirez
Arthur C. Ramirez
Ayala Jorg Ramirez
Carlos B. Ramirez
Emilio Antonio Ramirez
Epifanio C. Ramirez
Ernest E. Ramirez
Ezequiel H. Ramirez
Fidel Ramirez
Frank R. Ramirez
George A. Ramirez
Ignacio Ramirez
Jesus J. Ramirez
Jose M. Ramirez, Jr.
Jusino Ism Ramirez
Lopez Rami Ramirez
Lupe H. Ramirez
Pablo Ramirez
Reynaldo S. Ramirez
Santos Ramirez
Reinaldo Ramirez-Ramos
Ayala Andres Ramos
Cruz Luis M. Ramos
Daniel T. Ramos
Diaz Pedro Ramos
Echevarria P. Ramos
Fred M. Ramos
Isaiah Ramos
Israel Ramos
Jesse S. Ramos
Joseph D. L. C. Ramos
Juan Ramos
Lawrence Ramos
Martin M. Ramos
Ortiz Narcis Ramos
Pablo Ramos
Pablo Ramos
Rodriguez Jo Ramos
Roman Jesus Ramos
Torres Orlan Ramos
Francisco Ramos-Rivera
Dieter Rampendahl
Robert L. Ramsaur
Arlis W. Ramsay
Gerald C. Ramsay
Gilbert Howard Ramsdell
Howard W. Ramser, Jr.
Billy G. Ramsey
Donald E. Ramsey
Donald L. Ramsey
Irvanule Ramsey
James C. Ramsey
James N. Ramsey, Jr.
Lee R. Ramsey
Max D. Ramsey
Nolan R. Ramsey
Robert D. Ramsey, Jr.
Robert E. Ramsey
Robert James Ramsey
Sam Ramsey
Thomas Eugene Ramsey
Troy Odus Ramsey
Richard C. Ramsier
Dan Ranallo
Benjamin Rand
Robert C. Rand
Burton Wayne Randall
Charles H. Randall, Jr.
Daniel C. Randall
Earlan V. Randall
Elgin Vogala Randall
Fred Randall
Lester N. Randall
Rudolph M. Randall
Fred Randle
Evans Randolph, Jr.
George H. Randolph
John B. Randolph
Philip S. Randolph, Jr.
Raymond R. Randolph

William Henry Ranes
Algrit H. Raney
Donald D. Raney
William P. Raney
Richard C. Ranfranz
Samuel J. Rangatore
Eulalio N. Rangel
Frederick W. Ranger
Raymond L. Ranger
Paul J. Ranieri
Charles D. Rankin
David L. Rankin
Millage Rankin
Robert Rankin
Thomas D. Rankin
George C. Rankins
Henry Ransom, Jr.
Irwin G. Rapaport
John B. Rapee
Curtis C. Raper
Lindy John Raphiel
William George Rapien
Argul D. Rapier
Clinton D. Raplee
Luigi J. Rapone, Jr.
Raoul Raposa
Paul Milton Rapp
Jack W. Rapps
Milon E. Rardon
Robert T. Rarick
Rolan Dean Rarick
Warren Jackson Rarick
John J. Rascher
Albert Edward Rase, Jr.
Jay B. Rash
Wilburn H. Rash
Willie Rasha
Norman L. Rask
Donald E. Raske
Alfred J. Raskin
Allen Elmer Rasmussen
John E. Rasmussen
John N. Rasmussen
Kenneth Rasmussen
Ray L. Rasmussen
Roland A. Rasmussen
Robert Rasor
Robert John Raspanti
Walter J. Rassat
Joseph John Ratay
Griffith J. Iii Ratcliffe
Henry Brownell Rathbone
Ralph G. Rathburn
Harold G. Ratlieff
Harold Ratliff
Ishmeal Ratliff
Jerry H. Ratliff
Ora W. Ratliff
Leonard Ratter
Joseph C. Ratti
Harry Lester Rau
William L. Rau
Kaye Eugene Rauch
Robert M. Rauen
Ray R. Raught
Charles L. Rausch
Christopher Rausch
Eugene R. Rausch
Daniel J. Raven
Edward J. Raven, Jr.
Edward R. Ravenel, III
David L. Ravenell
Kenneth E. Ravitz
Frank Lee Rawlings
Patrick J. Rawlings
Robert E. Rawlins
Charles W. Rawls
Herbert L. Rawls, Jr.
Holman Calvin Rawls, Jr.
Chester Rawrynkiewicz
Albert Rawson
Alton G. Ray
Charles H. Ray
Dempsey E. Ray
Donald Vaughan Ray
Duaard Lee Ray
Durward Allen Ray
Earl R. Ray
Edward G. Ray
Floyd J. Ray
Gerald L. Ray
Harold C. Ray
Harold R. Ray
James Ray
James Edward Ray
Junior L. Ray
Lewis L. Ray
Loyd C. Ray
Napoleon Ray

Roy Ray, Jr.
William Albert Ray, Jr.
William Harriman Ray
Daniel J. Raybuck
Jerry J. Rayburn
Robert L. Rayburn
Le Roy J. Raye
Edward J. Rayles
Alphonse H. Raymond
Donald Roy Raymond
Ernest Raymond, Jr.
Gerald Westley Raymond
Gerard J. Raymond
Louis A. Raymond
Mahlon Lloyd Raymond
Nathaniel Raymond
Robert F. Raymond
Robert J. Raymond
Robert Lovejoy III Raymond
George Raymore
Ralph O. Raynes
Arthur Hayes Raynor
William Durwood Raynor
Fred M. Rea
Carl E. Reabe
Gordon John Read
Robert V. Read
William T. Read, Jr.
Donald L. Reade
Lavern Erenest Readle
Richard B. Ready
Billy E. Reagan
Billy J. Reagan
John Kevin Reagan
Joseph P. Reagan
Leland O. Reagan
Thomas W. Reagan
Walton R. Reagan
Robert Reager
John B. Reahl
Ernest J. Reale
Bruce A. Ream
John N. Ream, Jr.
Bruce L. Reames
Robert H. Reames
Graham L. Reams
Howard Reamsnyder
Michael J. Reardon
Chester F. Reas, Jr.
Herman Reasby
Harley N. Reasoner
Kyle Reasor
Robert C. Reasor
Charlie E. Reaves
David J. Reaves
James W. Reaves
Ralph Eugene Reaves
Lawrence Peter Rebagliati
Gary E. Rebbin
John J. Reber, Jr.
Charles Louis Rebeske
Ralph Elroy Rebman
Michael Gordon Rebo
Fritz J. Rebsom
William I. Rebuck
John W. Rector
Horn William Red
Mitchell Redcloud
Billy J. Redd
Donald R. Redd
Mark Redd
James V. Redden
Billy F. Reddick
Frank T. Reddick
Leroy H. Reddick
John R. Reddin
Frank M. Redding, Jr.
George H. Redding
Richard F. Redding
Chester W. Redford
Mark Franklin Redford, Jr.
Thomas J. Redgate
Philip August Redigonda
James B. Rediker
Adam Joseph Redmerski
Hugh Irwin Redmon
Eugene Daniel Redmond
Michael J. Redmond
Henry Richards Redner, Jr.
Robert Daniel Redner
Leon C. Redus
Charles L. Reece
James D. Reece
Amzie O. Reed
Archie L. Reed
Cecil Reed
Charles E. Reed
Charles E. Reed
Charles R. Reed

Clarence Reed
Elvie J. Reed
Francis Reed, Jr.
Franklin J. Reed
Freddy T. Reed
George E. Reed
Gerre N. Reed
Granville E. Reed
Harold Wilbert Reed
Harry R. Reed
Harry William Reed
Howard R. Reed
Hubert C. Reed
Joseph E. Reed
Junior E. Reed
Kenneth E. Reed
Laurence A. Reed
Lee Bright Reed
Loren Dee Reed
Melvin Reed
Myron H. Reed
Nathaniel Reed
Paul D. Reed
Paul R. Reed
Ples Reed, Jr.
Ralph Waldo Reed
Ray W. Reed
Raymond Cleo Reed
Richard E. Reed
Robert A. Reed
Robert Dugger Reed
Robert E. Reed
Ronald W. Reed
Samuel Reed
Sylvanus F. Reed
Thomas C. Reed
Thomas C. Reed
Thomas Edward Reed
Wayne W. Reed
William H. B. Reed
Howard R. Reeder
Jack N. Reeder
James A. Reeder
Martin L. Reeder
Stanley G. Reeder
Claude Edward Reedy
William A. Reedy
Robert Dale Reem
David Reese
Eugene S. Reese
Grady D. Reese
Jodie S. Reese
John E. Reese
John Reese, Jr.
Kenneth F. Reese
Lafayette M. Reese
Leon Reese
Richard Gene Reese
Richard T. Reese
William N. Reese, Jr.
Willie Reese
Donald William Reeser
Edwin B. Reeser
Jack B. Reesor
Harry J. Reeve
Charles M. Reeves
Clifford M. Reeves
Daryl D. Reeves
Ernest Julius Reeves, Jr.
George R. Reeves
Otto Reeves
Paul I. Reeves
Richard W. Reeves
Thiel M. Reeves
Herbert J. Reevis
Emerson L. Reffner
Melville Eugene Reffner
Humberto Regalado
Francis Aloysius Regan
John Lynn Regan
Robert W. Regan
Thomas J. Regan
Thomas J. Regan, Jr.
William Edward Regan, Jr.
Alton R. Register
Harvey L. Register
Joe A. Regmund
Ernest Regney, Jr.
Robert D. Regnier
John Robert Regulski
Harry Marshall Rehm
Robert J. Rehm
Robert M. Rehor
Clarence R. Reich
George Lee Reich
Kenneth W. Reich
James A. Reichard
Paul Richard Reiche
Norm Reichenberger

Edward L. Reick
Alexander Reid, Jr.
Alfred A. Reid
Alva Louis Reid, Jr.
Arones V. Reid
Edgar L. Reid
Elbert Josephus Reid, Jr.
Eugene A. Reid
Harold Reid, Jr.
Henry S. Reid
Hugh C. Reid
Lawrence A. Reid
Lloyd W. Reid
Lyle E. Reid
Norman L. Reid
Patrick C. Reid
Thomas A. Reid
Thomas E. Reid
Wallace Jordan Reid
James K. Reider
Quin P. Reidy
Raymond N. Reifers
Thomas Edward Reifsteck
Robert W. Reigle
John J. Reihner
Robert F. Reil
Thomas P. Reiley
Yale R. Reilich
Charles P. Reilly
Edmund Hubert Reilly
John P. Reilly
Thomas Francis Reilly, Jr.
Francis J. Reimer
Kenneth F. Reimer
Walter F. Reimer
Lee F. Reimert
Charles M. Rein
Warren M. Reinbold
Marcus G. Reinhard
John Reinhardt, Jr.
John P. Reinhardt
Vernon C. Reinhardt
William Reinhardt
Duane C. Reinhart
Noel F. Reinhart
John Charles Reinhold, Jr.
Elton W. Reinisch
Lawrence Louis Reinke
Harold Eugene Reins
Jack Walter Reinsmith
George Francis Reis
William W. Reiser
Morris Fredric Reisinger
Ralph W. Reisinger
Walter L. Reisinger
Francis R. Reiswitz
Edward J. Reiter
George Joseph Reitmeyer
Robert N. Reitmeyer
Donald Ray Reitsma
Harry W. Sr Reitze
George E. Relihan
Richard G. Relva
Herman L. Rembert
Clarence Remer
Raymond Edwin Remers
Joseph Warren Remine
Ray Remorin
Don Ray Remsnyder
Walter Remus, Jr.
Lloyd D. Renander
Manuel J. Rendon
Jerry H. Renew
Edward S. Reney
Jack Renfro, Jr.
Clarence E. Renfrow
Norman E. Renfrow
James M. Renne
Anthony W. Renneberg
Robert A. Renneman
James Edward Renner
Jose G. Renner
Thomas R. Renner
Meinhardt Rennich
Donald G. Renstrom
John Renteria
James D. Rentschler
Barney C. Rentz
Archie J. Reon
Charles A. Repkie
James O. Replogle
Junior W. Repp
Quentin L. Requa
Loyd A. Resch
Hugo E. Ress, Jr.
Arthur E. Ressor
Michael D. Restaino
Gerard L. Restel
Cruz Monserr Resto

Robert L. Retherford
Morris L. Rethmeier
William H. Rettinger
Leander J. Rettler
Roy Retzloff
Harlan R. Reuter
Wallace Ralph Reuter
John Franklin Revell
Dewey E. Rewis, Jr.
Robert H. Rexius
Willard J. Rey
De Jesus Elc Reyes
Falcon Adela Reyes
Guadalupe R. Reyes
Guillermo Reyes
Humberto L. Reyes
Ildefonzo Reyes
John T. Reyes
Juventino G. Reyes
Medina Anton Reyes
Rivera Luis Reyes
Ruiz Benigno Reyes
Velez Armand Reyes
William Reyes
Marcos Reyes-Rodriguez
Arnold V. Reyna
Heriberto Loya Reyna
Archie L. Reynolds
Arthur D. Reynolds
Arthur Ray Reynolds
Bernard C. Reynolds
Charles John Reynolds, Jr.
Edward R. Reynolds
Elwood D. Reynolds
Henry Reynolds
Herbert W. Reynolds
James C. Reynolds
James H. Reynolds
James T. Reynolds
John A. Reynolds, Jr.
Johnnie Reynolds
Lindberg Reynolds
Melvin E. Reynolds
Merle W. Reynolds
Paul Ray Reynolds
Philip Anthony Reynolds
Promus Fletcher Reynolds
Russell F. Reynolds
Stanley W. Reynolds
Theodore A. Reynolds
Van W. Reynolds
Virgil Lee Reynolds
William G. Reynolds
William H. Reynolds
William H. Reynolds
William L. Reynolds
William Roy Reynolds
Winferd L. Reynolds
Adolph C. Reynoso
Billy J. Rhea
Vernon Ray Rhine
Charles Walter Rhinehart
Charles Junior Rhoades
Eckard A. Rhoades
James F. Rhoades
George M. Rhoadman, Jr.
Edward W. Rhoads
Eugene D. Rhoads
John Kyler Rhoads
Robert E. Rhoads
Robert L. Rhoads
Vivan Wallace Rhoads
Eugene C. Rhode
Ralph Rhodehamel
Donis E. Rhoden
Alvin M. Rhodes
Billy J. Rhodes
Charles M. Rhodes
Clyde Rhodes, Jr.
Elden P. Rhodes
Harold L. Rhodes
Hugh Arnold Rhodes
James A. Rhodes
James D. Rhodes
James E. Rhodes
Jay Ruffus Rhodes
John R. Rhodes, Jr.
Johnnie B. Rhodes
Norman N. Rhodes
Paul Robins Rhodes
Roy D. Rhodes
Stanley Q. Rhodes
Victor H. Rhodes
William Douglas Rhodes
Clifton M. Rholetter
Eugene E. Rhyner
Bartolome S. Ribac
Larry D. Ribble
Salgado Carl Ribot

George S. Riccardo
Albert M. Ricci
Anthony A. Ricci
Daniel Ricci
Sirio A. Ricci
Carl D. Rice
Carlton J. Rice
Charles Irwin Rice, Jr.
Chester Rice
Clifton L. Rice
Curtis R. Rice
Curtis R. Rice
Donald Rice
Donald R. Rice
Edgar Dale Rice
Fred L. Rice
Harold E. Rice
Harold P. Rice
Herbert Rice, Jr.
Homer Rice
Howard Rice
James Rice
Jimmy M. Rice
John Andrew Rice
John R. Rice
Joseph Jerome Rice
Robert Edward Rice
Ronald Rice
Houston N. Rich
Richard Usher Rich
Ronald D. Rich
Teddy W. Rich
Theodore L. Rich
Earl J. Richard
Elmer Gene Richard
Elmer Powers Richard
Ernest B. Richard
Robert E. Richard
Roland R. Richard
Arthur D. Richards
Arthur L. Richards
Charles A. Richards
Clark M. Richards
Dewayne Fayette Richards
Donald R. Richards
Edward F. Richards
Flint B. Richards
George E. Richards
George I. Richards
Hunter J. Richards
Isiac E. Richards
Joice C. Richards
Joseph T. Richards
Kenneth S. Richards
Leonard Bertrem Richards
Leonard L. Richards
Louis J. Richards
Lowell E. Richards
Milford D. Richards
Ralph Leslie Richards
Sumner Eugene Richards
Alexand Richardson
Amos E. Richardson
Ardys Lee Richardson
Arthur Richardson
C. B. Richardson
Charles Richardson
Clark B. Richardson
David G. Richardson
Dean E. Richardson
Donald Richardson
Dwight Richardson
Earl R. Richardson
Edward Richardson
Eugene Richardson
Glen C. Richardson
Harold Richardson
Jack Richardson
Jake Rans Richardson, Jr.
James Albert Richardson
James F. Richardson
James H. Richardson
James N. Richardson
Joe Ballard Richardson
John W. Richardson
Leslie Richardson
Leslie K. Richardson, Jr.
Lester Richardson
Lue Donal Richardson
Marlin L. Richardson
Martin Richardson
Oneil B. Richardson
Orvil C. Richardson
Otha Richardson
Paul E. Richardson
Peter Bowen Richardson
Prater H. Richardson, Jr.
Robert Richardson
Robert Richardson

Rolland Richardson
Rufus S. Richardson
Walter Richardson
Wayne L. Richardson
Wilbert Richardson
William Richardson
Sammie J. Richburg
Jules A. Riche
Harlen E. Richerson
John Richetta
Aggie L. Richey
Leland Ralph Richey
Afton L. Richison
Charles R. Richmond
Clyde E. Richmond
Edward G. Richmond
Gordon F. Richmond
James R. Richmond
Robert E. Richmond
Alfred D. Richner
Leroy A. Richter
Johnnie D. Richters
N. L. Rickard
Ross R. Rickard
Clyde J. Rickards
Eugene T. Ricke
Glen Howard Rickelton
Adam L. Rickenbach
Harry A. Ricker
Cornelius L. Rickert
Ernest L. Rickert
Thomas L. Rickett
Clarence E. Rickl
Charles E. Ricklefs
Vincent R. Rickman
Kenneth J. Rickrode
Eugene H. Ricks
Frank Rico
Thomas John Ricotta
Frederick Riddagh
Dock L. Riddle
Hoyle Trentun Riddle
James A. Riddle
James W. Riddle
Richard A. Riddle
Charle Riddlebaugh
James R. Riddley
William G. Ridel
Hugh A. Ridenour, Jr.
Alexander David Rider
John H. Rider
Richard Glenn Rider
Billy J. Ridge
Kenneth L. Ridge
Junior V. Ridgeway
Robert E. Ridgeway
Floyd A. Ridgley, Jr.
Maurice D. Ridgway
Robert J. Ridings
Lawrence Riedmann
Edward R. Riedy
Oliver P. Riels
Dale R. Ries
Robert John Ries
Paul E. Riess
Edwin A. Rietz
John K. Riffle
Paul Bryant Riffle
Lionel W. Rigaud
Edward W. Rigdon
Meryl G. Riggenbach
Clifton R. Riggins
Earl L. Riggins, Jr.
George Riggins
Gene F. Riggle
Karl L. Riggle
Wayne E. Riggleman
Bobby L. Riggs
Bryan K. Riggs
Herschel M. Riggs
John F. Riggs
Ray L. Riggs
Roy T. Riggs
William Russel Riggs
Louie James Rightmire
Raymond J. Rightmyer, Jr.
George Le Tell Rights
Edward J. Rigley
John P. Rigney
Keith E. Rigney
Roger Bradley Rigney
Alvin S. Rigsby
Chester E. Rigsby
James D. Rigsby
Harold Edward Riker, Jr.
Oscar V. Rikke
George C. Riles
Alfred Riley
Charles David Riley

Charles L. Riley
Donald L. Riley
Francis A. Riley
George Riley
George P. Riley
Glen Alton Riley
Howard C. Riley
James Franklin Riley
James H.
John F. Riley
Joseph F. Riley
Kenneth V. Riley, Jr.
Lawrence T. Riley
Philip Irving Riley
Ray O. Riley
Reginald A. Riley
Reginald Alvin Riley
Robert William Riley
William F. Riley
Harold L. Rinard
Ernest L. Rinehart
Willard A. Rinehart
William Edgar Rinehart
Claude L. Riner, Jr.
Luther C. Riner
Raymond S. Rines
Charles A. Ring
Conyard L. Ring
Emmett Weaver Ring
Ralph E. Ring
Charles E. Ringer
Donald M. Ringer
Raymond F. Ringo
Howard Rinkes, Jr.
Kenneth M. Rinkes
Victor J. Rioli
Richard Riordan
Barbosa Willi Rios
Felix Rios
Florencio Rios
Jesse M. Rios
Leopoldo Rios
Morales Gaspa Rios
Ortiz Manuel Rios
Gordon N. Ripatranzone
Julian R. Ripley
Lawrence Thomas Ripley
Irving Rippen
James A. Rippin
Forrest Don Risch
Robert L. Risher
George A. Rising
Walter J. Risk
Stanley K. Risner
Alfred L. Rist
Vinel Rist, Jr.
Harst Rister
Robert W. Ritchey
Robert B. Ritchie
Leroy A. R. Ritenour
Herbert Edward Ritter
Jackie L. Ritter
Joel N. Ritter
John G. Ritter
Robert D. Ritter
Robert M. Ritter
Ronald Ritter
Stanley C. Ritter
Thomas W. Ritter
Wallace Ritter
George Rittereiser
Theodore E. Rittko
Jack Donald Ritz
Louis Rivardo
Jesus Rivas
John S. Rivas
Arnold David Rivedal
Andrew C. Rivera
Andy M. Rivera
Angel A. Rivera
Angel H. Rivera
Aruz Rafael Rivera
Benitez Ang Rivera
Cancel Hora Rivera
Carlos E. Rivera
Carrion Fra Rivera
Colon Jose Rivera
Crespo Isma Rivera
Fernando Rivera, Jr.
Floyd Rivera
Ildefonso A. Rivera
Jorge L. Rivera
Jose H. Rivera
Jose T. Rivera
Juan Rivera
Juan F. Rivera
Julio Rivera
Leocadio Rivera
Leoncio P. Rivera

Luis P. Rivera
Mercado Mig Rivera
Miguel Rivera
Oquendo Gui Rivera
Ortiz Adolf Rivera
Paul Rivera, Jr.
Pedro A. Rivera
Rivera Luis Rivera
Ruben Rivera
Serrano Eli Rivera
William P. Rivera
Juan Rivera-Carrillo
Roberto Rivera-Claudio
Gilberto Rivera-Cruz
Victor Miguel Rivera-Diaz
Israel Rivera-Galarza
Reyes Rivera-Gonzalez
Raul Rivera-Rodriguez
Roberto Rivera-Tapia
Armando F. Rivero
Darcy M. Rivers
Edwin Eugene Rivers
J. L. Rivers
James Joseph Rivers
John Ezekiel Rivers
Marion Rivers
Melvin C. Rivers
Norman O. Rivers
Richard E. Rivers
David A. Rives
Joel Orlander Rives
Robert H. Rivet
Frank Victor Riviello
Reginald F. Riviere
James C. Rix
Michael Rizdy
Joseph A. Rizzi
Edward J. Rizzo
Guido Rizzo
John Rizzo, Jr.
Leo Anthony Rizzuto
Bob M. Roach
Charles E. Roach
Eric Roach
Glenn V. Roach
James Jerome Roach
Jorge F. Roach
Wendell E. Roach
Harold S. Roadenizer
Clifford E. Roalf
Carroll Roane
George R. Roark
Gerald Hugh Roark
Harold E. Roark
Michael Robanke
Norman Joseph Robare
Donald Earl Robarge
Paul N. Robarge
John B. Robart
James S. Robason
Charles E. Robb
Charles L. Robb
Floyd J. Robb
Thomas M. Robb
Albert R. Robbins
Charles F. Robbins
Edward B. Robbins
Fenton B. Robbins
Gerald T. Robbins
Leonard C. Robbins
Ray N. Robbins
Robert Ford Robbins
Wayne Robbins
William B. Robbins
Eugene A. Robenolt
George J. Robenson
Donald A. Roberge
Robert J. Roberge
Allen M. Roberson
Edward L. Roberson
Eugene Roberson
Harry P. Roberson
Jack Alexander Roberson
John H. Roberson
Lloyd E. Roberson
Teddy E. Roberson
Wayne Roberson
Will Roberson, Jr.
Willie J. Roberson
Frank Joseph Roberta
Joseph M. Roberti
Albert S. Roberts
Arlys I. Roberts
Aubrie Roberts
Carl W. Roberts
Charles C. Roberts
Clarence C. Roberts
Clayton L. Roberts
Clayton Leroy Roberts

Curtis E. Roberts
Donald R. Roberts
Earl E. Roberts
Edmund C. Roberts
Ernest R. Roberts
Eugene I. Roberts
Everett R. Roberts
Finis W. Roberts
Freddie J. Roberts
George B. Roberts
George E. Roberts
Gerald R. Roberts
Gordon A. Roberts
Gordon G. Roberts
Henry D. Roberts
Hobson J. Roberts
Howard M. Roberts
Hudson Roberts, Jr.
Ivan Roberts
Jack Roberts
James B. Roberts
James Joseph Roberts
James Richard Roberts
Jeff Roberts, Jr.
John Edward Roberts
John Luverne Roberts
John W. Roberts
Joseph A. Roberts
Kenneth J. Roberts
Kenneth N. Roberts
Leonard W. Roberts
Marion O. Roberts
Martin Robert Roberts
Omer Roberts, Jr.
Pinkney Roberts, Jr.
Ralph Edward Roberts
Randall C. Roberts
Rayger G. Roberts
Raymond L. Roberts
Robert E. Roberts
Robert I. Roberts
Robert L. Roberts
Robert S. Roberts
Roy L. Roberts
Russell H. Roberts
Stephen G. Roberts
Willard F. Roberts, Jr.
William J. Roberts
William M. Roberts
William M. Roberts
Allan R. Robertson
Charles Robertson
Clonnie Robertson
Corbett B. Robertson
Dewey E. Robertson, Jr.
Donald L. Robertson
Earnest R. Robertson
Edward Robertson
Ernest C. Robertson
Herbert Robertson
Howard L. Robertson
James L. Robertson
James P. Robertson
James R. Robertson
John A. Robertson
Joseph K. Robertson
Paul E. Robertson
Samuel A. Robertson
Thomas R. Robertson
Vernon W. Robertson
William Robertson
William Lewis Robertson
John J. Robichaud
Lawrence J. Robidoux
Wilfred C. Robidoux
Joseph A. Robillard, Jr.
Eugene R. Robinette
Frank O. Robinette
Robert F. Robinette
Gordon L. Robins
Alfred Gene Robinson
Alvin Robinson
Barnette Robinson
Billy J. Robinson
Calvin T. Robinson
Charles S. Robinson
Donald W. Robinson
Eddie Robinson
Edward Robinson, Jr.
Ernest Robinson
Frank Robinson
George Robinson
George A. Robinson
George N. Robinson
Gerald G. Robinson
Glen A. Robinson
Gordon P. Robinson
Homer Robinson, Jr.
James Robinson

James B. Robinson
James E. Robinson
James H. Robinson
James N. Robinson
James W. Robinson
Jasper Robinson
Jimmie Robinson
Joe Robinson
Joe M. Robinson
John Robinson, Jr.
John W. Robinson
Joseph C. Robinson
Joseph W. Robinson
Kenneth C. Robinson
Leland S. Robinson
Leon Robinson
Louis Robinson
Marvin L. Robinson
Max D. Robinson
Max E. Robinson
Ralph G. Robinson
Rex Franklin Robinson
Robert E. Robinson, Jr.
Robert H. Robinson
Robert R. Robinson
Robert W. Robinson
Robert W. Robinson
Robert Winfred Robinson
Roy Robinson
Samuel F. Robinson
Stanley E. Robinson
Walter G. Robinson
Walter R. Robinson
Wilbur J. Robinson
Wilda E. Robinson
William Robinson
William A. Robinson
William J. Robinson
William L. Robinson
Bert D. Robirds
Leland W. Robison
Malcolm A. Robison
Paul L. Robison
Richard Lloyd Robison
Robert L. Robison
Robert W. Robison
Ramon Cordero Robledo
Carlos L. Robles
Dejesus Ism Robles
Frank P. Robles
Robert Earl Robling
John Robnett
Burt A. Robson
Donald G. Robson
Raymond C. Robson
Donnie F. Roby
Frank C. Rocha
Lawrence M. Rocha
Roberto Delgado Rocha
Harold A. Rochan
Jose Diego Roche-Torres
Robert H. Rocheford
James C. Rochelle
Duane F. Rochester
Hubert Rochester
Francis J. Rochon
Arthur H. Rock
Edward Joseph Rock
Jasper Rock, Jr.
Robert Rockenbauch
Harry W. Rocklage, Jr.
Clyde T. Rockwell
Jackie H. Rockwell
Richard Roclawski
Paul E. Rocus
Jack W. Rodarme
Manuel R. Rodarte
David Leo Rodden
Arthur D. Roddy
Hugh J. Roddy
Hoye L. Rodeheaver
Billie J. Rodeischak
Vernon F. Rodel
Ralph A. Rodemer
Tracy N. Roden
Earl Francis Roderick
Bernard Joseph Rodger
Billy V. Rodgers
Charles E. Rodgers
Franklin E. Rodgers
Gary Lincoln Rodgers
George W. Rodgers
James T. Rodgers
Jerome H. Rodgers
Lawrence C. Rodgers
Leonard T. Rodgers
Robert R. Rodgers
Robert S. Rodgers
Samuel J. Rodkey

Marvin L. Rodman
Robert J. Rodman
Daryl Erwin Rodney
Theodore E. Rodney
Calvin L. Rodrigue
Edward Rodrigues
Abelardo Rodriguez
Adam B. Rodriguez
Alejandr Rodriguez
Alfonso Rodriguez
Alfredo Rodriguez
Alicea N. Rodriguez
Anthony Nick Rodriguez
Arthur Rodriguez
Battisti Rodriguez
Bermudez Rodriguez
Bonifaci Rodriguez
Borrero Rodriguez
Clifford Rodriguez
Del Toro Rodriguez
Diego L. Rodriguez
Earl G. Rodriguez
Elpidio Rodriguez, Jr.
Emillio C. Rodriguez
Enrique Rodriguez
Enrique Rodriguez
Felipe Rodriguez
Gregorio Rodriguez
Henry Rodriguez
John Rodriguez
Jose M. Rodriguez
Jose Rios Rodriguez
Joseph R. Rodriguez
Julio R. Rodriguez
Leonardo Rodriguez
Lopez An Rodriguez
Lopez Fl Rodriguez
Lopez Ra Rodriguez
Lupe R. Rodriguez
Mario J. Rodriguez
Martin Rodriguez
Martinez Rodriguez
Matilde Rodriguez
Montanez Rodriguez
Narciso Rodriguez
Negron J. Rodriguez
Omar L. Rodriguez
Oquendo Rodriguez
Otero Al Rodriguez
Pedro Rodriguez
Pedro A. Rodriguez
Perez Ju Rodriguez
Rivera R. Rodriguez
Robert D. Rodriguez
Roberto Rodriguez
Roddy E. Rodriguez
Rodrigue Rodriguez
Rolando Rodriguez
Ruben Rodriguez
Ruben Cuellar Rodriguez
Santiago Rodriguez
Santiago Rodriguez
Theodore F. Rodriguez
Tony Phillip Rodriguez
Vargas J. Rodriguez
Samuel Rodriguez-Lopez
Alberto Rodriguez-Lozada
Roberto Rodriques
Hector R. Rodriquez
Samuel Rodriquez
Donald E. Rodstrom
James B. Rodway
Emory L. Roe
Ross Edward Roe
Roy E. Roe
Stephen K. Roe
Eddie L. Roebuck
Leon Roebuck
Chris L. Roed
Emanuel George Roehm
George E. Roehrich
Richard L. Roemer
Eugene Harold Roering
Norman E. Roesberry
Herman W. Roesch
Paul Roese
Richard L. Roeske
John Jennings Roessel
Alexander Roessler
David S. Roessler
Robert M. Roessler
Ernest Roessner
Adolphus W. Roffe
Albert Jerome Rogalla
Costanzo Rogato
Arthur H. Rogers
Benny D. Rogers
Carl R. Rogers
Charles F. Rogers

Charles L. Rogers
Cleveland Green Rogers
Clinton R. Rogers
Clyde N. Rogers
Daniel B. Rogers, Jr.
Daniel Frances Rogers
Donald C. Rogers
Donald W. Rogers
Eugene Rogers
Eugene Jerome Rogers
Floyd A. T. Rogers
Frank Joseph Rogers
Frederick G. Rogers
George S. Rogers
Gerald E. Rogers
Glenn R. Rogers
Harold F. Rogers
Harry L. Rogers
Harvey W. Rogers
James D. Rogers
James E. Rogers, Jr.
Jone Rogers
Joseph Lee Rogers
Kenneth E. Rogers
Kenneth G. Rogers
Lloyd G. Rogers
Paul Howard Rogers
Ralph D. Rogers
Randolph R. Rogers
Raymond C. Rogers
Raymond Rogers, Jr.
Richard M. Rogers
Robert James Rogers
Robert L. Rogers, Jr.
Rube Rogers
Sylvester Rogers
Theodore A. Rogers
Tommie E. Rogers
Vincent Frank Rogers
Warren Winfield Rogers
William H. Rogers
William J. Rogers
Willie L. Rogers
Wyllis P. Rogers
Thomas G. Rogerson
Walter W. Roggow
Joseph R. Roginskie
Ray A. Rognas
Theodore Rogosky
Louis J. Rohanna
Paul Leander Rohr
William Rohr
Kenneth Rohrbacher
Lawrence Rohrback
Jim L. Rohrbaugh
Gaylen Floyd Rohwer
Nils M. Rojas
Raymond A. Rojas
Rivera Cloti Rojas
Juan Rojas-Reyes
John Edward Roland
Alex Rolek
Harold J. Rolfe, Jr.
George Roller
Johnson T. Rolles
Henry L. Rolling
Charles W. Rollins
Claud Rollins
Falle T. Rollins
Grady L. Rollins
Laurence E. Rollins
Samuel S. Rollins
William Rollins
Donald E. Rolls
Hernandez Ju Rolon
Juan A. Rolon
Brull Carlos Roman
Edward J. Roman
Ernesto T. Roman
Frank M. Roman
Joseph Roman
Joseph J. Roman
Louis Henry Roman
Marrero Pabl Roman
Morales Ange Roman
Paul A. Roman
Raphael Roman
Reichard D. Roman
Richard Romanchik
Frank P. Romandetti
John V. Romanek
Michael Romanelli
Stephen J. Romanick
Aime Romano
Francis M. Romano
Philip S. Romano
Raymond J. Romano
Earnest I. Romans
Richard J. Romanus

Daniel F. Romeo
James Joseph Romeo
Peter R. Romeo
Reginald E. Romeo
Vincenzo D. Romeo
Adam M. Romero
Antonio Romero
Aristeo Romero
Cales Celio Romero
Charles B. Romero
Charles Patrick Romero
Eddie J. Romero
Gilbert J. Romero
Humberto Romero
Joe C. Romero
Jose L. Romero
Manuel J. Romero
Manuel Torrio Romero
Martin Z. Romero
Miguel A. Romero
Nelson R. Romero
Rosendo G. Romero
John D. Romine
Luther V. Rominger
Carmen A. Romito
Angel Peter Romo
Arturo Romo
Cristobal Romo
Fernando V. Romo
Jose Romo
Kenneth Rompalski
Clarence M. Ronan
Harold J. Ronan
Richard Ronczkowski
James John Rone
William Bryan Rone
Otto L. Roneker, Jr.
Nils O. Ronnquist
Robert V. Rood
Roy Franklin Rooffener
Ernest E. Rooker
Daniel Francis Rooks
John H. Rooks
Robert L. Rooks
Robert Rooksberry
James Vincent Rooney
Robert Frederick Rooney
Robert J. Rooney
Donald H. Roop
George F. Roos
Henry Olaf Roos
Jerry Mikesell Roos
Richard E. Roosa
Franklin Roosevelt
Howard L. Root
Jack F. Root
Leo R. Root
Voorhees S. Root, Jr.
Billy J. Roper
Chester J. Roper
Earl G. Roper
Hillard Marshall Roper
Leon Jose J. Roque
Ramon Roque-Pena
William L. Roques
Talvin J. Roraus
James E. Rorie
Frank D. Rorrer
George H. Rosa
Hector P. Rosa
Juan A. Rosa
Santiago Rosa
Guillermo Rosa-Rivera
Rosado Pedr Rosado
Jose V. Rosado-Bravo
Adolfo G. Rosales
Frank L. Rosales
James C. Rosamond
James R. Rosamond
De Jesus A. Rosario
Eliu Rosario
Melendez F. Rosario
Morales Ju Rosario
Santos Hum Rosario
Domingo R. Rosas
Frank R. Rosas
Muniz Emilio Rosas
Anthony Rosati
Raymond J. Rosbeck
Edward D. Roscoe
Albert Eugene Rose
Arthur J. Rose
Damon L. Rose
Darrow A. Rose
Douglas W. Rose
Edward M. Rose
Edward E. Rose
Fred Rose, Jr.
Gene Stuart Rose

Gilbert G. Rose, Jr.
Glenn A. Rose
Harvey L. Rose
Herman Rose
James S. Rose
Leonard E. Rose
Nokomis J. Rose
Paul E. Rose
Robert Allen Rose
Sydney C. Rose
William Rose
William Wilber Rose
Wiley D. Roseberry
George F. Rosecrants
Norman Rosecrants
William H. Roseler
Hershel H. Rosell, Jr.
Gloyd Elwood Rosen, Jr.
Michael Rosen
Karl R. Rosenbach
Sol Rosenberg
Warren S. Rosenberger
Herman Rosenblatt
Norman Meyer Rosenblatt
Harvey Rosenblum
Valdean Rosenboom
Sam Rosenfeld
Dick Rosengrant
Alfred M. Rosenthal
Alvin Stanford Rosenthal
Fred D. Rosenthal
George A. Rosenthal
Jerome C. Rosenthal
Richard Blaine Rosenvall
Floyd R. Rosette
Victor J. Rosetto
Donald L. Rosevink
William E. Roshia
Robert W. Roshon
Melvin G. Roskelley
Edward E. Roslof
Andrew C. Ross
Arden D. Ross
Arthur Lee Ross
Arthur Sr Ross
Bernard Herman Ross
Calvin L. Ross
Carol B. Ross
Charles D. Ross
Charley C. Ross
Delmer W. Ross
Donald Ray Ross
Edward F. Ross
Forrest S. Ross, Jr.
Guy Ross, Jr.
Haldean Ross
Harold E. Ross
Harold Leslie Ross
Harrison S. Ross
James Ross
John E. Ross
John H. Ross
Joseph B. Ross
Kenneth W. Ross
Mcelree A. Ross
Paul Clement Ross
Raymond E. Ross
Raymond T. Ross
Richard C. Ross
Richard Chaney Ross
Richard Ross, Jr.
Robert A. Ross
Robert Earl Ross
Robert Lewis Ross
Tenney K. Ross
Thomas Ross
Tommy Eugene Ross
Ulysses Ross
Walter A. Ross, Jr.
William M. Ross
Joseph N. Rossano
Dewey Rossel
Richard Dale Rosser
William T. Rosser
Andrew Rossetti, Jr.
Armand G. Rossi
Normand S. Rossignal
Kenneth A. Rossin
Gerald V. Rossiter
Walte Rosteutscher
Dominick B. Rostine
James A. Rostollan
Marvin H. Roswell
Joseph W. Roszak
Robert L. Roszek
John E. Rotarius
Teddy E. Roten
Claren Rotenberger
Bernard F. Roth

Joseph H. Roth
Oscar F. Roth
Richard Roth
Robert E. Roth
George J. Rothenberger
Charles R. Rother
Robert Lee Rother
Donald K. Rothermel
Donald G. Rothlauf
Thomas E. Rotramel
James F. Roudebush
Arthur L. Rought
Ernest R. Rouleau
Terrell Ray Roulston
John Henry Roumiguiere
James A. Round
Edward P. Rounds
Jimy R. Roundtree
Willie Roundtree
Allen Lon Rountree
Fred Brinson Rountree
Charles W. Rouse
David C. Rouse
Delbert G. Rouse
John D. Rouse
Roy E. Rouse
Ulysee Rouse
Robert L. Roush
Richard B. Roussel
Joseph R. Roussin
Edward U. Routh
Howard D. Routt
Salvador J. Rovello
Harold J. Rovira, Jr.
Joseph T. Rowan
Walter D. Rowatt
Thomas W. Rowden, Jr.
Donald Eugene Rowe
Edward Earl Rowe
Elmer A. Rowe
James R. Rowe
Johnny Rowe
Lewis H. Rowe
Morrilton C. Rowe
Othel H. Rowe
Phillip L. Rowe
Richard Carl Rowe
Rodney R. Rowe
Viles C. Rowe
William E. Rowe
William F. Rowe
Willie Rowe
Harold M. Rowell
James E. Rowell
Carl W. Rowland
Ernest J. Rowland
Eugene Edward Rowland
Jimmy Rowland
Milford N. Rowland
Raymond F. Rowland
William T. Rowland
Louis Rowlette
David A. Rowley
Don E. Rowley
Harold C. Rowley
Waynord W. Rowley
Arvis F. Roy
Charles Anthony Roy
Elliott Roy
Floyd Alexander Roy
Francis Roy
Hayward J. Roy
Leonard Edmond Roy
Murphy Roy
Paul J. Roy
Robert S. Roy
William Edward Roy
William F. Roy
Leff V. Royal
Marvin Royal
Solomon R. Royal
Willie Royal
Eugene E. Roybal
Hinton C. Royce
Ernest R. Roye
Bill D. Royer
Charles B. Royer
Ted Grover Royer
Robert D. Royster
Casmere J. Rozanski
John M. Rozear, Jr.
Francis Anton Rozeski
Richard B. Roznowski
Raymond E. Rozyka
Oscar Rubart, Jr.
Charles D. Rubel
Leopoldo Rubert
Donald J. Rubideaux
Arroyo Luis Rubio

Benjamin Rubio
Juan Charles Rubio, Jr.
James C. Ruble
Thomas E. Ruble
Charles A. Rublee
Daniel Gregory Ruby, Jr.
Gene Robert Ruby
George E. Ruchty
Robert G. Rucinski
Hurley B. Rucker
John Dooley Rucker
Oscar R. Rucker
Otis G. Rucker, Jr.
Emil John Rucki
Fred Otto Rudat
Adler Earl Ruddell
James C. Ruddell, Jr.
Francis J. Rudden
William F. Rudder
Jack E. Ruddick
Bobby J. Ruddle
Thomas E. Ruddock
Robert F. Ruder
Frederick A. Rudge
Allan Keith Rudolph
Delmar W. Ruediger
William H. Rueger
John F. Rufener
Walter E. Ruff
Joseph Ruffule
Roy L. Rufus
Herbert E. Rugar
Ciro J. Ruggero
Allen Ward Ruggles
Harold T. Ruggles
Vern O. Rugh
Earl Oswald Ruhlin
William Francis Ruhlman
Duane Nelson Ruid
Donald E. Ruiter
Albert A. Ruiu
Armando Ruiz
De Porras Sar Ruiz
Eugene Louis Ruiz
John G. Ruiz
Jose P. Ruiz
Leopoldo L. Ruiz
Norberto Ruiz
Victor M. Ruiz
Ronald P. Ruka
Joseph T. Rule
Lawrence G. Rule
Willard A. Rule
Lester R. Rulik
Louis H. Rulon
Carlton M. Rumley
John E. Rummel
Jerome Alexander Runcie
Clarence C. Rundle
Glenn W. Runge
Cecil A. Runk
Frank J. Runnels, Jr.
Leroy J. Runner
Freeman C. Runnett
Edward J. Runt, Jr.
Robert W. Rupe
Waldemar Frederick Rupp
Richard M. Ruppenthal
Dennis R. Rush
Eugene Francis Rush
John Earl Rush
Malcolm L. Rush
Marion A. Rush
Billy O. Rushing
Charles V. Rushing
Harry Eugene Rushing
Larry W. Rushing
Donald J. Rushmore
Alvin J. Rushton
James B. Rushton
Richard George Lero Rusk
James Ruska
Earl Russ
George D. Russ
John Mathew Russ
Norman P. Russ
Robert C. Russ
Leo P. Russavage
Clifford Vernon Russel
David Eugene Russel
Eugene Robert Russel
Herman Russel
Jasper Virgil Russel, Jr.
Louis Edward Russel
Michel Baines Russel
Tom Franklin Russel
Beverly E. Russell
Charles A. Russell
Charles P. Russell

Earl Russell
Emmitt Russell
Ernest F. Russell
Eugene E. Russell
Frank S. Russell
Gordon C. Russell
Herman M. Russell
Hoyt O. Russell
Jack P. Russell
James P. Russell
John H. Russell
John T. Russell
John W. Russell
Leonard E. Russell
Michel B. Russell
Robert G. Russell
Robert John Russell
Robert McFadden Russell
Thomas Richard Russell
Walter R. Russell
William Robert Russell
Fred Russenberger
Henry W. Russey
Ramos Jose O. Russi
Anthony Louis Russo
John Francis Russo
Joseph F. Russo
Rocco Russo
Vincent J. Russo
Charles Vernon Rust
Dennis A. Rust
Donald W. Rust
Helmar O. Rusth
John R. Ruth
Louis S. Ruth
Johnie B. Rutheford
Alvin N. Rutherford
Daniel Rutherford
Hillard Rutherford
Kenneth Rutherford
Carroll O. Ruthstrom
Salvato Rutigliano
Albert J. Rutkowski
Anthony Rutkowski
Elvin A. Rutland
Charles J. Rutledge
Fostine R. Rutledge
James Rutledge
Wade E. Rutledge
Walter Kenneth Rutledge
William K. Rutledge
Willie M. Rutledge
Jessie W. Rutliff
Robert L. Rutt
Claude E. Rutter
Luther E. Rutter
Luther Lee Rutter, Jr.
Wayne C. Ruud
Lawrence V. Ruvolo
Frank Ruzon
Edwin C. Ryals
Arthur A. Ryan
Clifford L. Ryan
Darrell E. Ryan
Howard Ryan
James Ryan
Jim J. Ryan
John J. Ryan
John O. Ryan
Lawrence J. Ryan, Jr.
Leeroy R. Ryan
Richard Allan Ryan
Robert A. Ryan
Robert W. Ryan
Thomas F. Ryan
Thomas Joseph Ryan
Thomas K. Ryan
Travis L. Ryan
Vincent M. Ryan, Jr.
William H. Ryan
William J. Ryan
Donald C. Rybiski
Jule C. Rybolt
Phillip W. Rydberg
Daniel F. Ryder
Roy Gilbert Rydin
James Davis Rye
John P. Ryhter
Loren Rylance
William Harvey Ryman
Thomas J. Ryncavage
Richard W. Rysavy
Frank C. Rysiawa
Paul T. Rzeczowski
Raymond A. Rzepecki

— S —

Martin A. Saar

Ignacio A. Saavedra
Agapito Sabando
Kerry C. Sabanty
Fortunato A. Sabatino
Michael E. Sabel
Guisseppe Sabella
Bernard J. Sabin
Robert C. Sabine
Elmer J. Sabino
Jerry Sabino
Jose P. Sablan
John Sablyar
Emery J. Sabo
James Sabo, Jr.
George A. Sabourin
Albert V. Sacca
Pascal Sacco
Joseph D. Saccullo
Howard S. Sachs
Glenn Sachteleben
George Bishop Sacson
Richard E. Sad
Eugene Saddler
Eugene J. Sadek
William R. Sadewasser
Leon R. Sadler
Joseph J. Sady
Ralph V. Saenz
Joseph H. Safford
Fausto Sagadraca
Rolf John Sagdahl
Samuel Stanley Sage
Robert F. Sager
Elpidio M. Sagisi
Joseph J. Sahtila
Clarence C. Sain
Masaya Saito
Tsugio Saito
Allen T. Sakamoto
James N. Sakamoto
Hans P. Saks, Jr.
Doss L. Saladin
Carlos Luis Salaices
Arroyo Hec Salaman
Gregorio B. Salas
Carlos R. Salazar
Donaciano Salazar
Estevan Salazar
Eugene Martinez Salazar
Frank Ralph Salazar
Joe Salazar, Jr.
John Manuel Salazar
Richard Salazar
Sastines Salazar
John J. Salazer
Enrique A. Salcido
Robert Salcido
Juan Saldana
Roberto Saldana
Chester J. Salecki
Anthony Ray Salena
Aivars K. Salenieks
John W. Salerno
Joseph Salerno, Jr.
Frank Salgado, Jr.
Angel Salgado-Torres
Alejandro Enrique Salinas
James Salisbury
Owen E. Salisbury
John Stanley Saliski
Floyd B. Sallee
Raymond Sallee
Booker T. Salley
Donald W. Salmon
Jack R. Salmon
Richard Salomon
Joseph S. Salony
Aldin B. Saloway
David W. Salsbery
Alfred L. Salter
Earl C. Saltz
Ralph J. Salvati
Richard Salvatore
Robert J. Salvie
Billy J. Salyer
Scott W. Salyer
John D. Salzbrenner
Floyd Wheeler Salze
Joseph S. Samayoa
Paul Sambol, Jr.
Stanley J. Samczyk
Ambers B. Sammons
Randall G. Sammons
Van B. Sammons
Jack Clinton Samms
Stanley Samolinski
Jose M. Samora
Harold N. Sample
William B. Sample

Albert Randolph Sampson
George L. Sampson
James Edward Sampson
James W. Sampson
Orie D. W. Sampson, Jr.
Richard Sampson
Rudolph Sampson
Frank J. Samsa
Denzil Gene Samsel
Jessie A. Samson
John S. Samson
George Samuel, Jr.
Wickcliff J. Samuel
Antoine T. Samuels
Columbus Samuels
Santo San Kitts
Pedro San Miguel
Angel S. Sanabria
Enrique Sanabria
Donald D. Sanborn
James E. Sanborn
John L. Sanborn
Linwood B. Sanborn
Charles Sanchez
Colon Virg Sanchez
Gilberto L. Sanchez
Gregorio G. Sanchez
Herrera Ar Sanchez
James R. Sanchez
Jesse B. Sanchez
Jorge Sanchez
Jose Sanchez
Jose J. Sanchez, Jr.
Kenneth L. Sanchez
Leo Carlos Sanchez
Richard Sanchez
Robert M. Sanchez
Rodriguez Sanchez
Rodriguez Sanchez
William Sanchez
William Sanchez
William Q. Sanchez
Rafael Sanchez-Lopez
Juan Sanchez-Mendez
Pablo Sanchez-Torres
Victor M. Sanchez-Villegas
Elmer H. Sand
Hans R. Sand
James F. Sand
James B. Sandefur
Mathew George Sand
George W. Sanderbeck
Bobby M. Sanders
Charles O. Sanders
Donald C. Sanders
Earl C. Sanders
Earl Jackson Sanders, Jr.
Earl Sanders, Jr.
Eddie Sanders
Frederick Sanders
Gene A. Sanders
Gerald E. Sanders
Harry William Sanders
J. D. Sanders
Jack D. Sanders
James Sanders
James B. Sanders
James S. Sanders
James R. Sanders, Jr.
John P. Sanders
John W. Sanders
John W. Sanders
Joseph M. Sanders
Leonard C. Sanders
Mcdonald Sanders
Ozell Sanders
Richard G. Sanders
Sidney Maurice Sanders
Tony M. Sanders
Wade C. Sanders
Weldon Sanders
William L. Sanders
Francis Sanderson
Gerald R. Sanderson
Lewis O. Sanderson
Robert J. Sanderson
Alfred T. Sandford
Floyd A. Sandlin
Harry Till Sandlin
James E. Sandlin
Albino Sandobal
Alberto Sandoval
Antonio Sandoval
Frank Luna Sandoval
Isaac Sandoval
Joe Z. Sandoval
Leopold Sandoval
Paul Leo Sandoval
Phil Sandoval

Philip G. Sandoval
Robert Sandretzky
Calvin G. Sandrock, Jr.
Charles Clark Sands
Ralph E. Sands
William T. Sands
Nestor C. Sandstrom
Roy Sandvik
Anthony G. Sandwell
Barnie L. Sanford
Charles D. Sanford
De Alton H. J. Sanford
Isadore Sanford
Royal W. Sanford
William H. Sanford
Donald A. Sangsland
Caswell L. Sangster, Jr.
William C. Sankey, Jr.
Joseph Daniel Sanko
Joseph J. Sansalone
Domenci J. Santa-Maria
Rudy J. Santacruz
Concepcion Santana
Luis F. Santana
Martinez L. Santana
Martinez M. Santana
Joseph Santarsiero
Anthony C. Santella
Ernest S. Santesse
Frank Santi
Alvarado Santiago
Angel Santiago
Angel L. Santiago
Aponte Do Santiago
Bonilla E. Santiago
Crespo Fa Santiago
Gilbert Santiago
Juan Santiago
Luis Santiago
Navarro F. Santiago
Ruiz Carm Santiago
Jose E. Santiago-Ortiz
Ramon Santiago-Rosario
Andrew Santibanez
Joseph F. Santillo
Herman Santistevan
Richard Santistvan
Louis Santopietro
Edward F. Santora
George J. Santore
Cruz Doming Santos
Cruz Jesus Santos
Davila Mari Santos
Delmo Santos
Jimenez Ern Santos
Joaquin S. Santos
Manuel Santos
Rivera Manu Santos
Rosa Gualbe Santos
Salgado Iso Santos
Santiago Ag Santos
Norberto Santos-Rivera
Nicolas Santos-Rosario
Robert D. Sanzi
James S. Sapack
Elroy R. Sapia
Charles R. Sapp
Clifford N. Sapp
Philip Sarabia
Michael J. Saraco
Albin P. Sarafin
Steve Sarapa, Jr.
Manuel Sarate
Arnold L. Sardeson
Harold J. Sargeant
Arthur S. Sargent
Claud C. Sargent, Jr.
Earl Sargent
Harry L. Sargent, Jr.
David Sarine
Melvin Edwin Sarkilanti
Felipe Sarmiento
Achille Carl Sarno, Jr.
John E. Sarno
Mike Saroian
Richard H. Sarpola
Henry B. Sarrail
Elliott Bland Sartain, Jr.
Robert W. Sarver
Minoru Sasaki
Takeshi Sasaki
Leoris Sasser
Ralph Sasser
Pietro Satalino
Robert M. Satchell
Thomas J. Satchell
Neil M. Sather
Shoji Sato
Gonzalo Sator

Leo C. Satter
Glenn Satterfield
Paul Veston Satterfield
Roger Satterfield
William Monroe Satterfield
Freeman D. Satterlee
Lee Saucier
Charles F. Sauer
Jon E. Sauer
Warren E. Sauer
Clarence Sauerbrei
Leo R. Saul
Jack Saum
Andrew A. Saunders
Edward Saunders
Frederick A. Saunders
Harry J. Saunders
Harry L. Saunders
Jack J. Saunders
James B. J. Saunders
James M. Saunders
John E. Saunders
John H. Saunders
Louis A. Saunders
Norbert B. Saunders
Richard A. Saunders
Theodore Saunders
Joseph E. Sauve
James Aloysius Savage
James T. Savage
Merle L. Z. Savage
Leo Paul T. Savard
Joseph V. Savarese
Paul Lloyd Savery
Dwight E. Saville
John Peter Savitski, Jr.
Edward J. Savko
Harold Joseph Savoie
Leo R. Savoie
Euclide J. Savoy, Jr.
Chester E. Sawicki
John J. Sawickis
Victor Sawina
Doil B. Sawyer
Earl H. Sawyer, Jr.
George A. Sawyer
George J. Sawyer
Kenneth E. Sawyer
Leo J. Sawyer
Levi L. Sawyer
Philip H. Sawyer
William A. Sawyer
Robert Eugene Sawyers
Gerald H. Saxton
Gilbert D. Saxton
Harvey F. Saxton
Harold M. Saylor
Herman Saylor
Derrell B. Sayre
Fred Beecher Sayre
Herbert G. Sayre
Arthur Sazo
Frederi Scacchetti
Peter J. Scaccia
Tony Scaffidi
Joseph Scalesi, Jr.
Garland R. Scalf
Joe R. Scalf
William M. Scalf
Anthony N. Scalzo
Herbert Leo Scanlon, Jr.
James C. Scanlon
Robert E. Scanlon
Robert H. Scanlon
Laurence Scarberry
James H. Scarbor
Henry T. Scarboro
George Scarborough
Harry E. Scarborough
Jack K. Scarborough
Darrell W. Scarbrough
Francis Scarlett
William C. Scarsellone
Hugo Vernor Scarsheim
Rudolph M. Scateni
Harry M. Schaad, Jr.
Howard C. Schaap
Paul E. Schad
Bruce Allen Schaefer
Charles H. Schaefer
Donald L. Schaefer
George J. Schaefer
Joseph A. Schaefer
Paul Laverne Schaefer
Robert E. Schaefer
Robert Edward Schaefer
Carl Lamar Schaeffer
Malcolm J. Schaeffer
Walter J. Schaekel

Edward F. Schafenacker
Clark D. Schaffer
Gaylord Leo Schaffer
Raymond P. Schaffer
Marion F. Schaffert
Melvin R. Schamber
Ronald Schamberger
Russell D. Schanck
Paul R. Schanhofer
Carlton F. Schankin
Addison Schantz, Jr.
William Schardein
Henry C. Scharlott
Richard Scharmack
Charles E. Schatz
Doyle Schatz
Raymond H. Schatz
Robert R. Schatz
Frederick Schauer
Gilbert Jack Schauer
Douglas F. Schauf
William Schaufler
Albert E. Schawlem
James C. Scheck
George W. Scheetz
Richard H. Scheffer
Elmer H. Scheffler
Ray W. Scheibe
Edward Patrick Scheider
Carl J. Scheidt
Robert G. Scheirer
Willia Schellenger
Ervin A. Scheller
John Schellhammer
Frank J. Scheltens
Charles F. Schemmel
William C. Schemmel
Robert Lenard Schenck
Everett D. Schenk
Henry A. Schenk
Leonard Scheper
Hubert C. Scherdin
Edward Donald Scherer
John F. Scherer
Seymour Scherer
Walter George Scherer, Jr.
Francis Scherman
Mayna Schermerhorn
Rober Schermerhorn
Verno Schermerhorn
Herbert A. Scherzinger
Gerald Alan Schick
Paul Gerhardt Schick
Robert Arnold Schick
Vernon G. Schieffer
Catesby E. Schiele
Theodore Schierman
Robert J. Schifano
Albert F. Schildmeyer
Paul W. Schildt
James Schillicutt
Ferdin Schillinger
Glen D. Schiltz, Jr.
Jack W. Schindler
John Schine, Jr.
Harvey T. Schinkal
George R. Schipani
Robert R. Schirmer
Lyle E. Schiro
Peter Martin Schiro
Russell Schlabaugh
Arthur Henry Schlansky
Raymond G. Schlecht
Charles B. Schlegel
Delmond W. Schlegel
Earl E. Schlegel
Lee Geoffrey Schlegel
Joseph W. Schlette
Clement Schlimgen
Carl J. Schlitz
Walter J. Schlomer
Carl S. Schlossman
Kenneth A. Schlotfeldt
Robert Schlotfeldt
Allen Francis Schlueter
Henry F. Schlueter
Melvin A. Schmatz
Raymond Schmelzer
Eugene O. Schmid
John Robert Schmid
Walter D. Schmid
Arthur E. Schmidt
Carl P. Schmidt
Carrol E. Schmidt
Duane C. Schmidt
Frank L. Schmidt
Frank X. Schmidt
George C. Schmidt
Henry Schmidt, Jr.

Myron L. Schmidt
Oris Julius Carl Schmidt
Raymond F. Schmidt
Robert C. Schmidt
Robert Harry Schmidt
Walter Stanley Schmidt
Wesley J. Schmidt
Gordon Louis Schmieder
Vernon E. Schmiedl
David John Schmit
Alphonse R. Schmitt
Edward Schmitt
Edward Schmitt
Francis G. Schmitt
Herbert H. Schmitt
John Gilbert Schmitt
Max R. Schmitt
Robert G. Schmitt
Warren Wendolem Schmitt
Joseph F. Schmitz
Raymond Schmoldt
James E. Schmollinger
Floyd M. Schmouder
John R. Schmutz
William A. Schnader, Jr.
Andrew Schneider
Arley B. Schneider
Christop Schneider
Donald Charles Schneider
Edward Charles Schneider
Edward J. Schneider
Erville Schneider
Gus T. Schneider
James Anthony Schneider
John C. Schneider
John E. Schneider
Joseph W. Schneider
Leon J. Schneider
Leonard Schneider
Myron Lee Schneider
Roger F. Schneider
Rolline E. Schneider
Walter O. Schneider
William Schneider
Norman William Schneidt
Paul W. Schnepper
Fred Jake Schnorr, Jr.
Gilbert E. Schnurr
Robert H. Schoel
Christia Schoeller
Robert G. Schoening
Glenn S. Schoenmann
Ruben Schoenwald
Marion K. Schoffner
Blair Schoffstoll
George A. Schofield, Jr.
John D. Scholes
Herbert Leslie Scholl
Donald E. Scholten
Julius J. Scholtz
William G. Scholze
Louis Schonberger
William D. Schonder, Jr.
Magnus Donald Schone
Willia Schoolcraft
Curtis B. Schooley
Ernest William Schooley
James M. Schooley, Jr.
Ralph H. Schooley
Saint Schoolfield
Charles E. Schoonover
Dan Dwain Schoonover
George Schoonover
Howard Dane Schoonover
Richard L. Schott
William A. Schott
George L. Schoulthies
Delmar L. Schowengerdt
Edward Schrader, Jr.
Gordon W. Schrader
Reuben Schraeder
Donald R. Schramm
Olan B. Schrank
Paul M. Schrecengost
David A. Schreffler
Robert C. Schreiber
Allen W. Schreiner
Glenn A. Schreiner
Henry D. Schriefer
Elmer L. Schriever
John C. Schrobilgen
Floyd M. Schroeder
Gordon T. Schroeder
Guy M. Schroeder
James R. Schroeder
Maynard Schroeder
Robert I. Schroeder
Fredrick E. Schroen
Merl A. Schroy

Robert L. Schubbe
Emanuel R. Schubert
Ronald R. Schuchert
George Alfred Schuck
Richard Fred Schuckman
Alford E. Schuft
Dwain Albert Schuh
Edward R. Schuh
Peter J. Schuil
Clair C. Schuknecht
Willard F. Schuldt
Eugene Schuler
Ralph H. Schuler, Jr.
Fred Schuller
James Robert Schulte
John T. Schulte, Jr.
Roy A. Schulte, Jr.
Bertram E. Schultz
Daniel J. Schultz
Emil Schultz
Floyd Schultz
John A. Schultz
John Emmett Schultz, Jr.
Richard J. Schultz
Robert E. Schultz
Robert William Schultz
Charles Allen Schulz
Walter M. Schulz
Paul E. Schulze
Paul R. Schulze
Richard T. Schum
Henry J. Schumacher
Arthur Henry Schuman
John Henry Schuman
Walter Schuman
John C. Schumann
Ralph E. Schumitsh
Horace I. Schumpert
Gerald O. Schunke
Richard W. Schunke, Jr.
Ward Schupbach
Gerald G. Schuring
Clarence Leo Schuster
Eugene A. Schuster
Merlin N. Schuster
Kenneth E. Schutt
Edward Anthony Schwab
James K. Schwach
Francis D. Schwager
Charles Clinton Schwartz
Donald A. Schwartz
Dwain E. Schwartz
Edward J. Schwartz
Harold A. Schwartz
Lon Schwartz
Raymond R. Schwartz
Robert C. Schwartz
Herman Schwartzkopff
Brandt E. Schwarz
Herbert B. Schwatka
John Schwed, Jr.
Clifford Schwegler
John Joseph Schwegman
William Schweiger
Bobby Schweingruber
Raymond K. Schweitz
William M. Schweitzer
Harold G. Schwemer
Eugene C. Schwend
Raymond Paul Schwerer
Arthur A. Schwind
Paul R. Schwoegl
Daniel Sciannameo
Henry A. Scipioni
Clifton Eugene Scites
William J. Sciulli
Joseph G. Sclafani
Dominic N. Scocchera
Lowell Dean Scofield
Randolph Taylor Scoggan
Bobby G. Scoggins
James L. Scoggins
David W. Scogin
James W. Scolf
Pilton Scoon
A. V. Scott
Amos L. Scott
Benjamin W. Scott
Bennie L. Scott
Bruce Erwin Scott, Jr.
Charles D. Scott
Charles L. Scott
Charles Lee Scott
Charles William Scott
Cletis E. Scott
Conrad William Scott
Cornelius Elliott Scott
Darrell H. Scott
Edward Scott, Jr.

Elmer A. Scott
Felix Scott
Floyd C. Scott
Floyd E. Scott
Floyd Edward Scott
Frank B. Scott, Jr.
Frank J. Scott
Fred E. Scott
Gerald Francis Scott
Gerald L. Scott
Grattin Scott
Henry Scott
James C. Scott
James R. Scott
Jessie L. Scott
Jimmie Scott, Jr.
Joe B. Scott
John Scott
John J. Scott
Lawrence H. Scott
Leonard Scott, Jr.
Lester W. Scott
Lowell L. Scott
Marle D. Scott
Melvin A. Scott
Neil Roger Scott
Osa Scott, Jr.
Richard Charles Scott, Jr.
Richard Dale Scott
Richard L. Scott
Richard W. Scott
Robert D. Scott
Robert F. Scott
Robert Frederick Scott
Robert G. Scott
Robert L. Scott
Robert R. Scott
Robert T. Scott
Robert W. Scott
Sammie R. Scott
Samuel E. Scott
Samuel L. Scott
Stanley V. Scott
Thomas E. Scott
Will Scott
William Donald Scott
William E. Scott
William J. Scott
Wilmer O. Scott
Henry Scotti
Edmund G. Scoullar
Bernard E. Scovell
James M. Scriber
Frederick Scribner
Jerrold R. Scribner
John R. Scrogey
Walter J. Scroggin
Robert D. Scruggs
Edward B. Scullion
Francis J. Scully
William Scully
William G. Scurr
Conrad Jack Seabloom
Larry L. Seaborn
Donald T. Seabourn
Albert Seabrook
Israel Seabrooke
Richard John Seadore
Altie F. Seagle
John R. Seagle
Richard David Seagoe
William O. Seal
Earl F. Seale, Jr.
Billy Seals
Earl E. Seals
Leonard H. Seals
Otis C. Seals
Hoyt Leguin Sealy, Jr
John E. Seaman
Keith D. Seaman
Leroy D. Seaman
Robert L. Seaman
Albert G. Seamon
James D. Seamster
Dalton J. Searcy
Delbert G. Searle
Clyde H. Sears
Donald F. Sears, Jr.
Jerome F. Sears
John A. Sears
Warren Sears
Arthur Leo Seaton
Edward Gordon Seaton
Edward H. Seavey
Earl M. Seay
Robert J. Sebacher
Brown Sebastian
Donald L. Sebastian
Henry H. Sebastian

Logan Sebastian
George Sebest
Alfonso N. Sebia, Jr.
Louis Joseph Sebille
Donald R. Sechman
Gene Sechman
Forest B. Seckman
Elmer W. Secore
Chester T. Secrease
Felipe T. Sedillo
Reynaldo Sedillos
Joseph George Sedlak
Donald G. Sedlow
Clell O. See
Irving L. Seeberg
Boone Seegers
Raymond W. Seegert
Phillip White Seeley
Jack C. Seelinger
Clifford Eugene Seeman
William L. Seery
Robert Lester Seese
Herman J. Seesengood
Dale L. Seeman
Thomas Robert Segar
William R. Seggie
Albert J. Seghetti
Oscar G. Segobia
John Pinto Segrede, Jr.
Richard James Seguin
George P. Segura
Lloyd J. Segura
James A. Seibold
Raymond Gerald Seidel
Robert W. Seidel
Alvin A. Seifert
Chester J. Seifert
Joseph C. Seigle
George D. Seiler
John H. Seip
James F. Seitz
Bernard K. Seitzinger
Walter Louis Seivers, Jr.
Charles R. Selby
Donald Harold Selby
Lloyd F. Selby
Ray D. Selby
Arthur W. Seldon, Jr.
Robert L. Seldon
Walter K. Selenger
Leonard T. Selenski
Albert Arthur Self
Charles L. R. Self
Orville C. Self
Richard A. Self
Samuel D. Self
Louis G. Selig, Jr.
Stanley S. Selinger
Lester C. Selke
Benjamin J. Sell
Frederick Paul Sell
Larry Eugene Sell
Ramos Israel Sella
Jack Herman Selle
J. L. Seller
A. L. Sellers
Dallas Sellers
Donald E. Sellers
Ellis Sellers
Floyd H. Sellers
Harold G. Sellers
Leroy O. Sellers
Lonnie J. Sellers
Regis Aloysivs Sellers
Roger E. Sellers
Thomas M. Sellers
William J. Sellers
Leonard Sellickson
Roald E. Sellie
Charles Harvey Sells
Gail F. Sells
Harold Sells
Clifford Gene Selman
Richard Seloover
Oscar Seltzer
Vernon L. Selvester
Floyd S. Selvidge
Maynard Arthur Selvog
James M. Selzer
John Elsworth Semar
George J. Semetges
Pedro Semidey
Vincent C. Seminara
Deloy G. Semingson
George Semosky, Jr.
Albert Rudolph Semple
John Semulka, Jr.
Henry T. Senaha
John F. Senay

Robert B. Senell
George Albert Senior
Martin Senkowski
Floyd L. Senter, Jr.
Robert Reed Senter
Donald W. Sentz
Charles H. Senz
John Francis Senzig, Jr.
Clayton Sepulvado
Torres A. Sepulveda
Antonio Sequeira
Allen A. Sequin
Joseph Serback
Custer Serbascewicz
Tony Sercel, Jr.
Donald S. Sereika
Marlin F. Serhagl
Anthony D. Serna
Frank Joseph Serna
Jesse Serna
Samuel Serpe
Orsini Jorge Serra
Daniel V. Serrano
Serrano An Serrano
Valentin I. Serrano
Jose M. Serratto
Daniel J. Serre
Eugene A. Serre
Luther D. Serwise
Chester P. Sescilla
Lepe Sesepasara
Philip K. Sesler
Myron Frederick Sestak
Robert Sestito
Arthur Setaro, Jr.
Harry E. Sethman
Michael Sethnovic
Marvin R. Setter
Alain Leroy Settle
Raymond J. Settle
Gerald A. Settles
Norman C. Setzer
Charles E. Setzler
William B. Sevening
Leon J. Severan
Marvin D. Severe
Robert Norman Severson
Dean H. Sevey
Wilfred J. Sevigny
David R. Seward
Stanley James Seward
Thomas E. Seward
Charles L. Sewell
David C. Sewell
Leonard T. Sewell
Nathul Sewell
William G. Sewell
Jack R. Sexson
Oliver Clyde Sexson
Boyd S. Sexton
Carol William Sexton
Talmage J. Sexton
Karle Frederick Seydel
Ralph J. Seyler
Lawrence D. Seymore
Martin F. Seymour
Paul R. Seymour
Thomas B. Seymour
Allen Shackelford
Howard J. Shackelford
Reginald F. J. Shackleford
Frederick Shadden
John Phillip Iii Shaddick
Ronald Edwin Shaddock
John F. Shadel
Romus Shadid
Alan Michael Shadis
Edgar L. Shadrick
Kenneth Shadrick
Willard J. Shafer
Wylie Philip Shafer
George L. Shaffer
Harold R. Shaffer
Jack W. Shaffer
Robert R. Shaffer
William A. Shaffer
William E. Shaffer
William H. Shaffer
Frankie W. Shaffier
Paul Shaffron
Billy E. Shahan
Floyd Shahan
Leroy Shannon Shahan
Stanford G. Shahan
Forrest S. Shambaugh
Robert F. Shambaugh
John Albert Shammo
George Shamoon
Jack B. Shanahan

Jeremiah David Shanahan
Earl H. Shanaver
Andrew B. Shane
Larry R. Shane
Richard H. Shane
Richard L. Shaner
George J. Shank
Joel Shanklin
John W. Shanklin, Jr.
Harold W. Shanks
Robert D. Shanks
Carl G. Shannon
John D. Shannon
Joseph M. Shannon
Larry Shannon
Robert E. Shannon
Robert James Shannon
Thomas J. Shannon
Wilma Shannon
Jack Gordon Shanyfelt
Henry C. Iii Sharland
John F. Sharon
Braxton W. Sharp
Charles R. Sharp
Donald W. Sharp
Felix G. Sharp
J. D. Sharp
Jack D. Sharp
James W. Sharp
John Thomas Sharp
Nathaniel M. Sharp
Oral R. Sharp
Raleigh T. Sharp
William J. Sharp
William W. Sharp, Jr.
Alin L. Sharp
Harry Sharpe
Lawrence Curfew Sharpe
Robert Vincent Sharpe
Walter Joseph Sharpe
Harry M. Sharpless
Martin J. Sharron
Richard M. Sharrow
Joseph C. Shattas
William Jerome Shauf
John R. Shaughnessy
Lyle L. Shaul
Benjamin K. Shaver
Donald E. Shaver
Gerald C. Shaver
Irvin E. Shaver
Robert L. Shavers
Abner V. Shaw
Albert L. Shaw
Billy D. Shaw
Charles W. Shaw
Clarence H. Shaw
David W. Shaw
Donald D. Shaw
Eugene Marvin Shaw
Eulas M. Shaw
Glenace H. Shaw
James C. Shaw
James F. Shaw
James P. Shaw
Kenneth R. Shaw
Lee Shaw, Jr.
Lionel Shaw
Marvin K. Shaw
Ralph Lee Shaw
Robert E. Shaw
William F. Shaw
William Hamilton Shaw
William R. Shaw
Willie C. Shaw
Leo C. Shawanesse
James A. Shawver
Roy C. Shawver
Charles Shay
Jackie L. Shay
John B. S. Shay
John J. Shay, Jr.
Nealon C. Shay, Jr.
Andrew B. Shea
James W. Shea, Jr.
Jeremiah J. Shea
Richard T. Shea, Jr.
Warren D. Sheafor
Patrick Sheahan
Alan D. Shearer, Jr.
Velmer Shearer
William L. Shebloski, Jr.
George Gene Shecklen
Rodney C. Sheckler
Harold Shedd
Robert W. Shee
Robert Lee Sheed
Erwin W. Sheehan
Francis L. Sheehan

Gerald D. Sheehan
John Francis Sheehan
John G. Sheehan
Robert Emmett Sheehan
William F. Sheehan
William J. Sheehan, Jr.
Wilbur K. Sheehy, Jr.
Gordon A. Sheeks
Glenn K. Sheely
John Edward Sheets
Doren Paul Sheffield
James L. Sheffield
Robert E. Sheffield
Abraham Sheftel
Charles Shehorn, Jr.
George W. Shelby
James A. Shelby
Donald F. Sheldon
James H. Sheldon
John A. Shelemba
Fred P. Shelgren
George A. Shell
Glenn E. Shell, Jr.
Virgil Charles Shelley, Jr.
Ralph J. Shellhaas
John H. Shelly
John Carlton Shelnutt
Lawrence E. Shelork
Harry Shelquist, Jr.
Charlie Shelton
Chester W. Shelton
Eddie L. Shelton
George Shelton, Jr.
Gilman Lee Shelton
Harry D. Shelton
James D. Shelton
Jim Shelton, Jr.
John Shelton
Leslie Taylor Shelton, Jr.
Lyle R. Shelton
Philip D. Shelton
Roy Shelton
William B. Shelton
Joseph F. Shemelewski
Thomas E. Shemwell
Robert Shenault
Frederick Berlin Shenk
Henry Hess Shenk
Reynard E. Shenton
Clarence E. Shepard
Floyd Shepard
Harold R. Shepard
James Robert Shepard
Leon M. Shepard
Ollie E. Shepard
Robert A. Shepard
Howard Shepherd
J. M. Shepherd
John H. Shepherd
Perry Shepherd, Jr.
Robert F. Shepherd
Robert Neale Shepherd
Thomas A. Shepherd
Warren Maxwell Shepherd
Gerald Ivin Shepler
Brian Frederick Sheppard
Charlie C. Sheppard
Claude L. Sheppard
James W. Sheppard
Lowell B. Sheppard
Robert L. Sheppard
Tally J. Sheppard
Carl E. Sheraden
Toney J. Sherard
Robert Sherbineau
Frank W. Sheridan
John L. Sheridan
Richard B. Sheridan
William L. Sheridan
Louis F. Sheriff
John B. Sherlock
Albert Sherman
Andrew E. Sherman
Earl W. Sherman
Frank Foster Sherman
Harry H. Sherman, Jr.
Leroy James Sherman
James H. Sherrell
Allen Sherry, Jr.
John Martin Sherry
Vernon W. Sherry
Gordon R. Shertzer
Charles W. Sherwood
Eugene E. Sherwood
Francis E. Sherwood
Howard T. Sherwood
Louis H. Sherwood
Sheldon A. Sherwood
William H. Sherwood

Franklin Shetters
Mathew Shevrovich
John William Shewmaker
Hiroshi Shibao
Nobumi Shibao
Chauncey E. Shick
Hilton G. Shick
Andrew Shields
Charles P. Shields
Elvin Baker Shields
Everette Lee Shields, Jr.
Mark Shields
Mark L. Shields
Thomas Lester Shields
Wayne N. Shields
William E. Shiffer
William F. Shifflet
Charles Shifflett
Herbert Shifflett
Doyle W. Shiley
Lawrence Y. Shima
Robert Shimabukuro
Shingo Shimabukuro
Calvin T. Shimata
Kenneth Shimogawa
Toshio Shimonoya
Dale D. Shinabarger
Donald A. Shinabery
Bert Shinault
Robert M. Shinde
Edward A. Shine
Joseph E. Shine
Larry Ross Shiner
Albert J. Shinkus
Robert N. Shipe
Earl D. Shipers
Allen Dean Shipley
Charles T. Shipley
Gene E. Shipley
Clyde W. Shipman
Frederick J. Shipman
Howard I. Shipman
Lowell D. Shipman
William D. Shipman
Jack E. Shipp
Leonard W. Shipp
Maxwell Jonah Shipp
Truman O. Shipp
Willard H. Shipp
Charles H. Shippen
Charles C. Shipps
John G. Shipton
Roy Edward Shirey, Jr.
Alton E. Shirley
Fred D. Shirley
Gerald R. Shirley
Robert Wayne Shirley
Alton L. Shirtz
Nobuo Shishido
Takashi Shishido
Glen R. Shisler
William Anthony Shiveree
Tommy E. Shivers
Jack M. Shockley
Raymond Rence Shockley
Charles H. Shoe
Edward Leroy Shoemaker
Francis E. Shoemaker
Harold W. Shoemaker
John W. Shoemaker
William Shoemaker
Charles H. Shoffit
Sidney Shoifet
Ervin S. Sholes
Clarence J. Shook
John William Shook, Jr.
Lonnie R. Shook
Henry G. Shoop
William G. Shope
George Arnold Shore, Jr.
Ira W. Shore, Jr.
William G. Shore
Billie J. Shores
William Clarence Shores
James G. Shorman
Clifford T. Short
George S. Short
Herschel G. Short
James M. Short
John W. Short
Marvin E. Short
Paul H. Short
R. V. Leo Short
Raymond Uriah Short
Richard L. Short
Thomas L. Short
Thomas W. Short, Jr.
James R. Shortell
Percival Shorten

Jack A. Shorter
James W. Shorter
Raymond A. Shortino
Walter Shorts
John P. Shott
Robert G. Shoulders
Edgar R. Shoults
Erwin T. Showalter
Raymond H. Showalter
J. M. Shows
Louis C. Shrader
Jack Howard Shramek
Charles D. Shreeve
Clarence Edmond Shreve
Delbert Shreve
Harold R. Shreve
Jim C. Shreves
Richar Shrewsberry
Arthur J. Shropshire
James E. Shropshire, Jr.
Charles T. Shroyer
Dorse W. Shryock
Andrew C. Shuck
Herbert D. Shuck
Howard R. Shuck
William Edward Shuck, Jr.
Earl V. Shuckhart
Carl Shuford
Billy Shuler
Molton A. Shuler, Jr.
Jerry L. Shullenberger
Irving Shulman
Rembert D. Shults
Thurman Milton Shults
Colin Shultz
Homer H. Shultz
Herbert C. Shuman
Bendum D. Shumate
Elmer L. Shumate
Harry S. Shunkamolah
James P. Shunney
Jerry Earl Shup
Glen L. Shupe
Gene E. Shupp
Howard M. Shupp, Jr.
Lee J. Shur
Wayne C. Shurbet
William David Shurts
Hubert W. Shurtz
David W. Shute
Raymond James Shute
Philip Shutman
Bion Q. Shutts
Richard Joseph Shvonski
Henry H. Shy
Leslie A. Shy
Eugene F. Shyne
Arthur Elmer Sias, Jr.
John A. Sibley
Willard J. Sibley
Edmundas G. Sicas
Leslie A. Siciliano
Donald H. Siddell
Jimmy Carter Sides
William Sides, Jr.
Alfred Harry Sidney
Peter M. Sidorka
Anthony R. Sidoti
Werner Franklin Sieber
Richard Henry Sieckmann
Walter J. Sieczka
Russell A. Sieder
Edwin P. Siedler
Ralph E. Siefring
Merle W. Siegersma
Earl V. Siegmund
Donald H. Sielaff
Clarence A. Siemers
Curtis L. Siemers
Sigmund Siemies
Walter E. Siemon
Pablo Sierra
Paul M. Siers
J. Donald Siesky, Jr.
John M. Siewielski
Thomas E. Sifling
Daniel T. Sifuentes
Harvey B. Sigers
Richard George Sigg
Robert L. Siggins
William R. Sigler
Albert W. Sigley, Jr.
Thomas J. Sigley
Harold G. Sigmon
Edmund G. Sigmund
Jesus G. Siguenza
William R. Sigwart
Marvin M. Sihrer
David T. Siira

Daniel K. Sikes
Jackie Page Sikes
Olen J. Sikes
Joseph C. Sikora
Michael Sikora, Jr.
Leonard Sileo
Willie J. Siler
Charles E. Silfies
James Richard Silk
Estil Silkwood
Maurice R. Sills
David Silva
Enfre Silva
Eugene W. Silva
Jesus A. Silva
Madura Cesar Silva
Ramiro F. Silva
Santiago Rau Silva
Thomas Conlin Silva
Alfred Silver
Clarence P. Silver
Stewart Burt Silver
Roger M. Silvernail
J. S. Silvers
Arnold Norman Silverstein
Joseph F. Silvia
Joseph M. Silvia
Joseph A. F. Simard
Robert C. Simard
Rofino Simbre
Leland K. Sime
Rudolph C. Simeone
Lester G. Simeral
Joe D. Simerly
Eugene N. Simiele
Lawrence Henry Simmon
Albert E. Simmons
Allen E. Simmons
Allen W. Simmons
Bryan Eugene Simmons
Calvin C. Simmons
Clarence A. Simmons
Coryden J. Simmons
Douglas N. Simmons
Earl S. Simmons
Edward L. Simmons
Eldred R. Simmons
Gene Simmons
George E. Simmons
Glen D. Simmons
Irvin O. Simmons, Jr.
James R. Simmons
Jesse E. Simmons
John W. Simmons
Johnnie L. Simmons
Joseph Simmons
Joseph D. Simmons
Leon F. Simmons
Louis T. Simmons
Millard E. Simmons
Robert J. Simmons
Robert J. Simmons
Robert W. Simmons
Ronald P. Simmons
Ross D. Simmons
Roy Simmons
Thomas Simmons
Thurman Nelson Simmons
Vernie D. Simmons
Wallace Simmons, Jr.
William A. Simmons
William D. Simmons
William R. Simmons
Willie H. Simmons
Clemmie Simms
Wilbert Simms
Frank P. Simon
James B. Simon
Pete W. Simon
Stanley A. Simon
Bruce Thomas Simonds
Joseph H. Simoneau
Calvin H. Simons
Randolph Simons
Robert L. Simons
Donald H. Simonson
Ernest V. Simonson
Marshall Edwin Simonson
Herman I. Simpkins
Benjamin C. Simpson, Jr.
Charles L. Simpson
Grant W. Simpson
Homer I. Simpson
Issac Simpson, Jr.
James C. Simpson
James D. Simpson
John Eugene Simpson, Jr.
John M. Simpson
Lee A. Simpson

Lewis Simpson
Matthew A. Simpson
Orville L. Simpson
Richard Harold Simpson
Robert L. Simpson
Samuel Simpson
Samuel R. Simpson
William F. Simpson, Jr.
William W. Simpson
Carroll J. Simrell
Alfred Sims
Alfred R. Sims
Claude T. Sims
David Sims
Derwood W. Sims
Ernest E. Sims
Ernest L. Sims
Frank Sims
Holly B. Sims
Ray Sims
Richard Emery Sims
Robert W. Sims
Shelby T. Sims
Truman D. Sims
Clifford Sinclair
Fairris F. Sinclair
Frederick Sinclair
George Alfred Singer, Jr.
Karl G. Singer
Gerald Singletary
Charles Singleton
Jesse C. Singleton
John P. Singleton
Marion L. Singleton
Paul L. Singleton
Robert Singleton
William Singleton
William E. Singleton
Harvey E. Singley
Walter Siniawski
Nichol Siniscalchi
Edward B. Sinkler
Charles F. Sinnett
Lutrell M. Sinnett
Brumitt G. Sinor
Gerald T. Sinz
Robert J. Sipes, Jr.
Gene H. Sippel
Henry M. Sipsey
Gamez R. Siqueiros
Angelo Siragusa
William F. Sirera
Donald S. Sirman
Reno G. Sirois
Benny Sirski
Samuel Sisco
Homer L. Sisk, Jr.
Joe C. Sisk
Robert W. Sisk
Bennie Sisneros
Dennis Orlando Sisneros
Andrew Sissack
Clyde E. Sissom
Charles T. Sisson
Joseph F. Sisson, Jr.
Thomas L. Sisson
Frank Sistrunk
William S. Sitman
William Lavern Sittig
Lester R. Sitton, Jr.
Ernest Siudzinski
Robert L. Sivage
Bill T. Sizemore
Charles E. Sizemore
Clifford Sizemore
Zemria V. Sizemore
John R. Sjodin
Robert E. Sjolander
Howard R. Skaalerud
Clide E. Skaggs
Edwin Skaggs
Glen Willard Skaggs
James H. Skaggs
Perry A. Skaggs
Richard M. Skapyak
Carter Morrison Skare
Clarence R. Skates
John O. Skaug
Theodore M. Skeals, Jr.
Donald N. Skean
Calvin L. Skeen
Kenneth L. Skeen
Robert E. Skeen
Irvin K. Skeens
Lonald D. Skeens
Robert S. Skees
John Theodore Skelley
John Clifton Skelton
Charles M. Skero

Gerald A. Skerry
Peter B. Skiba
Walter L. Skiba
Chester A. Skibicki
Doyle R. Skidmore
Forrest G. Skidmore
Melvin B. Skidmore
Phillip C. Skiles
Roger B. Skillings
Rollin W. Skilton
Henry J. Skinger
Charles Edward Skinner
Earl L. Skinner
Kenneth L. Skinner
Lewis F. Skinner
Lindell Skinner
Preston Skinner
Robert K. Skinner
Russell J. Skinner
Sherrod E. Skinner, Jr.
James E. Skipper
Gardie Skivington
Donald C. Skoglund
George M. Skogstad
Steve Skorich
Robert B. Skowron
Charles Skrobanek
Joseph J. Skwierawski
Walter Louis Skwiercz
Clarence Virgil Slack, Jr.
George D. Slack
Carl C. Slade
William Bonner Slade
Earnest Newton Slagle
Kenneth E. Slagle
Leonard P. Slagle
Robert W. Slaick
James J. Slane
Donald G. Slaney
Peter F. Slansky
Ray Emerson Slasor
Waymon Slaten
Christopher Slater
Donald K. Slater
James A. Slater
Richard J. Slater
Thomas Slater
Harry L. Slates
Raymond E. Slattery
Robert Thomas Slattery
Hayden W. Slatton
Andrew J. Slaughter
Dewitt L. Slaughter
James A. Slaughter
Julius Edward Slaughter
Larry E. Slaughter
Lum L. Slaughter
Charles W. Slaven
Glen Leroy Slavicek
William A. Slayback
Richard Stanislaw Sleboda
Merle T. Sledd
William Sledge
Albert L. Sleet
Herbert N. Sleeth
Gerald G. Slemmer
Donald C. Slemp
James C. Slemp
Marvin Elwood Sleppy
Delbert Carl Slider
Wallace L. Slight
Fredrick J. Slipka
Alfred C. Sliter
Edward Sliva, Jr.
Carl T. Sloan
Donald E. Sloan
Harold Sloan
James Sloan
Laurence E. Sloan
Lawrence H. Sloan
John A. Sloat
Richard F. Sloat
Norbert J. Slomba
Raymond A. Sloop
Clifford O. Sloppy
Alvin E. Sloss
Robert Bernard Slotabec
Ivan Brust Slote
Donald E. Sloughfy
Amos L. Sluder
David P. Sluder
Louis E. Slusarski
William R. Sluss
Martin H. Slutsky
Donald Dean Sly
Willie W. Sly
Anthony F. Slysz
Fred G. Smack
James W. Smaglik

Earl W. Small
Richard E. Small
Roscoe D. Small
Stephen Smallbone
Alfred August Smalley
Everett F. Smalley
Gail W. Smalley
Lloyd Buchanan Smalley
Robert E. Smalley
David M. Smalls
William Smallstey
George L. Smallwood
Howard I. Smallwood
Raymond Smallwood
Charles F. Smarr
George A. Smart
Gerald R. Smart
James Smart
Norman Smart
Otto W. Smart
Paul L. Smart
Richard Franklin Smartt
Walter A. Smead
Bobby Joe Smedley
Edward Eugene Smedley
Richard E. Smelcer
Andrew K. Smelik
Robert E. Smeltzer
Nickolas Smerkar
Glen E. Smethers
Arthur Lee Smickley
James J. Smile
James R. Smiley
Kenneth H. Smiley
Paul Authur Smiley
Albert D. Smith
Albert Eugene Smith
Albert W. Smith
Alfred E. Smith
Alfred J. Smith
Alfred Smith, Jr.
Allen L. Smith
Allen W. Smith
Amon K. Smith
Anthony Keemon Smith
Anthony M. Smith
Archie Smith, Jr.
Archie Leonard Smith
Arnold G. Smith
Arthur B. Smith
Asa William Smith
August O. Smith
Ben T. Smith, Jr.
Benjamin F. Smith
Benjamin L. Smith
Bernard Smith
Bernard L. Smith
Billy Doyle Smith
Billy E. Smith
Billy G. Smith
Billy J. Smith
Billy R. Smith
Billy Ray Smith
Bobby J. Smith
Bobby L. Smith
Calvin Smith
Carl D. Smith
Carl E. Smith
Carl S. Smith
Carlton J. Smith
Cecil E. Smith
Cecil E. Smith
Cecil J. Smith
Chadwick Boyd Smith
Charles Smith
Charles B. Smith, Jr.
Charles D. Smith
Charles E. Smith
Charles H. Smith, Jr.
Charles J. Smith
Charles L. Smith
Charles M. Smith
Charles R. Smith
Charlie V. Smith
Clarence Smith
Clarence D. Smith
Clarence W. Smith
Claude E. Smith
Claude Smith, Jr.
Claude R. Smith
Claudine E. Smith
Clifford H. Smith
Clifton E. Smith
Clifton E. Smith, Jr.
Clyde D. Smith
Clyde J. Smith
Crist W. Smith
Curtis Latham Smith

Curtis N. Smith
Danny R. Smith
Darrel Otto Smith
David Barr Smith
David E. Smith
David Junior Smith
David L. Smith
David M. Smith
David R. Smith
Dayle Le Roy Smith
De Witt R. Smith
Dean C. Smith
Delbert W. Smith
Delma B. Smith
Denford R. Smith
Denver J. Smith
Dewain Donald Smith
Don Smith
Donald Allen Smith
Donald Edward Smith
Donald F. Smith
Donald Francis Smith
Donald G. Smith
Donald G. Smith
Donald L. Smith
Donald L. Smith
Donald L. Smith
Donald L. Smith
Donald M. Smith
Donald R. Smith
Donald R. Smith, Jr.
Donnelly Frank Smith
Douglas Elliott Smith
Douglas Marshall Smith
Douglas Y. Smith
Doyle E. Smith
Doyle L. Smith
Duane W. Smith
Earl Smith
Earl J. Smith
Earl K. Smith
Ed L. Smith, Jr.
Edgar E. Smith
Edgar F. Smith
Edward F. Smith
Edward H. Smith
Edward J. Smith
Edward M. Smith
Edward Walter Smith
Elijah Smith, Jr.
Elmer D. Smith
Elmore Charles Smith
Emmitte Smith
Ernest E. Smith
Ernest M. Smith
Eugene Smith
Eugene E. Smith
Eugene W. Smith
Floyd A. Smith
Francis Keith Smith
Francis R. Smith
Francis T. Smith
Frank H. Smith
Frank J. Smith
Franklin Smith, Jr.
Fred Smith
Fred H. Smith, Jr.
Frederick O. Smith
Frederick T. Smith
Gabriel J. Smith
Garrard L. D. Smith
Gene J. Smith
Genejo Smith
George A. Smith
George C. Smith
George C. Smith
George E. Smith
George E. Smith
George J. Smith
George R. Smith
George Ullman Smith
Gerald Smith
Gerald George Smith
Gerald Jay Smith
Gerald Kermit Smith
Gerald Lee Smith
Gerald Lorian Smith
Gilbert R. Smith
Glen F. Smith
Gordon Oliver Smith
Gordon R. Smith
Graham Smith
Grover C. Smith
H. J. Smith
Harold A. Smith
Harold B. Smith
Harold E. Smith
Harold L. Smith
Harold L. Smith

Harper H. Smith
Harrison Smith, Jr.
Harry B. Smith
Harry S. Smith
Harry W. Smith
Harvey E. Smith
Herbert David Smith
Herbert Leroy Smith
Herbert Windfld Smith, Jr.
Howard A. Smith
Howard E. Smith
Howard Emmerson Smith
Howard F. Smith
Howard R. Smith
Ira B. Smith
Isaac Smith
Ivory V. Smith
J. D. Smith
Jack A. Smith
Jack O. Smith
Jack R. Smith
James Alfred Smith, Jr.
James Bruce Smith
James C. Smith
James C. Smith
James Dela Smith, Jr.
James E. Smith
James E. Smith
James E. Smith
James E. Smith, Jr.
James Edward Smith, Jr.
James F. Smith
James Harold Smith
James H. Smith
James K. Smith
James L. Smith
James L. Smith
James M. Smith
James M. Smith
James Marvin Smith
James R. Smith
James R. Smith
James T. Smith
James W. Smith
James W. Smith
Javery Edler Smith
Jerrold R. Smith
Jesse C. Smith
Jessie Alvin Smith
Jimmie Reed Smith
Jimmy D. Smith
Joe W. Smith
John Smith
John A. Smith
John B. Smith
John C. Smith
John C. Smith
John D. Smith
John E. Smith
John F. Smith
John H. Smith
John H. Smith
John L. Smith
John L. Smith
John Louis Smith
John R. Smith
John S. Smith
John W. Smith
John W. Smith
John W. Smith
John W. Smith
Joseph C. Smith
Joseph L. Smith
Joseph S. Smith
Joseph W. Smith
Kenneth B. Smith
Kenneth L. Smith
Kenneth Lee Smith
Kimball E. Smith
Laurence M. Smith
Laverne N. Smith
Lawrence Smith
Lawrence A. Smith
Lawrence A. Smith
Lawrence A. Smith
Lawrence J. Smith
Leland F. Smith
Leland R. Smith
Leonard G. Smith
Leonard H. Smith
Leonard J. Smith, Jr.
Leonard Leroy Smith
Leotis Q. Smith
Levere E. Smith
Lewis B. Smith
Linton Carlton Smith, Jr.
Lloyd G. Smith
Loren Dickerson Smith
Louis K. Smith
Louis L. Smith

Lowell E. Smith
Luis Smith
Lyman J. Smith
Manuel Y. Smith
Marcel Albert Smith
Marion L. Smith
Marvin W. Smith
Maurice K. Smith
Melvin H. Smith
Moses Smith
Myron D. Smith
Myron James Smith
Orvil Smith
Otis Carl Smith
Paul A. Smith
Paul H. Smith
Paul R. Smith
Paul T. Smith
Paul V. Smith
Peron Smith
Philip C. Smith
Ralph Arthur Smith
Ralph F. Smith
Ray Smith
Ray C. Smith
Ray W. Smith
Raymon L. Smith
Raymond A. Smith
Raymond Todd Smith
Reginald D. Smith
Richard E. Smith
Richard E. Smith
Richard F. Smith
Richard Wayne Smith
Richard Yorke Smith
Robert Smith
Robert Smith
Robert A. Smith
Robert Brandon Smith
Robert E. Smith
Robert Emmett Smith
Robert Eugene Smith
Robert Eugene Smith
Robert F. Smith
Robert J. Smith
Robert J. Smith
Robert J. Smith
Robert J. Smith
Robert K. Smith
Robert L. Smith
Robert L. Smith
Robert Leslie Smith
Robert N. Smith
Robert Samuel Smith
Robert William Smith
Roderick C. Smith
Roger A. Smith
Roger B. Smith
Roger W. Smith
Ronald Smith
Ronald M. Smith
Ronnie T. Smith
Roy Crafton Smith
Roy E. Smith
Roy H. Smith
Roy L. Smith
Roy L. Smith
Rudy B. Smith
Rufus A. Smith
Russell Everett Smith
Sam H. Smith
Samuel Smith
Samuel A. Smith
Sanford J. Smith
Shadrach B. Smith
Sherry J. Smith
Sherwin V. Smith
Steve Smith, Jr.
Thaddeus L. Smith
Theodore G. Smith
Theodore J. Smith
Therlo G. L. Smith
Thomas A. Smith
Thomas C. Smith
Thomas F. Smith
Thomas J. Smith
Thomas J. Smith
Thomas O. Smith
Tommy Henry Smith
Travis Smith
Troy N. Smith
Vernon Dean Smith
Virgil J. Smith
Walter B. Smith
Walter L. Smith, Jr.
Walter L. Smith, Jr.
Walter M. Smith
Warren C. Smith

Wendall C. Smith, Jr.
Wendell E. Smith
Wesley F. Smith
Wilbur L. Smith
Wilford B. Smith
Willard E. Smith
William Bartlett Smith, Jr.
William D. Smith
William D. Smith
William D. Smith
William E. Smith
William E. Smith
William E. Smith
William Eugene Smith
William G. Smith, Jr.
William H. Smith
William H. Smith
William H. Smith
William H. Smith
William J. Smith
William J. Smith
William L. Smith
William L. Smith
William L. Smith
William Lewis Smith
William S. Smith
William Sproat Smith, Jr.
Willie Smith
Willie M. Smith
Willis Preston Smith
Winford D. Smith
Ernest L. Smither
Ferman T. Smithers
James N. Smithers
Donald Smithson
Porter Joe Smithson
Elton E. Smoak
Harvey H. Smoak
Richard T. Smock
Raymond Smolinski
Frank S. Smolinsky
Billie A. Smoot
Marion Kent Smotherman
C. O. Smothermon, Jr.
Chaffine Smothers
Comer Smothers
Loyd Smothers
Richard T. Smotts
George B. Smudski
William H. Smugi
Walter Joseph Smyk, Jr.
James G. Smyros
William R. Smyth
Adolph E. Snarski
Paul E. Snavely, Jr.
Elmer L. Snay
Lawrence L. Snead
Lawrence A. Snedden
Albert Sneed
Eother L. Sneed
Floyd Sneed
William C. Sneed
Delbert R. Snell
James W. Snell
James W. Snell
Charles H. Snelling
Nolan Harry Snelling
Philip Snethen
Norman Snidenbach
Alfred E. Snider
Arlon P. Snider
Carl G. Snider, Jr.
Delmar R. Snider
Glenn A. Snider
John Kennard Snider
Robert I. Snider
David M. Sniderman
Raymond J. Sniezyk
Edward M. Sniffen
John Snipe
Edgar T. Snipes, Jr.
Floyd W. Snipes
Leon S. Snipes
Joseph M. Snock, Jr.
Robert Ronald Snoddy
Cecil Allen Snodgrass
D. C. Snodgrass
James F. Snodgrass
Robert C. Snodgrass
Russell L. Snook
Alan S. Snouffer
Billy J. Snow
Earl M. Snow
Ronald Snow
Homer L. Snowden
Thomas G. Snowden
Charles F. Snyder
Charles H. Snyder
David B. Snyder
David L. Snyder

Donald E. Snyder
Edward C. Snyder
Elwood M. Snyder
Fred M. Snyder
George T. Snyder
Gerald Dudley Snyder
Ivan J. Snyder
Jackson E. Snyder
John M. Snyder, Jr.
Leo M. Snyder
Mervin B. Snyder
Raymond A. Snyder
Ronald Forrest Snyder
Walter A. Snyder
Walter Henry Snyder, Jr.
William H. Snyder
Edwin A. Soares
Ernest A. Sobeck, Jr.
Argene J. Sobehart
Robert Leroy Sobey
Albert T. Sobieraj
Eugene R. Sobrek
Ernest T. Socha
Joseph J. Socha
Adolph G. Sodemann
Billy Gene Soden
Herbert N. Soden
Marvin W. Soderstrom
Ralph Soderstrom
Rudolph W. Soellner
Charles R. Sohler
John A. Sokol
Harry S. Soladay
Milnor L. Solberg
Raymond Curtis Solberg
Joseph J. Solem
Morris Albert Solem
Adelaido M. Solis
Raymond C. Solis
Ricardo F. Solis
Joe A. Soliz, Jr.
Matilde Soliz
Joseph Ray Sollars
John G. Sollie
Thomas F. Solometo
Arnold D. Solomon
Leslie H. Solomon
Richard W. Solomon
Robert Solomon
Edward J. Solway
John Soman
Raymond Someillan
Charles L. Somers
James E. Somers
Donald William Somerville
Smith S. Somerville
Stephen Ray Somjai
Eugene Franklin Sommer
Hugh N. Sommer, Jr.
Paul H. Sommer
Edward Sommerfeld
Edward G. Sommerfield
Wayne B. Sommerfield
Jerry W. Sommers
William H. Sommers
Cecil Sommerville
Glen Allen Somsen
John E. Somsky, Jr.
John Eugene Songer
William Sonnamaker
Louis Sonnier, Jr.
Frank H. Sonoski
Walter R. Soots
Ralph E. Sooy
Joseph Sopak
Joseph A. Sopko
Carl Edward Soreide
Eugene Roy Sorensen
Lyle Allen Sorensen
Mainerd Atwell Sorensen
Dean R. Sorenson
George A. Sorenson
Grigorij Sorin
Louis M. Sormrude
Anthony T. Sorrentino
Donald Anthony Sorrentino
Lawrence R. Sorum
Cayetano Sosa
William E. Sosebee
John N. Sotelo
Antonio M. Soto
David B. Soto
George Jimmie Soto
Jose Soto
Peter S. Soto, Jr.
Santos Soto
Tony Soto
Francis Philip Soucie
Alva L. Souers

William Soukup, Jr.
Clement R. Sousa
Ian Soutar
Bobby Gene South
Ernest C. South
James W. Southard
William E. Southard
James Southerland
John E. Southerland
Lyndel Southerland
Garland Southwood
Richard Southworth
Roy H. Southworth
Lawrence Souza
Melvin Souza
Dewey L. Soward
Robert G. Sowder
Lester Irving Sowell
Benjamin F. Sowers
Douglas H. Sowers
Kenneth C. Sowers
Lewis W. Sowles
Richard J. Spaar
Francis B. Spaeth
Michael Spagnola
Antonio Spagnuolo
William C. Spaid
Charles Ogan Spain
Charlie J. Spain
Francis E. Spain
John B. Spain
Robert L. Spain
Dempsey Spainhour
William C. Spalding
Charles Ormand Spallone
George L. Spangenberg
Arthur H. Spangler
Donald E. Spangler
Donald G. Spangler
John Spann
Joseph F. Spann
Robert A. Sparkman
Bobby C. Sparks
Charles S. Sparks
Donald D. Sparks, Jr.
Harold Sparks
Horace Sparks
Huil Denver E. Sparks
James E. Sparks
James R. Sparks
James T. Sparks
John E. Sparks
Robert H. Sparks
Ronald C. Sparks
Ronald Morh Sparks
Walker J. Sparrow
Charles Ray Spath
Warren W. Spaulding
Thomas Bernard Speaker
Cloid V. Speakman
Paul F. Spear
Spero G. Spear
Columbus Spearman
Harry L. Spearman
Donald E. Spears
Elton M. Spears
Henry F. Spears
Leonard L. Spears
Paul Spears
Woodroe W. Spears
Wilfred G. Specht
Harry E. Speck
Richard Speech, Jr
George Speedy, Jr.
Kelton Speegle
Russell L. Spegal
Chester F. Speicher
Clifton T. Speicher
Robert A. Speicher
Harry Speight
Igene Speight
David B. Spellman
John C. Spellman
Govan L. Spells
Carl Madison Spence
Donald B. Spence
Grover C. Spence, Jr.
John W. Spence
Joseph Spence
Marvin James Spence
Richard L. Spence, Jr.
Albert William Spencer
Chapman T. Spencer
Charles Richard Spencer
Floyd S. Spencer
Harold G. Spencer
John K. Spencer
Kenneth H. Spencer
Lloyd Spencer

Mickey R. Spencer
Olaf Spencer, Jr.
Thomas W. Spencer
Robert W. Sperbeck
Lewis F. Sperduto
Donald G. Sperl
Peter Spernyak
Carl P. Sperondio
Elliott E. Sperry
Elmer G. Sperry
Orville K. Spicer
John A. Spidal
George E. Spiegel
Elmo M. Spiller
William R. Spiller
Jack L. Spillman
Joseph Anthony Spina
Frederick G. Spindler
Willie F. Spinks
Eugene Spinosa
Richard H. Spirat
Rudolph J. Spisko
Bryan Spitler, Jr.
Clarence Edward Spitz
Everett W. Spitzer
James R. Spitzer
Bobby E. Spivey
Bernard L. Splittstoesser
Christian J. Spoerl, Jr.
Lee F. Spoffard
Richard Spon
Gerald K. Sponsler
Peter Spontik
Manuel J. Spoon
Herbert Spoonemore
Glen L. Spooner
Philip A. Spooner
Clarence Spoonhour
Bear Ignat Spotted
Glen L. Spradley
Cecil A. Spradlin
Clyde D. Spradlin
William G. Spradlin
Earl F. Spradling
Wilbur R. Spradling, Jr.
David J. Spraggs
Robert E. Spragins
George Smith Sprague
Oscar L. Sprague
Harry W. Spraker, Jr.
Homer J. Sprankle
Sherwood Spratlin
Robert W. Springborn
Marvin R. Springer
William Springer
Elvern Springfield
Myron H. Springsteen, Jr.
Clyde A. Springston
Warren H. Sprinkle
Alvin Sprock
Donald J. Sprong
Harold R. Sproul
Clarence E. Sprouse
Jesse E. Sprouse
Thomas C. Sprouse
Curtis B. Sprow
John A. Spruell
Johnnie H. Spruell
John Mitchell III Spudick
John W. Spurlock
Robert L. Spurlock
Stuart Lee Spurlock
Stanley J. Spychaj
James S. Spyre
John M. Squier
George F. Squiggins
Charles L. Squires
James W. Squires
Rodney L. Srb
Joseph L. Srebroski
George J. Srogoncik
Anthony D. Srok
Johnnie A. Sronce
Merril L. Sronce
Howard St Bernard
Benjamin St Clair
David E. St Clair
George A. St Clair
Willie A. St Clair
Aldon J. St Germain
Lionel St Germain
Paul E. St Julien
Joseph R. St Louis
Carroll St Martin
Robert Ronald St Mary
John D. St Onge
Joseph D. St Onge
Narcisse D. St Onge
Roger A. St Pierre

Robert St Thomas
John P. Staat
Raymond A. Staats
James W. Stables
Victor J. Staccone
Alton R. Stacey
Patrick J. Stack
Ralph S. Stackig, Jr.
C. B. Stacy
Clyde T. Stacy
Gene E. Stacy
Herbert Stacy
James I. Stacy, Jr.
Lenox Stacy
Ralph Wells Stacy, Jr.
Rex F. Stacy
Roland B. Iii Stacy
Kenneth R. Stadler
Frank G. Staffen
Dayton J. Stafford
Dorin S. Stafford
Jack N. Stafford
Richard Stafford
Robert Everett Stafford
Thomas C. Stagg
Westervelt Charles Stagg
William C. Staggs
William F. Stagnoli
Howard R. Stahala
Paul K. Stahl
Philip B. Stahley
Jack J. Stai
Melvin R. Stai
T. A. Stainbrook, Jr.
Calvert Loraine Stair
George K. Stairs
Clifford E. Stalkfleet
Roy G. Stallard
Walter E. Stallard
Ernest E. Stallings
Jack W. Stallings
Vernon D. Stallings
Harold Stallsworth
Charles Stalnaker
Nason D. Stalnaker
Virgil L. Stambaugh
Francis H. Stamer
Harold C. Stamm
Roy Stamm
John Edward Stammel
Mack Stamper, Jr.
Paul Stamper
Wayne E. Stamper
Albert William Stampfel
Jimmie Stampley
Clyde J. Stanback
Joseph E. Stancel
Orlin Stanchfield
Lee R. Stancil
Curtis Stand
Richard Standaert
Albert C. Standish
Jessie Standridge
Edward J. Stanek
Raymond D. Stanfill
James C. Stanford
Jessie M. Stanford
Harry Stang, Jr.
William E. Stangl
Edward J. Stanicki
Frank J. Stankevich
Gerald Norman Stanko
Theodore Stanks
Frank Krisin Stankus
Clancy D. Stanley
Glen James Stanley
Grady Stanley
James J. Stanley
John Stanley
Kenneth Stanley
Lee R. Stanley
Otha P. Stanley
Pat M. Stanley, Jr.
Richard L. Stanley
Vernon Ivan Stanley
William Alfred Stanley
Dock L. Stanphill
Verlyn L. Stanphill
William H. Stansbury
Frank I. Stansel
Donald William Stanton
Earl D. Stanton
Frederick Stanton
Gerald L. Stanton
Gordon R. Stanton
Hartswell Stanton
James O. Stanton
Jessie R. Stanton
John B. Stanton

Charles Ramsay Stapler
Carl Willis Staples
Jakey F. Staples
Arthur E. Stapleton
Austin Stapleton
David Francis Stapleton
Edward D. Stapleton
James R. Stapleton
Joseph W. Stapleton
Thomas P. Stapleton
Charles William Stapp
Rodey D. Stapp
Charles L. Starcher
Ollie V. Starcher
John Shirley Starck
William F. Staric
Gaylord W. Stark
Kenneth R. Stark
Louis Carroll Stark, Jr.
Louis K. Stark
Marshall W. Stark
Olen C. Stark
Robert J. Stark
Clyde M. Starkey
Herman F. Starkey
Jack R. Starkey
Junior D. Starkey
Lewis B. Starkey
Lloyd Henry Starkey
William R. Starkey
Ward L. Starkweather
Clyde Ronald Starling
Robert C. Starling
Delbert L. Starnes
Raymond S. Starnes
James Leonard Starr
Norman F. Starr
Robert I. Starr
Raymond Starzee
Raymond Earl Stash
Walter Staskiewicz
Douglas States
Angelo Stathes
James Francis Statia
Lavern D. Statler
Loren Staton
Robert W. Staub
John Carl Stauber
Bill James Stauffer
Kenneth G. Stauffer
Robert L. Stauffer
Roger Neil Stauffer
Bernard Ulrich Stavely
Paul M. Stavnitzky
Lester C. Stavos
Stephen Staysich
Joseph Stdko
Alvin L. Stebbins
George F. Stebbins
Arthur Robert Stebner
Ronald C. Stec
Richard Edmund Steckel
Daniel A. Stedman
Gerald F. Stedman
Larry R. Steed
Nelson Steedley
James B. Steel
Robert D. Steel
Arthur J. Steele
Aurthor G. Steele
Auther R. Steele
Charles H. Steele
Charles Oscar Steele
Clyde D. Steele
Darrell R. Steele
Dean A. Steele
Harold M. Steele
Homer Dean Steele
James A. Steele
John Augusta Steele
John W. Steele
Lloyd E. Steele
Nathan Steele, Jr.
Robert Coultas Steele
Robert R. Steele
Ronald E. Steele
Walter Steele
William Steele, Jr.
C. J. Steelman
Gerald D. Steen
Ivan M. Steenbergh
John C. Stefanac
Louis T. Stefanak
Stanley John Stefaniak
Frank Stefas
Daniel F. Steffen
Donald E. Steffen
Alvin J. Steffensen
William R. Steger

Edwin C. Steigerwalt
Gerald D. Stein
Richard James Stein
Robert Anthony Stein
Robert J. Stein
Roger A. Stein
Ernest W. Steinberg
Joseph D. Steinberg
James Anthony Steiner
Jack Charles Steinharter
Anthon Steinhauser
Harold Steinhilber
Obed N. Steininger
Robert E. Steinle
Dale C. Steinmetz
John E. Steinson
Italo L. Stella
John A. Stelline
Henry J. Stelmasiak
Robert J. Stelter
John J. Stempkowski
Paul B. Stemrick
Allen Gene Stenerson
William A. Stengel
John Clinton Stenger
John F. Stenger
Robert T. Stenson
John Jay Stenz
Lawrence F. Stenzel
Paul E. Stephan
Henry J. Stephany
James William Stephen
Mose Stephen, Jr.
Arnold E. Stephens
Carlton C. Stephens
Cleo Stephens
Dale L. Stephens
Dan Stephens, Jr.
Daniel T. Stephens
Don Richard Stephens
Elmore J. Stephens
George R. Stephens
Harry E. Stephens
Harvey Stephens, Jr.
James F. Stephens
James F. Stephens, Jr.
James M. Stephens
James W. Stephens
Jerome Stephens
Leon B. Stephens
Ralph Stephens
Raymond G. Stephens
Robert D. Stephens
Russell L. Stephens
Wesley Stephens
William M. Stephens
Albert Stephenson
Billy Clyde Stephenson
Chester Stephenson
Floyd A. Stephenson, Jr.
James E. Stephenson
James E. Stephenson
James Lee Stephenson
Virgil E. Stephenson
Dallas W. Stephey
Nicholas Stephno
George Stepina
David C. Stepp
Harlan L. Stepp
Mermon J. Stepp
Frank S. Sterczek
Harold W. Sterling
Donald Eugene Stern
John M. L. Stern, Jr.
John T. Sternard
Robert E. Sternard
Alton G. Sterner
Walter W. Sterner
Glenwood Stettler
Percy Lee Steuart
Barnard Stevens
Billy J. Stevens
Claud N. Stevens
Claude Otis Stevens, Jr.
Cleve R. Stevens
Crocket B. Stevens
Edward R. Stevens
Frank L. Stevens
J. T. Stevens, Jr.
James Stevens
James A. Stevens
James E. Stevens
James P. Stevens
Leo Stevens
Leonard Ray Stevens
Lionel F. Stevens
Lynn Stevens
Richard C. Stevens
Robert B. Stevens

Robert Stevens, Jr.
Robert L. Stevens
Simon J. Stevens
Thaddeus F. Stevens
William Stevens
William E. Stevens
William T. Stevens
Billie G. Stevenson
Bobby R. Stevenson
Carl Cecil Stevenson
Charles Stevenson
Charles Stevenson
Frank James Stevenson
James A. Stevenson, Jr.
Jeffery Stevenson
Kenneth Stevenson
Max B. Stevenson
Robert E. Stevenson
William Stevenson
James F. Steverson
David D. Steward
L. V. Steward
Alexander Stewart
Bernard A. Stewart
Bill J. Stewart
Carl Norman Stewart
Charles F. Stewart
David L. Stewart
Donald Stewart
Duane B. Stewart
Earl B. Stewart
Edward F. Stewart
Eugene W. Stewart
George E. Stewart
Gerald W. Stewart
Graham Stewart
Harold E. Stewart
Harry M. Stewart, Jr.
Henry C. Stewart
Howard Stewart
Howard J. Stewart
Huell J. Stewart, Jr.
Isiah Stewart
James E. Stewart
James E. Stewart
James W. Stewart
James Walter Stewart
John W. Stewart, Jr.
Joseph Elmer Stewart
Kenneth C. Stewart
Leon S. Stewart
Orestus M. Stewart
Raymond A. Stewart, Jr.
Richard H. Stewart
Richard H. Stewart
Robert Edwin Stewart
Robert F. Stewart
Robert J. Stewart
Ronald Loren Stewart
Roy Stewart
Rudolph Stewart
Russell D. Stewart
Stanley Stewart
Thomas K. Stewart
Udell V. Stewart
Victor L. Stewart
Victor W. Stewart
Wallace Delford Stewart
Walter Lee Stewart
Warren E. Stewart
Weldon F. Stewart
Weldon W. Stewart
William H. Stewart
William James Stewart
William L. Stewart
William S. Stewart
William T. Stewart
Wilson W. Stewart
Arnold E. Stibelman
Billy L. Stice
Reno D. Stice
William W. Stickler
Gary S. Stickles
Asa David Stidger
Carl Stidham
Henry Stidham
Henry Clifton Stidham
Lloyd D. Stidham
Ernest J. Stiefel
Lawrence H. Stigge
Earl C. Stiles
George W. Stiles
Jerry D. Stiles
Paul G. Stiles
Vernon Lester Stiles
Edgar H. Still
William Raymond Still
Daniel John Stiller
Charles Robert Stilwell

Robert J. Stim
George W. Stimpson
Percy E. Stine, Jr.
Kent W. Stinger
Guyton Stingley
Billie J. Stinnet
Bob F. Stinnett
Clem Lee Stinnett
Edward N. Stinnett
William R. Stinnett
Herman E. Stinnette
Charlie Stinson
Paul Stipandic, Jr.
Ellwood C. Stirm, Jr.
Richard N. Stirr
George C. III Stith
Doil R. Stitzel
John A. Stiver
Felix Charles Stock
Robert Cicero Stockard
Benny George Stockert
Lee Carl Stockholm, Jr.
Charles E. Stocklen
Richard W. Stockman
Douglas Stockstill
Cecil R. Stockton
Lee E. Stockton
Jesse H. Stockwell
Roy L. Stockwell
Walter Stodolsky
Walter T. Stoeber, Jr.
George Stoeckl, Jr.
Jerome H. Stoffel
Claude L. Stokes
Earle Vincent Stokes
Fred J. Stokes
Joe L. Stokes
John M. Stokes
Kenneth H. Stokes
Reginald H. Stokes
Robert W. Stokes
Sherman M. Stokes
Walter C. Stokes
Richard W. Stokum
Thomas H. Stoliker
Earl Daniel Stoll
Edward Joseph Stoll
James W. Stoll
Dale R. Stollberg
Bertram L. Stolze
Bernard J. Stone
Bob G. Stone
Charles A. Stone
Charles A. Stone, Jr.
Charlie C. Stone
Edward J. Stone
Edward M. Stone, Jr.
Frederic E. Stone
Harold J. Stone
Harry W. Stone, Jr.
John F. Stone
John G. Stone
Kelly L. Stone
Lafe E. Stone
Lawrence M. Stone
Lloyd H. Stone
Marion H. Stone
Neil R. Stone
Oliver Stone, Jr.
Paul H. Stone
Richard M. Stone
Richard T. Stone
Robert L. Stone
Robert Nathan Stone
William H. Stone
Clarence D. Stoneking
Joseph Oscar L. Stonelake
James W. Stoner
Jay R. Stoner
Milton Elsworth Stoner
Oliver Stoney, Jr.
Harvel Stooksberry
Dewey Stopa
Paul Norman Storaasli
Louis J. Storck
William E. Storck
Dallas R. Storey
Leroy Gene Storey
Alva J. Stork
John L. Storment
Harold A. Storms
Harvey H. Storms
Joseph E. Storti
Donald R. Story
Donald Wilbur Story
Glen Frederick Story
Leroy A. Story
Luther H. Story
Martin L. Story

372

Charles H. Stotler
Isaac D. Stotler, Jr.
Beverly R. Stott
Billy J. Stotts
Frank A. Stout
Harold C. Stout, Jr.
James H. Stout
Johnnie Oval Stout
Philip D. Stout
Richard L. Stout
Russell B. Stout
Dawn Joseph Stovall
Jack Stovall
John R. Stovall
John R. Stovall, Jr.
Benny R. Stover
Max R. Stover
Ralph Stover
Marvin E. Stoy
John J. Strack
Anthony Stracuzzi
Charles Glasgow Strahley
George A. Straight
Robert B. Straight
Lawrence N. Strainic
John D. Stransky
Edward L. Stratton
Franklyn H. Stratton
Ralph B. Stratton
Tex R. Straub
Deryle G. Straughn
Donald F. Strauser
Lloyd F. Strauser
Delmer Eugene Strawhorn
Paul P. Strawser
Robert L. Strawson
Joseph Straza
Johnnie Street
Karl J. Streeter
Richard Sherwin Streeter
James S. Streetman
Joseph M. Streetman
Donald O. Streicher
Donald N. Streight
Thomas Stretsbery
Guy Henry Streuven
Edward Stribling
Asa W. Strickland, Jr.
George Strickland
Jimmie Archless Strickland
Joe F. Strickland
John C. Strickland
John Strickland, Jr.
John M. Strickland
Marvin B. Strickland
Pete Strickland
Terrell Strickland
Williams W. Strickland
Woolard F. Strickland
Charles Stricklen
Donald W. Strickler
Paul C. Strickler
Richard Strickler
Clarence Stricklin
Richard Earl Strider
Leon C. Strieff
Joseph W. Striegel
Paul W. Strine
Gene Stringer
Harry C. Stringer
Richard J. Stringer
Leona Stringfellow
John Thomas Stritch
William F. Stritzke
Lawrence H. Strobel
William E. Strobel
Edward D. Strocky
Charles O. Stroemer
Ignatz James Strogis, Jr.
Frederick W. Strohm
Paul Daniel Strohmeyer
Carl A. Strom
John O. Strom
Ronald Duane Strommen
Cornelius Strong, Jr.
Dale H. Strong
Forrest T. Strong
Gordon M. Strong
Richard P. Strong
William A. Strong
Eugene Edward Strope
Dale Lemoine Stropes
Armour D. Strother
Keith A. Strotman
Arthur H. Stroud
Wayne A. Stroud
Jack D. Stroup
James R. Stroup
Ray C. Stroup

Roy A. Stroup
Clinton J. Strouse
Clifford D. Strout
Josep Strubczewski
Britton R. Struble
Henry M. Struemph
Ralph A. Struewing
Charles Struthers
James W. Struthers
Charles M. Stryker
James N. Stryker
Edward C. Strylowski
Henry T. Strzelecki
Donald A. Stuart
Donald C. Stuart
James F. Stuart
Jerome Carroll Stuart
Billy O. Stubblefield
Evart R. Stubbs
Kenneth R. Stuck
Richard L. Stuck
Lyle D. Stucker
Donald L. Stuckey
Frederick Stuckey
Oscar N. Stucki
Roland S. Studley
Robert B. Studnick
Willard Stuffelbeam
Stanwood Stufflebeam
George R. Stuhan
Charles E. Stuller
Hamer S. Stumbo
Orville L. Stumbo
Samuel T. Stumbo
Roy Stumbough, Jr.
Donald Paul Stump
James T. Stump
John Louis Stumpf
Marion F. Stumpf
Charles Sturdivant
Gene Alfred Sturgeon
Ralph C. Sturgill
Donald Richard Sturm
Ronald G. Sturm
William Sturm
R. Van Deren Sturtevant
Wilfred A. Stusse
Francis E. Stutlien
Henry R. Stutte
Joe D. Stutts
Robert C. Styslinger
Angel L. Suarez
Asher B. Sublett
John R. Sucich
Mathew Sucich
Edgar W. Suckow
Jerome A. Sudut
William Henry Suffern, Jr.
John E. Suggs
John P. Suggs
Dennis P. Sugrue
Edmund W. Suhren
Robert T. Suitor
Peter P. Sukley
Frank Sulier
Frank J. Suliman
Hugh L. Sullens
George Simon Sulliman
Charles P. Sullivan
Clinton V. Sullivan
Dave Paul Sullivan
David C. Sullivan
Edgar Sullivan
Edward T. Sullivan
Francis R. Sullivan
Frank E. Sullivan
Gerald James Sullivan
Harold J. Sullivan
Harrison Sullivan
Jack Sullivan
James A. Sullivan
James C. Sullivan
James D. Sullivan
James F. Sullivan
James Joseph Sullivan
John L. Sullivan
John L. Sullivan
Joseph J. Sullivan
Joseph W. Sullivan
Lacy L. Sullivan
Leonard J. Sullivan
Lloyd Spencer Sullivan
Louis Gene Sullivan
Maurice Patrick Sullivan
Peter F. Sullivan
Ralph F. Sullivan
Robert A. Sullivan
Robert E. Sullivan
James E. Sulser

Norbert C. Sulzer
Robert P. Summeries
L. D. Summerlin
Marshall J. Summerlin, Jr.
Allen Summers
Donald George Summers
Eddie C. Summers
John F. Summers
Thomas J. Summers
Charles Summerton
Arthur Carr Summs
James D. Summy
William Bryant Sumner
William G. Sumner
James E. Sumners
Bill S. Sumpter
Cleve Sumpter
Delbert L. Sumpter
Jerry Eugene Sumpter
Marvin J. Sumpter
Jack D. Sumrall
John E. Sumrall
Jerry D. Sumrow
Robert D. Sumter
Celestine H. T. Sun
James N. Sund
Roland V. Sund
Harry W. Sunday
Leonard E. Sundberg
Larry D. Sundquist
Edward I. Sunkel
Roy L. Sunsdahl
Marshall Suntzenich
Earnest E. Surber
Harold Paul Surber
James A. Surber
Ralph Edmonds Surber
Joseph Bernard Surette
Robert J. Surprenant
Norman G. Susice
William Howard Susong
Paul J. Suter
Conley H. Suther
Kenneth Sutherland
Kenneth Sutherland
Raymond Sutherland
Charles T. Sutlief
Laverne A. Sutliff
Conard E. Sutphin
Harold A. Sutphin
Allen L. Sutton
Andrew M. Sutton
Daniel H. Sutton
Frederick G. Sutton
George C. Sutton
Harry C. Sutton
Harry E. Sutton
James B. Sutton, Jr.
John R. Sutton
Johnie Sutton
Leslie R. Sutton
Lloyd L. Sutton
Merle Edward Sutton
Ralph W. Sutton
Raymond D. Sutton
Walter Edmond Sutton
Willard Reimer Sutton
William F. J. Sutton
Robert M. Suvada
Herbert H. Suzuki
Robert J. Svacha
George Svec
Henry Svehla
George A. Svicarovich
Richard L. Svitek
Troy W. Swain
Vincent Swain, Jr.
James E. Swainbank
Francis R. Swainson
Roger G. Swalm
Stanley H. Swalm
Edward J. Swan
Gerald Lee Swan
Gene E. Swanger
Philip O. Swank
Joel D. Swanner
Ernest A. Swanson
Ernest Clarence Swanson
Eugene Howard Swanson
John A. Swanson
Richard P. Swanson
Roy W. Swanson
Russell E. Swanson
William Swanson
William R. Swarmer
Fred D. Swart
Alfred Lander Swarthout
Franklin T. Swartz
Robert L. Swartz

Kermit G. Swavely
Kenneth D. Swearengen
George Swearingen
William Swearingen
Edward Swearinger
Joseph V. Sweat
Lester Keith Sweat
Quinton B. Sweat
Earl Arthur Sweatt
Floyd C. Sweatt
Walter M. Sweatt
Edward E. Sweeney
Errett L. Sweeney
John R. Sweeney
Robert J. Sweeney
Kieth A. Sweet
Merlin R. Sweet
Randall R. Sweet
Richard L. Sweet
Donald William Sweetall
Charles Sweetwood
Robert J. Sweezey
Carl L. Sweigart
Carroll W. Sweiger
William C. Sweitzer
Bruce Andrew Sweney
Wilbur W. Sweney
David H. Swenson
James E. Swenson
Kenneth Swenson
Paul David Swenson
Richard Lee Swenson
Melvin A. Swett
Theodo Swiczkowski
Edward Swiechowski
Andrew C. Swiers, Jr.
Jack Swift, Jr.
Thomas C. Swift
Chauncey W. Swiger
David L. Swihart
Harold M. Swihart
Oscar B. Swindall
Henry C. Swindell
Clarence W. Swiney
Duane Adelbert Swinford
Beverly Allison Swingle
Ivan E. Swingle
Benny S. Swiniarski
Clarice C. Swinney
Stanley Swinsinski
James E. Swinson
Carl E. Swint
Edward Deane Swisher
Forrest D. Swisher
James Allen Swisher
John Swisher
Robert L. Swisher
Contee L. Switzer
Jesse Clark Swoape
Herman T. Swofford
Gayle L. Swope
George A. Swope
Wallace C. Swope
Adam Swornog
Delbert V. Swygart
Donald L. Sybrant
Robert Austin Sydnor
Forest Dene Sykes
William U. Sykes
Thomas G. Sykora
Adrian J. Sylva
Caesar Sylvester
James Sylvester
Richard Sylvester
Thomas A. Symington, Jr.
Albert L. Symon
John O. Symons
Robert Syndergaard
Edmund Synski
Robert R. Sypniewski
Stanley L. Sypniewski
Joseph Sysak
Edward Szaflarski
Maxymilian Szafran
Robert J. Szayway
Anthony A. Szczepanski
Frank Szelinski
Michael G. Szollosy
Thaddeus S. Szukala
Edwin W. Szwabo
John Joseph Szwjkos
Robert Szwajkowski
Thaddeus T. Szweda
Stanley Szymanski
Raymond Szymovicz

— T —

Edward G. Taasevigen

Edwin Felix Tabaczynski
Elpidio Tabangcura
Herlindo Tabares
Victor Tabarrini
Bennie E. Tabb
William H. Tabert
Richard Tablante
Charles A. Tabor
James L. Tabor
Stanley E. Tabor
Horace S. Tabusa
Flabiano T. Tacazon
Rocco Taccio, Jr.
Ralph F. Tacheny
Harold G. Tacke
Donald F. Tackett
Raymond Tackett
Wilbur T. Tackett
Kenneth A. Tackus
Joseph A. Taddeo, Jr.
Alton L. Tadlock
Alvin J. Tadlock
Alvin R. Tadlock
Estel V. Tadlock
Iva B. Tadlock
Donald L. Taets
Elias B. Tafoya
George Tafoya
John M. Tafoya
James Richard Taft
Kenneth E. Taft, Jr.
Marvin Taft
Paul B. Taft
Edward John Taggart
Melvin E. Taggart
Robert B. Taggart
Meech Tahsequah
Rudolph A. Tainio
Luke B. Tainpeah
Charles T. Tait
Mant M. Tait
Robert James Tait
Theodore Takafuji
Sam O. Takahara
George Takahashi
Richard M. Takahashi
Tohoru T. Takai
Herbert T. Takamatsu
Mitsugi B. Takamoto
Nobuyuki Takeshita
Harry F. Takeuchi
Jack H. Taktakian
Bernard D. Takvam
John C. Talarico
Cesara Talavera
Edward A. Talbert
Claude E. Talbot
Edgar Howard Talbot
Jack F. Talbot
Charles J. Talbott
Charles E. Taliaferro
Dennis Lynn Taliaferro
Glen J. Talkington
Donald Walfred Tall
Kenneth Paul Tallant
Robert Tallentire
Bobbie L. Talley
Doyal Talley
James W. Talley
James Willis Talley
Leonard M. Talley
Robert Talley, Jr.
Russell D. Talley
Sidney D. Talley, Jr.
George R. Tallman
John E. Tallman
James M. Tallon
Howard Tallsalt
Clare Tallwhiteman
Matthew Tally
Prudencio Talon
Charles Y. Tamaru
Kaname R. Tamashiro
Refugio C. Tamayo
Dominic Tamberino
Darel E. Tamplin
Herbert E. Tamplin
Osamu Tamura
Bedros Manoog Tanealian
Eugene Duane Tangeman
Marcial M. Tangente
Glenn L. Tangman
Clarence A. Tangney
Cecil R. Tankersley
James N. Tanksley
Tildon Edward Tanksley
Charles M. Tannehill
Arlond M. Tanner, Jr.
Bobby D. Tanner

David H. Tanner
James H. Tanner
Marlin Arthur Tanner
George H. Tanonaka
Kiyoshi Tanouye
Yukiwo Tanouye
Joseph Gerard Tansey
Roger M. Tansey
Issiah Tansil
Paul J. Tanski
Henry L. Tansley
Leonard Earl Tant
Morris E. Tanton
Neil F. Tantoro
Joseph Taormino
Donald Edward Tapia
Luis Tapia
Thomas L. Tapley
John H. Tapper
Jack G. Tapscott
Richard L. Tarantino
Harold Michal Tardio
Harvey Tarkow
Antoni Tarnas
Herbert Tarnopol
John P. Taro
Floyd A. Tarpley
Joe H. Tarpley
Allan Maurice Tarr
Philip P. Tarr
Douglas E. Tarry
Ebb L. Tarry
Richard Tartar
Raymond M. Tartt
Leslie W. Tarver
Wilbur Thomas Tarwater
Theodore M. Tasker
John R. Tasset, Jr.
Rudolph Tatalovich
Michael Robert Tatar
George G. Tatarakis
Dick G. Tate
Harry E. Tate
Hershel Leon Tate
Jack Tate
James R. Tate
John A. Tate
John Edward Tate
Thomas E. Tate
Willie D. Tate
Glen W. Tatem
Raymond W. Tatro
Richard D. Tatro
David Franklin Tatum
James Tatum
Richard Tauzell
Fernandes Tavares
Tony Tavares
William Tavres
Nicholas R. Taweel
William S. Tawes
Alan Chandler Taylor
Allen R. Taylor
Alton Erwin Taylor, Jr.
Archibald H. Taylor
Arvil L. Taylor
Benny C. Taylor
Billie Eugene Taylor
Billy B. J. Taylor
Bobby D. Taylor
Carl E. Taylor
Charles Augusta Taylor
Charles S. Taylor
Charlie Taylor
Clark E. Taylor
Claude R. Taylor
Clifford A. Taylor
David F. Taylor
David Scott Taylor
Dean E. Taylor
Delbert L. Taylor
Donald H. Taylor
Donald M. Taylor
Douglas L. Taylor
Earl W. Taylor
Earnest A. Taylor
Earnest D. Taylor
Edward J. Taylor
Edward J. Taylor
Elbert M. Taylor
Ervin John Taylor
Everett W. Taylor
Francis E. Taylor
Gene S. Taylor
George D. Taylor
German V. Taylor
Glenn H. Taylor
Grover C. Taylor, Jr.
Harry L. Taylor

Harvey Taylor, Jr.
Harvey M. Taylor
Henry H. Taylor
Herman R. Taylor
Howell Taylor, Jr.
Hoyte R. Taylor
Ira N. Taylor
Ira N. Taylor
Irvin Earle Taylor
Jack O. Taylor
James E. Taylor
James E. Taylor
James Franklin Taylor
James H. Taylor
James H. Taylor
James K. Taylor
James L. Taylor
James M. Taylor
James P. Taylor
James P. Taylor
James Robert Taylor
Joe D. Taylor
John A. Taylor
John A. Taylor
John C. Taylor, Jr.
John Howard Taylor
John J. Taylor
John Joseph Taylor
John M. Taylor
Lawrence Ivan Taylor
Lawrence K. Taylor
Leonard E. Taylor
Lester Ray Taylor, Jr.
Linnard M. Taylor
Marvin E. Taylor
Marvin L. Taylor
Michael A. Taylor
Michael U. Taylor
Mott Taylor, Jr.
Murl L. Taylor
Norman J. Taylor
Olin Johnson Taylor
Oscar L. Taylor
Owen R. Taylor, Jr.
Paul Kenneth Taylor
Porter W. Taylor
Ralph E. Taylor
Raymond Taylor, Jr.
Raymond L. Taylor
Raymond S. Taylor
Richard B. Taylor
Richard J. Taylor
Richard Smith Taylor
Riley S. Taylor
Robert E. Taylor
Robert V. Taylor
Robert W. Taylor
Robert W. Taylor
Ronald G. Taylor
Roy Taylor
Ted C. Taylor
Thomas A. Taylor
Verl P. Taylor
Warren Herbert Taylor
Wayne D. Taylor
William E. Taylor
William E. Taylor
William Edward Taylor, Jr.
William F. Taylor
William G. Taylor
William K. Taylor
William Marshall Taylor
William R. Taylor
William R. Taylor
Worth W. Taylor
Mark Taynton, Jr.
George K. Tayrien
Boyd Thomas Teague
Cordice Isaac Teague
Harold G. Teague
James Wesley Teague
Kennith J. Teague
Clifford K. Teasel
William J. Teasley
John William Tedford
Robert A. Tedford
Gail R. Teegarden
Byron Conway Teel
Clair F. Teeter
Joseph Leo Teeters
Aaron Tegay
Donald Dean Tegt
Paul Tehero, Jr.
James Cuhna Teixeira
Robert J. Tell, Jr.
Augustine Tellez
Luis A. Tellez
Rudolph Tellez
Alan Edward Tellin

Marvin Temple
Wesley E. Temple
Amos Cleveland Temples
Douglas E. Templeton
William E. Templin
Roderick K. Tenaglier
Shinji Tengan
Howard C. Tenley
Francis H. Tenn
Claude E. Tennant
Oliver Tennell
Albert Gilbert Tenney
James E. Tennille
Billy E. Tennison
Charles D. Tennison
Durward J. Tennyson
Eduardo T. Tenorio
Ramon B. Tenorio
Henry S. Tenzar
Julius S. Tepakeyah
Wee Clayton Ter
Roberto Teran
Frank Terczak
Vicent Charles Terino
Theodore M. Terkos
Joseph W. Terman
Peter Ternes
Peter J. Terranova
Andrew J. Terrell
Benjamin F. Terrell
James Terrell, Jr.
Joseph A. Terrell
Lelmon J. Terrell
Ray Terrell
William Terrell
Donald Terrio
Joseph T. Territo
Bryant A. Terry
Donald W. Terry
Espy Terry, Jr.
George Terry
George W. Terry
Harold L. Terry
Herbert R. Terry
Hubert Terry
Jimmie Terry
Lewis J. Terry
Minter Charles Terry
Paul E. Terry
Paul J. Terry
Ralph R. Terry, Jr.
Robert W. Terry
Roger E. Terry
Simon Terry
Van N. Terry
Lyle C. Terwilliger
Roger C. Teske
Donald Tessendorff
Ronald R. Tessier
Willard N. Tessin
Walter Remus Testerman
Joseph J. Teti
William J. Teuchert
Bernard Tew
Earl Clayton Tew
Edward A. Tews
Charles B. Thacker
Columbus H. Thacker
Robert L. Thacker
Robert N. Thacker
Roy A. Thacker
Roy L. Thacker
Lyle K. Thaller
George Thamel
Chester E. Tharp
George W. Tharp
Billy Ray Thatcher
Floyd E. Thatcher
Willis William Thatcher
Maurice E. Thaxton
George Lytle Thayer
James B. Thayer
Leo W. Thayer
John Francis Thees
Calvin M. Theis
Kenneth A. Theis
Kenneth J. Theisen
Norbert J. Theisen
Nicholas E. Theodorow
David Curtis Theophilus
Conrad Walter Theriault
Romeo G. Theriault
Herman Lee Theriot
Hubert J. Theriot
Sylvester Theriot
Donald A. Therkelsen
David L. Therrien
John R. Theurer
Delmar Louis Thevenet

Arthur J. Thibault
Joseph L. Thibault
Arthur E. Thibeault
Allen G. Thibert
George W. Thibodeau
Clement Thibodeaux, Jr.
Irvin J. Thibodeaux
Joseph Thibodeaux
Lucian J. Thibodeaux
Andreas C. Thiel
Bobby J. Thiele
Jack J. Thieme
William H. Thien, Jr.
Walter E. Thierfelder, Jr.
Joel Aloysius Thinnes
Jack H. Third
Lote Thistlethwaite
Harland C. Thoen
Albert E. Thomas
Alexander A. Thomas
Alfred W. Clem Thomas
Alonzo T. Thomas
Archie E. Thomas
Arnold L. Thomas
Carl W. Thomas
Charles C. Thomas
Charles F. Thomas
Charles W. Thomas
Charlie N. Thomas
Donald J. Thomas
Donald R. Thomas
Edmund R. Thomas
Ernest R. Thomas
Everett E. Thomas
Ezell Thomas
Francis D. Thomas
Francis Robert Thomas, Jr.
Frank W. Thomas
Fred Thomas
Freddie B. Thomas
Garland C. Thomas
Garland R. Thomas
George H. Thomas
George Harry Thomas
Gerald Thomas
Gerald Thomas
Gerald S. Thomas
Glenn D. Thomas
Gordon William Thomas
Harvey H. Thomas
Hazel Thomas
Henry Thomas
Herman L. Thomas
Hosea Thomas
Howard F. Thomas
Howell G. Thomas, Jr.
Issaih R. Thomas
Jack Allen Thomas
Jack H. Thomas
Jackson Thomas
Jake R. Thomas
James Thomas
James Clark Thomas
James E. Thomas
James F. Thomas
James Grover Thomas
James H. Thomas
James Thomas, Jr.
James Thomas, Jr.
James W. Thomas
Jerry D. Thomas
Jerry R. Thomas
John A. Thomas
John F. Thomas
John H. Thomas
Johnny W. Thomas
Joseph Thomas
Joseph Thomas, Jr.
Keith Douglas Thomas
Kenneth D. Thomas
Kenneth W. Thomas
Leland C. Thomas
Leonard Thomas
Lewis Albert Thomas, Jr.
Lloyd Thomas
Lloyd E. Thomas
Marion L. Thomas
Mitchell C. Thomas
Morbourn Anton Thomas
Morris M. Thomas
Neal E. Thomas
Orville R. Thomas
Phillip Thomas
Phillip Roger Thomas
Ralph Hunter Thomas
Richard E. Thomas
Richard F. Thomas
Richard N. Thomas
Robert A. Thomas

Robert C. Thomas, Jr.
Robert H. Thomas
Robert Harry Thomas
Robert J. Thomas
Robert V. Thomas
Roosevelt T. Thomas
Roy H. Thomas
Roy L. Thomas
Samual Thomas
Samuel Thomas, Jr.
Troy L. Thomas
Walter Elijah Thomas
Wardell M. Thomas
William B. Thomas
Willie E. Thomas
Willie E. Thomas
Willie L. Thomas
Willie M. Thomas
Willis Thomas
Joseph E. Thomason
Eulis D. Thomasson
Forrest J. Thomasson
Eugene John Thome
William A. Thome
George Frank Thommes
Herbert Thompkins
Reuben Thompkins
Albert Thompson
Albert A. Thompson
Amos M. Thompson
Arlie O. Thompson
Aubrey E. Thompson
Bekay Thompson
Ben Thompson
Benjamin F. Thompson
Bernie E. Thompson
Billy Thompson
Charles Russell Thompson
Clarence Thompson
Clarence Thompson
Cleveland Thompson
Dale D. Thompson
Donald O. Thompson
Donald W. Thompson
Duane Thompson
Edward J. Thompson
Edward L. Thompson
Elmore M. Thompson
Elwood John Thompson
Ernest E. Thompson
Eugene H. Thompson
Eugene R. Thompson
Fletcher R. Thompson
Floyd Thompson
Frank H. Thompson
Franklin B. Thompson
Frederick B. Thompson
Gene A. Thompson
George M. Thompson
Gerald T. Thompson
Harley George Thompson
Harmon A. Thompson
Harold D. Thompson
Harold M. Thompson
Harold S. Thompson
Harwood H. Thompson
Hereford Thompson
Howard Thompson
Howard R. Thompson
Howard S. Thompson
J. D. Thompson
James E. Thompson
James K. Thompson
James L. Thompson
James O. Thompson
James R. Thompson
James R. Thompson
James W. Thompson
Jerry A. Thompson
Jim Harvey Thompson
John E. Thompson
John E. Thompson
John Elbert Thompson
John Franklin Thompson
John R. Thompson
John W. Thompson
Johnnie Thompson
Joseph C. Thompson
Kenneth T. Thompson
Lee J. Thompson
Leonard Thompson
Leonard F. Thompson
Leslie C. Thompson
Lorenzo D. Thompson
Maynard H. Thompson
Morris F. Thompson
Norman R. Thompson
Ogden N. Thompson
Paul David Thompson

Percy L. Thompson
Philip R. Thompson
Ralph A. Thompson
Raymond Thompson
Richard D. Thompson
Richard E. Thompson
Richard Harry Thompson
Robert E. Thompson
Robert E. Thompson
Robert E. Thompson
Robert F. Thompson
Robert K. Thompson
Rodney D. Thompson
Roland D. Thompson
Ronald L. Thompson
Sequoyah Thompson
Spencer J. Thompson
Thomas B. Thompson
Warren E. Thompson
Wayne L. Thompson
Weston H. Thompson
Will Allen Thompson
William Thompson
William A. Thompson
William E. Thompson
William Edward Thompson
William H. Thompson
William R. Thompson
Allen E. Thomsen
Charles D. Thomson
Donald J. Thomson
Gordon W. Thomson
Hugh Kerr Thomson
John C. R. Thomson
John Norman Thomson
Joseph A. Thomson
Keith Edward Thomson
Malcolm M. Thomson
Thomas Lyon Thomson, Jr
Edward Edvert Thorn
John B. Thorn
Devaun Lyle Thornberry
Clyde Thornburg
Harold H. Thorne
Marion Elisha Thornhill, Jr.
Bobby J. Thornton
Bobby O. Thornton
Brian Bernard Thornton
Clayton H. Thornton
Cordus H. Thornton
Donald M. Thornton
Edward D. Thornton
Jack Raymond Thornton
Jack S. Thornton
Kenneth Adrian Thornton
Larry G. Thornton
Lonnie Thornton
Raymond R. Thornton
Richard R. Thornton
Theodore Thornton
William B. Thornton
Robert J. Thorp
Robert J. Thorp
Bill Daniel Thorpe
Ernest L. Thorpe, Jr.
Jake R. Thorpe
Richard Bertram Thorpe
Robert S. Thorpe, Jr.
Walter E. Thorpe, Jr.
Will Roy Thorpe, Jr.
George S. Thorsen
Dunca Thorsteinson
Robert Lee Thosath
Chester T. Thrailkill
Robert C. Thrane
James Ernest Thrash
Billy L. Thrasher
Edward J. Thraum
Delmer Threadgill
Woodie B. Threat
Fred Threet
William E. Threlkeld
Housto Throgmartin
James A. Thrower
Elton L. Thunander
Alvin D. Thurman
Henry T. Thurman, Jr.
Jackie L. Thurman
James B. Thurman
John Edward Thurman
Lester Paul Thurman
Ruben Thurman, Jr.
Ralph R. Thurmond
Ralph G. Thurner
Richard F. Thursie
John Wilson Thurston
Russell E. Thurston
Donald Edward Thwaites
James A. Thweatt

Darrell J. Tibben
Charles O. Tibbetts
Gerald Keith Tibbit
Marvin W. Tibbits
Clarence E. Tibbs
Connie L. Tibbs
Don E. Tibbs
Jessie T. Tibbs
Robert E. Tibbs
Charles L. Tice
Clinton C. Tice
Robert W. Tichnell
Stanley Milner Tick
Dewey L. Tidwell
Gerald Gladden Tidwell
James A. Tidwell
Reuben W. Tiegs
Raymond W. Tieman
Allen Richard Tiernan, Jr.
John J. Tiernan
Austin Joseph Tierney, Jr.
Edmund W. Tierney
Jack Tierney
Michael J. Tierney
Wesley E. Tietge
Albert Rowe Tiffany
Max G. Tiger
Thomas J. Tighe
Antonio D. Tijerina
Phillip Wayne Tilch
Henry C. Tilden
Melvin H. Tilden
William A. Tilghman
Peter Tilhof
Horace Nelson Tiller
Ernest L. Tillett
Herbert L. Tilley
Louis Henry Tilley
William L. Tilley
Bernard J. Tillman
Charles W. Tillman
George D. Tillman
Gerald David Tillman
Herbert E. Tillman
Johnston C. Tillman
Richard H. Tillman
Howard Winfield Tillotson
Jared E. Tillotson
Clark M. Tilton
David Timberlake
Wallace L. Timm
James E. Timmerberg
Theodore Timmerman
John W. Timmins, Jr.
Claude C. J. Timmons
Eugene Leroy Timmons
Robert L. Timmons
William E. Timmons
Irvin Myles Tindall
Leo J. Tindall
Edward T. Tindell
James Tindell, Jr.
Bobby A. Tingle
Clarence H. Tingle
Paul L. Tingle
Arden L. Tinnel
Cecil E. Tinsley, Jr.
Earl G. Tinsley
George M. Tinsley
Wallace A. Tinsman
Donald E. Tippery
Wiley J. Tipton
Cortes Juli Tirado
Eugene L. Tirado
Serrano Ama Tirado
Jose M. Tirado-Gacia
Charles Rayford Tircuit
Andrew J. Tischler
Leonard Mickel Tiscia, Jr.
Charles E. Tisdale
Clarence A. Tish, Jr.
George E. Tishner
Herbert R. Tison
Leonidas L. Titchnell
Raymond Harvey Titley
Albert D. Titman
Alfred J. Titone
Eugene L. Titsworth
David B. Titus
David O. Titus
Donald George Titus
Harold Jack Titus
James R. Titus
Robert Eli Titus
Robert O. Titus
Dale M. Tjaden
Alexander Toatley
Arnold Rudolph Tobias
Stanley P. Tobias

374

James Edward Tobin
Robert W. Tobin
Roy J. Tobin
Walter H. Tobin, Jr.
Anthony F. Tobio
Louis Tocci
Joseph A. Tocco
Joseph T. Tocco
Silvio N. Tocco
Peter V. Todaro
Albert Erwin Todd
Augustus Edward Todd
Blanton Todd
Duane A. Todd
Frederick E. Todd
Leo C. Todd
Leon D. Todd
Leonard Vernon Todd, Jr.
Marion H. Todd
Phillip J. Todd
Richard H. Todd
Joseph H. Toecus
Donald J. Togni
Howard M. Tohill
Lawrence S. Tohill
Melvin Toho
Ivan Tokartschuk
Richard R. Tokunaga
Donald Timothy Toland
Barney A. Tolbert
Alton L. Toler
Robert S. Toler
Walter Toler
Lowell Tollefsrud
Marion E. Tolleson
Ted L. Tolleson
Harry C. Tolley
Robert E. Tolliver
Richard L. Tom
Sun K. Tom
Daniel Takashi Toma
Frank S. Toman
Waclaw A. Tomaszewski
William Rawle Tome
Harold M. Tomer
Glenn E. Tomes
Haruo Tomita
Andrew A. Tomkovich
Edward Junior Tomlin
Charles Tomlinson
Lawerence Tomlinson
Marvin E. Tomlinson
Maurice Tomlinson
Simpson Tomlinson
William Tomlinson
Daniel D. Tompkins
Richard A. Tompkins
William J. Tompkins, Jr.
Edward B. Tonander
Raul A. Sr Tonche
George A. Tondreau
Peter Fortunato Tonellato
Edward E. Toner
Joseph F. Toner
Raymond C. Toner
Clarence Toney
William H. Toney
David A. Tong
William J. Tonker
Joseph R. Toohey
Orlin R. Toohey
Marck Loos Tooker, Jr.
Ronald H. Tooker
Arnold E. Toole
Robert Philip Toole
Charles R. Toombs
Jewell A. Toombs
Joseph D. Toomey
Albert E. Toon
Winfred Basil Toone
William Wilbur Toops
John Topolancik
Edward F. Toraitis
George W. T. Torbett
Guy F. Torchia
Robert J. Toress
James Edward Torgeson
George Torhan
Louis C. Toribio
Frank W. Torigian
Casey N. Torikawa
Richard Torkelson
George Toro
Hernandez Jos Toro
Issac Del Toro
Ramon P. Toro
Jacob Torosian
Howard P. Torpy
Ferman L. Torrence

Titus R. Torrence
Fernando Torrent
Angel M. Torres
Anselmo Torres
Bello Franc Torres
Caban Jose Torres
Donald Torres
Elias E. Torres
Ernest E. Torres
Ernesto Torres
Ernesto J. Torres
Fuentes Ang Torres
George Torres
Joe Torres
Jose Torres
Jose C. Torres
Lugo Manuel Torres
Luis P. Torres
Luna Angel Torres
Marcelo Torres
Nicholas Torres
Orellana Jo Torres
Ortiz Anton Torres
Pablo Torres
Pete Torres
Phil Torres
Ralph Lopez Torres
Roberto R. Torres
Rodriguez G. Torres
Roselio J. Torres
Russell G. Torres
Segarra Wil Torres
Torres Remi Torres
Walter Torres
Jorge Torres-Green
E. Torres-Rodriguez
Samuel Torres-Rodriguez
Donald Richard Torstad
Charles Tortorici
Frank Tosetti
Edward J. Toth
James C. Toth
John R. Toth
Sigmond L. Toth
Mical M. Totland
Edward John Toto
Douglas Eugene Totten
Gene D. Totten
Robert A. Totty
Regis M. Tougas
Lester E. Toulmin, Jr.
Irving Tourtelotte
Julian Tamayo Tovar
Jesus I. Toves
Donald E. Tovsen
Frank Tow
George W. Tow
Jessie Towe, Jr.
Joseph N. Towell
Ellis E. Towery
James Ellingwood Towle
James L. Towles
Edwin Jack Town
Charles E. Towne
Roosevelt Towns
Albert M. Townsend
Clifford Townsend
Delmar A. Townsend
James H. Townsend
James L. Townsend
James M. Townsend
Randolph Townsend
Thomas S. Townsend
Hugh A. Townsley
Grover C. Towry
Edwin R. Tracy
John H. Tracy
Robert W. Tracy
Theodore P. Tracy
Jack Dale Trader
Leroy A. Trader
Daniel J. Trahan
John W. Trail, Jr.
Joseph H. Trail
John Train, Jr.
Atlee Bryn Trainer
Henry Taft Trainum, Jr.
Otto C. Trakberger
Roger N. Trall
George B. Trammell
James Trammell
Joseph L. Trammell
William D. Trammell
Elijah Trannon, Jr.
Andrew L. Trano
Archie Peyton Trantham
Warren G. Trantham
Lawrenc Trapanotto
Eugene O. Trask

Nelson E. Trask
Jesse J. Traughber
Donald Chris Trausch
John E. Trautman
Arthur A. Trautmann
Edward J. Trautwein
Joseph Raymond Travers
William S. Travers
Arthur H. Traverso
Chester B. Travis
Edward J. Travis
Gilbert M. Travis
Henry C. Third Travis
John T. Travis
Rollin G. Travis
William F. Traxler
James M. Traylor
Edgar J. Treacy, Jr.
Joseph Edward Treadway
Peter Treadway
Richard A. Treadway
John E. Treanor, Jr.
George F. Treder
Gordon Thomas Tredoar
Thomas E. Tredway
William A. Treece
James Lee Treester
David Orozco Trejo
Refugio Trejo
Clayton A. Treloar
Aurel N. Tremblay
Paul N. Tremblay
David K. Trembley
Richard G. Trembley
Richard R. Trenholm
Don L. W. Trent
Donald C. Trent
Donald M. Trent
Ira V. Trent
James L. Trent
James O. Trent
Jebru Trent
John C. Trent
Arthur A. Trentt
James E. Trepanier
Joseph Trepasso
Kenneth W. Treptau
Agustin Trevino, Jr.
Alfredo T. Trevino
Gabriel Trevis
George C. Trexler
Rayfield A. Trexler
Joseph R. Tria
Julian Tribble
Richard S. Tribble
Robert J. Tricomi
John A. Tricomo
William L. Trietsch
John A. Trigg, Jr.
Gregory W. Triggs
James B. Triggs
Jim S. Trimble
Thomas William Trimble
William J. Trimble
Joe B. Trimm, Jr.
John Edward Trimm
William P. Trinen
Joseph F. Trinkaus
John H. Trinkle
James J. Trione
Delmer L. Triplett
Lowell C. Triplett
Ray Tripp
William A. Tripp
Clarence W. Trivett
Robert M. Trivett
Billie J. Trobough
Gerald D. Troccola
Maximo A. Troche
Vance E. Trogdon
Harold Trolle
Alva F. Trombly, Jr.
George Trompak, Jr.
William B. Trompics
Robert D. Troncin
Ernest H. Tronier
James Oliver Trosclair
Lawrence J. Trosclair, Jr.
Eugene F. Tross
Robert C. Trotman
Donald Kenneth Trotter, Jr.
John Edward Trotter
Robert A. Troufield
Howard A. Troup
Ben Dick Trout
Earl M. Trout, Jr.
Harry C. Trout, Jr.
Alfred Jackson Trovilo
Billy R. Trow

Truman D. Trowbridge, Jr.
Cornelius Trowel
Paul Theodore Troxell, Jr.
Donald O. Troxler
Carl K. Troy
George F. Troy
Joel J. Troy
Joseph W. Troy
Lawrence E. Troy
John J. Truan
Cecil S. Truax, Jr.
Kenneth A. Truax
Reed A. Truax
Donald W. Trubee
Norman F. Trudeau
Roger Trudeau
Edward D. Trueblood
Hubert P. Trueblood
Paul H. V. Trueheart
Robert Daniel Truelock
Bobby L. Truelove
Harold Truesdale
Furman Maxey Truett
Ray E. Truett
John S. Truhan
Anthony J. Truisi
Granville H. Truitt
Howard E. Truitt
Thomas Truitt
Biviano Trujillo
Domingo Trujillo
Isidro E. Trujillo
John D. Trujillo
Melecio H. Trujillo
Robert M. Trujillo
Tony E. Trujillo
Welton P. Trull, Jr.
Glen K. Trulock
Glenn E. Truman
Thomas E. Truman
John H. Trusckewicz
Arthur E. Truslow
Elwood M. Truslow
John Truter
Kenneth T. Trutna
Arthur H. Truxes, Jr.
Emil Trynoski
Lawrence Andrew Tryon
Nickolas J. Tsaknis
William Tschuschke
James Tsitsinos
Thomas Tsoukras
Jack S. Tsuboi
Sueo Tsunoda
Nicola A. Tucci
Walter M. Tuck
William C. Tuck
Boyd E. Tucker
Clifford Tucker
Daniel H. Tucker
Donald H. Tucker
Drexell Eugene Tucker
Earl J. Tucker
Francis J. Tucker
Frank B. Tucker
George E. Tucker
Herbert Tucker
J. D. Tucker
John L. Tucker
Junior R. Tucker
Lloyd L. Tucker
Luke James Tucker, Jr.
Ray D. Tucker
Richard F. Tucker
Robert J. Tucker
Robert L. Tucker
Stanley R. Tucker
Thomas W. Tucker
Willie L. Tufts
Richard J. Tugman
John Tuin
James G. Tulip
William Allen Tulk, Jr.
George A. Tull
Ralph E. Tull
Travis Lloyd Tull
Thomas J. Tullo
John Franklin Tulloch, Jr.
John Ruben Tully
Thomas Eugene Tumey
Carl D. Tumlinson
George E. Tunin
Adolph Tunstall, Jr.
Stanley Turba
Jack Howard Turberville
Michaux Turbeville
Clarence Turcott
Edmund J. Turcotte
Ray C. Turcotte

Lawrence G. Turczyn
George E. Turek
Daniel A. Turgeon
Arthur T. Turingan
Ned Turk, Jr.
Dorsey V. Turley
James E. Turley
Herbert C. Turman
Jeff Turman
John H. Turman
James D. Turnbull
Robert J. Turnbull
Allen D. Turner
Allen T. Turner
Berry W. Turner
Billy A. Turner
Charles W. Turner
Charlie Turner
Clemon Turner
Cooper T. Turner
Corbet L. Turner
David C. Turner
Donald E. Turner
Edwin P. Turner
Elmer Carlton Turner, Jr.
Ernest K. Turner
Eugene C. Turner
Gerald O. J. Turner
Hallie K. Turner
Harold Peter Turner
Herbert Turner
Howard L. Turner
James H. Turner
James L. Turner
James Roy Turner
James W. Turner
Joe Henderson Turner
Joseph L. Turner
Larry Denis Turner
Lester S. Turner
Lorenzo Turner
Marvin Turner
Melvin L. Turner
Raymond Alfred Turner
Richard C. Turner
Richard L. Turner
Robert G. Turner
Robert William Turner
Ronald L. Turner
Roy David Turner
Roy Frederick Turner
Thomas J. Turner
W. D. Turner
Wallace W. Turner
Weldon G. Turner
William H. Turner
William T. Turner
Winston Turner
Winston M. Turner
James P. Turney
Waldo W. Turney, Jr.
David A. Turovh
Richard Franklin Turpin
Maurice Alfred Tuthill
Leon H. Tutt
Allen H. Tuttle
Frederick H. Tuttle
James K. Tuttle
Kenneth E. Tuttle
Lloyd C. Tuttle
Mathew Tuttle
Raymond John Tuttle
Raymond Lee Tuttle
Harry D. Tuxhorn
Vito C. Tuzzolino
Harold Anton Twedt
Benjamin F. Twiddy
Lloyd D. Twidt
Harry G. Twiford
Charles C. Twigg
Gene A. Twitchell
Wallace Twitchell
James N. Twitty
Jack O. Tye
Leonard E. Tye
Robert Edward Tykarski
Benjamin M. Tyler
Charles E. Tyler
Charles R. Tyler
Elmer J. Tyler
Emile Tyler
Harry M. Tyler
Kenneth E. Tyler
Maxine Tyler
Robert L. Tyler
Rodney Tyler
Adam P. Tymowicz
Joseph E. Tynan
Avery B. Tyndall, Jr.

Bradford E. Tyndall
Jake Tyner, Jr.
John T. Tyner
James B. Tynes
Jesse Tyra
Anthony J. Tyrala
Noah H. Tyree, Jr.
Stanley L. Tyrell
Frederick Tyrrell
Paul E. Tyrrell
Lester Tyson

— U —

Lester J. Uber
James E. Udd
Lester L. Udenberg
Noboru Uehara
Seiho Uejo
Mitsuo Uemura
Paul A. Uherchik
Edward M. Uhl
Roger L. Uhll
Jerry E. Uhls
Joseph W. Ujek, Jr.
Yukio Ujimori
William L. Ulbrich
Onis L. Ulerick
Valerian Ulinski
Chauncey Ludwig Ullman
William Ullman
La Vern C. Ullmer
Richard R. Ulrey
Curt W. Ulrich
Herman A. Ulrich
Louis M. Ulrich
William F. Umbarger
Ernest Junior Umbaugh
Robert E. Umbel
Robert Edward Umhoefer
John F. Umlauf
Alfred Underbaggage
William Underdown
Virgil E. Underhill
Robert Logan Undersinger
Donald A. Underwood
George Curtis Underwood
Guy L. Underwood, Jr.
Harold L. Underwood
Herbert Underwood
Homer H. Underwood
Ralph F. Underwood
Ralph F. Underwood
Ray C. Underwood
Roy S. Underwood
Troy D. Underwood
Kenneth W. Unger
Henry J. Unkel, Jr.
Archie M. Uno
Halbert Caloway Unruh
Roy Dean Unruh
Walter Unruh
Lawrence A. Unsell
Akira Uota
James B. Upchurch
Ernest Harold Upmeyer
James B. Upschulte
Huey Edward Upshaw
Willie D. Uptain
John W. Uptegrove
Richard R. Upton
Konomu Ura
Takaya Uragami
Manuel S. Uranga
Antonio Yanes Urbalejo
Isidro D. Urbano
Joseph P. Urbanorwicz
Edward Urbanowski
Darold D. Urbanski
Herman E. Urch
Edward E. Uria
Joe D. Uribe
John Uribe
William Urick
Richard M. Urmanski
Burdett C. Urness
Hughie D. Urquhart
Leroy C. Urquhart
Faustino Urro
Jerry Ursini
James E. Uselton
Curtis Usher
Ronald Clarence Usher
William R. Usnik
Terah A. Usry
Robert F. Ustick
Joseph H. Utard
Clifford L. Utter
Wilbur E. Utter

375

Stephen T. Uurtamo
Manuel J. Uvalle
Robert T. Uyeda
Alfred S. Uyehara
Takeo Uyehara
Francis A. Uzzo

— V —

Frank E. Vaage
Daniel J. Vaccaro
Fredrick W. Vach
Elphege Vadenais
Andrew Vaganka
John W. Vagg
Robert J. Vahlsing
William F. Vahlsing
Alber Vaillancourt
John Vaillancourt
Josep Vaillancourt
Leo J. Vaillancourt
Maxwell W. Vails
Lloyd C. Vajen
William Valachovic
Gilbert U. Valdenegro
Benito V. Valdez
Bernard T. Valdez
Ernest Valdez
Manuel Valdez
Rudy E. Valdez
Solomon Valdez, Jr.
Angel M. Valdiviez
Concepcio Valencia
Louis Valenciano
Cirildo Valencio
Joseph F. Valencourt
Fred Ange Valentin
Irizarry Valentin
Ralph J. Valentin
Earl Lester Valentine, Jr.
Eugne Valentine
James Nelson Valentine
Nicholas J. Valentine
Robert F. Valentine
William Valentine
Adolpho A. Valenzuela
Alfredo Valenzuela
Joe Mascareno Valenzuela
Tony L. Valenzuela
Bob S. Valera
Celestino D. Valera
Dominick V. Valle
Mario F. Valle
Emil J. Vallecorse
David Thomas Vallejo
Juan B. Vallesteros
Eugene Steven Vallo
Nello Valorosi
Charles Van Allen
Loyd A. Van Allen
Joachim Van Ameyde
Frank Van Antwerp
Edward Van Arsdale
Wilbur Van Bremen
William Van Brook
Richar Van Buskirk
Leo F. Van Camp
Richard Van Cleave
Deldt Ray J. Van Den
Harold Van Denburg
Gerald F. Van Denhende
Linde John Van Der
Patrick W. Van Dewerker
Donald F. Van Dine
Dale E. Van Draska
William G. Van Dunk
Edward L. Van Dusen
Bryant Van Dyke
George Van Dyke
Wallace W. Van Dyke
Charle Van Elsberg
James A. Van Fleet, Jr.
Mon Van Fradenburg
Donald Louis Van Frayen
John G. Van Goethem
Charles Clive Van Gorden
Julius L. Van Gundy
Henry W. Van Harn
Marshal Van Hoesen
Joseph J. Van Hook
Robert E. Van Hook
Howard G. Van Horn
Irving H. Van Horn
Robert L. Van Horn
John Edgar Van Housen
Frederick Donald Van Lehn
John E. Van Loh, Jr.
Paul Ernest Van Loo
Herbert Van Meter

Solomon L. III Van Meter
Russell Edward Van Natta
Theodore Van Natta
James J. Van Ness
Richard Van Newhouse
Marvin Van Ningen
Thomas Van Norden
Lester Henry Van Nort
Gilbert A. Van Nostrand
Harold Alfred Van Nostrum
Robert Dan Van Note
Charles E. Van Osdol
Kenneth F. Van Ost
William O. Van Pelt
Leslie Van Poucke
Robe Van Quakebeke
Bernard E. Fred Van Raay
Thomas Louis Van Riper
Samuel Van Saders
Frank Louis Van Sickle, Jr.
Eugene R. Van Steenvoort
Donald Glenn Van Til
James Arthur Van Veen
Paul Edward Van Voorhis
Ronald D. Van Wees
Charles R. Van Wey
Fred J. Van Why
Calvin A. Van Winkle
Clayton E. Van Wyk
Leonard J. Vanata
Asa E. Vance
Charles E. Vance
Doral A. Vance
William R. Vance
Zeb W. Vance, Jr.
Clayton W. Vandarwarka
Berghe Dona Vanden
Gordon Vandenbush
Burg Vernon Vander
Gast James Vander
Charles Vanderkooi
Jacob Vanderlaan
George Vanderloop
Douglas G. Vandermyde
Richar Vanderploeg
Willia Vandervoort
Lawrence M. Vanderwilt
Joseph Vandeventer
Richard E. Vaneekhoven
Ralph J. Vangsness
Clarence Vanhoose
Robert G. Vanhoose
William B. Vanhoy
Pompey J. Vanicola
Ralph Vanlear, Jr.
Harvey Thomas Vann
Russell E. Vannatta
Andrew Vanness
Kenneth T. Vannett
William Horace Vanney
Gilbert Vannosdall
James Vannoy
James M. Vannoy
Robert L. Vanover
Martin D. Vanoy
Thomas R. Sr Vantre
William H. Vanwey
Joseph B. Varcelli
Avelardo Varela
Julio S. Varela
Frank P. Varga
Flor Vargas
Grafals Ren Vargas
Rivera Guil Vargas
Julius John Vargo
Richard J. Vargo
Charles A. Varkett
James O. Varnell, Jr.
Alvin L. Varner
Edmund S. Varner
Gene C. Varner
John William Varner
Melvin Dene Varner
Thomas H. Varner
Basil Varney, Jr.
Billy F. Varney
Gerald L. Varney
Jon D. Varney
Robert E. Varney
Christopher Y. Vars
Patrick J. Varvel
Fernando Vasaldua
Henri J. Vaschetto
Balint Vash
Donald Vashon
Zane Morley Vasold
Albert M. Vasquez
Albert S. Vasquez
Arturo Vasquez

John V. Vasquez
Jose Vasquez
Jose J. Vasquez
Rumaldo R. Vasquez
Robert E. Vass, Jr.
H. T. Vaughan
Jack Eugene Vaughan
Samuel L. Vaughan
William E. Vaughan
Wilson H. Vaughan
Aubrey Dean Vaughn
Bill Mack Vaughn
Billie V. Vaughn
Carl D. Vaughn
Cleveland Vaughn, Jr.
Donald C. Vaughn
Glenn W. Vaughn
Grayson S. Vaughn
Hayden Gale Vaughn
Ira L. Vaughn
Jack Dennis Vaughn
Orville L. Vaughn
Robert T. Vaughn
Thomas H. Vaughn
Walter F. Vaughn
William Columbus Vaughn
William R. Vaughn
Winford L. Vaughn
Billy D. Vaught
Joseph F. Vavroch
John Michael Vaydich
Cruz Joaqu Vazquez
De Jesus E. Vazquez
Diaz Pablo Vazquez
Hilario C. Vazquez
Jorge L. Vazquez
Joseph T. Vazquez
Juan R. Vazquez
Rivera H. Vazquez
Rodriguez Vazquez
Ronald J. Vecchie
John Veckly, Jr.
Joseph S. Veckov
Walter C. Vedaa
Albert W. Veenstra
Joseph H. Veevaete
Enrique Vega, Jr.
Epifanio Vega
Perdomo Juan Vega
Ricardo Vega
Rivera Jose A. Vega
Rodriguez Fra Vega
Thomas P. Vega
Victor M. Vega
Vincent A. Vega
Albert Joseph Vegas
L. D. Veillon
Cecil T. Veit
Freddie Joe Veit
Frank G. Vejar
Manuel N. Vela
Frank A. Velasco
Angelo M. Velasquez
Jorge Velazquez
Jorge N. Velazquez
Lopez Is Velazquez
Pedro Velazquez
Richard Veld
Augusto Arma Velez
Rodolfo Velez
Santiago Lem Velez
Luis Velez-Montes
Miguel A. Velez-Santiago
Joseph Phillip Vella
Vincent P. Vella
Richard G. Velles
George Vellias
Antonio Velo
Charles D. Vender
Frank Joseph Venditti
John Robert Venditto
James Joseph Venes
Robert J. Venetz
Vincent Venezia
Harold W. Venson
Marcial T. Vera
Miguel A. Vera
Ramos Juan A. Vera
Tony S. Vera
Fred L. Verant
Robert Verardi
Carl Joseph Verbanac
William Cristian Verburg
Albert L. Vercolen
Clarence Henry Verett, Jr.
Eliseo C. Vergara
Ira H. Verill
William Vermillion
George E. Vernon

Harold Mark Vernon, Jr.
Raymond A. Vernon
Marco J. Verrant
Howard P. Verret
Steve J. Vertcnik
Ronald Lary Vertz
Lambert T. Vervoort, Jr.
Curtis E. Vestal
John William Vester
Cecil T. Vesy
Donald H. Vetowich
Robert M. Vetter
Joseph S. Veverka
Arnold Robert Vey
Nick Vezakis, Jr.
William A. Vezzoli
Maurice L. Viaene
Dallas W. Vian
James E. Viars
Joseph E. Viator
Robert Vicaldo
Steve Vich
Calvin C. Vick
Donald G. Vick
Gordon R. Vick
John Steven Vick
Kenneth N. Vick
Charles Vickers
Ivey E. Vickers
Wendell Vickers
Charles J. Vickery
Roy M. Vickery
Irwin L. Victor, Jr.
Olegario Vidaurri
Paul B. Vidock
Albert W. Vidrine
Marvin E. Viel
Frank Viera, Jr.
Isidoro Viera-Rodriguez
Harold A. Vierra
Edris A. Viers
Arturo Vigil
Enrique Vigil
Filbert J. Vigil
Isaac L. Vigil
Jose G. Vigil
Juan B. Vigil
Orace M. Vigil
Pablo J. Vigil
Rudolph F. Vigil
Henry F. Vigneau
Jakie J. Vignes
Lopez Abraham Vila
Raymond A. Vilage
Ruben Vilches
Robert Leland Viles
Herman F. Villa
John Rojas Villa
Paul Villa
George H. Villacres
Davila D. Villafane
Luis A. Villafane
G. Villafane-Vazquez
Robert C. Villalva
Gelio J. Villani
Gilbert Villanueva
Joaquin Villanueva
Alfonso Villareal
Raul S. Villareal
Cristob Villarreal
Jesus Villarreal
Juan L. Villarreal
Julio Villarreal, Jr.
Ernest Villaverde
Angel Villegas
Antonio B. Villela
Pedro G. Villereal
Nazario Lui Villot
Peter Vilutis, Jr.
Leroy D. Vinar
Albert A. Vincent
Donald F. Vincent
Edward C. Vincent
Frank H. Vincent
Raymond M. Vincent
William E. Vincent
Otha R. Vinceson
Salvatore Vinci
Cecil Vines
Thomas Franklin Vines, Jr.
Murray N. Vineyard
Robert J. Vineyard
John Vingione, Jr.
Jack L. Vining
Lawrence Edward Vink
John P. Vinkenberg
George E. Vinnedge
Donald C. Vinson
Earnest L. Vinson

Bobby Dean Vinyard
Herbert F. Vinyard
William Edward Violante
Joseph C. Violette
Robert James Violette
David G. Viramontes
Miranda Ro Virella
Anthony Paul Virgadamo
Peter A. Viscuso
Alphard R. Vismor
Robert J. Vitello
Joseph Vittori
Manuel Joseph Viveiros
Herbert D. Vizena
Irvin F. Vizenor
Harold A. Vizina
Roy Vizuete
Mitchell Vlahovich
Charles B. Vodicka
Jerry Dean Voelm
Jake Neil Voermans
Osman Voga, Jr.
Bruce O. Vogel
Joseph C. Vogel
Raymond William Vogel, Jr.
William Vogel, Jr.
Delbert E. Vogeli
Leo S. Vogen, Jr.
Leonard Paul Vogt
James Void
Edward Frederick Voight
John H. Voight
Paul T. Voight, Jr.
Rufus E. Voigt
Richard Voisine
John E. Voit
Robert J. Volack
Jerome A. Volk
Louis T. Volk
Virgil H. Volk
Fred W. Volkman
Andrew Emil Vollo
Sam A. Volpe
Richard H. Volz
Eschen David Von
Robert L. Vonallmen
Haar James Vonder
Victor G. Voorhees
William Robert Voorhees
Carl F. Vorbeck
Tony Voreh
Charles A. Vorel, Jr.
Alexander Vorobey
William H. Vorpagel
Harold B. Vortherms
Preston W. Vortish
Bernard W. Vos
Harry G. Vosburgh
Arthur Voss
Eugene F. Voss
Fred G. Voss
Gustave Roger Voss, Jr.
Harvey R. Voss
William Anthony Voss
Arthur R. Vossen
John W. Vought
Dallas Vowell
Herbert H. Vowell
Andrew I. Voyles
Eugene R. Voyles
Ray F. Voyles
William E. Voyles
Robert S. Vozar
Robert Vradenburgh
Anthony Vranic
James C. Vreeland
James George Vretis
Daniel Vukasovich
Edward R. Vydra

— W —

Cleo F. Wachel
Gus Wachenschwanz
Thomas G. Wachtman
William T. Wackermann
Cecil Alden Waddell
Edward L. Waddell
Donald L. Waddoups
Alexander Wade, Jr.
Charles C. Wade
Don Edgar Wade
Duerell Wade
Everett H. Wade
Freeman Mcmillan Wade
George A. Wade
John G. Wade
Leonard L. Wade
Mearl L. Wade

Samuel H. Wade
Tim E. Wade
Troy H. Wade
Vernon L. Wade
Vincent M. Wade
Willie R. Wade
Eddie G. Wadford
Billy F. Wadkins
Jimmie Lester Wadkins
La Grant L. Wadman
Donald E. Wadsworth
Freeman Wadsworth
John W. Wadsworth
William Wadsworth
Stanley E. Wafle
Everett W. Waford
Floyd R. Wagaman
James J. Wagenshutz
Dan H. Wagers
Joseph P. Wagers
Bille E. Waggoner
George Earl Waggoner
Burton A. Wagner
Carl R. Wagner
Danny L. Wagner
Donald L. Wagner
Gene L. Wagner
George J. Wagner, Jr.
Harold Lee Wagner
James R. Wagner
Miles E. Wagner, Jr.
Nicholas J. Wagner
Oscar W. Wagner
Paul Amrine Wagner
Paul R. Wagner
Ralph P. Wagner
Rex E. Wagner
Richard H. Wagner
Robert A. Wagner
Robert B. Wagner
Sim Wagner
Theodore A. Wagner
William Edward Wagner
William George Wagner
James C. Wagoner
Robert G. Wagoner
Melvin Waguespack
Martin J. Wahl
Richard L. Wahlert
Edward C. Wahlgren
Homer L. Waid
William H. Waid
Vincent E. Waidman
Ardean R. Wailes
Daniel E. Wain
Elmer G. Wainman
Lloyd E. Wainscott
Billy J. Wainwright
John K. Wainwright
Robert Ernest Wainwright
Stanford M. Wait
Kenneth E. Waite
Rex L. Waite
James H. Waites
Charles E. Waits
Louis E. Waiwaiole
Franklin Wakefield
Joseph W. Wakefield
Neal V. Wakely
Roland A. Wakenight
Joe R. Walbeck
Joseph Michael Walck
Casimir F. Walczak
John G. Walczak
Arnold Waldbillig
Charles J. Walden
Max M. Waldherr
Roman J. Waldkirch
Robert E. Waldman
Eugene L. Waldo
Edward S. Waldoch
Wilbur E. Waldon
Lloyd L. Waldrip
Clifton W. Waldron
Alton Waldrop
Arthur T. Waldrop
Jack N. Waldrup
Harry L. Walega
John L. Walenty
Owen Leslie Walgamotte
Raymond Waligorski
Arnold E. Walk
John H. Walk
William W. Walk
Archie Walker
Benjamin M. Walker
Bobby G. Walker
Charles E. Walker
Charles Walker, Jr.

David S. Walker
Don Walker
Donald Morris Walker
Earl F. Walker
Earl W. Walker
Eddie Walker
Emile Alan Walker
Francis J. Walker
Frank Mc Nally Walker
Glenn R. Walker
Guy J. Walker
Harold R. Walker
Harold Thomas Walker
Henry L. Walker
Howard Joseph Walker
Hugh W. Walker
Ishmael W. Walker
Jack Earl Walker
Jack L. Walker
Jack O. Walker
James Walker
James D. Walker
James I. Walker
James K. Walker, Jr.
James S. Walker
James T. Walker
James W. Walker
James Young Walker
Javy C. Walker
Jesse L. Walker
Joe C. Walker
Joe W. Walker, Jr.
John A. Walker
John Edward Walker
Kenneth E. Walker
Lawrence R. Walker
Leo Walker
Leonard Lawrence Walker
Leroy Manly Walker
Lester R. Walker
Lloyd B. Walker
Louie D. Walker
Noah Walker
Ralph B. Walker
Richard D. Walker
Robert B. Walker
Ross M. Walker
Teddy J. Walker
Thomas S. Walker
Tommy C. Walker
Walter Allen Walker
Walter L. Walker
Walton H. Walker
Wendell H. Walker
William E. Walker
William E. Walker
William H. Walker
William J. Walker
William Sterling Walker
Willie A. Walker
Arthur Hinton Wall
Doyle B. Wall
Paul A. Wall
Telma W. Wall, Jr.
Willie J. Wall, Jr.
Alvin L. Wallace
Bill S. Wallace
Carl E. Wallace
Carlson E. Wallace
Charles A. Wallace
Clarence M. Wallace
Clyde L. Wallace
Donald E. Wallace
Earl Wallace, Jr.
Elbert P. Wallace
Emil E. Wallace
Eugene Jurgen Wallace
Floyd Wallace
George W. Wallace
Grady Wallace
Harry R. Wallace
Henry Knox Wallace
Howard E. Wallace
J. I. Wallace
Jack D. Wallace
James A. Wallace
James M. Wallace
John W. Wallace
Mitchell Allen Sr Wallace
Pendleton W. Wallace
Ray E. Wallace
Robert J. Wallace
Robert L. Wallace
Willard D. Wallace
William K. Wallace
Zechariah Wallace
David Wallach
Joseph Creighton Wallack
William W. Wallack

Kenneth P. Wallan
James A. Wallen
James T. Wallen
Richard Earl Wallen
Charles H. Waller
Freemon C. Waller
Joseph E. Waller, Jr.
William D. Waller
William J. Waller, Jr.
William Wallgren
Howard Keith Walling
Vincon Walling
Calvin Wallingford
James L. Wallis
Roger Wallis
Joseph R. Wallman
Gordon Stewart Walls
James L. Walls
Jesse J. Walls
Max E. Walls
Robert W. Walls
William M. Walls
John S. Walmsley, Jr.
Marlin N. Walraven
Bernard J. Walsh
David Charles Walsh
Donald E. Walsh
James Emory Walsh
James J. Walsh
John Joseph Walsh
John P. Walsh
Robert C. Walsh
Robert F. Walsh
William R. Walsh
Calvin Pugh Walston
Jesse E. Walston
Stephen Walston
Francis G. Walter
John G. Walter
Stephen C. Walter
Charle Walterhouse
Billy Walters, Jr.
Dale E. Walters
Dallas J. Walters
David F. Walters
Earnest L. Walters
Frank B. Walters, Jr.
Fred T. Walters
George N. Walters
George W. Walters
James C. Walters
Kenneth E. Walters
Leland R. Walters
Marvin O. Walters
Robert K. Walters
William F. Walters
Charles P. Walthour
Cedric W. Waltman
Bobby B. Walton
Carl E. Walton
Curtis L. Walton
Gussie Vay Walton
Harold L. Walton
John Laurice Walton
Lloyd R. Walton, Jr.
Lucius Prewett Walton
Elmer E. Waltz
Leonard M. Walz
Ralph L. Walz
Henry L. Wamble
Jacob H. Wambrodt
Martin E. Wampler
Shuller Wanamaker
Ralph R. Wance
Frank P. Wancoski, Jr.
Harold E. Wandover
John Anderson Wands
Leroy Wands
Donald Victor Wanee
Harold N. Wanned
Robert Lee Wanner
Donald Eugene Wanoreck
Charles L. Waples
Henry A. Warblow, Jr.
Alfred Joseph Ward
Burlin W. Ward
Calvin Benjamin Ward
Charles E. Ward
Charles H. Ward
Delmer R. Ward
Donald E. Ward
Donald J. Ward
Donald K. Ward
Edward W. Ward
Frank M. Ward
Fred Alvin Ward
Gene C. Ward
Harold B. Ward, Jr.
Herbert Ward

James B. Ward
James E. Ward
James F. Ward, Jr.
James Henry Ward
Jessie Ward
Jessie T. Ward
John H. Ward
John Lawrence Ward
John Robert Ward
Johnnie T. Ward
Kenneth C. Ward
Leon Ward
Lester J. Ward
Lowell M. Ward
Melvin R. Ward
Norman L. Ward
Otis E. Ward
Robert Ward
Robert A. Ward
Samuel E. Ward
Thomas J. Ward
Virgil E. Ward
William Alfred Ward, Jr.
William D. Ward, Jr.
William F. Ward
William J. Ward
Willie E. Ward, Jr.
Joseph J. Warda, Jr.
Raymond E. Wardell
Doyle R. Warden
Jack W. Wardlaw
Joseph S. Wardynski
Fred Wardzinski
Cecil O. Ware
Clarence E. Ware
Harry W. Ware
James Ware
Raymond O. Ware
Robert L. Ware
Stanford Ware
William D. Ware
David Warfield
Edward F. Warfield
Lloyd R. Warfield
George Albert Wark, Jr.
James Veryle Wark
Jessie P. Warlick
Will Warlie
Jacob H. Warmbrodt
David F. Warmoth
Alfred E. Warmouth
Bennie R. Warner
Bruce Herrick Warner
Carl J. Warner
Charles L. Warner
Dewayne H. Warner
James K. Warner
Kenneth F. Warner
Leonard K. Warner
Marvin L. Warner
Norman C. Warner
Paul C. Warner
Robert Harold Warner
William Warner
Donald A. Warning
Walter W. Warnke
David W. Warnock
John N. Warny
George Francis Waropay
Harold T. Warp
Ernest G. Warram
Clarence J. Warren
Courtney Van Warren
Edgar Odell Warren
Everett Warren
George A. Warren
George J. Warren
Jack W. Warren
James O. Warren
Larry D. Warren
Leonard E. Warren
Martin W. Warren
Maurice D. Warren
Paul Eugene Warren
Richard L. Warren
Robert P. Warren
Samuel Warren
T. P. Warren
Valent Warrichaiet
John Edward Warrick
Raymond P. Warrick
Van Warrick
James D. Warriner
Rufus C. Warrior, Jr.
Walter T. Warshal
Dillon E. Warthan
Billie F. Warwick
William B. Warwick
Carl Leodis Washburn, Jr.

Clarence E. Washburn
George H. Washburn
James F. Washburn
John Gilbert Washburn
Melvin G. Washburn
Charles Washington
Curtis Washington
Hansel Washington
John H. Washington
John M. Washington
Johnny Washington
Joseph Washington
Junius Washington
Lott H. Washington
Perry L. Washington
Peter E. Washington
Preston Washington
R. A. Washington
Rufus Washington
Timothy Washington
Walter Washington
William Washington
Richard L. Wasiak
Edwin Wasielewski
Richard C. Wasinger
Leroy Waskiewicz
Richard J. Wasko
John R. Wasson
Nick Wasylyshyn
Andrew R. Watada
Richard M. Watanabe
Carl W. Waterbury
Albert Waterhouse
Paul Waterloo
Allan Joseph Waterman
Glen E. Waterman
Eunis G. Waters
Fred Waters
Harold L. Waters
John L. Waters
Luther N. Waters
Raymond Lee Waters
Willie Waters
Billy S. Watford
Albert Watkins
Benjamin F. Watkins, Jr.
Calvin C. Watkins
David D. Watkins
Eddie M. Watkins
George Riley Watkins
Harold B. Watkins
Jack G. Watkins
John E. Watkins
Lewis George Watkins
Louis Watkins
Melvin Watkins
Milton K. Watkins
Norman E. Watkins
Randall J. Watkins
Roy R. Watkins
Samuel K. Watkins
Travis E. Watkins
William H. Watkins
Willie J. Watkins
Wooster Watkins
John W. Watlington
Billie B. Watson
Byron Eugene Watson
Cecil H. Watson
Charles Watson
Charles W. Watson
Clarence E. Watson
Clarence R. Watson
Clifton H. Watson
Clifton Nathaniel Watson
Eugene F. Watson
Frank Watson
George Richard Watson
Glen L. Watson
Glenn E. Watson
Glenwood F. Watson, Jr.
Harold B. Watson
Harold Watson, Jr.
Harold L. Watson
Henry L. Watson
Howard R. Watson
James D. Watson
John F. Watson, Jr.
John W. Watson
Kenneth R. Watson
Lawrence John Watson
Leo Watson
Leonard Watson
Leonard S. Watson
Michael R. Watson
Numa A. Watson, Jr.
Robert B. Watson
Robert Bruce Watson
Robert E. Watson

Rolfe M. Watson
Samuel E. Watson
Stephen A. Watson
Theodore S. Watson
Thomas Henry Watson
Tubby Brian Watson
Vernon Watson
Walter Conrad Watson
Walter John Watson
Wayne T. Watson
Willard K. Watson
William B. Watson
William E. Watson
William G. Watson
William H. Watson
William John Watson
William W. Watson
George W. Watt
John F. Watt, Jr.
Lawrence J. Watt
Spencer R. Watt
Thomas F. Watt
Cecil H. Watters
David E. Watters
Willis Watters
Delmer C. Watterson
Fred L. Watterson
Irving Watterson
Arnold Watts
Bigelow Watts, Jr.
Bobbie E. Watts
Cleveland E. Watts
Eddie Watts
Enoch Watts
Franklin H. Watts
George F. Watts, Jr.
Hugh Watts, Jr.
Ishmael Watts
Jack K. Watts
James E. Watts
Orville L. Watts
Roy H. Watts, Jr.
Sammy A. Watts
William F. D. Watts
Willie Watts, Jr.
Ray O. Wauer
Leo J. Wawro
Jerome H. Wax
Robert I. Wax
Donald E. Waxler
George Way
Herbert H. Waymer
Eldon D. Waymire
William H. Waynick
Elmer C. Wear
Dale E. Wears
N. D. Weary
Henry Weatherford
Sydney W. Weatherford
William R. Weatherman
Logan C. Weathers
Arthur Joe Weaver
Carlos D. Weaver
Charles A. Weaver
Charles E. Weaver
Clyde W. Weaver
Curtis H. Weaver
Curtis P. Weaver, Jr.
David L. Weaver
Edward P. Weaver
Edward T. Weaver
Gene E. Weaver
James Monroe Weaver
Jasper P. Weaver
Jeff L. Weaver
John L. Weaver
Larry A. Weaver
Paul D. Weaver
Raymond E. Weaver
Robert F. Weaver
Robert R. Weaver, Jr.
Robert S. Weaver
Roger J. Weaver
Roger L. Weaver
Wadie Weaver, Jr.
William G. Weaver
Danna L. Webb
Delno V. Webb
Donald E. Webb
Donald F. Webb
Donald K. Webb
Donald W. Webb
Edward Arvil Webb
Edwin F. Webb
Henry L. Webb
James D. Webb
Jerald C. Webb
John Bailey Webb
Jonas B. Webb

Kenneth O. Webb
Louis A. Webb
Ralph B. Webb
Shirley R. Webb
St Clair Webb, Jr.
Stanley S. Webb
Donald E. Webbe
Donald W. Webber
Jack E. Webber
James K. Webber
Albert George Weber
Gerhardt H. Weber
Grant Weber
Guillermo Weber
John C. Weber
John E. Weber
John F. Weber
Leonard F. Weber
Murray Weber
Paul Weber, Jr.
Richard A. Weber
Calvin A. Webster
Donald L. Webster
Donald L. Webster
Donald N. Webster
Floyd D. Webster
George W. Webster
Harold D. Webster, Jr.
Herbert E. Webster
Jack M. Webster
Jacob Webster, Jr.
Joseph O. Webster
Lee R. Webster
Lewis F. Webster
Marvin L. Webster
Warren III Webster
William A. Webster
William E. Webster
Henry J. Weckerly
Willie H. Wedgeworth
Cecil Wedworth
Harold J. Weed
Berl D. Weekley
Garnett L. Weeks
Grady Marvin Weeks
Homer G. Weeks
Keith W. Weeks
Otis B. Weeks
Richard A. Weeks
Roy Weeks
Vester W. Weeks
Henry Mcgee Weems
Randall M. Weems
Amos D. Weese
Henry Douglas Weese
Raymond A. Weesner
Paul D. Wegleitner
Richard Lee Wegner
Robert W. Wegner
Chester J. Wegrzyn
George E. Wehage
Jerome H. Wehage
John J. Wehinger
William H. Wehland
William P. Wehrle
William R. Weiand
Frederick Weichler
Bernard E. Weichman
Maurice Henry Weidemann
Ronald J. Weider
Benjamin D. Weidner
Jesse Weidner, Jr.
Merle R. Weidner
Norman Weidy
Arthur A. Weigand
William Weigeshoff
Ronald William Weik
Cook Weikle, Jr.
Richard Maurice Weil
Raymond H. Weiland
Charles E. Weimer
Howard R. Weingarth
George Weingartner
James Weingartner
Melvin Weinraub
Donald G. Weir
James P. Weir
Charles J. Weiser
Wilfred A. Weisheit
James Weisinger
Carl P. Weiss
Clarence H. Weiss
Irving S. Weiss
Melvin Weiss
Sherwin B. Weiss
Herman Weissman
Stanley J. Weissman
Jack Weister
Charles A. Weitekamp

William R. Weitman
Charles W. Weizel
Adon Harry Welch
Arthur R. Sr Welch
Daniel B. Welch
Dillon F. Welch
Douglas L. Welch
Elton Welch
Gobel J. Welch
Harry E. Welch
James D. Welch
James L. Welch
Lonnie F. Welch
Richard G. Welch
Robert D. Welch
Robert L. Welch
Robert Raymond Welch
William C. Welch, Jr.
Williard Martin Welch
John Edward Welches
Harvey J. Welcomer
Robert S. Welding
Elbert Weldon
Harold D. Weldon
James C. Weldon
Olebia G. Weldon
James Richard Welfare
Ernest V. Welker
Eugene P. Welker
Harold M. Welker
Robert E. Welker
Raymond B. Wellbrock
Frank Perrenot Weller
Jerry L. Weller
Randolph W. Weller
Winfred N. Weller
Raymond E. Welley
Henry Welling, Jr.
Harvey Francis Wellman
Joseph E. Wellman
Arthur L. Wells, Jr.
Bernard Wells
Bobby L. Wells
Calvin D. Wells
Curtis J. Wells
Denver L. Wells
Elmer L. Wells
Frederick A. Wells
George Thomas Wells, Jr.
George W. Wells
Harry I. Wells
Harvey L. Wells
James E. Wells
James R. Wells
Joseph Wells
Lawrence A. Wells
Nile Leroy Wells
Ray Edward Wells
Robert Wells
Thomas Franklin Wells
Thomas J. Wells
Willard D. Wells
William L. Wells
Willie Wells
Edward H. Welsch
James W. Welsch
Donald L. Welsh
Harley Welsh
James Douglas Welsh
Neal W. Welsh
Roy W. Welsh
Royce A. Welsh
Donald G. Wemple
Glenn D. Wenck
Raymond D. Wendell
Ernest A. Wendling
George Vincent Wendling
Wilbert Wendricks
Arlin H. Wendt
Jake F. Weng
Marvin R. Wenger
Roman L. Weninger
Charles Wenn
Robert Griffiths Wensley
Chester Wentko
David C. Wently
Jerome Daniel Wentworth
Leigh M. Wentworth
Mark A. Wentworth
Durward E. Wentz
Walter L. Wentz
Dave W. Wentzel
Carl R. Wentzell
Edward W. Wenzel
Frank John Wenzel
Rodney D. Wenzel
Charles P. Wenzl
Alvin F. Werbe
James F. Werber

Glen E. Werhan
Donald Werkheiser
James W. Werkman
Charles E. Werkmeister
Forrest R. Werley
Lowell Lee Werling
Richard J. Werme
Alan R. Werndli
Francis E. Wertz
Clement L. Wery
Ernie E. Wescott
Gerald E. Wescott
John W. Weske
Walter Howard Wesley
Herman R. Wesling
Donald F. Wessel
Lee C. Wesson
Benny L. West
Carl West
Carl Amos West
Carl Emmons West
Charles E. West
Charles Edgar West
Clarence Edward West
Cleveland West
Dallas G. West
David L. West
Donald L. West
E. George West
Edward H. West
George West, Jr.
Henry F. West
Howard Junior West
John W. West
Kenneth Leslie West
Kenneth R. West
Leonard L. West
Milton Morris West
Paul R. West
Radford Carter West
Randell West
Richard D. West
Richard T. West
Roy Lee West
Stanley R. West
William H. West
William Sherrell West
Willis N. West
Leslie Enes Westberry
William H. Westbrook
David C. Westbrooks
Eliot R. Westcoat
John C. Westcott
Jack R. Westel
Melvin Peter Wester
Pervis Wester
Robert Wester
James Royce Westerman
Kenneth Westerman
Samuel V. Westerman
Dirck D. Westervelt
Howard W. Westervelt, Jr.
John F. Westfall
Sten E. Westin
Virgil E. Westlund
Roy R. Westmoreland
Willi Westmoreland
Donald Eugene Weston
Robert J. Weston
Tony Weston
Vernon C. Weston
Phillip B. Westphal
Jonnie J. Westphall
James P. Westry
William Robert Westwood
Bobby T. Wethington
Howell Wethington
Eugene V. Wetzel
Franklin W. Wetzell
Joseph Wetzig
Raymond Wewason
Elwood E. Weyandt
Clifton A. Weyerman
Daniel T. Whalen
Delbert J. Whalen
Frederick W. Whalen
John R. Whalen
Kenneth J. Whalen
Michael T. Whalen
Richard D. Whalen
Elwin Irving Whaley
Henry N. Whaley, Jr.
Norman L. Whaley
Roy L. Whaley
Willard J. Whaley
Granvil Harry Whalin
Charles Leroy Whatley
Ithiel E. Whatley
David G. Wheat

Charles W. Wheatley
Ray R. Wheaton
Vernon D. Wheeldon
Carol Gilbert Wheeler
David F. Wheeler
Donald L. Wheeler
Donald W. Wheeler
Floyd L. Wheeler, Jr.
Harry F. Wheeler
James D. Wheeler
James J. Wheeler
Jesse James Wheeler
John H. Wheeler
John N. Wheeler
Lowell T. Wheeler
Ordis J. Wheeler
Robert Lockridge Wheeler
Robert N. Wheeler
Robert W. Wheeler
Sebastian Wheeler
Vernon Odell Wheeler, Jr.
Wilfrid Iii Wheeler
William A. Wheeler
Charles V. Wheeling
Charles W. Wheelwright
Francis E. Whelan
Leonard James Whelan
Robert John Wherley
Ralph J. Whetstine
Richard G. Whible
Francis J. Whidden
Reginald W. Whiddon
William H. Whigham
Howard K. Whipkey
Francis J. Whipple
Nois L. Whisenant
Robert L. Whisler
William L. Whisler
James Whisman, Jr.
Hugh D. Whitacre
Charles E. Whitaker
Clyde E. Whitaker
Donald L. Whitaker
Francis Whitaker
Gilbert Whitaker
Norman L. Whitaker
Odell Whitaker
Earl A. Whitbeck
Cyrus J. Whitby
Albert W. White
Arlo L. Whit
Billy Ray White
Burl D. White
Carl White, Jr.
Carl L. White
Carl W. White
Cecil W. White
Charles A. White
Chester A. White
Claude Vincent White
Dale I. White
Dalton J. White
Daniel M. White
David J. White
David N. White
David R. White
Dean Walker White
Delbert L. White
Donald C. White
Donald Curtis White
Donald H. White
Donald H. White
Donald R. White
Dwight C. White
Edgar T. White
Edward A. White
Edward F. White
Elvis J. White
Eugene White
Frank M. White
Franklin H. White
Graceon H. White
Harlan A. White
Harold Edward White
Harry E. White, Jr.
Howard E. White
Hughie A. White
J. W. White
Jackie J. White
James A. White
James B. White
James E. White
James H. White
James R. Edward White
James S. White
James W. White
Jimmie M. White
John Edward White
John G. White, Jr.

John H. White
John White, Jr.
John Patrick White
Kenneth R. White
Leroy J. White
Lightning P. White
Llewellyn White
Lonnie R. White
Martin E. White
Merle E. White
Noel E. White
Odell White
Patrick A. White
Paul F. White
Perry O. White
Prechea C. White
Ray White, Jr.
Fort Smith, AR
Raymond P. White
Richard A. White
Richard C. White
Richard E. White
Robert Edward
Robert H. White
Robert J. White
Robert L. White
Robert Lee White
Roy White
Rudolph A. White
Ruthers White
Sherman H. White
Sidney Matthews White
Stanley H. White
Thomas P. White
Waddell White
Walton R. White
Will C. White
William A. White
William D. White
William E. White
William F. White
William G. White
William J. White, Jr.
William K. White
William L. White
Willie E. White, Jr.
Wilmer C. White
Arthur J. Whitebear
Orbia Whitecotton
Roy N. Whited
Wesley L. Whited
Dana L. Whitehead
Joseph C. Whitehead
Lee Whitehead, Jr.
Marvin L. Whitehead
Minter W. Whitehead
Robert L. Whitehead
Wallace Whitehead
William Whitehurst
Floyd R. Whiteman
Marshall E. Whiteman
Martin H. Whiteman
Richard D. Whiteman
William S. Whiteman
William Francis Whitemore
James Whitener
Joe B. Whitener, Jr.
Gerald B. Whiterock
Joseph C. Whitesell
Billy E. Whiteside
Cole E. L. Whiteside
Joseph E. Whiteside
Eric Whitfield, Jr
Howard Whitfield
Samuel E. Whitfield
Charles H. Whitford
James Willis Whitford, Jr.
Jesse E. Whitford
Charles P. Whitler
William R. Whitlock
Leeroy Whitlow
Bobby H. Whitman
Lankford L. Whitman
Walter M. Whitman
William Henry Whitman
Harold W. Whitmer
Robert M. Whitmire
Andrew A. Whitmore
Donald Ray Whitmore
George H. Whitney
Ralph Henry Whitney
Robert Hickson Whitney, Jr.
Theron H. Whitneybell
Lynn Barry Whitsett
Walter E. Whitsett
Alfred Whitson
John Byron Whitson, Jr.
Robert M. Whitson

John T. Whitt
Alton Whittaker
Billie Whittaker
Edward Horold Whittaker
Eugene Whittaker
Melvin T. Whittaker
James D. S. Whittemore
John S. Whittemore
James A. Whitten
Joe E. Whitten
Robert E. Whitten, Jr.
Ivan D. Whittenburg
Walter Whittington
Jack D. Whittle
Everett Whitworth
Worthaw Whitworth
Vernon I. Whorley
Vinton O. Whyde
Joseph R. Wiatrak
Gilber Wibbenmeyer
Paul J. Wichman
Robert J. Wichman
Morris J. Wick
Robert L. Wickham
Robert D. Wickline
Leigh W. Widel
William J. Widener
William L. Widner
Marvin Wiebelhaus
Walter Wieckowski
James Lowell Wiedau
Owen Charles Wiederhold
Carl F. Wiegand
Thaddeus J. Wiegel
Robert Leroy Wiegman
Christian Wieland
James E. Wielert
William C. Wiener
Chester W. Wierzbicki
Joseph Wierzbicki
Theodore W. Wieseke
James M. Wiewel
Robert L. Wigen
Ralph A. Wigert, Jr.
Don M. Wiggins
Frederick H. Wiggins
H. P. Wiggins
Harold Wiggins
Jim P. Wiggins, Jr.
John G. Wiggins
Marvin L. Wiggins
Mervyn L. Wiggins
Samuel Wiggins
Robert G. Wight
James M. Wightman
Howard Wigley
James M. Wigley
Carlie A. Wike
James W. Wike
Willie C. Wilbanks
Julian L. Wilbourn
William H. Wilbur
Robert W. Wilburn
Charlie Wilcher, Jr.
Thomas R. Wilcosky
Charles B. Wilcox
Conrad D. Wilcox
Dale Robert Wilcox
Duane W. Wilcox
Harland N. Wilcox
Harry James Wilcox
Harry K. Wilcox
Joe D. Wilcox
Kenneth E. Wilcox
Lawrence A. Wilcox
Lyman L. Wilcox
Ralph S. Wilcox
Robert B. Wilcox
Stanton Granville Wilcox
Vernon A. Wilde
Harold D. Wilder
Harold G. Wilder
James B. Wilder
Robert De Witt Wilder
Luther M. Wildes
Jesse Wildman
Johnny R. Wilds
John M. Wildy
Irwin D. Wilensky
Rossie E. Wiles
Albert L. Wiley
Donald E. Wiley
Farrel K. Wiley
Kenneth Dale Wiley
William J. Wiley
William W. Wiley
Arville E. Wilfong
Charles C. Wilhelm
Clarence E. Wilhelm

John Henry Wilhelm
Maurice E. Wilhelm
Edward John Wilhide
Charles E. Wilhite
Oron T. Wilhite
Raymond Conrad Wilk
Jack T. Wilke
Desmond K. Wilkerson
Eddie Wayne Wilkerson
Gordon M. Wilkerson
John A. Wilkerson
Nelson Howe Wilkerson
R. C. Wilkerson
Charles W. Wilkes
David C. Wilkes
Donald Wilkes
Philip J. Wilkes
Franklin H. Wilkey
Harold Gene Wilkie
Marlin A. Wilkie
Beauford E. Wilkins
Bertram D. Wilkins
Cleophas Wilkins
Joseph H. Wilkins
Joseph Murray Wilkins
Paul W. Wilkins
Ralph C. Wilkins
Robert Blair Wilkins
Francis Wilkinson
Franklin Wilkinson
James L. Wilkinson
William Wilkinson
Edward E. Wilkosz
Louis V. Wilkowski
Van L. Wilks
Francis J. Will
Fred Willaims
Franklin Louis Willams
George Willard, Jr.
Joseph W. Willardo
Harold E. Willecke
George W. Willett
Richard R. Willett
Robert M. Willett
Eddie M. Willette
Omer T. Willette
Frank Bud Willhite
Everett Ray Willhoite
Albert Raymond William
Hardy L. William
James H. William
Johnnie William
Kenneth P. William
Albert Williams
Alexander Williams
Allen V. Williams
Alvin C. Williams
Amos Williams
Andrew D. Williams
Arthur A. Williams
Arthur I. Williams
Arthur L. Williams
Arthur L. Williams
Augustus Williams
Averill Williams
Basil A. Williams
Bertram E. Williams
Billy J. Williams
Billy J. Williams
Bob H. Williams
Buck Williams
C. Lee Williams
Carl Williams
Charles Williams
Charles A. Williams
Charles D. Williams
Charles E. Williams
Charles J. Williams
Charles J. Williams
Charles K. Williams
Charles L. Williams
Charles O. Williams
Charleston Williams
Chester L. Williams
Clarence Williams
Clarence Williams
Clarence Williams, Jr.
Claude M. Williams
Clyde Williams
Clyde S. Williams
Coleman B. Williams
Curlester Williams
Dale E. Williams
Dan R. Williams
Darwin M. Williams
Delmont Williams
Donald E. Williams
Donald K. Williams
Donald R. Williams, Jr.

378

Donald Roy Williams
Douglas B. Williams
Earl E. Williams
Earl J. Williams
Eddie Williams
Eddie Williams, Jr.
Edward Allen Williams
Edward Julius Williams
Edward P. Williams, Jr.
Edward W. Williams
Ellis E. Williams
Everett Lee Williams
Ezra Williams
Fleming Williams
Floyd B. Williams
Franklin Williams
Franklin L. Williams
Fred Williams
Frederick Russell Williams
George H. Williams
George M. Williams, Jr.
Gerald E. Williams
Gerald F. Williams
Gerald M. Williams
Gerald R. Williams
Grover Lois Williams
Hardy L. Williams
Harold G. Williams
Harry E. Williams
Harvey C. Williams
Henry L. Williams
Henry M. Williams
Herbert H. Williams
Herman Williams
Hubert A. Williams
Hubert T. Williams
Hura K. Williams
Isiah Williams
Ivan F. Williams
Jack K. Williams
Jack Pryer Williams
Jack R. Williams
Jack Vernon Williams
James A. Williams
James B. Williams
James C. Williams
James E. Williams
James E. Williams
James H. Williams
James I. Williams
James J. Williams, Jr.
James M. Williams
James Marvin Williams, Jr.
James O. Williams
James R. Williams
James Robert Williams
James W. Williams
Jasper D. Williams
Jerome Francis Williams
Jim E. Williams
John David Williams
John H. Williams
John J. Williams
John Williams, Jr.
John Williams, Jr.
John M. Williams
John Milton Williams
John N. Williams, Jr.
John R. Williams
Johnnie Williams, Jr.
Johnny B. Williams
Johnny Williams, Jr.
Joseph H. Williams
Kenneth B. Williams
Kenneth E. Williams
Kenneth G. Williams
Kenneth O. Williams
Kenneth P. Williams
Lamson Paul Williams
Lawrence Williams
Lawrence Williams
Lawrence H. Williams
Leo H. Williams
Leonard Williams
Leonard J. Williams
Leslie Conrad Williams
Lester David Williams
Lewis Williams
Lewis D. Williams
Luis F. Williams
Marshall M. Williams, Jr.
Marvin Williams
Marvin M. Williams
Maurice Williams
Mc Kinley Williams
Melvin Edward Williams
Merlyn Keith Williams
Milton L. Williams
Morris Williams

Nathaniel Williams
Neil Rodney Williams
Nelson E. Williams
Olen B. Williams
Oliver S. Williams
Oscar Williams
Otis C. Williams
Owen Foch Williams
Paul Ervin Williams
Paul R. Williams
Percy E. Williams
Ralph B. Williams
Ray G. Williams
Raymond Clair Williams
Relda H. Williams
Reynolds Williams
Richard D. Williams
Richard George Williams
Richard M. Williams
Robert Williams
Robert Allen Williams
Robert Allen Williams
Robert E. Williams
Robert H. Williams
Robert H. Williams
Robert H. Williams
Robert Joseph Williams
Robert K. Williams
Robert L. Williams
Robert L. Williams
Robert L. Williams
Robert M. Williams
Robert R. Williams
Roman J. Williams
Ronald Duane Williams
Ronald R. Williams
Roosevelt Williams
Roosevelt Williams
Roosevelt Williams
Sam D. Williams
Simmuel L. Williams
Stanely R. Williams
Stevens Williams
Talmage C. Williams
Thomas Williams
Thomas B. Williams
Thomas W. Williams
Tommie Joe Williams
Tony N. Williams
Truman H. Williams
Walter N. Williams
Wilford H. Williams
Willard F. Williams
William Williams
William E. Williams
William M. Williams
William P. Williams
Willie Joseph Williams
Willie Williams, Jr.
Willie S. Williams
Willie V. Williams
Winston W. Williams
Bennie Williamson
Bob Williamson
Charles Williamson
Charles Williamson
Claud H. Williamson
Daniel Williamson
Eugene Williamson
Flavius Joseph Williamson
George H. Williamson
Herbert Williamson
James Williamson
James H. Williamson
John Williamson, Jr.
Kenneth E. Williamson
Melvill Williamson
Melvin Williamson
Richard Williamson
Robert Williamson
Wallace Lee Williamson
Ila J. Willie
John Williford
Billie Willingham
Joseph Willingham
Thomas Willingham
Adam M. Willis
Albert E. Willis, Jr.
Bert L. Willis
Carlos E. Willis
Cecil M. Willis
Charles A. Willis
Cornell F. Willis
Doyle D. Willis
Ernest A. Willis
Frank Willis
Gaylord B. Willis
George W. Willis
Howard Willis

James G. Willis, Jr.
Jess E. Willis
Louis R. Willis
Paul J. Willis
Perry Walon Willis
Robert Willis
Robert F. Willis
Sylvester Willis
James E. Willison
Richard Charles Willmann
Lee E. Willmsen
Earl C. Willoughby
Monroe Willoughby
Ray Willoughby
Richard E. Willoughby
Glen Earl Willow
Gene W. R. Willrich
Carlton R. Wills
Earl E. Wills
Elbert F. Wills
Eugene E. Wills
James W. Wills, Jr.
Joseph D. Wills, Jr.
Victor L. Wills
Virgil V. Wills
Joseph H. Willson, Jr.
James L. Wilmoth
Robert W. Wilmoth
Fred D. Wilmuth
William H. Wilner
Marvin Wilsie
Albert Wilson
Amos Wilson
Arthur C. Wilson, Jr.
Aubrey Wilson
Benjamin Wilson
Bernard O. Wilson
Bobby Ray Wilson
Bruce S. Wilson
Charles B. Wilson
Charles E. Wilson
Charles E. Wilson
Charles G. Wilson
Charles H. Wilson
Charles Wilson, Jr.
Charles L. Wilson
Charles L. Wilson
Charles R. Wilson
Clarence O. Wilson
David H. Wilson
Donald E. Wilson
Donald Harold Wilson
Donald J. Wilson
Donald W. Wilson, Jr.
Douglas C. Wilson
Duane E. Wilson
Earl T. Wilson
Earnest G. Wilson
Edward J. Wilson
Elmer T. Wilson
Ernest E. Wilson
Floyd Leo Wilson
Forest M. Wilson
Francis E. Wilson
Frank Wilson, Jr.
Frederick D. Wilson
Garvin Wilson
Gary R. Wilson
General J. Wilson
George F. Wilson
George W. Wilson, Jr.
George W. Wilson, Jr.
Gerald H. Wilson, Jr.
Gerald N. Wilson
Gilmer W. Wilson
Hallie W. Wilson, Jr.
Harold D. Wilson
Harold F. Wilson
Harry L. Wilson
Henry C. Wilson
Herbert Wilson
Hollis Granville Wilson
Homer C. Wilson
Howard A. Wilson, Jr.
Hugh C. Wilson
Hurley Wilson
Isaac Wilson
James Wilson
James C. Wilson
James E. Wilson
James E. Wilson
James H. Wilson
James L. Wilson
James M. Wilson
James Martin Wilson
James R. Wilson
James Swayne Wilson, Jr.
James V. Wilson
James W. Wilson

James Waters Wilson
Jerry Wilson
Jerry D. Wilson
Jesse Wilson
Jesse E. Wilson
John B. Wilson
John D. Wilson, Jr.
John R. Wilson
John R. Wilson
Jonn B. Wilson
Joseph F. Wilson
Juan B. Wilson
Kenneth R. Wilson
Leroy E. Wilson
Leroy W. Wilson
Leslie G. Wilson
Linwood F. D. Wilson
Louis R. Wilson
Loyd Junior Wilson
Merble E. Wilson
Paul A. Wilson
Ralph E. Wilson, Jr.
Ray Wilson
Raymond C. Wilson
Richard E. Wilson
Richard G. Wilson
Richard L. Wilson
Richard R. Wilson
Robert D. Wilson
Robert D. Wilson
Robert E. Wilson
Robert E. Wilson
Robert L. Wilson
Robert V. Wilson
Rodney H. Wilson
Roy Cornelius Wilson, Jr.
Roy S. Wilson, Jr.
Rubin B. Wilson
Rudolph Wilson
Russell Charles Wilson
Samuel A. Wilson
Silas W. Wilson
Sylvester Wilson
Thomas Wilson, Jr.
Thomas P. Wilson
Wallace Wilson
Walter Wilson, Jr.
Warren W. Wilson
William C. Wilson
William Dean Wilson
William G. Wilson
William H. Wilson
William H. Wilson
Winston D. Wilson
John T. Wilt
William Walter Wilt
Albert J. Wiltrout
Joseph G. Wilusz
William Hurt Wimbish
John W. Wimbley, Jr.
Leroy H. Winans
Royce W. Winarski
James A. Winborn
Ben L. Wince
Charles L. Winchell
Otto B. Winchell
Eddie Winchester
Gordon Winchester
John L. Winchester
William J. Winchester
James F. Winckler
Henry J. Windecker
Alvin A. Winder
Willie E. Windham
Max E. Windle
Clifford J. Windom
Francis Charles Windover
William Gordon Windrich
William Plumer Windus, Jr.
Edward J. Wine
Robert L. Wine
George H. Wines
Thomas Henry Wines, Jr.
Leroy C. Winfield
Ralph E. Winfield
Samuel F. Winfield
Elmer V. Wing, Jr.
Phillip Randolph Wing
Richard L. Wing
Wilbur S. Wing
William Wing
Lewis M. Wingard
Charles Wingfield
Horace Wingfield
Jack M. Winick
Gene L. Winiecki
Benjamin Winikoff
Marshall Winkfield
Frank N. Winkle, Jr.

Billie G. Winkler
Harlan R. Winkler
Marvin J. Winkler
Walter W. Winkler
Archie D. Winn
Harry Winn, Jr.
Gerald W. Winner
Richard A. Winnie
William P. Winnington, Jr.
Howard W. Winrader, Jr.
Horace T. Winslett
Kenelm Winslow, Jr.
Harold G. Winsor
Henry G. Winstead
Otho T. Winstead
Edward R. Winston
Huston Winston
James R. Winston
Arthur F. Winter
Frederick W. Winter
Gerald A. Winter
Peter Paul Winter
Samuel G. Winter
Wilbert L. Winter
Clarence R. Winters
Donald F. Winters
Melvin Percy Winters
Norman P. Winters
Van W. Winters
William W. Winters
Ralph E. Winthrop
David Wireman
William Wirotzious
Samuel Wirrick
Clarence J. Wirschinger
Frederick B. Wirt
Merl D. Wirt
Howard Steward Wirth
Raymond E. Wirth
Harold D. Wirtz
William J. Wirtz, Jr.
Warren Bacon Wisdom
Arthur F. Wise
Bruce P. Wise
Earl E. Wise
Earl Vincent Wise
Edward L. Wise
Esley Wise
Gordon L. Wise
Harold A. Wise
James D. Wise
Luther Wise
Paul Wise
William L. Wise
Carl E. Wisecup
Jack V. Wiseman
Milton Lane Wiseman
Paul E. Wiseman
Ernest J. Wisenor
Albert Wisher
David J. Wishon, Jr.
John L. Wiskoski
Albin J. Wisneski
Phillip Francis Wisneski
Adolph Daniel Wisniewski
Felix J. Wisniewski
Albert V. Wiswell
J. D. Witcher
Cleland Davis With
Francis K. Witherell
Earl L. Witherow
Robert L. Withers
Donald E. Witherspoon
Gordon Witherspoon
Joseph P. Witherspoon
Robert H. Witherspoon
John T. Witkowski
Stanley J. Witkowski
Aloysius Witschen
Elbert Jackson Witt
Paul E. Witt
Ray Witt
Robert Virgil Witt
Wallace D. Witt
Harold H. Witte
Richard Earl Wittekind
William Wittenmyer
Albert J. Wittman
William Wittreich
Fredrick Charles Wittwer
Jack J. Witwer
Clayton J. Wixson
Bruce J. Woda
Henry A. Woelk
William Bernard Woerman
James H. Woest
Lawrence R. Wofford
John S. Wohlford
Harold Woiski

Donald I. Woitas
Alex Wojciechowski
Laurence Wojciechowski
Richard L. Wojeski
Frank P. Wojnowiak
Mathew Wojtowicz
Eugene Augustine Wokaty
Norman F. Wolbert
Wallace L. Wold
George L. Woldike
Donald Edward Wolf
James Vincent Wolf
Kenneth Frederick Wolf
Leland Henry Wolf
Melvin G. Wolf
Siegfried J. Wolf
Thomas R. Wolf
Thomas W. Wolf
Wendell D. Wolf
William Charles Wolf
David L. Wolfe
Don Wolfe
Edward Wolfe
George E. Wolfe
Glenn H. Wolfe
James Edward Wolfe
Jerry D. Wolfe
Lawrence Ervin Wolfe, Jr.
Lloyd E. Wolfe
Lowell Thomas Wolfe
Melvin E. Wolfe
Robert E. Wolfe
Robert O. Wolfe
Samuel L. Wolfe
Thomas F. Wolfe
Donald C. Wolff
Roy A. Wolff
Russell Jack Wolfgram
Billy Wolford
Everett Wolford, Jr.
John C. Wolford
Ransome Wolford, Jr.
Samuel N. Wolfsdorf
Elliott Dexter Wolfsen
Edward J. Wolgemuth
Carl Benedict Wolin
John George Woliung
Joseph J. Wolk
Bryant H. Womack
Clarence Womack
Edward R. Womack
King S. Womack
Marion M. Womack
Robert W. Womack
William C. Womack
William Francis Womack
Dress Patric Woman
Kan W. Wong
William K. C. Wong
Edward Wontkowski
Theodore R. Woo
Arlton H. Wood
Bobby J. Wood
Charles E. Wood
Donald K. Wood
Donald Owen Wood
Fernie Wood
Fred W. Wood
Gene A. Wood
George C. Wood
Gerald S. Wood
Harold E. Wood
Harold H. Wood
Harold T. Wood
Harvey J. Wood
James Filmore Wood
James L. Wood
Joe F. Wood
Joseph E. Wood
Junior R. Wood
Kenneth E. Wood
Lyle E. Wood
Marvin R. Wood
Melvin Clinton Wood
Milton Vernon Wood
Ottie Logan Wood
Paul E. Wood
Paul L. Wood
Raymond G. Wood
Robert H. Wood
Robert M. Wood
Ronald C. Wood
Roy Wilbur Wood
Thomas D. Wood
Thomas F. Wood
Tom J. Wood
Virgile Leon Wood
Wallace Norman Wood
Walter R. Wood

William A. C. Wood, Jr.
William E. Wood
William G. Wood
William King Wood
William L. Wood
Wyatt L. Wood
Charles A. Woodall
Charles R. Woodall
William F. Woodall
William T. Woodall
Cecil V. Woodard
Earle L. Woodard
Harold L. Woodard
James Roscoe Woodard
Joel G. Woodard, Jr.
Roger Clinton Woodard
Russell E. Woodard
Fred Woodburn
Harnold D. Woodbury
Wesley R. Woodbury
Frank E. Woodcock
Albert D. Woodcox
Preston B. Woodell
Harry Woodfolk, Jr.
William R. Woodhall
Alphonso Woodlief
Thurman K. Woodlief
Russell H. Woodman
James J. Woodmansee
Elmer James Woodring, Jr.
Floy A. Woodring
Raymond L. Woodring
Edward C. Woodroof
Benjamin H. Woodruff, Jr.
Charles L. Woodruff
David Woodruff
Delbert D. Woodruff
Robert Seymour Woodruff
William M. Woodruff
Allen Woods
Denton Bishop Woods
Donal L. Woods
Earl E. Woods
Frederick E. Woods
George Woods
George H. Woods
Harold Everett Woods
Isaac T. Woods
Jacob Woods
James E. Woods
James W. Woods
Jimmie D. Woods
Joseph H. Woods
Juliga Woods, Jr.
Luther J. Woods
Resteen Woods, Jr.
Robert Woods
Robert Eugene Woods
Roger L. Woods
Thomas B. Woods, Jr.
Tommy Woods
Wilfred E. Woods
William E. Woods
William J. Woods
D. W. Woodson
Guy Woodson
Lewis B. Woodson
Ernest A. Woodward
Francis Woodward
Richard H. Woodward
Robert A. Woodward
William K. Woodward
William L. Woodward
Richard A. Woodworth
Bobby J. Woody
Everett H. Woody
Everett J. Woody
George D. Woody
Charles W. Woolam
Thomas Woolcocks
Claude Wooldridge
Omar E. Wooldridge
Clyde Lee Woolery, Jr.
Loren Willis Woolever
William L. Woolford
Harry H. Woolley
Jack L. Woolley
Douglas S. Woolman
Eugene T. Woolridge
James M. Woolsey
Lowell W. Woolsey
Ernest F. Woolum
Clair D. Woomer
Audrey H. Wooster
Arthur J. Wooten
Cecil L. Wooten
Edwin E. Wooten
Franklin D. Wooten
Ray D. Wooten

Thomas B. Wootteon
Arthur J. Worden
Dow F. Worden
Harry Raymond Worden
Walter Worhach
Charles Workman
Donald G. Workman
John Charles Workman
Lyman W. Workman
Charles L. Worley
Donald B. Worley
Donald B. Worley
Ely E. Worley, Jr.
Forest Edward Worley
Frank Worley
Jack E. Worley
Ronald Worley
Theodore Worley
Clark E. Worline
Philip W. Worm
Thelbert Bernard Wormack
Henry G. Worman
Richard C. Wormwood
Edward J. Worosz
Leonard E. Worrell
Melbern W. Worrell
Pat Augusta Worsham
Vance Olland Worster
Warren W. Worster
George Warren Worth, Jr.
Marcellus D. Worth
Philip L. Worth
Walter E. Worthen
Henry Worthington
Holly Worthy
Jack Worthy
Samuel Benjamin Worthy
John M. Wortman, Jr.
Fred B. Worzala
Gerald E. Wotring
Frank J. Wozniak, Jr.
William M. Wozniak
Paul D. Wrather
John G. Wray
Carlton Alton Wren, Jr.
Allen Wright
Benjamin H. Wright
Billie Dean Wright
C. W. Wright, Jr.
Carl S. Wright
Cecil R. Wright
Charles Francis Wright
Chester A. Wright
Clyde M. Wright
Dale W. Wright
David Van Ness Wright
Dewey Eugene Wright
Donald Wright
Donald D. Wright
Edward C. Wright
Emerson J. Wright
Floyd Wright
Fred L. Wright, Jr.
Gene E. Wright
George H. Wright
George M. Wright
Gerald Wright
Henry F. Wright
Howard A. Wright
Hull Le Roy Wright
Jack M. Wright
James A. Wright
James B. Wright
James H. Wright
James L. Wright
James W. Wright
Jasper Lafayette Wright
Jay E. Wright
John B. Wright
John F. Wright
John H. Wright
John L. Wright
Joseph R. Wright
Kenneth Earl Wright
Kenneth W. Wright
Lewis C. Wright
Martin Joseph Wright
Marvin L. Wright
Melvin G. Wright
Millard R. Wright
Morris B. Wright, Jr.
Onzie L. Wright
Paul L. Wright
Paul T. Wright
Preston A. Wright
Raymond Wright, Jr.
Richard E. Wright
Richard K. Wright
Robert A. Wright

Robert J. Wright, Jr.
Robert L. Wright
Roy C. Wright
Roy E. Wright
Roy N. Wright
Spurgeon Wright
Sylvester Wright
Theodore Wright
Theodore J. Wright
William G. Wright
William H. Wright, Jr.
William J. Wright
Willie K. Wright
William Wrightsel
Richard Harold Wrobel
Josep Wrzesniewski
Fred N. Wujcik
John R. Wulf
Paul Henry Wulf
Marvin Wunderlich
Walter A. Wuotila
Robert E. Wurtsbaugh
Clyde A. Wurtz
David H. Wustrack
Andrew G. Wutz
Alfred E. Wyatt
Billy D. Wyatt
Carl D. Wyatt
Dillard C. Wyatt
Duane Wyatt
Herbert G. Wyatt
Richard S. Wyatt
Roy Wyatt
Ruble W. Wyatt
Wilmer T. Wyatt
James W. Wyche
Ernest W. Wyckoff
John P. Wyda
Homer H. Wyles
George R. Wylie
George H. Wyman
Kenneth Lamont Wyman
Robert Darrel Wymer
Ronald Wyn
Martin D. Wynalda
James E. Wynn
Merritt L. Wynn
Robert Day Wynn
Roy F. Wynn
William Delnoe Wynn
Oliver Wynne
Frederick E. Wysocki

— Y —

Kenneth Fred Yablinsky
Frank A. Yablonski
Lawrence M. Yaeger
Ramond A. Yafrate
Richard F. Yagac
Armour R. Yahn
Donald E. Yahnke
Arthur D. Yaich
Muneo Yaka
Nobuji Yamagata
Tsugio Yamaguchi
Yeiji Yamaguchi
Timothy Shito Yamakawa
Taketo Yamane
Harold S. Yamasaki
Joichi Yamashita
Juan Yanas
Clellan Yancey
Jerry M. Yancey
Robert G. Yancey
John A. Yanecko
Felix M. Yanez
Joe G. Yanez
James A. Yanisch
Dennis W. Yankee
Jerome O. Yankowitz
Mike Yanovik
Valentine J. Yanta
Donald A. Yap
David Yarbrough
Harold L. Yarbrough
Lige Yarbrough
Melvin Leon Yarbrough
Nelson W. Yargar
William F. Yarnell
Bertram Joseph Yaroch
Ralph Frederick Yarosh
Alexander Yarosky
Gerald V. Yarrish
John P. Yarusso
Donald T. Yasko
Gary K. Yasunaka
Ben J. Yates
Bobby K. Yates

Donald Jesse Yates
Edward J. Yates
George W. Yates
Gordon C. Yates
Jackie C. Yates
John C. Yates
Melvin O. Yates
Ray B. Yates
Richard Lawrence Yates
Wiley A. Yates
William J. Yates
Billy G. Yaw
Bruce J. Yax
Mike J. Ybarra
Erik Faddersboll Yde
Manuel Ydrogo
Manuel John Yduate, Jr.
Bruce J. Yeager
Frank Earl Yeager
Ralph F. Yeager
Thomas Michael Yeager
Raymond E. Yeargle
Lemaster B. Yearwood
Corbett Yeater, Jr.
Lawrence O. Yeater
Richard Yee
Ernest W. Yehle, Jr.
James H. Yeley
Leo B. Yelle
John Paul Yellen
Bernard Yelsky
Claud Allen Yelton
Harold Eugene Yelton
Thomas W. Yelton
V. S. Yelverton
Dale Yenger
Eddie E. Yengich
James E. Yenor
Michael Yercich, Jr.
Ray N. Yerdon
George R. Yerger, Jr.
Richard A. Yernaux
Thomas Yesenko
Charles R. Yetsko
Walter L. Yetter
Wilburn R. Yielding
Earl D. Yinger
John Ylinen
Walter Ernest Yockey
George Jacob Yohe
Thomas H. Yokomichi
Tetsumi Yokooji
Katashi Yokotake
Jack W. Yon
Lyle F. Yonge
Vincent A. Yonta
Robert B. Yonts
Stanley W. Yoppini
Arthur A. York
Blaine G. York
Charles Kenneth York
Clebron M. York
James D. York
Joe L. York
Melvin D. York
Ray A. York
Richard William York
Warren Monroe York, Jr.
William E. York
Willie M. York
Kanji Yoshida
Elmer J. Yoshihara
Thoshihar Yoshikawa
Tatsuo Yoshino
Edward F. Yost
Eugene W. Yost
Leroy T. Yost
Oscar C. Yost
Vernon R. Yost
Donald P. Younce
Bear Jasper Young
Bernard Maurice Young
Bobby Eugene Young
Carlton H. Young
Charles H. Young
Clifford Lee Young
Curtis R. Young
David A. Young
Donald R. Young
Earnest M. Young
Edward Young
Erwin C. Young, Jr.
Eugene Young
Francis E. Young
Frank A. Young
Freddie W. Young
George A. Young
Gerald R. Young
Gilbert F. Young
Harry Thomas Young
Howard W. Young
Jack L. Young

Jack R. Young
James C. Young
James E. Young, Jr.
James T. Young
Jimmie Dale Young
Joe C. Young
John C. Young
John D. Young
John M. Young
John R. Young
Joseph P. Young, Jr.
Jules Edwin Young
Kenneth Young
Kenneth E. Young
L. D. Young
Lee R. Young
Leroy C. Young
Leslie Young, Jr.
Merle W. Young
Nelson Edward Young
Norman Young
Orville T. Young
Paul Young
Paul A. Young
Paul H. Young
Ralph C. Young
Ralph G. Young
Ralph Leo Young, Jr.
Raymond C. Young
Richard W. Young
Robert C. Young
Robert H. Young
Robert J. Young
Robert L. Young, Jr.
Russell V. Young
Thomas Young
Walter R. Young
William H. Young
William J. Young
William T. C. Young
Charles Youngblood
James Louis Youngblood
Curtis Younger
Donald D. Younger
William R. Younger
Wilbur H. Youngman, Jr.
Wayne R. Youngquist
John James Youngsman
Amodore Yount, Jr.
Burl Richard Youse
Lawrence R. Yovino
Fermin M. Yparraguirre
Tony F. Yuhasz
John C. Yuill, Jr.
Don Yumori
George Yuritic
Mandell Yuster
Walter John Yuszkiewics

— Z —

Edward Zabilowski
Lester Zabriskie, Jr.
Obidee Zackery
Michael B. Zaczyk
Steve A. Zagurskie
Eugene C. Zahm
James H. Zahorik
Anthony C. Zahra
Robert W. Zak
Arthur J. Zakalyk
Floyd F. Zakrzewski
Richard Zakrzewski
Joseph A. Zalar
Teddy A. Zalba
Joey Lawrence Zaldain
George Zaleha
Anthony Michael Zalek, Jr.
George E. Zaleski
Paul E. Zaleski
Albert A. Zalner
Arthur Zamarripa
Anselmo Zamora
Louis E. Zamora
Alphonse Zampier
Jerry Joseph Zanetti
Primo A. Zanni
Donald L. Zanovich
Samuel V. Zanten
Victor J. Zapata
Anthony J. Zappetti
Thomas E. Zarada
Manuel G. Zaragoza
Alexander Zaremba
Rupert Zarin
Albert V. Zarzetski
Nicholas Zatezalo
Paul Zatzek
Freddie Zavala
John C. Zavalick
Frank J. Zawacki
Charles P. Zawadski
Richard C. Zawlocki
Miguel A. Zayas

Pedrogo Jorg Zayas
William Edward Zbella
John J. Zdybel
Donald D. Zea
John W. Zebrowski
Victor P. Zecchin
Ralph E. Zecchini
Ralph Zecco
John H. Zech
Ernest A. Zecha, Jr.
Chester Zeciciskey
Donald F. Zednik
Joseph Patrick Zeigler
George T. Zeiher
Donald Jack Zeinert
Charles Zeitler
Bernard M. Zekucia
Alfred Zelazo
Tom Zeleles
James J. Zeleznik
Leland Zelinsky
Eugene G. Zelkowski
Robert E. Zellars
Robert William Zeller
William Frederick Zeltman
Marvin H. Zempel
Delbert Laney Zengarling
Donald E. Zentner
Frederick O. Zentner
Charles E. Zepp
David M. G. Zerbach, Jr.
Richard G. Zerbian
Joseph C. Zerbo
Robert L. Zeumault
Casemir Joseph Ziarko
Joseph R. Zich, Jr.
Rolf L. Zickel
William F. Zidelski
Laverne J. Ziebarth
Alfred O. Ziegler
Paul M. Zielinski
Raymond R. Ziemecki
Jack R. Ziemer
George F. Ziesch
Lawrence Zigerelli
Edward E. Zimbelman
Donald J. Zimdahl
Raymond J. Zimmer
Thomas E. Zimmer
John Henry Zimmerlee, Jr.
Carl H. Zimmerman
Eugene H. Zimmerman
Gerald G. Zimmerman
Gleason Zimmerman
Johnnie Zimmerman
Luther B. Zimmerman
Michael Zimmerman
Myles W. Zimmerman
Robert Zimmerman
Walter L. Zimmerman
Sebastian Zimmitti
Siegfried Zimniuch
Ralph L. Zinck
Anthony Zingarella
Charles E. Zinkan
Francis J. Zinkus
Warren Arnold Zinn
Lawrence Joseph Zinner
Jack E. Zipfel
Ronald M. Zirbel
Jack A. Zirkle
Charles Lad Zmeskal
William M. Zoellick
Felix J. Zolkowski
Jack Raymond Zoller
David E. Zollman
Aloysius L. Zonca
Ralph Zonta
Harold W. Zook
Walter L. Zopf
Darrell W. Zorn
Gordon J. Zorn
Richard C. Zseltvay
Robert L. Zubrod
Salvatore J. Zucca
Anthony J. Zukas
George Michael Zukowski
Richard Anthony Zukowski
Robert J. Zulke
Anthony P. Zullo
Charles Zumar
Roger E. Zunk
Harry R. Zupke
Ignatius S. Zupparo
Edwin J. Zurek
Roland H. Zurfluh
Raymond A. Zurla
Vernie A. Zurn
Albert I. Zurovetz
Billy G. Zuspan
Jack C. Zuver
Robert L. Zuver
Lewis William Zwarka
Louis J. Zwilling
Melvin T. Zychowicz

Korean War Veteran's Memorial Index

Numbers

1st Cavalry Division 27, 29, 30, 34, 43, 44, 50, 51, 53, 55, 57, 62, 64, 67, 68, 76, 94, 104, 125, 143, 144, 151, 157, 162, 163, 264, 266, 282, 294, 299

1st Division (ROK) 44, 50, 63, 65, 67, 71, 72, 73, 74, 94, 98, 113, 155,

1st Infantry Division (NKPA) 52

1st Marine Brigade 37

1st Marine Division 47, 48, 49, 66, 80, 81, 82, 86, 88, 105, 110, 117, 123, 150, 154, 158, 159, 160, 161, 164, 165, 176, 178, 261, 262, 264, 265, 266, 267, 268, 269, 271, 272, 276, 277, 280, 281, 282, 283, 284, 285, 286, 288, 289, 290, 292, 293, 295, 296, 298

1st Marine Provisional Brigade 152, 169

1st Marine Regiment 49, 87, 91

1st Royal Tank Regiment 142

2d Cavalry Division 94

2d Division 44, 98, 103, 104, 118, 128, 133, 141, 145

2d Division (ROK) 125

2d Infantry Division 74, 163, 170, 179, 183, 264, 270, 273, 278, 279, 280, 286, 288, 290, 292, 293, 294, 295, 297

2d Marine Division 150

3d Battalion (Australian) 63, 64

3d Bomb Group 296

3d Division 97, 100, 102, 113, 118, 147

3d Division (NKPA) 27, 29, 45

3d Division (ROK) 44, 62, 104

3d Field Army (CCF) 91

3d Infantry Division 90, 91, 96, 158, 165, 174, 183, 184, 185, 190, 262, 267, 270, 271, 277, 279, 283, 284, 287

4th Division (NKPA) 31, 43

4th Field Army (Chinese) 71

5th Air Force 26, 129, 130, 134, 267, 291

5th Cavalry 29, 45, 51, 53, 62, 63, 68, 95, 104, 117, 125, 144, 151, 152, 157, 266

5th Division (ROK) 104, 167, 171, 176

5th Infantry Regiment 273

5th Marine Regiment 81, 85

5th Marines 36, 37, 38, 48, 49, 82, 88, 150, 152, 153, 154

5th Regimental Combat Team 37, 51, 66, 110, 115, 154

6th Division (NKPA) 30, 31, 33, 37, 58

6th Division (ROK) 62, 65, 67, 94, 98, 115, 117, 125, 139, 162

7th Cavalry 62, 157, 158

7th Division 49, 58, 90, 97, 103, 145, 168, 176

7th Division (NKPA) 40, 58

7th Division (ROK) 121

7th Infantry Division 49, 66, 81, 88, 96, 98, 151, 157, 159, 160, 166, 178, 262, 270, 275, 281, 288, 290, 291

7th Infantry Regiment 272

7th Marine Regiment 85

7th Marines 82, 90, 160, 162

7th Regiment (ROK) 79

8th Army 26, 29, 30, 34, 37, 40, 45, 47, 50, 55, 58, 59, 60, 62, 63, 64, 70, 71, 72, 73, 74, 75, 76, 77, 79, 91, 92, 93, 94, 97, 98, 99, 100, 102, 105, 107, 110, 112, 117, 118, 119, 121, 123, 125, 126, 128, 129, 136, 139, 140, 143, 146, 152, 153, 154, 155, 156, 165, 168, 172, 174, 179, 180, 182, 185, 188, 189

8th Cavalry 29, 51, 62, 67, 68, 157, 162, 187

8th Division (ROK) 104, 139, 164

8th Engineer Combat Battalion 263

8th Field Artillery Battalion 115

8th Fighter-Bomber Wing 280

8th Ranger Company 116

9th Division (ROK) 184

9th Infantry 44, 54, 74, 110, 124, 145, 163, 164, 276

11th Division (ROK) 139, 185

11th Marines 150

12th Division (NKPA) 44, 54

12th Regiment (ROK) 162

13th Infantry Division (NKPA) 52, 54

15th Division (NKPA) 44

15th Infantry 110, 165, 166

16th Regiment (NKPA) 27

17th Infantry Regiment 166, 167, 168, 190, 274

17th Regiment (ROK) 49

19th Infantry Regiment 27, 44, 261, 263

21st Infantry Regiment 23, 44, 168, 169

23rd Command Post 75

23rd Infantry 74, 104, 122, 170, 172

23rd Infantry (Night) 45

24th Cavalry Division 55

24th Division 25, 27, 31, 34, 43, 44, 50, 55, 57, 63, 65, 71, 98, 100, 105, 107, 110, 113, 115, 129, 153, 168

24th Division Artillery 57, 68

24th Infantry Division 38, 155, 157, 163, 172, 173, 174, 186, 190, 268, 269, 276, 279, 289

24th Infantry Regiment 73

24th Reconnaissance Company 27

25th Division 26, 29, 30, 37, 40, 54, 58, 74, 98, 102, 110, 113, 136, 160, 172, 180

25th Infantry Division 152, 156, 157, 175, 185, 265, 268, 275, 276, 281, 289, 294, 295, 297, 299

25th Recon. Company 58

26th Regiment (ROK) 160

27th Commonwealth Brigade 63

27th (Wolfhound) Infantry Regiment 33, 44, 74, 115

27th Army (CCF) 91

27th Brigade (Argylls) 63

27th British Commonwealth Brigade 50, 56, 65, 71

27th Chinese Army 83

27th Infantry Regiment 174, 175, 180, 181, 266, 283

28th Infantry Regiment 274

29th Brigade Battalion (Glouchesters) (British) 77, 113

29th Infantry Regiment 31, 32

31st Infantry 58, 82, 145, 169, 176, 177, 297

31st Infantry Regiment 273

31st Tank Company 82

32d Infantry 82, 156, 178, 179

34th Infantry 24, 25, 169, 179, 180

35th Infantry 38, 39, 55, 73, 74, 94, 95, 96, 115, 174, 180, 181, 182, 285

36th Regiment (ROK) 121

38th Field Artillery Battalion 43, 78

38th Infantry 54, 74, 75, 182, 183

40th Army (CCF) 104

40th Infantry Division 143, 188, 191, 192, 263, 265, 294

42d Army (CCF) 72

45th Infantry Division 143, 144, 152, 156, 157, 163, 271

52d Field Artillery Battery 23

54th Massachusetts Infantry 246

57th Field Artillery Battalion 82, 83

59th Division (CCF) 115

60th Division (CCF) 115

61st Field Artillery Battalion 75

63d Field Artillery Battalion 27

64th Tank Battalion 90, 110

65th Infantry 114, 183, 184

65th Regimental Combat Team 185

66th Army (CCF) 104

70th Tank Battalion 57, 58

72d Tank Battalion 278

73d Tank Battalion 49

77th Field Artillery Battalion 60, 141

82nd Airborne Division 107

89th Tank Battalion 58, 73

90th Field Artillery Battalion 38, 115

99th Field Artillery Battalion 163

105th Armored Division (NKPA) 45, 49

159th Field Artillery 39

160th Infantry 186

176th Field Artillery Battalion 115

179th Infantry 187

180th Infantry 187, 188

187th Airborne RCT 64, 71, 94, 100, 103, 104, 118, 119, 133, 147, 162, 188, 202, 273, 274, 298

223d Infantry 190

224th Infantry 191

239th Regiment (NKPA) 64

279th Infantry 191

315th Air Division (Combat Cargo) 133

503d Field Artillery 74

555th FA Battalion 38

555th Artillery Battalion 116

555th Field Artillery Battalion 155, 157

987th Field Artillery Bn. 115

A

ABMC 235, 240

Abrell, Charles G. 261

Acheson, Dean 20, 59

Ackerly, Sgt. James 107

Adams, General 240

Adams, Stanley T. 261

Alfonso, Capt. Al 44

Alfred, Col. Lee L. 154

All Wars Memorial To The Colored Soldiers And Sail 246

Allen, Capt. Norman 51

Almond, General "Ned" 49, 119

Almond, Maj. General Edward M. 47

American Battle Monuments Commission 198, 200, 205, 206, 216, 217, 221, 232

American Expeditionary Forces Memorial 206

American Legion 205

Amur 17

Anju 74, 75, 76, 78, 94

Ansong 25

Anui 31

Argyll and Sutherland Highlanders 56, 142

Armstrong, Senator William 198

Arnett, Corporal 73

Arnold, Henry 6, 258

Ash Woods 207, 208, 209, 213, 219, 243, 245, 250

Asia 13, 18

Atherton, Charles 6, 209, 219

Australian Battalion 117

Austria 14

Avery, Sgt. F/C Warren 98

Ayres, Lt. Col. Harold B. 26

B

Badger, Col. Frederick C. 6, 203, 217, 222, 223, 234

Bair, S/Sgt. Chester 84

Baker, Lt. Robert W. 58

Barber, Captain 87

Barber, William E. 261

Barker, Charles H. 262

Barr, Gen. David G. 82

Barre 243, 253

Barton, Capt. R O. 129, 130

Battle Mountain 40, 41

Battle of Bloody Angle 125

Battle of Cannae 71

Battle of the Chosin Reservoir 82

Baugh, William B. 262

Baxter, Pfc. Floyd 123

Beacon 239, 243, 255

Beardsley, John 6, 235, 251, 255

Belgian Battalion 113, 184

Bell, Jerry 6, 244

Benford, Edward C. 262

Bennett, Emory L. 262

Bergee, S/Sgt. Lee 50

Berlin 12

Berlin Airlift 14

Berry, Capt. Sidney 95

Korean War History from Turner Publishing

Turner Publishing Company is the largest publisher of military association histories in the United States with nearly 300 titles. The following are a few selections that feature Korean War History:

Korean War Veterans Association
Complete history of the Korean War with many never-before published combat action photographs. Special "war stories" as told by veterans who served in Korea. The history of the founding and activities of the Korean War Association and nearly 800 personal veteran's biographies, roster, indexed. $49.95 plus $5.00 s/h, 9x12" hardbound, 256 pages.

Korean War Ex-Prisoners of War
A detailed and impassioned look into the lives and the struggles of the prisoners of America's forgotten war. Includes astonishing photos, personal descriptions recounting the hardships of daily routines and victorious homecomings. Features maps showing locations of many prison camps. $42.50 plus $5.00 s/h, 9x12" hardbound, 128 pages.

Chosin Few, North Korea
November-December 1950
"Hell did indeed freeze over once upon a time and we were there," President Harry Truman said. The soldiers of the Changjin Reservoir were extraordinary heroes. It was the "Frozen Chosin" to 15,000 soldiers who spent two weeks fighting their way out of a trap set by 120,000 Chinese troops. This book tells how it actually happened with breathtaking photographs, fascinating text and first-person anecdotes which outline the campaign fought in the frozen wastes of the Changjin Reservoir. $49.95 plus $5.00 s/h, 9x12", 340 pages.

1st Cavalry Division - Korea
An unabridged reprint of the original book produced by the Division documenting the history of the 1st Cavalry Division in Korea. Each unit is represented with a narrative of combat action and crisp photo reproductions. $54.95 plus $5.00 s/h, 9x12" hardbound, 304 pages.

1st Marine Division
The complete history of one of the proudest of the proud—the 1st Marine Division. Experience the captivating story of the Leathernecks throughout WWII, North China, Korea, Vietnam, the Cold War, and Kuwait. Documentary photos, "war stories" by Marines, Association history, index, roster, and personal biographies of hundreds of vets with service and current photos. $49.95 plus $5.00 s/h. 9x12"hardbound, 208 pages, release date: 1997

3rd Infantry Division
Journey with the Third Infantry Division as it fights its way through WWI, WWII, and Korea. The history of the Society of the Third Infantry Division is included along with a memorial roster of those who gave their lives while serving. Incredible photographs accompany the manuscript to tell the complete story. Also included are biographies of the "Rock of the Marne" veterans. $49.95 plus $5.00 s/h, 9x12" hardbound, 120 pages.

5th Marine Division
Experience the hardships and victories of the 5th Marine Division during WWII, Korea, and Vietnam. This commemorative history book also includes maps, charts, outstanding photos, and special battle stories written by the 5th's veterans. $49.95 plus $5.00 s/h, 9x12" hardbound, 128 pages.

Skirmish: Red, White and Blue
The history of the 7th U.S. Cavalry covering the period from 1945 to 1953 by author Edward L. Daily. A historical rendering of the 7th Cav during Occupation Duty in Japan after WWII and combat actions during the Korean War taken from official records in the National Military Archives. Hundreds of action photos, maps, Medal of Honor recipients, and more. $24.95 plus $5.00 s/h. 81/2x11" softbound, 128 pages.

7th Cavalry in Korea
The historical account was written by a Korean War veteran and former prisoner of war. It is the story of an ordeal sustained by the flesh and blood of United Nations, American, and Republic of Korea soldiers, not to mention the innocent and defenseless refugees. Superior photos, maps, casualty list, military symbols, weapons glossary, and the roster of the 7th U.S. Cavalry Association. $39.95 plus $5.00 s/h, 8 1/2x11" hardbound, 128 pages.

7th Infantry Division
Join the 7th in WWII as they combat the elements and the enemy from the Aleutians, Leyte, Ryukus and on to Okinawa in WWII, to Korea with the 7th Infantry's "Light Fighters" as they participate in the Panamanian Invasion. Maps, charts and hundreds of photos. $49.95 plus $5.00 s/h, 9x12" hardbound, 120 pages.

25th Infantry Division, Volume I and II.
Volume I: Extensive coverage from Guadalcanal to Korea's Nevada Complex and on to Vietnam's Cu Chi. Includes never-before-published photographs and biographies of Medal of Honor recipients.
Volume II: A special 50th Anniversary edition commerorating the 25th Infantry Division and its founding celebration at Schofield Barracks, HI. Covers the division from Vietnam through 1991. $47.50 each plus $5.00 s/h. Each 9x12" hardbound, each 208 pages.

31st Infantry "Dixie" Division
History of the 31st Division from its involvement in the jungle warfare of the Philippines in WWII, Korea, and through to today. Many historic photos with personal stories depicting vivid battle scenes from those who were there. $49.95 plus $5.00 s/h. 9x12" hardbound, 104 pages.

32nd Infantry Division
Chronicles the amazing exploits of the *Red Arrow Division* from being WWI's first U.S. Division on German soil, to the first U.S. offensive action in the Southwest Pacific in WWII. Described are also the important roles the Division played in Korea and the Berlin Crisis. Indexed with Roster. $52.50 plus $5.00 s/h. 9x12" hardbound, 160 pages.

35th Infantry Division
Complete history of the 35th Division from WWI, WWII, Korea, through the present. President Truman served with this division as a young lieutenant; battle accounts and biographies by 35th unit veterans. Describes the continued lineage into National Guard service in Kansas, Nebraska, Colorado, Missouri and Kentucky; hundreds of outstanding photographs; very important comprehensive listing of American military cemeteries and memorials of the 35th Division and KIAs in Europe. $49.95 plus $5.00 s/h. 9x12" hardbound, 112 pages.

65th Infantry Division
Published during the 50th Anniversary of the Halberdiers! Follow the path of the 65th to war. From its formation in 1943 and its deployment to battle-scarred France and Germany in 1945, its deployment to Korea, to the present day. Features a bibliography and dozens of outstanding photos. $39.95 plus $5.00 s/h. 9x12" hardbound, 88 pages.

187th Airborne (RCT)
The Rakkasans are the only U.S. Airborne unit to see action throughout WWII, Korea, Vietnam, and Desert Storm. Has over 1,000 photographs and a detailed narrative by Col. William Weber. Charts, tables and maps, a roster of RAKKASAN Association members as well as a roster of current active-duty personnel is included. Indexed. $49.95 plus $5.00 s/h. 9x12" hardbound, 292 pages.

Coast Guard Combat Veterans
This is the complete history of the Coast Guard from WWI to Operation Desert Storm. Vivid photographs compliment the fascinating personal stories of combat on the high seas. Contains the Coast Guard Song, Association membership, roster, SINBAD, and hundreds of biographies. $49.95 plus $5.00 s/h. 9x12" hardbound, 144 pages.

Legacy of the Purple Heart
This book helps to preserve the legacy of the veterans who were awarded the Purple Heart. Thousands of photographs, biographies of Purple Heart veterans, and more than 22,000 names of recipients who were combat wounded. The first two editions are sold out; however, a third edition is currently being published. $49.95 plus $5.00 s/h. 9x12" hardbound, 128 pages.

For more information, contact:
Turner Publishing Company
1-800-788-3350
P.O. Box 3101
Paducah, KY 42002-3101

Notes

Notes